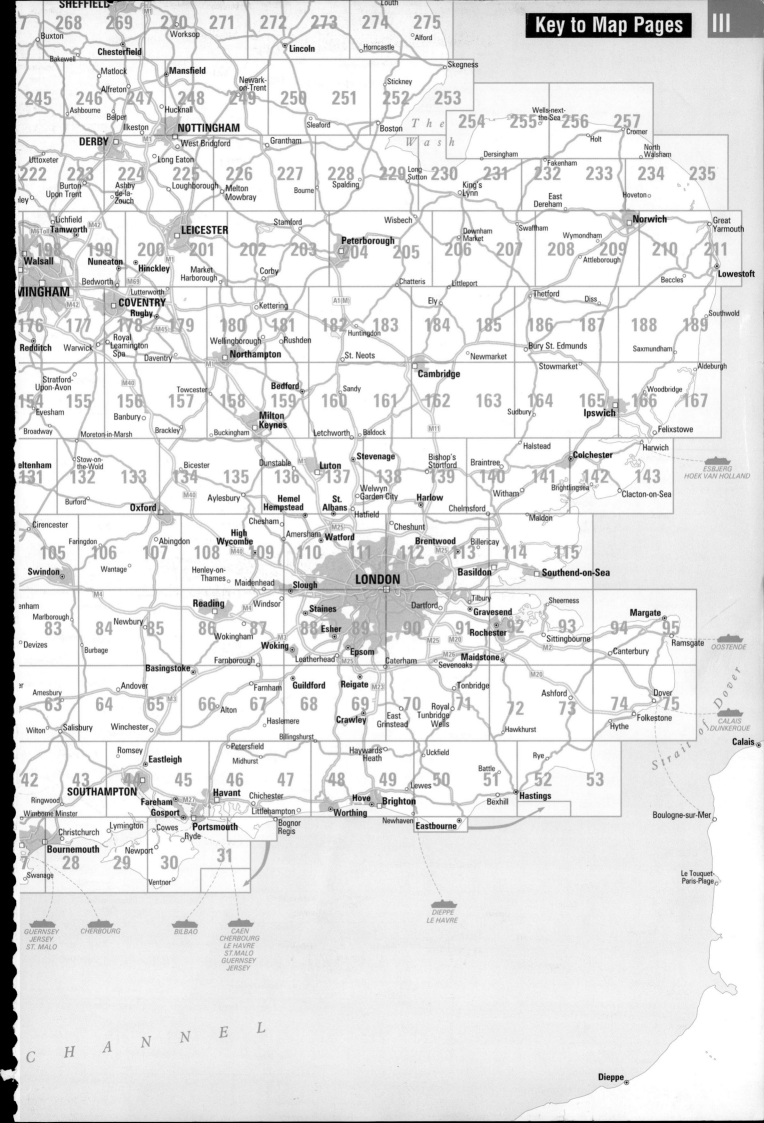

# Key to Map Pages

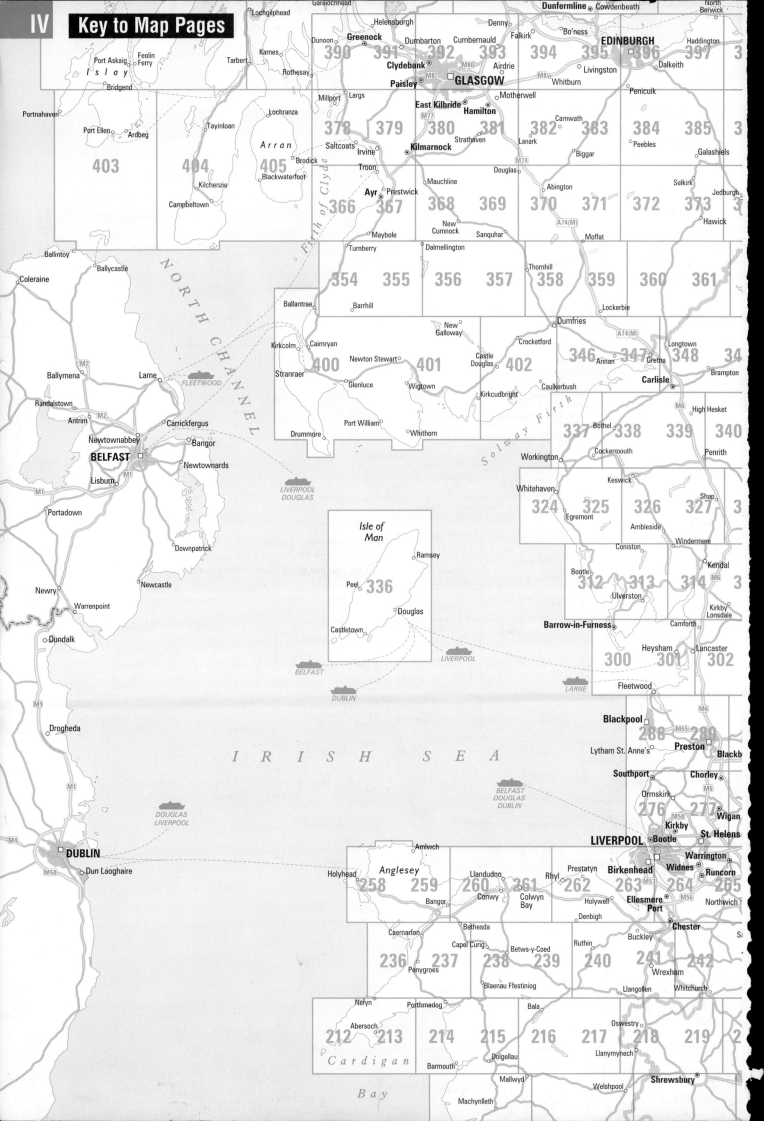

**NORTH CHANNEL**

**Firth of Clyde**

*Islay*

*Arran*

**403** **404** **405**

**390** **391** **392** **393** **394** **395** **396** **397**

**378** **379** **380** **381** **382** **383** **384** **385**

**366** **367** **368** **369** **370** **371** **372** **373**

**354** **355** **356** **357** **358** **359** **360** **361**

**400** **401** **402** **346** **347** **348** **34**

**337** **338** **339** **340**

**324** **325** **326** **327** **3**

**312** **313** **314** **3**

**300** **301** **302**

*Isle of Man*

**336**

*IRISH SEA*

**288** **289**

**276** **277**

**258** **259** **260** **261** **262** **263** **264** **265**

**236** **237** **238** **239** **240** **241** **242**

**212** **213** **214** **215** **216** **217** **218** **219** **2**

*Anglesey*

*Cardigan*

*Bay*

*Solway Firth*

EDINBURGH

GLASGOW

DUBLIN

BELFAST

LIVERPOOL

FLEETWOOD

LIVERPOOL DOUGLAS

BELFAST

DUBLIN

LARNE

DOUGLAS LIVERPOOL

BELFAST DOUGLAS DUBLIN

Lochgilphead, Garelochhead, Dunfermline, Cowdenbeath, North Berwick, Helensburgh, Denny, Bo'ness, Haddington, Dunoon, Greenock, Dumbarton, Cumbernauld, Falkirk, Kames, Kilmacolm, Clydebank, Airdrie, Livingston, Dalkeith, Tarbert, Rothesay, Paisley, Motherwell, Whitburn, Penicuik, Millport, Largs, East Kilbride, Hamilton, Carnwath, Saltcoats, Irvine, Strathaven, Lanark, Biggar, Peebles, Galashiels, Kilmarnock, Douglas, Abington, Selkirk, Jedburgh, Brodick, Ayr, Prestwick, Mauchline, Troon, Hawick, New Cumnock, Sanquhar, Moffat, Maybole, Turnberry, Dalmellington, Thornhill, Lockerbie, Ballantrae, Barrhill, New Galloway, Crocketford, Dumfries, Longtown, Kirkcolm, Cairnryan, Newton Stewart, Castle Douglas, Annan, Gretna, Brampton, Stranraer, Glenluce, Wigtown, Kirkcudbright, Caulkerbush, Carlisle, High Hesket, Drummore, Port William, Whithorn, Bothel, Penrith, Workington, Cockermouth, Whitehaven, Keswick, Shap, Egremont, Ambleside, Windermere, Coniston, Kendal, Bootle, Ulverston, Kirkby Lonsdale, Barrow-in-Furness, Carnforth, Heysham, Lancaster, Fleetworth, Ramsey, Peel, Douglas, Castletown, Blackpool, Lytham St. Anne's, Preston, Blackb, Southport, Chorley, Ormskirk, Wigan, Kirkby, St. Helens, Bootle, Warrington, Widnes, Runcorn, Birkenhead, Ellesmere Port, Northwich, Chester, Amlwch, Llandudno, Prestatyn, Holyhead, Conwy, Rhyl, Holywell, Denbigh, Bangor, Colwyn Bay, Buckley, Bethesda, Ruthin, Wrexham, Caernarfon, Llangollen, Whitchurch, Capel Curig, Betws-y-Coed, Blaenau Ffestiniog, Llanymynech, Nefyn, Porthmadog, Bala, Oswestry, Abersoch, Dolgellau, Welshpool, Barmouth, Mallwyd, Shrewsbury, Machynlleth, Ballintoy, Ballycastle, Coleraine, Ballymena, Larne, Randalstown, Antrim, Carrickfergus, Newtownabbey, Bangor, BELFAST, Newtownards, Lisburn, Portadown, Downpatrick, Newry, Newcastle, Warrenpoint, Dundalk, Drogheda, DUBLIN, Dun Laoghaire

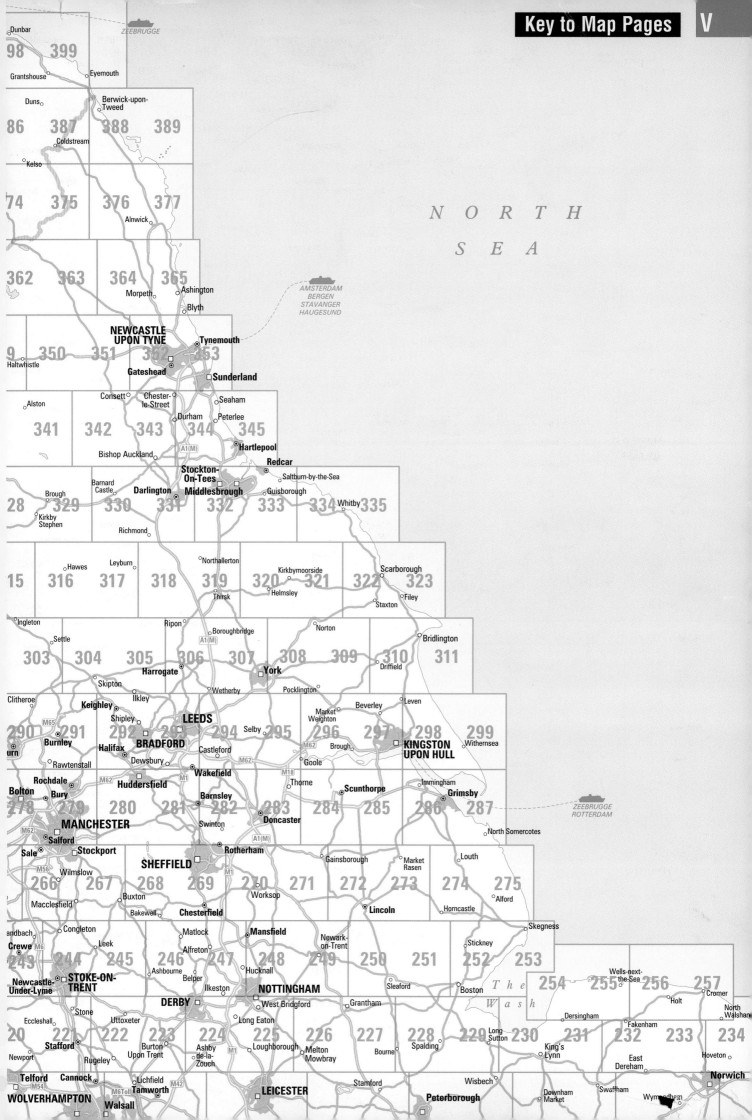

Dunbar

98 399

Grantshouse Eyemouth

Duns

Berwick-upon-Tweed

86 387 388 389

Coldstream

Kelso

74 375 376 377

Alnwick

ZEEBRUGGE

362 363 364 365

Morpeth Ashington

Blyth

NORTH SEA

AMSTERDAM BERGEN STAVANGER HAUGESUND

NEWCASTLE UPON TYNE Tynemouth

9 350 351 352 353

Haltwhistle

Gateshead Sunderland

Alston

Consett Chester-le-Street Seaham

341 342 343 344 345

Durham Peterlee

Bishop Auckland Hartlepool

A1(M) Redcar

Stockton-On-Tees Saltburn-by-the-Sea

Barnard Castle Darlington Middlesbrough Guisborough

28 329 330 331 332 333 334 Whitby 335

Brough

Kirkby Stephen Richmond

Hawes Leyburn Northallerton Kirkbymoorside Scarborough

15 316 317 318 319 320 321 322 323

Thirsk Helmsley Filey

Staxton

Ingleton Ripon Norton Bridlington

Settle A1(M) Boroughbridge

303 304 305 306 307 308 309 310 311

Harrogate York Driffield

Skipton Wetherby Pocklington

Clitheroe Ilkley Leven

Keighley Beverley

Shipley Market Weighton

290 291 292 LEEDS 294 Selby 295 296 297 298 299

Burnley Halifax BRADFORD Castleford Brough KINGSTON Withernsea

urn Dewsbury M62 Goole UPON HULL

Rawtenstall M1

Rochdale M62 Huddersfield Wakefield Thorne Immingham

Bolton Bury Barnsley Scunthorpe Grimsby

278 279 280 281 282 283 284 285 286 287

MANCHESTER Swinton Doncaster ZEEBRUGGE ROTTERDAM

M62 A1(M)

Salford North Somercotes

Sale Stockport Rotherham

Wilmslow Gainsborough Market Rasen Louth

SHEFFIELD M1

M56 266 267 268 269 270 271 272 273 274 275

Buxton Worksop Alford

Macclesfield Bakewell Chesterfield Lincoln Horncastle

andbach Congleton Matlock Mansfield Newark-on-Trent Skegness

Crewe M6 Leek Alfreton Stickney

243 244 245 246 247 248 249 250 251 252 253

Newcastle-Under-Lyme STOKE-ON-TRENT Ashbourne Belper Hucknall Sleaford Boston Wells-next-the-Sea 254 255 256 257

Newport Stone Ilkeston NOTTINGHAM The Cromer

DERBY West Bridgford Grantham Wash Holt North Walsham

Eccleshall Uttoxeter Long Eaton Dersingham Fakenham

20 221 222 223 224 225 226 227 228 229 230 231 232 233 234

Stafford Burton Ashby Loughborough Melton Bourne Spalding Long King's East Hoveton
Upon Trent de-la- Mowbray Sutton Lynn Dereham
Zouch M1

Rugeley Norwich

Telford Cannock Lichfield Tamworth Stamford Wisbech Swaffham Wymondham

M54 M42 Downham

WOLVERHAMPTON LEICESTER PETERBOROUGH Market

M6 Toll

Walsall

STROMNESS

*Outer Hebrides*

Port Nis

Siabost

450 451

Stornoway Port Nan Giuran

*Lewis*

442 443 444

Durness

Melvich Scrabster

Tongue

Laxford Bridge

Kinloch Kinbrace

Huisinis

Lochinver Helmsdale

Tairbeart (Tarbert)

Ledmore Lairg Brora

448 449 438 439 440 441

Roghadal

Aultbea Ullapool Kincardine Dornoch

Gairloch Braemore Tain

*North Minch*

Loch nam Madadh (Lochmaddy)

*North Uist*

Kilmaluag

Invergordon

*Moray*

Clachan na Luib

Uig Evanton Nairn Forres

447

Dunvegan

Achnasheen Muir of Ord Inverness

Portree Shieldaig

Tobha Mor

*South Uist*

430 431 432 433 434

Lochcarron

*Skye*

Sligachan Kyle of Lochalsh Drumnadrochit

Loch Baghasdail (Lochboisdale)

Kyleakin Tomatin Grantown-on-Spey

Broadford

Shiel Bridge Invermoriston Aviemore

446

Bagh a Chaisteil (Castlebay)

*Little Minch*

Armadale Fort Augustus

Mallaig Newtonmore

422 423 424 425 426

*Inner Hebrides*

Lochailort Spean Bridge Dalwhinnie

Spittal of Glenshee

Fort William

Kilchoan Strontian Blair Atholl

Arinagour Glencoe Pitlochry

Tobermory Aberfeldy

Lochaline

414 415 416 417 418 419

Scarinish Salen Bridge of Orchy

Connel Killin Amulree

*Mull* Oban Dalmally St. Fillans

*Firth of Lorn*

Fionnphort Crianlarich Crieff

Strathyre Auchterarder

Kilmelford Greenloaning

Inveraray Tarbet

Kilmartin

408 409 410

Scalasaig

Lochgilphead Garelochhead Stirling Alloa

406 407 Buchlyvie

Dunfermline

*Jura* Helensburgh Denny Bo'ness

Dunoon Falkirk

Tarbert Kames Dumbarton Cumbernauld

390 391 392 393 394

Greenock Airdrie

Port Askaig Clydebank

Feolin Ferry Rothesay Paisley GLASGOW Whitburn

Bridgend *Islay*

Millport Largs Motherwell

East Kilbride Hamilton

Portnahaven

Lochranza 378 379 380 381 382

Port Ellen Tayinloan Saltcoats Strathaven Lanark Carnwath

Ardbeg Irvine Kilmarnock Biggar

403 404 405 *Arran* Troon Douglas

Brodick Mauchline Abington

Kilchenzie Blackwaterfoot 366 367 368 369 370

*Firth of Clyde*

Campbeltown LARNE Ayr Prestwick New Cumnock Sanquhar

Maybole Turnberry Dalmellington

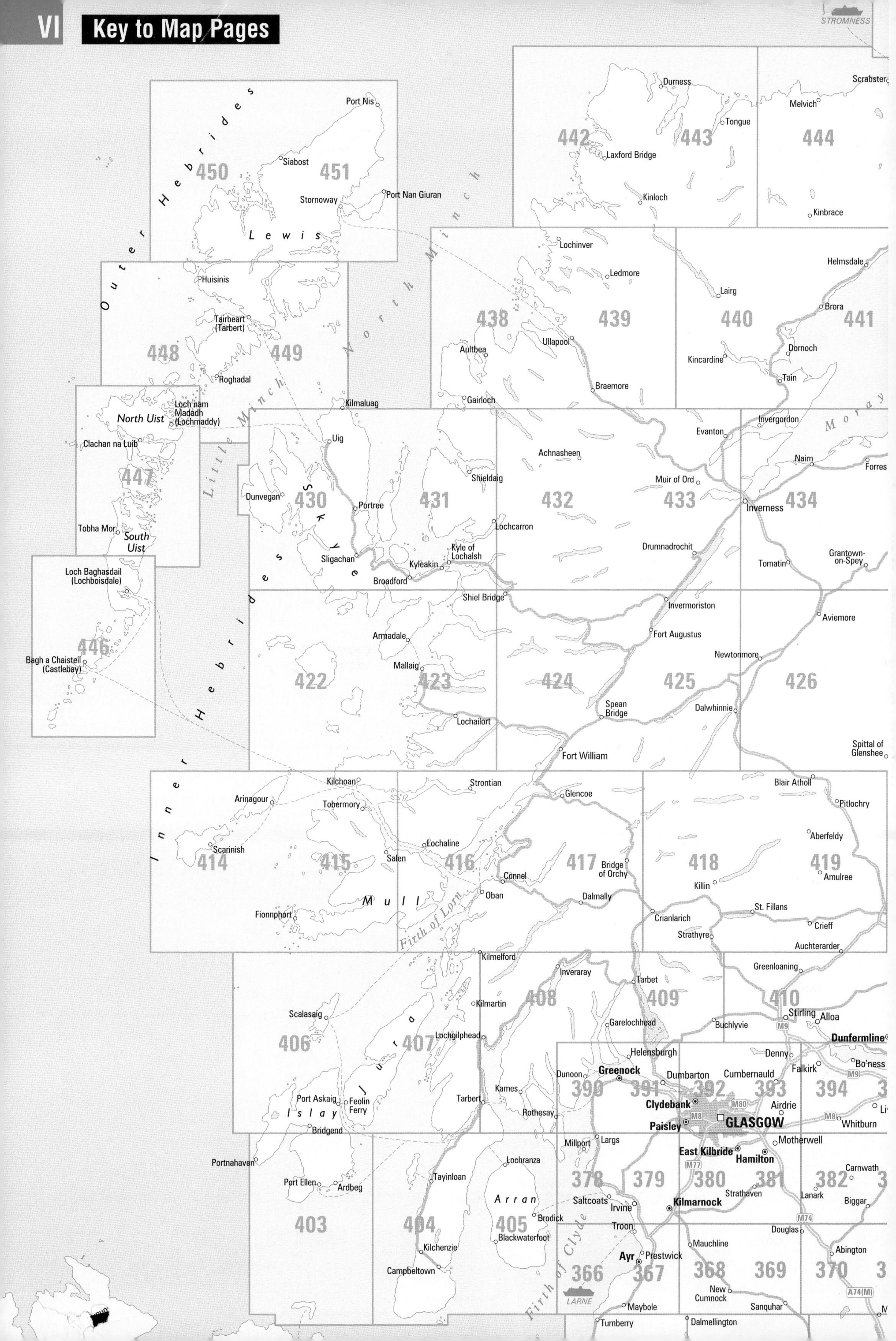

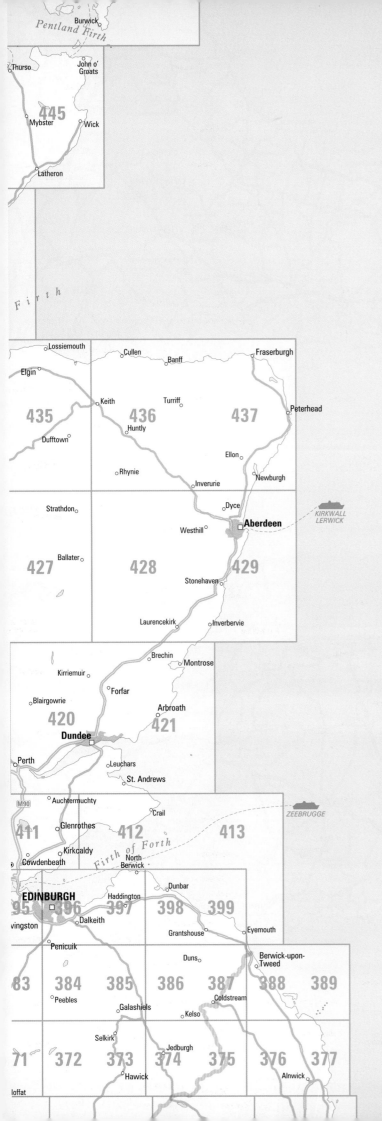

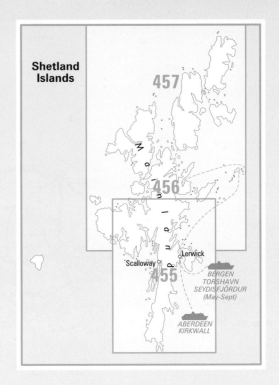

**Shetland Islands**

457

456

455

Scalloway

Lerwick

*BERGEN TORSHAVN SEYDISFJÖRDUR (May-Sept)*

*ABERDEEN KIRKWALL*

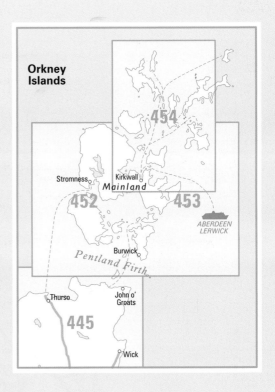

**Orkney Islands**

454

Stromness

Kirkwall

*Mainland*

452

453

*ABERDEEN LERWICK*

Burwick

*Pentland Firth*

Thurso

John o' Groats

445

Wick

*N O R T H*

*S E A*

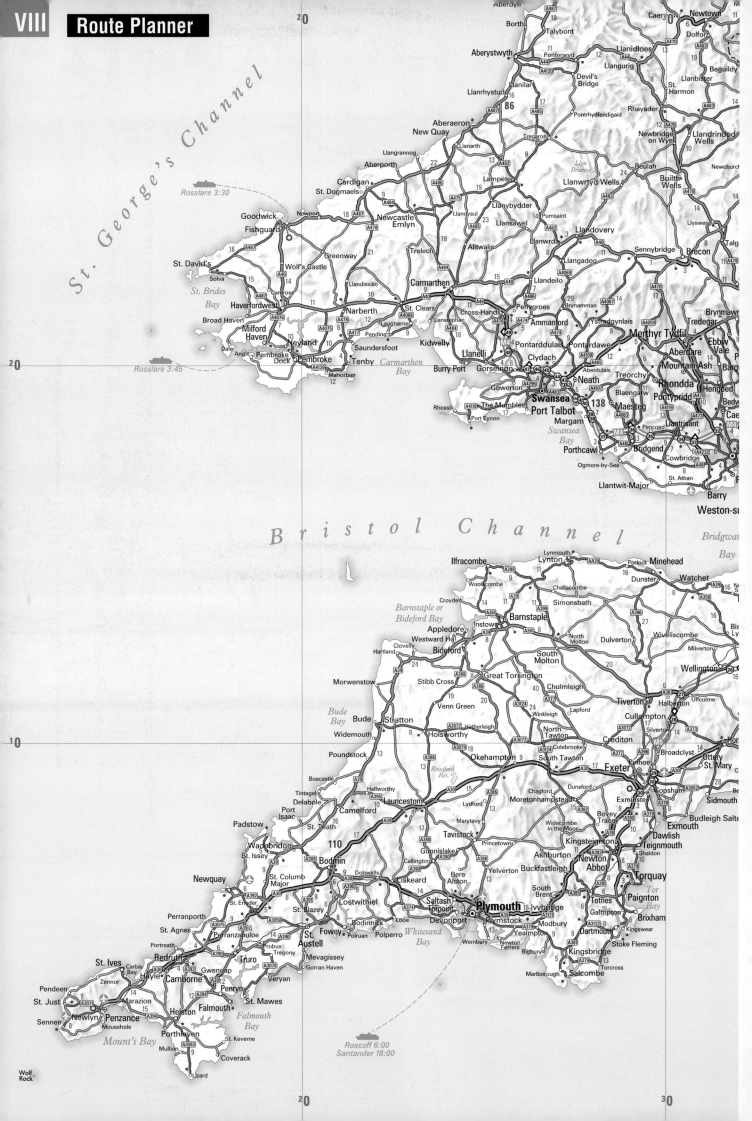

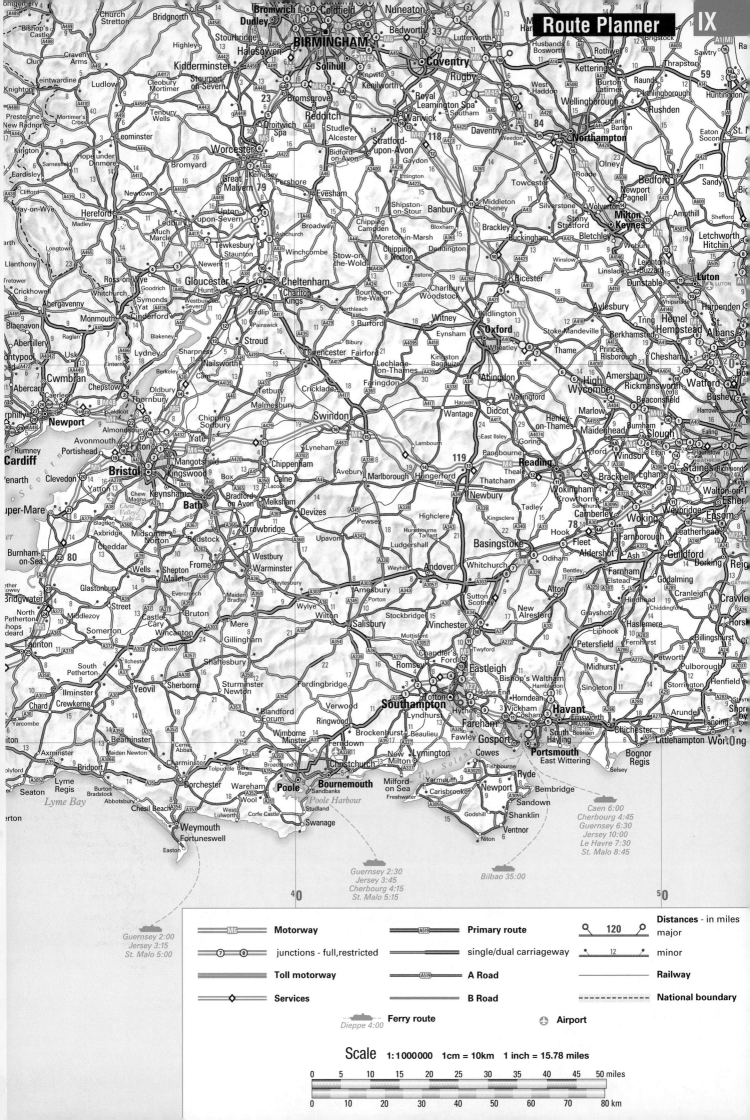

**Scale** 1:1000000  1cm = 10km  1 inch = 15.78 miles

| Motorway | Primary route | **Distances** - in miles |
| junctions - full, restricted | single/dual carriageway | 120 major |
| Toll motorway | A Road | 12 minor |
| Services | B Road | Railway |
| | Ferry route | National boundary |
| | | Airport |

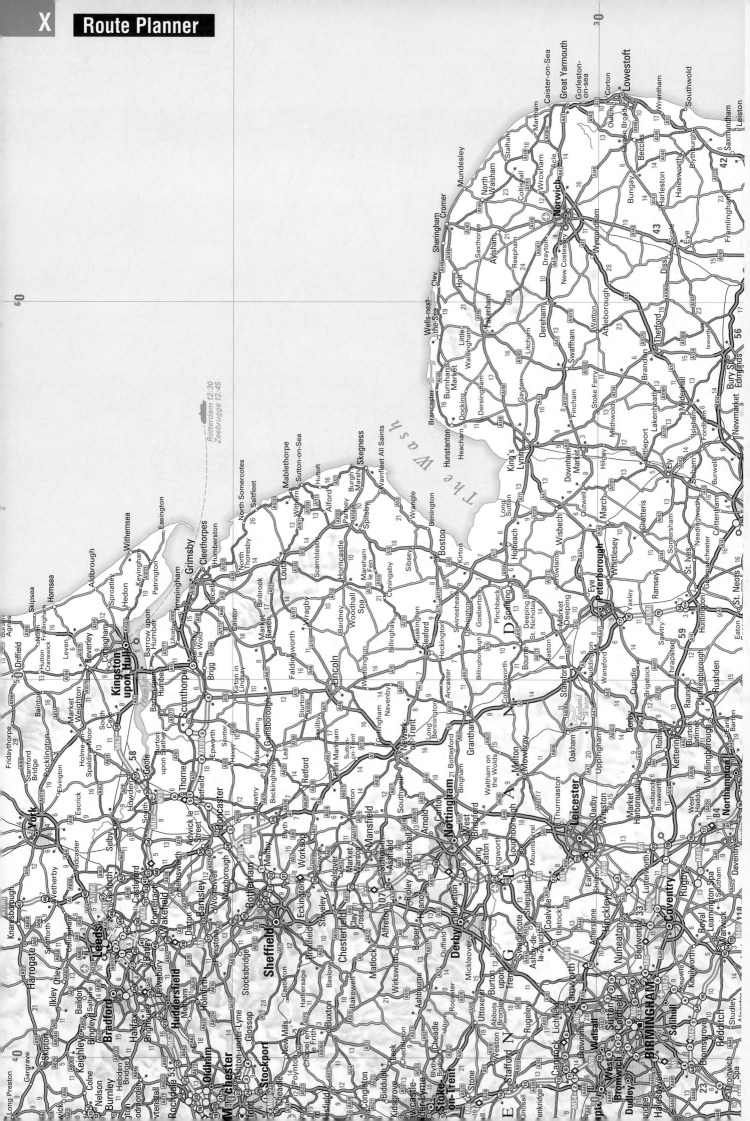

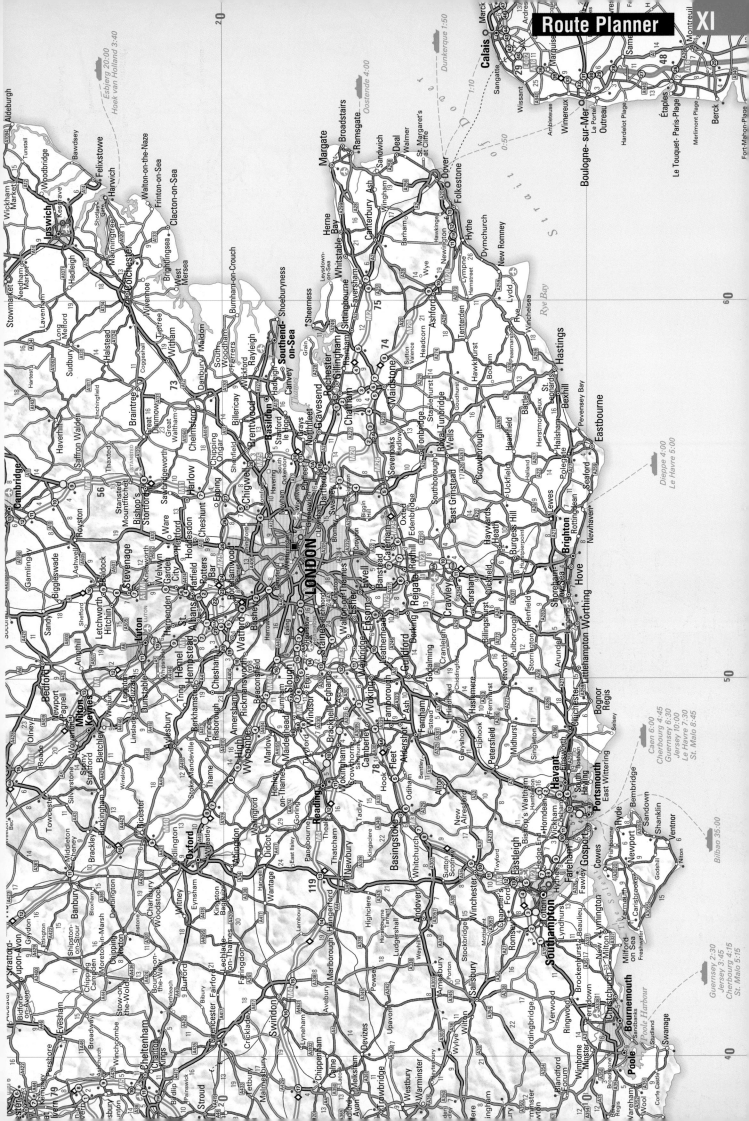

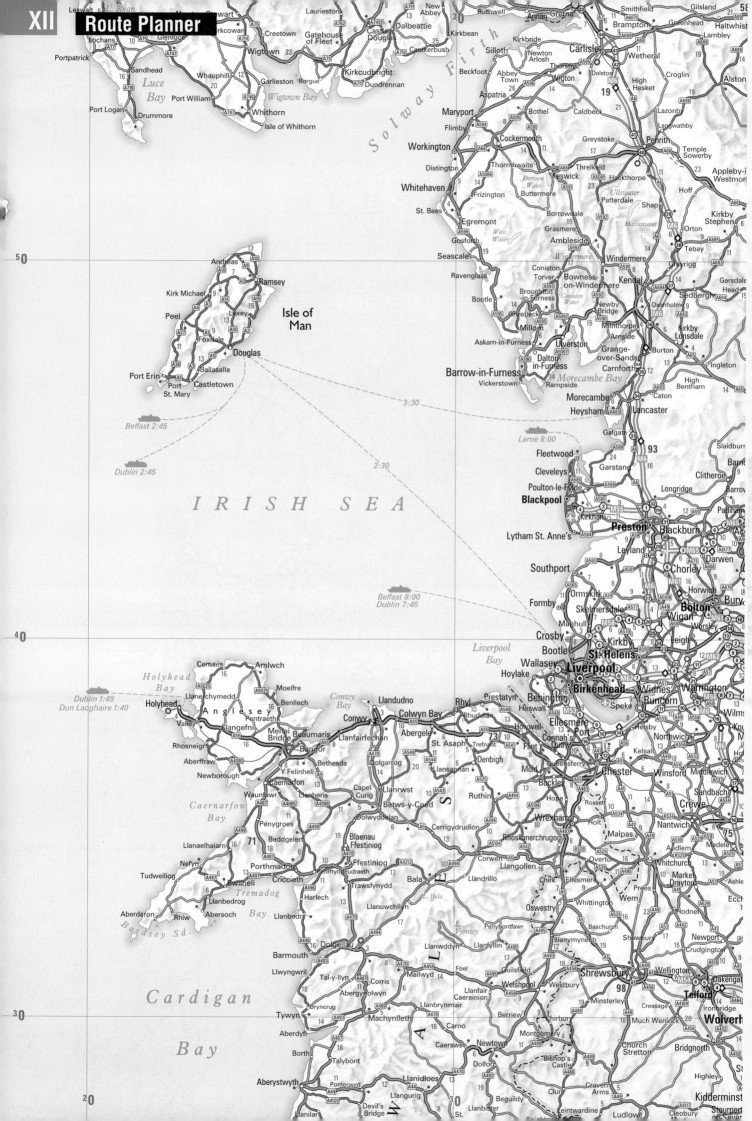

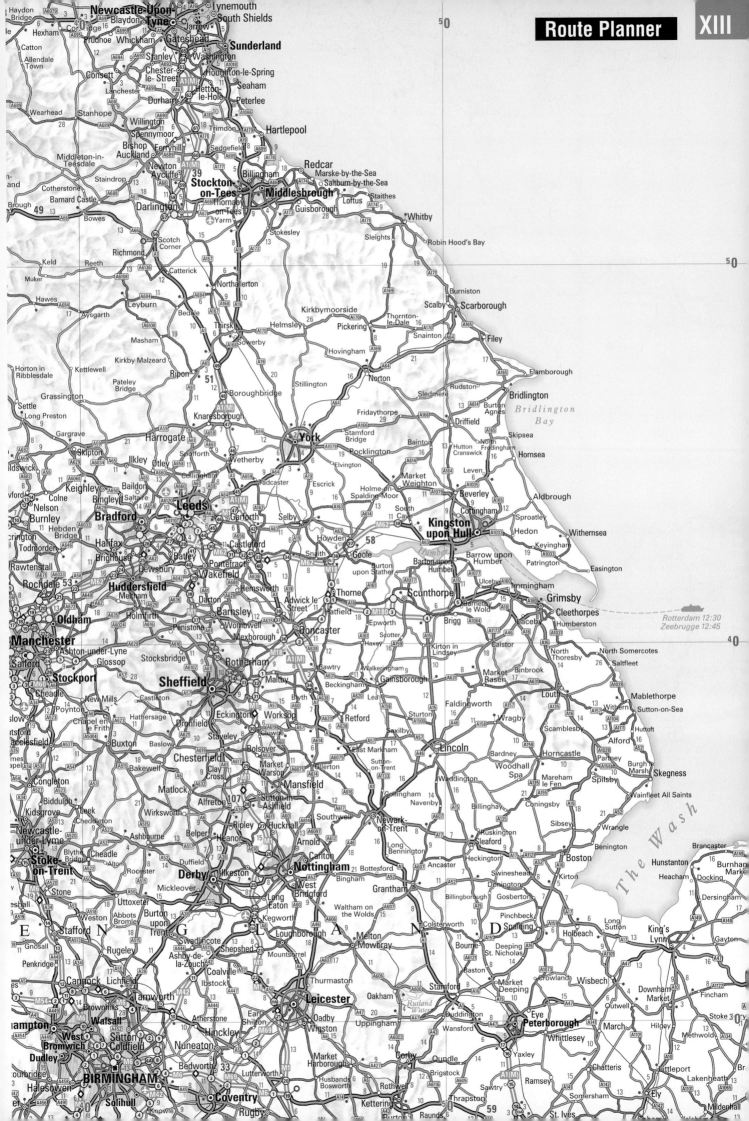

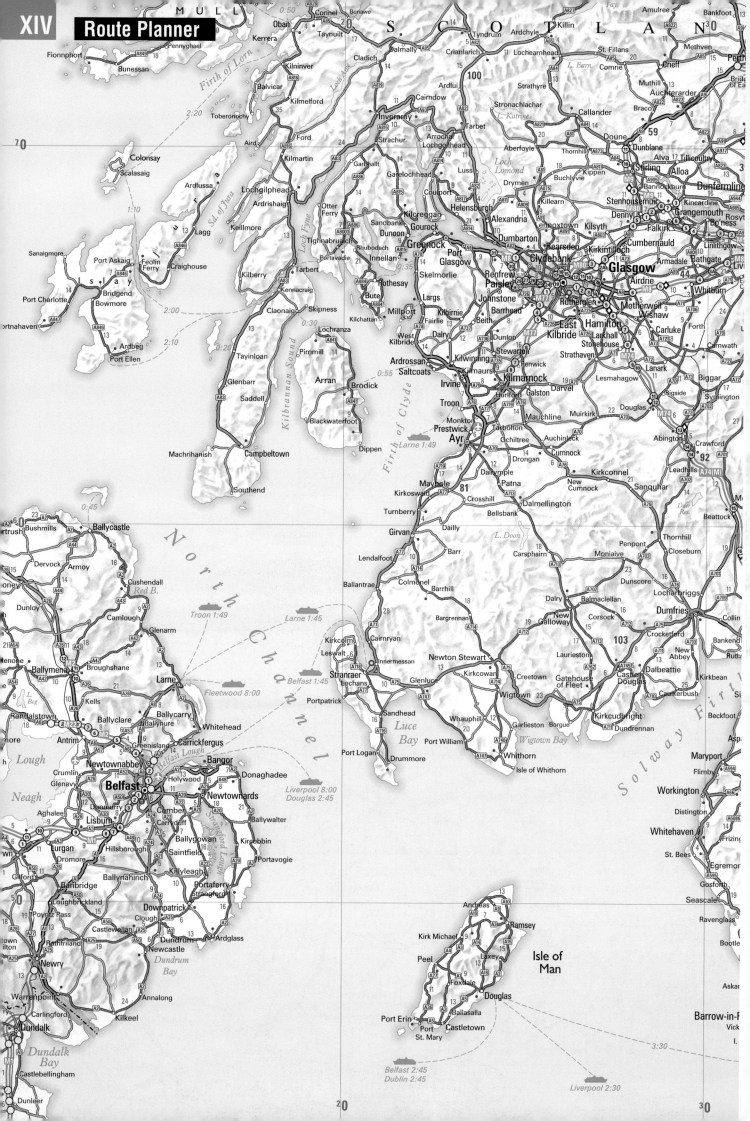

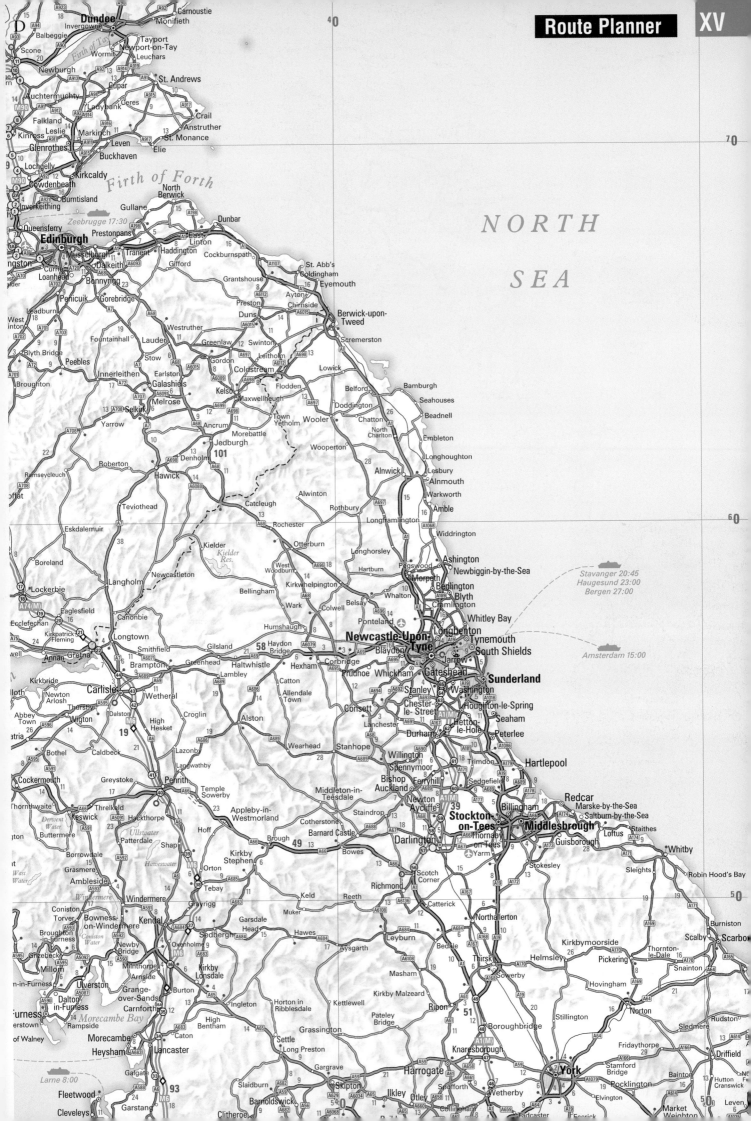

D

NORTH

SEA

*Firth of Forth*

*Firth of Tay*

*Morecambe Bay*

Dundee
Edinburgh
Newcastle-Upon-Tyne
Sunderland
Middlesbrough
Stockton-on-Tees
York
Carlisle
Kendal
Lancaster
Harrogate

Zeebrugge 17:30
Stavanger 20:45
Haugesund 23:00
Bergen 27:00
Amsterdam 15:00
Larne 8:00

101
58
19
49
39
51
93

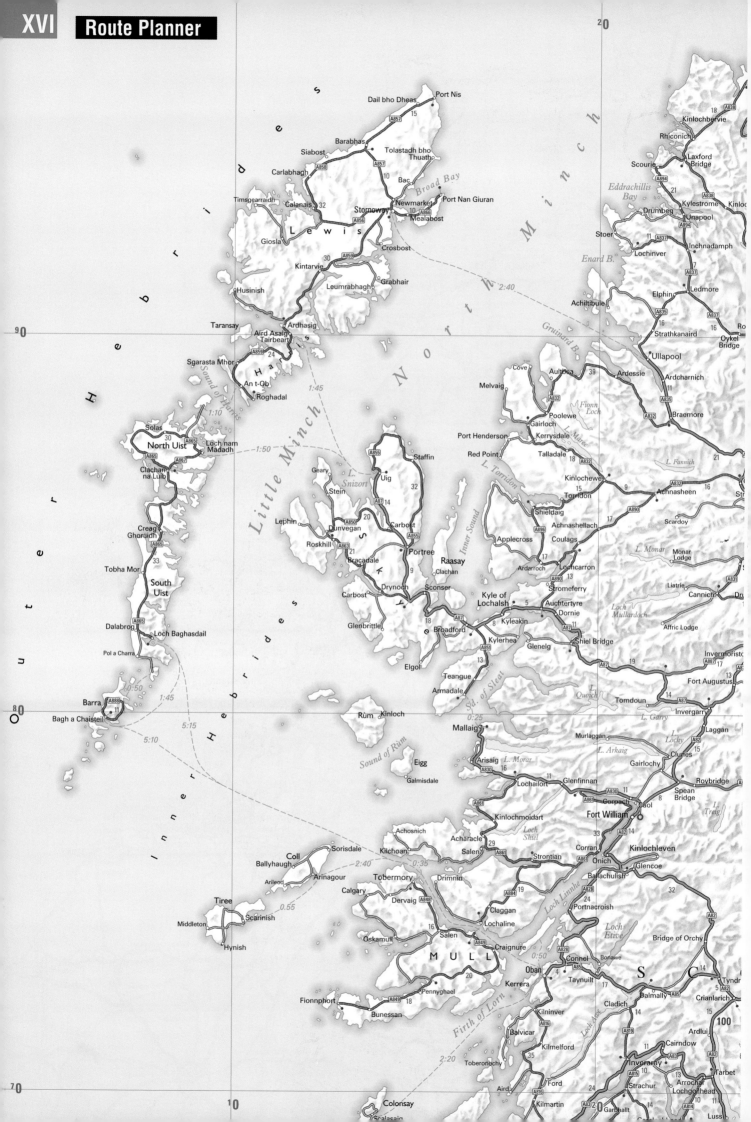

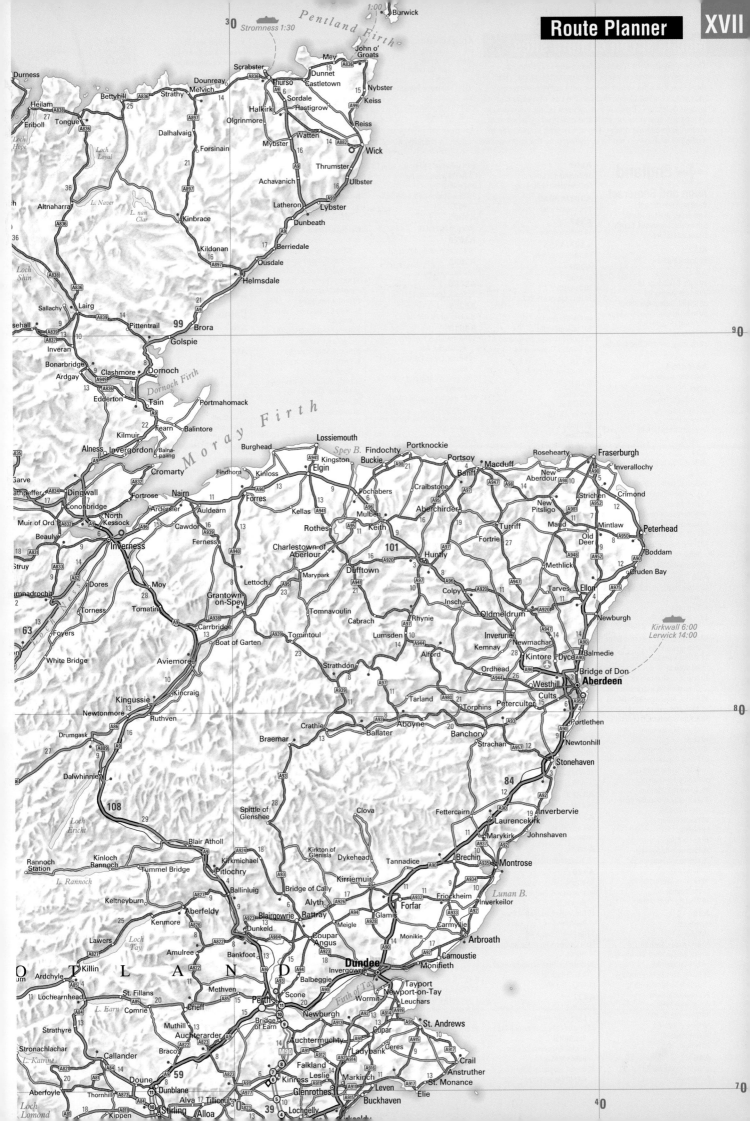

# Mobile speed camera sites

The vast majority of speed cameras used on Britain's roads are operated by safety camera partnerships. This table lists the sites where each safety camera partnership may enforce speed limits through the use of mobile cameras or detectors. These are usually set up on the roadside or a bridge spanning the road and operated by a police or civilian enforcement officer. The speed limit at each site (if available) is shown in red type, followed by the approximate location in black type.

## Abbreviations

| | |
|---|---|
| adj | adjacent |
| btwn | between |
| j/w | junction with |
| nr | near |
| NSL | National Speed Limit |
| o/s | outside |
| rdbts | roundabouts |
| twds | towards |

## England

### Avon and Somerset
Bath and North East Somerset, Bristol, North Somerset, Somerset, South Gloucestershire

**M32**
60 Bristol Stadium

**A4**
30 Bath, Newbridge Rd
30 Bristol, Anchor Rd
30 Bristol, Totterdown Bridge
50 Nr Keynsham, Keynsham Bypass jct A4175 Durley Hill
50 Portway
30 Portway, nr A4176 Bridge Valley Rd

**A4/B4054**
30 Bristol, Avonmouth Rd

**A30**
50 Cricket St Thomas
30 East Chinnock
40 Roundham
40 Yeovil, Hospital Rdbt
30 Yeovil, Sherborne Rd

**A37**
30 Bristol, Wells Rd (nr jct Airport Rd)
30 Bristol, Wells Rd (nr St Johns La)
60 Chilthorne Domer (east)
50 Emborough
30 Gurney Slade (north)
60 Lydford to Bristol
40 Lydford to Yeovil
60 Fosse Way, north of Podimore Rdbt
30 Shepton Mallet

**A38**
40 Aztec West, nr Bradley Stoke Way
30 Bathpool
40 Bedminster Down, Bridgwater Rd
40 Bristol, Bedminster Down Rd nr Bishopsworth Rd
30 Bristol, Bedminster Down Rd/West St
30 Bristol, Cheltenham Rd/ Gloucester Rd, nr Cranbrook Rd
30 Bristol, Gloucester Rd nr B4052 Ashley Down Rd
30 Bristol, Stokes Croft nr Bond St
40 Churchill – Langford
40 Cross
30 East Reach/Toneway
40 Filton, Gloucester Rd (north) nr B4057 Gypsy Patch Lane
50 Heatherton Grange
40,30 North Petherton
40 Patchway, Gloucester Rd nr Highwood Rd
50 Pawlett (south)
50 Redhill
30 Rooks Bridge (east)
30 Taunton – Bridgwater
30 Taunton, Wellington Rd (inbound)
30 Taunton, Wellington Rd (outbound)
30 West Huntspill (north)

**A39**
30 Ashcott
30 Bilbrook
30 Bridgwater, Bath Rd
30 Bridgwater, North Broadway nr A38 Taunton Rd
30 Bridgwater, North Broadway/ Broadway/Monmouth St
30 Chewton Mendip
40 Coxley nr Wells
50 Green Ore (south)
40 Horsey, Bath Rd
30 Quantock Rd
30 Walton

**A46**
60 Bath to Wickwar Rd
40 Dunkirk

**A303**
50 Buckland St Mary
50 Downhead nr Ilchester

**A303/A3088**
70 Cartgate Rdbt

**A357**
30 Templecombe

**A303/A358**
60 Southfields Rdbt

**A358**
60 Ashill
30 Donyatt
30 Henlade, nr M5 jct 25
40 Hornsbury Mill
40 Pen Elm (south)
30 Staplegrove Rd
30 Taunton Deane, Priorswood Rd
30 Taunton, Greenway Rd

**A359**
30 Mudford (north)

**A361**
30 Doulting
40 Durston
60 Frome Bypass
30 Othery
30 Pilton
30 West Pennard

**A362**
40 Terry Hill

**A367**
30 Bath, Green Park Rd
30 Bath, Bear Flat
30 Radstock, Wells Rd

**A369**
40 Abbots Leigh
60 Easton-in-Gordano, Martcombe Rd nr M5 jct 19

**A370**
30 Cleeve Village
30 Congresbury, Station Rd, Bristol Rd
30 Flax Bourton nr B3130
40 Long Ashton Bypass, Bristol End
50 West Wick, Somerset Avenue, west of M5 jct 21
30 Weston-super-Mare, Beach Rd
50 Weston-super-Mare, Herluin Way nr Winterstoke Rd
50 Weston-super-Mare, Somerset Avenue (central reservation)
50 Weston-super-Mare, Somerset Avenue, jct Moor Lane
30 Weston-super-Mare, Winterstoke Rd

**A371**
30 Draycott
40 Priestleigh (south)
30 Winscombe, Sidcot Lane nr jct A38,

**A372**
30 Aller

**A378**
30 Curry Rivel
40 Wrantage

**A403**
40 Avonmouth Docks

**A420**
30 Bristol, Lawrence Hill
30 Kingswood, Two Mile Hill Rd, Regent St
30 Old Market, nr Temple Way/ Bond St
30 Redfield, Church Rd
30 St George, Clouds Hill Rd/Bell Hill Rd
30 Warmley, High St London Rd nr A4175 Bath Rd
60 Wick, Tog Hill

**A432**
30 Bristol, Fishponds Rd nr B4048 Lodge Causeway
30 Bristol, Fishponds Rd nr B4469 Royate Hill
30 Bristol, Fishponds Rd with B4469 Muller Rd
30 Bristol, Stapleton Rd nr jct A4320 Easton Way

40 Hambrook, Badminton Rd nr A4174 Avon Ring Rd
40 Kendleshire
30 Yate, Station Rd/B4059 Stover Rd

**A3027**
30 North St/East St

**A3029**
40 Bristol, Avon Bridge

**A3039**
30 Devonshire Rd

**A3088**
30 Yeovil, Lysander Rd

**A3259**
30 Monkton Heathfield

**A4018**
30 Bristol, Black Boy Hill/ Whiteladies Rd
30 Bristol, Cribbs Causeway jct 17 M5
30 Bristol, Westbury Rd nr B4054 North View
30 Bristol, Whiteladies Rd into Queens Rd
30 Westbury on Trym, Falcondale Rd

**A4044**
30 Bristol, Temple Way/Redcliffe Way

**A4081**
40 Catbrain

**A4162**
30 Bristol, Sylvan Way/Dingle Rd/Canford Lane

**A4174**
50 Avon Ring Rd nr jct 1 M32
30 Bristol, Hartcliffe Way
40 Bristol, Hengrove Way/Airport Rd nr Creswicke Rd
30 Bromley Heath
50 Filton, Filton Rd/Avon Ring Rd nr Coldharbour Lane
40 Filton, Station Rd, nr Great Stoke Way

**A4320**
30 Bristol, at A4 Bath Rd nr Sandy Park Rd

**B3124**
30 Clevedon, Walton Rd

**B3130**
30 Nailsea, Stockway (north)/ Chapel Avenue
30,40 Wraxall

**B3133**
30 Clevedon, Central Way

**B3139**
30,40 Mark Causeway
30 Chilcompton

**B3140**
30 Berrow, Coast Rd

**B3141**
30 East Huntspill

**B3151**
30 Compton Dundon
30 Ilchester
30 St, Somerton Rd

**B3153**
30 Keinton Mandeville (east Somerton)

**B3170**
30 Shoreditch Rd

**B3440**
30 Weston-super-Mare, Locking Rd/Regent St/Alexandra Parade

**B4051**
30 Bristol, Park Row/Perry Rd

**B4054**
30 Sea Mills, Shirehampton Rd

**B4056**
30 Bristol, Northumbria Drive/ Linden Rd/Westbury Park
30 Bristol, Southmead Rd nr Pen Park Rd
30 Bristol, Southmead Rd nr Wellington Hill

**B4057**
30 Bristol, Crow Lane nr A4018 Passage Rd
30 Gypsy Patch Lane nr Hatchet Rd

50 Winterbourne Rd nr B4427 Gloucester Rd

**B4058**
30 Bristol, Frenchay Park Rd
30 Winterbourne, Winterbourne Hill/High St

**B4059**
30 Yate, Goose Green Way

**B4060**
30 Yate, Station Rd/Bowling Hill/Rounceval St

**B4061**
30 Thornbury, Bristol Rd

**B4465**
30 Mangotsfield, Broad St

**B4465**
30 Staple Hill, Staple Hill Rd/High St nr Forest Rd

**Unclassified**
30 Bristol, Bishopsworth, Whitchurch/Hareclive Rd
30 Bristol, Bishport Avenue
30 Knowle Bristol, Broadwalk
30 Bristol, Hengrove, Hawkfield Rd nr A4174 Hartcliffe Way
30 Bristol, Kingsway
30 Bristol, Long Cross, Lawrence Weston
30 Bristol, Stoke Hill/Stoke Rd nr Saville Rd, Clifton
30 Bristol, Sturminster Rd
30 Bristol, Whitchurch Lane nr Dundry Rd
30 Little Stoke, Little Stoke Lane
30 Taunton, Cheddon Rd
30 Taunton, Chestnut Drive
30 Taunton, Lisieux Way
30 Taunton, Trull Rd
30 Watergore, Harp Rd
30 Yeovil, Combe St

### Bedfordshire and Luton

**A5**
60 Battlesden
50 Dunstable
40 Hockcliffe
60 Kensworth

**A6**
30 Clapham, High St
60 Gravenhurst, Barton Rd
30 Kempston, Ampthill Rd
30 Luton, New Bedford Rd
60 Pulloxhill, Barton Rd
60 Silsoe

**A421**
50 Brogborough
60 Link Rd
60 Wootton, south of Fields Rd

**A428**
30 Bedford, Bromham Rd
30 Bedford, Goldington Rd

**A505**
30 Dunstable, Luton Rd
60 Leighton to Linslade Bypass
30 Luton, Dunstable Rd
30 Luton, Park Viaduct

**A507**
30 Ridgemont (East)
30 Ridgemont (West)
60 Shefford, nr New Rd

**A603**
30 Bedford, Cardington Rd
30 Bedford, Lovell Rd
40 Willington

**A1081**
30,40,70 Luton, Capability Green, Airport Way
30,60 Luton, Gipsy Lane, Airport Way

**A4146**
40 Leighton Buzzard, Billington Rd

**A5120**
40 Houghton Regis, Bedford Rd
40 Toddington, nr Jct 12 M1

**A5134**
30 Kempston, High St

**B530**
60 Houghton Conquest

**B1040**
30 Biggleswade, Potton Rd

**Unclassified**
30 Bedford, Cardington Rd
30 Bedford, Park Avenue
30 Bedford, Roff Avenue
30 Bedford, Wentworth Drive
30 Biggleswade, Potton Rd
30 Bromham, Stagsden Rd
30 Bromham, Village Rd
30 Clapham, Highbury Grange

30 Cranfield, High St
30 Eaton Bray, Bower Lane
30 Flitwick, Ampthill Rd
30 Flitwick, Dunstable Rd
30 Harlington, Goswell End Rd
30 Heath and Reach, Woburn Rd
30 Houghton Regis, Parkside Drive
30 Kempston, Bedford Rd
30 Kempston, High Street
30 Leighton Buzzard, Heath Rd
30 Luton, Crawley Green Rd
30 Luton, Grange Avenue
30 Luton, Leagrave High St
30 Luton, Marsh Rd
30 Luton, New Bedford Rd
30 Luton, Park Viaduct
30 Luton, Waller Avenue
30 Luton, Whitehorse Vale
30 Slip End, Markyate Rd
30 Upper Caldecote, Hitchin Rd

### Berkshire
see Thames Valley

### Buckinghamshire
see Thames Valley

### Cambridgeshire

**A10**
Littleport

**A14**
East/Westbound

**A15**
New Fletton, London Rd

**A141**
Clews Corner
Warboys
Wimblington/Doddington Bypass

**A142**
Soham Bypass
Witchford Bypass

**A505**
Whittlesford

**A605**
Elton, Bullock Rd
Kings Dyke

**A1073**
Eye Green, Peterborough Rd

**A1123**
Bluntisham, Needingworth Bypass
St Ives, Houghton Hill
Wiburton Village

**A1134**
Cambridge

**A1303**
Cambridge

**A1307**
Bartlow crossroads
Hills Rd
Linton Bypass

### Cheshire

**A50**
30 Grappenhall, Knutsford Rd
30 Knutsford, Manchester/Toft Rd
30 Warrington, Long Lane

**A54**
60 & 70   Ashton, Kelsall Rd

**A56**
40 Lymm, Camsley Lane

**A57**
40 Paddington, New Manchester Rd

**A523**
30 Poynton, London Rd

**A532**
30 Crewe, West St

**A533**
40 Middlewich, Booth Lane

**A537**
50 Macclesfield, Buxton Rd nr Wildboarclough

**A5019**
30 Crewe, Mill St

**A5032**
30 Whitby, Chester Rd

**A5034**
60 Mere, Mereside Rd

**A5104**
30 Chester, Hough Green

**B5071**
30 Crewe, Gresty Rd

**B5078**
30 Alsager, Sandbach Rd North

**B5082**
30 Northwich, Middlewich Rd

**B5132**
30 Ellesmere Port, Overpool Rd

**B5153**
30 Mill Lane/Hollow Lane (speed indicator sign)

**B5463**
30 Little Sutton, Station Rd

**B5470**
30 Macclesfield, Rainow Rd

**Unclasssified**
30 Burtonwood, Lumber Lane
30 Ellesmere Port, Overpool Rd
30 Fearnhead, Harpers Rd
30 Hough Green, Prescot Rd
30 Howley, Battersby Lane
40 Runcorn, Astmoor Rd
30 Runcorn, Boston Avenue
30 Runcorn, Clifton Rd
30 Runcorn, Halton Rd
30 Runcorn, Heath Rd
30 Runcorn, Northwich Rd
30 Runcorn, Warrington Rd
30 Vale Royal, Woodford Lane (St John's Drive)
30 Whitecross, Lovely Lane
30 Widnes, Birchfield Rd
30 Widnes, Hough Green Rd
40 Winsford, Bradford Rd

### Cleveland
Darlington, Hartlepool, Middlesbrough, Redcar and Cleveland

**A171**
50 Redcar, Charltons

**A172**
40 Middlesbrough, Morton Rd from crossroads to St Lukes
30 Middlesbrough, Morton Rd from Longlands to St Lukes
40 Middlesbrough, Stokesley – from Guisborough Rd jct to Captain Cooks Crescent

**A177**
50,60 Stockton, Durham Rd

**A178**
30 Seaton Carew, The Front

**A179**
30,40,50 Hartlepool, Easington Rd/Powlett Rd

**A689**
50 to 40  Hartlepool, from Sappers Corner

**B1380**
40 Middlesbrough, Ladgate Lane
30 Redcar, Eston

**Unclassified**
30 Hartlepool, Catcote Rd
40,30 Hartlepool, Coronation Drive
30 Hartlepool, Elwick Rd
30 Hartlepool, King Oswy Drive
30 Hartlepool, Owton Manor Lane and Wynyard Rd
30 Hartlepool, Oxford Rd
30 Hartlepool, Raby Rd
30 Hartlepool, Seaton Lane
30 Hartlepool, Station Lane
30 Hartlepool, Throston Grange Lane
30 Hartlepool, Winterbottom Avenue
30 Middlesbrough, Acklam Rd
40 Middlesbrough, Acklam Rd from Blue Bell to the Crematorium
30 Middlesbrough, Mandale Rd
30 Middlesbrough, Ormesby, Normanby Rd
30 Middlesbrough, Ormesby Rd
30 Middlesbrough, Trimdon Avenue
30 Redcar, Bankfields Rd
30 Redcar, Carlin How
30 Redcar, Church Lane
30 Redcar, Dormanstow, Broadway
30 Redcar, Flatts Lane
30 Redcar, Greenstones Rd
30,40 Redcar, Kirkleatham Lane
30 Redcar, Marske High St
30 Redcar, Normanby Rd
30 Redcar, Ormesby Bank
30 Redcar, Redcar Lane
30 Redcar, Redcar Rd
30 Redcar, Stanghow Rd
30 Redcar, West Dyke Rd
30 Stockton, Thornaby, Acklam Rd
40 Stockton, Bishopton Avenue
30 Stockton, Bishopton Rd West
30 Stockton, Thornaby, Cunningham Drive
30 Stockton, Darlington Lane
30 Stockton, Harrogate Lane
30 Stockton, Junction Rd

XVIII

30 Stockton, Thames Rd
30 Stockton, Thornaby Rd
30 Stockton, Whitehouse Rd
30 Stockton, Eaglescliffe, Yarm Rd

## Cumbria
### M6
70 Brunthwaite
70 Capplerigg
70 Cowperthwaite
70 Tebay
### A6
60 Garnett Bridge/Hollowgate
30 Kendal, Milnthorpe Rd
30 Kendal, Shap Rd
30 London Rd
30 Penrith, Scotland Rd
60 Thiefside
### A7
60 Westlinton Crossroads
### A65
30 Kendal, Burton Rd
40 Kirby Lonsdale, Devils Bridge
60 Kirkby Lonsdale, Hollin Hall to
  Hornsbarrow
### A66
60 Brigham/Broughton to Chapel
  Brow
60 Crackenthorpe
60 Dubwath/Bass Lake
60 Sandford Rd Ends
60 Troutbeck/Mungrisdale
60 Warcop, Brough Hill
### A69
60 Aglionby
60 Scarrow Hill
### A74
70 Kendal, Floriston
### A590
60 Bouth Rd Ends
60 Haverthwaite/Backbarrow
70 Heaves/Levens/Gilpin
60 Newlands
### A592
30,40 Rayrigg Rd
### A595
60 Broughton, Wreaks End
30 Carlisle, Wigton Rd
60 Red Dial, Greenhill Hotel
60 West Woodside/Curthwaite Jct
40 Whitehaven, Loop Rd
### A596
60 Micklethwaite
### A683
60 Middleton to Cautley
### A685
30 Kendal, Appleby Rd
### A686
60 Edenhall to Meathaw Hill
### A5087
30 Ulverston
### B5277
30 Grange, Lindale Rd
### B5299
40 Carlisle, Dalston Rd
### Unclassified
30 Carlisle, Durdar Rd / Blackwell
  Rd
30 Barrow in Furness, Abbey Rd
30 Barrow in Furness, Michelson Rd

## Derbyshire
### A6
30 Allestree
  Alvaston
  Alvaston to Raynesway
  Ashford in the Water
30 Bakewell
30 Belper
  Belper to Ambergate
  Buxton to Dove Holes
  Cromford
  Darley Dale
30 Derby, London Rd
  Dove Holes
  Dove Holes to Chapel
  Duffield
  Furness Vale to Newtown
  Homesford Cottage to Cromford
  Matlock
  Matlock Bath
  Milford to Belper
  Northwood
  Rowsley to Bakewell
  Shardlow to Derby
50 Taddington to Buxton
### A52
30 Derby, Ashbourne Rd
  East of Brailsford
40 Mackworth

---

Shirley Hollow
### A57
  Snake Rd
### A511
  Swadlincote, Ashby Rd East
### A514
  Hartshorne
30 Swadlincote
40 Swadlincote to Hartshorne
30 Ticknall
### A515
  Alsop-en-le-Dale
  Sudbury
### A516
  Derby, Uttoxeter New Rd
  Derby, Uttoxeter Rd
### A601
30 Derby, Abbey St
### A608
30 Heanor, Heanor Rd
30 Smalley
### A609
30 Ilkeston, Nottingham Rd
30 Kilburn to Horsley Woodhouse
  Stanley Common
### A610
40 Codnor Gate
### A615
  Tansley to Wessington
### A616
30 Clowne
30 Creswell
### A617
40 Bramley Vale
40 Glapwell to Pleasley
### A619
  Eastmoor
### A623
  Peak to Barmoor Clough
  Peak Forest
30 Stoney Middleton
### A624
50 Chunal to Little Hayfield
  Glossop
  Hayfield to Chinley
### A628
  Tintwistle to Boundary
### A632
30 Bolsover
  Hady to Calow
30 Matlock
### A5250
30 Derby, Burton Rd
30 Littleover, Burton Rd
### A6005
30 Draycott to Breaston
  Long Eaton, Derby Rd
  Spondon, Derby Rd
  Spondon, Nottingham Rd
### A6007
30 Codnor to Heanor
### A6096
30 Kirk Hallam, Ladywood Rd
### A6175
30 Holmewood
30 North Wingfield
### B600
  Somercotes
### B5010
  Sandiacre, Derby Rd
### B5353
30 Newhall, Park Rd
### B6019
  South Normanton
### B6051
30 Chesterfield, Newbold Rd
30 Newbold, Newbold Rd
### B6052
30 Whittington
### B6057
  Chesterfield, Sheffield Rd
### B6062
30 Chinley
### B6179
  Denby
30 Little Eaton
40 Lower Kilburn
50 Lower Kilburn to Little Eaton
30 Ripley to Marehay
### B6540
30 Long Eaton, Tamworth Rd
### Unclassified
  Bolsover, Shuttlewood Rd
30 Charlesworth, Long Lane
30 Chesterfield, Boythorpe Rd
30 Derby, Blagreaves Lane
30 Derby, Kedleston Rd
30 Derby, Stenson Rd
  Mickleover, Station Rd

---

30 Shardlow, London Rd
40 Stenson Fields, Stenson Rd
30 Swadlincote, Hearthcote Rd

## Devon and Cornwall
### A30
60 Chiverton Cross
70 Highgate (Eastbound)
70 Highgate Hill
40 Exeter, Sowton
60 Temple
### A38
70 Bittaford Straight, Wrangaton
70 Deep Lane
70 Lee Mill, Lee Mill On-slip
70 Lower Clicker Tor
70 Overbridge, Smithaleigh
70 Smithaleigh, Smithaleigh
  Overbridge
70 Wrangaton, Bittaford Straight
### A39
60 Barras Moor
30 Camelford, Valley Truckle
40 Perranarworthal, nr Truro
### A361
50 Barnstaple, Ashford
30 Barnstaple, Eastern Avenue
40 Braunton, Knowle
30 Braunton, Knowle (Westerland)
30 Wrafton
### A374
40 Plymouth, Plymouth Rd
  (Inbound)
40 Plymouth, Plymouth Rd
  (Outbound)
30 Torpoint, Anthony Rd
### A376
30 Ebford
30 Exmouth, Exeter Rd
### A377
30 Copplestone
30 Crediton, Western Rd
30 Exeter, Alphington Rd
### A379
30 Brixton Village
30 Paignton, Dartmouth Rd
30 Starcross
30 Starcross, The Strand
30 Teignmouth, Teignmouth Rd
30 Torquay, Babbacombe Rd
30 Yealmpton
### A380
40 Kingskerswell, Newton Rd
### A381
30 Newton Abbott, East St
### A385
30 Paignton, Collaton St Mary,
  Totnes Rd
30 Totnes, Ashburton Rd
### A386
60 Chubb Tor
30 Plymouth, Outland Rd
60 Plymouth, Roborough Down
40 Plymouth, Tavistock Rd
### A388
30,40 Callington, Kelly Bray
### A390
60 Penstraze
60 Sticker Bypass
### A394
40 Kenneggy Downs
### A396
30 Rewe
30 Stoke Canon, Exeter Rd
### A3015
30 Exeter, Topsham Rd
### A3047
30 St Ives, Carbis Bay
30 Camborne, Pool, Trevenson Rd
30 Camborne, Tuckingmill
### A3058
30 St Austell, Trewoon
### A3064
30 Plymouth, St Budeaux Bypass
### A3075
60 Newquay, Rosecliston
### B3165
30 Raymonds Hill, Crewkerne Rd
### B3174
30 Ottery St Mary, Barrack Rd
### B3183
30 Exeter, Heavitree Rd
30 Exeter, New North Rd
### B3212
30 Exeter, Dunsford Rd
30 Exeter, Pinhoe Rd
### B3213
30 Wrangaton Village, nr South
  Brent

---

### B3233
30 Barnstaple, Bickington Rd
### B3250
30 Plymouth, North Hill
### B3284
60 Liskey
30 Perranporth, Liskey
30 Chudleigh, Station Hill
### B3396
30 Plymouth, Milehouse Rd
### Unclassified
30 Avonwick Village
30 Buddle Lane, Exwick Rd
30 Elburton, Haye Rd
30 Exeter, Exwick Lane
30 Fraddon Village, nr Indian
  Queens
60 Goss Moor, Castle an Dinas
30 Honicknowle, Shakespeare Rd
30 Ivybridge, Exeter Rd
40 Monkton Village
30 Paignton, Colley End Rd
30 Paignton, Preston Down Rd
30 Plymouth, Beacon Park Rd
30 Plymouth, Church Hill
30 Plymouth, Devonport Rd
30 Plymouth, Eggbuckland Rd
30 Plymouth, Glen Rd
30 Plymouth, Honicknowle Lane
30 Plymouth, Honicknowle Lane
  (North)
30 Plymouth, Lipson Rd
30 Plymouth, Mannamead Rd
30 Plymouth, Molesworth Rd
30 Plymouth, North Prospect Rd
40 Plymouth, Novorrossiysk Rd
30 Plymouth, Pomphlett Rd
30 Plymouth, St Levan Rd
30 Plymouth, Southway Drive
30 Plymouth, Tamerton Foliot Rd
30 Plymouth, Union St
30 Plymouth, Weston Park Rd
30 Plymouth, Wolseley Rd (Both
  Directions)
30 Plympton, Glen Rd
30 St Judes, Grenville Rd
30 Saltash, Callington Rd

## Dorset
### A30
70 Babylon Hill
40 Shaftesbury, Long Cross
### A31
40 Winterbourne Zelston
### A35
60 Bridport, Cross Dykes nr
  Whiteway Cross
60 btwn Morden Mill & Slepe
70 Christchurch Bypass
60 Dorchester, Friary Press
60 Kingston Russell
60 Lyndhurst Rd
50 Lytchett Minster, Bakers Arms
30 Poole, Upton Rd
40 Sea Rd South
60 Vinney Cross
### A37
60 Holywell Cross
60 Long Ash Lane
60 Staggs Folly
### A338
50 Cooper Dean, Wessex Way
70 Spur Rd
### A348
40 Bear Cross, Ringwood Rd
### A349
40 Poole, Gravell Hill
### A350
50 Holes Bay Rd to Sterte Rd
60 Poole Rd
70 Poole, Upton Country Park
30 Stourplane, Shashton Rd
### A352
30 Wool, Dorchester Rd
### A354
30 Dorchester Rd Manor Rdbt
40 Redlands, Dorchester Rd
60 Ridgeway Hill, Dorchester Rd
30 Upwey, Dorchester Rd
30 Weymouth, Buxton Rd
30 Whitechurch, Winterbourne
### B3065
30 Poole, Pinecliff Rd
30 Poole, The Avenue
### B3073
40 West Parley, Christchurch Rd
30 Wimborne, Oakley Hill
### B3074
30 Poole, Higher Blandford Rd
### B3081
30 Ebblake, Ringwood Rd

---

### B3082
60 Bradbury Rings, Blandford Rd
### B3092
n/a Gillingham, Colesbrook
### B3157
30 Lanehouse Rocks Rd
50 Limekiln Hill
30 Portesham
### B3369
30 Poole, Sandbanks Rd
30 Poole, Shore Rd
### Unclassified
30 Blandford, Salisbury Rd
30 Bournemouth, Branksome Wood
  Rd
30 Bournemouth, Crabery Avenue
30 Bournemouth, Littledown
  Avenue
30 Bournemouth, Southbourne
  Overcliff Drive
30 Poole, Old Wareham Rd
30 Portland, Weston Rd
40 Staplehill, Wimbourne Rd
30 Upton, Poole Rd
30 Weymouth, Chickerell Rd

## Essex
### A12
  Braintree, Overbridge nr
  Kelvedon Interchange
### A13
30 Castle Point, High St (Hadleigh
  twds London)
30 Leigh on Sea, London Rd
  Southend, Bournes Green Chase
  Southend, North Shoebury
  Southend, Southchurch
  Boulevard
### A113
30 Epping, High Rd
### A120
  Little Bentley, Pellens Corner
### A121
30 Epping, High Rd
30 Loughton, Goldings Hill (j/w
  Monkchester Close)
  Loughton, High Rd
  Waltham Abbey, Farm Hill Rd
  Waltham Abbey, Sewardstine Rd
### A126
30 Grays, London Rd
30 Tilbury, Montreal Rd
### A128
  Chipping Ongar, High St
30 Ingrave/Herongate, Brentwood
  Rd
### A129
30 Basildon, Crays Hill
  Billericay, Southend Rd
  Rayleigh, London Rd
30 Wickford, London Rd
  Wickford, Southend Rd
### A130
30 Canvey Island, Long Rd
  South Benfleet, Canvey Way
### A133
30 Elmstead Market, Clacton Rd
### A133
  Little Bentley, Colchester Rd
### A134
40 Great Horkesley, Nayland Rd
### A137
30 Lawford, Wignall St
### A1016
30 Chelmsford, Waterhouse Lane
### A1017
30 Sible Hedingham, Swan St
### A1023
30 Brentwood, Chelmsford Rd
30 Brentwood, London Rd
30 Brentwood, Shenfield Rd
### A1025
40 Harlow, Third Avenue
### A1060
  Little Hallingbury, Lower Rd
### A1090
30 Purfleet, London Rd
30 Purfleet, Tank Hill Rd
### A1124
30 Colchester, Lexden Rd
### A1158
30 Westcliff on Sea, Southbourne
  Grove
### A1168
30 Loughton, Rectors Lane
### A1169
40 Harlow, Southern Way
### A1205
40 Harlow, Second Avenue

---

### B170
  Loughton, Roding Lane
  Chigwell, Chigwell Rise
### B172
  Theydon Bois, Coppice Row
### B173
  Chigwell, Lambourne Rd
### B184
40 Great Easton, Snow Hill
### B186
30 South Ockendon, South Rd
### B1002
30 Ingatestone, High St
### B1007
30 Billericay, Laindon Rd
40 Chelmsford, Stock Rd
### B1007
30 Billericay, Stock Rd
### B1008
30 Chelmsford, Broomfield Rd
### B1013
30 Hawkwell, High Rd
30 Hawkwell, Main Rd
30 Hockley/Hawkwell, Southend
  Rd
  Rayleigh, High Rd
30 Rayleigh, Hockley Rd
### B1014
30 South Benfleet, Benfleet Rd
### B1018
30 Latchingdon, The St
30 Maldon, The Causeway
### B1019
30 Hatfield Peveral, Maldon Rd
### B1021
  Burnham on Crouch, Church Rd
### B1022
30 Colchester, Maldon Rd
30 Heckfordbridge, Maldon Rd
30 Maldon, Colchester Rd
30 Tiptree Heath, Maldon Rd
### B1027
30 Clacton-on-Sea, Valley Rd/Old
  Rd
30 St Osyth, Pump Hill
40 Wivenhoe, Brightlingsea Rd
### B1028
30 Wivenhoe, Colchester Rd
30 Wivenhoe, The Avenue
### B1033
30 Kirby Cross, Frinton Rd
### B1335
40 South Ockendon, Stifford Rd
### B1352
  Harwich, Main Rd
### B1383
30 Newport, London Rd
  Stansted Mountfitchet,
  Cambridge Rd
### B1389
30 Witham, Colchester Rd
30 Witham, Hatfield Rd
### B1393
30 Epping, Palmers Hill
### B1441
30 Clacton-on-Sea, London Rd
### B1442
30 Clacton-on-Sea, Thorpe Rd
### B1464
30 Bowers Gifford, London Rd
### Unclassified
40 Alresford, St Osyth Rd
30 Aveley, Purfleet Rd
  Aveley, Romford Rd
30 Barstable, Sandon Rd
30 Basildon, Ashlyns
40 Basildon, Cranes Farm Rd (j/w
  Honywood Rd)
  Basildon, Crayhill Rd
30 Basildon, Felmores
  Basildon, London Rd, Wickford
30 Basildon, Vange Hill Drive
30 Basildon, Whitmore Way
30 Basildon, Wickford Avenue
30 Billericay, Mountnessing Rd
30 Bowers Gifford, London Rd
30 Braintree, Coldnailhurst Avenue
30 Brentwood, Eagle Way (nr j/w
  Clive Rd twds Warley Rd)
30 Buckhurst Hill, Buckhurst
  Way/Albert Rd
30 Canvey Island, Dovervelt Rd
30 Canvey Island, Link Rd
30 Canvey Island, Thorney Bay Rd
  Chadwell St Mary, Brentwood
  Rd
30 Chadwell St Mary, Linford Rd
30 Chadwell St Mary, Riverview
30 Chelmsford, Baddow Rd
30 Chelmsford, Chignall Rd
30 Chelmsford, Copperfield Rd
  Chelmsford, Galleywood Rd

XIX

30 Chelmsford, Longstomps Avenue
30 Clacton-on-Sea, St Johns Rd
30 Clacton, Kings Parade
30 Clacton, Marine Parade East
30 Colchester, Abbots Rd
30 Colchester, Avon Way
30 Colchester, Bromley Rd
Colchester, Ipswich Rd
30 Colchester, Old Heath Rd
30 Colchester, Shrub End Rd
30 Corringham, Southend Rd
30 Corringham, Springhouse Rd
Danbury, Maldon Rd
30 Daws Heath, Daws Heath Rd
30 Eastwood, Green Lane j/w Kendal Way
30 Eastwood, Western Approaches j/w Rockall
30 Grays, Blackshots Lane
30 Grays, Lodge Lane
Grays, London Rd (nr Angel Rd)
Grays, London Rd (nr Bransons Way)
40 Harlow, Abercrombie Way, twds Southern Way
40 Harlow, Howard Way
30 Hullbridge, Coventry Hill
30 Laindon, Durham Rd
30 Laindon, Nightingales
30 Laindon, Wash Rd
Langdon Hills, High Rd
30 Leigh on Sea, Belton Way East
30 Leigh on Sea, Belton Way West
30 Leigh on Sea, Blenhelm Chase
30 Leigh on Sea, Grand Parade/Cliff Parade
30 Leigh on Sea, Hadleigh Rd
30 Leigh on Sea, Highlands Boulevard
30 Leigh on Sea, Manchester Drive
30 Leigh on Sea, Mountdale Gardens
30 Leigh on Sea, Western Rd
30 Loughton, Alderton Hill
30 Loughton, Loughton Way
Loughton, Valley Hill
30 Maldon, Fambridge Rd
30 Maldon, Holloway Rd
30 Maldon, Mundon Rd
30 Pitsea, Rectory Rd
30 Prittlewell, Kenilworth Gardens
30 Prittlewell, Prittlewell Chase
30 Rayleigh, Bull Lane
Rayleigh, Downhall Rd
30 Rayleigh, Trinity Rd, nr Church Rd
30 Rochford, Ashingdon Rd
30 Rochford, Rectory Rd
Rush Green, St Osyth Rd
30 Shoeburyness, Ness Rd
30 South Woodham Ferrers, Hullbridge Rd
30 South Woodham Ferrers, Inchbonnie Rd
30 Southend on Sea, Lifstan Way
30 Southend, Bournemouth Park Rd
30 Southend, Hamstel Rd
Southend, Western Esplanade/ Westcliff on Sea
30 Southend, Woodgrange Drive j/w Sandringham Rd
30 Springfield, New Bowers Way
30 Stanford le Hope, London Rd
30 Tendring, Burrs Rd, Clacton
Tendring, Harwich Rd, Wix Arch Cottages to Cansey Lane
Theydon Bois, Piercing Hill
30 Thorpe Bay, Barnstaple Rd
30 Thorpe Bay, Thorpe Hall Avenue
Waltham Abbey, Paternoster Hill
Weeley Heath, Clacton Rd
30 West Thurrock, London Rd
30 Westcliff on Sea, Chalkwell Avenue
30 Westcliff on Sea, Kings Rd
30 Wickford, Radwinter Avenue
30 Witham, Powers Hall End
30 Witham, Rickstones Rd

## Gloucestershire
**A38**
40 Twigworth
**A40**
60 Andoversford
50 Churcham
60 Farmington
40 Gloucester Rd
60 Hampnett
60 Hazleton
60 Northleach
60 The Barringtons
60 Whittington Area

**A46**
30 Ashchurch
40 North of Nailsworth
**A48**
60 Stroat
**A417**
70 Burford Jct
40 Corse, Gloucester Rd
70 Dartley Bottom
40 Lechlade
30 Maisemore
40 North of Hartpury
**A419**
40 Oldends Lane to Stonehouse Court
**A429**
60 Nr Bourton-on-the-Water
40 Fossebridge
**A430**
40 Hempsted Bypass
**A435**
60 Colesbourne
**A436**
60 Jct with B4068
**A4013**
30 Gloucester, Princess Elizabeth Way
30 Gloucester, Princess Elizabeth Way (Arle)
**A4019**
50 Uckington
**A4136**
40 Brierley
40 Coleford, Lower Lane
40 Harrow Hill
40 Little London
**A4151**
40 Steam Mills
**A4173**
30 nr St Peters School
**B4008**
40 Hardwicke, Bristol Rd south of Tesco rdbt
30 Olympus Park Area, Bristol Rd
30 Stonehouse, Gloucester Rd
**B4060**
30 Katharine Lady Berkeley's School
**B4215**
50 South east of Rudford
50 South of Newent Bypass
**B4221**
30 Picklenash School
40 Kilcot Village
**B4226**
60 Speech House
**B4228**
30 Coleford, Old Station Way
40 Perrygrove
**B4231**
30 Bream, Coleford Rd
**B4633**
30 Cheltenham, Gloucester Rd
**Unclassified**
30 Gloucester, Abbeymead Avenue
30 Gloucester, Barrow Hill
30 Gloucester, Chesterton Lane
30 Gloucester, Parkend Fancy Rd
30 Gloucester, St Georges Rd
30 Gloucester, Swindon Lane
30 Gloucester, Wymans Lane
30 Lydney, Highfield Rd
40 Minchinhampton Common
30 Siddington
40 Tewkesbury, Gloucester Rd

## Greater Manchester
**A6**
Manchester, Stockport Rd
Salford, Manchester Rd
**A34**
Manchester, Birchfield Road
**A49**
Marus Bridge, Warrington Rd
**A56**
Bury, Bury New Rd
Bury, Walmersley Rd
Bury, Whalley Rd
**A57**
Manchester, Hyde Rd
Salford, Liverpool Rd
Tameside, Manchester Rd
**A58**
Bury, Bury & Bolton Rd
Bury, Rochdale Rd
**A62**
Manchester, Oldham Rd
Oldham, Oldham Rd
Oldham, Oldham Way

**A575**
Salford, Walkden Rd
**A580**
Salford, East Lancashire Rd
**A627**
Oldham, Chadderton Way
Oldham, Ashton Rd
**A662**
Manchester, Ashton New Rd
**A663**
Oldham, Broadway
**A664**
Manchester, Rochdale Rd
**A665**
Bury, New Rd
Bury, Radcliffe New Rd
**A666**
Bolton, Blackburn Rd
Bolton, St Peter's Way
Salford, Manchester Rd
**A667**
Bury, Ringley Rd West
**A5103**
Manchester, Princess Parkway/ Road
**A6010**
Manchester, Alan Turing Way
**A6044**
Prestwich, Sheepfoot Lane
Prestwich, Hilton Lane
**A6053**
Radcliffe, Dumers Lane
**A6104**
Blackley, Victoria Avenue
**B6196**
Ainsworth, Church Street
Ainsworth, Cockey Moor Rd
**B6213**
Tottington, Turton Rd
**B6214**
Greenmount, Brandlesholme Rd
Holcombe, Helmshore Rd
Holcombe Brook, Longsight Rd
**B6226**
Horwich, Chorley Old Rd
**Unclassified**
Ashton on Mersey, Ashton Lane
Bolton, Chorley Old Rd
Bolton, Hardy Mill Rd
Bolton, Hulton Lane
Bolton, Lever Park Avenue
Bolton, Plodder Lane
Bolton, Stitch Mi Lane
Bredbury, Ashton Rd
Bury, Croft Lane
Bury, Higher Lane
Bury, Stand Lane
Bury, Walshaw Rd
Manchester, Blackley New Rd
Manchester, Kingsway
Manchester, Mancunian Way
Oldham, Abbey Hills Rd
Oldham, Manchester Rd
Rochdale, Bagslate Moor Rd
Rochdale, Broad Lane
Rochdale, Bury Old Rd
Rochdale, Caldershaw Rd
Rochdale, Edenfield Rd
Rochdale, Halifax Rd
Rochdale, Heywood Old Rd
Rochdale, Hollin Lane
Rochdale, Manchester Rd
Rochdale, Queens Park Rd
Rochdale, Shawclough Rd
Rochdale, Smithybridge Rd
Rochdale, Todmorden Rd
Rochdale, Wildhouse Lane
Salford, Belvedere Rd
Salford, Langley Rd
Stockport, Birdhall Lane
Stockport, Bridge Lane
Stockport, Buxton Rd
Stockport, Chester Rd
Stockport, Councillor Lane
Stockport, Dialstone Lane
Stockport, Harrytown
Stockport, Jacksons Lane
Stockport, Kingsway
Stockport, Longhurst Lane
Stockport, Marple Rd
Stockport, Sandy Lane
Stockport, Schools Hill
Stockport, Strines Rd
Stockport, Styal Rd
Stockport, Wellington Rd North
Tameside, Mossley Rd
Tameside, Mottram Old Rd
Tameside, Mottram Rd
Tameside, Stamford Rd
Tameside, Stamford Street
Trafford, Church Rd

Trafford, Edge Lane
Trafford, Glebelands Rd
Trafford, Hope Rd
Trafford, Mosley Rd
Trafford, Norris Rd
Trafford, Park Rd
Trafford, Seymour Grove
Trafford, Warburton Lane
Trafford, Westinghouse Rd
Wigan, Almond Brook Rd
Wigan, Bickershaw Lane
Wigan, Bolton Rd
Wigan, Chaddock Lane
Wigan, Chorley Rd
Wigan, Crow Orchard Rd
Wigan, Lily Lane
Wigan, Newton Rd
Wigan, Pemberton Rd
Wigan, Scot Lane
Wigan, Victoria Street
Wigan, Wigan Rd

## Hampshire and Isle of Wight
**A3**
70 Liphook
30 Petersfield
**A27**
40 Fareham (east and west bound)
30 Fareham, Portchester Rd (eastbound)
30 Fareham, Portchester Rd (westbound)
30 Fareham, The Avenue
**A30**
30 Blackwater
30 Hook, London Rd
**A32**
30 West Meon
**A33**
50 Basingstoke
50 Chandlers Green
50 Sherfield on Loddon
50 Southampton, Millbrook Rd (western end of Flyover to Regents Park Rd)
30 West Quay Rd
**A35**
50 Totton
**A325**
40 East Hampshire (south)
70 Farnborough, Farnborough Rd
40 Rushmoor (north)
**A334/B2177**
40 Wickham
**A335**
30 Eastleigh
**A337**
30 New Forest (east)
40 New Forest (west)
**A338**
40 New Forest (south and north bound)
**A339**
60 Lasham
**A340**
30 Basingstoke
30 Tadley
**A343**
30 Hurstbourne Tarrant
**A3020**
40 Blackwater Rd
**A3024**
40 Bursledon Rd
30 Northam Rd to southern river bank
**A3054**
30 Newport, Fairlee Rd
30 Wootton / Lushington Hill, High St
**B3037/A335**
30,40 Eastleigh
**B3055**
40 New Forest
**B3395**
30 Sandown, Culver Parade
**Unclassified**
30 Apse Heath
30 Binstead Hill
30 Brading, High St New Rd
30 East Cowes, Victoria Grove/ Adelaide Grove
30 East Cowes, York Avenue
40 Fareham, Western Way
30 Fleet, Reading Rd South
30 Newport, Staplers Rd/Long Lane
30 Portsmouth, Northern Rd (north and south bound)
40 Southampton, The Avenue (north and south bound)

30 Swanick, Swanick Lane
50 Totton / Redbridge, Redbridge Flyover

## Herefordshire
see West Mercia

## Hertfordshire
**A119**
30 Hertford, North Rd
**A409**
30 Bushey, Heathbourne Rd
**A411**
30 Bushey, London Rd
30 Elstree, Barnet Lane
30 Watford, Hempstead Rd
**A414**
40 Hemel Hempstead, St Albans Rd
40 Hertford, Hertingfordbury Rd
**A505**
30 Hitchin, Cambridge Rd
**A600**
30 Hitchin, Bedford Rd
**A602**
40 Hitchin, Stevenage Rd
40 Stevenage, Broadhall Way
40 Stevenage, Monkswood Way
**A1000**
40 Bishops Stortford, Barnet Rd
**A1057**
40 Hatfield, St Albans Rd West
30 St Albans, Hatfield Rd
**A1170**
30 Turnford, High Rd
**A4125**
40 South Oxhey, Sandy Lane
30 Watford, Eastbury Rd
**A4145**
30 Watford, Tolpits Lane
**A4147**
30 Hemel Hempstead, Leverstock Green Rd
**A4251**
30 Bourne End, London Rd
**A5183**
30 St Albans, Frogmore Rd
**A6141**
60 Letchworth, Letchworth Gate
**B156**
30 Cheshunt, Goffs Lane
**B176**
30 Cheshunt, High Street
**B197**
30 Baldock, London Rd
30 Stevenage, North Rd
**B462**
30 Bushey, Aldenham Rd
**B487**
30 Harpenden, Hatching Green, Redbourn Lane
40 Hemel Hempstead, Queensway
**B488**
40 Tring, Icknield Way
**B556**
30 Potters Bar, Mutton Lane
**B1004**
30 Bishops Stortford, Windhill
**B1197**
30 Hertford, London Rd
**B1502**
30 Hertford, Stansted Rd
**B4505**
30 Bovingdon, Chesham Rd
**B4630**
30 St Albans, Watford Rd
**B5378**
30 Elstree, Borehamwood, Allum Lane
40 London Colney, Shenleybury
**B6426**
30 Hatfield, Cavendish Way
**Unclassified**
30 Cheshunt, Hammond St Rd
30 Hemel Hempstead, Bennetts End Rd
30 Hemel Hempstead, High Street Green
30 Hemel Hempstead, Long Chaulden
30 Hoddesdon, Essex Rd
30 Letchworth, Pixmore Way
30 Royston, Old North Rd
30 South Oxhey, Hayling Rd
30 St Albans, Sandpit Lane
30 Stevenage, Clovelly Way
30 Stevenage, Grace Way
40 Stevenage, Gresley Way
30 Watford, Radlett Rd
30 Watford, Whippendell Rd

30 Welwyn Garden City, Heronswood Rd
30 Welwyn Garden City, Howlands

## Humberside
**East Riding of Yorkshire, Hull, North East Lincolnshire, North Lincolnshire**
**M180**
NSL North Lincolnshire, West of River Trent
**A18**
NSL North East Lincolnshire, Barton St Central
NSL North East Lincolnshire, Barton St North
NSL North East Lincolnshire, Barton St South
30 North Lincolnshire, Wrawby
**A63**
50 East Riding, Melton
40 Hull, Castle St
40 Hull, Daltry St Flyover
**A161**
30 Belton
**A163**
30 Holme on Spalding Moor
**A164**
30 Leconfield
**A165**
30 Beeford
40 East Riding, Coniston
30 Freetown Way
40 Holderness Rd
30 Skirlaugh
**A180**
NSL Great Coates Jct
**A614**
40 Holme on Spalding Moor
30 Middleton on the Wolds
NSL Shiptonthorpe, north of rdbt
NSL Shiptonthorpe, south of rdbt
**A1033**
40 Thomas Clarkson Way
30 Thorngumbald, Main St
30 Withernsea
**A1077**
30 Barton
**A1079**
50 Barmby Moor
30 Bishop Burton
30 Hull, Beverley Rd (Desmond Ave to Riverdale Rd)
40 Hull, Beverley Rd (Sutton Rd to Mizzen Rd)
**A1084**
30 Brigg, Bigby High Rd
**A1174**
30 Dunswell
30 Woodmansey
**B1206**
30 Barrow, Wold Rd
**B1230**
40 Gilberdyke
40 Newport
**B1398**
40 Greetwell
**Unclassified**
30 Ashby, Grange Lane South
30 Ashby, Messingham Rd
30 Belton, Westgate Rd
30 Beverley, Hull Bridge Rd
30 Bilton, Main Rd
30 Bridlington, Kingsgate
30 Bridlington, Quay Rd/St John's St
30 Broughton, High St
30 Cleethorpes, Clee Rd
30 East Halton, College Rd
30 Goole, Airmyn Rd
30 Grimsby, Cromwell Rd
30 Grimsby, Great Coates Rd
30 Grimsby, Laceby Rd
30 Grimsby, Louth Rd
30 Grimsby, Waltham Rd
30 Grimsby, Weelsby Rd
30 Hessle, Beverley Rd
30 Hornsea, Rolston Rd
30 Howden, Thorpe Rd
30 Hull, Anlaby Rd
40 Hull, Boothferry Rd
30 Hull, Bricknell Avenue
40 Hull, Greenwood Avenue
30 Hull, Hall Rd
30 Hull, John Newton Way/Bude Rd
30 Hull, Leads Rd
30 Hull, Marfleet Lane
30 Hull, Marfleet Lane/Marfleet Avenue
30 Hull, Priory Rd
30 Hull, Saltshouse Rd

40 Hull, Spring Bank West
30 Hull, Wawne Rd
30 Humberston, Tetney Rd
30 Immingham, Pelham Rd
NSL Laceby Bypass
30 Preston, Station Rd
30 Scunthorpe, Ashby Rd
30 Scunthorpe, Cambridge Avenue
30 Scunthorpe, Cottage Beck Rd
40 Scunthorpe, Doncaster Rd
30 Scunthorpe, Luneburg Way
40 Scunthorpe, Queensway
30 Scunthorpe, Rowland Rd
30 South Killingholme, Top Rd
30 Yaddlethorpe, Moorwell Rd

## Kent and Medway

**A2**
70 Canterbury
60 Dover, Guston
70 Dover, Lydden
40 Medway, London Rd

**A20**
70,40 Dover, Dover Rd/Archcliffe
40,50 Tonbridge and Malling, London Rd

**A21**
70 Sevenoaks Bypass
60 Tonbridge and Malling, Castle Hill
60 Tunbridge Wells, Key's Green

**A25**
30 Sevenoaks, Seal Rd

**A26**
40 Tonbridge and Malling, Maidstone Rd

**A28**
40 Ashford, Ashford Rd

**A224**
30 Sevenoaks, Tubs Hill

**A225**
30 Sevenoaks, Sevenoaks Rd

**A226**
50 Gravesham, Rochester Rd/Gravesend Rd through Chalk
50 Gravesham, Rochester Rd/Gravesend Rd through Shorne
40 Gravesham, Rochester Rd/Gravesend Rd through Higham

**A227**
30 Gravesham, through Culverstone Green
40 Gravesham, through Istead Rise
30 Gravesham, through Meopham Green

**A228**
40 Medway, Ratcliffe Highway

**A229**
50 Maidstone, Bluebell Hill
40,30 Maidstone, Linton Rd/Loose Rd
30 Medway, City Way
40 Tunbridge Wells, Angley Rd (Hartley Rd)

**A249**
70 Maidstone, Chalky Rd/Rumstead Lane, South St
70 Swale, Chestnut St

**A253**
30 Thanet, Canterbury Rd West

**A256**
70 Dover
30 Dover, London Rd
40 Thanet, Haine Rd

**A258**
50 Dover, Dover Rd

**A259**
40 Shepway
60 Shepway, Guldeford Lane
30 Shepway, High St

**A262**
30 Ashford, High St

**A268**
30 Tunbridge Wells, Queen St

**A289**
50 Medway, Medway Tunnel
70 Medway, Wainscott Bypass

**A290**
30 Canterbury, Blean

**A291**
30 Canterbury, Canterbury Rd

**A292**
30 Ashford, Mace Lane

**A2033**
30 Shepway, Dover Rd

**A2990**
60 Canterbury, Old Thanet Way

**B258**
30 Dartford, Barn End Lane

**B2015**
40 Nettlestead Green, Maidstone Rd

**B2017**
30 Tunbridge Wells, Badsell Rd

**B2067**
60 Ashford, Ashford Rd
30 Ashford, Woodchurch Rd

**B2071**
30 Shepway, Littlestone Rd

**B2097**
30 Rochester, Maidstone Rd

**B2205**
30 Swale, Mill Way

**Unclassified**
30 Canterbury, Mickleburgh Hill
30 Canterbury, Rough Common Rd
30 Dartford, Ash Rd/Hartley Rd
30 Gravesham, Sole St
30 Medway, Beechings Way
30 Medway, Esplanade
30 Medway, Maidstone Rd
30 Medway, St End Rd
30 Medway, Walderslade Rd
30 Sevenoaks, Ash Rd/Hartley Rd
30 Swale, Lower Rd
30 Thanet, Shottendane Rd

## Lancashire

**A6**
40 Broughton, Garstang Rd (north of M55)
30 Chorley, Bolton Rd
30 Fulwood, Garstang Rd (south of M55)
30 Fulwood, Garstang Rd, north of Blackpool Rd
30 Lancaster, Greaves Rd
50 Lancaster, Scotforth Rd nr Burrow Lane Bailrigg
30 Preston, North Rd
30 Preston, Ringway

**A56**
30 Colne, Albert Rd
30 Colne, Burnley Rd
30 Nelson, Leeds Rd

**A59**
60 Gisburn, Gisburn Rd
50 Hutton, Liverpool Rd
30 Preston, New Hall Lane

**A65**
40 Lancaster, Cowan Bridge

**A570**
40 Scarisbrick, Southport Rd, Brook House Farm

**A581**
40 Ulnes Walton, Southport Rd

**A583+A5073**
30 Blackpool, Whitegate Drive/Waterloo Rd

**A583+B5266**
30 Blackpool, Church St/Newton Drive

**A584**
30 Blackpool, Promenade
30 Lytham, West/Central Beach
30 Warton, Lytham Rd

**A584+A587**
30 Blackpool, Promenade/Fleetwood Rd

**A587**
30 Blackpool, East/North Park Drive
30 Cleveleys, Rossall Rd/Crescent East

**A588**
60 Pilling, Head Dyke Lane
60 Wyre, Lancaster Rd, Cockerham at Gulf Lane

**A666**
30 Darwen, Blackburn Rd
30 Darwen, Bolton Rd nr Cross St
30 Darwen, Duckworth St

**A671**
30 Read, Whalley Rd

**A674**
30 Cherry Tree, Preston Old Rd

**A675**
50 Belmont, Belmont Rd (south of village)
50 Darwen, Belmont Rd, north of Belmont Village
60 Withnell, Bolton Rd (Dole Lane to Calf Hey Bridge)

**A680**
40 Edenfield, Rochdalee Rd

**A682**
60 Barrowford, Gisburn Rd nr Moorcock Inn

**B2015**
40 Crawshawbooth, Burnley Rd
60 Gisburn, Gisburn Rd
60 Gisburn, Long Preston Rd

**A683**
30 Lancaster, Morecambe Rd

**A5073**
30 Blackpool, Waterloo Rd

**A5085**
30 Lane Ends, Blackpool Rd

**A5209**
30 Newburgh, Course Lane/Ash Brow

**A6068**
50 Barrowford, Barrowford Rd

**A6114**
30 Burnley, Casterton Avenue

**A6177**
50 Haslingden, Grane Rd West of Holcombe Rd
50 Hyndburn, Haslingden Rd/Elton Rd

**B5192**
30 Kirkham, Preston St

**B5251**
30 Chorley, Pall Mall

**B5254**
30 Lostock Hall, Leyland Rd/Watkin Lane
30 South Ribble, Leyland Rd

**B5256**
30 Leyland, Turpin Green Lane

**B5269**
40 Goosnargh, Whittingham Lane

**B6231**
30 Oswaldtwistle, Union St

**Unclassified**
60 Belmont, Egerton Rd
30 Blackburn, East Park Rd
30 Blackburn, Whalley Old Rd, west of Railway Bridge
30 Blackpool, Dickson Rd, Queens St to Pleasant St
30 Briercliffe, Burnley Rd
30 Darwen, Lower Eccleshill Rd
60 Galgate, Bay Horse Rd
30 Nelson, Netherfield Rd
30 Preston, Lytham Rd
30 Preston, St Georges Rd
30 St Anne's, Church Rd to Albany Rd, nr High School

## Leicestershire and Rutland

**A1**
70 Empingham, Great North Rd
70 Stretton, Great North Rd

**A5**
60 Hinckley, Watling St (B578 to M69)
50 Hinckley, Watling St (M69 to A47)
70 Sharnford, Watling St (Highcross to B4114)

**A6**
40 Birstall, Loughborough Rd
40 Leicester, Abbey Lane
30 Leicester, London Rd (Knighton Drive)
30 Loughborough, Derby Rd
40 Oadby, Glen Rd/Harborough Rd

**A47**
60 Barrowden, Peterborough Rd
60 Bisbrooke, Uppingham Rd
30 Earl Shilton, Hinckley Rd
40 Houghton on the Hill, Uppingham Rd
30 Leicester, Hinckley Rd
30 Leicester, Humberstone Rd
50 Morcott, Glaston Rd
50 Skeffington, Uppingham Rd
50 Tugby, Uppingham Rd

**A50**
70 Hemmington to Lockington
40 Leicester/Glenfield, Groby Rd/Leicester Rd
30 Woodgate

**A426**
30 Dunchurch, Rugby Rd
50 Dunton Bassett, Lutterworth Rd
40 Glen Parva, Leicester Rd
60 Lutterworth, Leicester Rd
60 Whetstone, Lutterworth Rd

**A444**
60 Fenny Drayton, Atherstone Rd
30 Twycross Village, Main St
60 Twycross, Norton Juxta

**A447**
60 Cadeby, Hinckley Rd
40 Ravenstone, Wash Lane

**A512**
30 Loughborough, Ashby Rd
40 Shepshed, Ashby Rd Central

**A563**
30 Leicester, Attlee Way
30 Leicester, Colchester Rd/Hungarton Boulevard
30 Leicester, Glenhills Way
40 Leicester, Krefield Way
30 Leicester, New Parks Way

**A594**
30 Leicester, St Georges Way

**A606**
60 Barnsdale, Stamford Rd
60 Leicester, Broughton/Old Dalby
60 Tinwell, Stamford Rd

**A607**
40 Leicester, Melton Rd
30 Melton, Norman Way
70 Thurmaston, Newark Rd
60 Waltham on the Wolds, Melton Rd
60 Waltham/Croxton Kerrial, Melton Rd

**A4304**
40 Market Harborough, Lubbenham Hill

**A5199**
30 Leicester, Welford Rd
30 Wigston, Bull Head St
30 Wigston, Leicester Rd

**A5460**
40 Leicester, Narborough Rd

**A6004**
30 Loughborough, Alan Moss Rd

**A6030**
30 Leicester, Wakerley Rd/Broad Avenue

**A6121**
30 Ketton, Stamford Rd

**B568**
30 Leicester, Victoria Park Rd

**B581**
30 Broughton Astley, Broughton Way

**B582**
30 Blaby, Little Glen Rd

**B590**
30 Hinckley, Rugby Rd

**B591**
60 Charley, Loughborough Rd

**B676**
60 Freeby, Saxby Rd

**B4114**
40 Enderby/Narborough, Leicester Rd/King Edward Avenue
30 Leicester, Sharnford

**B4616**
30 Leicester, East Park Rd

**B4666**
30 Hinckley, Coventry Rd

**B5003**
40 Norris Hill, Ashby Rd

**B5366**
30 Leicester, Saffron Lane

**B5350**
30 Loughborough, Foreset Rd
30 Loughborough, Nanpantan Rd

**Unclassified**
30 Barrow upon Soar, Sileby Rd
30 Blaby, Lutterworth Rd
30 Ibstock, Leicester Rd
30 Leicester, Fosse Rd South
30 Shepshed, Leicester Rd

## Lincolnshire

**A15**
60 Ashby Lodge
60 Aswarby

**A15-B1191**
60 Dunsby Hollow

**A16**
60 Boston, Boston Tytton Lane
40 Burwell
60 Deeping Bypass
60 Grainsby to Holton-le-Clay
60 North Thoresby

**A17**
60 Fleet Hargate
60 Hoffleet Stow
60 Moulton Common

**A50**
60 Thulston, London/Shardlow Rd

**A52**
60 Bridge End
60 Horbling and Swaton
60 Ropsley

**A153**
40 Billinghay
50 Tattershall

**A158**
50 Scremby to Candlesby

**A631**
60 Hemswell
60 West Rasen, Dale Bridge

**A6005**
40 Breaston to Long Eaton

**B1188**
30 Branston
60 Canwick, Highfield House
60 Potterhanworth

## London

**M11**
Chadwell

**M25**
Egham
Elmbridge, Byfleet
Hillingdon
Hillingdon, Colnbrook
Runneymeade
Spelthorne
Wraysbury

**A3**
Kingston Bypass
Wandsworth, Kingston Rd

**A4**
Hounslow, Brentford, Great West Rd
Hounslow, Great West Rd

**A5**
Barnet, Hendon Broadway
Brent, Edgware Rd

**A10**
Enfield, Great Cambridge Rd
Hackney, Stamford Hill

**A13**
Barking and Dagenham, Alfreds Way
Barking and Dagenham, Ripple Rd
Dagenham, Ripple Rd
Newham, Alfreds Way

**A20**
Bexley, Sidcup Rd
Bromley, Sidcup Bypass
Greenwich, Sidcup Rd

**A21**
Lewisham, Bromley Rd

**A22**
Croydon, Godstone Rd

**A40**
City of Westminster, Westway
Ealing, Perivale
Ealing, Western Avenue
Hammersmith and Fulham, Westway
Hillingdon, Ruislip, Western Avenue

**A110**
Enfield, Enfield Rd

**A124**
Newham, Barking Rd

**A205**
Richmond upon Thames
Richmond upon Thames, Upper Richmond Rd West

**A213**
Bromley, Croydon Rd

**A214**
Wandsworth, Trinity Rd

**A215**
Croydon, Beulah Hill

**A217**
Croydon, Garratt Lane

**A219**
Hammersmith and Fulham, Scrubs Lane

**A222**
Bromley, Bromley Rd

**A232**
Sutton, Cheam Rd

**A298**
West Barnes, Bushey Rd

**A312**
Hillingdon

**A315**
Hounslow, High St

**A406**
Barking and Dagenham, Barking Relief Rd
Barnet, North Circular Rd
Redbridge, Southend Rd

**A501**
Camden, Euston Rd

**A503**
Haringey, Seven Sisters Rd

**A3220**
Wandsworth, Latchmere Rd

**A4006**
Brent, Kenton Rd

**B178**
Barking and Dagenham, Ballards Rd

**B272**
Sutton, Foresters Rd

**B278**
Sutton, Green Lane

**B279**
Sutton, Tudor Drive

**Unclassified**
Barnet, Oakleigh Rd South
Bexley, Abbey Rd
Bexley, Bellegrove Rd
Bexley, Erith Rd
Bexley, Faraday Avenue
Bexley, King Harolds Way
Bexley, Lower Rd
Bexley, Penhill Rd
Bexley, Pickford Lane
Bexley, Well Hall Rd
Bexley, Woolwich Rd
Brent, Crest Rd
Brent, Hillside
Brent, Kingsbury Rd
Brent, Kingsbury, Fryent Way
Brent, Sudbury, Watford Rd
Brent, Wembley, Watford Rd
Brent, Woodcock Hill
Bromley, Beckenham Rd
Bromley, Burnt Ash Lane
Bromley, Crystal Palace Park Rd
Bromley, Elmers End Rd
Bromley, Main Rd
Bromley, Sevenoaks Way
Bromley, Wickham Way
City of Westminster, Great Western Rd
City of Westminster, Millbank
City of Westminster, Vauxhall Bridge Rd
Croydon, Addiscombe, Long Lane
Croydon, Brigstock Rd
Croydon, Coulsdon, Coulsdon Rd
Croydon, Coulsdon, Portnalls Rd
Croydon, Thornton Rd
Ealing, Greenford, Greenford Rd
Ealing, Horn Lane
Ealing, Lady Margaret Rd
Ealing, Ruislip Rd
Ealing, Southall, Greenford Rd
Ealing, Uxbridge Rd
Eastcote, Field End Rd
Enfield, Fore St
Forest Hill, Stanstead Rd
Forest Hill, Stanstead Rd
Greenwick, Beresford St
Greenwick, Court Rd
Greenwick, Creek Rd
Greenwick, Glenesk Rd
Greenwick, Rochester Way
Greenwick, Rochester Way
Greenwick, Woolwich Church St
Hackney, Clapton Common
Hackney, Seven Sisters Rd
Hackney, Upper Clapton Rd
Hammersmith and Fulham, Fulham Palace Rd
Hammersmith and Fulham, Uxbridge Rd
Hammersmith and Fulham, Westway
Haringey, Belmont Rd
Haringey, Bounds Green Rd
Haringey, Seven Sisters Rd
Haringey, White Hart Lane
Harrow, Alexandra Avenue
Harrow, Harrow View
Harrow, Harrow Weald, Uxbridge Rd
Harrow, Honeypot Lane
Harrow, Porlock Avenue
Harrow, Watford Rd
Havering, Chase Cross Rd
Havering, Eastern Avenue
Havering, Eastern Avenue East
Havering, Hall Lane
Havering, Hornchurch, Parkstone Avenue
Havering, Ockenden Rd
Havering, Romford, Brentwood Rd
Havering, Wingletye Lane
Hillingdon, Cowley, Cowley Rd
Hillingdon, Cowley, High Rd
Hillingdon, Harefield, Church Hill
Hillingdon, Hayes, Kingshill Avenue

Hillingdon, Hayes, Uxbridge Rd
Hillingdon, Northwood Hills, Joel St
Hillingdon, Park Rd
Hillingdon, Stockley Rd
Hillingdon, Uxbridge, Cowley Rd
Hounslow, Bedfont, Hatton Rd
Hounslow, Great West Rd
Hounslow, Hanworth, Castle Way
Hounslow, Harlington Rd West
Islington, Holloway Rd
Islington, Seven Sisters Rd
Islington, Upper St
Kensington and Chelsea, Barlby Rd
Kensington and Chelsea, Chelsea Embankment
Kensington and Chelsea, Chesterton Rd
Kensington and Chelsea, Holand Park Avenue
Kensington and Chelsea, Holland Villas Rd
Kensington and Chelsea, Kensington Park Rd
Kensington and Chelsea, Kensington Rd
Kensington and Chelsea, Ladbroke Grove
Kensington and Chelsea, Latimer Rd
Kensington and Chelsea, Royal Hospital Rd
Kensington and Chelsea, Sloane St
Kensington and Chelsea, St Helens Gardens
Kingston upon Thames, Kingston Rd
Kingston upon Thames, Manor Drive North
Kingston upon Thames, Richmond Rd
Lambeth, Atkins Rd
Lambeth, Brixton Hill
Lambeth, Brixton Rd
Lambeth, Clapham Rd
Lambeth, Herne Hill Rd
Lambeth, Kennington Park Rd
Lambeth, Kings Avenue
Lambeth, Streatham High Rd
Lewisham, Brockley Rd
Lewisham, Brownhill Rd
Lewisham, Burnt Ash Hill
Lewisham, Lee High Rd
Lewisham, Lewisham Way
Lewisham, Westwood Hill
Merton, Central Rd
Merton, Colliers Wood, High St
Merton, Hillcross Avenue
Merton, London Rd
Merton, Martin Way
Merton, Ridgway Place
Merton, West Barnes Lane
Newham, Barking Rd
Newham, Romford Rd
Newham, Royal Albert Dock, Spine Rd
Newham, Royal Docks Rd
North Dagenham, Rainham Rd
Redbridge, Hainault, Manford Way
Redbridge, Woodford Avenue
Redbridge, Woodford Rd
Richmond upon Thames, Kew Rd
Richmond upon Thames, Sixth Cross Rd
Richmond upon Thames, Uxbridge Rd
Southwark, Albany Rd
Southwark, Alleyn Park
Southwark, Brenchley Gardens
Southwark, Camberwell New Rd
Southwark, Denmark Hill
Southwark, Kennington Park Rd
Southwark, Linden Grove
Southwark, Old Kent Rd
Southwark, Peckham Rye
Southwark, Salter Rd
Southwark, Sunray Avenue
Streatham, Streatham High Rd
Sutton, Beddington Lane
Sutton, Cheam Common Rd
Sutton, Maiden Rd
Sutton, Middleton Rd
Tower Hamlets, Bow Rd
Tower Hamlets, Cambridge Heath Rd
Tower Hamlets, Homerton High Rd
Tower Hamlets, Manchester Rd
Tower Hamlets, Mile End Rd

Tower Hamlets, Upper Clapton Rd
Tower Hamlets, Westferry Rd
Waltham Forest, Chingford Rd
Waltham Forest, Hoe St
Waltham Forest, Larksall Rd
Wandsworth, Battersea Park Rd
Wandsworth, Garratt Lane
Wandsworth, Upper Richmond Rd
Woolwich, Woolwich Church St

## Merseyside

**A57**
Liverpool, East Prescot Rd
**A58**
St Helens, Prescot Rd
**A506**
Liverpool, Longmoor Lane
**A551**
Wirral, Leasowe Rd
**A553**
Wirral, Laird Street
**A561**
Liverpool, Speke Rd/Speke Boulevard
**A562**
Liverpool, Parliament Street/ Upper Parliament Street
**A572**
St Helens, Common Rd
**A580**
Liverpool, Townsend Avenue
St Helens, East Lancashire Rd
**A5038**
Sefton, Southport Rd/Liverpool Boundary to Oxford Rd
Sefton, Southport Rd/Oxford Rd to Northfield Rd
**A5080**
Liverpool, Bowring Park Rd/Roby Rd
**A5098**
Liverpool, Hornby Rd
**Unclassified**
Liverpool, Great Homer Street
Liverpool, Green Lane
Liverpool, Lower House Lane/ Dwerry House Lane
Liverpool, Muirhead Avenue
Liverpool, Netherfield Rd North
Liverpool, Utting Avevnue East
Sefton, Park Lane
Wirral, New Chester Rd

## Norfolk

**A10**
Stow Bardolph
Tottenhill/Watlington
**A11**
Attleborough Bypass
Ketteringham
Roundham
Snetterton
Wymondham/Bestthorpe
**A47**
East Winch
Emneth
Honington/Easton
Lingwood/Acle
Mautby/Halvergate
Narborough
Postwick
Pullover Rdbt
Scarning
Swaffham/Sporle
Terrington St John
Tuddenham
Wendling/Framsham
**A140**
Aylsham
Dickleburgh Moor
Erpingham
Long Stratton/Tivetshall St Mary
Newton Flotman
Newton Flotman/Saxlingham Thorpe
Norwich, Harford Bridge
Roughton village
Scole Bypass
St. Faiths
**A143**
Billingford/Brockdish
**A148**
Bodham
Fakenham Bypass
King's Lynn, Grimston Rd
Pretty Corner
Thursford

**A149**
Caister Bypass
Catfield
Catfield/Potter Heigham
Hunstanton
Kings Lynn/Nth Runcton
Knights Hill
Little Snoring
Roughton (N and S Repps)
Sandringham
Wayford Bridge East
Wayford Bridge West/ Smallburgh

## Northamptonshire

**A5**
60 DIRFT to County Boundary
60 Norton/Whilton Crossroads
30/40 Towcester Racecourse to A43
**A6**
60 Burton Latimer Bypass
**A14**
70 Kelmarsh
70 Kelmarsh Junctions 7-10
**A43**
60 Laxton Turn to A47 Duddington
60 Mawsley to A14 Junc 8 (inc Mawsley Spur)
70 Towcester to M1 Junc 15a
**A45**
60 M1 Junc 16 to Weedon
60 Stanwick to Raunds
**A361**
60 Byfield to Chipping Warden
**A422**
60 Brackley West to A43
**A428**
60 East Haddon
30/60 Great Houghton to Yardley Hastings
**A508**
30 Northampton, Plough Gyratory
30 Northampton, St Georges Avenue to Holly Lodge Rd
30 Northampton, St Peters Way to St Georges Avenue
30/60 Stoke Bruerne to A5
70 Wootton Flyover to M1 Junc 15
**A509**
60 Wellingborough to Isham
**A605**
40/60 Thrapston to Warmington
**A4256**
30 Daventry, Eastern Way
**A4500**
40/60 Great Billing to Earls Barton
30 Northampton, Abington Park to York Rd
30 Northampton, Park Avenue to Booth Lane South
30 Northampton, Weedon Rd to Duston Rd
**A5076**
40 Mere Way
40 Northampton, Great Billing Way South
**A5193**
30/40 Wellingborough, London Rd
**A6003**
50/60 Kettering to Corby
**A6014**
40/60 Corby, Oakley Rd
**B569**
50 Irchester to Rushden
**B576**
60 Desborough to Rothwell
**B4038**
30/60 Kilsby, Rugby Rd
**B4525**
40/60 Welsh Lane
**B5385**
60 Watford to West Haddon
**Unclassified**
30 Brackmills Industrial Estate
30 Northampton, Grange Rd

## Northumbria
**Gateshead, Newcastle-upon-Tyne, North Tyneside, Northumberland, South Tyneside, Sunderland**

**A1**
60 Berwick Bypass, Dunns Jct (N)
**A68**
60 Colt Crag
**A69**
60 Haltwhistle Bypass
70 Hexham, Two Mile Cottage

**A167**
30 Newcastle, Stamfordham Rd
**A182**
30 Sunderland, Houghton Rd
**A183**
30 Broadway, Chester Rd
**A186**
40 Denton Burn, West Rd
30 Newcastle, City Rd at Beamish House
40 Newcastle, West Rd at Turret Rd
30 Newcastle, Westgate Rd at Elwick Row
**A189**
70 Cramlington, High Pitt
70 Cramlington, Spine Rd
30 South Gosforth, Haddricks Mill Rd
**A191**
30 Benton, Whitley Rd
30 Fenham, Springfield Rd
**A193**
30 Wallsend, Church Bank
**A194**
40 Simonside, Newcastle Rd
**A196**
30 Blackclose Bank
**A690**
30 Sunderland, Durham Rd
50 Sunderland, Stoneygate, Houghton, Durham Rd
**A692**
30 Gateshead, Church Street
**A694**
30 Gateshead, Rowlands Gill, Station Rd
40 Gateshead, Winlaton Mill (Spa Well Rd)
**A695**
60 Gateshead, Crawcrook Bypass
40 Prudhoe Jct B6395

30 Belsay Village
60 Blaxter Cottages
60 Kirkwhelpiington
60 Otterburn Monkridge
**A697**
60 Morpeth, Heighley Gate
60 Wooperton
**A1018**
30 Sunderland, Ryhope Rd, Irene Avenue
**A1058**
30 Newcastle, Jesmond Rd at Akenside Terrace
**A1068**
30 Amble Ind Est
**A1147**
30 Stakeford, Gordon Terrace
**A1171**
30 Cramlington, Dudley Lane
**A1290**
30 Sunderland, Southwick, Keir Hardie Way
**A1300**
30 South Tyneside, Nook, Prince Edward Rd
**A6085**
40 Newcastle, Lemington Rd
**A6127**
30 Gateshead, Barley Mow, Durham Rd
**B1286**
30 Sunderland, Burdon Rd
30 Sunderland, Tunstall Bank
**B1288**
40 Gateshead, Leam Lane/A195
**B1296**
30 Gateshead, Sheriffs Highway, QE Hospital
30 Gateshead, Sheriffs Highway, Split Crow Rd
**B1297**
30 South Tyneside, Blackett Street
**B1298**
30 South Tyneside, Boldon Colliery, New Rd
**B1301**
30 South Tyneside, Dean Rd (John Clay St)
30 South Tyneside, Laygate, Eglesfield Rd
**B1316**
30 North Shields, Lynn Rd
**B1318**
30 North Tyneside, Seaton Burn, Bridge St
**B1404**
30 Sunderland, Seaham Rd

**B1426**
30 Gateshead, Felling, Sunderland Rd
**B1505**
30 North Tyneside, West Moor, Great Lime Rd
**B6315**
30 Gateshead, High Spen, Hookergate Lane
**B6317**
30 Gateshead, Ryton, Main Rd
30 Gateshead, Whickham Highway
**B6318**
60 Whitchester, Military Rd
60 Whittington Fell, Military Rd
**B6324**
40 Newcastle, Stamfordham Rd southeast of Walbottle Rd
**B6918**
30 Newcastle, Woolsington Village
**Unclassified**
30 Ashington, Barrington Rd
30 Ashington, Station Rd
30 Benton, Coach Lane
30 Gateshead, Askew Rd West
30 Gateshead, Blaydon, Shibdon Bank
30 Gateshead, Chopwell, Mill Rd
30 Gateshead, Crawcrook, Greenside Rd
30 Gateshead, Felling, Watermill Lane
30 Gateshead, Whickham, Fellside Rd
30 Hebburn, Campbell Park Rd
70 Nafferton
60 Newcastle, Dinnington Rd North Brunton Lane
40 Newcastle, West Denton Way east of Hawksley
30 North Shields, Norham Rd
50 South Tyneside, Harton Lane
40 South Tyneside, Hedworth Lane, Abingdon Way
30 Sunderland, Allendale Rd
30 Sunderland, Burdon Lane
40 Sunderland, Farringdon, North Moor Lane
40 Sunderland, North Hylton Rd, Castletown Way
30 Sunderland, Parkway at Barrington Drive
30 Sunderland, St Aidens Terrace at the Vicarage
30 Sunderland, Silksworth Rd, Rutland Avenue
30 Sunderland, Springwell Rd
30 Sunderland, Warwick Terrace
30 Wallsend, Battle Hill Drive
30 Whiteleas, Nevinson Avenue

## Nottinghamshire

**A1(T)**
70 East Markham (Northbound)
**A52(T)**
40 Clifton Boulevard
**A60**
30 Carlton in Lindrick
30 Mansfield, Nottingham Rd
60 Market Warsop/Cuckney Nottingham, Bellar Gate to Woodthorpe Drive
Nottingham, London Rd
50 Ravenshead
30 South, Nottingham
**A609**
30 Nottingham, Ilkeston Rd/ Wollaton Rd/Russell Drive
**A610**
30 Nottingham, Bobbers Mill
**A611**
30 Annelsey, Derby Rd
30 Nottingham, Hucknall Rd
**A612**
30 Southwell, Nottingham Rd
**A614**
60 Arnold, Burnt Stump
**A617**
40 Mansfield, Chesterfield Rd South
**A620**
40 Retford, Welham Rd
**A631**
50 Beckingham Bypass
50 Beckingham, Flood Plain Rd
50 Beckingham, nr Wood Lane
60 Gringley to Beckingham, nr Mutton Lane
50 West of Beckingham

**A6005**
30 Nottingham, Castle Boulevard/ Abbey Bridge/Beeston Rd
**A6008**
30 Nottingham, Canal St
**A6130**
30 Nottingham, Gregory Boulevard
30 Nottingham, Radford and Lenton Boulevards
**A6200/A52**
30 Nottingham, Derby Rd
**B679**
30 West Bridgford, Wilford Lane
**B682**
30 Nottingham, Sherwood Rise/ Nottingham Rd/Vernon Rd
**B6004**
40 Arnold, Oxclose Lane
**B6010**
30 Giltbrook, Nottingham Rd
**B6011**
30 Hucknall, Annesley Rd/ Nottingham Rd/Portland Rd
**B6020**
30 Rainworth, Kirklington Rd
**B6040**
30 Worksop, Retford Rd
**B6166**
30 Newark on Trent, Lincoln Rd/Northgate
**B6326**
40 Newark on Trent, London Rd
**Unclassified**
30 Newark, Balderton, Hawton Lane
30 Nottingham, Beechdale Rd/Wigman Rd
30 Nottingham, Bestwood Park Drive
Nottingham, Radford Boulevard/Lenton Boulevard
30 Nottingham, Ridge Way/Top Valley Drive

## Oxfordshire
see Thames Valley

## Shropshire
see West Mercia

## Somerset
see Avon and Somerset

## South Yorkshire

**A18**
60 Doncaster, Slay Pits to Tudworth, Epworth Rd
40 Doncaster, Carr House Rd/Leger Way
**A57**
40,60 Anston, Sheffield Rd/ Worksop Rd
60 Rotherham, Worksop Rd
60 Sheffield, Mosborough Parkway
**A60**
60 Tickhill, Doncaster Rd
30,60 Tickhill, Worksop Rd
**A61**
30 Cutting Edge, Park Rd
30,40 Sheffield, Chesterfield Rd/Chesterfield Rd South
30,40 Sheffield, Halifax Rd
30 Sheffield, Penistone Rd
**A614**
60 Thorne, Selby Rd
**A618**
40 Wales Bar, Mansfield Rd
**A628**
30,40 Barnsley, Cundy Cross to Shafton Two Gates
40,60 Barnsley, Dodworth
40 Penistone, Barnsley Rd
**A629**
60 Barnsley, Wortley
30 Burncross, Hallowed Rd/ Burncross Rd
40 Rotherham, New Wortley Rd
30,40 Rotherham, Wortley Rd/Upper Wortley Rd
**A630**
30,40,60 Dalton/Thrybergh, Doncaster Rd
30,40,60 Doncaster, Balby Flyover to Hill Top
40 Doncaster, Wheatley Hall Rd
40,50 Rotherham, Centenary Way
**A631**
40 Brinsworth, Bawtry Rd
30,40 Hellaby/Maltby, Bawtry Rd/Rotherham Rd
50 Rotherham, West Bawtry Rd

40 Wickersley/Brecks, Bawtry Rd

**A633**
30 Athersley South, Rotherham Rd
40 Monk Bretton, Rotherham Rd
30 Wath upon Dearne, Sandygate
30,40 Wombwell, Barnsley Rd

**A635**
30,40,60 Barnsley, Doncaster Rd/Saltersbrook Rd

**A638**
40 Doncaster, Bawtry Rd
40,50 Doncaster, Great North Rd/York Rd

**A6022**
30 Rotherham, Swinton

**A6101**
40 Sheffield, Rivelin Valley Rd

**A6102**
30,40 Hillsborough/Deepcar, Manchester Rd/Langsett Rd

**A6109**
40 Rotherham, Meadow Bank Rd

**A6123**
40 Rotherham, Herringthorpe Valley Rd

**A6135**
40 Sheffield, Ecclesfield Rd/Chapeltown Rd

**B6059**
30,40 Rotherham, Kiveton/Wales

**B6089**
40 Thorn Hill/Greasbrough, Greasbrough Rd/Greasbrough St

**B6096**
30 Barnsley, Wombwell to Snape Hill

**B6097**
30,60 Wath upon Dearne, Doncaster Rd

**B6100**
30 Barnsley, Ardsley Rd/Hunningley Lane

**B6411**
30 Thurnscoe, Houghton Rd

**B6463**
60 Tickhill, Stripe Rd

**Unclassified**
30 Armthorpe, Hatfield Lane/Mill St
30 Armthorpe, Nutwell Lane
30 Barnsley, Pogmoor Rd
30 Bolton upon Dearne, Dearne Rd
30 Doncaster, Melton Rd/Sprotbrough Rd
30 Doncaster, Urban Rd
30,60 Edlington/Warmsworth, Broomhouse Lane/Springwell Lane
40,60 Finningley, Hurst Lane
30 Grimethorpe, Brierley Rd
30,60 Rotherham, Fenton Rd
30,40 Rotherham, Haugh Rd
30 Rotherham, Kilnhurst Rd
30 Stiainforth, Station Rd
40 Wath upon Dearne, Barnsley Rd
30 Wheatley, Thorne Rd

## Staffordshire

**A5**
60 A5127 to A38 – Wall Island to Weeford Island
60,70,60,30 btwn A34 Churchbridge and The Turf Pub Island (B4154)
50,40 from A38 to Hints Lane
70 from A461 to A5127 (Muckley Corner Island to Wall Island Lichfield/Tamworth)
60,70,60 Hanney Hay/Barracks Lane Island to Muckley Corner Island
50 M6 jct 12 to A460/A4601 Island
50,30 South Cannock, A460/A4601 to A34 Longford Island to A34 Bridgetown

**A34**
30 Cannock North, North of Holly Lane jct to A34/B5012 rdbt
30,50,30 Cannock South to County Boundary
30 Cannock South, A34 from south of jct of A5 Walstall Rd to north of jct with Jones Lane
40 Newcastle North, from Wolstanton Rd/Dimsdale Parade west Island to Milehouse Lane/B5367
30,40 Newcastle Rd btwn Hanford Island to London Rd Bowling Club

40 Newcastle South, Barracks Rd to Stoke City Boundary
70,40 Newcastle under Lyme to Talke, btwn Wolstanton Rd/Dimsdale Parade West Island to Jct of A500
30,40 Stafford South, from A449 jct to Acton Hill Lane Jct
40,30 Stone Rd from jct of Longton Rd/A5035 to Handford Island/A500
40,30 Stone Rd Redhill (A513/A34) island to Lloyds Island, Eccleshall Rd Talke, Jct A500 (Peacock Hay Rd) to Jct A5011

**A50**
30 Kidsgrove, btwn City Boundary and Oldcott Drive

**A51**
30,40,60 Lichfield, from A5127 Birmingham Rd to Heath Rd
50 Pasturefields, A51 from south of jct with Amerton Lane to south of Hoomill Lane
40,30 Rugeley North, from A51 jct with Bower Lane to island of A460 Sandy Lane and B5013 Elmore Lane
30,40 Rugeley South, from south of island of A460/Sandy Lane and B5013 Elmore Lane to Brereton Island
30 Tamworth, A51 Tamworth Rd/Dosthill Rd from south of jct with Peelers Way to jct with A51 Ascot Drive
60,40,50 Weston, btwn New Rd and 500m past Sandy Lane (going north)

**A52**
30 Stoke on Trent, Werrington Rd – btwn jct of B5040 to half mile east of Brookhouse Lane (Ashbank)
30,40 Stoke, Werrington Rd, btwn Brookhouse Lane and Kingsley Rd

**A53**
Blackshaw Moor btwn Thorncliffe Rd and Hazel Barrow Lane
40,30,40,60 Endon, from A53 Leek New Rd from jct with Nursery Avenue to jct with Dunwood Lane
60,40,30 Longsden, from A53 jct with Dunwood Lane to A53 jct with Wallbridge Drive

**A444**
30 Stanton Rd – St Peters Bridge to Derbyshire boundary

**A449**
70,40 Coven, btwn Station Drive by Four Ashes to just before M54 island
60,70 Gailey, btwn Rodbaston Drive and Station Drive
40 Penkridge, Lynehill Lane to 0.5mile north of Goodstation Lane
30 Stafford, Lichfield Rd to Gravel Lane Stourton btwn Ashwood Lower Lane and Dunsley Lane

**A454**
50 Trescott, Bridgenorth Rd btwn Brantley Lane and Shop Lane

**A460**
30 Rugeley, A460 from A51/A460 jct of Sandy Lane/Hednesford Rd to south of jct A460 Stile Cop Rd

**A511**
40,30 Burton North, btwn Anslow Lane to island of A5121
30 Burton South, island of A5121 to Brizlincote Lane (by Derbyshire boundary)

**A518**
30 Stafford, btwn M6 and Bridge St
30,40 Stafford, Riverway to Blackheath Lane

**A519**
40 Newcastle, Clayton Rd – from south of A519 Clayton Rd/Friars Wood and Brook Lane to rdbt on A519

**A520**
30 Sandon Rd btwn Grange Rd and A50

30 Weston Rd – from north of the A50 to City boundary (Park Hall) through Meir and Weston Coyney

**A4601**
30 Cannock, btwn A34 Walsall Rd jct to Longford Island A5
30 Old Hednesford Rd btwn jct with A5190 Lichfield Rd and jct with A460 Eastern Way
30,40 Wedges Mill, Longford Island twd jct 11 to just before Saredon Rd

**A5005**
Stoke on Trent, Lightwood Rd btwn A520 and A50

**A5035**
30 Trentham, Longton Rd btwn Trentham Rdbt A34 and A50 jct at Longton

**A5121**
50,40,30 Burton, from Island Junction with B5108 Branston to Borough Rd
30,40 Burton, from jct with Byrkley St, Horninglow to jct with Hillfield Lane

**A5127**
30 Lichfield, from jct with Upper St John St towards Streethay (incs change in speed limit over railway bridge)

**A5189**
40,30 Burton, btwn Wellington Rd jct along St Peters Bridge to Stapenhill Rd rdbt

**A5190**
30 Burntwood, Cannock Rd from Attwood Rd to Stockhay Lane Jct
30,40,60 Cannock, from Five Ways Island to Hednesford Rd

**B5044**
30 Silverdale, btwn Sneyd Terrace and the jct of the B5368 (Church Lane/Cemetery Rd)

**B5051**
30 btwn Sneyd Hill Rd and Brown Edge

**B5080**
30,40 Tamworth, Pennine Way btwn B5000 and Pennymoor Rd

**B5404**
40,30 Tamworth, from Sutton Rd to jct of A4091 (Coleshill Rd/Fazeley Rd)
30 Tamworth, Watling St btwn with A51 and A5

**Unclassified**
30 Burton, Rosliston Rd btwn A5189 St Peters Bridge and County Boundary by Railway Bridge
30 Cannock, Pye Green Rd
30 Cedar Rd btwn Crackley Bank and B5500 Audley Rd
30,40 Leek New Rd – btwn B5049 Hanley Rd and B5051 jct with A53 at Endon
30 Oxford Rd/Chell Heath Rd btwn A527 and B5051
30 Stoke on Trent, Dividy Rd – btwn B5039 and A52

## Suffolk

**A11**
50 Barton Mills Elveden
40 Elveden Cross Rds Elveden, Chalk Hall

**A12**
40 Blythburgh Kelsale
30 Little Glemham Lound
40 Melton Saxmundham

**A14**
Exning Rougham

**A134**
40 Barnham Long Melford
40 Nowton

**A137**
30 Brantham

**A140**
50 Thwaite

**A143**
30 Bury St Edmunds
30 Chedburgh
40 Stanton Bypass

40 Stradishall, Highpoint Prison

**A144**
30 Ilketshall St Lawrence

**A146**
50 Barnby Bends

**A1065**
40 Eriswell Mildenhall North of RAF Lakenheath

**A1071**
40 Boxford Hadleigh, Lady Lane

**A1092**
30 Cavendish
30 Clare
40 Glemsford, Skates Hill

**A1101**
30 Flempton

**A1117**
50 Lowestoft, Saltwater Way

**A1120**
30 Stonham Aspal

**A1156**
30 Ipswich, Norwich Rd

**A1302**
30 Bury St Edmunds

**A1304**
Newmarket, Golf Club

**B1078**
30 Barking
30 Needham Market

**B1106**
30 Fornham

**B1113**
40 Bramford

**B1115**
40 Chilton

**B1384**
30 Carlton Colville

**B1438**
30 Melton Hill

**B1506**
40 Kentford Moulton

**Unclassified**
30 Felixstowe, Grange Farm Avenue
30 Ipswich, Foxhall Rd
30 Ipswich, Nacton Rd
30 Kesgrave, Ropes Drive

## Surrey

**A3**
Grayshott to Cobham

**A23**
Salfords, Brighton Rd

**A24**
Mickleham

**A25**
Westcott to West Clandon

**A30**
Staines

**A31**
Hogs Back (Central and Eastern sections)

**A217**
Lower Kingswood to Banstead

**A242**
Reigate to Merstham

**A243**
Hook

**A246**
Guildford

**A248**
Chilworth

**A307**
Esher

**A308**
Staines

**A320**
Guildford to Staines

**A3016**
Hale

**A3100**
Guildford to Godalming

**B367**
Ripley

**B375**
Chertsey

**B380**
Mayford

**B385**
Woodham

**B386**
Windlesham

**B389**
Virginia Water

**B2030**
Caterham to Old Coulsdon

**B2031**
Caterham to Chaldon

**B2126**
Holmbury St Mary

**B2127**
Ewhurst

**B2130**
Godalming

**B3411**
Ash Vale

**Unclassified**
Effingham, Effingham Common Rd
Epsom, Longdown Lane South
Frith Hill, Charterhouse Rd
Hurtmore, Hurtmore Rd
Leigh, Apners Rd
Lightwater, Macdonald Rd
Staines, Kingston Rd

## Thames Valley
**Bracknell Forest, Buckinghamshire, Milton Keynes, Oxfordshire, Reading, Slough, West Berkshire, Windsor and Maidenhead, Wokingham**

**A5**
70 Wolverton
70 Bletchley

**A30(T)**
30 Sunningdale, London Rd

**A34**
70 Radley
70 Kennington

**A40**
60 Cassington
70 Forest Hills

**A41**
70 Buckland

**A44**
50 Kiddington with Asterleigh

**A338**
50 Hungerford

**A361**
30 Chipping Norton, Burford Rd
60 Little Faringdon

**A404**
70 Little Marlow, Marlow Bypass

**A413**
60 Swanbourne
60 Weedon
60 Hardwick
60 Wendover Bypass

**A421**
70 Tingewick Bypass
60 Wavendon

**A422**
50 Radclive cum Chackmore

**A509**
70 Newport Pagnell
60 Emberton Bypass

**A4074**
60 Dorchester
50 Nuneham Courteney

**A4095**
40 Freeland, Witney Rd

**A4130**
60 Nuffield
40 Remenham Hill

**A4155**
30 Shipiake

**A4260**
50 Shipton on Cherwell, Banbury Rd
60 Rousham, Banbury Rd
60 Steeple Aston

**B4009**
50 Ewelme

**B4011**
60 Piddington

**B4494**
60 Leckhampstead

**Unclassified**
30 Abingdon, Drayton Rd
30 Abingdon, Oxford Rd
30 Aylesbury, Buckingham Rd
30 Aylesbury, Gatehouse Rd
30 Aylesbury, Oakfield Rd
30 Aylesbury, Tring Rd
30 Aylesbury, Walton St
30 Aylesbury, Wendover Rd
30 Barkham, Barkham Rd
60 Beenham, Bath Rd
30 Blackbird Leys, Watlington Rd
30 Bletchley, Buckingham Rd
40 Bracknell, Bagshot Rd

50 Bracknell, Nine Mile Ride
30 Bracknell, Opladen Way
30 Buckingham, Stratford Rd
50 Burnham, Bath Rd
30 Chalfont St Peter, Gravel Hill
30 Chipping Norton, London Rd
40 Curbridge, Bampton Rd
30 Denham, North Orbital Rd
30 Denham, Oxford Rd
40 Earley, London Rd
30 Great Missenden, Rignall Rd
60 Hardmead, Newport Rd
30 Hazelmere, Sawpit Hill
30 High Wycombe, Holmers Farm Way
30 High Wycombe, Marlow Hill
30 High Wycombe, New Rd
30 High Wycombe, West Wycombe Rd
60 Hungerford, Bath Rd
30 Kidlington, Oxford Rd
60 Kintbury, Bath Rd
40 Long Crendon, Bicester Rd
30 Maidenhead, Braywick Rd
70 Milton Keynes, Woughton on the Green, Standing Way
30 Milton Keynes, Avebury Boulevard
30 Milton Keynes, Midsummer Boulevard
30 Milton Keynes, Silbury Boulevard
30 Monks Risborough, Aylesbury Rd
30 Oxford, Church Cowley Rd
30 Oxford, Headington Rd
30 Oxford, London Rd
30 Oxford, Windmill Rd
30 Reading, Berkeley Avenue
30 Reading, Castle Hill
30 Reading, Kings Rd
30 Reading, Park Lane
30 Reading, Vastern Rd
30 Reading, Wokingham Rd
30 Slough, Buckingham Rd
30 Slough, Cippenham Lane
40 Slough, London Rd
30 Slough, Parlaunt Rd
30 Slough, Sussex Place
60 Speen, Bath Rd
30 Stanford in the Vale, Faringdon Rd
40 Sunninghill, Brockenhurst Rd
30 Tiddington, Oxford Rd
40 Tilehurst, Bath Rd
30 Wantage, Charlton Rd
70 Winkfield, Bagshot Rd
30 Witney, Corn St
30 Wokingham, London Rd
60 Wroxton, Stratford Rd

## Warwickshire

**A5**
50 Grendon to Atherstone, Watling Street
60 Rugby, Churchover, Watling Street

**A44**
60 Little Compton, London Rd

**A46**
60 Stratford Northern Bypass, nr Snitterfield
70 Warwick, Stoneleigh, Kenilworth Bypass

**A47**
40 Nuneaton and Bedworth, The Longshoot

**A422**
30 Pillerton Priors, Banbury Rd
30 Stratford, Alcester Rd

**A423**
60 Farnborough, Southam Rd
60 Fenny Compton, Banbury Rd
60 Rugby, nr Marton, Oxford Rd
30 Rugby, Marton, Coventry Rd
60 south of Southam, Southam Rd

**A425**
30 Warwick, Radford Semele, Radford Rd

**A426**
30 Rugby, Dunchurch Rd
60 Stockton, Rugby Rd

**A428**
30 Rugby, Binley Woods, Rugby Rd
60 Rugby, Church Lawford, Coventry Rd
40 Rugby, Long Lawford, Coventry Rd

**A429**
60 Stretton on Fosse
30 Warwick, Coventry Rd
60 Wellesbourne, Ettington Rd

**A435**
40 Mappleborough Green

**A439**
50 Stratford, nr Fisherman's car park
50 Warwick Rd nr Hatton Rock

**A445**
40 Leamington Spa, Leicester Lane

**A446**
60 Allen End, London Rd
60 Bassetts Pole, London Rd

**A452**
60 Warwick, Greys Mallory, Banbury Rd
60 Warwick, Heathcote, Europa Way

**A3400**
30 Alderminster, Shipston Rd
40 Henley in Arden, Stratford Rd
60 Little Woldford, London Rd
30 Long Compton, Main Street
30 Newbold on Stour, Stratford Rd
50 Pathlow, Birmingham Rd
50 Wootton Wawen, Stratford Rd

**A4189**
60 Lower Norton, Henley Rd

**B439**
60 Cranhill, Evesham Rd

**B4035**
30 Upper Brailes, Main Rd

**B4065**
30 Ansty, Main Rd

**B4087**
30 Wellesbourne, Newbold Rd

**B4089**
30 Stratford, Alcester, Arden Rd

**B4098**
40 Corley, Tamworth Rd

**B4100**
60 Bishop's Tachbrook, north of Harwood's House
60 south of Gaydon, Banbury Rd

**B4101**
40 Tamworth in Arden, Broad Lane

**B4102**
30 Nuneaton, Arbury Rd

**B4109**
40 Bulkington, Coventry Rd

**B4111**
30 Nuneaton, Mancetter Rd

**B4112**
40 Nuneaton, Ansley Rd

**B4113**
30 Nuneaton, Coventry Rd

**B4114**
30 Ansley Common, Coleshill Rd
60 Church End, Coleshill Rd
60 Rugby, Burton Hastings, Lutterworth Rd

**B4429**
40 Rugby, Ashlawn Rd

**B4455**
60 Rugby, Fosse Way south of Princethorpe

**Unclassified**
30 Ash Green, Royal Oak Lane
30 Ash Green, St Giles Rd
30 Ash Green, Vicarage Lane
30 Butlers Marston, Kineton Rd
30 Coleshill, Station Rd
30 Exhall, School Lane
30 Lighthorne, Chesterton Rd
60 Monks Kirby, Coalpit Lane
30 Nuneaton, Donnithorne Avenue
30 Rugby, Vicarage Hill, Clifton Rd
40 Salford Priors, Station Rd
40 Sambourne, Middletown Lane
30 Warwick, Woodloes Park, Primrose Hill

## West Mercia
**Herefordshire, Shropshire, Telford and Wrekin, Worcestershire**

**A5**
NSL Aston
NSL Gobowen, Moreton Bridge
60 Montford Bridge
NSL West Felton

**A40**
50 Pencraig

**A41**
40,NSL Albrighton Bypass
NSL Chetwynd nr Newport
40 Tern Hill
NSL Whitchurch Bypass

**A44**
40 Wickhamford
30 Worcester, Bromyard Rd

**A46**
50 Beckford
NSL Evesham Bypass

**A49**
NSL Ashton
30 Dorrington
40 Herefordshire, Harewood End

**A417**
40 Ledbury, Parkway

**A438**
60 Staunton-on-Wye

**A442**
40 Crudgington

**A448**
30 Bromsgrove, Kidderminster Rd

**A456**
30 Blakedown
30 Newnham Bridge

**A458**
40 Morville
30 Much Wenlock

**A465**
NSL Allensmore

**A491**
50 Bromsgrove, Stourbridge Rd
NSL Hagley, Sandy Lane

**A528**
30 Shrewsbury, Ellesmere Rd

**A4103**
NSL Hereford, Lumber Lane/Lugg Bridge
40 Newtown Cross
50 Stiffords Bridge/Storridge

**A4104**
30 Welland, Drake St
30 Welland, Marlbank Rd

**A4110**
30 Hereford, Three Elms Rd

**A5064**
30 Shrewsbury, London Rd

**B4084**
40 Cropthorne

**B4096**
30 Bromsgrove, Old Birmingham Rd

**B4208**
30 Welland

**B4211**
30 Malvern, Barnards Green Rd

**B4368**
40 Hungerford

**B4373**
40 Telford, Castlefields Way
40 Telford, Wrockwardine Wood Way

**B4638**
30 Worcester, Woodgreen Drive

**B5060**
40 Telford, Castle Farm Way

**B5062**
60 Newport, Edgmond Rd
30 Shrewsbury, Sundorne Rd

**Unclassified**
30 Hadley, Britannia Way
30 Hereford, Yazor Rd
30 Kidderminster, Habberley Lane
30 Newport, Wellington Rd
30 Redditch, Bromsgrove Rd
40 Redditch, Coldfield Drive
30 Shrewsbury, Monkmoor Rd
30 Shropshire, Longden Rd (Rural)
40 Telford, Britannia Way

## West Midlands
**Birmingham, Coventry, Dudley, Sandwell, Solihull, Walsall, Wolverhampton**

**A5**
60 Brownhills, Watling St
50 Cannock, Watling St
60 Wall, Watling St

**A41**
40 Albrighton Bypass towards Wolverhampton
40,60 Albrighton, Albrighton Bypass towards Newport
30 Silhill, Warwick Rd

**A46**
70 Stoneleigh, Kenilworth Bypass

**A51**
30 Lichfield, Tamworth Rd
60 Weeford, Watling St

**A446**
60 Allens End, London Rd
60 Bassetts Pole, London Rd

**A449**
40 Coven, Wolverhampton Rd
60 Gailey, Wolverhampton Rd

**A452**
50 Smith's Wood, Collector Rd

**A4034**
30 Langley, Oldbury Rd

**A4036**
40 Netherton Woodside and St Andrew's, Pedmore Rd

**A4040**
30 Hodge Hill, Bromford Lane

**A4123**
40 Castle and Priory, Birmingham New Rd

**A4177**
60 Hasley Knob, Honiley Rd

**A5127**
30 Lichfield, Trent Valley Rd

**A4600**
40 Wyken, Ansty Rd

**B425**
30 Elmdon, Lode Lane

**B4065**
30 Ansty, Main Rd

**B4098**
40 Fillongley, Coventry Rd
60 Fillongley, Tamworth Rd

**B4101**
40 Tanworth, Broad Lane

**B4103**
30 Kenilworth, Castle Rd
30 Kenilworth, Clinton Lane

**B4109**
40 Bulkington, Coventry Rd

**B4114**
30 Hodge Hill, Washwood Heath Rd

**B4121**
40 Bartley Green, Barnes Hill
40 Weoley, Shenley Lane

**B4135**
30 Soho and Victoria, Heath Street

**Unclassified**
30 Ash Green, Royal Oak Lane
30 Ash Green, St Giles Rd
30 Ash Green, Vicarage Lane
30 Coleshill, Station Rd
30 Oxley, The Droveway
30 St Alphege, Widney Manor Rd

## West Yorkshire
**M606**
50 Mill Carr Hill Bridge

**A58**
40 Leeds, Easterly Rd

**A61**
40 Leeds, Alwoodley, Harrogate Rd
40 Leeds, Scott Hall Rd
40,60 Rothwell, Wakefield Rd

**A62**
30 Huddersfield, Manchester Rd
30 Kirklees, Birstall, Gelderd Rd
30 Slaithwaite, Manchester Rd

**A64**
40 Leeds, York Rd

**A65**
30 Guiseley, Otley Rd
40 Ilkley, Ilkley Rd

**A616**
40 Huddersfield, Woodhead Rd

**A629**
30 Cullingworth, Halifax Rd
50 Elland, Calderdale Way southbound
50 Halifax, Keighley Rd
30 Halifax, Ovenden Rd
30 Halifax, Skircoat Rd
30 Keighley, Halifax Rd
40 Shelley, Pennistone Rd

**A635**
30 Kirklees, Holmfirth, Holmfirth Rd

**A636**
30 Wakefield, Denby Dale Rd

**A638**
50 Ossett Bypass
30 Wakefield, Dewsbury Rd

**A640**
30 Huddersfield, Westbourne Rd

**A642**
30 Wakefield, Horbury, Northfield Lane

**A644**
30 Brighouse, Denholme Rd
30 Kirklees, Dewsbury, Huddersfield Rd
30 Mirfield, Huddersfield Rd

**A645**
30 Wakefield, Featherstone, Pontefract Rd
30 Wakefield, Featherstone, Wakefield Rd

**A646**
30 Calderdale, Cornholme, Burnley Rd
30 Calderdale, Luddenden Foot, Burnley Rd
30 Calderdale, Todmorden, Halifax Rd
30 Portsmouth, Burnley Rd jct Durn St
30 Todmorden, Halifax Rd jct Hallroyd Rd

**A647**
30 Bradford, Great Horton Rd
30 Clayton Heights, Highgate Rd
40 Pudsey, Bradford Rd

**A650**
30 Frizinghall, Bradford Rd

**A651**
30 Birkenshaw, Bradford Rd

**A652**
30 Batley, Bradford Rd
40 Birstall, Bradford Rd

**A653**
40 Leeds, Shaw Cross, Leeds Rd

**A657**
30 Shipley, Leeds Rd
30 Thackley, Leeds Rd

**A6025**
50 Elland, Elland Rd

**A6036**
30 Calderdale, Northowram, Bradford Rd

**A6037/A650**
40 Bradford, Shipley Airedale Rd

**A6038**
40 Baildon, Otley Rd
40 Esholt, Otley Rd

**A6120**
30 Leeds, Cross Gates, Station Rd

**A6177**
30 Bradford, Ingleby Rd
40 Bradford, Rooley Lane

**A6186**
30 Wakefield, Durkar, Asdale Rd

**B6124**
30 Wakefield, Batley Rd

**B6144**
30 Bradford, Haworth Rd Daisy Hill
30 Bradford, Toller Lane

**B6145**
30 Bradford, Thornton Rd

**B6265**
30 Stockbridge, Bradford Rd

**B6269**
30 Shipley, Cottingley Cliffe Rd

**B6273**
30 Wakefield, Kinsley, Wakefield Rd

**B6380**
30 Bradford, Beacon Rd

**Unclassified**
30 Bradford, Cutler Heights Lane
30 Bradford, Dick Lane
30 Bradford, Gain Lane
30 Bradford, Moore Avenue
30 Calderdale, Crag Lane
30 Huddersfield, Dalton, Long Lane
30 Leeds, Burley, Willow Rd/Cardigan Rd
30 Leeds, Horsforth, Low Lane
30 Leeds, Lawnswood, Otley Old Rd
30 Leeds, Sandford, Broad Lane
30 South Elmsall, Minsthorpe Lane
30 South Kirby, Minsthorpe
60 Walton, Wetherby Rd

## Wiltshire and Swindon
**M4**
70 east and west of jct 15
70 east and west of jct 16
70 east and west of jct 17

**A4**
40 Froxfield
60 West Overton

**A30**
40 Fovant
60 The Pheasant

**A36**
60 Brickworth
60 Hanging Langford
50 Knook
30 Salisbury, Wilton Rd
60 south of Whaddon
60 Stapleford to East Clyffe

**A303**
50 Chicklade
30 Parsonage Down
60 Willoughby Hedge

**A338**
40 Bosscombe
30 nr Little Woodbury
60 nr Southgrove Copse

**A342**
60 Chirton to Charlton
30 Ludgershall, Andover Rd
50 Lydeway

**A346**
60 Chiseldon Firs
60 Whitefield
30 Heywood
70 Pretty Chimneys

**A354**
40 Coombe Bissett

**A360/A344**
60 Airmans Corner

**A361**
60 Inglesham
60 nr Blackland Turning
70 nr jct with B3101
60 nr Shepherds Shore
30 Southwick
30 Trowbridge, Frome Rd
60 west of Beckhampton

**A363**
30 Bradford on Avon, Trowbridge Rd
30 North Bradley, Woodmarsh
40 Trowle Common

**A419**
70 Cricklade
70 nr Covingham
70 Widhill

**A420**
60 Giddeahall to Ford

**A3026**
40 Ludgershall, Tidworth Rd

**A3028**
40 Durrington, Larkhill Rd

**A3102**
30 Calme, Oxford Rd
30 Lyneham
30 Melksham, Sandridge Rd
30 Wootten Bassett

**A4259**
50 nr Coate
40 Swindon, Queens Drive

**A4361**
60 Broad Hinton
60 Uffcott Xrd
30 Wroughton, Swindon Rd

**B390**
60 Maddington Farm

**B3105**
30 Hilperton, Hill St/Marsh St

**B4006**
40 Swindon, Marlborough Rd

**B3098**
30 Bratton

**B3106**
30 Hilperton, Hammond Way

**B3107**
30 Bradford on Avon, Holt Rd

**B4006**
30 Stratton St Margaret, Swindon Rd
30 Swindon, Whitworth Rd

**B4040**
50 Leigh

**B4041**
30 Wootten Bassett, Station Rd

**B4143**
30 Swindon, Bridge End Rd

**B4192**
50 Liddington

**B4289**
40 Great Western Way nr Bruce St Bridges

**B4553**
40 Swindon, Tewkesbury Way

**B4587**
30 Swindon, Akers Way

**Unclassified**
30 Corsham, Park Lane
30 Swindon, Ermin St
30 Swindon, Merlin Way
30 Swindon, Moredon Rd
30 Trowbridge, Wiltshire Drive

## Worcestershire
see West Mercia

## Wales
### Mid and South Wales
**Blaenau Gwent, Bridgend, Caerphilly, Cardiff, Carmarthenshire, Merthyr Tydfil, Monmouthshire, Neath Port Talbot, Newport, Pembrokeshire, Rhondda Cynon Taff, Swansea, Torfaen, Vale of Glamorgan**

**M4**
70 2km east of Jct35
30 east of Jct36, nr Sarn
40 1.5km west of Jct37, nr Pyle
30 Llanmartin Overbridge
30 Toll Plaza

**A40**
40 Bancyfelin Bypass
30 Buckland Hall, Brecon to Abergavenny
30 Johnstown, Carmarthen to St Clears
30 Llanhamlach, Brecon to Abergavenny
50 Llansantffried Jct
30 Monmouth, Llangattock Lodge
30 Rhosmaen
30 Scethrog, Brecon to Abergavenny
30 Trecastle
40 Whitemill

**A44**
30 Forest Bends
30 Gwystre
30 Llanbadarn Fawr
30 Llanfihangel, Nant Melan
30 Rhydgaled, Sweet Lamb

**A48**
30 Baglan, Dinas Baglan
30 Berryhill
30 Bonvilston
40 Castleton
50 Cowbridge, Cowbridge Bypass
70 Langstone, Chepstow Rd
30 Llanddarog
30 Morriston, Clasemont Rd
30 Nantycaws
30 Parkwall, Parkwall Hill
30 north of Pont Abraham
30 Pontarddulais, Bolqoed Rd
30 Pontardualais, Carmarthen Rd
60 Pontardualais, Fforest Rd
30 Port Talbot, Margam Rd
30 Wenvoe, St Nicholas

**A410**
30 Porthcawl, The Porthway

**A422**
40 Cowbridge, Aberthin Rd

**A438**
30 Bronllys
60 Three Cocks

**A449**
30 north of Coldra
60 Llandenny
30 Llantrissent nr Usk

**A458**
60 Cefn Bridge
30 Llanfair Caereinion (Neuadd Bridge)
40 Trewem

**A465**
30 btwn Aberbaden and Llanfoist
40 Abergavenny, Ilanfoist
30 Abergavenny, Triley Mill
30 Glynneath Bank
30 Pandy
30 Resolven north
60 Rheola

**A466**
60 Llandogo
30 Monmouth, High Beech Rdbt to Old Hospital
30 Monmouth, Redbrook Rd
70 Monmouth, Whitecross Street
30 St Arvans to Livox Ends
40 Tintern

**A467**
30 Aberbeeg, Aberbeeg Rd
60 Abertillery, Aberbeeg Rd
40 Blaina, Abertillery Rd
70 Danycraig, Risca

**A468**
30 Machen Village
30 Rhiwderin, Caerphilly Rd

**A469**
30 Llanbradach, Lower Rhymney Valley Relief Rd

30 Tir-Y-Birth, New Rd

**A470**

30 Aberduhonw, south of Builth
30 Aberfan
30 Abernant, south of Builth
30 Beacons Reservoir
30 Cilfynydd
30 Erwood
30 Erwood South
30 Llandinam to Caersws Jct
30 Llanidloes to Llandinam
30 Llwyn y Celyn, Brecon to Merthyr
60 Llyswen
30 Newbridge to Rhayader, Argoed Mill
30 Newbridge on Wye
70 Rhydyfelin
30 nr Taffs Well
30 Ysgiog, south of Builth

**A472**

60 Hafodrynys, Hafod yr ynys Rd
30 Maes y cwmmer, Main Rd
30 Monkswood, Little Mill
30 Usk Bridge to Old Saw Mill
30 Ystrad Mynach to Nelson

**A473**

30 Bridgend, Bryntirion Hill
40 Bridgend, Coychurch Bypass
30 Bryncae, New Rd
30 Pencoed, Penybont Rd
30 Upper Boat, Main Rd

**A474**

60 Alltwen, Graig Rd
30 Briton Ferry, Briton Ferry Rd
40 Garnant, Glanffrwd Est Jct
40 Heol-y-Gors
60 Neath, Penywern Rd
30 Pontamman to Glanaman
60 Rhyd y Fro, Commercial St

**A475**

30 Lampeter, Pentrebach, County Rd
30 Llanwnen

**A476**

30 Carmel, Stag and Pheasant
30 Carmel to NSL at Temple Bar
30 Ffairfach, 30 mph to the Square
30 Gorslas, The Gate
40 Llannon, Erw Non Jct to Clos Rebecca Jct
30 Swiss Valley, Thomas Arms
30 Upper Tumble, Llannon Rd and Bethania Rd

**A477**

30 Llanddowror

**A478**

30 Clunderwen
30 Llandissilio, Nr school
30 Pentlepoir

**A482 & A475**

30 Lampeter

**A482**

30 Aberaeron, Lampeter Rd
30 Cwmann, North
30 Cwmann, South
30 Llanwrda

**A483**

30 Abbey Cwm Hir Jct
30 Ammanford, Penybanc Rd
30 north of Crossgates
30 south of Cwmgwili, Pontarddulais Rd
30 Ffairfach to Llandeilo Bridge
30 Garthmyl, Refail Garage
60 Garthmyl, Welshpool
30 Llandeilo, Rhosmaen St
30 Llandrindod, Midway Bends
30 Swansea, Fabian Way

**A484**

30 Bronwydd Village
30 Cenarth
50 Cwmffrwd
30 Cynwyl Elfed
30 Idole, from 200m s.w. of B4309 Jct south to NSL
30 Llanelli, Sandy Rd
60 Llanelli, Trostre Rdbt to Berwick Rdbt
30 Newcastle Emlyn
60 Pembrey
40 Pembrey, Lando Rd
60 Pentrecagel
30 Rhos
60 Saron

**A485**

40 Alltwalis
30 Cwmann, from the A482 Jct N
30 Llanllwni
30 Llanybydder
50 Peniel

**A486**

30 Llandysul, Well Street
30 New Quay

**A487 & A4120**

30 Aberystwyth, Southgate

**A487**

30 Aberaeron, Greenland Terrace
30 Bow Street
30 Eglwyswrw
30 Furnace
30 Llanarth, Alma Street
30 Llanfarian
70 Llanrhystud
30 Newgale
40 Newport
30 Penparc
30 Rhydyfelin
30 Rhydypennau
30 Talybont
30 Waunfawr, Penglais Hill

**A489**

30 Caersws Jct to Penstrowed
30 Kerry, County Rd, Glanmule Garage
30 Newtown, west of Hafren coll
30 Penstrowed to Newtown

**A490**

40 Llanffyllin

**A4042**

30 Llanover
50 Mamhilad

**A4043**

40 Abersychan, Cwmavon Rd

**A4046**

30 Ebbw Vale (nr Tesco's)
70 Ebbw Vale, College Rd
40 Waunllwyd, Station Rd

**A4047**

30 Brynmawr, Beaufort Hill and High St

**A4048**

30 Argoed
30 Blackwood (Sunnybank)
30 Cwmfelinfach Village
30 Hollybush
30 Pontllanfraith, Blackwood Rd

**A4050**

40 Barry, Jenner Rd

**A4054**

30 Cilfynydd, Cilfynydd Rd
30 Edwardsville, Nantddu
30 Merthyr Vale, Cardiff Rd
30 Mountain Ash, New Rd
40 Pontypridd, Pentrebach Rd
70 Upper Boat, Cardiff Rd

**A4055**

30 Barry, Gladstone Rd

**A4058**

30 Pontypridd, Broadway

**A4061**

40 Ogmore Vale, Cemetery Rd

**A4063**

30 Llangynwyd, Bridgend Rd
30 Penyfai, Bridgend Rd
30 Sarn Bypass

**A4066**

60 Broadway
30 Pendine, Llanmiloe
40 Pendine, Marsh Rd

**A4067**

30 Abercraf By-pass
30 Crai
40 Mumbles Rd

**A4068**

30 Cwmtwrch, Bethel Rd
30 Cwmtwrch, Heol Gleien

**A4069**

40 Brynamman, Brynamman Rd
30 Llandovery, Broad St
30 Llangadog, Station Rd

**A4075**

40 Pembroke

**A4076**

30 Hubberston, St Lawrence Hill
30 Johnston, Milford Rd
30 Johnston, Vine Rd
40 Steynton, Steynton Rd

**A4078**

30 Carew

**A4093**

40 Blackmill
70 Glynogwr
40 Hendreforgan, Gilfach Rd

**A4102**

30 Gellideg, Swansea Rd

**A4106**

30 Porthcawl, Bridgend Rd
30 Porthcawl, Newton Nottage Rd

**A4107**

70 Abergwynfi, High St

**A4109**

70 Aberdulias, Main Rd
30 Crynant, Main Rd
40 Glynneath
40 Seven Sisters, Dulais Rd

**A4118**

30 Fairwood Common

**A4119**

30 Cardiff, Llantrisant Rd
30 Groesfaen
30 Llantrisant, Mwyndy Cross

**A4139**

30 Pembroke, Orange Way
30 Pembroke Dock, Bush Street
30 Tenby, Marsh Rd

**A4216**

30 Cockett, Cockett Rd

**A4222**

30 Brynsadler, Cowbridge Rd
30 Cowbridge, Cardiff Rd
30 Maendy, Maendy Rd

**A4226**

30 Rhoose, Waycock Rd

**A4232**

30 Cardiff, Ely Link

**A4233**

30 Ferndale, The Parade

**B4181**

30 Bridgend, Coity Rd

**B4223**

30 Gelli, Gelli Rd
30 Ton Pentre, Maindy Rd
30 Ton Pentre, Pentwyn Rd

**B4235**

30 Gwernesney nr Usk

**B4236**

30 Llanfrechfa, Caerleon Rd

**B4237**

30 Maesglas, Cardiff Rd
30 Newport, opp Power Station, Risca Rd

**B4239**

30 Newport, Lighthouse Rd

**B4245**

30 Langstone, Magor Rd
30 Leechpool, Cartref to Uplands
30 Penpedairheol, Pengam Rd
40 Rogiet, Caldicot Rd
60 Rogiet, Green Farm

**B4246**

40 Abersychan, Varteg
60 Garndiffaith, New Rd

**B4248**

70 Blaenavon, Garn Rd

**B4251**

30 Abergavenny, Hereford Rd
40 Caerphilly, Kendon Hill

**B4265**

40 Llantwit Major, Llantwit Major Bypass
30 St Brides Major, Ewenny Rd
30 St Brides Major, St Brides Rd

**B4275**

30 Abercynon, Abercynon Rd

**B4278**

30 Dinas, Dinas Rd
30 Tonyrefail, Penrhiwfer Rd

**B4281**

30 Cefn Cribwr, Cefn Rd
30 Kenfig Hill, High St

**B4282**

30 Bryn, Measteg Rd
30 Maesteg, Bridgend Rd and Castle St

**B4283**

30 North Cornelly, Heol Fach

**B4290**

30 Jersey Marine, New Rd
30 Skewen, Burrows Rd
30 Skewen, Pen-yr-Heol and Crymlyn Rd

**B4293**

70 Trellech Village
40 Trellech, Monmouth Road

**B4295**

30 Crofty, New Rd
30 btwn Gowerton and Penclawdd
30 btwn Penclawdd and Llanrhidian

**B4296**

40 Waungren, Pentre Rd

**B4297**

30 Bynea, Lougher Bridge Rdbt to Station Rd Jct
30 Capel Hendre
60 Fforest
40 Llanedi
30 Llangennech, Cleviston Park Jct to Park Lane Jct
30 Llangennech, Pontardulais Rd
30 Llwynhendy, from Capel Soar to the Police Station

**B4301**

30 Bronwydd Village

**B4302**

30 Talley

**B4303**

30 Llanelli, Dafen Rdbt to Felinfoel Rdbt

**B4304**

40 Llanelli, Copperworks Rdbt to Morfa Rdbt
30 Llanelli, Lower Trostre Rd Rdbt to Trostre Rd Rdbt
60 Llanelli, New Dock Rd

**B4306**

40 Bancffosfelen, Heol Y Banc
50 Crwbin
40 Hendy, Heol Y Banc
30 Llangendeirn
30 Pontyberem, Llanon Rd

**B4308**

30 Penmynnydd

**B4309**

30 Cynheidre
60 Five Roads

**B4310**

30 Drefach, Heol Caegwyn

**B4312**

30 Llangain

**B4314**

30 Moorfield Road, Nr school
30 Pendine

**B4317**

30 Carway, East
30 Carway, West
70 Ponthenri, Myrtle Hill
30 Pontyberem, Heol Capel Ifan
30 Pontyberem, Station Rd

**B4320**

30 Hundleton

**B4322**

40 Pembroke Dock, Pembroke Rd

**B4325**

30 Llanstadwell, Honeyborough Rd
60 Neyland, High Street
60 Neyland, The Promenade

**B4328**

30 Whitland, Trevaughan

**B4333**

30 Cynwyl Elfed (North)
30 Hermon
30 Newcastle Emlyn, Aber-arad

**B4336**

60 Llandysul, Pont-tyweli
30 Llanfihangel Ar Arth

**B4337**

30 Llanybydder
30 Talsarn

**B4347**

30 Newcastle Village

**B4350**

60 Glasbury, Llwyn au bach

**B4436**

30 Bishopton, Northway
30 Killay, Goetre Fawr Rd
40 Kittle, Pennard Rd

**B4459**

30 Pencader

**B4471**

30 Llanhilleth, Oak Leaf Terrace, Commercial Rd

**B4478**

30 Beaufort, Letchworth Rd

**B4486**

30 Ebbw Vale, Steelworks Rd

**B4524**

30 Corntown, Corntown Rd

**B4538**

30 Cardigan

**B4556**

70 Blaenau, Penygroes Rd
70 Caerbryn
70 Pengroes, Norton Rd

**B4560**

40 Beaufort, Ebbw Vale, Llangynidr Rd

**B4591**

30 Highcross, Risca Rd
30 Pontymister, Risca Rd
30 Risca, opp Power Station, Risca Rd

**B4598**

30 Abergavenny, Horse and Jockey
30 Llancayo

**B4599**

30 Ystradgynlais

**B4603**

40 Clydach, Pontarddawe Rd
30 Ynystawe, Clydach Rd

**B4622**

30 Bridgend, Broadlands Link Rd

**B4623**

40 Caerphilly, Mountain Rd

**Unclassified**

40 Aberbargoed, Bedwellty and Coedymoeth Rd Jct
30 Abercwmboi, Park View Terrace
30 Abergwili, Ambulance Station to the Bypass Rdbt
60 Abersychan, Foundry Rd
60 Abertillery, Gwern Berthi
60 Abertillery, Roseheyworth Rd
30 Aberystwyth Town, Park Avenue
60 Ammanford, Dyffryn Rd
70 Ammanford, New Rd and Pantyffynnon Rd
30 Ammanford, layby outside Saron Church, Saron Rd
30 Barry, Buttrills Rd
30 Barry, Holton Rd
30 Barry, Winston Rd
40 Beddau, Bryniteg Hill
30 Beddau, Gwaunmiskin Rd
70 Betws, Betws Rd
30 Betws, Maesquarre Rd
30 Birchgrove, Birchgrove Rd
30 Blaenavon, Upper Coedcae Rd
30 Blaina, Bourneville Rd
30 Blaina, Farm Rd
30 Blaina, Surgery Rd
30 Brackla, Brackla Way
30 Bridgend, Pen-Y-Cae Lane
30 Bridgend Ind Est, Kingsway
30 Bridgend Ind Est, North Rd
30 Bridgend Ind Est, South Rd
30 Bridgend Ind Est, Western Avenue
30 Britton Ferry, Old Rd
40 Brynna, Brynna Rd
40 Caerleon, Ponthir Rd
30 Caerphilly, Lansbury Park Ring Rd
30 Caldicot, Chepstow Rd
30 Cardiff, Cherry Orchard Rd, M4 bridge site
30 Cardiff, Cyncoed Rd
30 Cardiff, Excalibur Drive
30 Cardiff, Heath, Maescoed Rd
30 Cardiff, Heol Isaf
30 Cardiff, Leckwith Rd
30 Cardiff, Newport Rd
30 Cardiff, Pencisely Rd
30 Cardiff, Penylan, Colchester Avenue
30 Cardiff, Rhiwbina Hill
30 Cardiff, Roath, Lake Rd East/West
30 Cardiff, St Fagans Rd
30 Cardiff, Wentloog Avenue
30 Cardiff, Willowbrook Drive
30 Carmarthen, Lime Grove Avenue and Fountain Head Tce
30 Cefn Glas, Merlin Crescent
30 Cefncoed, High St
30 Cefncoed, Vaynor Rd
30 Cefneithin
30 Chepstow, Mathern Rd
30 Church Village, Station Rd
40 Clydach, Vadre Rd
30 Coity, Heol Spencer
60 Coldharbour, Usk to Raglan Rd
30 Crumlin, Hafodyrynys Hill
40 Cwm Govilon, Bryn Awelon Rd
30 Cwmavon, Cwmavon Rd
30 Cwmbran, Greenforge Way
30 Cwmbran, Henllys Way
30 Cwmbran, Hollybush Way
30 Cwmbran, Llanfrechfa Way
30 Cwmbran, Maendy Way
70 Cwmbran, Pontnewydd, Chapel Street
30 Cwmbran, Thornhill Rd
30 Cwmbran, Ty Canol Way
30 Cwmbran, Ty Gwyn Way and Greenmeadow Way
30 Cwmbran, Upper Cwmbran Rd
30 Cwmgwili
70 Cwmgwili, Thornhill Rd
60 Deri, New Rd
30 Derwen Fawr, Rhy-Y-Defaid Drive
30 Dinas Powys, Pen-y-turnpike Rd
30 Dowlais, High St
50 Drefach, Heol Blawnhirwaun
30 Ebbw Vale, Newchurch Rd
30 Felinfoel, Llethri Rd
30 Fforest Fach, Carmarthen Rd
60 Fochrie, Olgivie Terrace
30 Forden
50 Gelli, Gelli Ind Est
30 Gelligaer, Church Rd
30 Gilwern, Cae Meldon (aka Ty Mawr Lane)
30 Glyncorrwg, Heol y Glyn
30 Gorseinon, Frampton Rd
70 Gorslas, Pengroes Rd
30 Grovesend
30 Haverfordwest, New Rd/Uzmaston Rd
30 Heol-Tai-Mawr
30 Hopkinstown, Hopkinstown Rd
30 Johnstown, St Clears Rd
50 Llanbradach, Coed y Brain Rd to Glyn Bedw
30 Llanelli, Denham Avenue
30 Llanelli, Heol Goffa
30 Llanfihangel Ar Arth (South)
30 Llangan
30 Llangyfelach, Swansea Rd
30 Llanharan, Brynna Rd
30 Llanhenock, Caerleon to Usk Rd – Apple tree farm
30 Llantwit Major, Llanmaes Rd
30 Maesteg, Heol-Ty-Gwyn
30 Maesteg, Heol Ty-Wyth
30 Malpas, Rowan Way
30 Merthyr Vale, Nixonvale
30 Merthyr Tydfil, Brecon Rd
30 Merthyr Tydfil, Goatmill Rd
30 Merthyr Tydfil, Gumos Rd
30 Merthyr Tydfil, Heolgerrig Rd
30 Merthyr Tydfil, Plymouth St
30 Merthyr Tydfil, Rocky Rd
30 Merthyr Tydfil, The Walk
30 Milford Haven, Priory Rd
40 Milford Haven, Thornton Rd
30 Monmouth, Devauden Village
60 Monmouth, Dixton Rd
30 Monmouth, Llangybi
70 Monmouth, Magor (West)
30 Morriston, Caemawr Rd
30 Mount Pleasant, Cardiff Rd
30 Mountain Ash, Llanwonno Rd
30 Mountain Ash, Miskin Rd
30 Nantgarw, Oxford St
30 Nantycaws Hill
30 Nash Village, West Nash Rd
60 New Tredegar, White Roase Way
30 Newbridge, Park Rd
30 Newport, Allt-Yr-Yn Avenue
30 Newport, Corporation Rd
40 Newport, Marshfield Rd
30 North Connelly, Fairfield Rd
30 Pant, Pant Rd
60 Pembroke Rd
30 Pencoed, Felindre Rd
30 Pendine
60 Pentrecagel
30 Penydarren, High Street
30 Pontardawe, Ynys-Meudwy Rd
40 Ponthir, Caerleon Rd
30 Pontllanfraith, Bryn Rd
60 Pontlottyn, Southend Terrace
30 Pontnewynydd, Plas Y Coed Rd
40 Pontyclun, Cowbridge Rd
60 Pontypool, Little Mill
40 Porthcawl, Fulmar Rd
30 Portskewett, Caldicot Rd
30 Rassau, Reservoir Rd
30 Rhymney, Llys Joseph Parry (nr Farmers Arms)
30 Rhymney, Wellington Way
30 Risca, Cromwell Rd
40 Risca, Holly Rd
30 Rogerstone, Pontymason Lane
30 Rogerstone, Tregwillym Rd
30 St Athan, Cowbridge Rd
50 Sandfields, Village Rd
30 Saron
30 Seven Sisters, Golwg-y-Bryn
30 Sully, Hayes Rd
30 Sully, South Rd
30 Swansea, Mynydd Newydd Rd, Caemawr Rd, Parry Rd, Vicarage Rd
30 Swansea, Pentregethin Rd
30 Tiers Cross
30 Tonteg, Church Rd
30 Tonyrefail, Gilfach Rd
30 Trebanos, Swansea Rd
30 Treboeth, Llangyfelach Rd
30 Tredegar, Merthyr Rd
30 Tredegar, Vale Terrace
30 Trehafod, Gyfeillion Rd
30 Trelewis, Gelligaer Rd
30 Usk, Maryport St
30 Usk, Porthycarne St
30 Whitland
30 Whitland, Market St
40 Whitland (East), Spring Gardens
30 Willowtow, Gwaun Helyg Rd
30 Ynysawdre, Heol-Yr-Ysgol
40 Ynysybwl, New Rd
30 Ystrad Mynah, Pengram Rd

## North Wales
### Ceredigion, Conwy, Denbighshire, Flintshire, Gwynedd, Isle of Anglesey, Powys, Wrexham

**A5**
30 Holyhead

**A5/A5025**
50 Holyhead to Llanfachraeth

**A470**
30,60 Conwy Valley
40,60 Dolgellau
40,60 (30 at rdbts) Llandudno to the A55
30,40,60 Tal-y-waenydd to Congl-y-wal (Blaenau)

**A483/A5**
60 Ruabon to Chirk

**A487**
30,40,50,60 Caernarfon to Dolbenmaen
30,40,60 Penmorfa to Gellilydan

**A494**
40,60 Bala to Glanrafon
30 Llyn Tegid, Bala
40,60 Ruthin to Llanferres

**A496**
30,40,60 Harlech to Llanbedr

**A499**
30,40,60 Pwllheli

**A525**
40,60 Denbigh to Ruthin
30,40,60 Llanfair Dyffryn Clwyd to Llandegla
30,60 Wrexham to Minera
30,40,60 Wrexham to Redbrook Maelor

**A534**
30 Holt Rd

**A539**
30,60 Llangollen, Mill St
30,40,60 Trevor to Erbistock

**A541**
30 Mold Rd
30,40,60,70 Mold to Caergwrle
30,40,60,70 Wrexham to Cefn-y-bedd

**A541/525**
30,40,60 St Asaph to Bodfari

**A545**
30,40 Menai Bridge to Beaumaris

**A547**
30,40,50 Colwyn Bay
30,40,60 Prestatyn to Rhuddlan
30 Rhyl, Vale Rd/Rhuddlan Rd

**A548**
30,40 Abergele to Kinmel Bay
30 Abergele, Dundonald Avenue
30,40,50,60,70 Gronant to Flint (Oakenholt)
30,40 Rhyl to Prestatyn

**A549**
30,60 Mynydd Isa to Buckley

**A550/B5125**
30 Hawarden

**A4086**
30,40,60 Cwm-y-glo to Llanrug

**A4212**
60 Graig Las/Tryweryn to Trawsfynydd

**A4244**
60 Ty Mawr to Cym-y-glo

**A5025**
30,40,50,60 Amlwch, Menai Bridge

**A5104**
30 Coed-Talon to Leeswood

**A5112**
30,40 Llandygai to Bangor

**A5119**
30,50,60 Mold to Flint

**A5152**
30,60 Bala
30 Chester Rd
30,40 Rhostyllen

**B4545**
30,40 Kingsland to Valley

**B5108**
30,60 Benllech

**B5109**
30 Llangefni

**B5113**
30 Colwyn Bay, Kings Rd/Kings Drive

**B5115**
30 Llandrillo, Llandudno Rd
30,40 Llandudno Promenade to Rhos Point

**B5118**
30 Rhyl Promenade

**B5120**
30 Prestatyn, Pendyffryn Rd

**B5129**
30,60 Kelsterton to Saltney Ferry

**B5420**
30 Menai Bridge

**B5425**
30,60 Llay, New Rd

**B5443**
30 Rossett

**Unclassified**
30,40 Johnstown
30,40 Kinmel Bay, St Asaph Avenue
30,40,60 Menai Bridge to Gwalchmai

---

# 🏴󠁧󠁢󠁳󠁣󠁴󠁿 Scotland

## Dumfries and Galloway
**A74(M)**
70 Cogries

**A7**
60 Langholm

**A76**
Auldgirth
60 Closeburn
30 Dumfries, Glasgow Rd Gateside

**A77**
60 Balyett
60 Cairnryan
60 Whiteleys

**A701**
30 Moffat
60 Mollinburn/St Anns

**A709**
60 Burnside

**A711**
50 Beeswing
30 Kirkcudbright

**A716**
60 Stoneykirk

**A718**
60 Craichmore

**B721**
30 Eastriggs

## Fife
**A91**
Deer Centre to Stratheden Jct
Guardbridge to St Andrews
Melville Lodges to St Andrews

**A92**
Cadham to New Inn
Cardenden Overbridge to Chapel
Cowdenbeath to Lochgelly
Crossgates to New Inn
Melville Lodges to Lindifferon
New Inn to Tay Bridge
Rathillet (south) to Easter Kinnear

**A823**
Dunfermline, Queensferryroad
Dunfermline, St Margaret Drive

**A907**
Dunfermline, Halbeath Rd

**A911**
Glenrothes to Leslie
Glenrothes to Milton

**A914**
Edenwood to Cupar
Forgan to St Michaels
Kettlebridge
New Inn to Cupar
Pitlessie to Clushford Toll

**A915**
Checkbar Jct to Percival Jcts

**A921**
Kirkcaldy, Esplanade
Kirkcaldy, High St/Path
Kirkcaldy, Rosslyn St
Kirkcaldy, St Clair St

**A977**
Kincardine, Fere Gait

**A985**
Culross (west) to C38 Valleyfield
Kincardine to Rosyth
Rosyth, Admiralty Rd
Waukmill to Brankholm

**B914**
Redcraigs to Greenknowes

**B942**
East of Collinsburgh

**B980**
Rosyth, Castlandhill Rd

**B981**
Cowdenbeath, Broad St
Gosshill to Ballingry
Kirkcaldy, Dunnikier Way

**B9157**
Bankhead of Pitheadle to Kirkcaldy
Orrock to East Balbairdie
Sheriff Rdbt to Kirkcaldy
White Lodge Jct to Croftgary

**Unclassified**
Buckhaven, Methilhaven Rd
Dunfermline, Townhill Rd
Glenrothes, Formonthills Rd
Glenrothes, Woodside Rd
Glenrothes, Woodside Way
Kirkcaldy, Hendry Rd
Leven, Glenlyon Rd
Methil, Methilhaven Rd

## Lothian and Borders
**East Lothian, Edinburgh, Midlothian, Scottish Borders, West Lothian**

**A8**
40 Edinburgh, at Ratho station

**A7**
60 Crookston
NSL Galashiels, Buckholmside to Bowland
30 Hawick Sandbed to Galalaw
30 Stow to Bowland

**A68**
30 Jedburgh
NSL Soutra Hill

**A70**
30 Edinburgh, Balerno between Bridge Rd and Stewart Rd

**A71**
30 Breich
30 Polbeth

**A72**
NSL Borders, Holylee nr Walkerburn
NSL Castlecraig nr Blyth bridge
30 Peebles, Innerleithen Rd

**A90**
40 Edinburgh, Southbound from Burnshot flyover to Cammo Rd

**A697**
30 Greenlaw and south approach
NSL Orange Lane
NSL Ploughlands to Hatchednize

**A697/8**
30 Coldstream

**A698**
NSL Ashybank
NSL Crailinghall

**A699**
40 Maxton Village

**A701**
NSL Blyth Bridge to Cowdenburn
30 Rachan Mill, Broughton to A72

**A702**
NSL Dolphinton to Medwyn Mains

**A703**
30 Eddleston and approaches
NSL Leadburn to Shiplaw
30 Peebles to Milkieston
30 Peebles, Edinburgh Rd

**A705**
30 between Whitburn and East Whitburn

**A706**
30 Whitburn, Carnie Place

**A720**
50 Edinburgh, City Bypass, east of Gogar Rdbt

**A899**
50 Edinburgh Lizzie Bryce Rdbt and Almond Interchange
50 South of Deer Park Rdbt

**A6091**
NSL Melrose bypass

**A6105**
30 Gordon and approaches

**B6374**
30 Galashiels, Station Bridge to Lowood Bridge

**Unclassified**
30 Edinburgh, Bruntsfield place btwn Thorneybauk and Merchiston place
40 Edinburgh, Comiston Rd btwn Oxgangs Rd and Buckstone Dr
40,60 Edinburgh, Frogston Rd west btwn Mounthooly loan and Mortonhall gate

## North East Scotland
**Aberdeen, Aberdeenshire, Moray**

**A90**
40 Aberdeen, Midstocket Rd to Whitestripes Avenue Rdbt
60 btwn bend at South of Leys and Bogbrae
60 btwn Bogbrae and north of Bridgend
70 btwn Candy and Upper Criggie
60 btwn Jct with B9032 and A98 at Fraserburgh
70 btwn Laurencekirk and north of Fourdon
70 btwn Mill of Barnes and Laurencekirk
60 btwn St Fergus and access Rd to Bilbo
70 Dundee to Aberdeen Rd at Jct with B9120 Laurencekirk
70 north of Newtonhill Jct to South of Schoolhill Rd
60 Peterhead and St Fergus, btwn A982 North Rd
70 Peterhead, btwn north of Bridgend and Blackhills
70 Portlethen to South Damhead (southbound), south of Schoolhill Rd
70 south of Schoolhill Rd, Portlethen to South Damhead (northbound)

**A92**
60 btwn Johnshaven and Inverbervie
60 btwn rdside of Kinneff and Mill of Uras

**A93**
30 Aboyne
40 at Banchory eastbound from Caravan Site
30 at Banchory westbound from Church
60 btwn Cambus O'May and Dinnet
60 btwn Dinnet to Aboyne
60 btwn Kincardine O'Neil and Haugh of Sluie

**A95**
30 Cornhill
60 btwn 30mph at Keith and Davoch of Grange

**A96**
60 btwn East Mill of Carden at B9002 Jct and north of Pitmachie
60 btwn Forgie and A98 Jct at Fochabers
60 btwn north of Pitmachie and Jct with A920 at Kirton of Culsalmond
30 Haudigain rdbt to Chapel of Stoneywood
60 Mosstodloch to Lhanbryde (East)
40 South Damhead to Midstocket Rd

**A98**
30 Banff
60 btwn Carnoch Farm Rd, Buckie and 30mph at Cullen
60 btwn Fochabers 30mph and Mill of Tynet
60 Buckle, btwn Mill of Tynet and Barhill Rd Jct

**A941**
60 btwn 30mph at Lossiemouth and 40mph at Elgin
60 btwn Clackmarras Rd and South Netherglen
60 btwn Glassgreen and Clackmarras Rd
60 from South Netherglen and Rothes

**A947**
60 btwn Mains of Tulloch Jct and Fyvie

**A947**
60 btwn Newmachar and Whiterashes

**A948**
60 btwn Ellon to Auchnagatt

**A952**
60 btwn New Leeds and Jct with A90 at Cortes

**B9040**
60 btwn Silver Sands Caravan Park to Jct with B9012

**B9089**
60 from Kinloss and crossroads at Roseisle Maltings

**Unclassified**
30 Aberdeen, Beach Boulevard to Links Rd
30 Aberdeen, Beach Boulevard to Wales Rd
30 Aberdeen, Great Northern Rd
30 Aberdeen, Great Southern Rd
30 Aberdeen, King St
30 Aberdeen, Springhill Rd
30 Aberdeen, St Machar Drive
40 Aberdeen, Wellington Rd
40 Aberdeen, West Tullos Rd

## Northern Scotland
**Highland, Orkney, Shetland, Western Isles**

**A9**
Altnasleanach by Inverness
Caulmaillie, Golspie, Sutherland
Cuaich by Dalwhinnie
Daviot, by Inverness
Fearn, by Tain
North Kessock jct (both directions)
North of Dalwhinnie junction nr Dalwhinnie
South of the Mound, by Golspie

**A82**
Altsigh Youth Hostel, by Inverness
Drumnadrochit, Temple Pier
Invergarry Power Station
Kingshouse Hotel, Glencoe
White Corries, Rannoch Moor, Lochaber

**A87**
West of Bunloyne jct

**A95**
by Grantown on Spey, Congash
Drumuillie by Boat of Garten
North of Cromdale

**A96**
East Auldearn jct, by Nairn
Gollanfield, by Nairn
Nairn, West Auldern Jct
West of Allanfearn jct, by Inverness

**A99**
Hempriggs, south of Wick

**A834**
Dingwall, nr Foddarty Bridge
Dingwall, Strathpeffer Rd

**A835**
Inverlael straight nr Ullapool

**A939**
Ferness to Grantown, Spey Rd

**B9006**
Sunnyside, Culloden, Inverness

## Strathclyde
**Argyll & Bute, East Ayrshire, East Dunbartonshire, East Renfrewshire, Glasgow, Inverclyde, North Ayrshire, North Lanarkshire, Renfrewshire, South Ayrshire, South Lanarkshire, West Dunbartonshire**

**M74**
Abington, Jct 13 (northbound)

**A70**
East Tarelgin

**A73**
Airdrie, Carlisle Rd

**A76**
New Cumnock, nr Lime Rd

**A78**
Fairlie, Main Rd

**A82**
Bridge of Orchy
Milton, Dunbarton Rd

**A85**
west of Tyndrum

**A89**
Airdrie, Forrest St

**A706**
South of Forth

**A730**
Rutherglen, Blairbeth Rd

**A737**
Dalry, New St/Kilwinning Rd

**A749**
East Kilbride Rd btwn Cathkin Rd and Cairnmuir Rd

**A807**
Bardowie, Balmore Rd

**A814**
Dunbarton, Cardross Rd

**A815**
nr Ardkinglass

**B768**
Rutherglen, Burnhill St

**B803**
Airdrie to Glenmavis, Coatbridge Rd

**B814**
Duntocher Rd

**B8048**
Kirkintilloch, Waterside Rd

**Unclassified**
Bargeddie, Glasgow Rd
Barrhead, Aurs Rd
Bishopbriggs, Woodhill Rd
Clydebank, Glasgow Rd
Coatbridge, Townhead Rd
Drymen Rd/Duntocher Rd
East Kilbride, Maxwelton Rd at Kirkoswald (South)
Johnstone, Beith Rd
Neilston, Kingston Rd
Newton Mearns, Mearns Rd
Paisley, Glasgow Rd nr Newtyle Rd
Rutherglen, Glasgow Rd
Rutherglen, Mill St
Troon, Craigend Rd

## Tayside
**Angus, Dundee, Perth & Kinross**

**A9**
60 Inverness to Perth road, nr Balnansteuartach
70 Perth to Inverness road, nr Inveralmond Industrial Estate
70 Stirling to Perth road, btwn Broom of Dalreoch and Upper Cairnie
70 Stirling to Perth road, Tibbermore jct

**A90**
40 Dundee nr Fountainbleau Drive, Forfar Rd
70 Dundee to Perth road, Walnut Grove to Inchyra
70 Dundee to Perth road, west of Longforgan village
50 Dundee, Kingsway
50 Dundee, Swallow rdbt to Strathmartine Rd rdbt

**A91**
60 Milnathort to Devon Bridge

**A92**
60 Arbroath to Montrose
30 Dundee btwn Arbroath Rd and Craigie Avenue, Greendykes Rd
40 Dundee, East Dock St

**A93**
60 Guildtown to Blairgowrie
60 Old Scone to Guildtown

**A94**
60 Scone to Coupar Angus

**A822**
60 Crieff to Braco

**A923**
60 Blairgowrie to Tullybaccart

**A933**
60 Colliston to Redford

**A935**
60 Brechin to Montrose

**A972**
40 Dundee, Kingsway East to Pitairlie Rd

**A977**
60 Kinross to Crook of Devon

**B961**
30 Dundee, Drumgeith Rd

**B996**
60 Kinross to Kelty

**Unclassified**
30 Dundee, Broughty Ferry Rd
30 Dundee, Charleston Drive
30 Dundee, Laird St
30 Dundee, Old Glamis Rd
30 Dundee, Perth Rd
30 Dundee, Strathmartine Rd

# Distance table

## How to use this table

Distances are shown in miles and kilometres with estimated journey times in hours and minutes.

For example: the distance between Dover and Fishguard is 331 miles or 533 kilometres with an estimated journey time of 6 hours, 20 minutes.

Estimated driving times are based on an average speed of 60mph on Motorways and 40mph on other roads. Drivers should allow extra time when driving at peak periods or through areas likely to be congested.

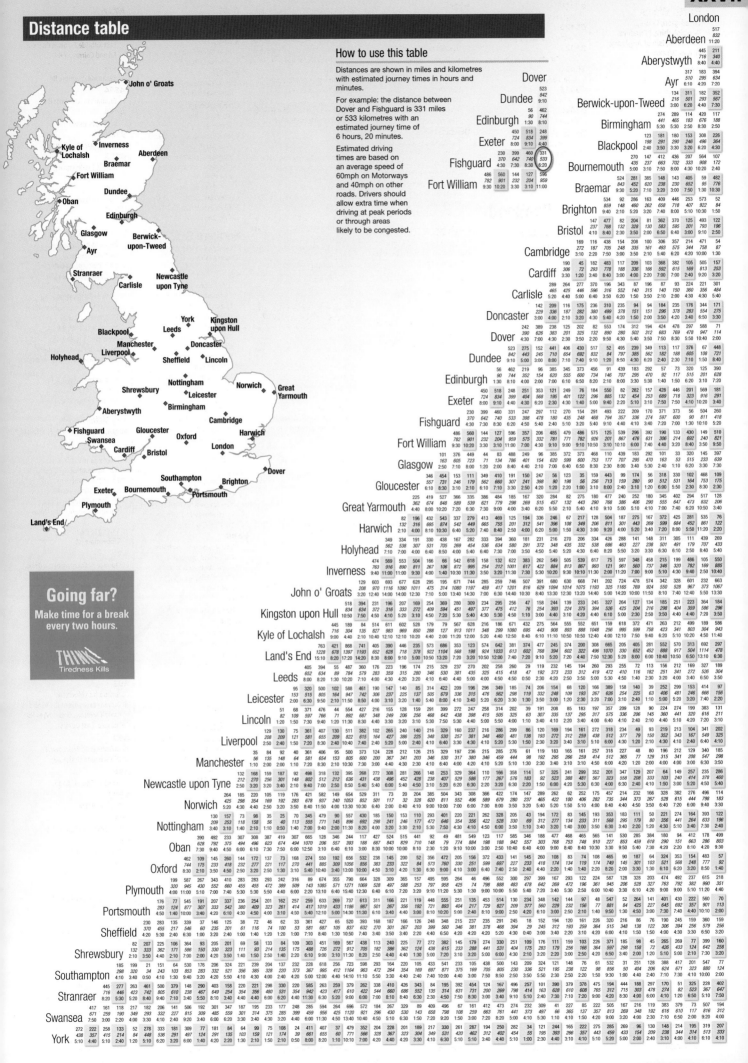

**Going far?**
Make time for a break every two hours.

THINK!
Tiredness Kills

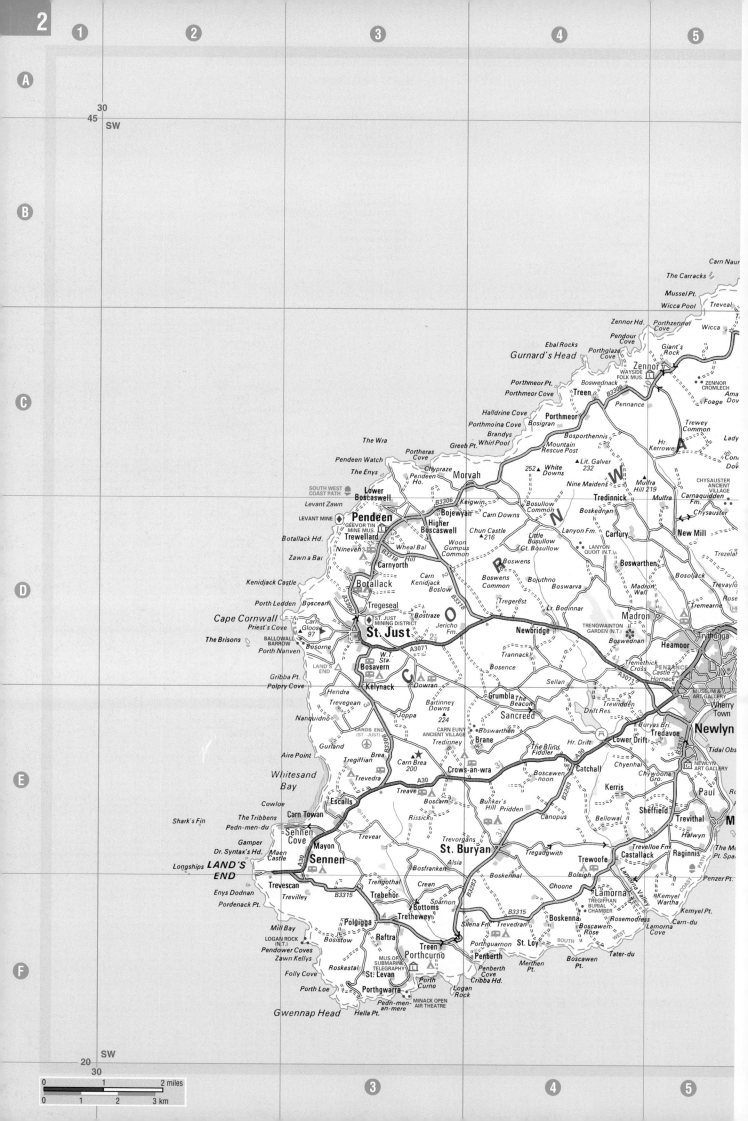

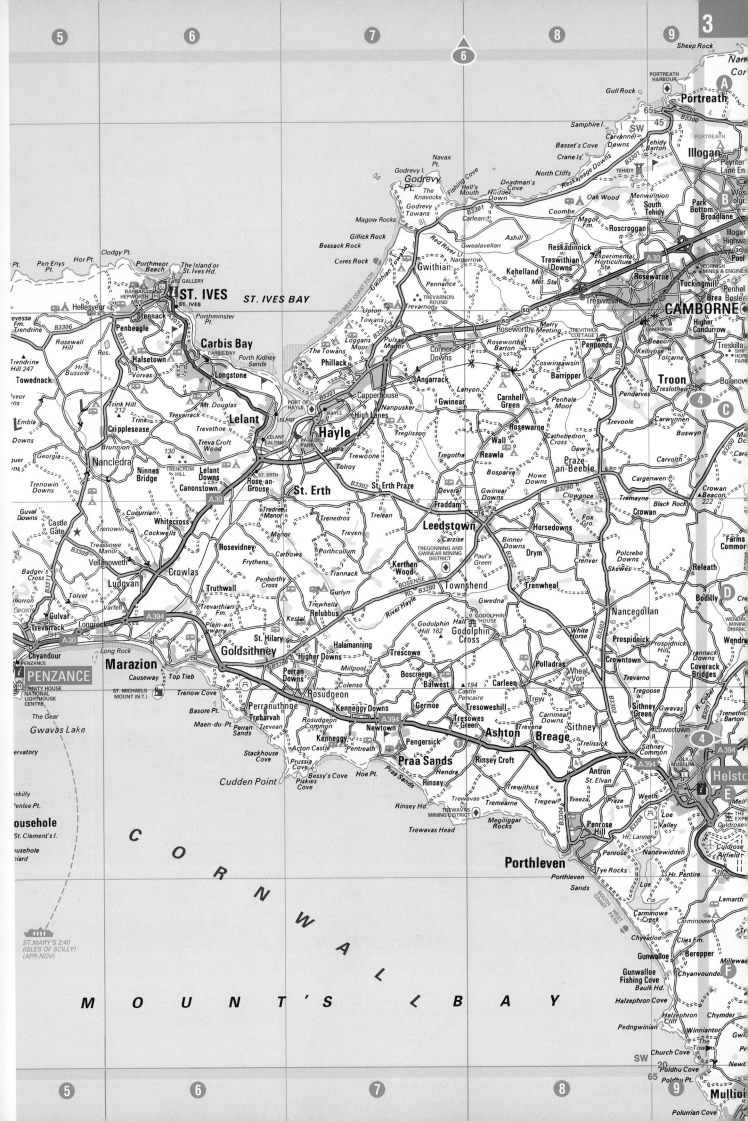

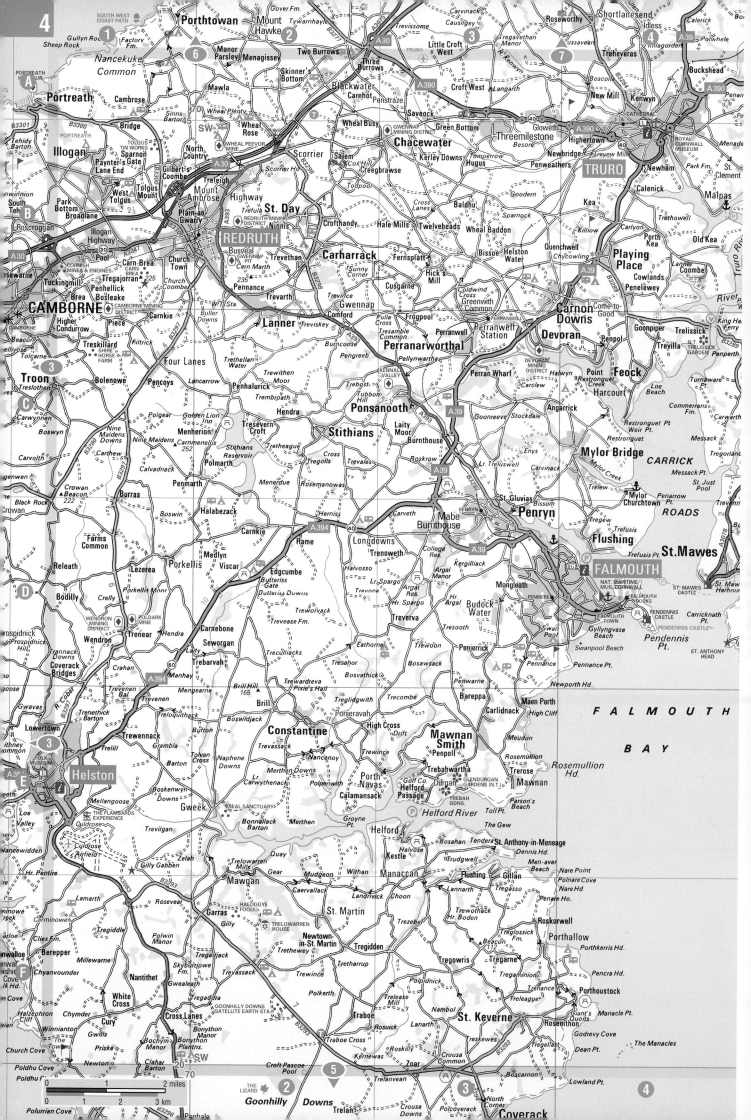

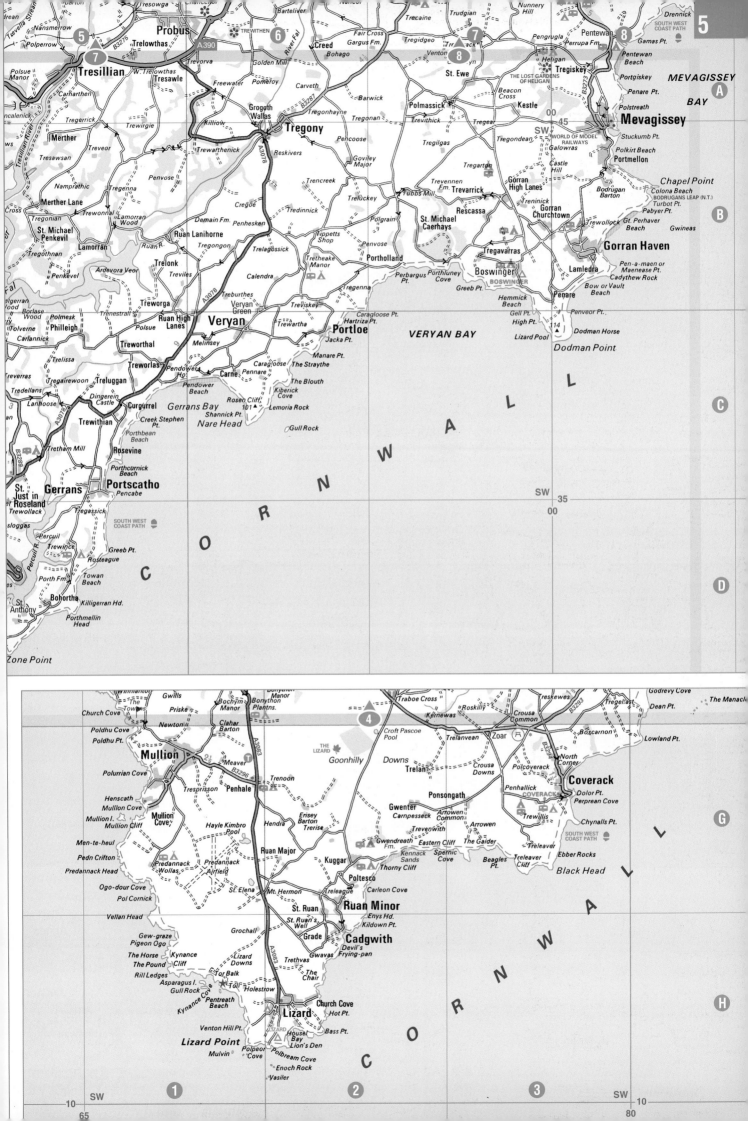

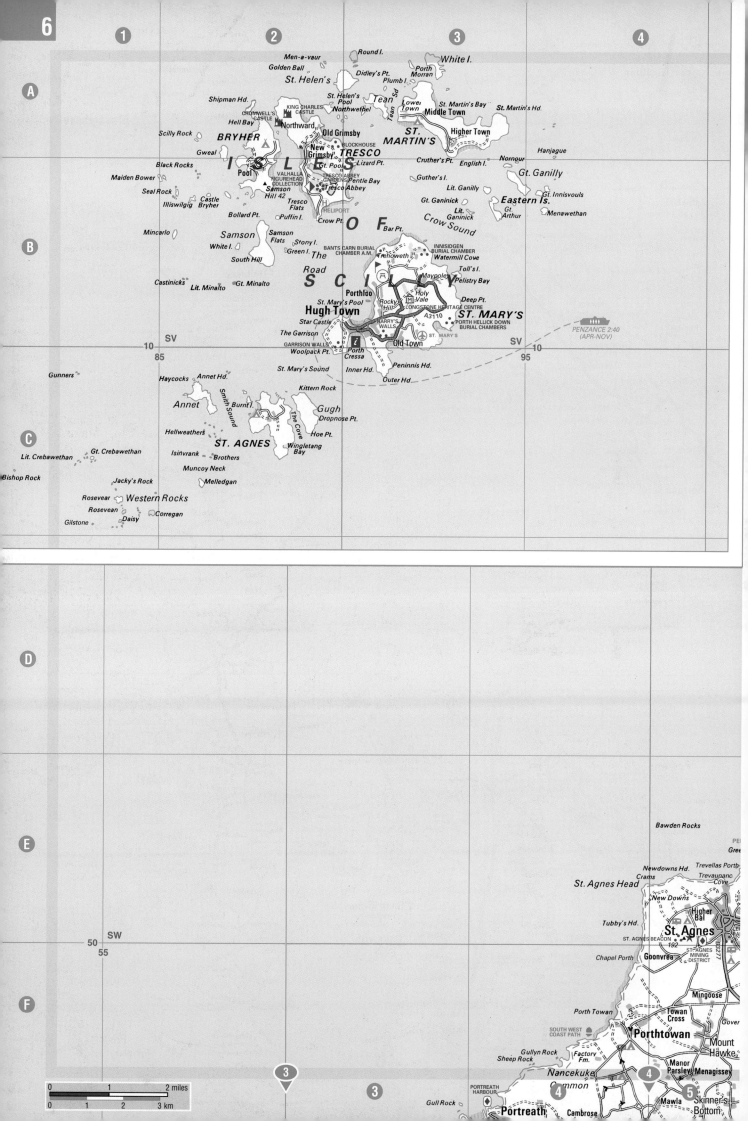

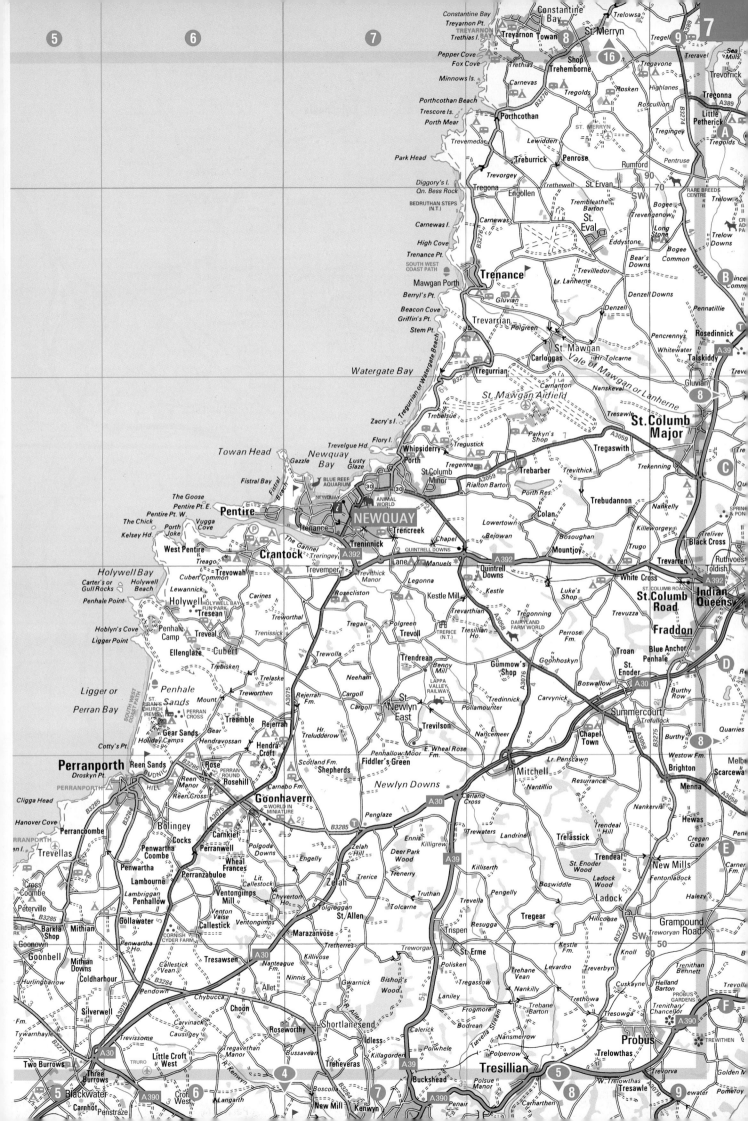

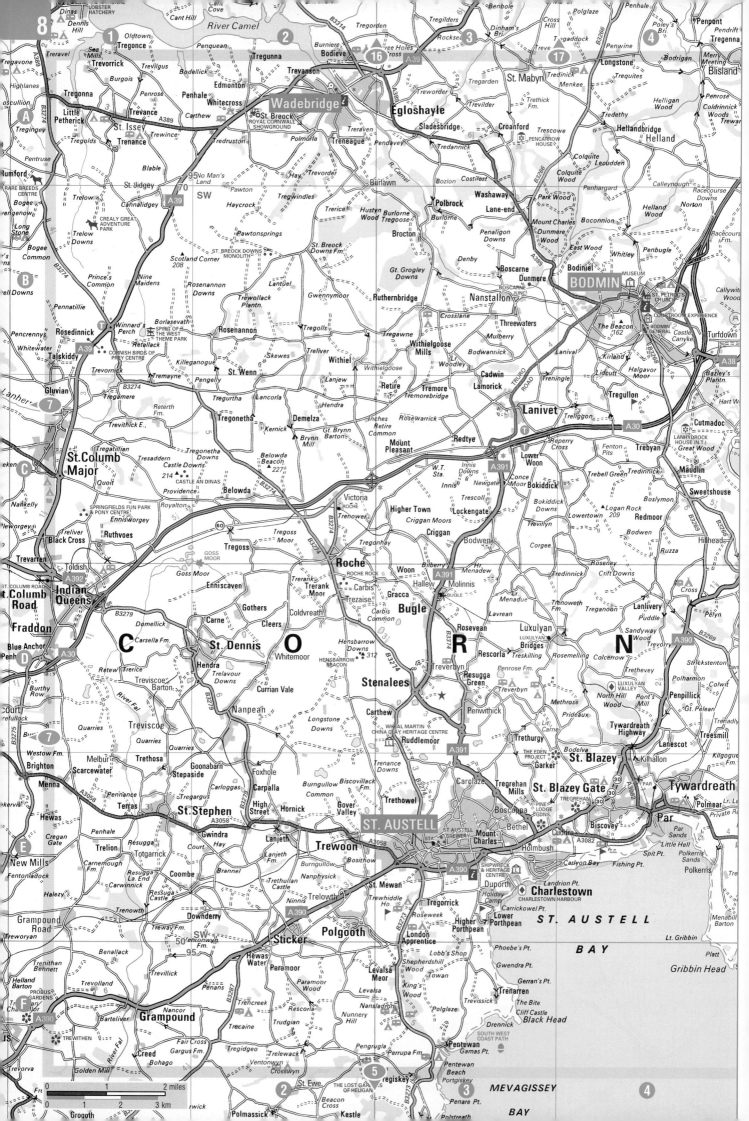

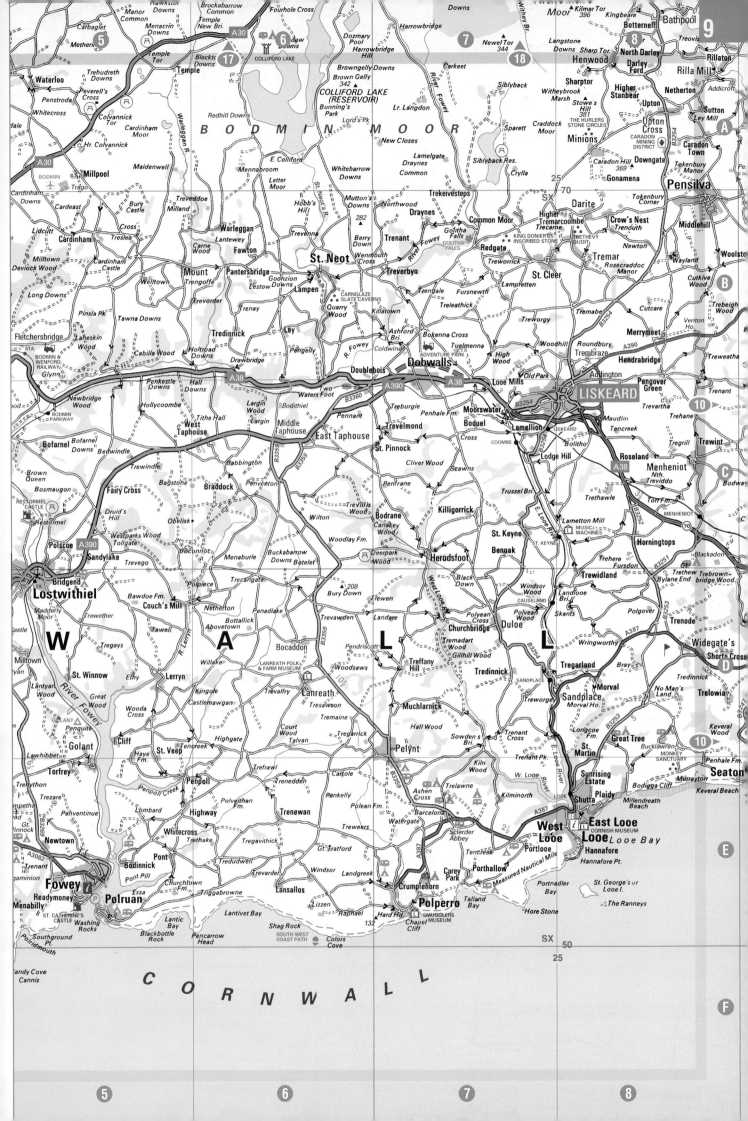

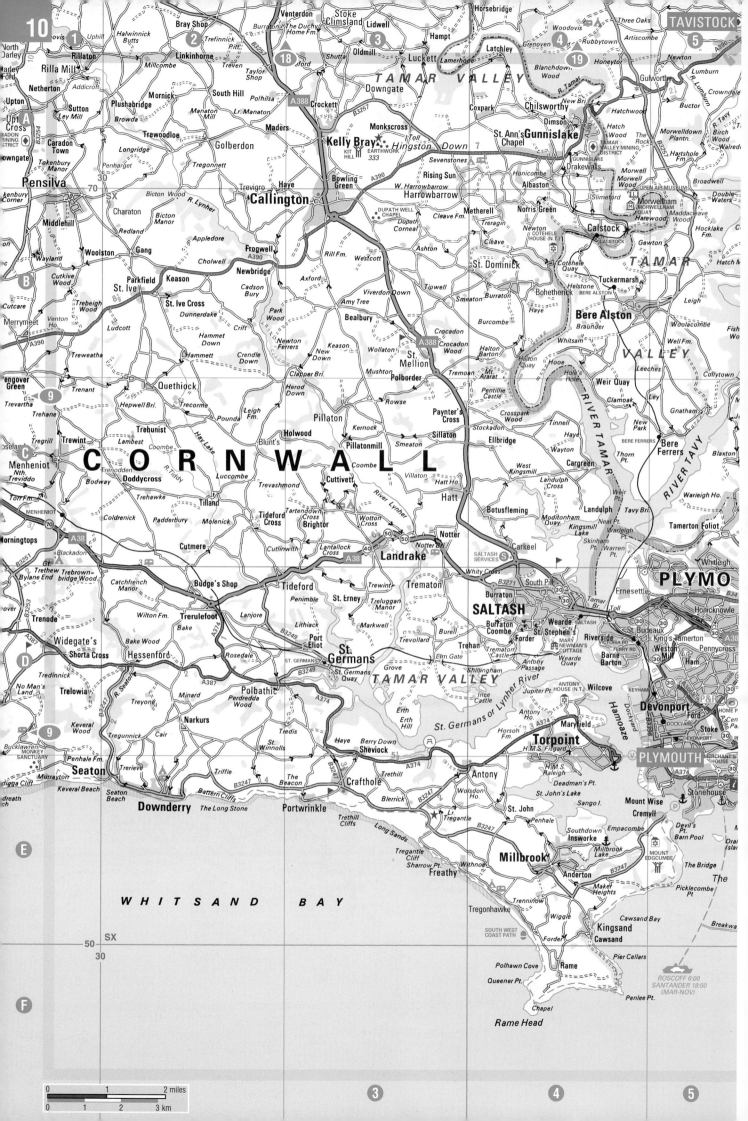

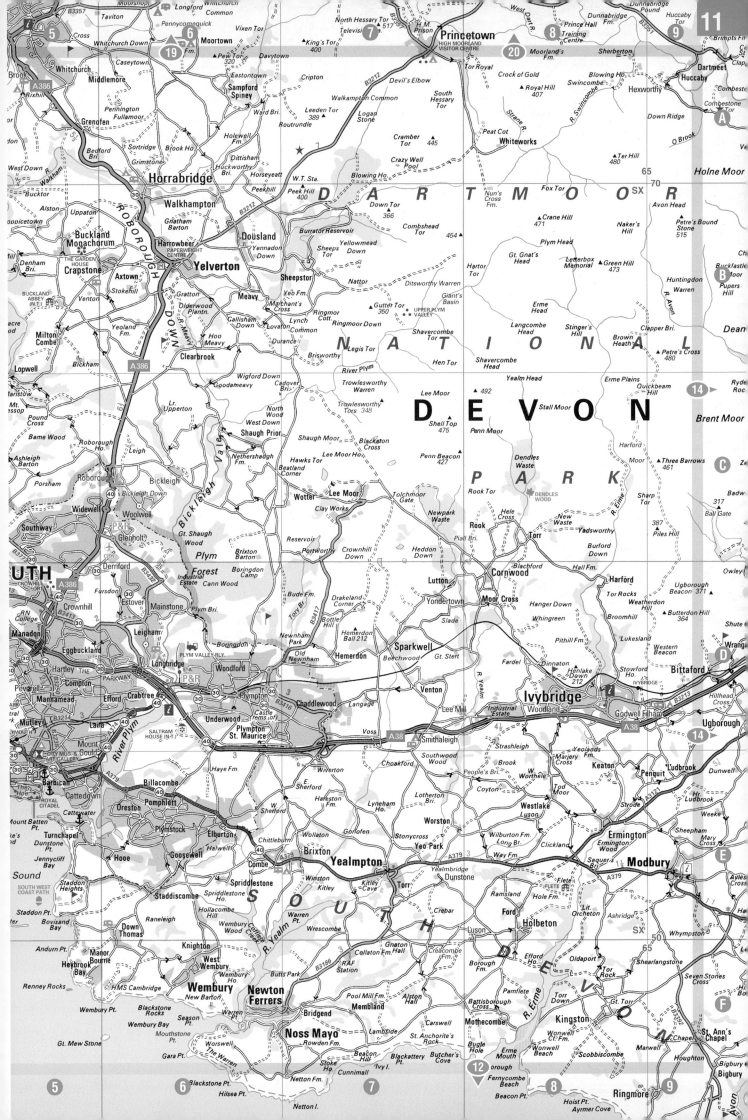

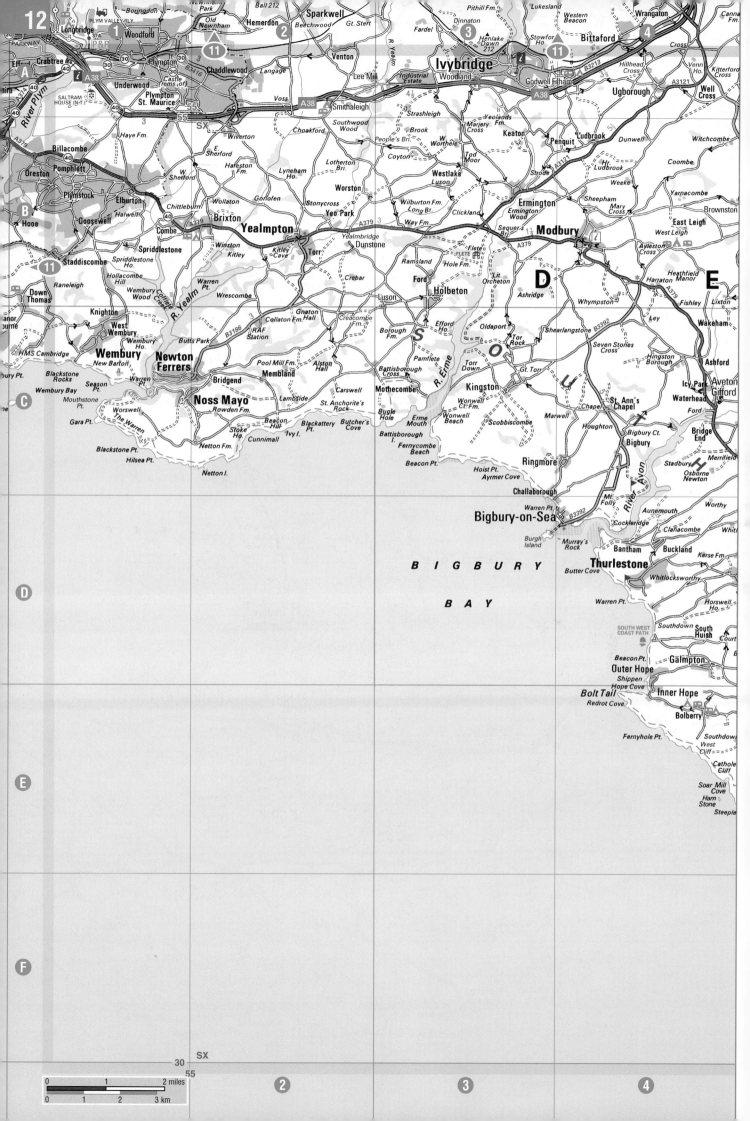

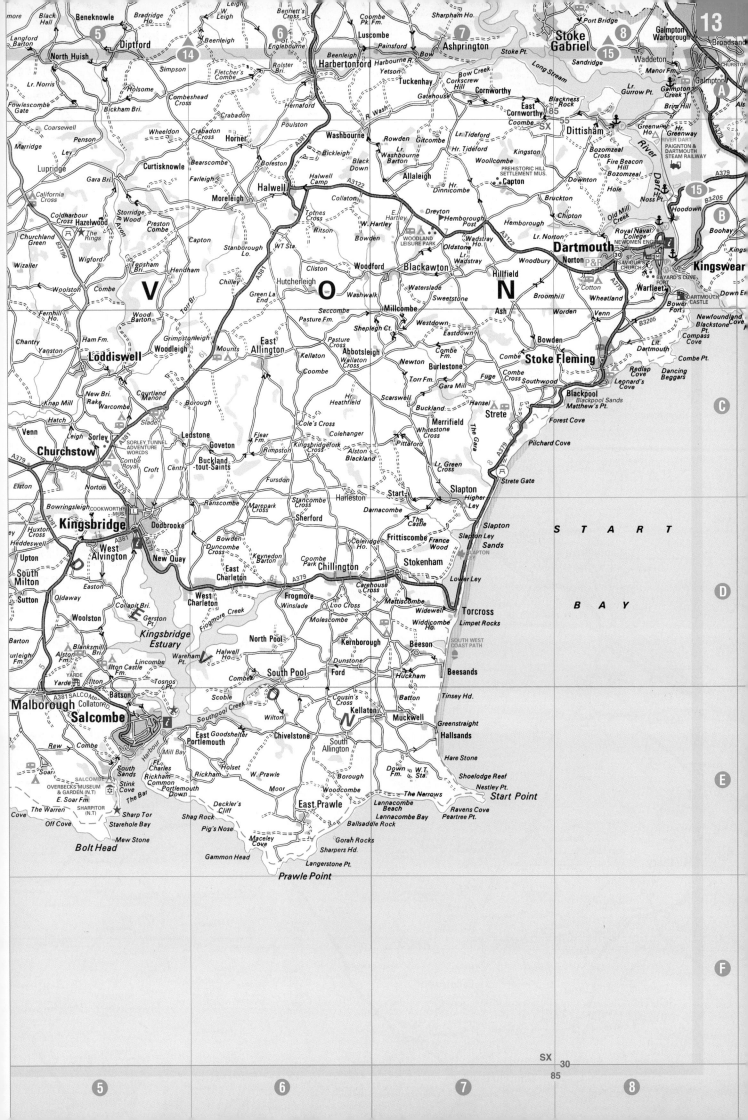

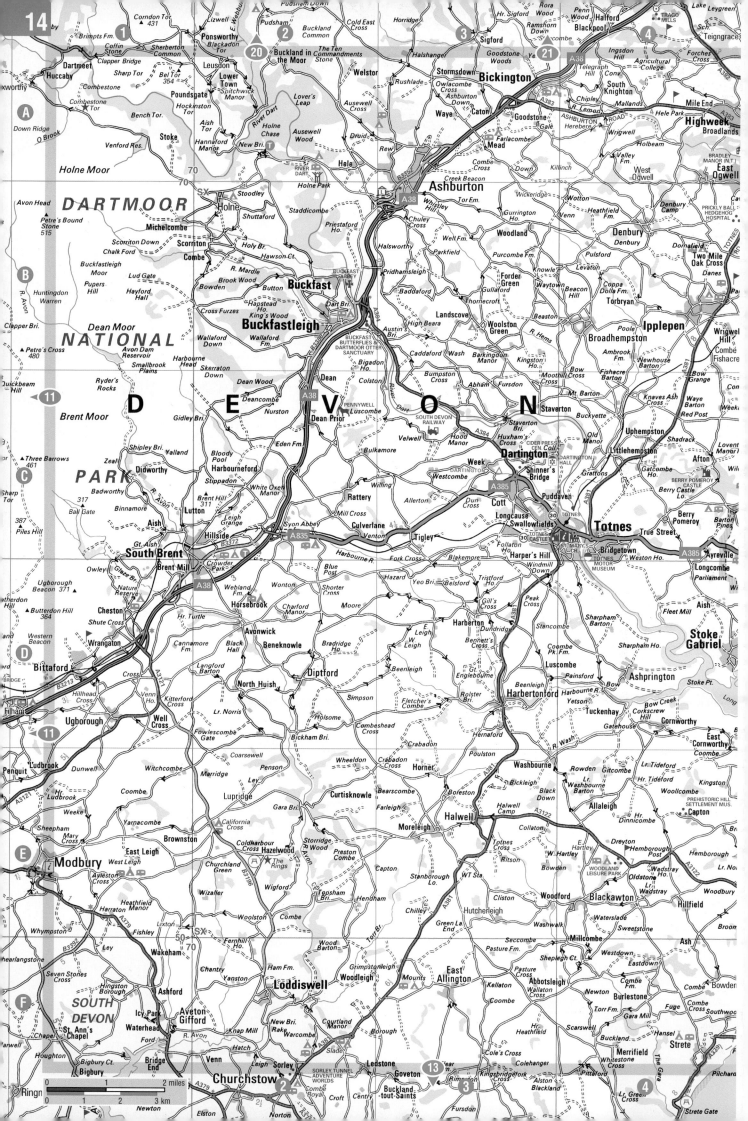

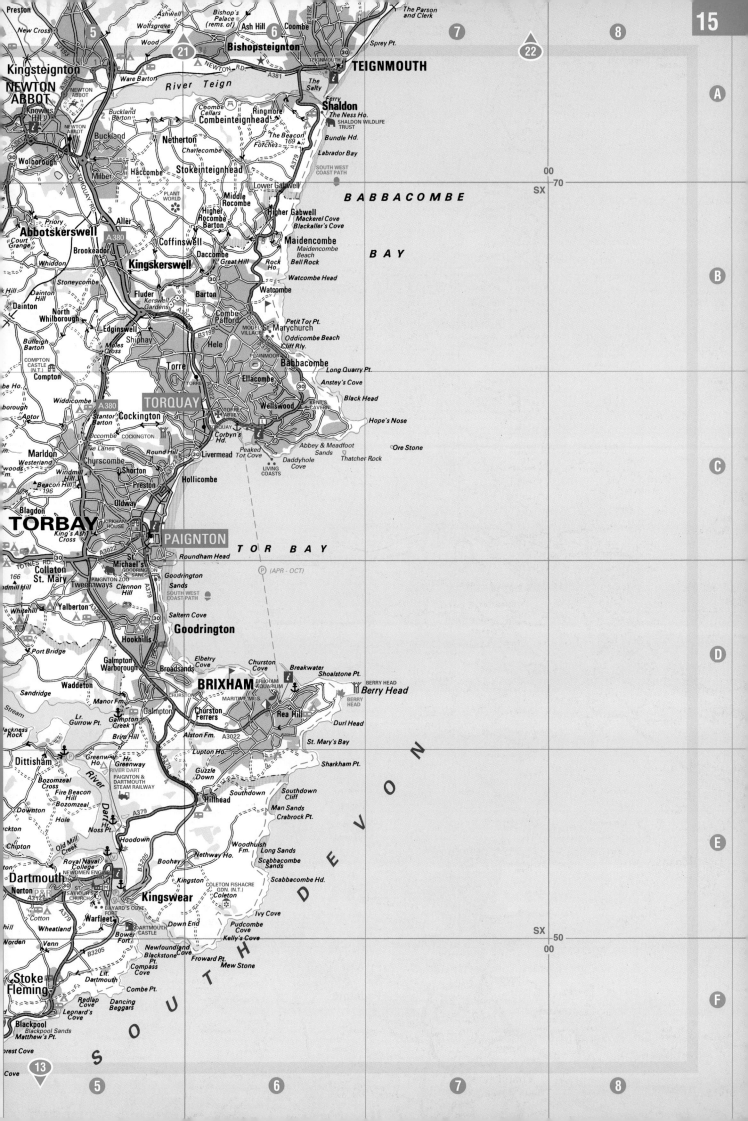

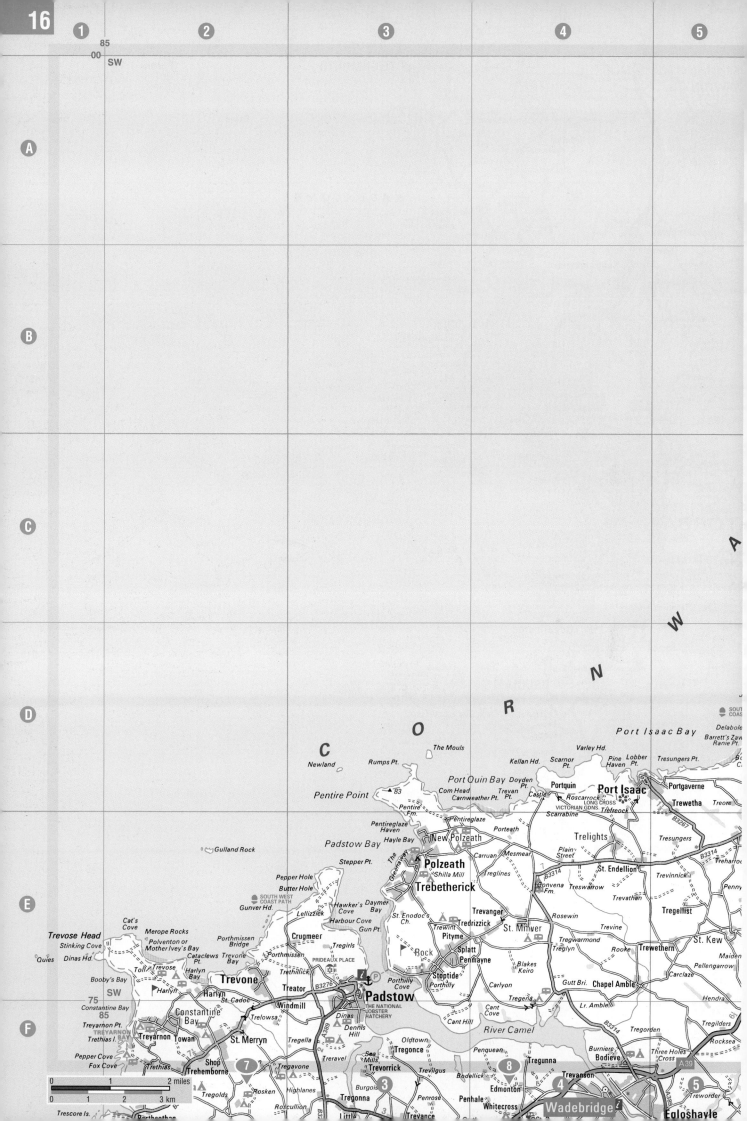

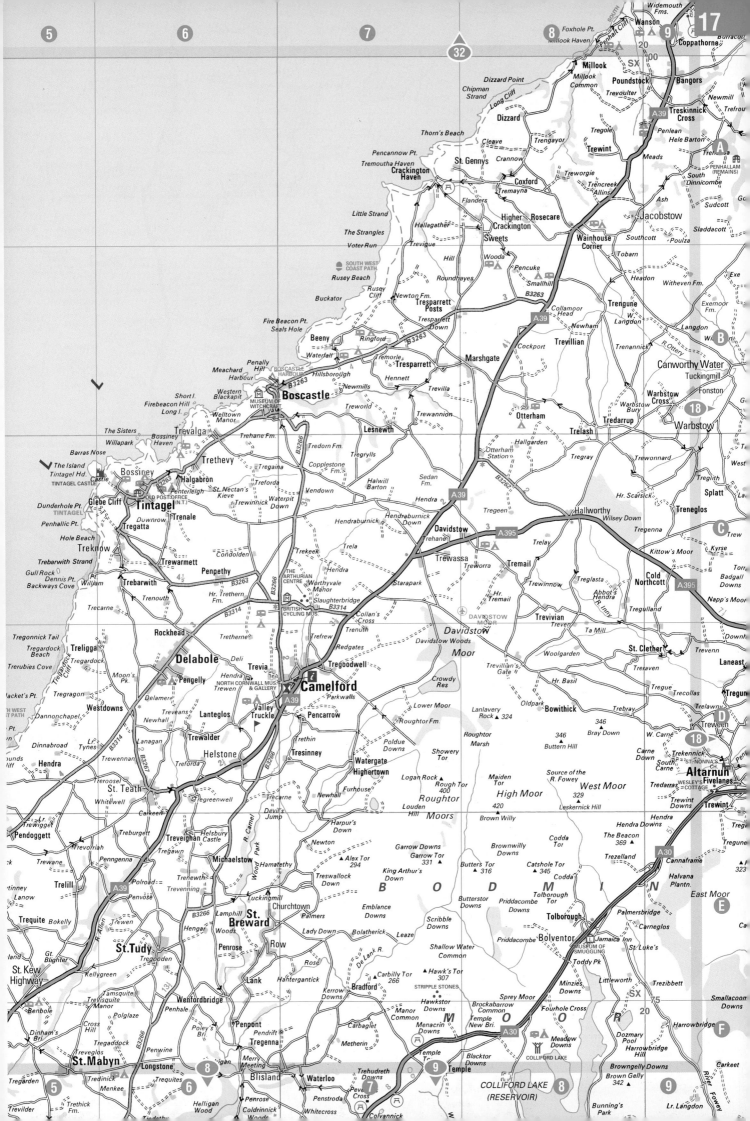

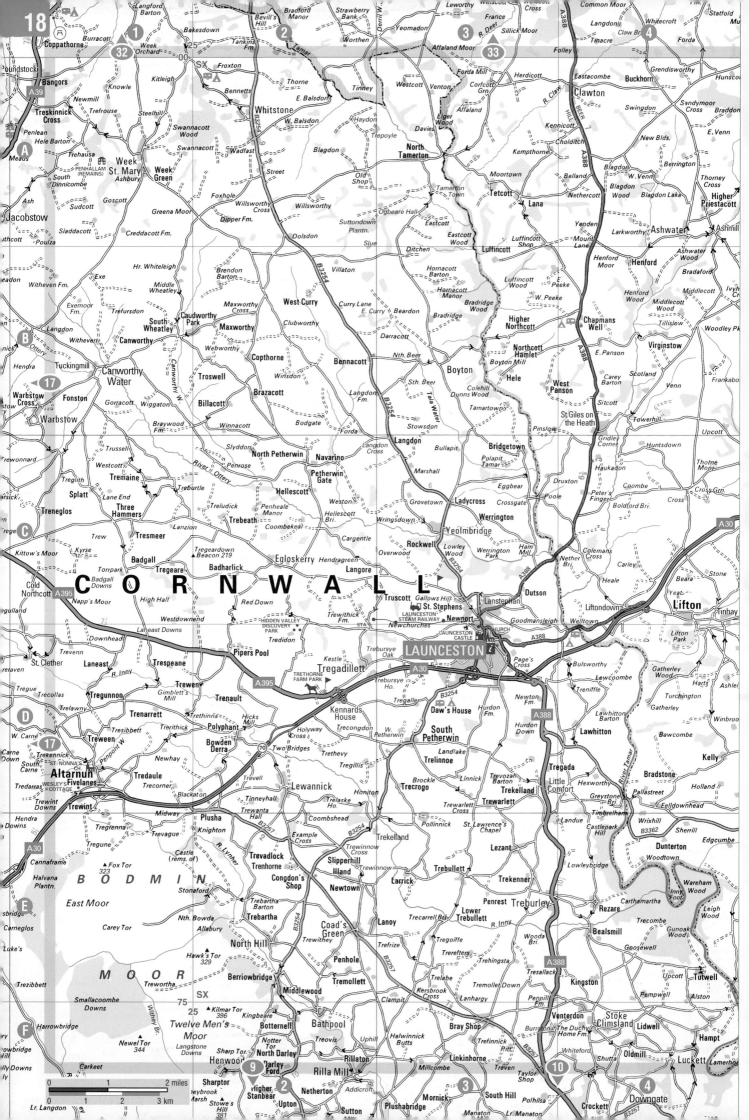

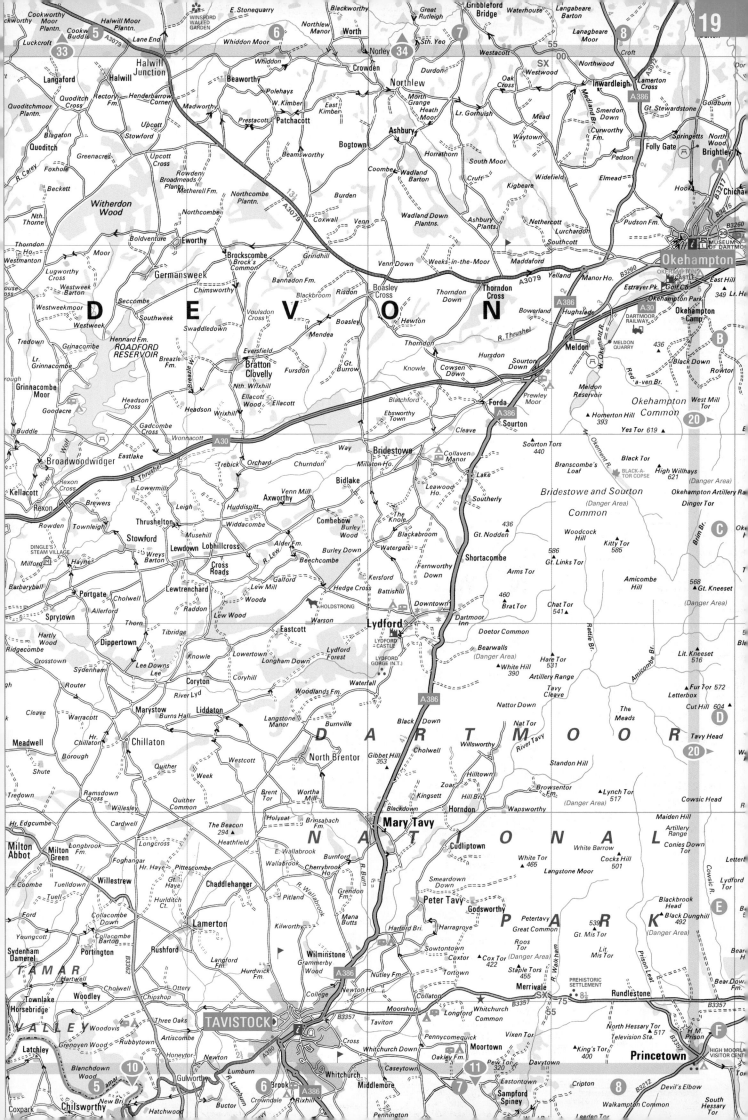

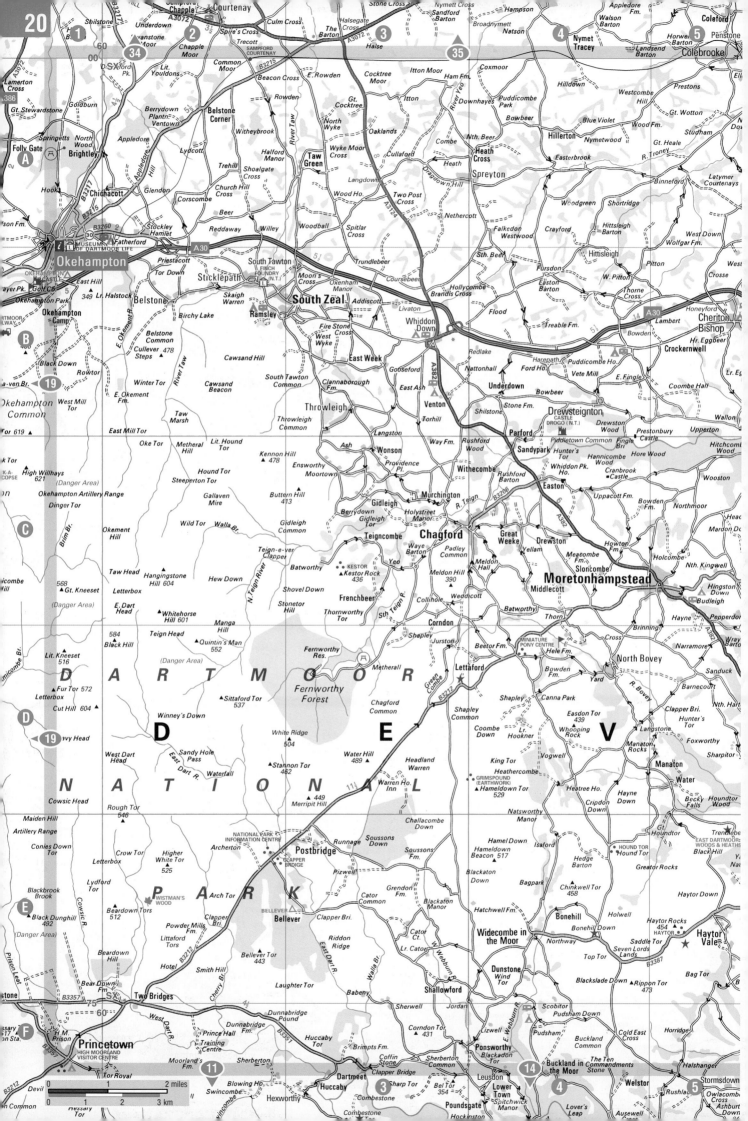

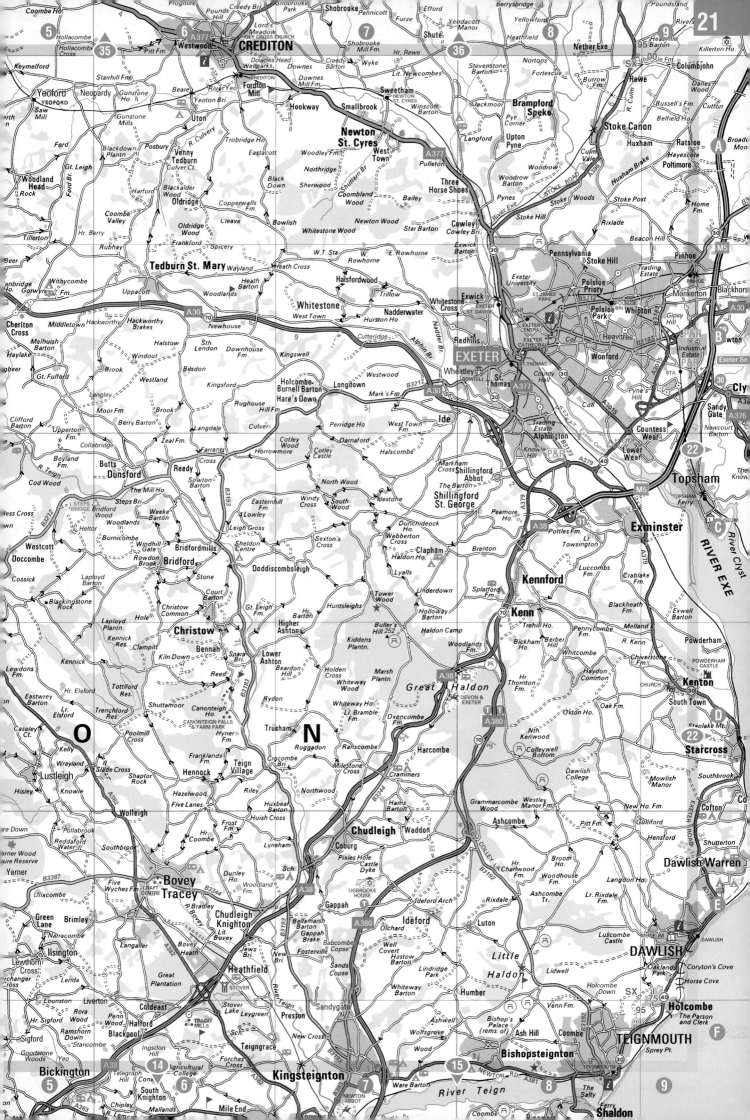

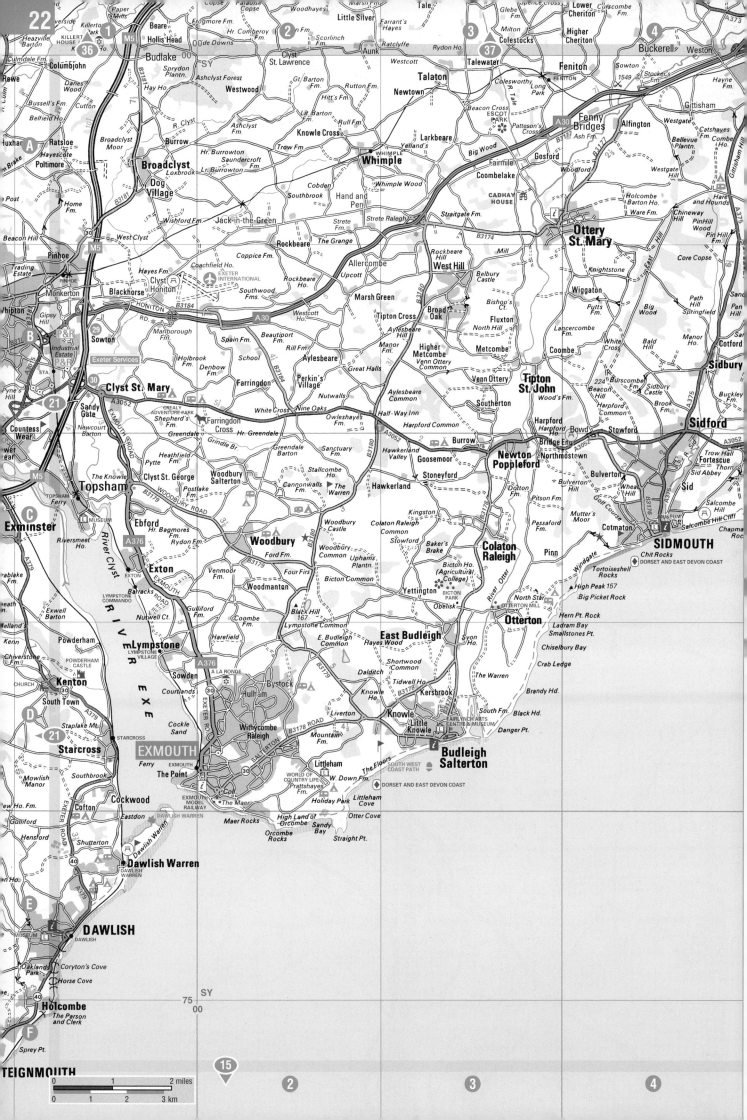

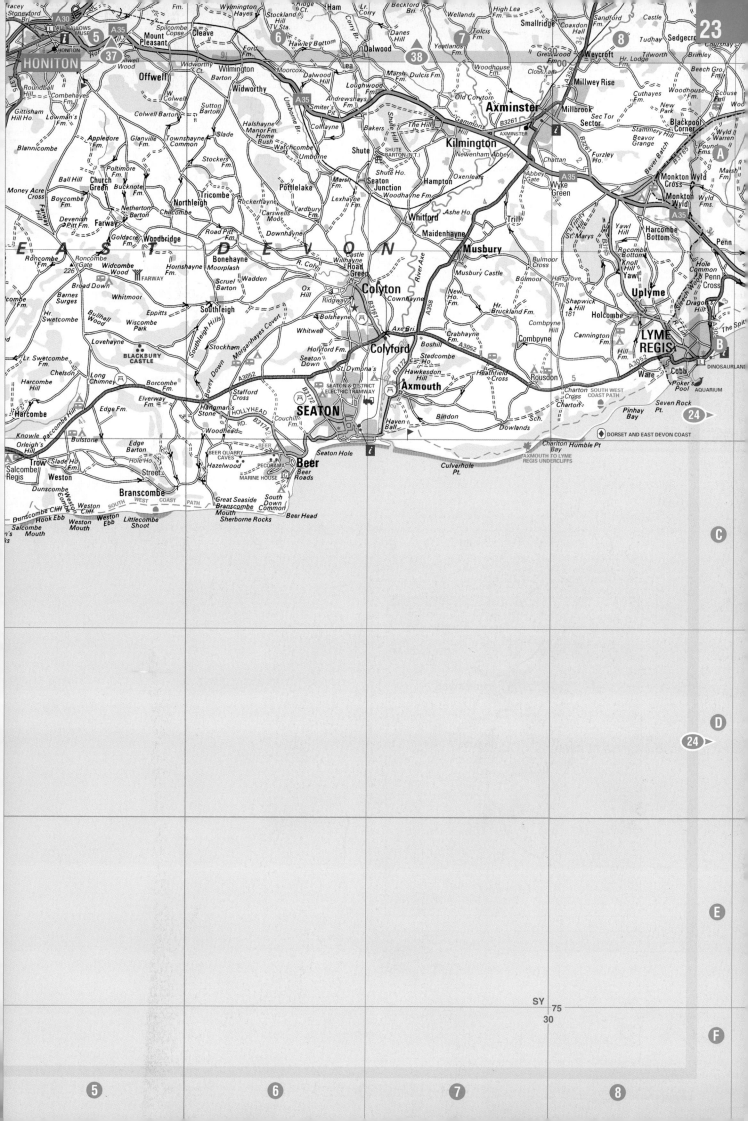

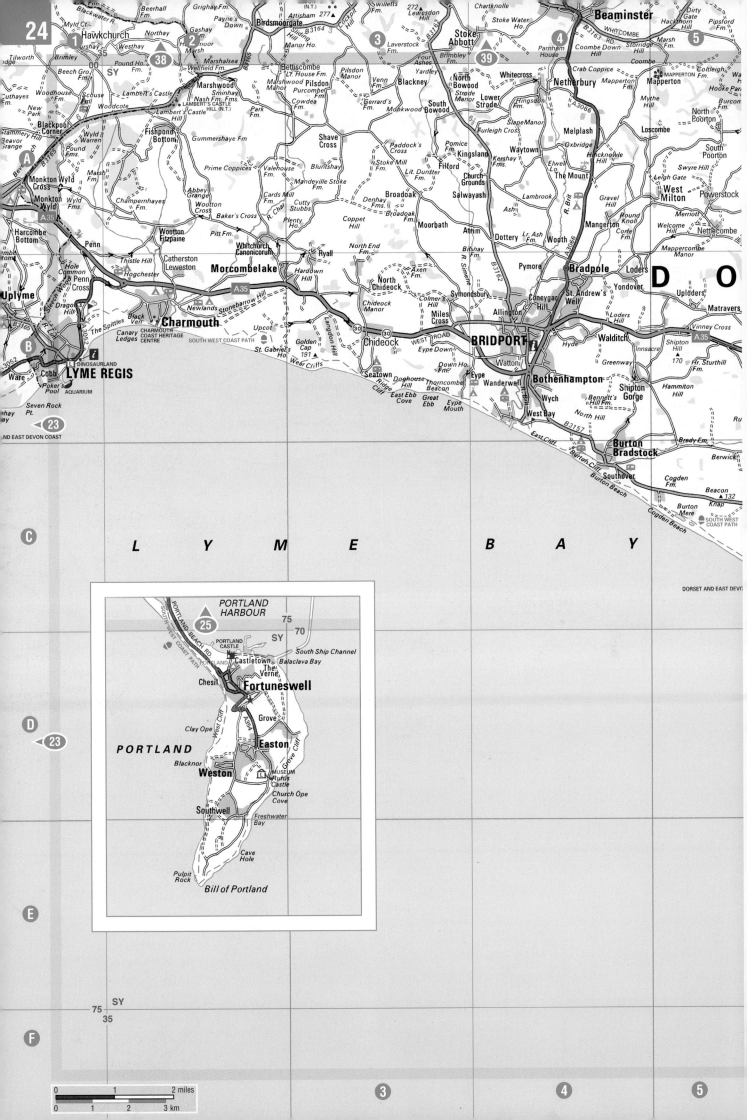

Hawkchurch
Blackwater R.
Beerhall Fm.
Grighay Fm.
Chartknolle
**Beaminster**
Dirty Gate
Hackthorn
Pipsford Fm.

Myld Ct.
Northay
Payne's Down
Birdsmoorgate
Attisham 277
Sliding Hill
Stoke Water Ho.
WHITCOMBE
B3163 RD.
Coombe Down Hill
Storridge Hill
Marsh Fm.

Tilworth
Brimley
Mudshay
Westhay
B3164
Cockpit Hill
Swilletts
Lewesdon Hill
**Stoke Abbott**
Parnham House
Crab Coppice
Coltleigh Fm.

Woodhouse Fm.
Scouse Farm
Lambert's Castle
Marshwood
Marshalsea
Wellfield Fm.
Bettiscombe
Laverstock Fm.
Four Ashes
Brimley Fm.
Netherbury
Mapperton
**Mapperton**
Hooke Park

Beech Gro. Fm.
Woodcote
Lambert's Castle Hill (N.T.)
Marshwood
Sminhay
Pilsdon
Manor Ho.
Venn Fm.
Blackney
North Bowood
Whitecross
Hingsdon
Oxbridge
Mythe Hill
North Poorton

Blackpool Corner
Wyld Warren
Fishpond Bottom
Nash Fm.
Park Fm.
Pilsdon Purcombe
Cowdale
Gerrard's
Monkwood
South Bowood
Strode Manor
Lower Strode
Slape Manor
**Melplash**
Loscombe

Stammery Hill
Beavor Grange
Pound Fm.
Wyld Fms.
Gummershaye Fm
Prime Coppices
Valehouse Fm.
Stoke Mill
Fifford
Kingsland
Pomice Fm.
Kershay Fms.
Furleigh Cross
Elwell Lo.
The Mount
South Poorton

**A** Monkton Wyld Cross
Monkton Wyld
A35
Champernhayes
Wootton Cross
Abbey Grange
Cards Mill Fm.
R. Char
Lit. Dunster Fm.
Church Grounds
Lambrook
Gravel Hill
Swyre Hill
Leigh Gate
**West Milton**
Powerstock

Harcombe Bottom
Penn
Thistle Hill
Hogchester
Catherston Leweston
Baker's Cross
Plenty Ho.
Cutty Stubbs
Broadoak
Denhay Fms.
Broadoak Fm.
Moorbath
Atrim
Dottery
Lr. Ash Fm.
Wooth
Ash
Mangerton
Corfe
Round Knoll
Welcome Hill
Merriott
Nettlecombe

Uplyme
Hole Common & Penn Cross
Dragon's Hill
The Spittles
Black Ven
Newlands
Stonebarrow Hill
Hardown Hill
Ryall
North End Fm.
North Chideock
Axen Fm.
R. Simene
Bilshay Fm.
Pymore
Coneygar Hill
St. Andrew's Well
**Bradpole**
Yondover
Loders
Mappercombe Manor

**B** Ware
Cobb
Poker's Pool
**LYME REGIS**
DINOSAURLAND
AQUARIUM
**Charmouth**
CHARMOUTH COAST HERITAGE CENTRE
Canary Ledges
Upcot
St. Gabriel's Ho.
Golden Cap 191
Langdon Hill
**Chideock**
Chideock Manor
Colmer's Hill
Miles Cross
Symondsbury
Allington
WEST ROAD
**BRIDPORT**
Loders Hill
Hyde
Waldìtch
Innsacre
Shipton Hill 170
Hr. Sturthill
A35
Vìnney Cross
Matravers
**Uploders**

SOUTH WEST COAST PATH
Wear Cliffs
Seatown
Ridge Cliff
Doghouse Hill
Thorncombe Beacon
East Ebb Cove
Great Ebb
Down Ho. Fm.
Eype Down
Eype Mouth
**Eype**
Wanderwell
Watton
**Bothenhampton**
Wych
Greenway
Bennett's Hill Fm.
Shipton Gorge
Hammiton Hill

Seven Rock Pt.
West Bay
North Hill
East Cliff
B3157
Southover
Burton Cliff
**Burton Bradstock**
Cogden Fm.
Bredy Fm.
Berwick

ND EAST DEVON COAST
Burton Beach
Burton Mere
Beacon Knap 132
Cogden Beach
SOUTH WEST COAST PATH

**L   Y   M   E      B   A   Y**

DORSET AND EAST DEVO

**PORTLAND HARBOUR**
SOUTH WEST COAST PATH
PORTLAND BEACH RD.
75
70
SY
PORTLAND CASTLE
South Ship Channel
**Castletown**
Balaclava Bay
The Verne
Chesil
**Fortuneswell**
Grove
**PORTLAND**
Clay Ope
West Cliff
A354
**Easton**
Grove Cliff
Blacknor
MUSEUM
Rufus Castle
Church Ope Cove
**Weston**
**Southwell**
Freshwater Bay
Cave Hole
Pulpit Rock
*Bill of Portland*

0      1      2 miles
0    1    2    3 km

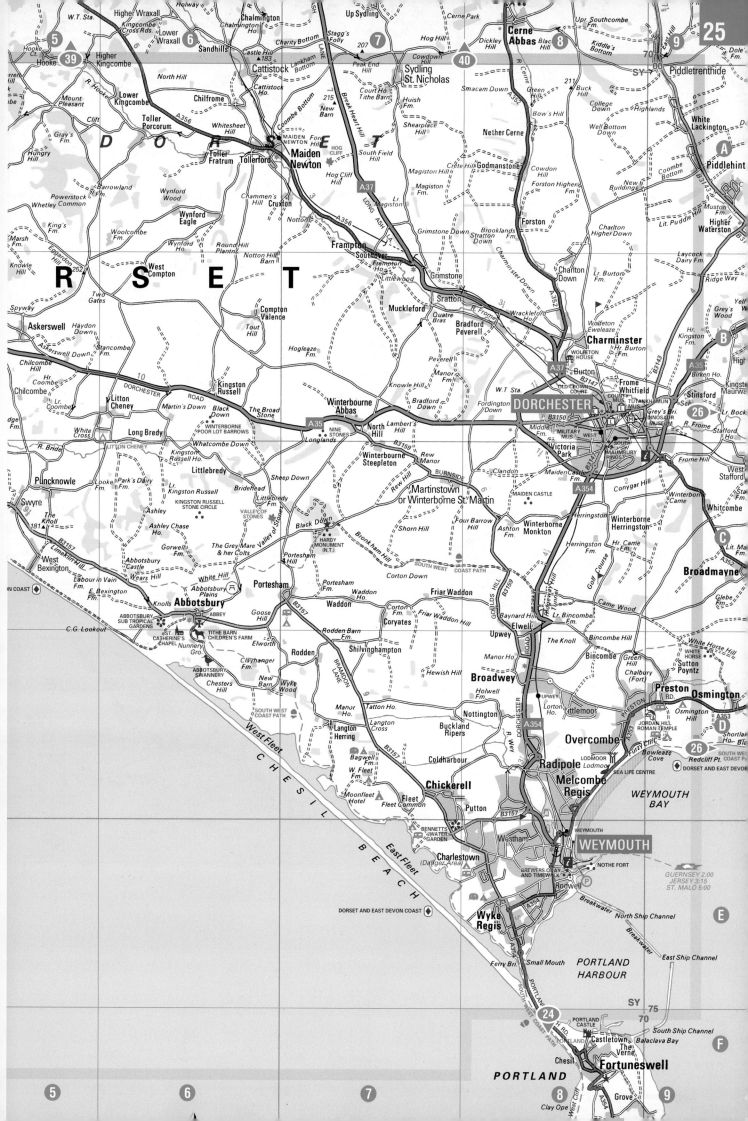

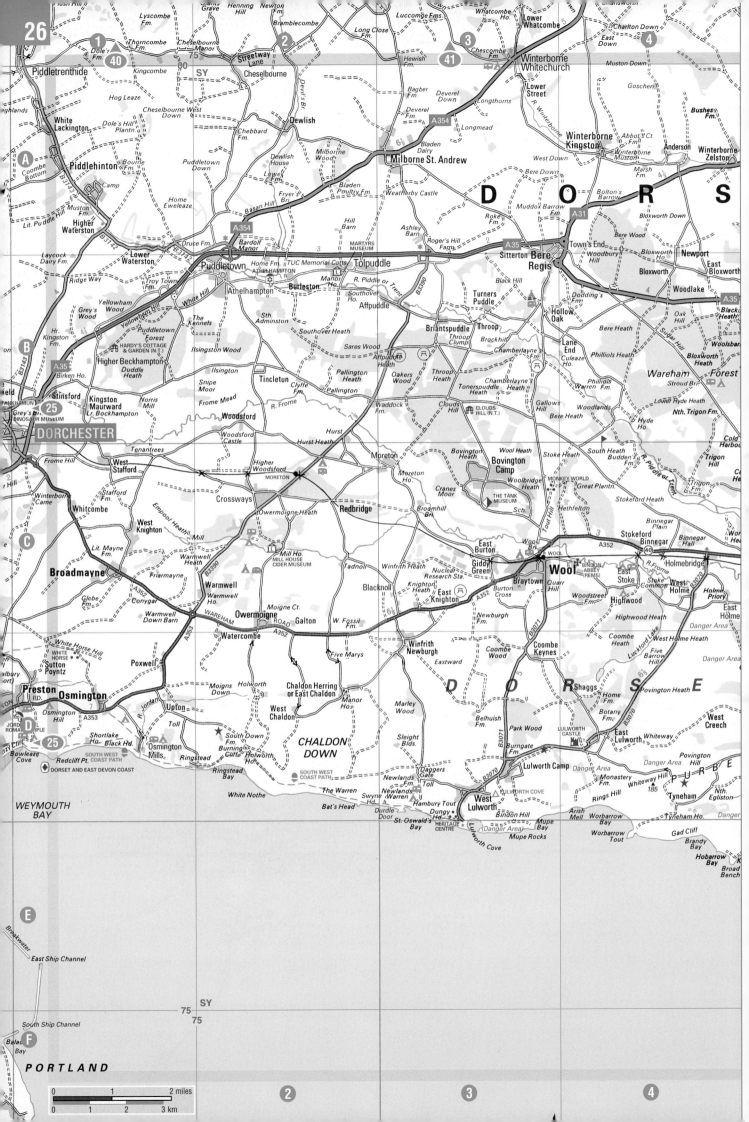

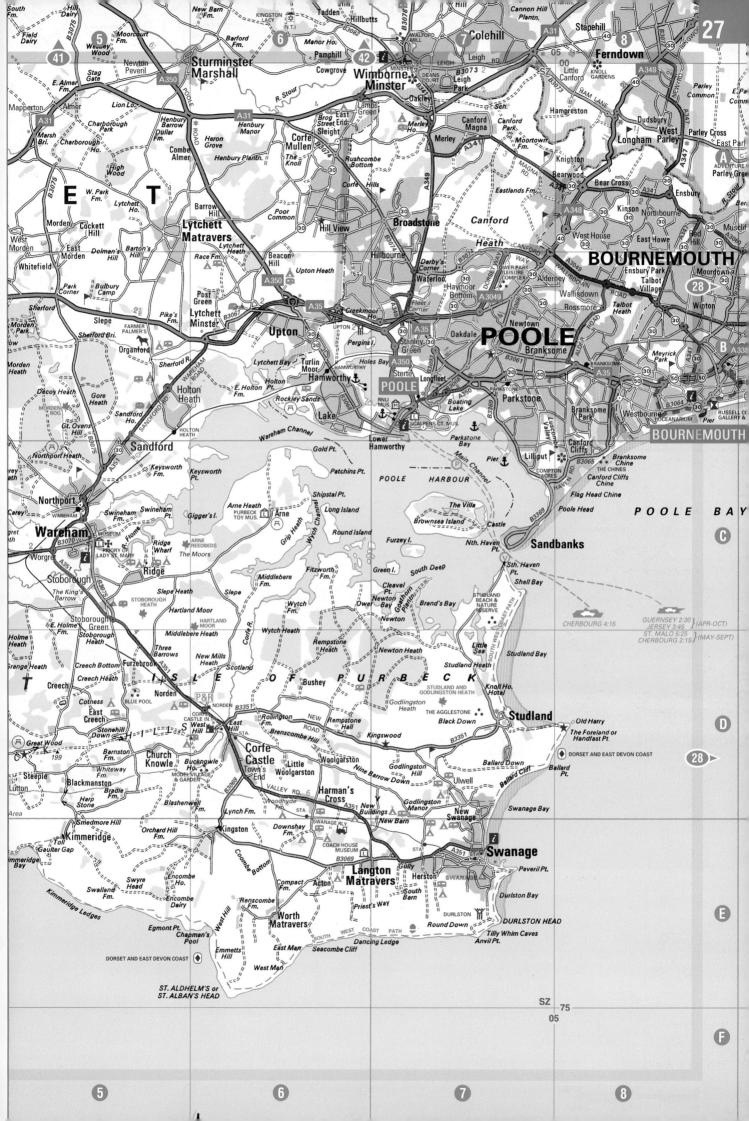

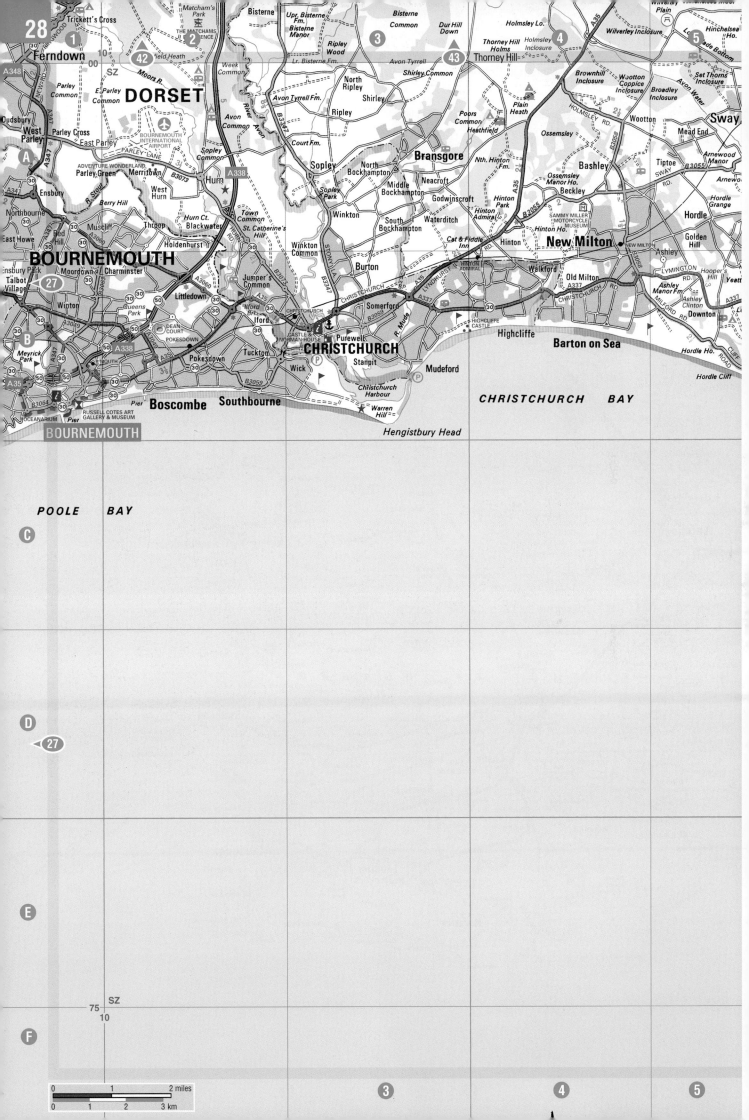

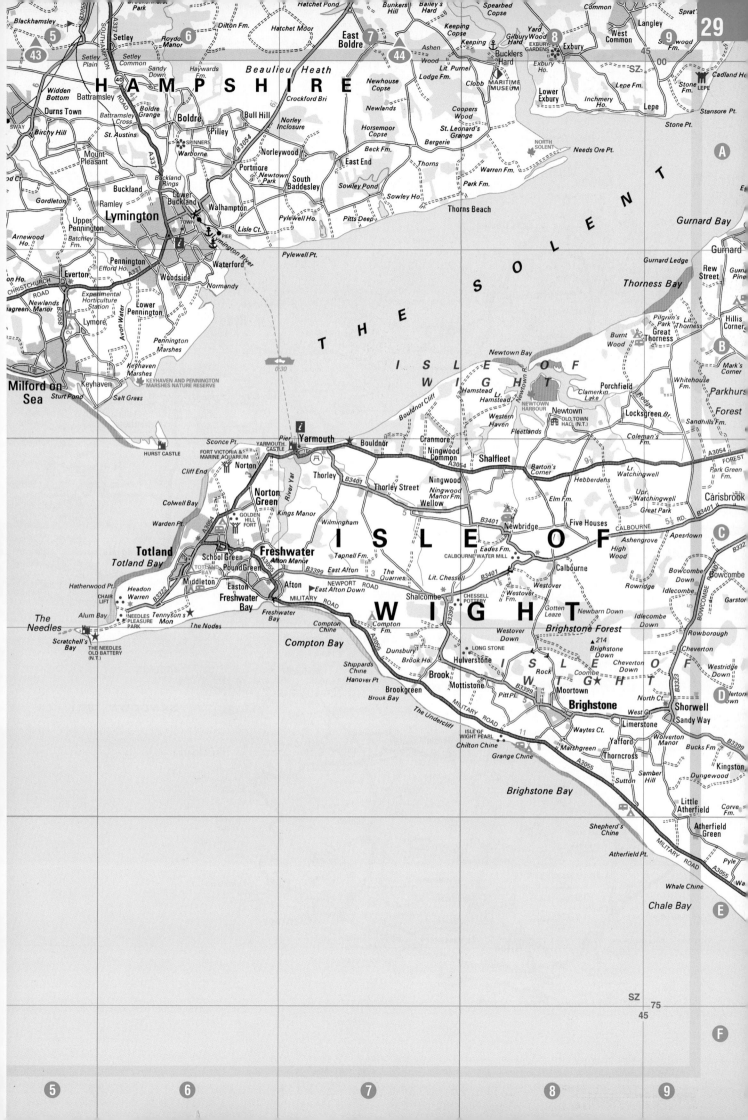

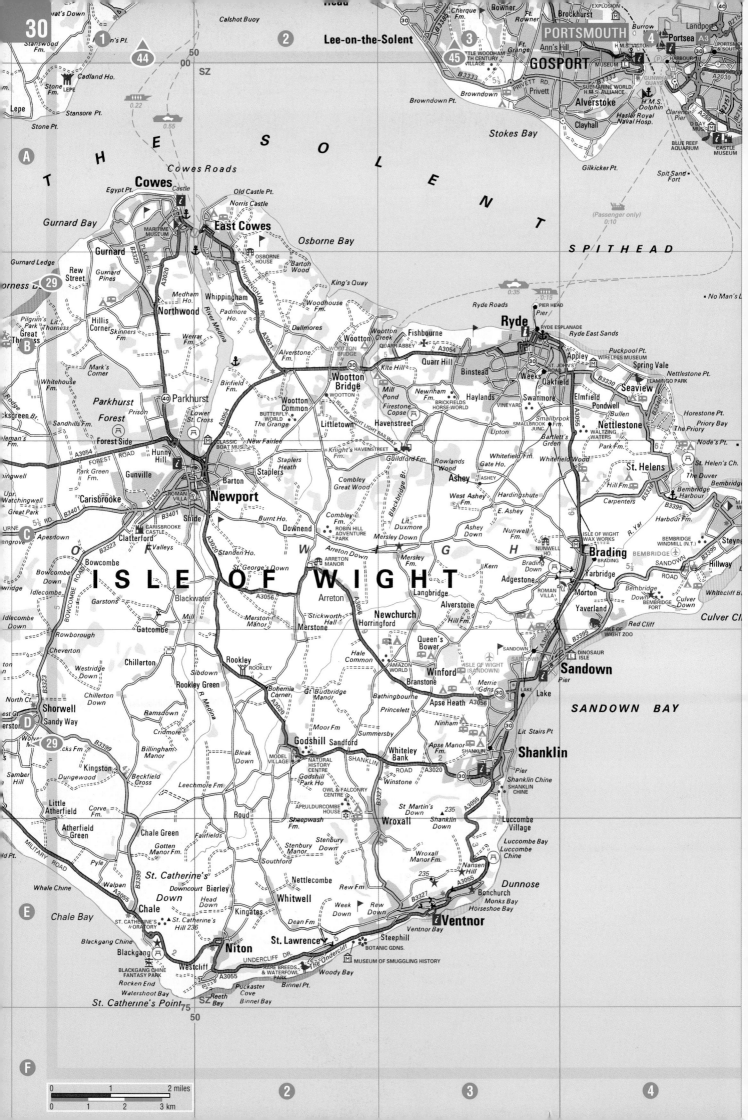

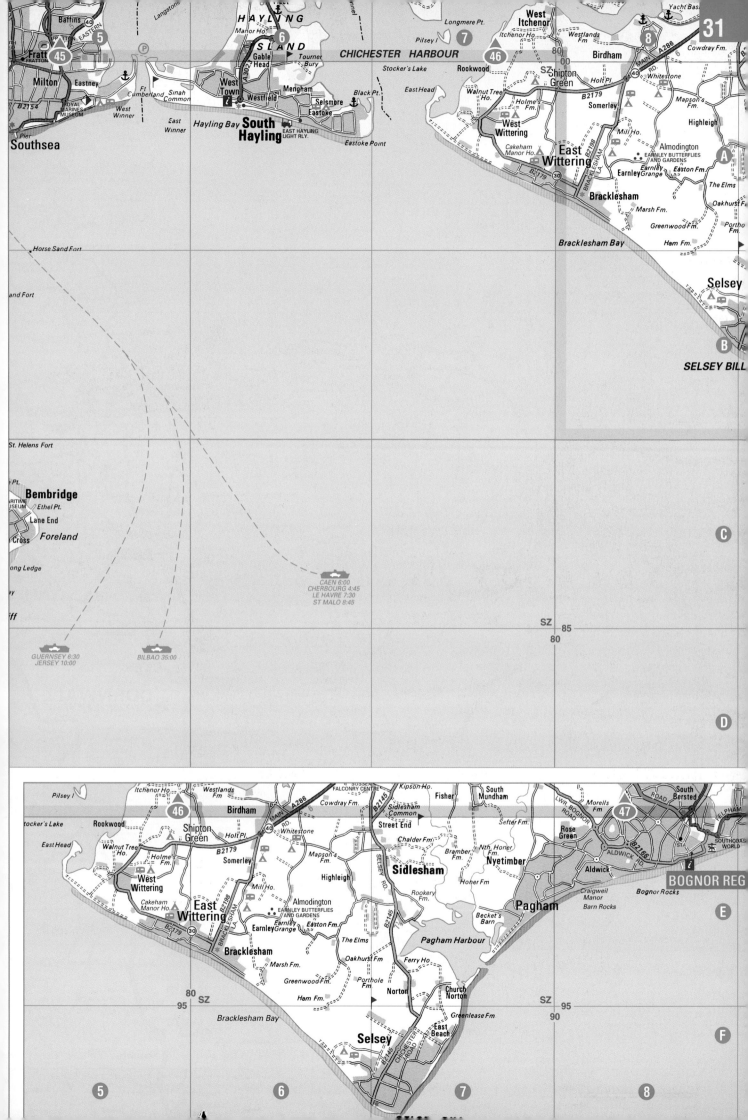

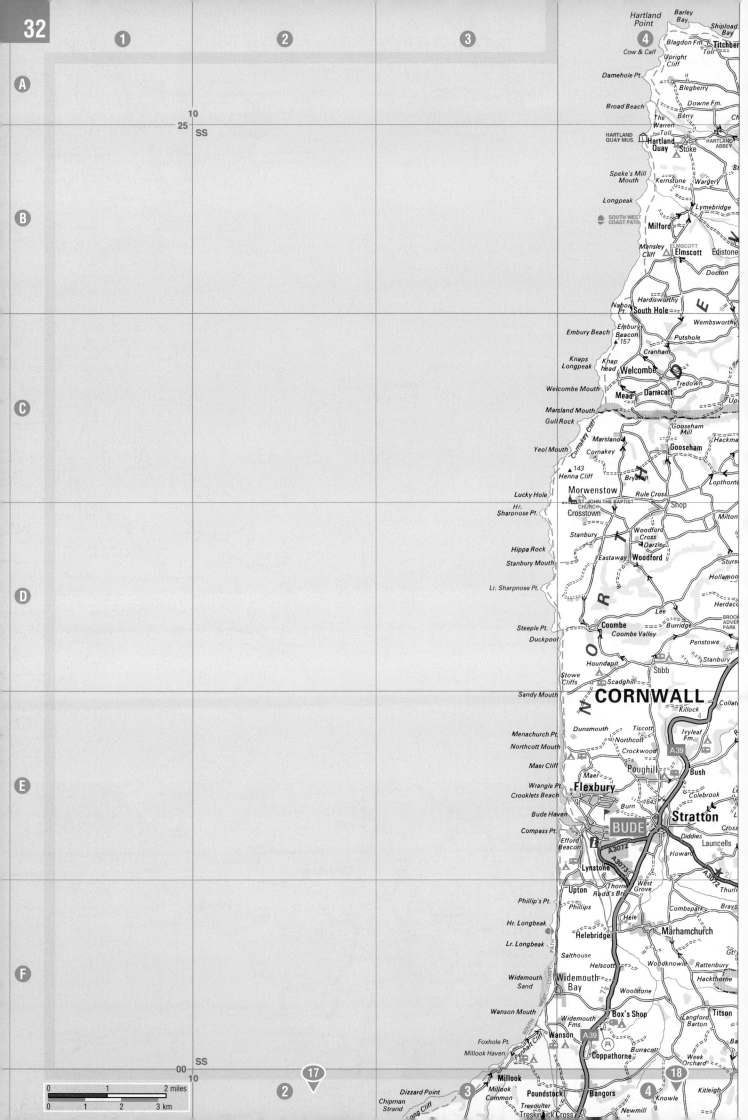

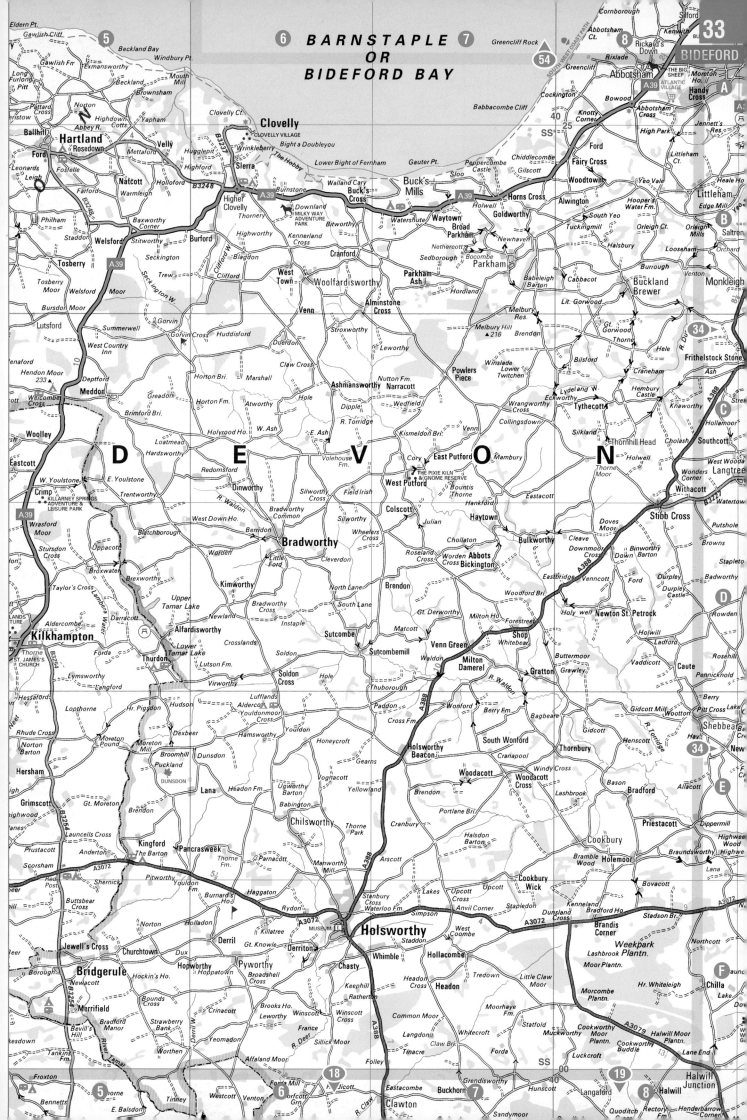

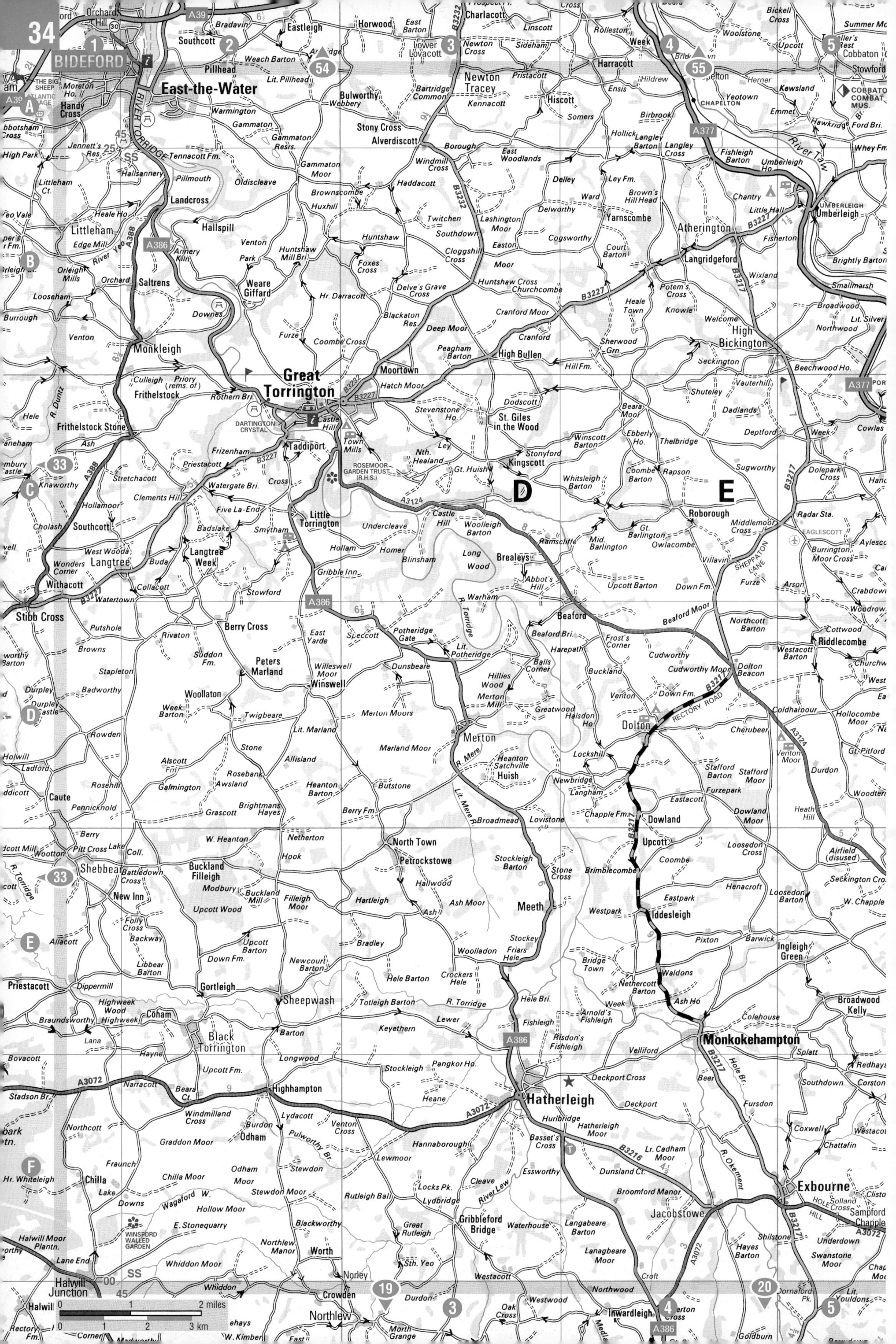

A39  A386  A388  A377  A3124  A3072  A361  B3217  B3227  B3232  B3216

East-the-Water
BIDEFORD
Handy Cross
THE BIG SHEEP
ATLANTIC VILLAGE
Moreton Ho.
Abbotsham Cross
High Park
Littleham Ct.
Yeo Vale
Heale Ho.
Jennett's Res.
Tennacott Fm.
Hallsannery
Pillmouth
Landcross
Oldiscleave
Orchard Hill
Bradavin
Southcott
Pillhead
Lit. Pillhead
Weach Barton
Warmington
Gammaton
Gammaton Resrs.
Gammaton Moor
Brownscombe
Huxhill
Haddacott
Windmill Cross
Bulworthy
Webbery
Bartridge Common
Eastleigh
Horwood
East Barton
Lower Lovacott
Newton Cross
Charlacott
Linscott
Sideham
Newton Tracey
Pristacott
Hiscott
Kennacott
Somers
Ensis
Hollick
Delley
Ward
Delworthy
Borough
East Woodlands
Stony Cross
Alverdiscott
Ley Fm.
Brown's Hill Head
Hildrew
Birbrook
Langley Barton
Langley Cross
Harracott
Chapelton
Yeotown
Herner
Kewsland
Emmet
Hawkridge
Ford Bri.
Whey Fm.
Umberleigh Ho.
Fisherton
UMBERLEIGH
Cobbaton
Stowford
Rolleston
Week
Woolstone
Upcott
Bickell Cross
Summer Mo.
Cobbaton Combat Mus.

Littleham
Edge Mill
River Yeo
Orleigh Mills
Orchard
Saltrens
Hallspill
Armery Kiln
Venton Park
Weare Giffard
Huntshaw Mill Bri.
Downes
Furze
Huntshaw
Foxes' Cross
Delve's Grave Cross
Coombe Cross
Huntshaw Cross
Churchcombe
Cranford Moor
Cranford
Sherwood Grn.
Heale Town
Potem's Cross
Knowle
Welcome
Wixland
Brightly Barton
Smallmarsh
Broadwood
Lit. Silver
Northwood
High Bickington
Seckington
Beechwood Ho.
Vauterhill
Shuteley
Dadlands
Deptford

Looseham
Burrough
Venton
Monkleigh
Culleigh
Priory (rems. of)
Frithelstock
Rothern Bri.
DARTINGTON CRYSTAL
Great Torrington
Castle Hill
Town Mills
ROSEMOOR GARDEN TRUST (R.H.S.)
Taddiport
Moortown
Hatch Moor
Peagham Barton
High Bullen
Hill Fm.
Dodscott
Stevenstone Ho.
St. Giles in the Wood
Winscott Barton
Ebberly Ho.
Thelbridge
Beara Moor
Roborough
Middlemoor Cross
Radar Sta.
EAGLESCOTT
Burrington Moor Cross
Cowlas
Week
Dolepark Cross

Hele
Frithelstock Stone
Ash
Hollamoor
Knaworthy
Stretchacott
Priestacott
Clements Hill
Frizenham
Watergate Bri.
Five La-End
Little Torrington
Undercleave
Homer
Castle Hill
Woolleigh Barton
Ley
Nth. Healand
Gt. Huish
Whitsleigh Barton
Kingscott
Stonyford
Coombe Barton
Rapson
Sugworthy

Cholash
Southcott
Badslake
Smytham
Hollam
Blinsham
Long Wood
Brealeys
Abbot's Hill
Ramscliffe
Mid. Barlington
Gt. Barlington
Owlacombe
Villavin
SHEPPATON LANE
Furze
Arson
Woodrow
Crabdown

West Wooda
Wonders Corner
Langtree
Buda
Langtree Week
Collacott
Watertown
Stowford
Gribble Inn
Warham
Torridge
Upcott Barton
Down Fm.
Beaford
Beaford Moor
Northcott Barton
Cottwood
Riddlecombe
Westacott Barton
Churchw.

Stibb Cross
Putshole
Rivaton
Berry Cross
East Yarde
Speccott
Potheridge Gate
Lit. Potheridge
Beaford Bri.
Frost's Corner
Harepath
Balls Corner
Buckland
Cudworthy
Cudworthy Moor
Dolton Beacon
Durrant
West
Ea.
Withacott
Browns
Suddon Fm.
Stapleton
Badworthy
Durpley
Durpley Castle
Woollaton
Peters Marland
Willeswell Moor
Winswell
Dunsbeare
Hillies Wood
Merton Mill
Greatwood
Halsdon Ho.
Venton
Down Fm.
Dolton
RECTORY ROAD
Coldharbour
Cherubeer
Hollocombe Moor
Venton Moor
Gt. Pitford
Durdon
Woodter

Rowden
Week Barton
Twigbeare
Lit. Marland
Stone
Allisland
Marland Moor
Butstone
Heanton Barton
Roseland
Awsland
Galmington
Brightmans Hayes
Grascott
Berry Fm.
Merton Moors
Merton
R. Mere
R. Mere
Heanton Satchville
Huish
Newbridge
Langham
Lockshill
Stafford Barton
Stafford Moor
Furzepark
Eastacott
Dowland
Dowland Moor
Heath Hill
Airfield (disused)
Seckington Cro.

Holwill
Ladford
Rosehill
Pennicknold
Caute
Berry
Pitt Cross
Lake
Coll.
Netherton
W. Heanton
Hook
North Town
Petrockstowe
Broadmead
Lovistone
Chapple Fm.
Upcott
Brimblecombe
Coombe
Looseden Cross
Henacroft
Looseden Barton
W. Chapple

Shebbear
Battledown Cross
Buckland Filleigh
Modbury
Buckland Mill
Filleigh Moor
Hartleigh
Stockleigh Barton
Stone Cross
Hallwood
Ash Moor
Ash
Meeth
Westpark
Eastpark
Iddesleigh
Pixton
Barwick
Ingleigh Green
Broadwood Kelly

New Inn
Folly Cross
Backway
Upcott Wood
Down Fm.
Newcourt Barton
Bradley
Woolladon
Stockey
Friars Hele
Crockers Hele
Hele Barton
Bridge Town
Waldons
Nethercott Barton
Week
Arnold's Fishleigh
Ash Ho.
Colehouse

Allacott
Libbear Barton
Gortleigh
Sheepwash
Totleigh Barton
Keyethern
R. Torridge
Hele Bri.
Fishleigh
Risdon's Fishleigh
Velliford
Monkokehampton
Splatt
Redhays

Priestacott
Dippermill
Highweek Wood
Highweek
Coham
Black Torrington
Barton
Lewer
Longwood
Pangkor Ho.
A386
Hatherleigh Moor
Basset's Cross
Lr. Cadham Moor
R. Okement
Coxwell
Westacot
Chattafin

Braundsworthy
Lana
Hayne
Upcott Fm.
Stockleigh
Heane
Highhampton
Windmilland Cross
Burdon
Odham
Lydacott
Venton Cross
Pulworthy Bri.
Hannaborough
Hatherleigh
Deckport Cross
Deckport
Hurlbridge
Dunsland Ct.
Broomford Manor
Jacobstowe
Exbourne
Sampford Chapple
Lit. Youldons

Bovacott
Stadson Br.
Narracott
Beara Ct.
Graddon Moor
Lewmoor
Essworthy
Cleave
R. Lew
Langabeare Barton
Langabeare Moor

Hr. Whiteleigh
Chilla
Fraunch
Chilla Moor
Odham Moor
Stewdon
Stewdon Moor
Locks Pk.
Lydbridge
Gribbleford Bridge
Waterhouse
Inwardleigh
Morton Cross
Hayes Barton
Shilstone
Underdown
Swanstone Moor

Downs
Hollow Moor
Wagafold W.
Blackworthy
Rutleigh Ball
Great Rutleigh
Northleigh Manor
Worth
Sth. Yeo
Westacott
Oak Cross
Goldburn

WINSFORD WALLED GARDEN
E. Stonequarry
Whiddon Moor
Whiddon
Norley
Crowden
Durdon
Morth Grange
W. Kimber

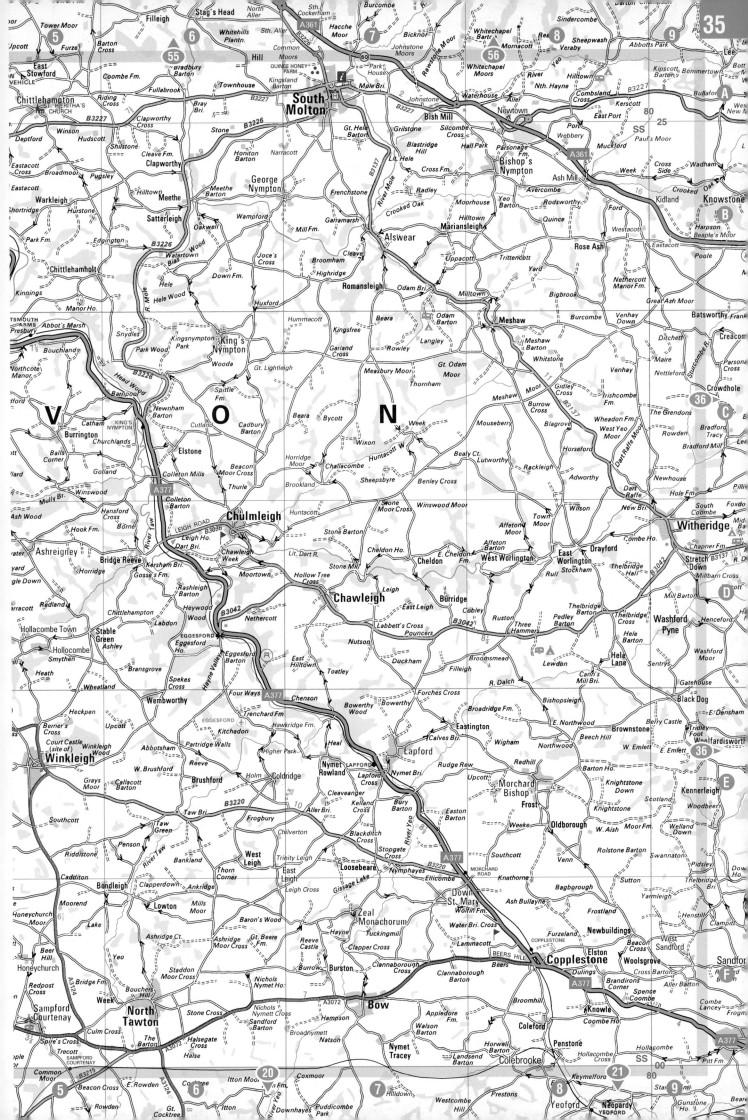

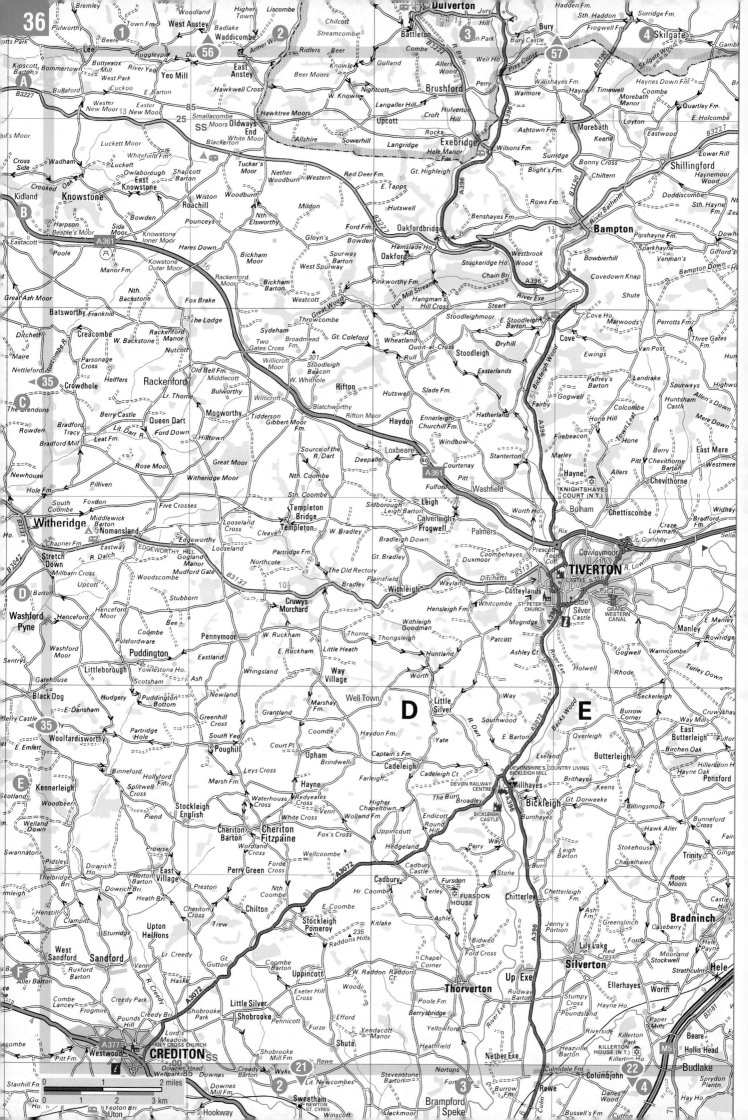

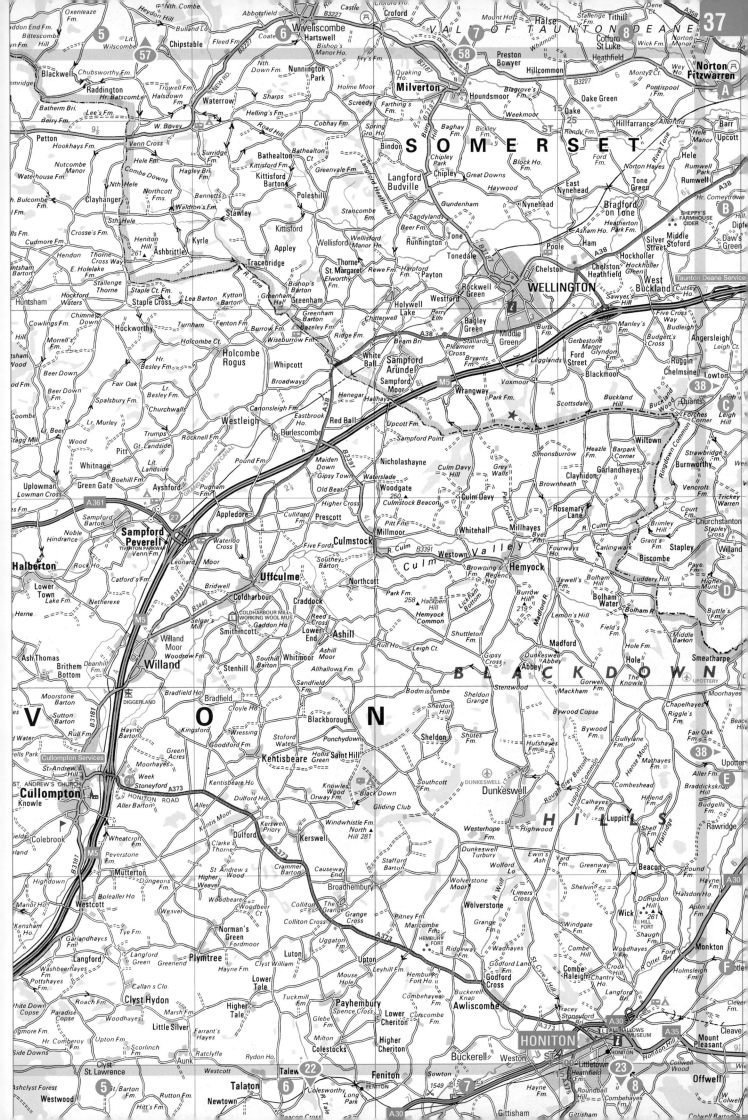

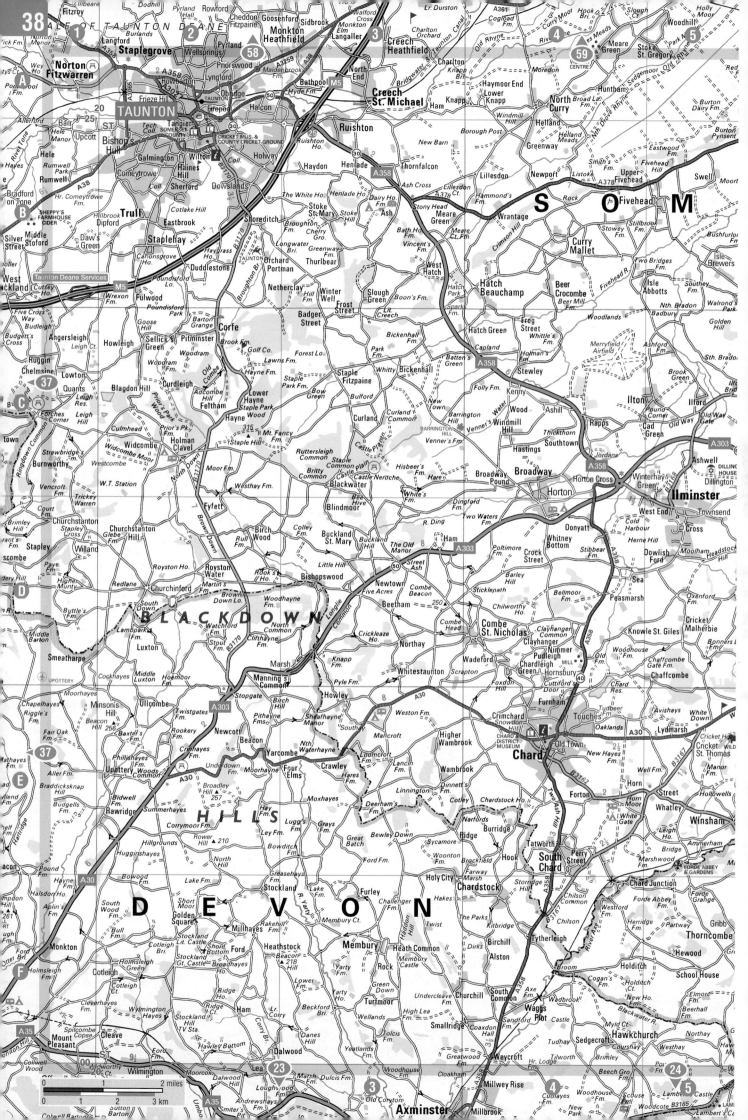

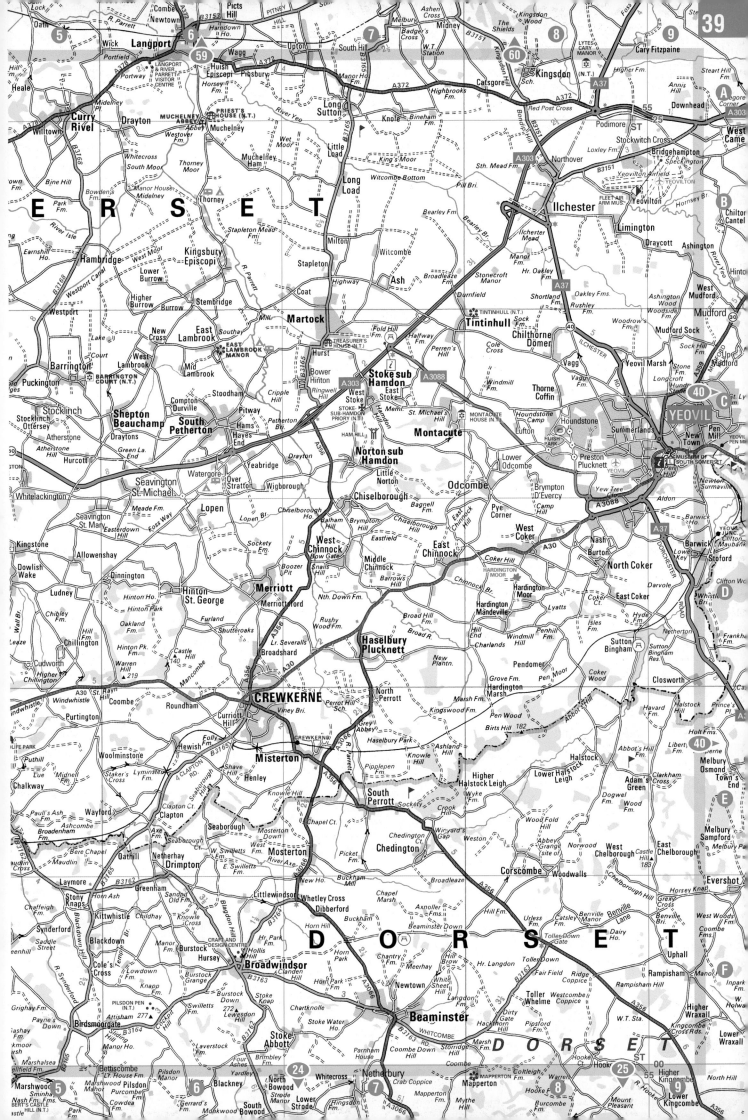

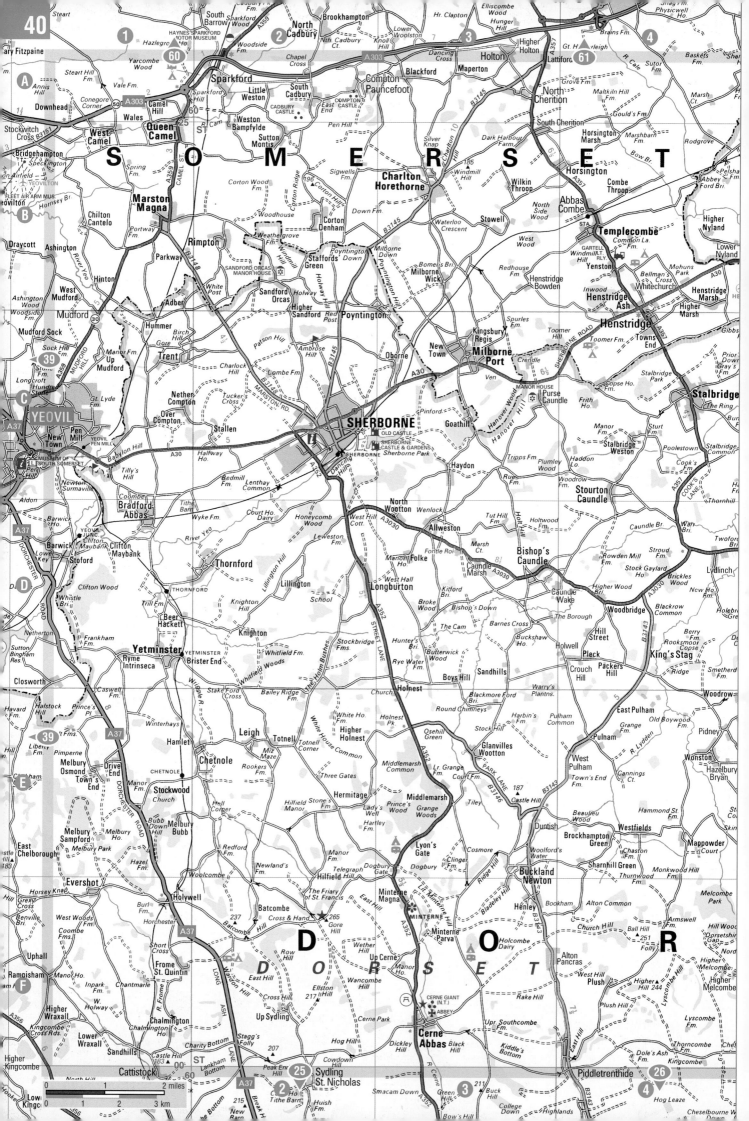

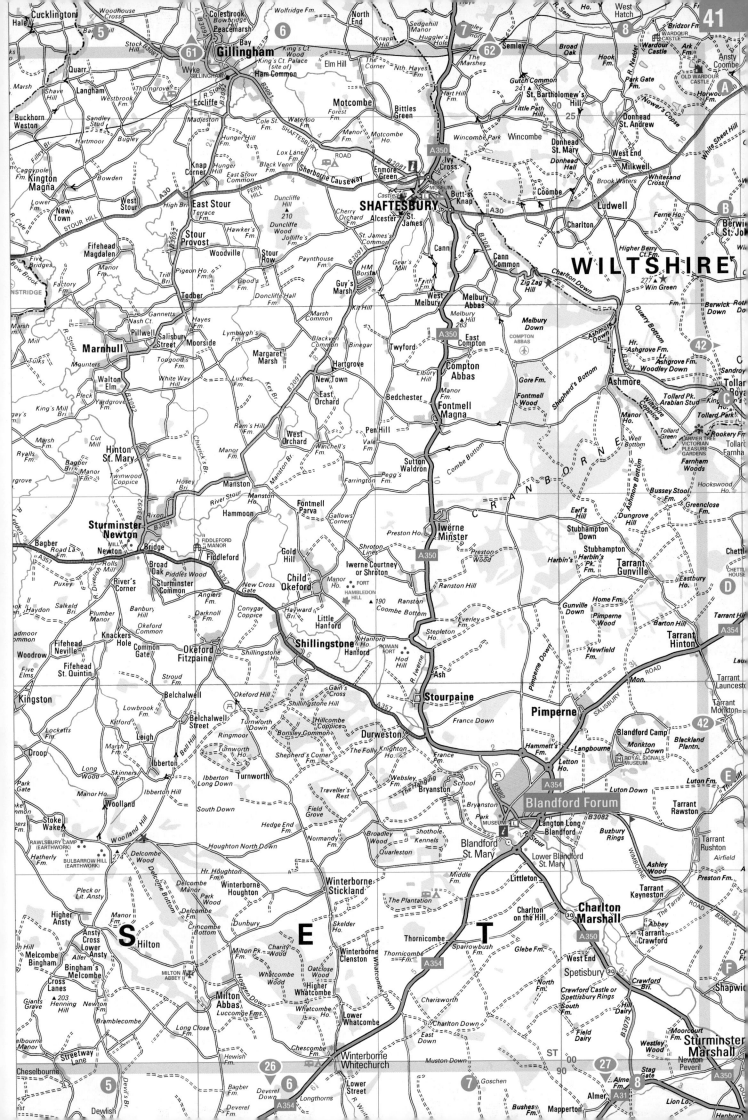

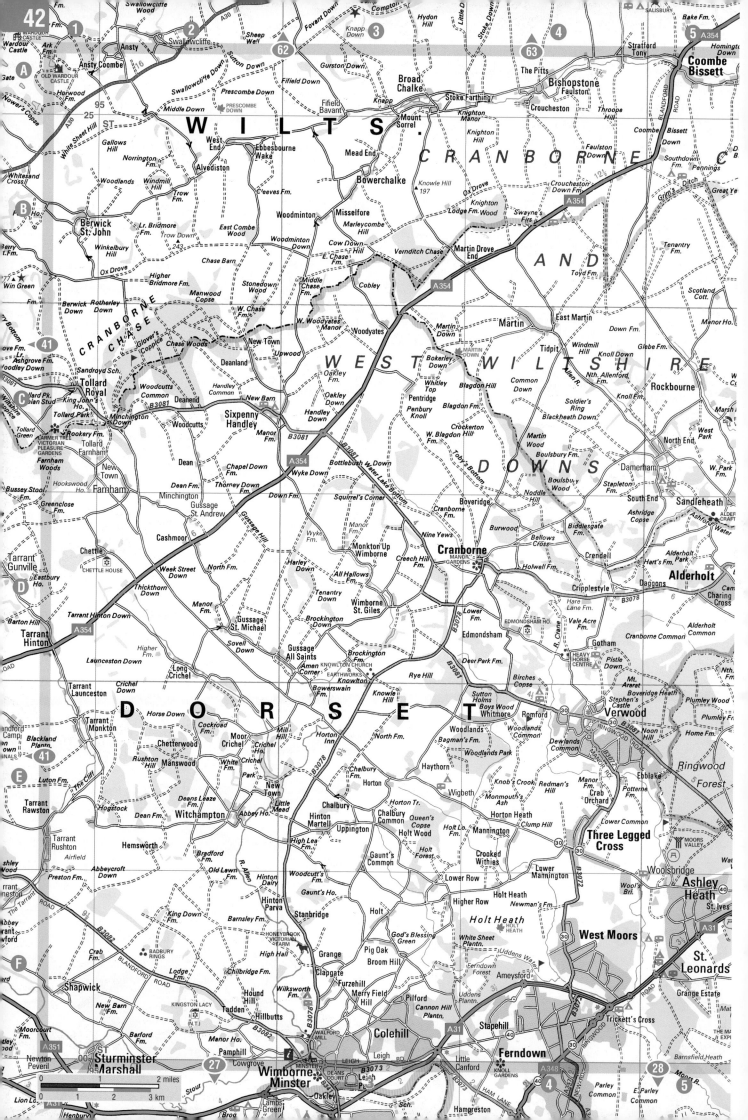

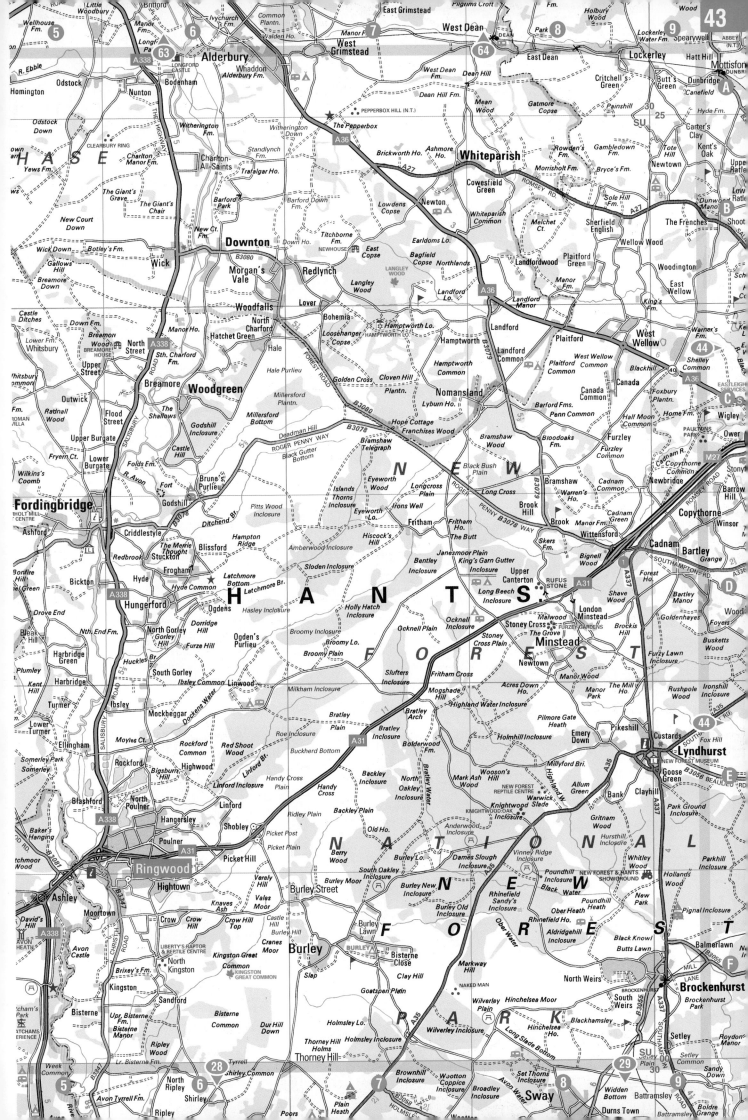

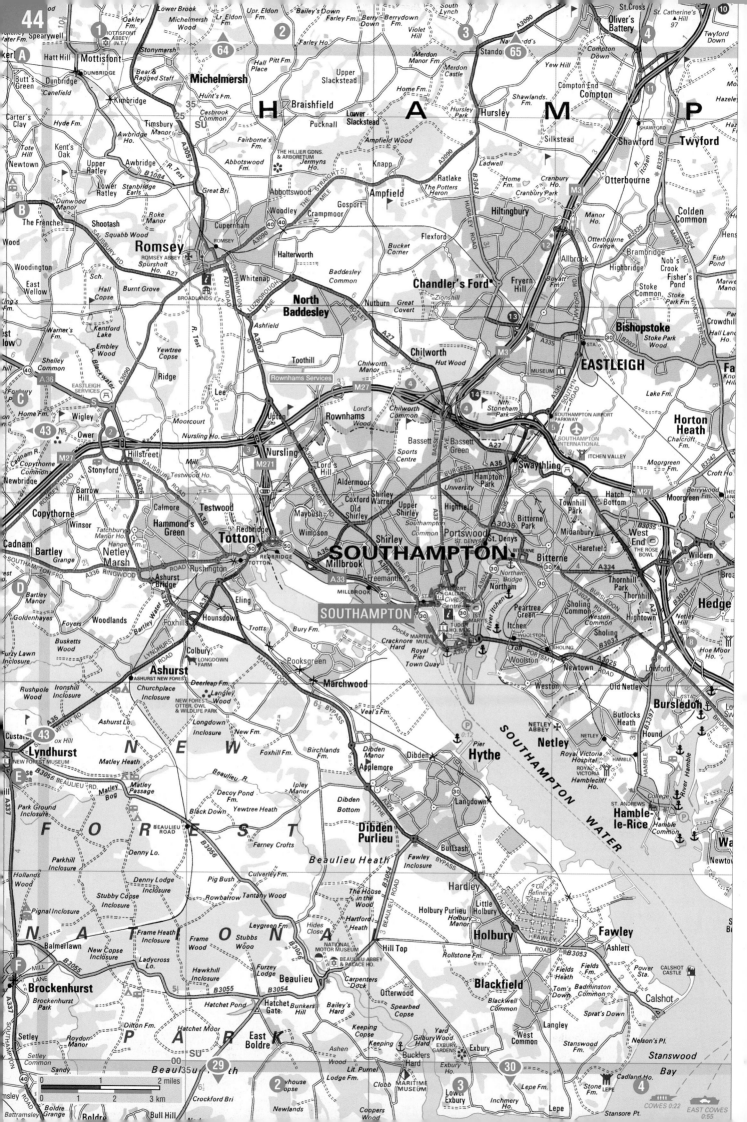

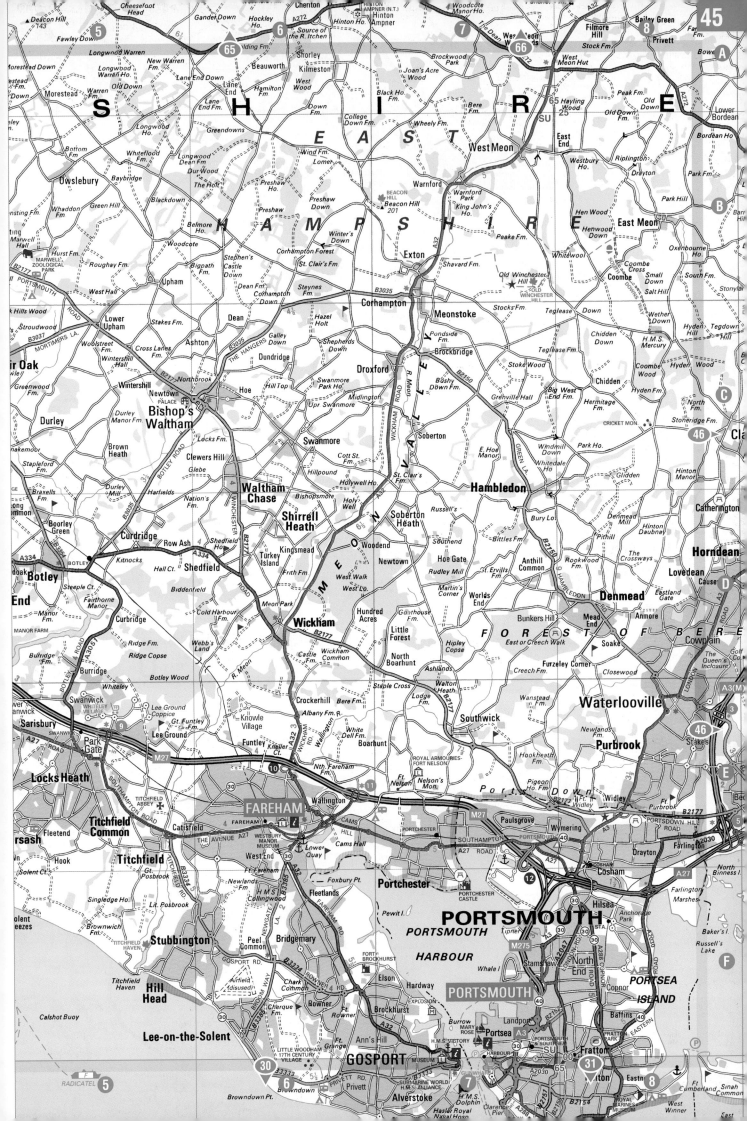

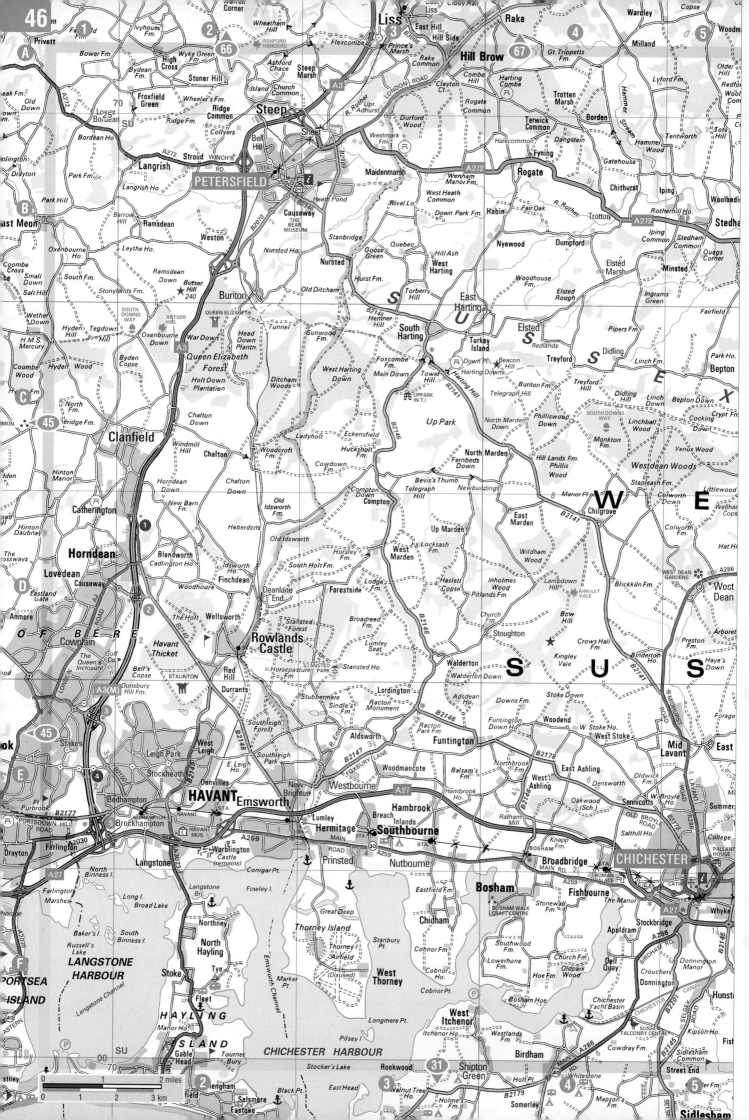

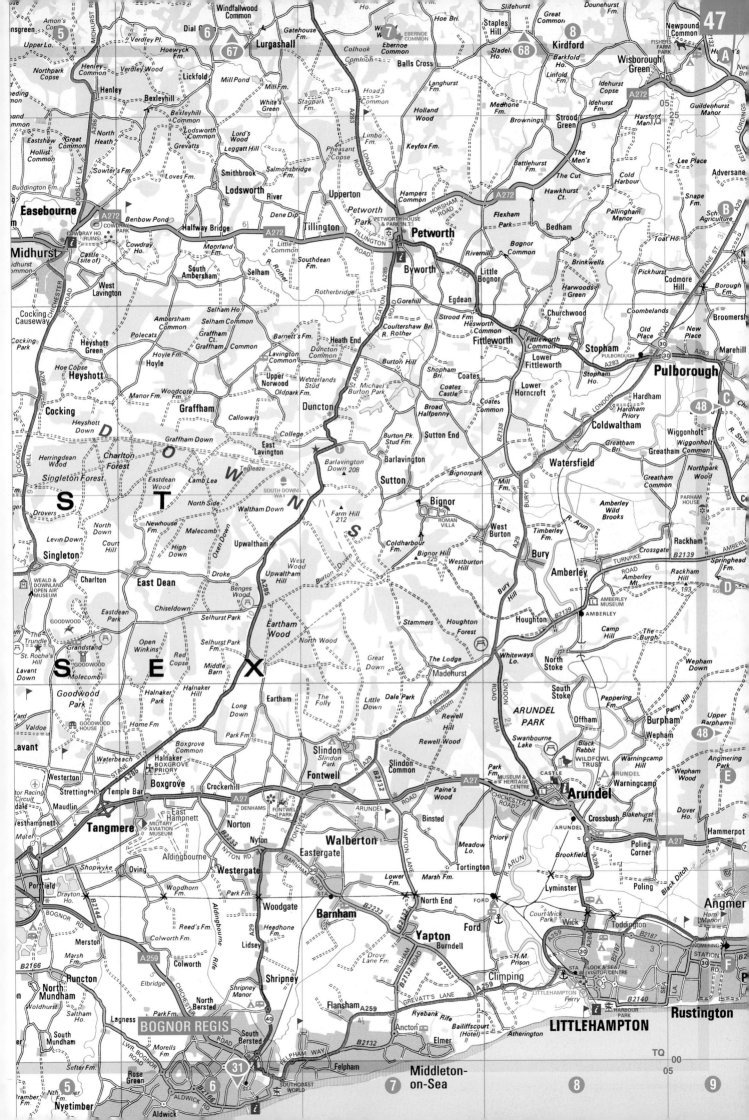

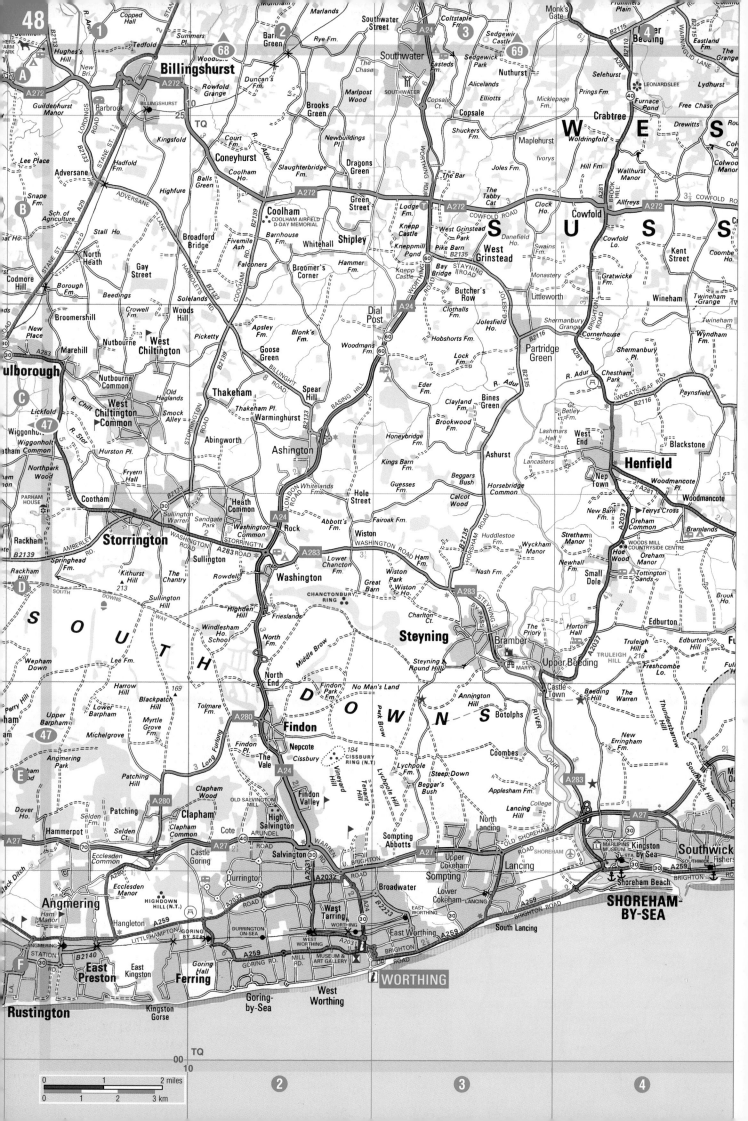

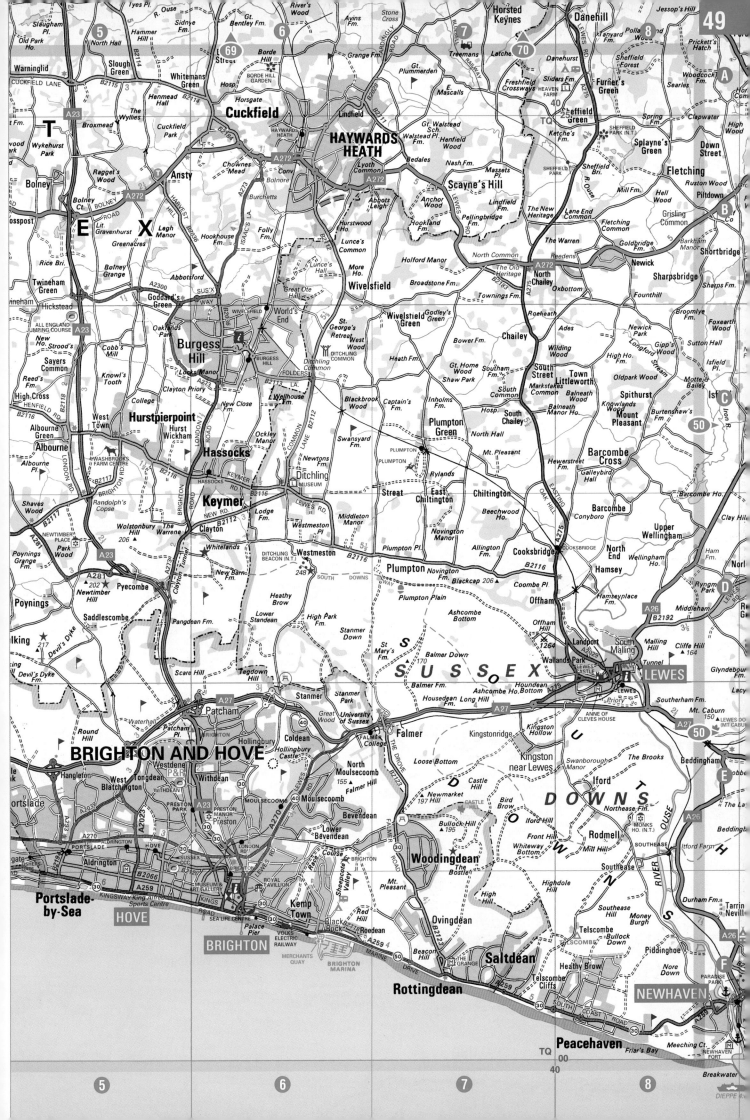

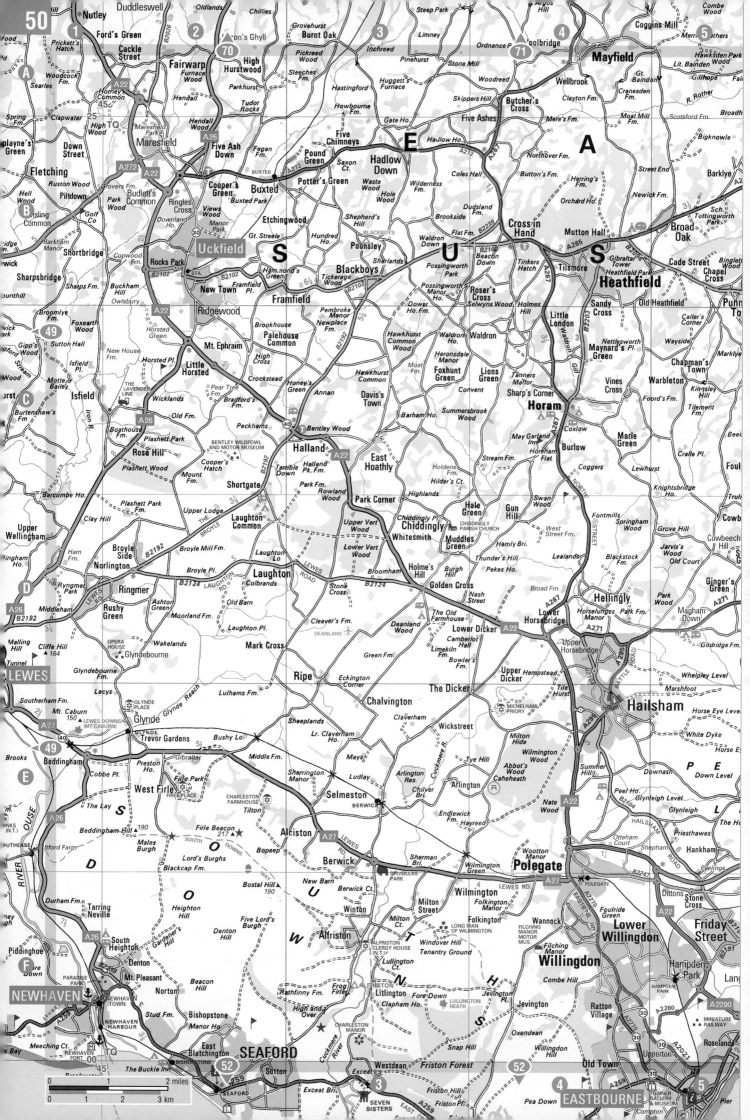

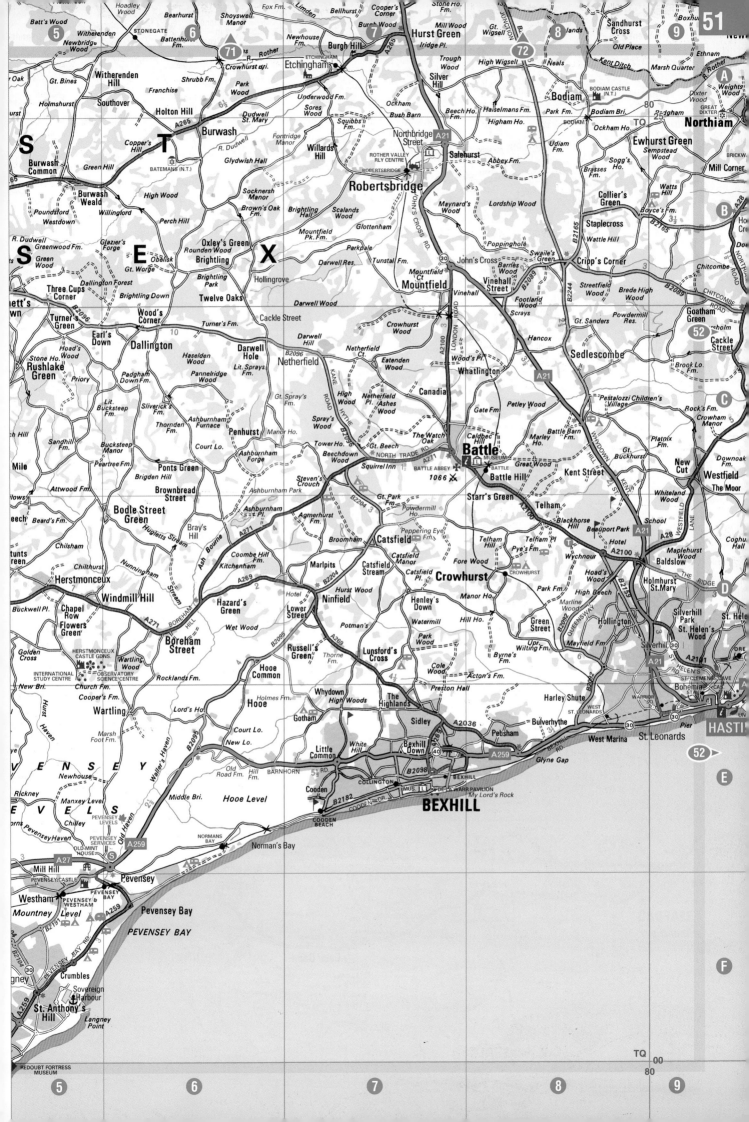

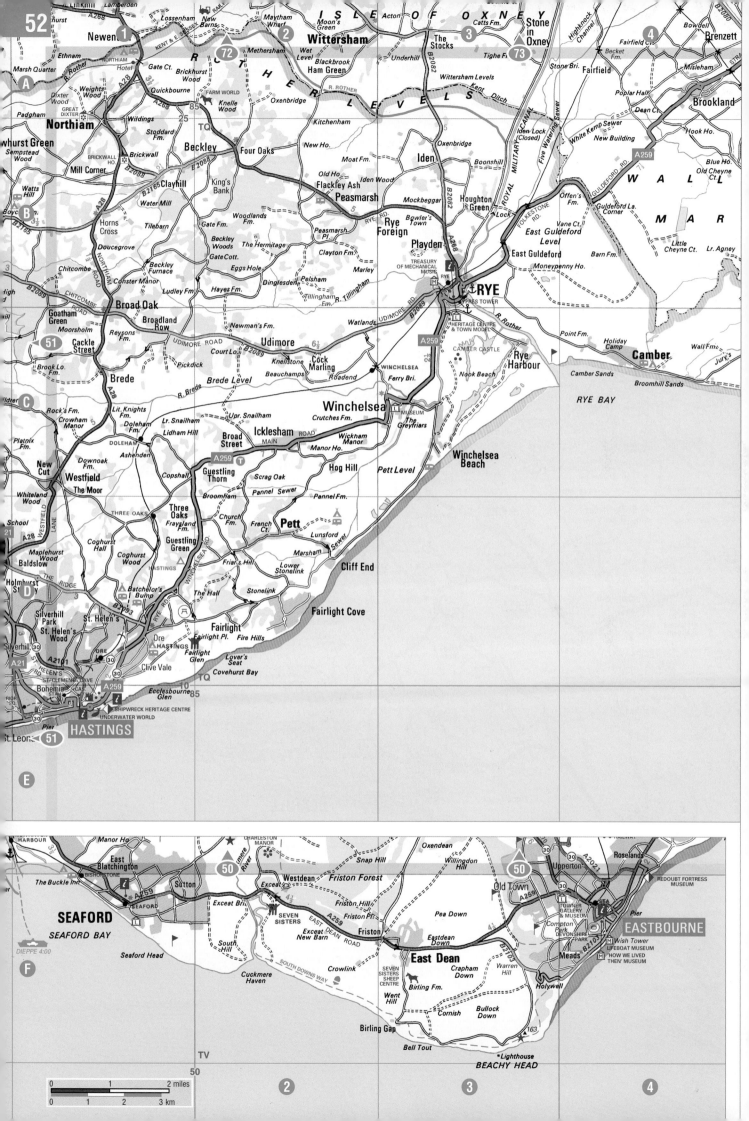

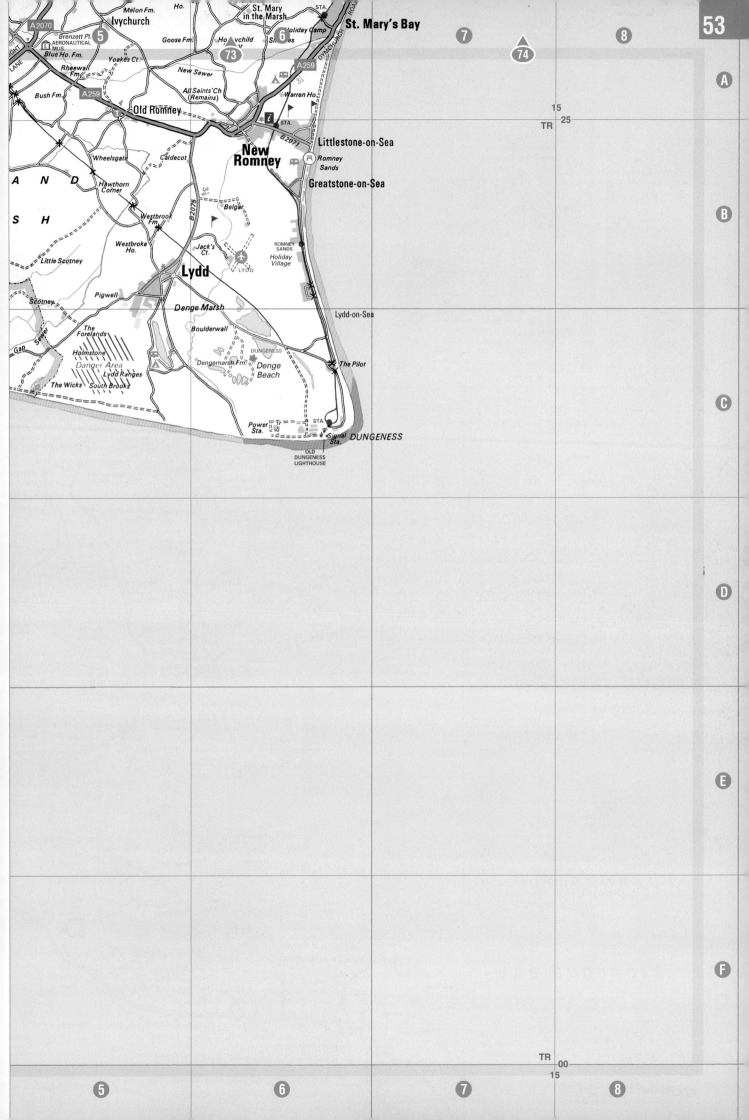

Ho.

Melon Fm.

St. Mary
in the Marsh

STA.

St. Mary's Bay

**Ivychurch**

Goose Fm.

Holiday Camp

7

8

A2070

Brenzett Pl.
AERONAUTICAL
MUS

5

Hallwchild
hor

Sh es

6

74

Blue Ho. Fm.

LANE

Yoakes Ct.

New Sewer

A259

3½

Rheewall
Fm.

All Saints'Ch
(Remains)

Warren Ho.

A

15

Bush Fm.

A259

Old Romney

STA.

TR  25

B2071

Littlestone-on-Sea

Wheelsgate

Caldecot

**New
Romney**

Romney
Sands

Greatstone-on-Sea

AND

Hawthorn
Corner

Westbrook
Fm.

B2075

Belgar

ROMNEY
SANDS
Holiday
Village

B

S

Westbroke
Ho.

Jack's
Ct.

LYDD

Little Scotney

**Lydd**

3½

Scotney

Pigwell

Denge Marsh

Lydd-on-Sea

Sewer

Gap

The Forelands

Boulderwall

Holmstone

DUNGENESS

The Pilot

C

Danger Area

Dengemarsh Fm.

Denge
Beach

Lydd Ranges

The Wicks

South Brooks

Power
Sta.

STA.

Signal
Sta.

DUNGENESS

OLD
DUNGENESS
LIGHTHOUSE

D

E

F

15

TR  25

5

6

7

8

TR  00

15

5

6

7

8

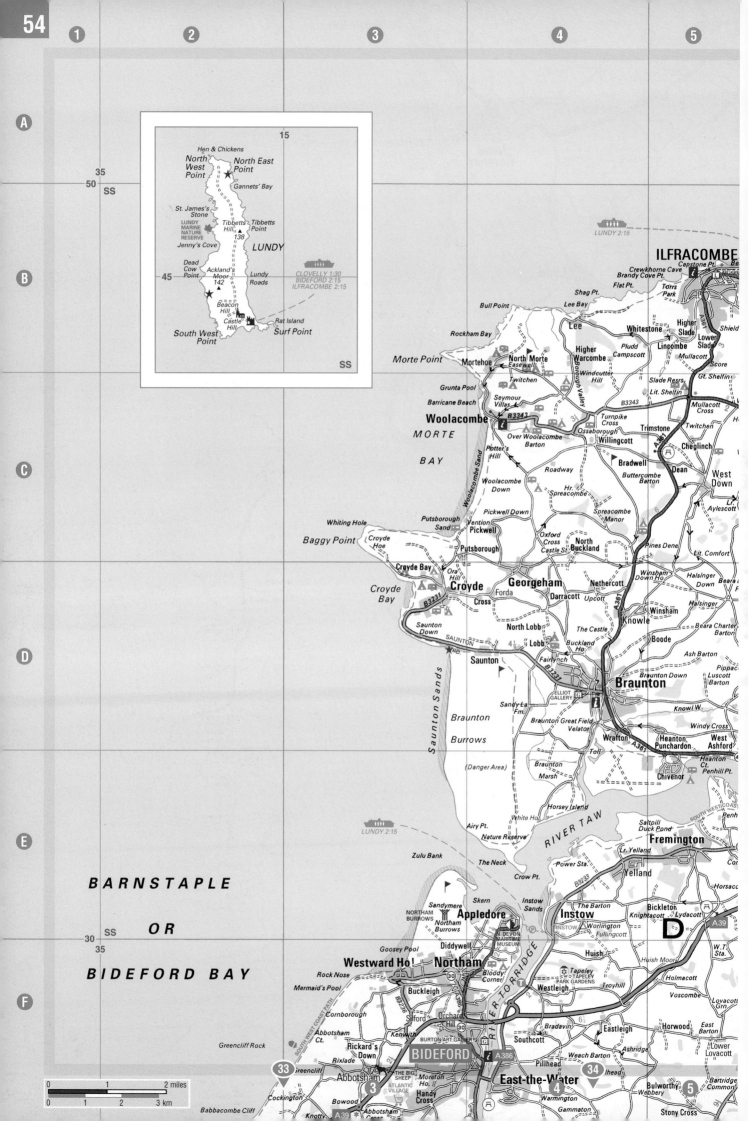

**1** **2** **3** **4** **5**

A

35
50
SS

**Hen & Chickens**
North West Point
North East Point
Gannets' Bay

St. James's Stone
LUNDY MARINE NATURE RESERVE
Tibbetts Hill
138
Tibbetts Point
LUNDY

Jenny's Cove

B

45

Dead Cow Point
Ackland's Moor 142
Lundy Roads

Beacon Hill 142
Castle Hill
Rat Island
South West Point
Surf Point

SS

CLOVELLY 1:30
BIDEFORD 2:15
ILFRACOMBE 2:15

LUNDY 2:15

**ILFRACOMBE**
Capstone Pt.
Crewkhorne Cave
Brandy Cove Pt.
MUSEUM
Shag Pt.
Flat Pt.
Torrs Park
Bull Point
Lee Bay
Higher Slade
Shield
Lee
Whitestone
Lower Slade
Rockham Bay
Pludd
Campscott
Lincombe
Mullacott
Score
Gt. Shelfin
Morte Point
Mortehoe
Higher Warcombe
Lit. Shelfin
Easewell
North Morte
Borough Valley
Windcutter Hill
Slade Resrs.
Mullacott Cross
Grunta Pool
Twitchen
B3343
Twitchen
Barricane Beach
Seymour Villas
Turnpike Cross
Trimstone
Cheglinch
**Woolacombe**
B3343
Over Woolacombe Barton
Ossaborough
Willingcott
Dean
West Down

*MORTE*

Potter's Hill
Bradwell
Buttercombe Barton

*BAY*

Roadway
Hr. Spreacombe
Lr. Aylescott
Woolacombe Down
Spreacombe Manor
Lit. Comfort
Whiting Hole
Putsborough Sand
Pickwell Down
Pines Dene
Baggy Point
Croyde Hoe
Vention
Pickwell
Oxford Cross
Castle St.
North Buckland
Winsham Down Ho.
Halsinger Down
Beara
Putsborough
Croyde Bay
Ora Hill
Netheracott
Winsham
**Croyde**
Georgeham
Halsinger
Croyde Bay
B3231
Croyde Cross
Forda
Darracott
Upcott
Knowle
Beara Charter Barton
Saunton Down
North Lobb
The Castle
Boode
Ash Barton
4½
Lobb
Buckland Ho.
Pippacc
Luscott Barton
Saunton
Fairlynch
Braunton Down
**Braunton**
Knowl W.
SAUNTON RD.
ELLIOT GALLERY
Sandy La. Fm.
Windy Cross
*Saunton Sands*
*Braunton*
Braunton Great Field
Velator
Wrafton
Heanton Puncharion
West Ashford
*Burrows*
Toll
Heanton Ct.
Penhill Pt.
Braunton Marsh
Chivenor

(Danger Area)

Horsey Island
White Ho.
Saltpill Duck Pond
Penh
SOUTH WEST COAST
*RIVER TAW*
Airy Pt.
Nature Reserve
**Fremington**
Zulu Bank
Power Sta.
B3233
Yelland
Lr. Yelland
Horsac
The Neck
Crow Pt.
The Barton
Bickleton
Lydacott
Knightacott
**Instow**
A39
INSTOW
Worlington
Fullingcott

*BARNSTAPLE*
Instow Sands
Huish
**D**
Skern
Sandymere
NORTHAM BURROWS
Northam Burrows
N. DEVON MARITIME MUSEUM
Huish Moor
Holmacott
*OR*
**Appledore**
Diddywell
Voscombe
30 SS
35
Goosey Pool
TAPELEY PARK GARDENS
Lovacott Grn.
*BIDEFORD BAY*
Rock Nose
Westward Ho!
**Northam**
Bloody Corner
Westleigh
Troyhill
East Barton
Mermaid's Pool
Buckleigh
Tapeley
Huish
Lovacott
Cornborough
Silford
Orchard Hill
Bradavin
Eastleigh
Ashridge
Greencliff Rock
BURTON ART GALLERY
Southcott
Weach Barton
Abbotsham Ct.
Kenwith
BIDEFORD
A386
Pillhead
Lower Lovacott
Rickard's Down
THE BIG SHEEP
Moreton Ho.
Ihead
33
Rixlade
Handy Cross
**East-the-Water**
34
Greencliff
Abbotsham
3
ATLANTIC VILLAGE
Bowood
4
Bulworthy Webbery
5
Babbacombe Cliff
Knotty
Cockington
A39
Handy Cross
Warmington
Stony Cross
Gammaton
Bartridge Common

0    1    2 miles
0  1  2  3 km

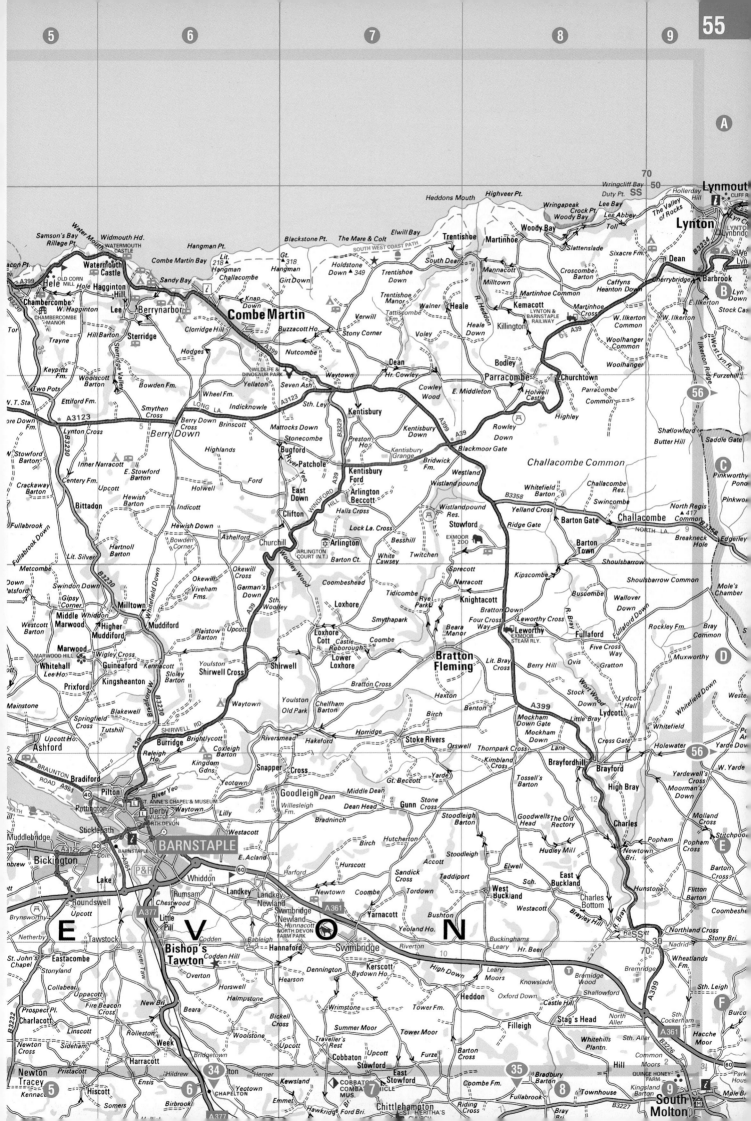

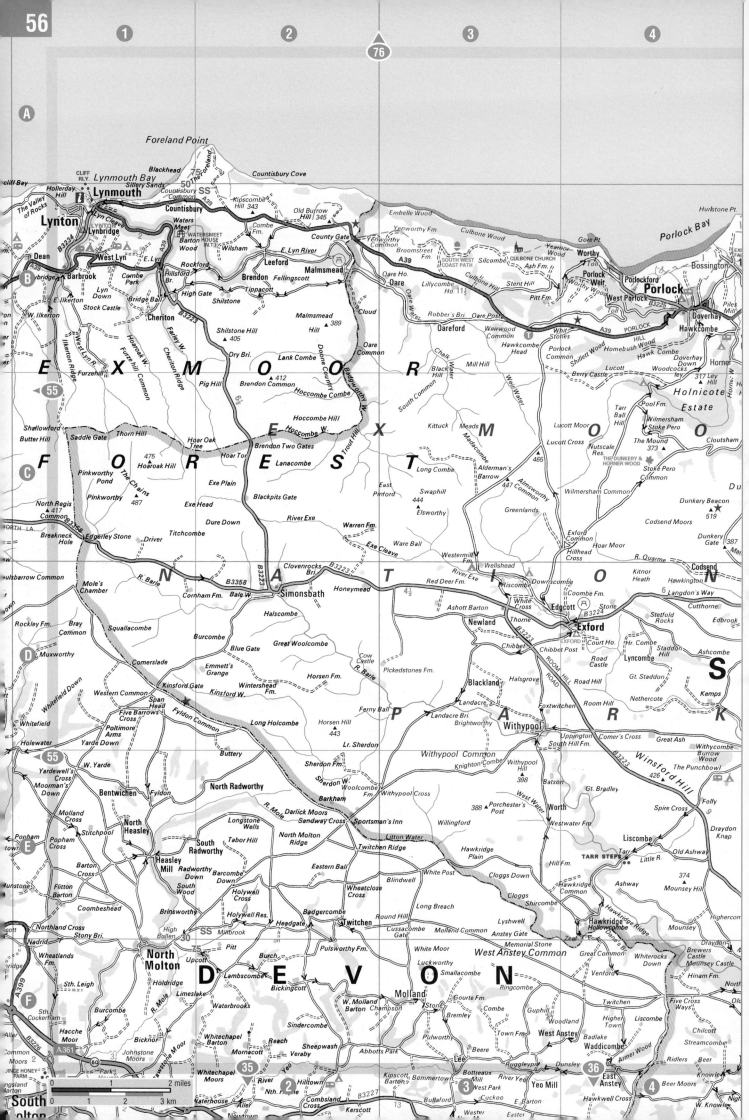

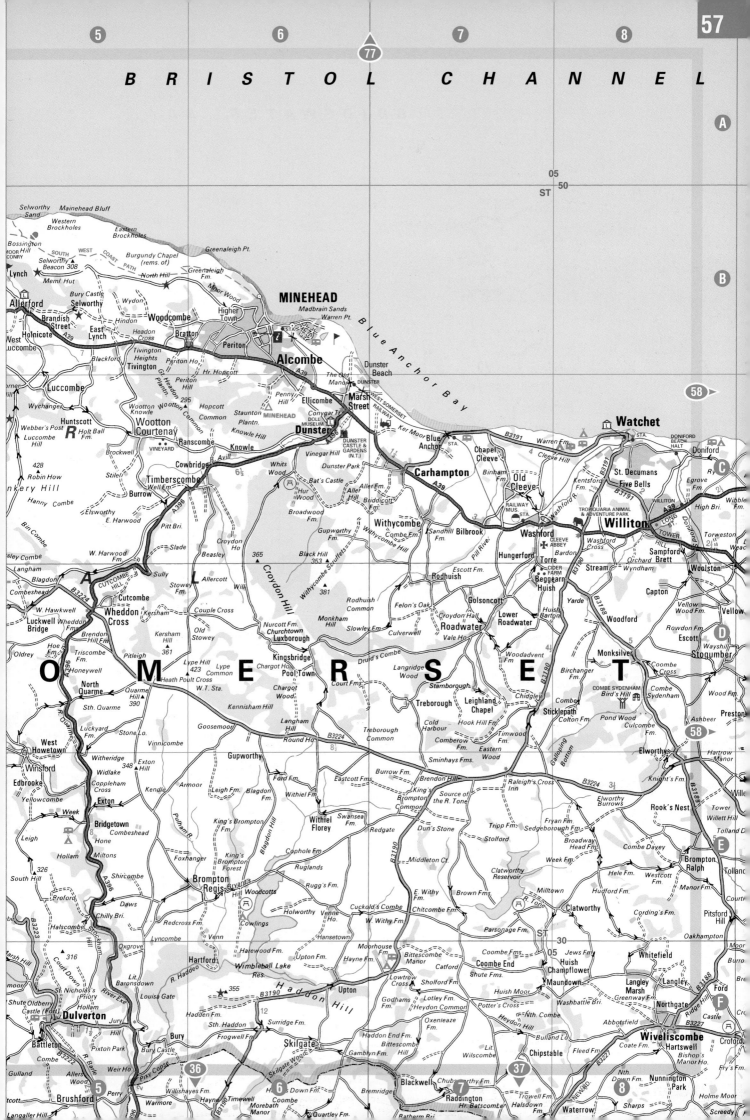

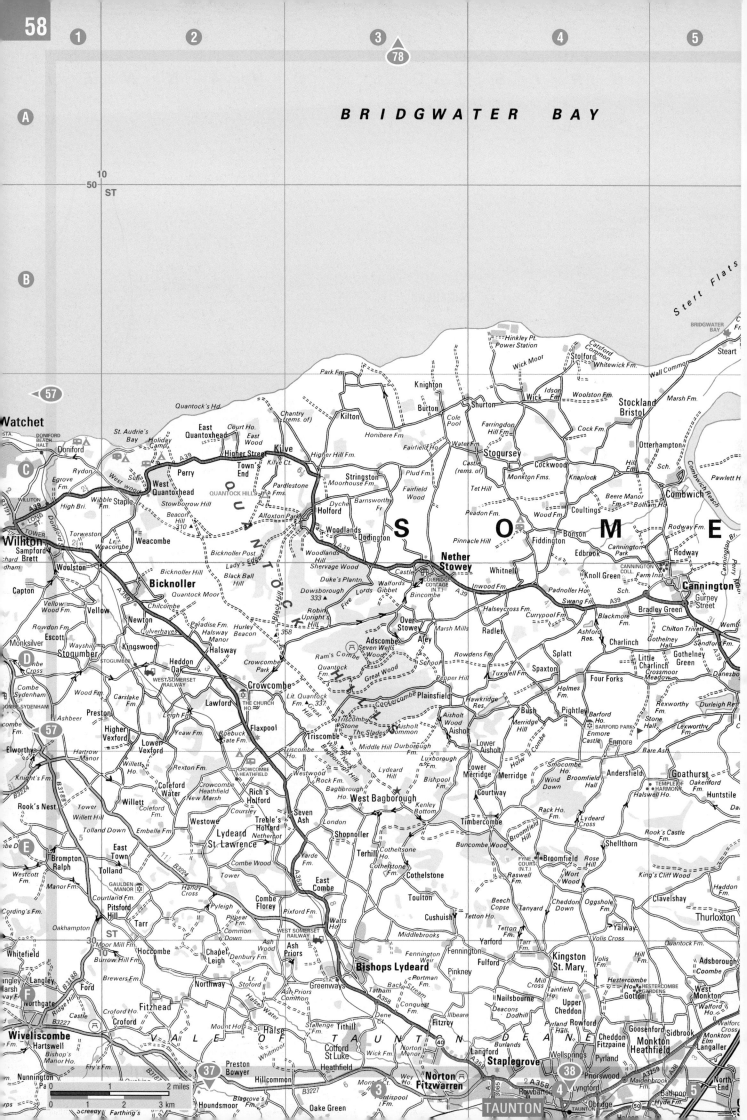

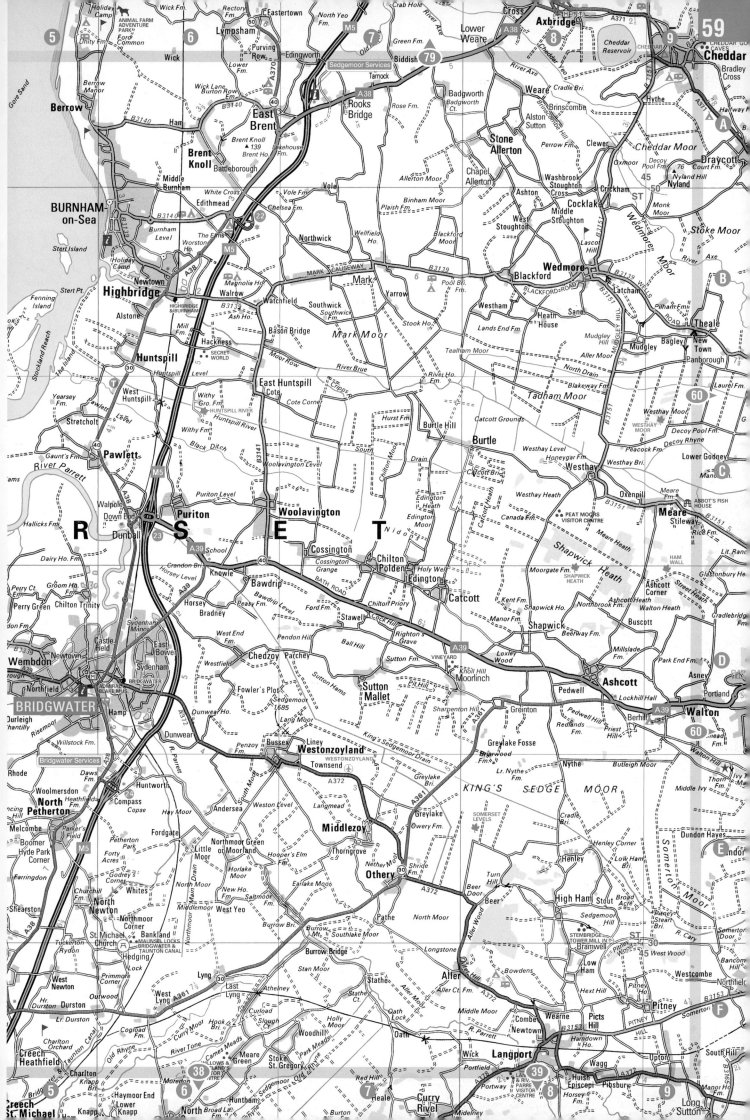

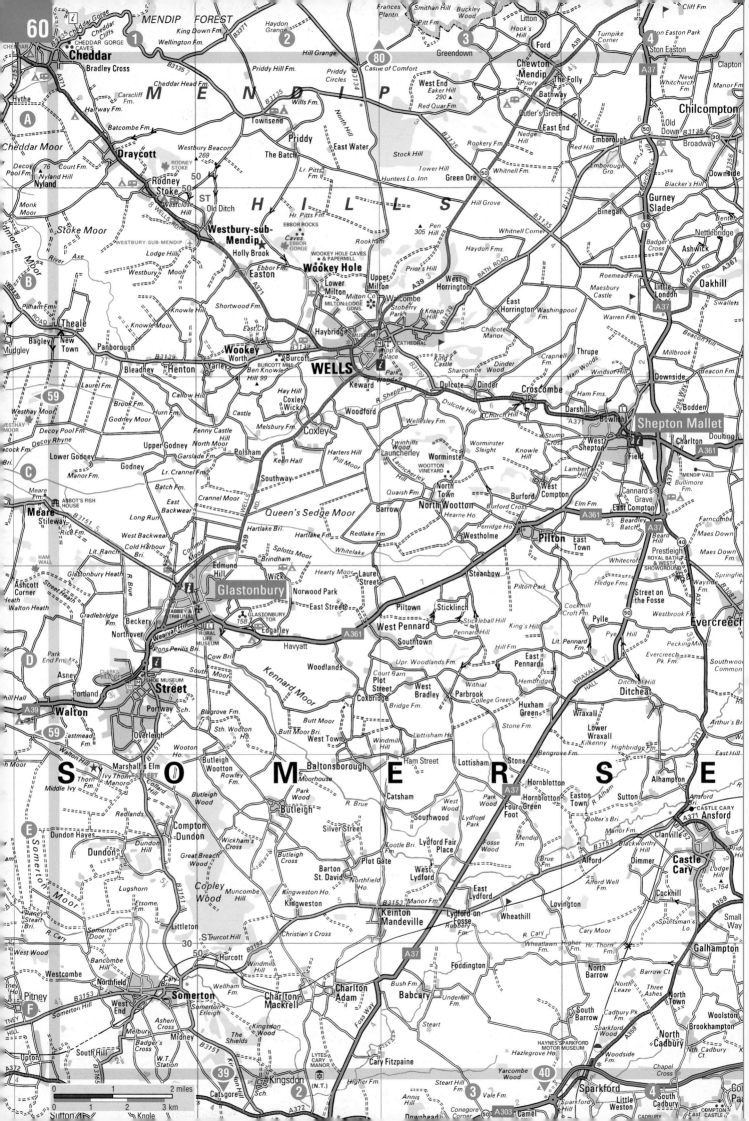

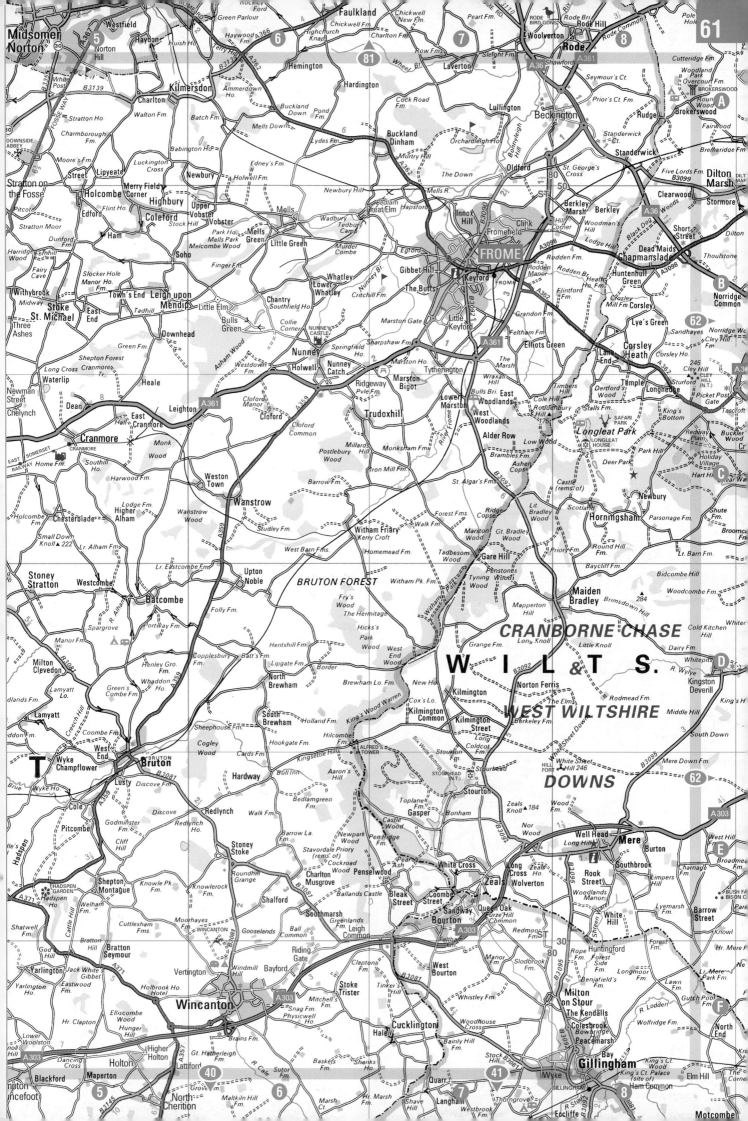

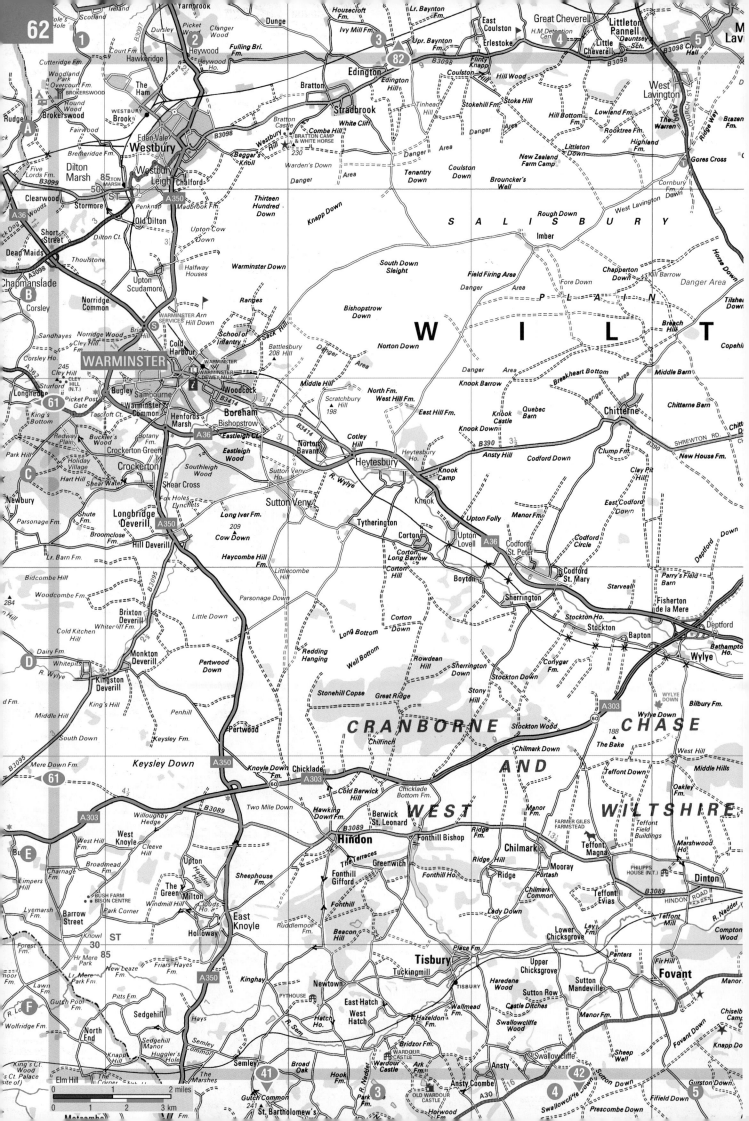

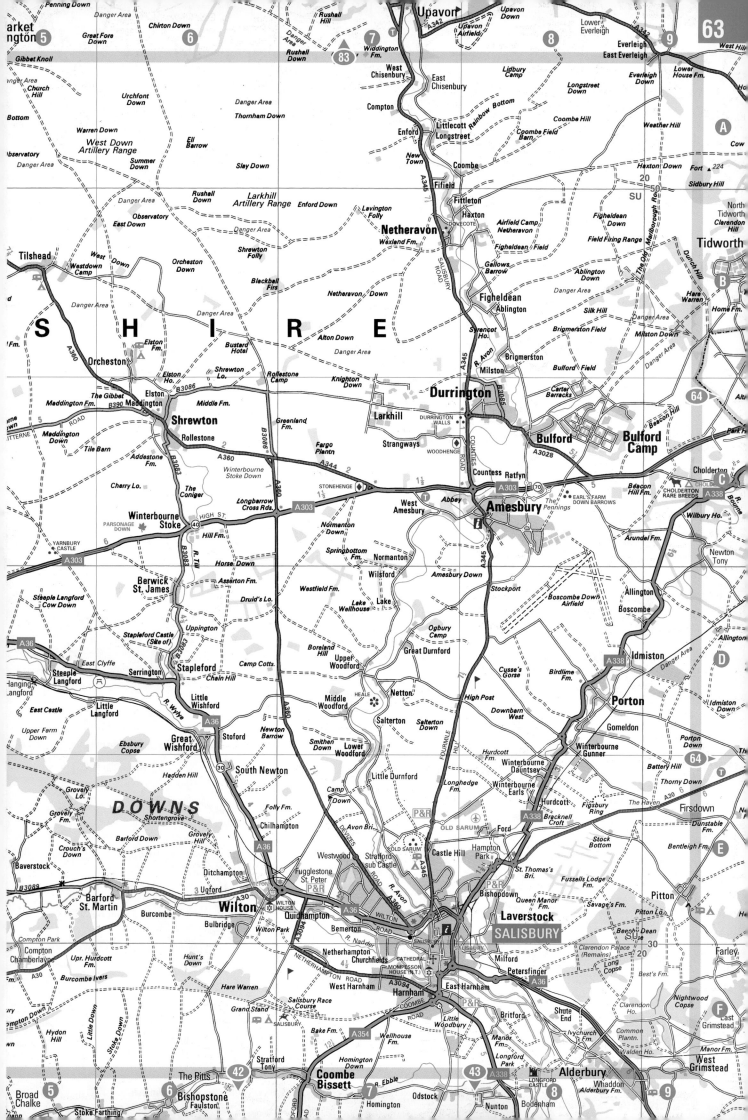

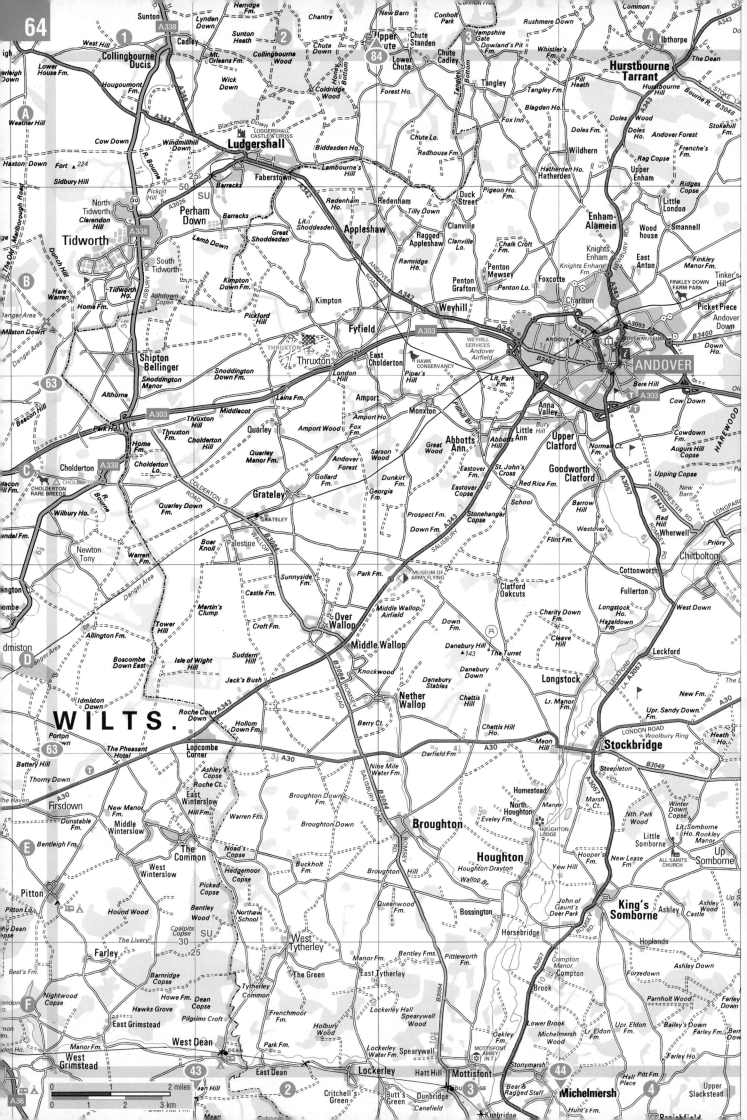

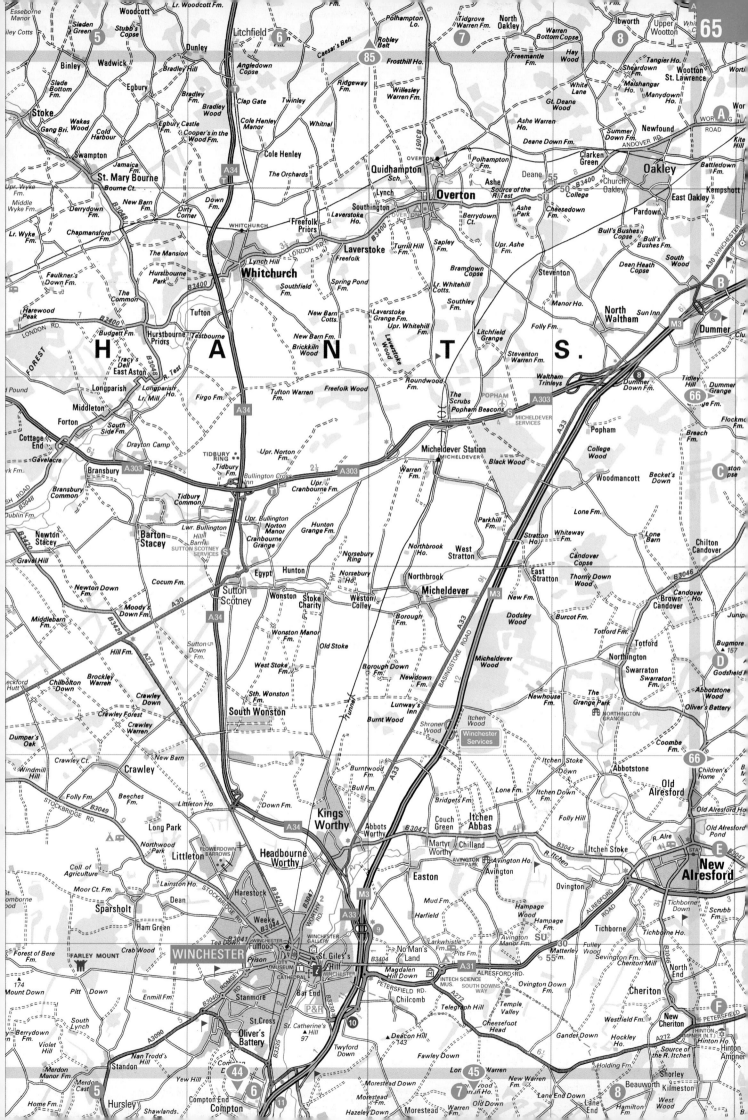

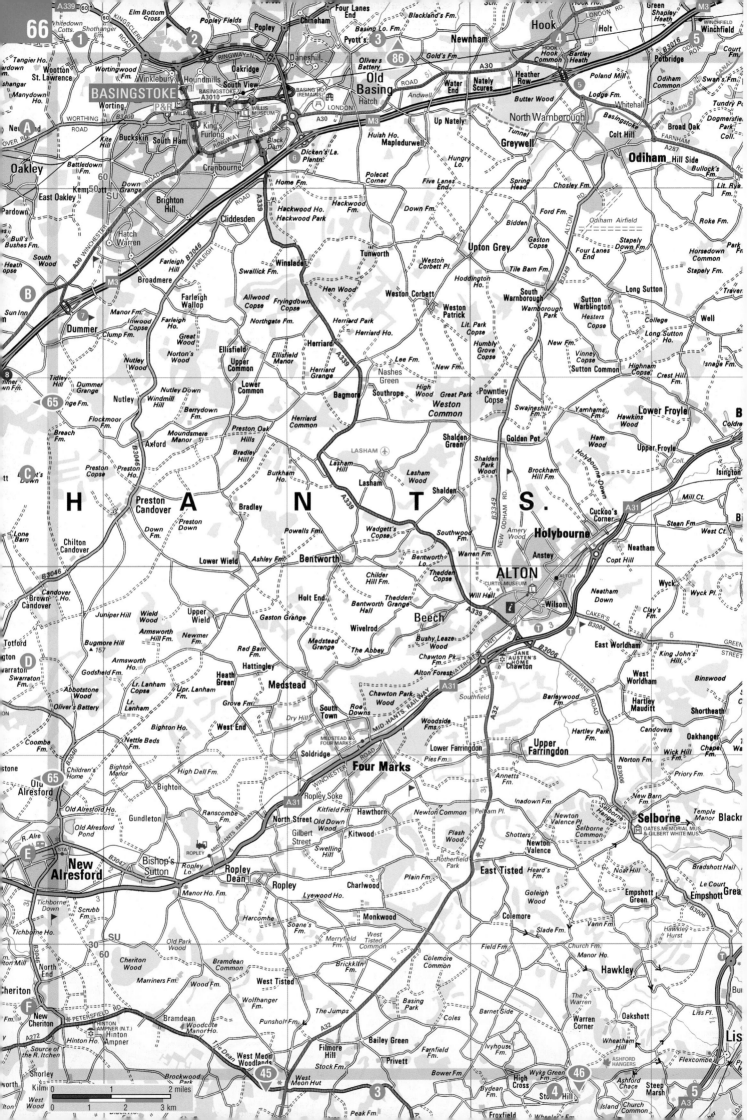

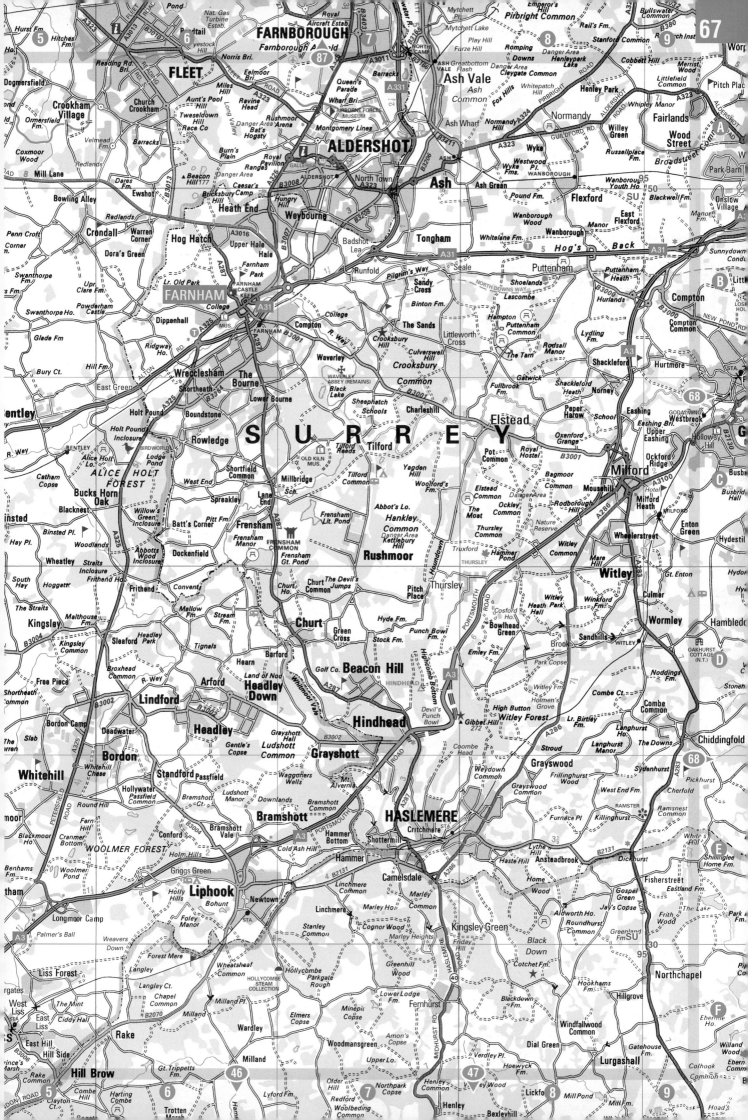

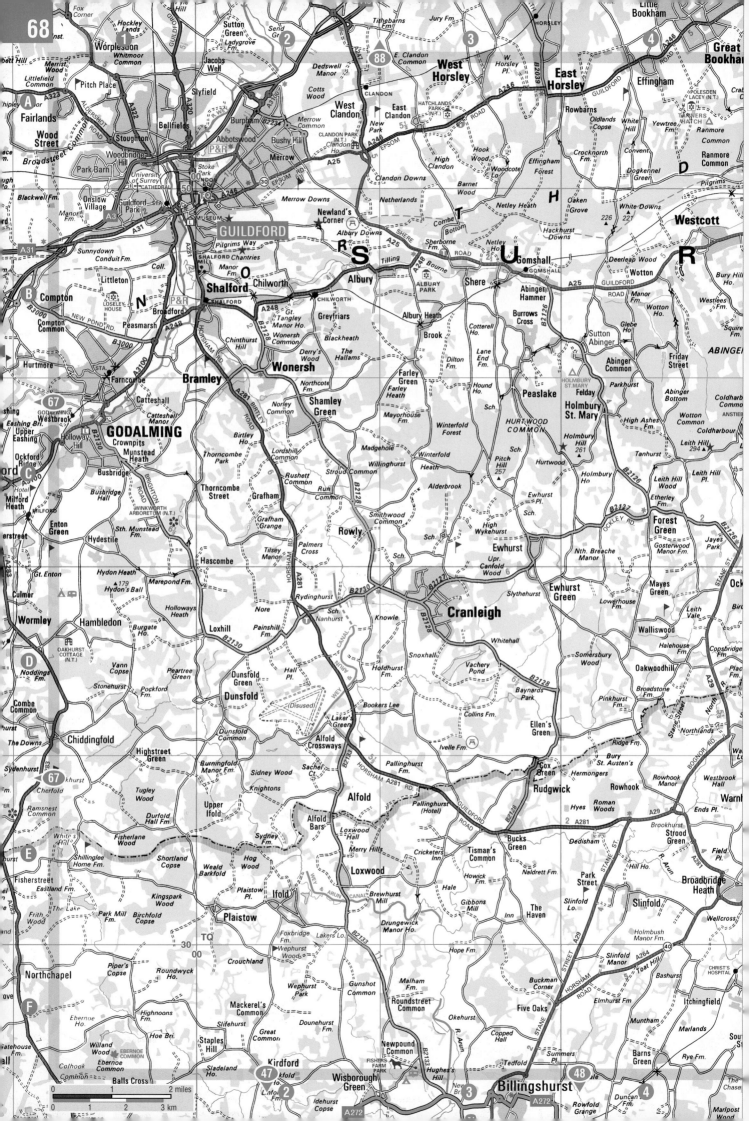

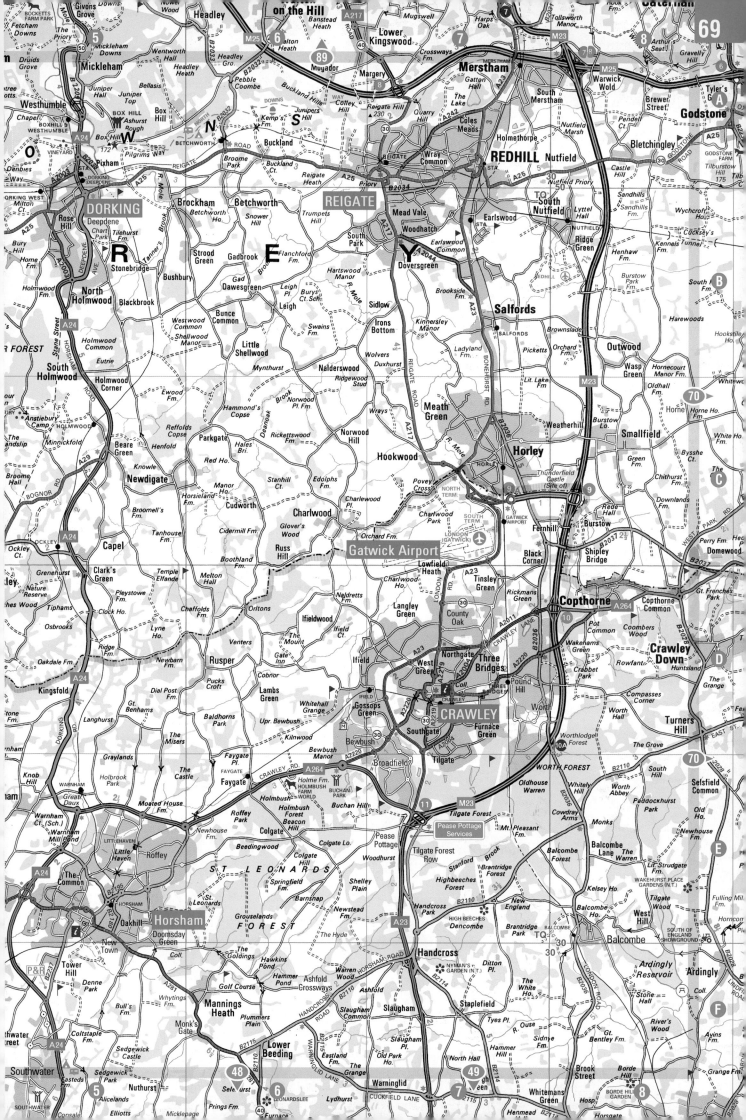

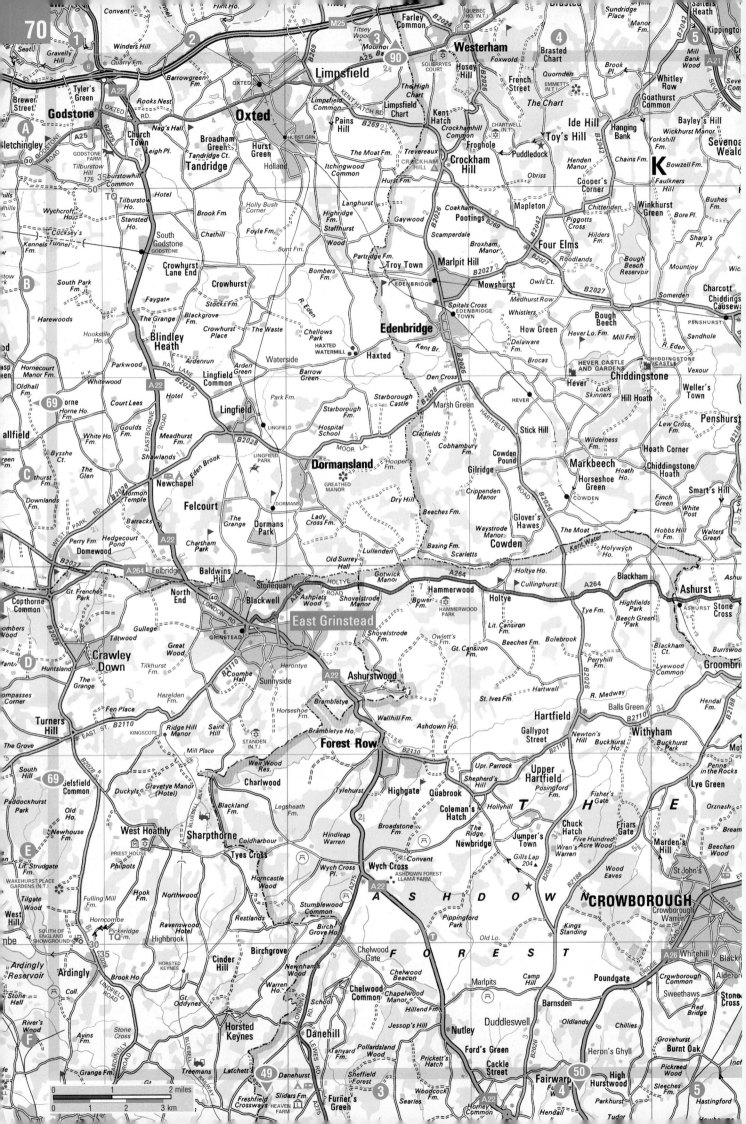

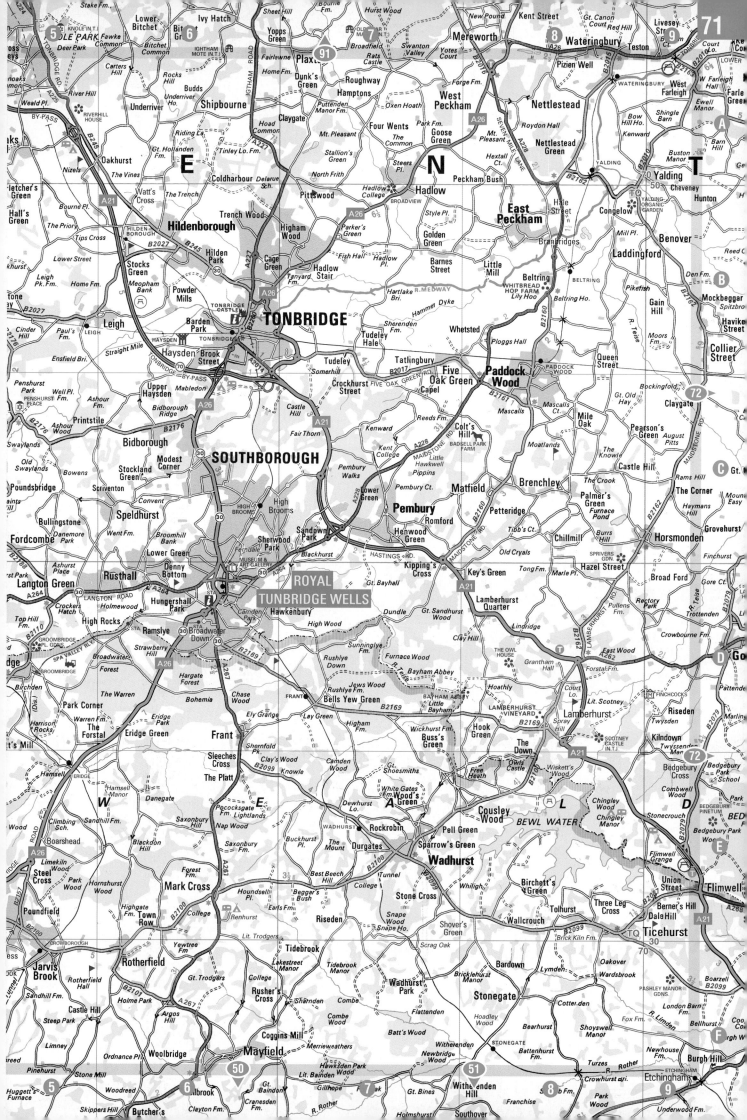

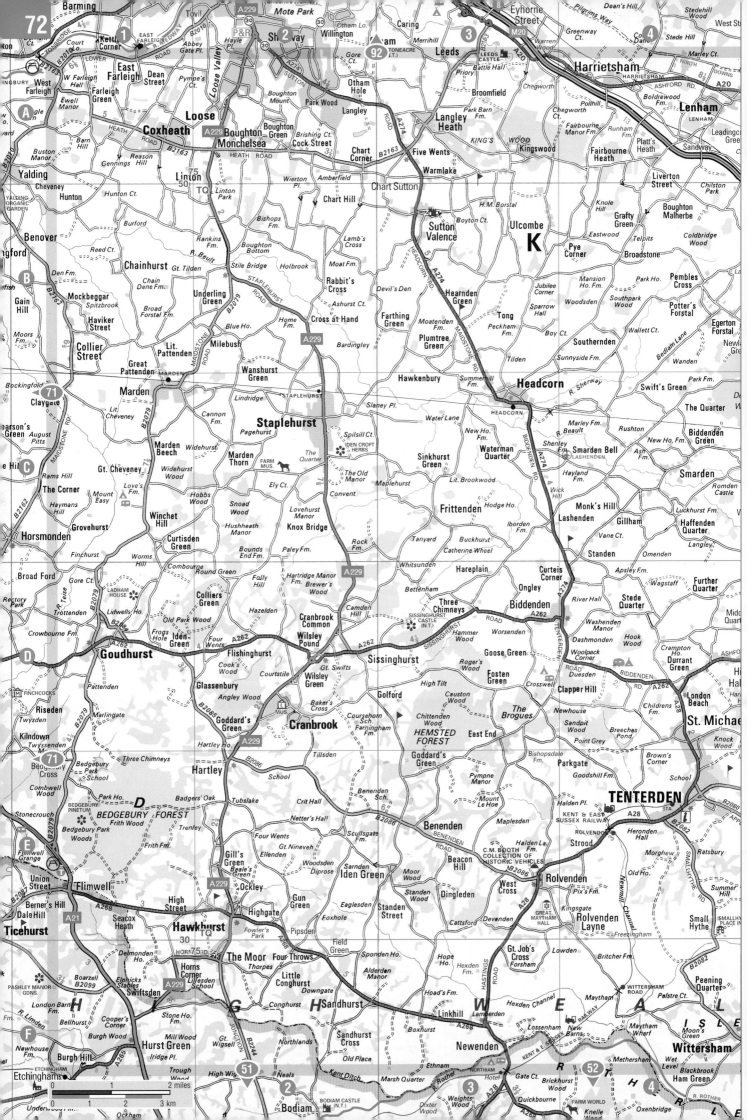

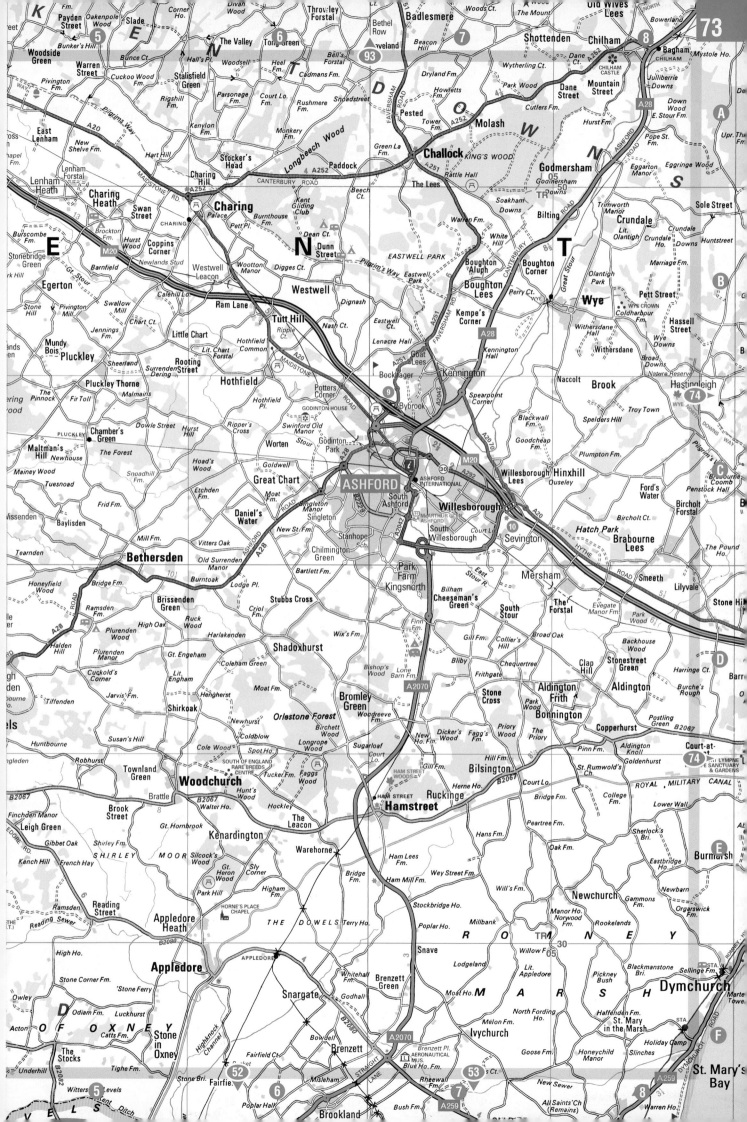

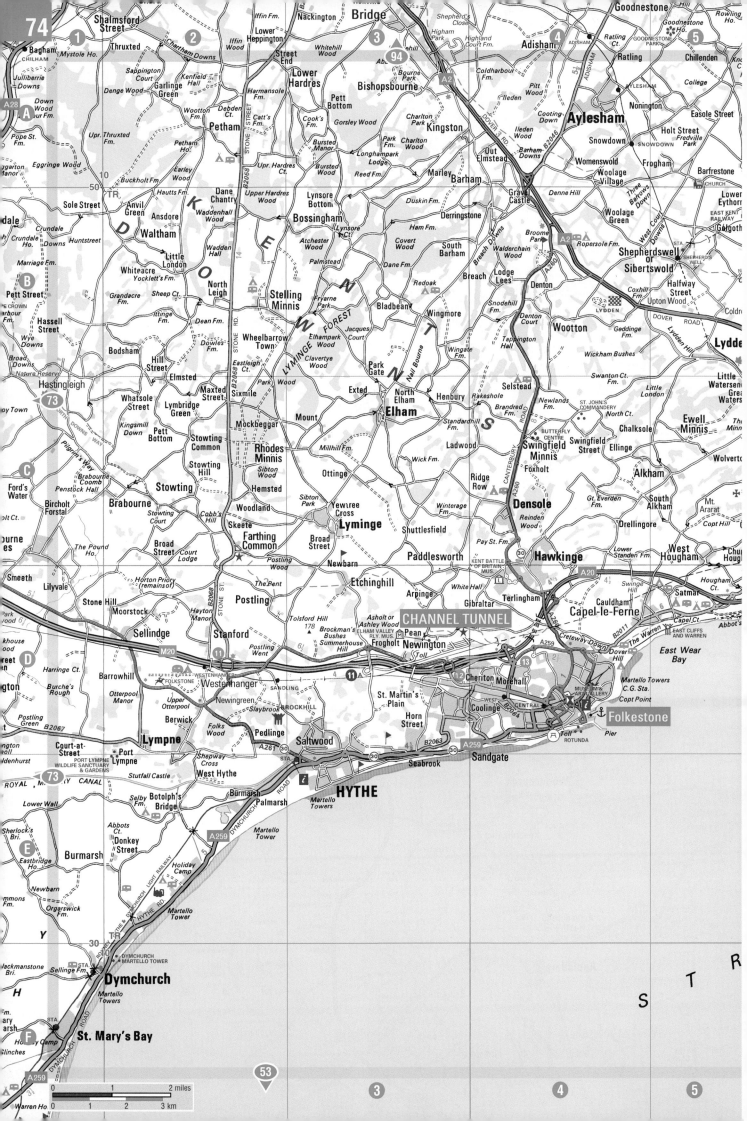

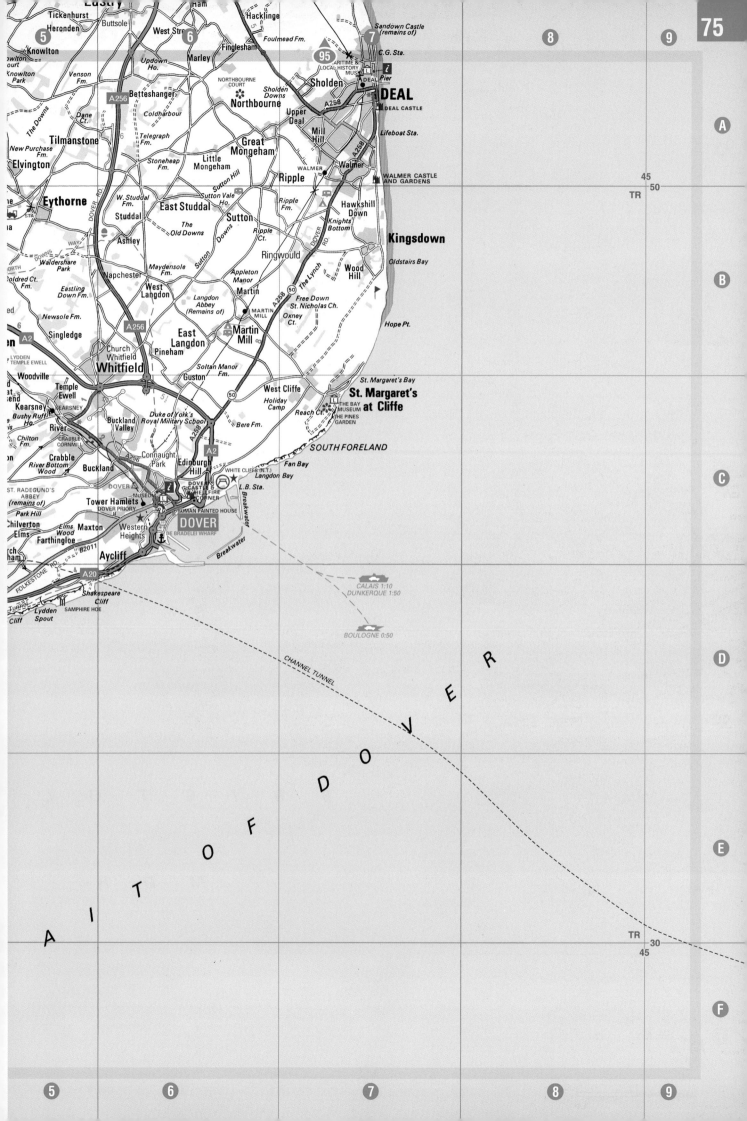

A

B

C

D

E

F

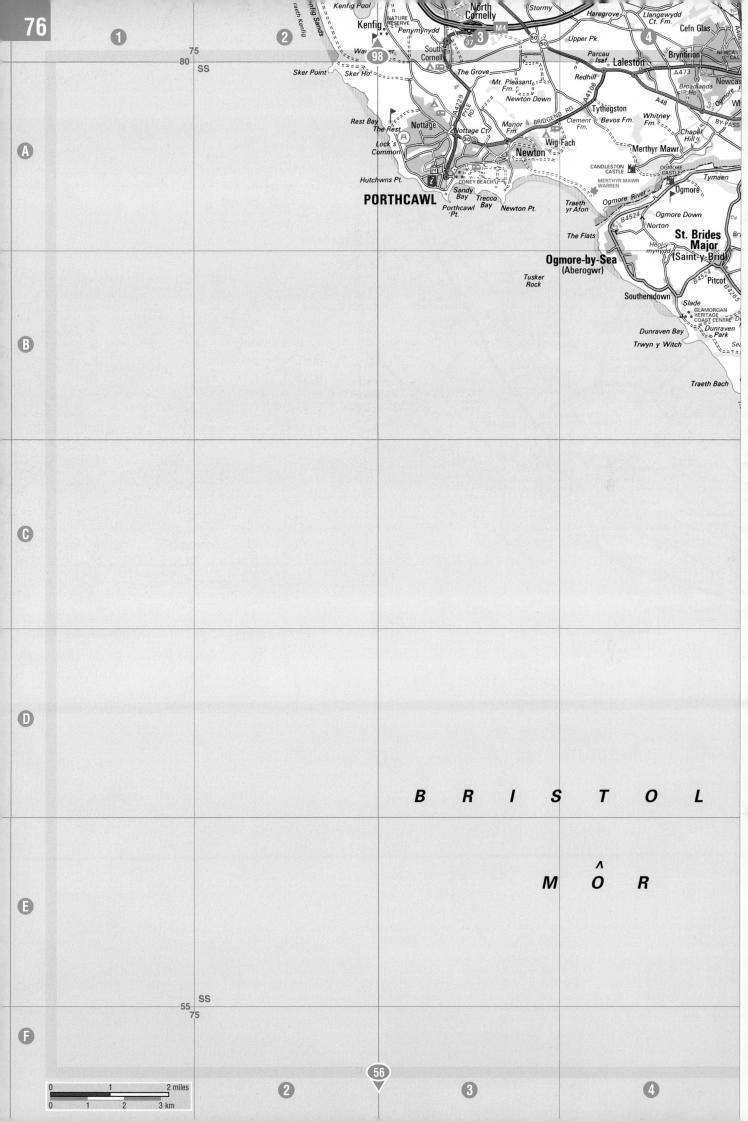

PORTHCAWL

Kenfig Pool
Kenfig
NATURE
RESERVE
Penymynydd
North
Cornelly
Stormy
Haregrove
Llangewydd
Ct. Fm.
Cefn Glas
South
Cornelly
Parcau
Isaf
Laleston
Bryntirion
Newcas
98
The Grove
Mt. Pleasant
Fm.
Redhill
Newton Down
Newton Down
Broadlands
Ho
Ogmore
Newcas
WY-PASS
Sker Point
Sker Ho
75
80
SS
raeth Kenfig
fig Sands
PYLE
RD.
BRIDGEND RD.
Tythegston
Clement
Fm.
Whitney
Fm.
Chapel
Hill
Rest Bay
The Rest
Nottage
Nottage Ct
Manor
Fm.
Bevos Fm.
Wig Fach
Lock's
Common
Newton
Merthyr Mawr
CANDLESTON
CASTLE
OGMORE
CASTLE
Tymaen
Hutchwns Pt.
CONEY BEACH
MERTHYR MAWR
WARREN
Ogmore
Sandy
Bay
Trecco
Bay
Newton Pt.
Traeth
yr Afon
Ogmore River
Ogmore Down
St. Brides
Major
(Saint-y-Brid)
Porthcawl
Pt.
The Flats
Norton
Pitcot
Ogmore-by-Sea
(Aberogwr)
Heol-y-
mynydd
Tusker
Rock
Southerndown
Slade
GLAMORGAN
HERITAGE
COAST CENTRE
Dunraven Bay
Dunraven
Park
Trwyn y Witch
Traeth Bach

B R I S T O L

M Ô R

56

0        1        2 miles
0    1    2    3 km

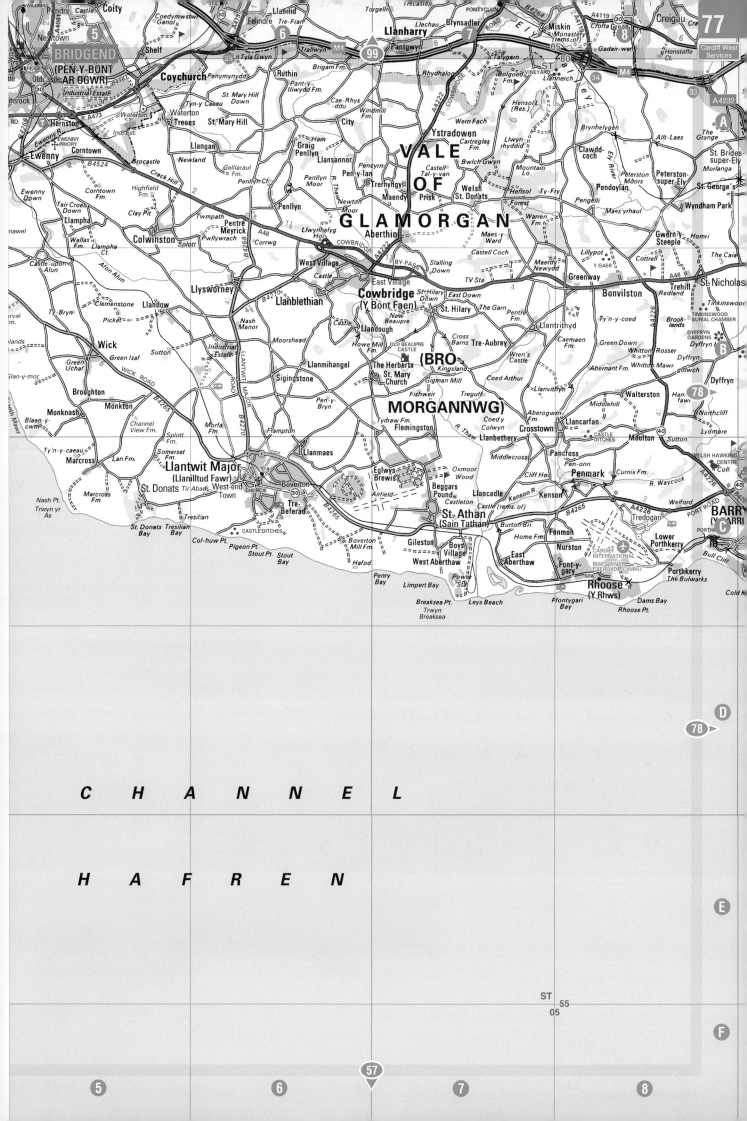

VALE
OF
GLAMORGAN

(BRO

MORGANNWG)

*C H A N N E L*

*H A F R E N*

BRIDGEND
(PEN-Y-BÔNT
AR OGWR)

Coity
Coychurch
Ewenny
Corntown
Cornton
Colwinston
Wick
Broughton
Monknash
Marcross
Llantwit Major
(Llanilltud Fawr)
St. Donats
Llanmaes
Boverton
Tre-Beferad
Llanbethian
Cowbridge
(Y Bònt Faen)
St. Hilary
Llandough
Llanmihangel
Sigingstone
St. Mary
Church
The Herberts
Flemingston
Llanmaes
Eglwys
Brewis
St. Athan
(Sain Tathan)
Gileston
Boys
Village
West Aberthaw
East
Aberthaw
Font-y-gary
Rhoose
(Y Rhws)
Llancarfan
Walterston
Moulton
Crosstown
Penmark
Llancadle
Fonmon
Nurston
Lower
Porthkerry
Porthkerry
BARRY
(Y BARRI)
Bonvilston
St. Nicholas
Peterston-
super-Ely
St. Brides-
super-Ely
Pendoylan
Llanharry
Llanharan
Miskin
Creigau

Llanlid
Felindre
Tre-Frân
Pantgwyn

78

40

99

57

34
33

M4

A48

A4232

A4226

A4119

A4264

B4265

B4270

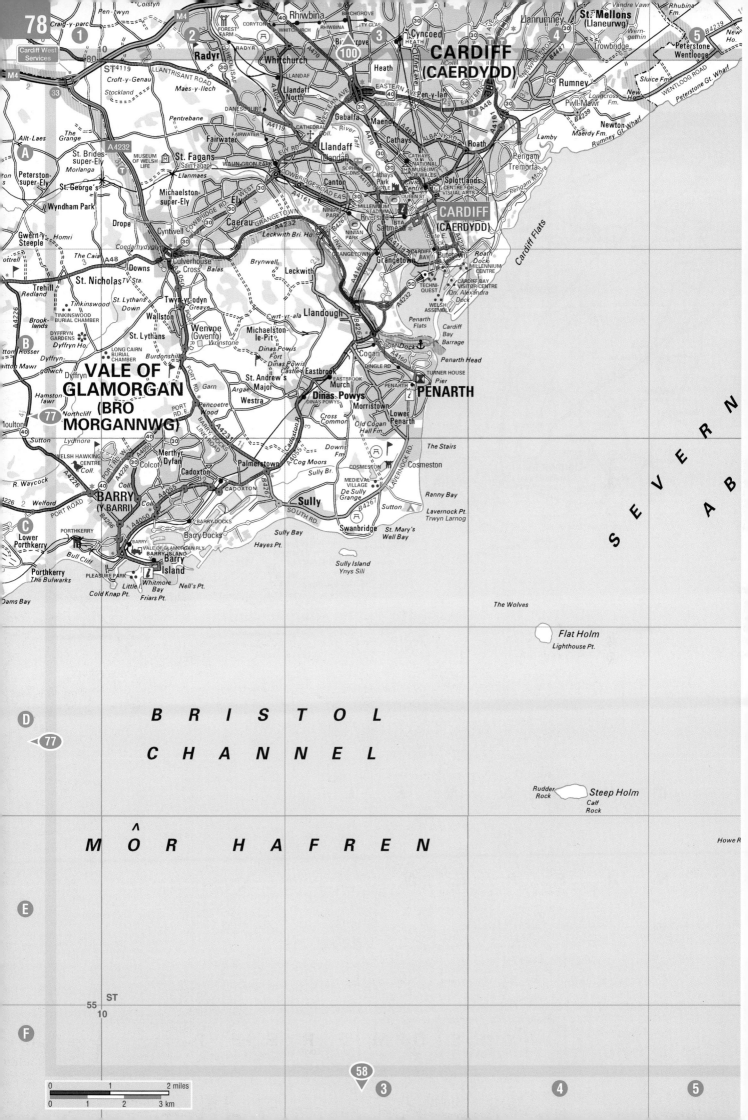

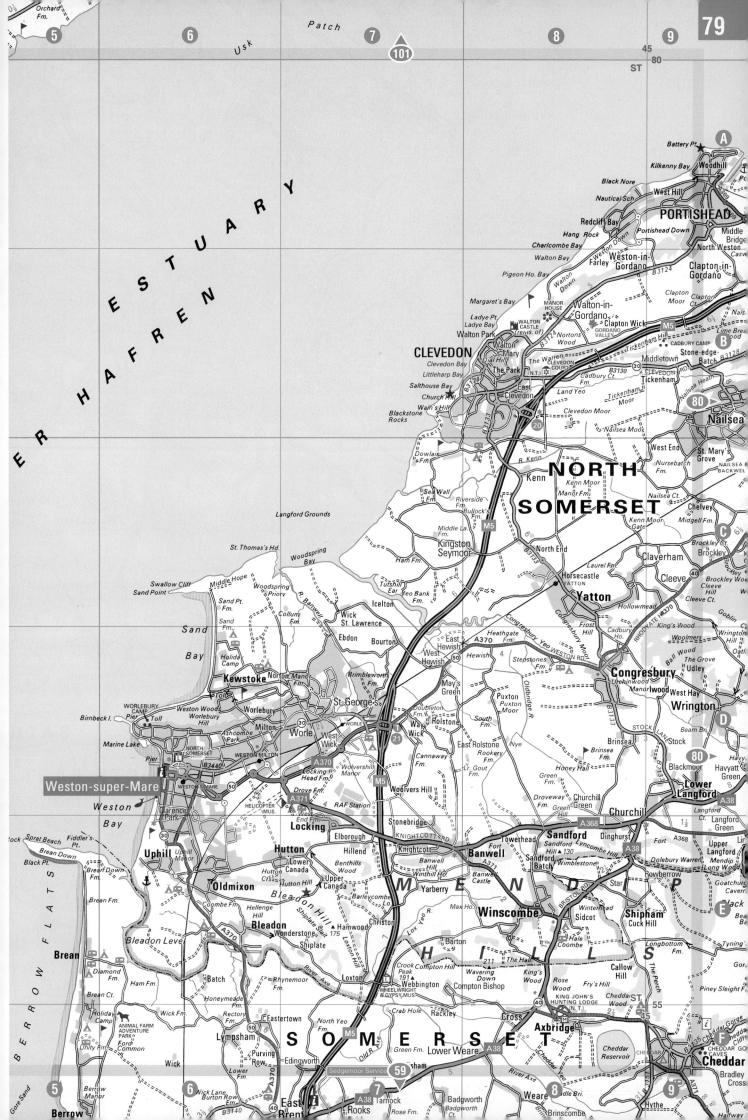

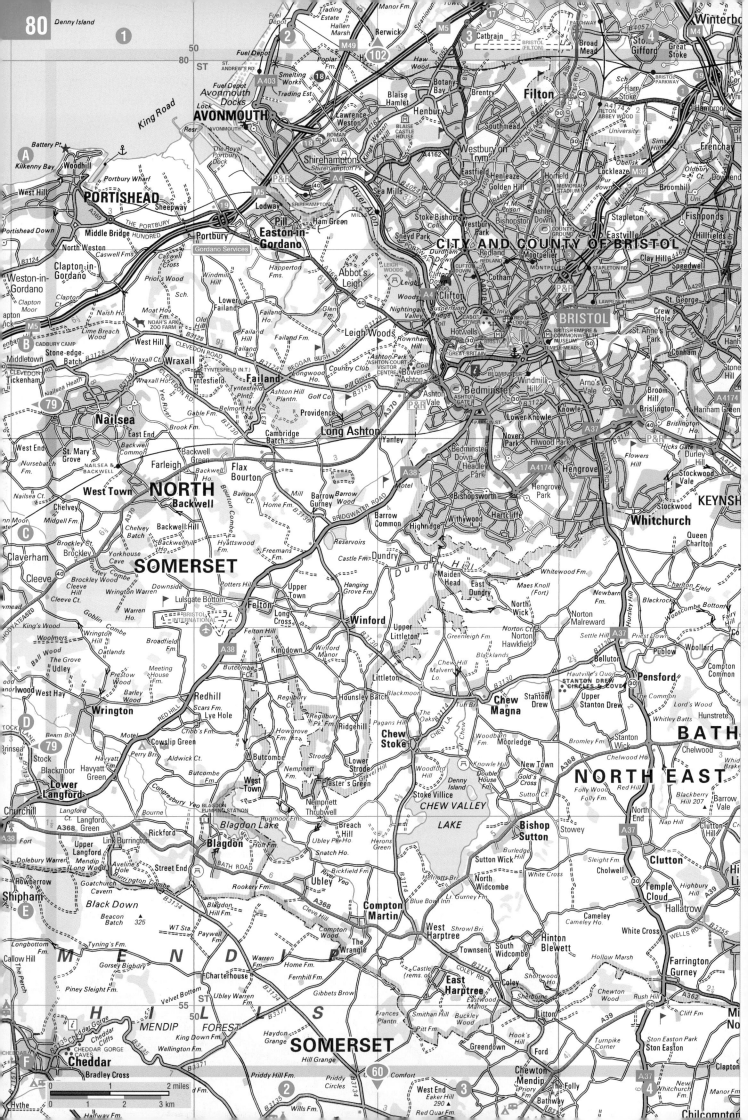

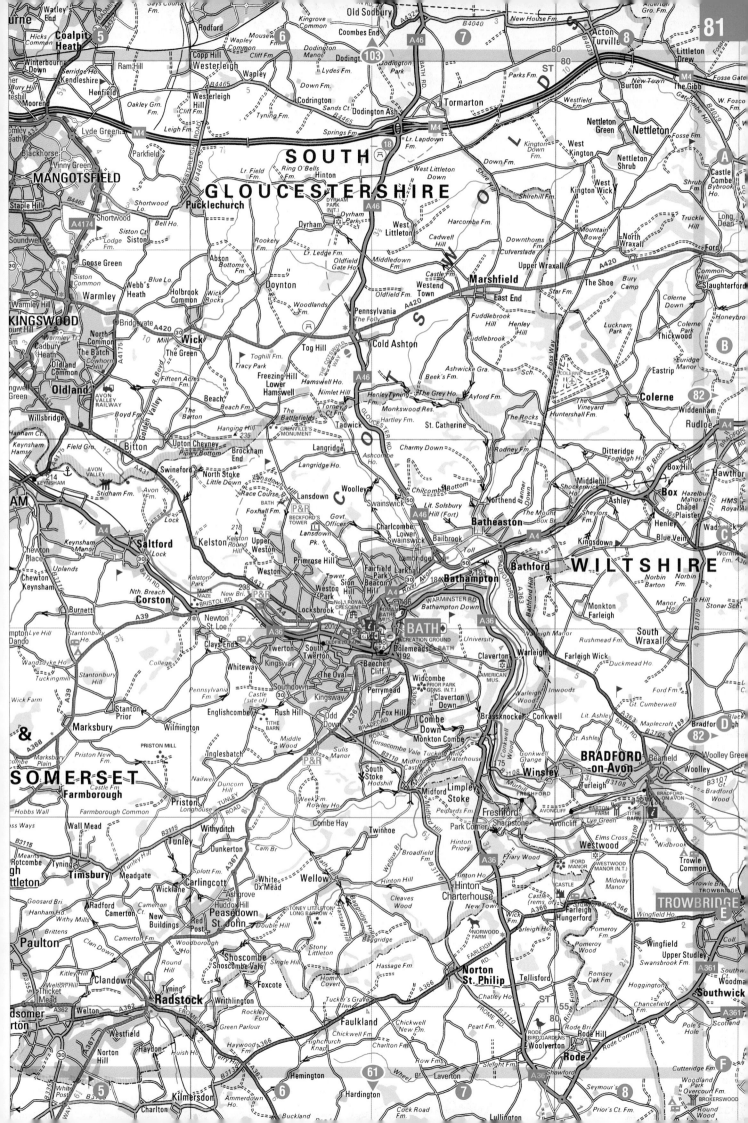

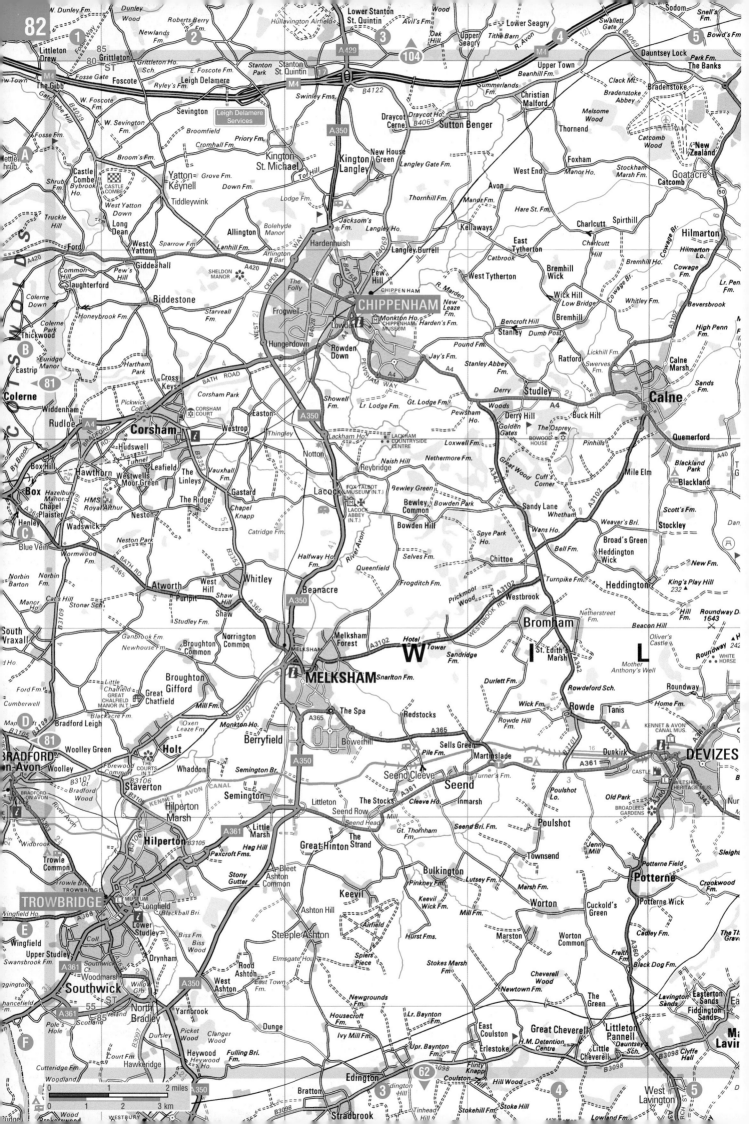

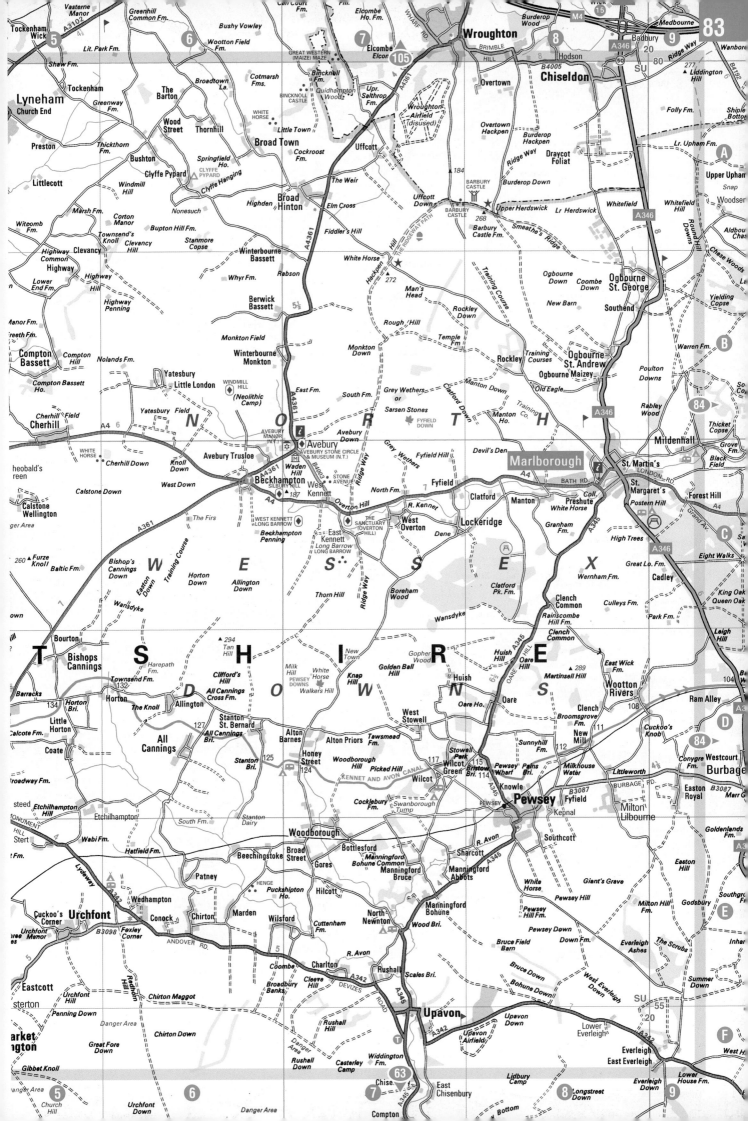

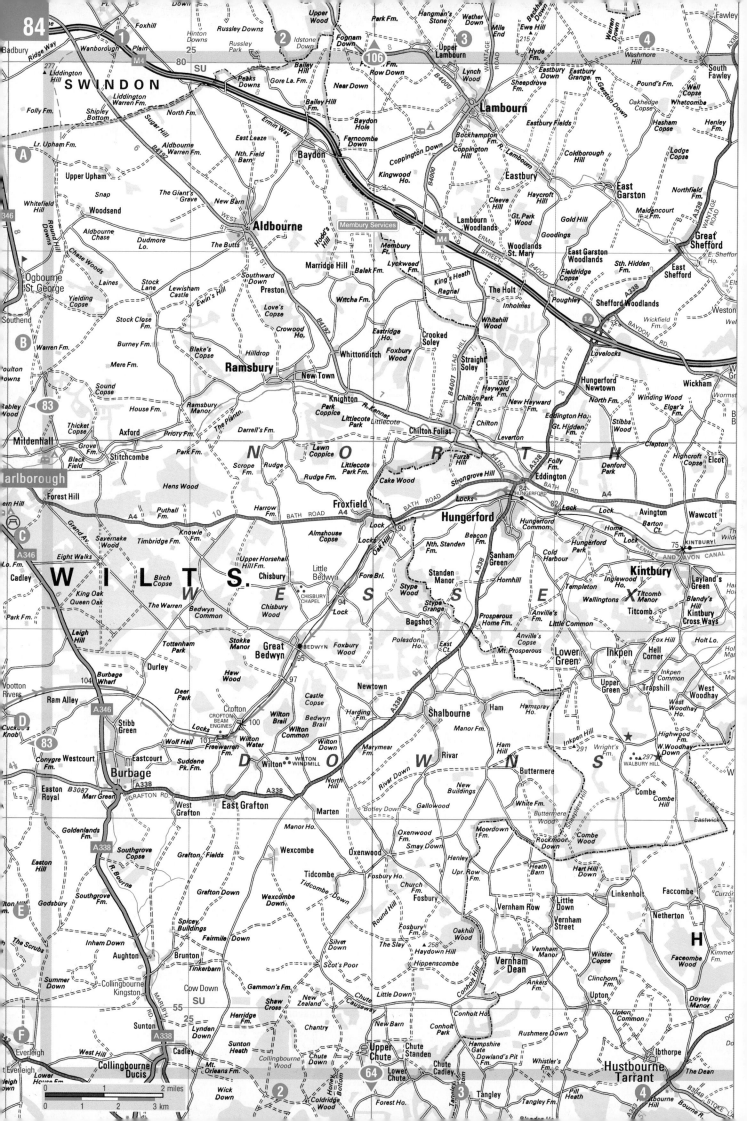

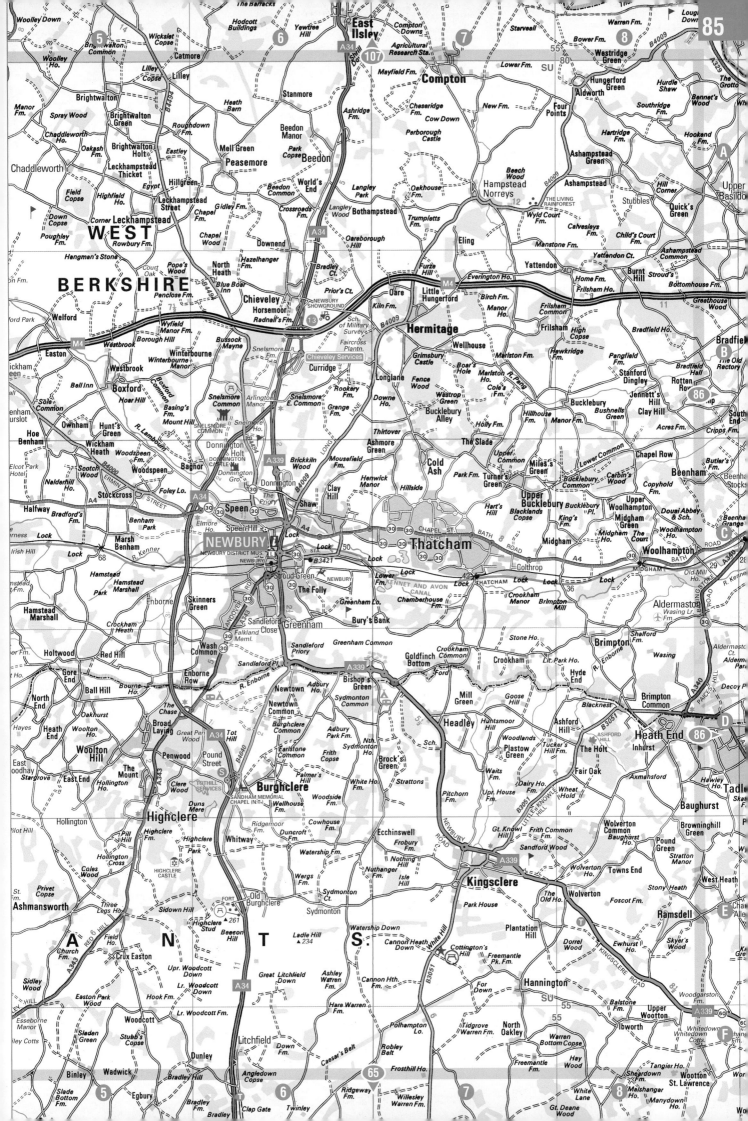

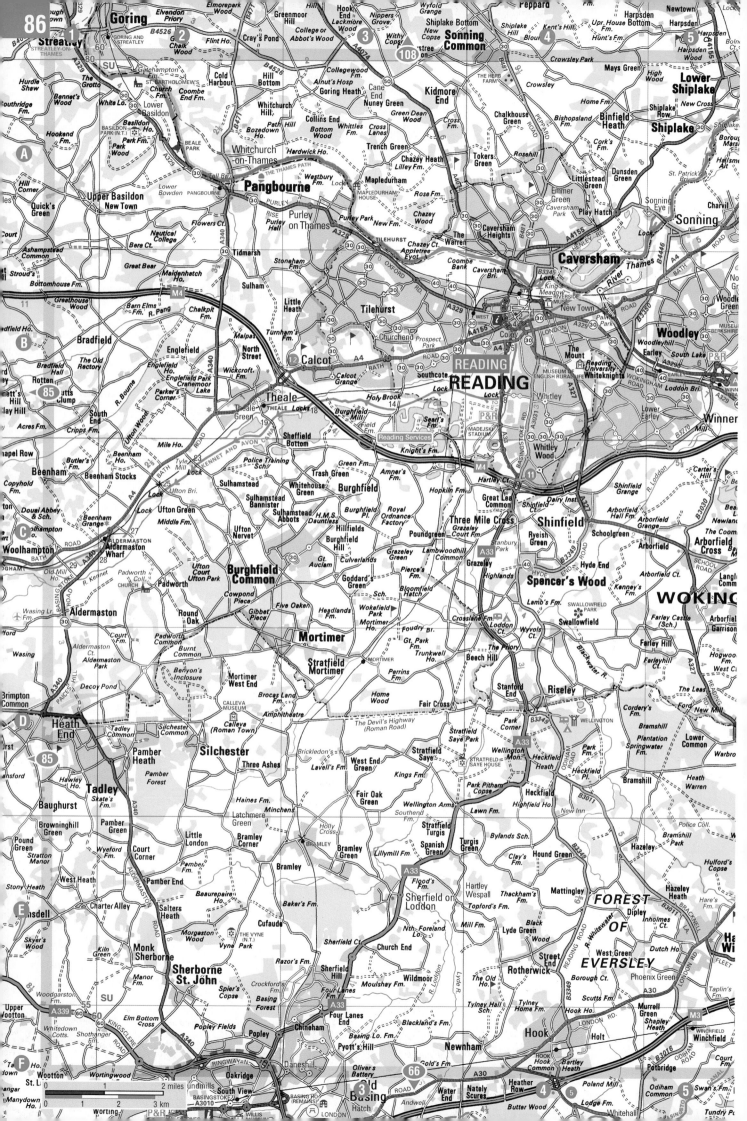

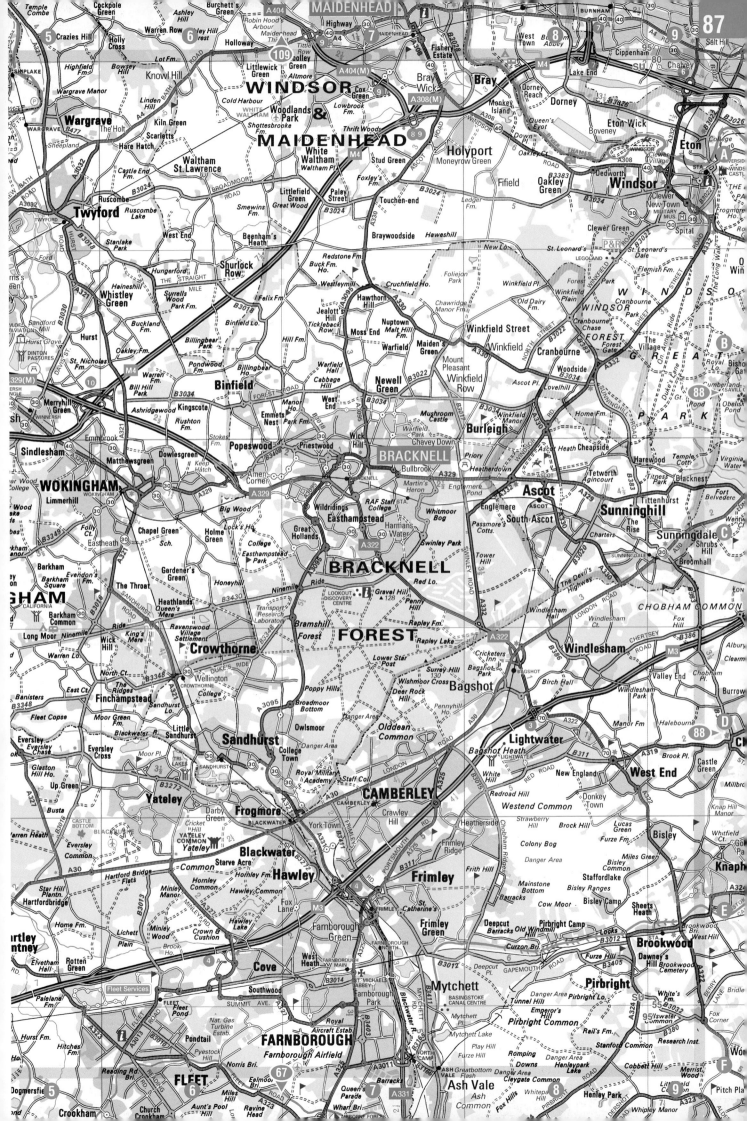

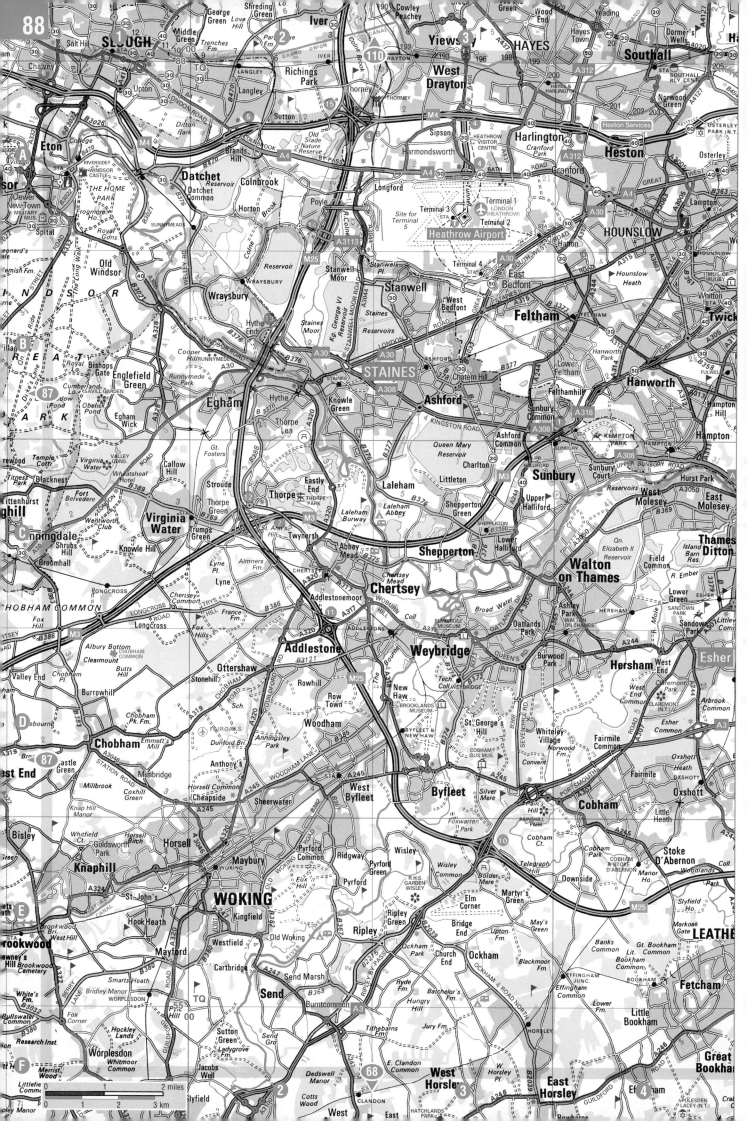

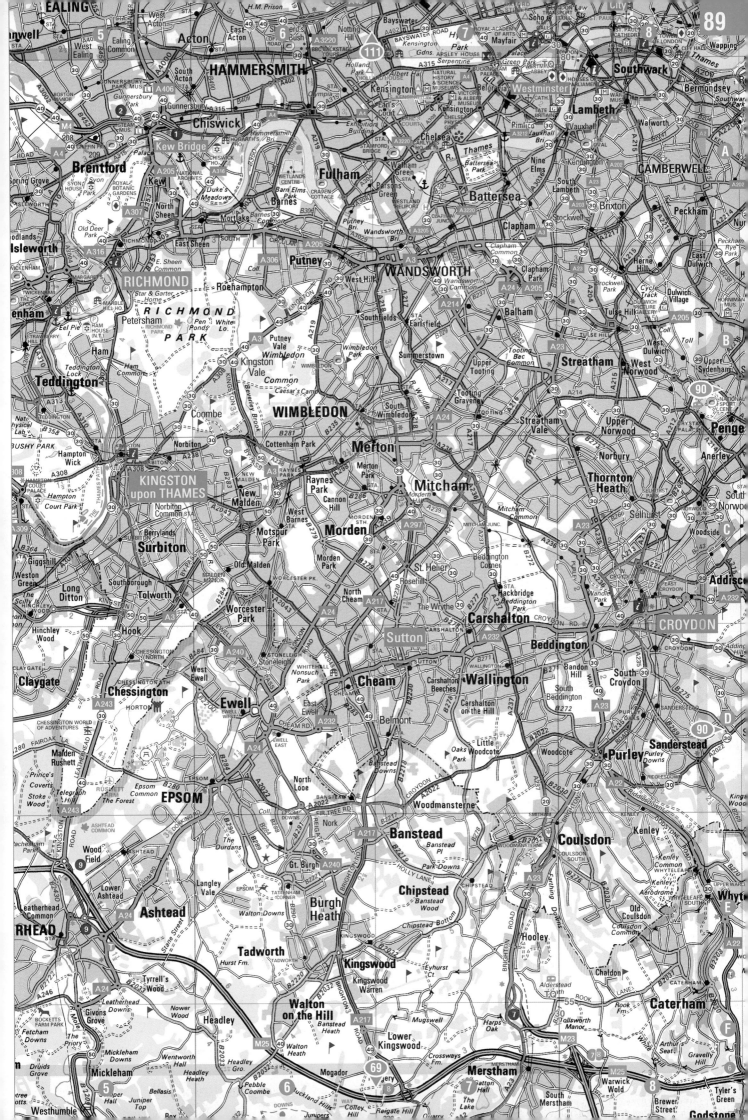

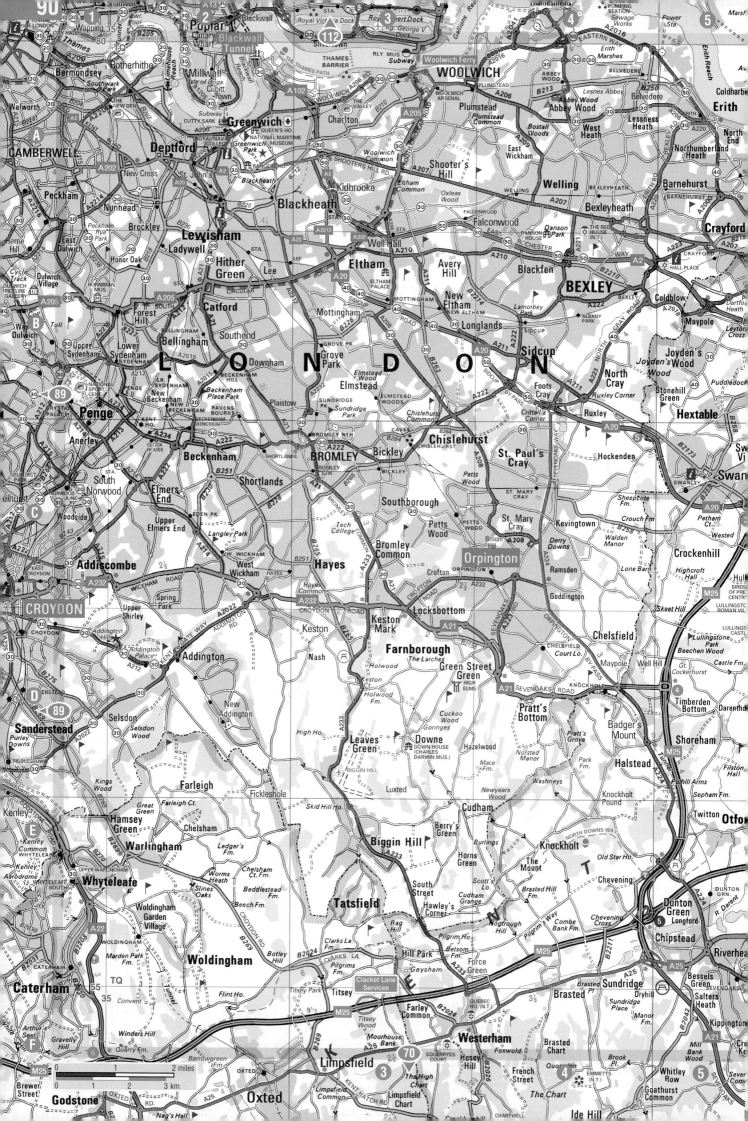

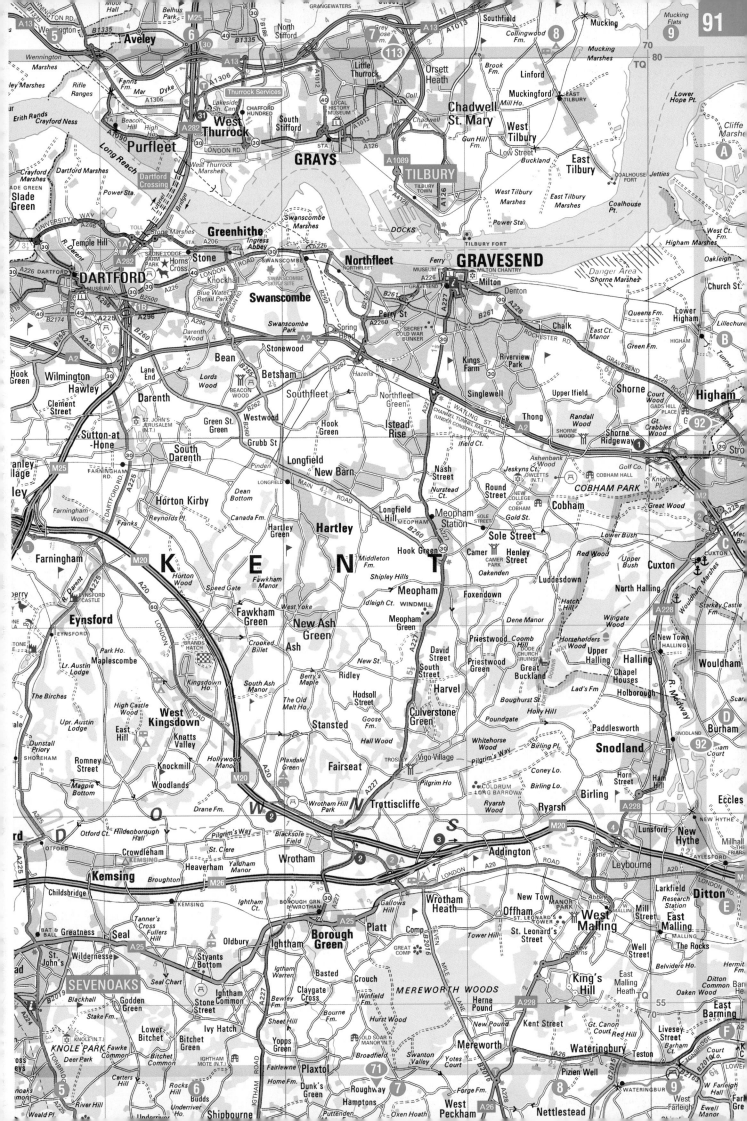

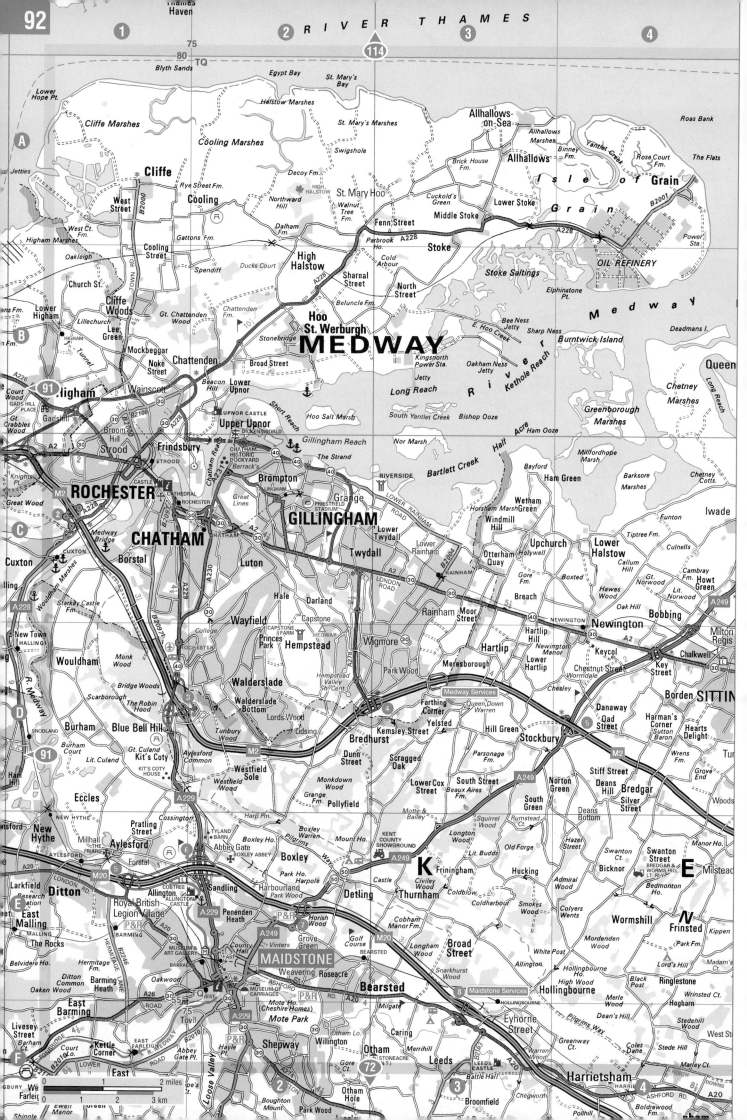

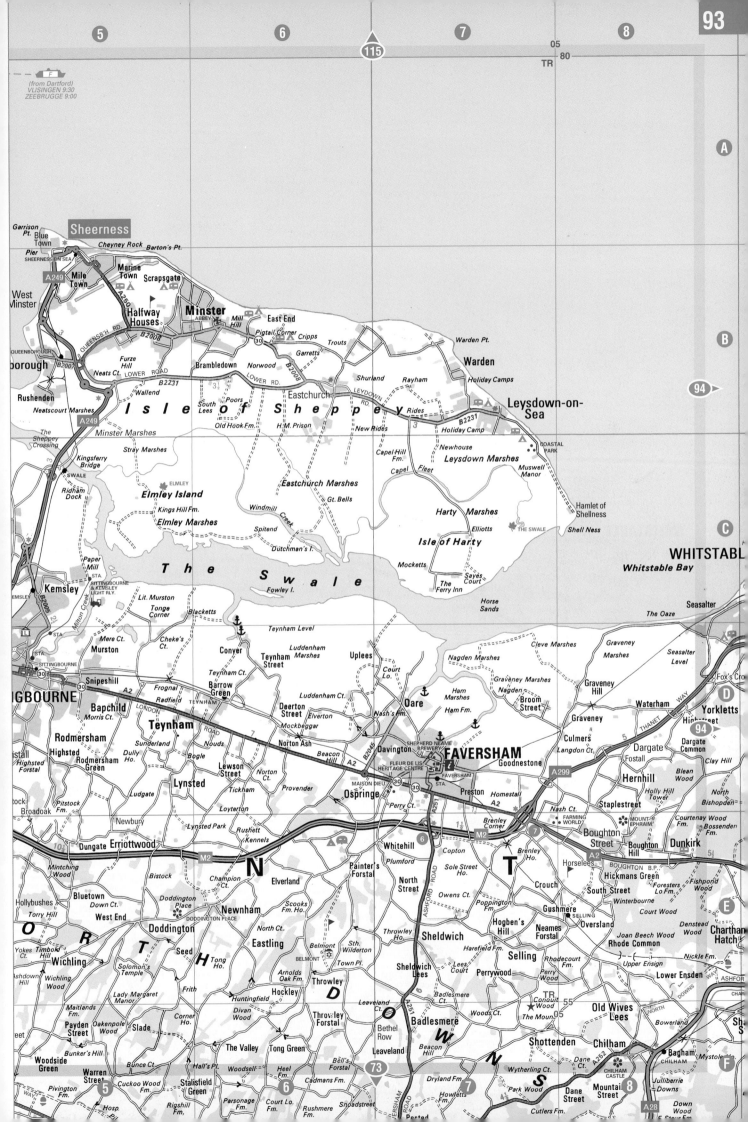

⑤ ⑥ ⑦ ⑧

115

05
80
TR

Ⓐ

94 ➤

Ⓑ

Ⓒ

Ⓓ

Ⓔ

Ⓕ

(from Dartford)
VLISINGEN 9:30
ZEEBRUGGE 9:00

Garrison Pt.  Blue Town
Sheerness
Cheyney Rock   Barton's Pt.
Pier
SHEERNESS ON SEA
A249  Mile Town
Marine Town
Scrapsgate
West Minster
QUEENSB'H RD.
Halfway Houses
Minster  East End
ABBEY  Mill Hill
Pigtail Corner  Cripps
Trouts
B2008
Garretts
borough
B2007
Queenborough
Furze Hill
Neats Ct.  LOWER ROAD
Brambledown  Norwood
B2231
Rushenden
Neatscourt Marshes
A249
South Lees  Poors
Old Hook Fm.
H.M. Prison
New Rides
Wallend
Eastchurch
LOWER RD.
B2008
LEYDOWN RD.
Rides
Shurland  Rayham
Warden Pt.
Warden
Holiday Camps
B2231
Leysdown-on-Sea
Holiday Camp
Newhouse
Capel Hill Fm.
Capel  Fleet
Leysdown Marshes
Muswell Manor
COASTAL PARK
Minster Marshes
The Sheppey Crossing
Kingsferry Bridge
Stray Marshes
Isle of Sheppey
Eastchurch Marshes
Gt. Bells
Harty Marshes
Hamlet of Shellness
SWALE
Ridham Dock
Elmley Island
ELMLEY
Kings Hill Fm.
Windmill Creek
Elliotts  THE SWALE
Shell Ness
Elmley Marshes
Spitend
Dutchman's I.
Isle of Harty
Mocketts
WHITSTABL
Paper Mill
Kemsley
KEMSLEY
B2005
Fowley I.
The Swale
Sayes Court
The Ferry Inn
Horse Sands
Whitstable Bay
Seasalter
The Oaze
Kemsley
STA.  SITTINGBOURNE & KEMSLEY LIGHT RLY.
Lit. Murston
Tonge Corner
Blacketts
Teynham Level
Conyer
Mere Ct.
Murston
Cheke's Ct.
STA.
SITTINGBOURNE
Snipeshill
IGBOURNE
A2
Bapchild  Morris Ct.
Teynham
Rodmersham
Highsted
Rodmersham Green
Highsted Forstal
stall
Broadoak
Pitstock Fm.
Teynham Ct.
Frognal  Radfield
TEYNHAM
Barrow Green
LONDON
Sunderland
Nouds
Dully Ho.
Bogle
Lewson Street
Lynsted
Ludgate
Teynham Street
Luddenham Marshes
Uplees
Deerton Street  Elverton
Luddenham Ct.
Mockbeggar
Norton Ash
Beacon Hill
B2045
Court Lo.
Nash's Fm.
Oare
ROAD
Tickham
Norton Ct.
Provender
Davington
SHEPHERD NEAME BREWERY
FLEUR DE LIS HERITAGE CENTRE
FAVERSHAM
MAISON DIEU
FAVERSHAM STA.
Preston
Ham Marshes
Ham Fm.
Nagden Marshes
Cleve Marshes
Graveney Marshes
Graveney
Nagden
Broom Street
Graveney Hill
Graveney Marshes
Seasalter Level
Waterham
THANET WAY
Fox's Cro
Yorkletts
Hinb-street
94 ➤
Dargate Common
Dargate
Fostall
Clay Hill
Blean Wood
North Bishopden
Hernhill
Holly Hill Tower
Staplestreet
MOUNT EPHRAIM
Langdon Ct.
Culmers
Goodnestone
A299
Homestall
A2
Nash Ct.
FARMING WORLD
Courtenay Wood
Bossenden Fm.
Ospringe
Perry Ct.
Brenley Corner
Brenley Ho.
M2
Boughton Street
Boughton Hill
A2
Dunkirk
Horselees
BOUGHTON B.P.
Lynsted Park
Rushett Kennels
Loyterton
Newbury
Dungate  Erriottwood
M2
N
Champion Ct.
Elverland
Whitehill
Copton
Plumford
Painter's Forstal
North Street
Sole Street Ho.
Owens Ct.
Poppington
Crouch
Hickmans Green
South Street
Winterbourne
Gushmere
Court Wood
Foresters Lo Fm.
Fishpond Wood
E
Mintching Wood
Bistock
Doddington Place
Bluetown  Down Ct.
Hollybushes
Torry Hill
West End
Doddington
DODDINGTON PLACE
North Ct.
Scooks Fm. Ho.
Newnham
Eastling
Belmont
BELMONT
Sth. Wilderton  Town Pl.
Throwley Ho.
Sheldwich
Hogben's Hill
Neames Forstal
Selling
Overland
Joan Beech Wood
Rhode Common
Denstead Wood
Chartham Hatch
O
R
T
H
Yokes Ct.  Timbold Hill
Wichling
ashdown Hill
Wichling Wood
Seed
Tong Hill
Solomon's Temple
Lady Margaret Manor
Frith
Arnolds Oak Fm.
Huntingfield
Divan Wood
Hockley
Throwley
Leaveland Ct.
Harefield Fm.
Sheldwich Lees
Lees Court
Perrywood
D
Perry Wood
Badlesmere Ct.
Woods Ct.
Rhodecourt Fm.
Upper Ensign
Lower Ensden
ASHFO
Old Wives Lees
Chartha
Sh
S
Maitlands Fm.
Payden Street
Oakenpole Wood
Slade
Bunker's Hill
Woodside Green
Warren Street
Pivington Fm.
Hosp.
Corner Ho.
The Valley
Tong Green
Bunce Ct.
Hall's Pl.
Cuckoo Wood Fm.
Stalisfield Green
Heel Fm.
Woodsell
Bell's Forstal
Throwley Forstal
Bethel Row
Leaveland
Badlesmere
Beacon Hill
Wytherling Ct.
Shottenden
Chilham
CHILHAM
CHILHAM CASTLE
Bagham
Mystole
Jullibernie Downs
Down Wood
A28
73
Cadmans Fm.
Dryland Fm.
Howletts
Park Wood
Mountain Street
Dane Street
A252
Dane Ct.
O
W
N
S
Rigshill Fm.
Parsonage Fm.
Court Lo. Fm.
Rushmere Fm.
Snoadstreet
Cutlers Fm.
Ported

⑤ ⑥ ⑦ ⑧

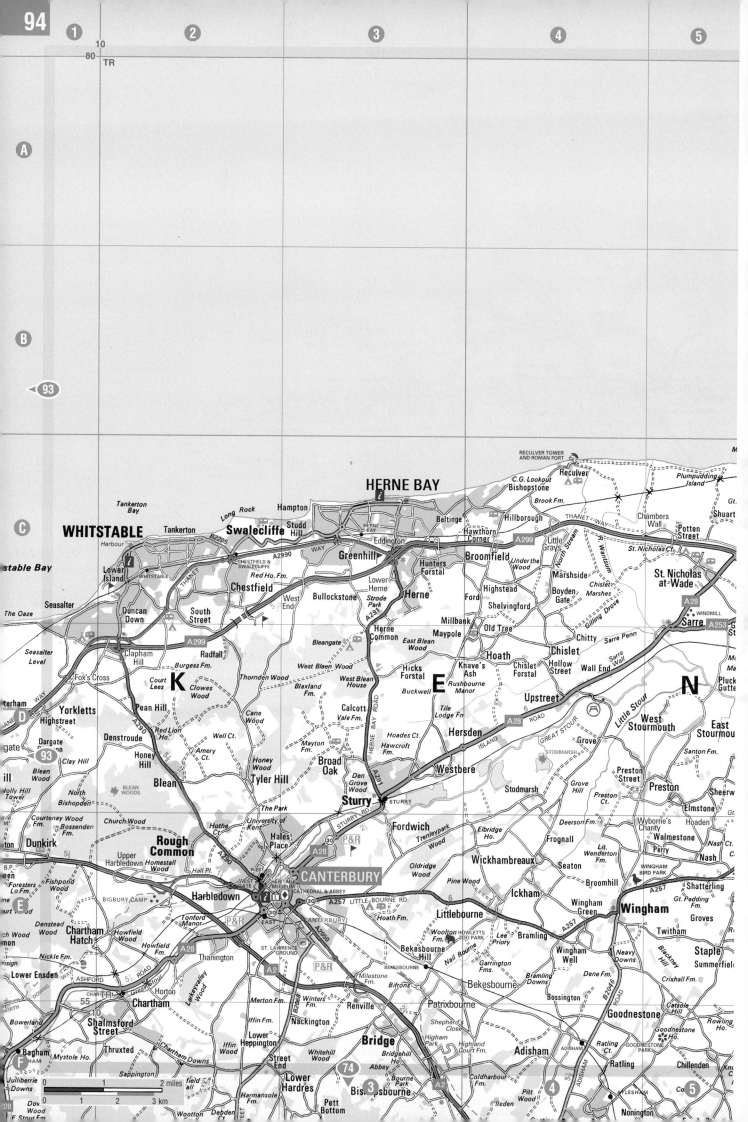

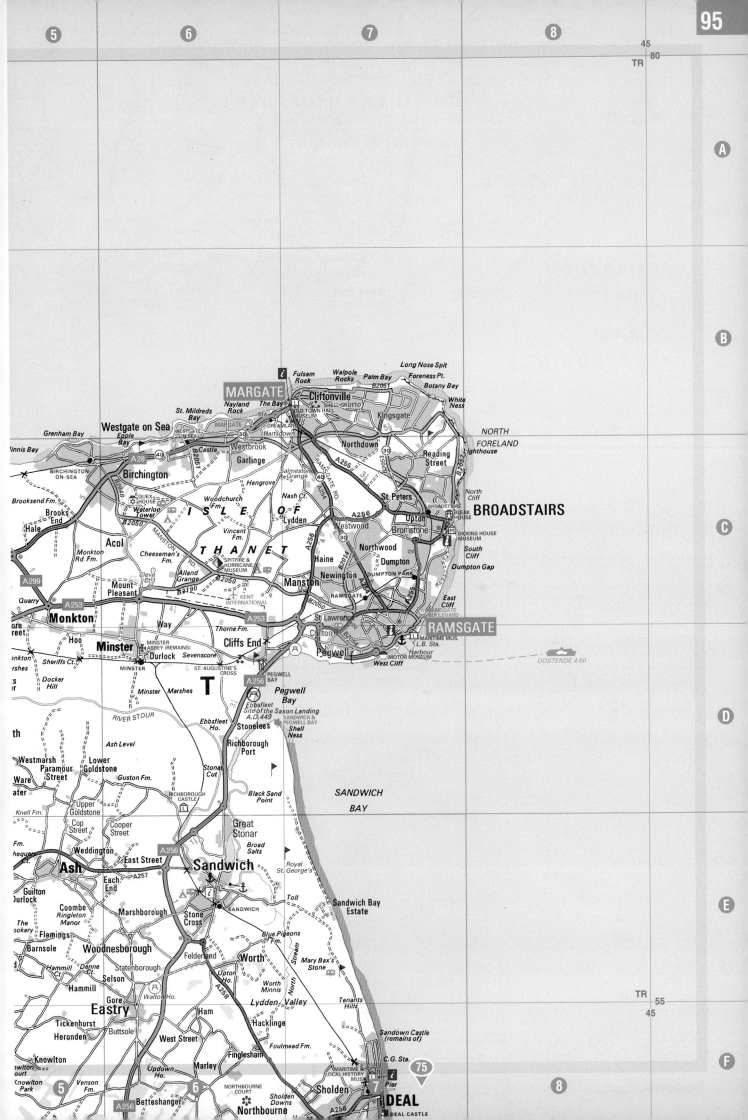

45
80
TR

A

B

MARGATE

Long Nose Spit
Fulsam Rock
Walpole Rocks
Palm Bay
Foreness Pt.
Botany Bay
B2051
St. Mildreds Bay
Cliftonville
SHELL-GROTTO
Kingsgate
White Ness
Nayland Rock
The Bay
OLD TOWN HALL MUSEUM
STA.
DREAMLAND
Grenham Bay
Epple Bay
Westgate on Sea
WESTGATE ON SEA
MARGATE
Hartsdown
Northdown
NORTH FORELAND Lighthouse
Minnis Bay
Westbrook
30
A255
31
Reading Street
Castle
Garlinge
Salmestone Grange
RAMSGATE RD.
40
A255
30
B2052
BIRCHINGTON-ON-SEA
A28
40
B2051
Birchington
Hengrove
A254
North Cliff
B204B
QUEX HOUSE
Woodchurch
Nash Ct.
St. Peters
BROADSTAIRS
Brooksend Fm.
Waterloo Tower
ISLE OF
Lydden
Westwood
A256
Upton
BLEAK HOUSE
Brooks End
B2050
A254
Bromstone
DICKINS HOUSE MUSEUM
Hale
Acol
THANET
A256
Haine
Northwood
South Cliff
Monkton Rd. Fm.
Cheeseman's Fm.
Vincent Fm.
B2014
Newington
Dumpton
Dumpton Gap
A299
Cleve Ct.
SPITFIRE & HURRICANE MUSEUM
Manston
DUMPTON PARK
Alland Grange
B2050
RAMSGATE
East Cliff
Quarry
A253
Mount Pleasant
B2190
KENT INTERNATIONAL
B2050
St. Lawrence
RAMSGATE BOULEVARD
RAMSGATE
Monkton
A253
Way
Thorne Fm.
A253
Chilton
B205
MARITIME MUS.
L.B. Sta.
Hoo
Cliffs End
Pegwell
OOSTENDE 4:00
Minster
MINSTER ABBEY (REMAINS)
Sevenscore
MOTOR MUSEUM
Harbour
Durlock
West Cliff
Sheriffs Ct.
ST. AUGUSTINE'S CROSS
A256
PEGWELL BAY
Docker Hill
MINSTER
Pegwell Bay
Minster
Minster Marshes
Ebbsfleet Site of the Saxon Landing A.D. 449
SANDWICH & PEGWELL BAY
RIVER STOUR
Ebbsfleet Ho.
Shell Ness
Ash Level
Stonelees
Richborough Port
SANDWICH BAY
Westmarsh
Lower Goldstone
Stonar Cut
Paramour Street
Guston Fm.
RICHBOROUGH CASTLE
Black Sand Point
Ware water
Knell Fm.
Upper Goldstone
Cop Street
Cooper Street
Great Stonar
Broad Salts
chequer Ct.
Weddington
A256
Royal St. George's
Ash
East Street
Sandwich
A257
Each End
SANDWICH
Sandwich Bay Estate
Guilton Durlock
Coombe
Ringleton Manor
Marshborough
Stone Cross
Toll
The Rookery
Flemings
Woodnesborough
Felderland
Blue Pigeons Fm.
Mary Bax's Stone
Barnsole
Worth
North Stream
Denne Ct.
Statenborough
Worth Minnis
Hammill Ct.
Selson
Upton Ho.
Tenants Hills
Hammill
Gore
A258
Lydden Valley
Eastry
Ham
Hacklinge
Walton Ho.
Tickenhurst
Heronden
West Street
Finglesham
Sandown Castle (remains of)
Buttsole
Knowlton
Foulmead Fm.
C.G. Sta.
nowlton Ct.
Updown Ho.
Marley
MARITIME & LOCAL HISTORY MUS.
75
Pier
Knowlton Park
Venson Fm.
NORTHBOURNE COURT
Sholden
DEAL
A256
Bettshanger
Sholden Downs
A258
DEAL CASTLE
Northbourne

TR
55
45

5       6       7       8

A

B

C

D

E

F

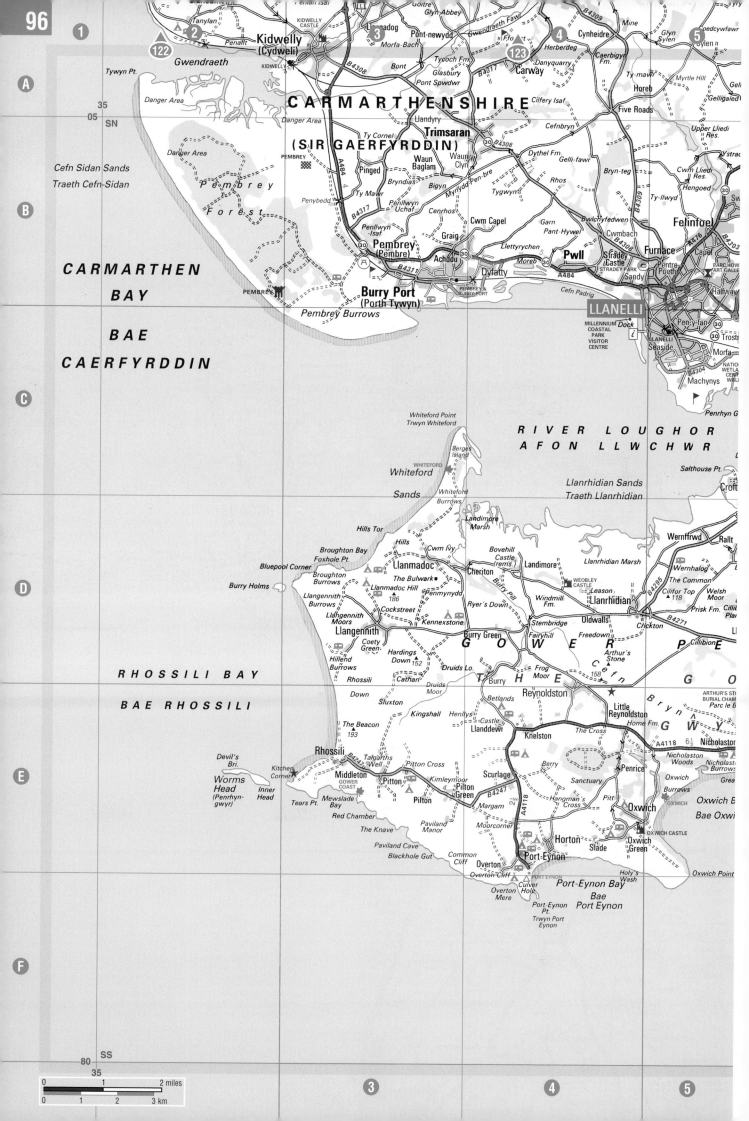

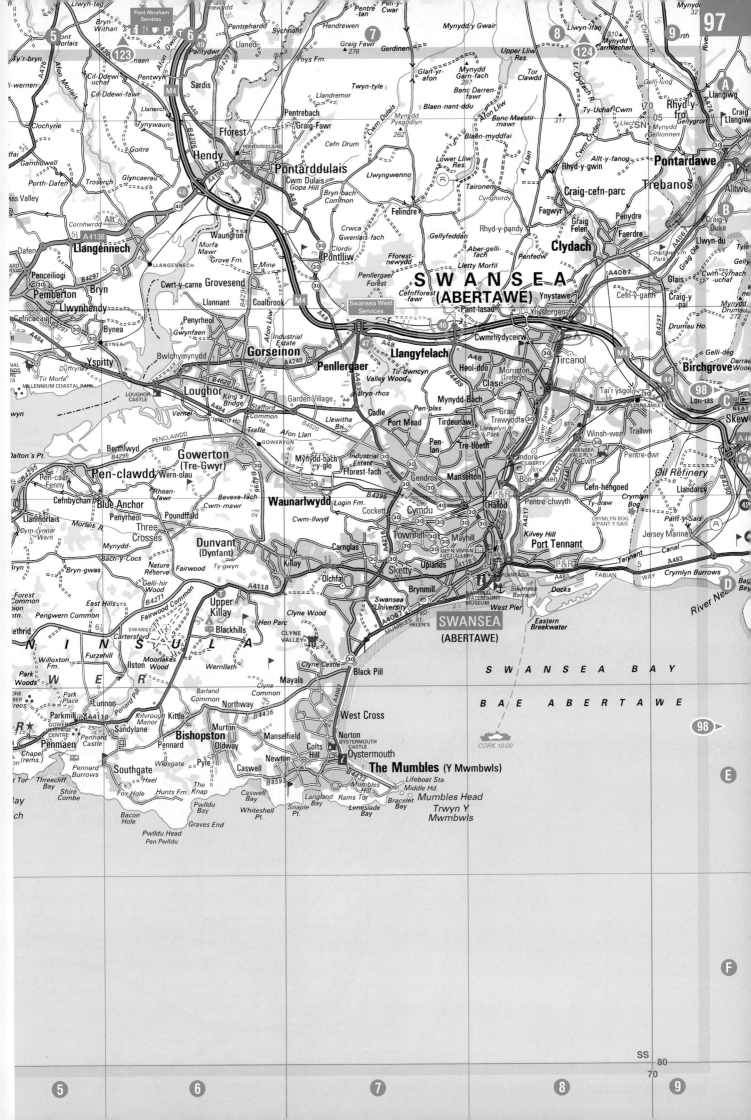

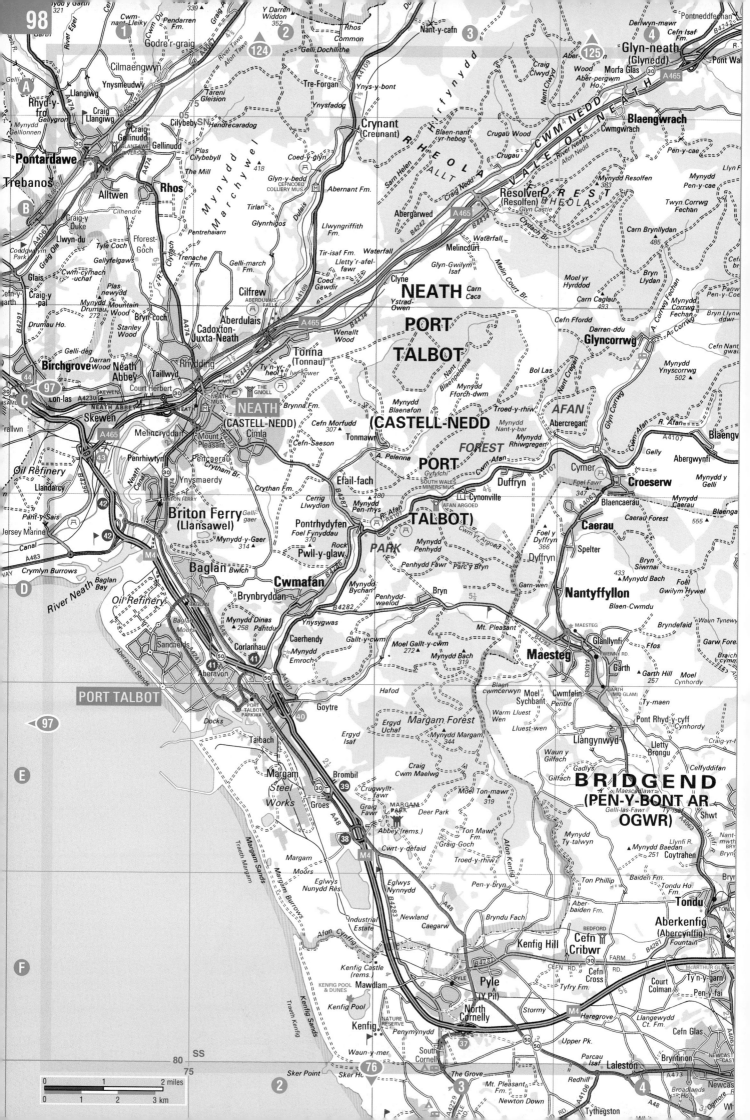

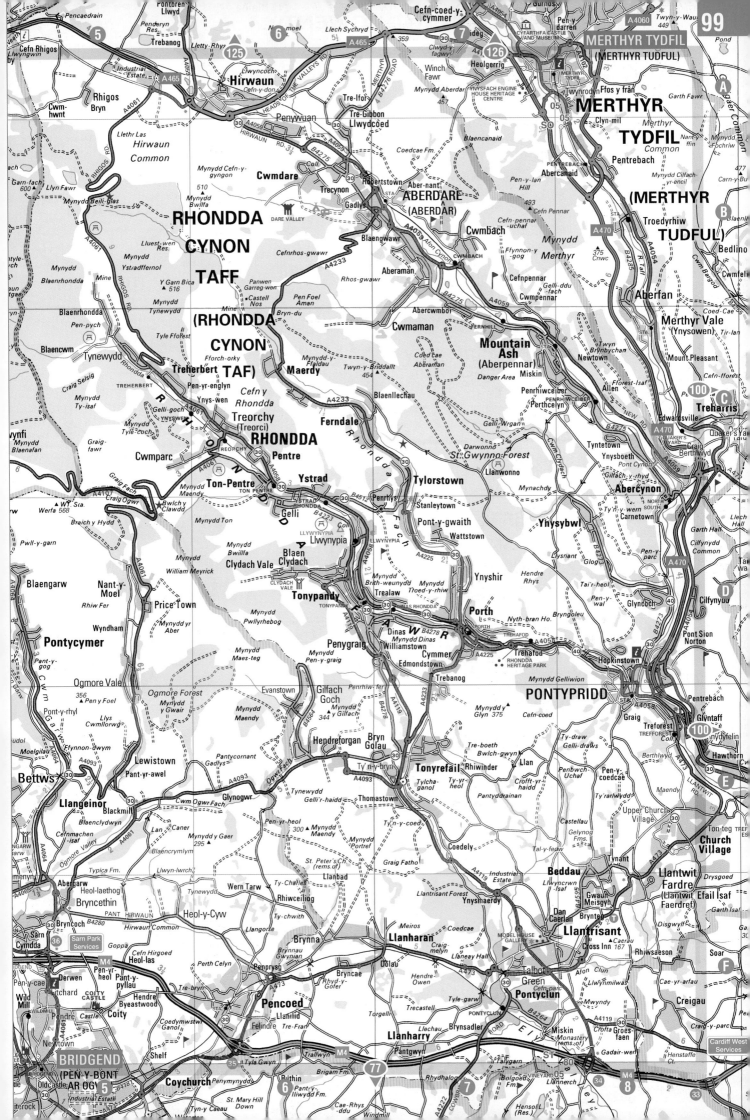

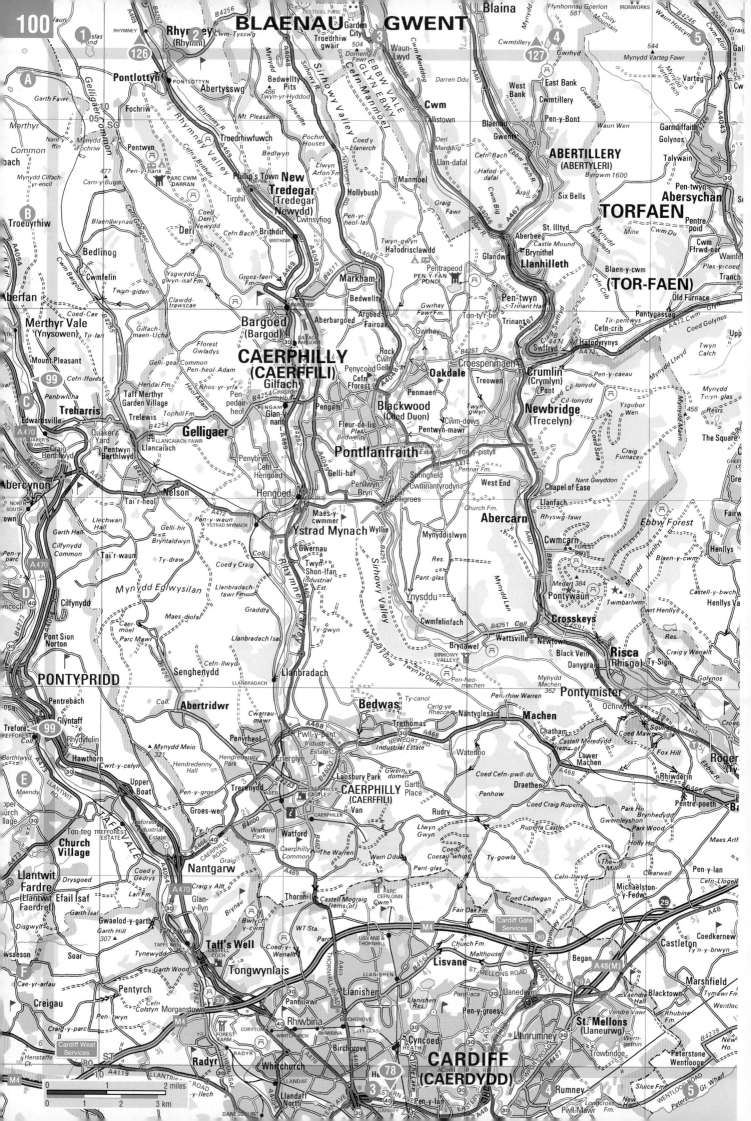

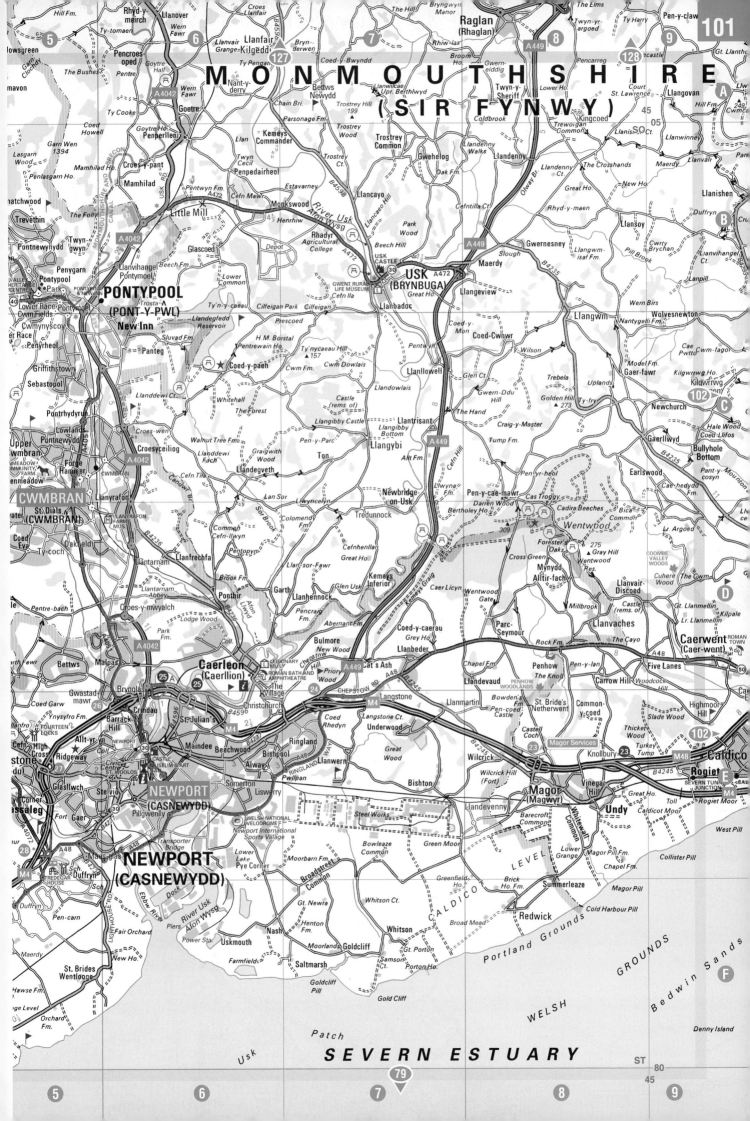

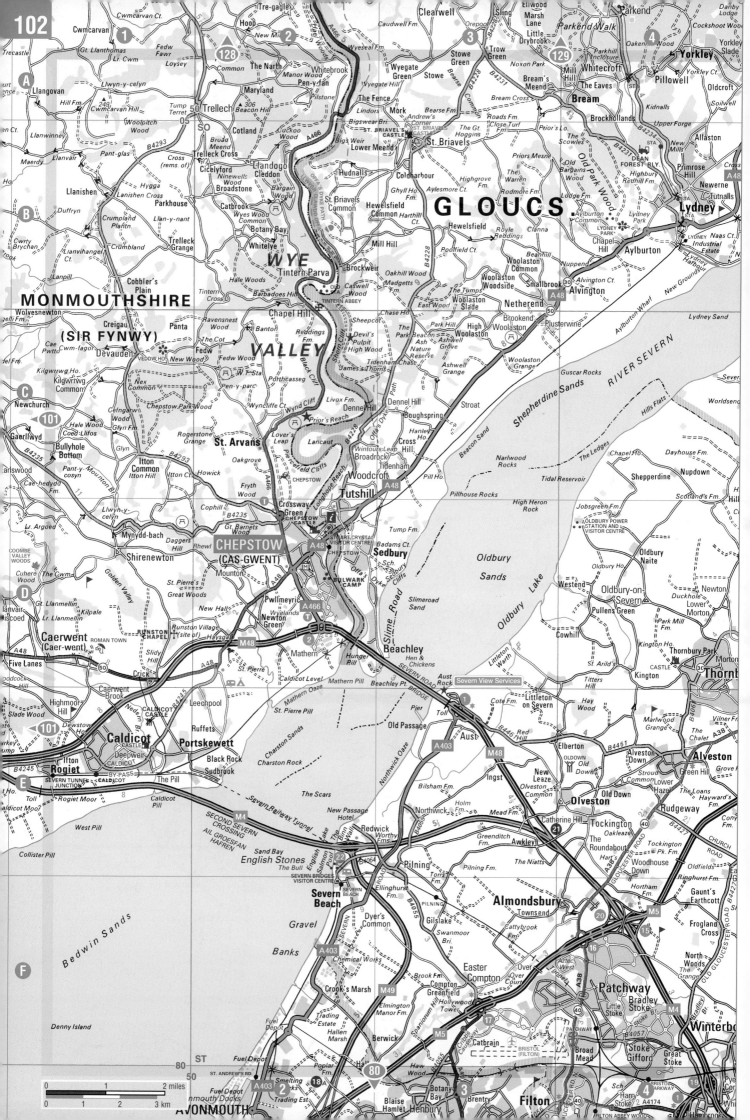

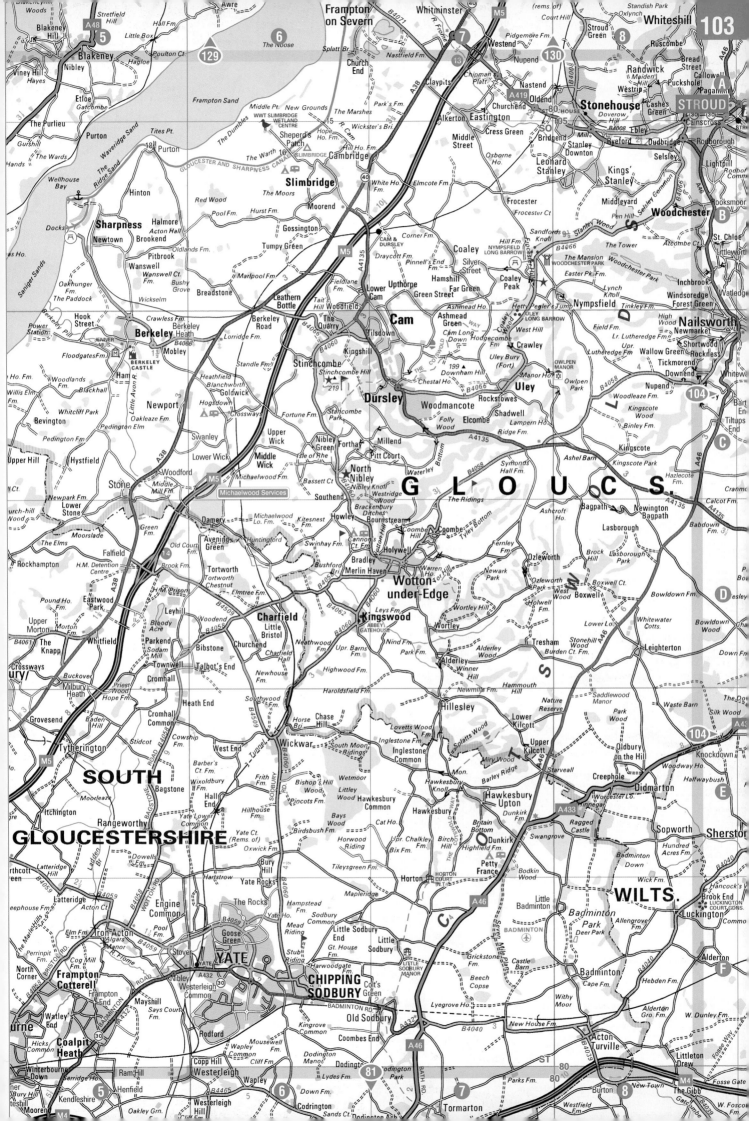

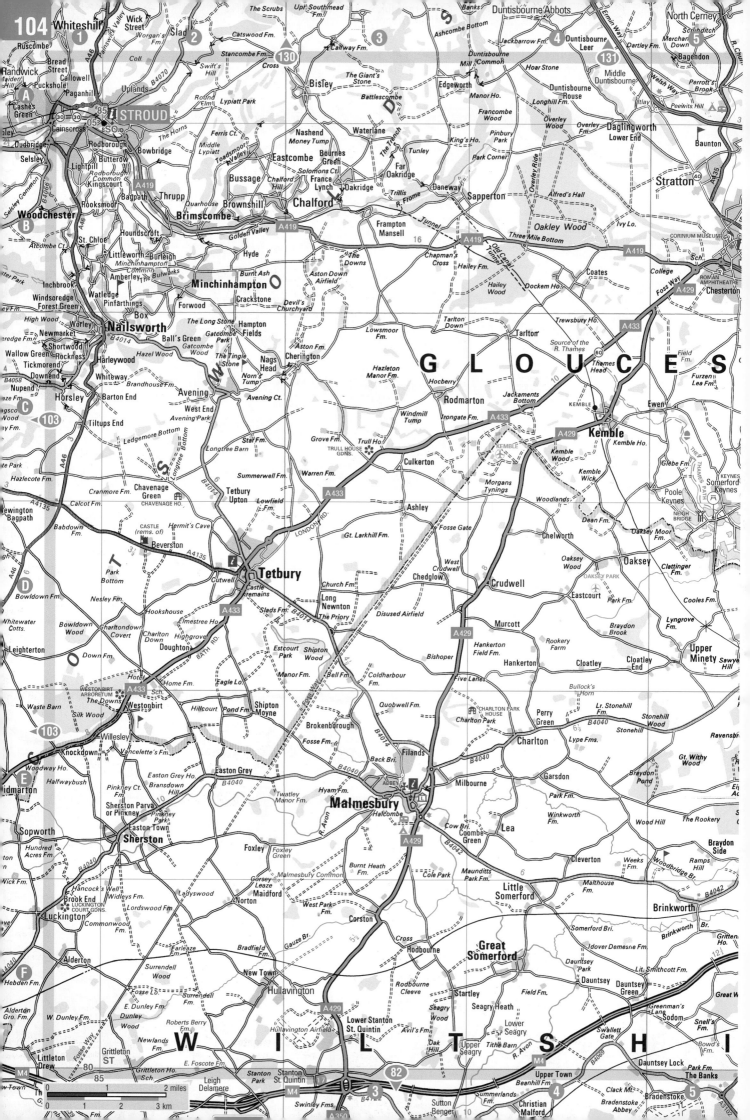

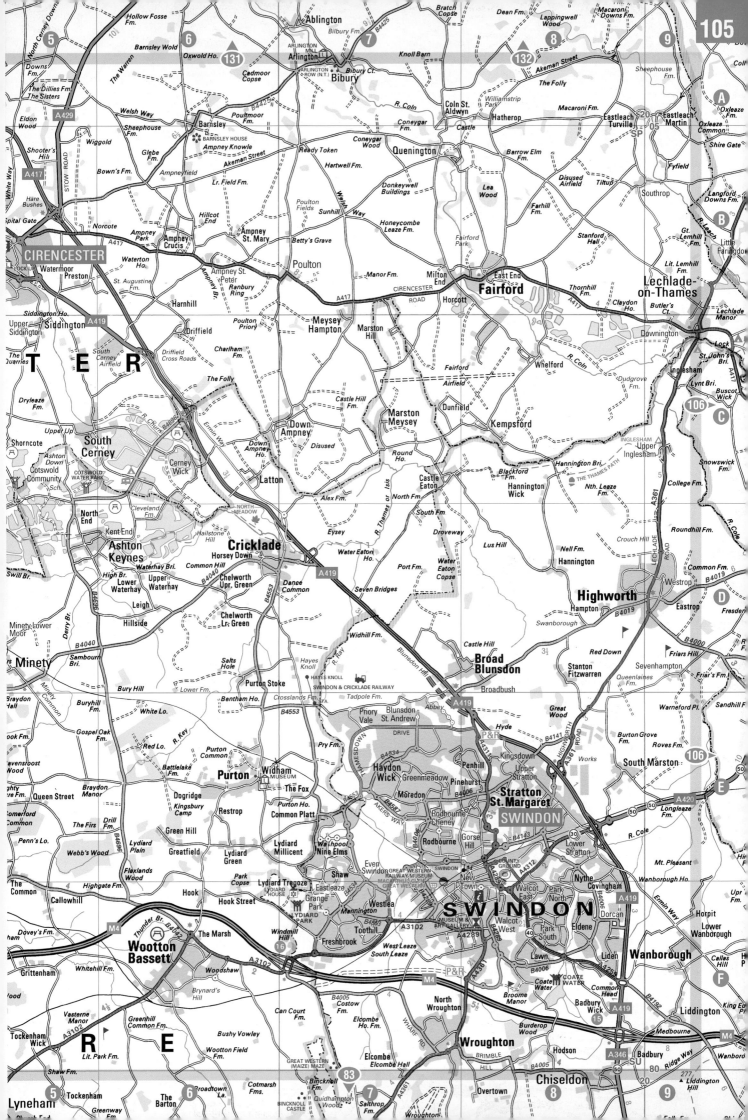

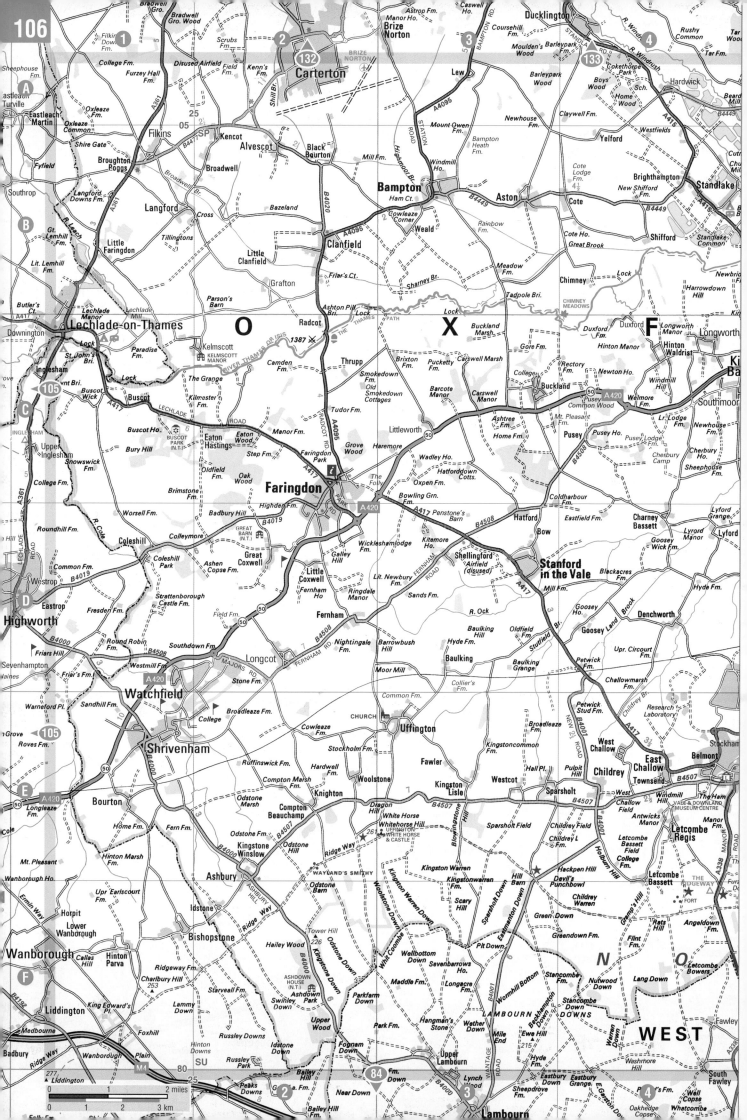

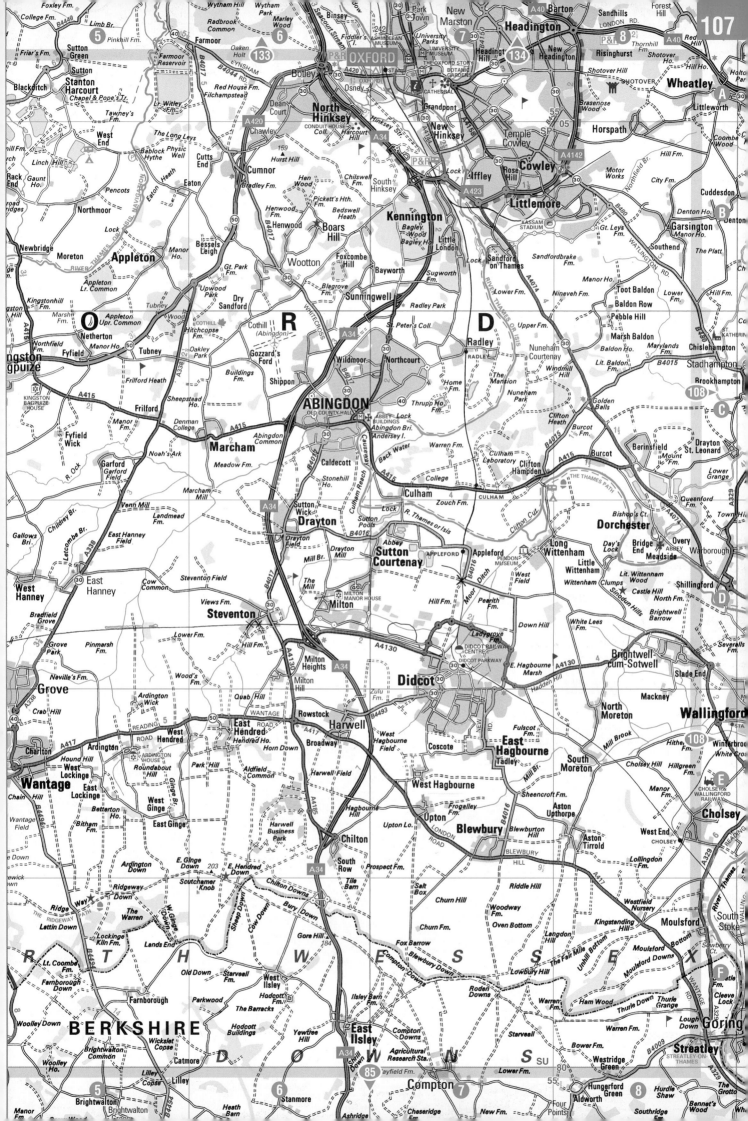

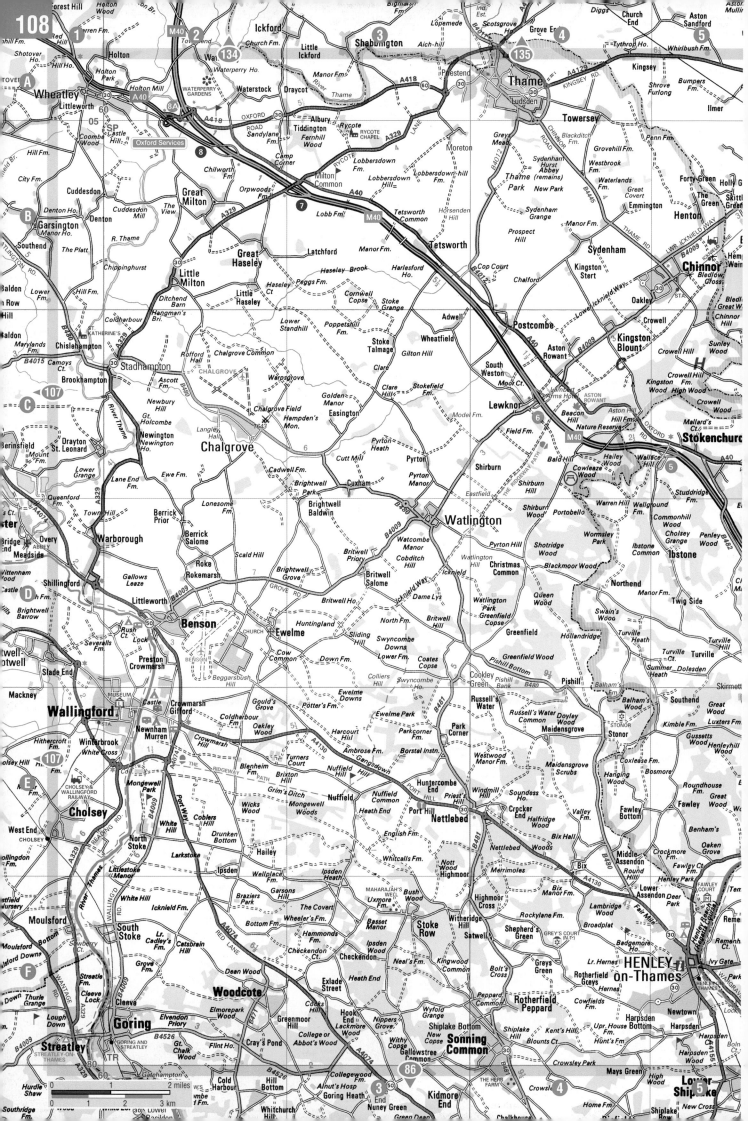

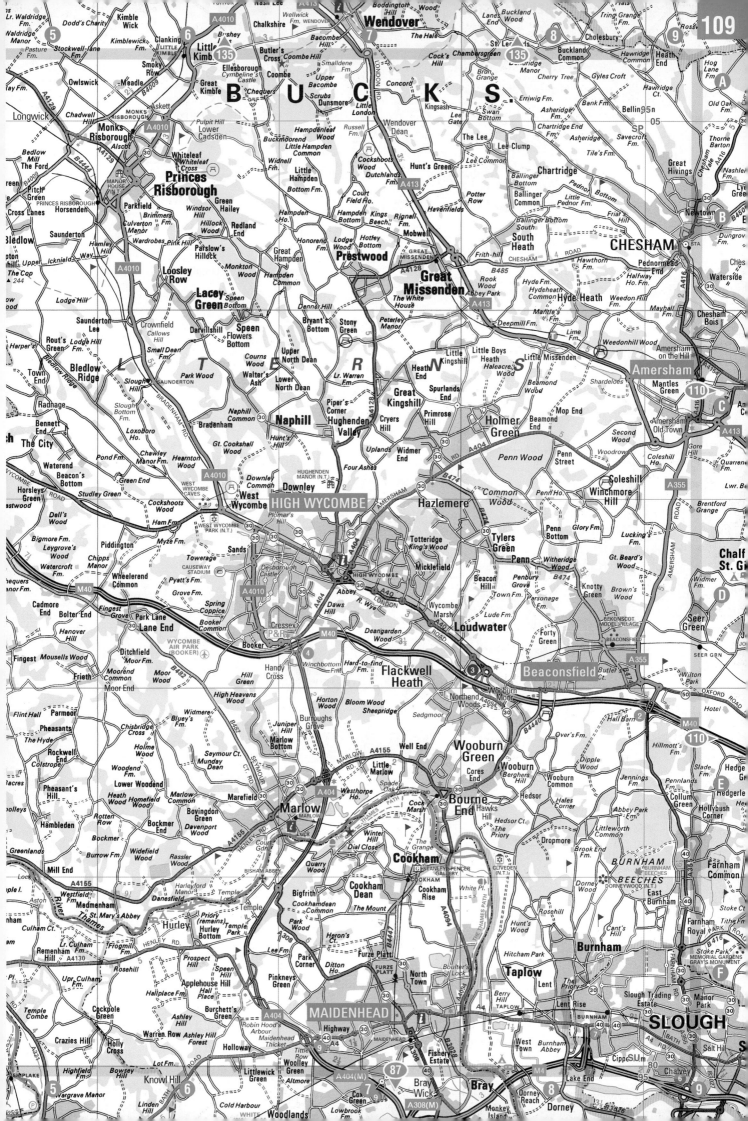

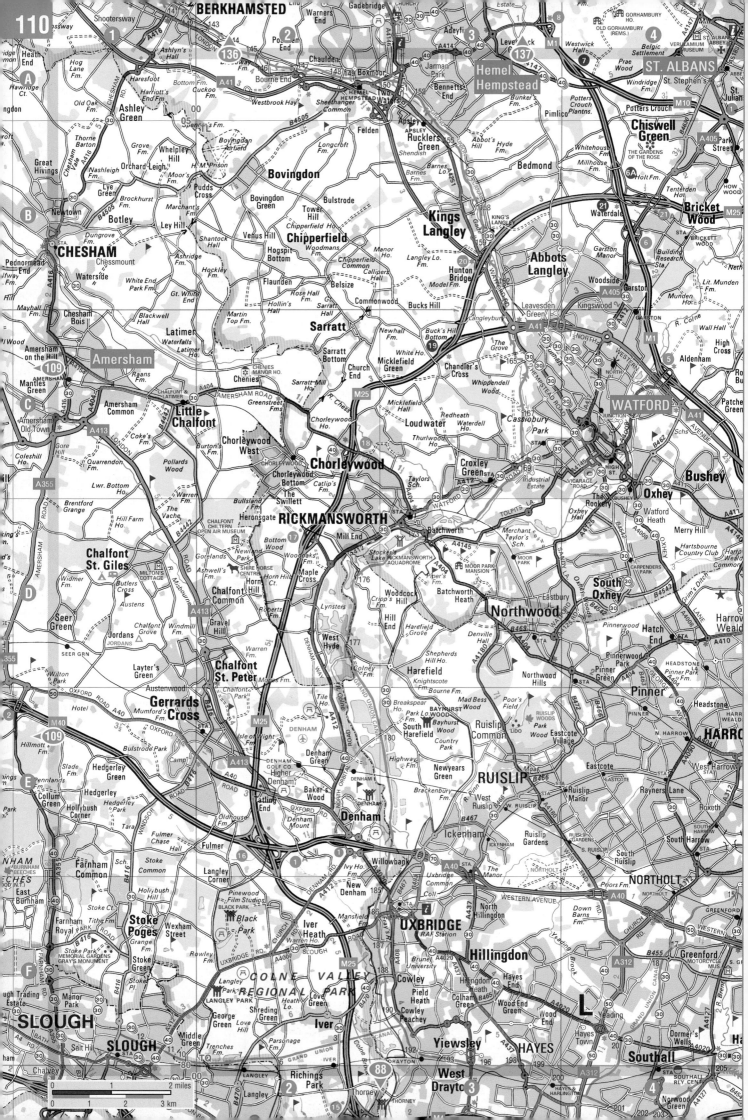

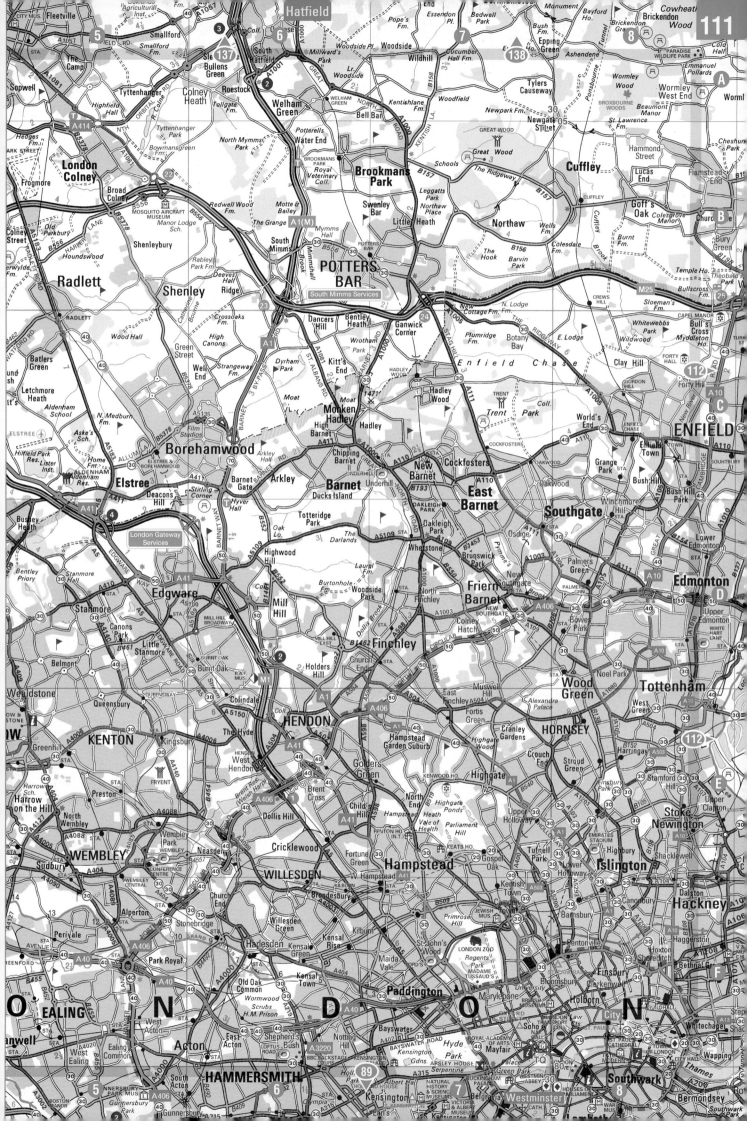

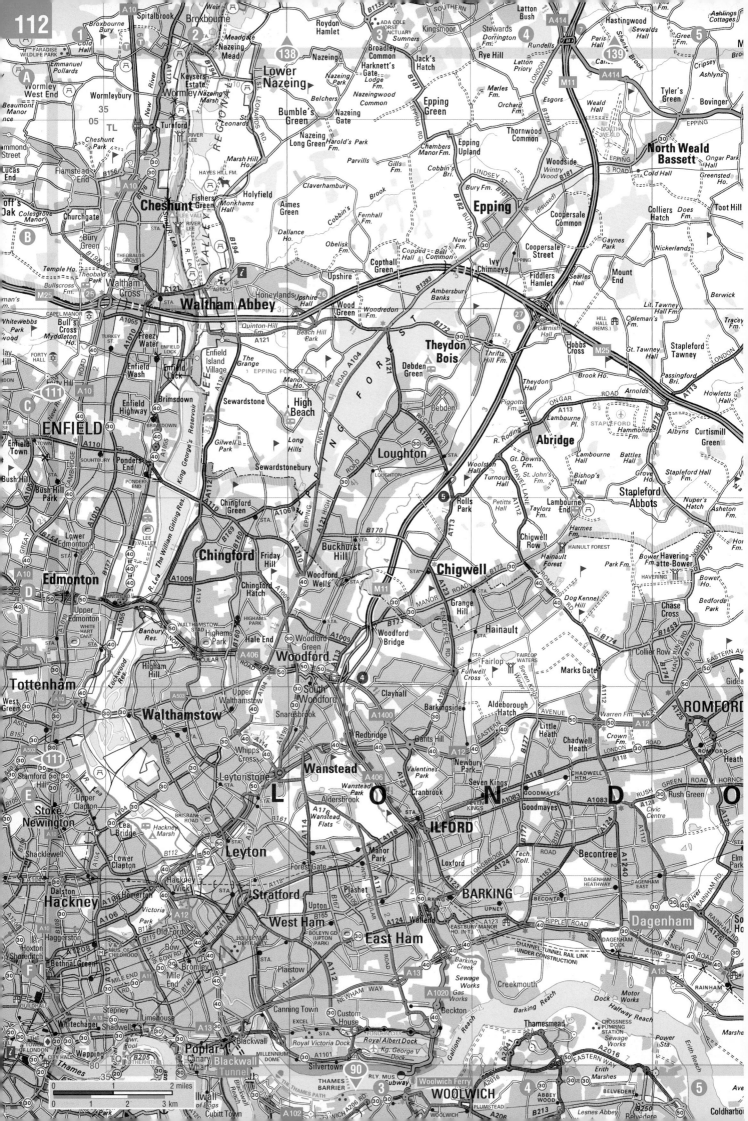

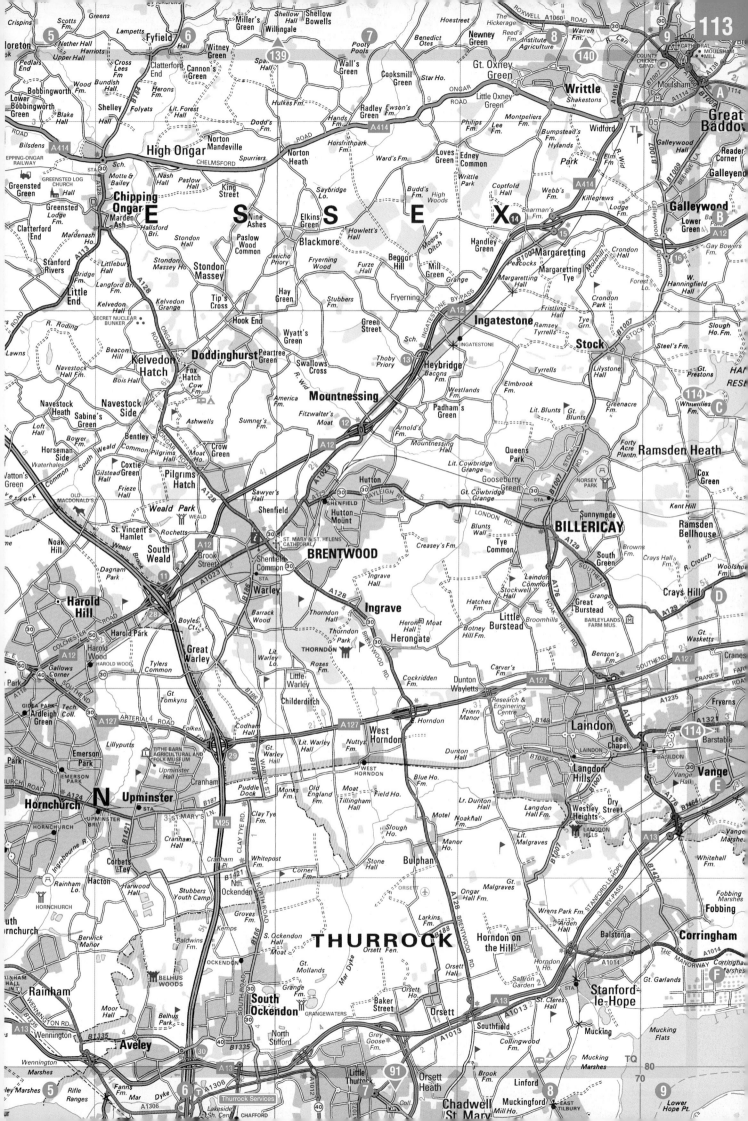

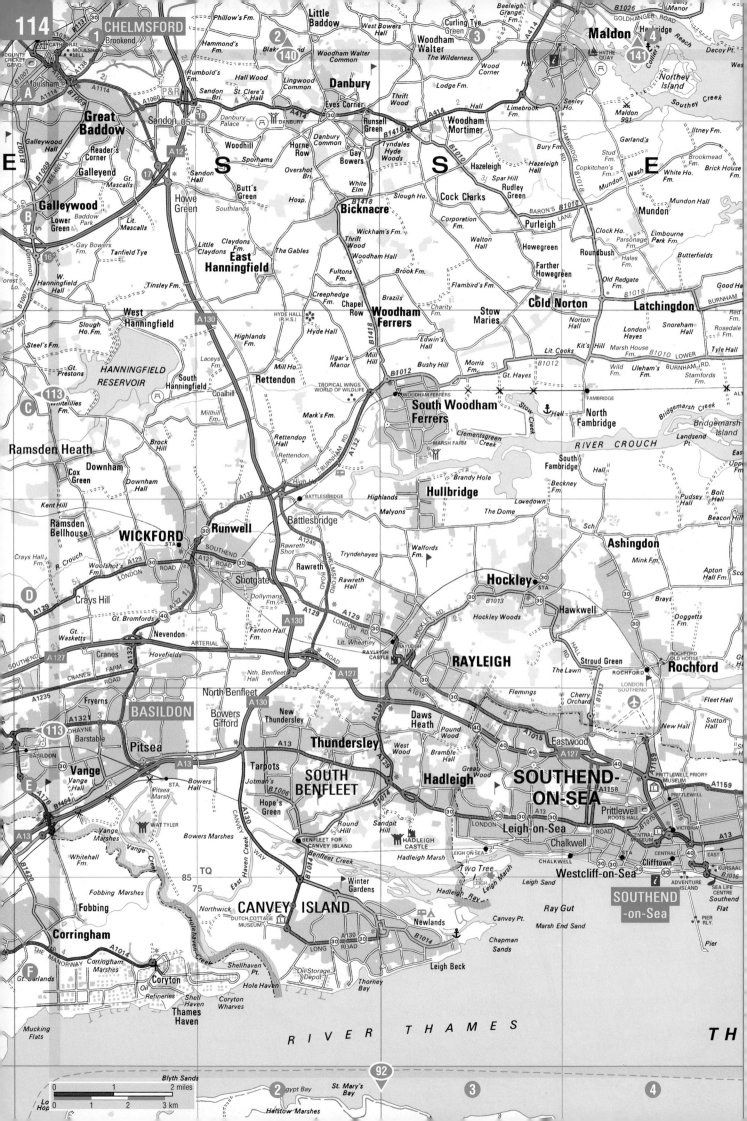

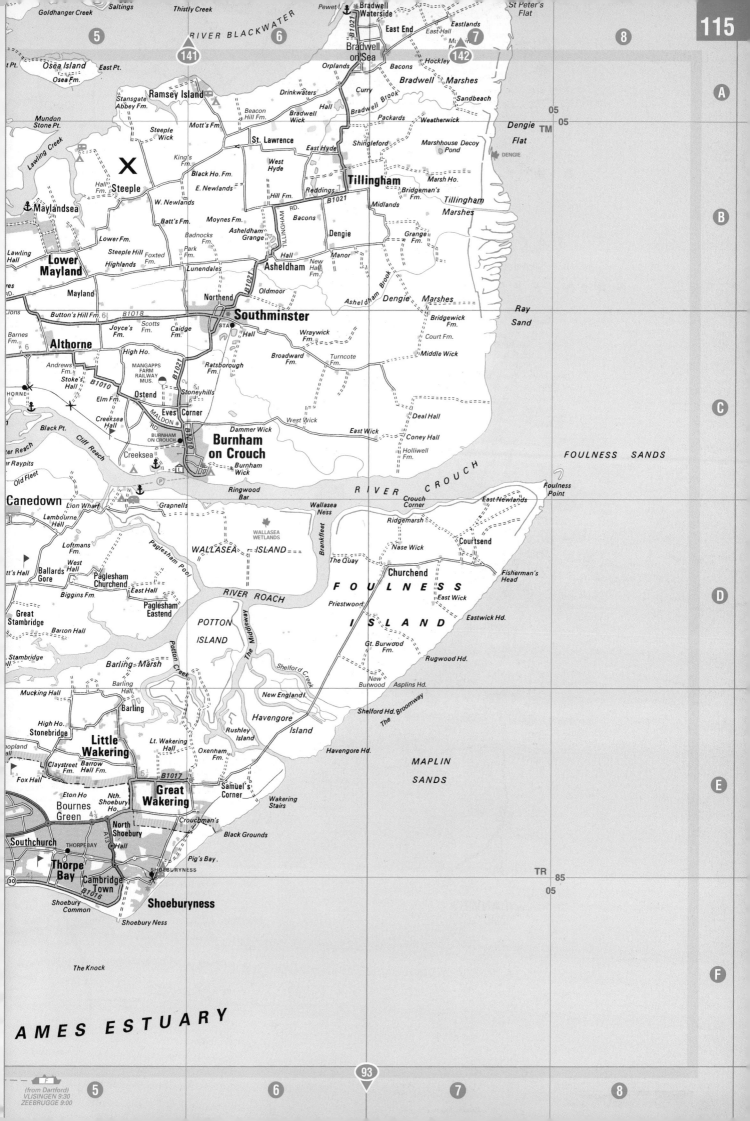

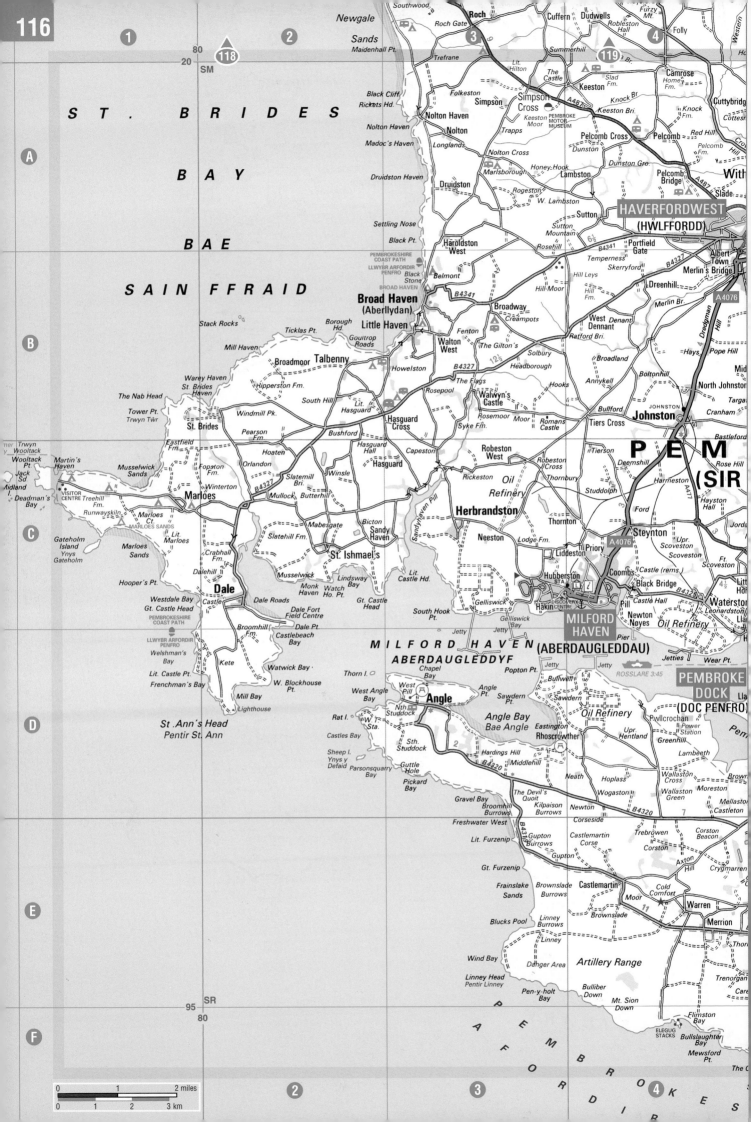

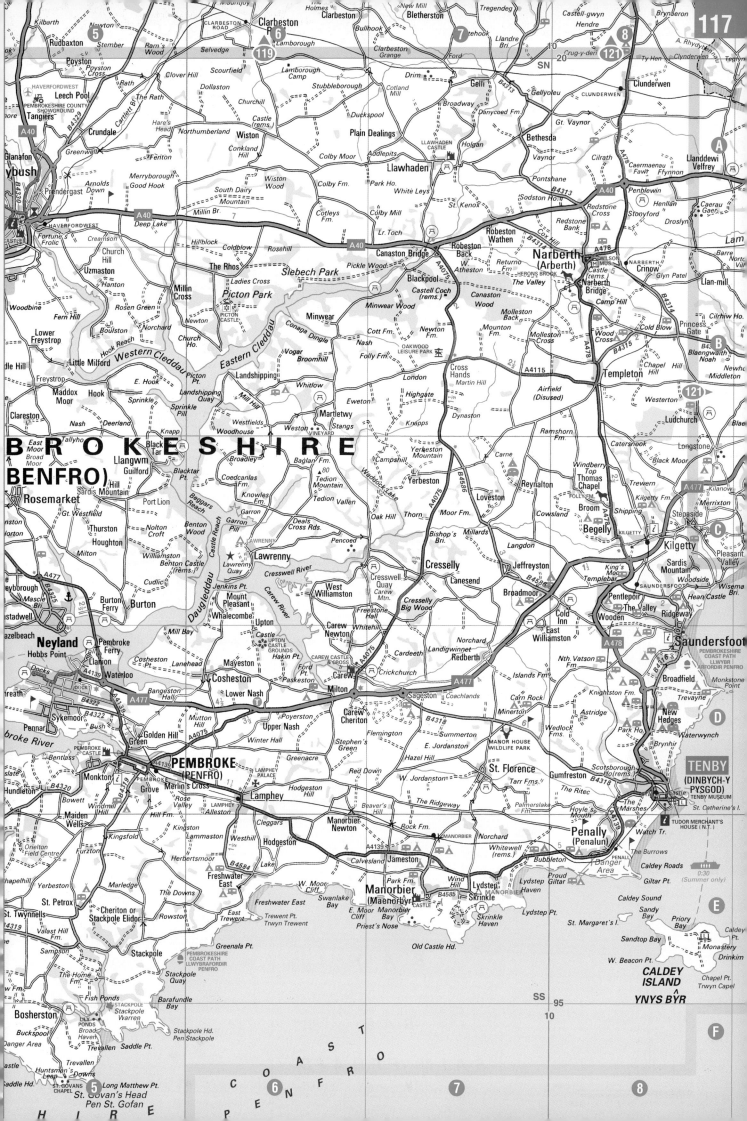

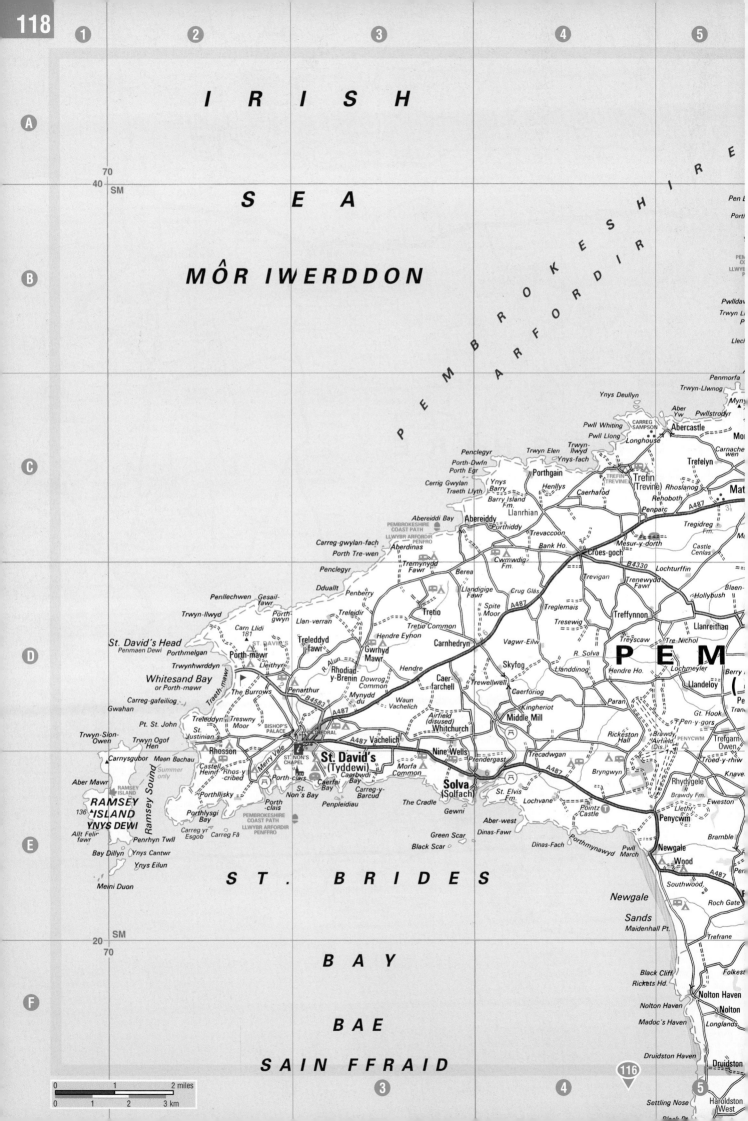

IRISH

SEA

MÔR IWERDDON

PEMBROKESHIRE ARFORDIR

70
40
SM

20
SM
70

ST. BRIDES

BAY

BAE

SAIN FFRAID

RAMSEY ISLAND
YNYS DEWI
136

St. David's Head
Penmaen Dewi

Whitesand Bay
or Porth-mawr

St. David's
(Tyddewi)

Solva
(Solfach)

Newgale

Newgale

Sands

Abercastle

Trefin
(Trevine)

Porthgain

Abereiddy

Croes-goch

PEM

Nolton Haven

Nolton

Druidston

0        1        2 miles
0    1    2    3 km

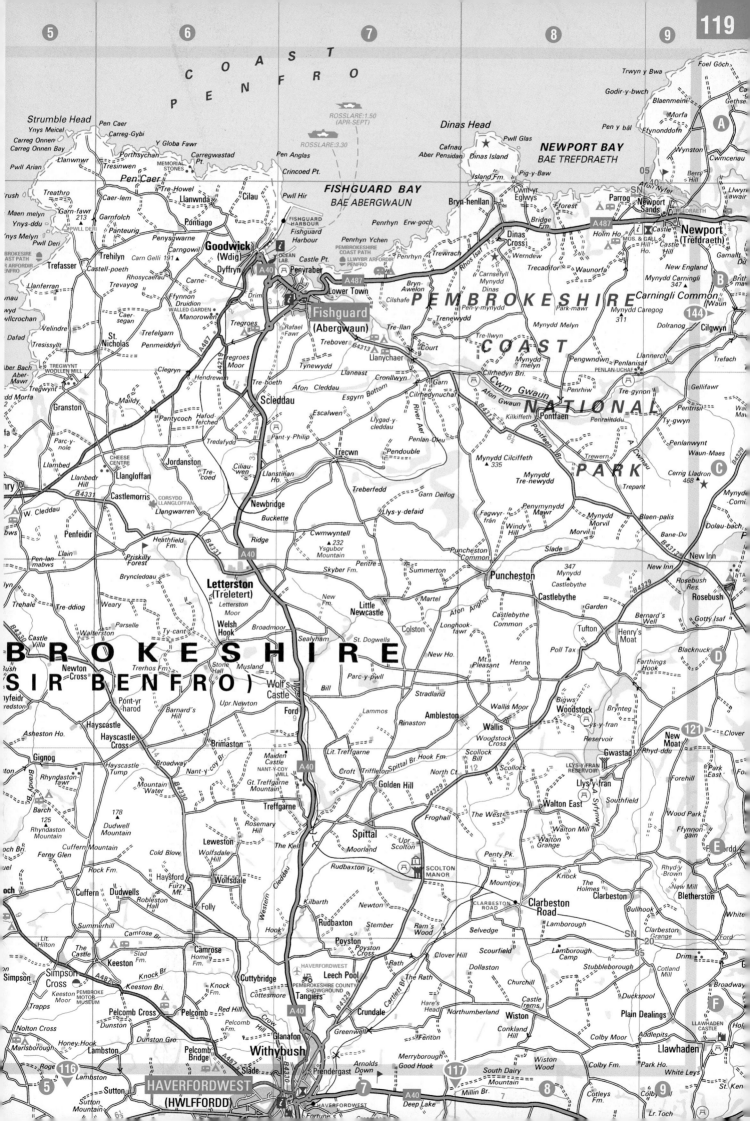

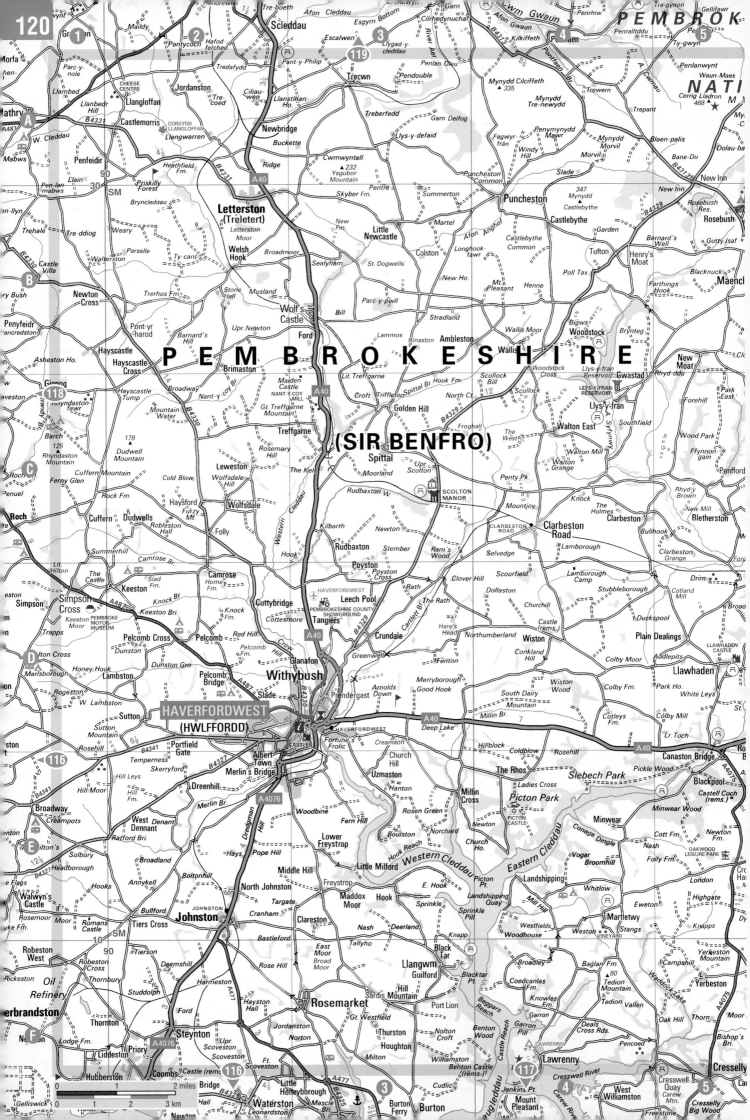

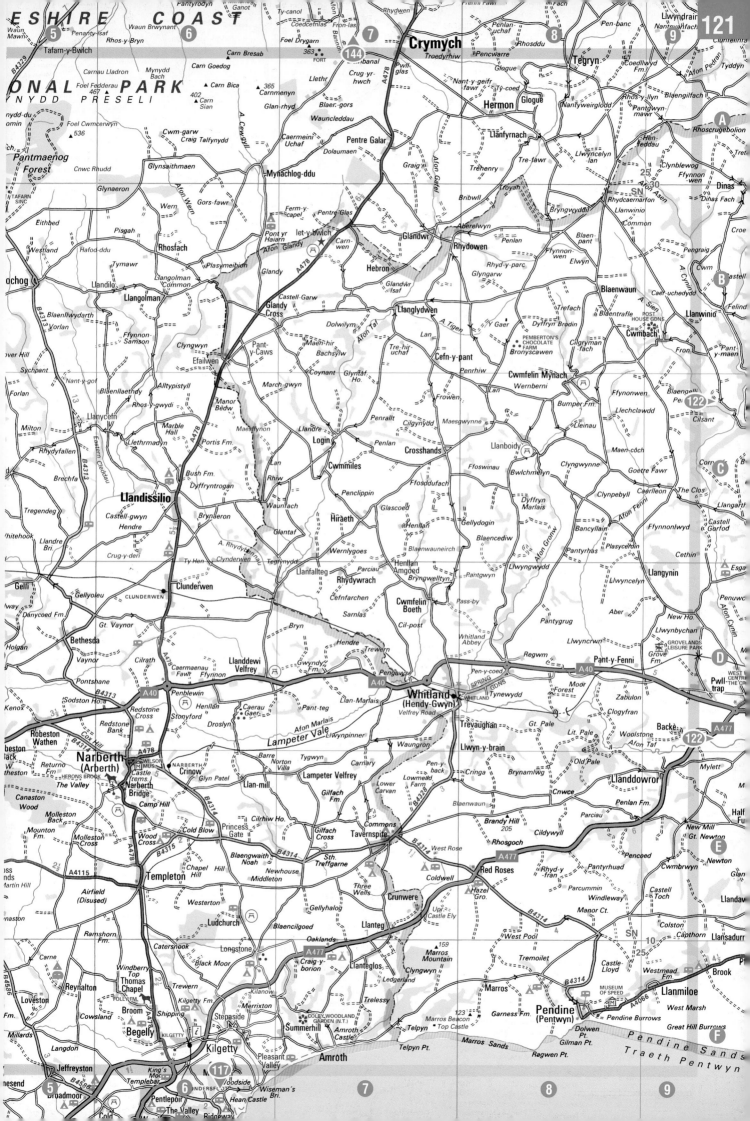

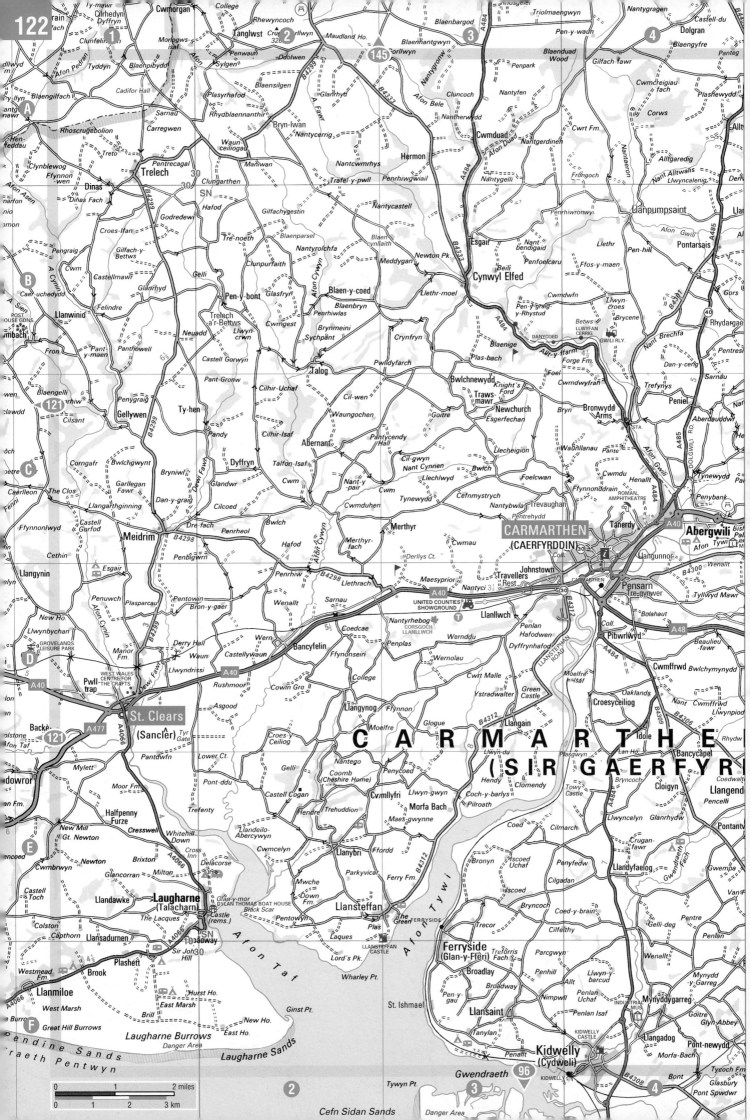

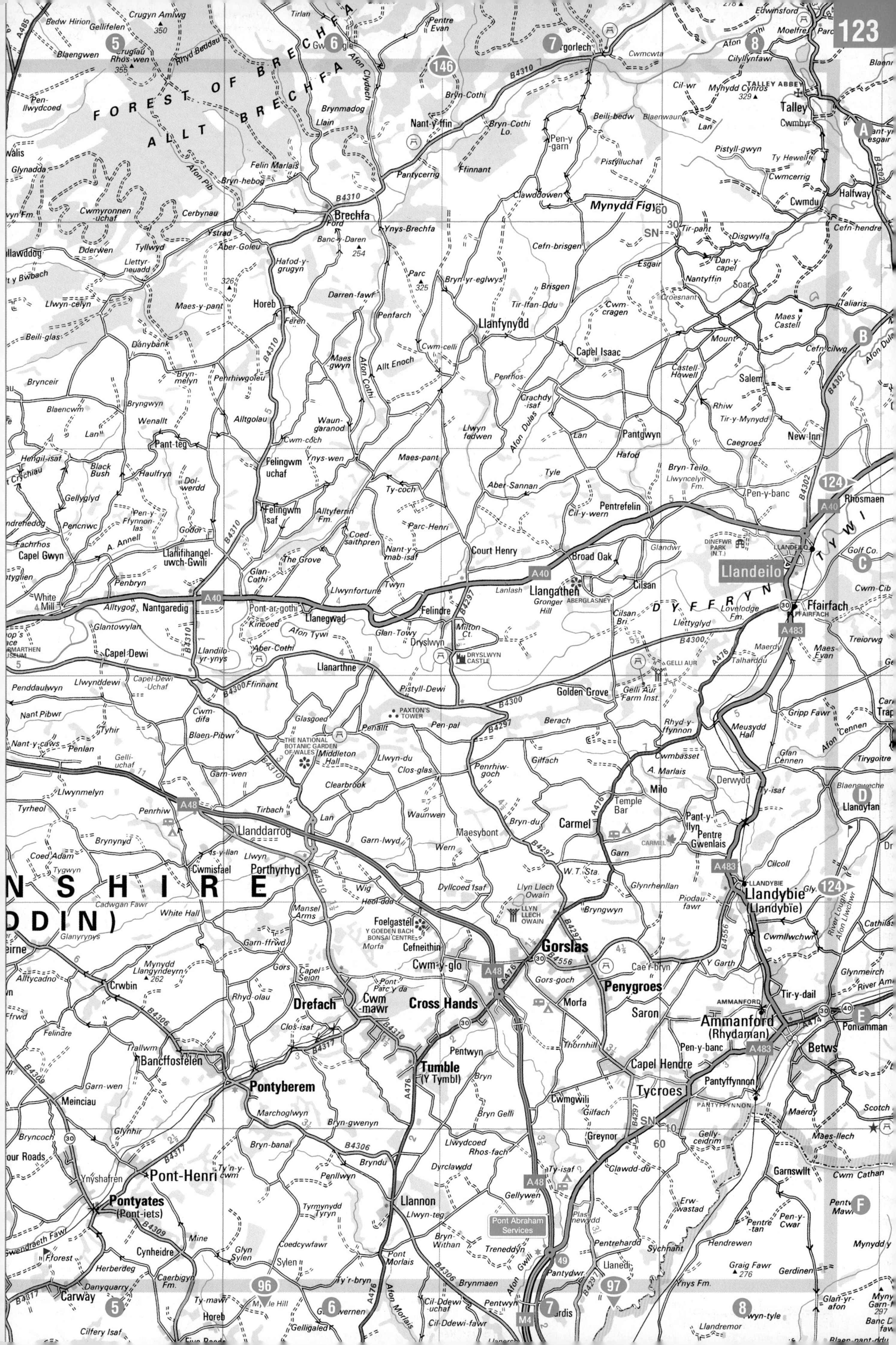

FOREST OF BRECHFA
ALLT BRECHFA

Bedw Hirion
Gellifelen
Crugyn Amlwg
350
Tirlan
Pentre Evan
Edwinsford
Moeltre
Blaenr
Crugiau Rhos-wen 355
Blaengwen
Rhyd Beddau
Gw gle
146
gorlech
Cwmcwta
Cilyllynfawr
Talley Abbey
Blaenr
Pen-llwydcoed
B4310
Bryn-Cothi
Cil-wr
Mynydd Cynros 329
Talley
Cwmbyr
Glynadda
Afon Clydach
Afon Pib
Brynmadog
Bryn-Cothi Lo
Beili-bedw
Blaenwaun
Lan
Pistyll-gwyn
Ty Hewell
Cwmcerrig
Halfway
Walis
Llain
Nant-y-ffin
Pen-y-garn
Pistylluchaf
Ty
nt-y esgair
Cwmryonnen-uchaf
Cerbynau
Ffinnant
Dan-y-capel
Cwmdu
Brechfa
Ford
Felin Marlais
Pantycerrig
Clawddowen
Mynydd Fig 60
Tir-pant
Nantyffin
Cefn-hendre
Bryn-hebog
Ystrad
Aber-Goleu
Banc-y-Daren 254
Ynys-Brechfa
Cefn-brisgen
SN 30
Esgair
Soar
Croesnant
Maes y Castell
Taliaris
Bryn-yr-eglwys
Brisgen
Cwm-cragen
Bryn melyn
Llanfynydd
Capel Isaac
Castell-Howell
Mount
Cefn cilwg
Afon Dula
Penrhos
Crachdy-isaf
Salem
Cwm-celli
Penrhos
Rhiw
Tir-y-Mynydd
New Inn
Caegroes
124
Rhosmaen
A40
Golf Co.
Court Henry
Broad Oak
A40
Llangathen
Llandeilo
Ffairfach
Dryslwyn
DYFFRYN
A483
TYWI

(CARMARTHENSHIRE)

Llanddarrog
A48
Porthyrhyd
Llandybie (Llandybie)
124

Cross Hands
Gorslas
Penygroes
Ammanford (Rhydaman)
Betws
A483
Tumble (Y Tymbl)
Tycroes
Pontyberem
Pontyates (Pont-iets)
Pont-Henri
Llannon
Pont Abraham Services
49
96
97
Carway
M4

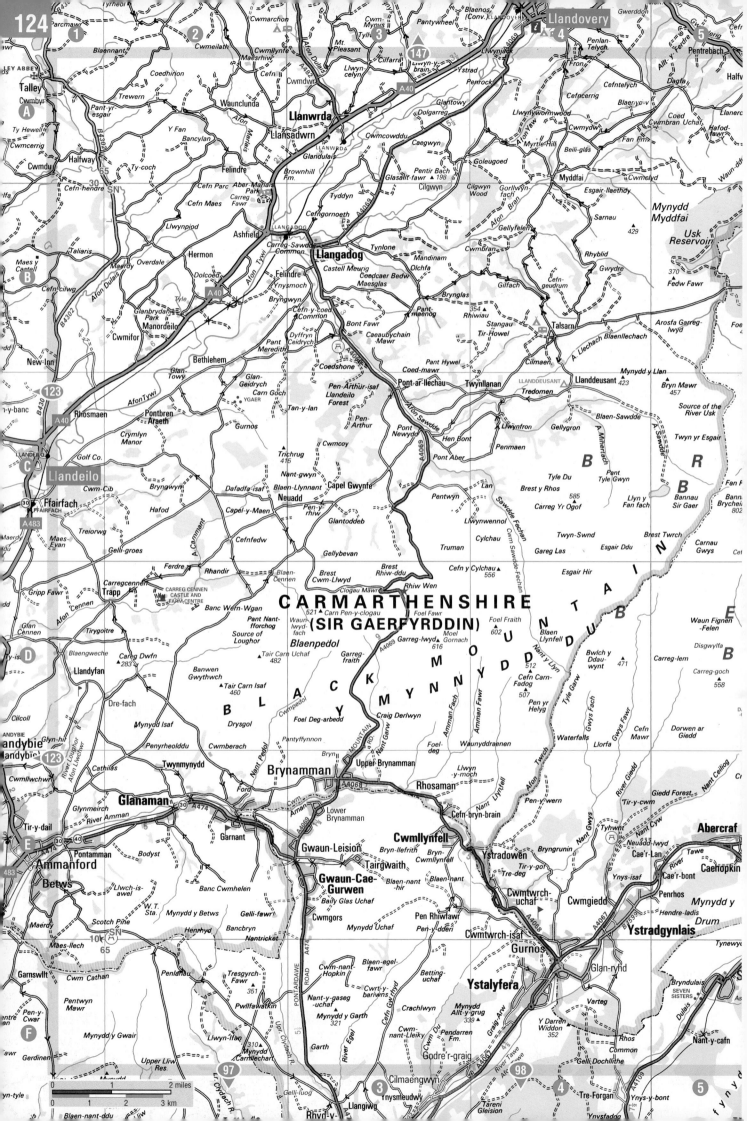

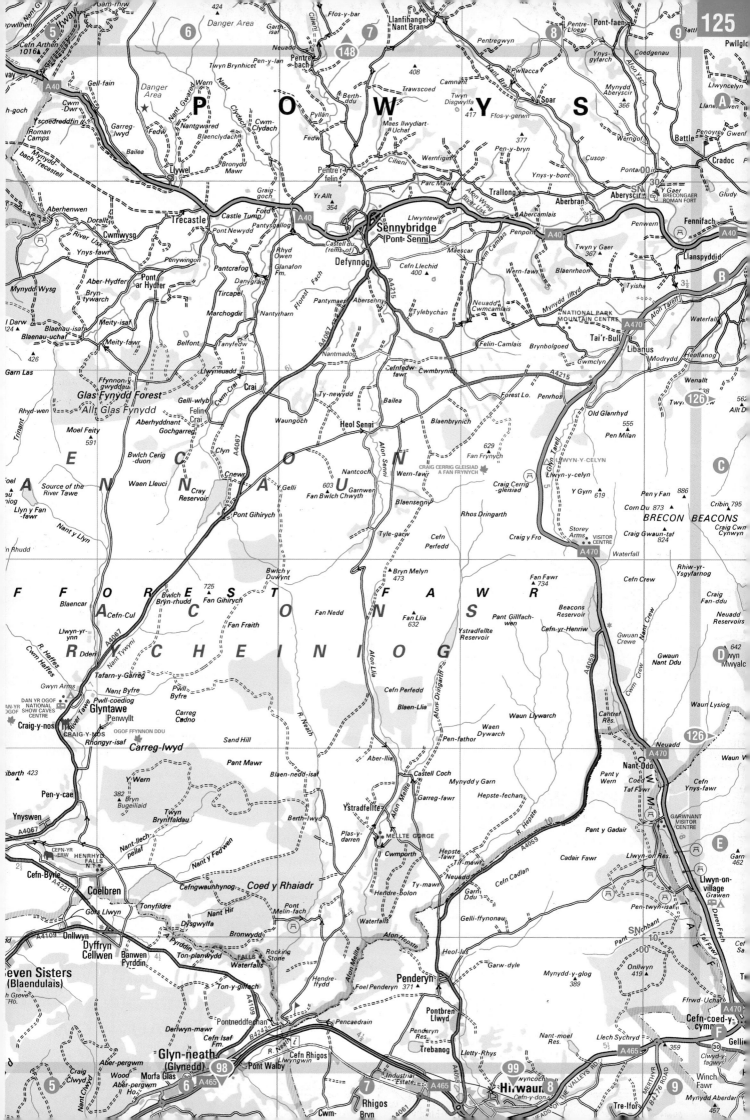

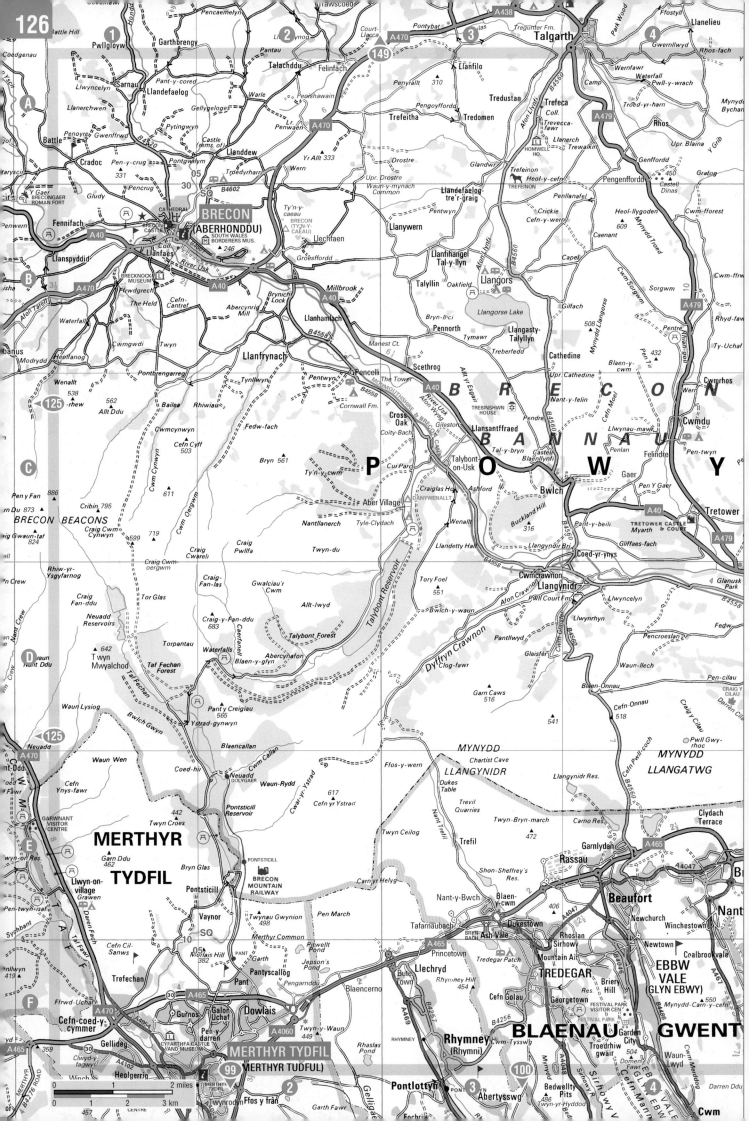

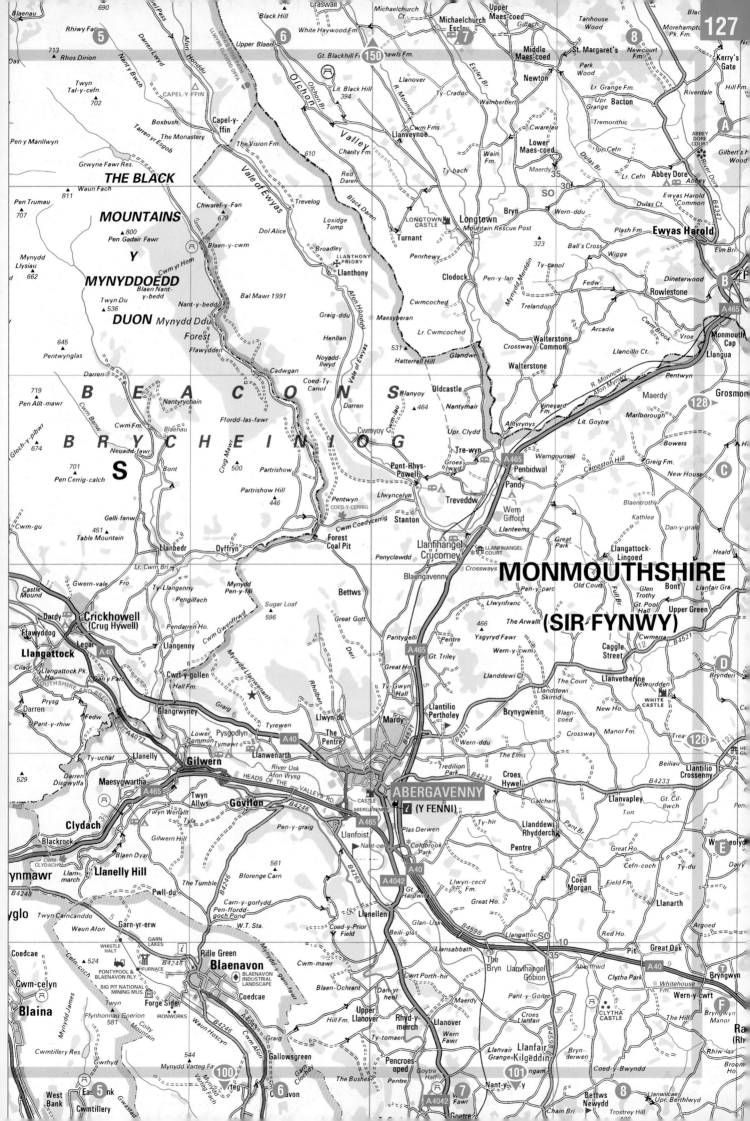

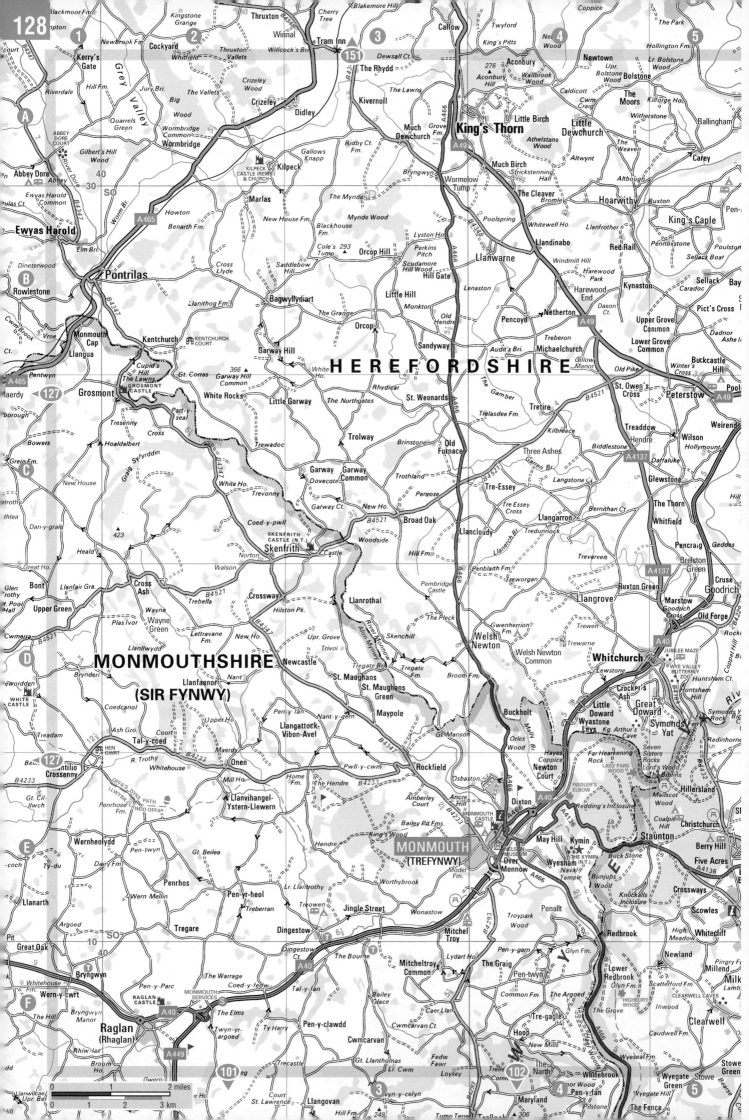

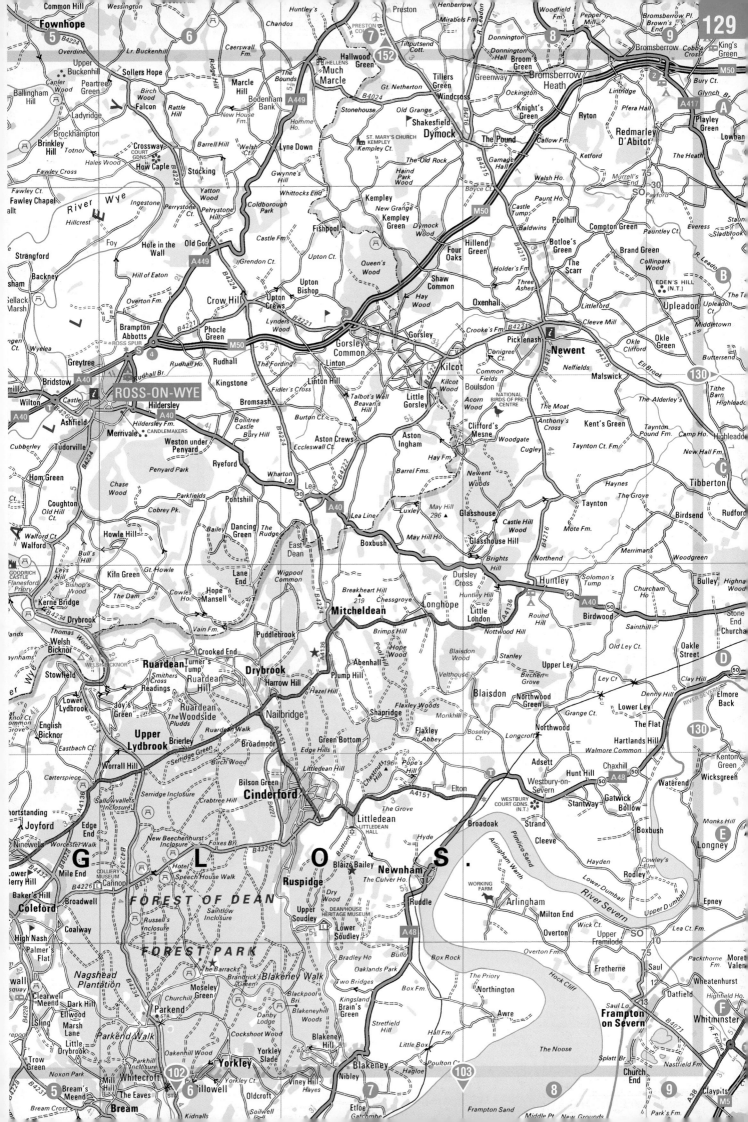

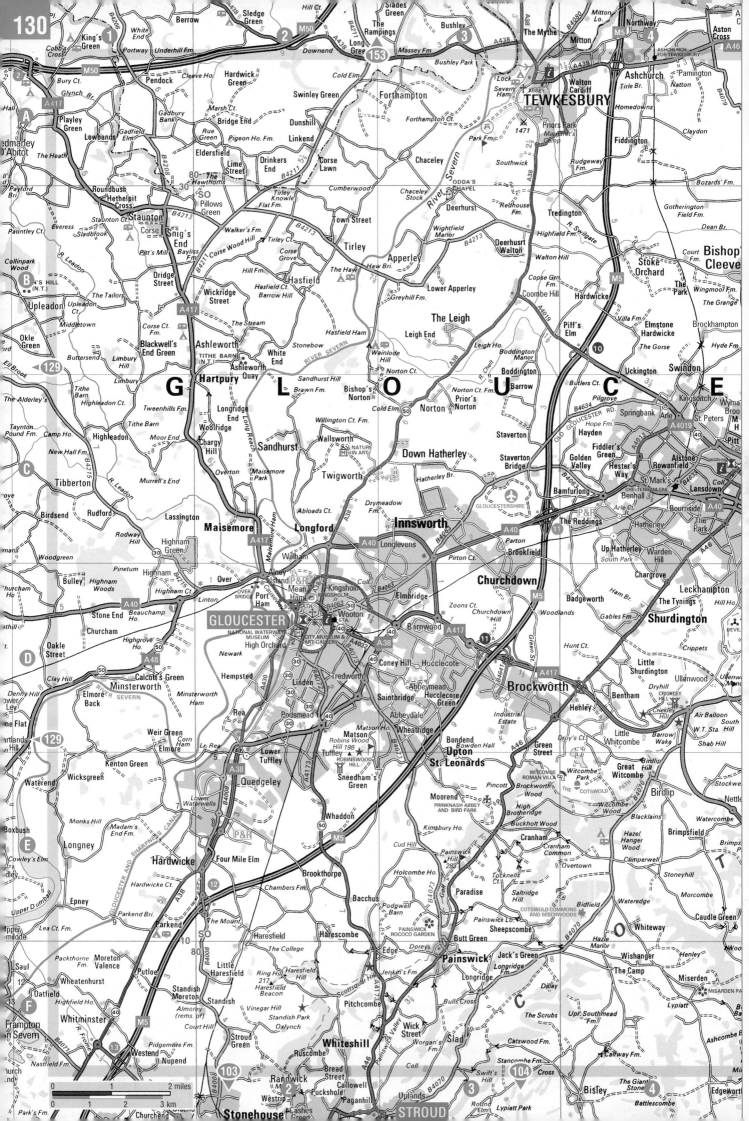

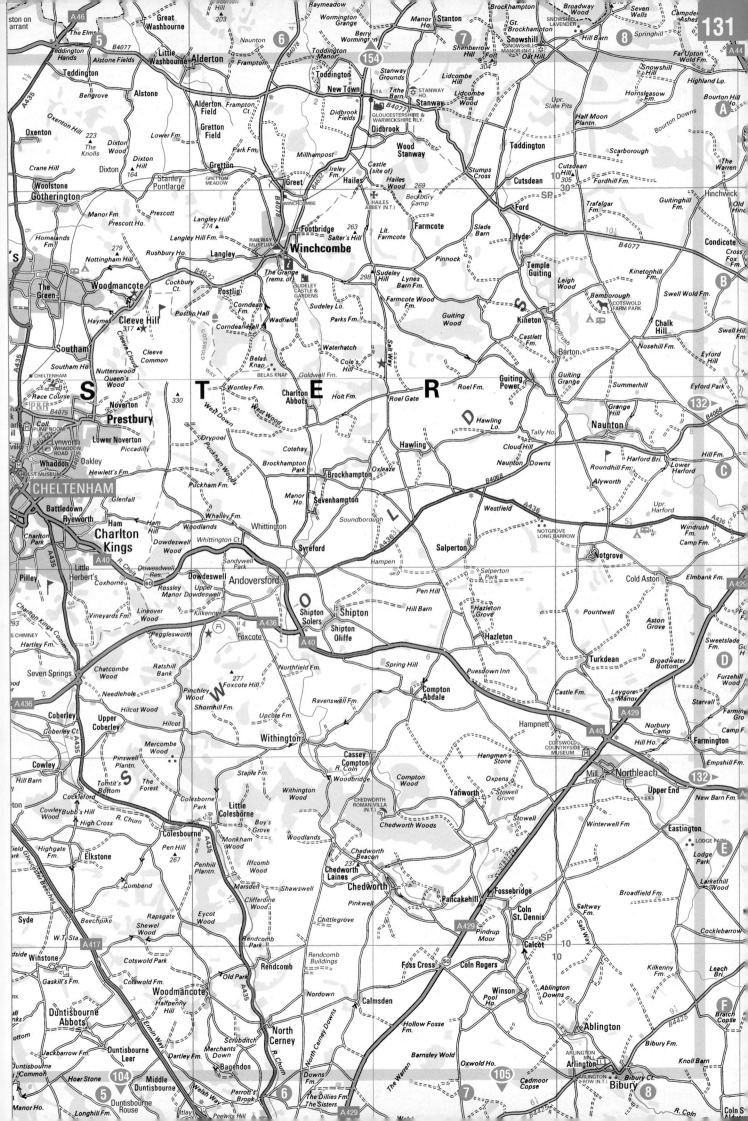

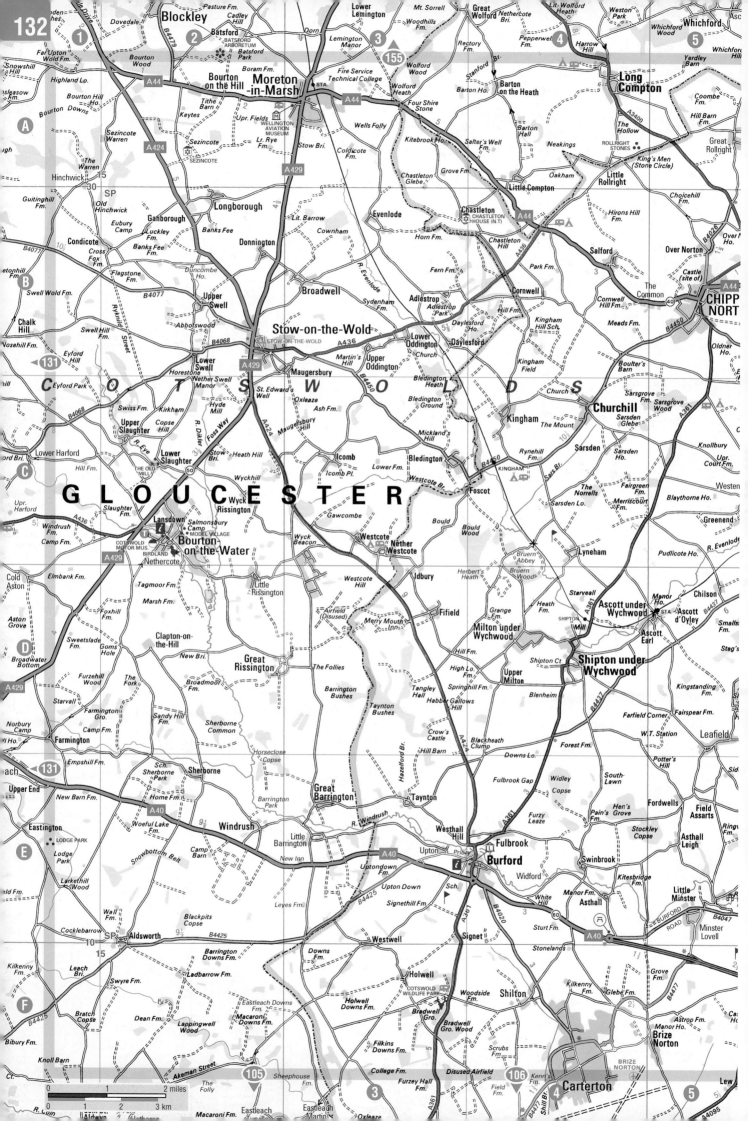

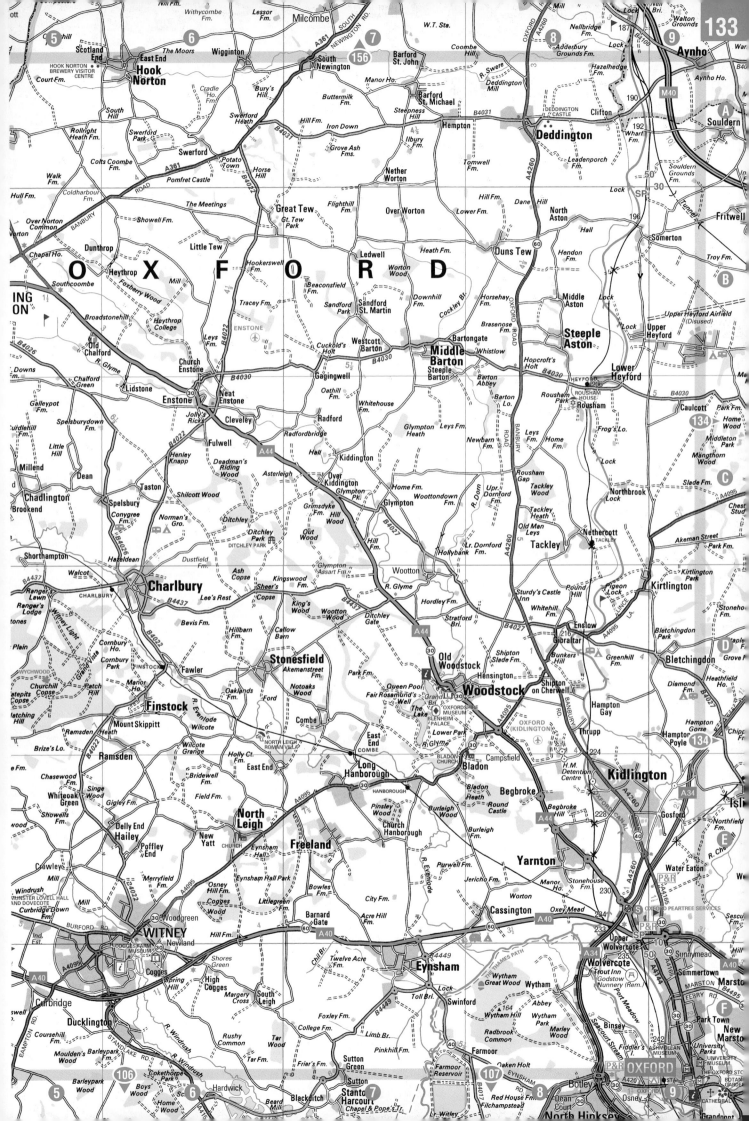

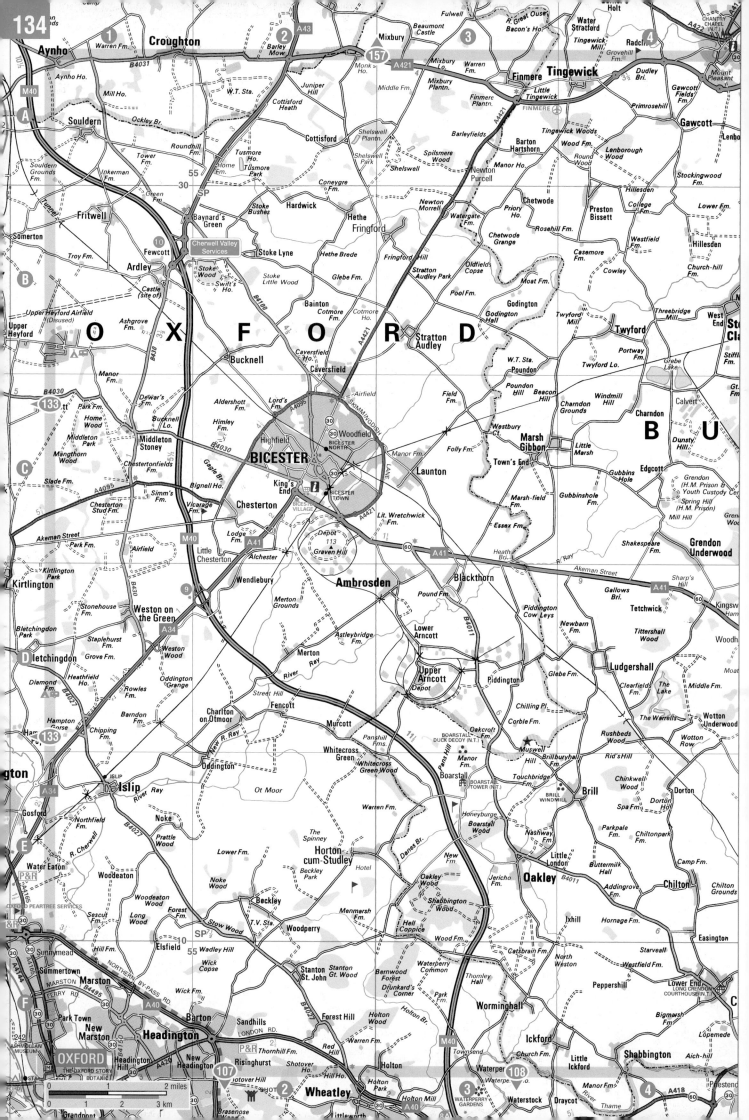

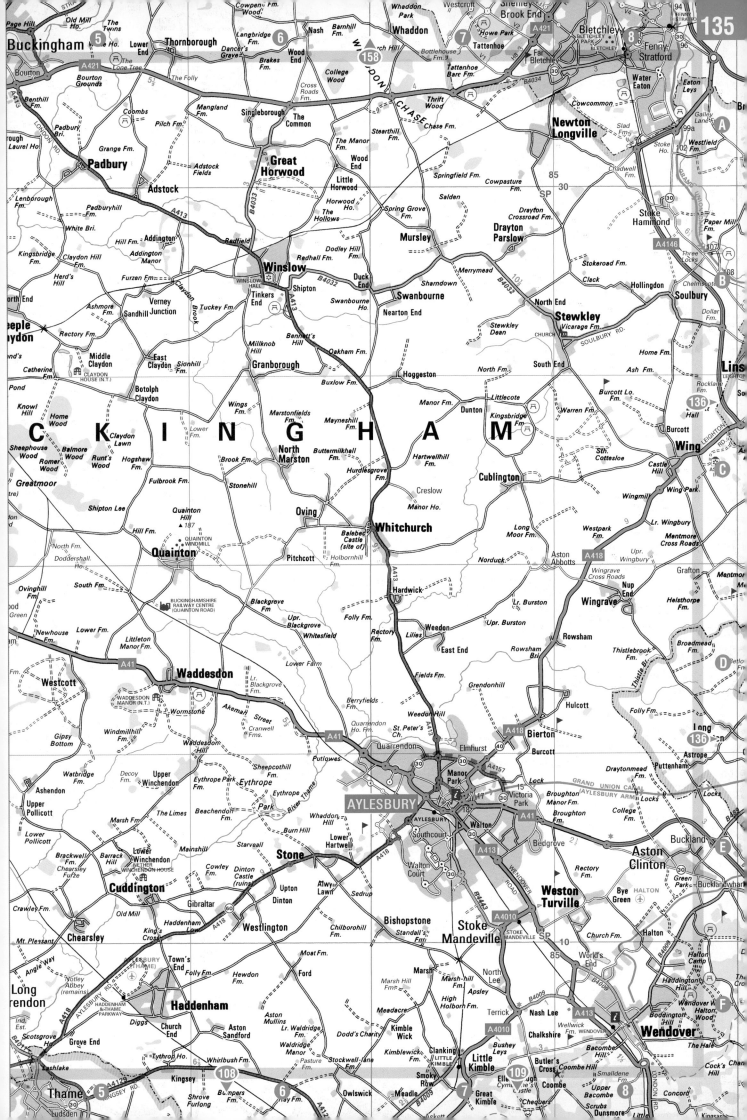

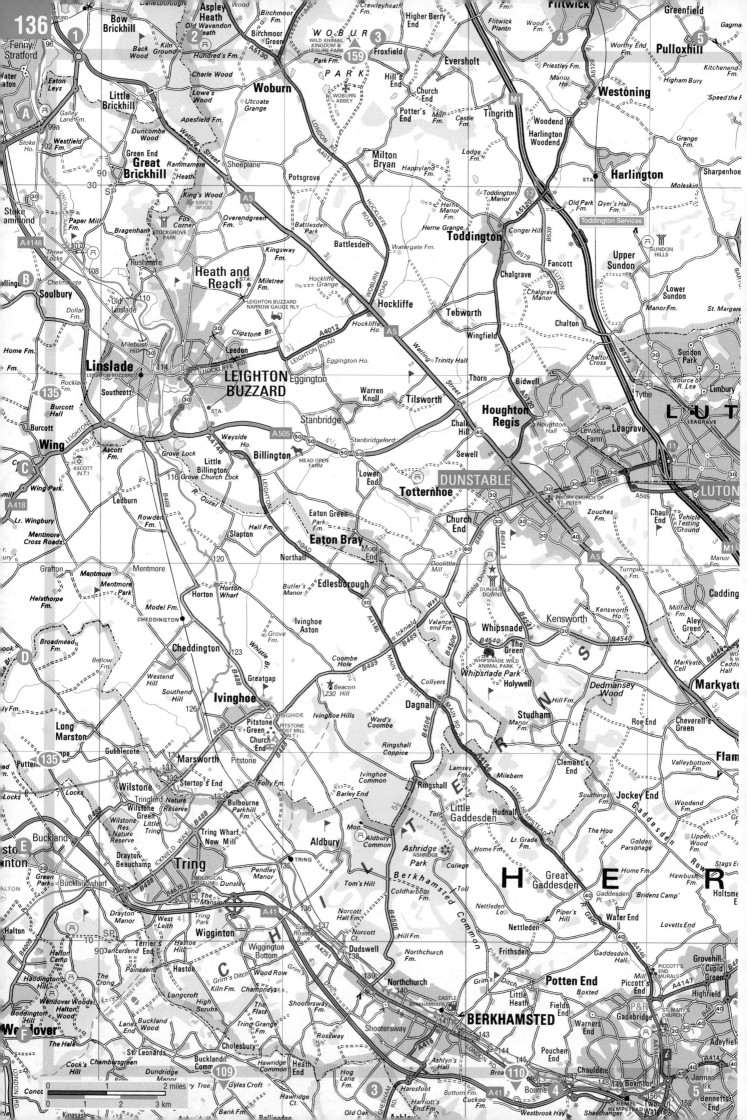

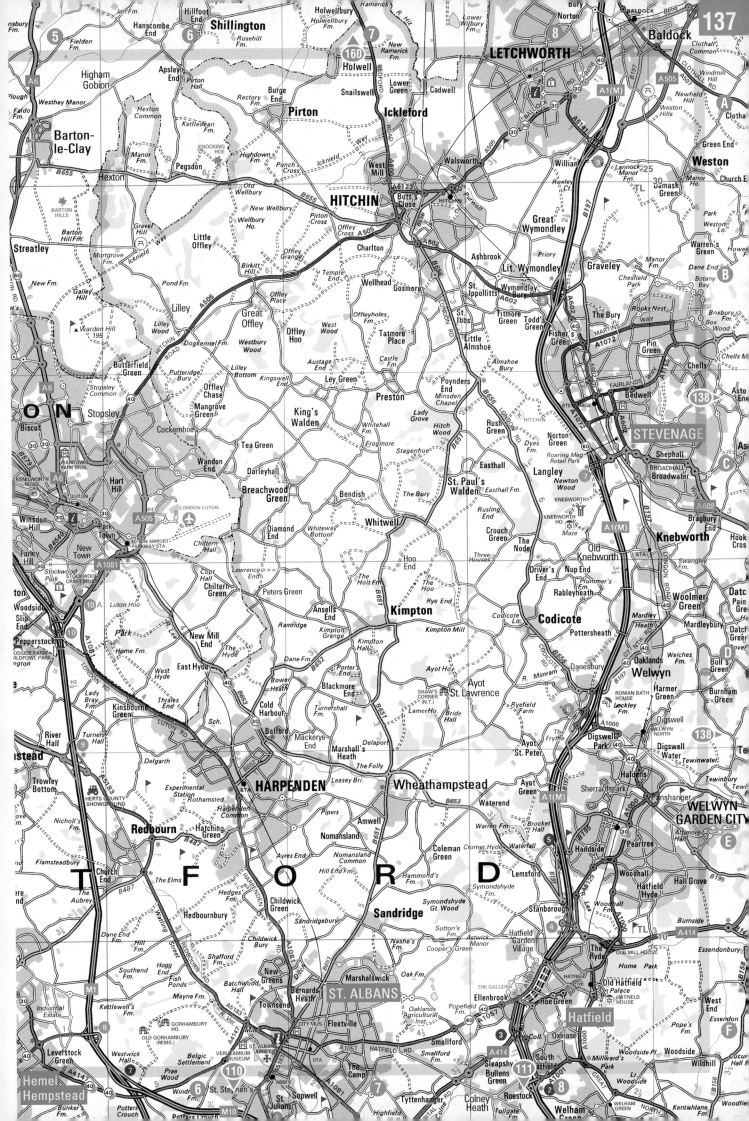

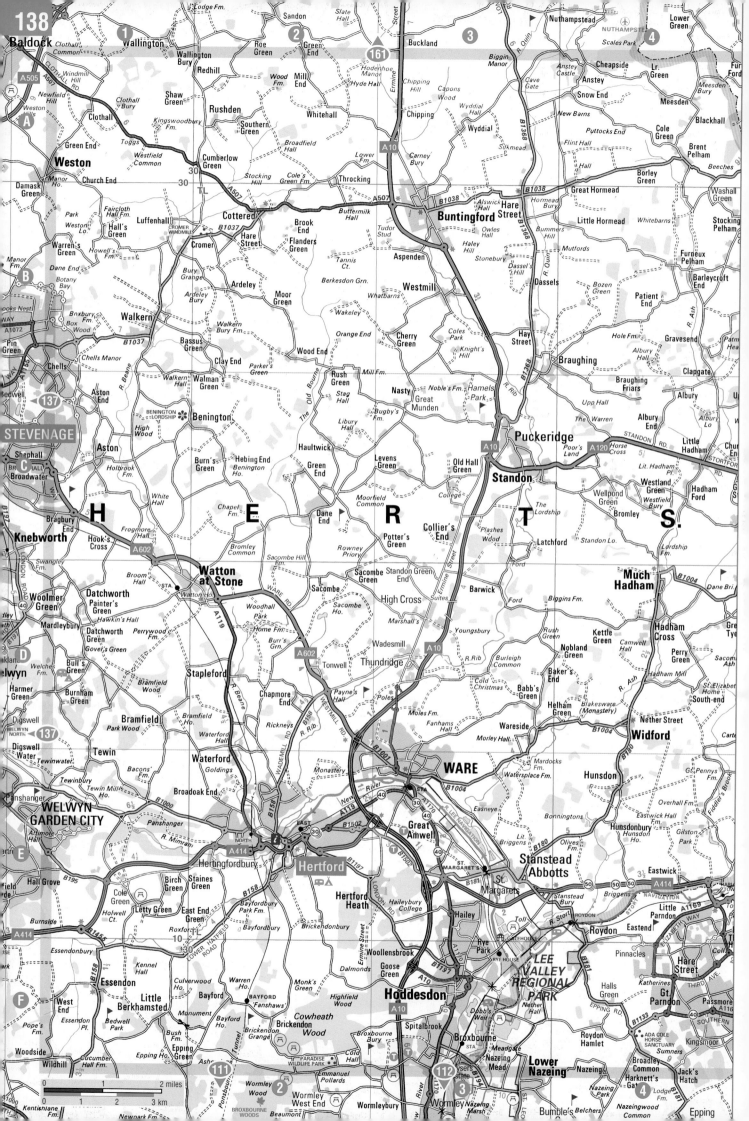

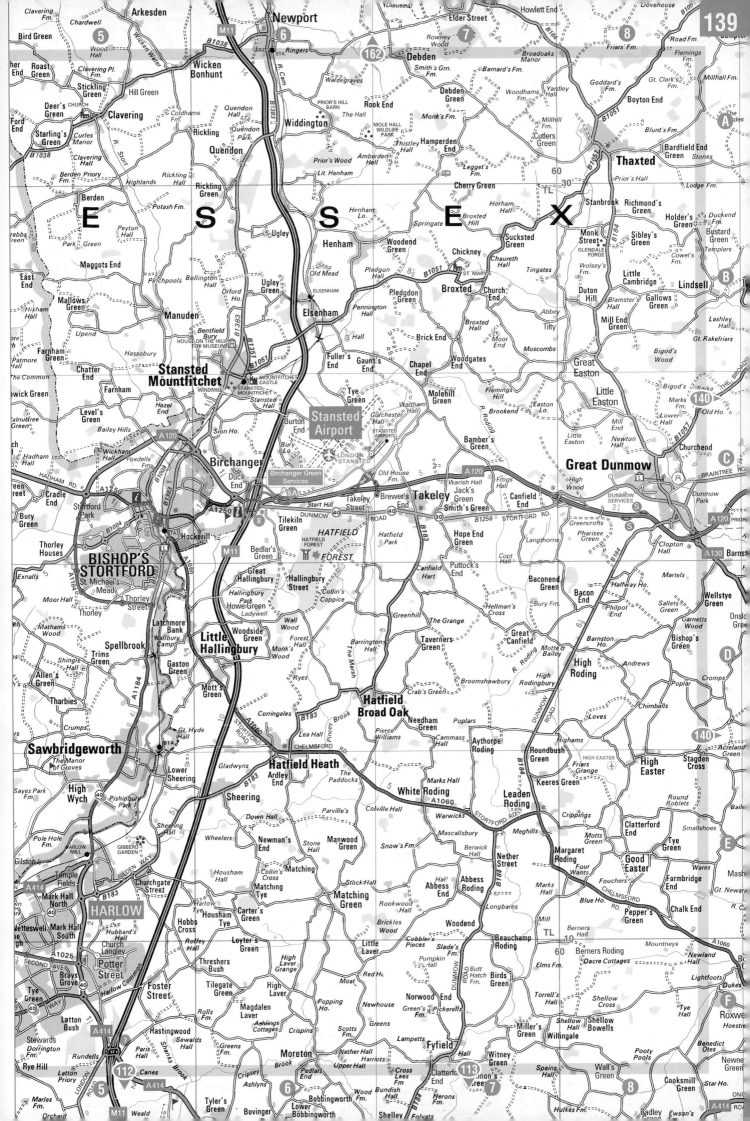

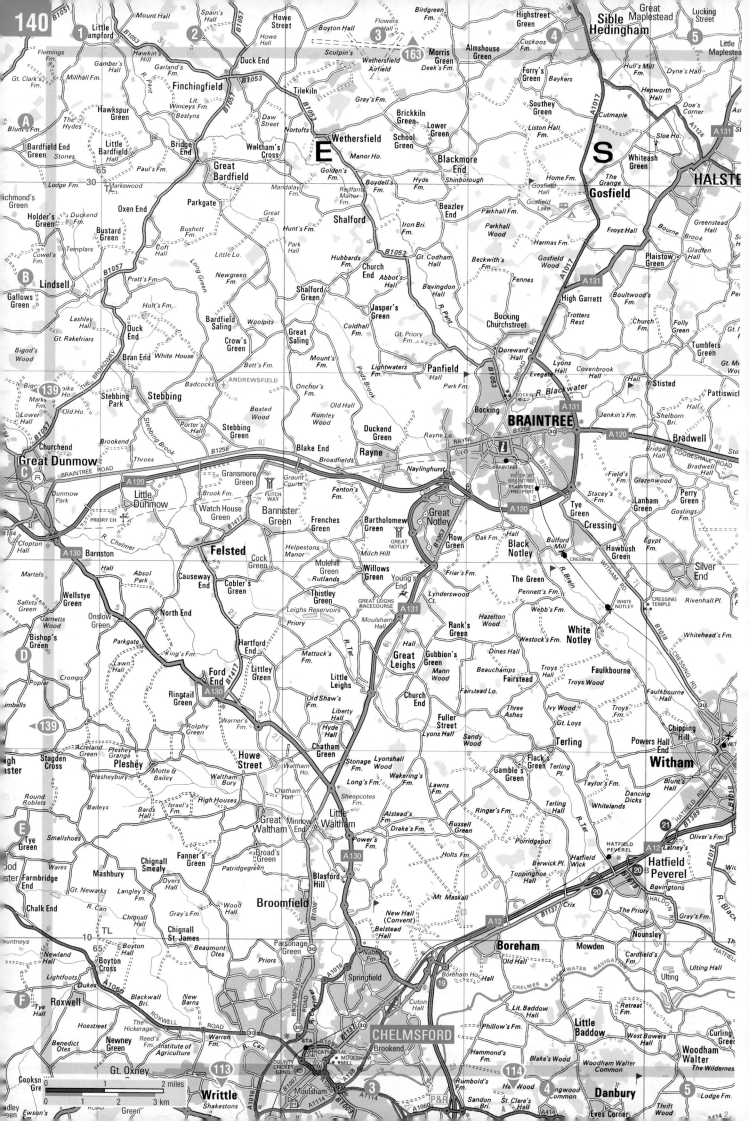

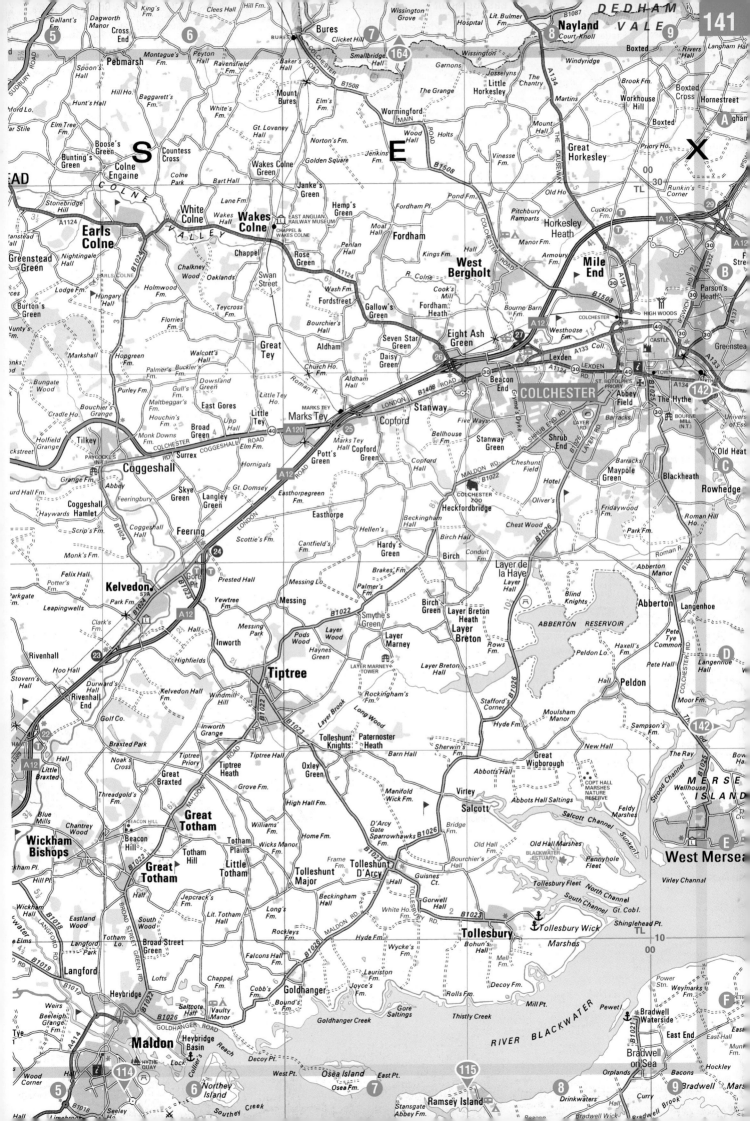

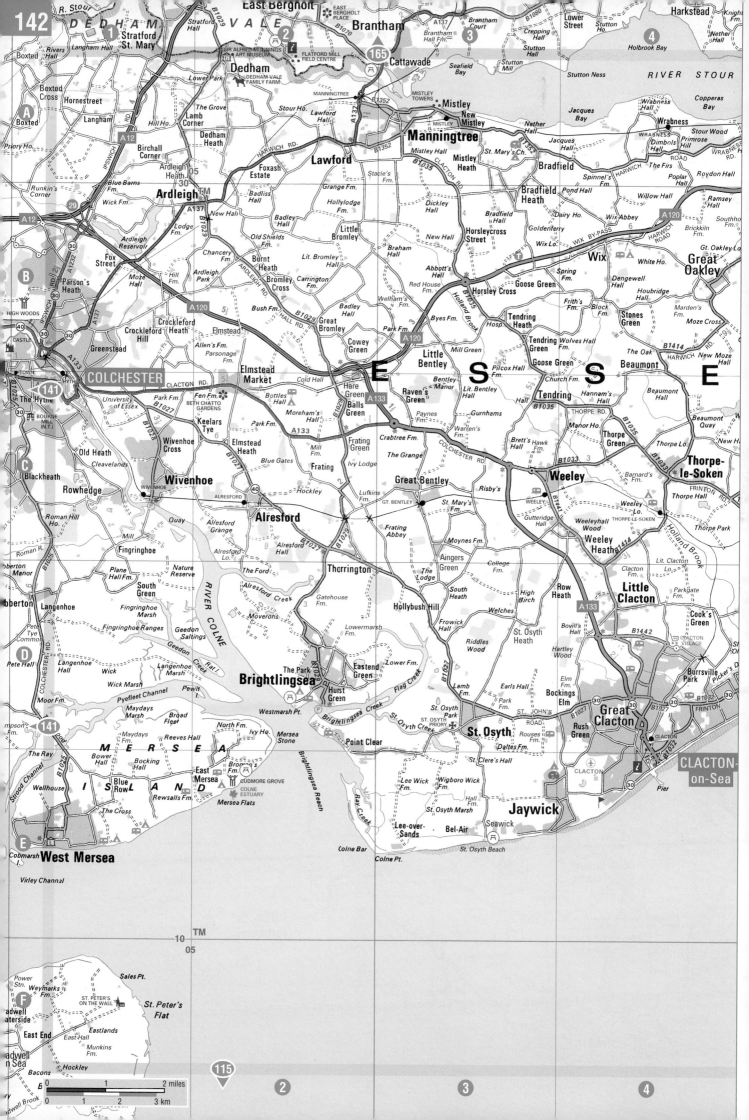

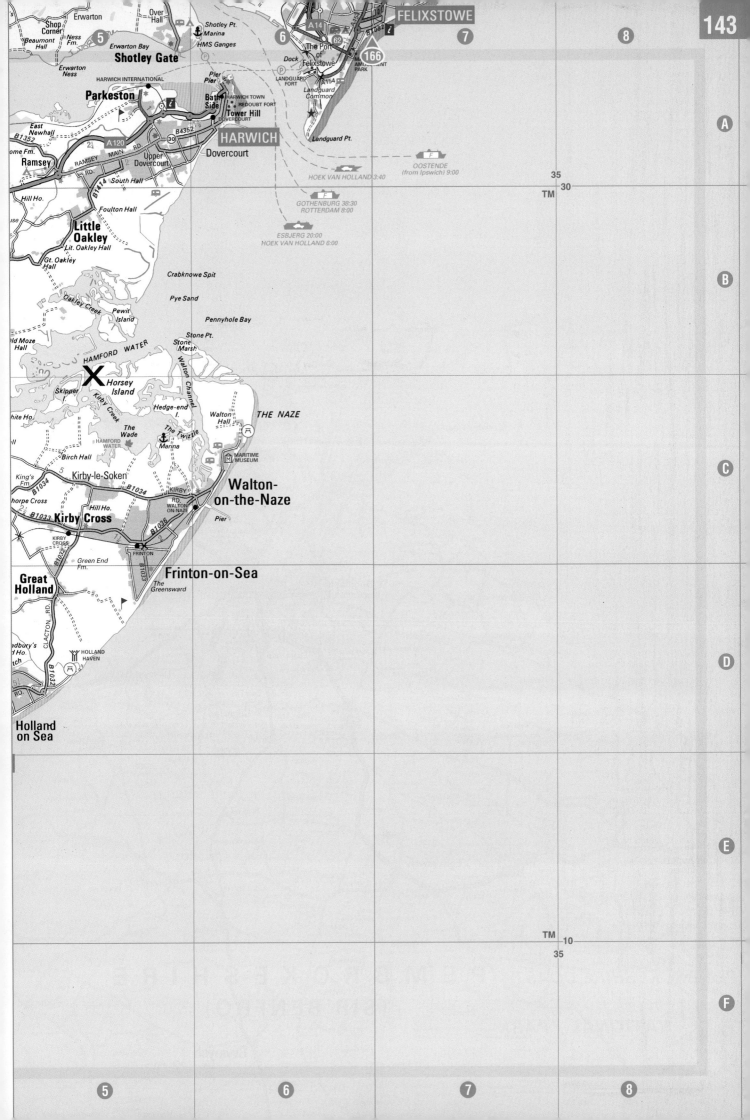

Over
Hall
Erwarton
Shop
Corner
Ness
Fm.
Erwarton Bay
Beaumont
Hall
Shotley Pt.
Marina
HMS Ganges
**FELIXSTOWE**
A14
**5**
Erwarton
Ness
**Shotley Gate**
**6**
62
B1082
**7**
**8**
The Port
of
Felixstowe
166
HARWICH INTERNATIONAL
**Parkeston**
Pier
Pier
Dock
P
LANDGUARD
FORT
Landguard
Common
AMUSEMENT
PARK
**A**
East
Newhall
B1352
Bath
Side
HARWICH TOWN
REDOUBT FORT
Tower Hill
DOVERCOURT
A154
Landguard Pt.
**Ramsey**
A120
RAMSEY
MAIN
RD.
30
B4352
Upper
Dovercourt
**HARWICH**
**Dovercourt**
Hill Ho.
B1414
South Hall
OOSTENDE
(from Ipswich) 9:00
35
30
TM
HOEK VAN HOLLAND 3:40
Foulton Hall
F
GOTHENBURG 38:30
ROTTERDAM 8:00
**Little**
**Oakley**
Lit. Oakley Hall
**B**
Gt. Oakley
Hall
ESBJERG 20:00
HOEK VAN HOLLAND 6:00
Crabknowe Spit
Oakley Creek
Pewit
Island
Pye Sand
ld Moze
Hall
Pennyhole Bay
Stone Pt.
Stone
Marsh
HAMFORD WATER
Walton Channel
X
Horsey
Island
Skipper
I.
Kirby Creek
Hedge-end
I.
Walton
Hall
**THE NAZE**
hite Ho.
The
Wade
The Twizzle
Marina
**C**
HAMFORD
WATER
Birch Hall
MARITIME
MUSEUM
King's
Fm.
**Kirby-le-Soken**
B1034
5
B1034
KIRBY
**Walton-**
**on-the-Naze**
horpe Cross
Hill Ho.
RD.
WALTON-
ON-NAZE
B1036
Pier
B1033
**Kirby Cross**
KIRBY
CROSS
B1034
FRINTON
Green End
Fm.
B1033
**Frinton-on-Sea**
**Great**
**Holland**
The
Greensward
CLACTON RD.
adbury's
d Ho.
HOLLAND
HAVEN
**D**
tch
B1032
**Holland**
**on Sea**
RD.
**E**
TM
10
35
**F**
**5**
**6**
**7**
**8**

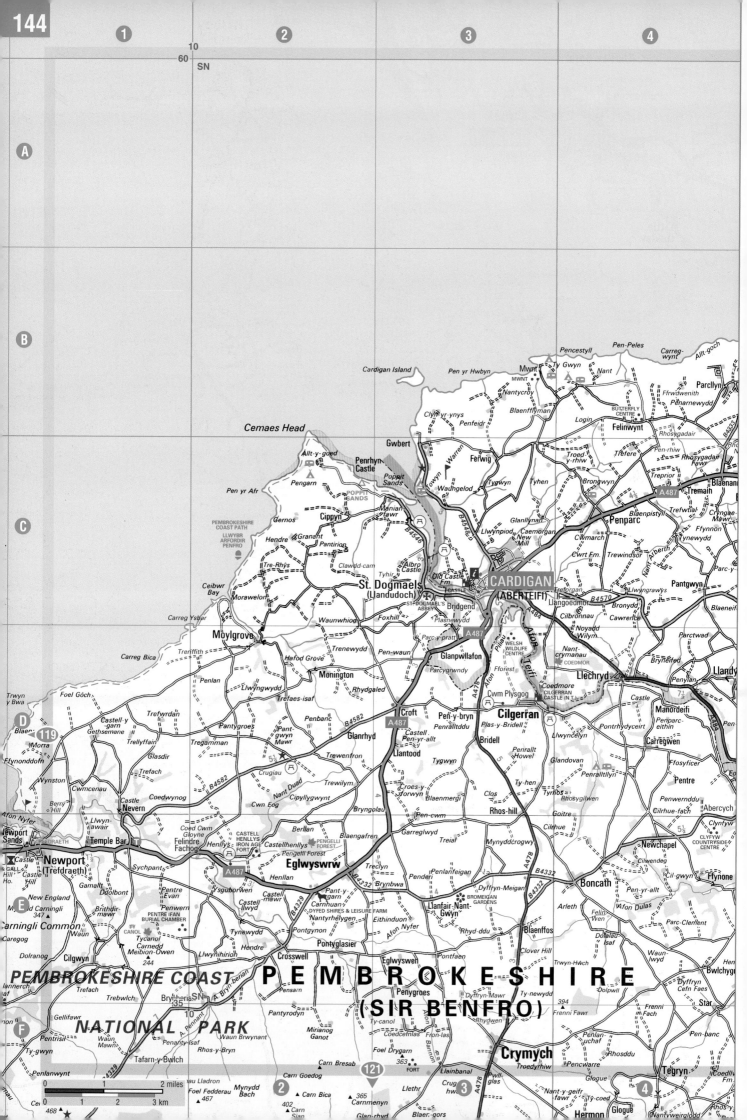

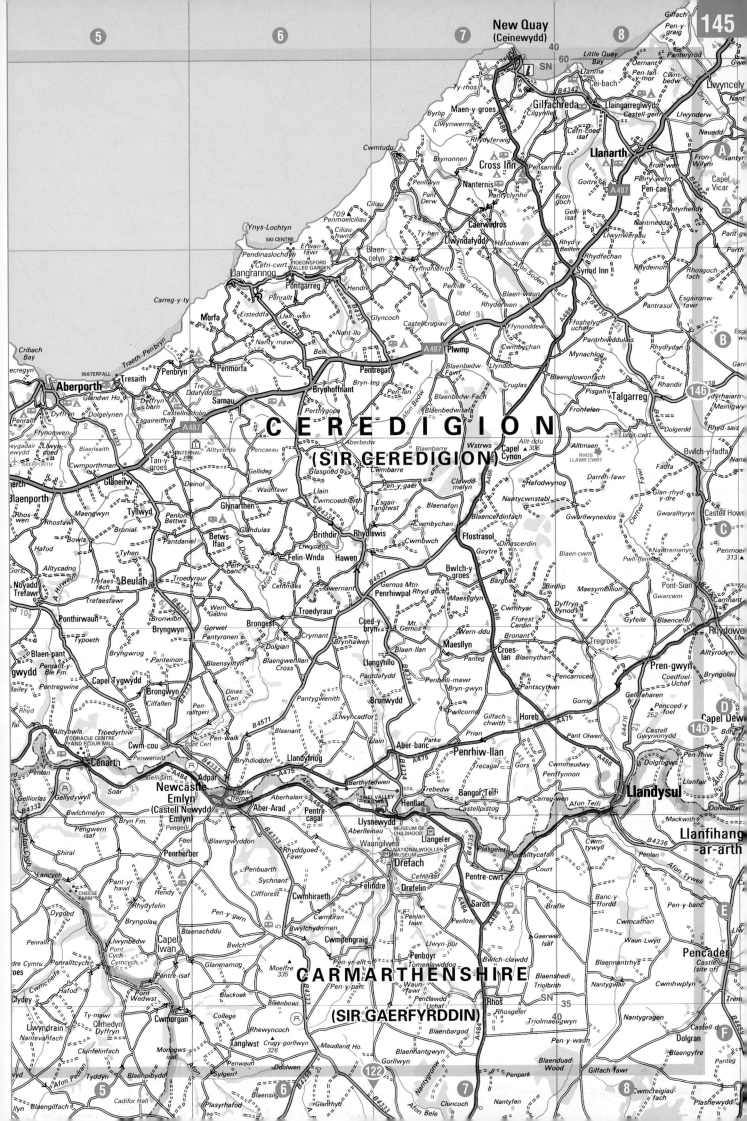

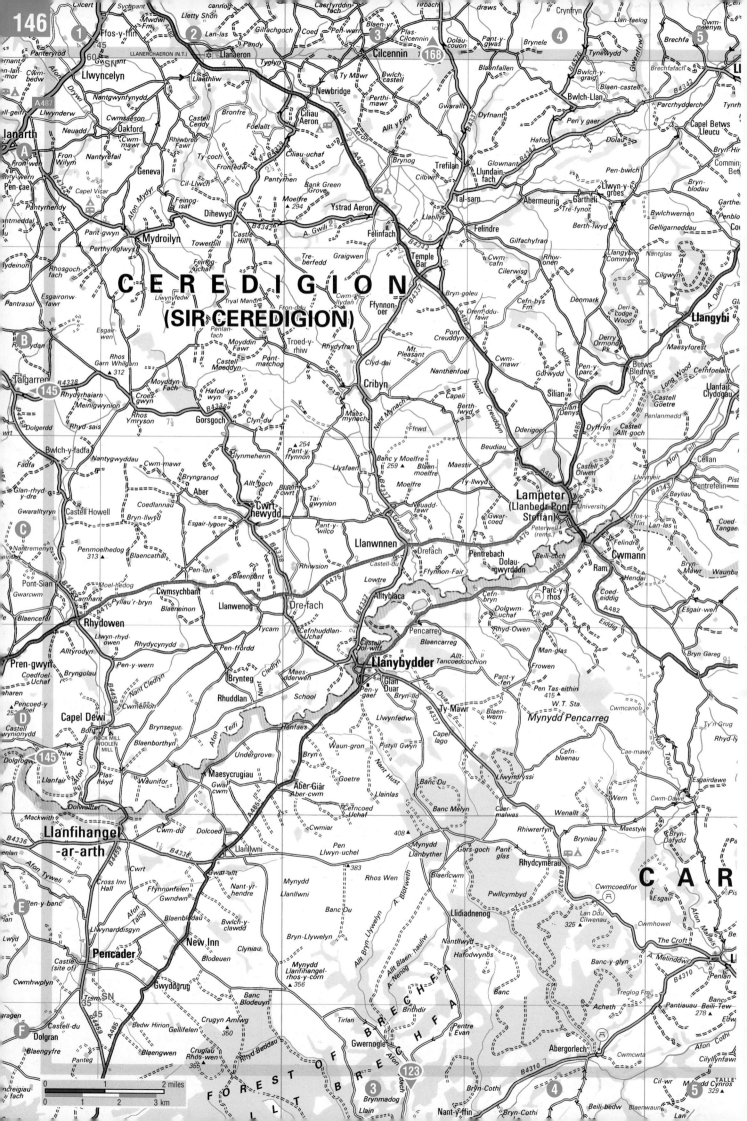

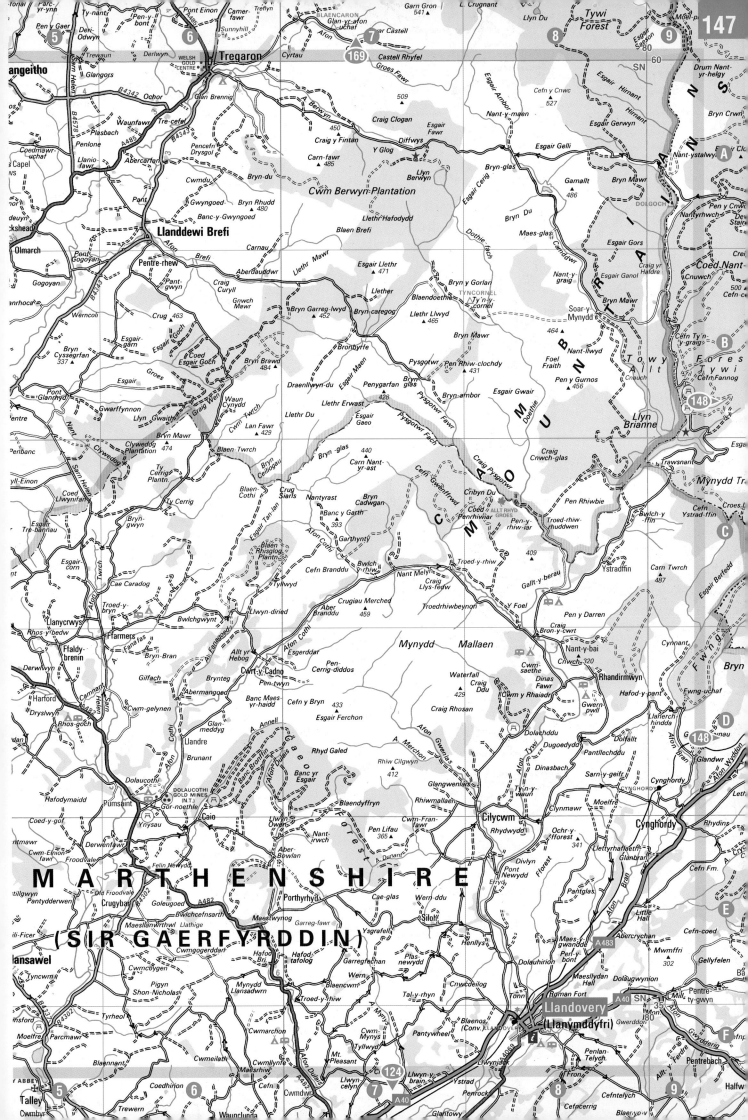

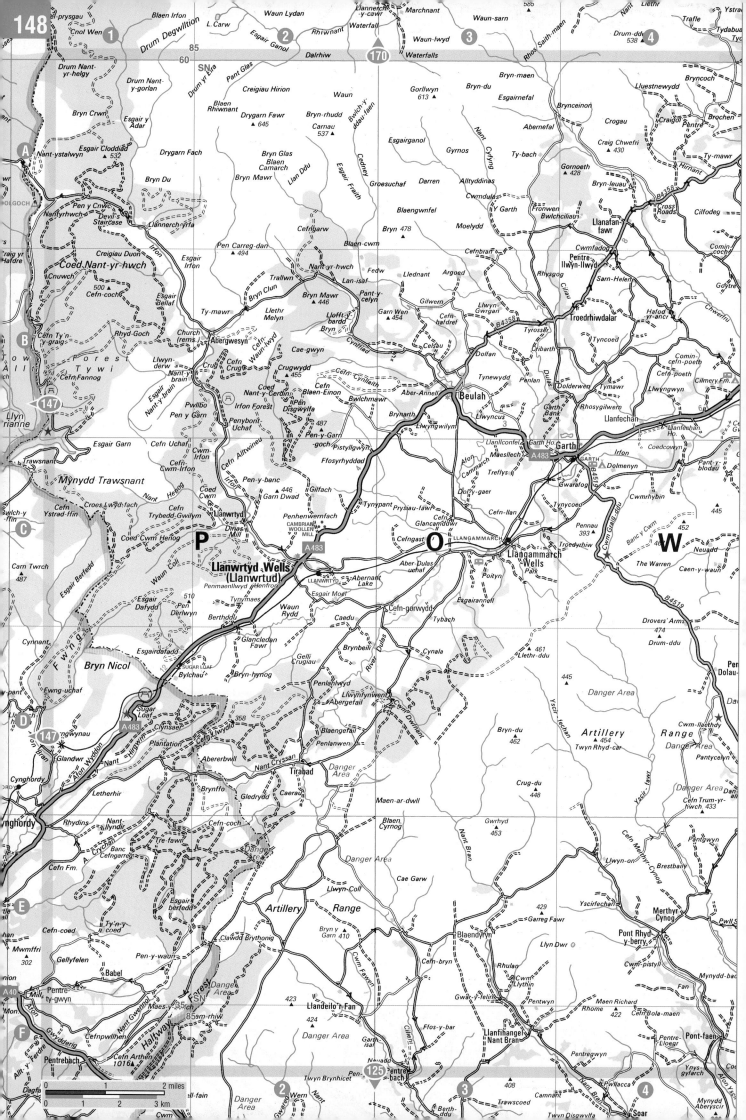

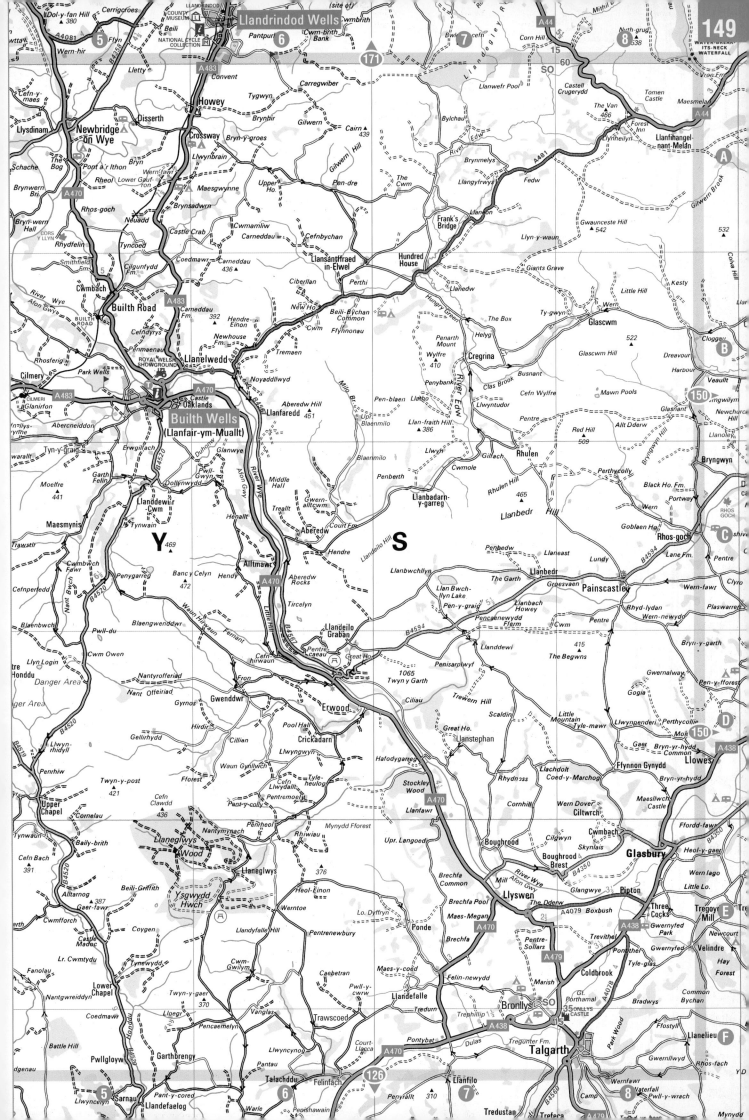

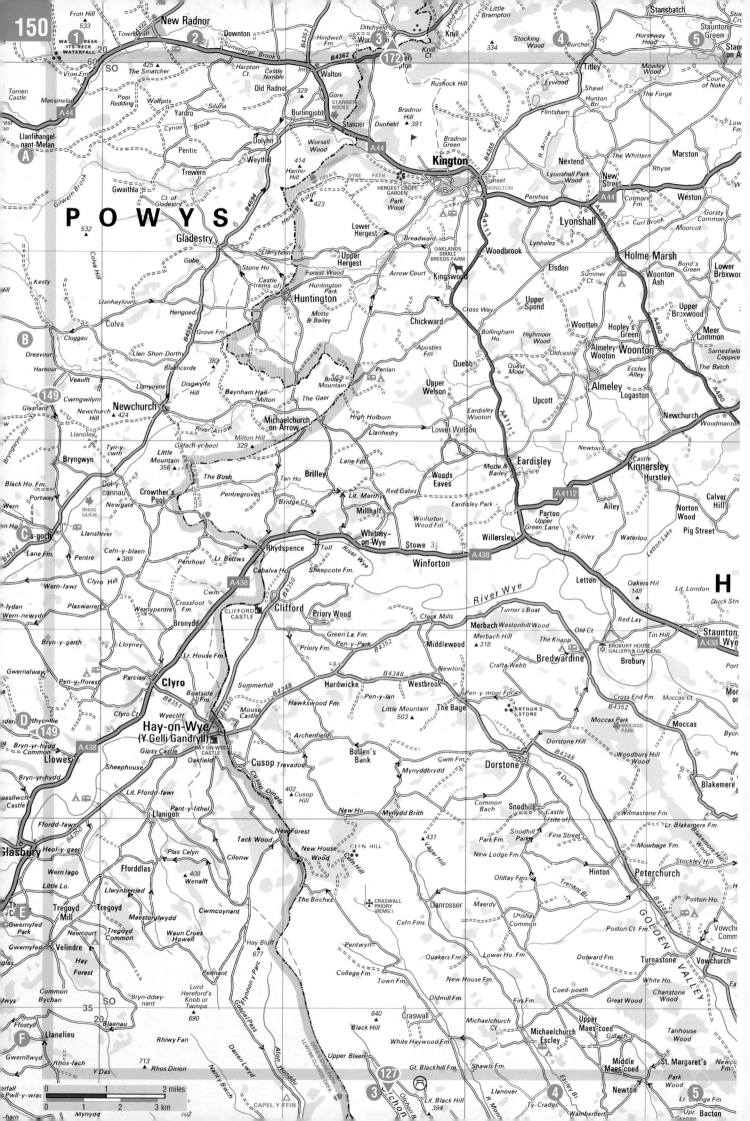

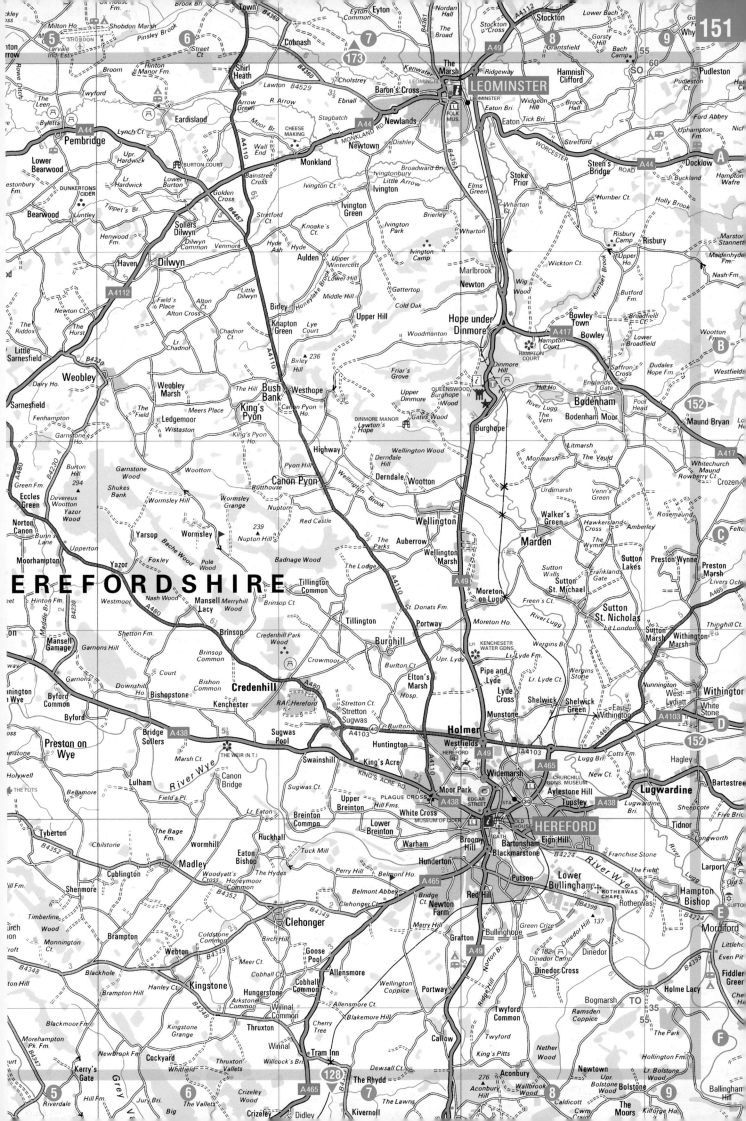

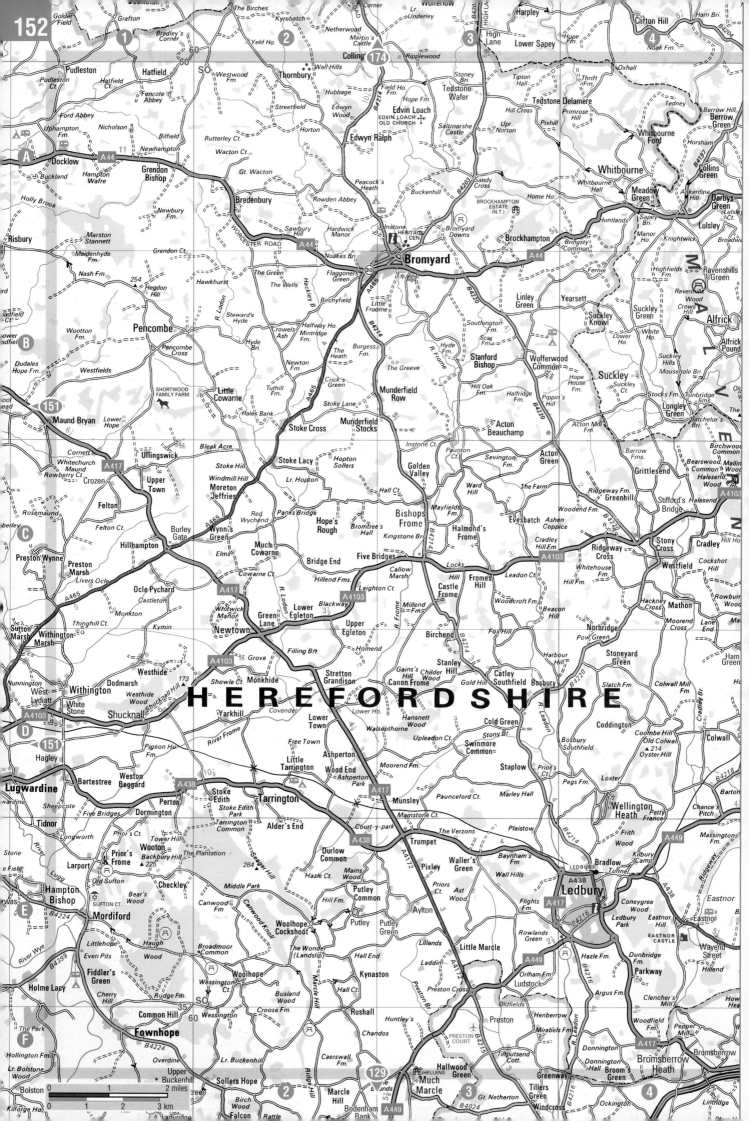

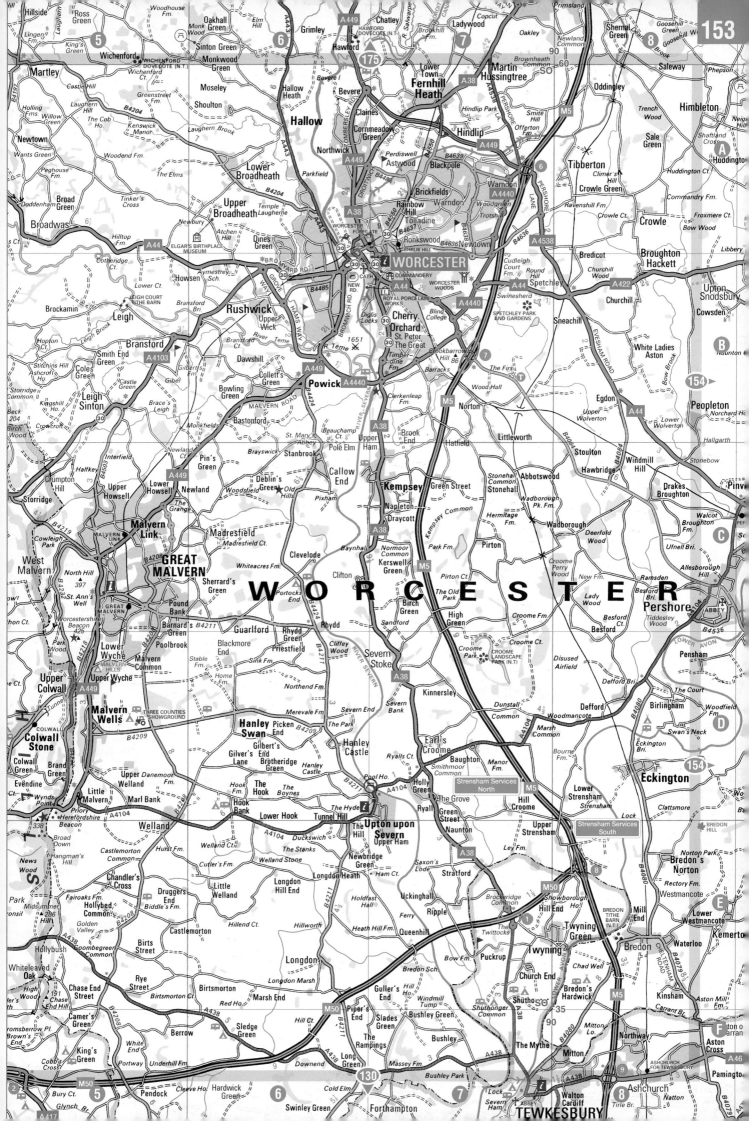

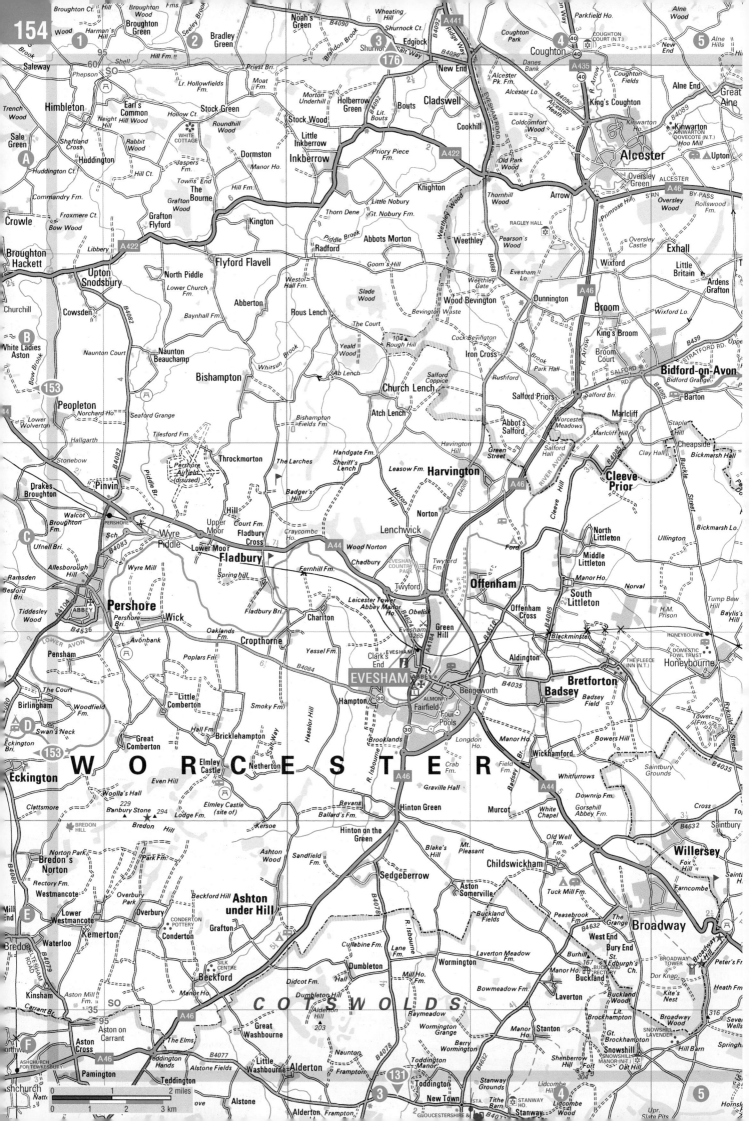

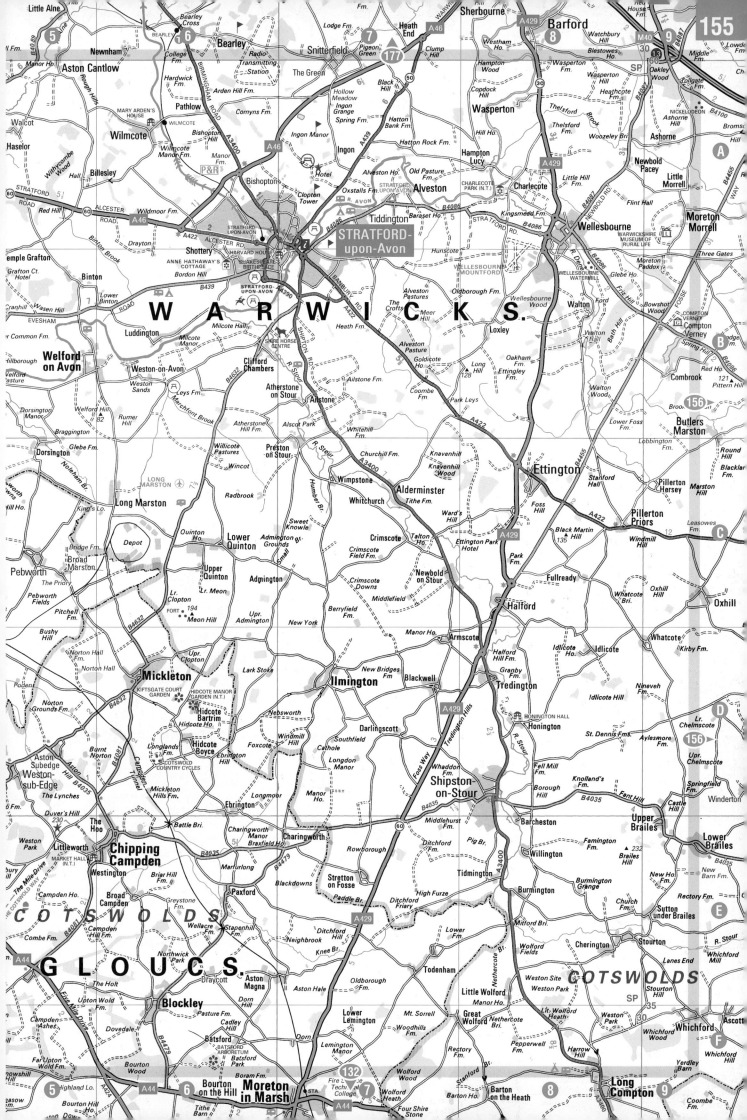

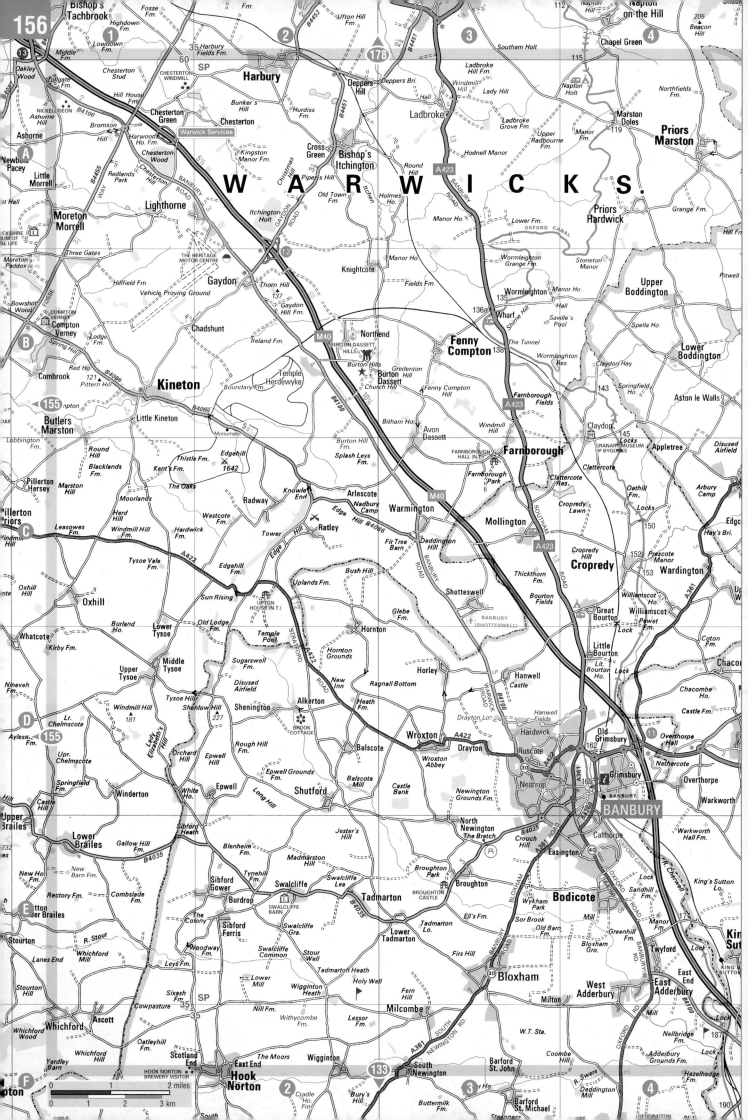

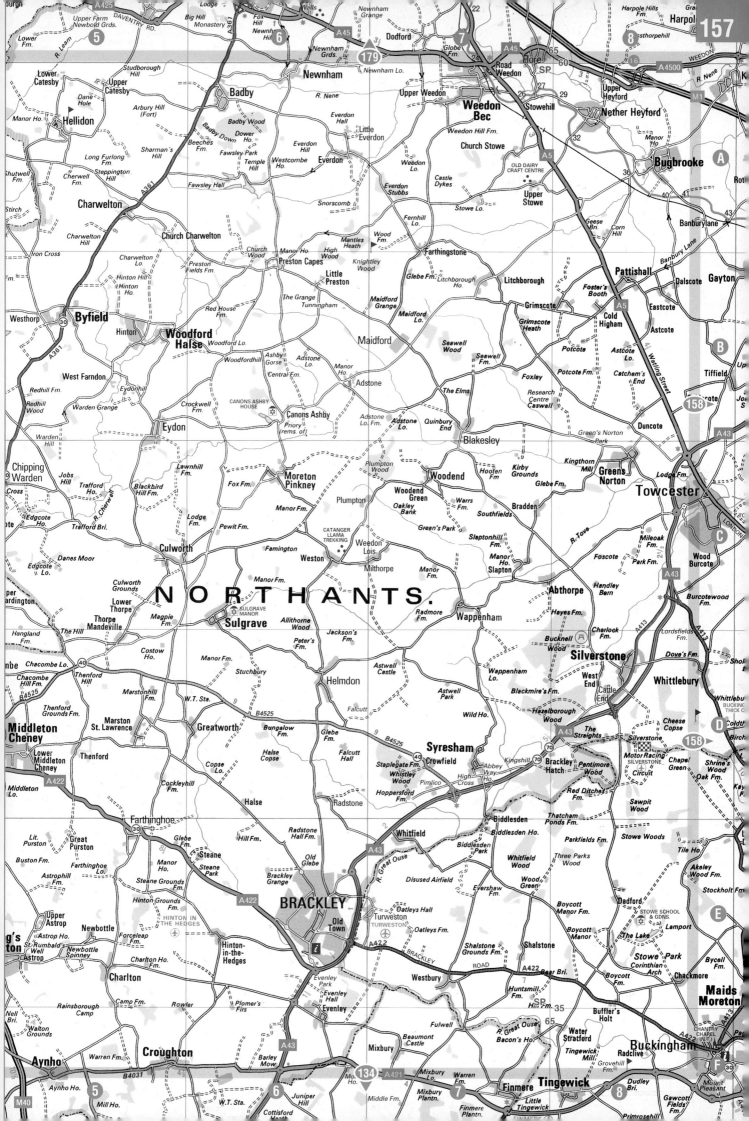

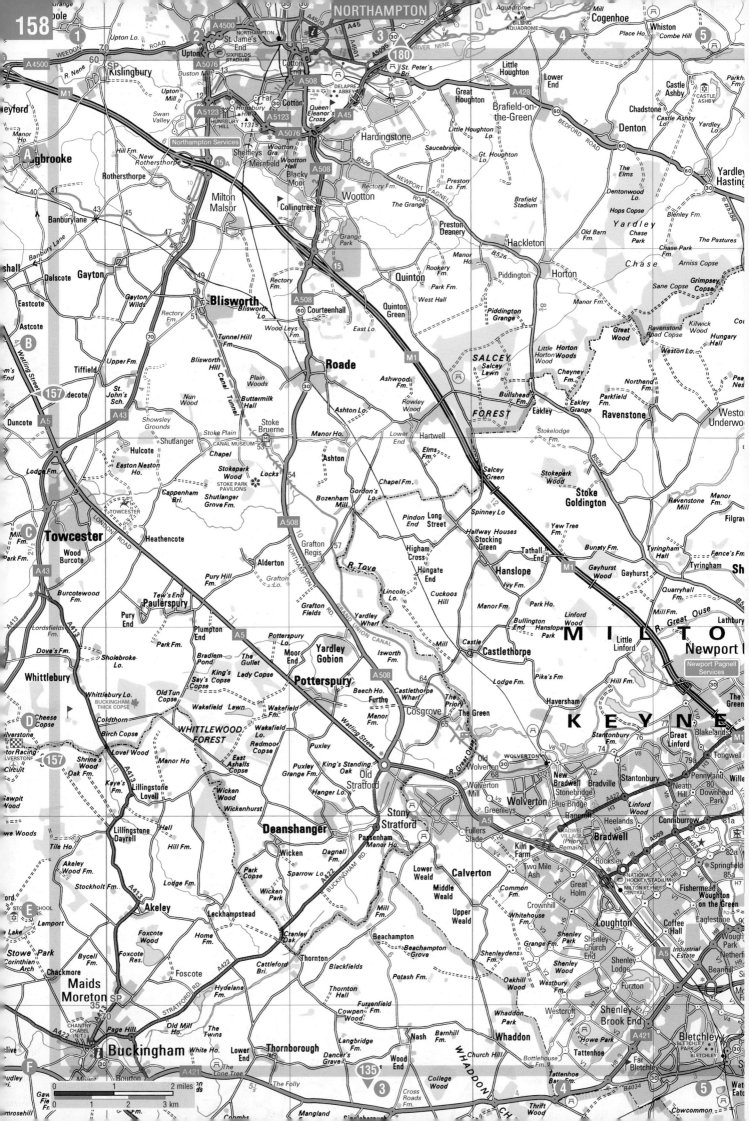

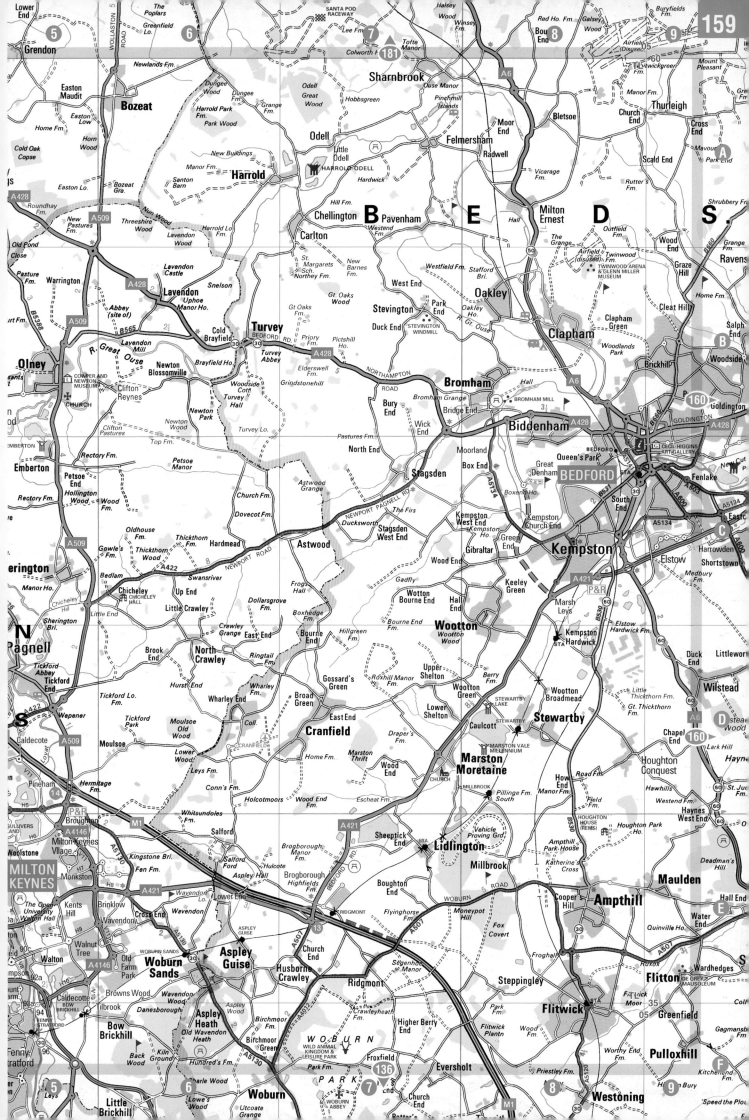

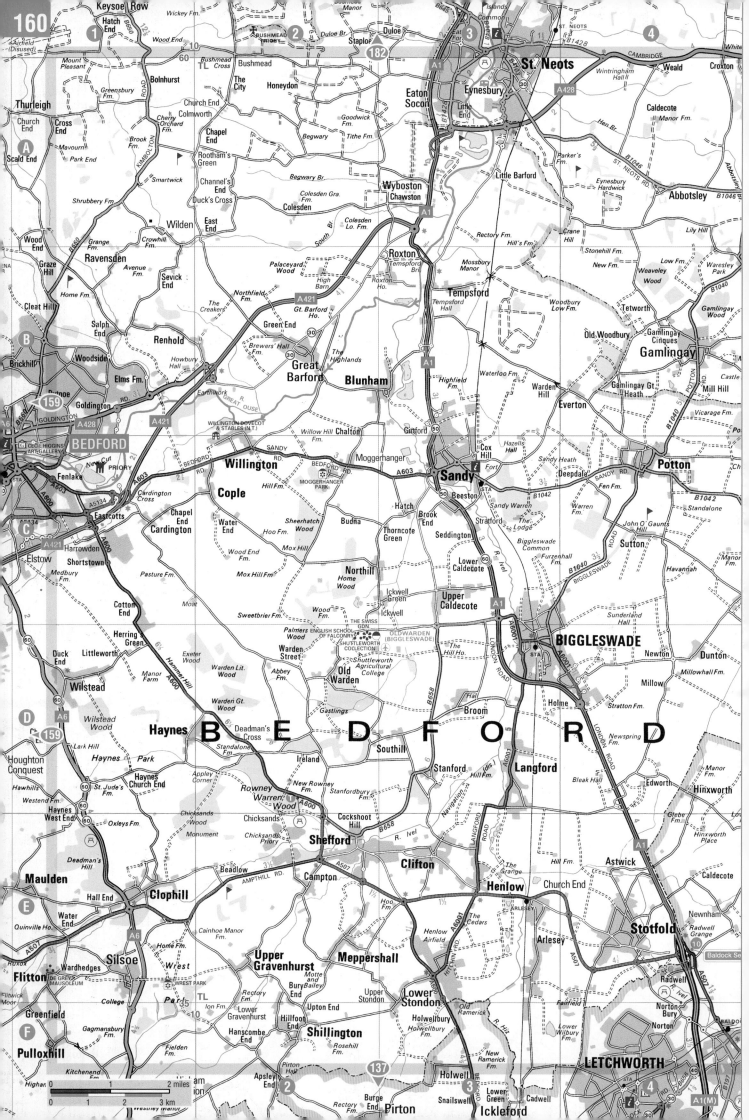

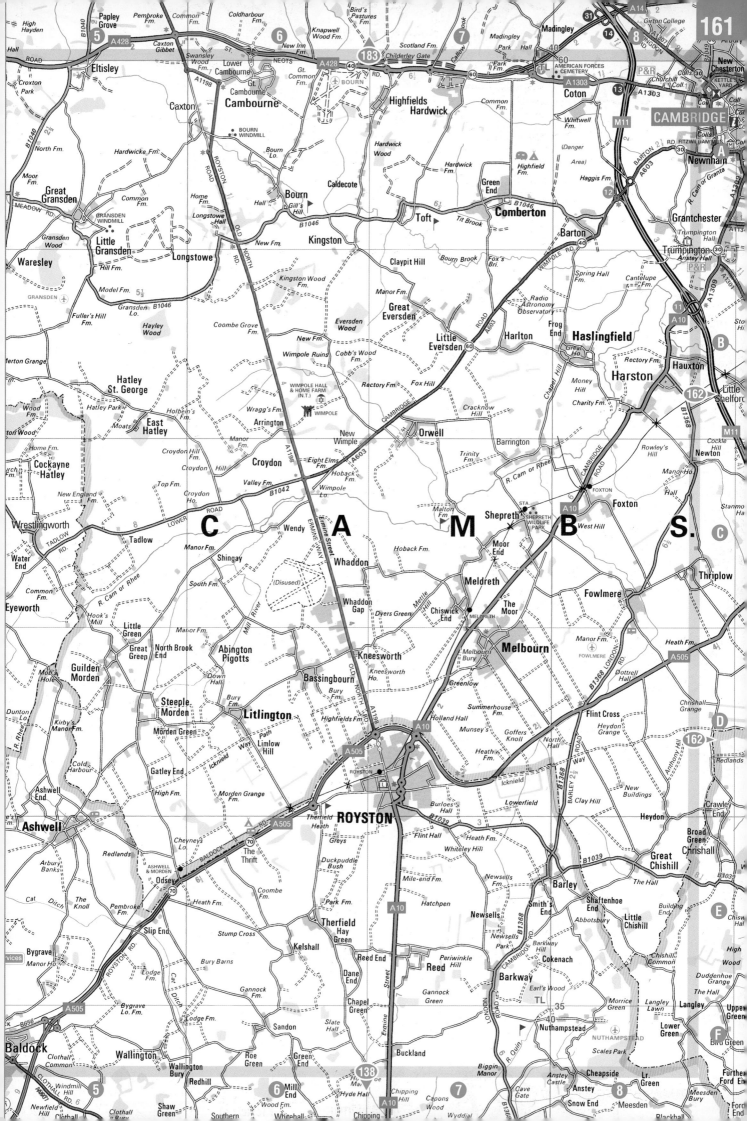

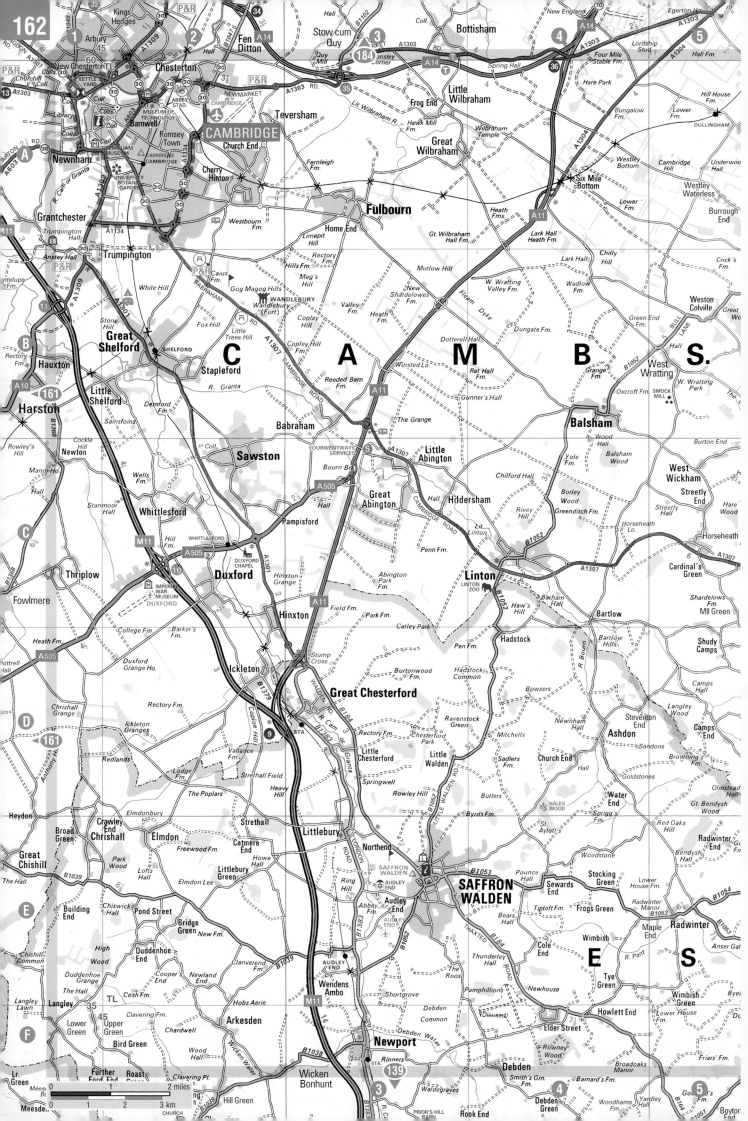

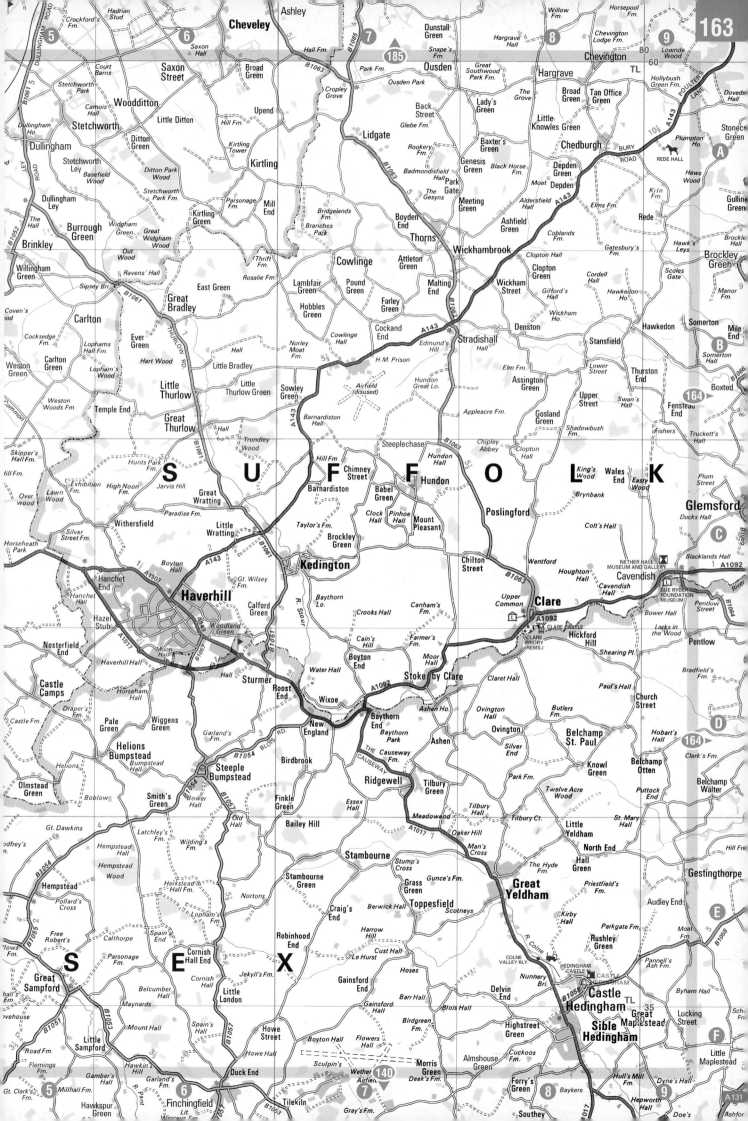

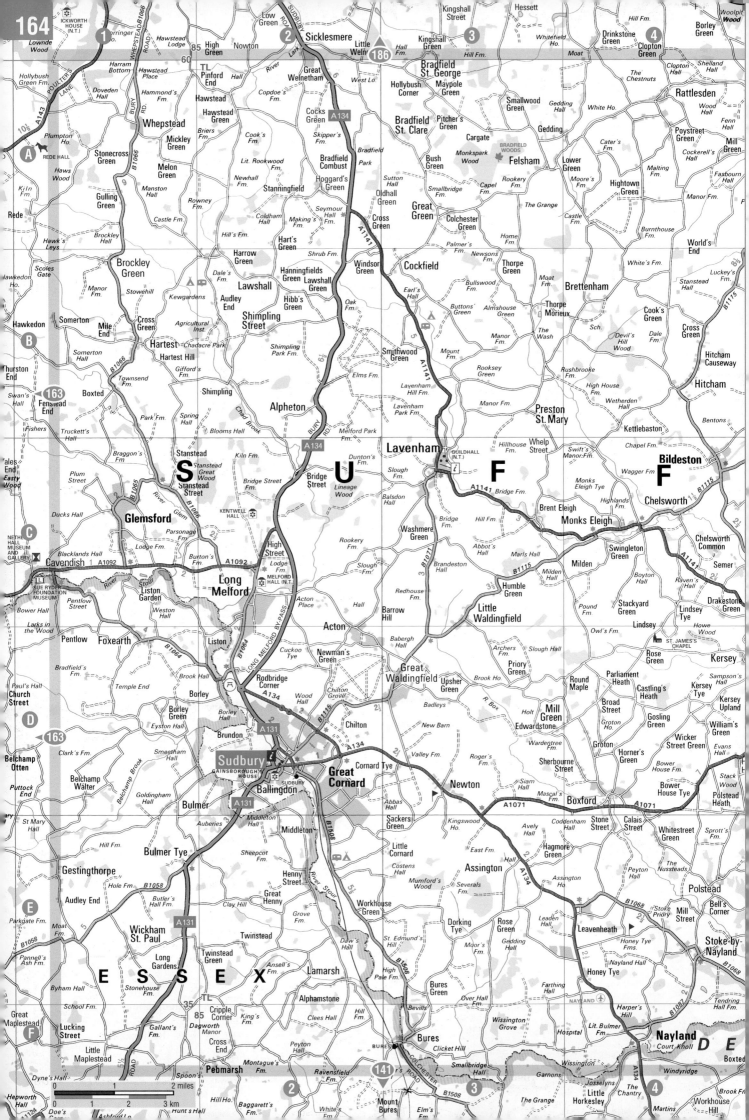

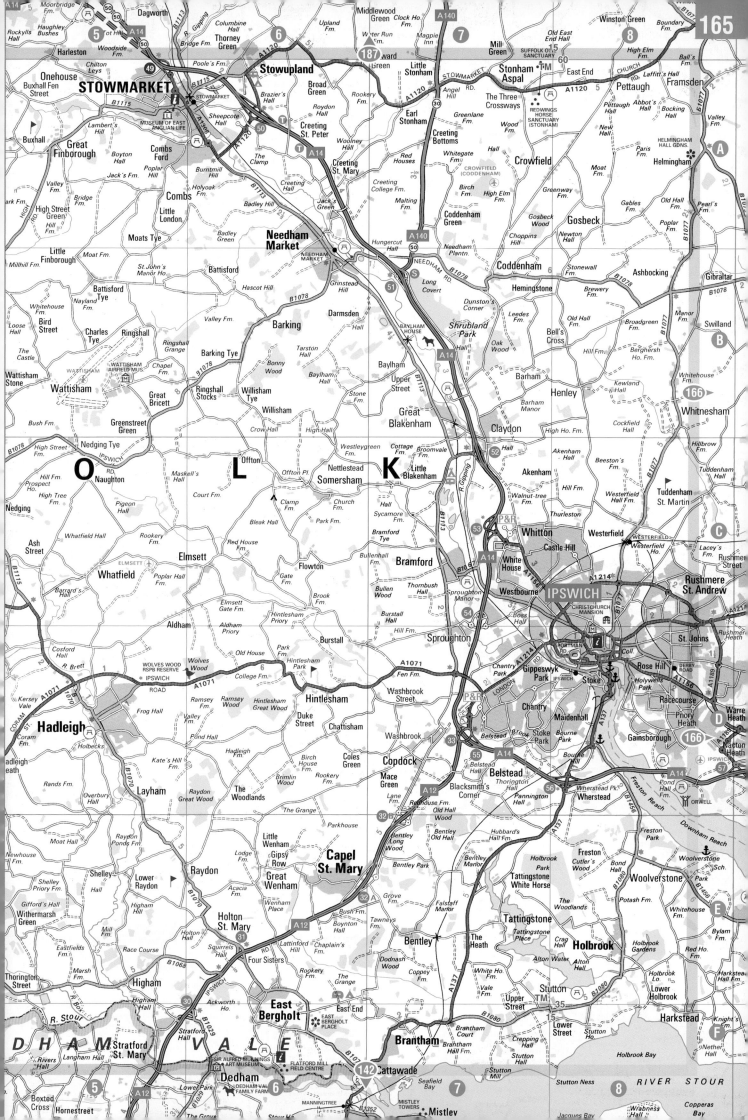

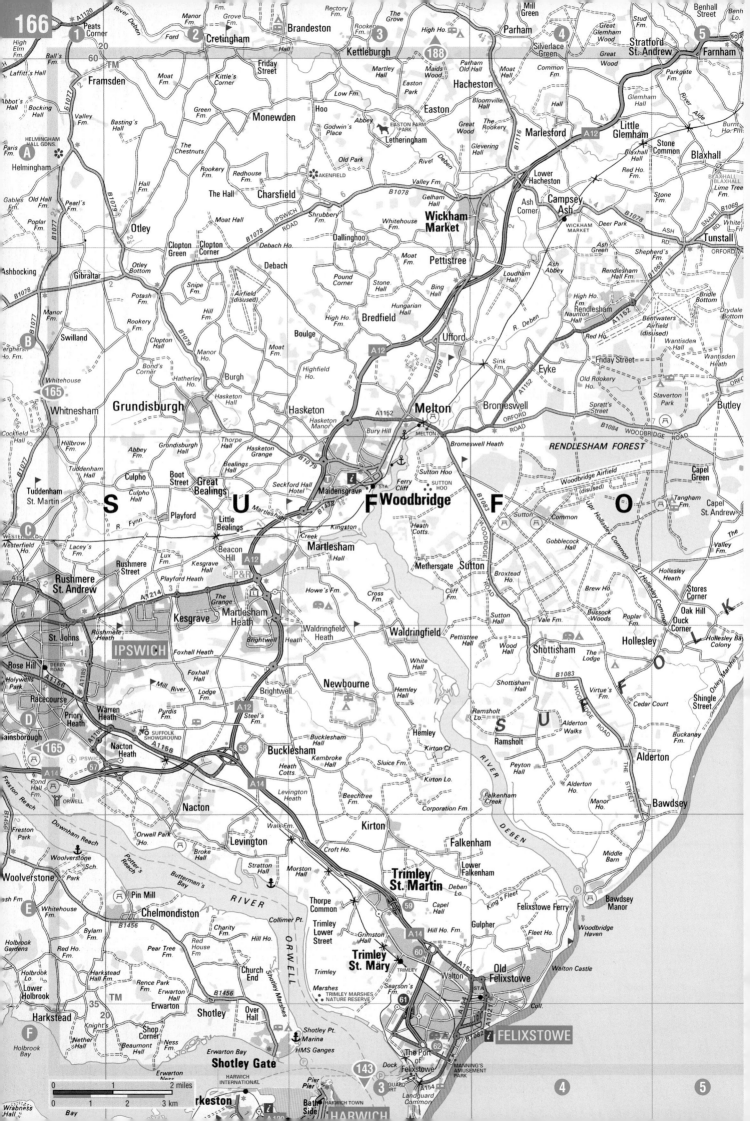

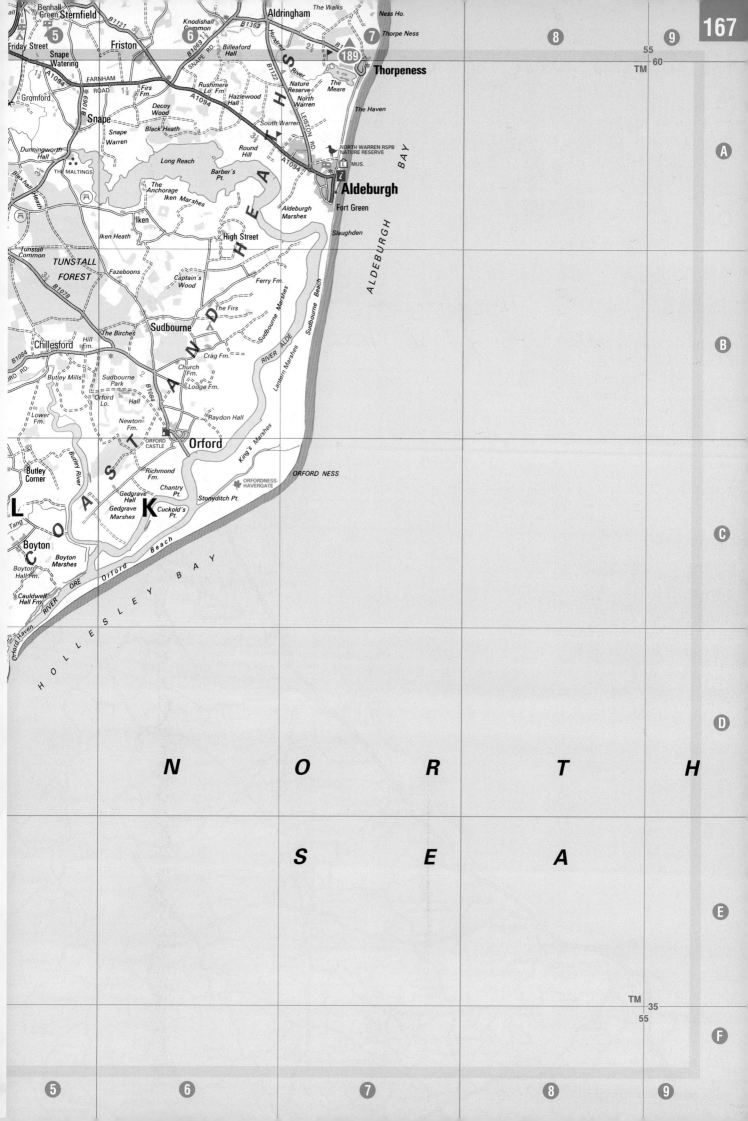

NORTH SEA

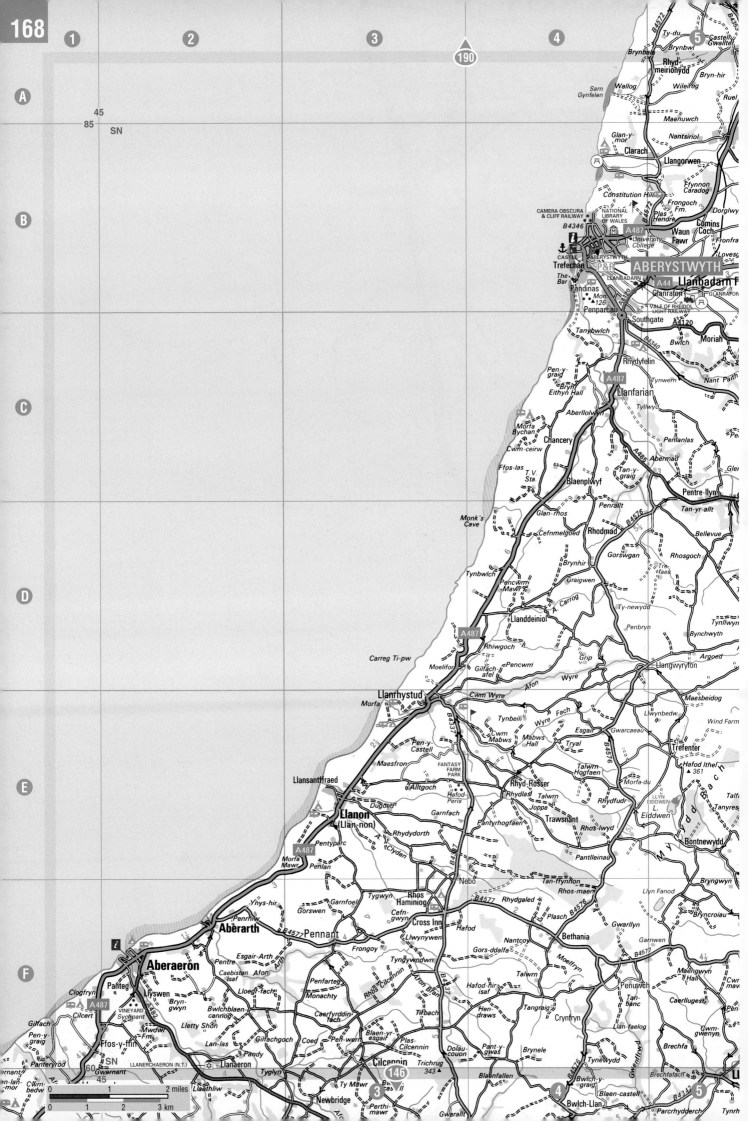

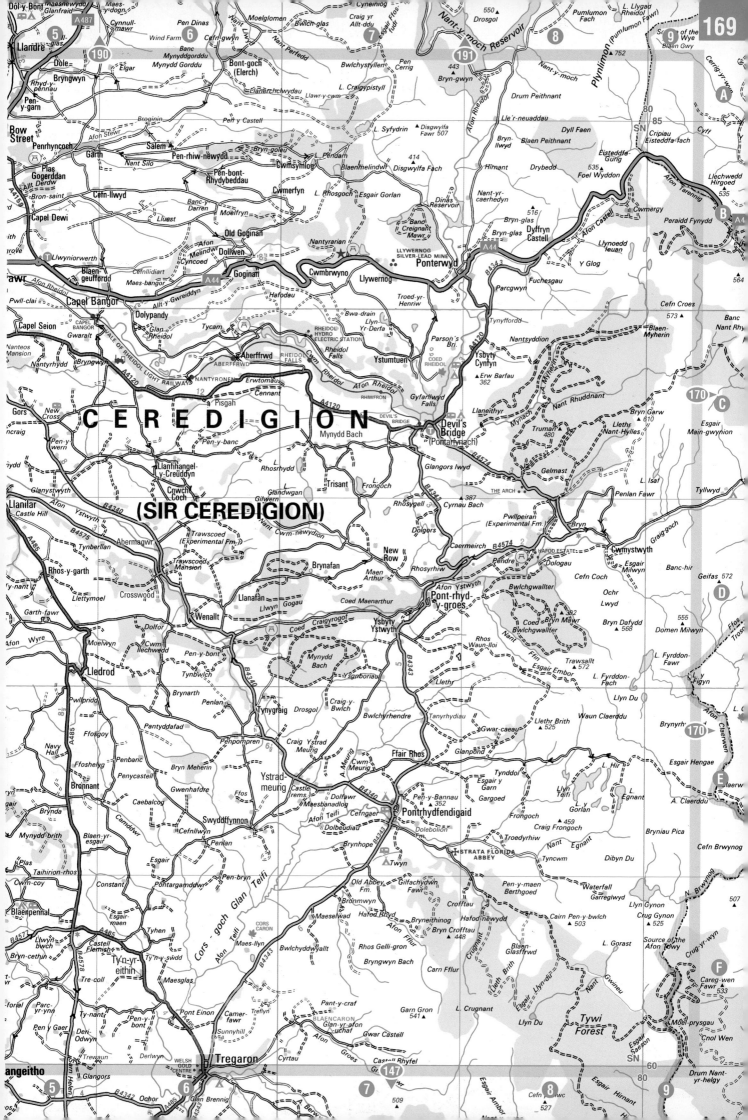

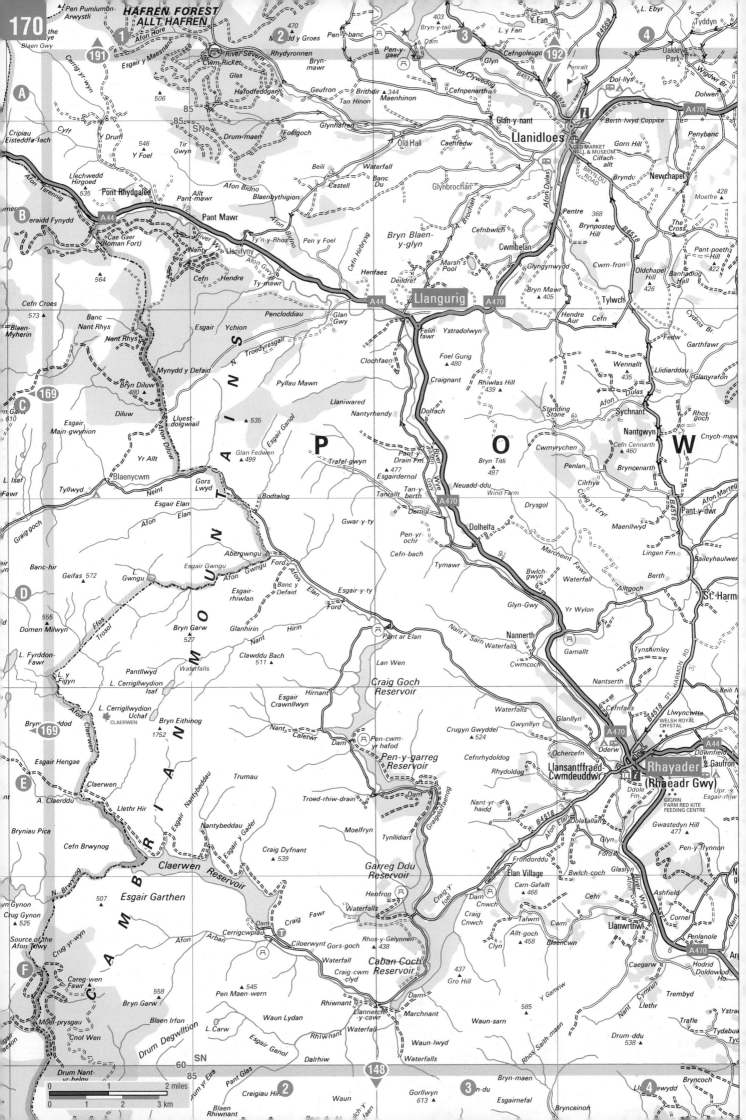

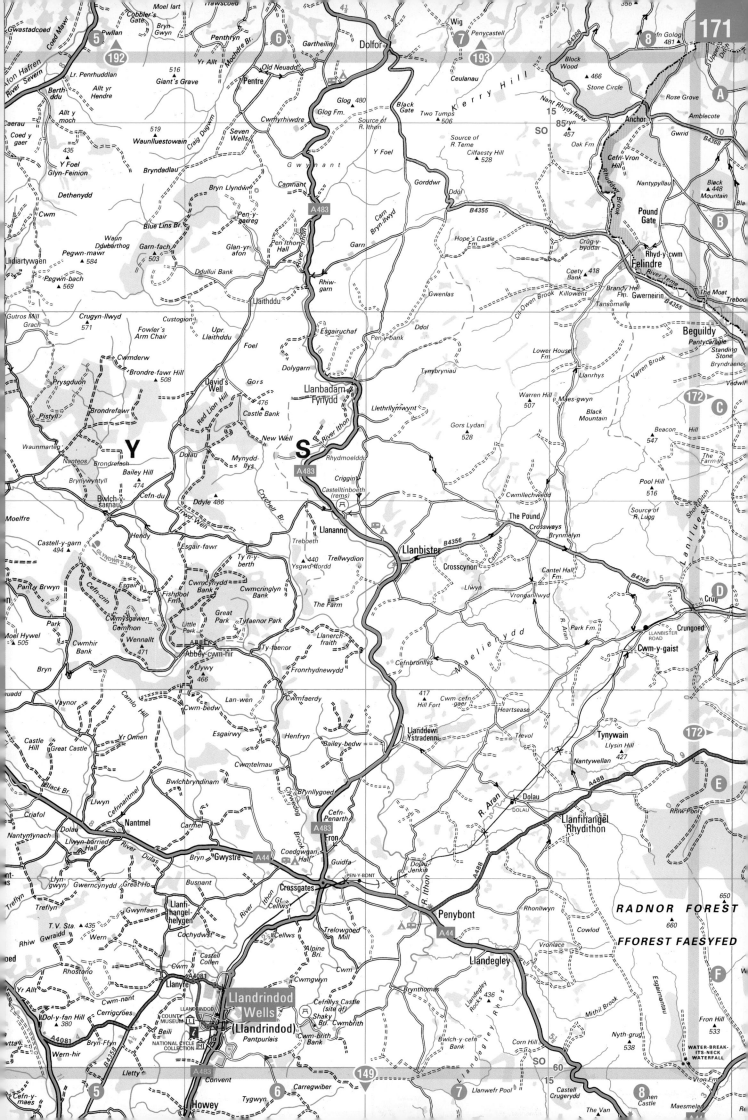

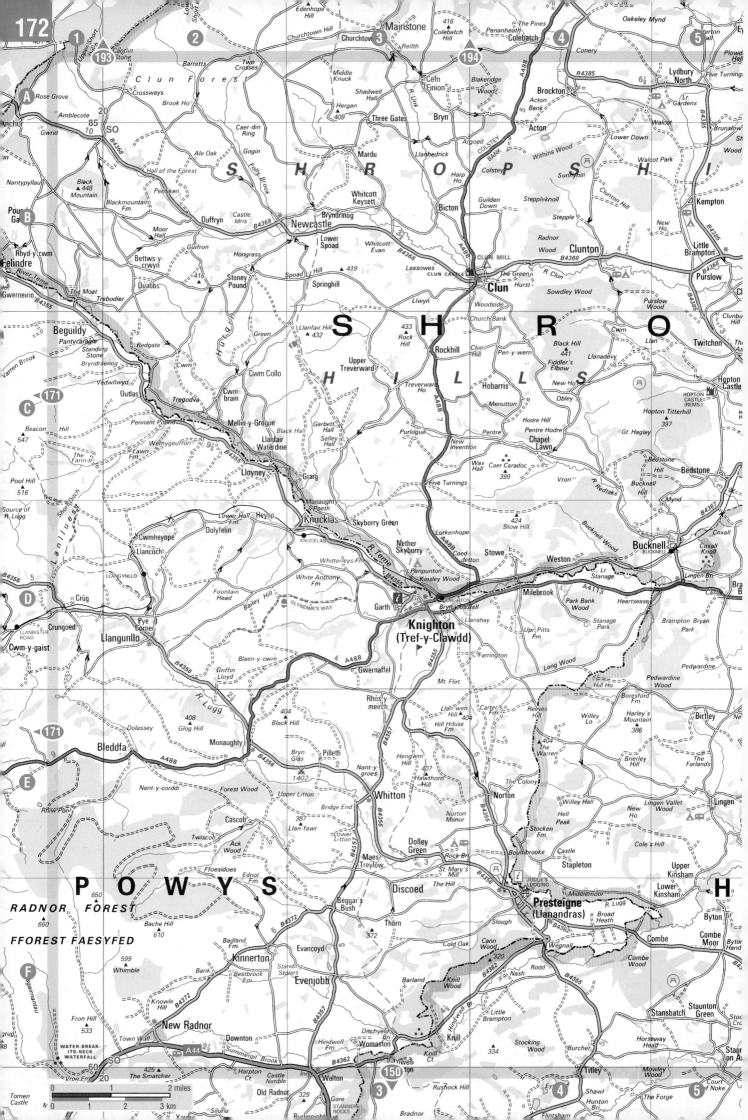

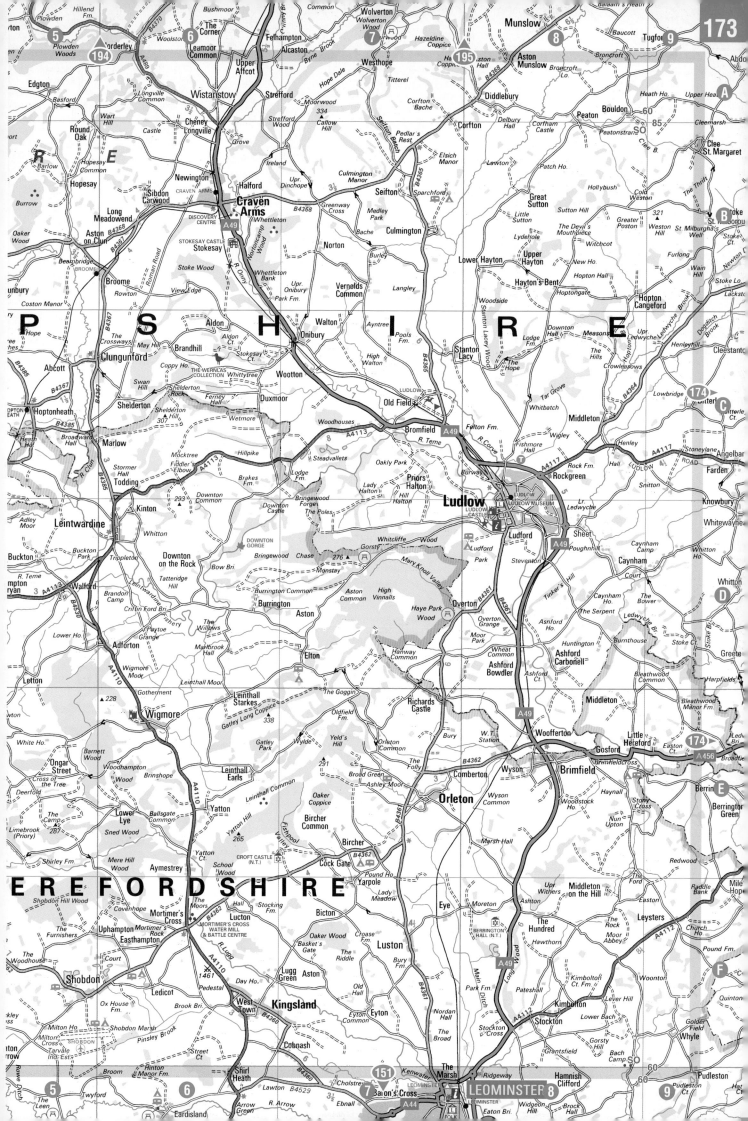

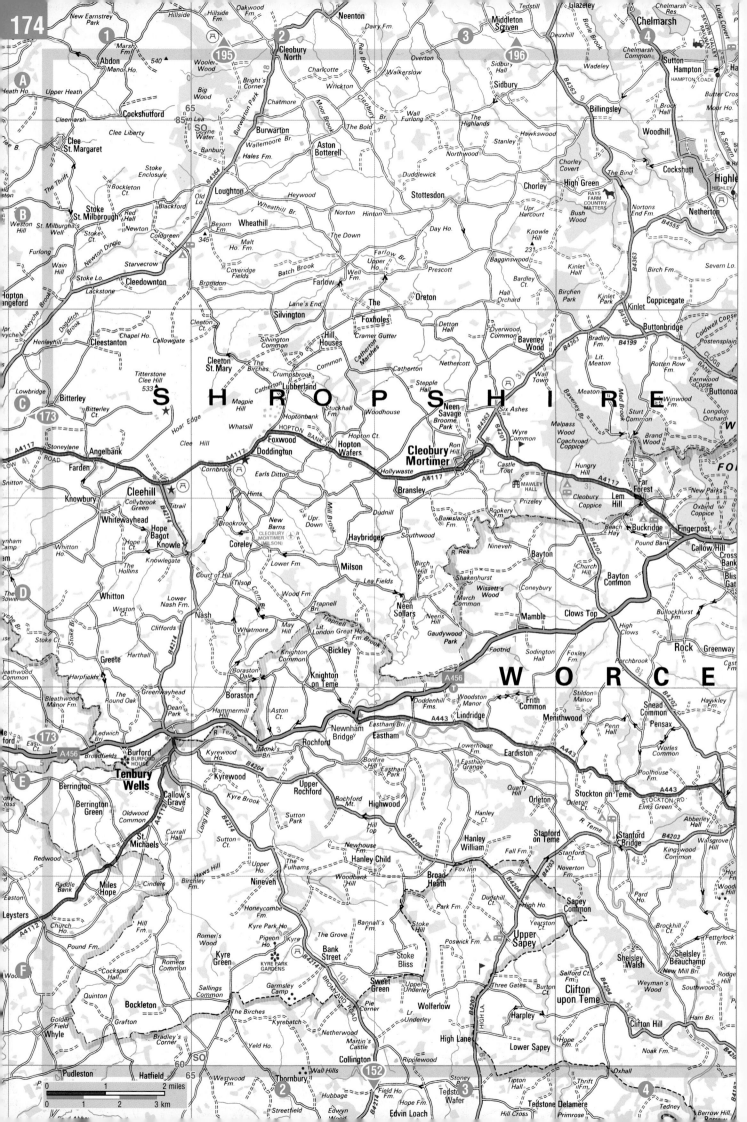

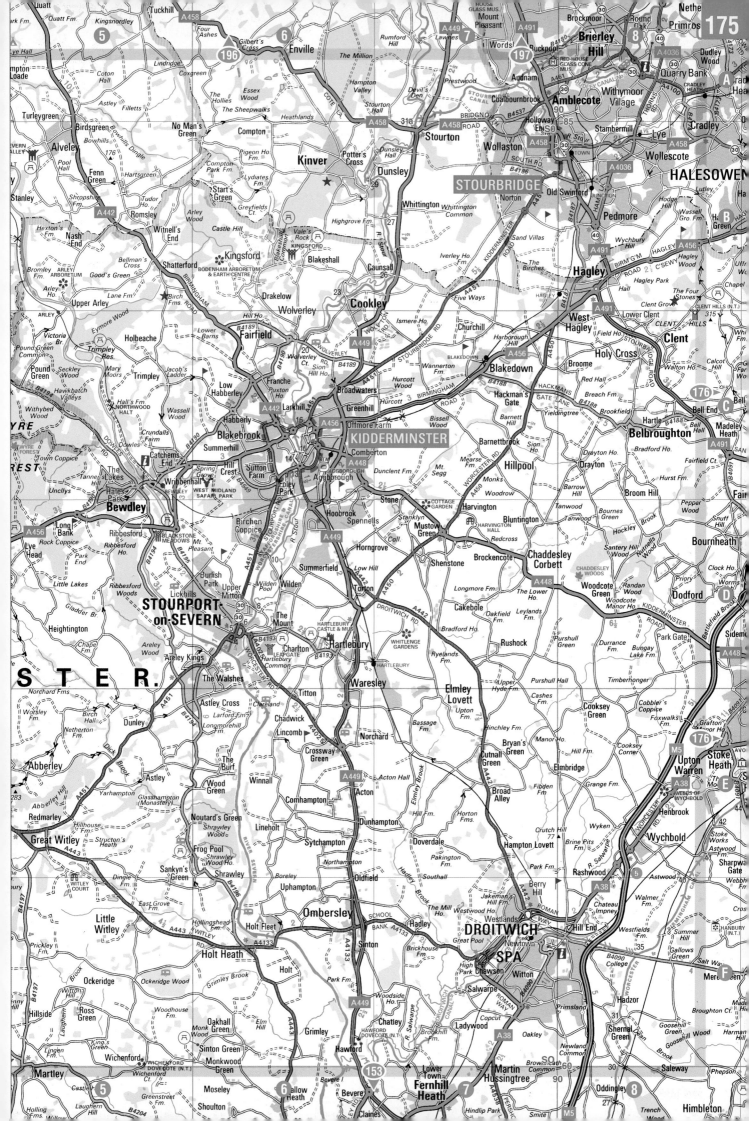

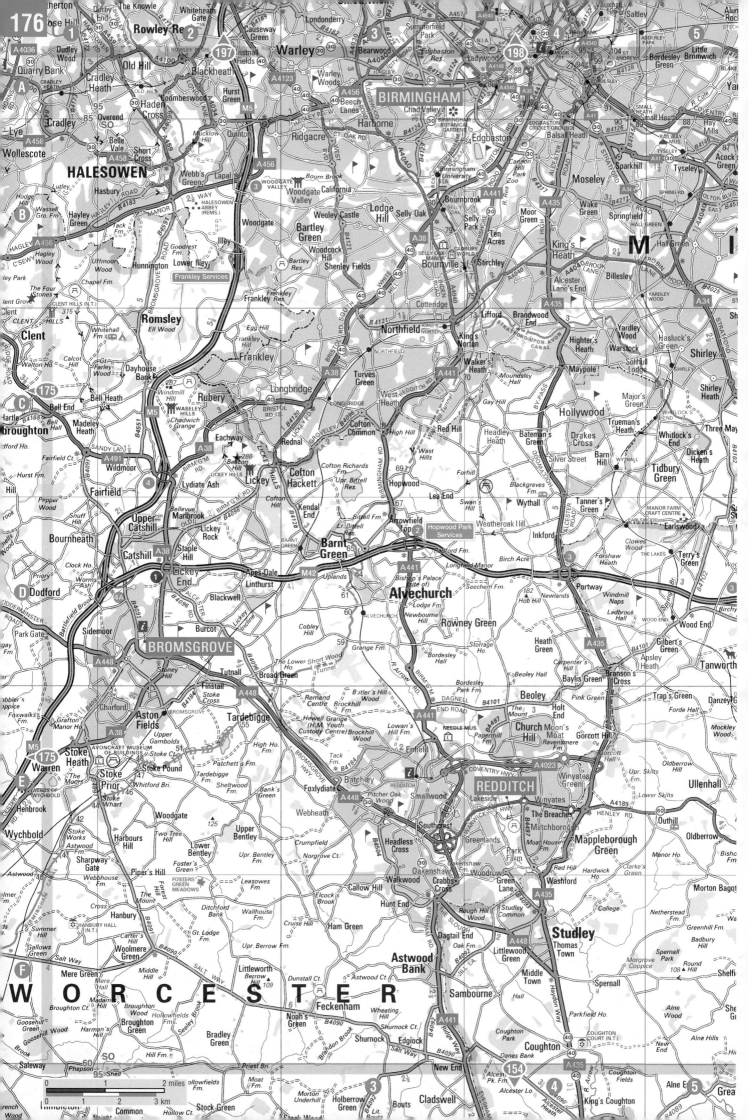

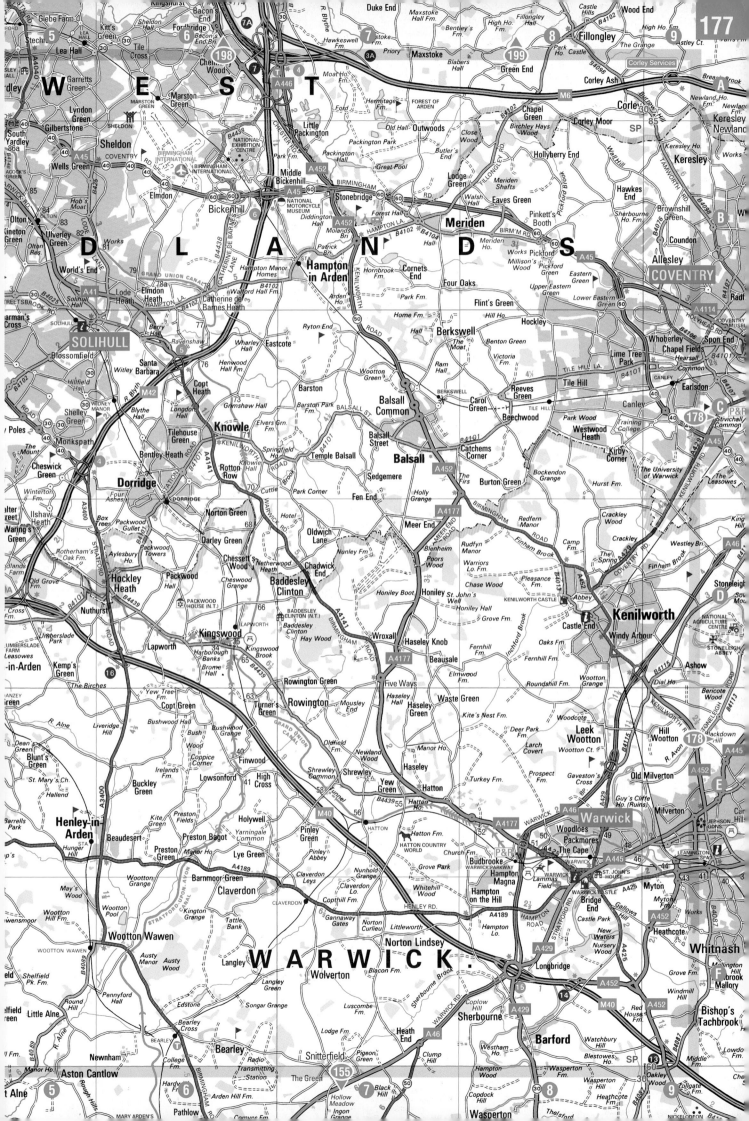

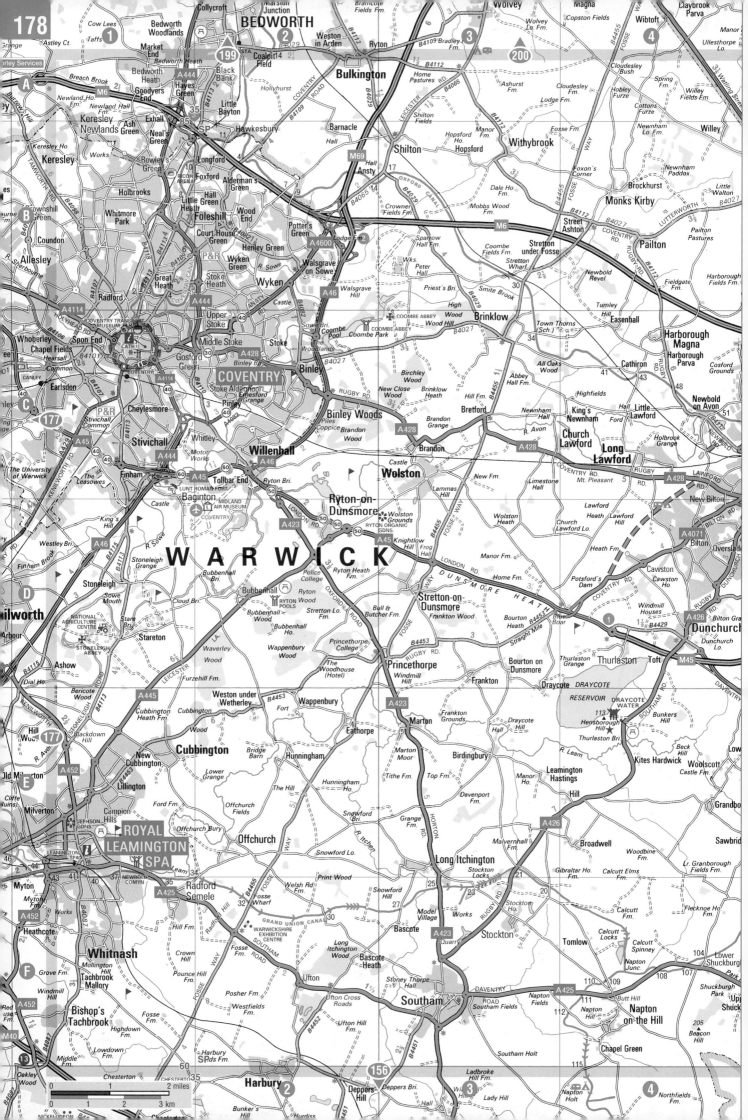

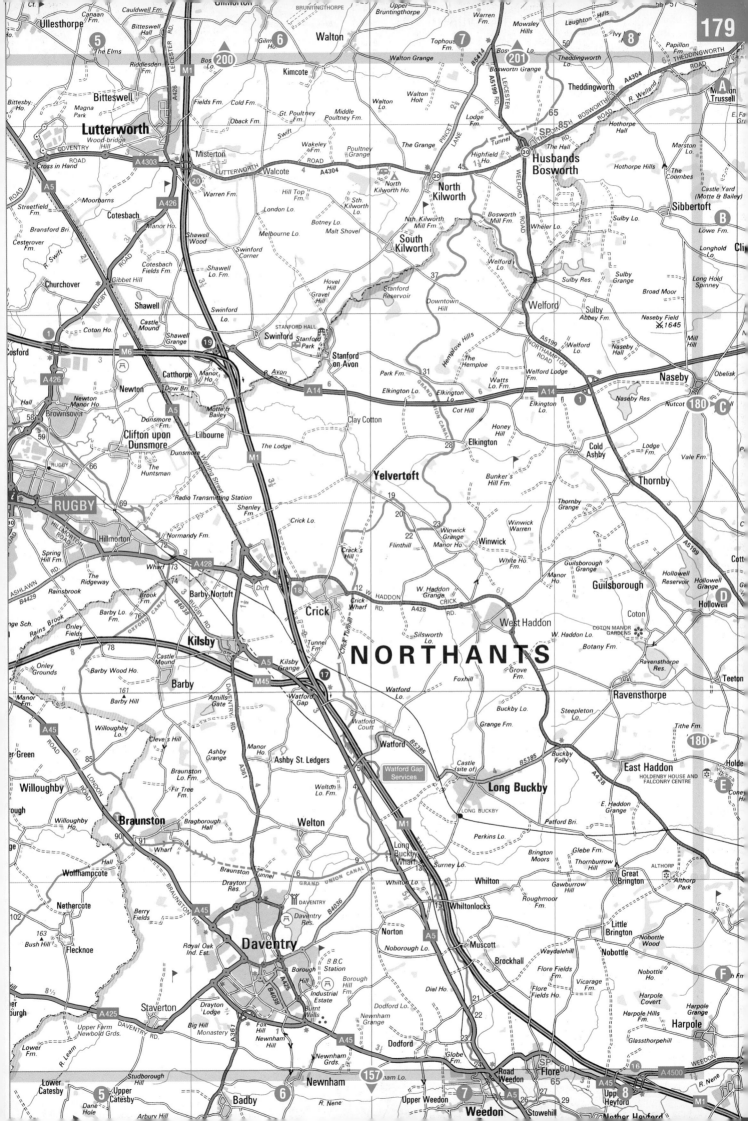

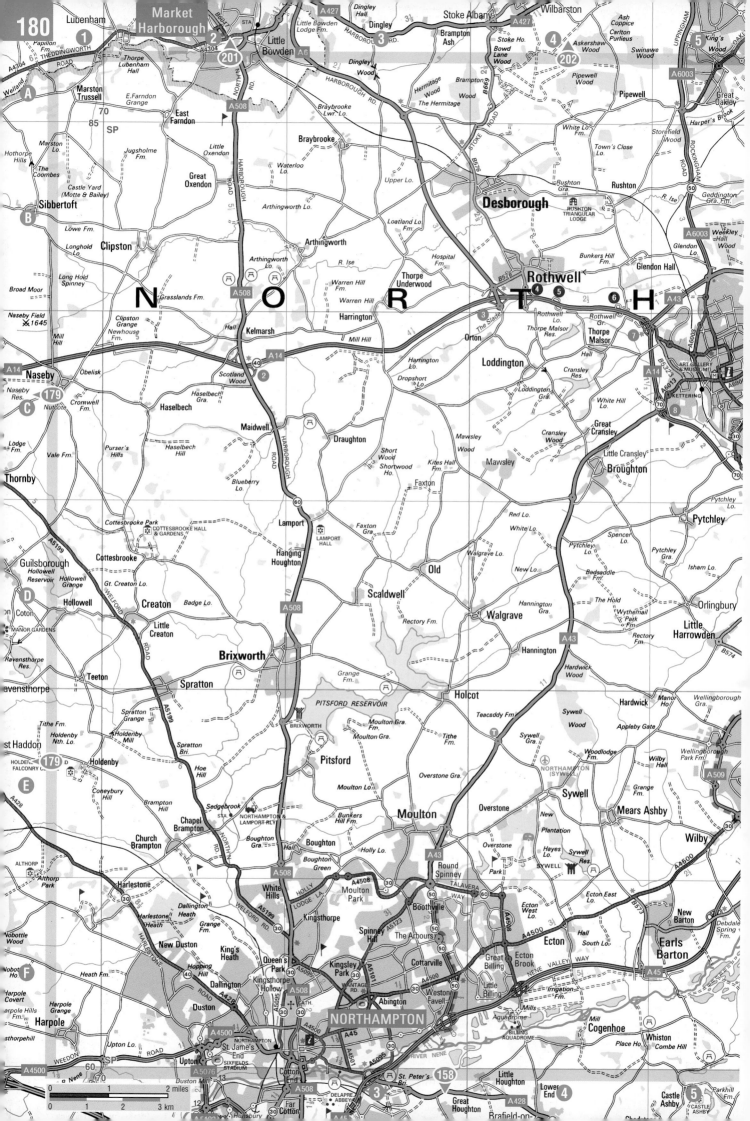

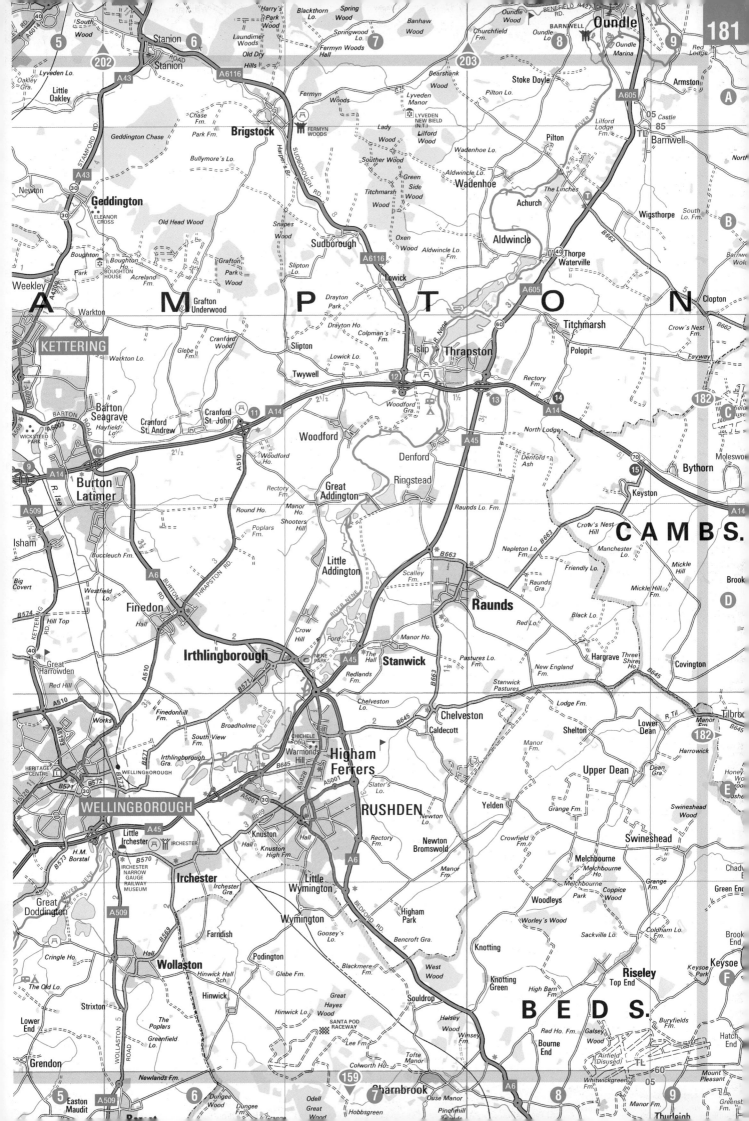

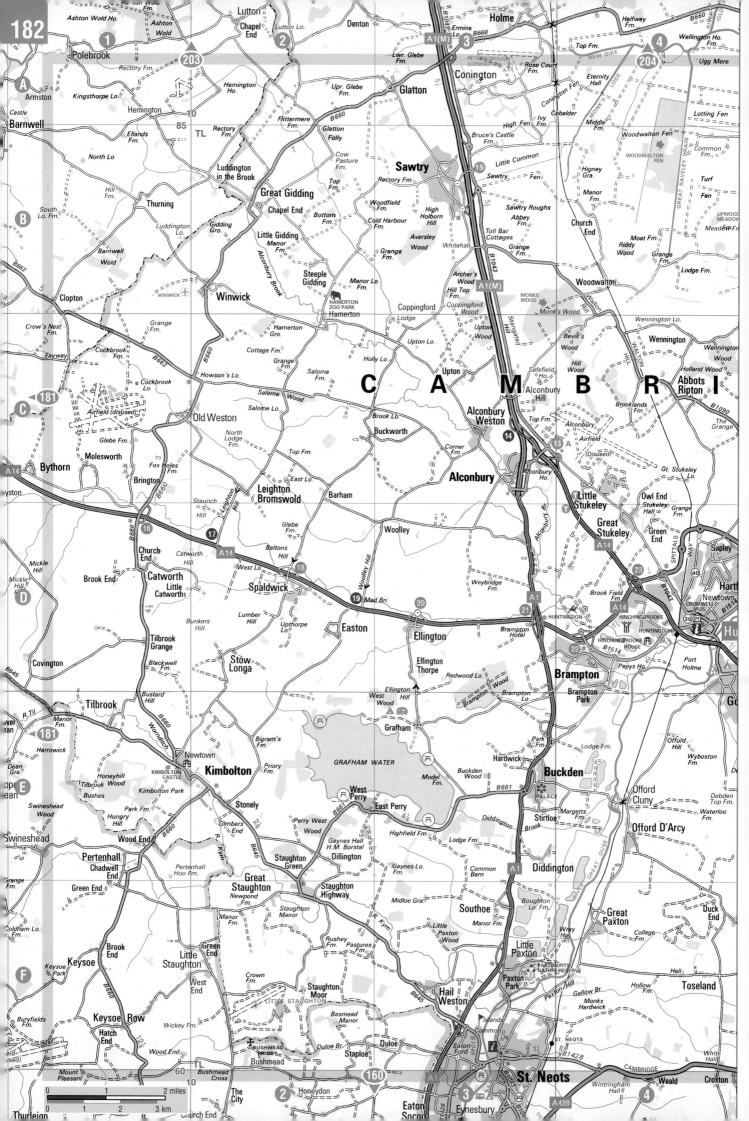

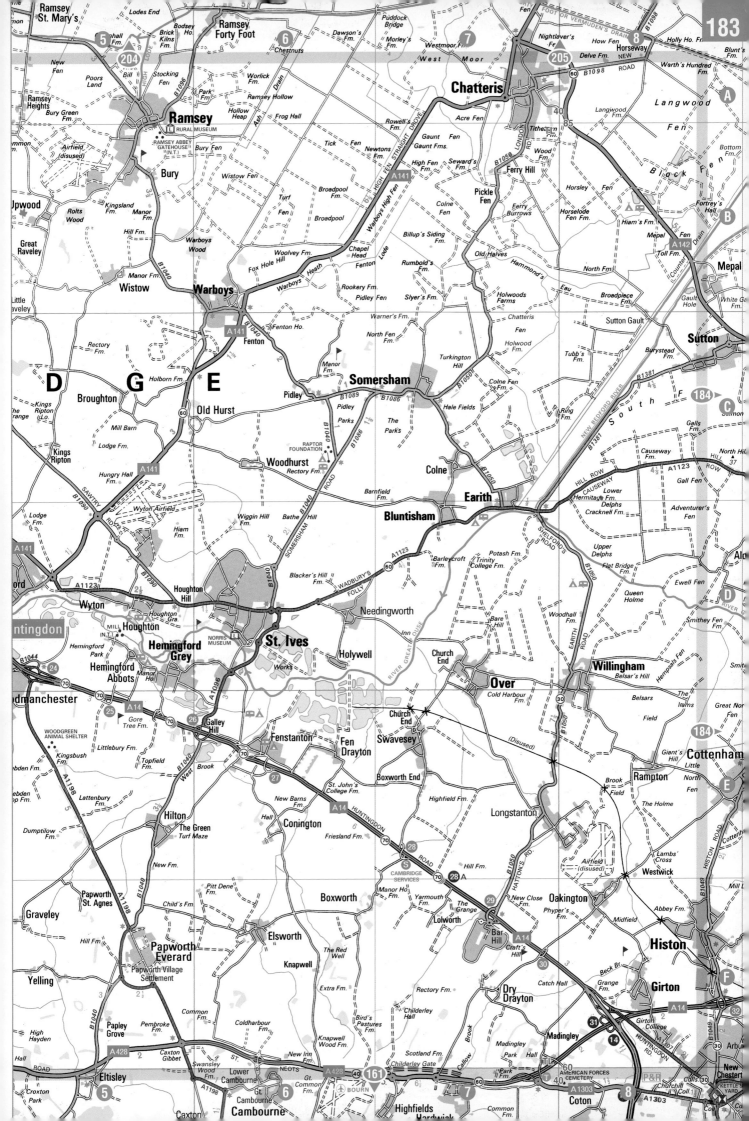

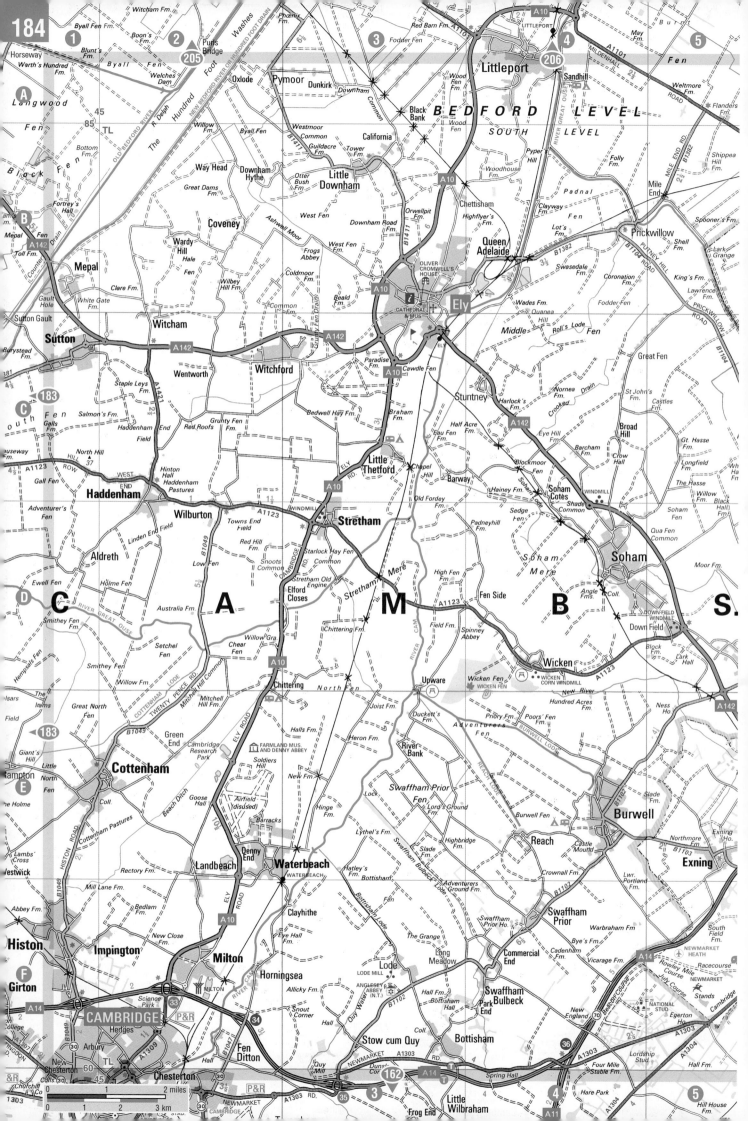

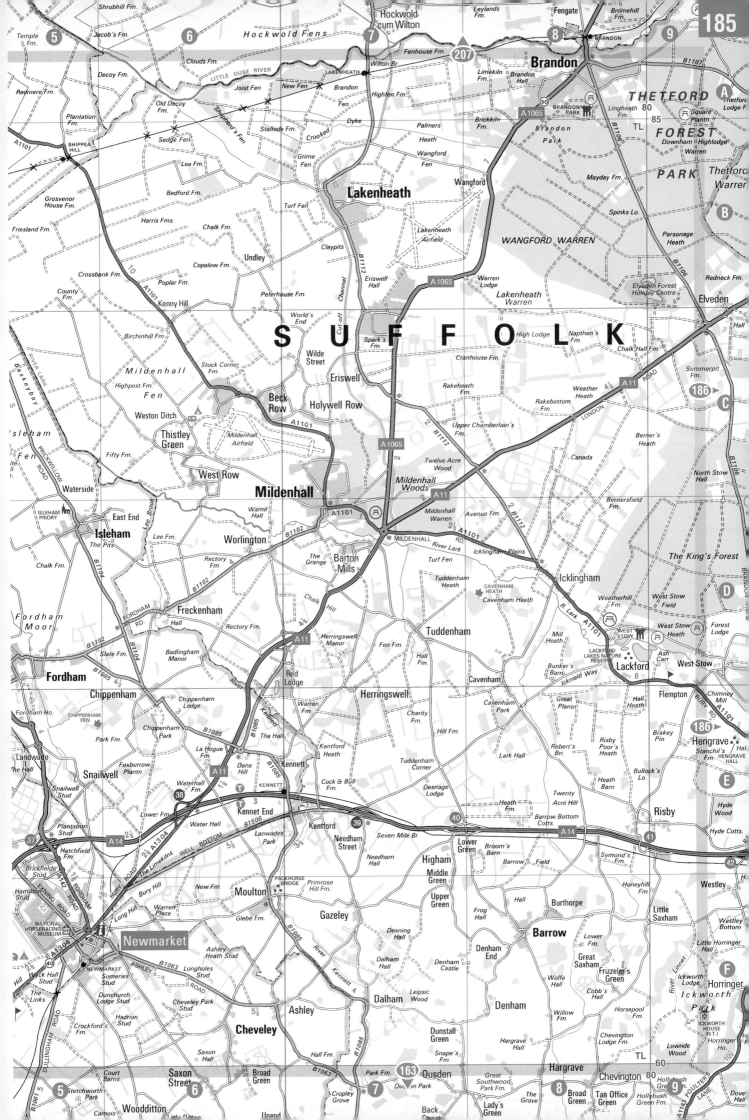

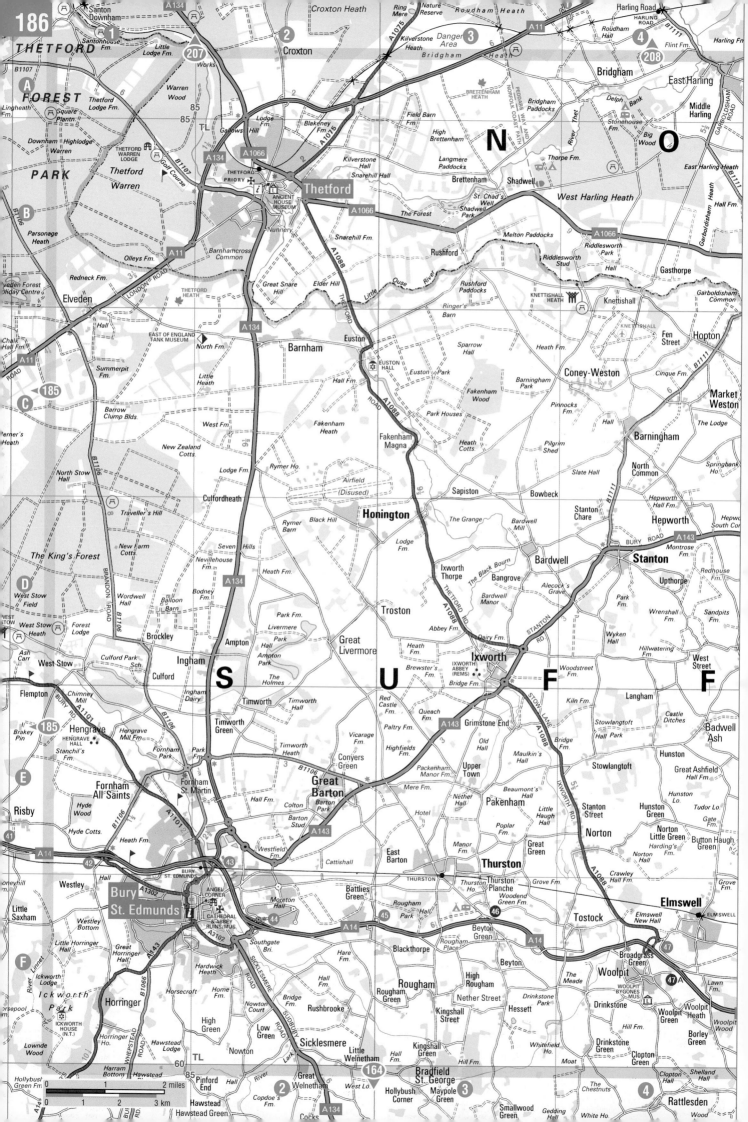

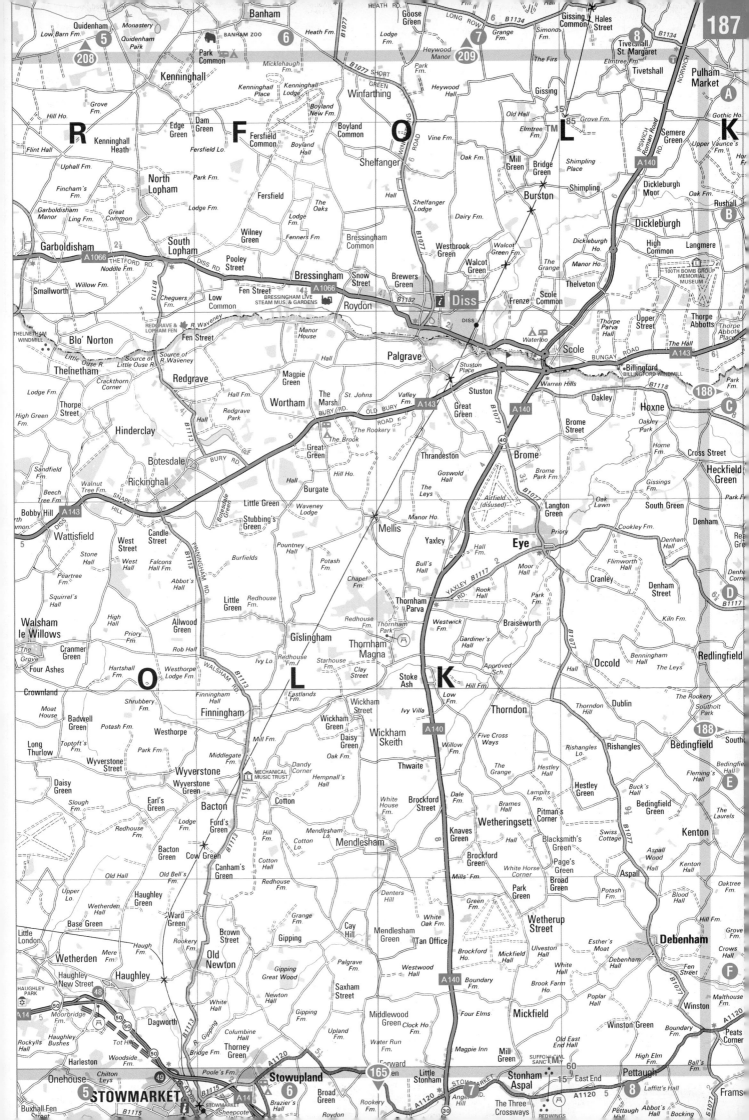

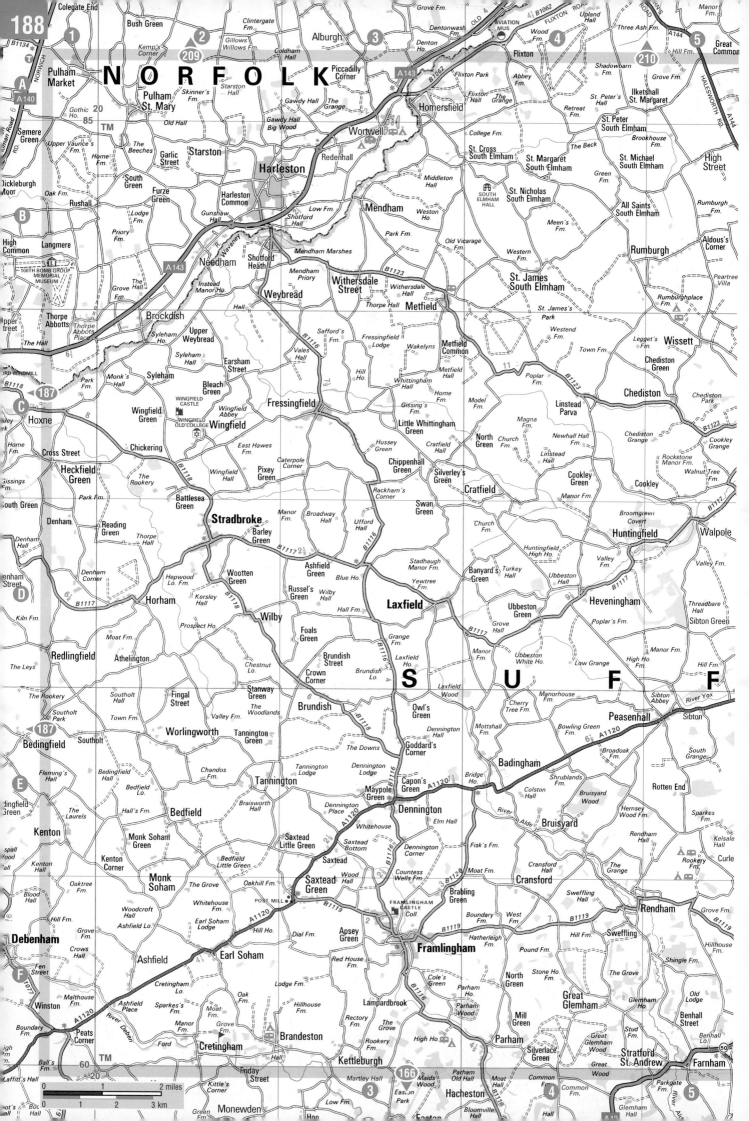

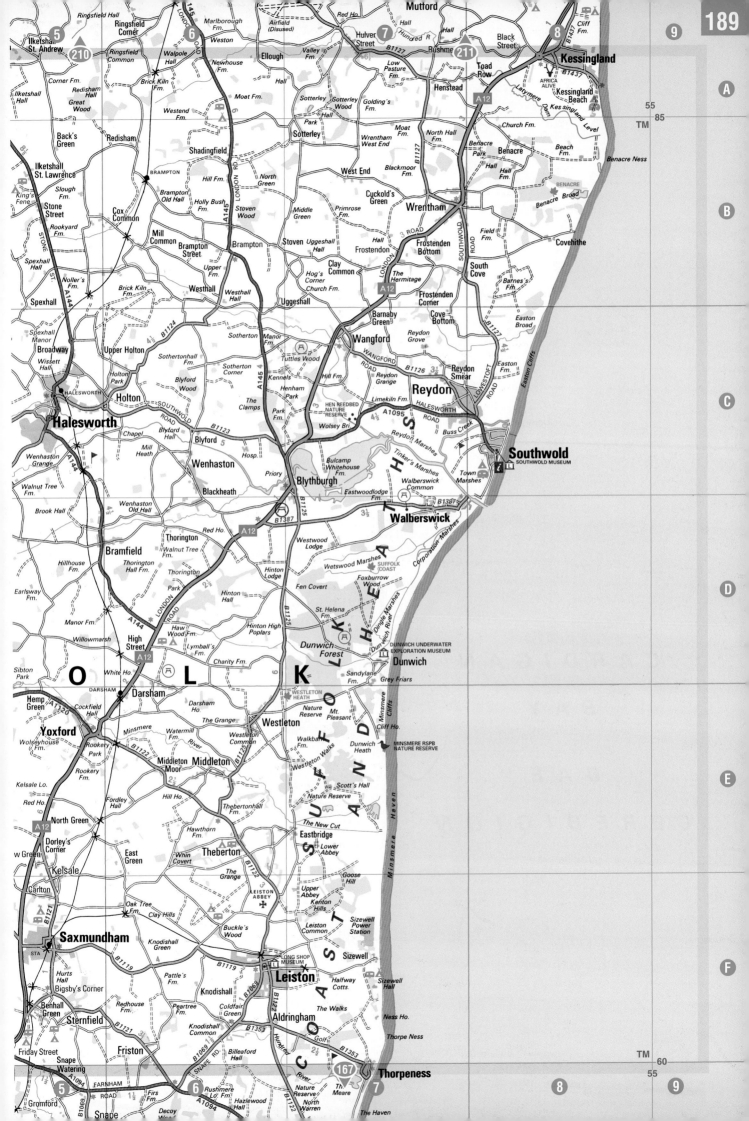

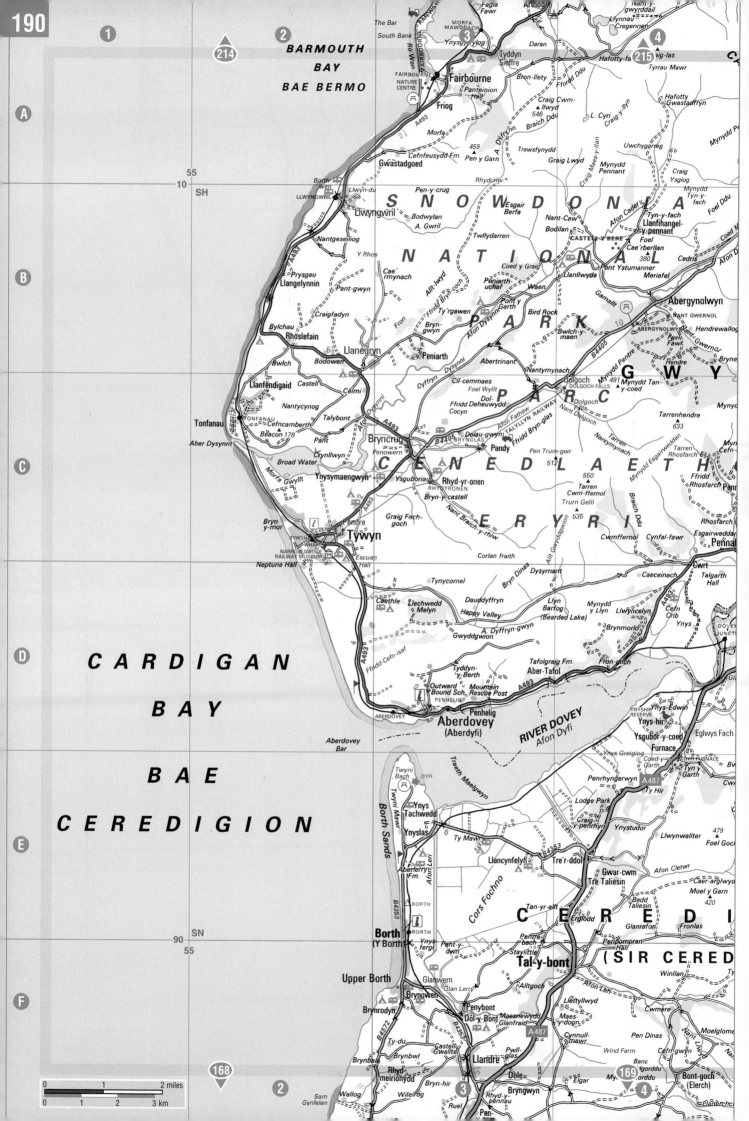

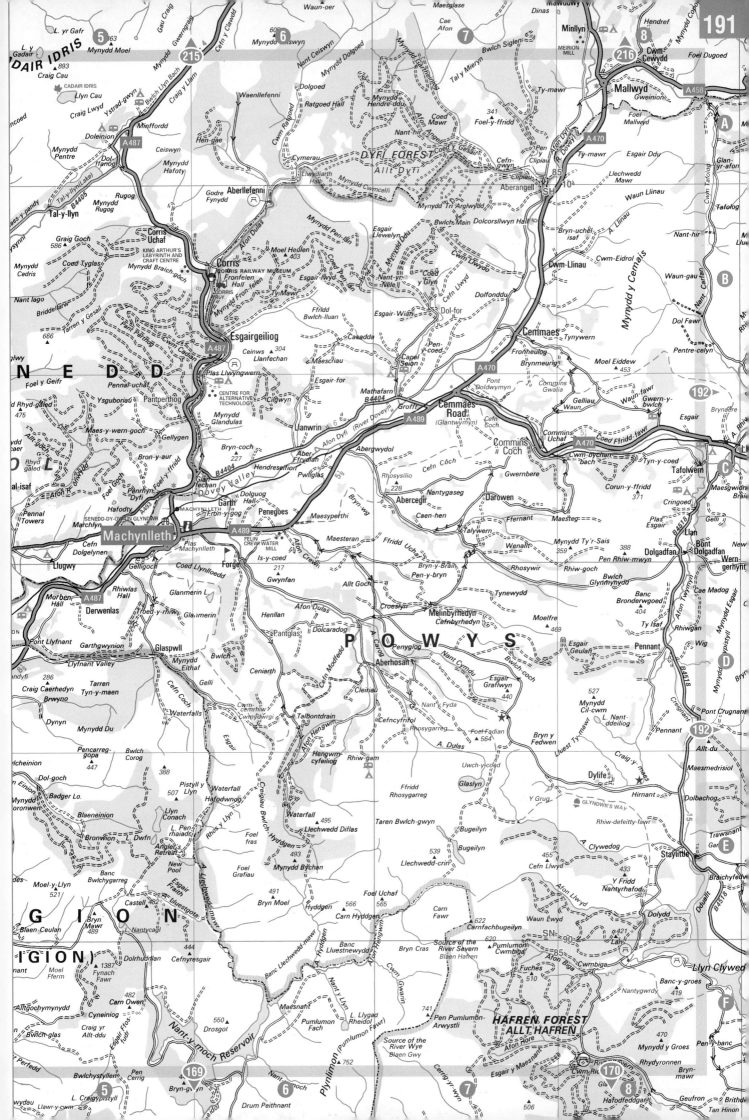

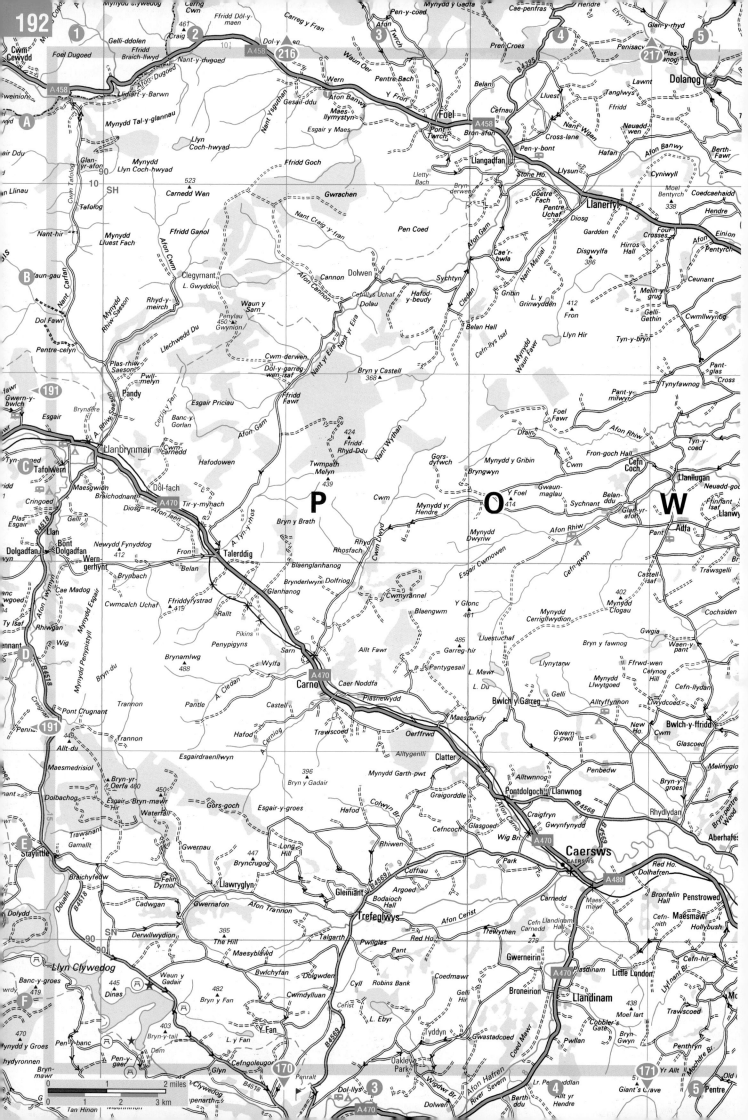

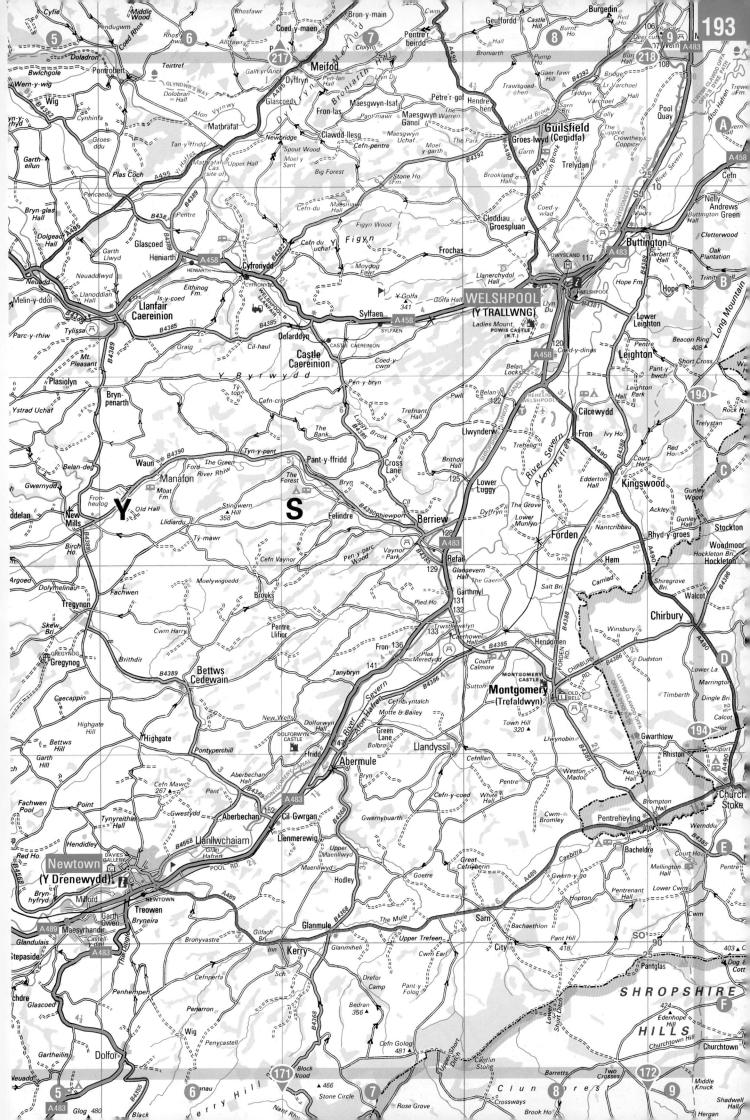

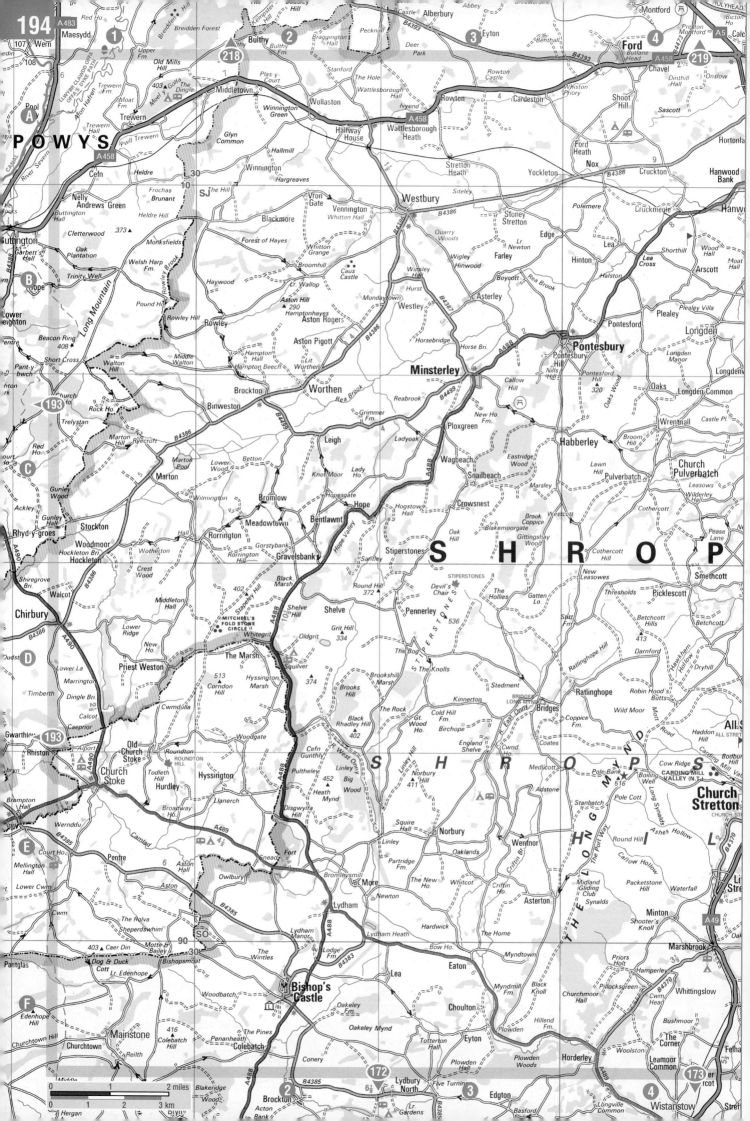

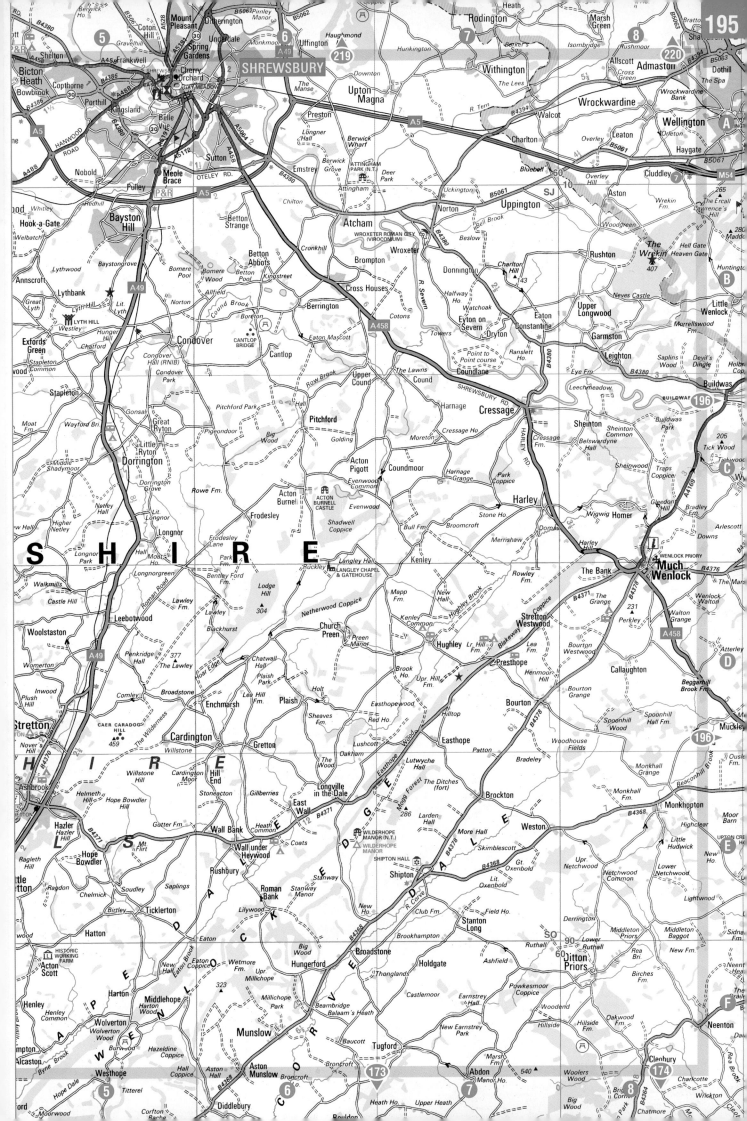

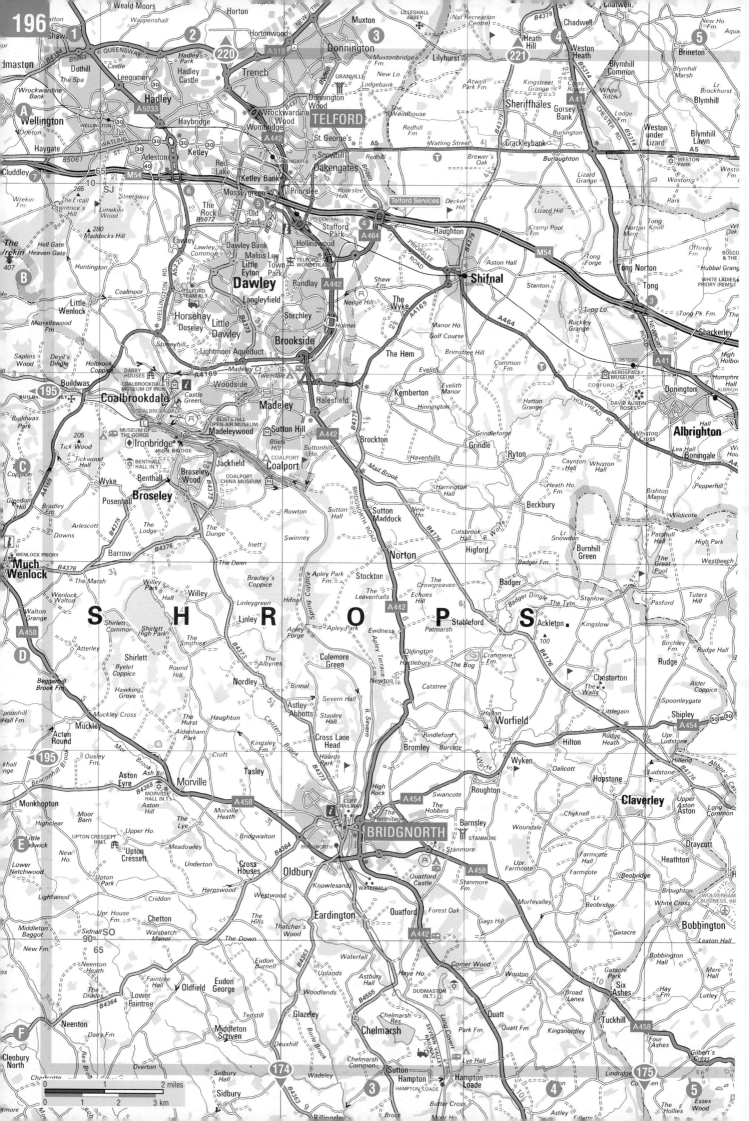

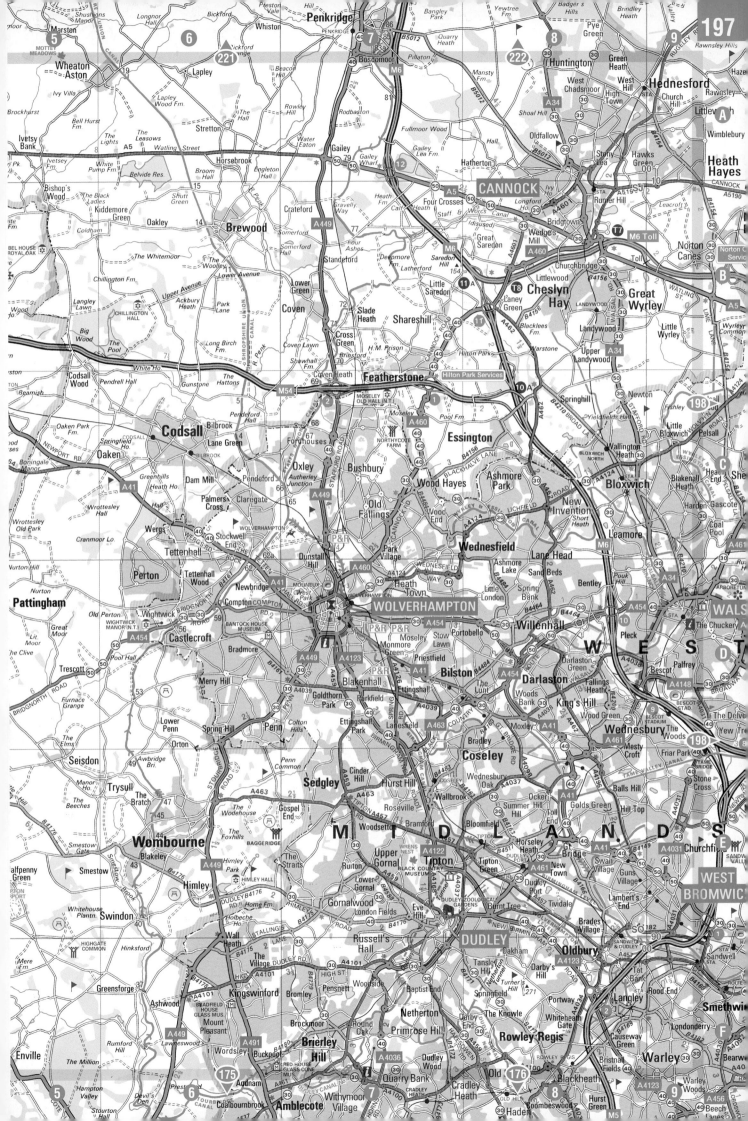

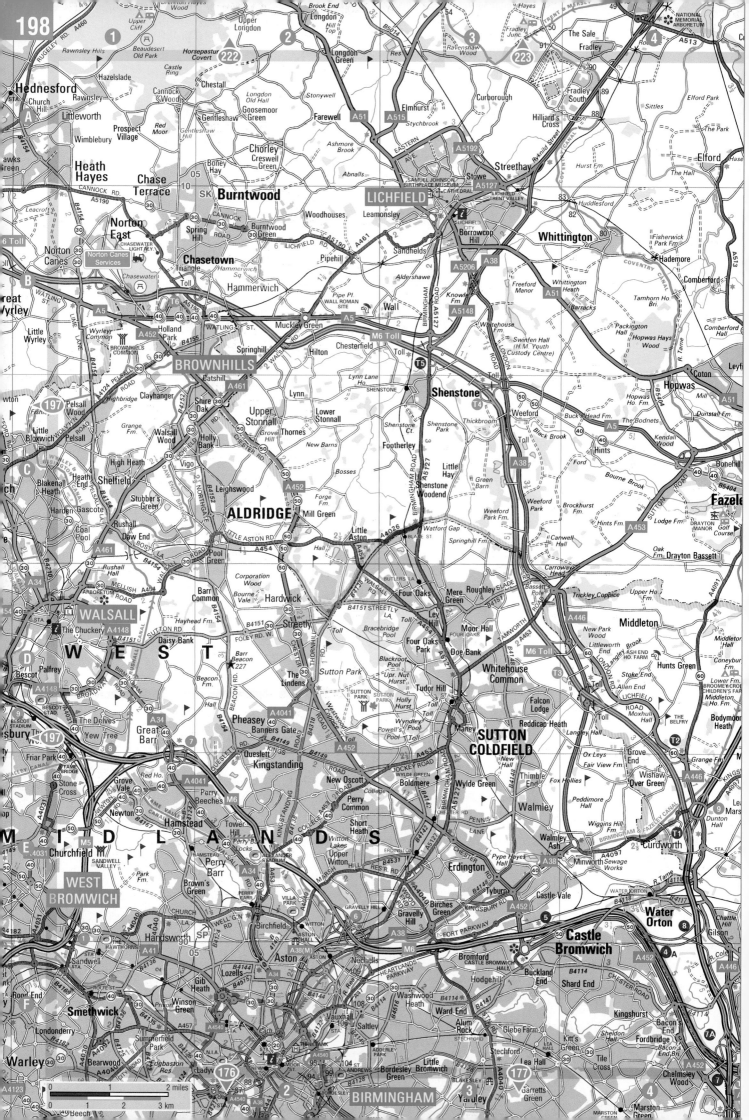

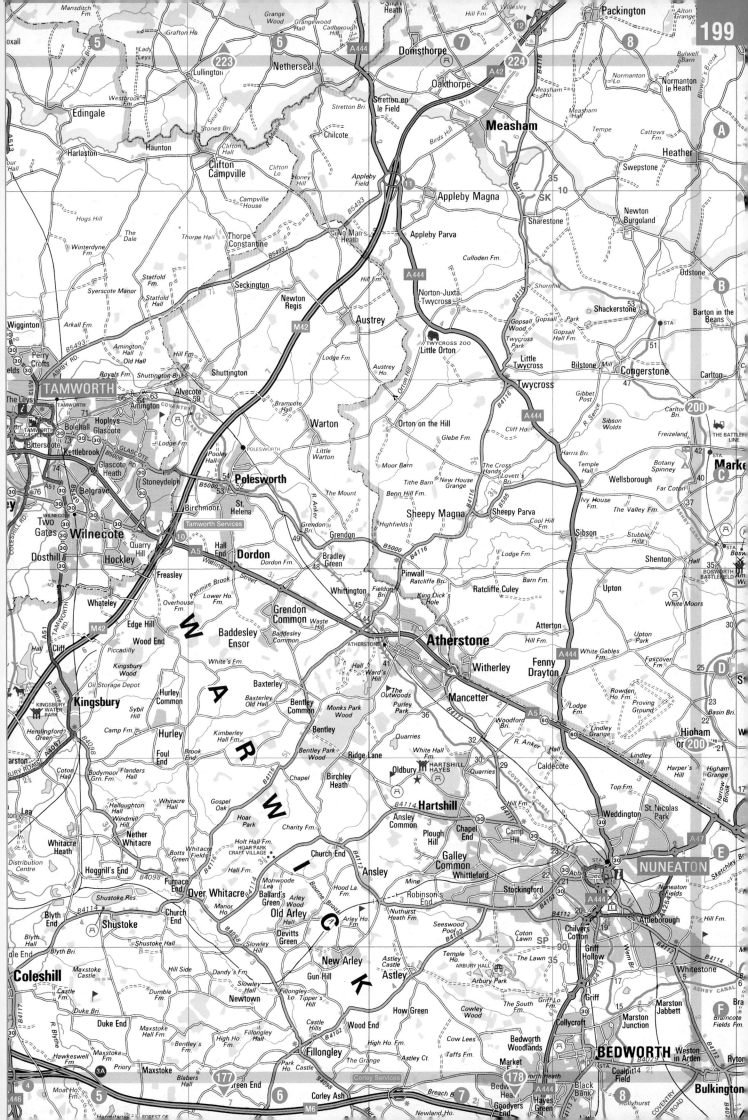

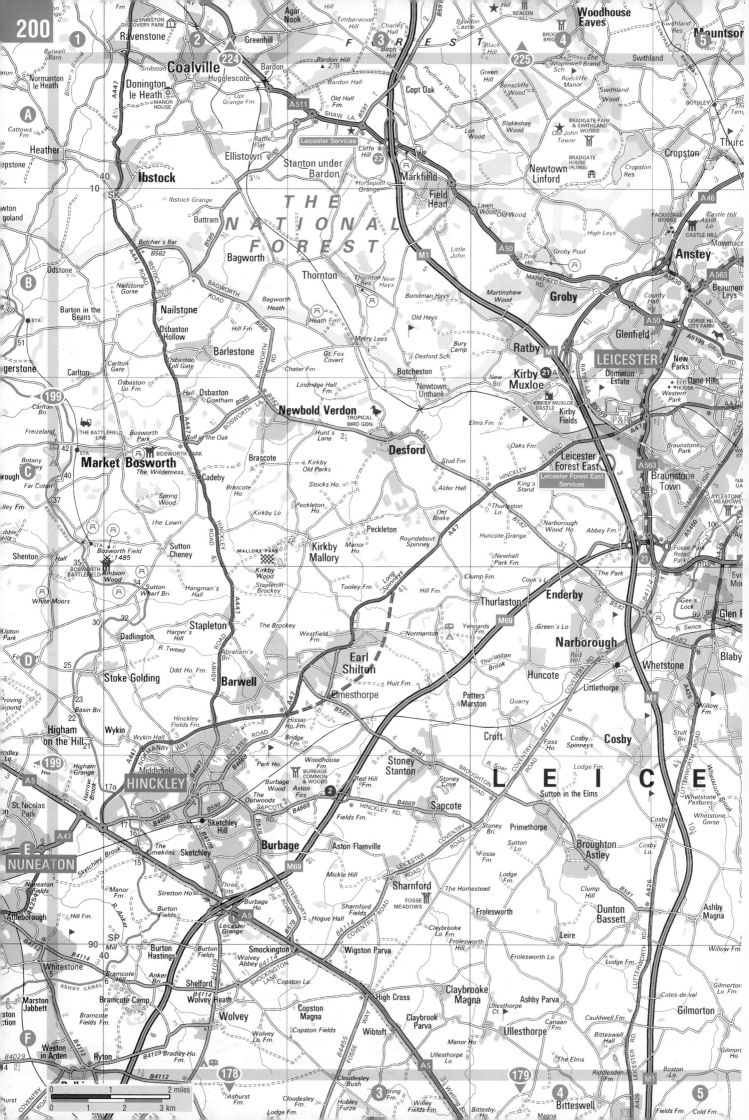

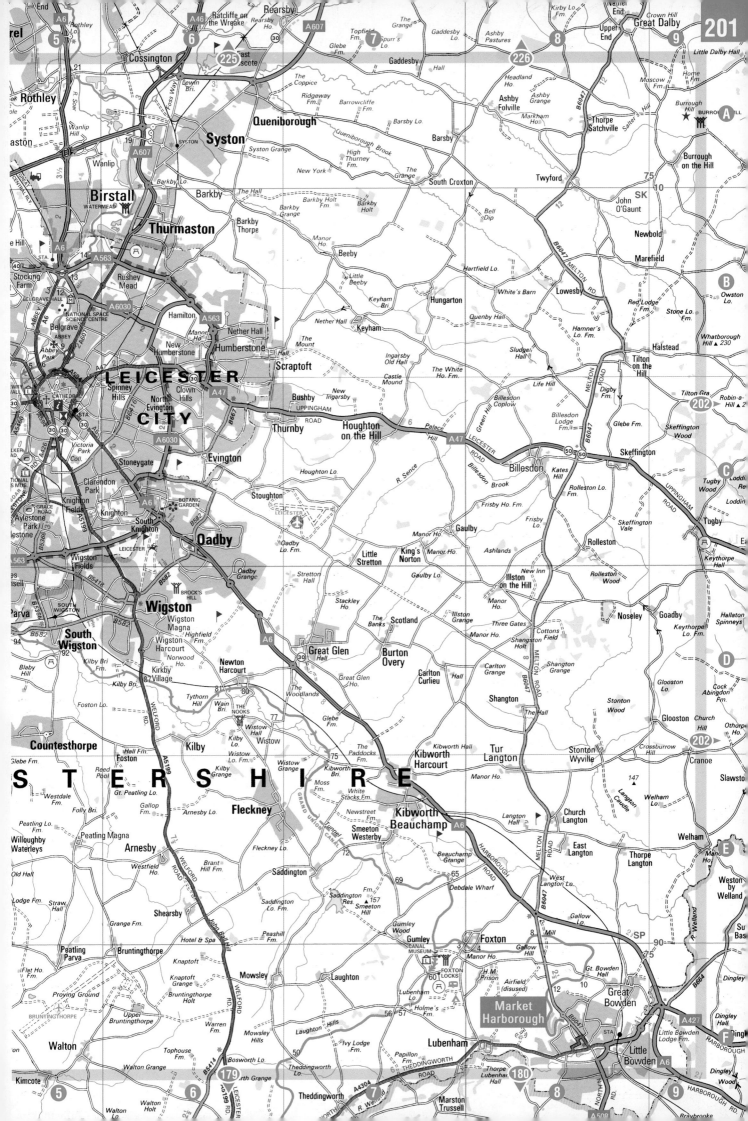

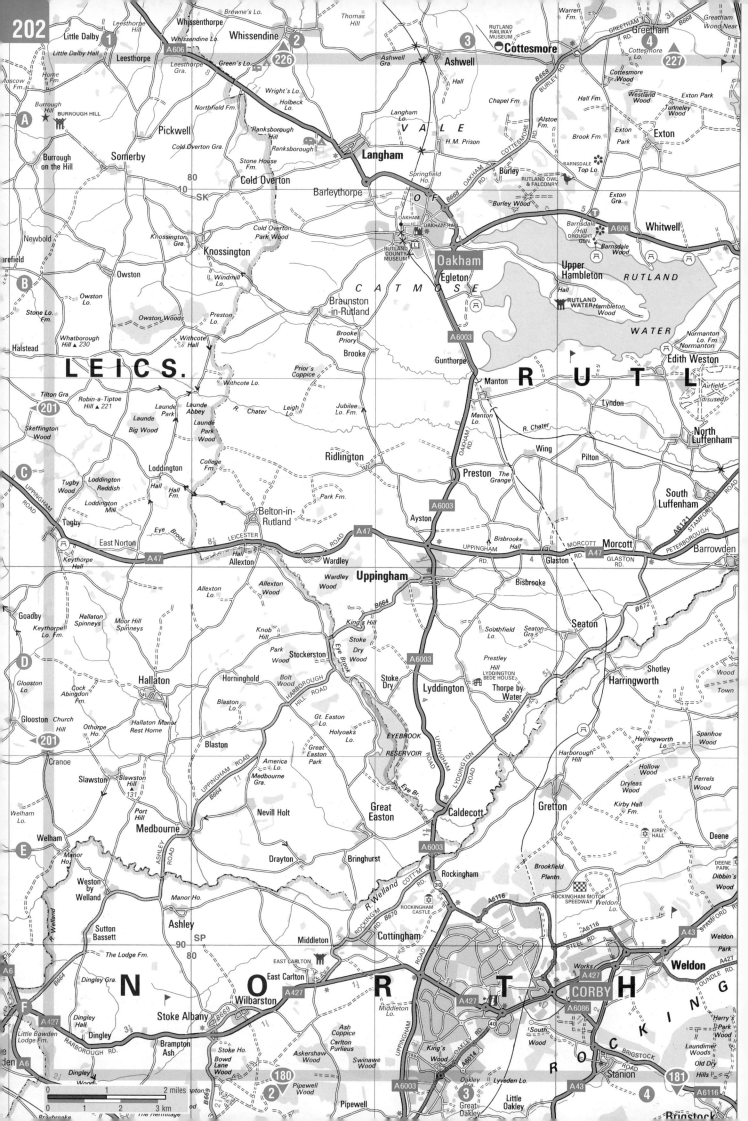

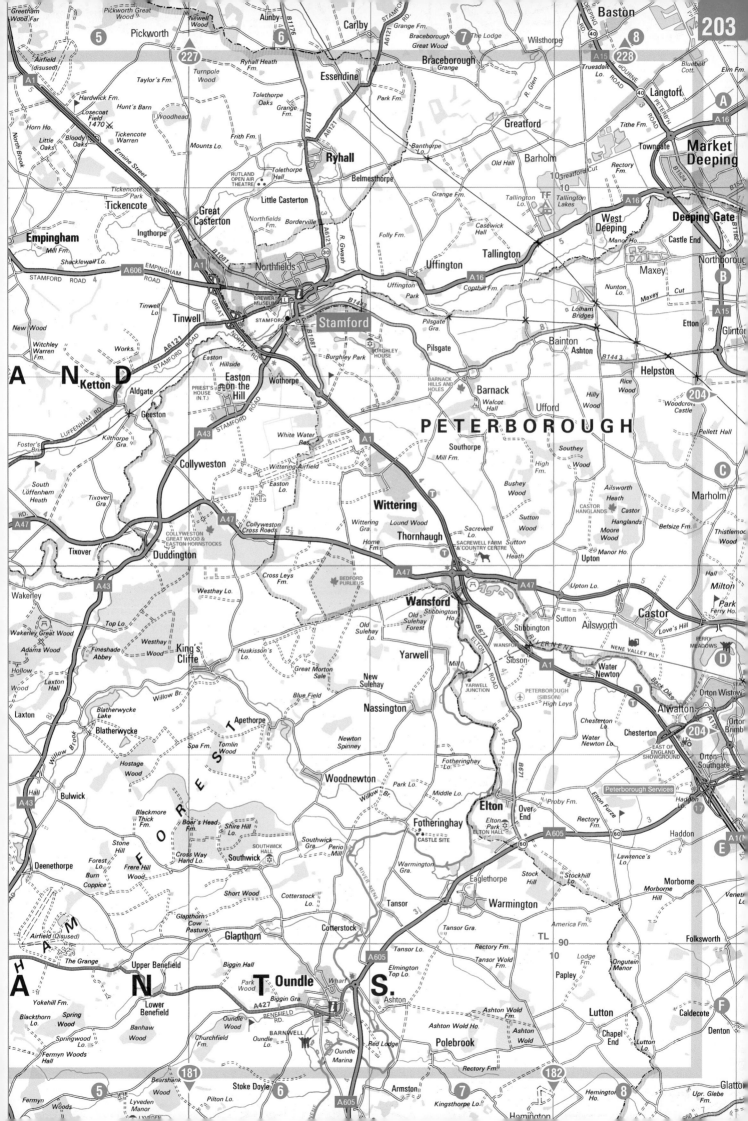

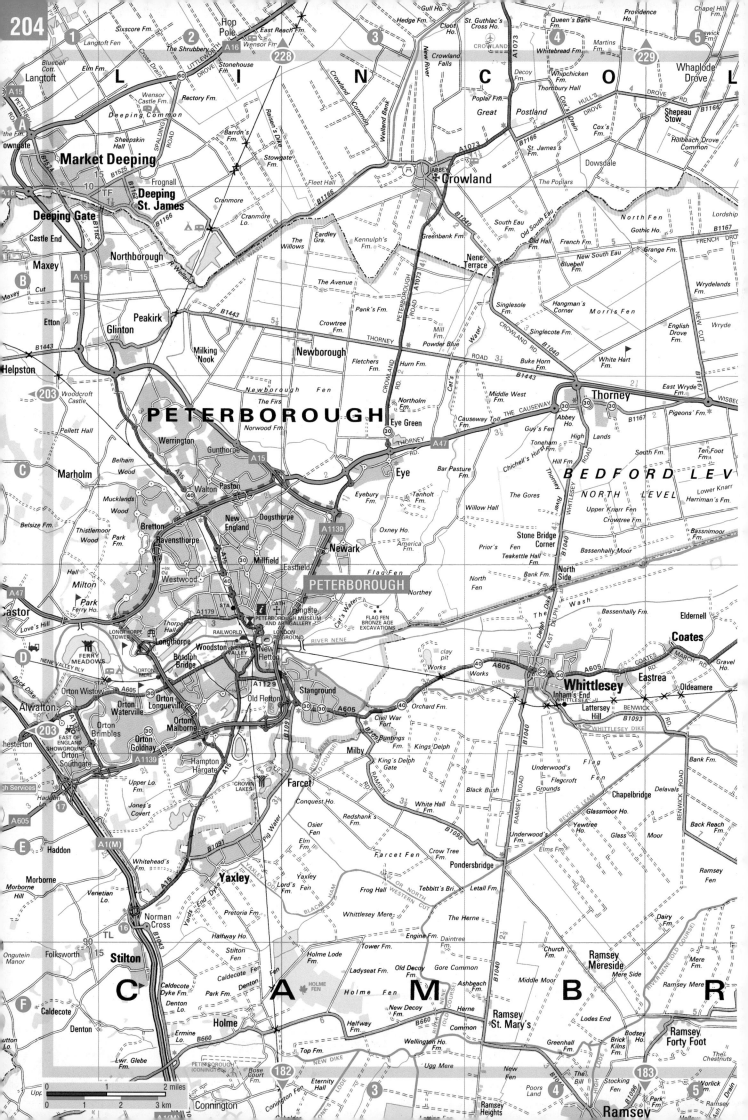

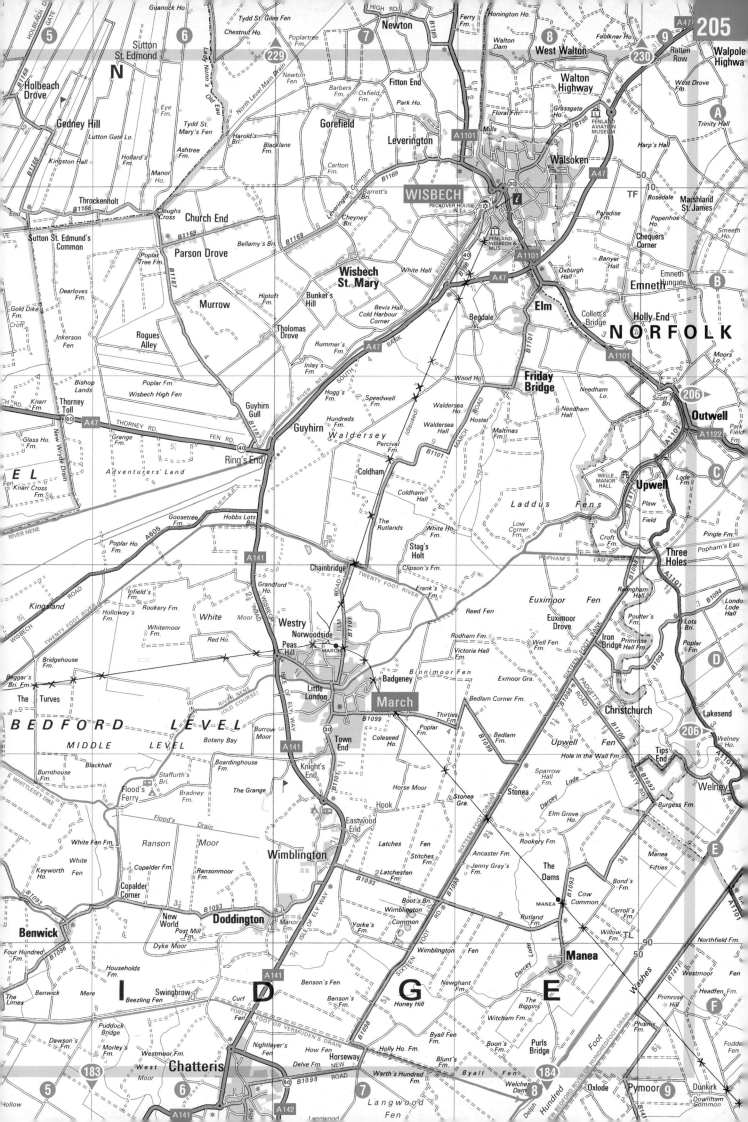

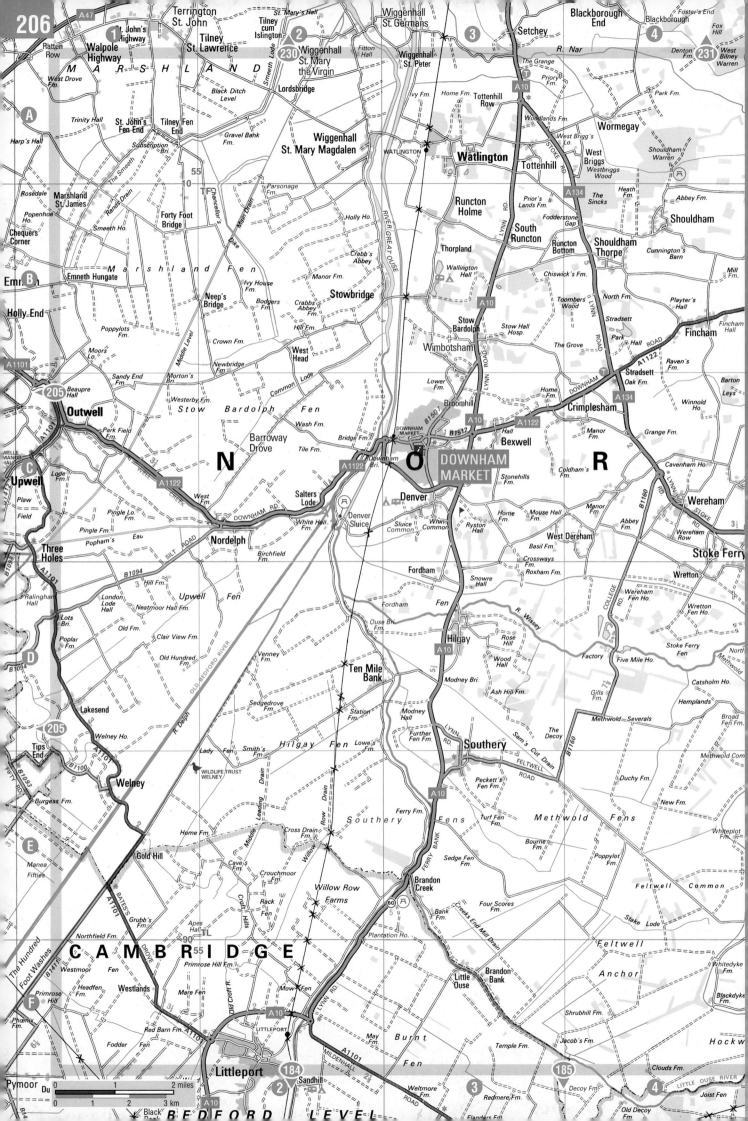

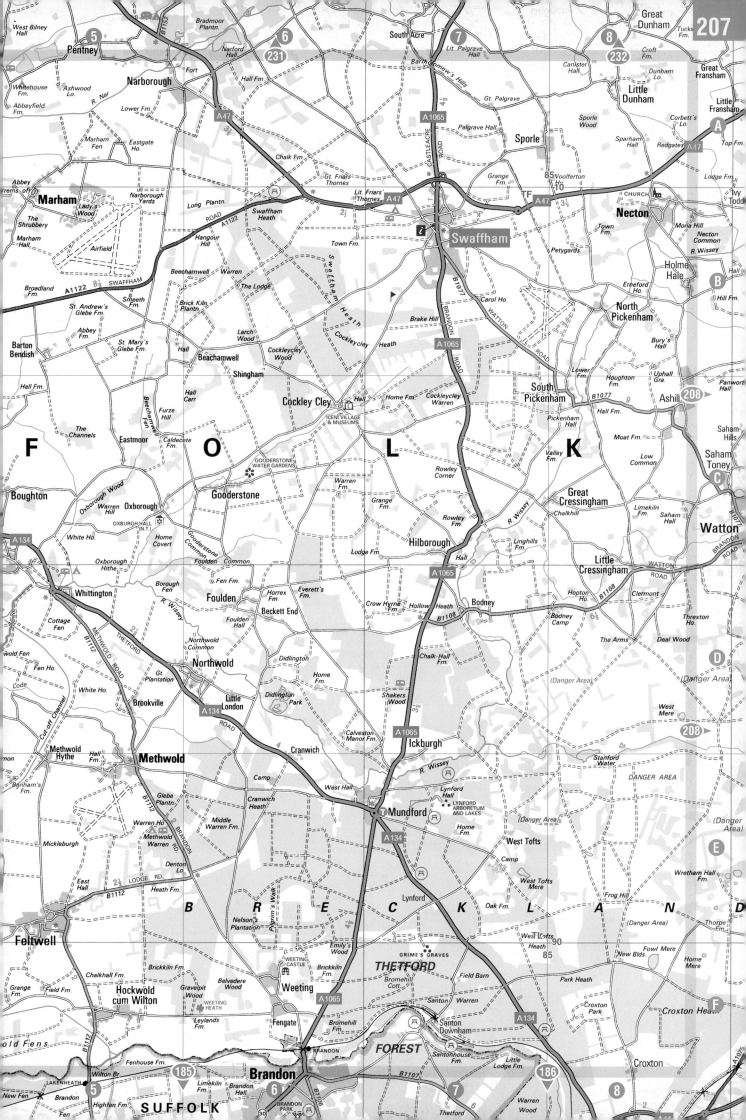

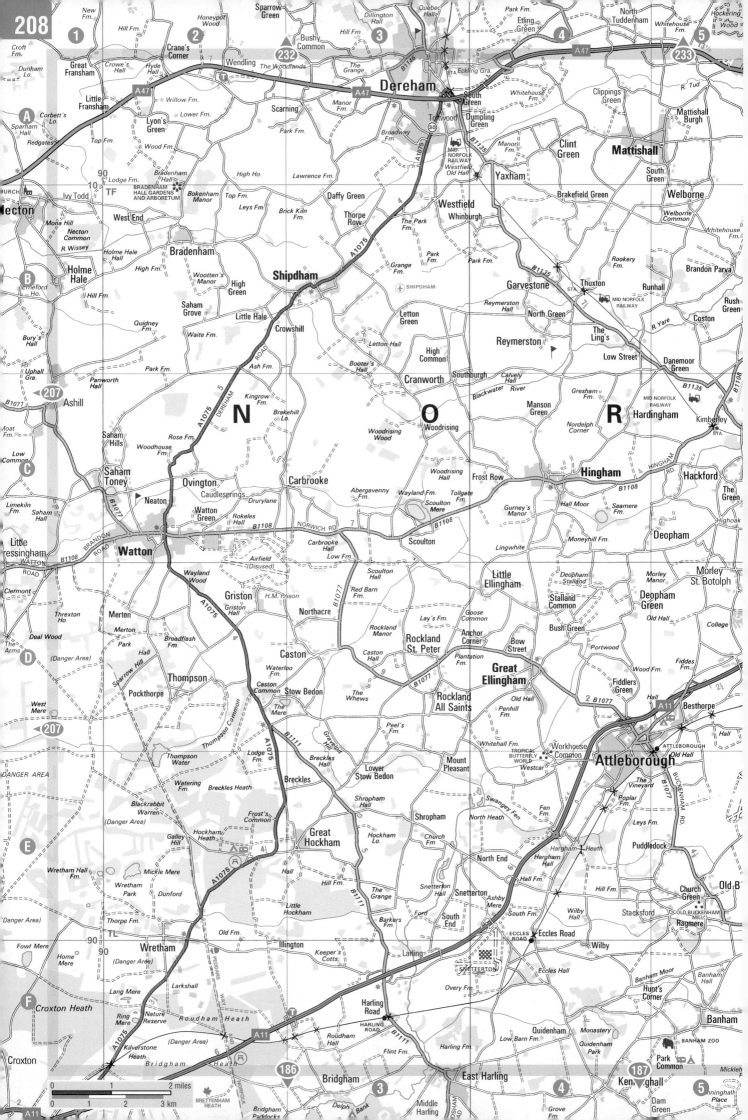

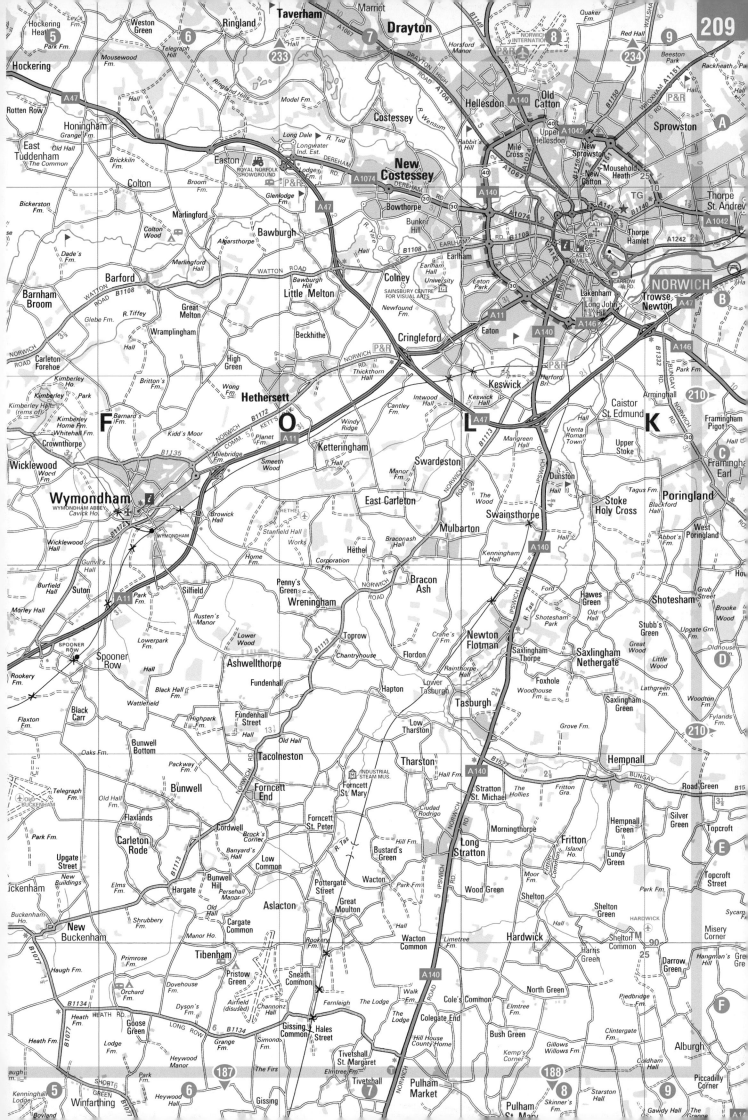

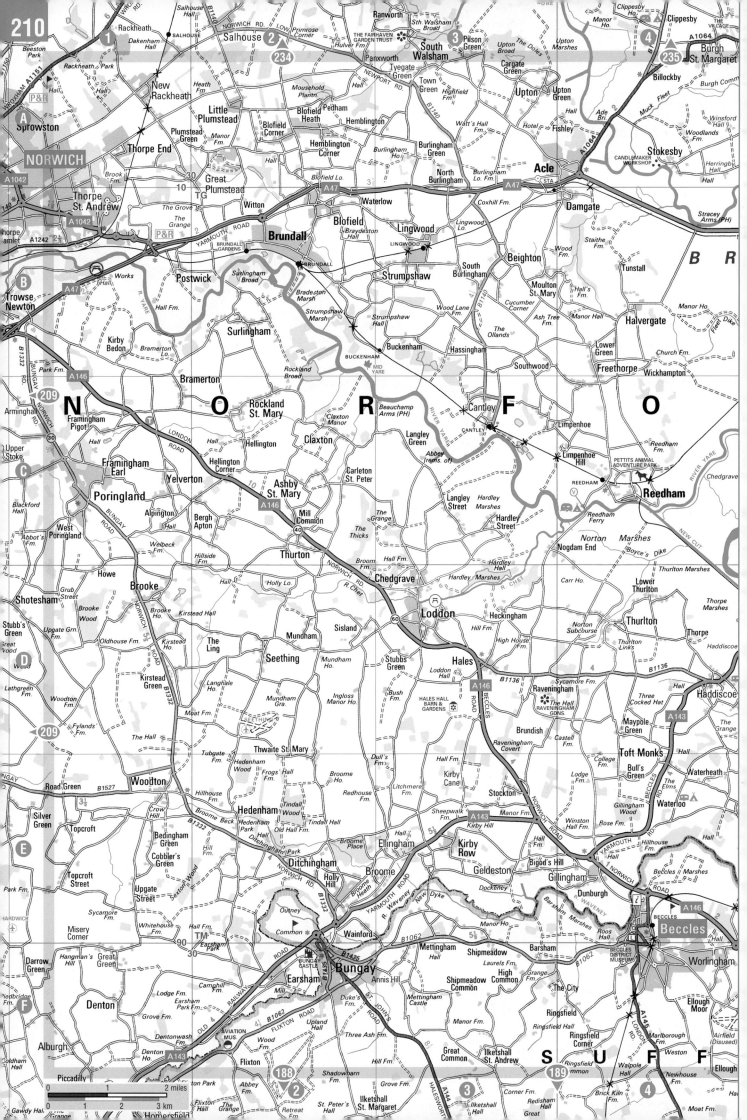

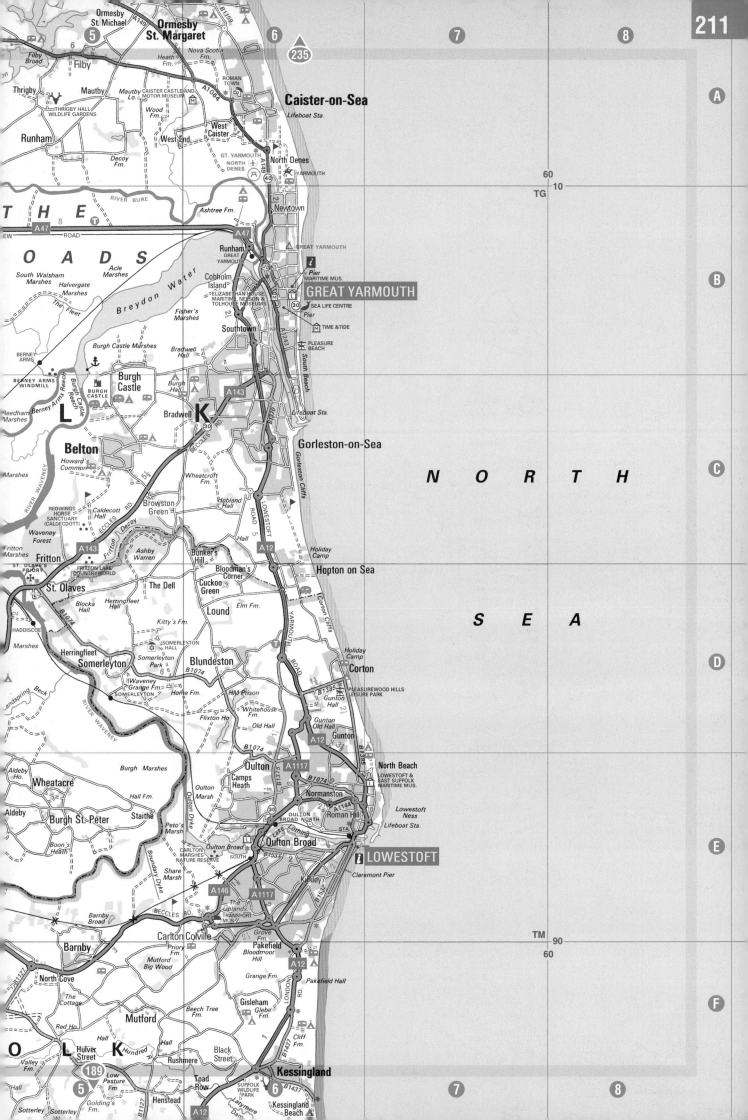

THE BROADS

Ormesby St. Michael
Ormesby St. Margaret
Filby
Filby Broad
Thrigby
Mautby
Mautby Lo.
THRIGBY HALL WILDLIFE GARDENS
Runham
Wood Fm.
Decoy Fm.
West End
West Caister
CAISTER CASTLE AND MOTOR MUSEUM
ROMAN TOWN
Heath Fm.
Nova Scotia Fm.
Caister-on-Sea
Lifeboat Sta.
GT. YARMOUTH NORTH DENES
North Denes
YARMOUTH
Newtown
RIVER BURE
Ashtree Fm.
NEW ROAD
Runham
GREAT YARMOUTH
Acle Marshes
South Walsham Marshes
Halvergate Marshes
The Fleet
Breydon Water
Fisher's Marshes
Cobholm Island
ELIZABETHAN HOUSE, MARITIME, NELSON & TOLHOUSE MUSEUMS
Pier MARITIME MUS.
GREAT YARMOUTH
SEA LIFE CENTRE
Pier
TIME & TIDE
Southtown
PLEASURE BEACH
South Beach
Berney Arms
BERNEY ARMS WINDMILL
Burgh Castle Marshes
Bradwell Hall
Burgh Hall
Burgh Castle
Burgh Castle
BECCLES RD.
Bradwell
Gorleston-on-Sea
Reedham Marshes
Belton
Howard's Common
Wheatcroft Fm.
Hobland Hall
Gorleston Cliffs
NORTH
Marshes
REDWINGS HORSE SANCTUARY (CALDECOTT)
Caldecott Hall
Browston Green
ECCLES RD.
Fritton Decoy
LOWESTOFT ROAD
Waveney Forest
Fritton Marshes
Fritton
FRITTON LAKE COUNTRYWORLD
Ashby Warren
Bunker's Hill
Bloodman's Corner
Holiday Camp
Hopton on Sea
ST. OLAVES PRIORY
St. Olaves
The Dell
Cuckoo Green
Lound
Elm Fm.
HADDISCOE
Blocka Hall
Herringfleet Hall
Kitty's Fm.
Corton Cliffs
SEA
RIVER WAVENEY
Marshes
Herringfleet
Somerleyton
SOMERLEYTON HALL
Somerleyton Park
Blundeston
Holiday Camp
Corton
Landspring Beck
Waveney Grange Fm.
SOMERLEYTON
Home Fm.
HM Prison
Whitehouse Fm.
Flixton Ho.
Old Hall
Gunton Hall
PLEASUREWOOD HILLS LEISURE PARK
Gunton Old Hall
Gunton
Burgh Marshes
Oulton
North Beach
LOWESTOFT & EAST SUFFOLK MARITIME MUS.
Aldeby Ho.
Wheatacre
Camps Heath
Normanston
Aldeby
Hall Fm.
Oulton Marsh
Roman Hill
Lowestoft Ness
Burgh St. Peter
Staithe
Oulton Dyke
OULTON BROAD NORTH
Lifeboat Sta.
Peto's Marsh
CARLTON MARSHES NATURE RESERVE
Oulton Broad SOUTH
Oulton Broad
Lake Lothing
LOWESTOFT
Boon's Heath
Share Marsh
Kirkley
Claremont Pier
Boundary Dyke
THE UPLANDS TRANSPORT MUS.
BECCLES RD.
Barnby Broad
Carlton Colville
Grove Fm.
Barnby
Priory Fm.
Pakefield
Bloodmoor Hill
North Cove
The Cottage
Mutford Big Wood
Grange Fm.
Pakefield Hall
Gisleham
Beech Tree Fm.
Red Ho.
Mutford
Black Street
Cliff Fm.
SUFFOLK
Hulver Street
Hundred
Rushmere
Valley Fm.
Low Pasture Fm.
Toad Row
Henstead
Kessingland
SUFFOLK WILDLIFE PARK
Sotterley
Golding's Fm.
Latymere Dam
Kessingland Beach

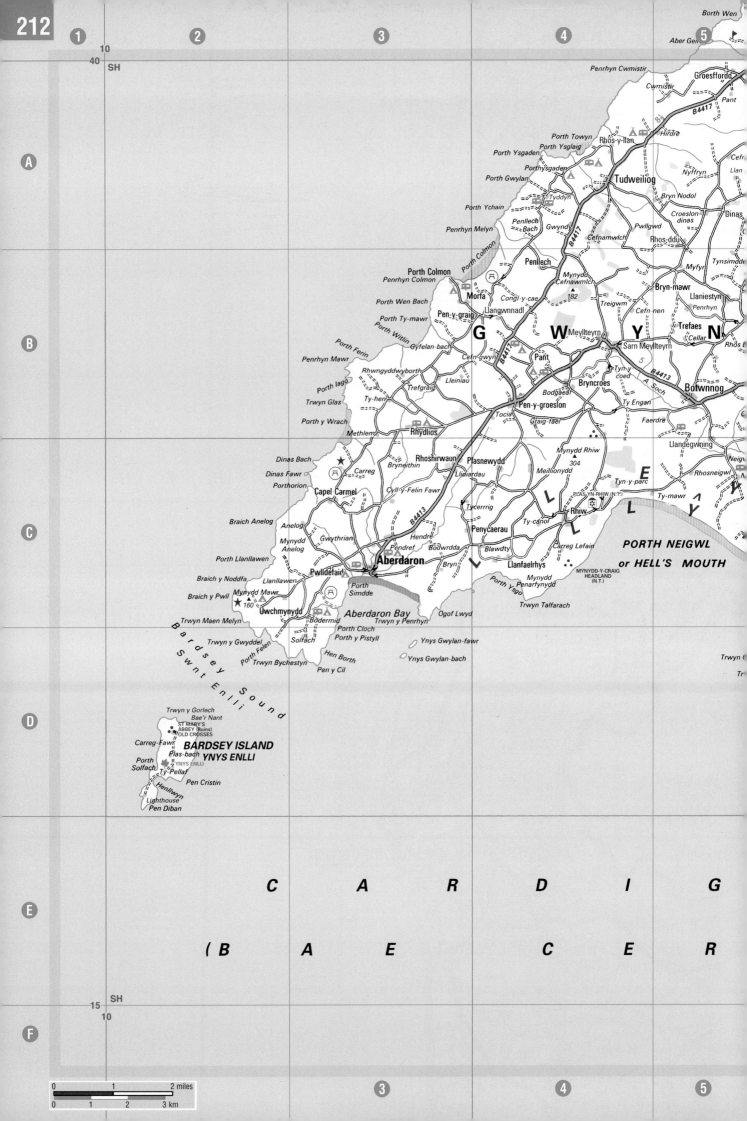

Borth Wen

Aber Gei

10
40 SH

Penrhyn Cwmistir
Cwmistir
Groesffordd
B4417
Pant
B4417
Hirdre

Porth Towyn
Rhos-y-llan
Porth Ysglaig
Porth Ysgaden
Cefr
Porthysgaden
Nyffryn
Llan
Porth Gwylan
Tudweiliog
Tyddyn
Bryn Nodol
Porth Ychain
Croeslon-
dinas
Dinas
Penrhyn Melyn
Penllech
Bach
Gwyndy
Pwllgwd
Rhos-ddu

**G**
Porth Colmon
Mynydd
Cefnamwlch
Tynsimdde
Porth Colmon
Penllech
182
Penrhyn Colmon
**W**
Myfyr
Morfa
Congl-y-cae
Treigwm
Bryn-mawr
**Y**
Porth Wen Bach
Llangwnnadl
Llaniestyn
Pen-y-graig
Meillteyrn
Cefn-nen
Penrhyn
**N**
Porth Ty-mawr
Cefnamwlch
Trefaes
Porth Witlin
Gyfelan-bach
Cellar
Rhos
Porth Ferin
Cefn-gwyn
Sarn Meillteyrn
Penrhyn Mawr
Rhwngyddwyborth
Lleiniau
Pant
Tyn y
coed
Botwnnog
Porth Iago
Bodgaeaf
B4413
A Soch
Trefgraig
Bryncroes
Trwyn Glas
Ty-hen
Ty Engan
Porth y Wrach
Pen-y-groeslon
Graig-fael
Faerdre
Methlem
Tocia
Rhydlios
Llandegwning
Dinas Bach
Rhoshirwaun
Plasnewydd
Mynydd Rhiw
Neig
Carreg
Bryneithin
304
Rhosneigwl
Dinas Fawr
Llidiardau
Meillionydd
Porthorion
Cyll-y-Felin Fawr
**E**
Ty-mawr
Capel Carmel
Tycerrrig
Tyn-y-parc
**L**
PLAS-YN-RHIW (N.T.)
Braich Anelog
Hendre
Ty-canol
Rhiw
**L**
Anelog
Gwythrian
Pendref
Bodwrdda
Penycaerau
Blawdty
Mynydd
Anelog
Bryn
**L**
Porth Llanllawen
Llanfaelrhys
**Y**
Braich y Noddfa
Llanllawen
MYNYDD-Y-CRAIG
HEADLAND
(N.T.)
Aberdaron
Mynydd
Penarfynydd
Braich y Pwll
Mynydd Mawr
Pwlldefaid
Porth Ysgo
**PORTH NEIGWL**
160
Porth
Simdde
**or HELL'S MOUTH**
Trwyn Maen Melyn
Uwchmynydd
Trwyn Talfarach
Bodermid
Aberdaron Bay
Trwyn y Penrhyn
Ogof Lwyd
Trwyn y Gwyddel
Porth Cloch
Ynys Gwylan-fawr
Trwyn (
Porth Felen
Porth y Pistyll
Tr
Trwyn Bychestyn
Hen Borth
Ynys Gwylan-bach
Pen y Cil
Solfach

Bardsey Sound
Swnt Enlli

Trwyn y Gorlech
Bae'r Nant
ST MARY'S
ABBEY (Ruins)
OLD CROSSES
**BARDSEY ISLAND**
Carreg-Fawr
**YNYS ENLLI**
Plas-bach
Porth
Solfach
YNYS ENLLI
Ty-Pellaf
Pen Cristin
Henllwyn
Lighthouse
Pen Diban

**C A R D I G G**

**( B A E C E R**

40 SH

15 SH
10

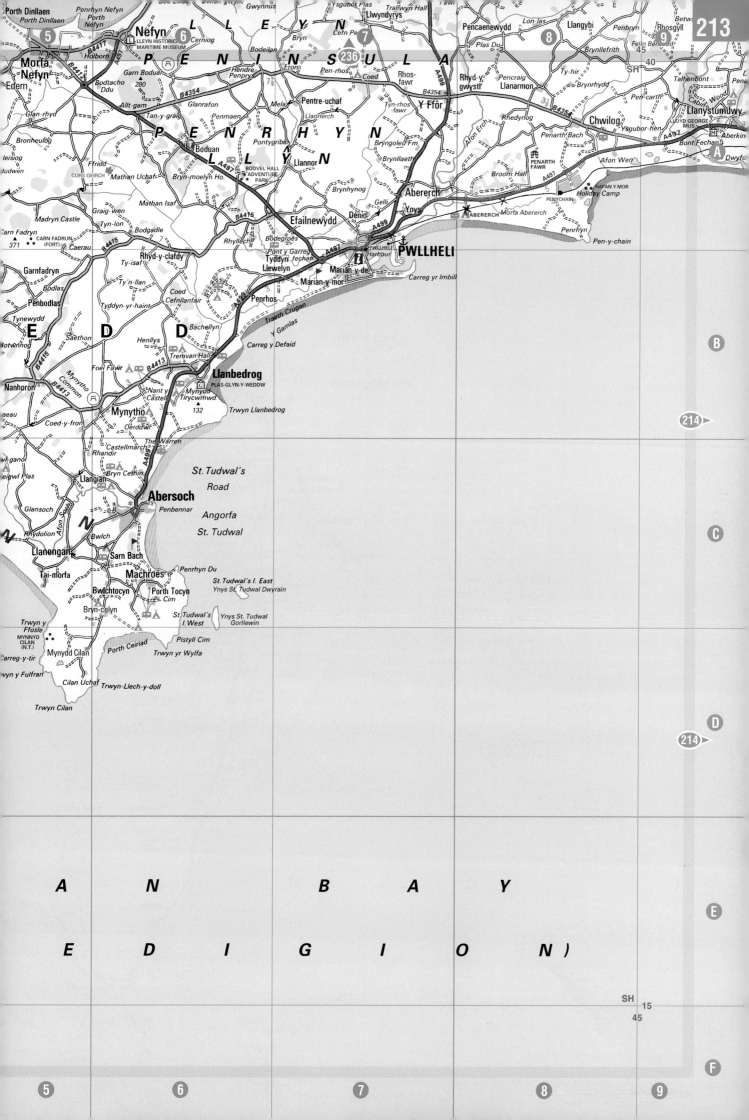

Porth Dinllaen
Porth Dinllaen

Penrhyn Nefyn
Porth
Nefyn

**Nefyn**

LLEYN

Gwynnus

Llwyndyrys

Trallwyn Hall

Y sgubor Plas

Pencaenewydd

Lon-las

Llangybi

Penrhyn

Rhosgyll

Felin Bendsed

45

SH

40

Cerniog

LLEYN HISTORIC
MARITIME MUSEUM

PENINSULA

Cefn Pe

Bryn

Bodeilan

Pen-rhos

Coed

Rhos-fawr

Plas Du

Ty-hir

Brynllefrith

Betw

Pena

Talhenbont

Llanystumdwy

Morfa
Nefyn

Holborn

Garn Boduan
280

Hendre
Penprys

Fron

236

Rhyd-y-
gwystl

Llanarmon

Pencraig
fawr

Brynrhydd

Pen-cartll

LLOYD GEORGE
MUS

Aberkin

Dwyfo

Bodtacho
Ddu

B4354

Glanrafon

Mela

Pentre-uchaf

Y Ffôr

B4354

Tyn-rhos
fawr

Afon Erch

Rhedynog

Penarth Bach

Chwilog

Ysgubor-hen

A497

Bont Fechan

A

Allt-gam

Tan-y-graig

Penmaen

Llannerch

Bryngoleu Fm

PENARTH
FAWR

HAFAN Y MOR
Holiday Camp

Afon Wen

Glan-rhyd

Edern

Bronheulog

Boduan

P E N R H Y N

Llannor

Brynllaethi

Abererch

Broom Hall

PENYCHAIN

Morfa Abererch

Penrhyn

Pen-y-chain

Fridd

Bryn-moelyn Ho.

BODVEL HALL
ADVENTURE PARK

Brynhynog

Ynys

ABERERCH

leisiog
ludwen

Mathan Uchaf

L L E Y N

Llanor

Gelli

Denio

Mathan Isaf

Bryn Cethin

B4415

Rhyllech

Bodegroes

Efailnewydd

A499

PWLLHELI
Harbour

**PWLLHELI**

Carreg yr Imbill

Madryn Castle

Graig-wen

Tyn-lon

Bodgadle

Pont y Garreg
fechan

Tyddyn
Llewelyn

Marian-y-de

Carn Fadryn
371

CARN FADRUN
(FORT)

Caerau

Ty-isaf

Rhyd-y-clafdy

Marian-y-mor

Garnfadryn

Bodlas

Ty'n-llan

Coed
Cefnllanfair

Penrhos

Traeth Crugan

Y Garnlas

Penbodlas

Tyddyn-yr-haint

Bachellyn

Carreg y Defaid

Tynewydd

Saethon

Henllys

Tremvan Hall

E D D D

otwnhog

Foel Fawr

B4413

**Llanbedrog**

PLAS-GLYN-Y-WEDDW

Nanhoron

Mynytho
Common

B4413

Nant y
Castell

Mynydd
Tirycwmwd
132

Trwyn Llanbedrog

Coed-y-fron

**Mynytho**

Oerddwr

The Warren

aeau

Castellmarch

St. Tudwal's

l-ganol

Rhandir

Road

eigwl Plas

Bryn Cethin

Angorfa

Llangian

Glansoch

**Abersoch**

Penbennar

St. Tudwal

Rhydolion

N

Bwlch

Tai-morfa

**Llanengan**

Sarn Bach

Penrhyn Du

St. Tudwal's I. East
Ynys St. Tudwal Dwyrain

Bwlchtocyn

**Machroes**

Porth Tocyn

Cim

Bryn-celyn

St. Tudwal's
I. West

Ynys St. Tudwal
Gorllewin

Trwyn y
Ffosle

MYNNYD
CILAN
(N.T.)

Pistyll Cim

Carreg-y-tir

Mynydd Cilan

Porth Ceiriad

Trwyn yr Wylfa

wyn y Fulfran

Cilan Uchaf

Trwyn-Llech-y-doll

Trwyn Cilan

A N B A Y

E D I G I O N )

SH
15

45

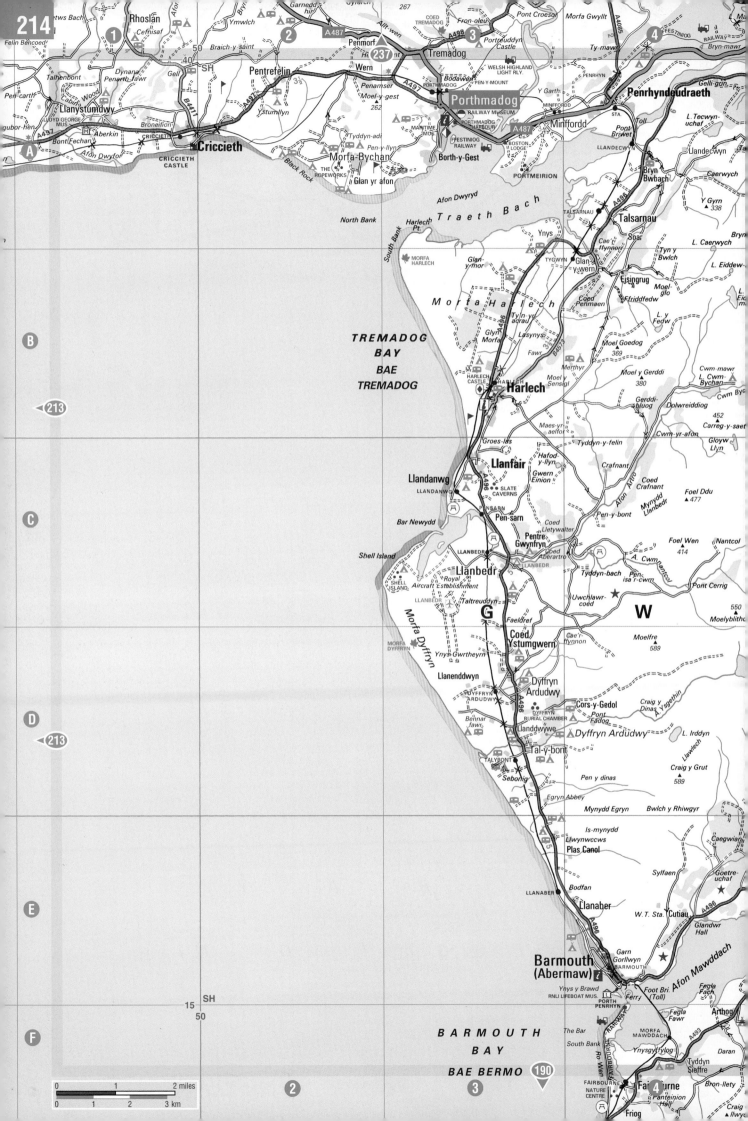

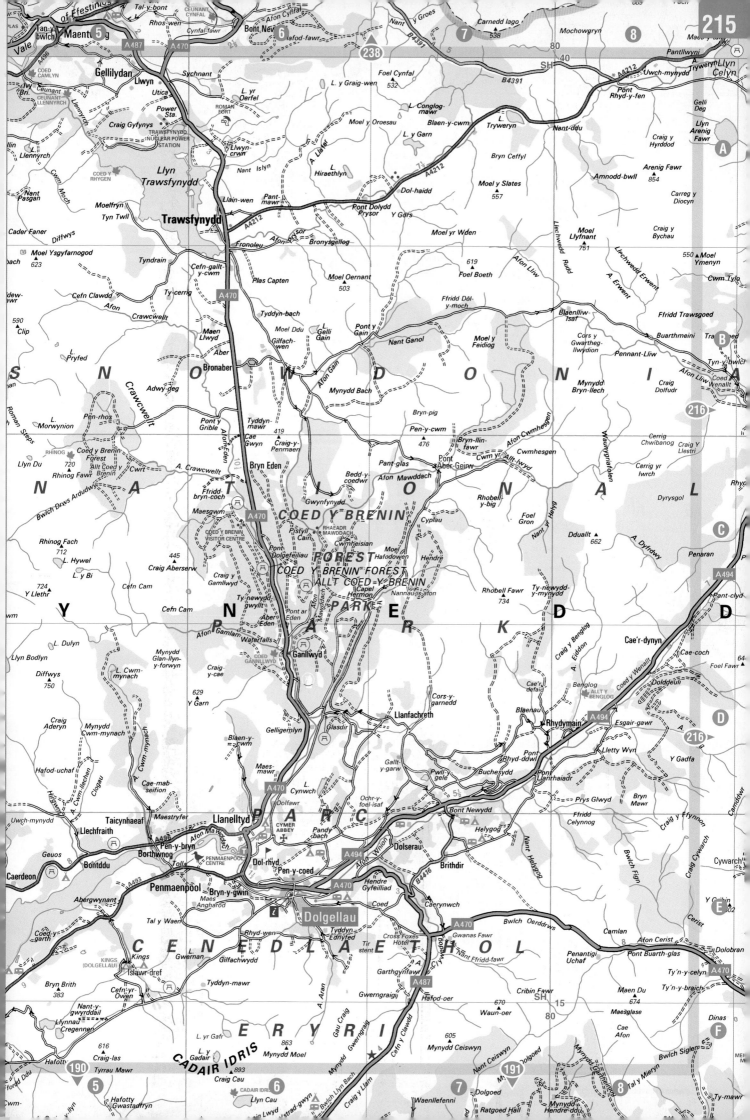

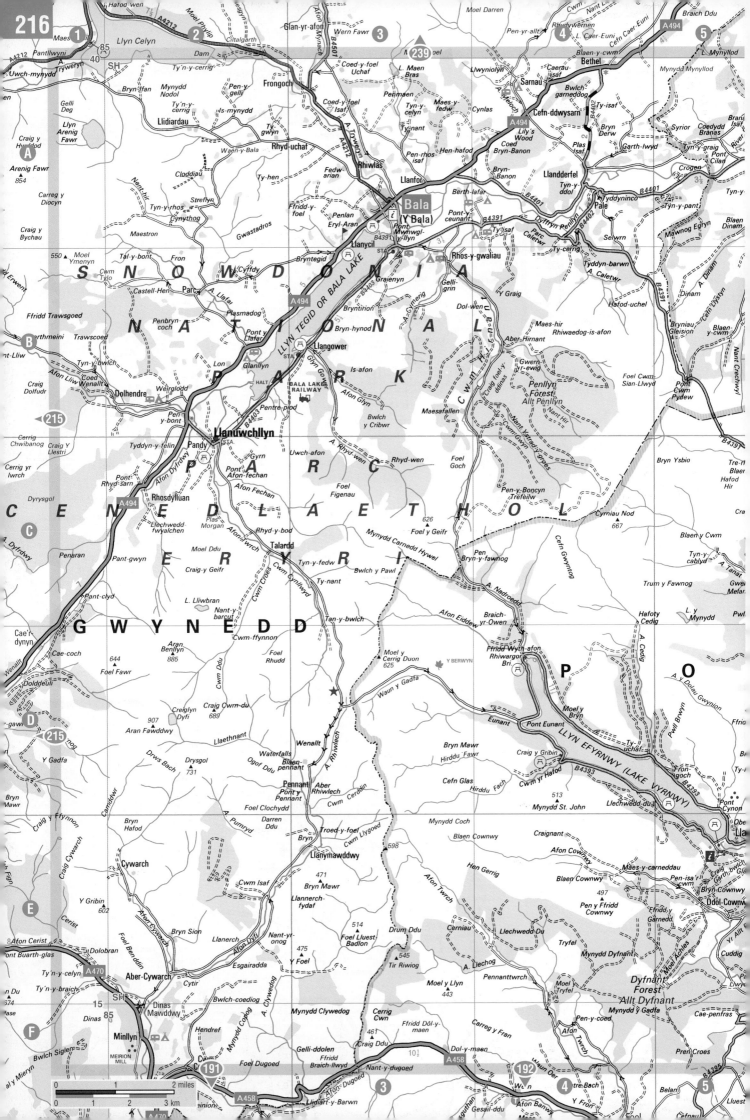

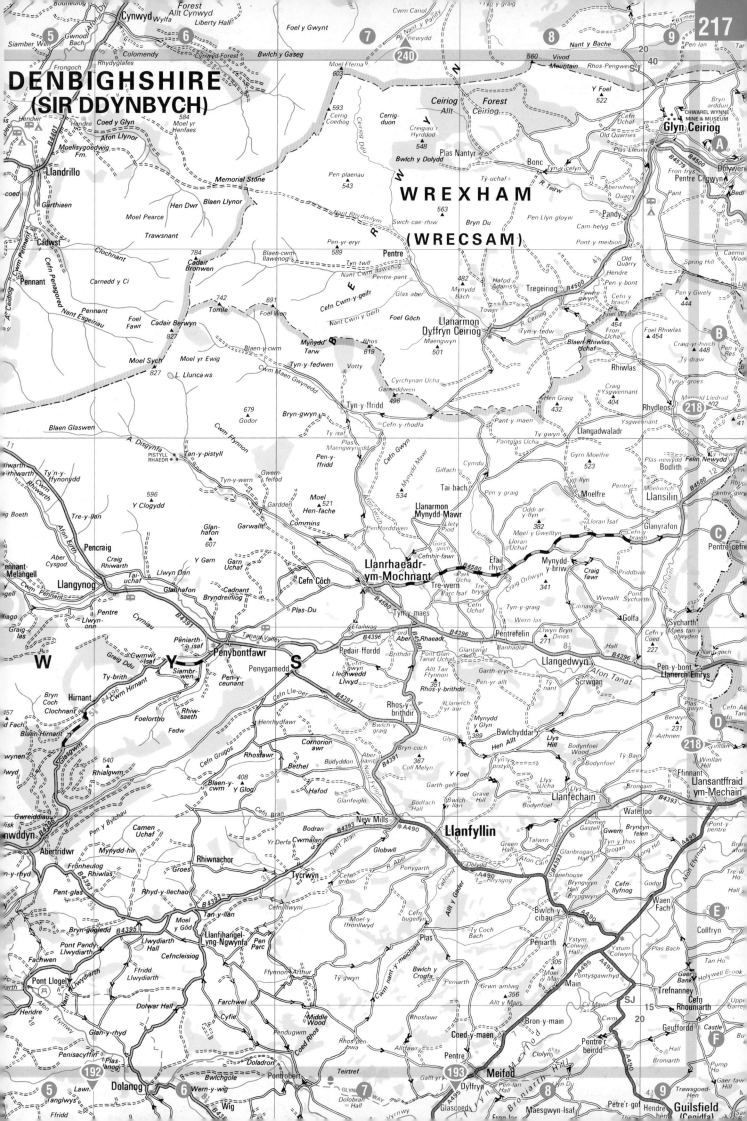

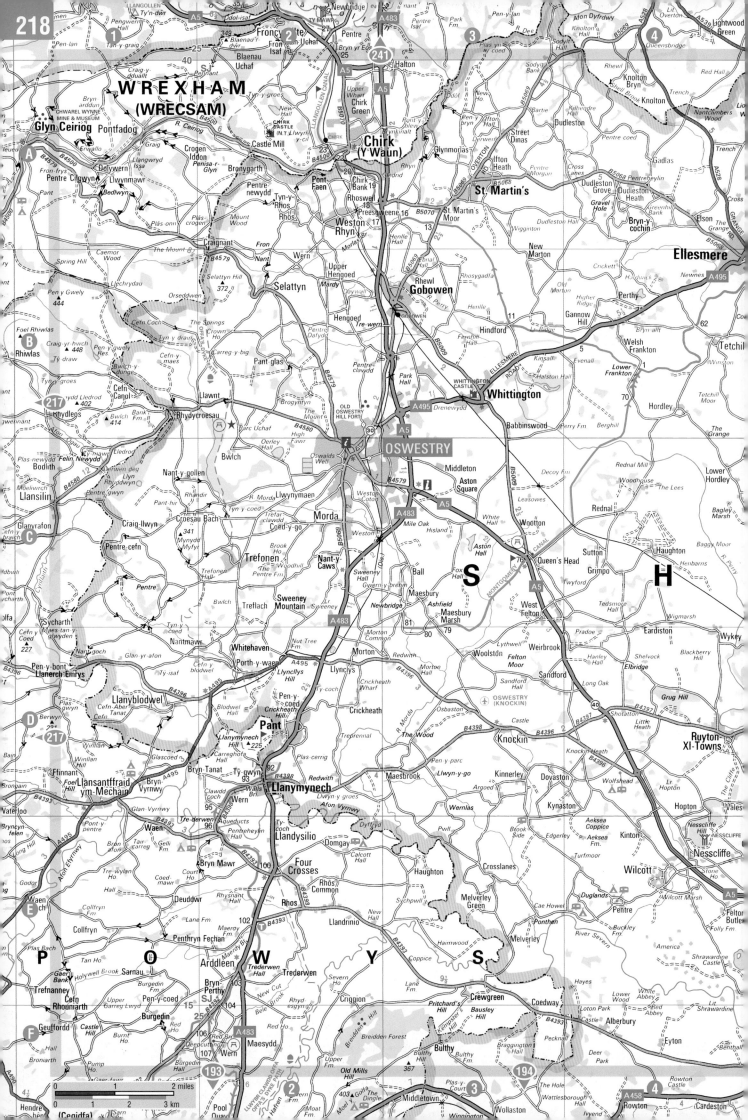

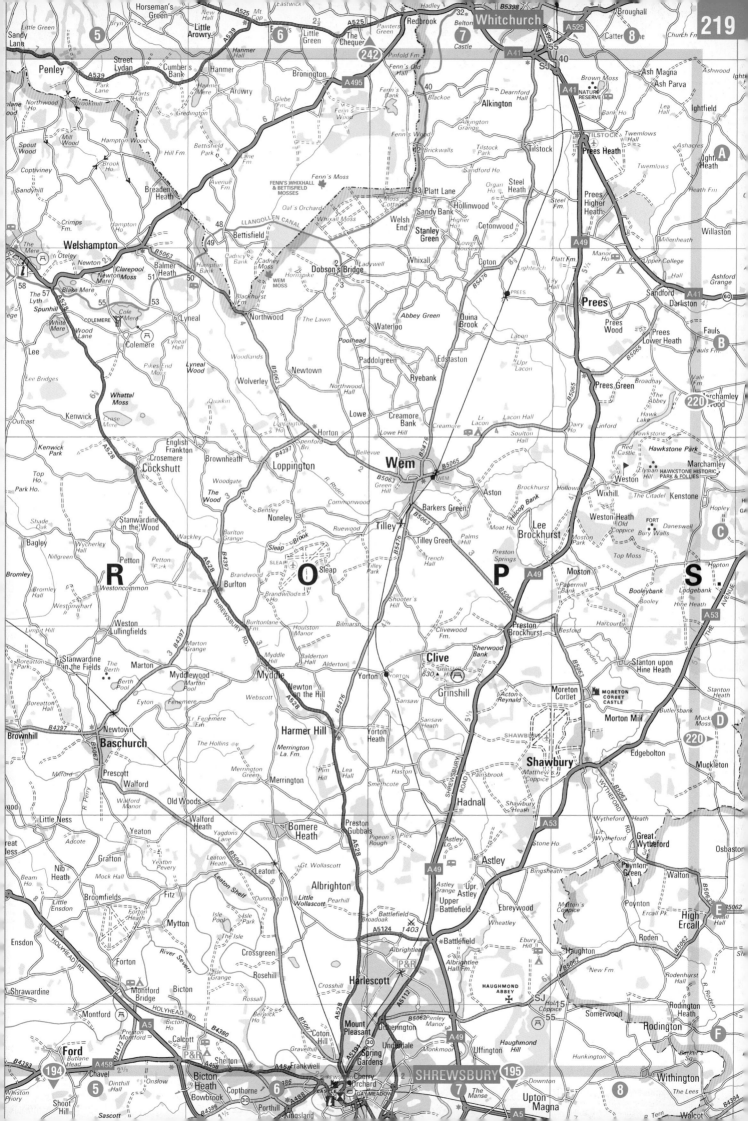

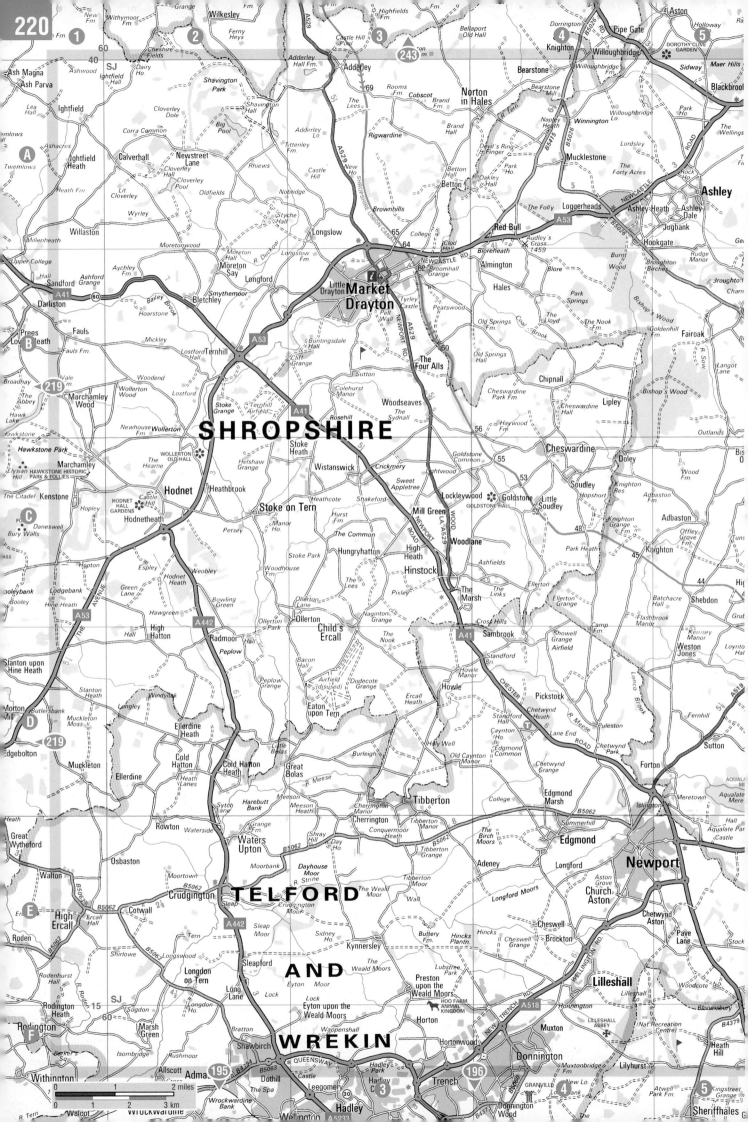

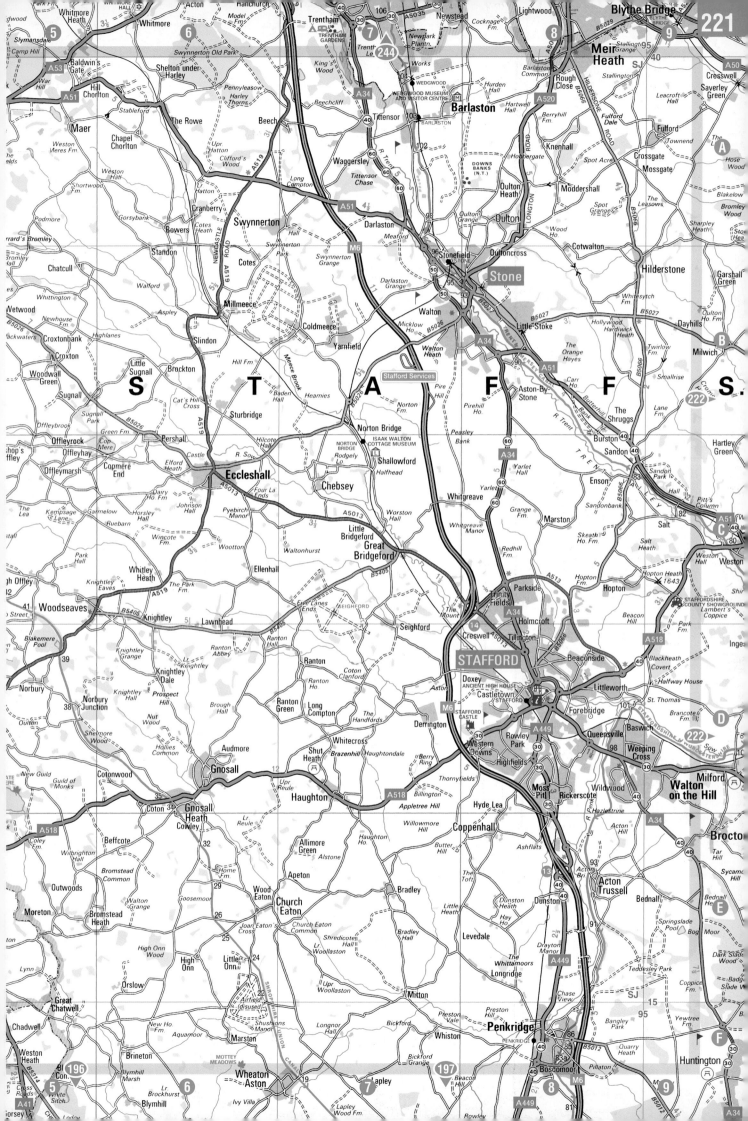

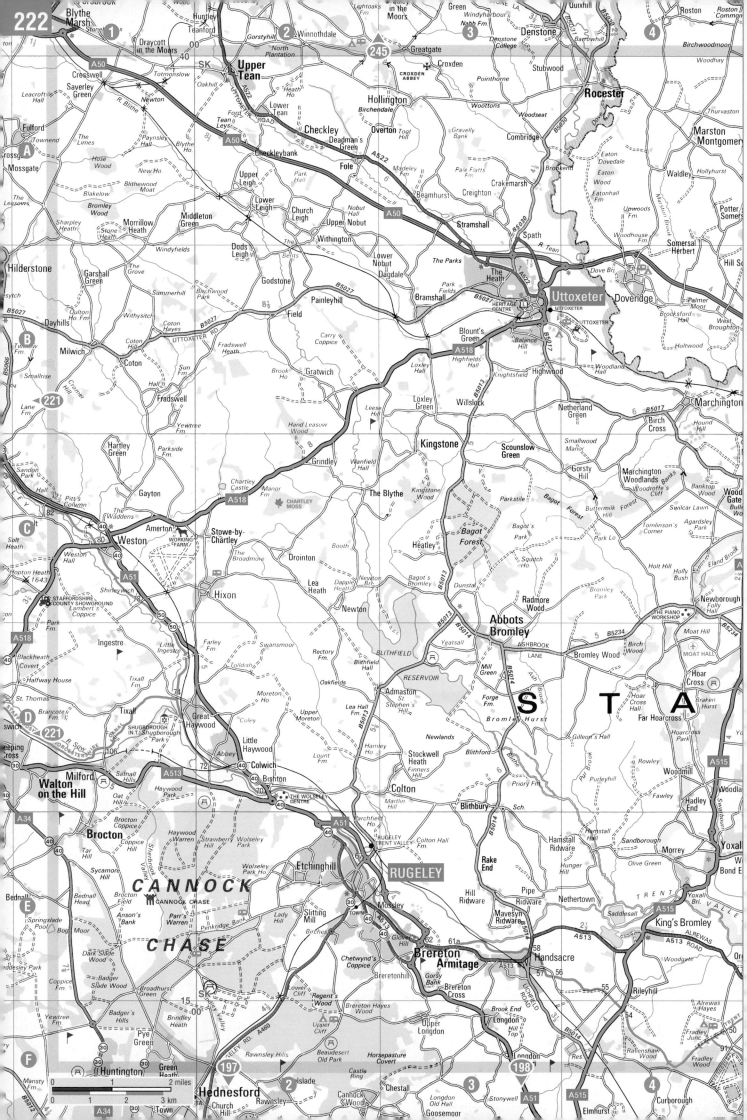

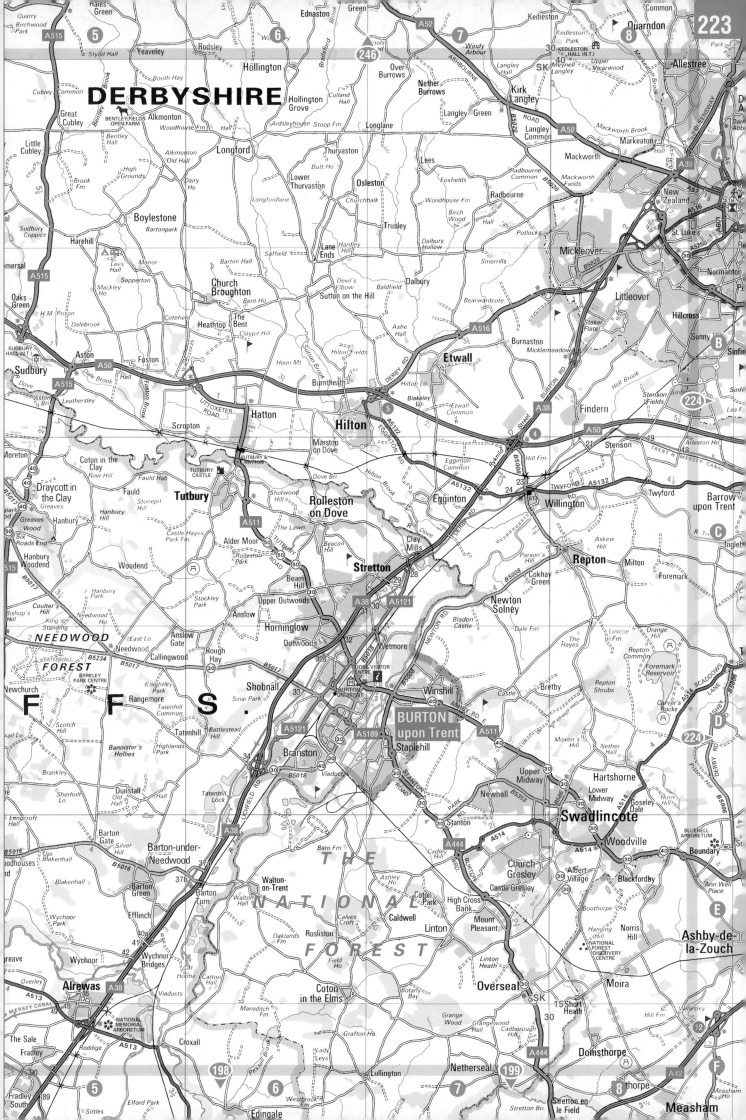

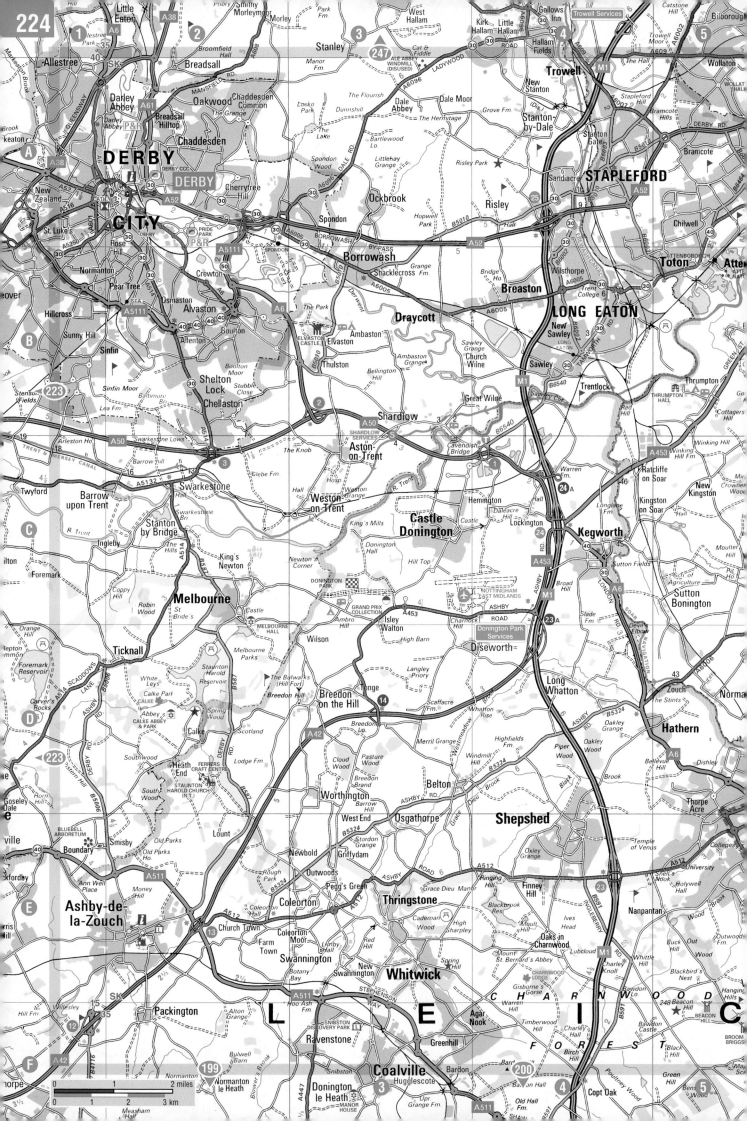

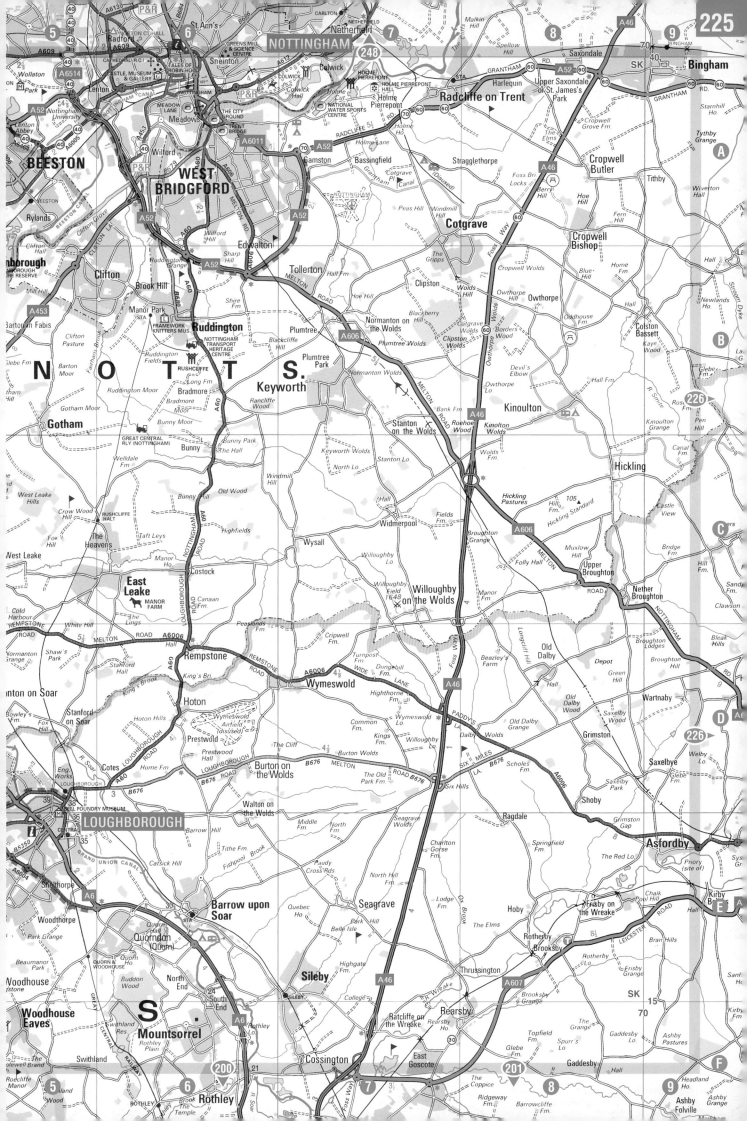

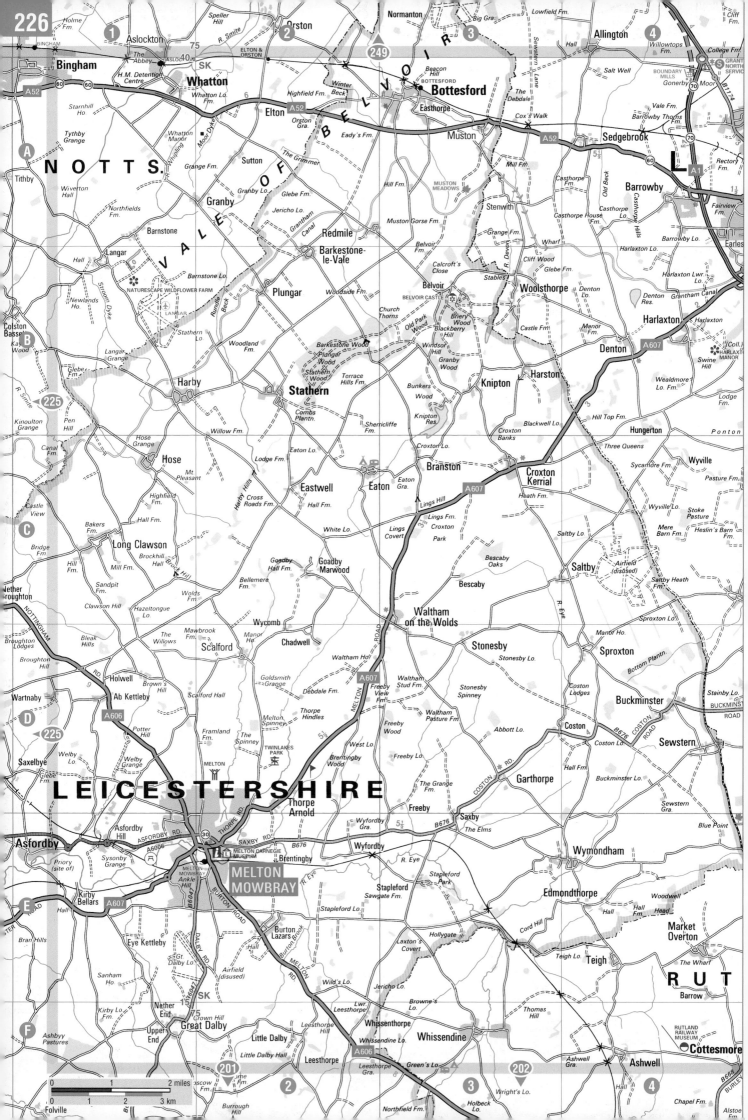

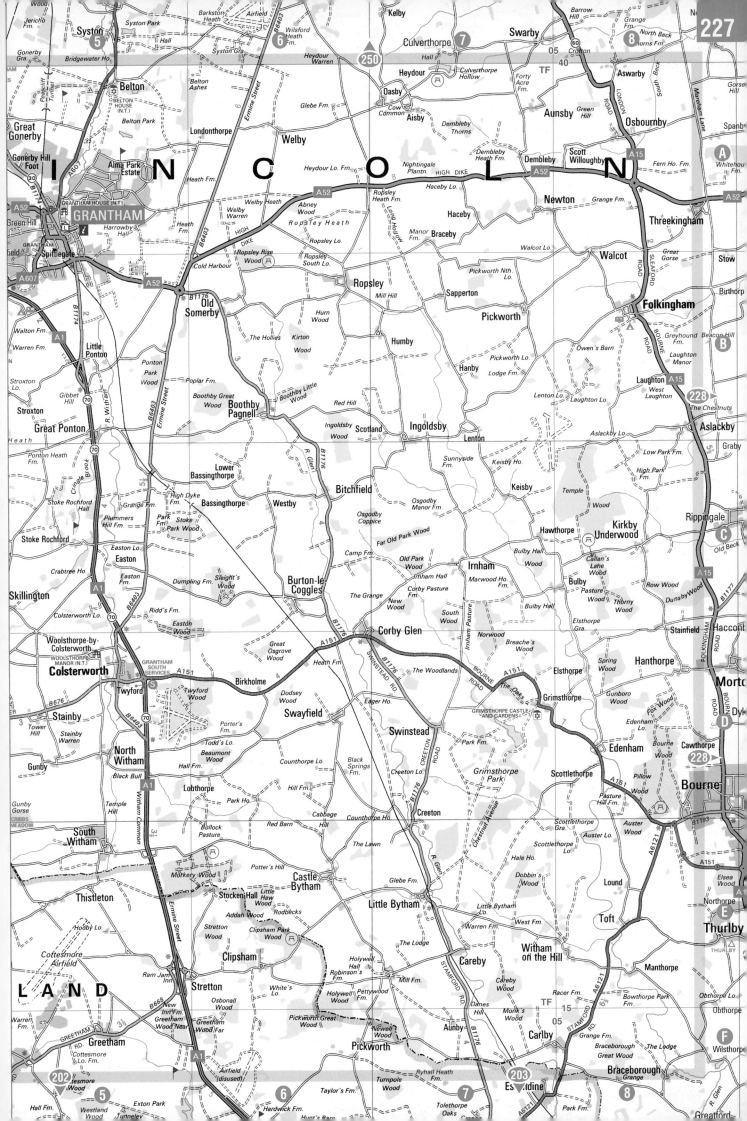

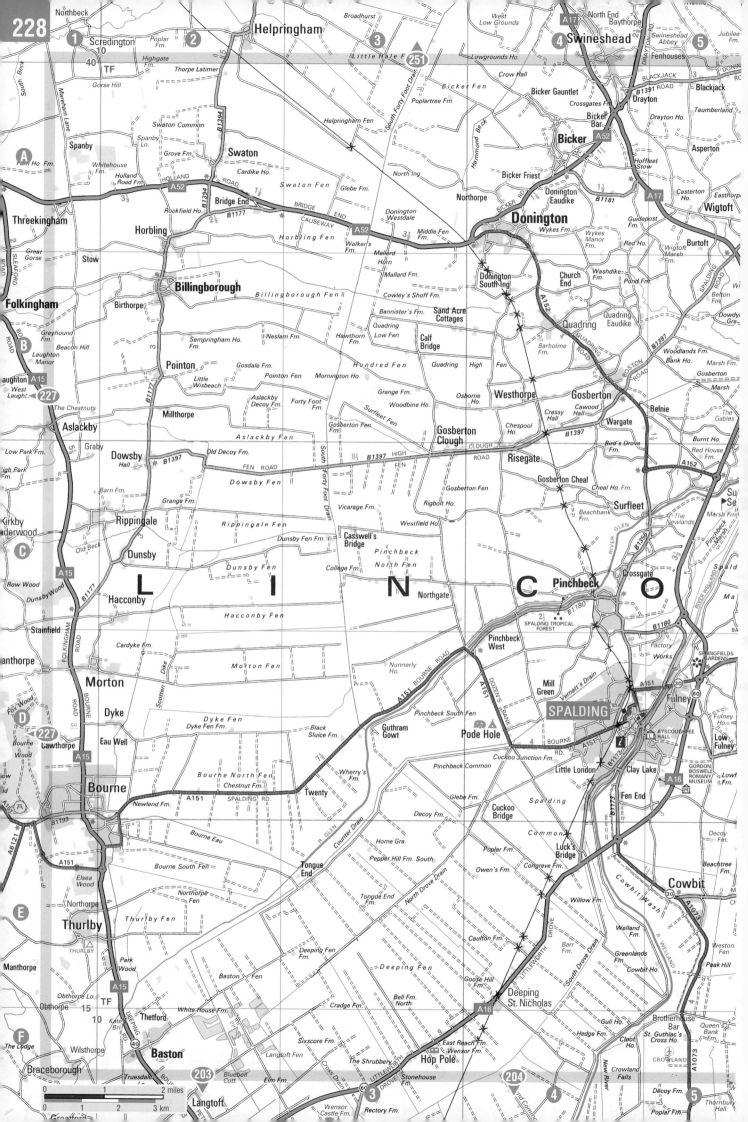

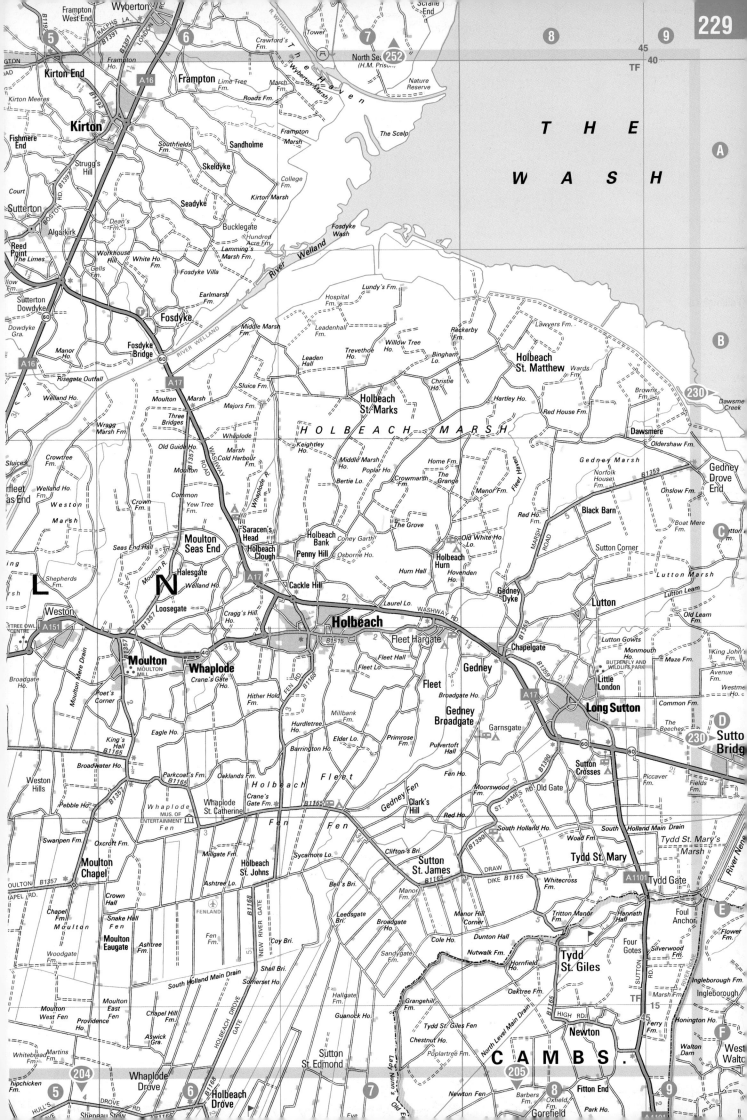

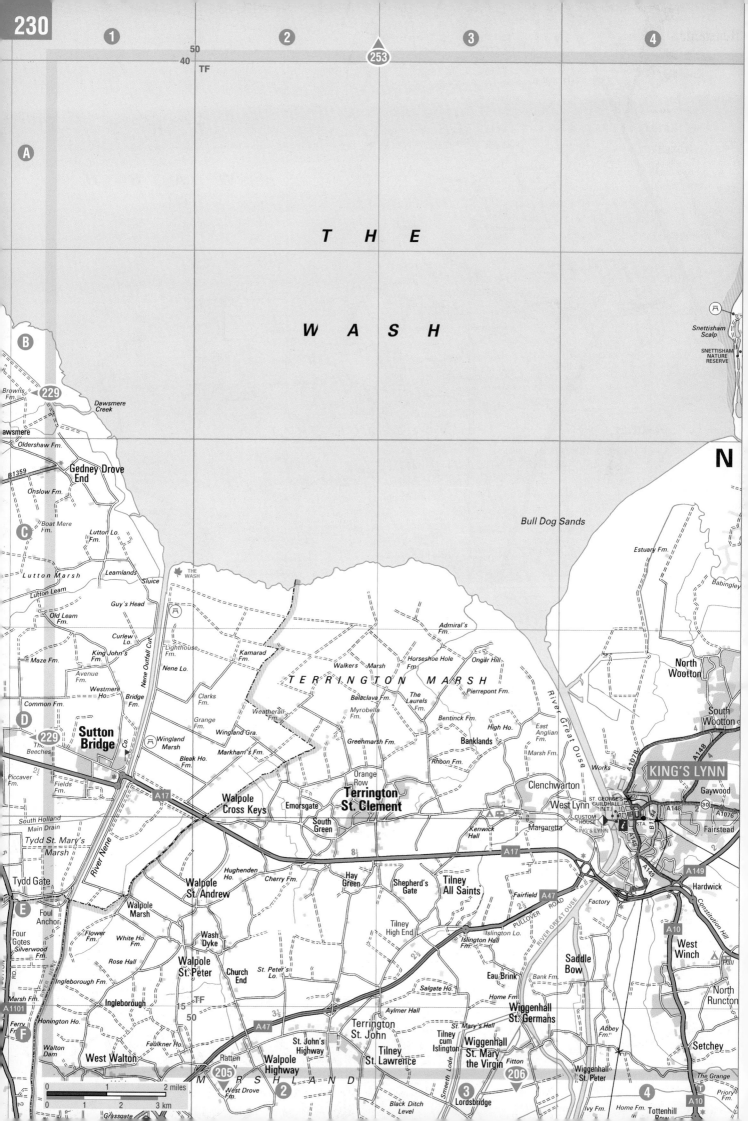

1    2    253    3    4

50
40
TF

A

B

T H E

W A S H

Snettisham
Scalp

SNETTISHAM
NATURE
RESERVE

Browns
Fm.    229

Dawsmere
Creek

awsmere

Oldershaw Fm.

B1359    Gedney Drove
End

Onslow Fm.

N

Boat Mere
Fm.

C    Lutton Lo.
Fm.

Bull Dog Sands

Estuary Fm.

Babingley

Leamlands

Lutton Marsh

Sluice    THE
WASH

Lutton Learn

Old Leam
Fm.    Guy's Head

Curlew
Lo.

Admiral's
Fm.

North
Wootton

Maze Fm.    King John's
Fm.    Lighthouse
Fm.    Kamarad
Fm.    Walkers   Marsh    Horseshoe Hole
Fm.    Ongar Hill

Avenue
Fm.    Nene Lo.    T E R R I N G T O N   M A R S H    Pierrepont Fm.

Westmere
Ho.    Clarks
Fm.    Balaclava Fm.    The
Laurels    Bentinck Fm.    High Ho.    East
Anglian
Fm.

River Great Ouse

South
Wootton

D    Common Fm.    Bridge
Fm.    Grange
Fm.    Weatherall
Fm.    Myrobella
Fm.    Greenmarsh Fm.    Banklands    Marsh Fm.    Works

Wingland Gra.    KING'S LYNN

229    Wingland
Marsh    Markham's Fm.    Rhoon Fm.    Clenchwarton    ST. GEORGE'S
GUILDHALL (N.T.)    Gaywood

The
Beeches    Bleak Ho.
Fm.    Orange
Row    West Lynn    A148    30    A1076

Sutton
Bridge    Co.    Terrington
St. Clement    Margaretta    CUSTOM
HOUSE    i    Fairstead

Piccaver
Fm.    Fields
Fm.    A17    Walpole
Cross Keys    Emorsgate    South
Green    KING'S LYNN    STA.

South Holland
Main Drain    Kenwick
Hall    229    A149    Hardwick

Tydd St. Mary's
Marsh    8½    A17

E    Tydd Gate    Hughenden
Ho.    Cherry Fm.    Hay
Green    Shepherd's
Gate    Tilney
All Saints    Fairfield    A47    Factory    A10

Foul
Anchor    Walpole
St. Andrew    PULLOVER ROAD    West
Winch

Four
Gotes    Walpole
Marsh    White Ho.
Fm.    Wash
Dyke    Tilney
High End    Islington Lo.    RIVER GREAT OUSE    North
Runcton

Silverwood
Fm.    Flower
Fm.    Rose Hall    Islington Hall    Saddle
Bow

Ingleborough Fm.    Walpole
St. Peter    Church
End    St. Peter's
Lo.    Salgate Ho.    Bank Fm.    Home Fm.

A1101    Ingleborough    15    TF    3½    Aylmer Hall    Eau Brink    Home Fm.    Wiggenhall
St. Germans    Abbey
Fm.    Setchey

50    Terrington
St. John    St. Mary's Hall    Wiggenhall
St. Mary
the Virgin    Fitton

F    Walton
Dam    A47    St. John's
Highway    Tilney
St. Lawrence    Tilney
cum Islington    Wiggenhall
St. Peter    Home Fm.    The Grange

West Walton    Ratten    Walpole
Highway    Priory
Fm.

0    1    2 miles    205    2    Black Ditch
Level    Lordsbridge    206    Tottenhill
Row    A10

0    1    2    3 km    M A R S H L A N D    West Drove
Fm.    3    4

Grossgate

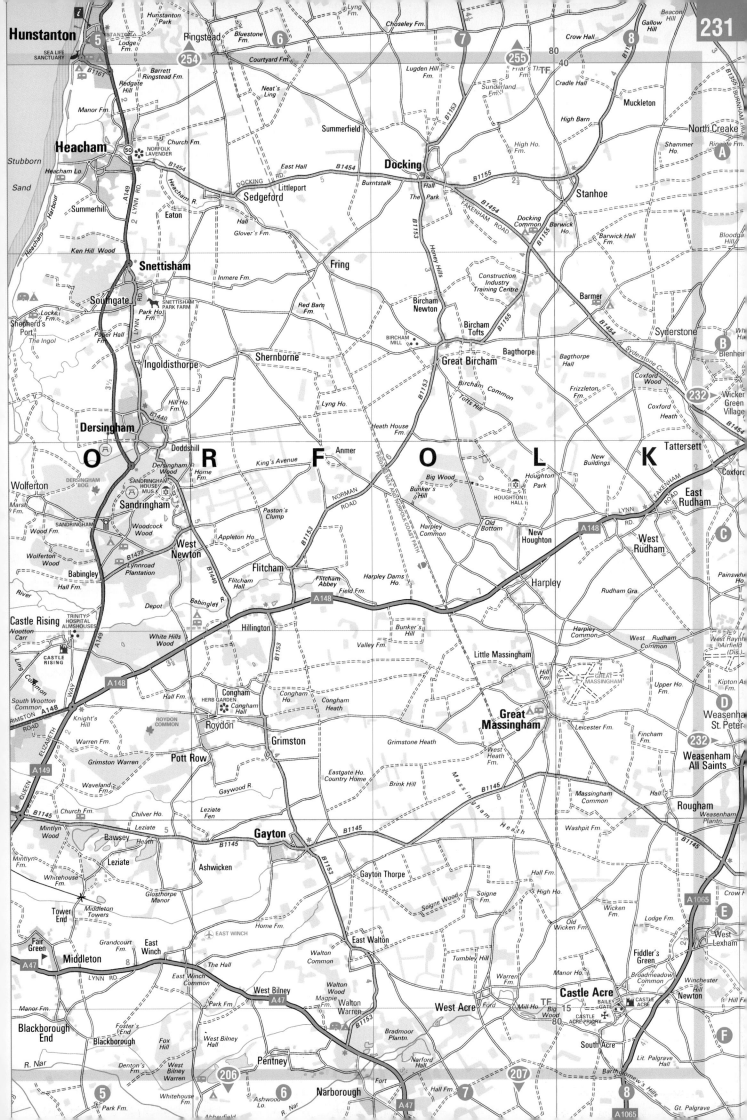

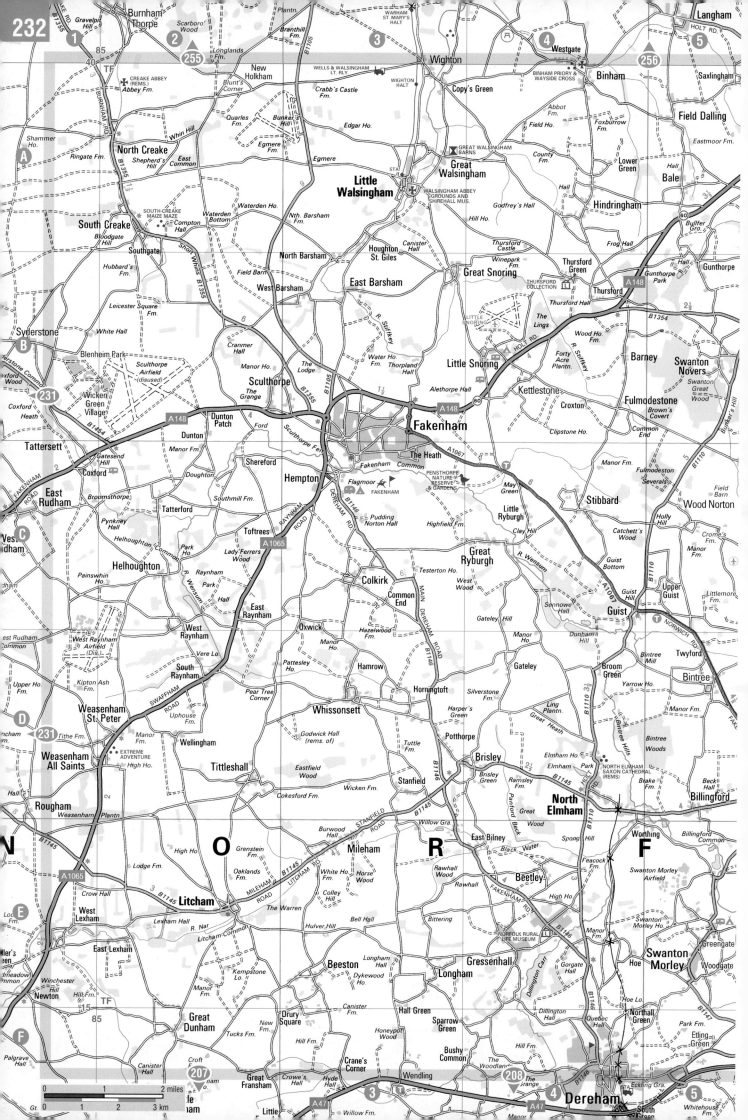

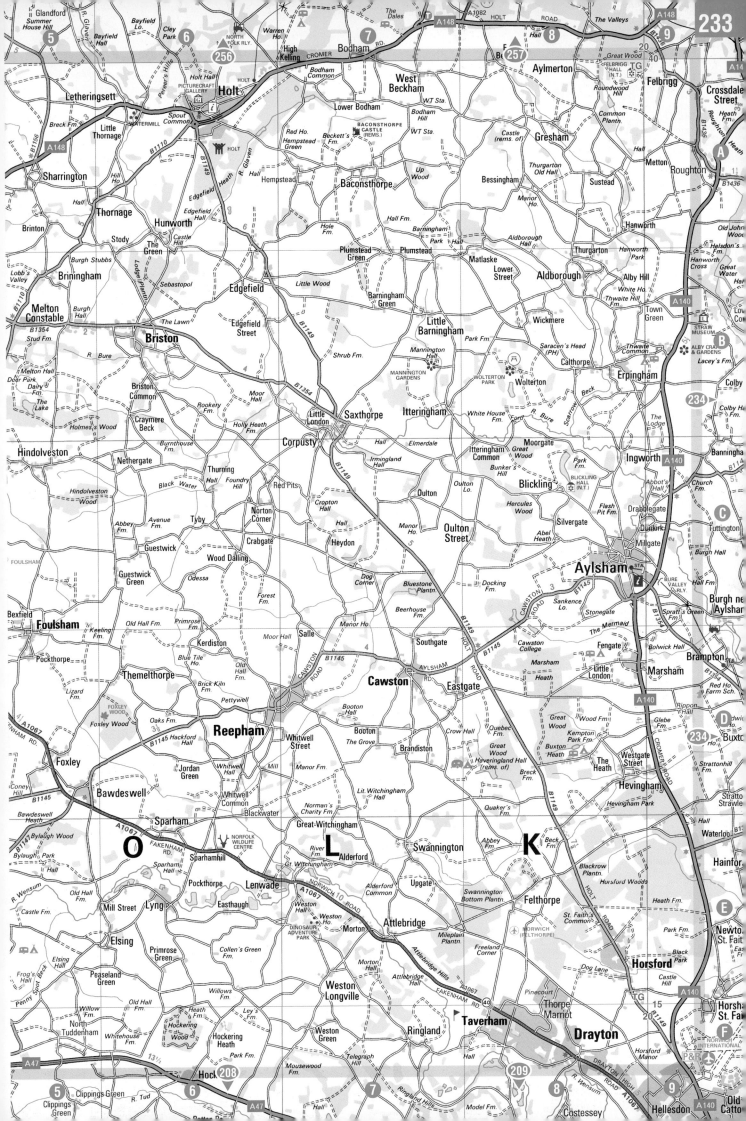

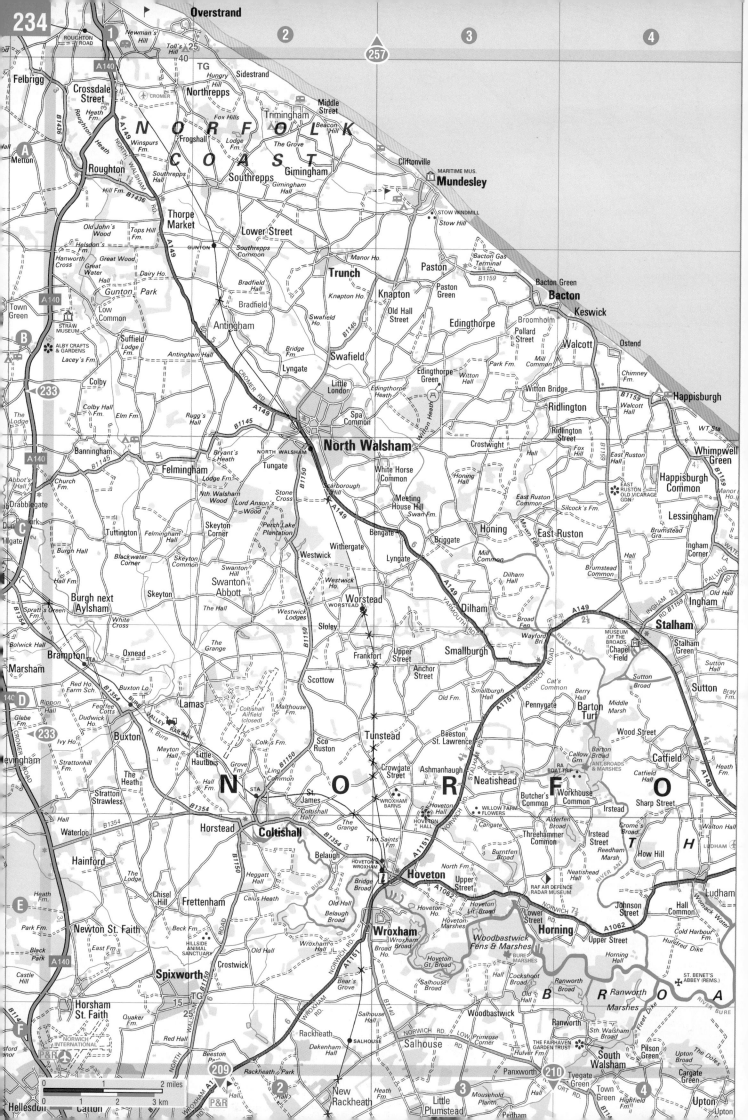

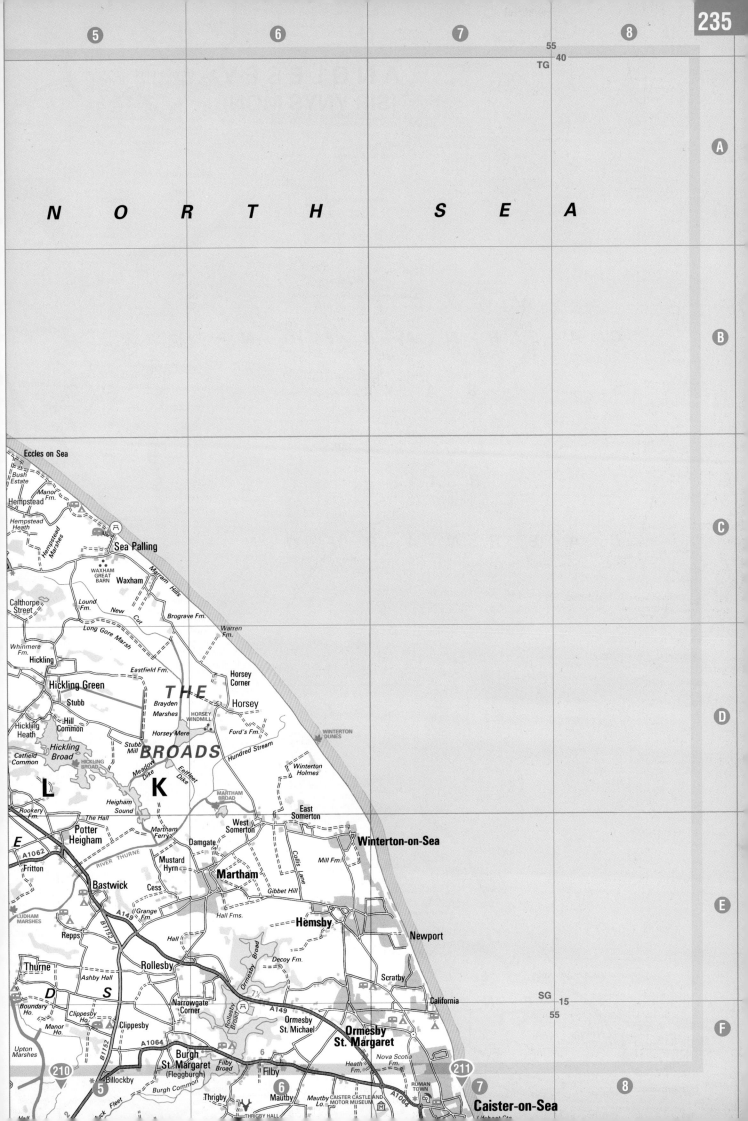

5    6    7    8

55
40
TG

**A**

**B**

**N  O  R  T  H    S  E  A**

**C**

Eccles on Sea
Bush Estate
Manor Fm.
Hempstead
Hempstead Heath
Sea Palling
WAXHAM GREAT BARN
Waxham
Marram Hills
Calthorpe Street
Lound Fm.
New Cut
Brograve Fm.
Warren Fm.
Whinmere Fm.
Long Gore Marsh
Hickling
Eastfield Fm.
Horsey Corner
Hickling Green
Stubb
Brayden Marshes
Horsey
**THE**
HORSEY WINDMILL
Hill Common
Horsey Mere
Ford's Fm.
WINTERTON DUNES
Hickling Heath
Stubb Mill
Hundred Stream
Catfield Common
Hickling Broad
HICKLING BROAD
**BROADS**
Winterton Holmes
**L**    **K**
Meadow Dike
Eelfleet Dike
Rookery Fm.
Heigham Sound
MARTHAM BROAD
East Somerton
Winterton-on-Sea
The Hall
West Somerton
Potter Heigham
Martham Ferry
Damgate
**E**
A1062
RIVER THURNE
Mustard Hyrn
Collis Lane
Mill Fm.
Fritton
**Martham**
Bastwick
Cess
Gibbet Hill
Grange Fm.
Hall Fms.
**E**
FLUDHAM MARSHES
A149
**Hemsby**
Repps
B1152
Hall
Newport
Thurne
Rollesby
Ashby Hall
Ormesby Broad
Decoy Fm.
Scratby
**D**  **S**
7½
California
SG
15
Boundary Ho.
Clippesby Ho.
Narrowgate Corner
A149
55
Manor Ho.
Clippesby
Ormesby St. Michael
Ormesby St. Margaret
Nova Scotia Fm.
**F**
Upton Marshes
B1152
A1064
Burgh St. Margaret (Fleggburgh)
Filby Broad
**Filby**
Heath Fm.
ROMAN TOWN
210
Billockby
Burgh Common
Thrigby
Mautby
Mautby Lo.
CAISTER CASTLE AND MOTOR MUSEUM
211
A1064
**Caister-on-Sea**
THRIGBY HALL
5    6    7    8

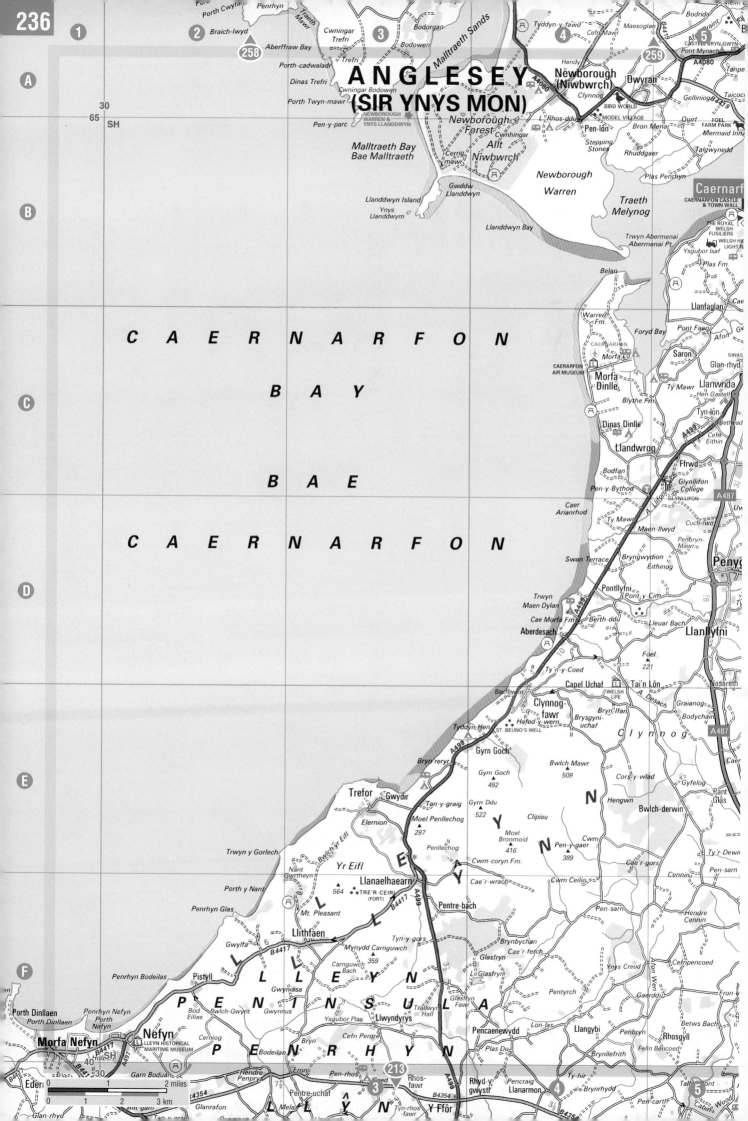

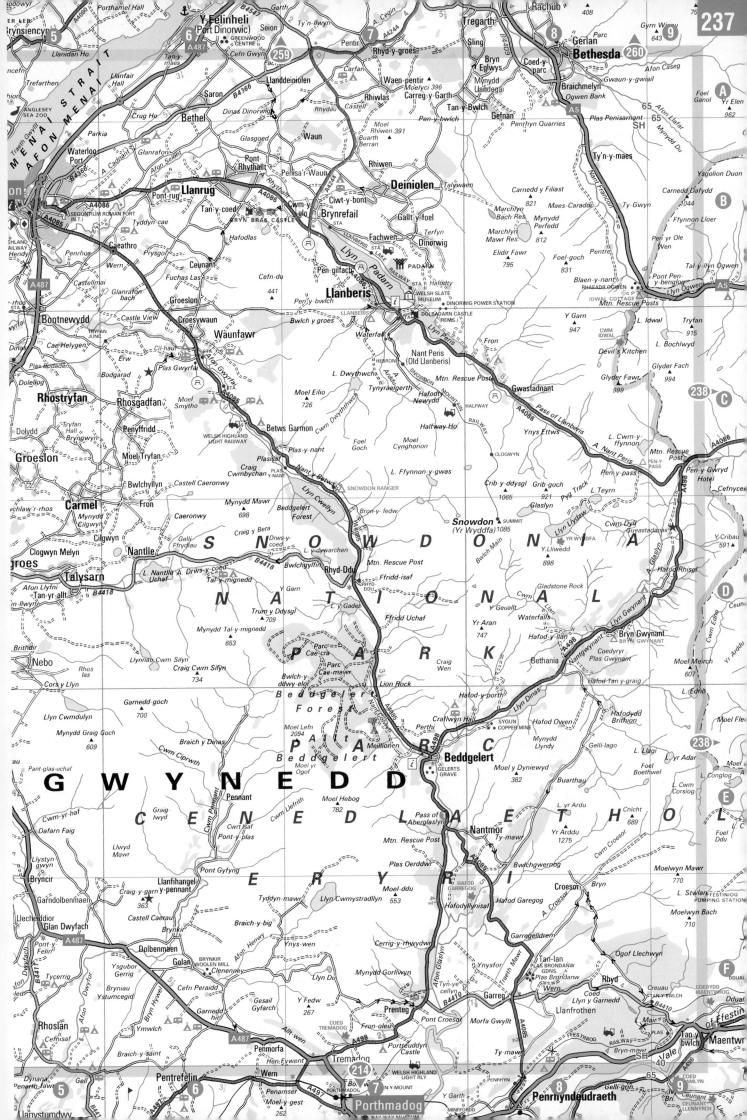

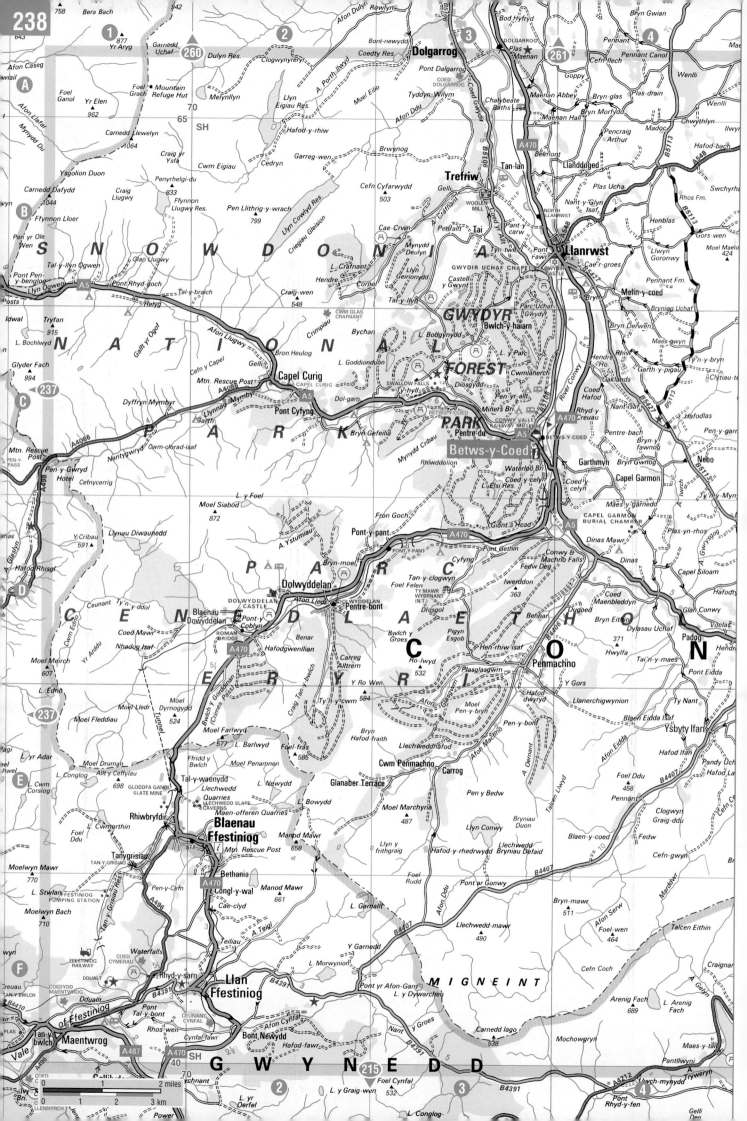

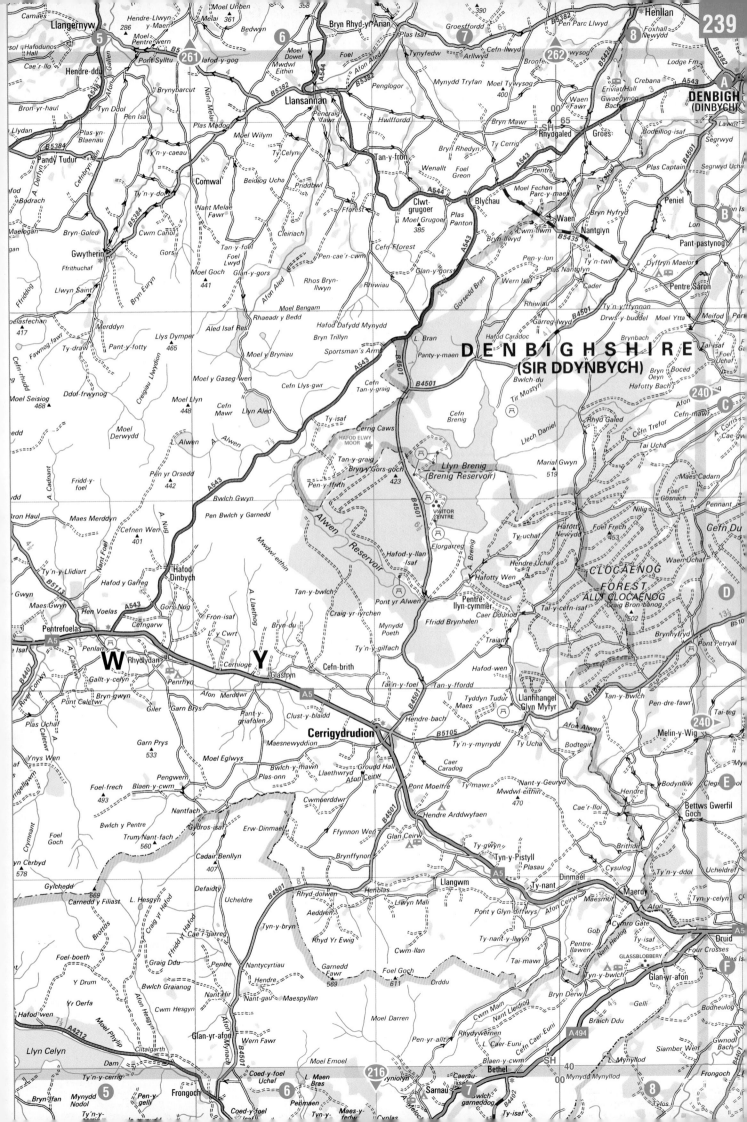

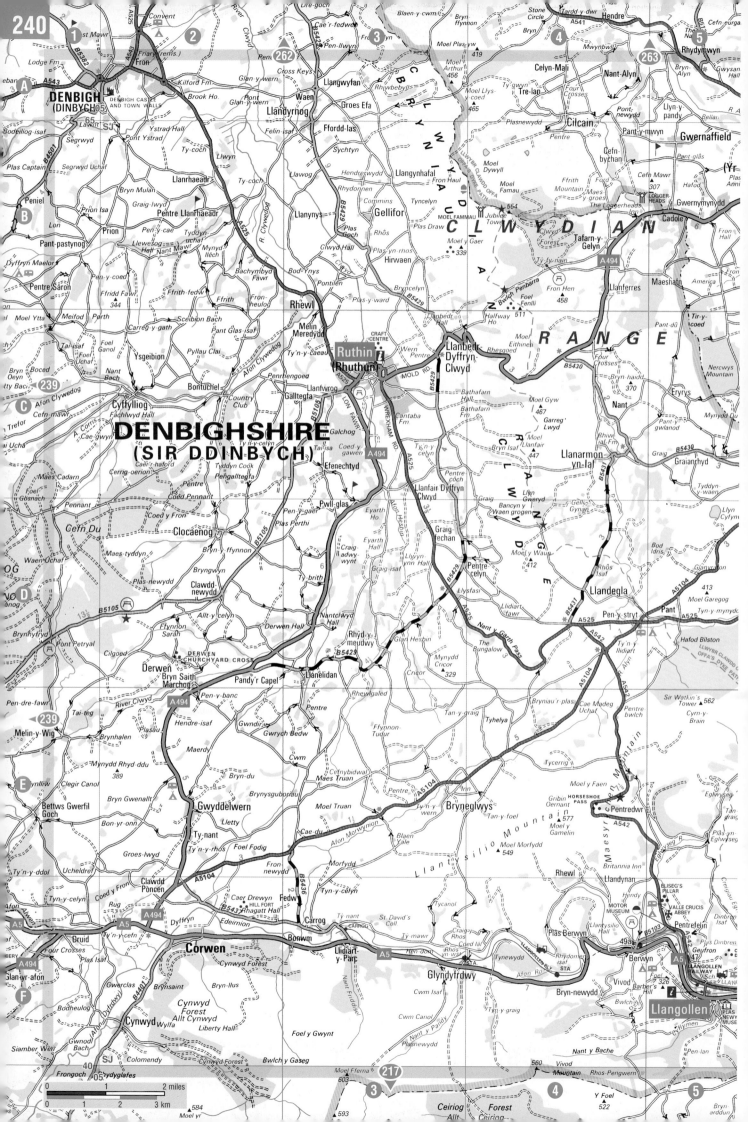

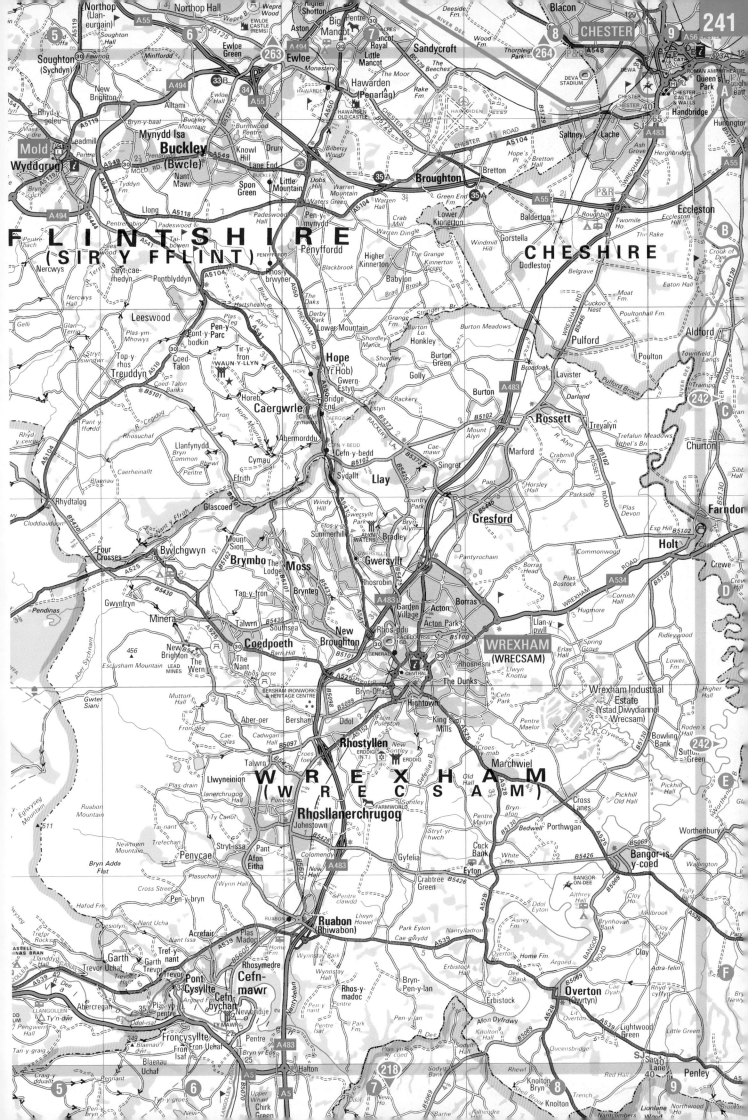

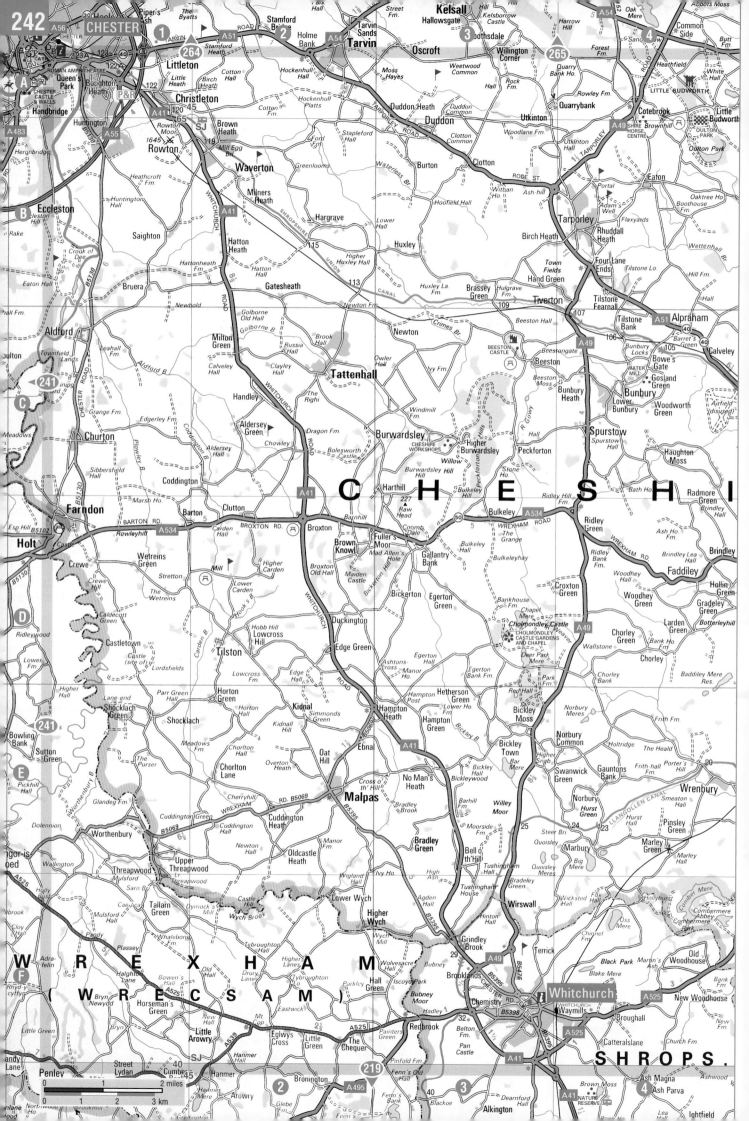

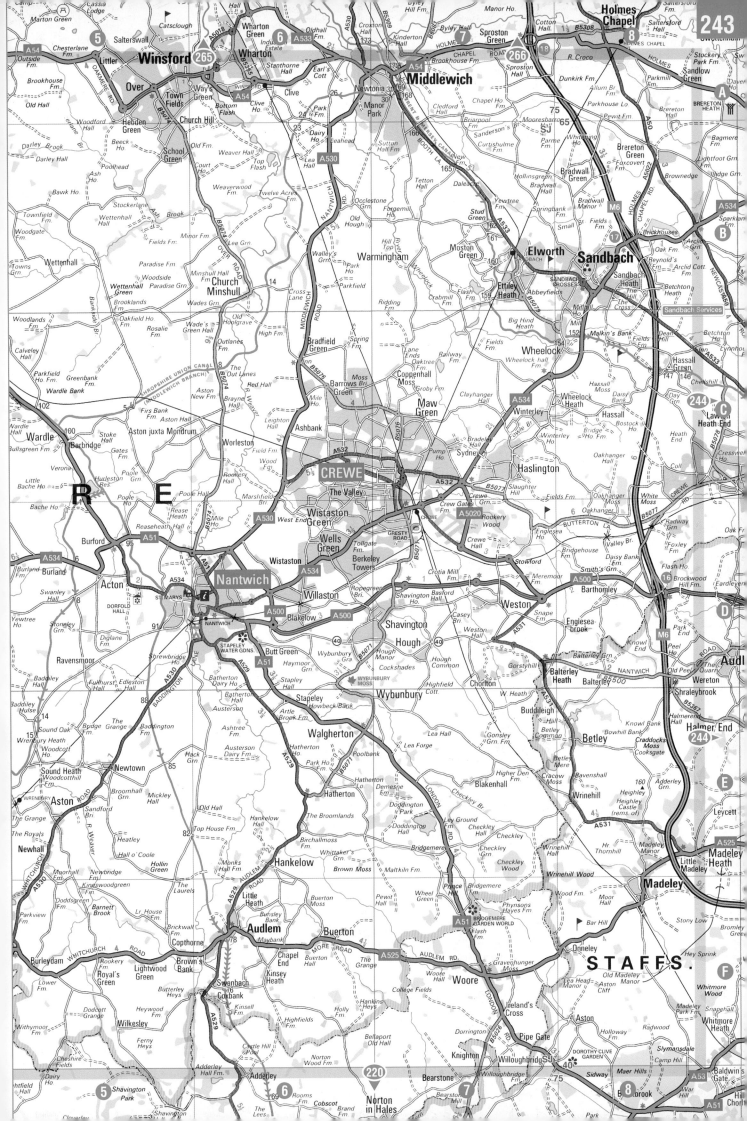

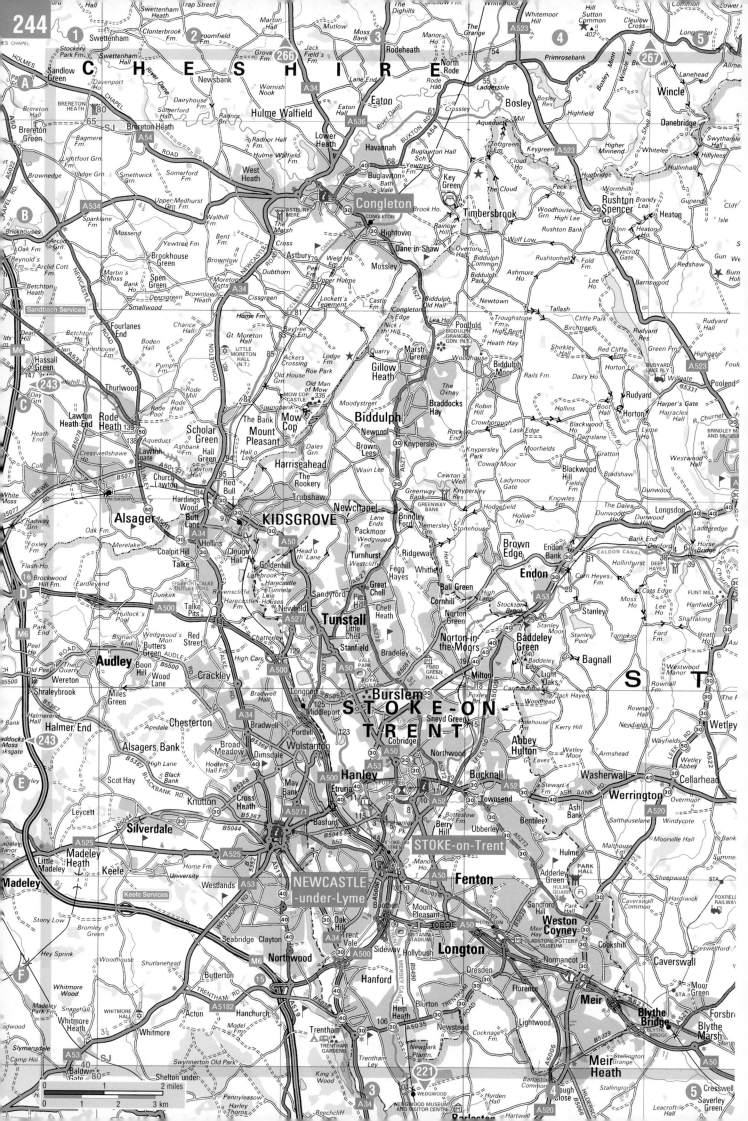

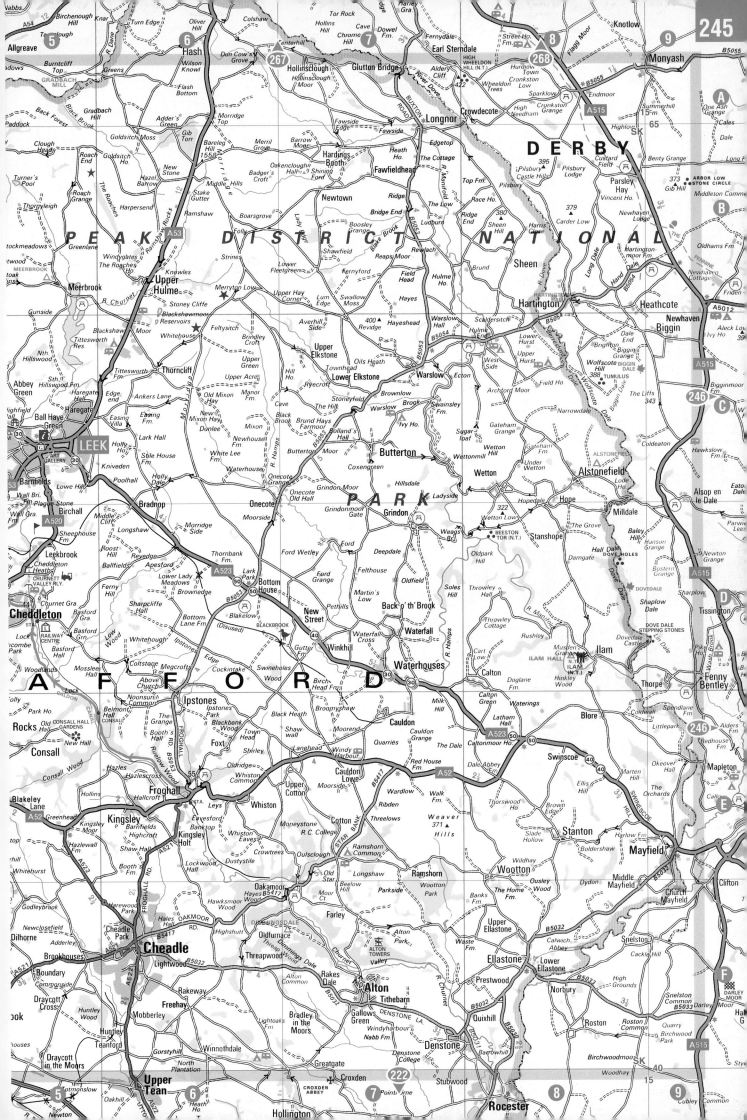

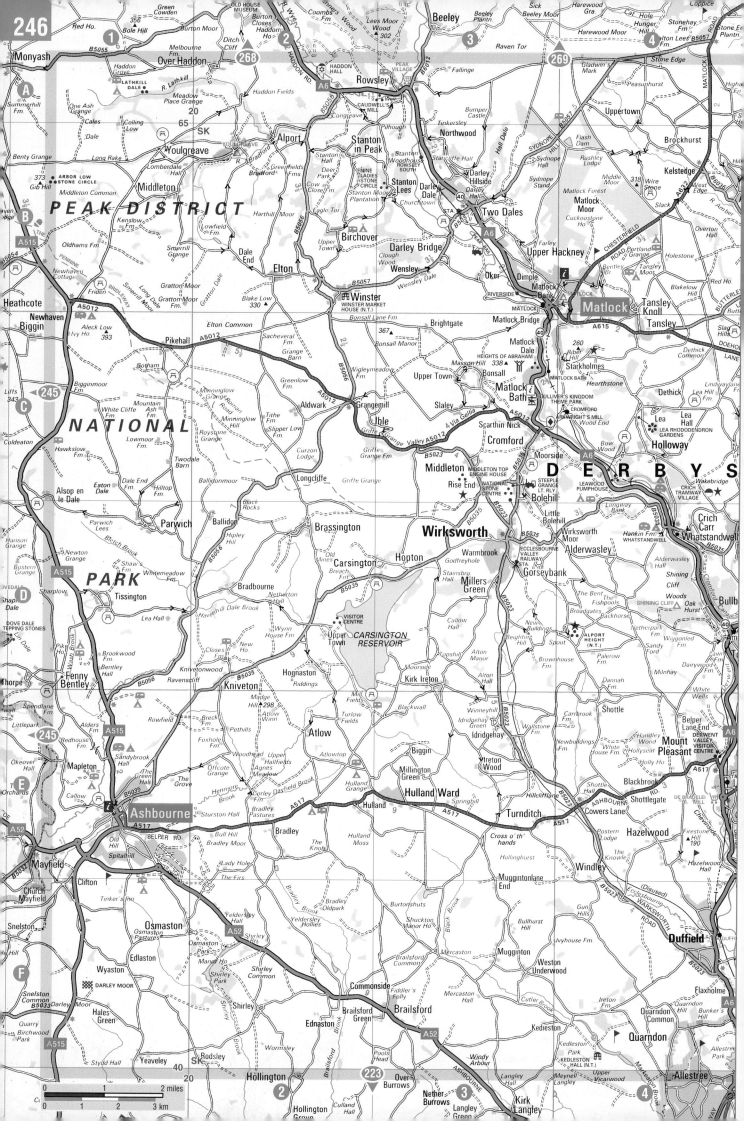

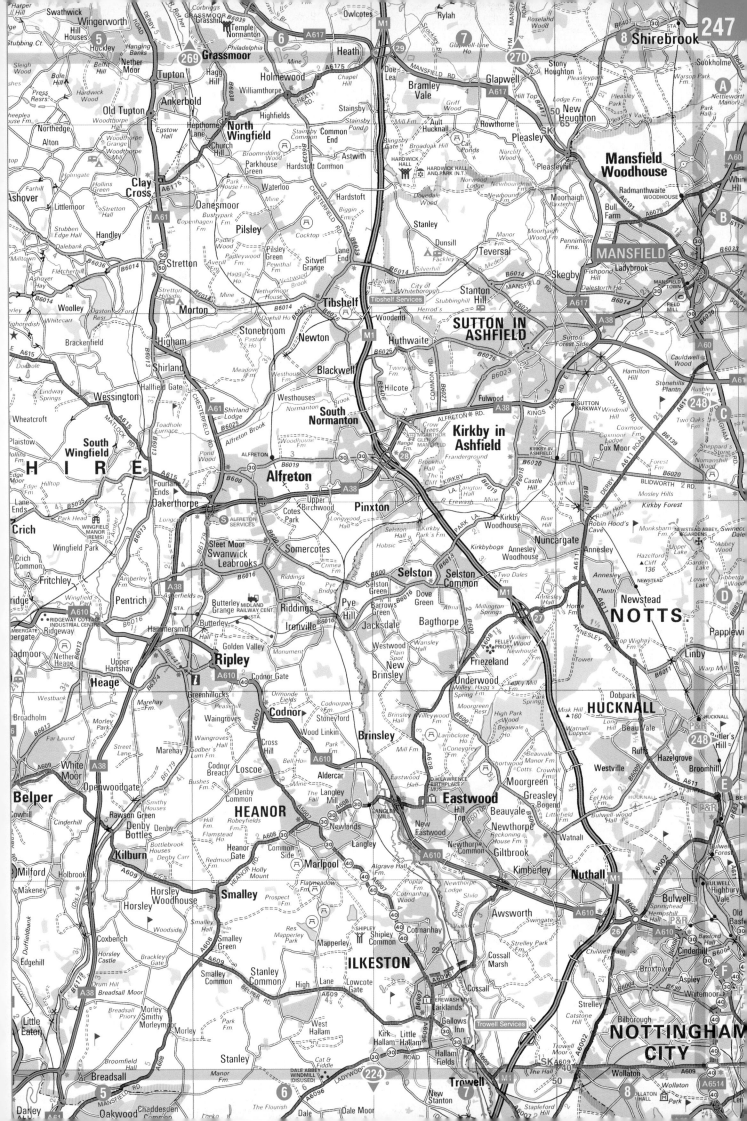

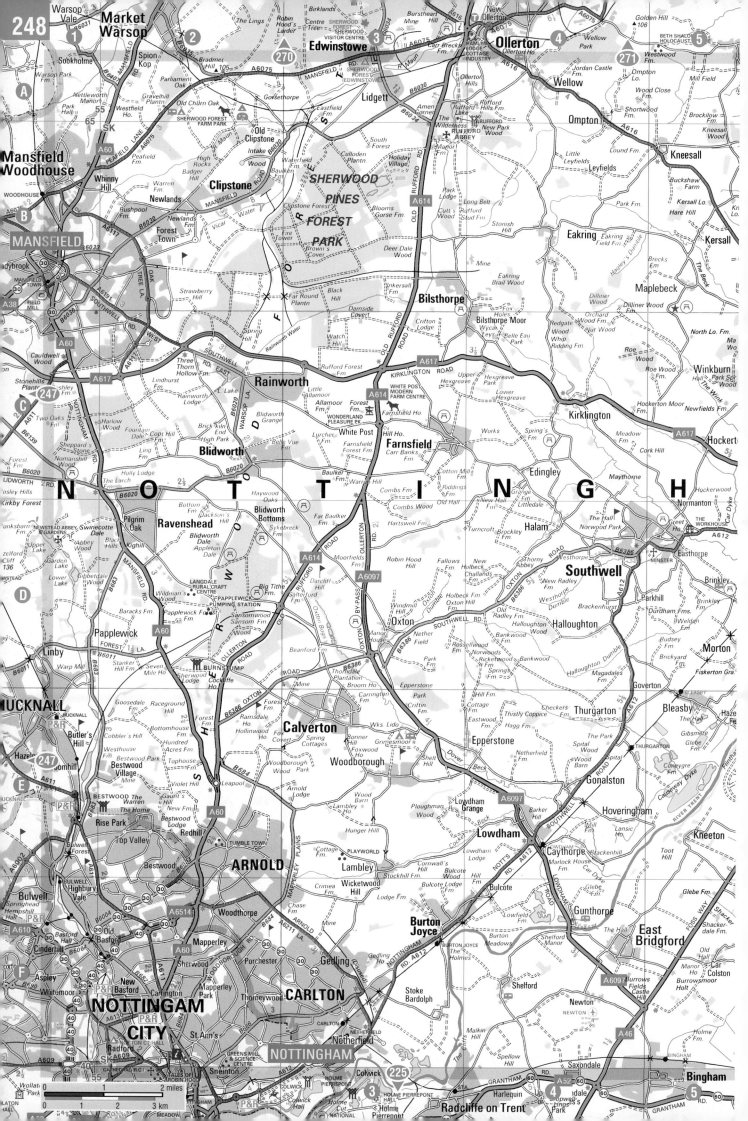

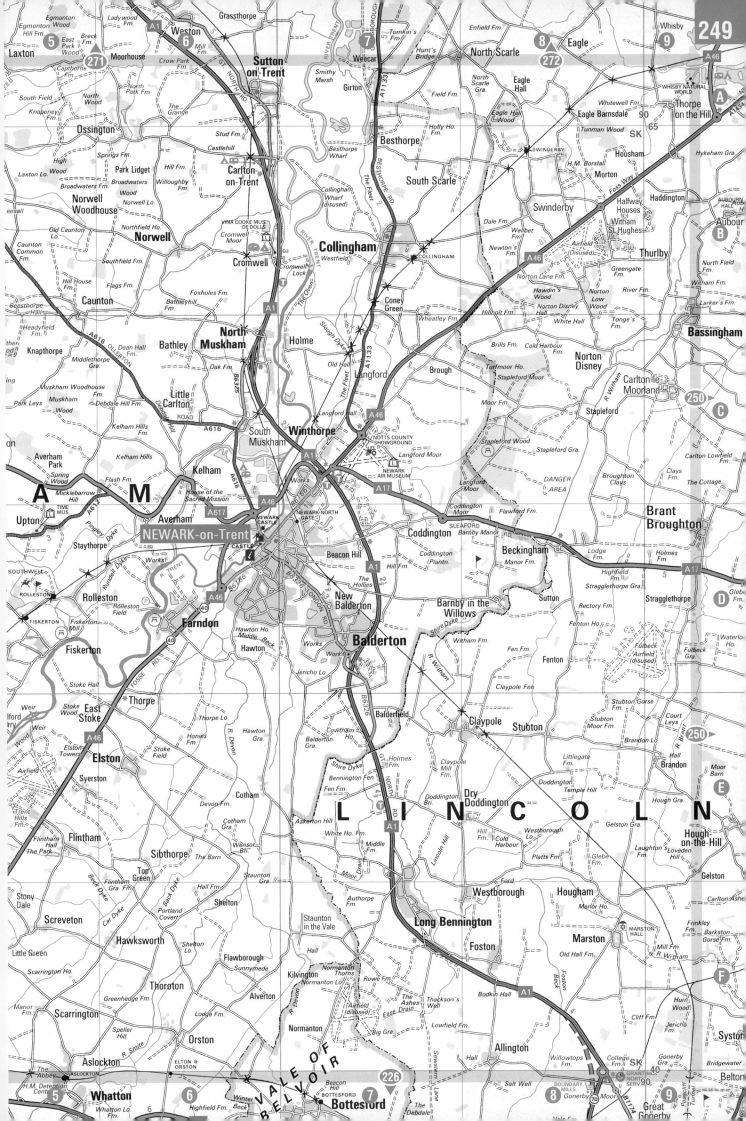

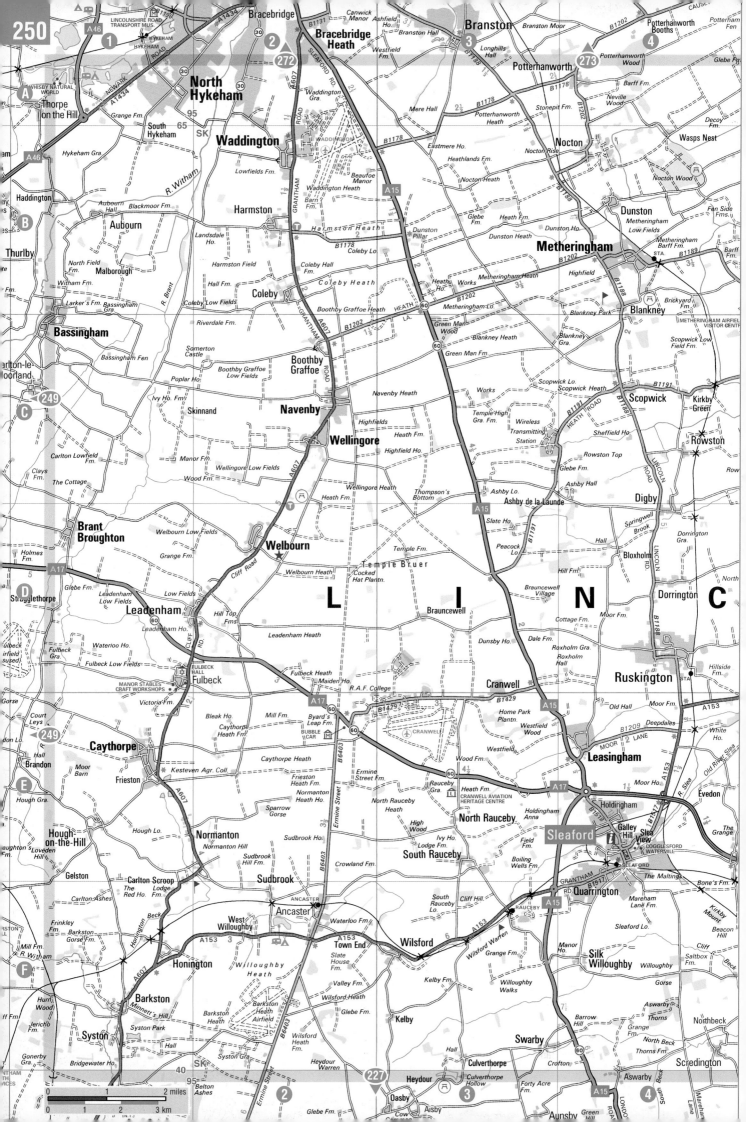

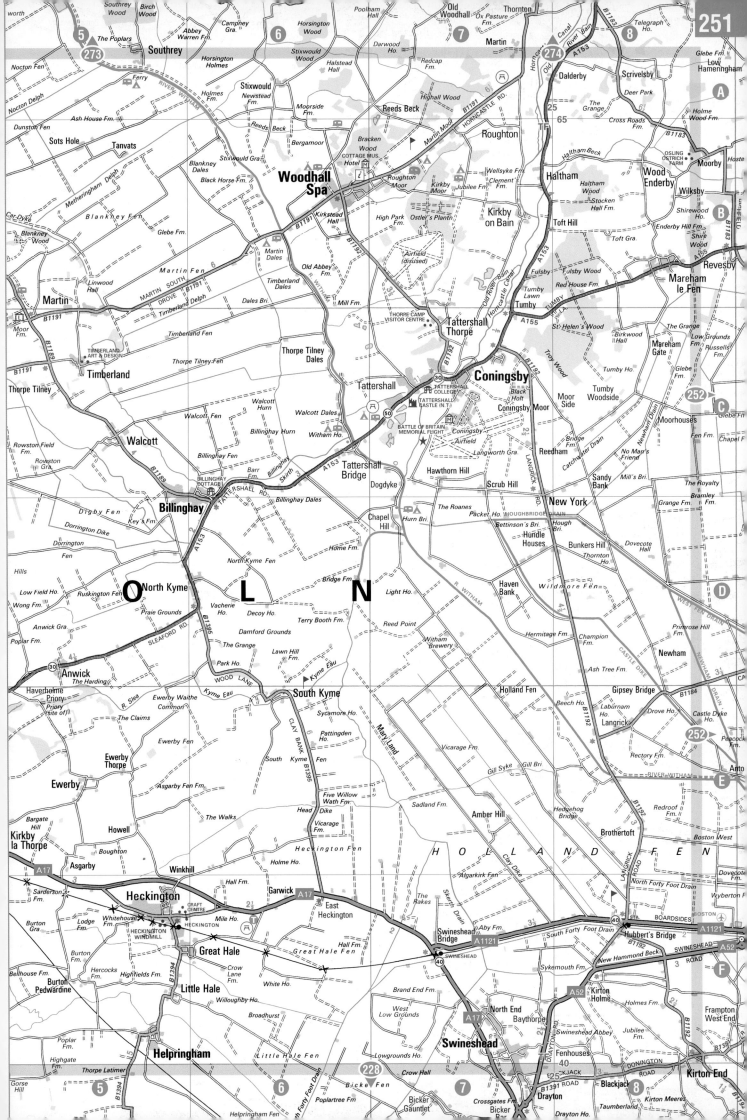

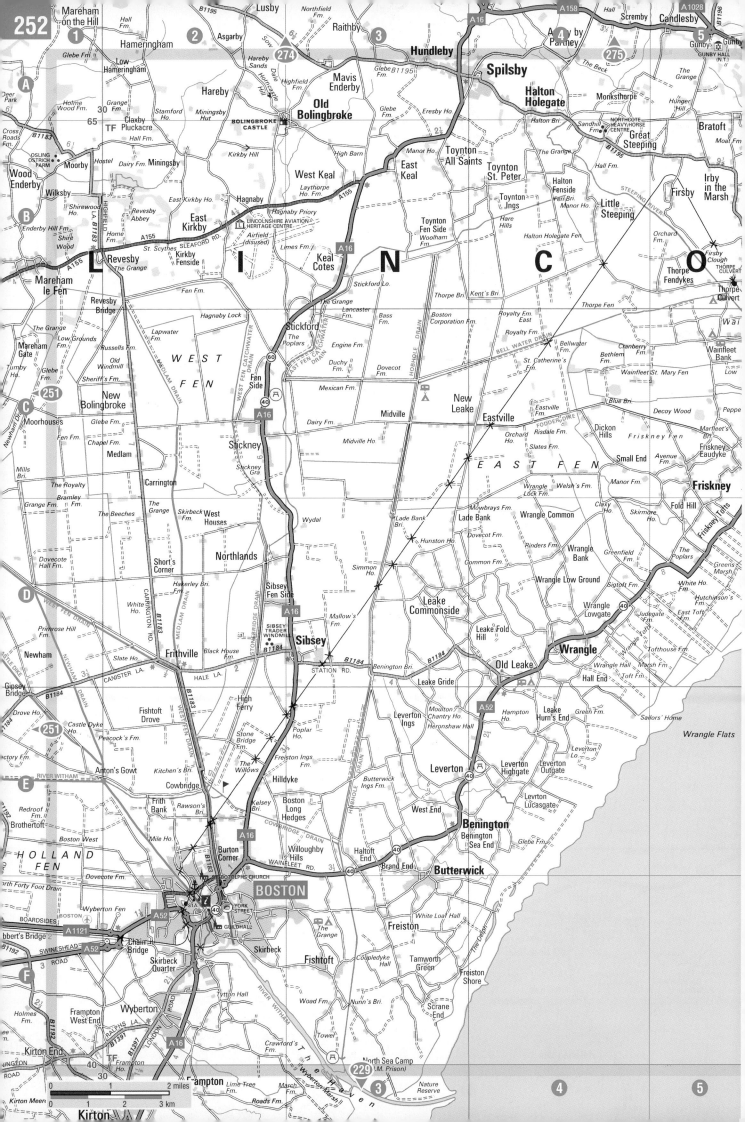

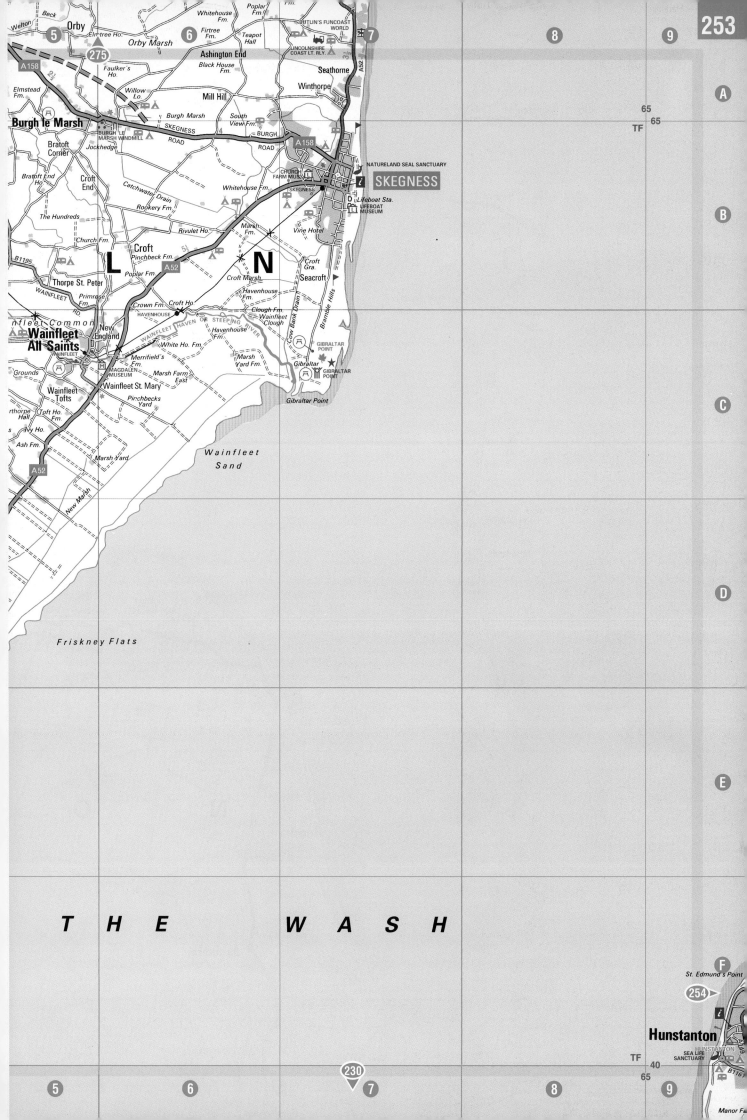

Welton
Beck
Orby
Elmtree Ho.
Orby Marsh
**A158**
**275**
Faulker's Ho.
Elmstead Fm.
Burgh le Marsh
Bratoft Corner
Jockhedge
BURGH LE MARSH WINDMILL
Whitehouse Fm.
Poplar Fm.
Firtree Fm.
Teapot Hall
Ashington End
Black House Fm.
Mill Hill
South View Fm.
Burgh Marsh
SKEGNESS ROAD
BURGH ROAD
**A158**
BUTLIN'S FUNCOAST WORLD
LINCOLNSHIRE COAST LT. RLY.
Seathorne
Winthorpe
**A52**

Bratoft End Ho.
Croft End
The Hundreds
Church Fm.
Catchwater Drain
Rookery Fm.
Whitehouse Fm.
Rivulet Ho.
Marsh Fm.
Vine Hotel

CHURCH FARM MUSEUM
SKEGNESS
NATURELAND SEAL SANCTUARY
*i* SKEGNESS
Lifeboat Sta.
LIFEBOAT MUSEUM

**B1195**
Croft
Pinchbeck Fm.
Poplar Fm.
**A52**
**L**   **N**
Thorpe St. Peter
Primrose Fm.
Crown Fm.
Croft Ho.
HAVENHOUSE
Croft Marsh
Havenhouse Fm.
Clough Fm.
Croft Gra.
Seacroft
Bramble Hills
WAINFLEET RD.
New England
WAINFLEET HAVEN OR STEEPING RIVER
Havenhouse Fm.
Wainfleet Clough
Cow Bank Drain
GIBRALTAR POINT
nfleet Common
Wainfleet All Saints
WAINFLEET
Merrifield's Fm.
MAGDALEN MUSEUM
White Ho. Fm.
Marsh Yard Fm.
Marsh Fm. East
Gibraltar
GIBRALTAR POINT
Grounds
Wainfleet St. Mary
Marsh Farm East
Gibraltar Point
Wainfleet Tofts
Pinchbecks Yard
rthorpe Hall
Toft Ho. Fm.
Ivy Ho.
**A52**
Ash Fm.
Marsh Yard
New Marsh
*Wainfleet Sand*

*Friskney Flats*

*T H E    W A S H*

St. Edmund's Point
**254**
*i*
**Hunstanton**
HUNSTANTON SEA LIFE SANCTUARY
**B116**
Manor F

**230**

65
65
TF
TF
40
65

5    6    7    8    9
A
B
C
D
E
F
5    6    7    8    9

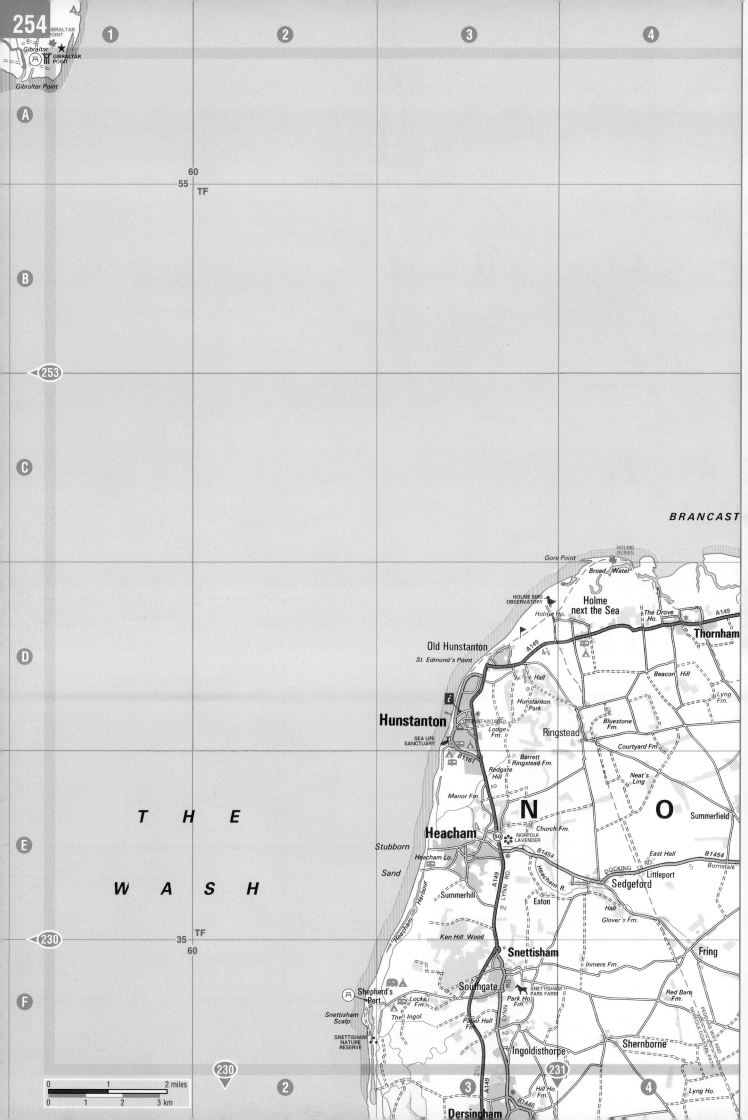

GIBRALTAR POINT

Gibraltar

GIBRALTAR POINT

Gibraltar Point

**1**  **2**  **3**  **4**

A

60
55
TF

B

253

C

BRANCAST

Gore Point

HOLME DUNES

Broad Water

HOLME BIRD OBSERVATORY

Holme Ho.

Holme next the Sea

The Drove Ho.

A149

Thornham

Old Hunstanton

St. Edmund's Point

Hall

Beacon Hill

Lyng Fm.

D

Hunstanton Park

Hunstanton

Ringstead

Bluestone Fm.

Lodge Fm.

Courtyard Fm.

SEA LIFE SANCTUARY

Barrett Ringstead Fm.

B1161

Redgate Hill

Neat's Ling

Manor Fm.

N O

Summerfield

**T H E**

Church Fm.

Heacham

NORFOLK LAVENDER

B1454

East Hall

B1454

Burnstalk

Stubborn

Heacham Lo.

DOCKING RD.

Littleport

E

**W A S H**

Sand

Heacham Harbour

Summerhill

A149

LYNN RD.

Heacham R.

Eaton

Sedgeford

Hall

Glover's Fm.

35
60
TF

230

Ken Hill Wood

Inmere Fm.

Snettisham

Fring

Shepherd's Port

Locke Fm.

Southgate

SNETTISHAM PARK FARM

Park Ho. Fm.

Red Barn Fm.

F

Snettisham Scalp

The Ingol

Paper Hall Fm.

NN RD.

PEDDARS WAY AND NORFOLK COASTAL PATH

SNETTISHAM NATURE RESERVE

Ingoldisthorpe

Shernborne

230

231

Hill Ho. Fm.

Lyng Ho.

A149

**2**  **3**  **4**

B1440

Dersingham

0    1    2 miles
0    1    2    3 km

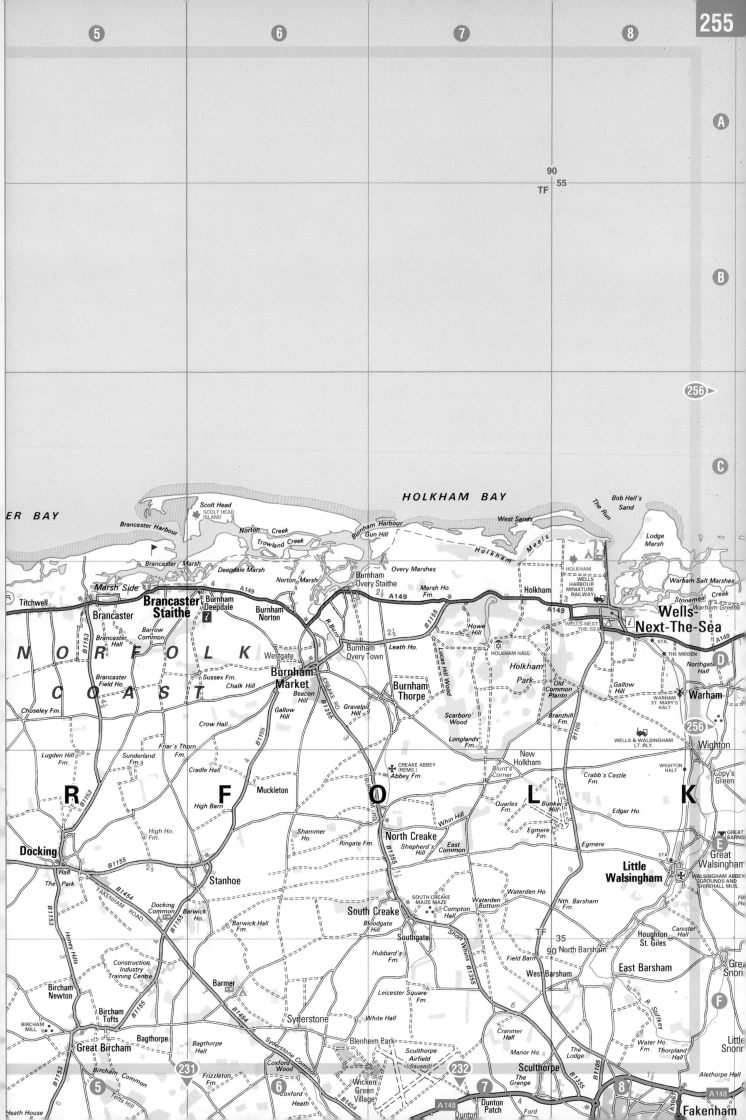

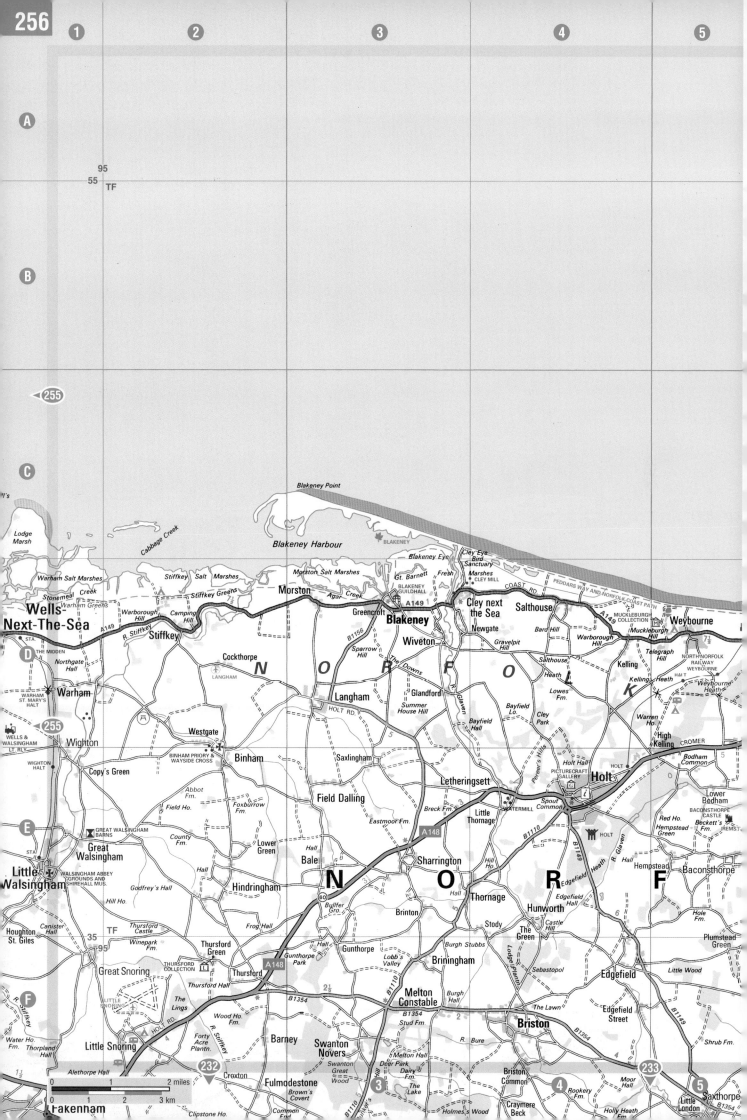

95
55 TF

◁ 255

Blakeney Point

Blakeney Harbour

Lodge Marsh

Cabbage Creek

Warham Salt Marshes

Stonemeal Creek

Stiffkey Salt Marshes

Stiffkey Greens

Morston Salt Marshes

BLAKENEY

Blakeney Eye

Cley Eye Bird Sanctuary

Marshes CLEY MILL

Fresh

Gt. Barnett

BLAKENEY GUILDHALL

COAST RD.

PEDDARS WAY AND NORFOLK COAST PATH

Morston

Agar Creek

Greencroft

Blakeney

A149

Cley next the Sea

Salthouse

A149

MUCKLEBURGH COLLECTION

Weybourne

Wells-Next-The-Sea

A149

Warborough Hill

Camping Hill

7½

Newgate

Wiveton

Bard Hill

Warborough Hill

Muckleburgh Hill

7½

R. Stiffkey

Stiffkey

Sparrow Hill

The Downs

Gravelpit Hill

Salthouse Heath

Kelling

Telegraph Hill

NORTH NORFOLK RAILWAY WEYBOURNE

H&T

STA.

THE MIDDEN

Cockthorpe

LANGHAM

Glandford

Summer House Hill

Lowes Fm.

Kelling Heath

Weybourne Heath

N　O　R　F　O　L　K

Northgate Hall

Warham

WARHAM ST. MARY'S HALT

Langham

HOLT RD.

R. Glaven

Bayfield Lo.

Cley Park

Warren Ho.

CROMER

High Kelling

◁ 255

Wighton

Westgate

BINHAM PRIORY & WAYSIDE CROSS

Binham

Saxlingham

Bayfield Hall

Holt Hall

PICTURECRAFT GALLERY

Holt

Bodham Common

WIGHTON HALT

Copy's Green

Abbot Fm.

Field Ho.

Foxburrow Fm.

Field Dalling

Percie's Hills

Letheringsett

WATERMILL

Spout Common

Lower Bodham

BACONSTHORPE CASTLE

Beckett's Fm.

GREAT WALSINGHAM BARNS

County Fm.

Breck Fm.

Little Thornage

A148

Holt

B1110

Red Ho.

Hempstead Green

REMST.

STA.

Great Walsingham

Hall

Lower Green

Bale

Eastmoor Fm.

Sharrington

Hill Ho.

B1149

Edgefield Heath

Hall

Hempstead

Baconsthorpe

Little Walsingham

WALSINGHAM ABBEY GROUNDS AND SHIREHALL MUS.

Godfrey's Hall

Hindringham

N　O　R　F

80

Thornage

Hall

Edgefield Hall

Hole Fm.

Hill Ho.

Bullfer Gro.

Brinton

Hunworth

Stody

Castle Hill

The Green

Edgefield

Little Wood

Plumstead Green

Houghton St. Giles

Canister Hall

35

TF

95

Thursford Castle

Frog Hall

Gunthorpe

Burgh Stubbs

Sebastopol

Winepark Fm.

THURSFORD COLLECTION

Thursford Green

Hall

Lobb's Valley

Briningham

The Lawn

Edgefield Street

B1149

Great Snoring

Thursford Hall

A148

Thursford

2½

B1354

Melton Constable

Burgh Hall

Lodge Plantn.

Shrub Fm.

LITTLE SNORING

The Lings

Wood Ho. Fm.

B1110

Briston

Water Ho. Fm.

Thorpland Hall

Little Snoring

Forty Acre Plantn.

R. Stiffkey

Barney

Swanton Novers

Stud Fm.

B1354

Moor Hall

Little London

Saxthorpe

B1354

1½

Alethorpe Hall

0 ——— 1 ——— 2 miles

0 — 1 — 2 — 3 km

232

Croxton

Fulmodestone

Swanton Great Wood

Melton Hall

Deer Park Dairy Fm.

R. Bure

Briston Common

233

Fakenham

Clipstone Ho.

Brown's Covert

Common End

The Lake

Holmes's Wood

Craymere Beck

Rookery Fm.

Holly Heath Fm.

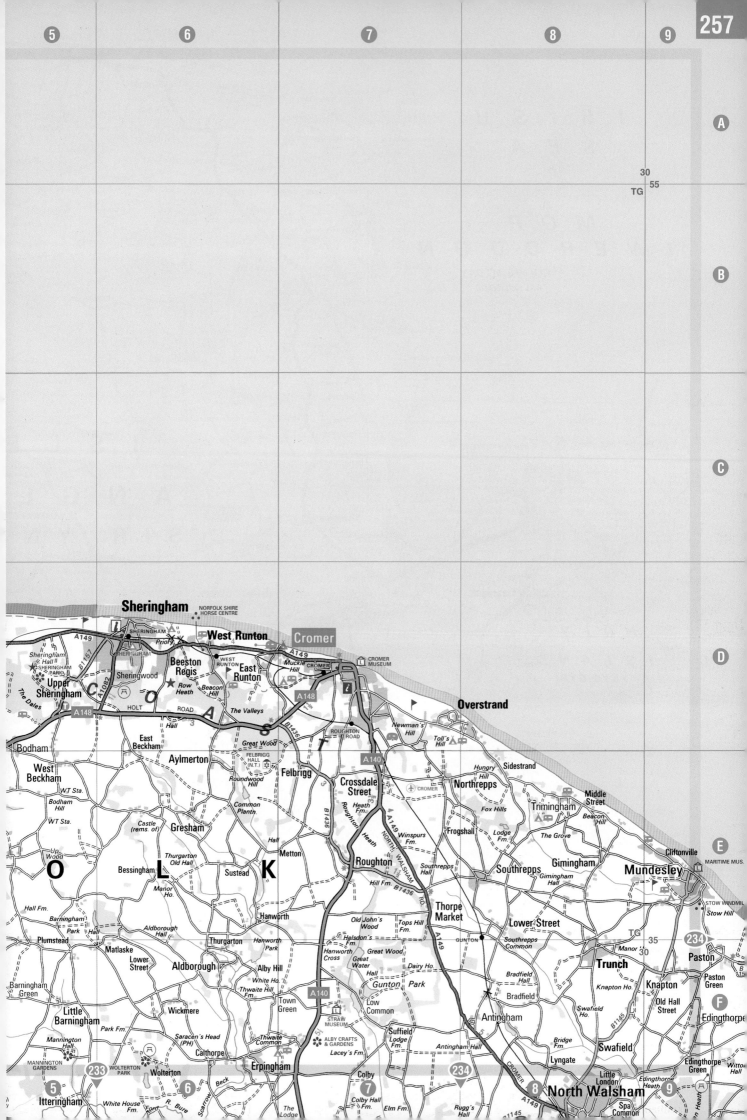

Sheringham
NORFOLK SHIRE
HORSE CENTRE
West Runton
Cromer
CROMER MUSEUM
Upper
Sheringham
Sheringham Hall
SHERINGHAM PARK
Sheringwood
Beeston Regis
Priory
WEST RUNTON
East Runton
Muckle Hill
CROMER
Overstrand
Bodham
East Beckham
Aylmerton
Felbrigg
FELBRIGG HALL (N.T.)
Roundwood Hill
Common Plantn.
Crossdale Street
Newman's Hill
Toll's Hill
Northrepps
Sidestrand
West Beckham
Bodham Hill
WT Sta.
Gresham
Metton
Hungry Hill
Frogshall
Fox Hills
Lodge Fm.
Trimingham
Middle Street
Beacon Hill
The Grove
Cliftonville
MARITIME MUS.
OLK
Bessingham
Thurgarton Old Hall
Sustead
Roughton
Winspurs Fm.
NORTH WALSHAM
Southrepps Hall
Southrepps
Gimingham
Gimingham Hall
Mundesley
STOW WINDMILL
Stow Hill
Hall Fm.
Barningham Park
Plumstead
Matlaske
Lower Street
Aldborough
Hanworth
Hanworth Park
Old John's Wood
Tops Hill Fm.
Thorpe Market
Lower Street
Trunch
Knapton Ho.
Knapton
Paston
Paston Green
Barningham Green
Little Barningham
Mannington Hall
MANNINGTON GARDENS
Wickmere
Alby Hill
White Ho.
Thwaite Hill Fm.
Town Green
Hanworth Cross
Great Wood
Great Water
Dairy Ho.
Gunton Park
GUNTON
Southrepps Common
Bradfield Hall
Bradfield
Swafield Ho.
Old Hall Street
Swafield
Lyngate
Edingthorpe
Itteringham
White House Fm.
Ford
R. Bure
Scarrow Beck
Wolterton
WOLTERTON PARK
Calthorpe
Erpingham
STRAW MUSEUM
ALBY CRAFTS & GARDENS
Lacey's Fm.
Low Common
Suffield Lodge Fm.
Colby
Colby Hall
Antingham
Antingham Hall
Bridge Fm.
Little London
Edingthorpe Heath
Edingthorpe Green
Witton Hall
North Walsham
Elm Fm.
Rugg's Hall
Spa Common

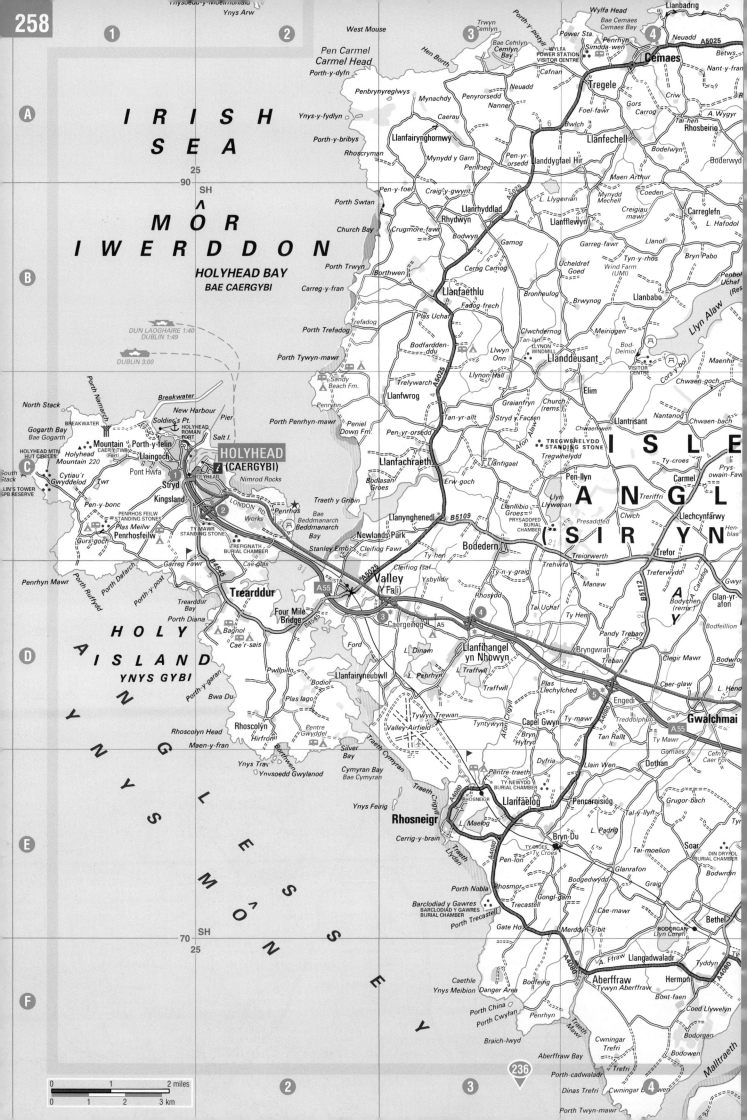

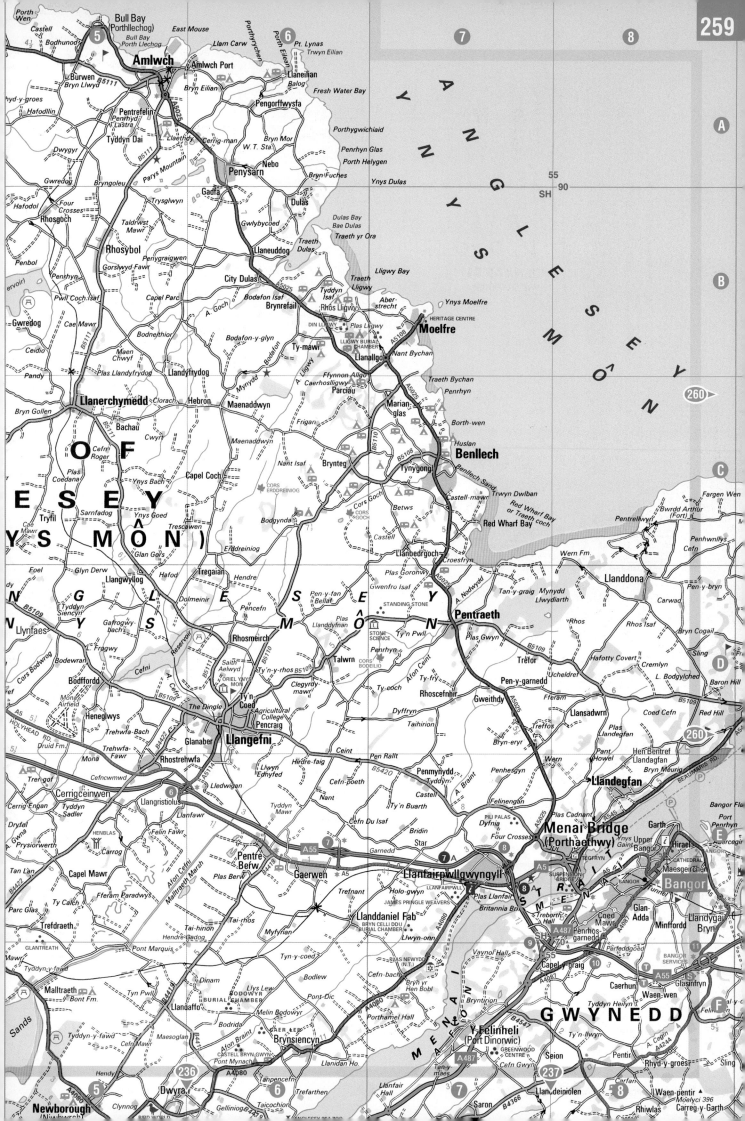

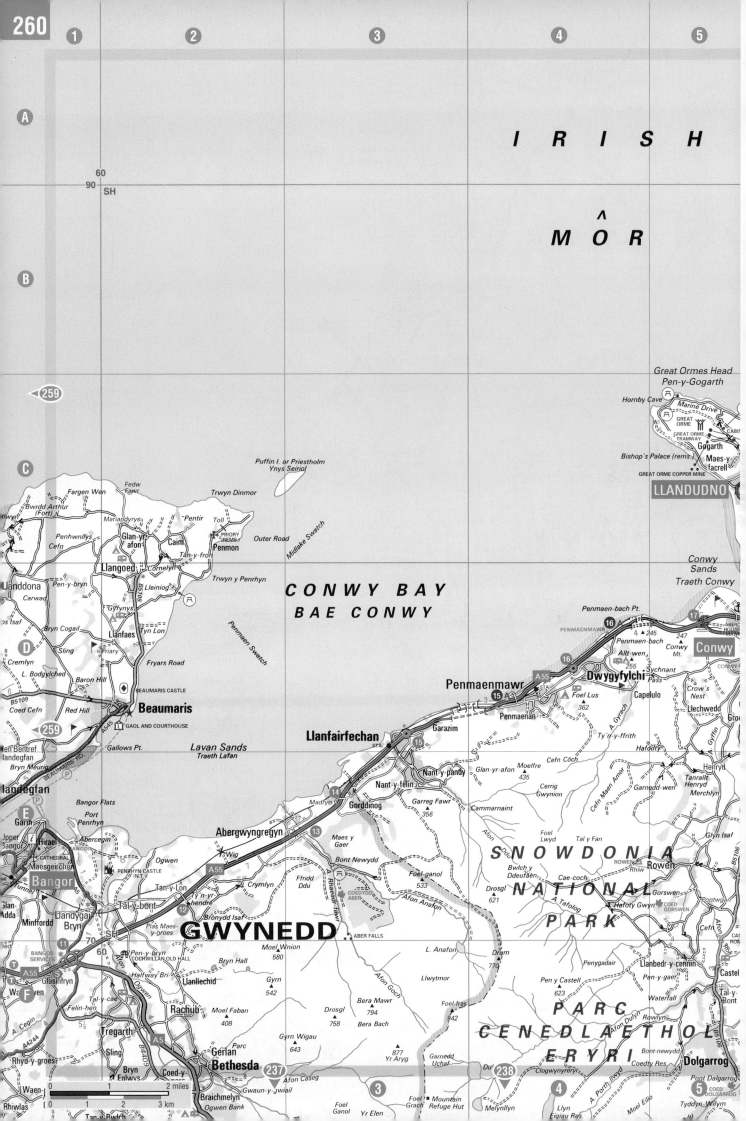

1    2    3    4    5

A

**I R I S H**

B

**M Ô R**

259

60
90
SH

C

Great Ormes Head
Pen-y-Gogarth
Hornby Cave
Marine Drive
GREAT
ORME
GREAT ORME
TRAMWAY
CABIN
Bishop's Palace (rems.)
Gogarth
Maes-y-facrell
GREAT ORME COPPER MINE

**LLANDUDNO**

Puffin I. or Priestholm
Ynys Seiriol

Fargen Wen
Fedw
Fawr
Trwyn Dinmor
Bwrdd Arthur
(Fort)
Mariandyrys
Pentir
Toll
Penhwnllys
Cefn
Glan-yr-
afon
Caim
PRIORY
(REMS)
Penmon
Conwy
Sands
Traeth Conwy
llwyn
Llangoed
Cornelyn
Tan-y-froh
Outer Road
Midlake Swatch
Llanddona
Pen-y-bryn
Carwad
B5109
Lleiniog
Trwyn y Penrhyn

**C O N W Y   B A Y**
**B A E   C O N W Y**

os Isaf
Bryn Cogail
Gyfynys
Llanfaes
Tyn Lon
Penmaen Swatch
Penmaen-bach Pt.
16
17
D
Sling
Friary
PENMAENMAWR
245
Conwy
Mt.
247
**Conwy**
Cremlyn
L. Bodgylched
Baron Hill
Fryars Road
Penmaen-bach
Allt-wen
255
Sychnant
Pass
ABER
HOUSE
Coed Cefn
Red Hill
B5109
A55
16
Dwygyfylchi
Foel Lus
362
Capelulo
Crow's
Nest
6
**BEAUMARIS CASTLE**
Penmaenmawr
15
Penmaenan
Llechwedd
Gro
**Beaumaris**
Llanfairfechan
Garazim
A. Gyrach
Ty'n-y-ffrith
Hafodty
259
GAOL AND COURTHOUSE
STA.
15
Garazim
Moelfre
435
Cerrig
Gwynion
Cefn Côch
Cefn Maen Amor
Garnedd-wen
Henryd
Tanrallt
Henryd
Merchlyn
en Bentref
landegfan
Gallows Pt.
**Lavan Sands**
Traeth Lafan
Nant-y-pandy
Glan-yr-afon
E
Bryn Meurig
Nant-y-felin
Garreg Fawr
356
Cammarnaint
landegfan
Bangor Flats
Port
Penrhyn
14
Madryn
Gorddinog
Foel
Lwyd
Tal y Fan
Glyn Isaf
Garth
Abercegin
Abergwyngregyn
13
Maes y
Gaer
**S N O W D O N I A**
Jpper
Bango
Hirael
Wig
Bont Newydd
Foel-ganol
533
Bwlch y
Ddeufaen
ROWEN
Rowen
CATHEDRAL
Ogwen
PENRHYN CASTLE
(N.T.)
Cae-coch
**N A T I O N A L**
Maesgeirchen
Ffridd
Ddu
COEDYDD
ABER
Drosgl
621
A Tafolog
Gorswen
Cefn
**Bangor**
Tan-y-Lôn
Crymlyn
Rhaeadr-fawr
Afon Anafon
Hafoty Gwyn
COED
GORSWEN
Pontwgan
Glan-
Adda
Llandygai
12
y'n-yr-
hendre
Brónydd Isaf
**P A R K**
Cefn
Minffordd
Bryn
Tal-y-bont
Plas Maes-
y-groes
**GWYNEDD**
ABER FALLS
Moel Wnion
580
L. Anafon
Drum
770
Penygadair
Llanbedr-y-cennin
11
70
60
SH
Pen-y-bryn
COCHWILLAN OLD HALL
Bryn Hall
Pen y Castell
623
Pen-y-gaer
Castel
BANGOR
SERVICES
Gyrn
542
Llwytmor
Waterfall
Tal-y-
Bont
T
A55
Glasinfryn
Halfway Bri
Llanllechid
Bera Mawr
794
Foel-fras
942
Afon Dulyn
Rowlyn
T
S
Tal-y-cae
PARC
Bont-newydd
Wa
F
Felin-hen
Drosgl
758
Bera Bach
Garnedd
Uchaf
**P A R C**
Clogwynyreryr
Coedty Res.
Dolgarrog
A Cegin
Rachub
Moel Faban
408
877
Yr Aryg
**C E N E D L A E T H O L**
A Porth llwyd
Pont Dalgarrog
Tregarth
Gyrn Wigau
643
**E R Y R I**
COED
DOLGARROG
Sling
Bryn
Eglwys
Gerlan
Parc
**Bethesda**
237
Afon Caseg
238
Llyn
Eigiau Res.
Tyddyn-Wilym
Rhyd-y-groes
A5
B4409
Coed-y-
pa
Gwaun-y-gwiail
Foel
Grach
Mountain
Refuge Hut
Melynllyn
Moel Eilio

0          1          2 miles
0     1     2     3 km

1    2    Braichmelyn    3    4    5
Waen-    Tan-y-Bwlch    Ogwen Bank    Foel
Rhiwlas    Ganol    Yr Elen

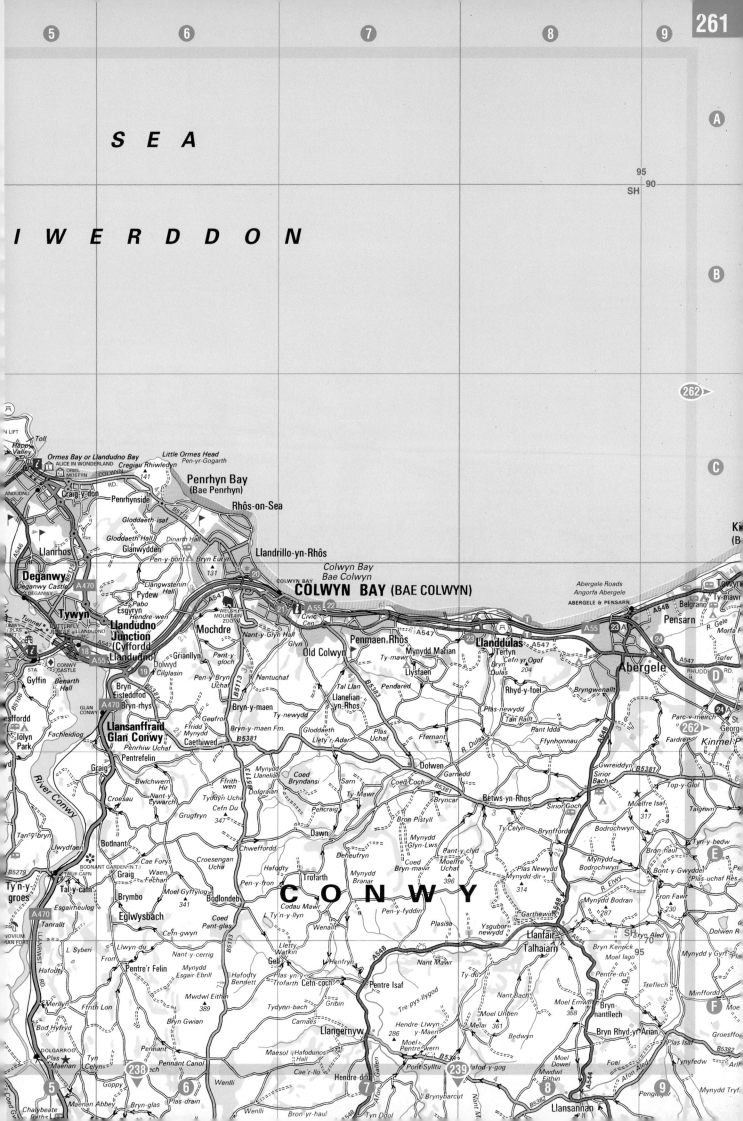

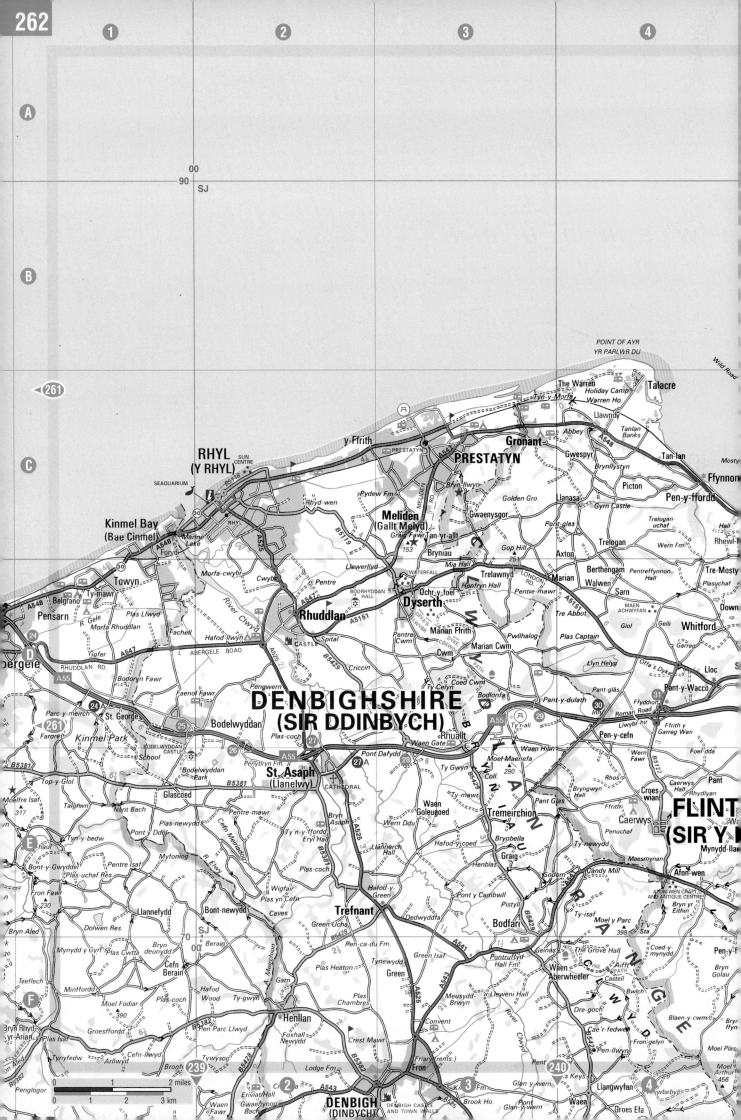

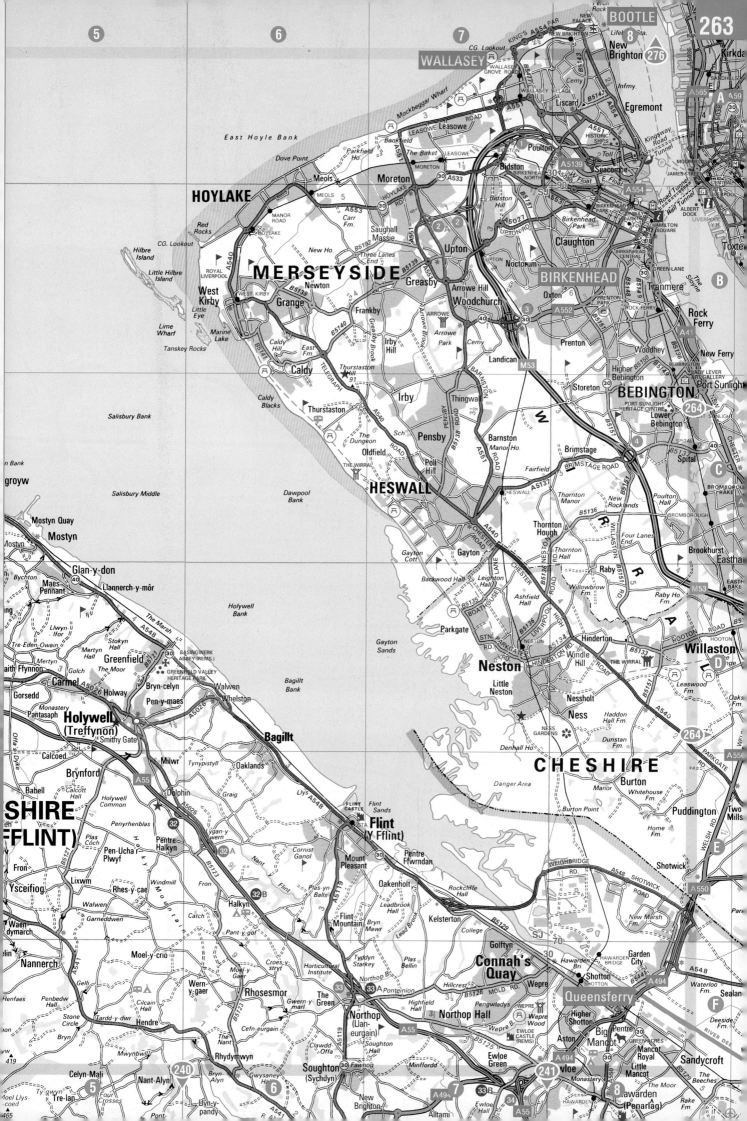

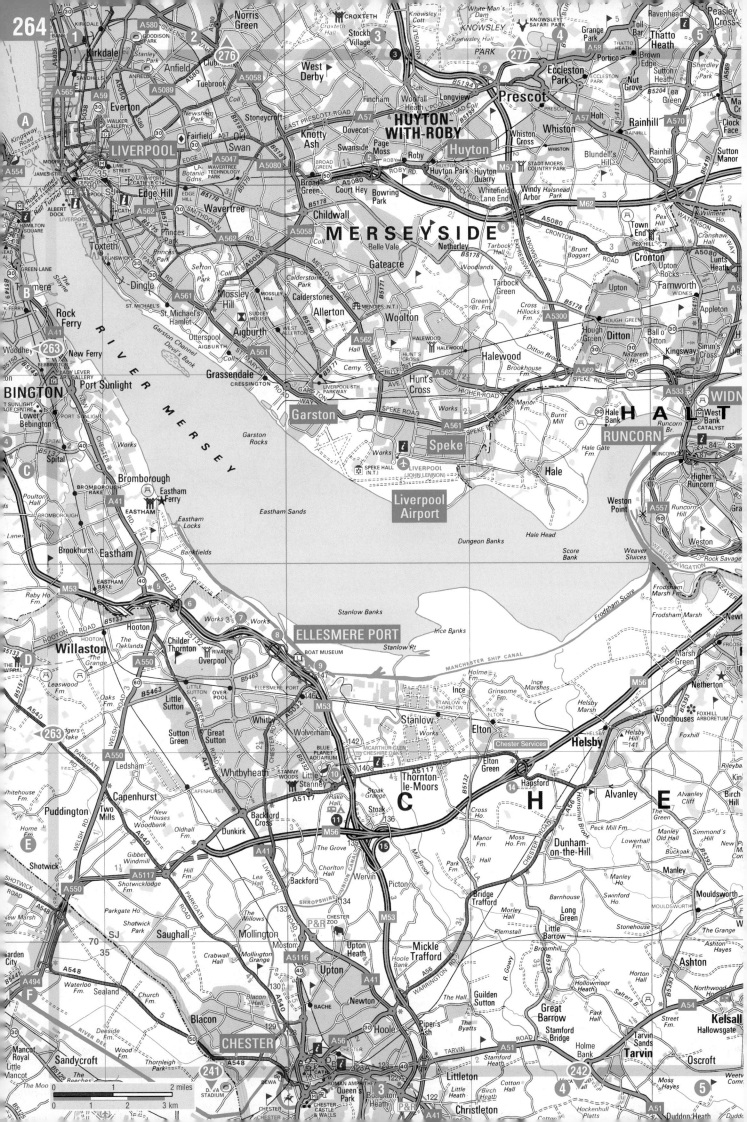

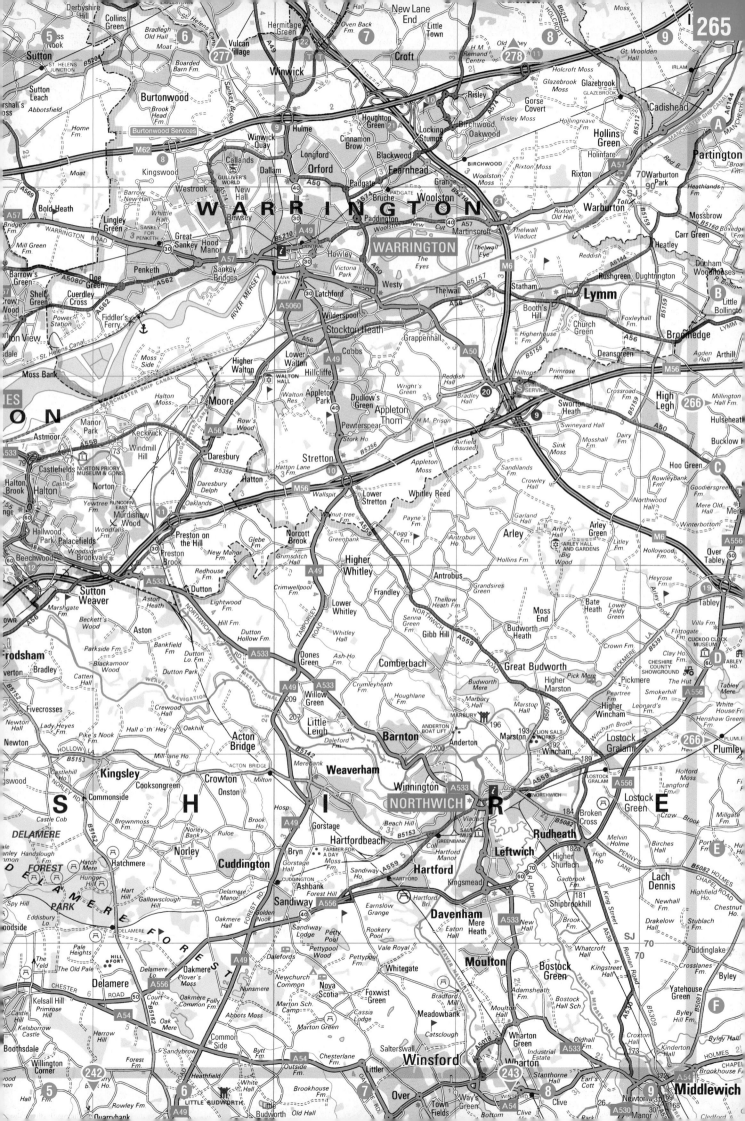

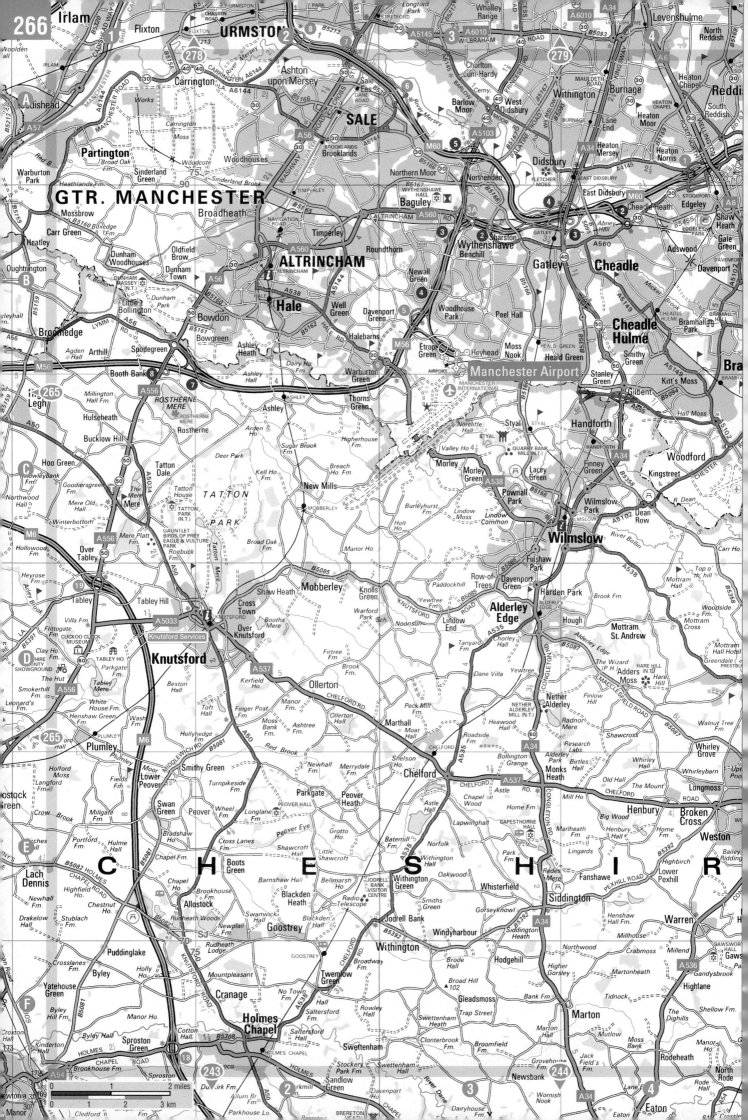

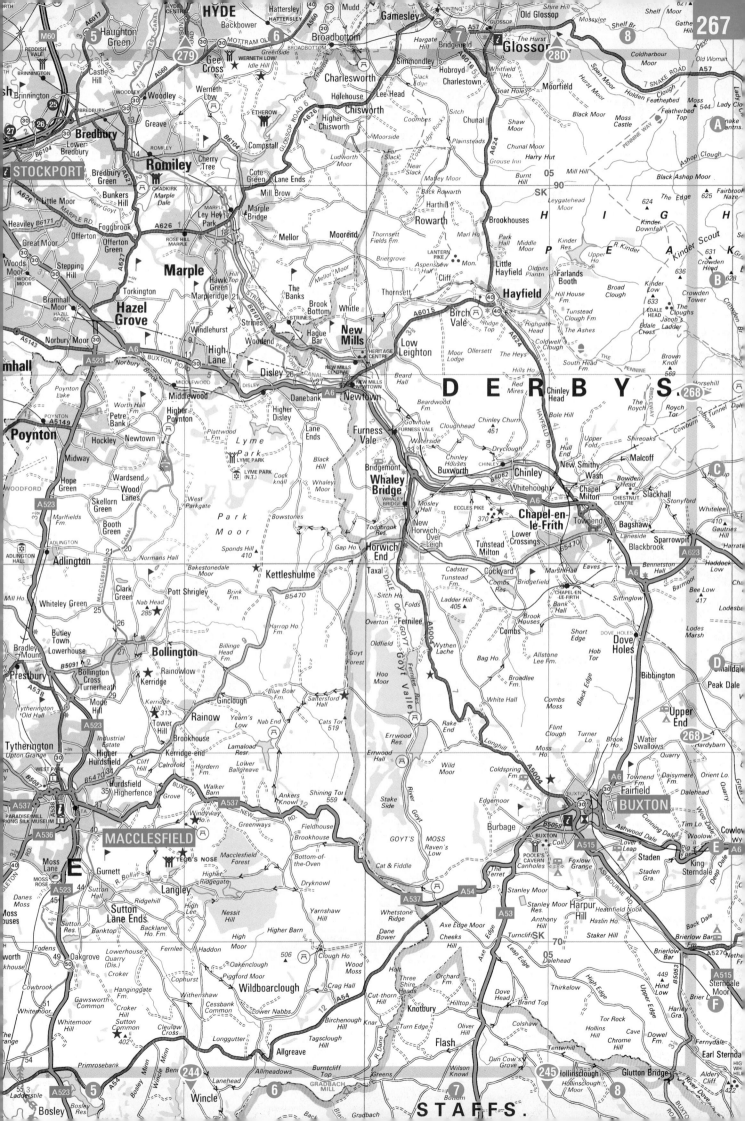

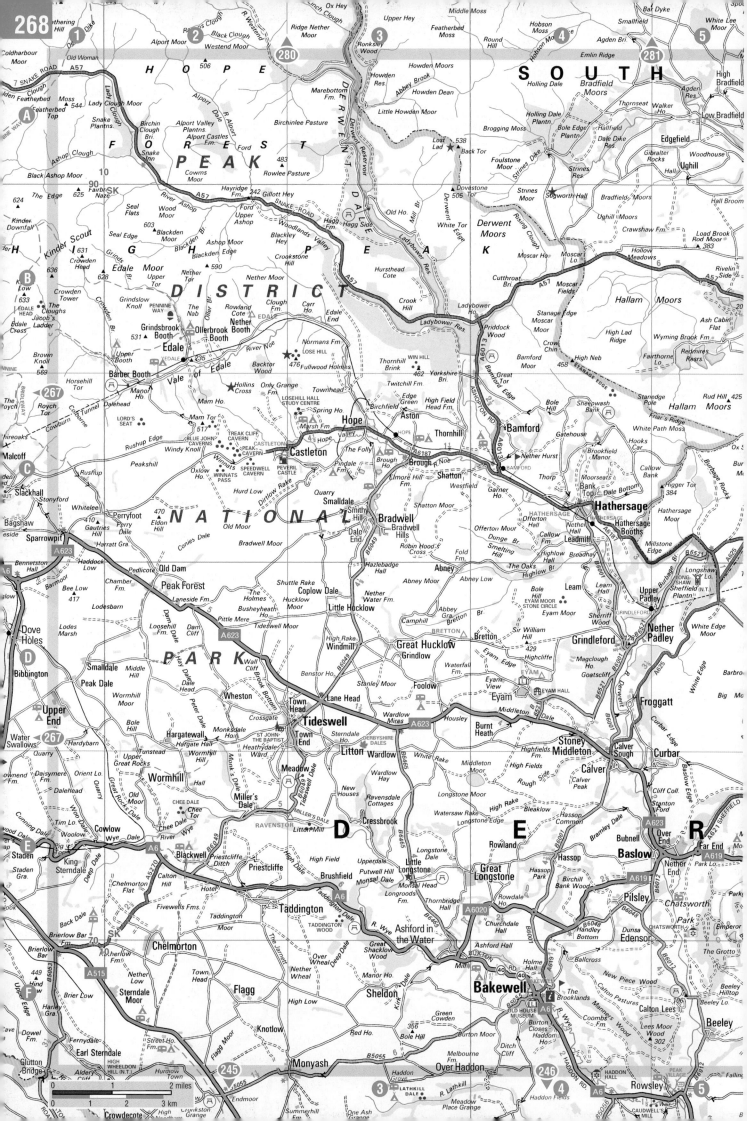

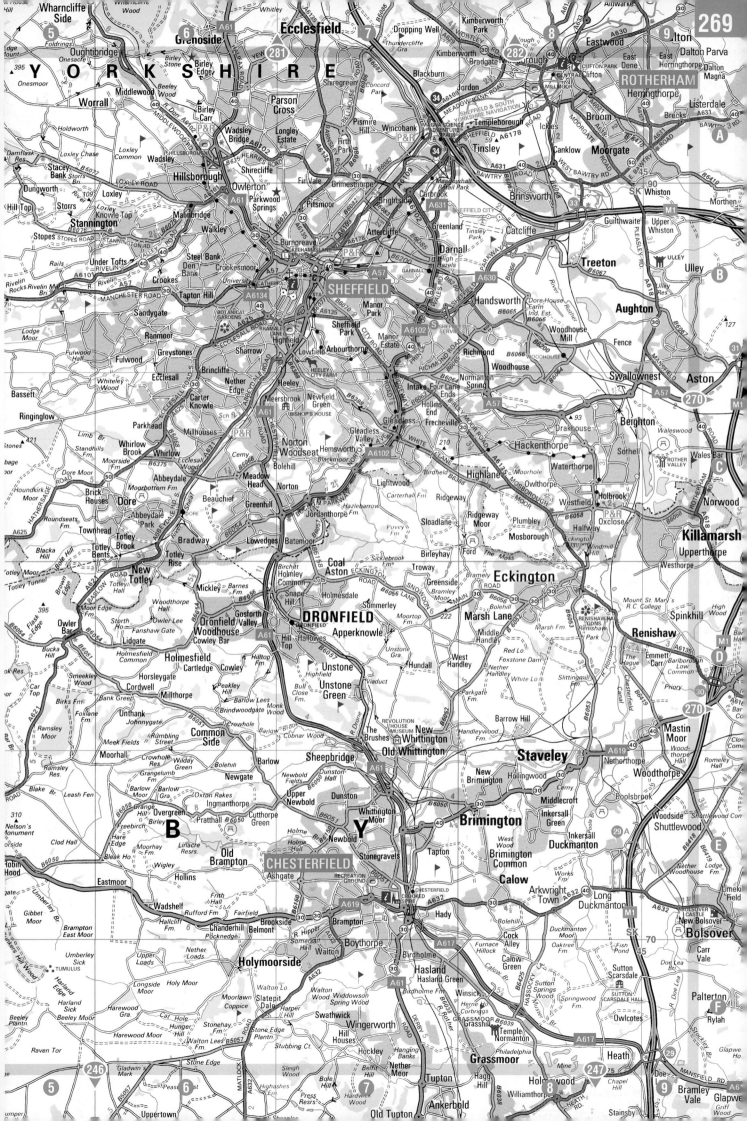

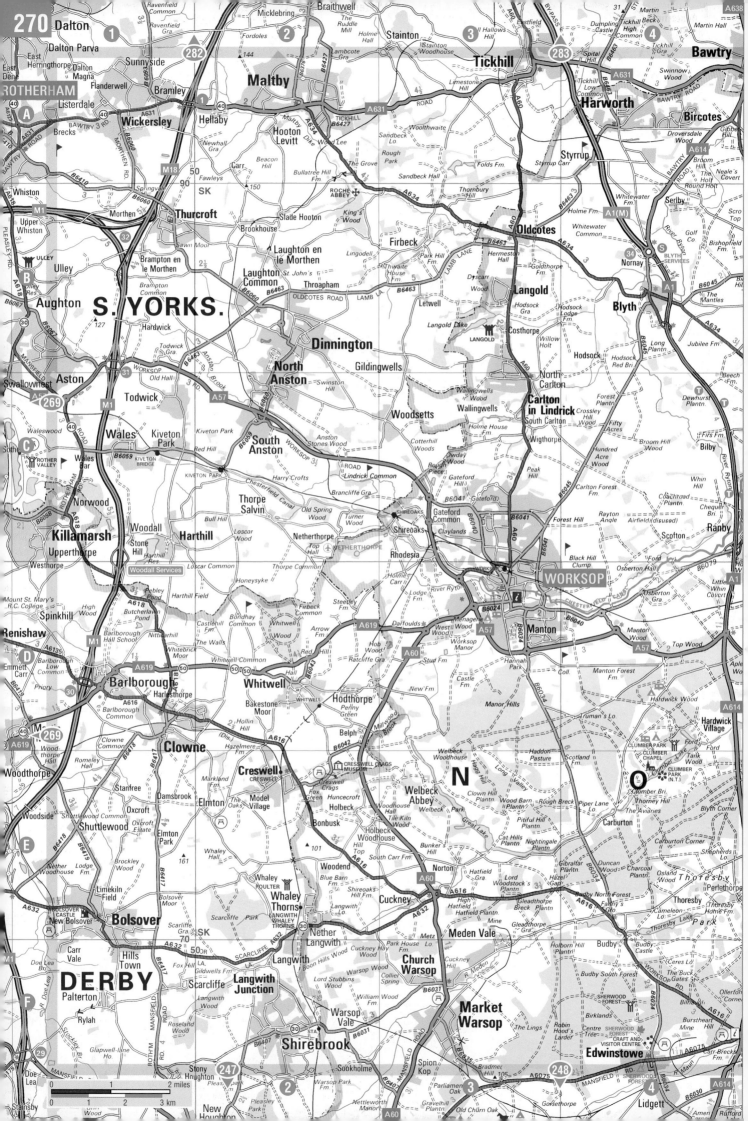

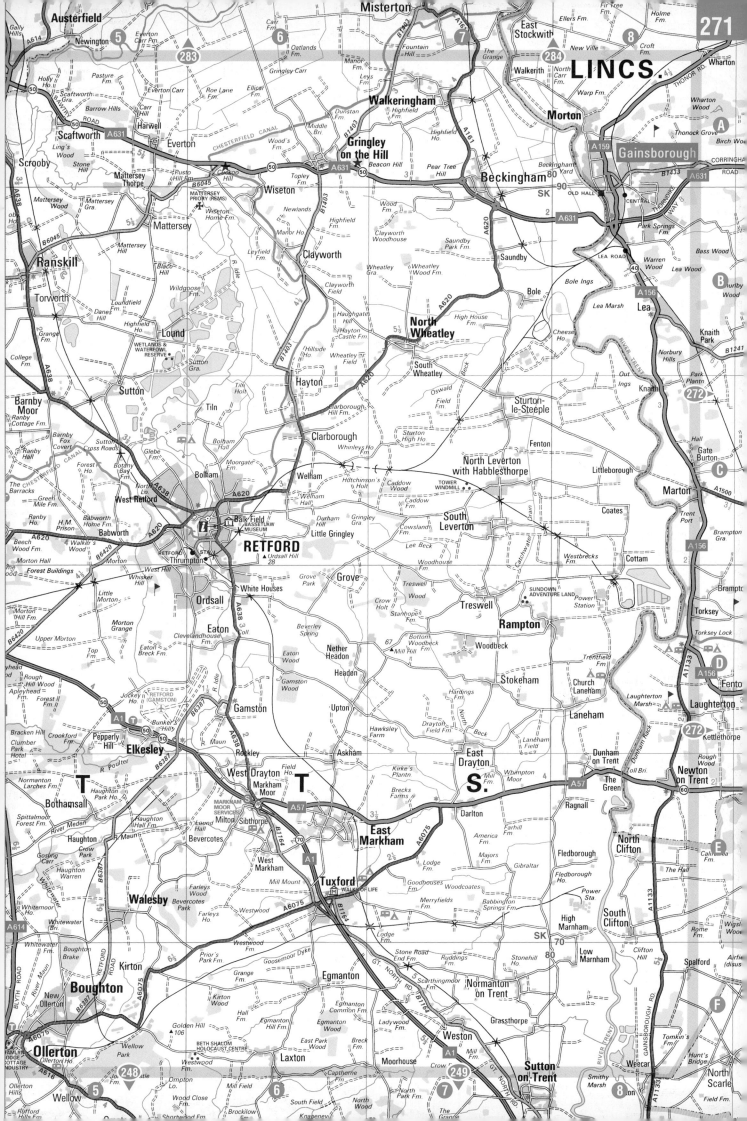

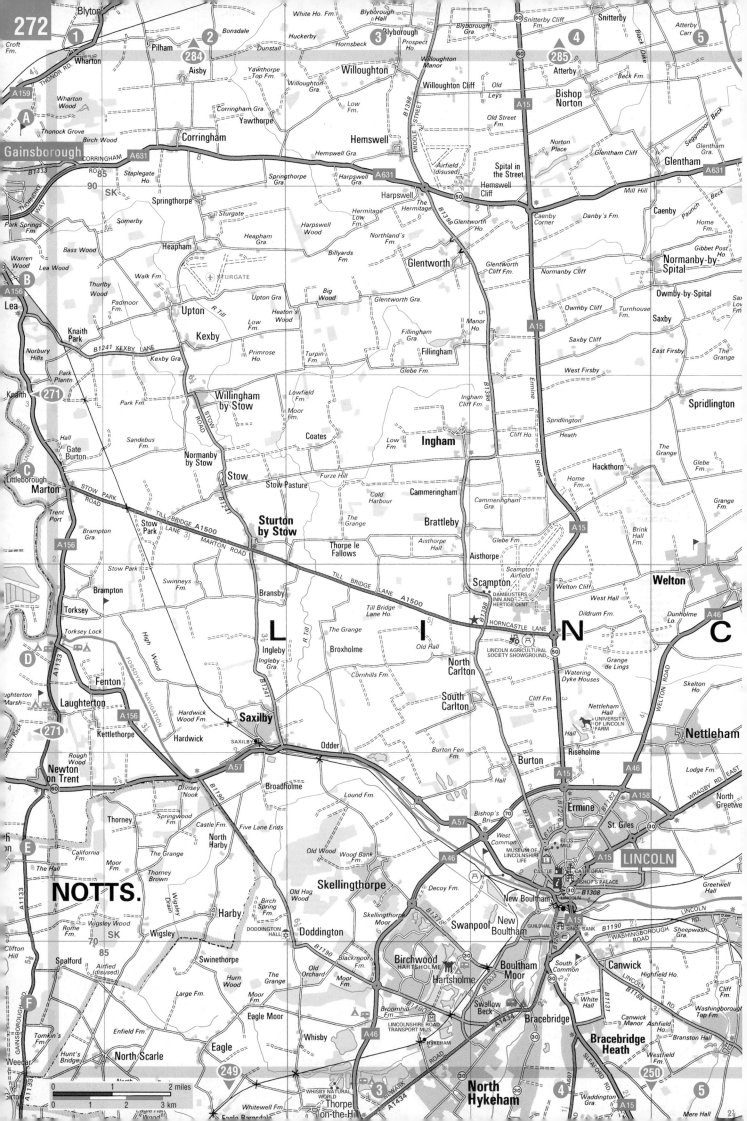

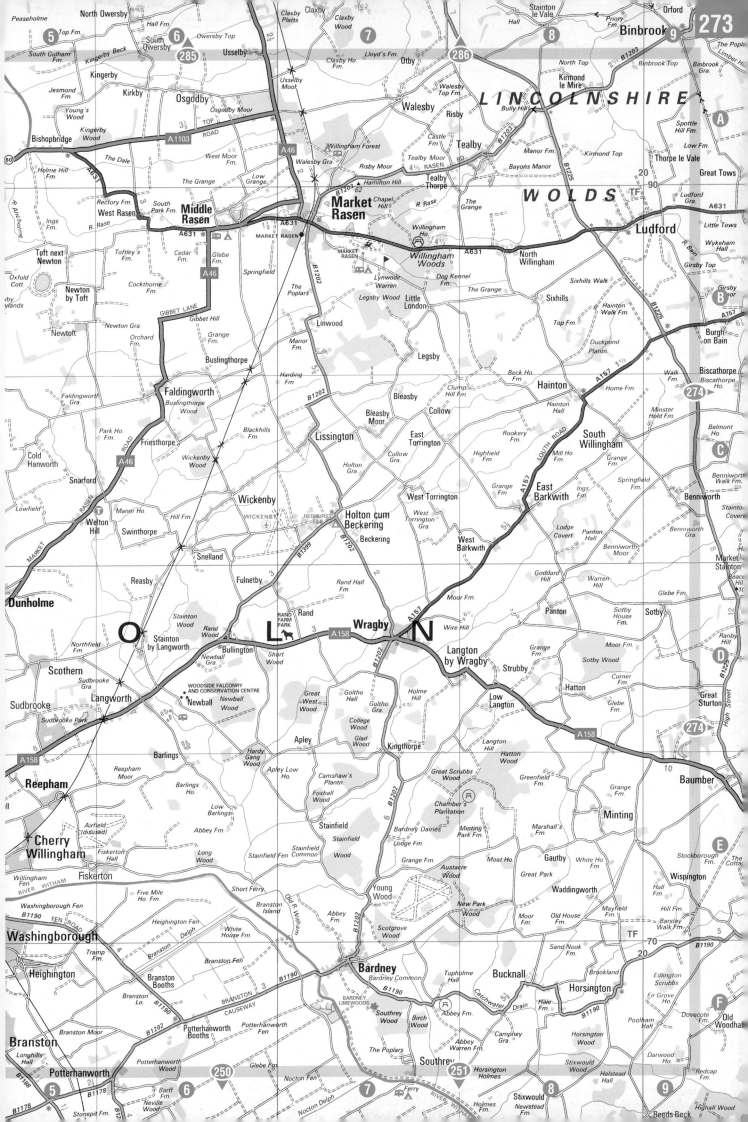

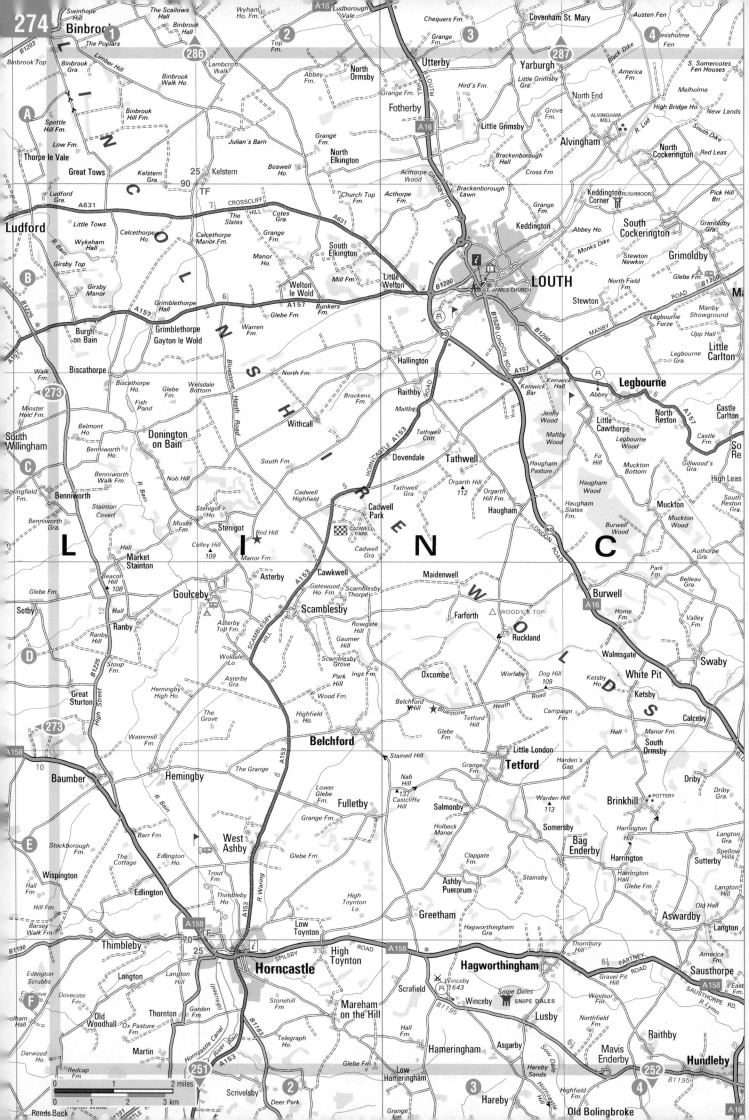

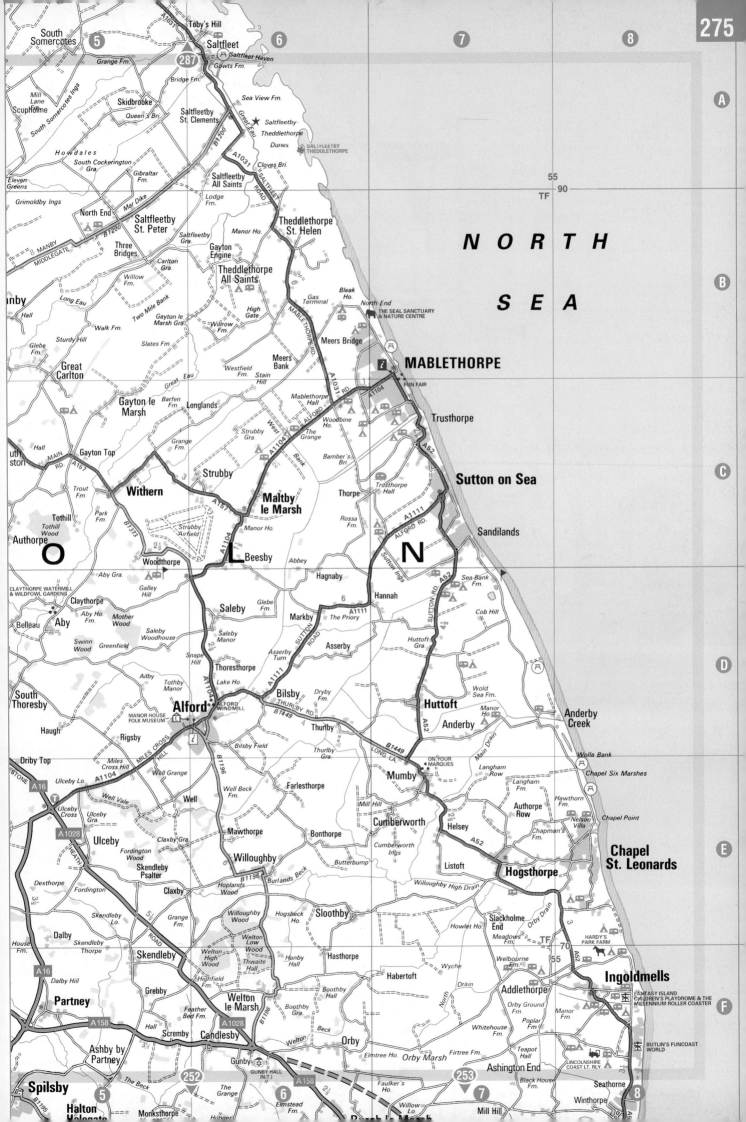

NORTH SEA

MABLETHORPE

Trusthorpe

Sutton on Sea

Sandilands

Huttoft

Anderby

Anderby Creek

Wolla Bank

Chapel Six Marshes

Chapel Point

Chapel St. Leonards

Hogsthorpe

Ingoldmells

FANTASY ISLAND CHILDREN'S PLAYDROME & THE MILLENNIUM ROLLER COASTER

BUTLIN'S FUNCOAST WORLD

Seathorne

Winthorpe

South Somercotes

Toby's Hill

Saltfleet

Saltfleet Haven

Gowts Fm.

Grange Fm.

Bridge Fm.

Sea View Fm.

Mill Lane Scupholme

Skidbrooke

Queen's Bri.

Saltfleetby St. Clements

Saltfleetby-Theddlethorpe Dunes

SALTFLEETBY THEDDLETHORPE

Howdales

South Cockerington Gra.

Gibraltar Fm.

Saltfleetby All Saints

Lodge Fm.

Eleven Greens

Grimoldby Ings

North End

Mar Dike

Saltfleetby St. Peter

Saltfleetby Gra.

Theddlethorpe St. Helen

MANBY

MIDDLEGATE

Three Bridges

Carlton Gra.

Gayton Engine

Theddlethorpe All Saints

nby

Hall

Long Eau

Willow Fm.

Gayton le Marsh Gra.

Willrow Fm.

Gas Terminal

Bleak Ho.

North End

THE SEAL SANCTUARY & NATURE CENTRE

Walk Fm.

High Gate

Meers Bridge

Sturdy Hill

Two Mile Bank

Slates Fm.

Meers Bank

Glebe Fm.

Great Carlton

Westfield Fm.

Stain Hill

Gayton le Marsh

Barfen Fm.

Longlands

Great Eau

Mablethorpe Hall

Woodbine Ho.

FUN FAIR

Hall

MAIN RD.

ston

Gayton Top

A157

Trout Fm.

Strubby Gra.

West Bank

The Grange

ALFORD

Bamber's Bri.

A52

Withern

Strubby

A1104

Maltby le Marsh

Manor Ho.

Thorpe

Trusthorpe Hall

Tothill

Park Fm.

Tothill Wood

Strubby Airfield

Rossa Fm.

A1111

ALFORD RD.

Authorpe

Woodthorpe

Beesby

Abbey

Hagnaby

Sutton Ings

CLAYTHORPE WATERMILL & WILDFOWL GARDENS

Aby Gra.

Galley Hill

Hannah

Sea Bank Fm.

Claythorpe

Saleby

Glebe Fm.

A1111

Cob Hill

Belleau

Aby

Aby Ho. Fm.

Mother Wood

Saleby Woodhouse

Markby

The Priory

Huttoft Gra.

Swinn Wood

Greenfield

Saleby Manor

Asserby

Wold Sea Fm.

South Thoresby

Ailby

Snape Hill

Thoresthorpe

Asserby Turn

Manor Ho.

A1104

Tothby Manor

Lake Ho.

A1111

Dryby Fm.

Anderby

Haugh

Alford

ALFORD WINDMILL

Bilsby

THURLBY RD.

B1449

A52

MANOR HOUSE FOLK MUSEUM

Rigsby

Thurlby

Thurlby Gra.

Driby Top

MILES CROSS HILL

Bilsby Field

LONG LA.

B1449

ON YOUR MARQUES

Mumby

Main Drain

Langham Row

Hawthorn Fm.

Nelson Villa

Stone

A16

A1104

Miles Cross Hill

Well Grange

Farlesthorpe

Langham Fm.

Chapman's Fm.

Ulceby Lo.

Well Beck Fm.

Mill Hill

Authorpe Row

Helsey

A52

Ulceby Cross

Well Vale

Well

Cumberworth

Ulceby Gra.

Fordington Wood

Mawthorpe

Bonthorpe

Cumberworth Ings

Listoft

Ulceby

Claxby Gra.

Willoughby

Butterbump

Dexthorpe

Skendleby Psalter

B1196

Hoplands Wood

Willoughby High Drain

Fordington

Claxby

Willoughby Wood

Sloothby

Orby Drain

HARDY'S PARK FARM

Dalby

Skendleby Lo.

Grange Fm.

Hogsbeck Ho.

Slackholme End

Welbourne

House Fm.

HEATH

Skendleby Thorpe

Welton High Wood

Howlet Ho.

Meadows Fm.

TF 70

55

Dalby Hill

A16

Skendleby

Welton Low Wood

Hanby Hall

Hasthorpe

Wyche

Grebby

Highfield Fm.

Thwaite Hall

Habertoft

Drain

Addlethorpe

Partney

ROAD

Welton le Marsh

Boothby Gra.

North

Orby Ground Fm.

Manor Fm.

Feather Bed Fm.

Boothby Hall

Whitehouse Fm.

Poplar Fm.

A158

Hall

Scremby

B1196

Orby

Elmtree Ho.

Orby Marsh

Teapot Hall

Ashby by Partney

Candlesby

The Beck

Welton

Beck

Firtree Fm.

LINCOLNSHIRE COAST LT. RLY.

Spilsby

A1028

GUNBY HALL (N.T.)

A158

Faulker's Ho.

Ashington End

Black House Fm.

Halton Holegate

Monksthorpe

The Grange

Elmstead Fm.

Willow Lo.

Mill Hill

B1195

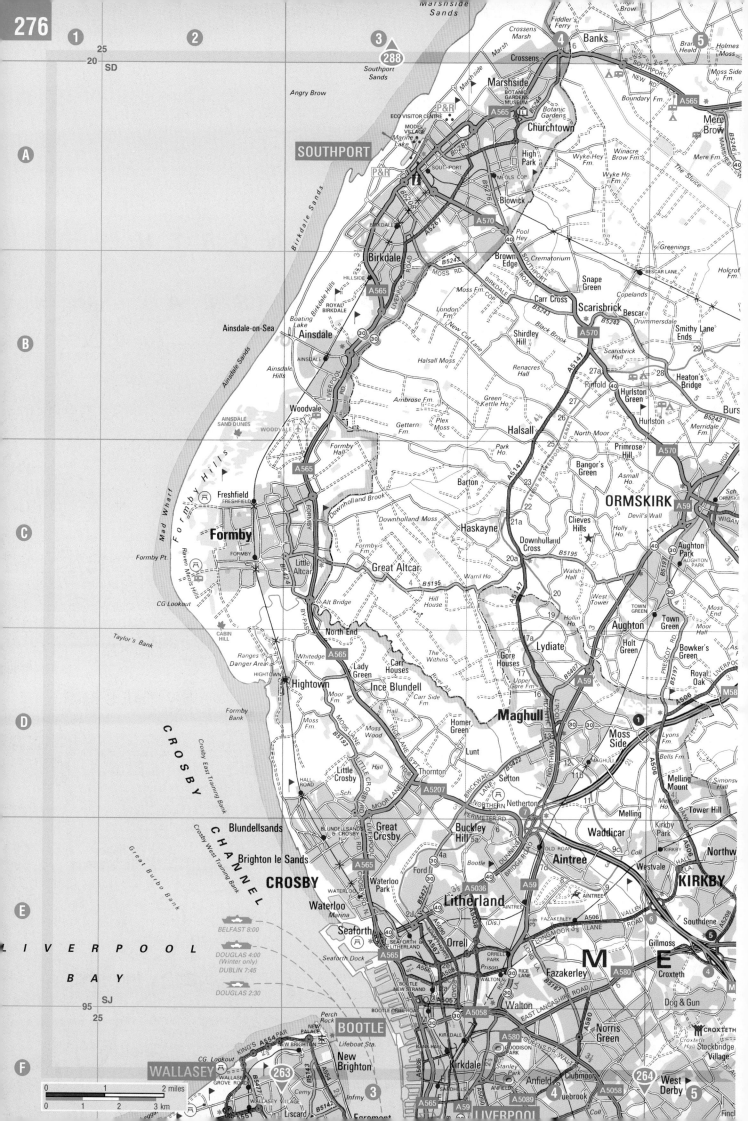

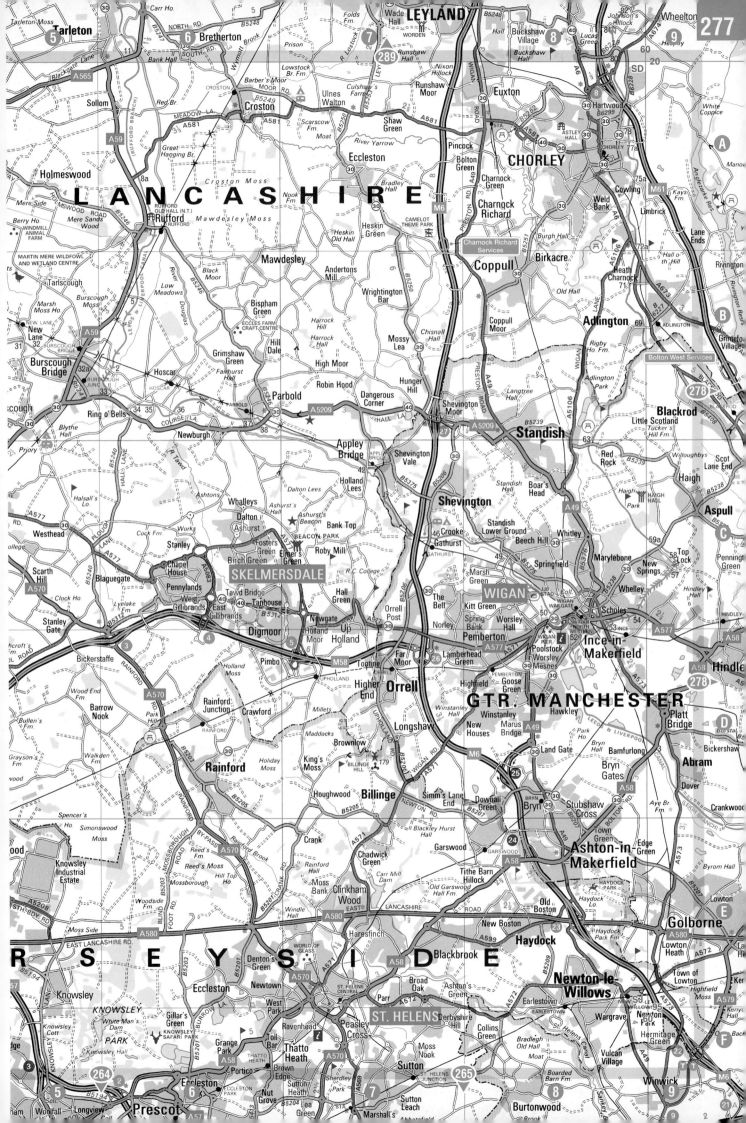

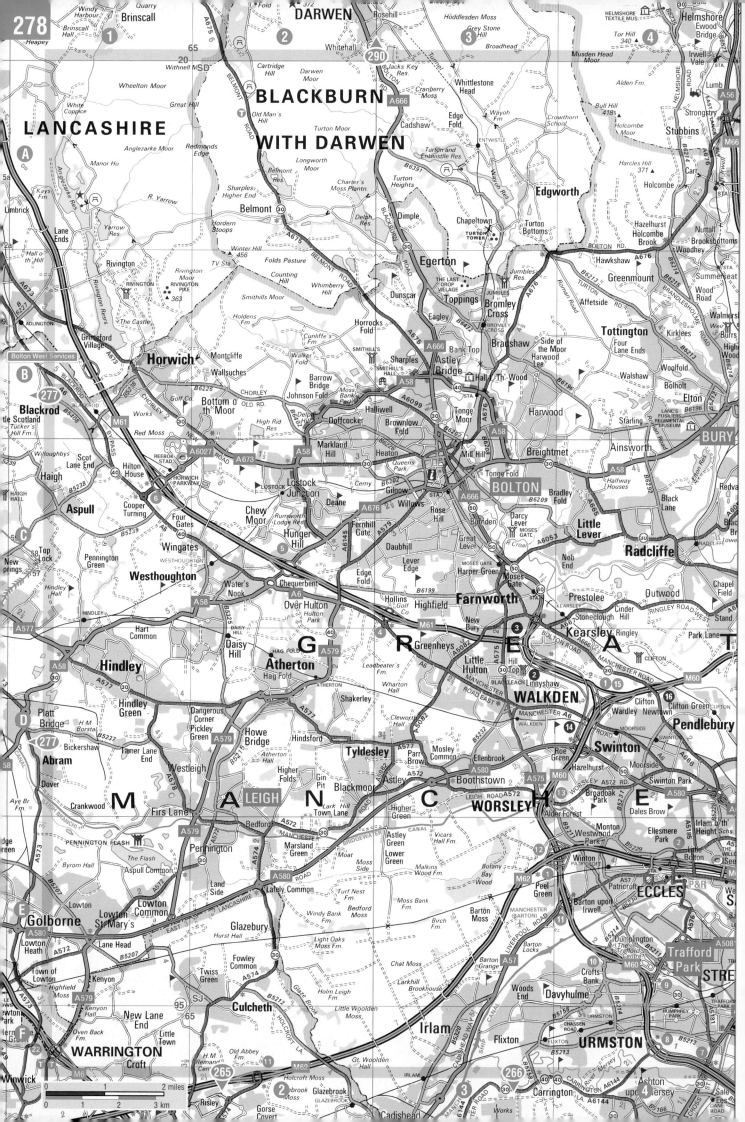

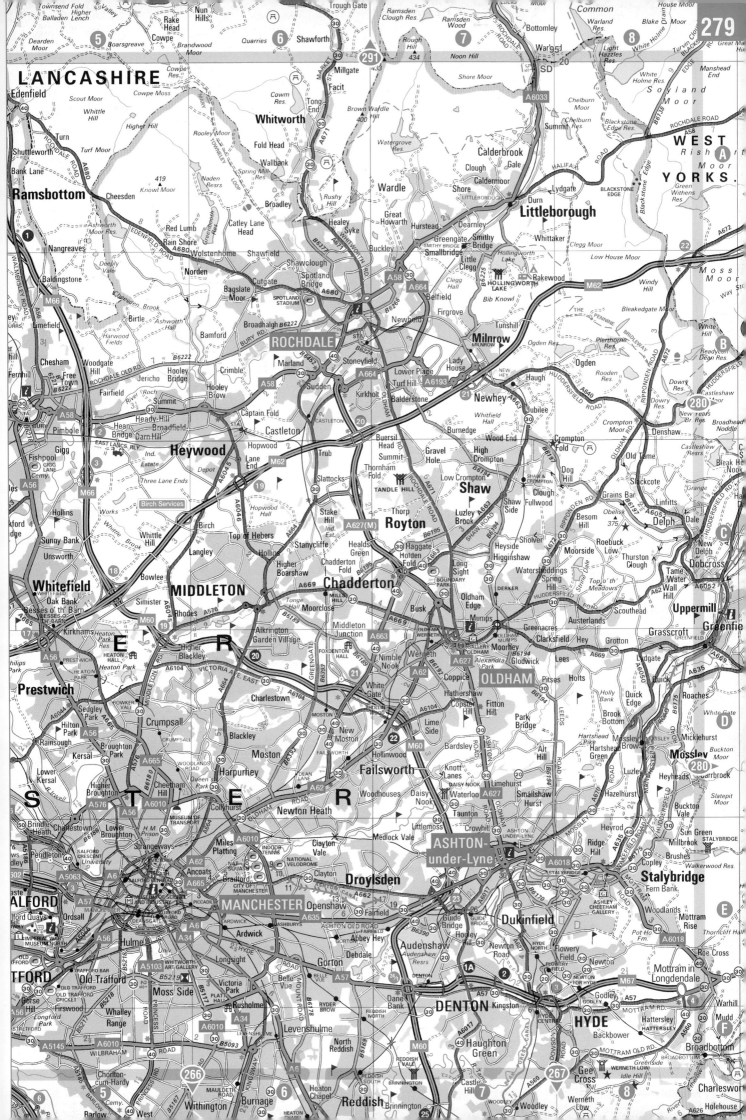

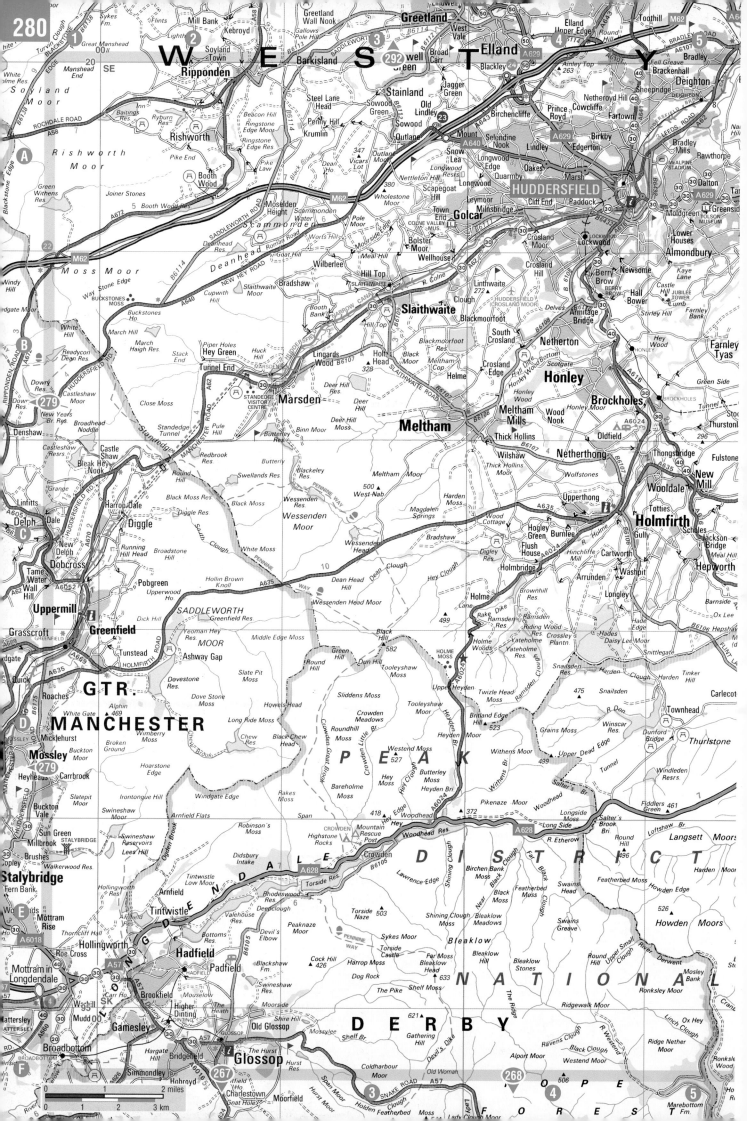

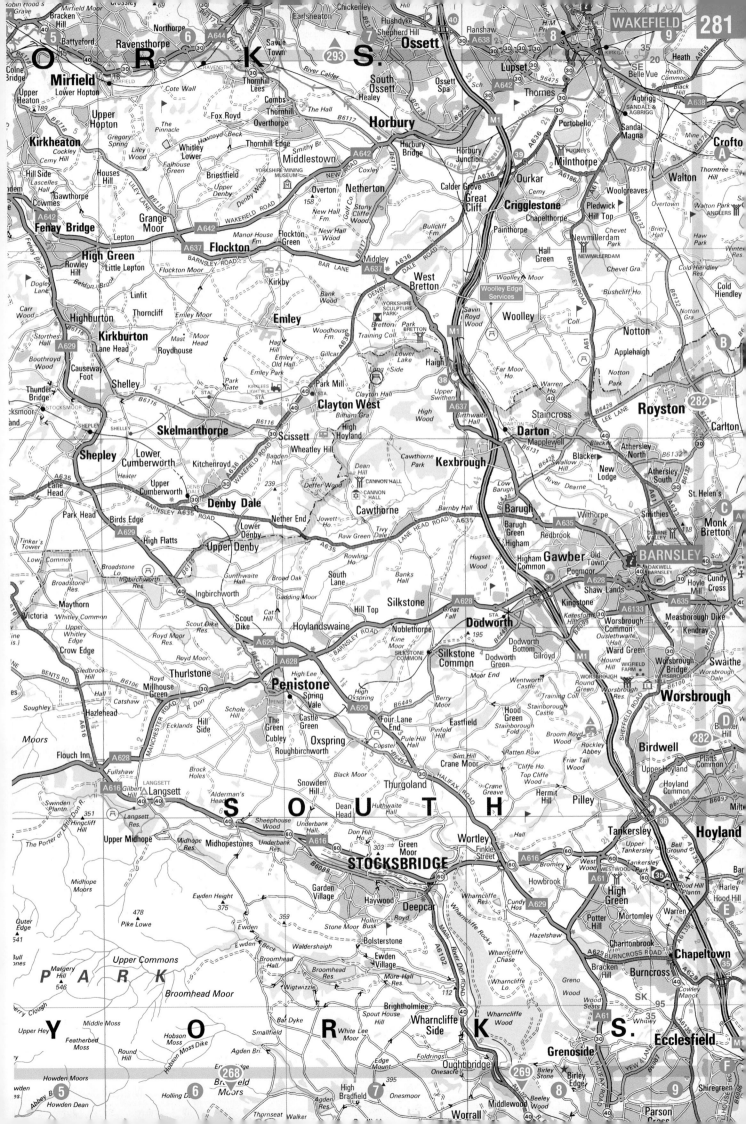

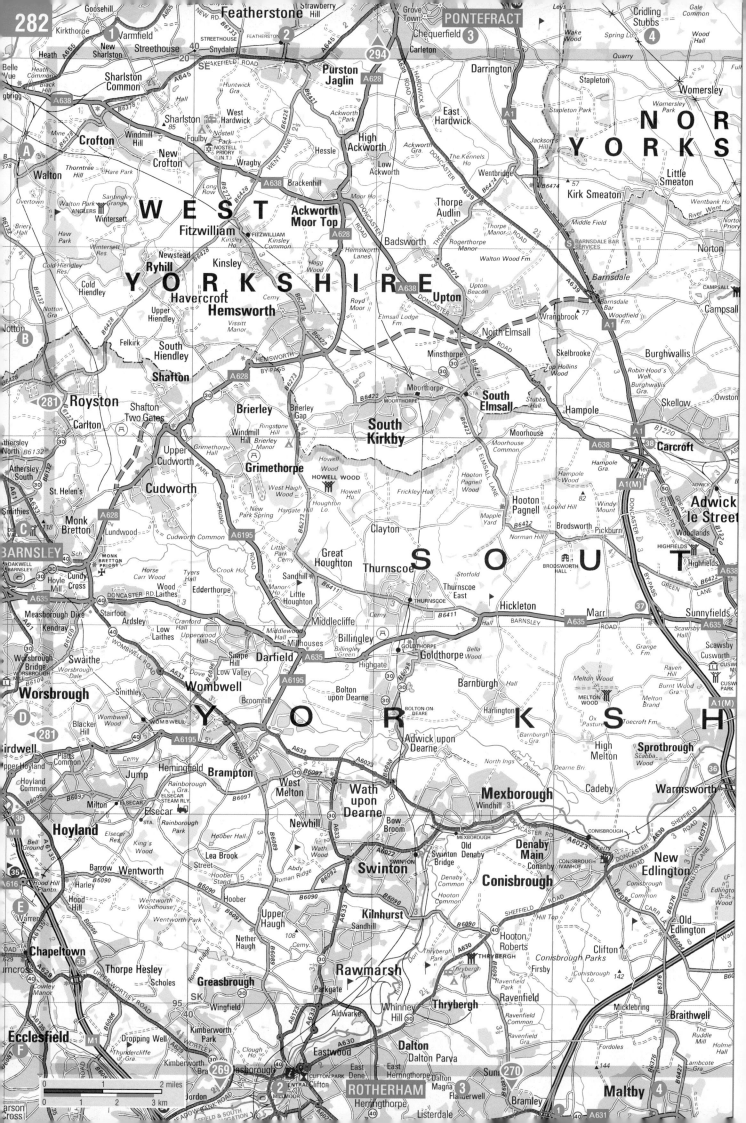

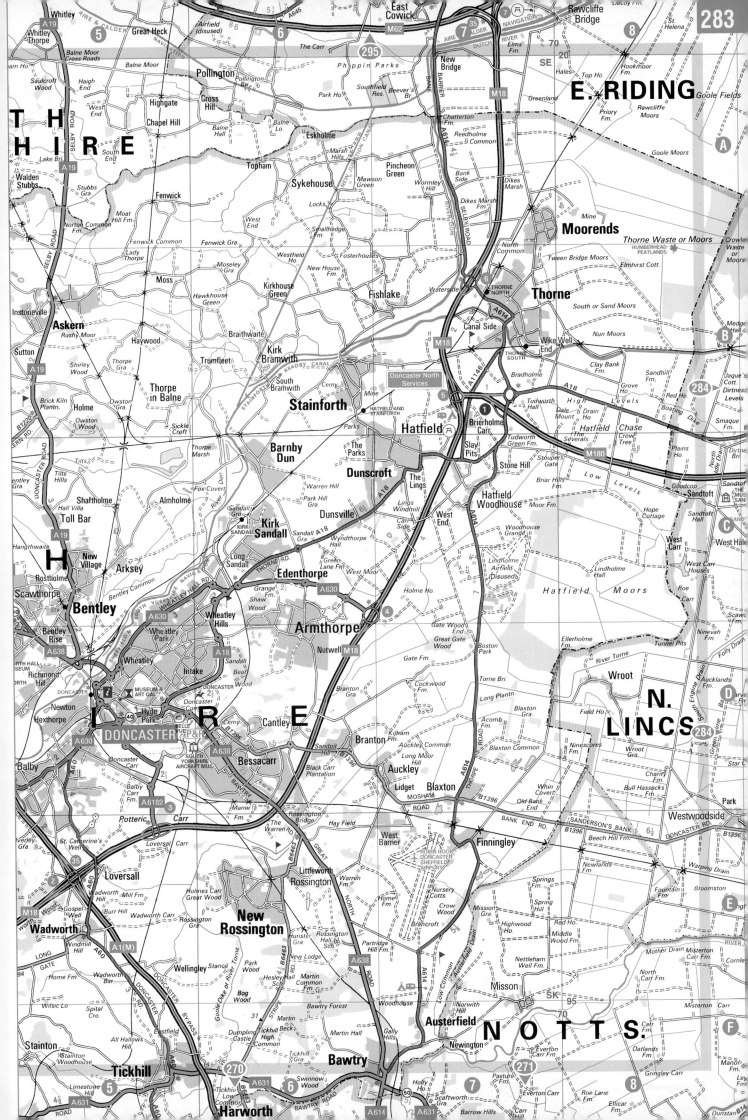

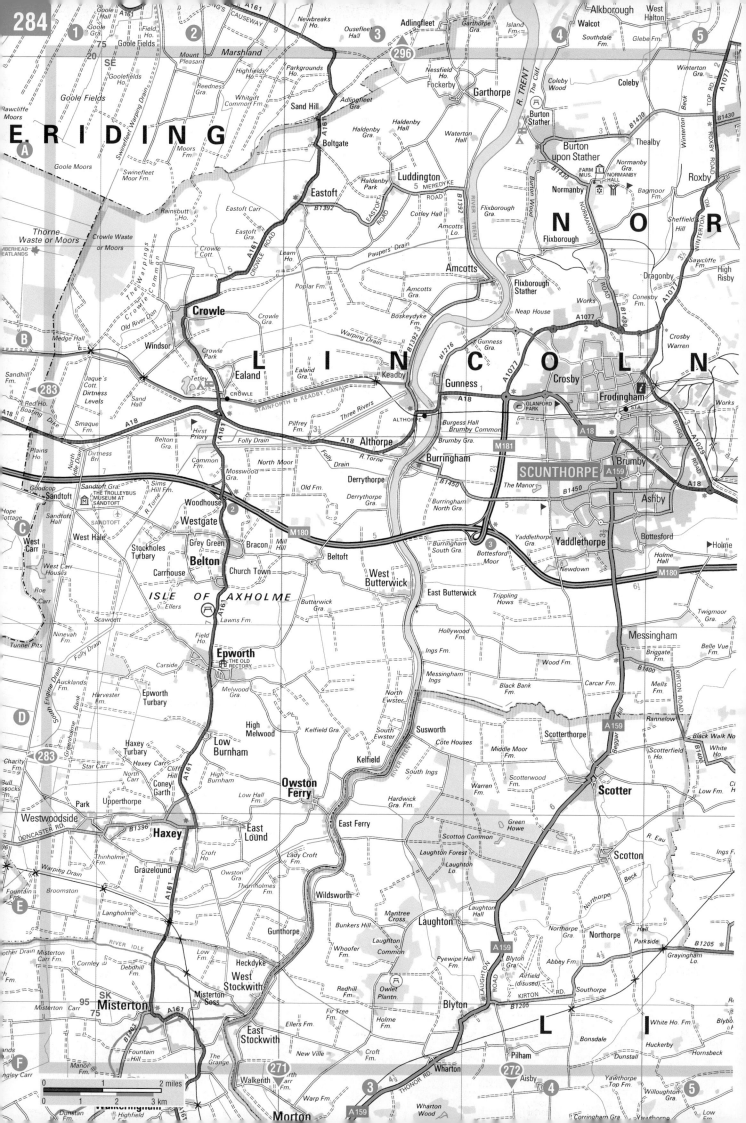

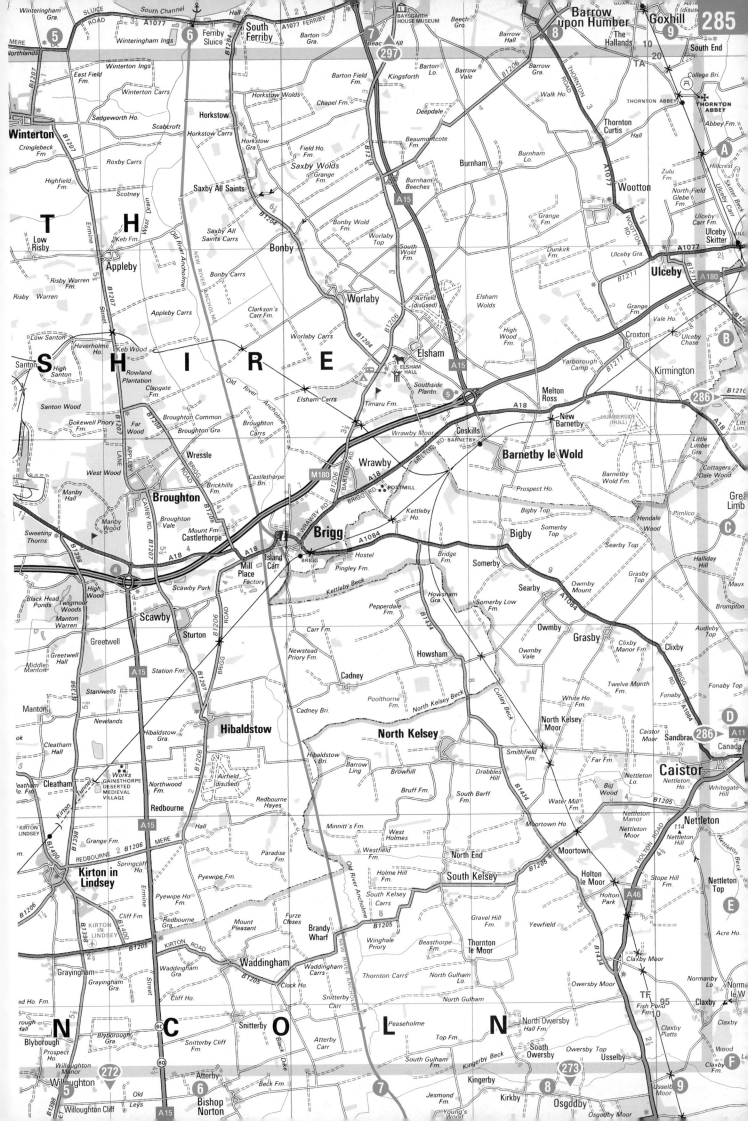

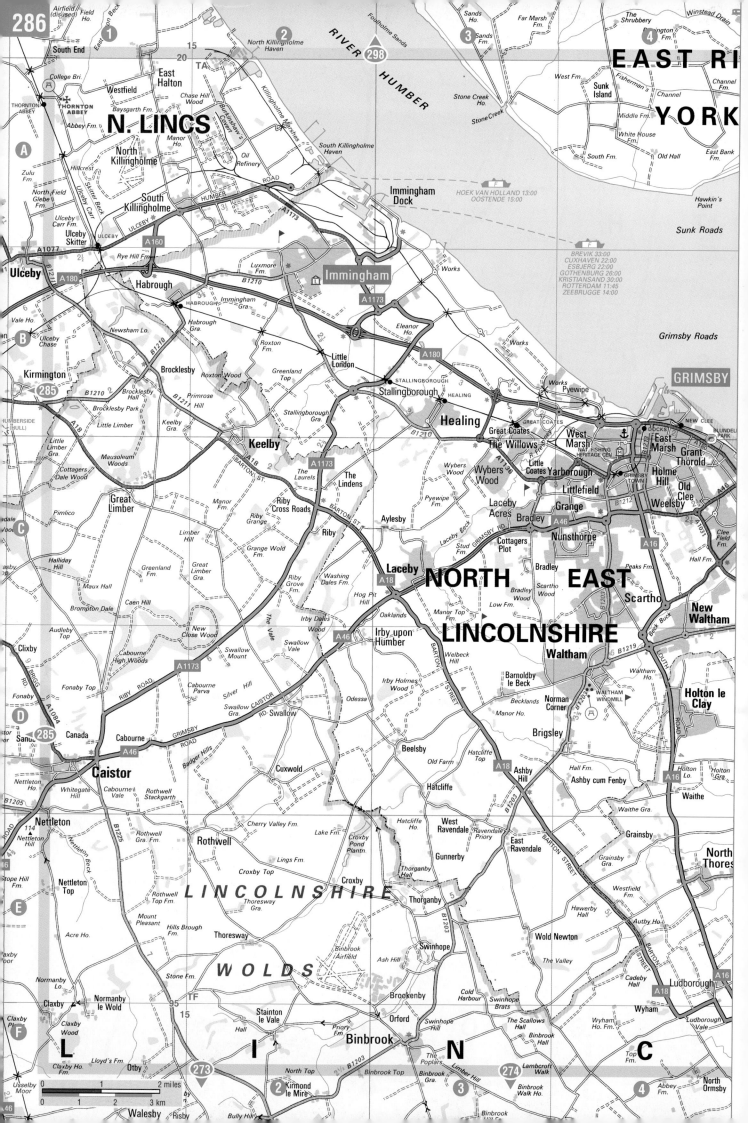

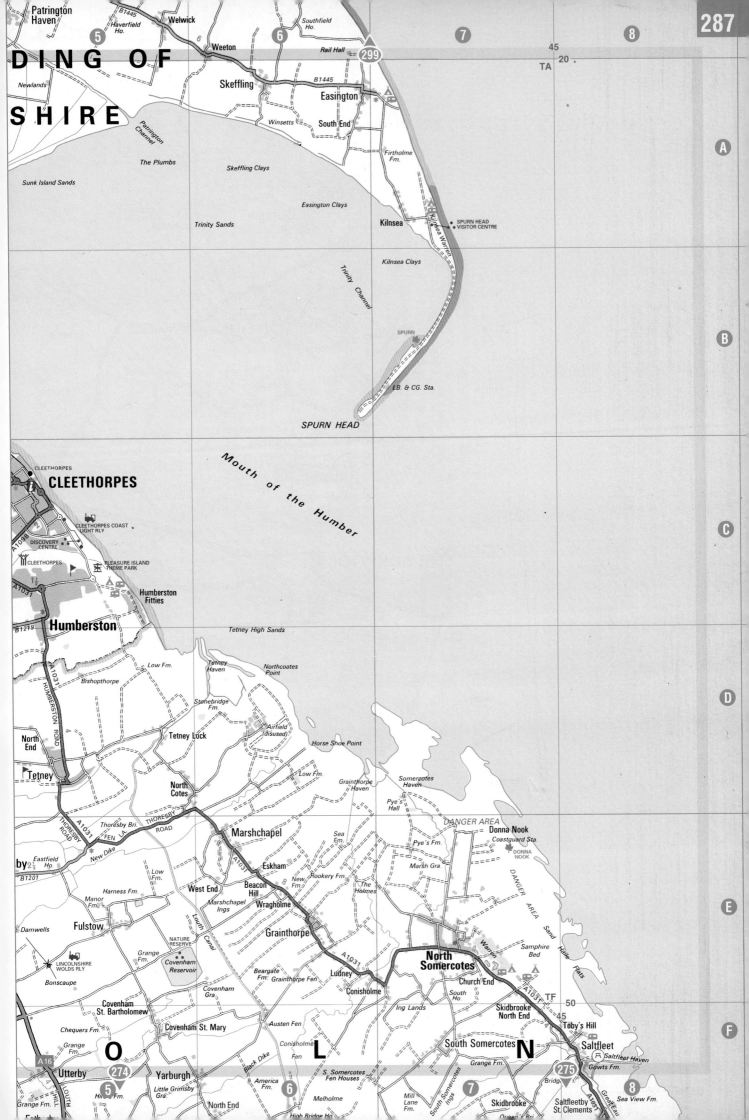

Patrington Haven
Haverfield Ho.
Welwick
Newlands
**DING OF**
Weeton
B1445
Skeffling
Southfield Ho.
Rail Hall
299
**SHIRE**
B1445
Easington
Patrington Channel
Winsetts
South End
The Plumbs
Sunk Island Sands
Skeffling Clays
Firtholme Fm.
Trinity Sands
Skeffling Clays
Easington Clays

Kilnsea Clays
Kilnsea
SPURN HEAD
VISITOR CENTRE
Kilnsea Warren

Trinity Channel

SPURN

LB. & CG. Sta.

*SPURN HEAD*

*Mouth of the Humber*

CLEETHORPES
CLEETHORPES COAST
LIGHT RLY
DISCOVERY CENTRE
CLEETHORPES
PLEASURE ISLAND
THEME PARK
Humberston Fitties
A1037
**Humberston**
Tetney High Sands
B1219
Low Fm.
Tetney Haven
Northcoates Point
Bishopthorpe
HUMBERSTON ROAD
Stonebridge Fm.
Airfield (disused)
Horse Shoe Point
North End
Tetney Lock
A1031
Tetney
Low Fm.
Low Fm.
Grainthorpe Haven
Somercotes Haven
North Cotes
Pye's Hall
THORESBY ROAD
Thoresby Bri.
THORESBY ROAD
FEN LA.
*DANGER AREA*
Donna Nook
New Dike
Marshchapel
Sea Fm.
Pye's Fm.
Coastguard Sta.
by
Eastfield Ho.
A1031
DONNA NOOK
B1201
Eskham
Hookery Fm.
Marsh Gra.
Harness Fm.
Low Fm.
Beacon Hill
New Fm.
DANGER AREA
Manor Fm.
West End
Marshchapel Ings
Wragholme
The Holmes
Sand
Damwells
Fulstow
Grainthorpe
Warren
Samphire Bed
Halte Flats
LINCOLNSHIRE WOLDS RLY
Grange Fm.
NATURE RESERVE
A1031
North Somercotes
Bonscaupe
Covenham Reservoir
Beargate Fm.
Grainthorpe Fen
Ludney
Church End
A103T
TF
Covenham St. Bartholomew
Covenham Gra.
Conisholme
South Ho.
Skidbrooke North End
Toby's Hill
Chequers Fm.
Covenham St. Mary
Austen Fen
Ing Lands
50
45
Grange Fm.
**O**
Conisholme Fen
**L**
**N**
Saltfleet
A16
Utterby
274
Yarburgh
Black Dike
America Fm.
S. Somercotes Fen Houses
**South Somercotes**
Grange Fm.
275
Saltfleet Haven
Gowts Fm.
Grange Fm.
Hills Fm.
North End
Little Grimsby Gra.
Melholme
Mill Lane Fm.
Skidbrooke
Saltfleetby St. Clements
Sea View Fm.
High Bridge Ho.

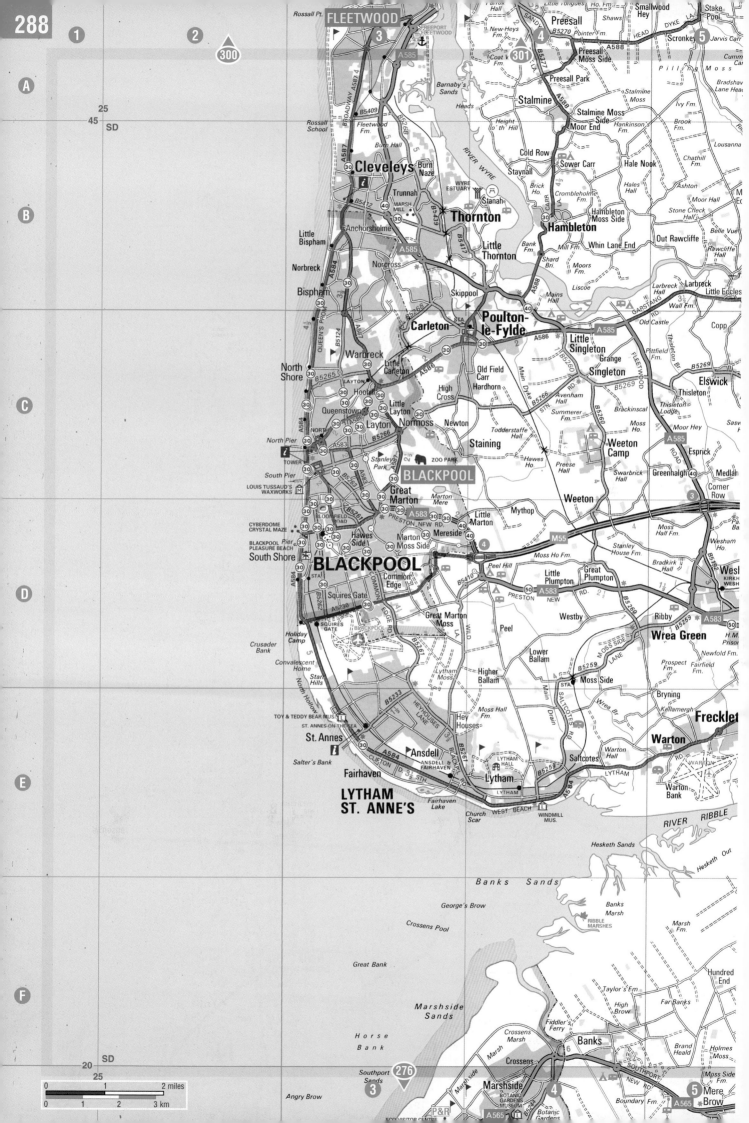

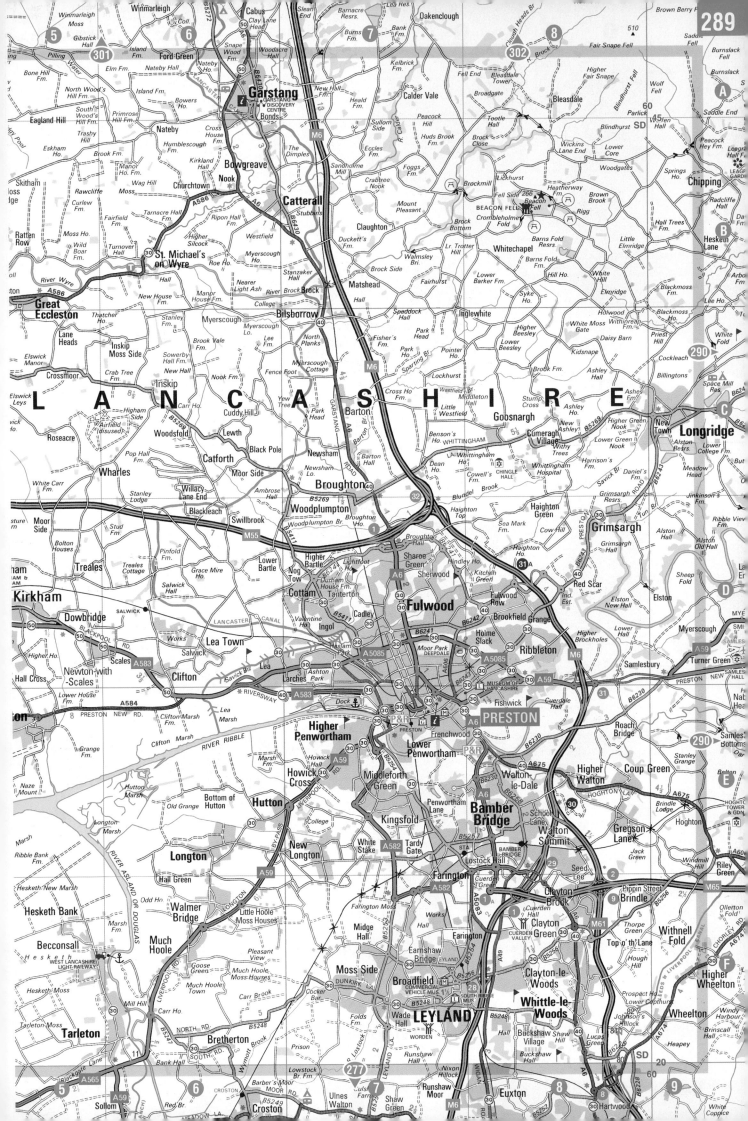

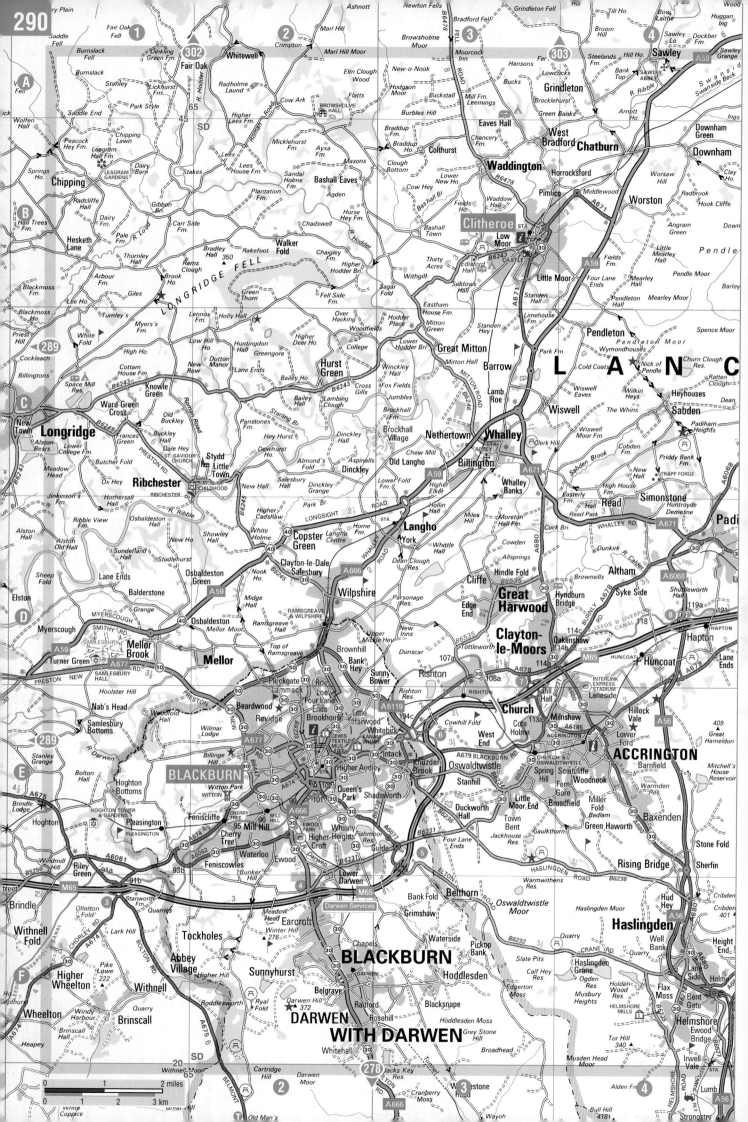

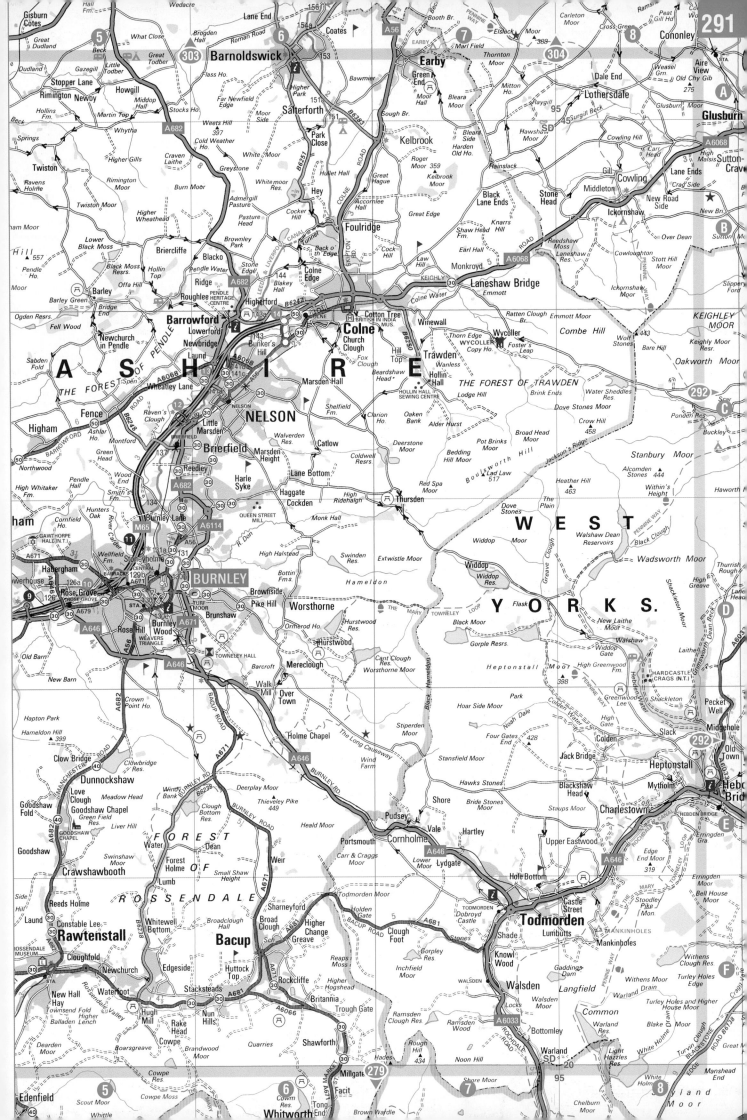

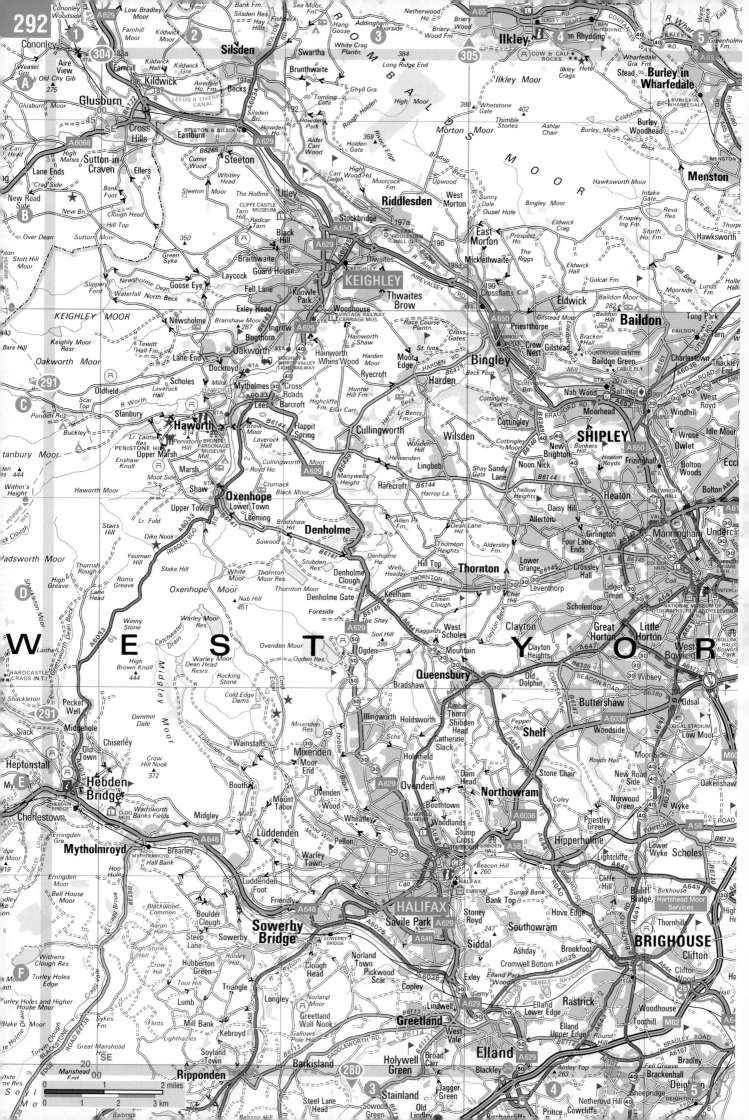

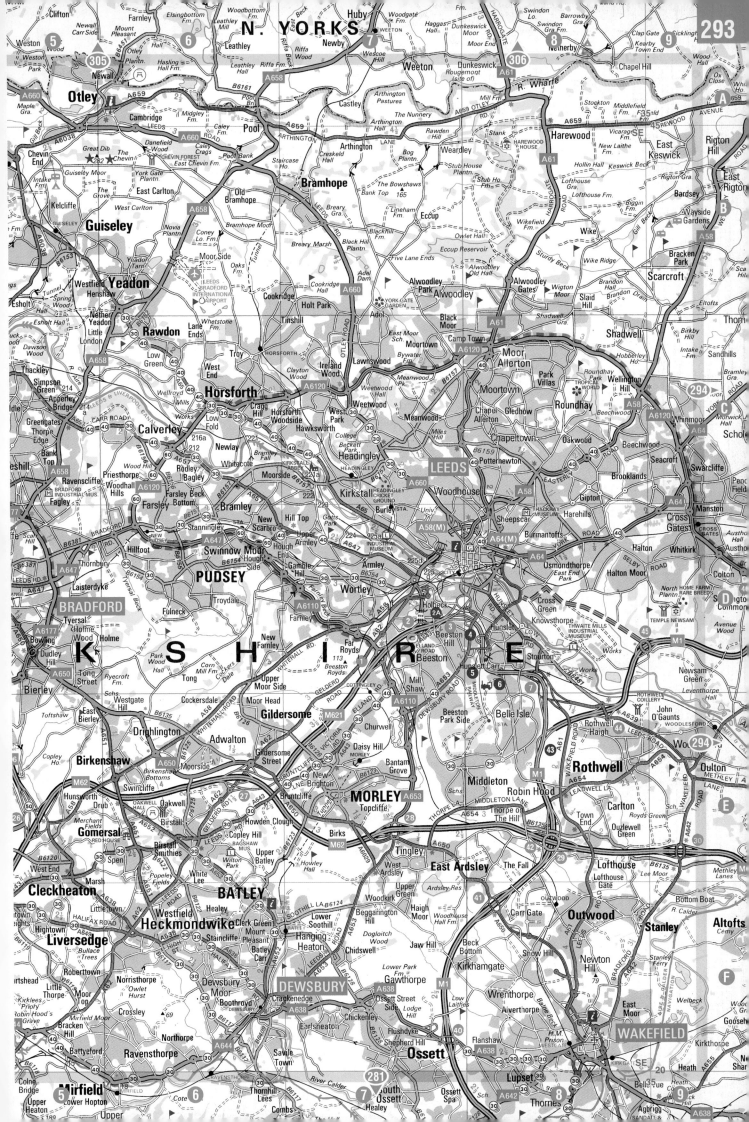

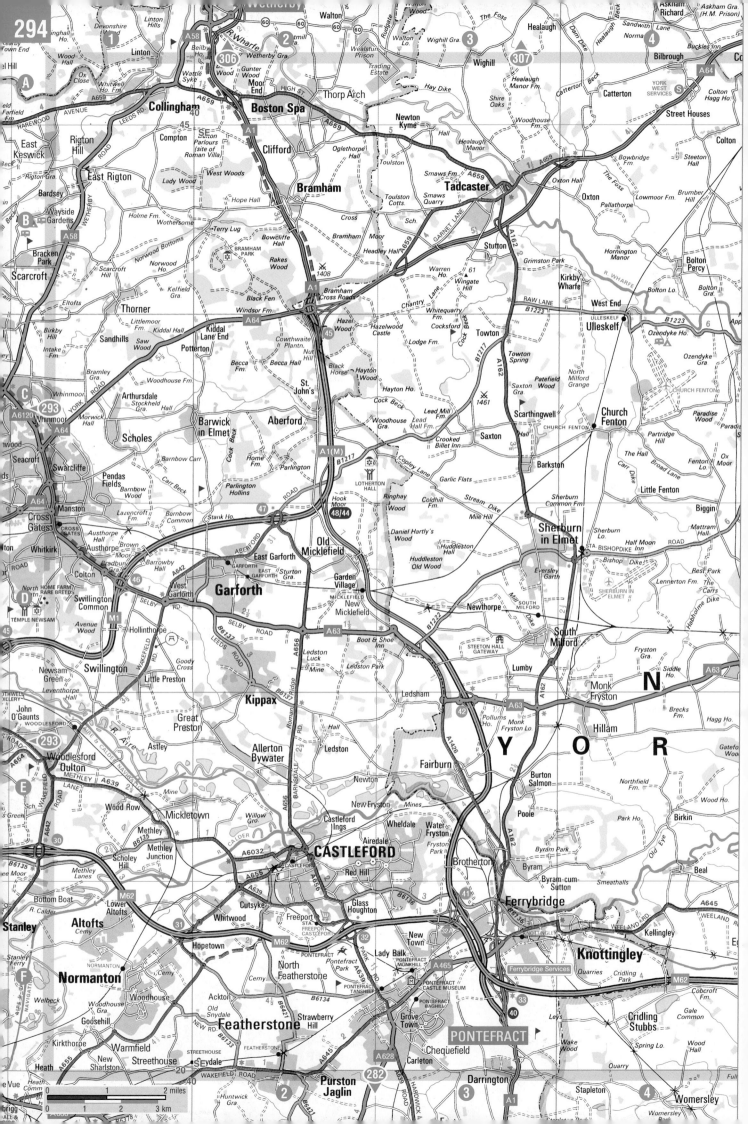

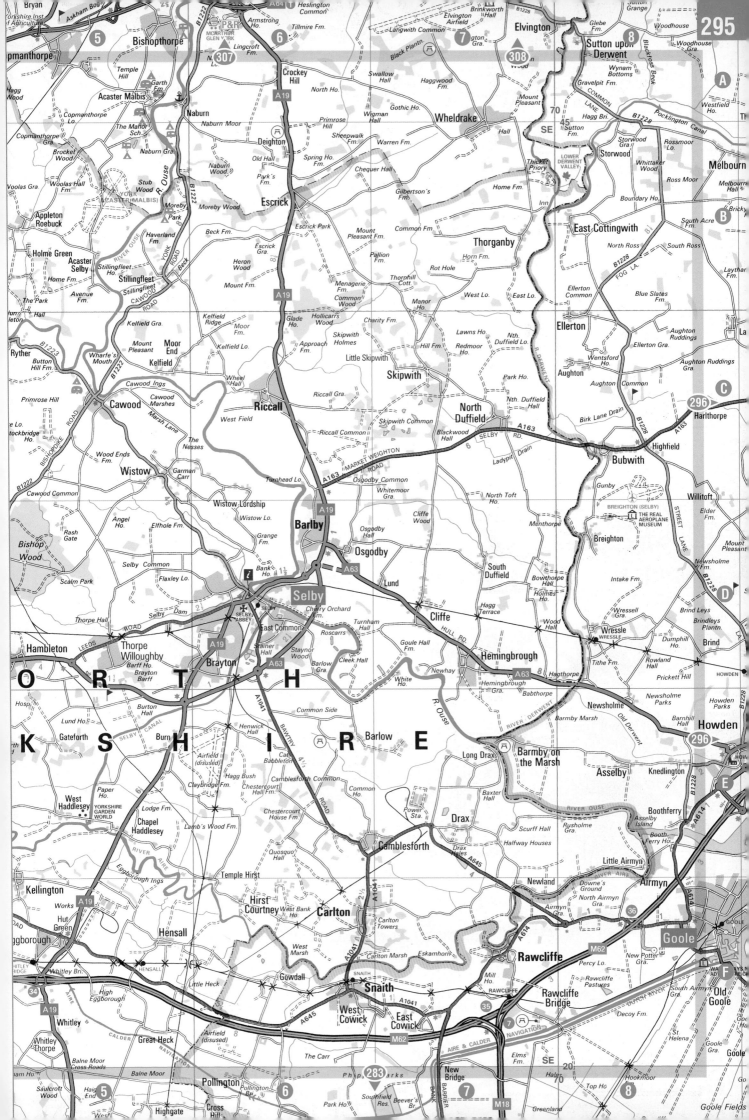

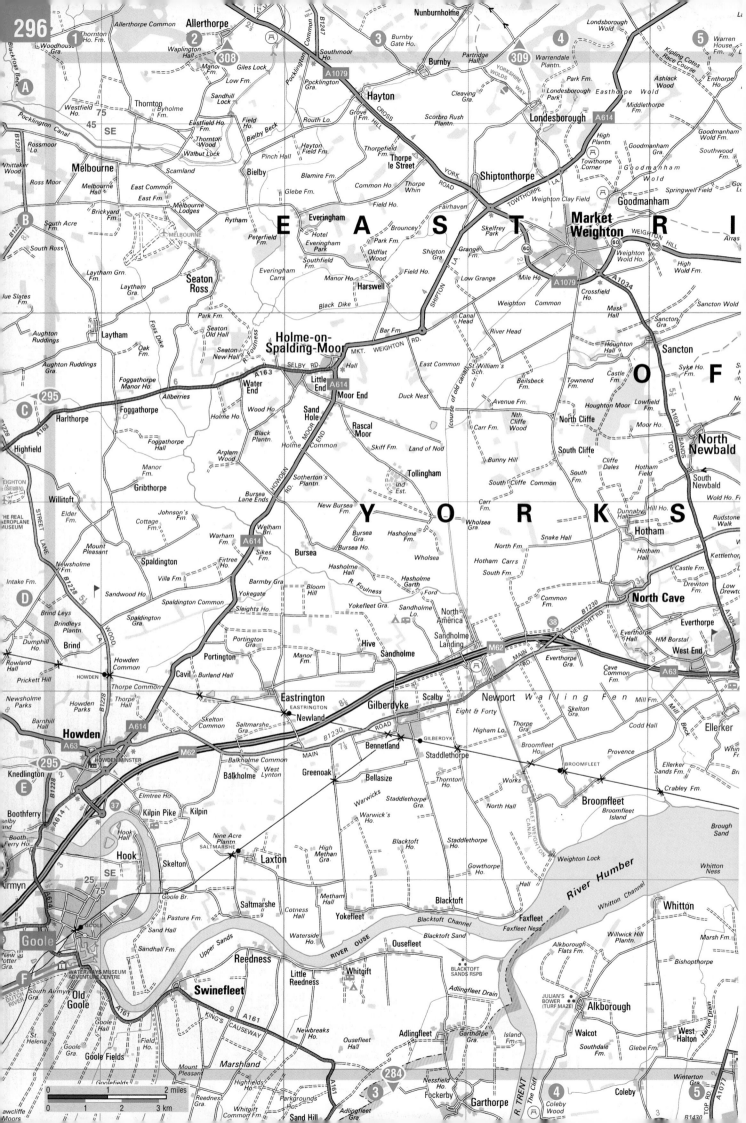

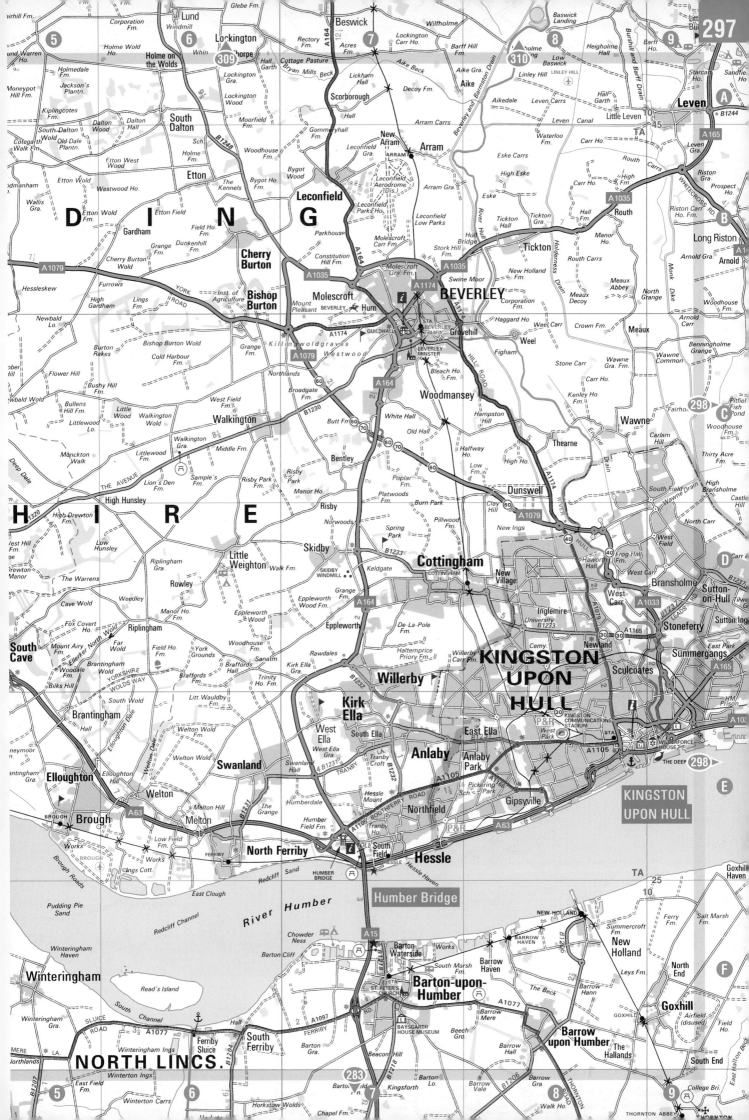

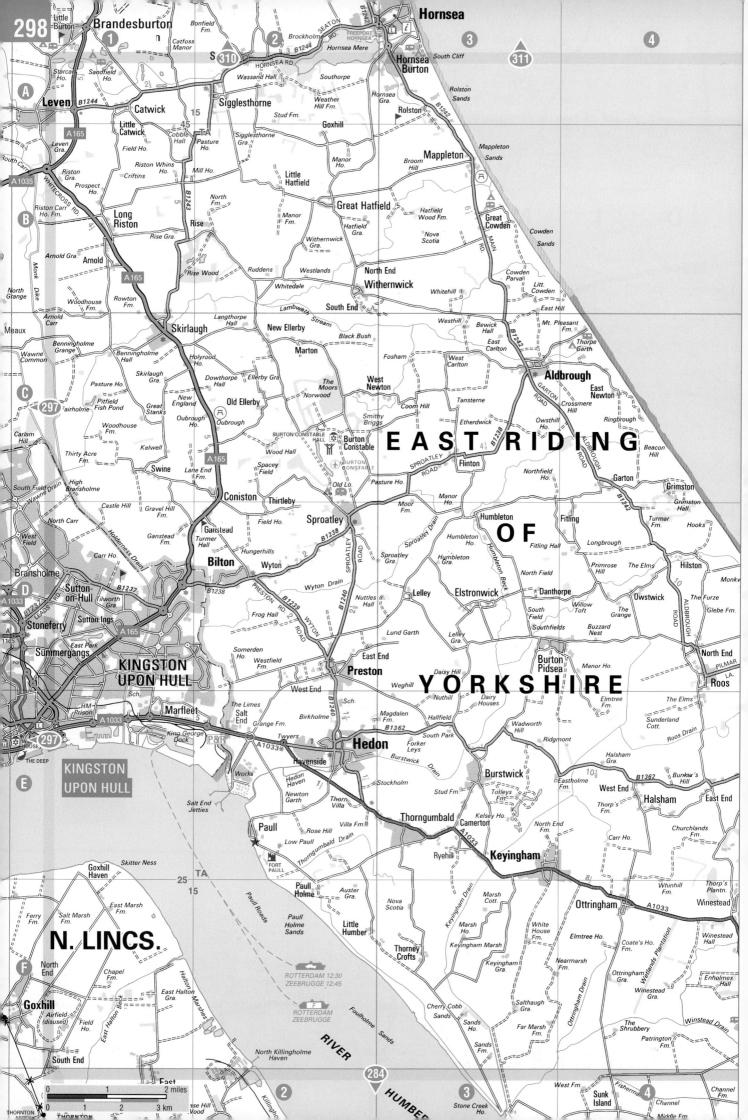

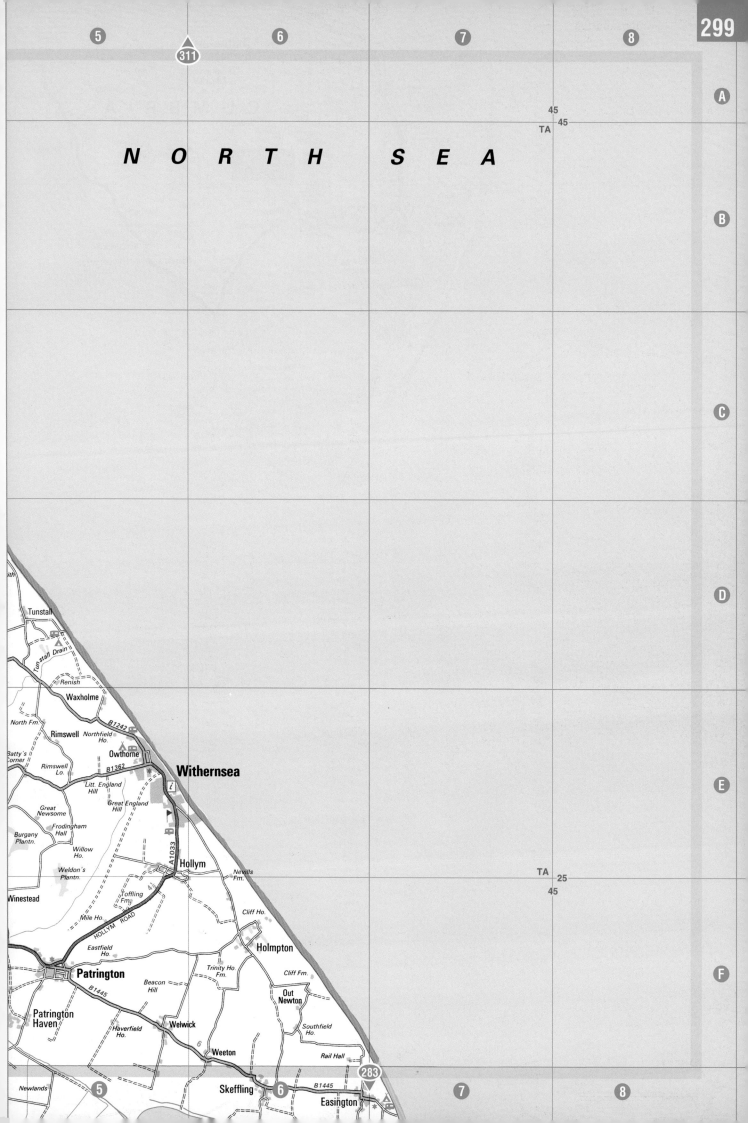

NORTH SEA

Tunstall
Tunstall Drain
Renish
Waxholme
North Fm.
Rimswell
B1242
Northfield Ho.
Batty's Corner
Rimswell Lo.
Owthorne
B1362
**Withernsea**
Litt. England Hill
Great Newsome
Great England Hill
Frodingham Hall
Burgany Plantn.
Willow Ho.
A1033
Weldon's Plantn.
Hollym
Nevills Fm.
Winestead
Toffling Fm.
Mile Ho.
HOLLYM ROAD
Cliff Ho.
Eastfield Ho.
Holmpton
**Patrington**
Trinity Ho. Fm.
Beacon Hill
Cliff Fm.
B1445
Out Newton
Patrington Haven
Haverfield Ho.
Welwick
Southfield Ho.
Weeton
Rail Hall
283
Newlands
Skeffling
B1445
Easington

311

TA 45 / 45

TA 25 / 45

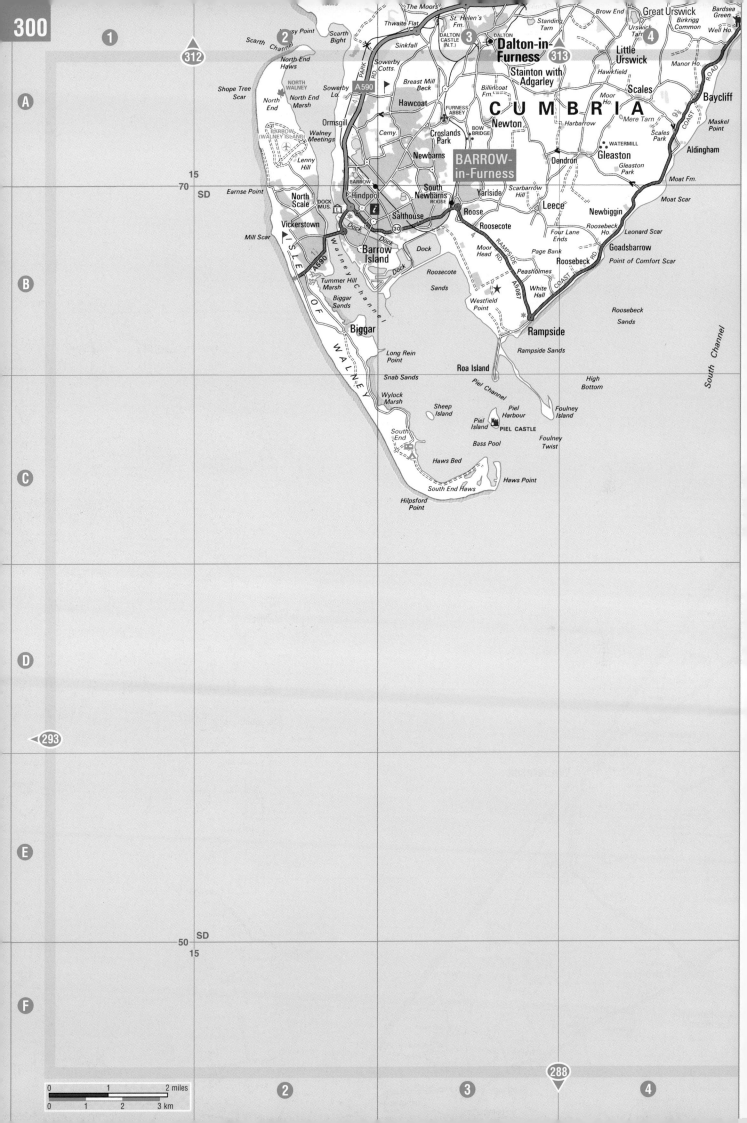

**1**

**2**

**3**

**4**

**A**

**B**

**C**

**D**

**E**

**F**

312

70 SD

15

293

50 SD

15

288

313

The Moors

St. Helen's Fm.

DALTON CASTLE (N.T.)

DALTON

**Dalton-in-Furness**

Brow End

**Great Urswick**

Birkrigg Common

Bardsea Green

Well Ho.

Urswick Tarn

**Little Urswick**

Manor Ho.

**Scales**

**Baycliff**

Standing Tarn

Thwaite Flat

Scarth Bight

Sinkfall

Scarth Channel

Ousey Point

Scarth Channel

North End Haws

Shope Tree Scar

NORTH WALNEY

North End Marsh

North End

Sowerby Cotts.

Sowerby Lo.

Breast Mill Beck

**Hawcoat**

Stainton with Adgarley

Hawkfield

Moor Ho.

Mere Tarn

Scales Park

Maskel Point

Aldingham

**C U M B R I A**

**Newton**

Billincoat Fm.

FURNESS ABBEY

Harbarrow

Ormsgill

Cerny.

**Croslands Park**

BOW BRIDGE

Gleaston Park

WATERMILL

**Gleaston**

Dendron

Moat Fm.

BARROW (WALNEY ISLAND)

Walney Meetings

**Newbarns**

**BARROW-in-Furness**

Moat Scar

Lenny Hill

Earnse Point

**North Scale**

DOCK MUS.

**Hindpool**

**South Newbarns**

ROOSE

**Roose**

Scarbarrow Hill

**Leece**

**Newbiggin**

SD

Mill Scar

**Vickerstown**

Dock

i

**Salthouse**

30

**Yarlside**

**Roosecote**

Roosebeck Ho.

Leonard Scar

Four Lane Ends

**Goadsbarrow**

Dock

**Barrow Island**

Dock

Dock

Page Bank

**Roosebeck**

Point of Comfort Scar

A590

Walney Channel

Tummer Hill Marsh

Moor Head

Peasholmes

White Hall

A5087

Biggar Sands

Roosecote Sands

Westfield Point

COAST RD.

RAMPSIDE RD.

Roosebeck Sands

I S L E   O F   W A L N E Y

**Biggar**

Long Rein Point

**Rampside**

Rampside Sands

Snab Sands

**Roa Island**

Piel Channel

High Bottom

South Channel

Wylock Marsh

Sheep Island

Foulney Island

South End

Piel Harbour

Piel Island

PIEL CASTLE

Foulney Twist

Bass Pool

Haws Bed

Haws Point

South End Haws

Hilpsford Point

0    1    2 miles

0    1    2    3 km

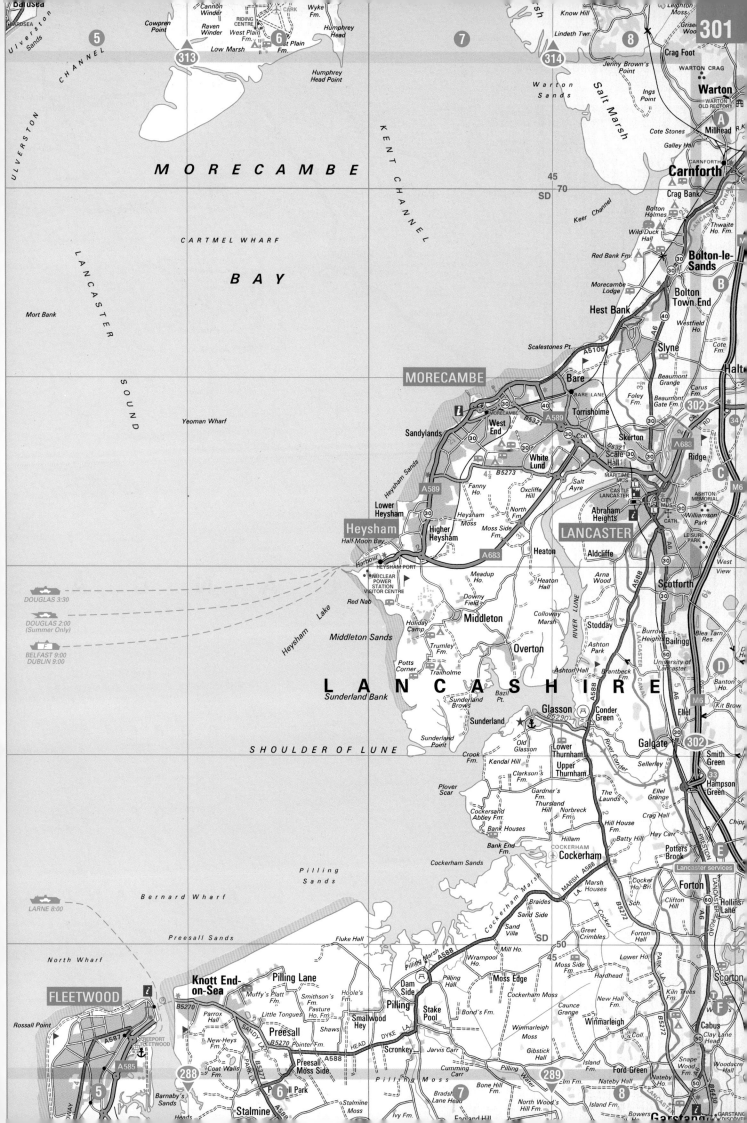

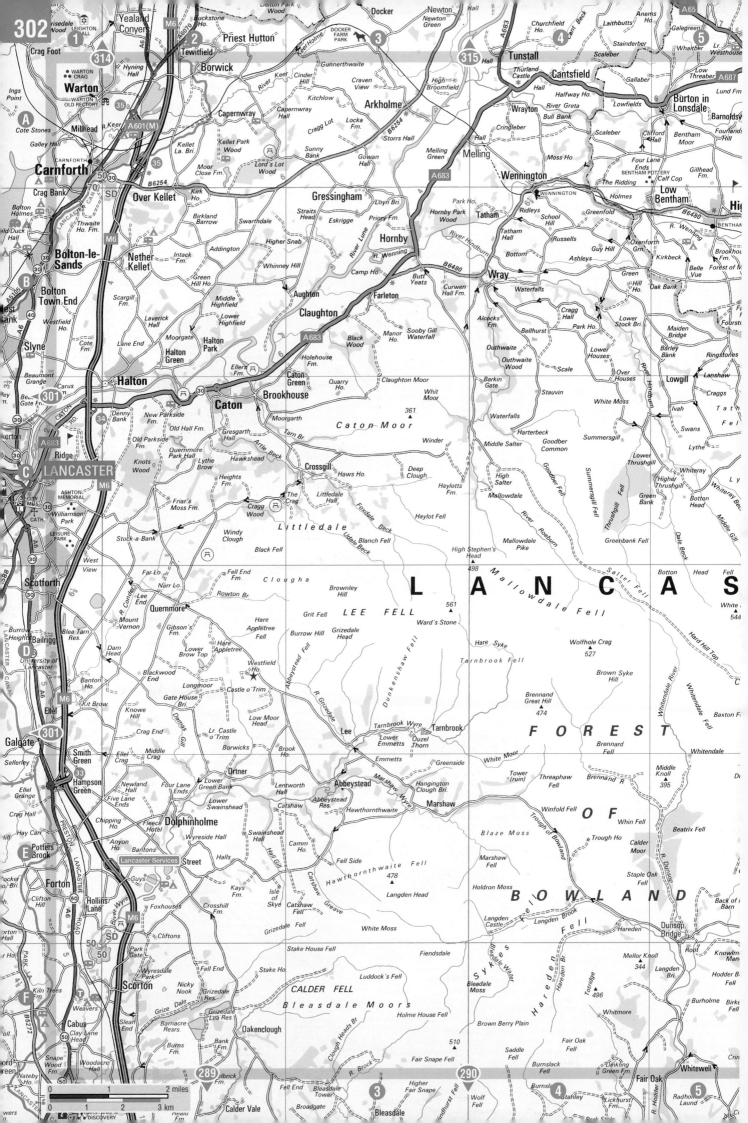

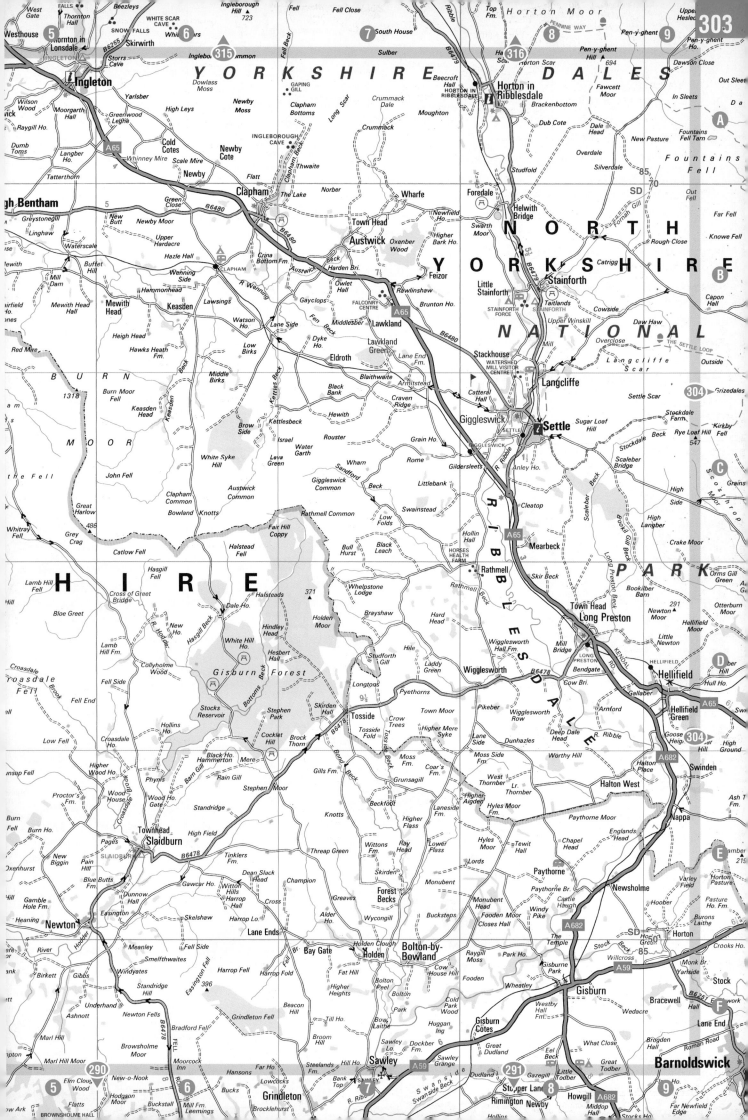

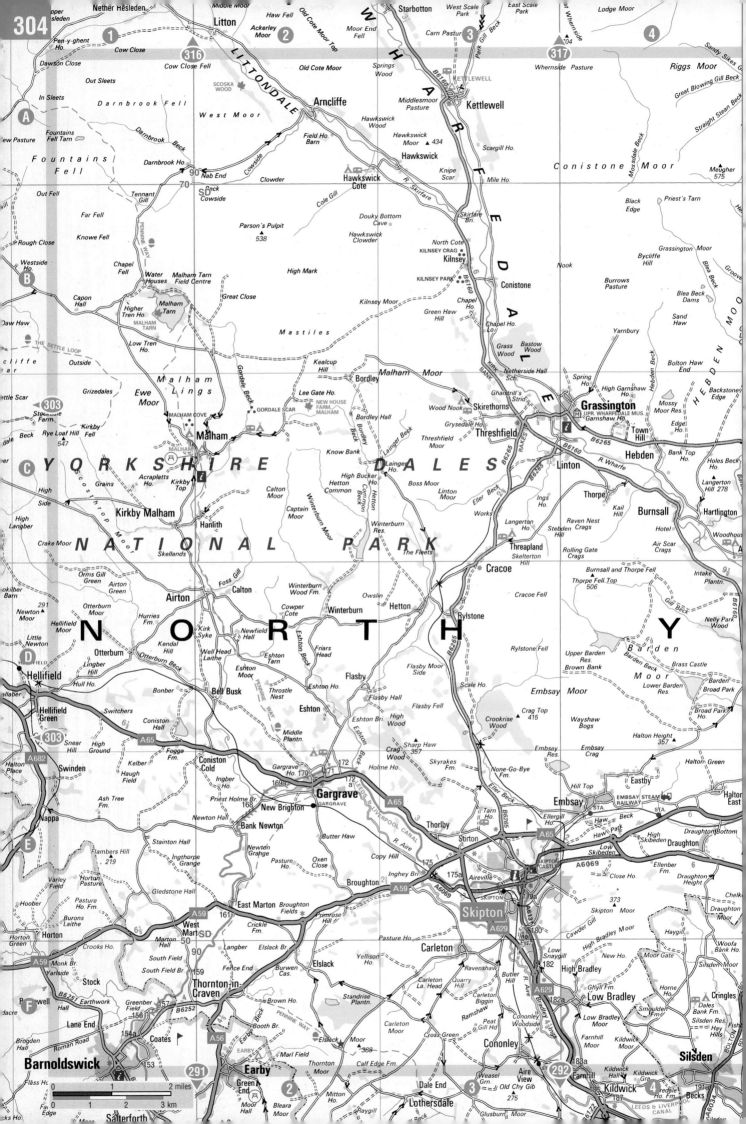

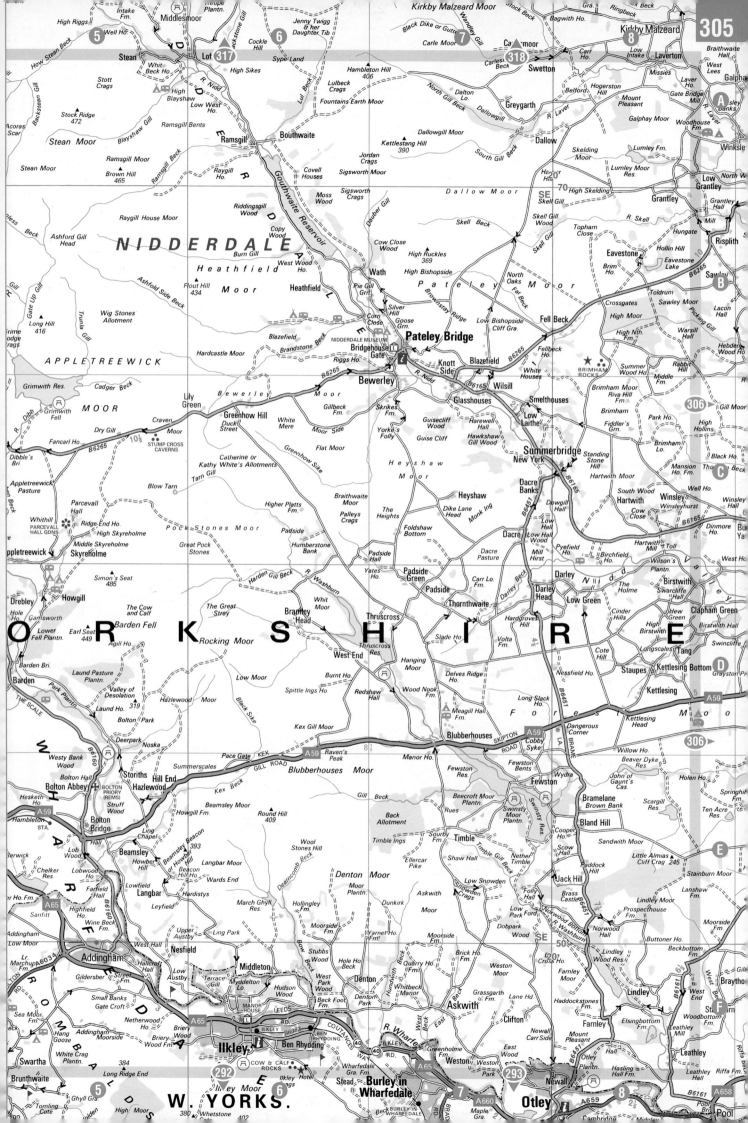

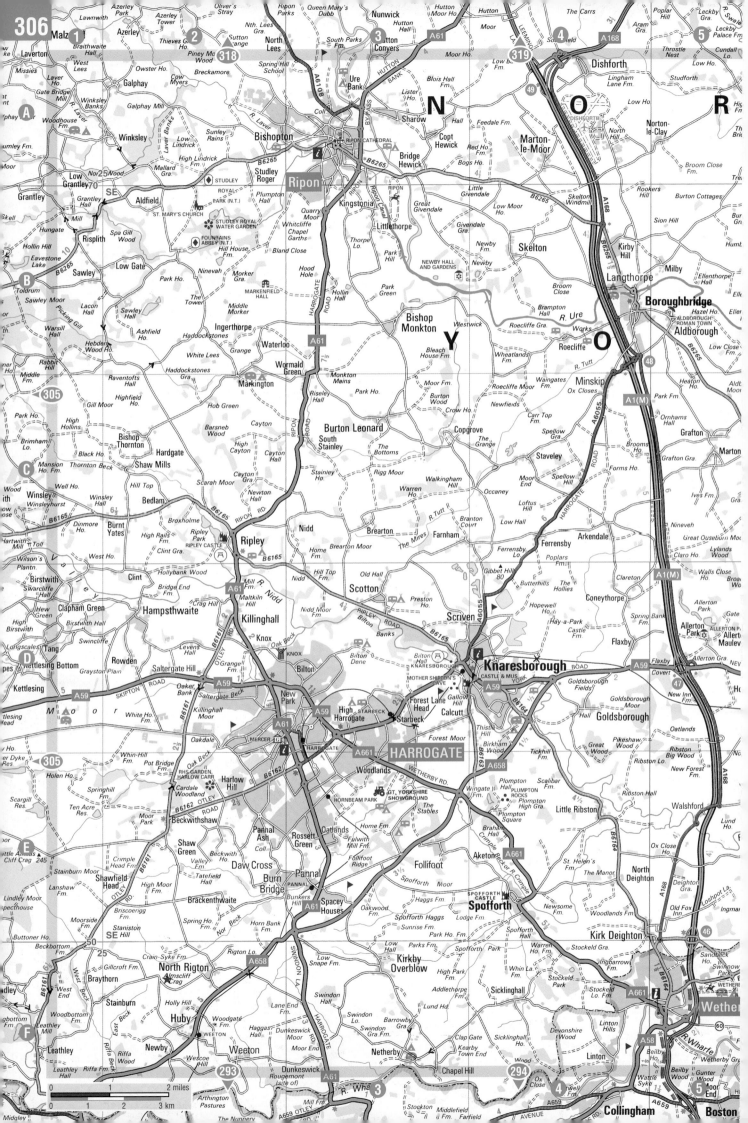

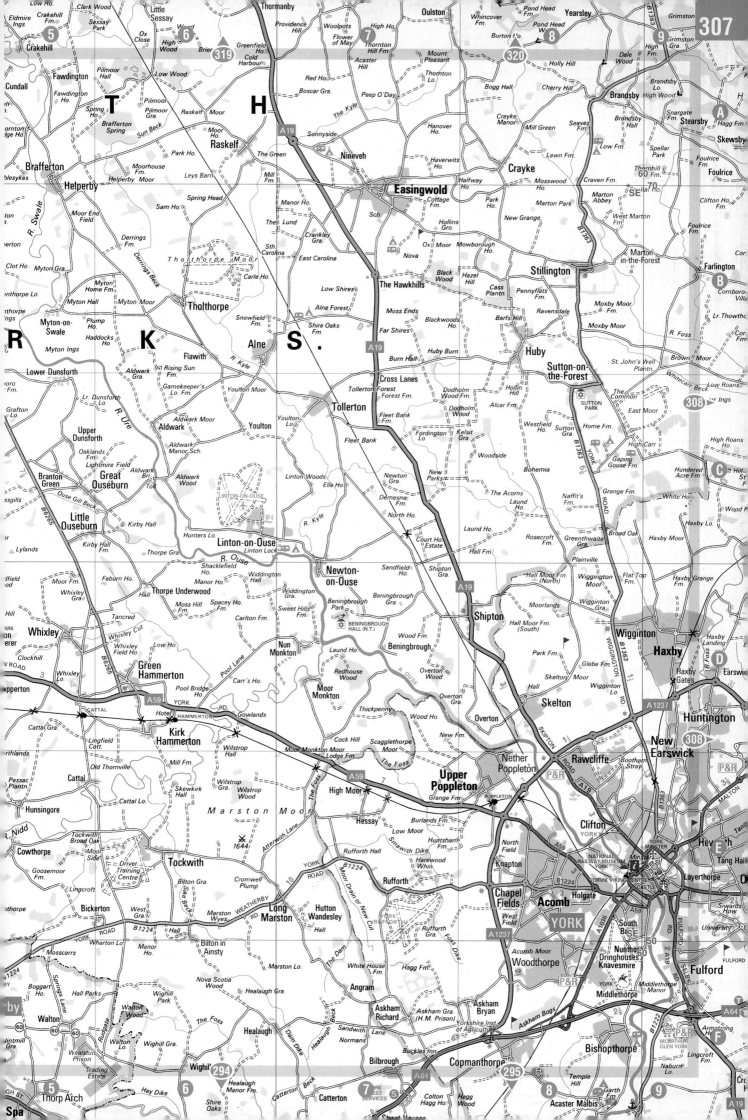

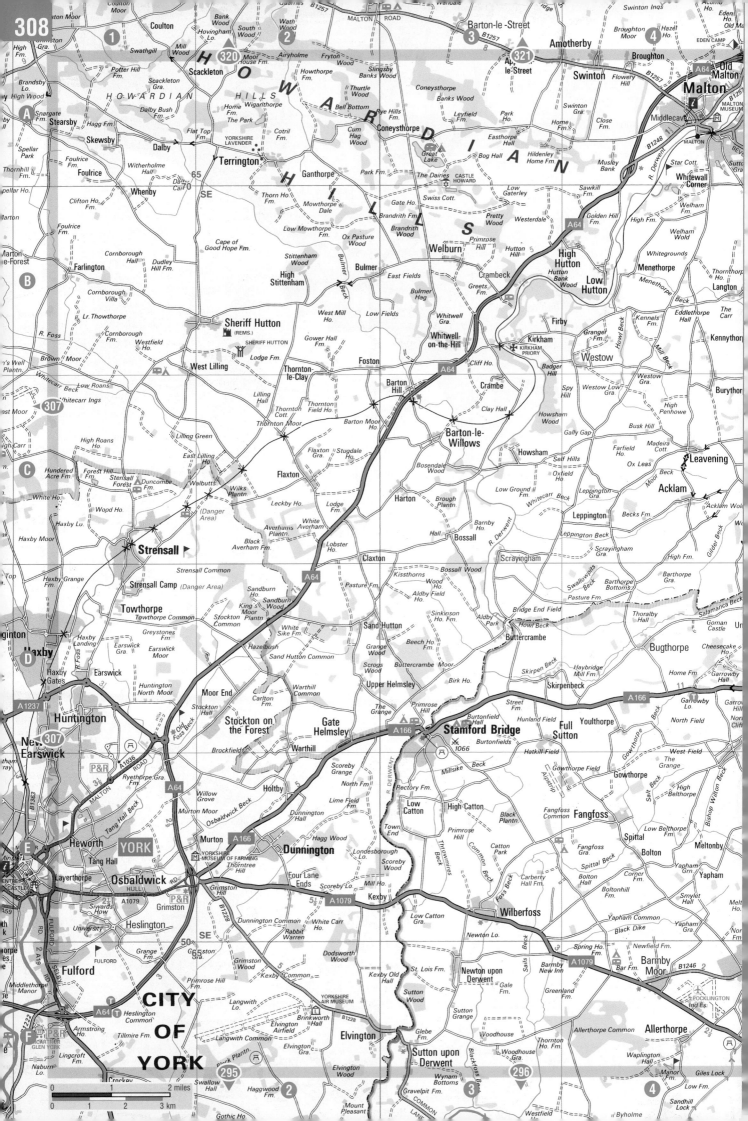

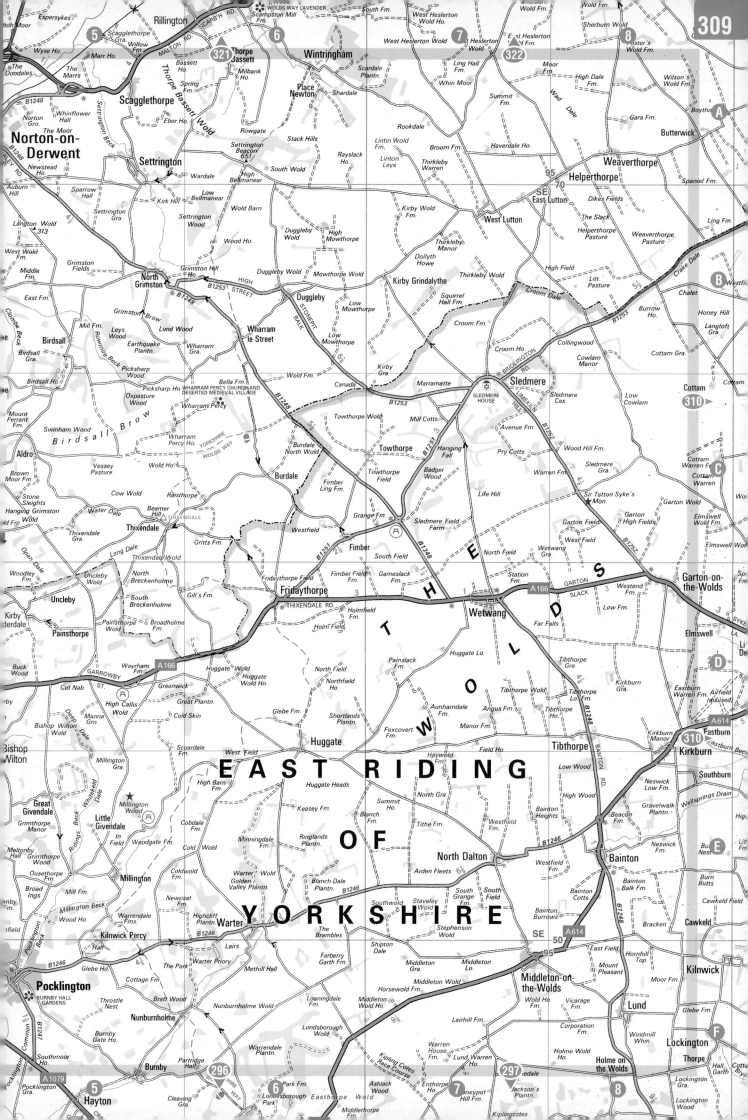

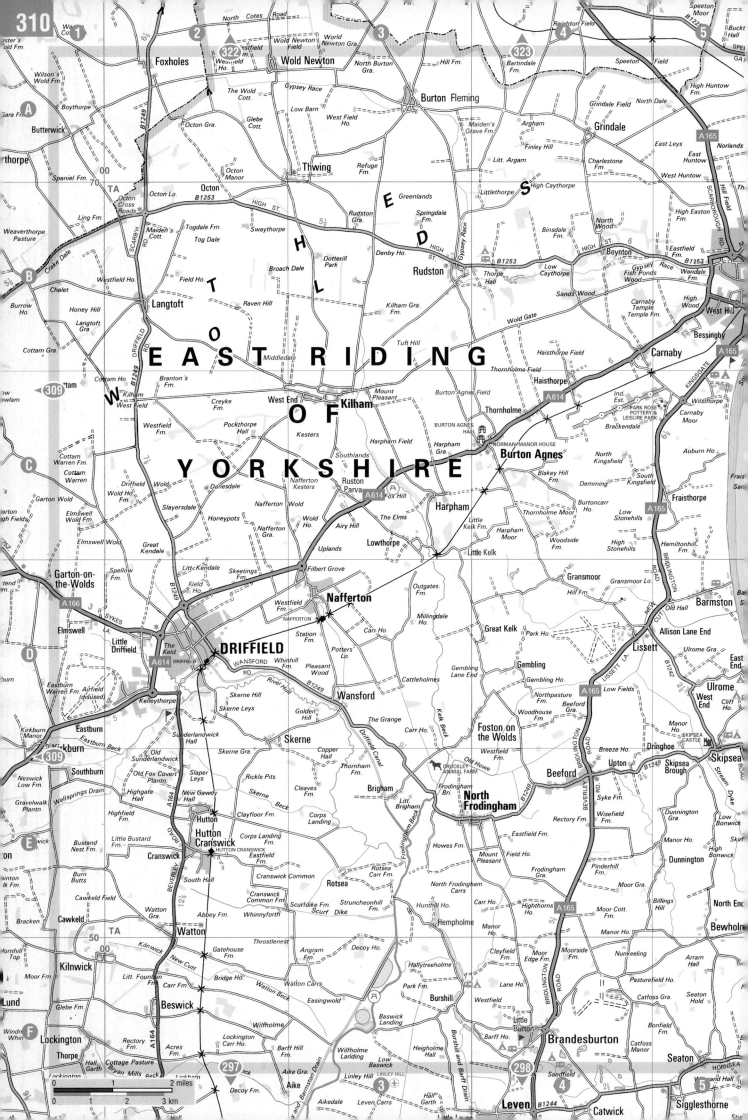

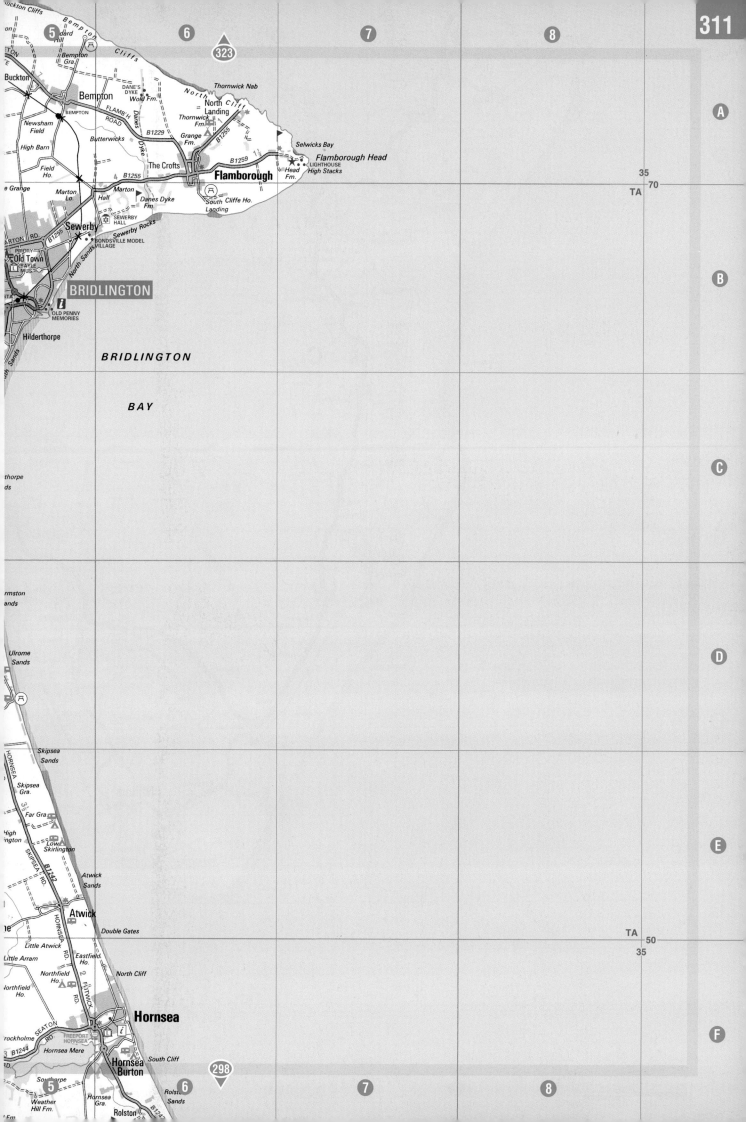

Buckton Cliffs
Bempton Cliffs
Bempton Hill
Buckton
Bempton
Newsham Field
High Barn
FLAMB'H ROAD
Butterwicks
BEMPTON GRA.
B1229
Danes Dyke
Wold Fm.
Dane's Dyke
North Landing
Thornwick Nab
Thornwick Fm.
North Cliff
Grange Fm.
B1255
Selwicks Bay
Flamborough Head
LIGHTHOUSE
High Stacks
Head Fm.
Grange
Marton Lo.
Hall
Marton
Danes Dyke Fm.
The Crofts
B1259
B1255
Flamborough
SEWERBY HALL
South Cliffe Ho.
Landing
Sewerby
MARTON RD.
B1255
PRIORY
Old Town
BAYLE MUS.
Sewerby Rocks
BONDSVILLE MODEL VILLAGE
North Sands
BRIDLINGTON
OLD PENNY MEMORIES
Hilderthorpe

BRIDLINGTON

BAY

thorpe
rds

rmston
ands

Ulrome Sands

Skipsea Sands
Skipsea Gra.
HORNSEA
Far Gra.
High ington
Low Skirlington
SKIPSEA RD.
B1242
Atwick Sands
Atwick
HORNSEA RD.
Double Gates
Little Atwick
Little Arram
Eastfield Ho.
Northfield Ho.
North Cliff
FILLINGWICK RD.
Northfield Ho.
Hornsea
SEATON RD.
Brockholme
FREEPORT HORNSEA
Hornsea Mere
South Cliff
B1244
Hornsea Burton
298
Southorpe
Hornsea Gra.
Rolston Sands
Weather Hill Fm.
Rolston
B1242

TA 70 35

TA 50 35

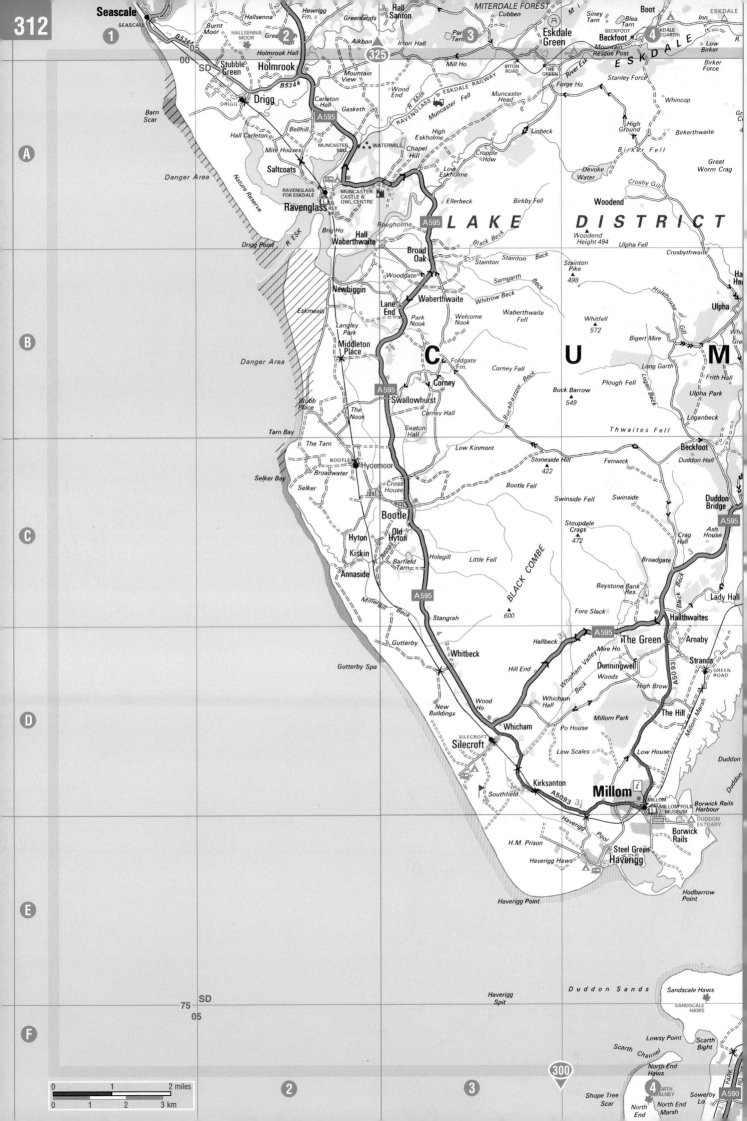

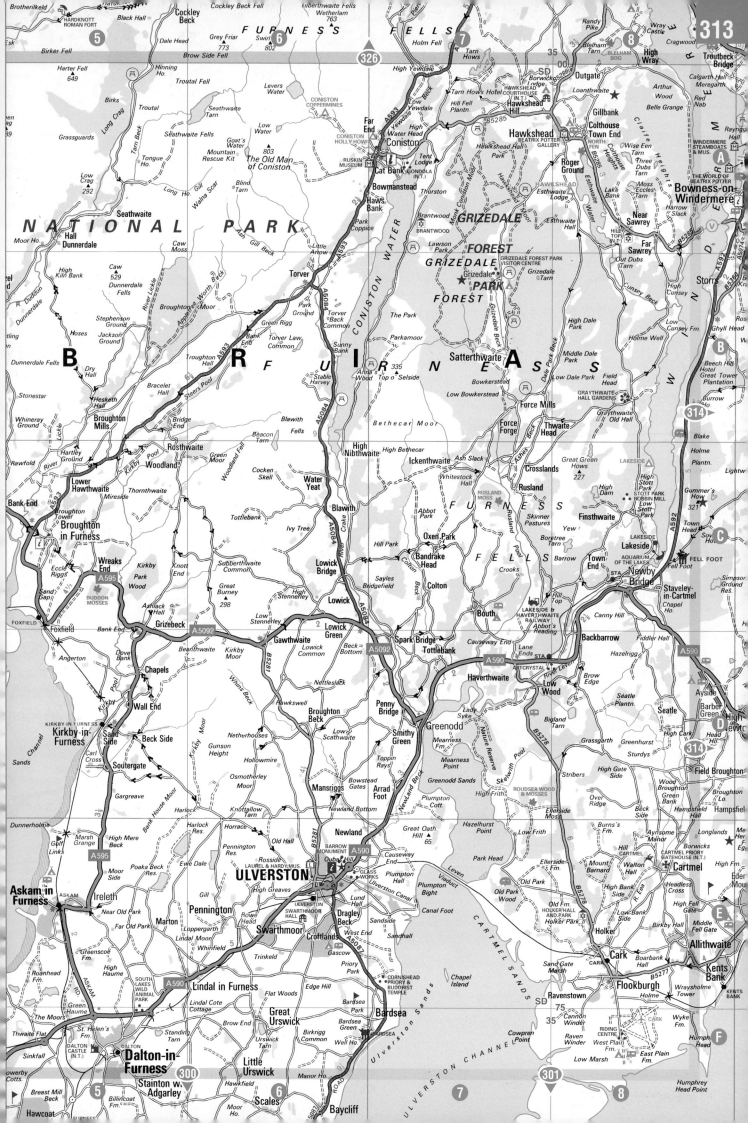

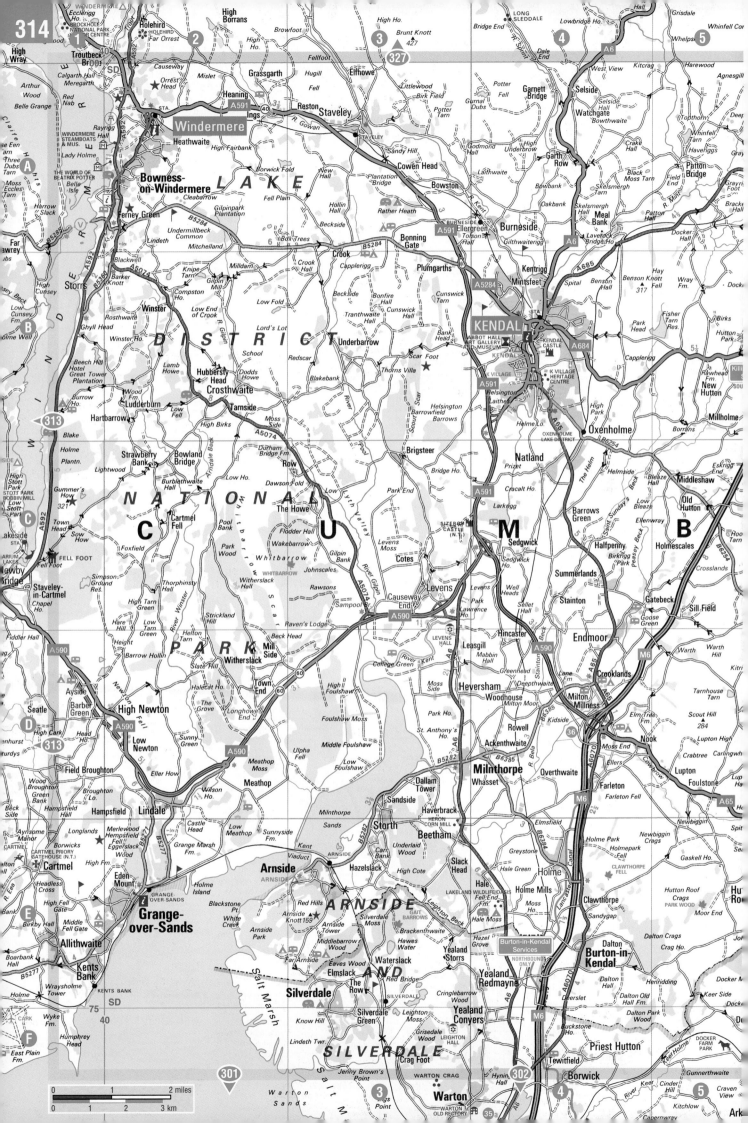

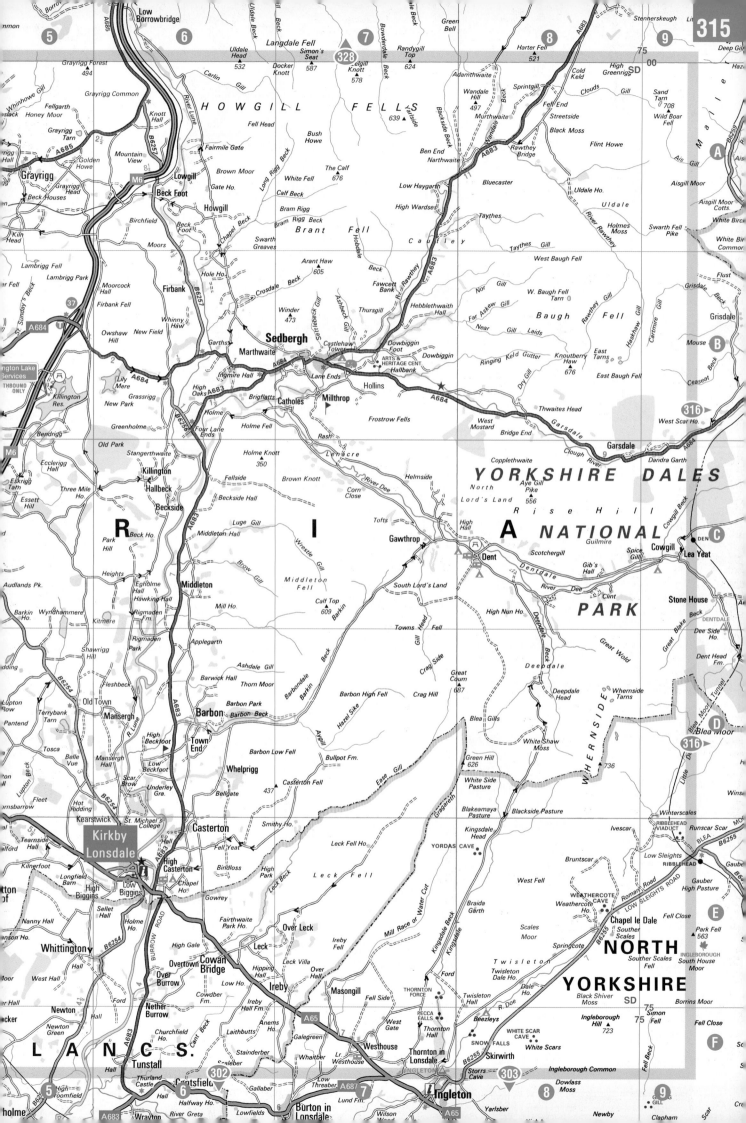

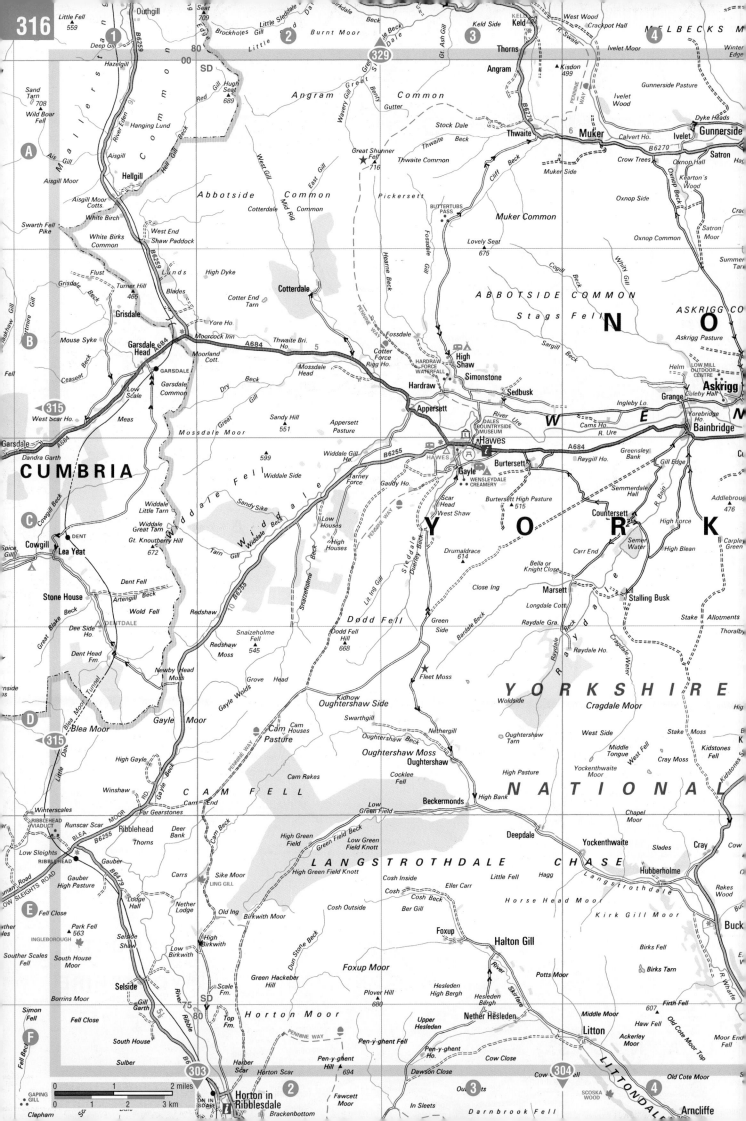

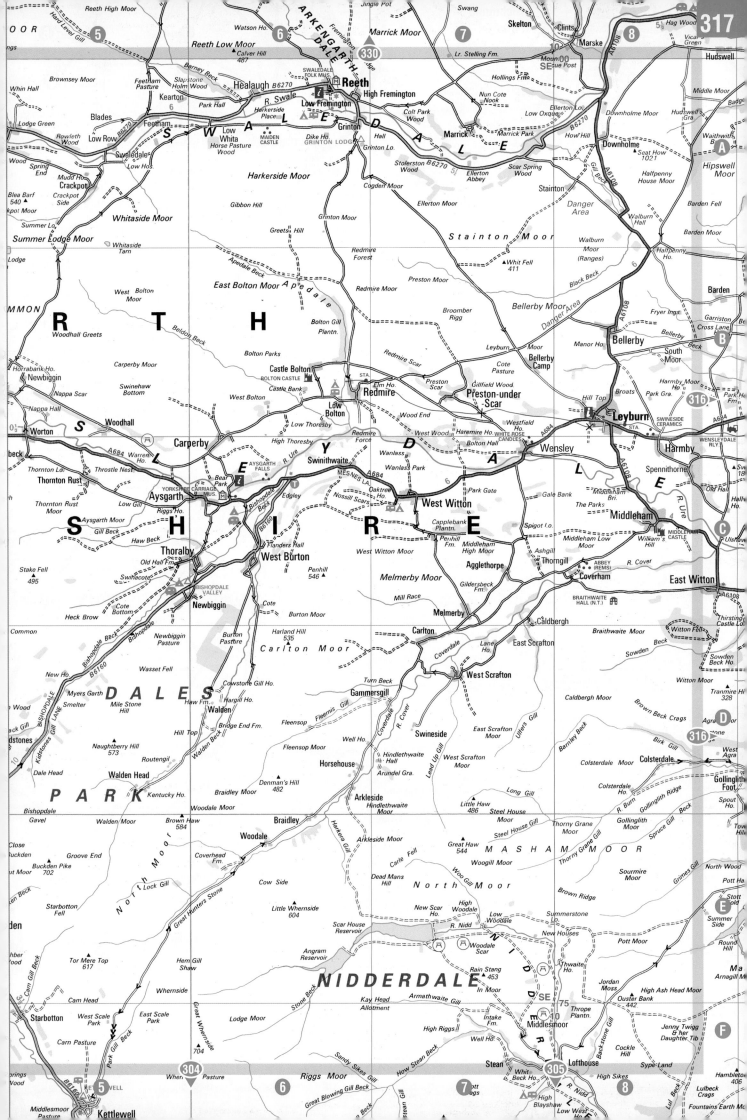

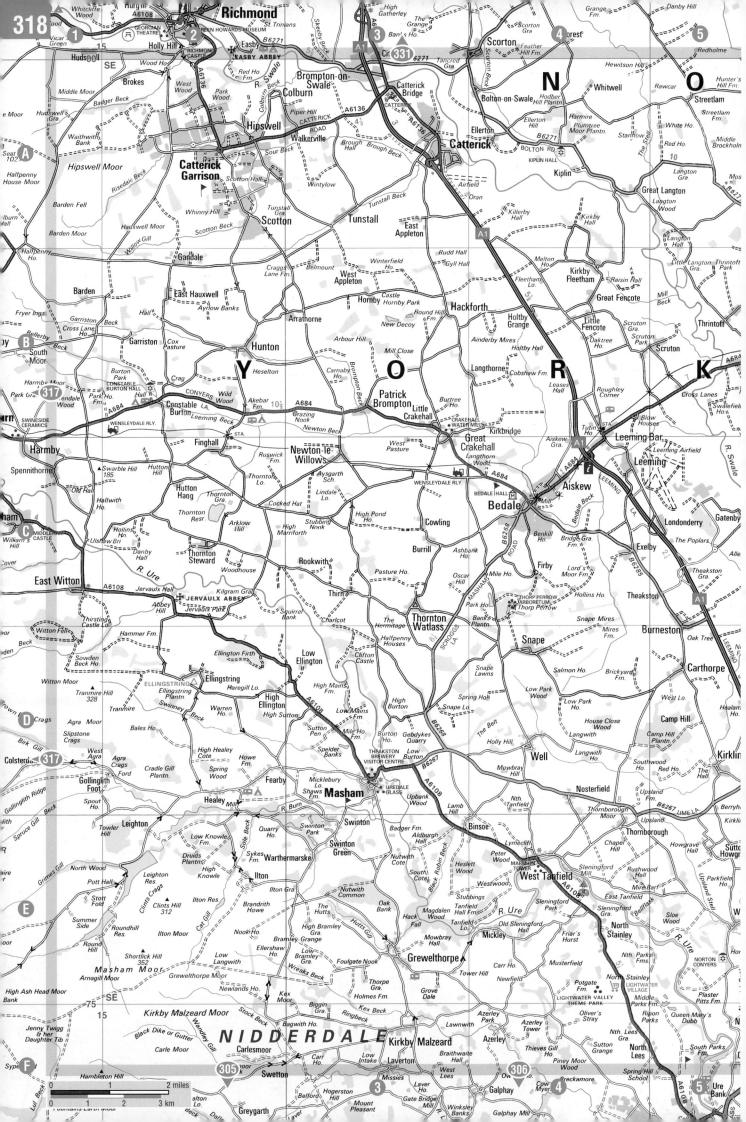

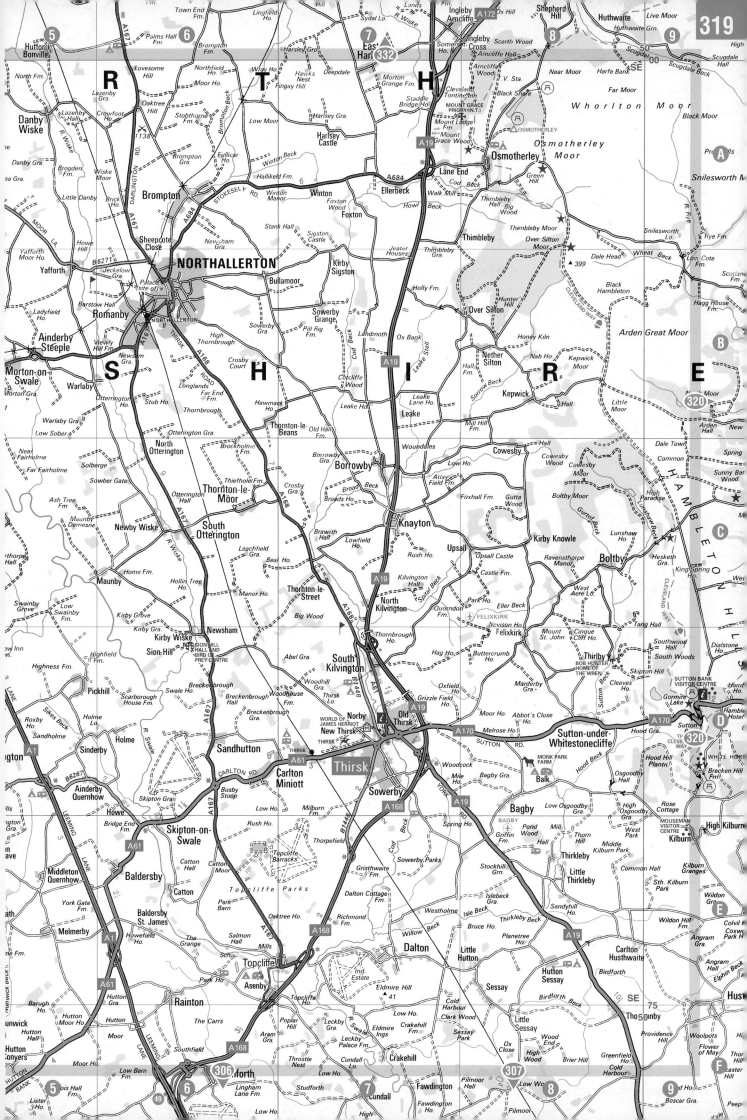

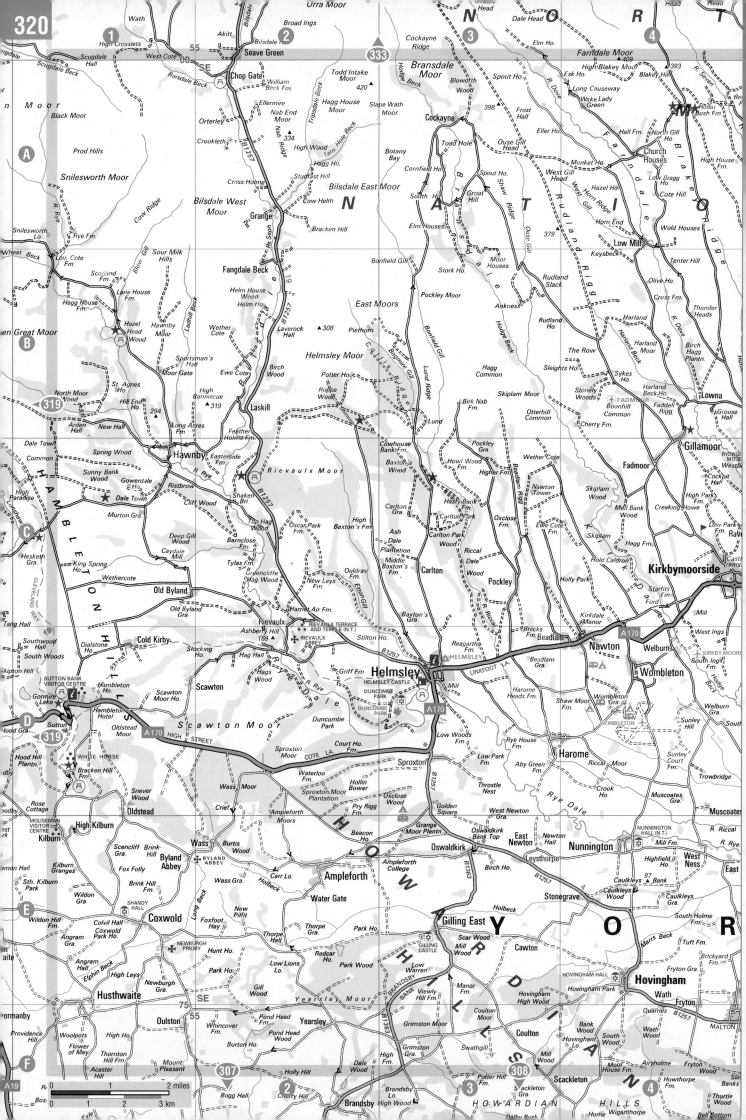

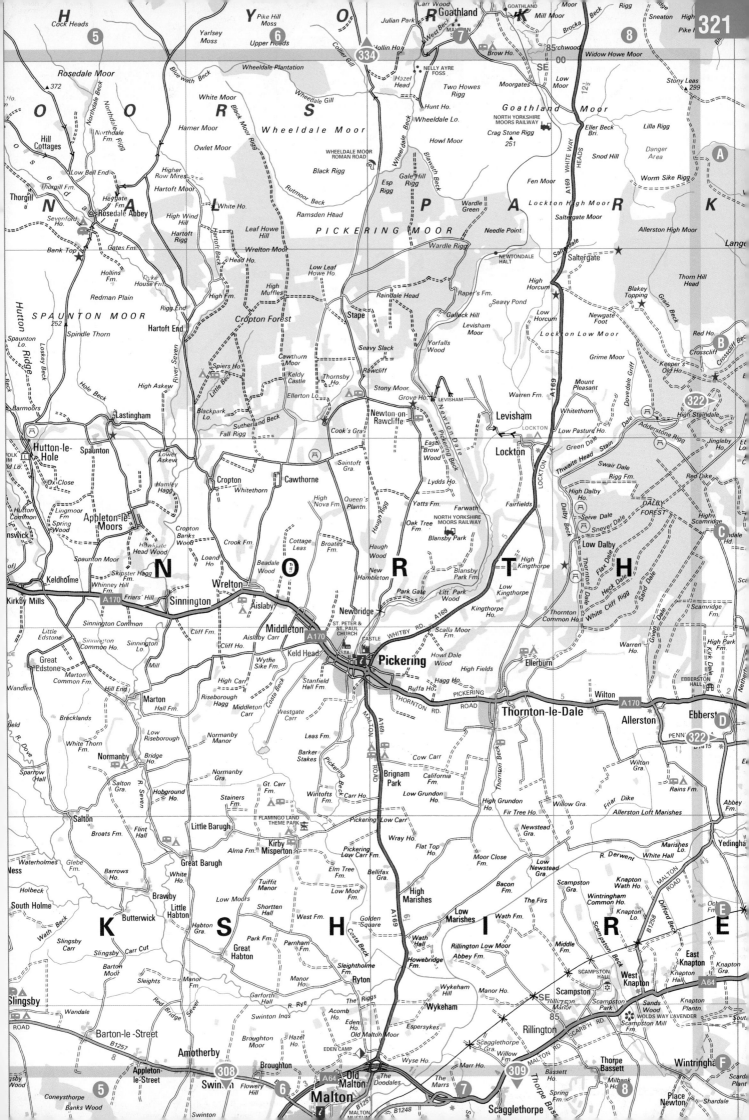

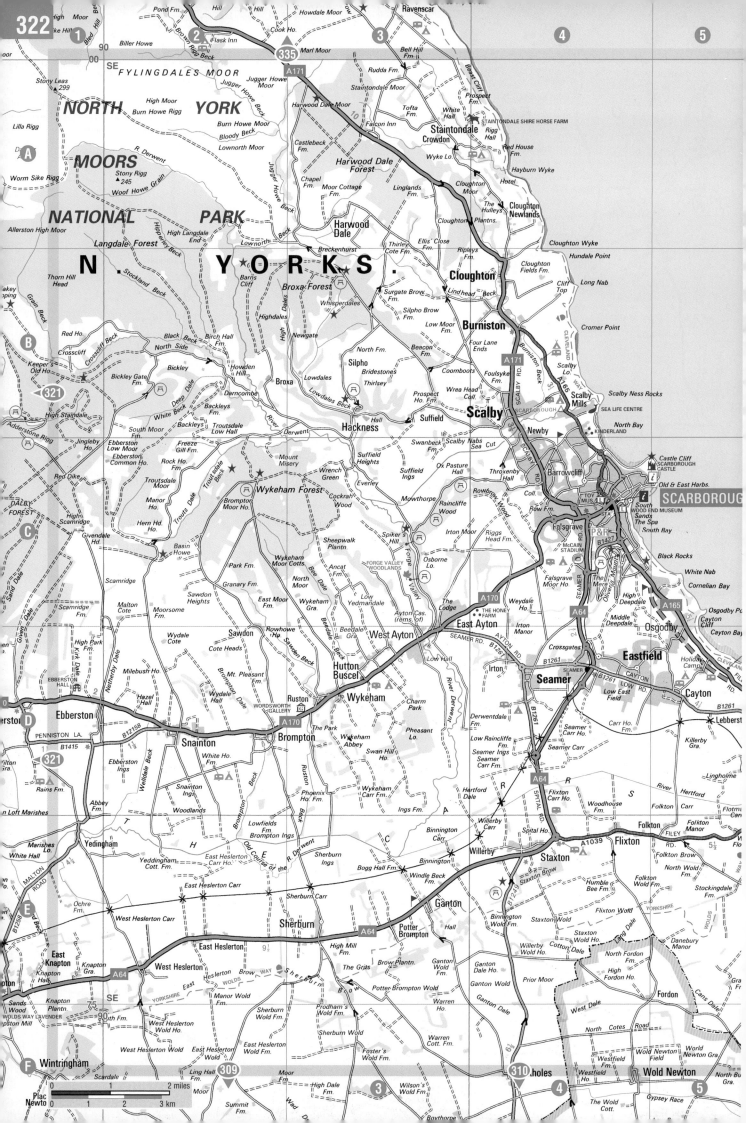

⑤ ⑥ ⑦ ⑧

25
TA 00

Ⓐ

Ⓑ

Ⓒ

ᴴ

*point*

*Yons Nab*

*Cunstone Nab*

*The Wyke*

Ⓓ

Ⓔ Redcliff Fm.

*Gristhorpe Cliff*

*Cliff Fm.*

*Club Point*

*North Cliff*

ton

Gristhorpe

Newbiggin

A1039

Filey Brigg

*Filey Sands*

Crayke Ho. Fm.

FILEY

**Filey**

*Magdalen Gra.*

Beacon Hill

*FILEY*

manby

Muston

A1039

Muston Sands

*FILEY BAY*

FLOTMANBY LANE

Muston Gra.

Vest tmanby

Pilmoor Fm.

The Dams

Royal Oak

Primrose Valley

Hunmanby Sands

Holiday Camp

Hunmanby Gap

Ⓔ

**Hunmanby**

Hunmanby Moor

Moor Fm.

Moor

Field Ho. Fm.

HUNMANBY

Moor Ho.

Reighton Sands

Hill Fm.

A165

Raincliff Ings

Speeton Sands

nge

South Dale

Graffitoe Fm.

Reighton

Speeton Hills

MOOR RD.

Howe Fm.

Dale Fm.

Speeton

Speeton Cliffs

TA 75
25

Buckton Cliffs

*Bempton*

Reighton Field

Speeton Moor

B1229

SPEETON GATE

Buckton Hall

Standard Hill

Bempton Gra.

Ⓕ

Hill Fm.

Bartindale Fm.

rton

Speeton Field

High Huntow Fm.

310

⑤ ⑥ ⑦ uckton ⑧

**Burton** Fleming

North Dale

Bempton

DANE'S DYKE

Wold Fm.

North Cliff

Thornwick Nab

311

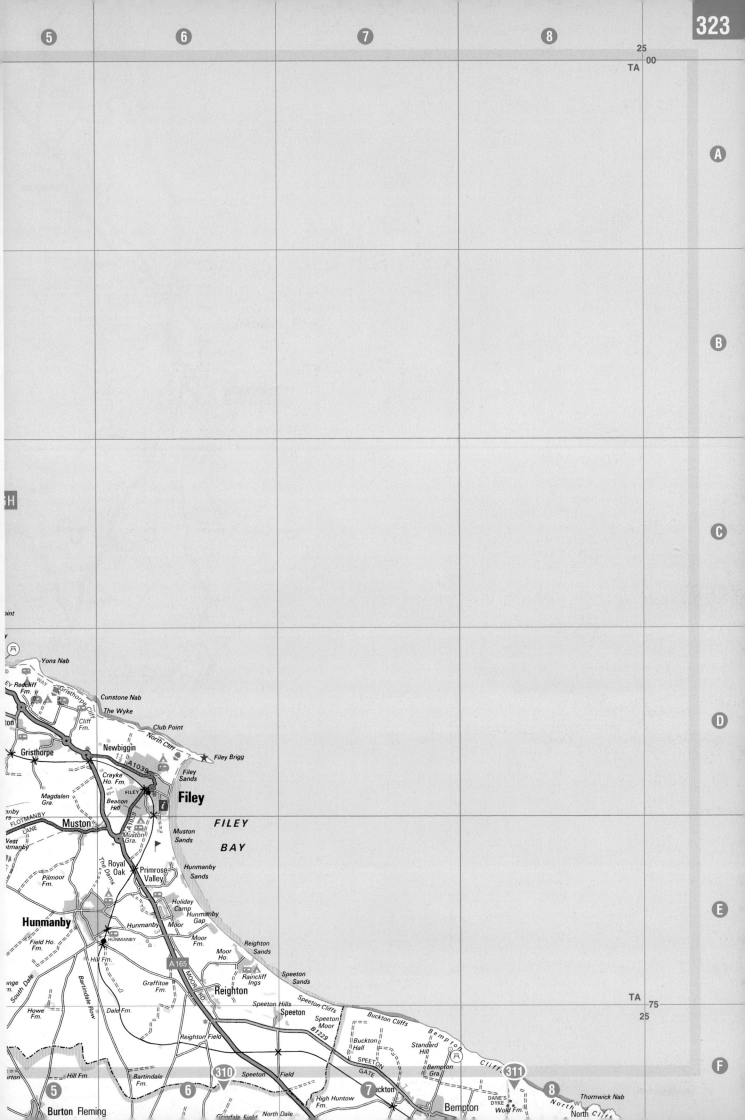

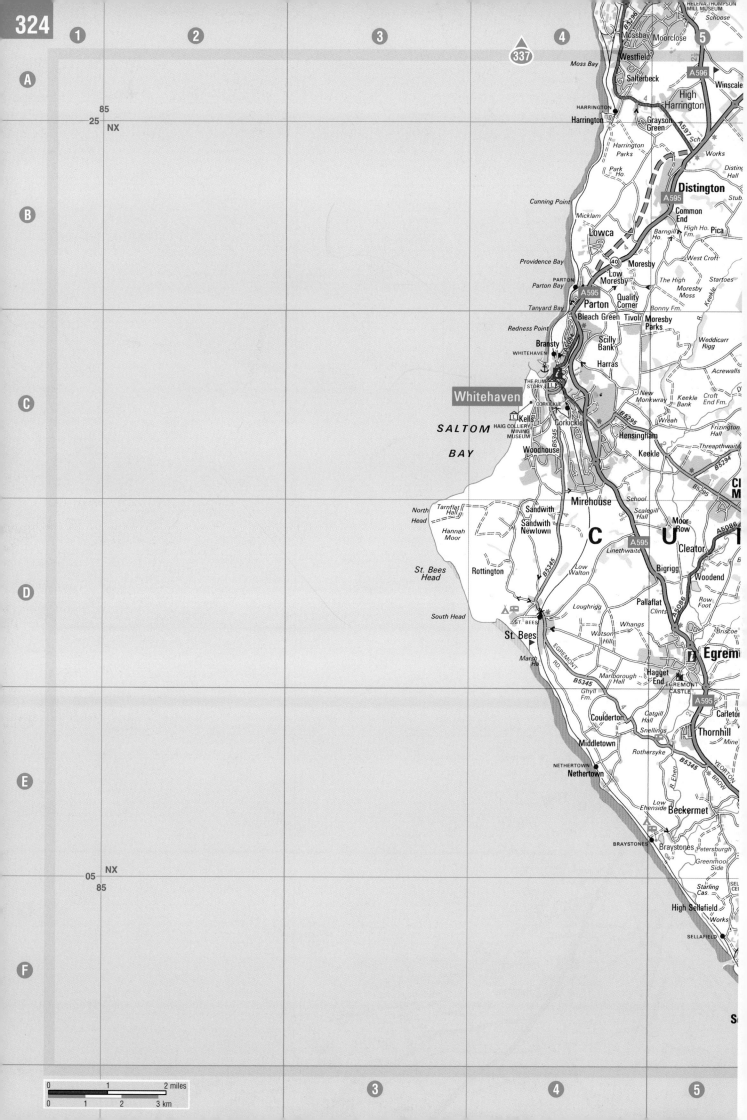

SALTOM

BAY

Whitehaven

St. Bees
Head

North
Head

South Head

HELENA THOMPSON
MILL MUSEUM
Schoose

Mossbay    Moorclose

Moss Bay

Westfield

Salterbeck

Winscale

High
Harrington

HARRINGTON

Harrington

Grayson
Green

Harrington
Parks

Works

Disting
Hall

Park
Ho.

Distington

Cunning Point

Micklam

High Ho.
Fm.

Common
End

Stub.

Lowca

Barngill
Ho.

Pica

Providence Bay

Moresby

West Croft

Startoes

Low
Moresby

The High
Moresby
Moss

Parton
Parton Bay

Quality
Corner

Bonny Fm.

Tanyard Bay

Parton

Bleach Green    Tivoli

Moresby
Parks

Redness Point

Scilly
Bank

Weddicarr
Rigg

Bransty

Acrewalls

WHITEHAVEN

Harras

THE RUM
STORY

New
Monkwray

Keekle
Bank

Croft
End Fm.

Frizington
Hall

CORKICKLE

Wreah

Threapthwaite

Kells

Corkickle

HAIG COLLIERY
MINING
MUSEUM

Hensingham

Keekle

Woodhouse

Mirehouse

School

Scalegill
Hall

Moor
Row

Cl
M

Tarnflat
Hall

Sandwith

C

U

I

Hannah
Moor

Sandwith
Newtown

Linethwaite

Cleator

St. Bees
Head

Rottington

Low
Walton

Bigrigg

Woodend

Pallaflat
Clints

Row
Foot

Loughrigg

Briscoe

Whangs

Egrem

ST. BEES

Watson
Hill

St. Bees

Marsh
Ho.

Hagget
End

EGREMONT
CASTLE

Marlborough
Hall

Carleton

Ghyll
Fm.

Thornhill
Mine

Coulderton

Catgill
Hall

Snellings

Middletown

Rothersyke

NETHERTOWN

Nethertown

Low
Ehenside

Beckermet

BRAYSTONES

Braystones

Petersburgh

Greenmoor
Side

Starling
Cas.

SEL
CEI

High Sellafield

Works

SELLAFIELD

S

337

A596

A597 Sch

A595

A595

A595

A595

B5296

A596

B5294

B5295

B5295

B5345

B5345

B5345

A5086

A5086

EGREMONT
RD.

R. Ehen

YEORTON
BROW

85
25
NX

05
NX
85

0        1        2 miles
0    1    2    3 km

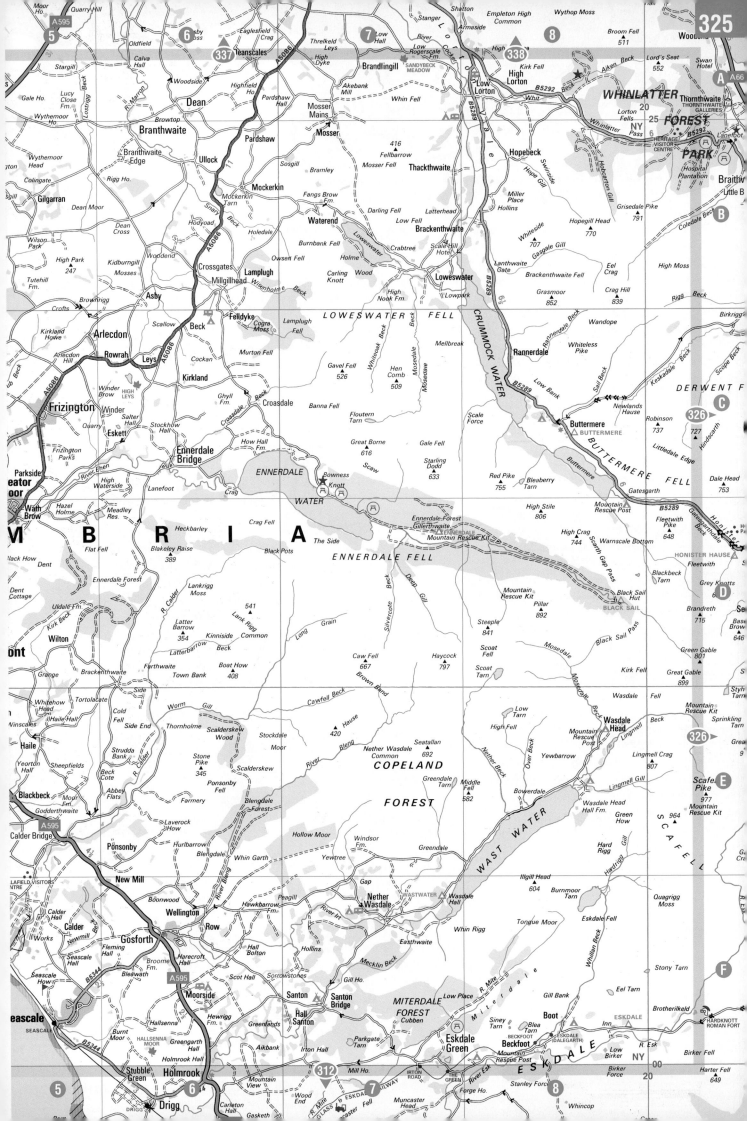

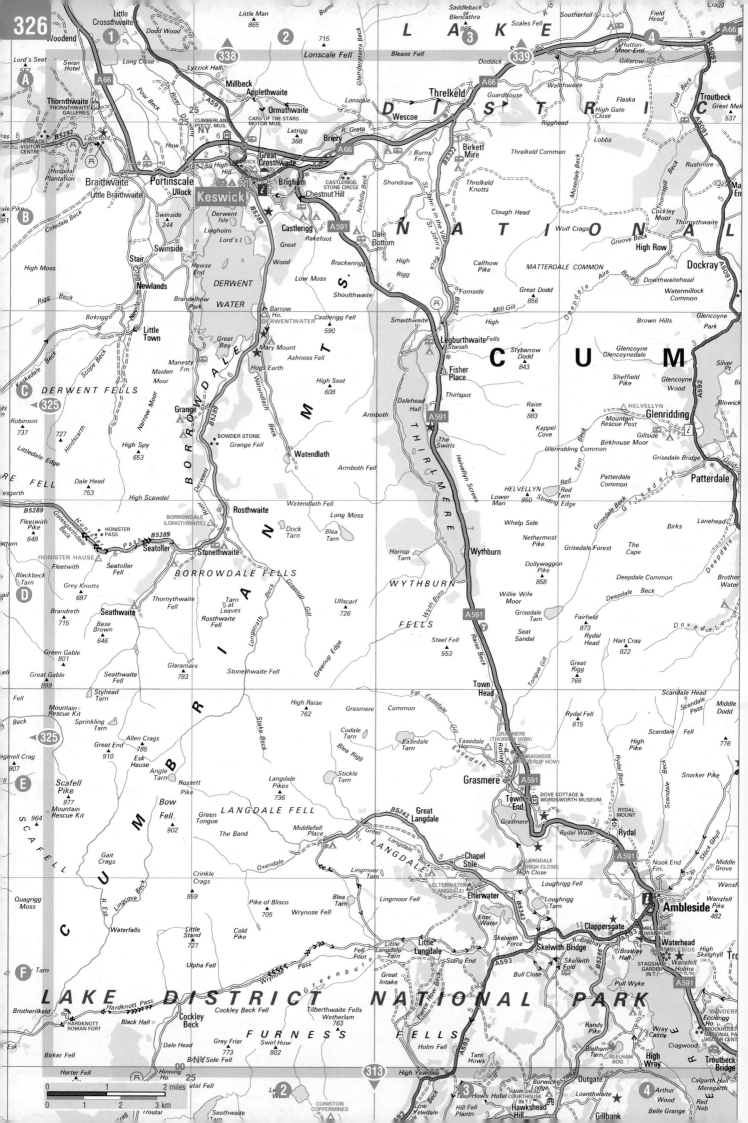

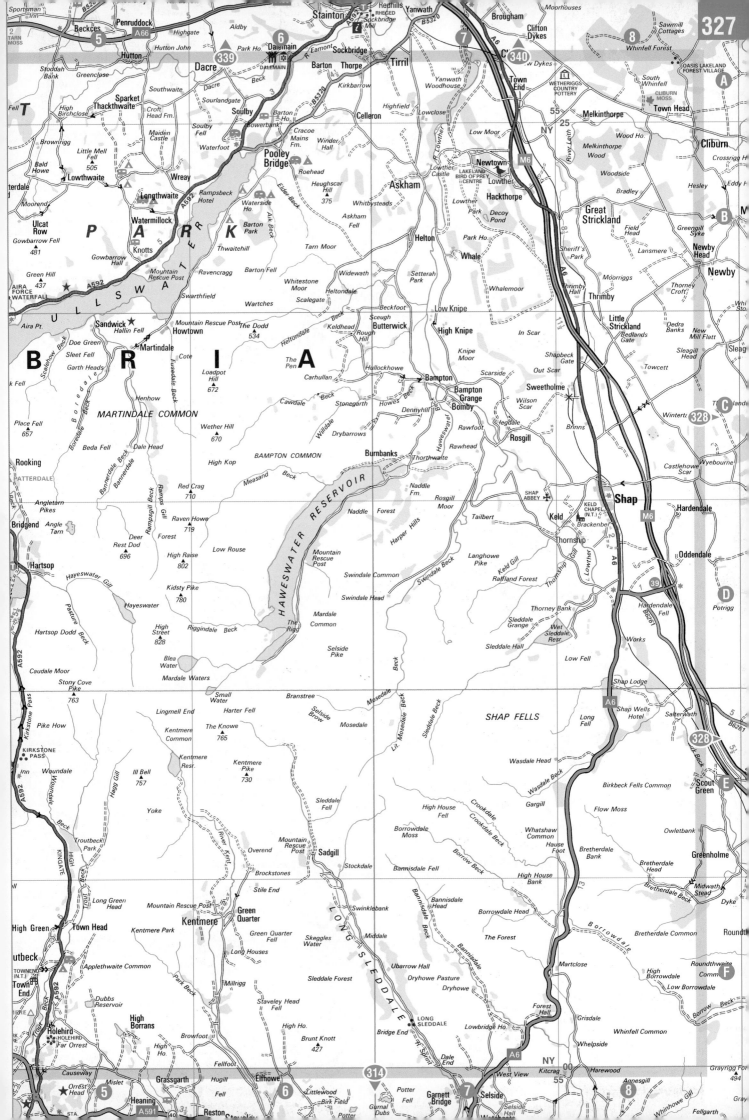

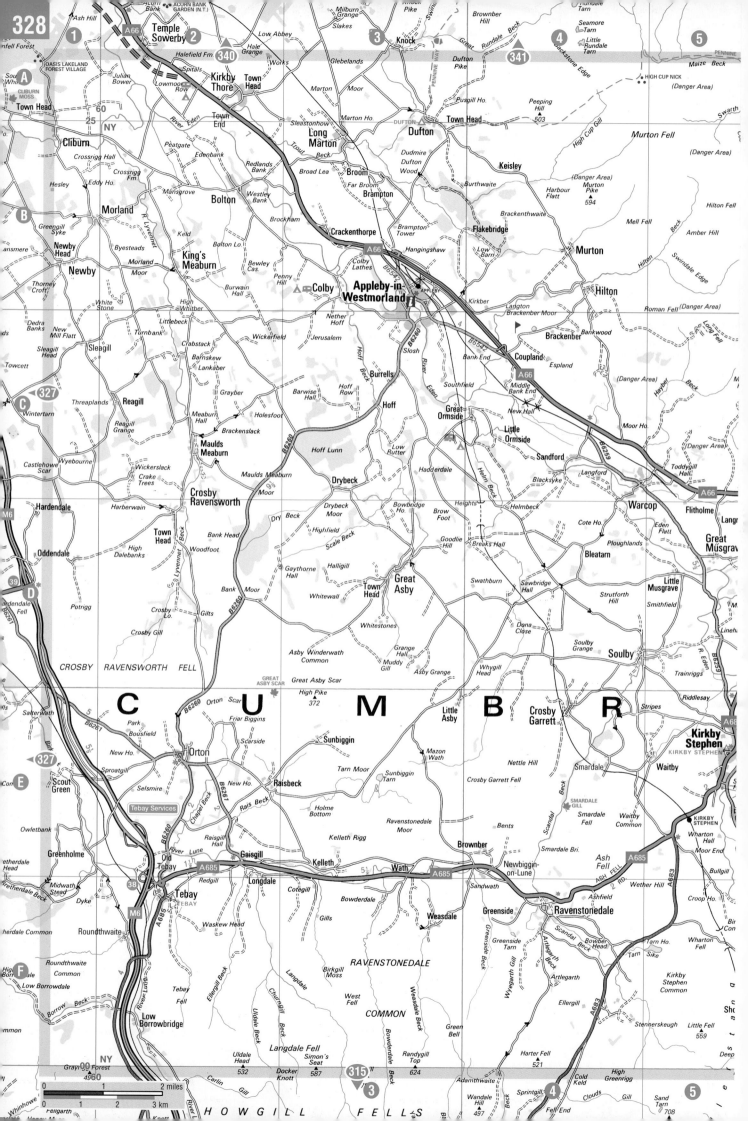

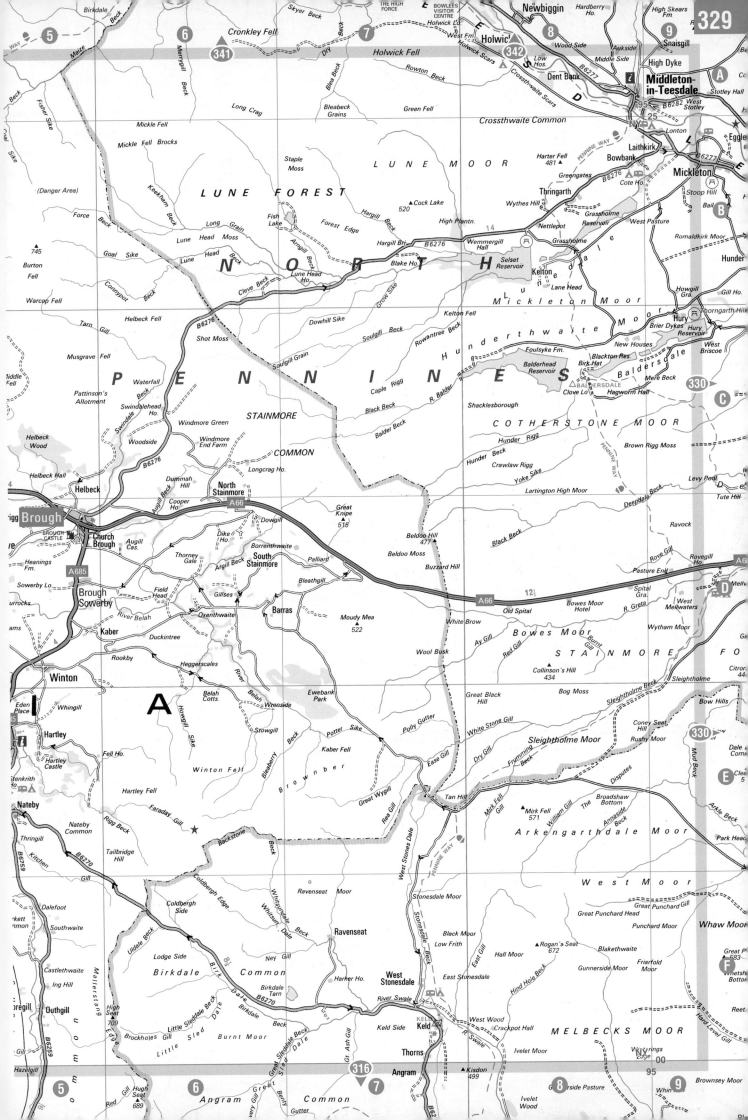

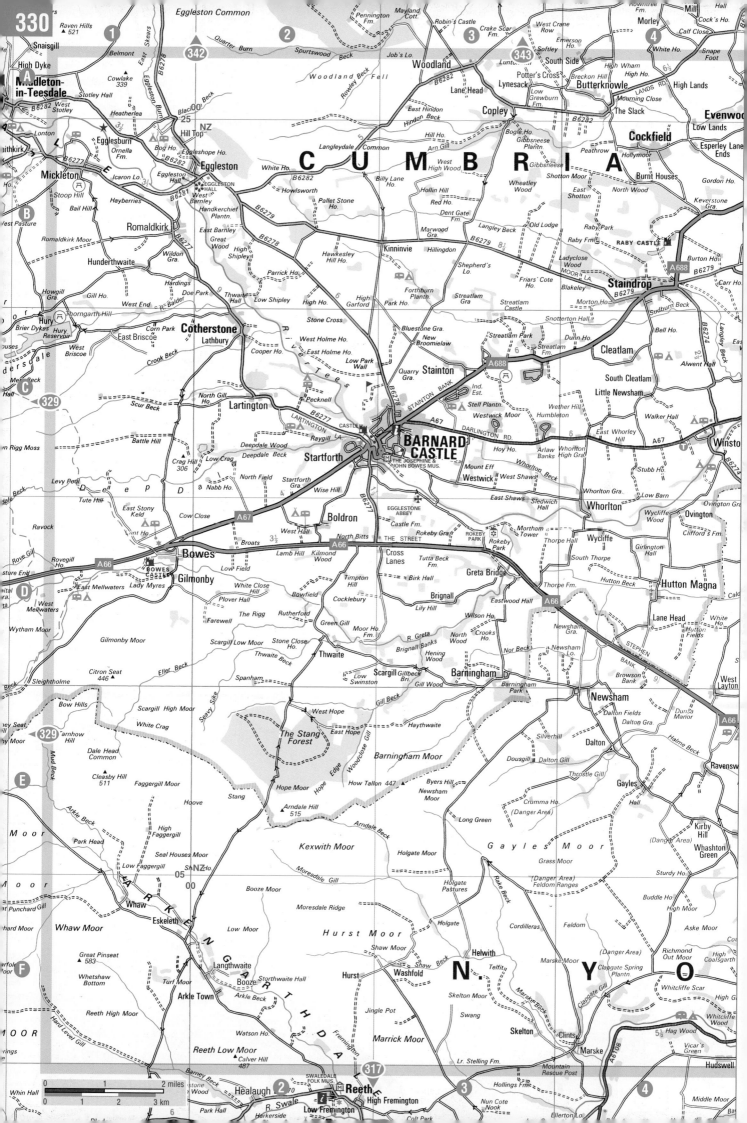

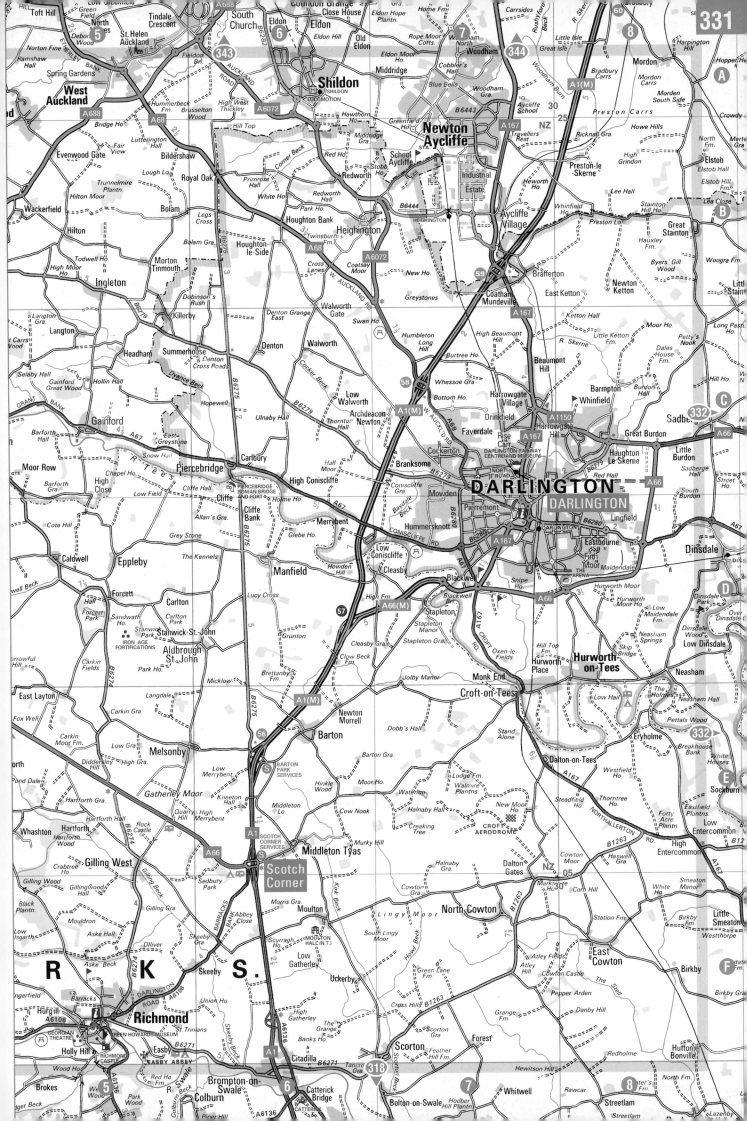

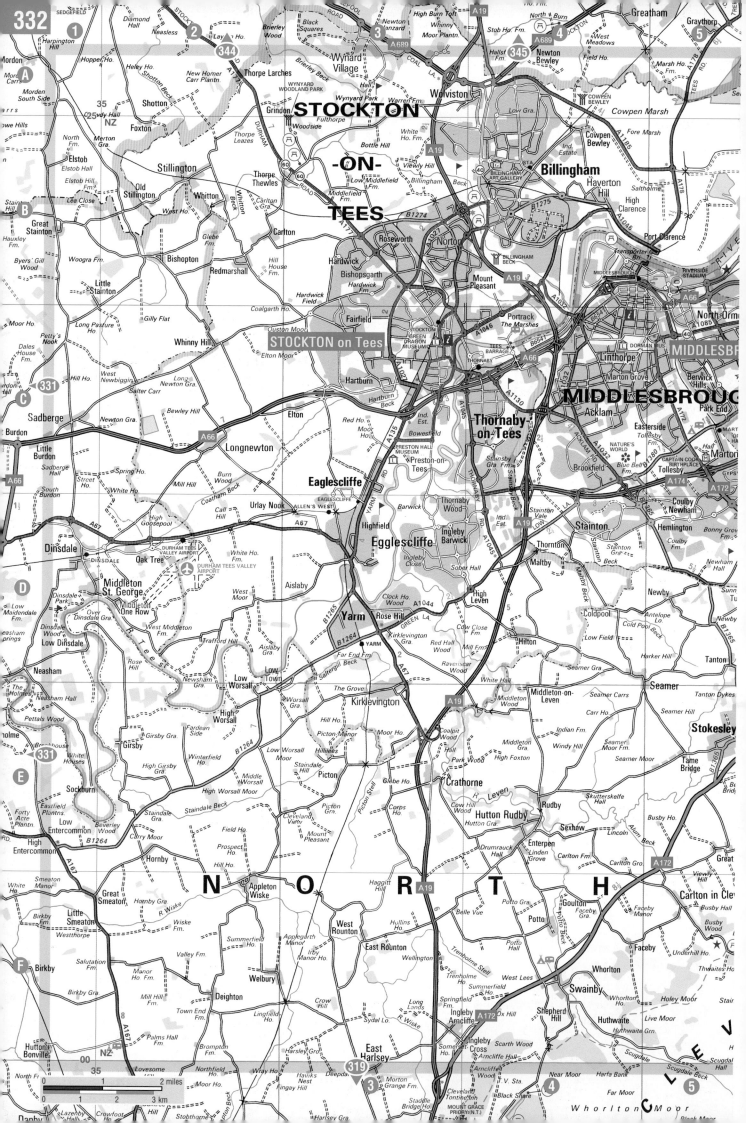

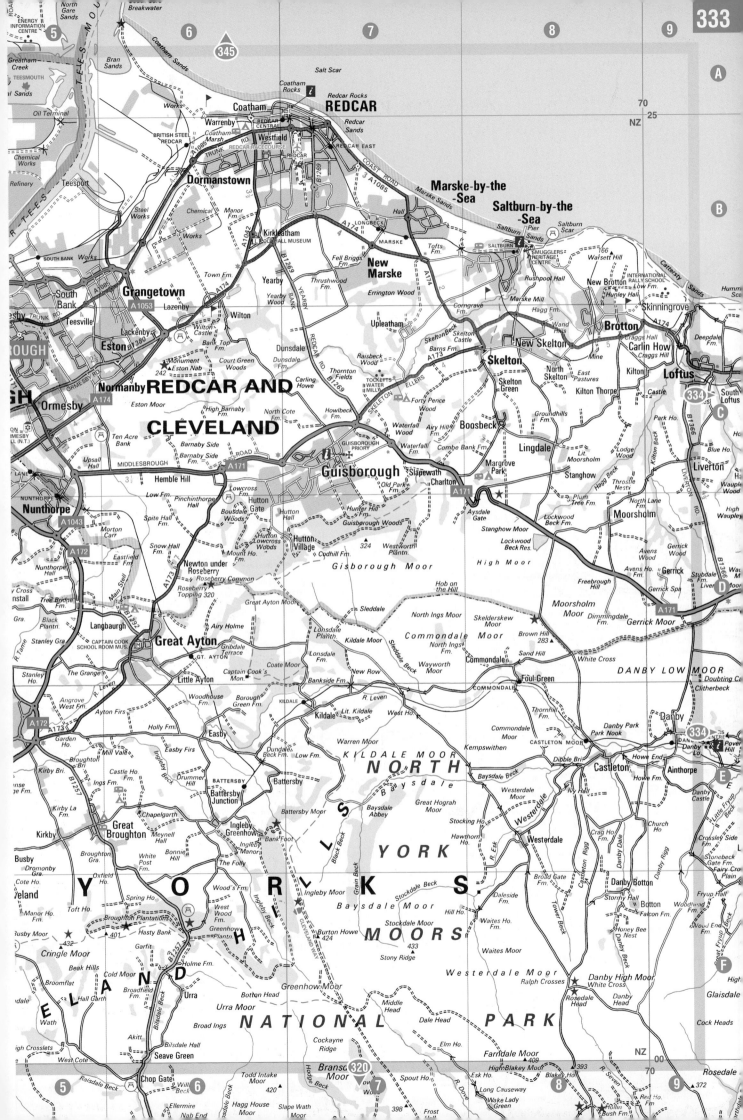

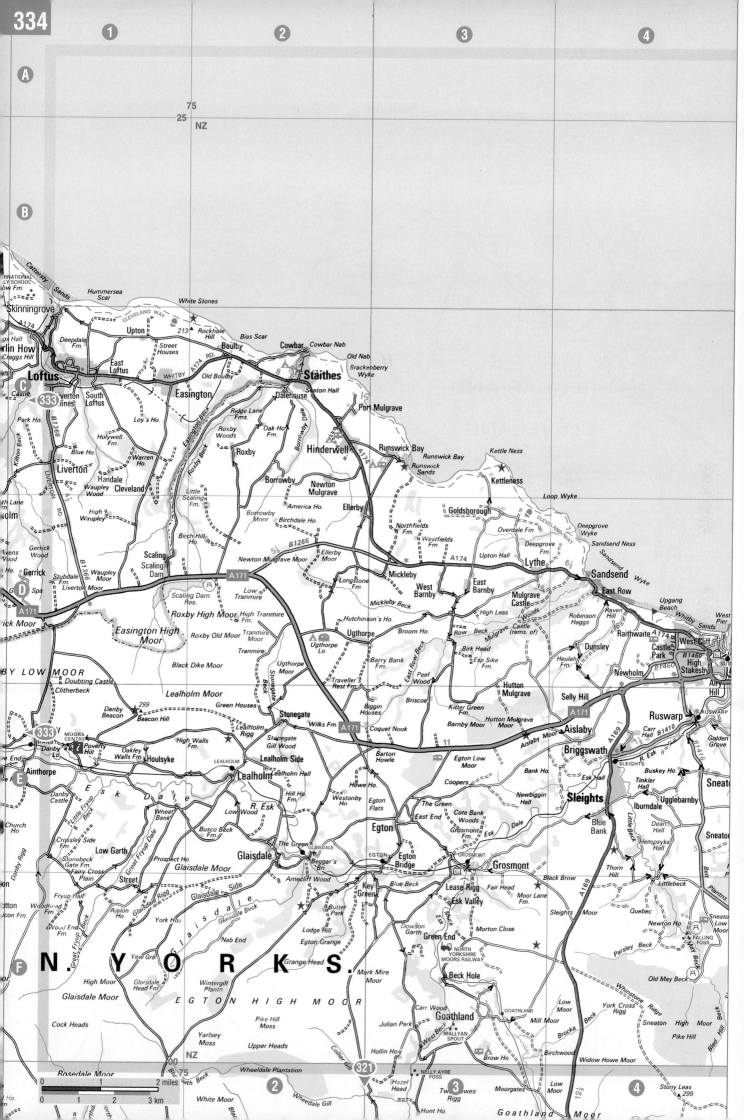

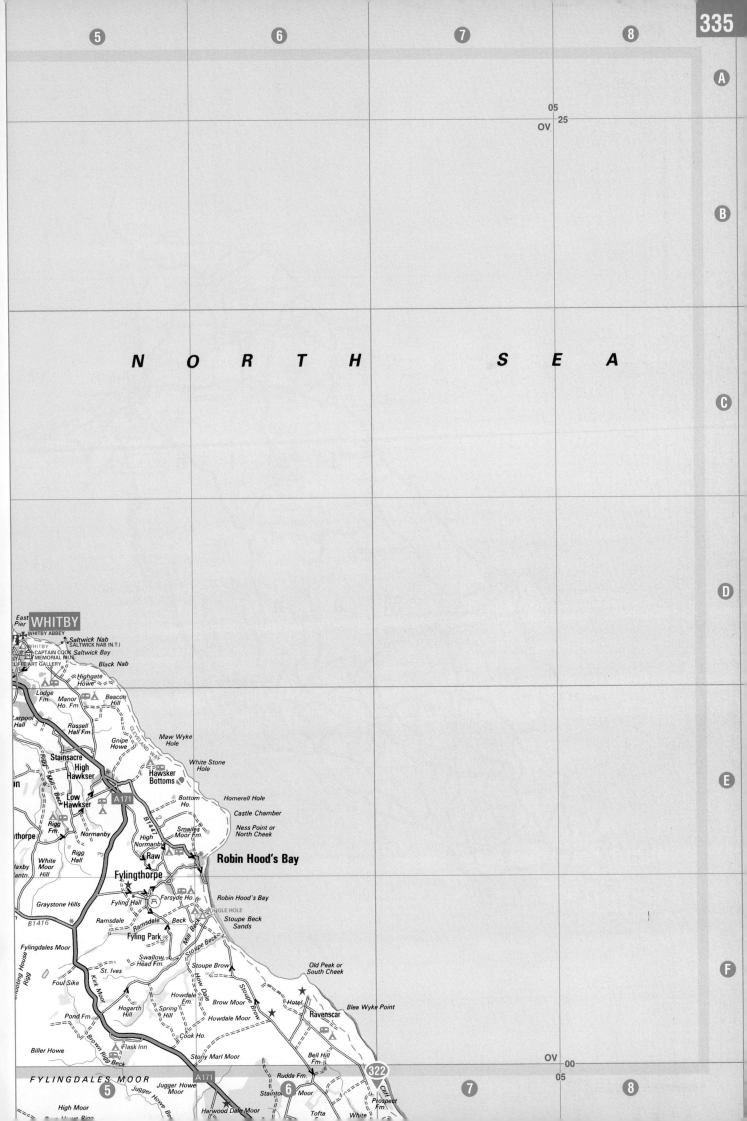

A

05
25
OV

B

N O R T H    S E A

C

D

East
Pier    WHITBY
WHITBY ABBEY
WHITBY    Saltwick Nab
CAPTAIN COOK    SALTWICK NAB (N.T.)
MEMORIAL MUS.    Saltwick Bay
...CLIFFE ART GALLERY    Black Nab
Highgate
Howe
Lodge    Manor    Beacon
Fm.    Ho. Fm.    Hill
Larpool
Hall    Russell    Maw Wyke
Hall Fm.    Hole
Gnipe
Stainsacre    Howe    White Stone
High    Hole
Hawsker    Hawsker
Bottoms
...n    Low    Bottom    Homerell Hole
Hawkser    Ho.
Rigg    Castle Chamber
Fm.    Smailes    Ness Point or
...thorpe    Normanby    Moor Fm.    North Cheek
Rigg    High
Hall    Normanby    Raw    Robin Hood's Bay
...laxby    White    Fylingthorpe
Moor    Graystone Hills    Farsyde Ho.    Robin Hood's Bay
...antn    Hill    Fyling Hall    BOGGLE HOLE
Ramsdale    Ramsdale    Beck    Stoupe Beck
B1416    Fyling Park    Sands
Fylingdales Moor    Swallow    Stoupe Brow    Old Peak or
...bbing House    Head Fm.    South Cheek
Rigg    St. Ives    Howdale    Hotel    Blea Wyke Point
Foul Sike    Fm.    Brow Moor
Hogarth    Spring    Howdale Moor    Ravenscar
Pond Fm.    Hill    Hill    Cook Ho.
Biller Howe    Flask Inn    Bell Hill
Stony Marl Moor    Fm.
OV
00
FYLINGDALES MOOR    A171    Rudda Fm.    322    05
Jugger Howe    Cliff
High Moor    Moor    Stainto... Moor    Prospect
Fm.
Harwood Dale Moor    Tofta
White

E

F

05
25
OV

00
05

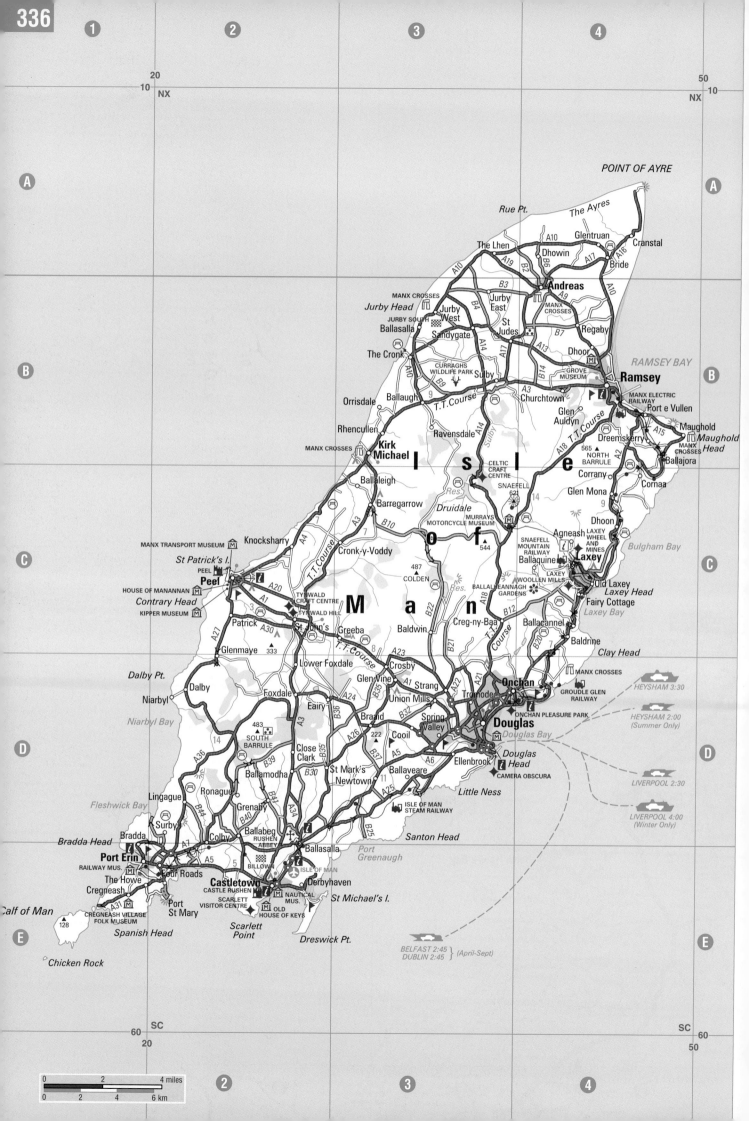

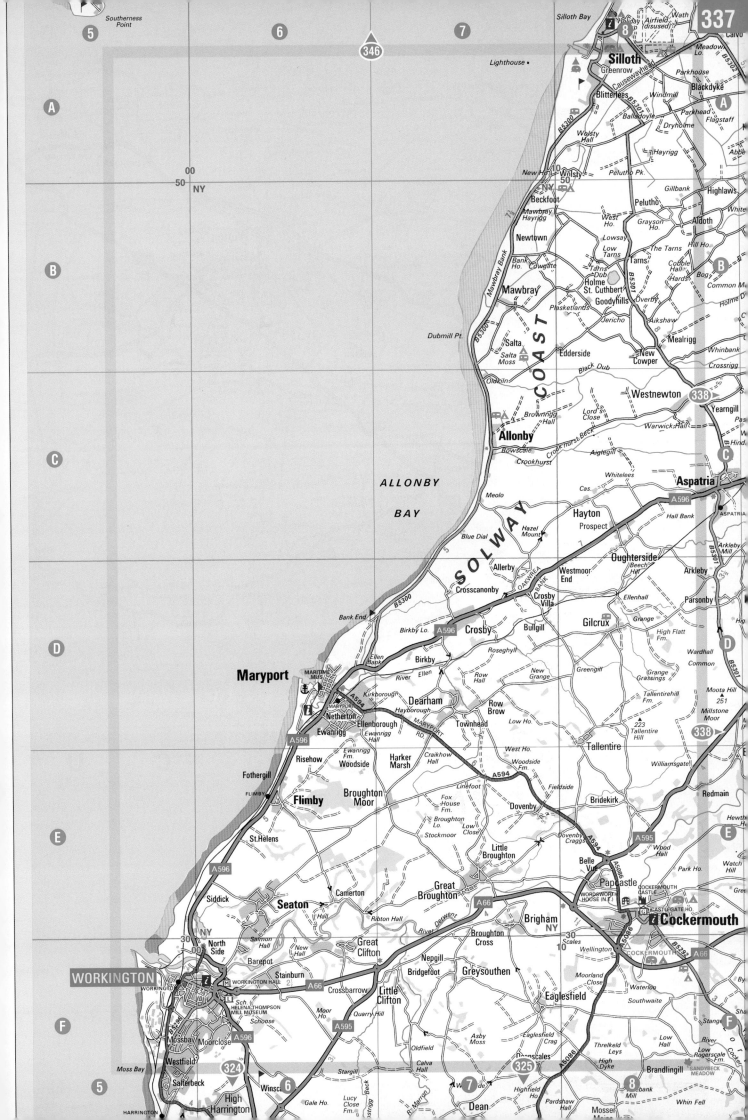

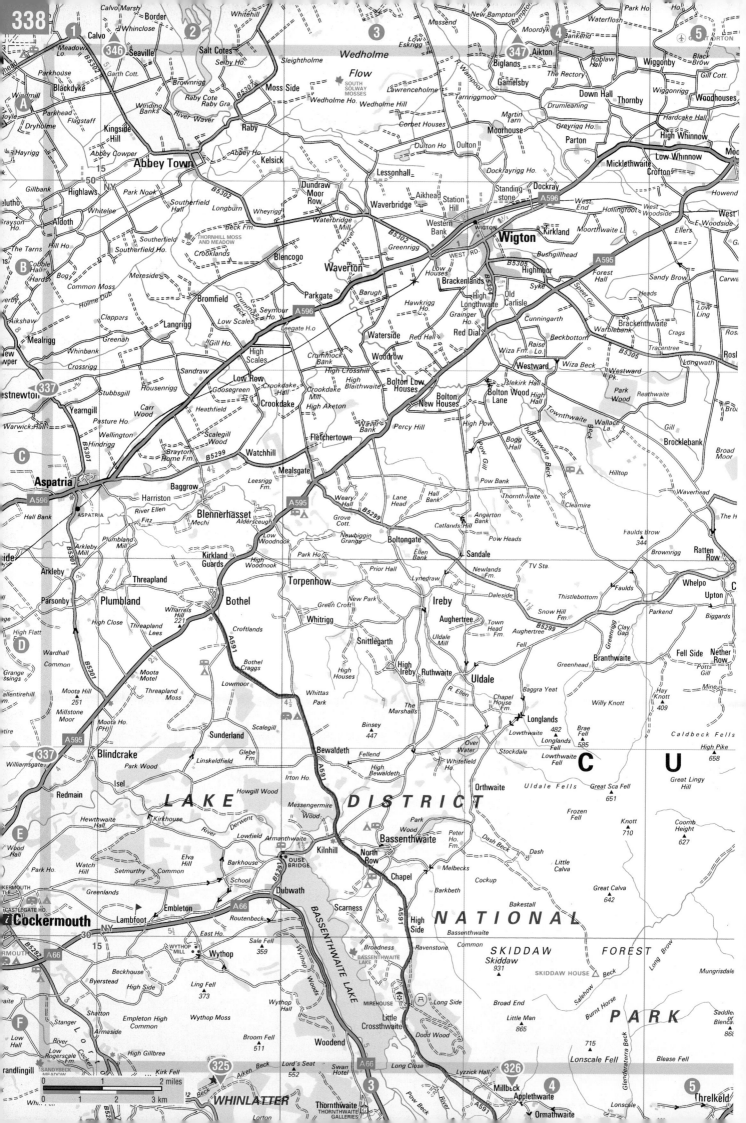

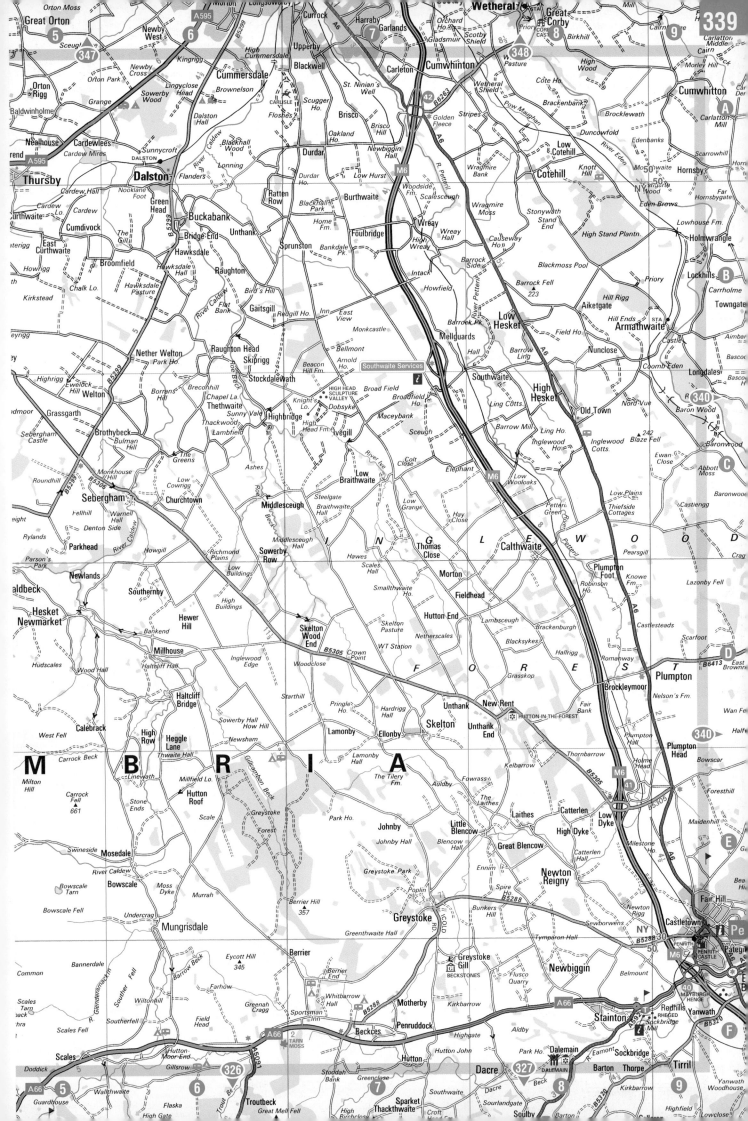

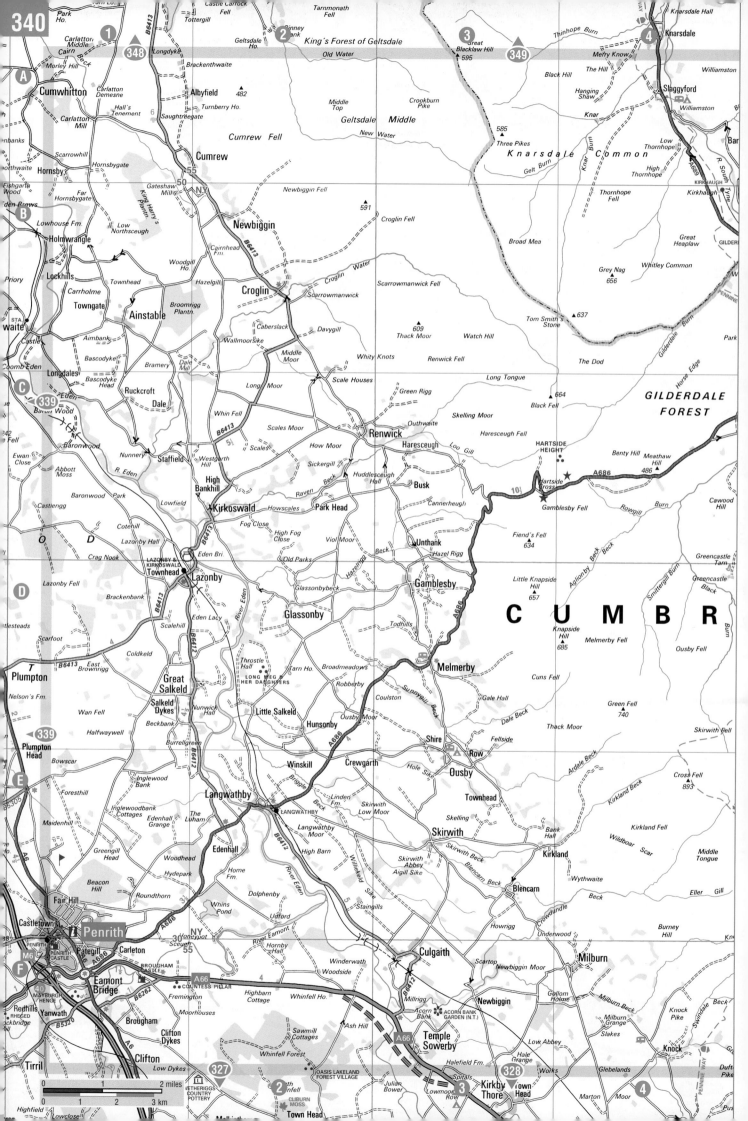

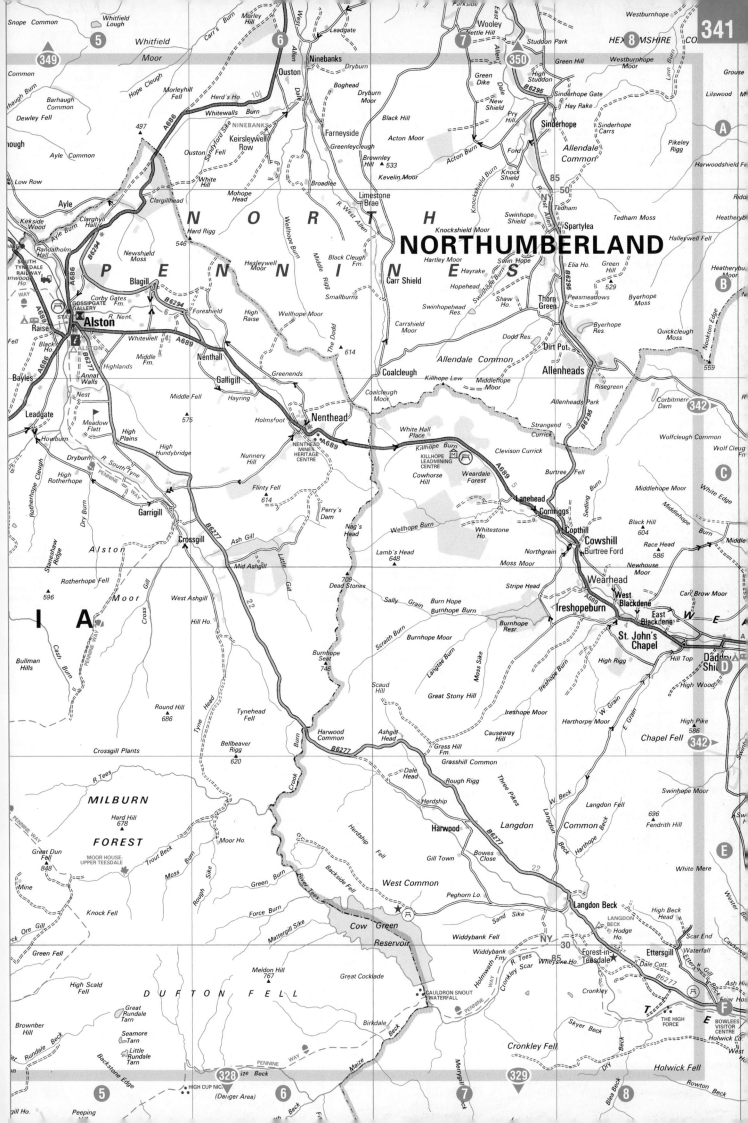

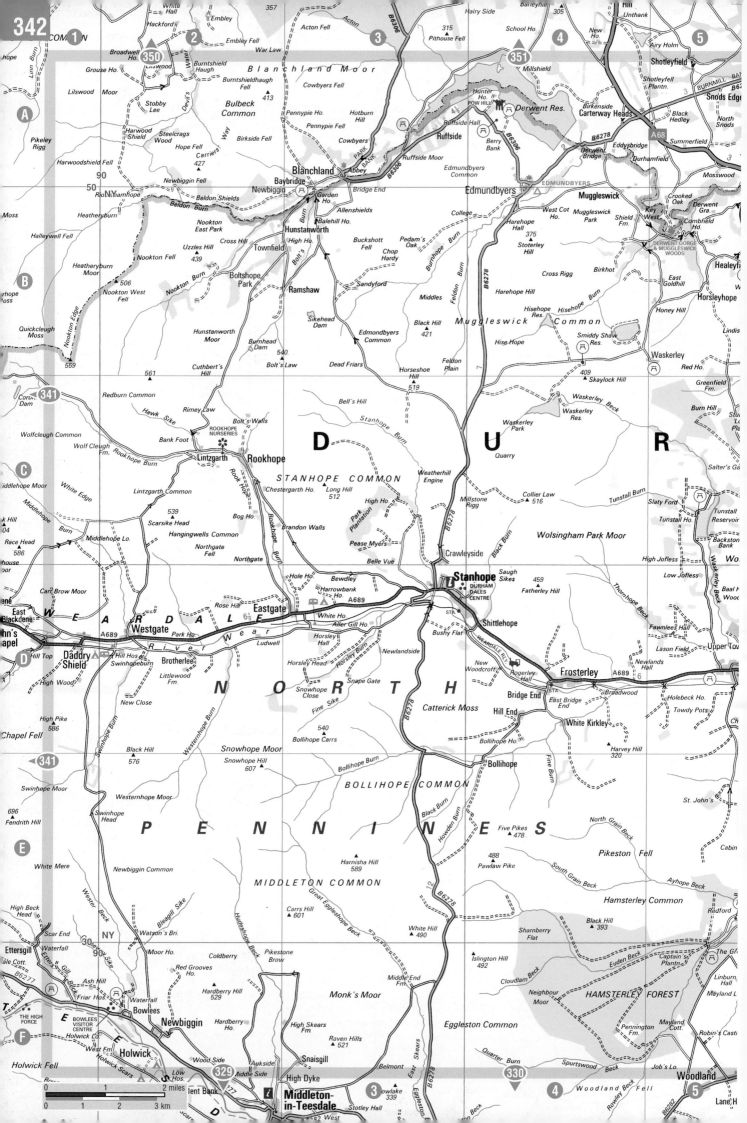

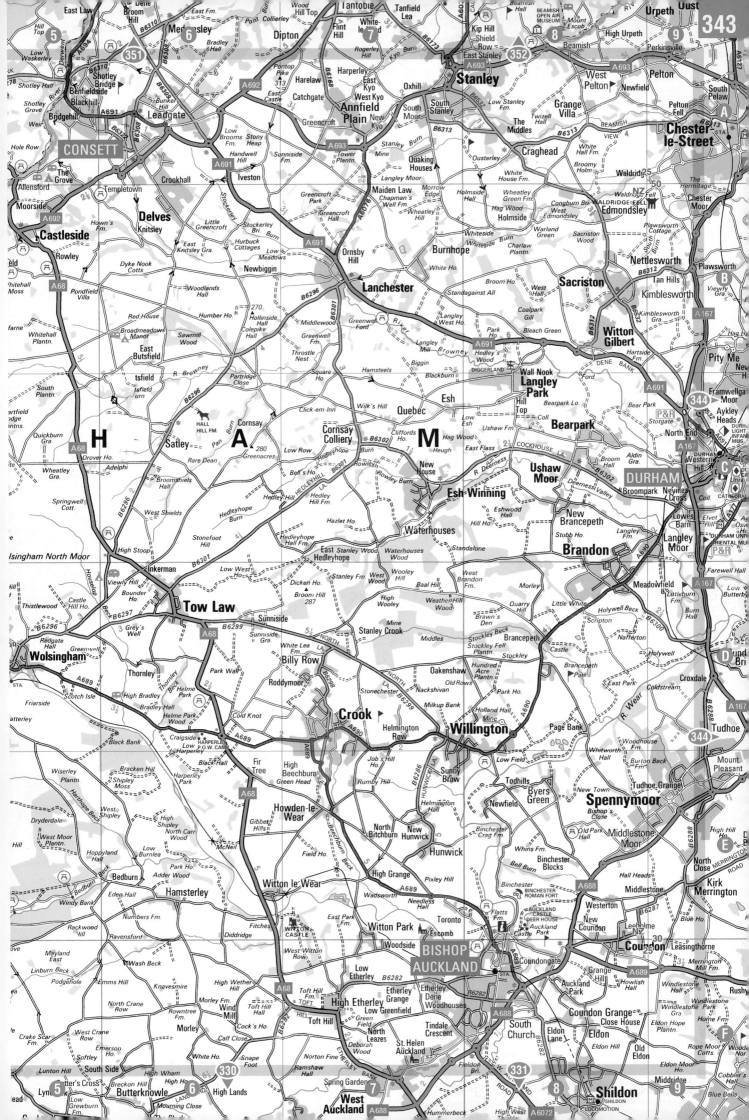

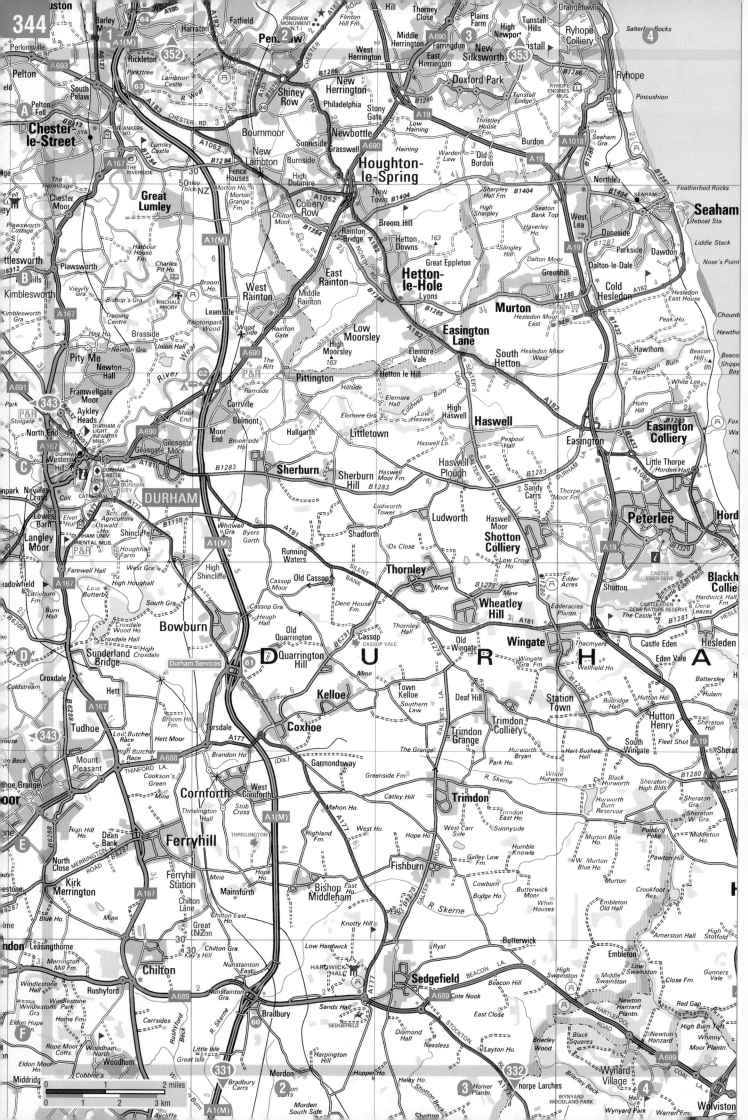

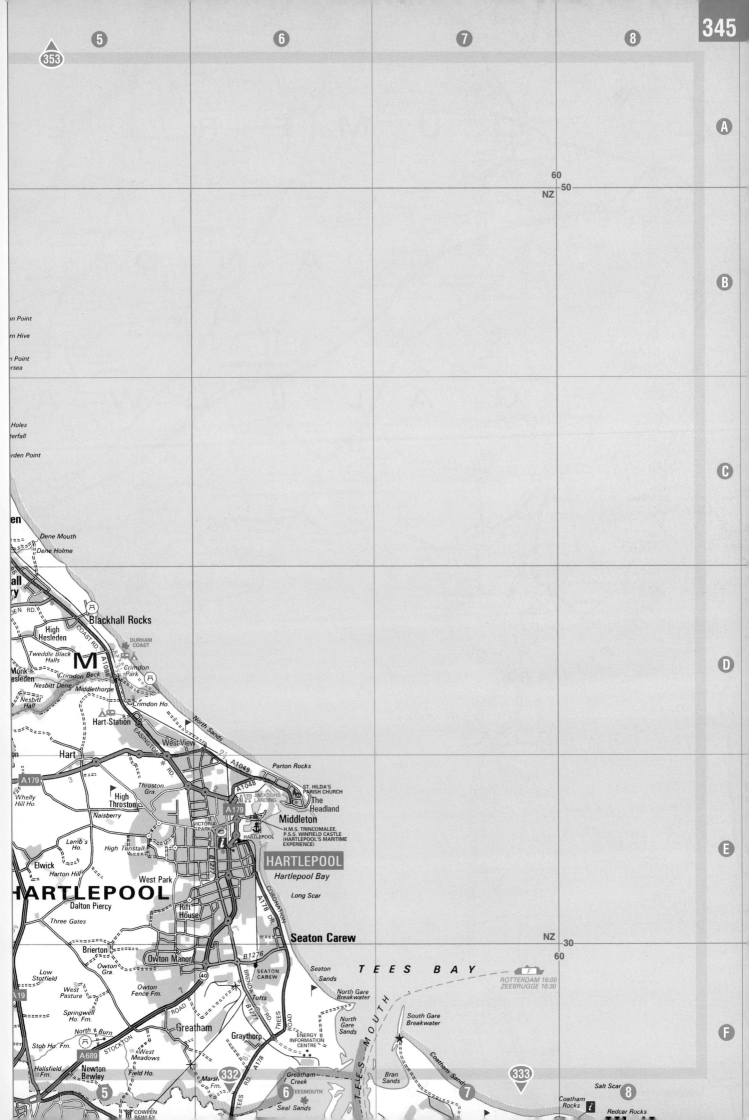

353

5    6    7    8

A

B

C

D

E

F

NZ 60 50

Dene Mouth
Dene Holme

Blackhall Rocks
High
Hesleden
DURHAM
COAST
Tweddle Black
Halls
Monk
esleden    Crimdon Beck    Crimdon
Park
Nesbitt Dene    Middlethorpe
Nesbitt    Crimdon Ho.
Hall
North Sands
Hart-Station    West-View
EASINGTON
Hart    A1049    Parton Rocks
A179    Throston
Gra.    A1048    ST. HILDA'S
PARISH CHURCH
Whelly    High    JACKSONS    The
Hill Ho.    Throston    LANDING    Headland
Naisberry    A179    Middleton
VICTORIA    H.M.S. TRINCOMALEE,
PARK    HARTLEPOOL    P.S.S. WINFIELD CASTLE
Lamb's    (HARTLEPOOL'S MARITIME
Ho.    High Tunstall    EXPERIENCE)
Elwick    West Park    HARTLEPOOL
Harton Hill    Hartlepool Bay
HARTLEPOOL    Riff
Dalton Piercy    House    Long Scar
Three Gates
Brierton    Seaton Carew
Low    Owton Manor    B1276
Stotfield    Owton
Gra.    Seaton
West    Owton    Sands
Pasture    Fence Fm.    Tofts    North Gare
Springwell    Breakwater
Ho. Fm.    North
North    Burn    Gare    North
Stob Ho. Fm.    Greatham    Sands    South Gare
West    Breakwater
A689    Meadows    Graythorp    ENERGY
Newton    Field Ho.    INFORMATION    Coatham Sands
Bewley    CENTRE
Hallsfield    Marsh    332    Greatham    Bran    Salt Scar
Fm.    Fm.    Creek    Sands    Coatham
5    6    TEESMOUTH    7    Rocks
COWPEN    Seal Sands    333    Redcar Rocks
BEWLEY

A1086    COAST RD.    EDEN RD.
A179    3    2½    ROAD
A19    2    CORONATION    A178 DR.
40    BRENDA    ROAD    B1276
B1277    TREES RD    STOCKTON    ROAD    A178
TEES    RD

T E E S   B A Y

ROTTERDAM 16:00
ZEEBRUGGE 16:30

T E E S M O U T H

NZ 30 60

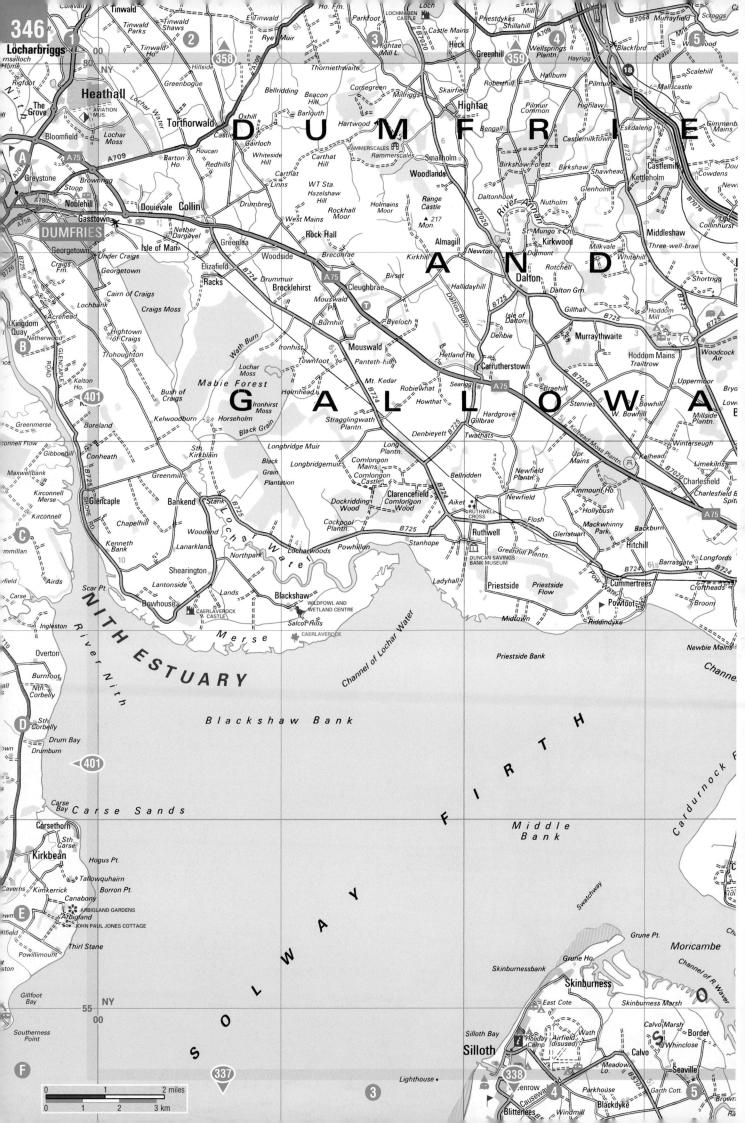

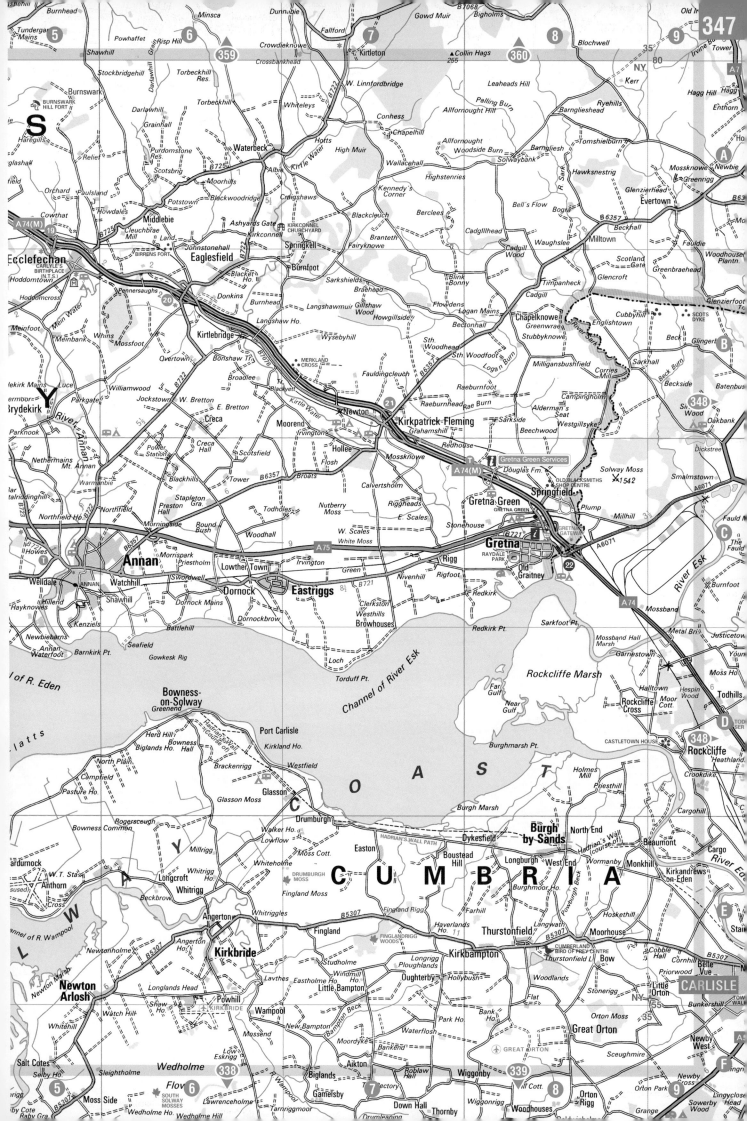

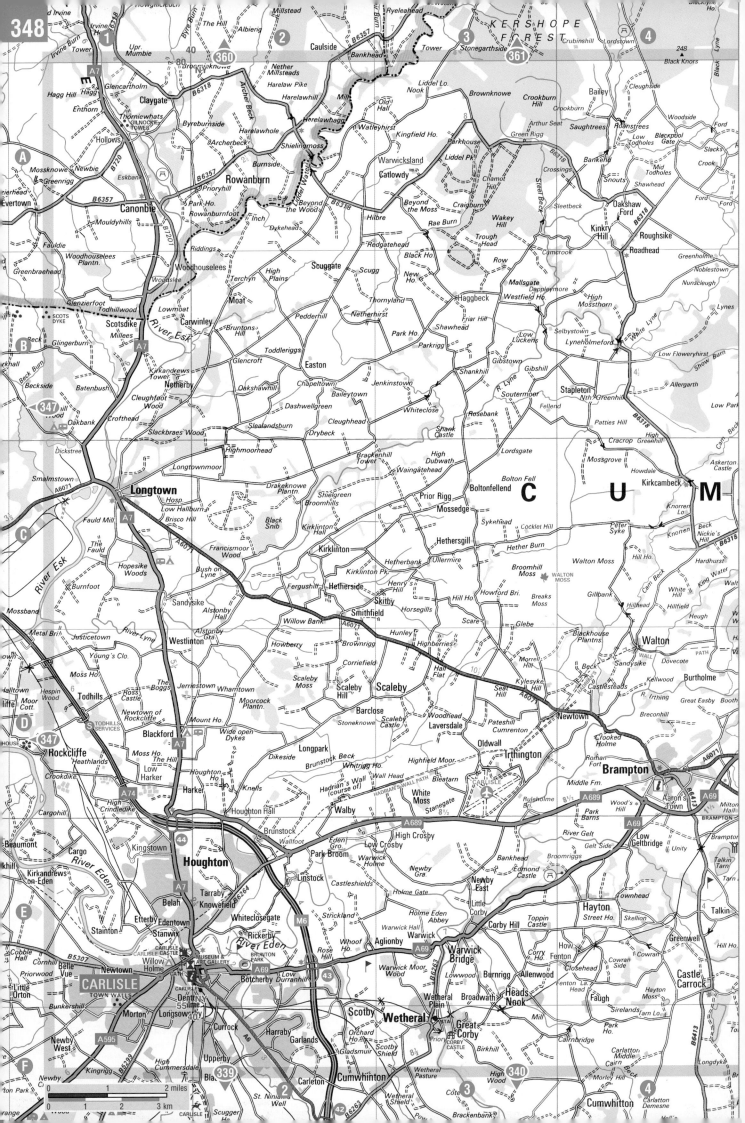

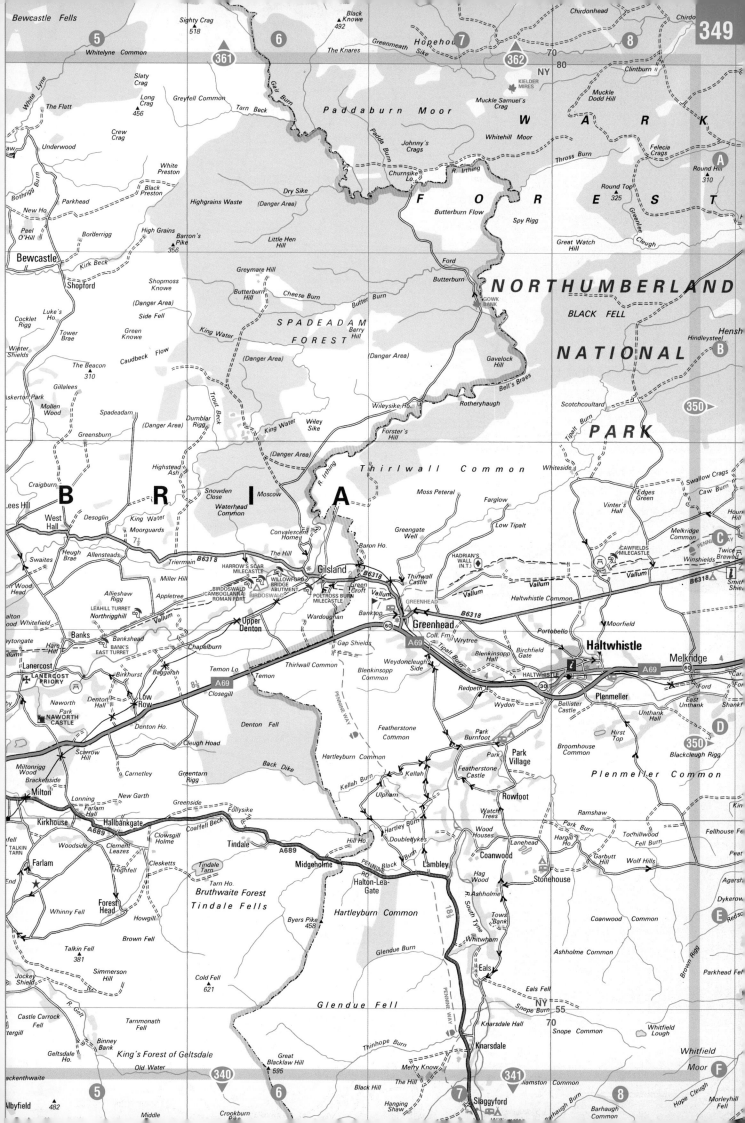

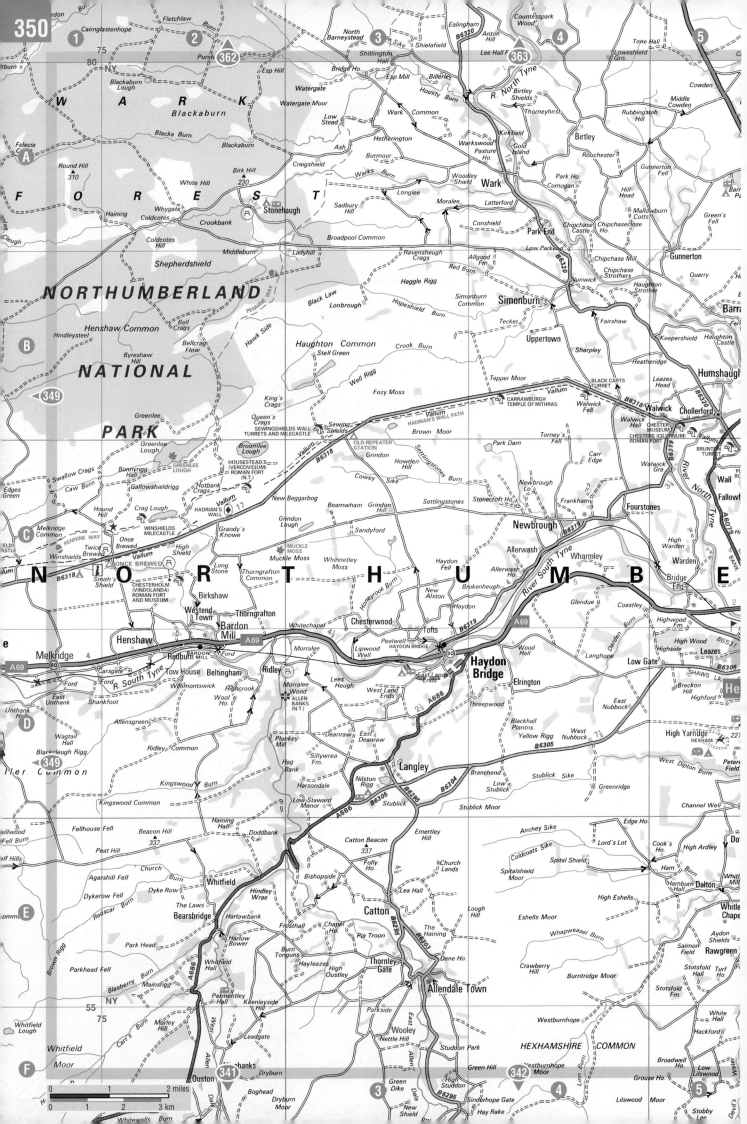

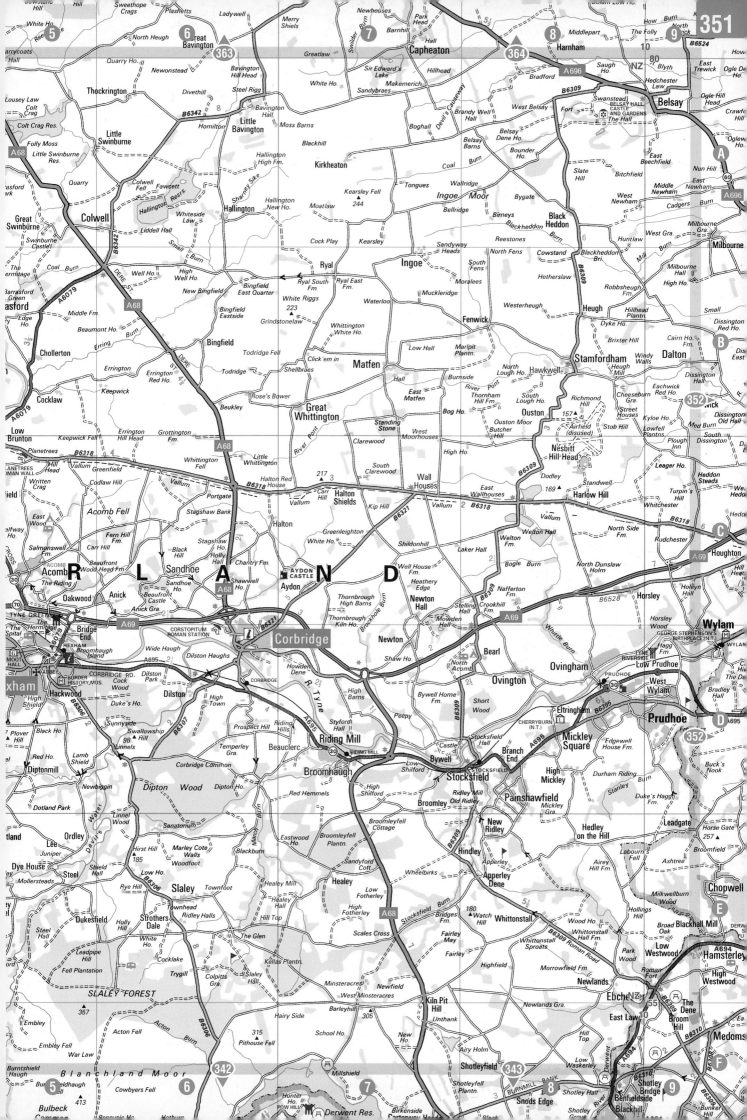

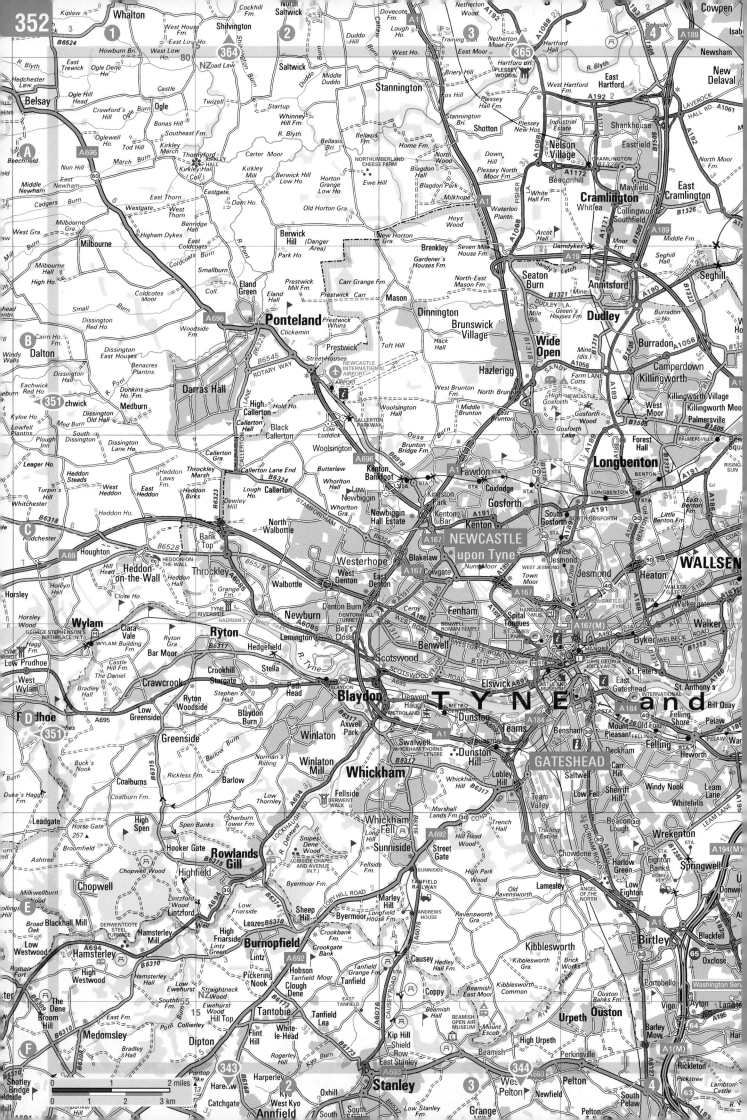

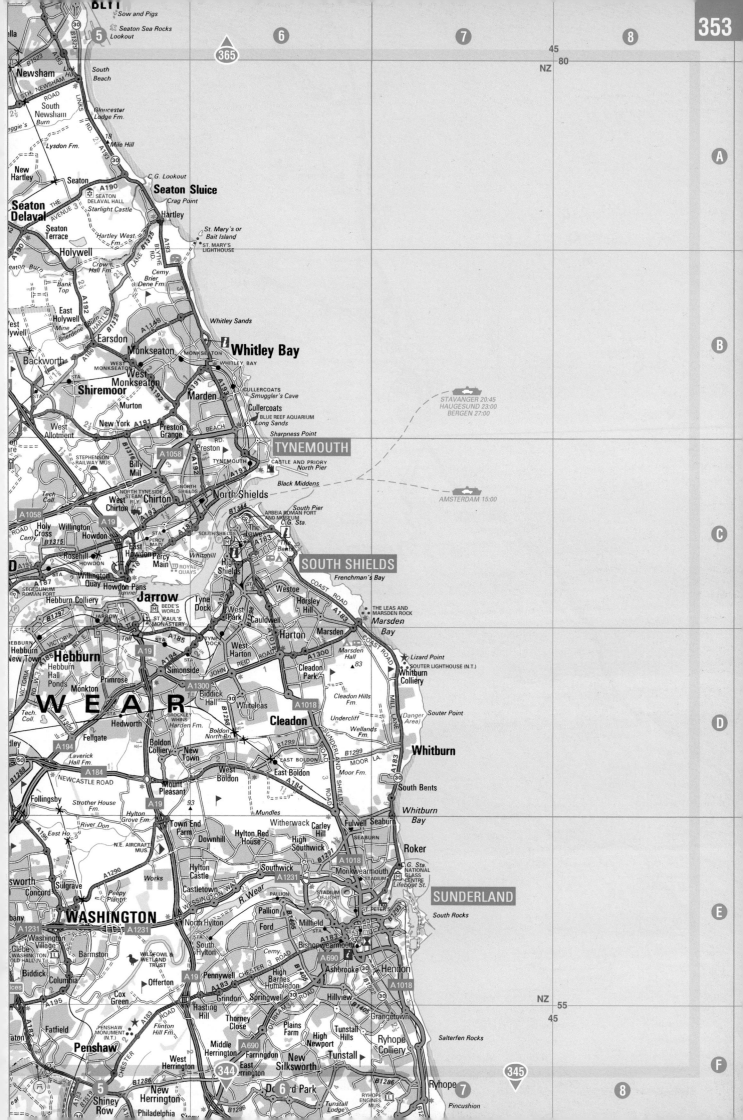

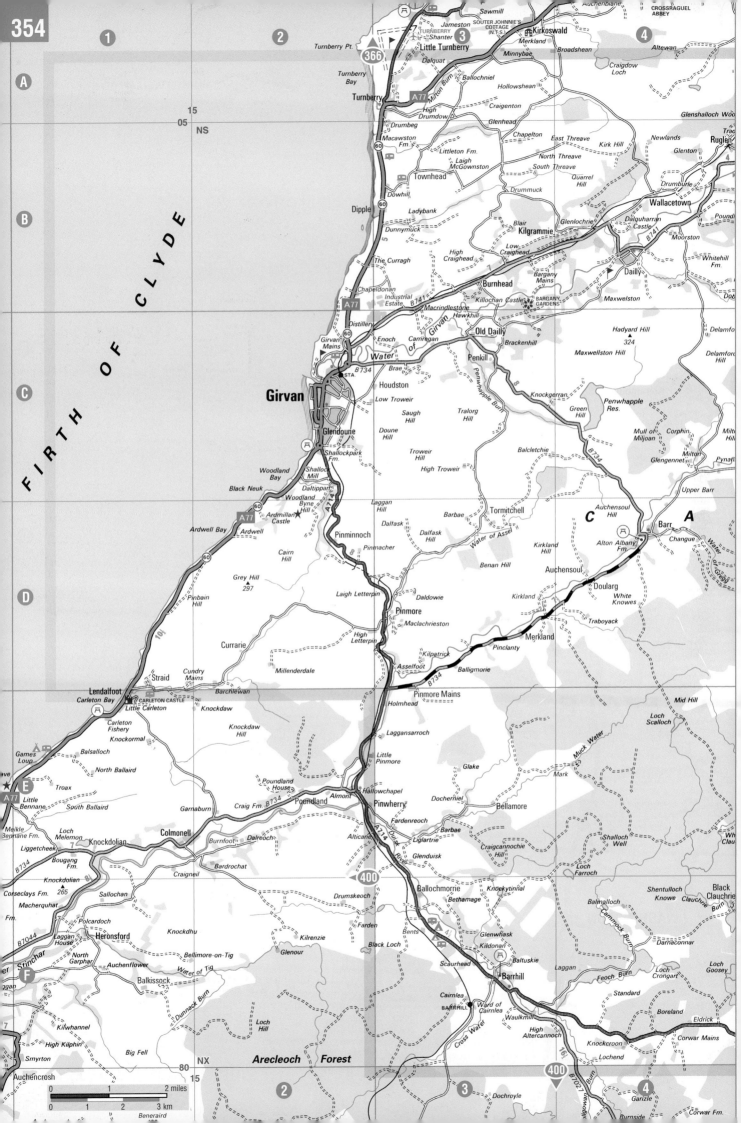

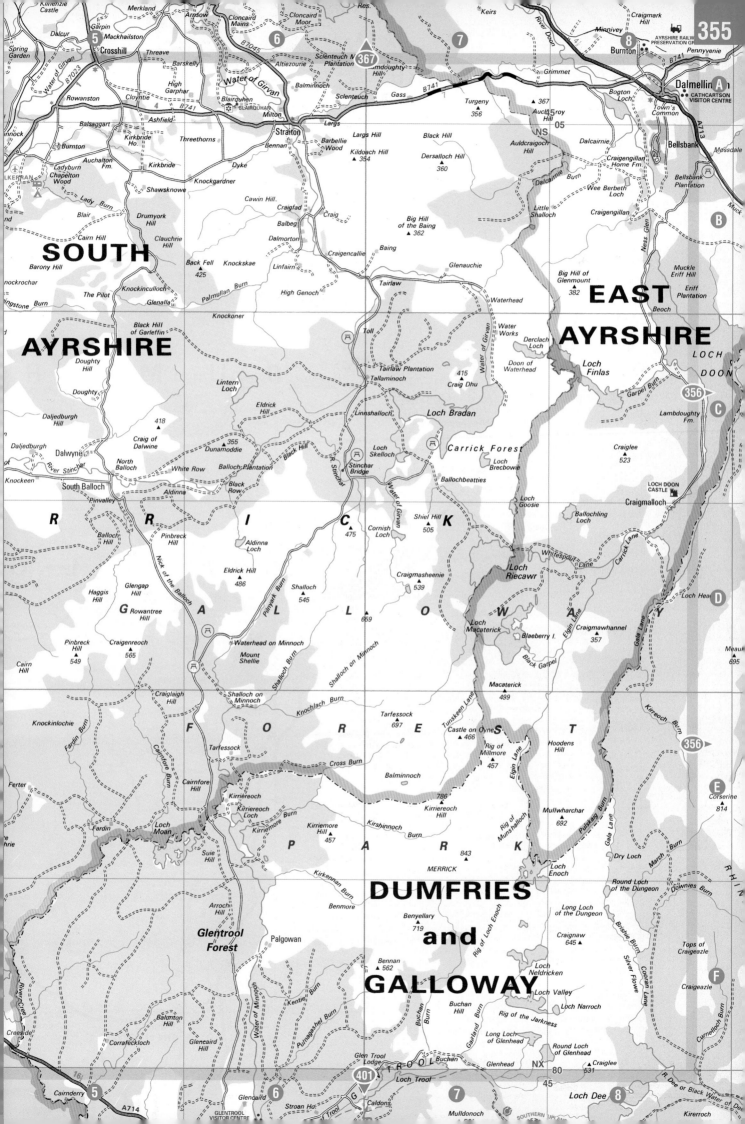

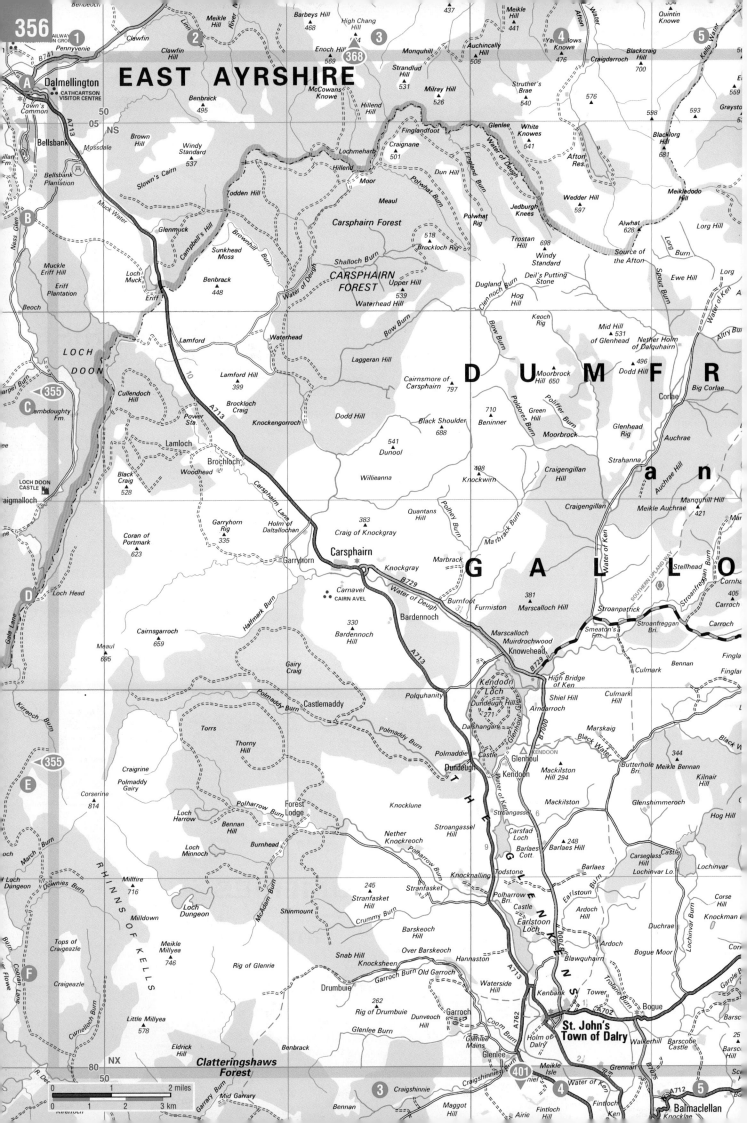

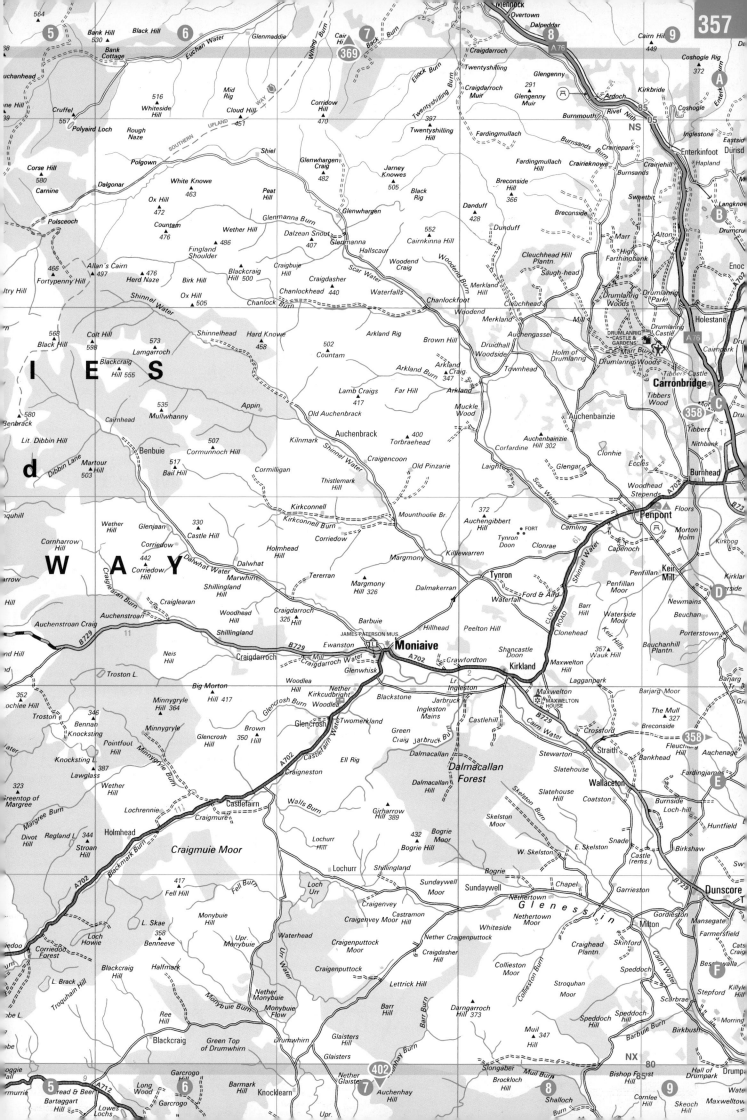

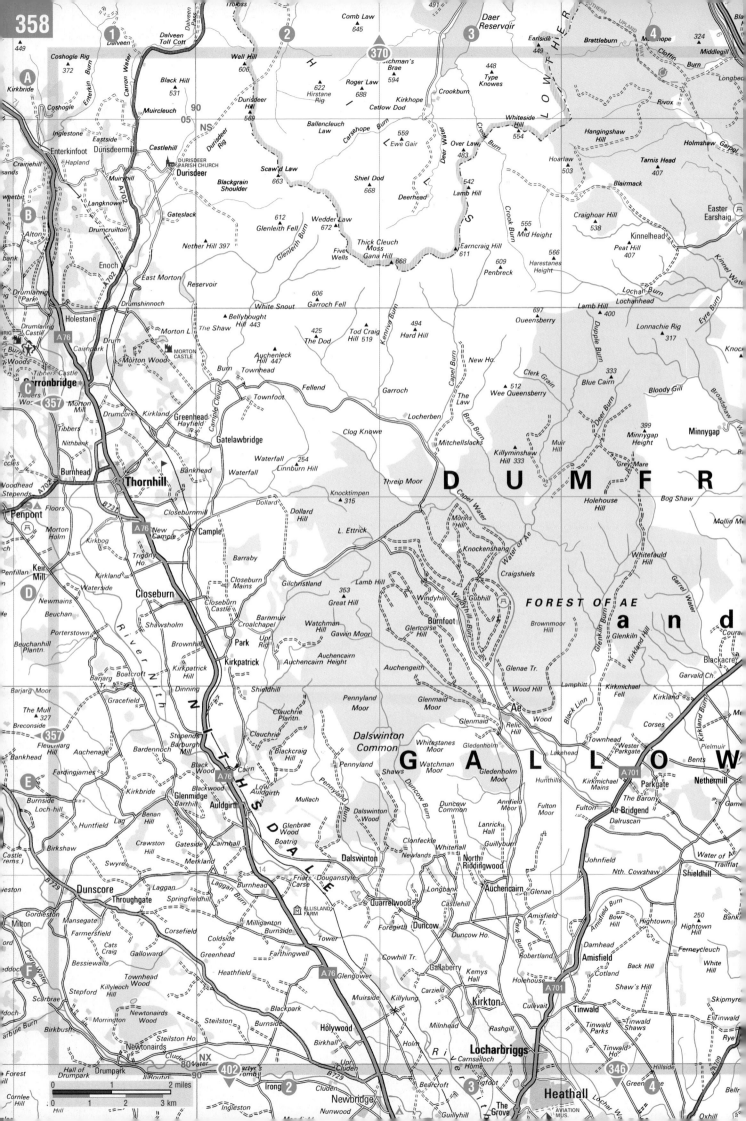

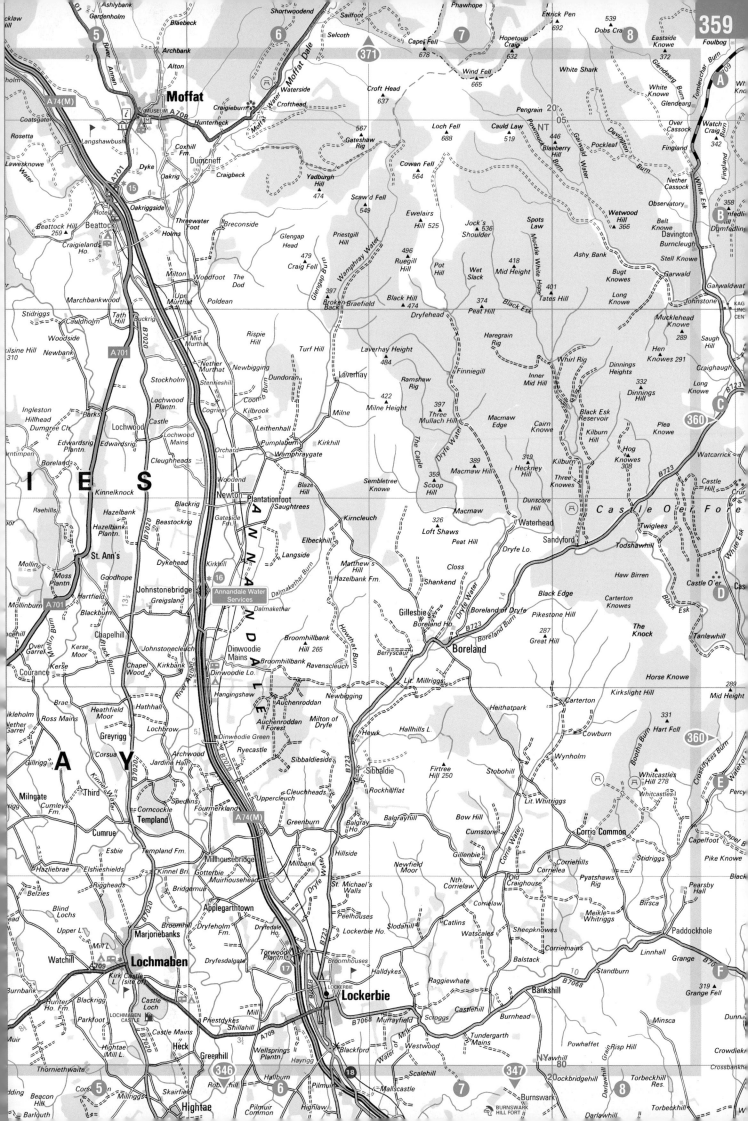

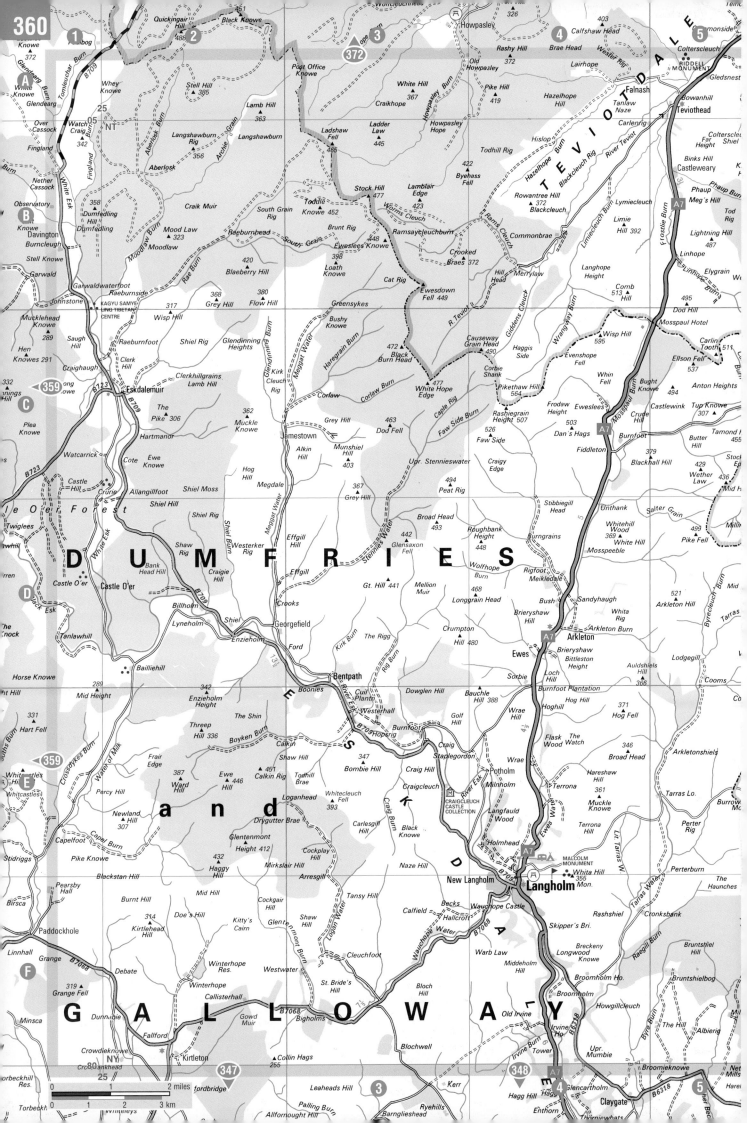

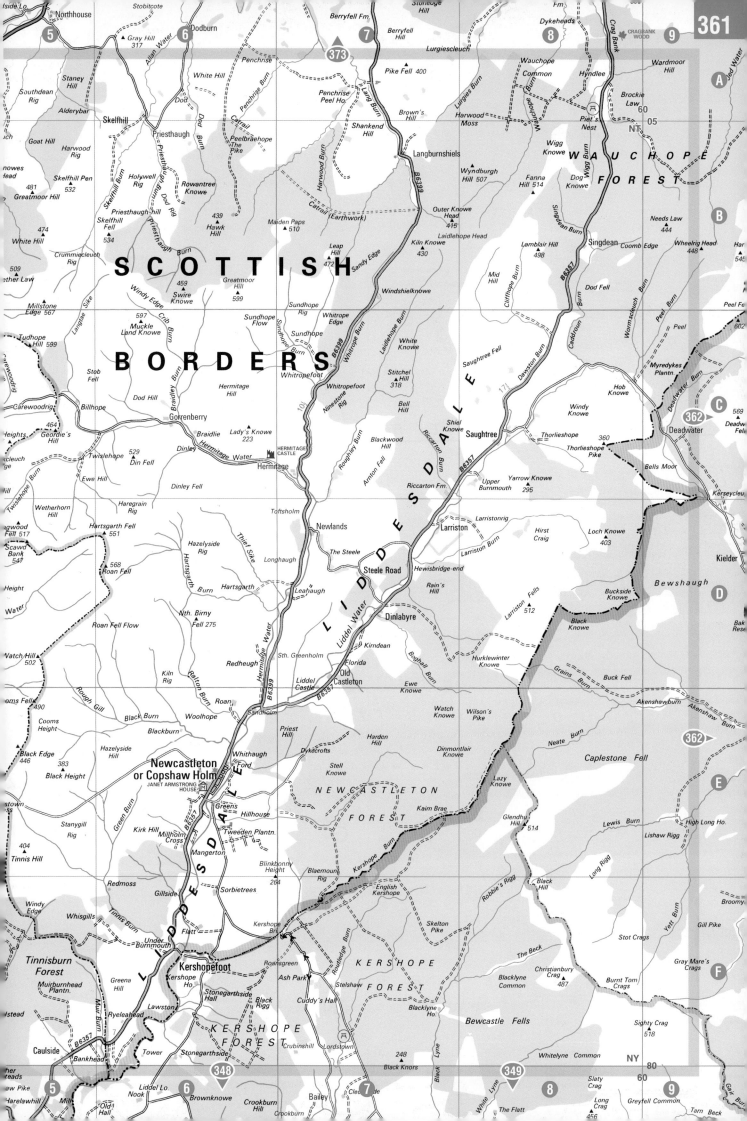

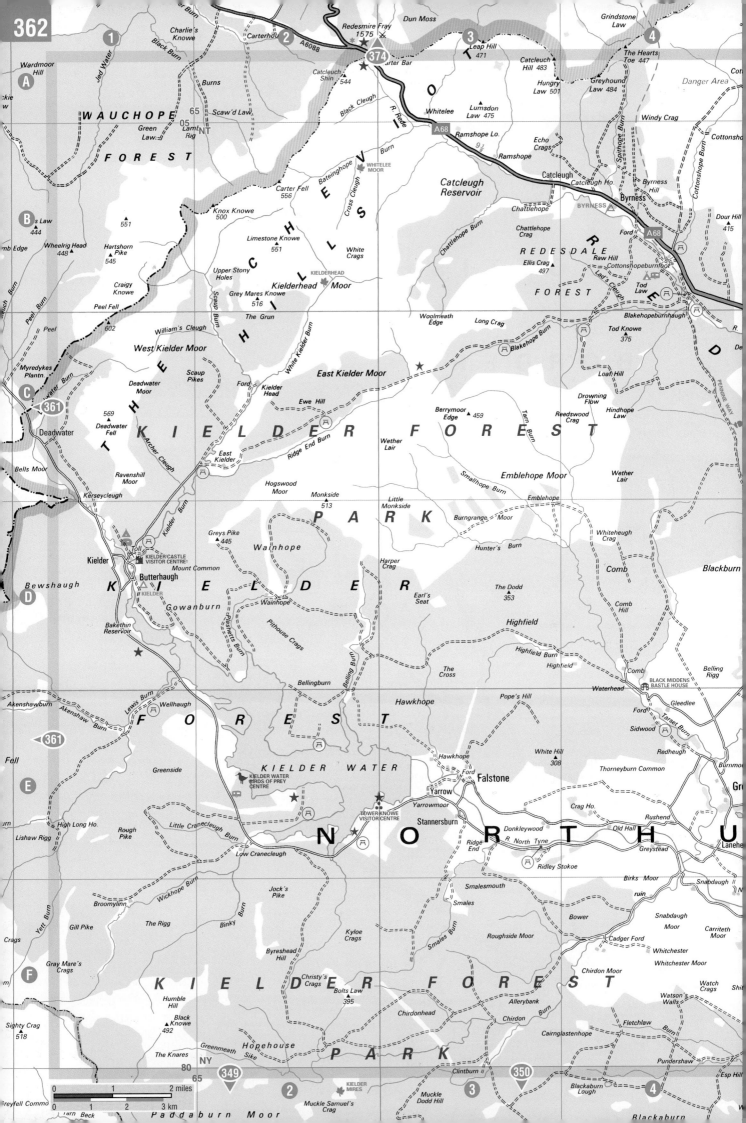

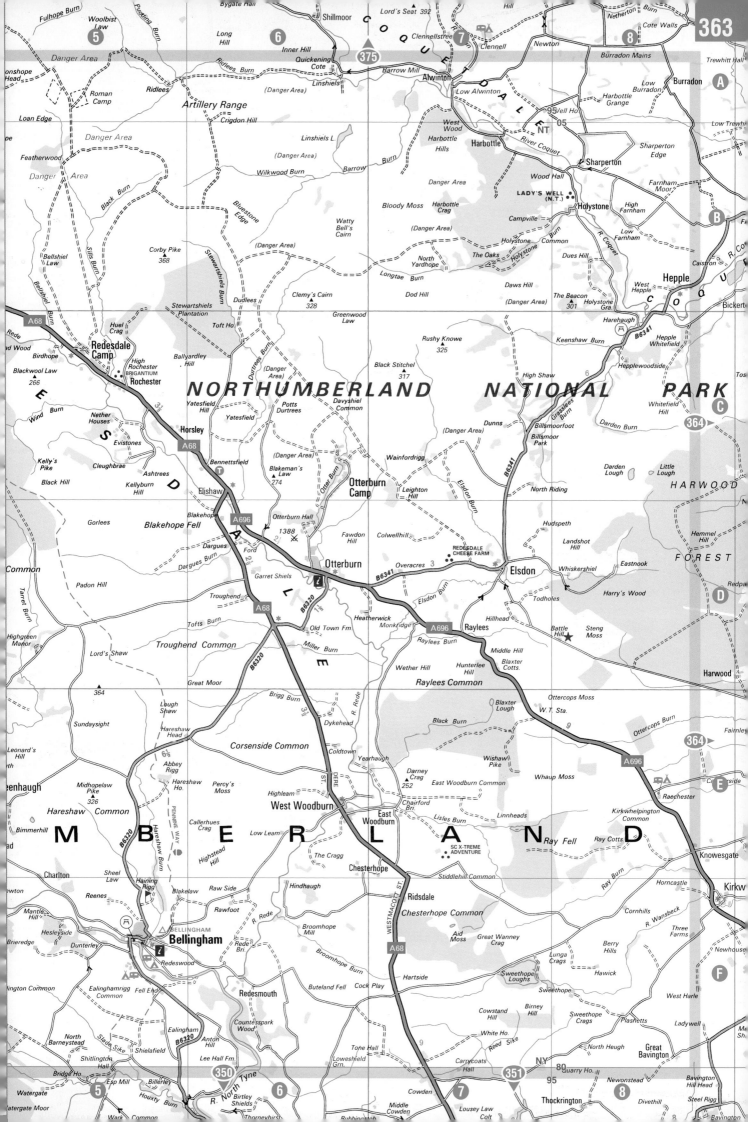

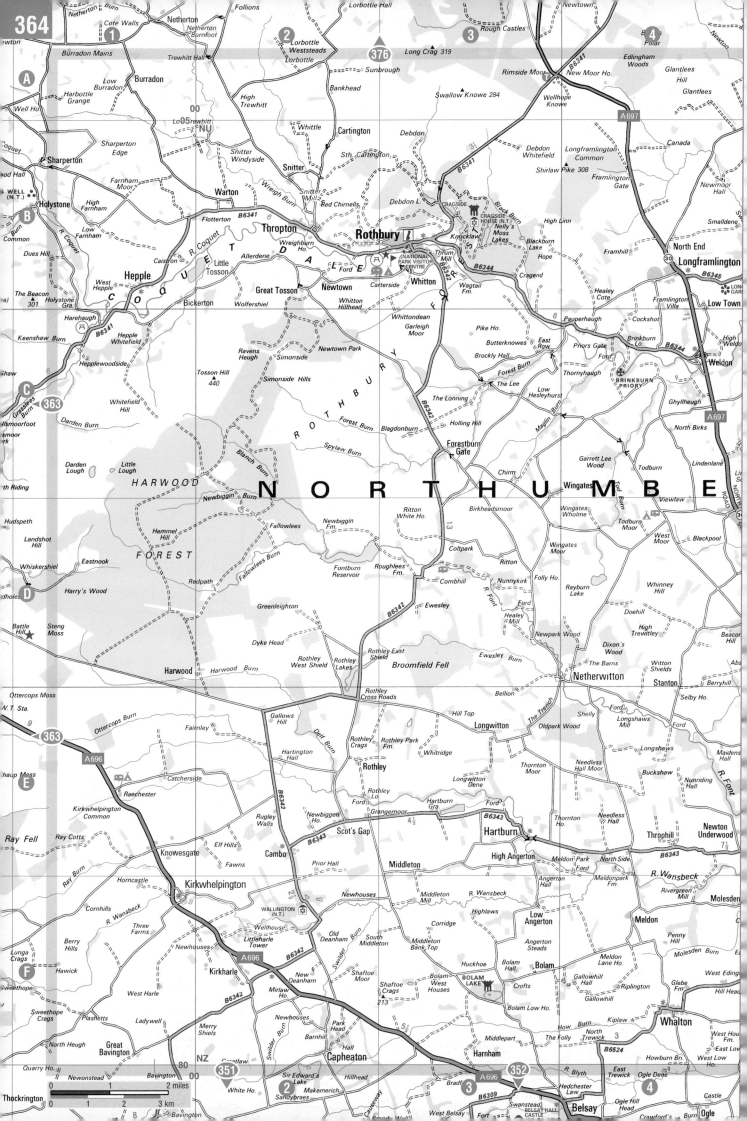

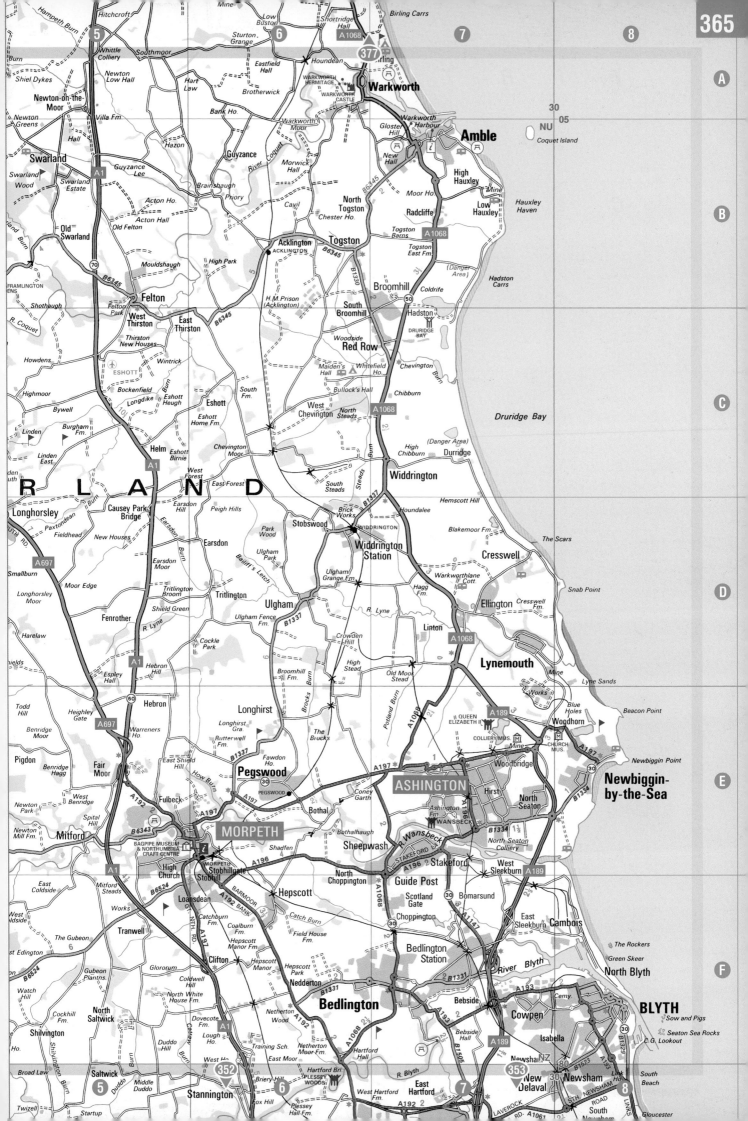

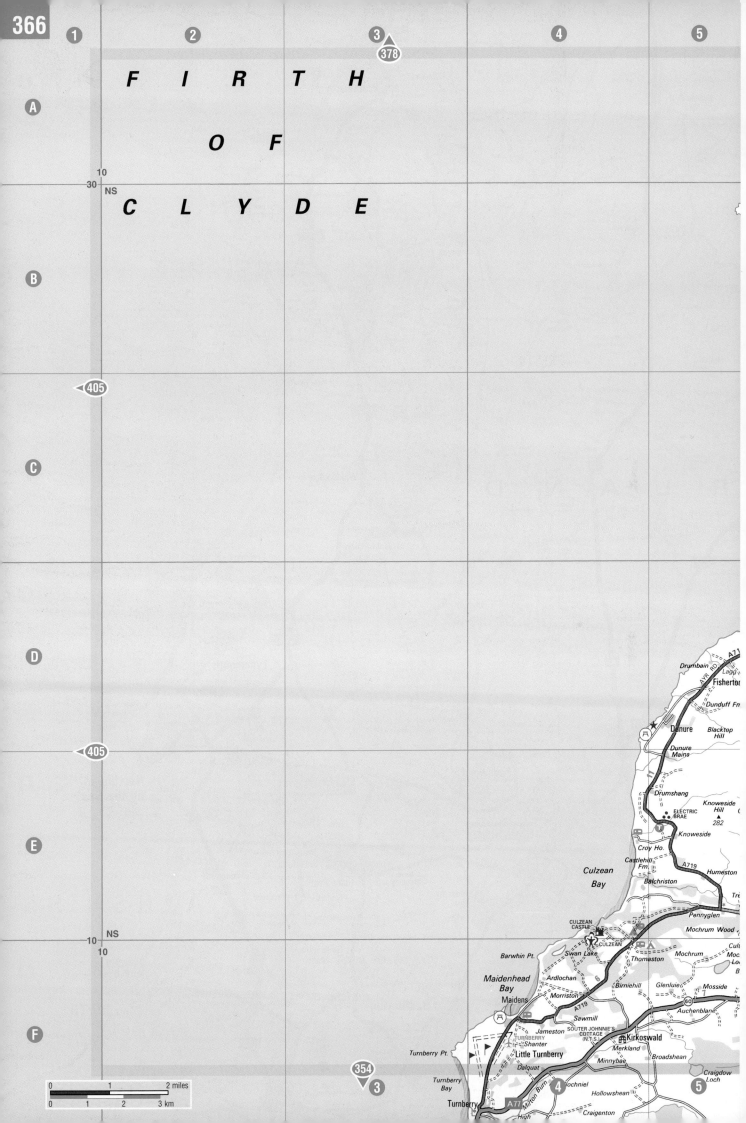

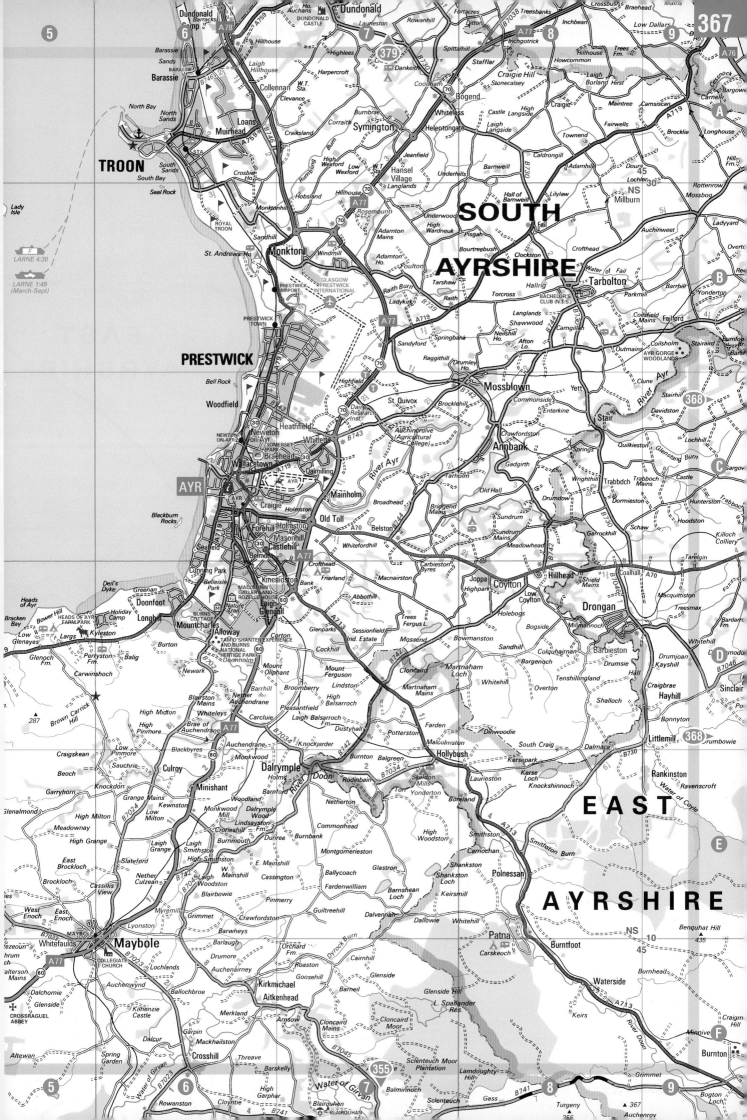

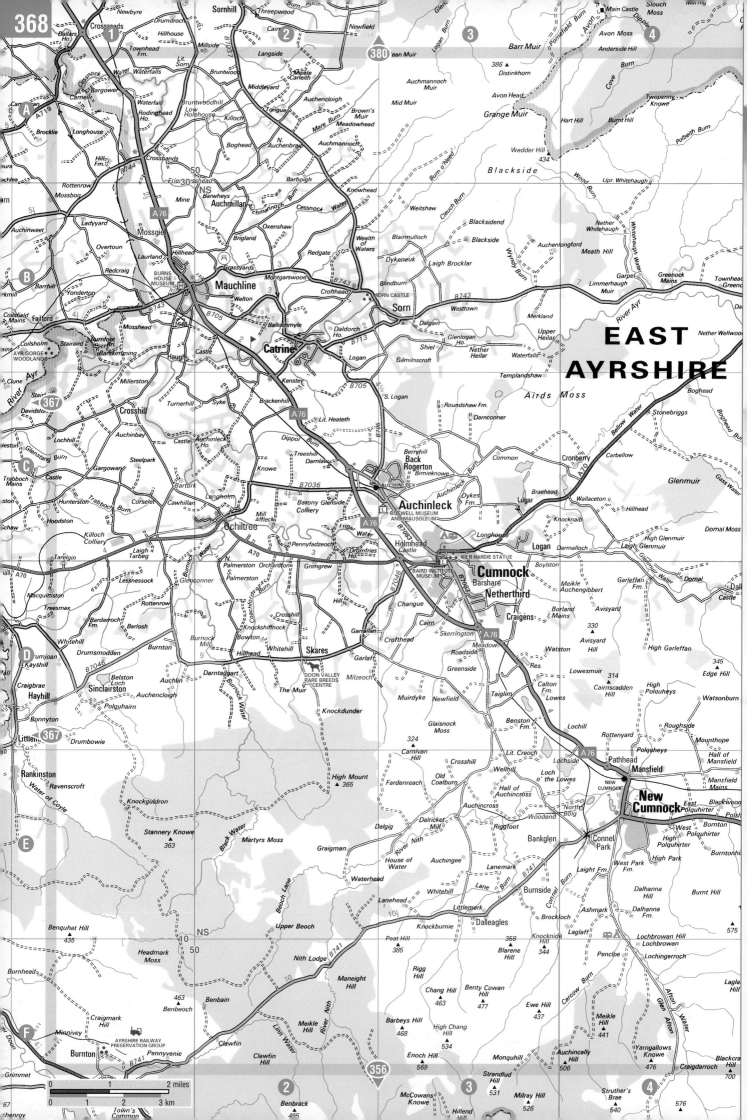

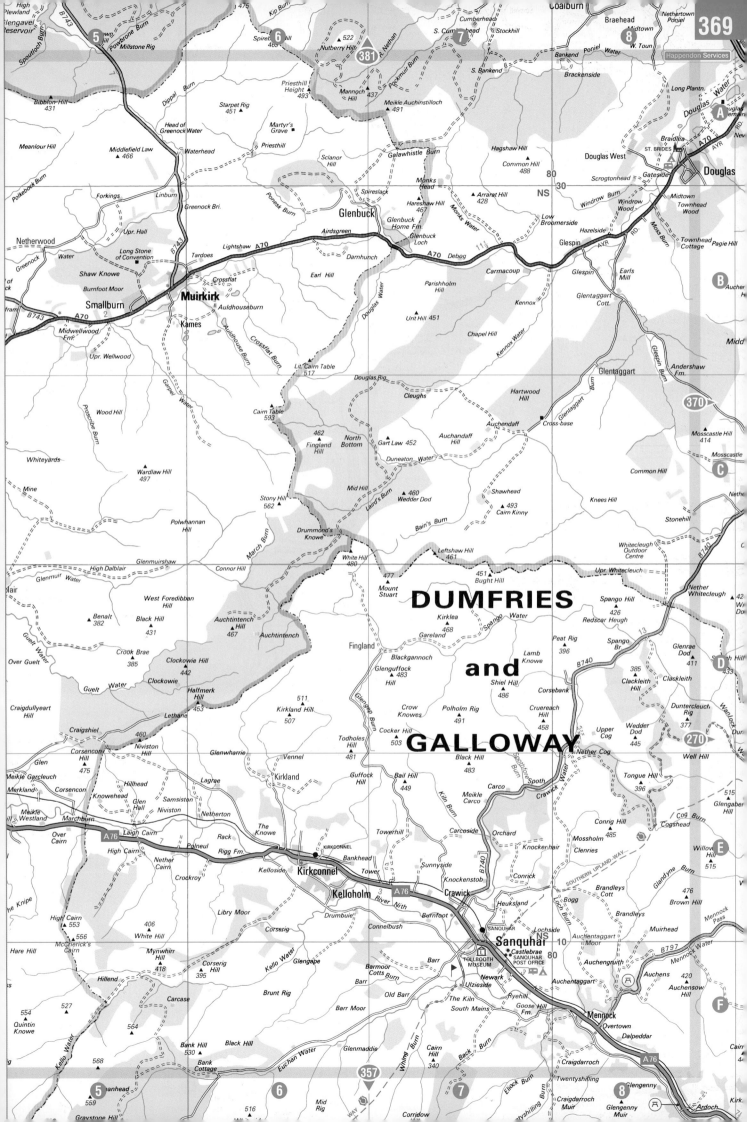

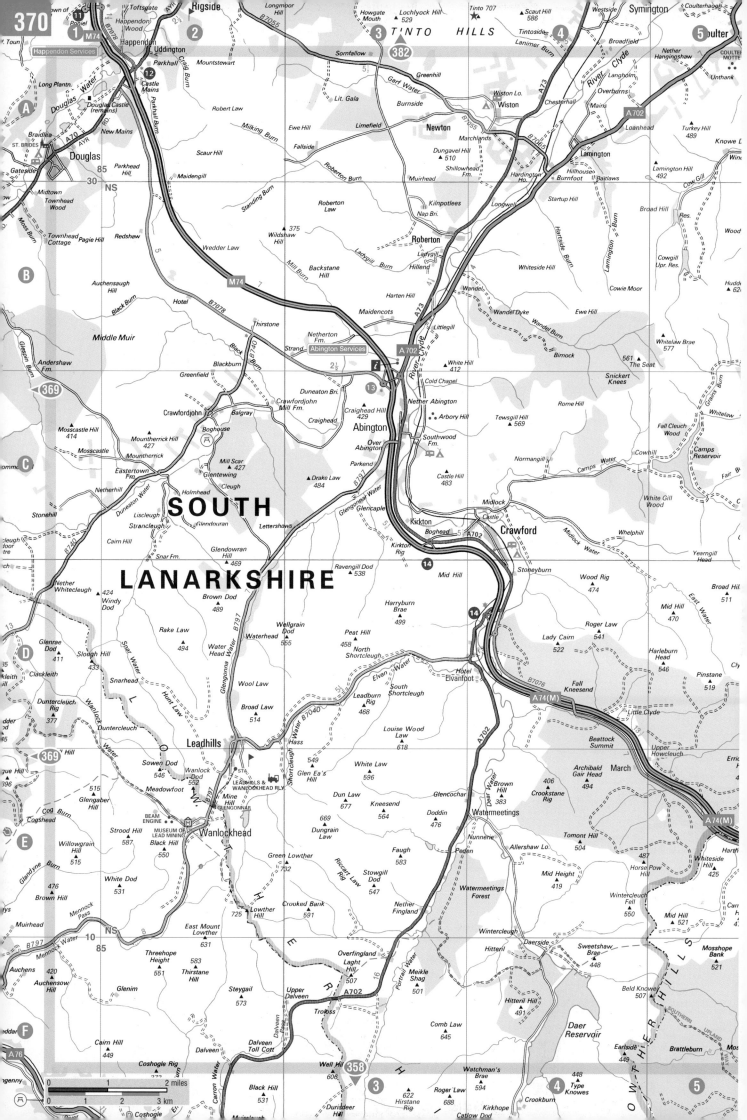

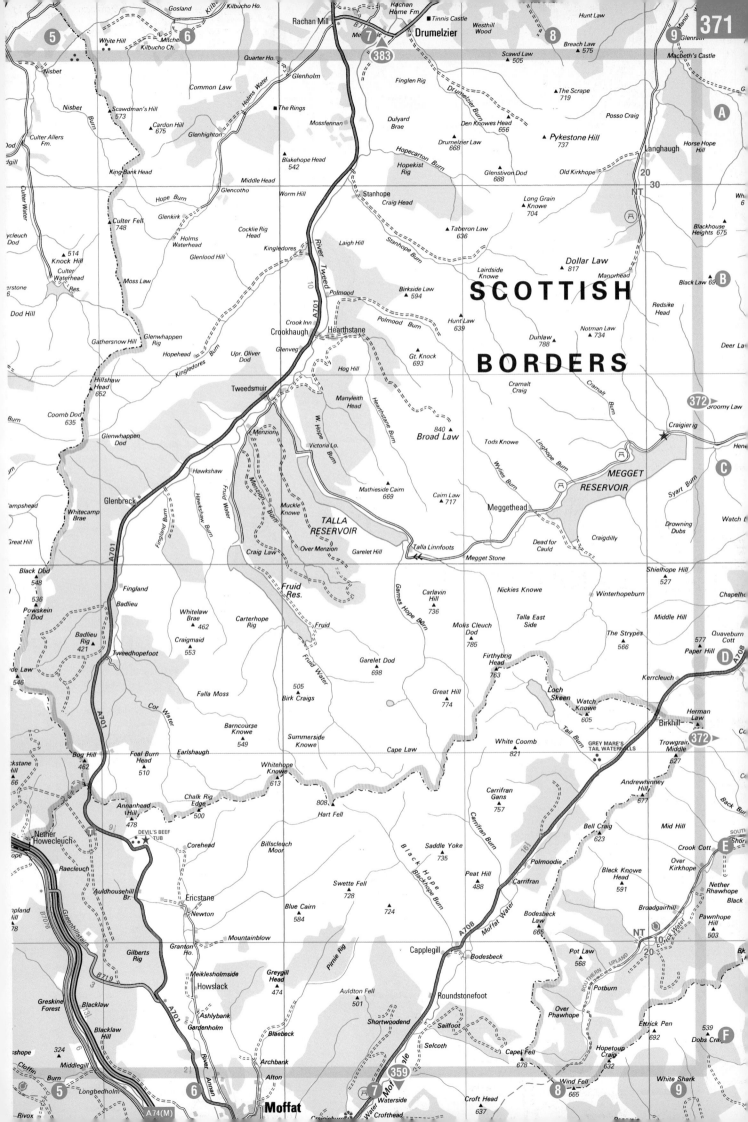

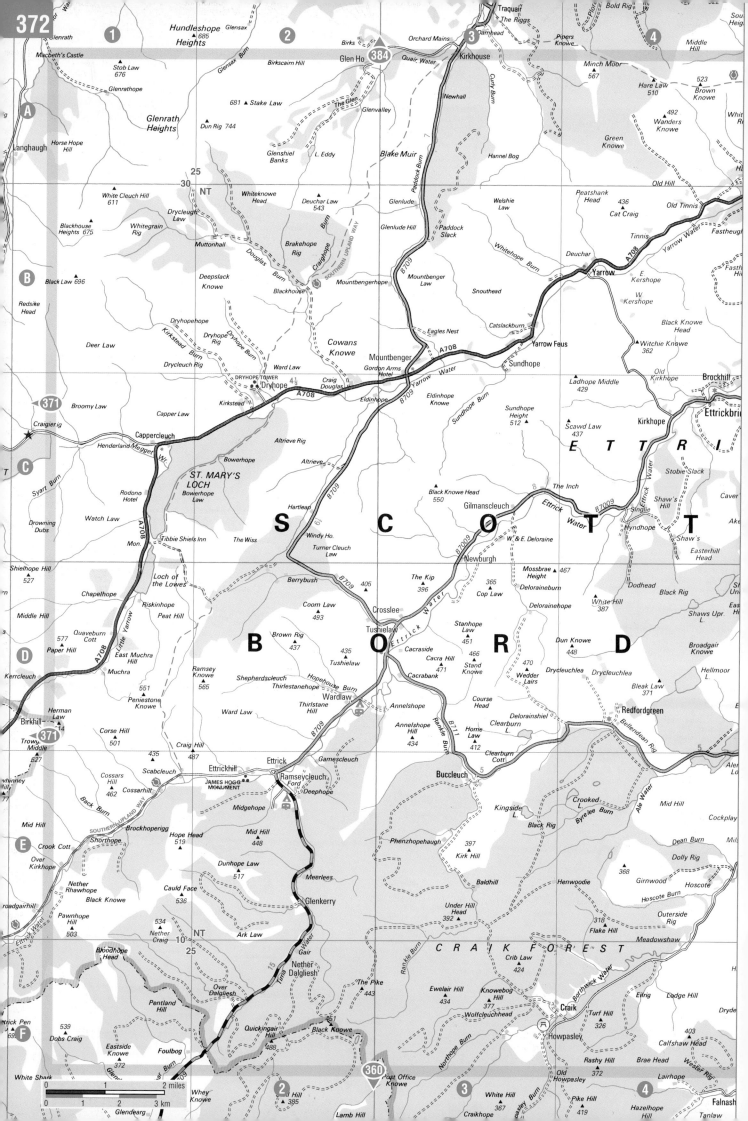

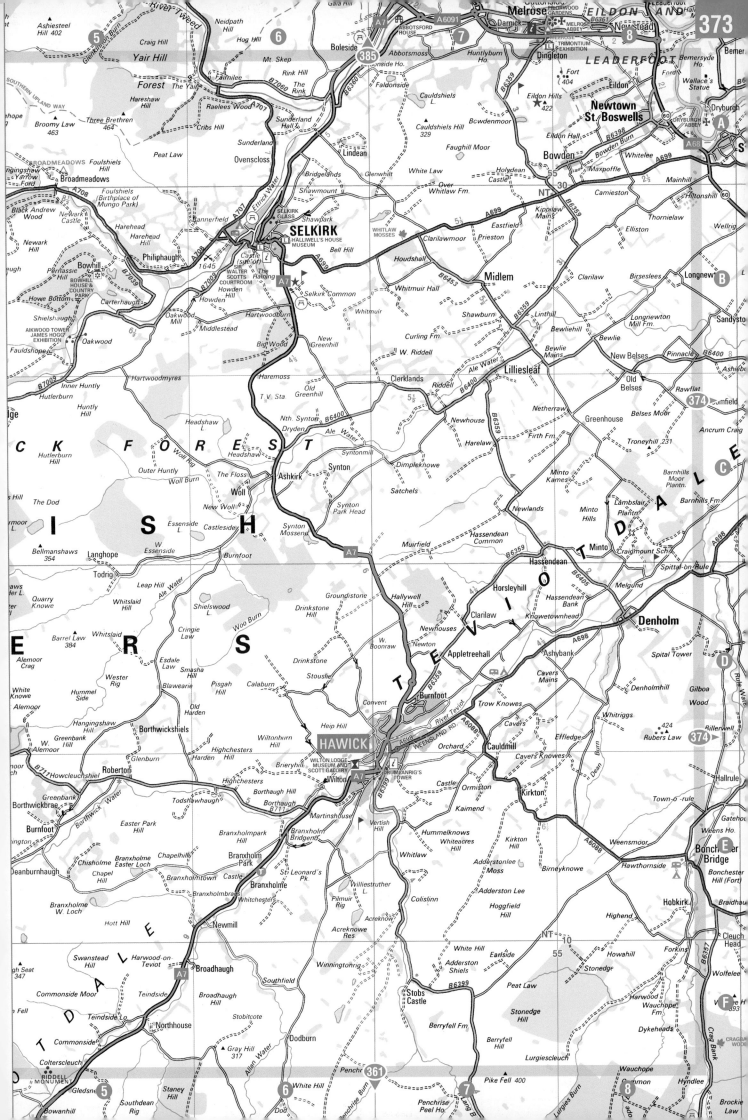

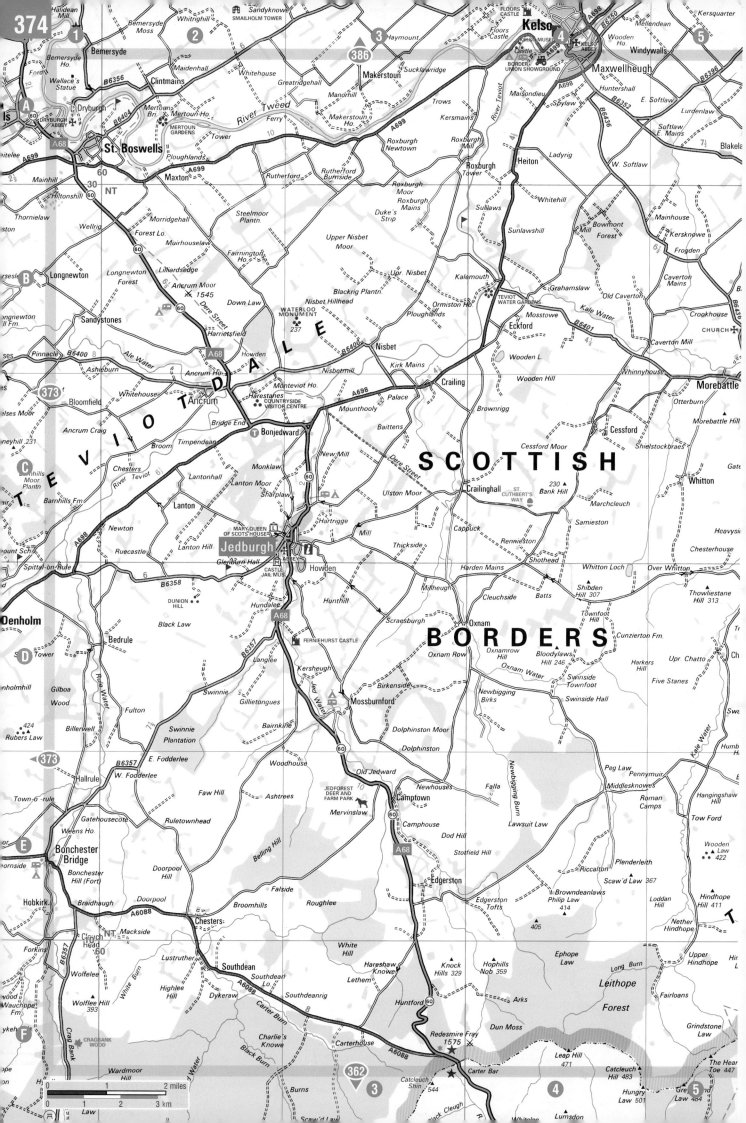

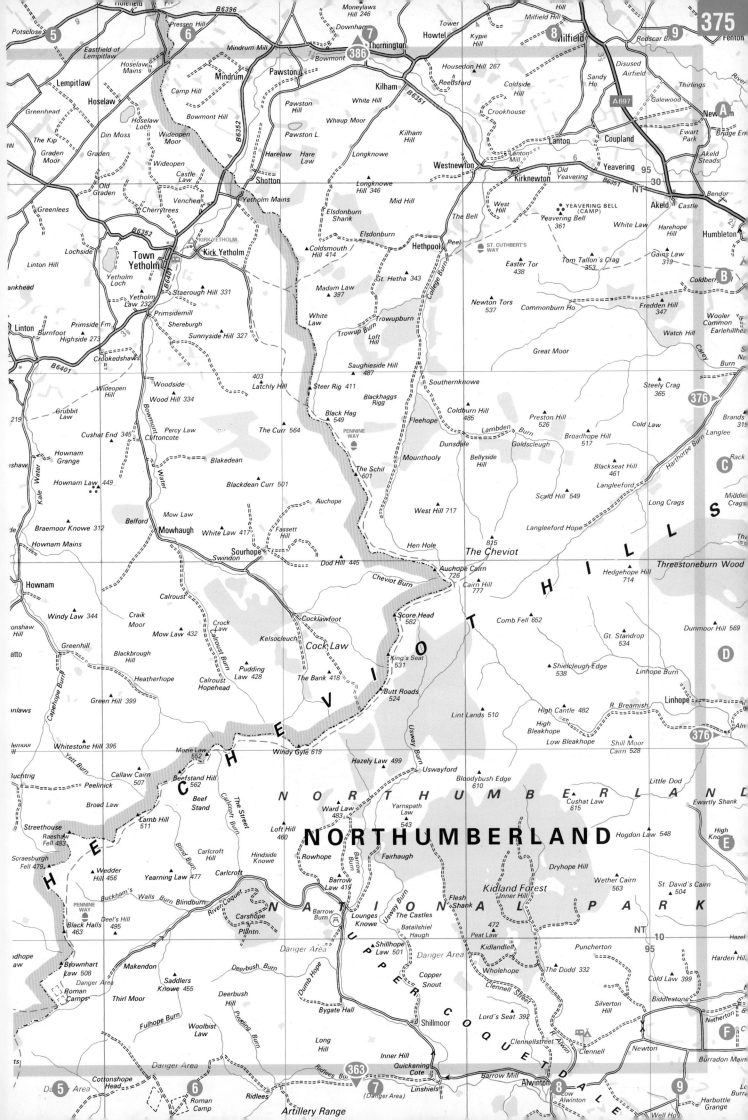

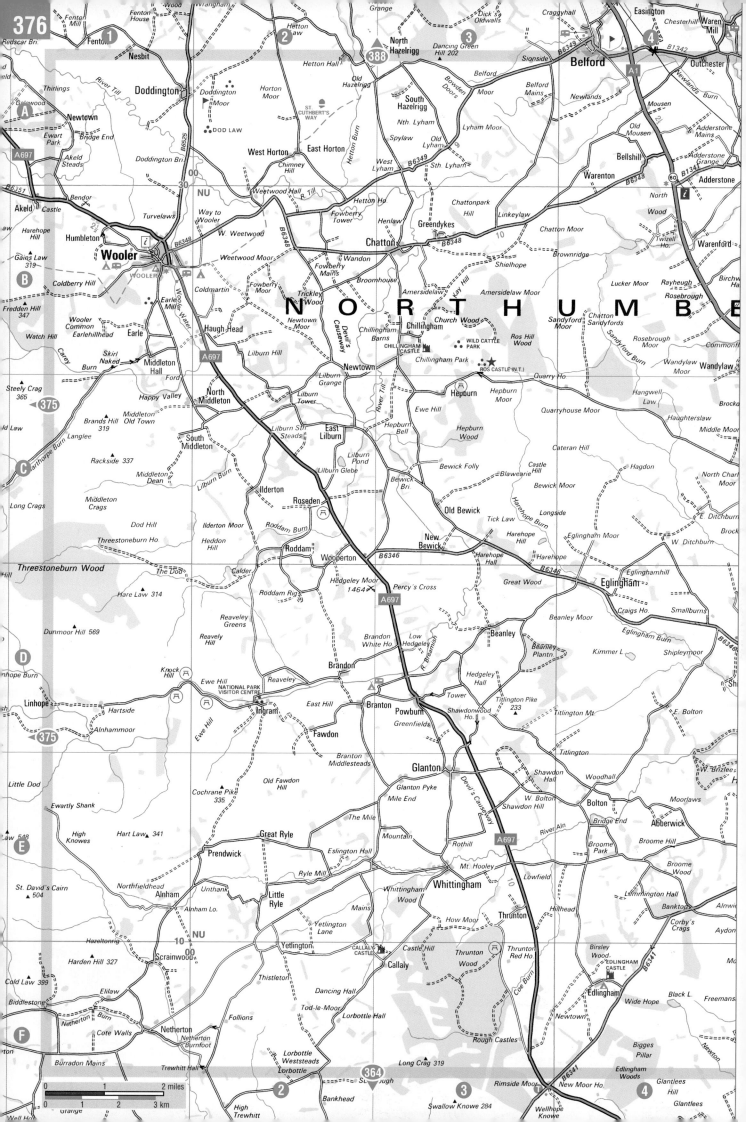

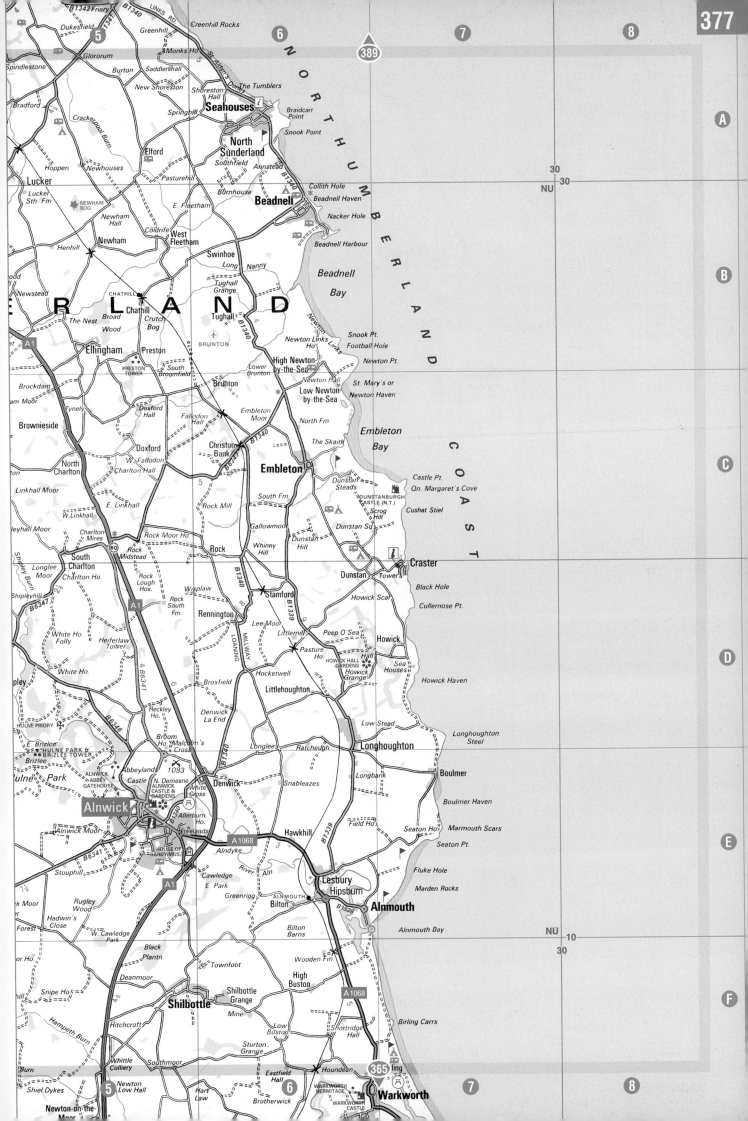

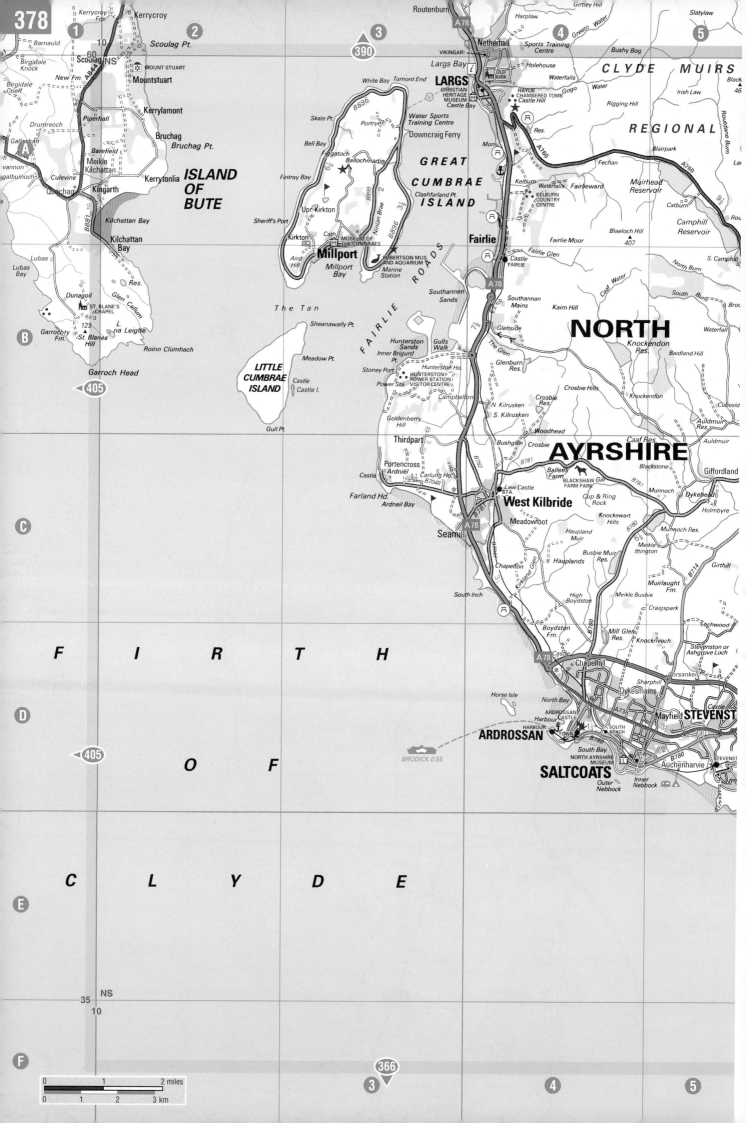

①　②　③　④　⑤

A78
390
VIKINGAR!
Netherhall
Largs Bay
OLD KIRK
LARGS
CHRISTIAN HERITAGE MUSEUM
Castle Bay
HAYLIE CHAMBERED TOMB
Castle Hill

Harplaw
Sports Training Centre
Bushy Bog
Greeto Water
Holehouse
Waterfalls
Gogo
Water
Slatylaw
Irish Law

CLYDE MUIRS

REGIONAL

Blairpark
Rigging Hill
Fechan
Catburn

Kerrycroy Fm.
Kerrycroy
Scoulag Pt.
Routenburn
Girtley Hill

Scoulag NS
60
10
Mount Stuart
MOUNT STUART
Mountstuart

Barnauld
Birgidale Knock
Birgidale Crieff
New Fm.
Drumreoch
Gallchan
A844

Piperhall
Kerrylamont
Bruchag
Bruchag Pt.
Barefield
Meikle Kilchattan
Kerrytonlia

ISLAND OF BUTE

White Bay
Tomont End
B896
Skate Pt.
Portryte
Bell Bay
Fintray Bay
Figgatoch
Ballochmartin
B899
6⅔
Ninian Brae
2
Clashfarland Pt.

GREAT CUMBRAE ISLAND

Res.
KELBURN COUNTRY CENTRE
Kelburn
Waterfalls
Fairlieward
Muirhead Reservoir

A760
Mon.

A760
9½

Blaeloch Hill
407
Camphill Reservoir

S. Camphill

Culevine
Quochag
Kingarth
B881
2

Kilchattan Bay

Upr. Kirkton
Sheriff's Port
Kirkton
Cath.
MUSEUM OF THE CUMBRAES
Aird Hill
Millport
Millport Bay
ROBERTSON MUS. AND AQUARIUM
Marine Station

B896
3½

Fairlie
Fairlie Glen
Castle FAIRLIE
Fairlie Moor

NORTH

Knockendon Res.
Baidland Hill
Waterfall

Lubas
Lubas Bay
Res.
Dunagoil
ST. BLANE'S CHAPEL
123
St. Blane's Hill
L. na Leighe
Glen Callum

Roinn Clùmhach
Garrochty Fm.
Garroch Head

405

The Tan
Sheanawally Pt.
Meadow Pt.

LITTLE CUMBRAE ISLAND
Castle I.
Castle I.
Gull Pt.

Southannan Sands
FAIRLIE ROADS

Southannan Mains
Glenside
Kaim Hill
Glenburn Res.
The Glen
Glenburn Res.

Knockendon

North Burn
South Burn

Cubesid

Hunterston Sands
Gulls Walk
Inner Brigurd Pt.
Stoney Port
Power Sta.
HUNTERSTON POWER STATION VISITOR CENTRE
Hunterston Ho.
Campbelton

N. Kilrusken
S. Kilrusken
Crosbie Res.
Crosbie Hills
Woodhead
Crosbie

Auldmuir Res.
Auldmuir

FIRTH

Goldenberry Hill
Thirdpart
Portencross
Ardniel
Castle
B7048
Carling Ho.
Farland Hd.
Ardneil Bay

AYRSHIRE

Ballees Farm
BLACKSHAW GILL FARM PARK
Law Castle STA.
Cup & Ring Rock
Knockewart Hills
Blackstone
Munnoch
Giffordland
Dykehead
Holmbyre

Seamill
A78
West Kilbride
B781
B781
B780
B780

Meadowfoot
Chapelton
Kirkland Glen
South Inch
Haupland Muir
Busbie Muir Res.
Haupands
High Boydston
Meikle Busbie
Munnoch Res.
Craigspark
Muirlaught Fm.
Girthill
Lochwood
Stevenston or Ashgrove Loch

OF

Boydston Fm.
Mill Glen Res.
Knockrivoch
Corsankell
Sharphill
Dykesmains

A78
Chapelhill
A738
Mayfield
STEVENST
Castle

Horse Isle
North Bay
ARDROSSAN CASTLE
HARBOUR
TOWN
SOUTH BEACH
STA.
B780

ARDROSSAN
South Bay
NORTH AYRSHIRE MUSEUM
SALTCOATS
Outer Nebbock
Inner Nebbock

STEVENST
Auchenharvie
B780
2

FIRTH OF CLYDE

BRODICK 0:55

405

F I R T H

O F

C L Y D E

NS
35
10

0　1　2 miles
0　1　2　3 km

①　②　③　④　⑤
Ⓐ　Ⓑ　Ⓒ　Ⓓ　Ⓔ　Ⓕ

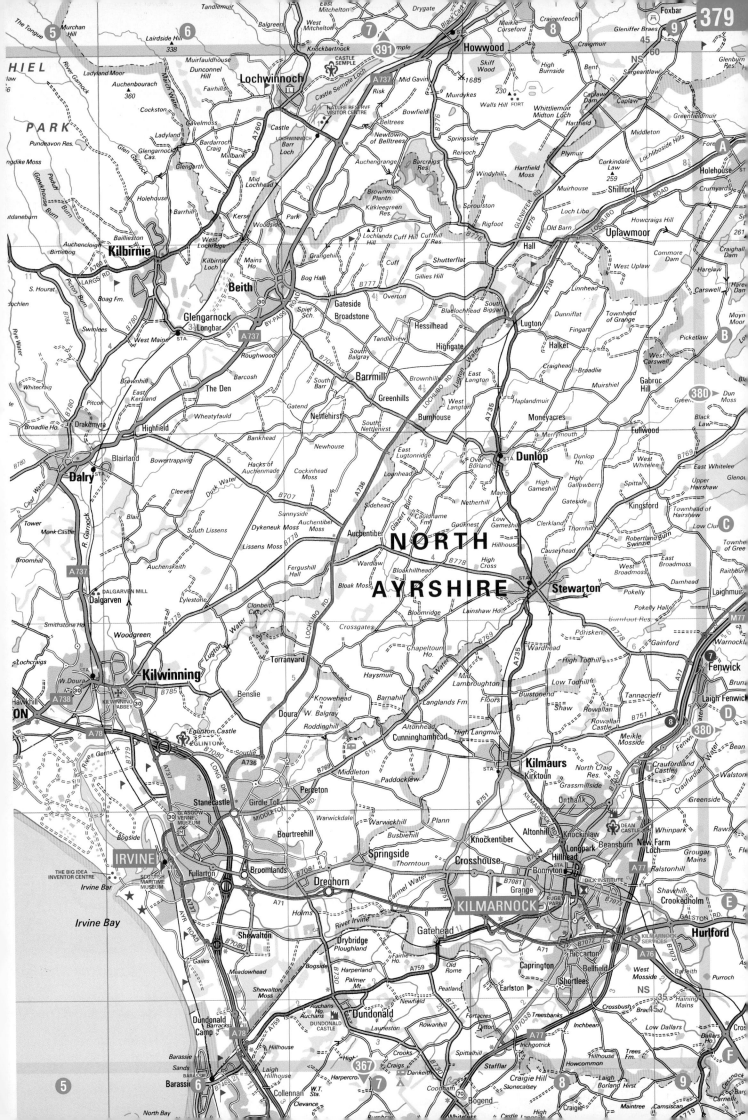

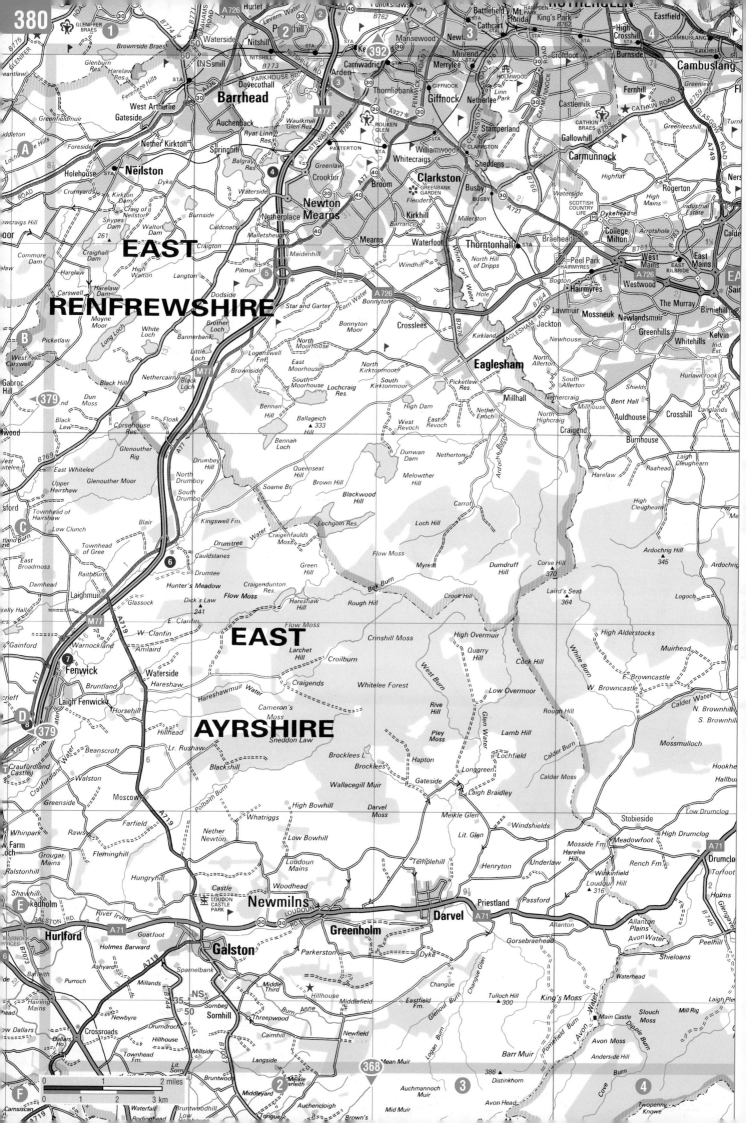

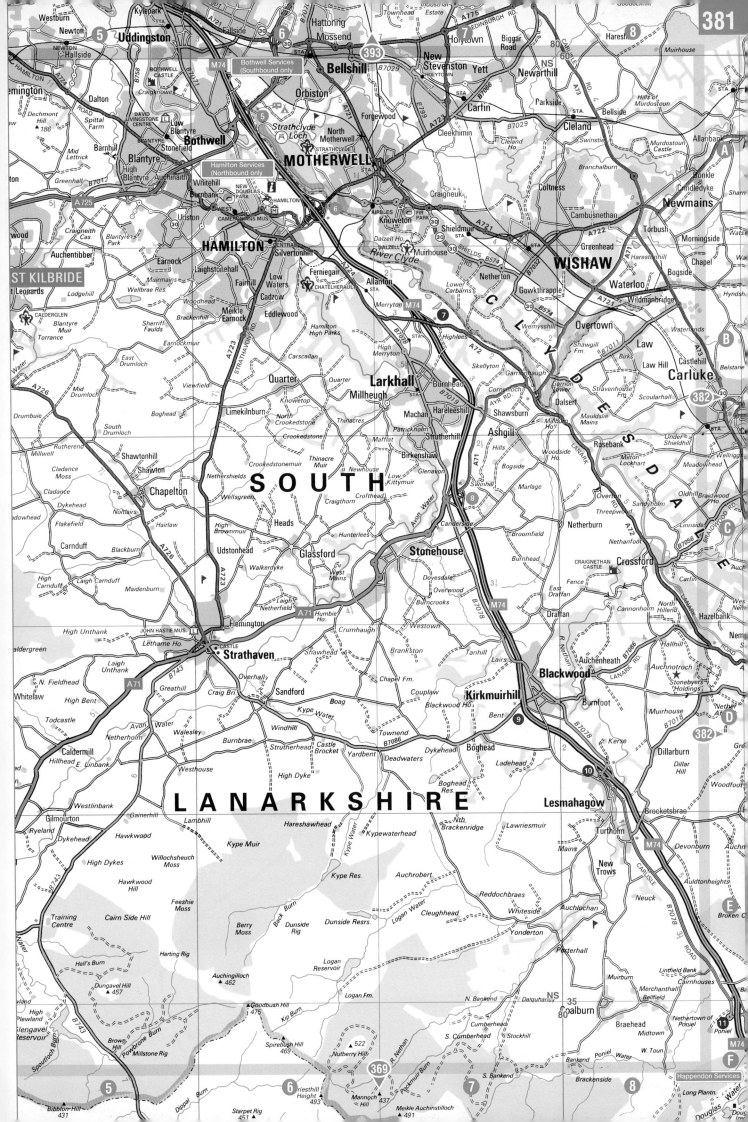

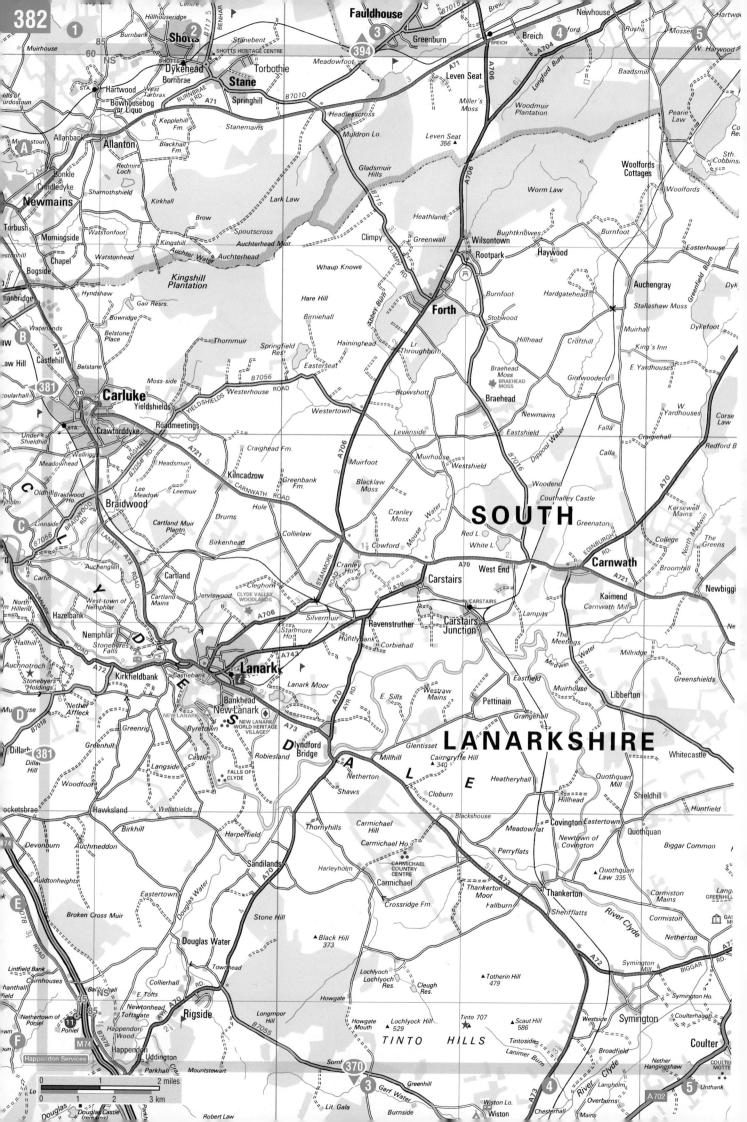

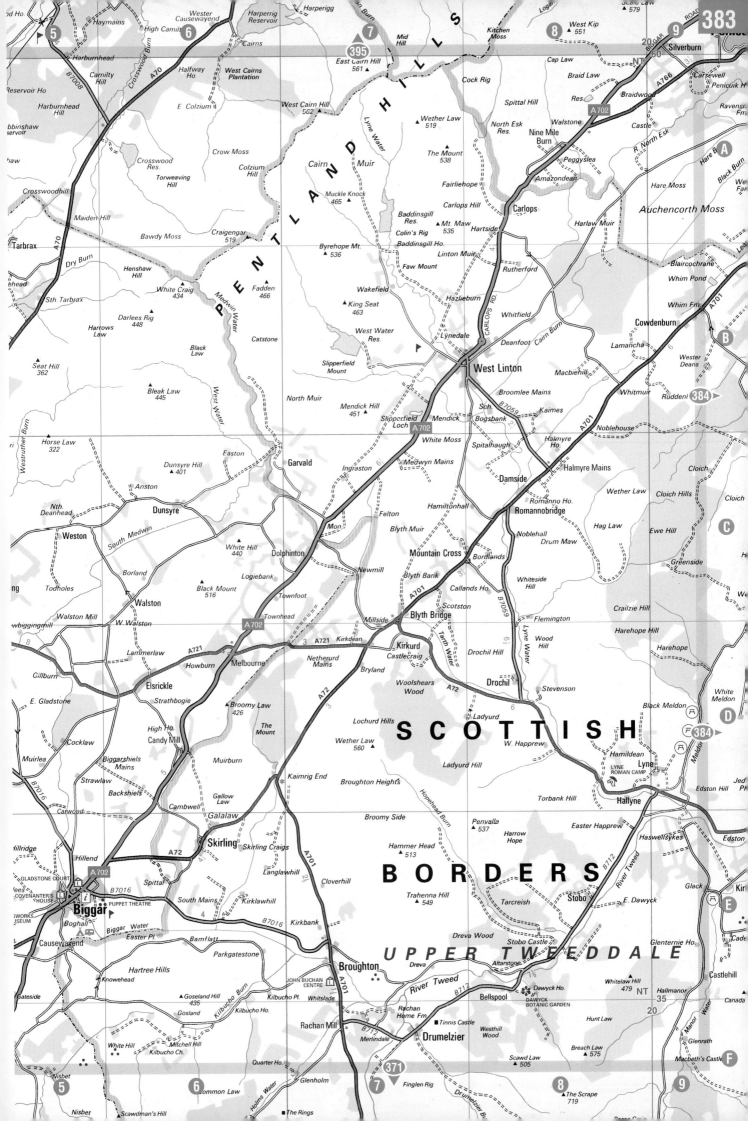

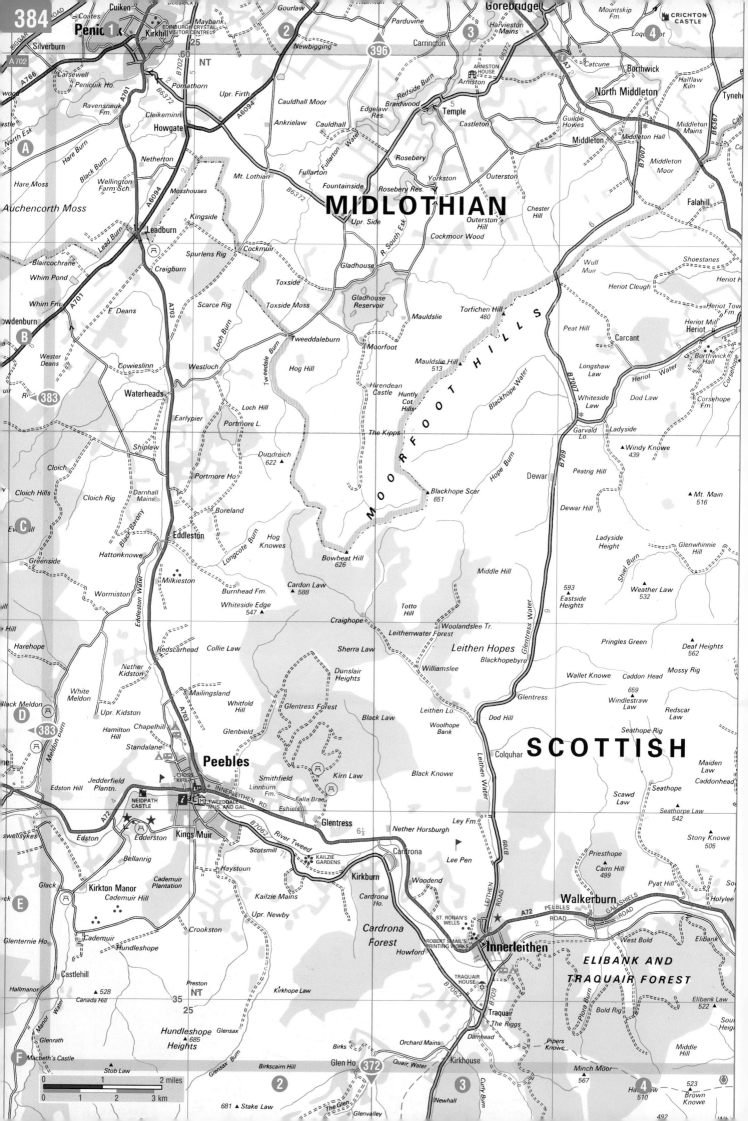

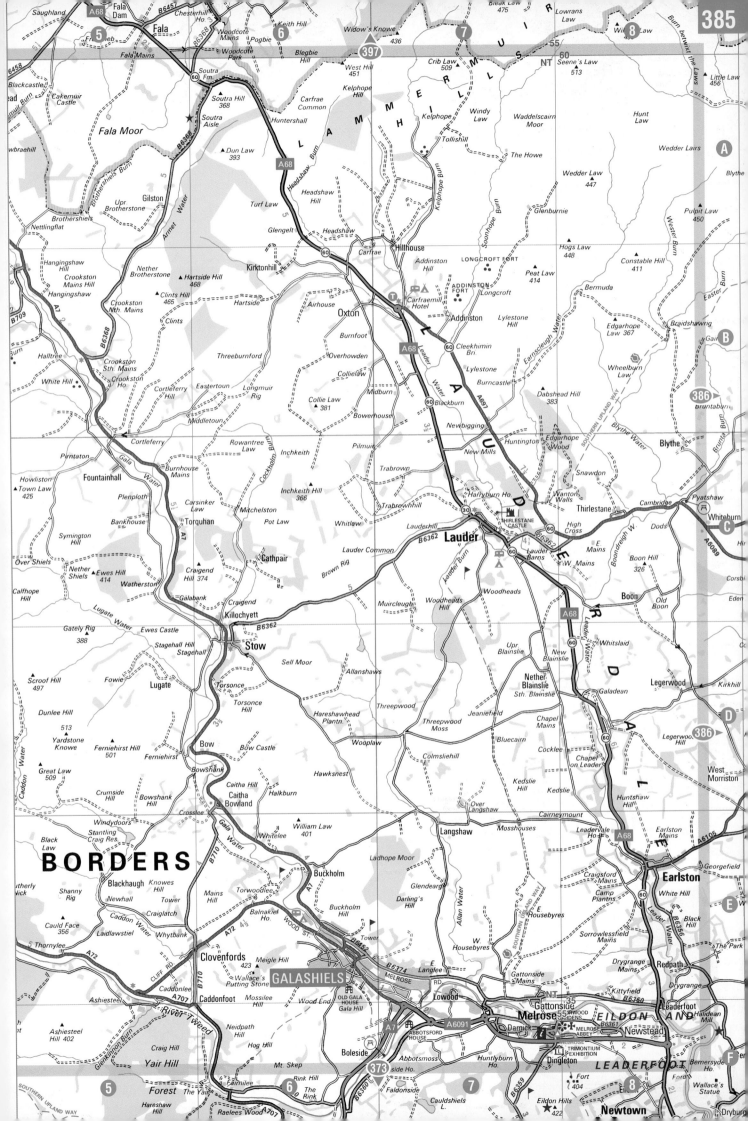

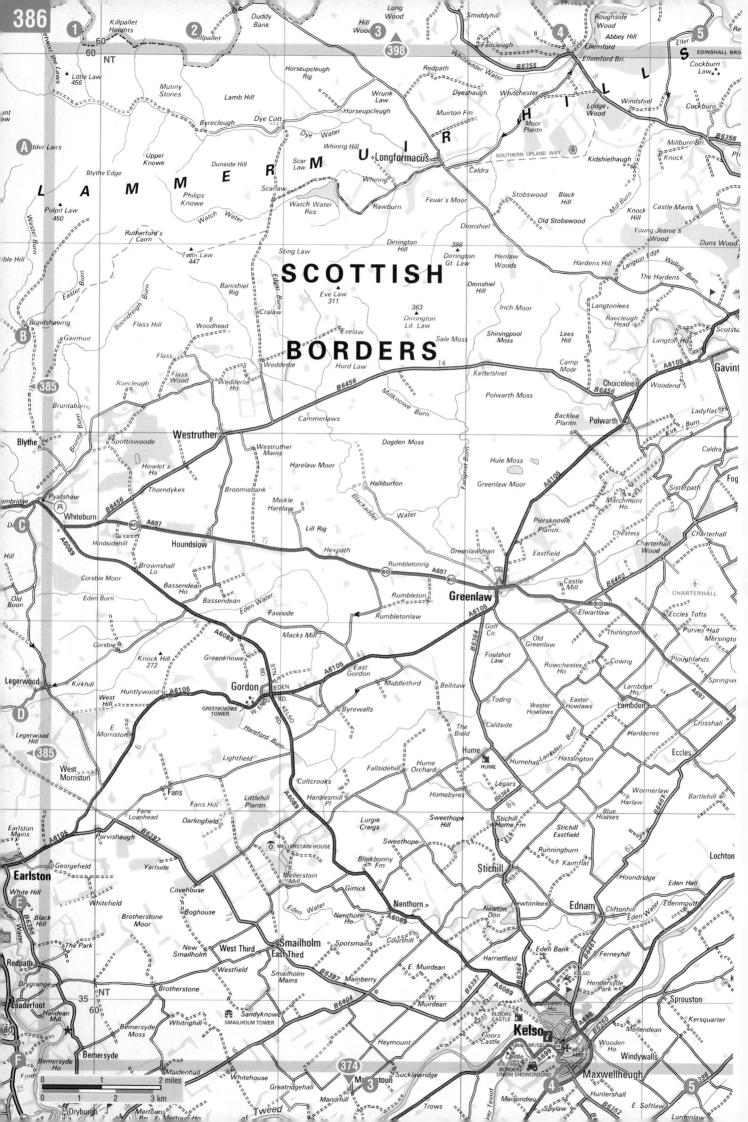

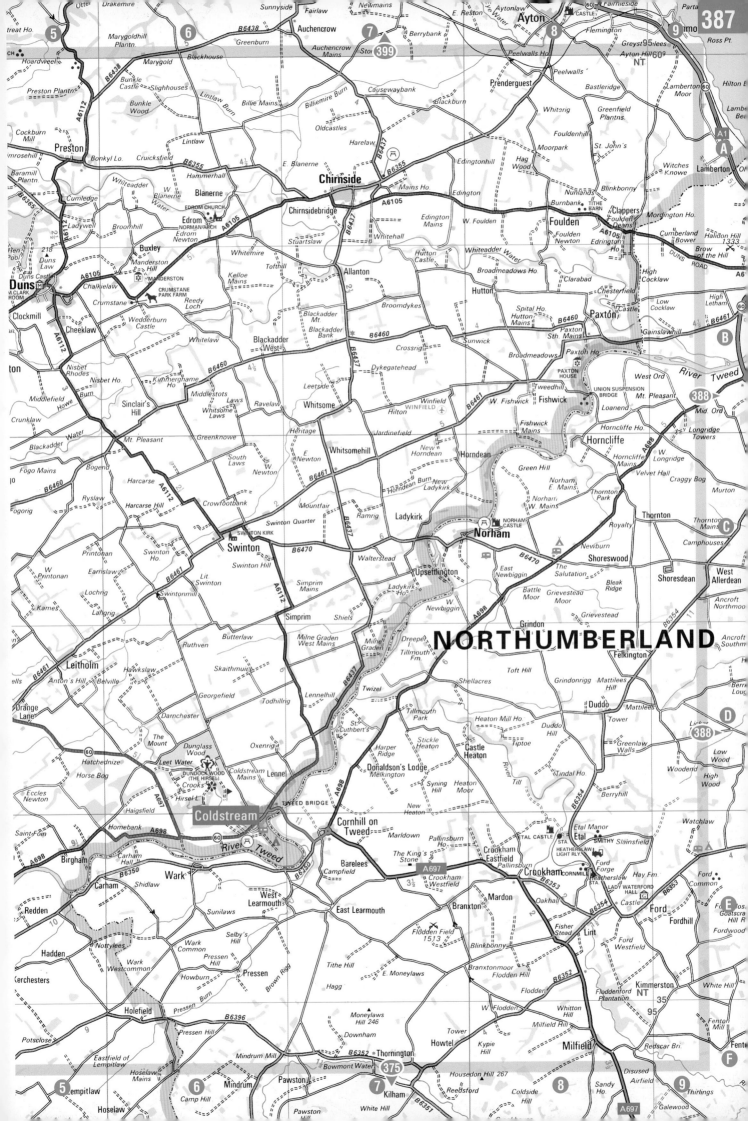

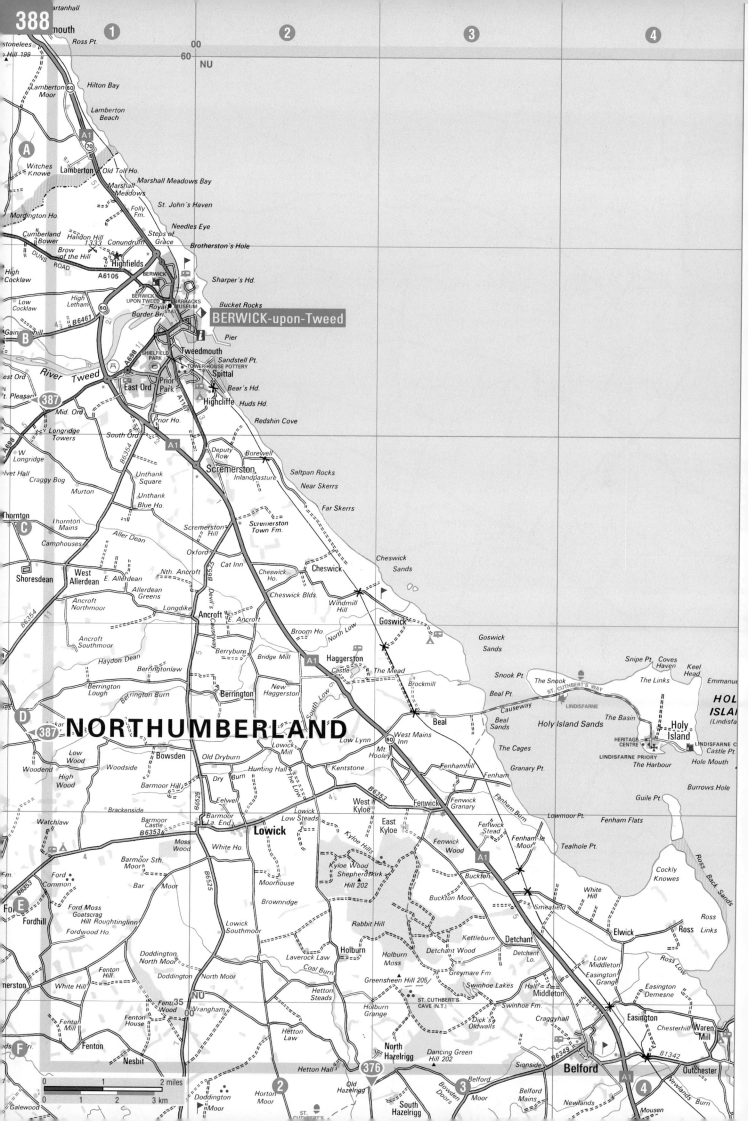

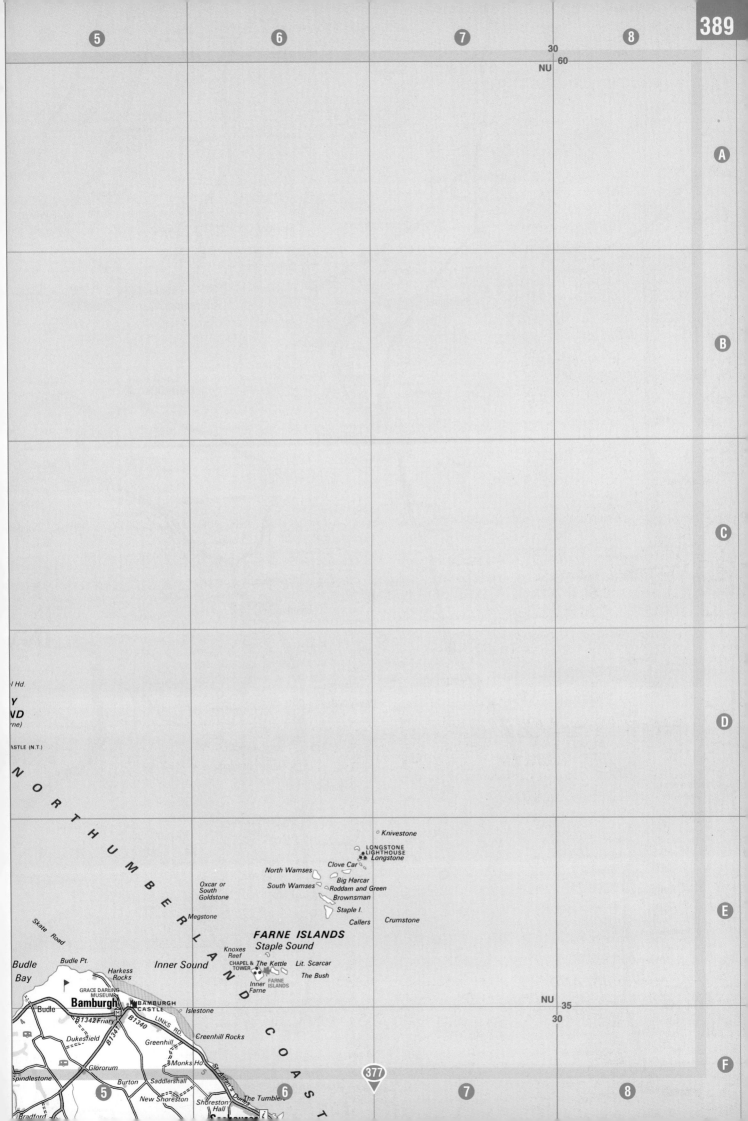

5    6    7    8

30
60
NU

A

B

C

/ Hd.

Y
ND
rne)

ASTLE (N.T.)

D

N O R T H U M B E R L A N D

○ Knivestone

LONGSTONE
LIGHTHOUSE
Longstone

Clove Car

North Wamses

Big Harcar

Oxcar or
South
Goldstone

South Wamses

Roddam and Green

Brownsman

Staple I.

Megstone

Callers        Crumstone

Skate Road

FARNE ISLANDS
Staple Sound

E

Budle Pt.

Inner Sound

Knoxes
Reef

Budle
Bay

CHAPEL & The Kettle

Lit. Scarcar

Harkess
Rocks

The Bush

Inner
Farne

FARNE
ISLANDS

GRACE DARLING
MUSEUM

Bamburgh      BAMBURGH
CASTLE

NU

Budle              Islestone

B1342 Friary

35
30

B1341      B1340      LINKS RD.

Dukesfield            Greenhill Rocks

Greenhill

Glororum      Monks Ho.

F

Spindlestone                St-Aidan's Dunes

377

Burton   Saddlershall        The Tumbler

5        New Shoreston        6        Shoreston        7        8
Hall
Bradford                        Seahouses      i

C O A S T

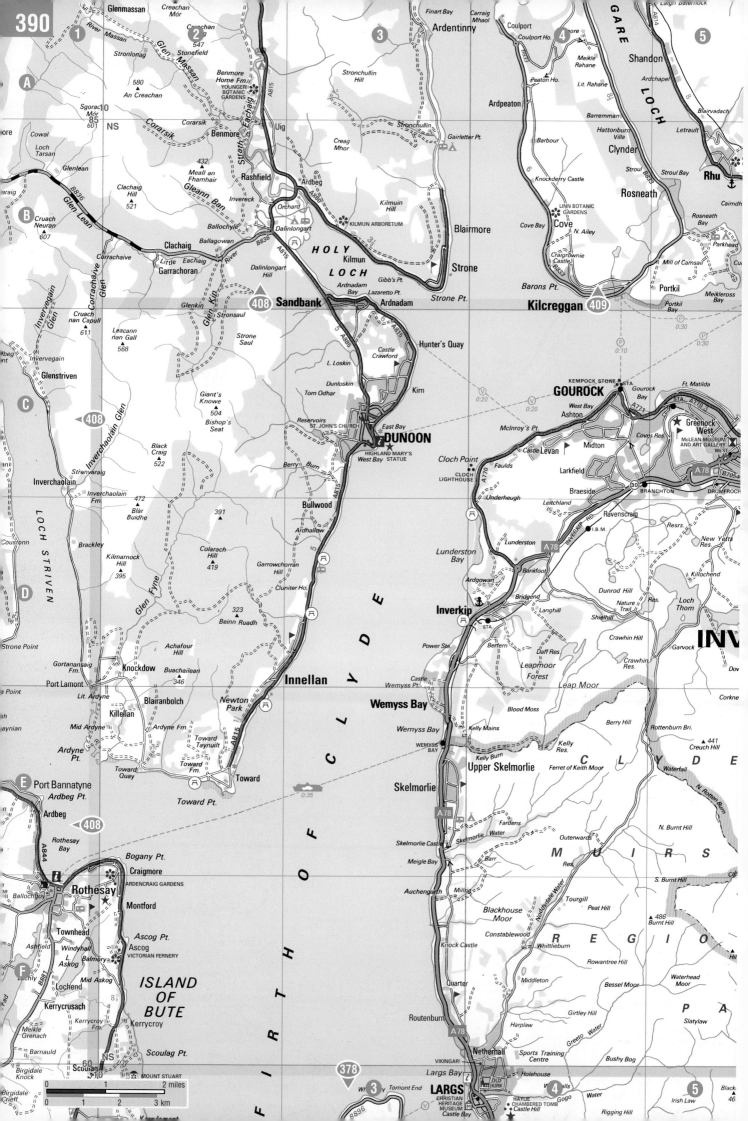

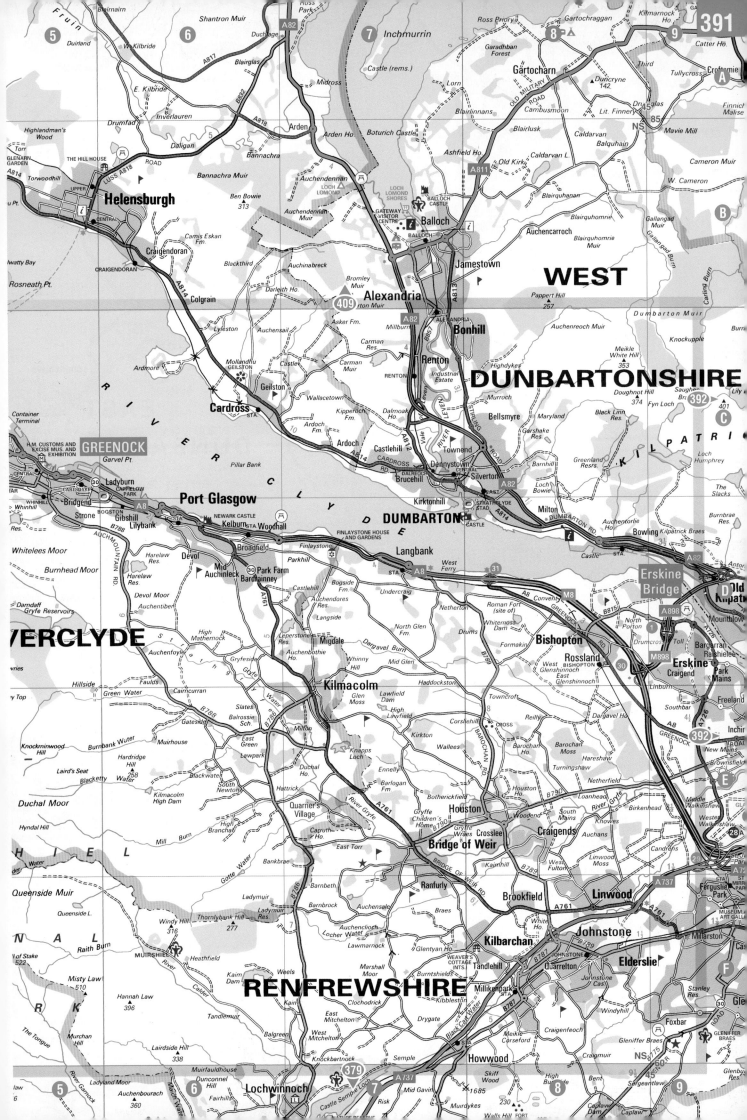

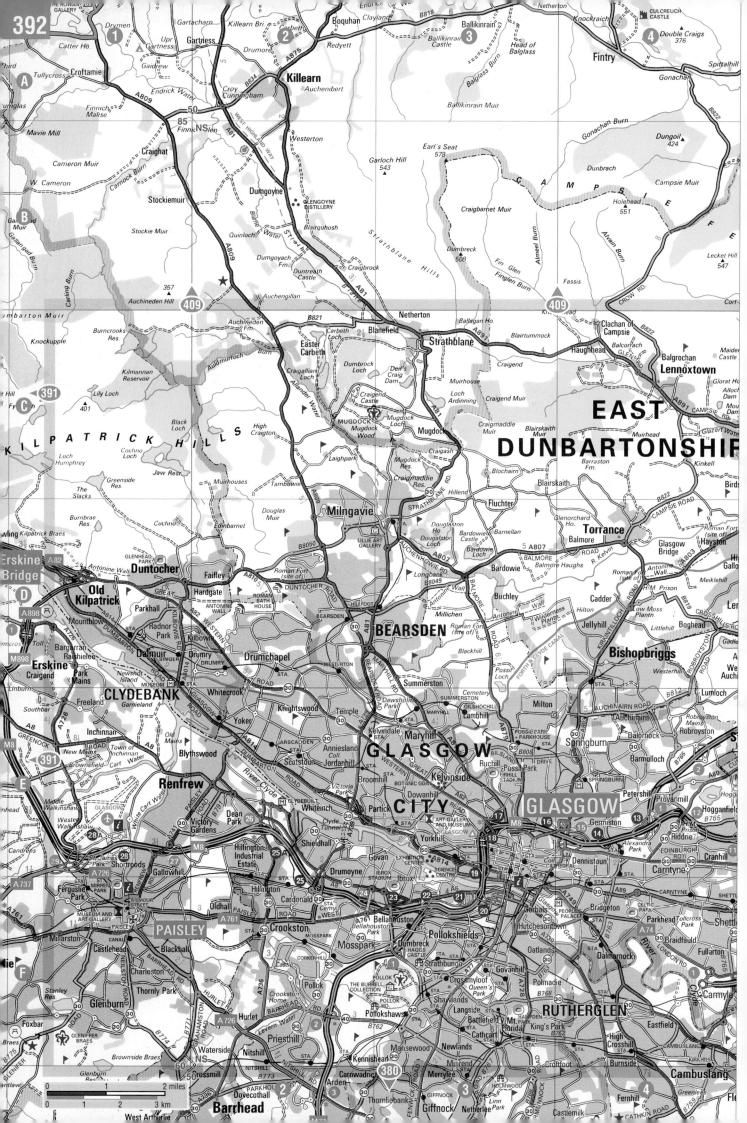

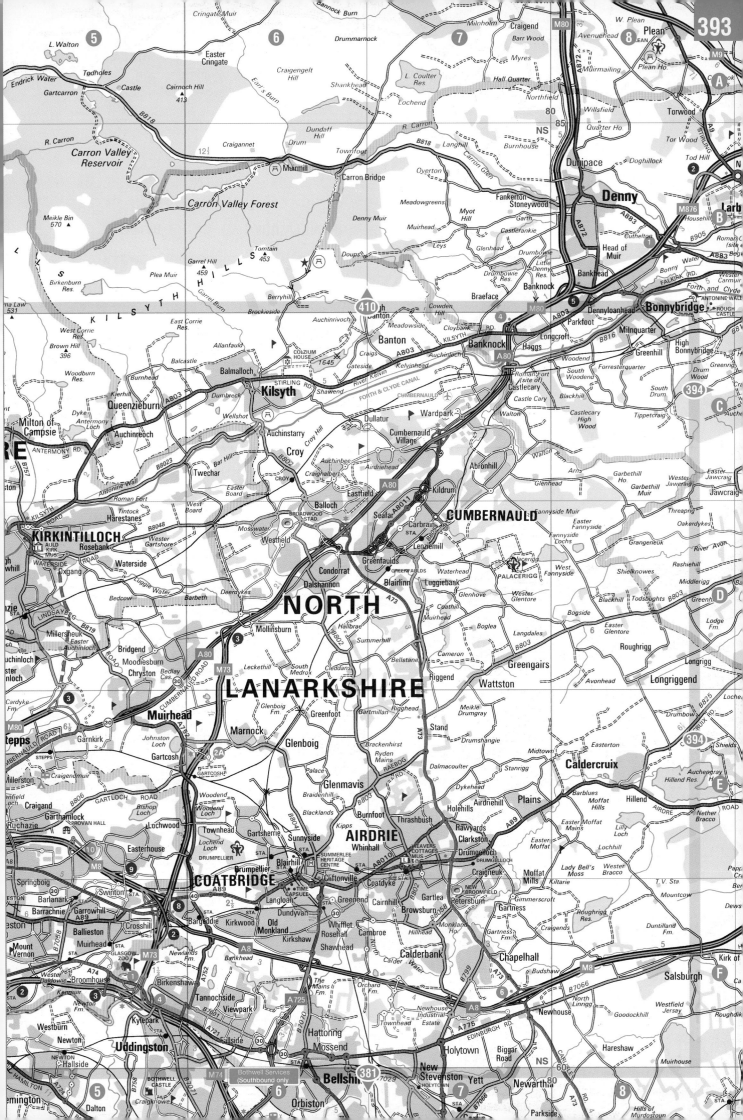

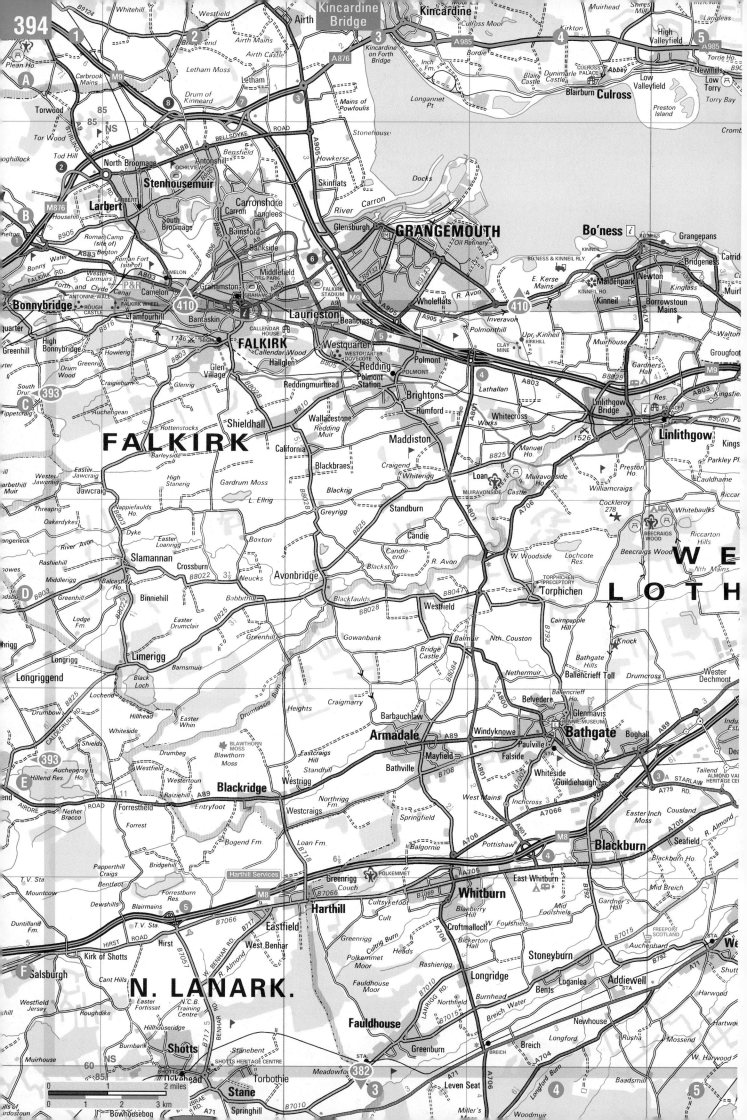

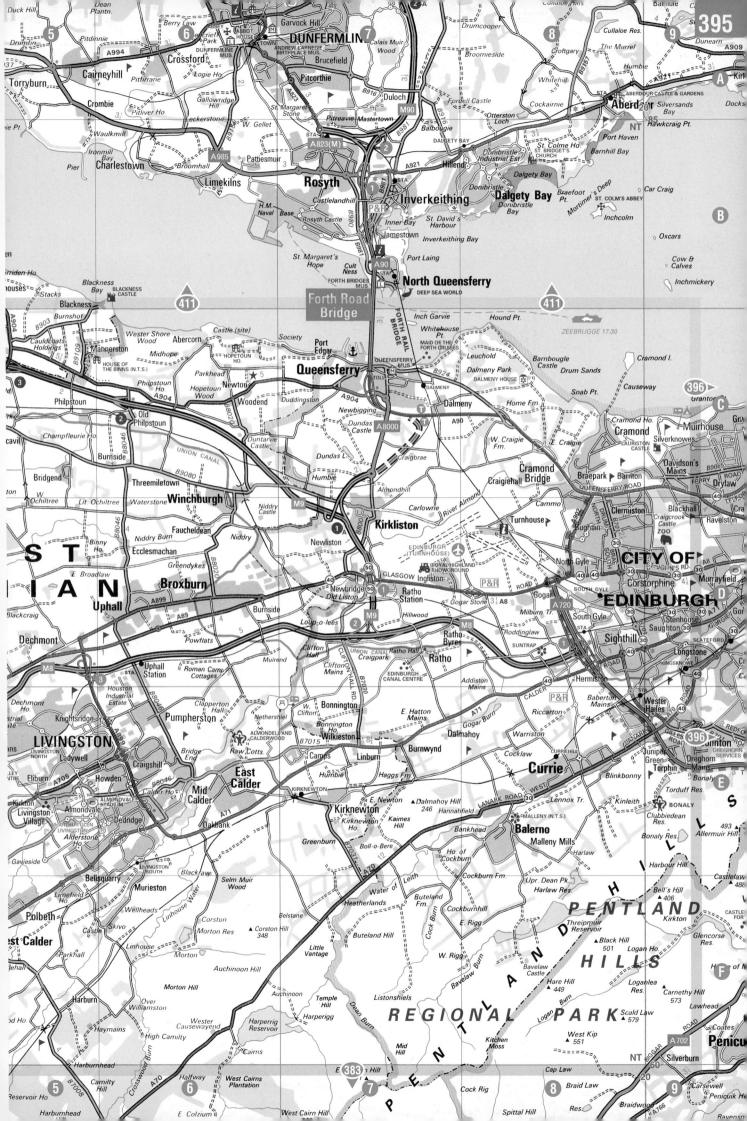

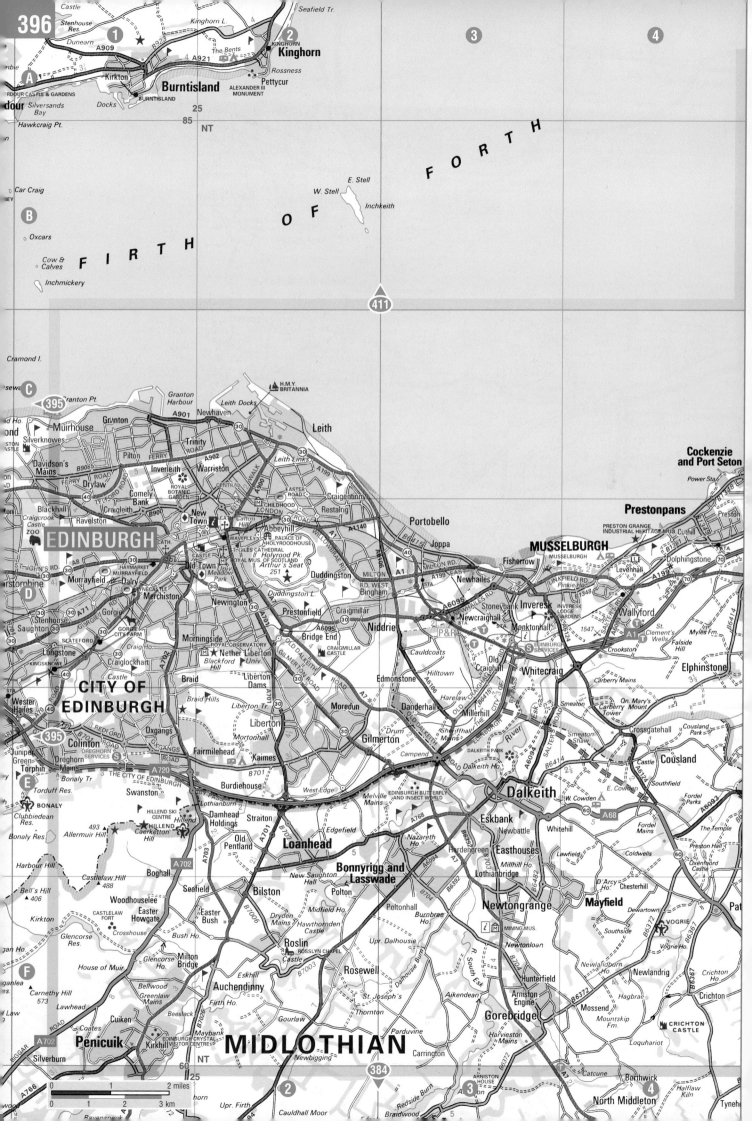

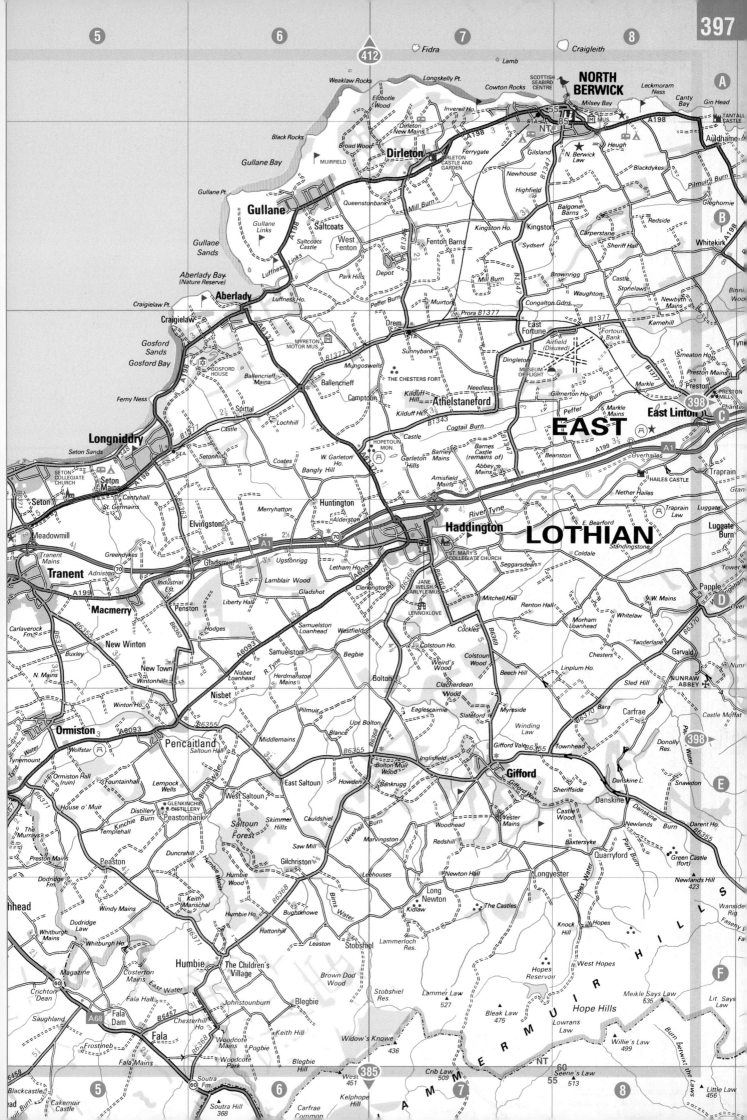

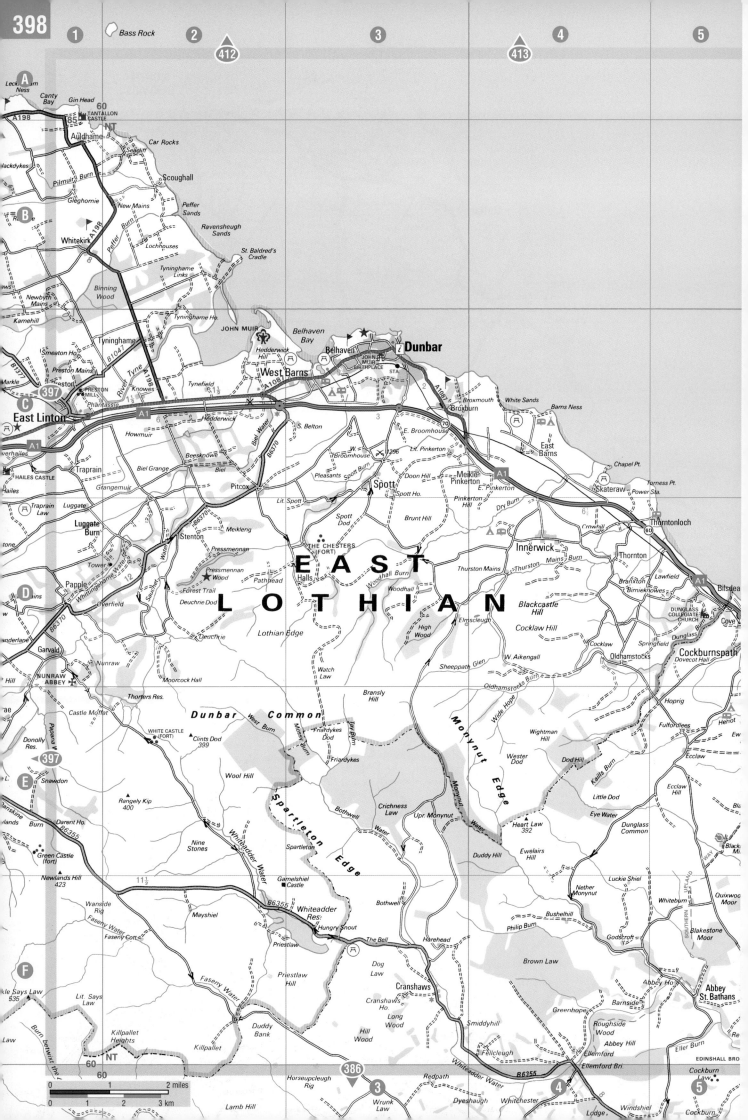

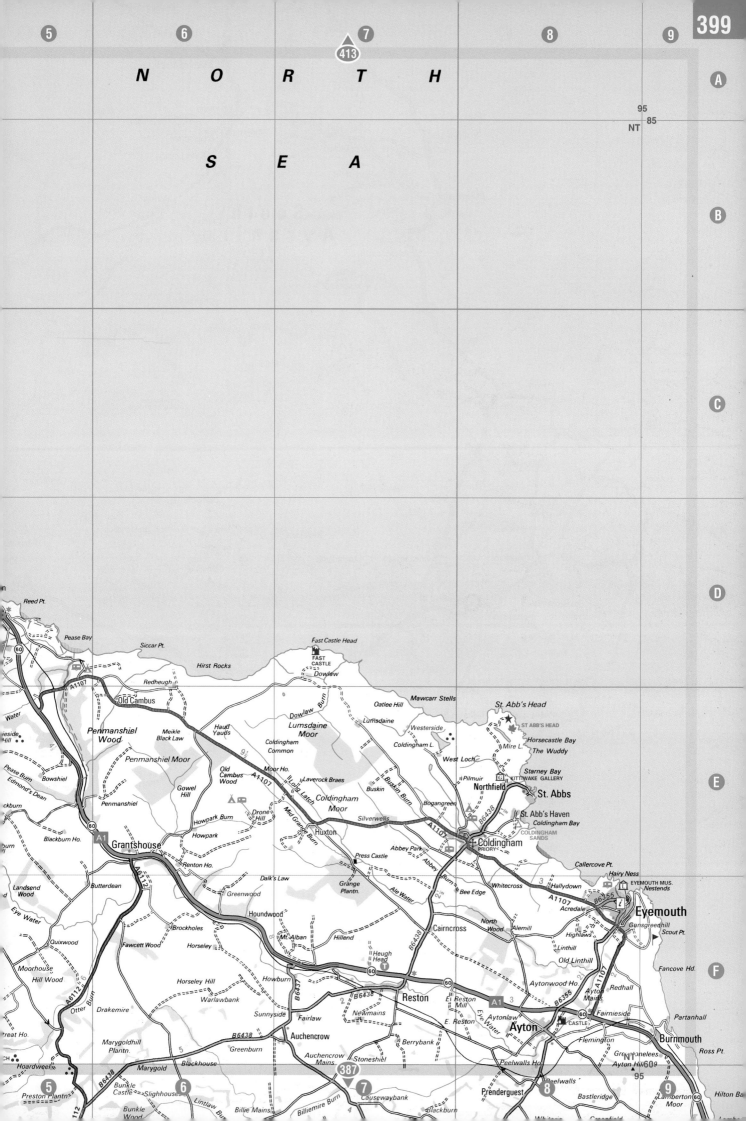

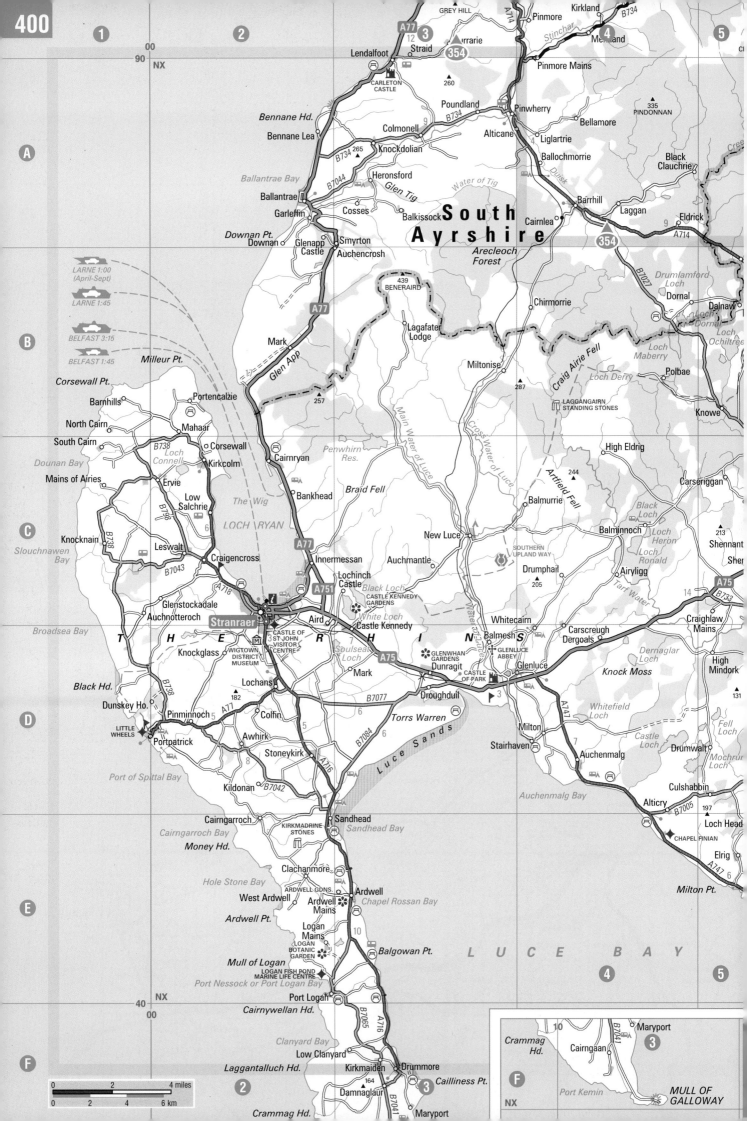

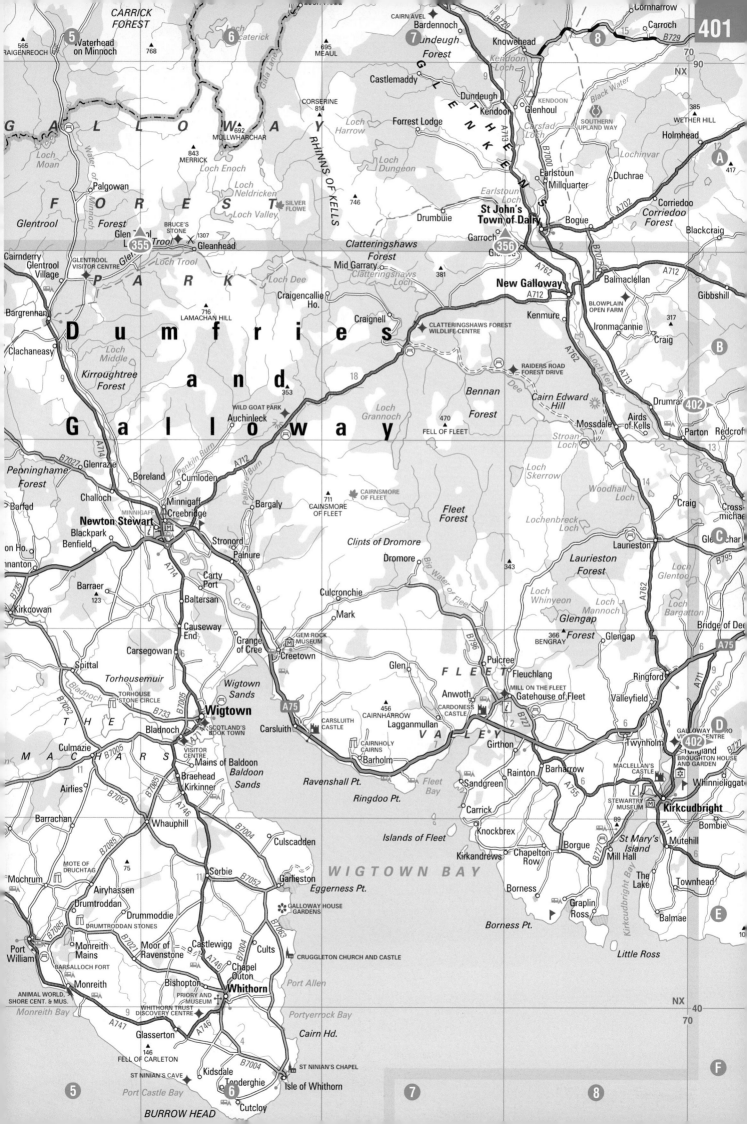

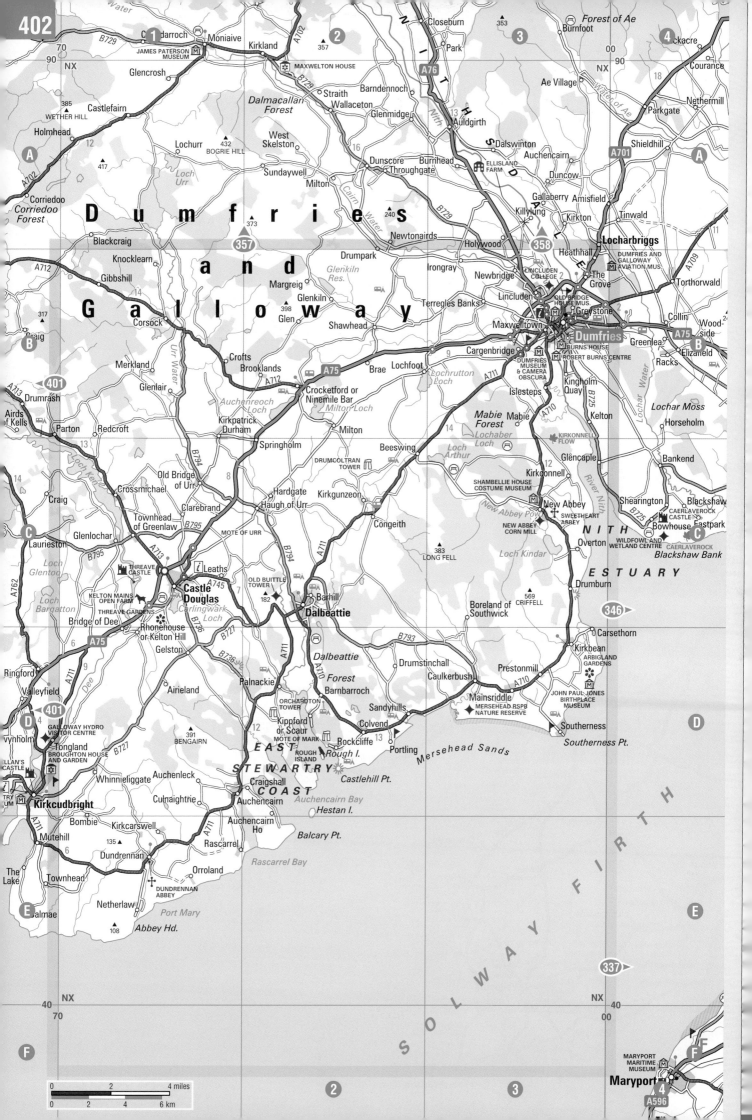

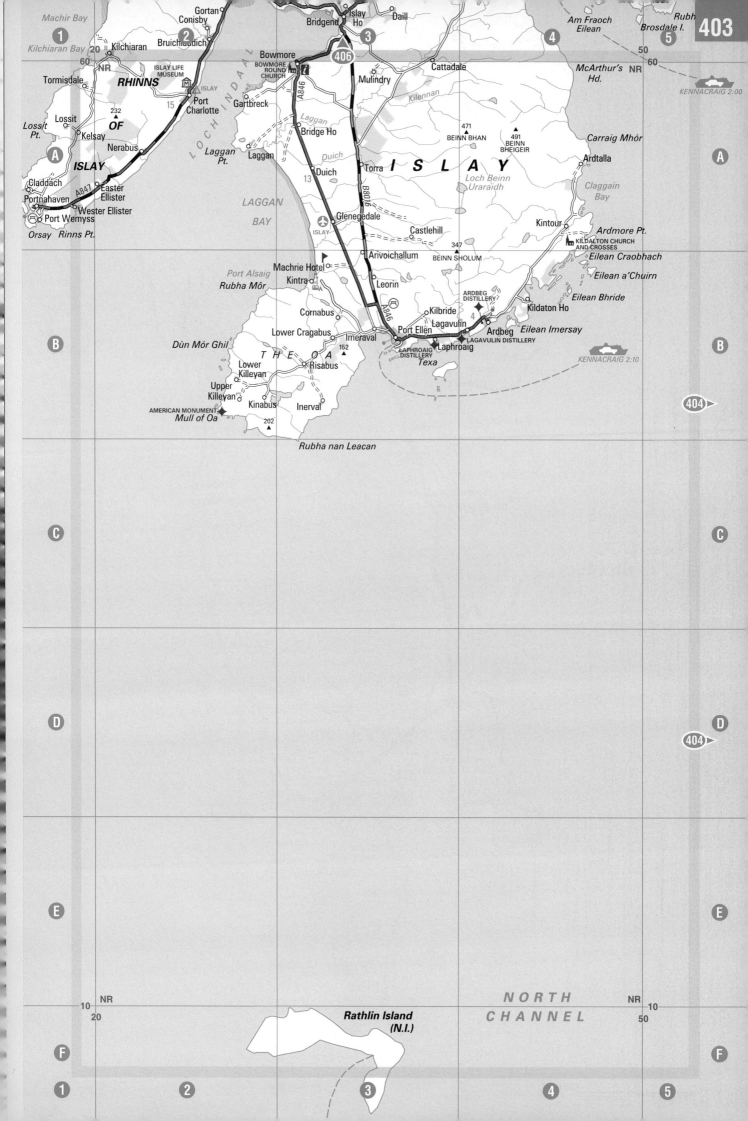

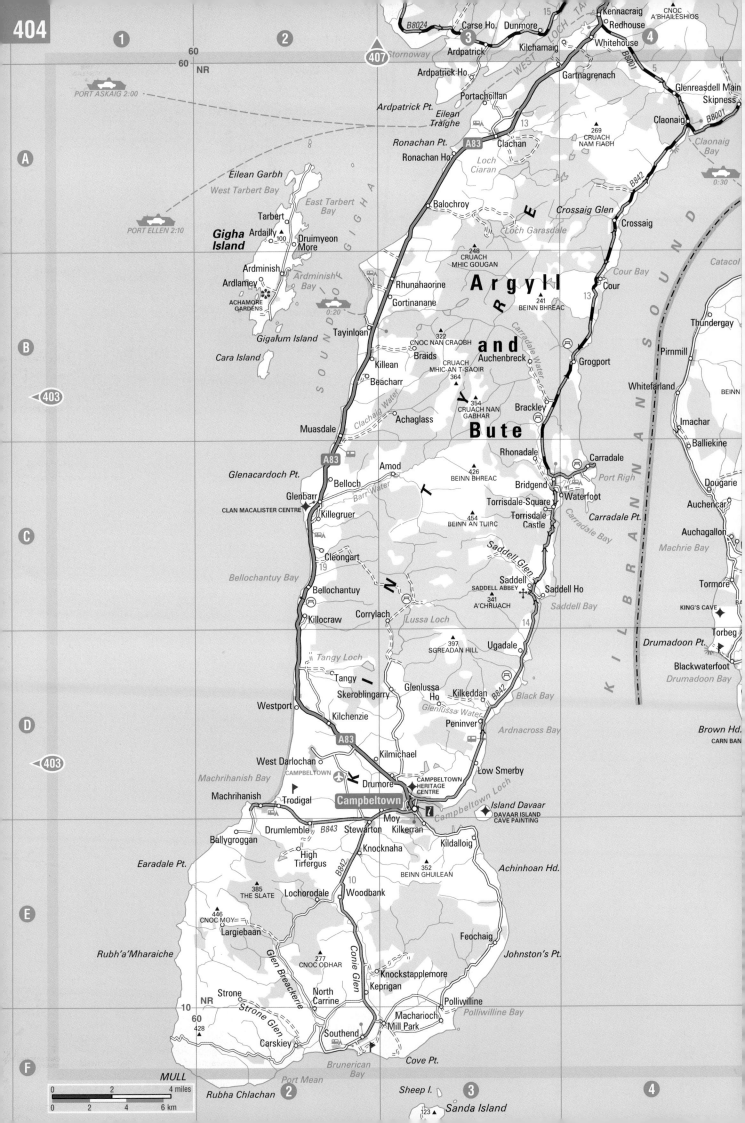

**Gigha Island**

Tarbert
Ardailly
Druimyeon More
Ardminish
Ardlamey
ACHAMORE GARDENS
West Tarbert Bay
East Tarbert Bay
Eilean Garbh
Ardminish Bay
Gigalum Island
Cara Island

Carse Ho.  Dunmore
B8024
Ardpatrick
407  Stornoway
Ardpatrick Ho.
Portachoillan
Ardpatrick Pt.
Eilean Traighe
Ronachan Pt.
Ronachan Ho.
A83  Clachan
Balochroy

Kilchamaig
Gartnagrenach
Kennacraig  Redhouse
Whitehouse
Glenreasdell Main
Skipness
Claonaig
B8001
B842
5
Loch Ciaran
269 CRUACH NAM FIADH
Crossaig Glen
Loch Garasdale
Crossaig

CNOC A'BHAILESHIOS

A r g y l l
a n d
B u t e

248 CRUACH MHIC GOUGAN
241 BEINN BHREAC
Cour
Cour Bay
13

Thundergay
Pirnmill
Whitefarland
BEINN
Imachar
Balliekine

Rhunahaorine
Gortinanane
322 CNOC NAN CRAOBH
Braids
CRUACH MHIC-AN T-SAOIR
364
354 CRUACH NAN GABHAR
Auchenbreck
Brackley
Grogport
Carradale Water

Tayinloan
Killean
Beacharr
Achaglass
Muasdale

Rhonadale
426 BEINN BHREAC
Carradale
Bridgend
Waterfoot
Torrisdale-Square
Torrisdale Castle
Port Righ
Carradale Pt.
Carradale Bay

Dougarie
Auchencar
Auchagallon
Machrie Bay
Tormore
KING'S CAVE

Glenacardoch Pt.
Belloch
Glenbarr
CLAN MACALISTER CENTRE
Killegruer
Cleongart
19
Bellochantuy Bay
Bellochantuy
Killocraw
Corrylach
Amod
Barr Water
Clachaig Water

454 BEINN AN TUIRC
Saddell Glen
Saddell
SADDELL ABBEY
341 A'CHRUACH
Saddell Ho.
Saddell Bay
14
Lussa Loch

Drumadoon Pt.
Torbeg
Blackwaterfoot
Drumadoon Bay
Brown Hd.
CARN BAN

Tangy Loch
Tangy
Skeroblingarry
Westport
Kilchenzie
A83
397 SGREADAN HILL
Ugadale
Glenlussa Ho.
Kilkeddan
B842
Glenlussa Water
Black Bay
Peninver
Ardnacross Bay

West Darlochan
CAMPBELTOWN
Drumore
Machrihanish
Trodigal
**Campbeltown**
Kilmichael
CAMPBELTOWN HERITAGE CENTRE
Low Smerby
Campbeltown Loch
Island Davaar
DAVAAR ISLAND CAVE PAINTING
Machrihanish Bay

Ballygroggan
Drumlemble
B843
Stewarton
Moy
Kilkerran
Kildalloig
Knocknaha
High Tirfergus
352 BEINN GHUILEAN
Achinhoan Hd.
Earadale Pt.

446 CNOC MOY
Largiebaan
385 THE SLATE
Lochorodale
Woodbank
Feochaig
Johnston's Pt.
Rubh'a'Mharaiche

277 CNOC ODHAR
Glen Breackerie
Conie Glen
Knockstapplemore
Keprigan
Polliwilline
Polliwilline Bay

Strone
North Carrine
Strone Glen
Macharioch
Mill Park
428
60
NR
10
Carskiey
Southend
Brunerican Bay
Cove Pt.
Port Mean
Rubha Chlachan
Sheep I.
Sanda Island
123

0  2  4 miles
0  2  4  6 km

403
403
60
60
NR
PORT ASKAIG 2:00
PORT ELLEN 2:10
0:20
0:30
15
WEST LOCH TARBERT
SOUND OF GIGHA
KILBRANNAN SOUND
Catacol
Claonaig Bay

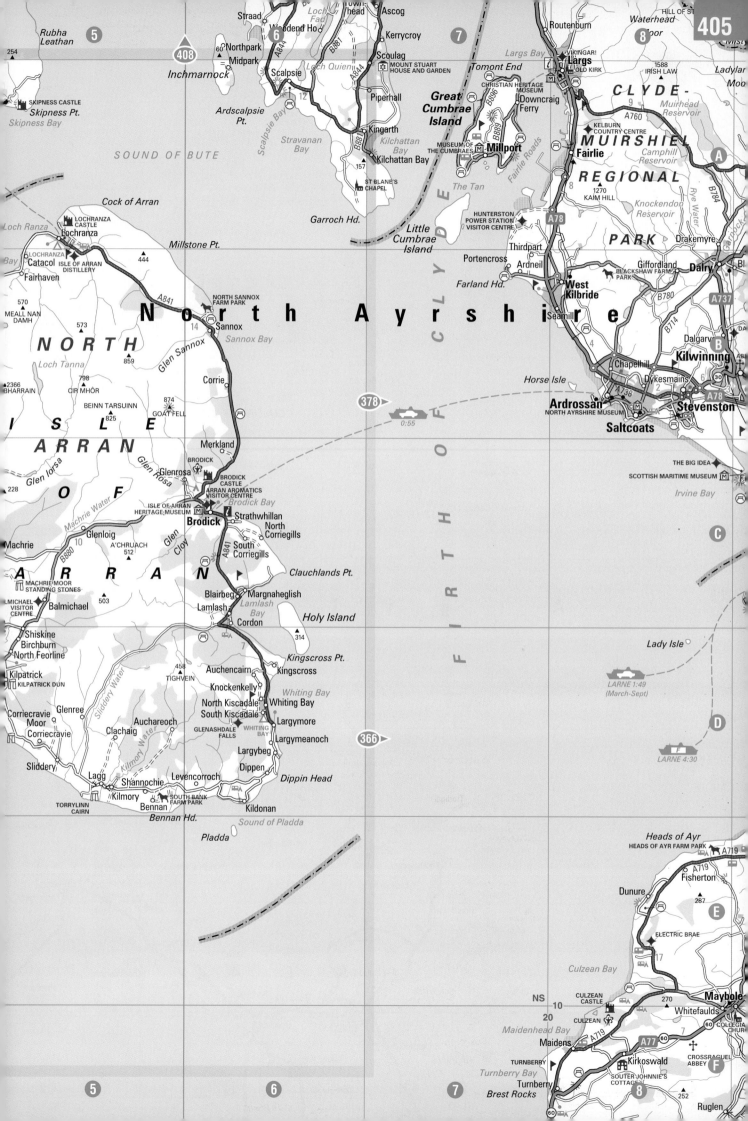

Rubha Leathan
254
⑤

408

Straad
Woodend Ho
⑥
A844
Northpark
60
Midpark
Scalpsie
Loch Quien
A844
12

Ascog
Loch Fad
head
Kerrycroy
Scoulag
MOUNT STUART HOUSE AND GARDEN
B881
⑦

Routenburn
Waterhead
Moor
HILL OF ST
⑧

Largs Bay
VIKINGAR!
Largs
Old Kirk
CHRISTIAN HERITAGE MUSEUM
B896
Downcraig Ferry
B889

1588
IRISH LAW

Ladylar
Moo

Inchmarnock

Ardscalpsie Pt.

Scalpsie Bay

Piperhall

B881
Kingarth
Kilchattan Bay
157
Kilchattan Bay

Great Cumbrae Island

MUSEUM OF THE CUMBRAES
Millport

CLYDE-
MUIRSHIEL
A760
KELBURN COUNTRY CENTRE
Fairlie
9
1270
KAIM HILL
8

Muirhead Reservoir

REGIONAL
Camphill Reservoir

Ⓐ

SOUND OF BUTE

Stravanan Bay

Garroch Hd.

ST BLANE'S CHAPEL

The Tan

Little Cumbrae Island

HUNTERSTON POWER STATION VISITOR CENTRE
A78

Knockendon Reservoir

Drakemyre
B784

SKIPNESS CASTLE
Skipness Pt.
Skipness Bay

Cock of Arran

LOCHRANZA CASTLE
Lochranza
Catacol
ISLE OF ARRAN DISTILLERY
Fairhaven
Bay
Loch Ranza

Millstone Pt.

Thirdpart
Portencross
Ardneil
Farland Hd.
Seamill

PARK

West Kilbride

B780

Giffordland
BLACKSHAW FARM PARK

Dalry
A737

Dalgarv

Ⓑ

570
MEALL NAN DAMH

NORTH
2366
BHARRAIN

444

859

573
798
CIR MHOR
BEINN TARSUINN
825

A841
NORTH SANNOX FARM PARK
14
Sannox
Glen Sannox
Sannox Bay

874
GOAT FELL

Corrie

B714
4
Chapelhill
A738
Kilwinning
6
30
Dykesmains
A78

ISLE
228
Glen Iorsa
Machrie Water

OF
Glenloig
A'CHRUACH
512
10
B880

Glen Rosa
Glenrosa
Merkland
BRODICK
BRODICK CASTLE
ARRAN AROMATICS VISITOR CENTRE
Brodick Bay
ISLE OF ARRAN HERITAGE MUSEUM
Brodick
Strathwhillan
North Corriegills
A841
South Corriegills

378
0:55

Horse Isle

Ardrossan
NORTH AYRSHIRE MUSEUM
Saltcoats

Stevenston

THE BIG IDEA
SCOTTISH MARITIME MUSEUM

Irvine Bay

Ⓒ

ARRAN
MACHRIE MOOR STANDING STONES
MICHAEL VISITOR CENTRE
Balmichael
503

Glen Cloy

Clauchlands Pt.

Blairbeg
Margnaheglish
Lamlash
Lamlash Bay
Cordon

Holy Island

Lady Isle

LARNE 1:49 (March-Sept)

Ⓓ

Shiskine
Birchburn
North Feorline
Kilpatrick
KILPATRICK DUN

Glenree
Corriecravie Moor
Corriecravie
Sliddery
Clachaig
Auchareoch

Sliddery Water

458
TIGHVEIN
Auchencairn
Knockenkelly
North Kiscadale
South Kiscadale
GLENASHDALE FALLS
WHITING BAY
Largybeg
Dippen
Levencorroch

314

7
Kingscross Pt.
Kingscross
Whiting Bay
Largymore
Largymeanoch

Kilmory Water

Lagg
Shannochie
Kilmory
Bennan
TORRYLINN CAIRN
SOUTH BANK FARM PARK

Dippin Head

366

LARNE 4:30

Ⓔ

Kildonan
Bennan Hd.

Sound of Pladda
Pladda

NS
10
20

Heads of Ayr
HEADS OF AYR FARM PARK
A719

Dunure
287
Fisherton

ELECTRIC BRAE

Culzean Bay

CULZEAN CASTLE
Culzean

Maidenhead Bay

A719
Maidens

270
Maybole
Whitefaulds

COLLEGIA
CHUR

Ⓕ

TURNBERRY
Turnberry Bay
Turnberry
Brest Rocks

KIRKOSWALD
SOUTER JOHNNIE'S COTTAGE
Kirkoswald

CROSSRAGUEL ABBEY

252
Ruglen

⑤
⑥
⑦
⑧

A

B

C

D

E

F

**1**

**2**

**3**

**4**

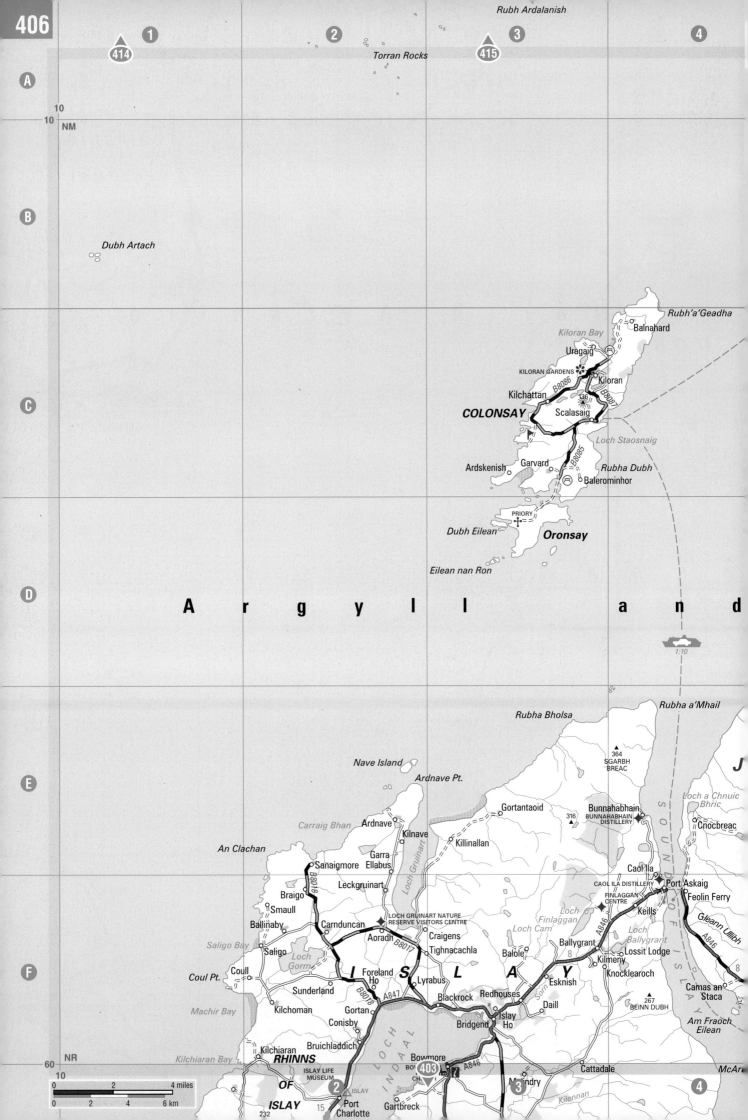

*Rubh Ardalanish*

*Torran Rocks*

10

10
NM

*Dubh Artach*

*Rubh'a'Geadha*

*Kiloran Bay*

Balnahard

Uragaig

KILORAN GARDENS

Kiloran

Kilchattan

B8086

B8087

**COLONSAY**

Scalasaig
136

*Loch Staosnaig*

Ardskenish

Garvard

B8085

*Rubha Dubh*

Balerominhor

*Dubh Eilean*

PRIORY

**Oronsay**

*Eilean nan Ron*

**A r g y l l a n d**

1:10

*Rubha a'Mhail*

*Rubha Bholsa*

364
SGARBH
BREAC

*Loch a Chnuic
Bhric*

*Nave Island*

Gortantaoid

Bunnahabhain

316
BUNNAHABHAIN
DISTILLERY

Cnocbreac

*Ardnave Pt.*

*Carraig Bhan*

Ardnave

Kilnave

Killinallan

SOUND OF ISLAY

*An Clachan*

Garra
Ellabus

Caol Ila

Sanaigmore

B8018

Leckgruinart

CAOL ILA DISTILLERY

Port Askaig

Braigo

FINLAGGAN
CENTRE

Feolin Ferry

Smaull

LOCH GRUINART NATURE
RESERVE VISITORS CENTRE

Keills

*Loch
Finlaggan*

A846

*Gleann Ullibh*

Ballinaby

Carnduncan

Craigens

Ballygrant

Lossit Lodge

A846

*Saligo Bay*

Aoradh

B8017

Tighnacachla

Balole

8

Kilmeny

*Loch
Ballygrant*

Saligo

*Loch
Gorm*

Foreland
Ho

Esknish

Knocklearoch

**I S L A Y**

Lyrabus

*Sorn*

**Y**

*Coul Pt.*

Coull

B8018

Blackrock

Redhouses

Daill

267
BEINN DUBH

Camas an
Staca

Sunderland

A847

8

Kilchoman

Gortan

Islay
Ho

Bridgend

*Am Fraoch
Eilean*

*Machir Bay*

Conisby

Bruichladdich

*Loch Indaal*

60
NR

KILCHIARAN

ISLAY LIFE
MUSEUM

**RHINNS**

*Kilchiaran Bay*

Bowmore
BO
CH

403

A846

Cattadale

*McAr*

10

**OF**

**ISLAY**

**2**

ISLAY

**3**

Mulindry

*Kilennan*

**4**

0    2    4 miles
0   2   4   6 km

Port
Charlotte

15

232

Gartbreck

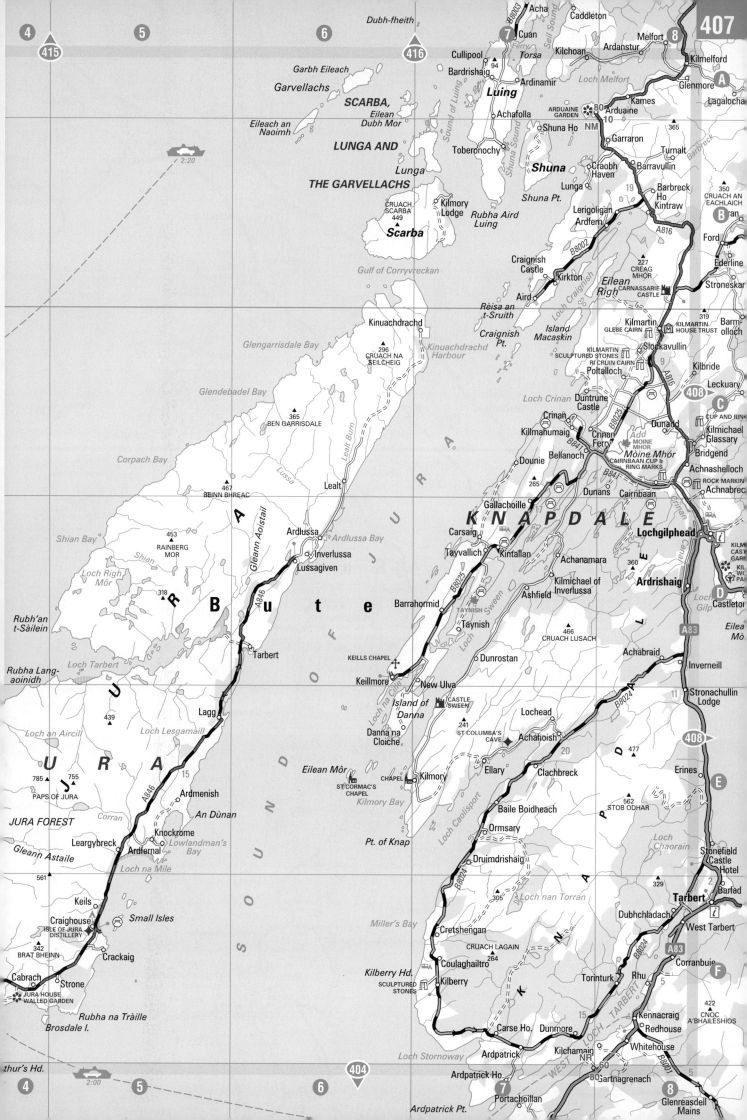

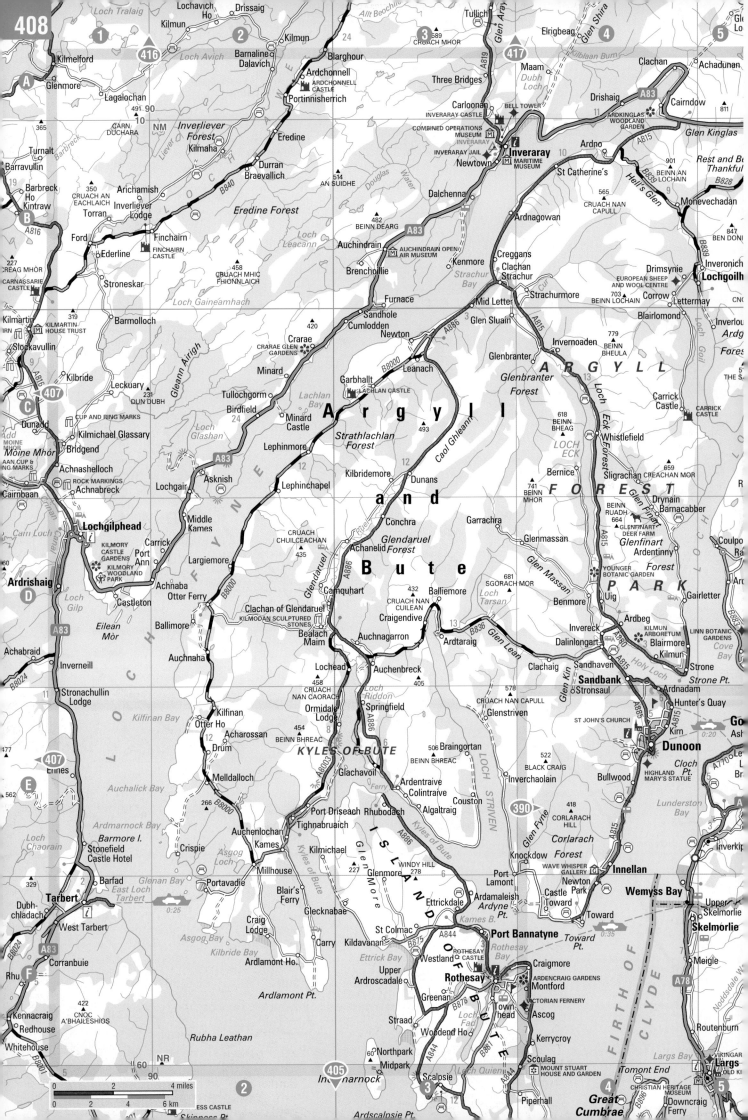

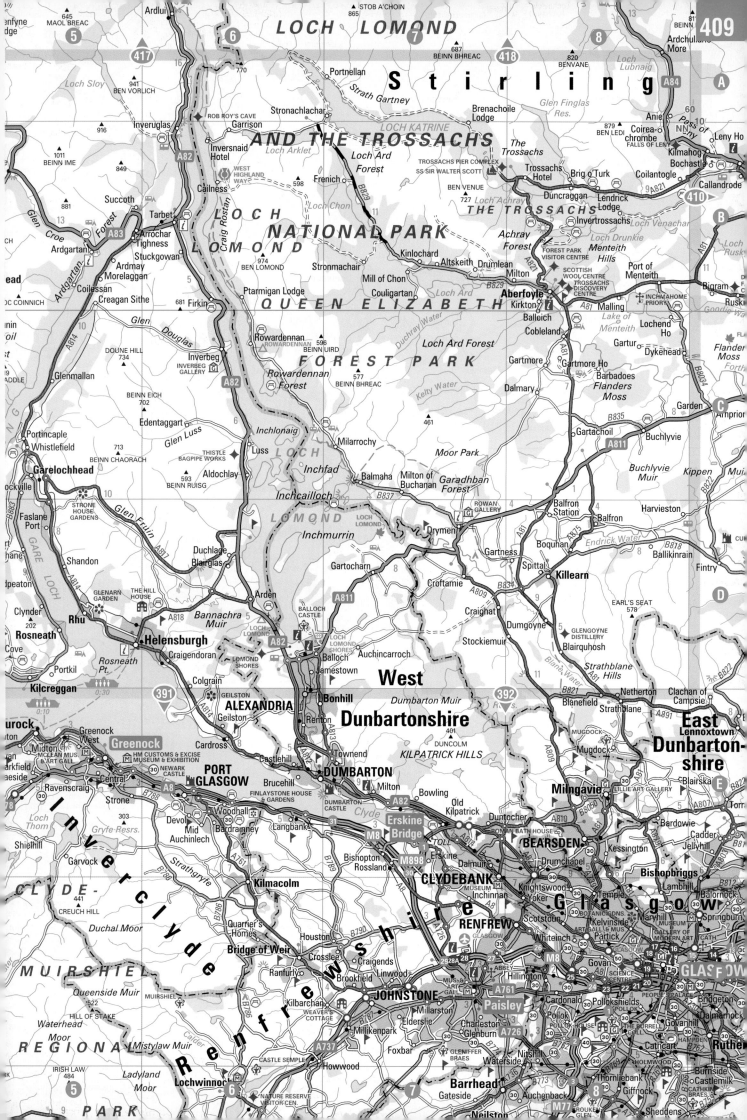

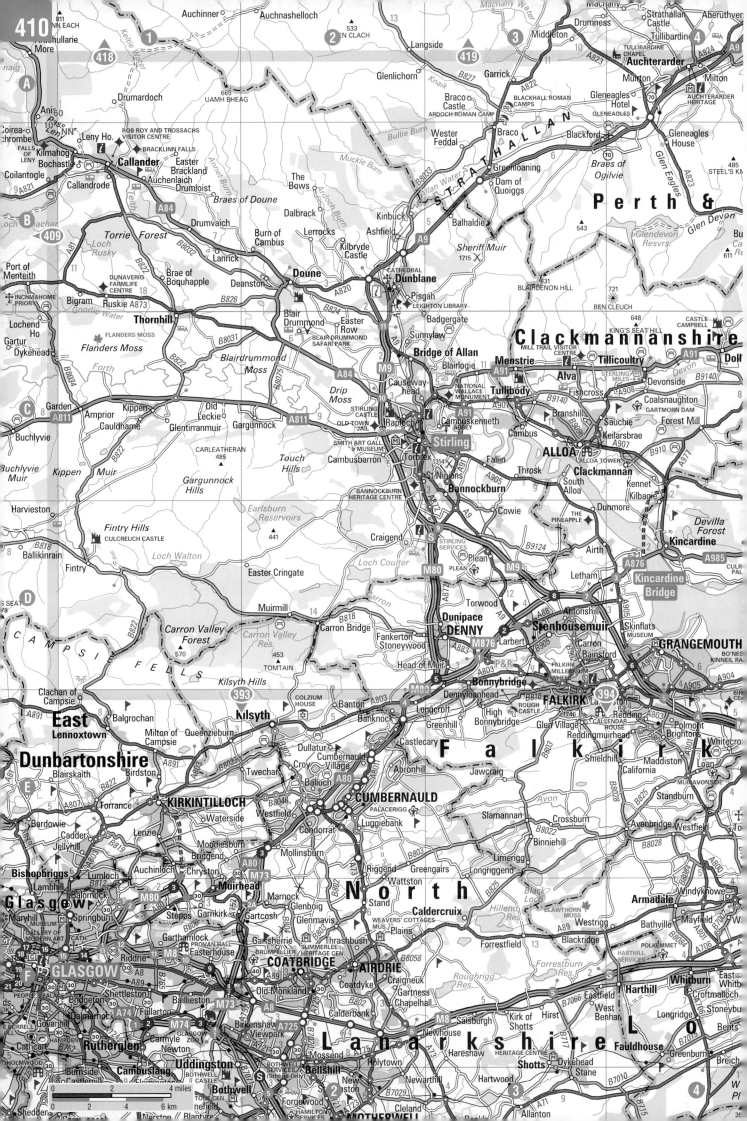

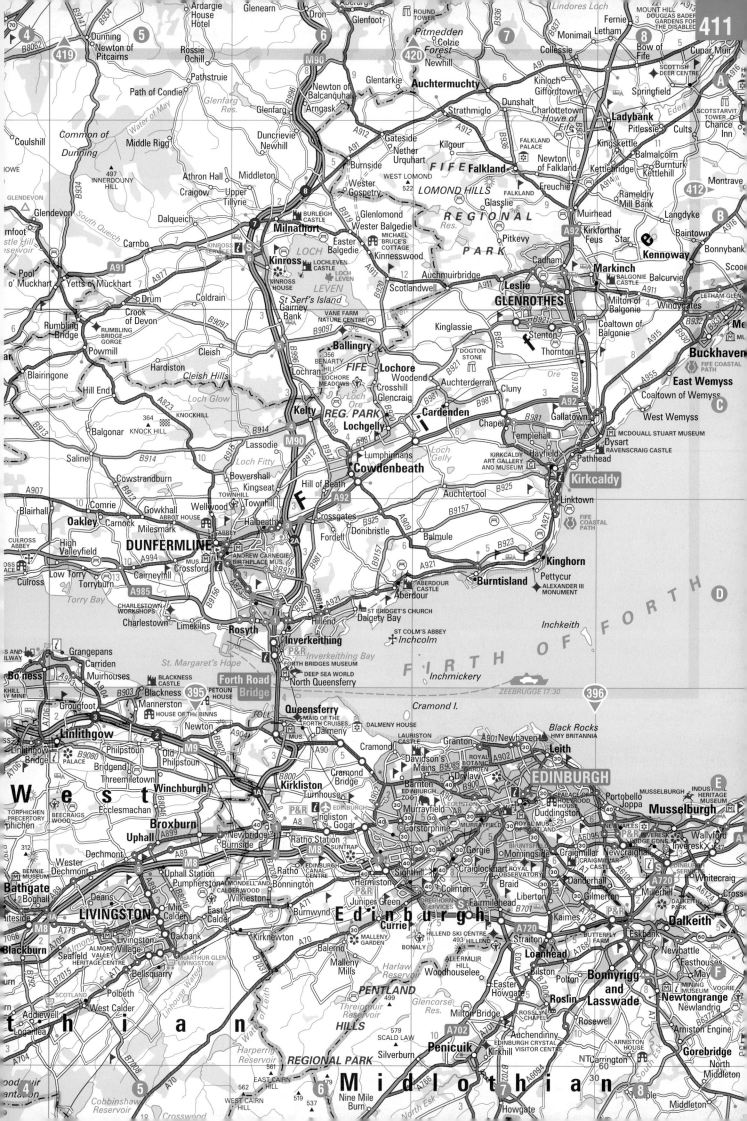

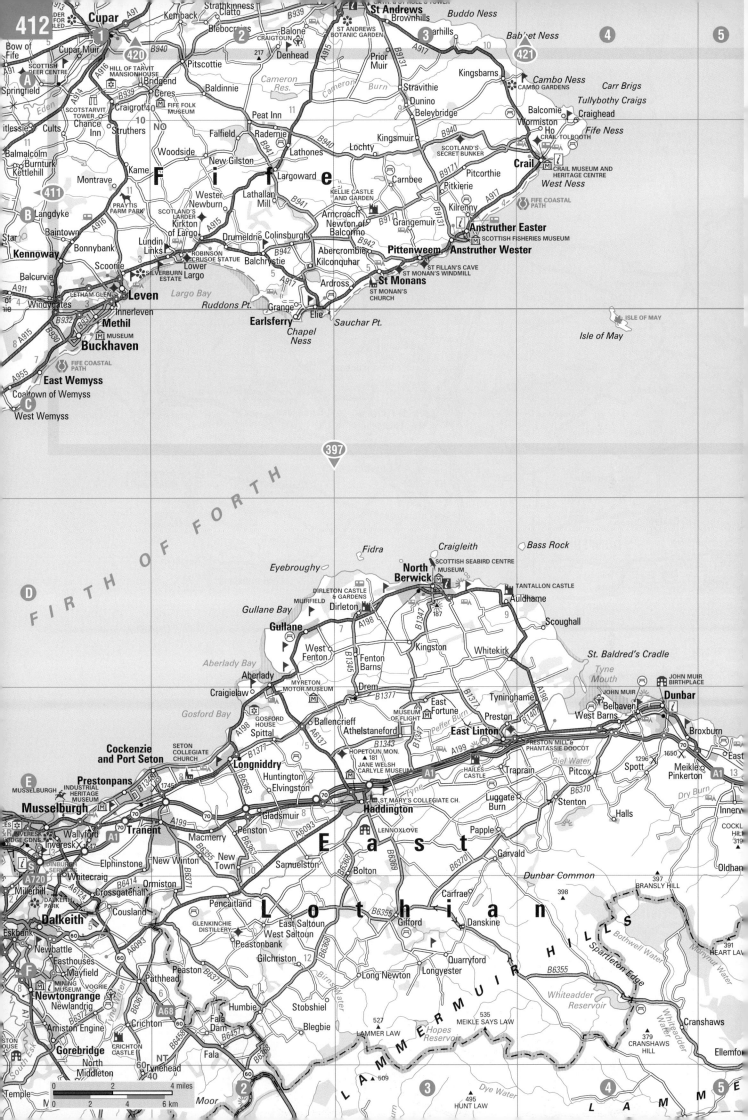

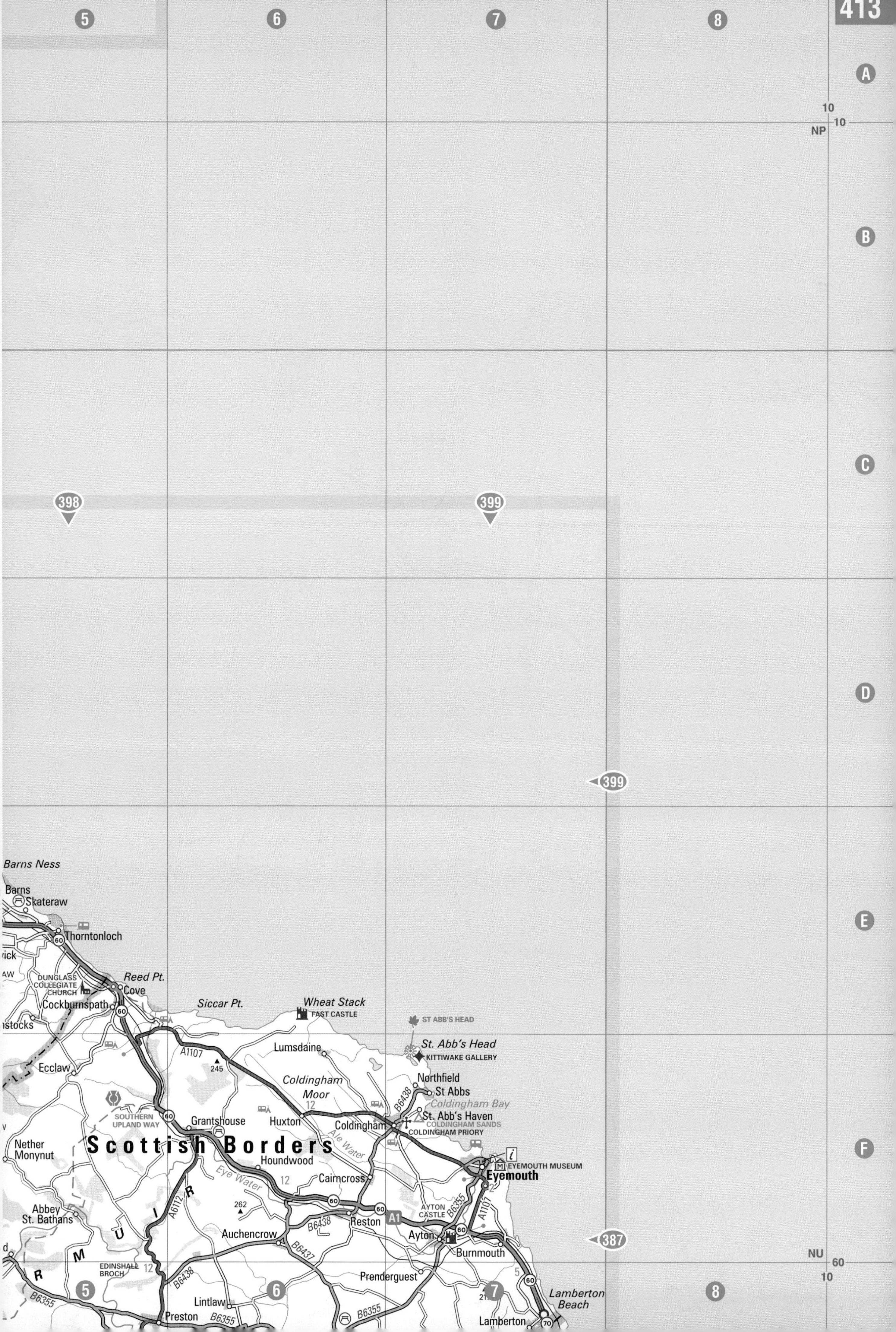

⑤ ⑥ ⑦ ⑧

Ⓐ

10
10
NP

Ⓑ

Ⓒ

③③⑧ ▽

③⑨⑨ ▽

Ⓓ

◁③⑨⑨

Ⓔ

*Barns Ness*

Barns
🏕 Skateraw

Thorntonloch

*Reed Pt.*
DUNGLASS
COLLEGIATE
CHURCH
Cove
Cockburnspath
*Siccar Pt.*
*Wheat Stack*
FAST CASTLE

🍁 ST ABB'S HEAD

Ecclaw
A1107
245
*Lumsdaine*
St. Abb's Head
◆ KITTIWAKE GALLERY

*Coldingham*
*Moor*
12
Northfield
B6438 St Abbs
*Coldingham Bay*
St. Abb's Haven
COLDINGHAM SANDS

SOUTHERN
UPLAND WAY
Grantshouse
Huxton
Coldingham
COLDINGHAM PRIORY

*Nether*
*Monynut*
# Scottish Borders
Houndwood
EYEMOUTH MUSEUM
*ℹ*
Ⓕ

*Eye Water*
12
Cairncross
Eyemouth

Abbey
St. Bathans
262
A6112
AYTON
CASTLE
Reston
A1
Ayton
B6438
◁③⑧⑦
60

EDINSHALL
BROCH
12
B6438
Prenderguest
Burnmouth
NU
60
10

⑤ ⑥ ⑦ ⑧
B6355
Lintlaw
B6437
B6355
*Lamberton*
*Beach*
Preston
Lamberton

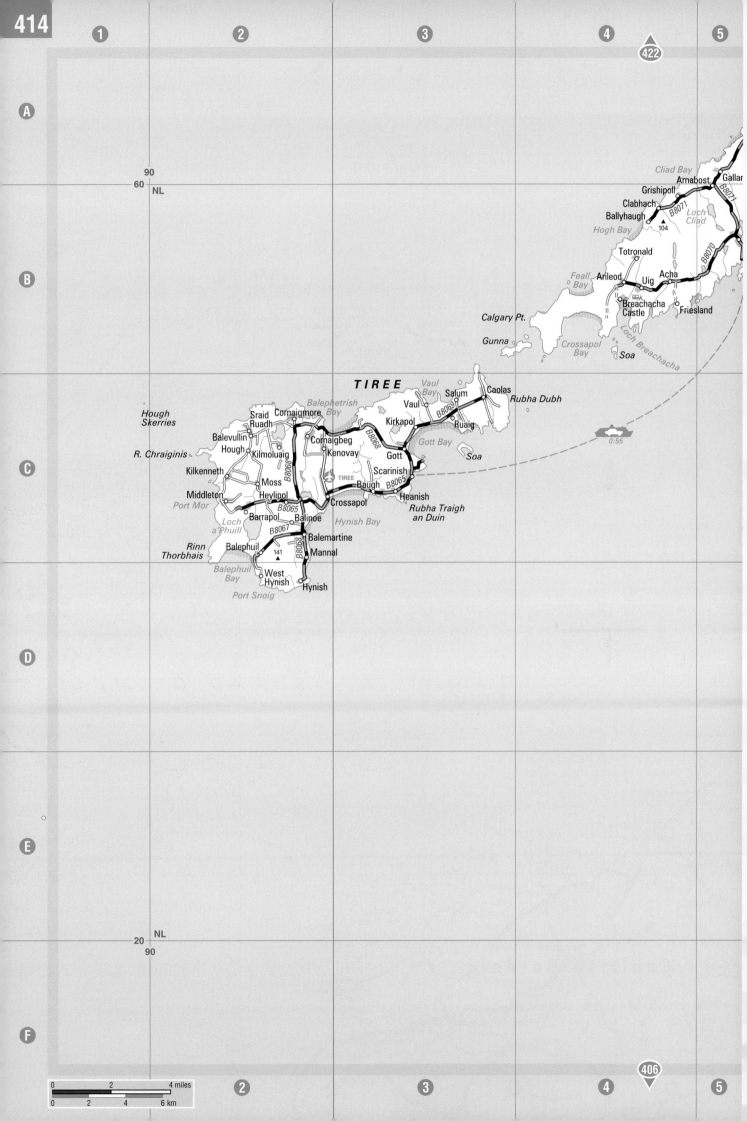

TIREE

Hough Skerries
Sraid Ruadh
Cornaigmore
Cornaigbeg
Balevullin
Hough
Kilmoluaig
Kenovay
R. Chraiginis
Kilkenneth
Moss
TIREE
Middleton
Heylipol
Baugh
Barrapol
Balinoe
Crossapol
Balephuil
Balemartine
Mannal
West Hynish
Hynish
Rinn Thorbhais
141

Vaul Bay
Salum
Vaul
Caolas
Rubha Dubh
Kirkapol
Ruaig
Gott
Gott Bay
Scarinish
Soa
Heanish
Rubha Traigh an Duin

Balephetrish Bay
B8068
B8069
B8065
B8067
B8068
B8065

Loch a'Phuill
Port Mor
Hynish Bay
Balephuil Bay
Port Snoig

Cliad Bay
Arnabost
Gallan
Grishipoll
Clabhach
Ballyhaugh
Loch Cliad
104
Hogh Bay
Totronald
Arileod
Uig
Acha
Feall Bay
Breachacha Castle
Friesland
Calgary Pt.
Gunna
Crossapol Bay
Soa
Loch Breachacha
B8071
B8070

422

90
60
NL

20
NL
90

0:55

406

0    2    4 miles
0   2    4    6 km

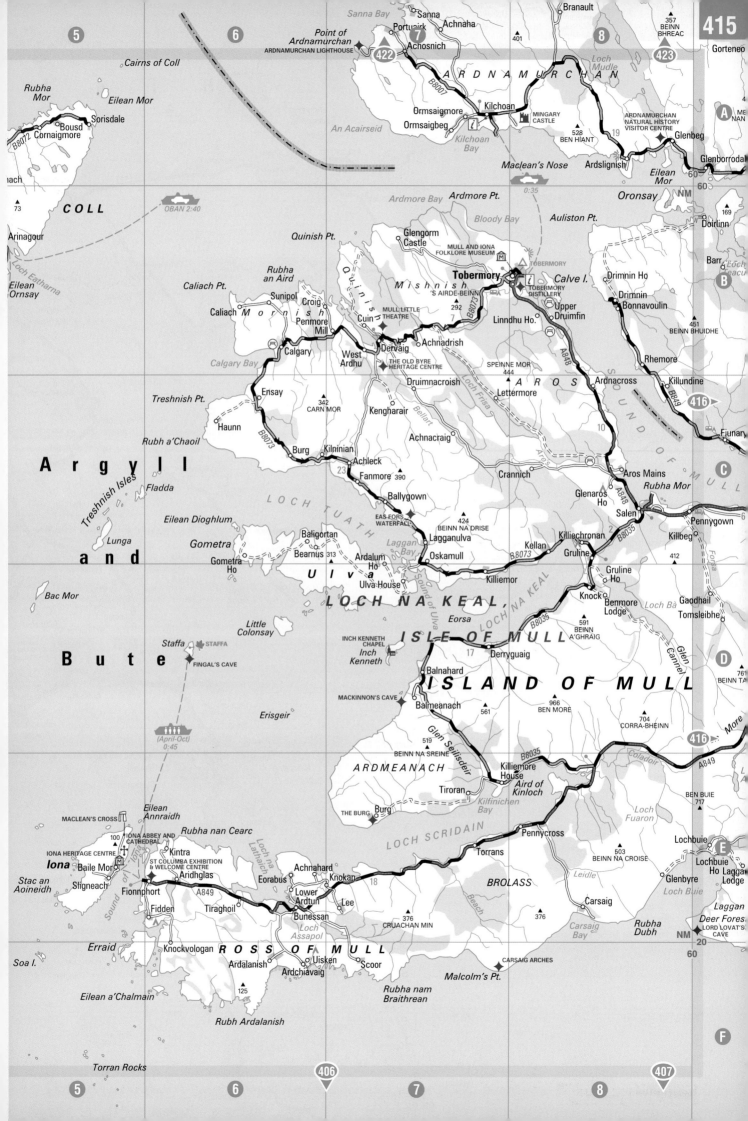

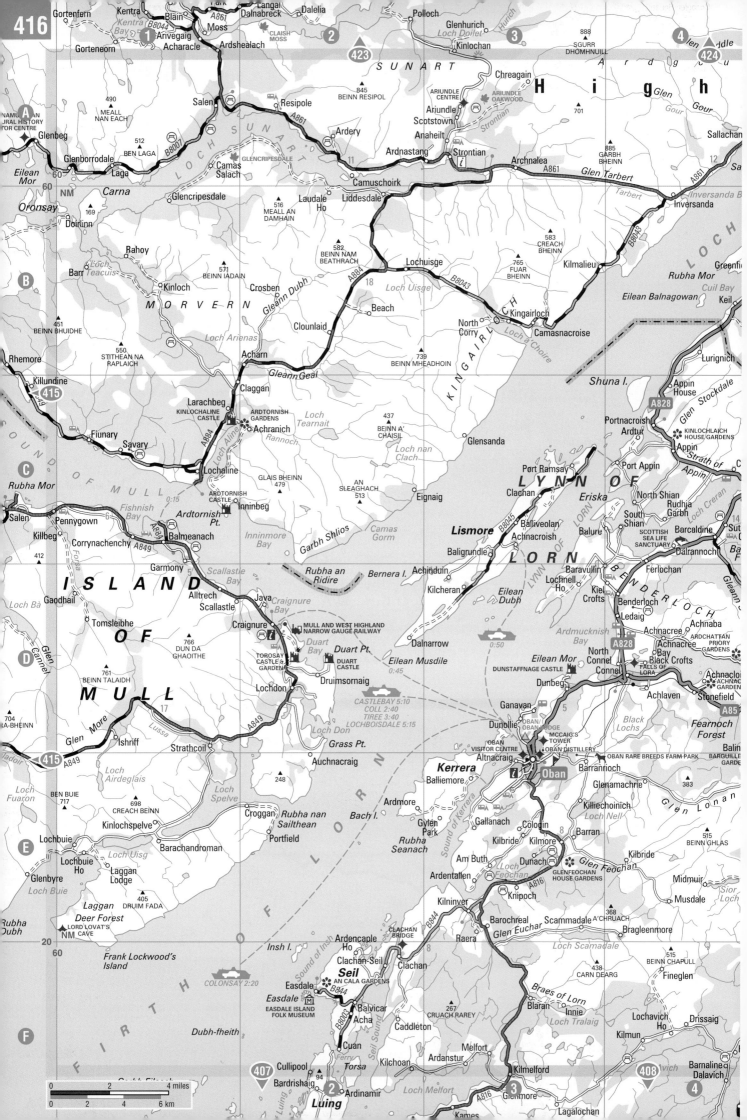

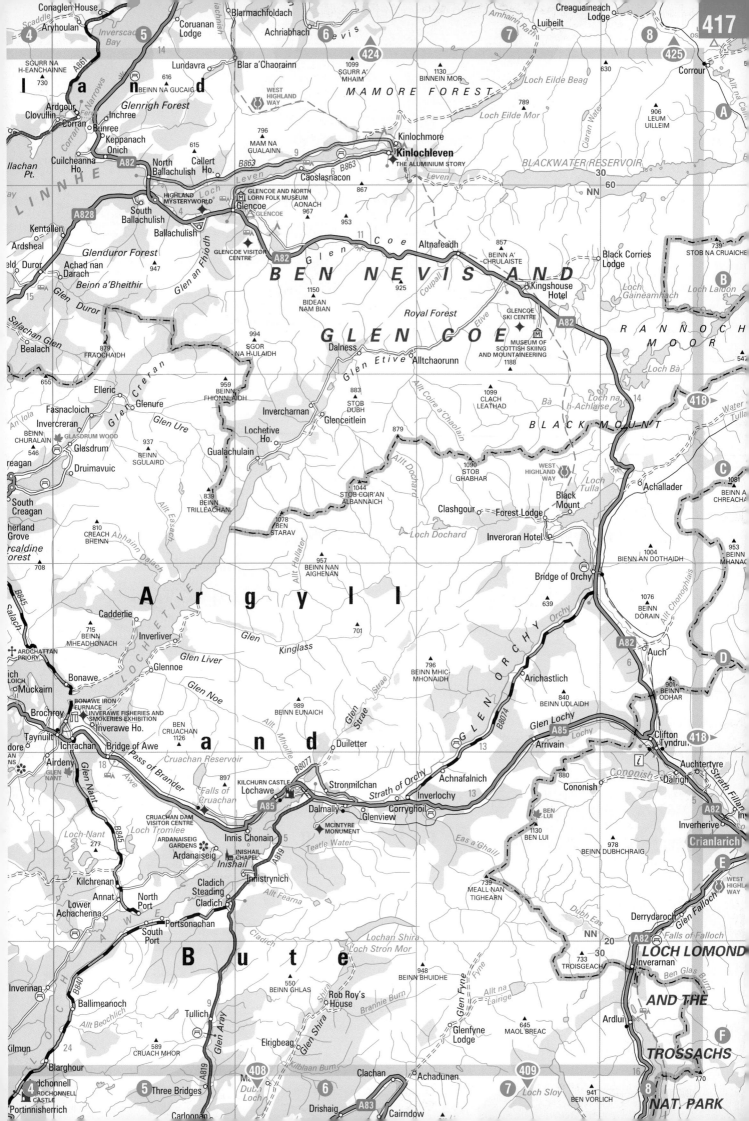

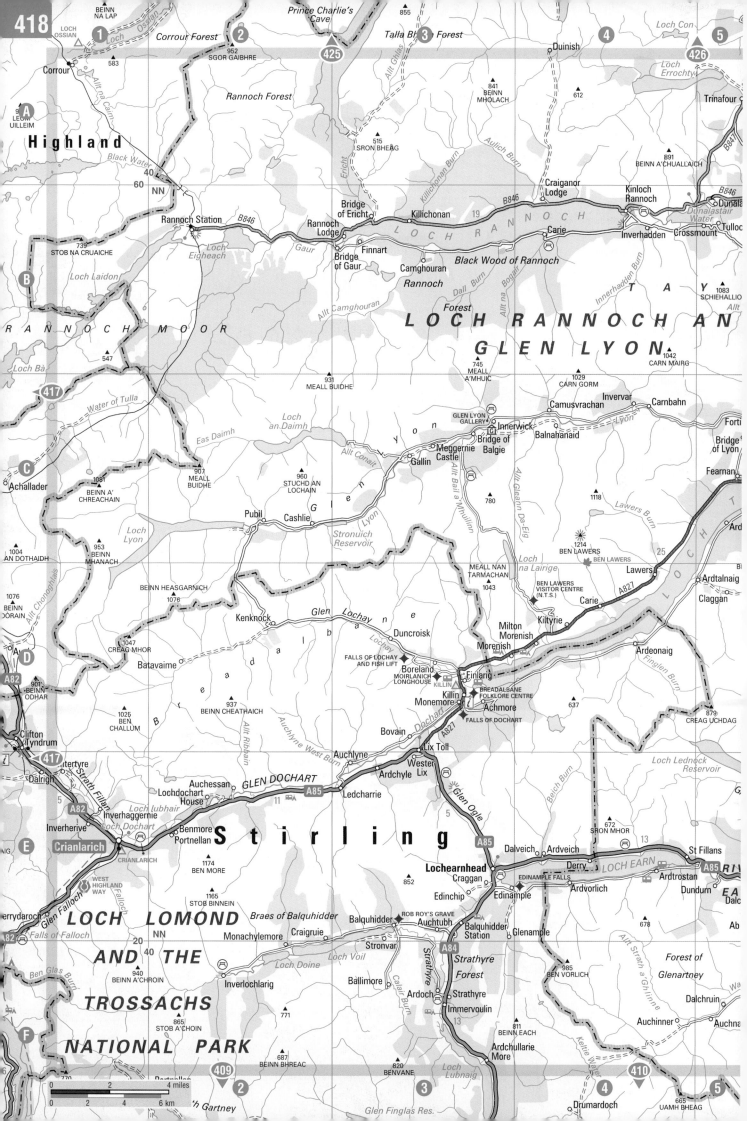

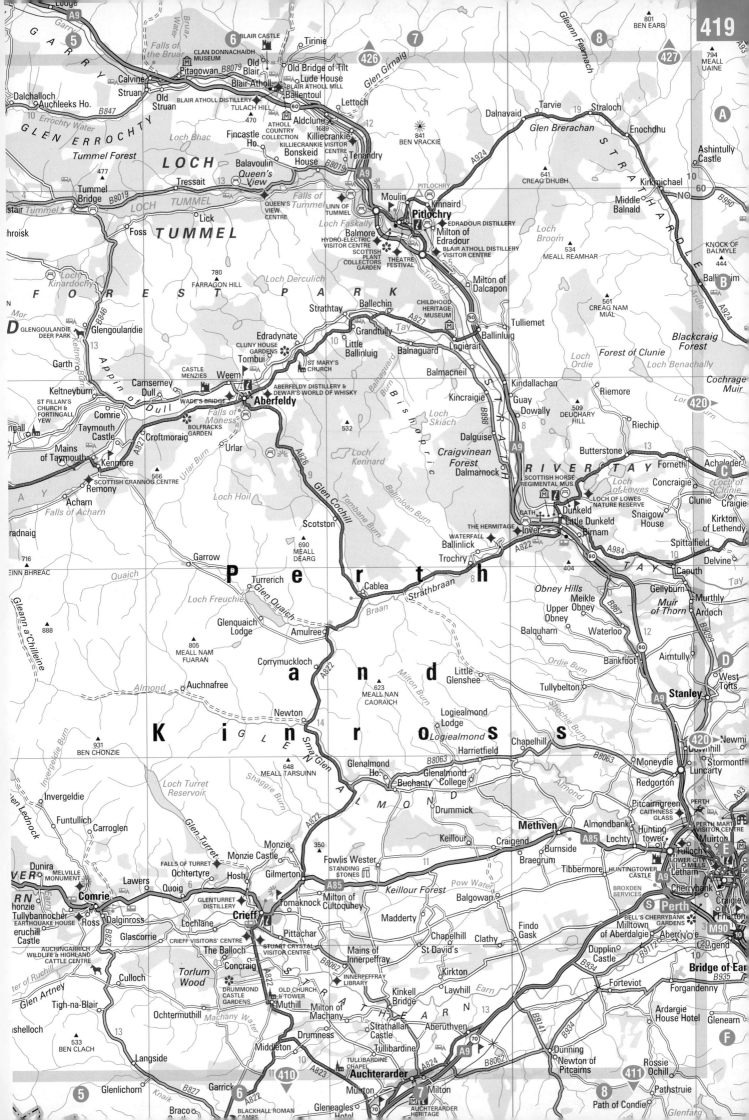

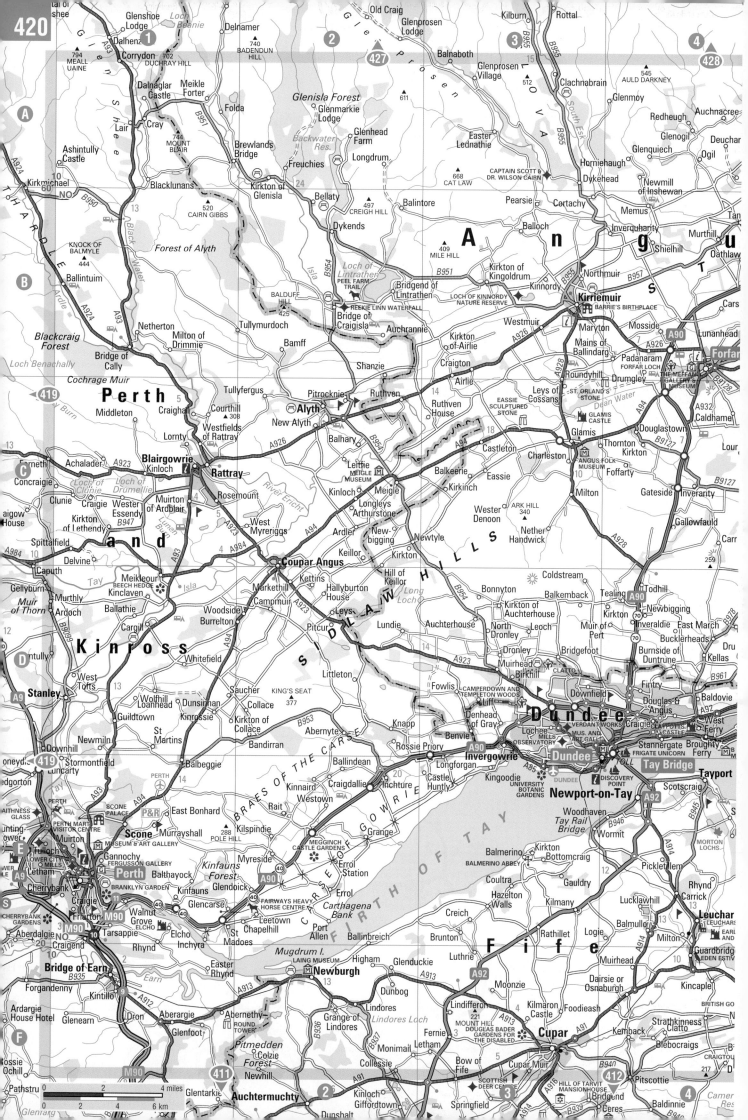

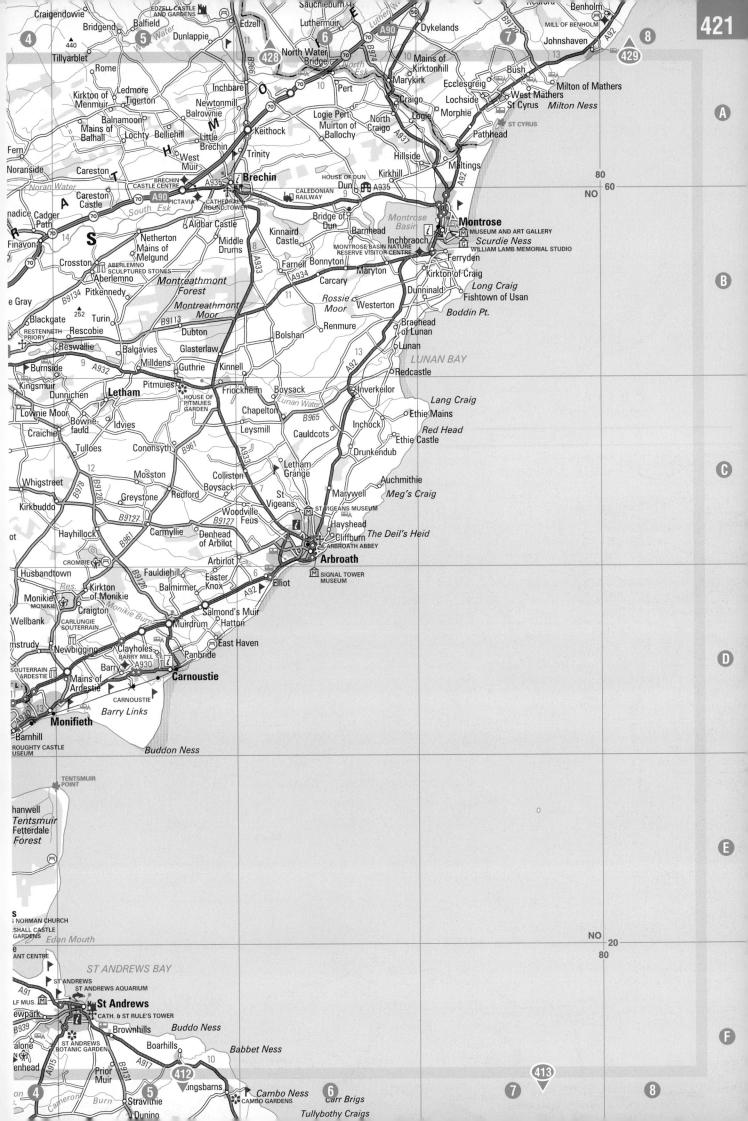

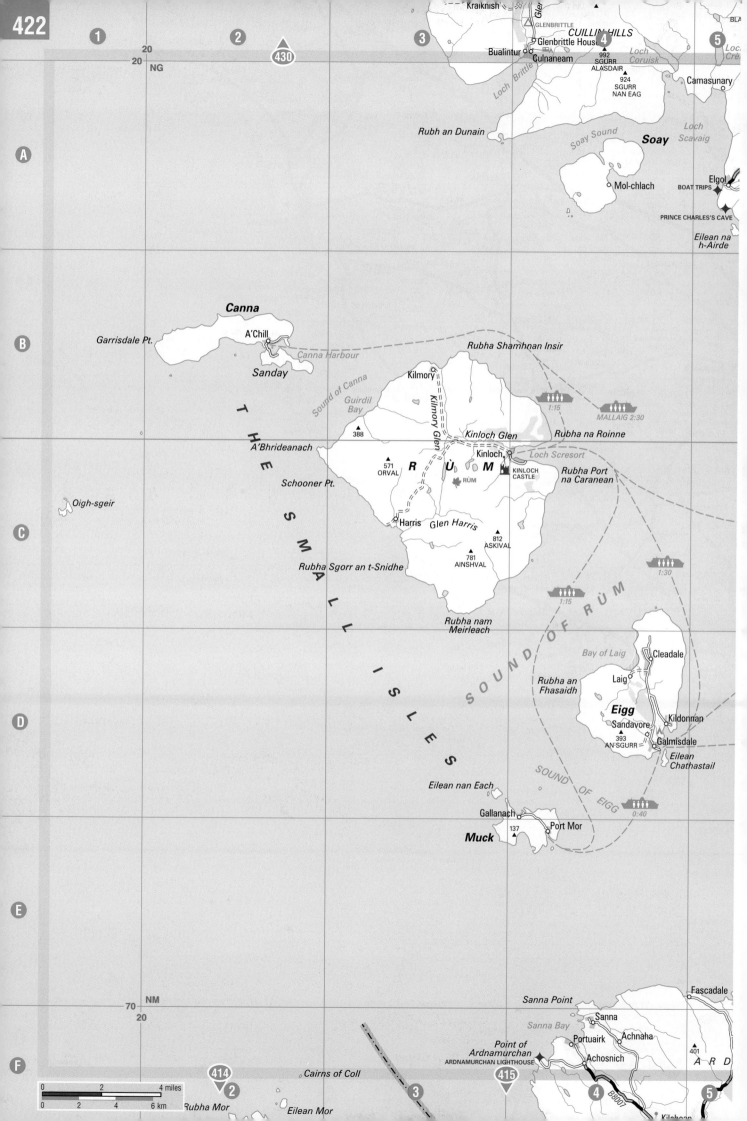

① ② ③ ④ ⑤

**NG**

Kraiknish
CUILLIN HILLS
Glenbrittle
Glenbrittle House
Bualintur
Culnaneam
992 SGURR ALASDAIR
Loch Coruisk
924 SGURR NAN EAG
Camasunary
Loch Scavaig
Rubh an Dunain
Soay Sound
**Soay**
Mol-chlach
BOAT TRIPS
Elgol
PRINCE CHARLES'S CAVE
Eilean na h-Airde

A

**Canna**
Garrisdale Pt.
A'Chill
Canna Harbour
*Sanday*
Rubha Shamhnan Insir
Kilmory
Sound of Canna
Guirdil Bay
1:15
MALLAIG 2:30
388
Kinloch Glen
Kinloch
Loch Scresort
Rubha na Roinne
A'Bhrideanach
571 ORVAL
R Ù M
RÙM
KINLOCH CASTLE
Kinloch Castle
Rubha Port na Caranean
Schooner Pt.
Harris
Glen Harris
812 ASKIVAL
1:30
Rubha Sgorr an t-Snidhe
781 AINSHVAL
Oigh-sgeir
1:15

B

T H E   S M A L L   I S L E S

C

S O U N D   O F   R Ù M

Rubha nam Meirleach
Bay of Laig
Cleadale
Rubha an Fhasaidh
Laig
**Eigg**
Kildonnan
Sandavore
393 AN-SGURR
Galmisdale
Eilean Chathastail
Eilean nan Each
SOUND OF EIGG
0:40
Gallanach
137
Port Mor
**Muck**

D

E

**NM**

Fascadale
Sanna Point
Sanna
Sanna Bay
Portuairk
Achnaha
401
A R D
Point of Ardnamurchan
ARDNAMURCHAN LIGHTHOUSE
Achosnich
B8007
Cairns of Coll
Rubha Mor
Eilean Mor
Kilchoan

F

0   2   4 miles
0   2   4   6 km

① ② ③ ④ ⑤
430
414 ②
415 ④

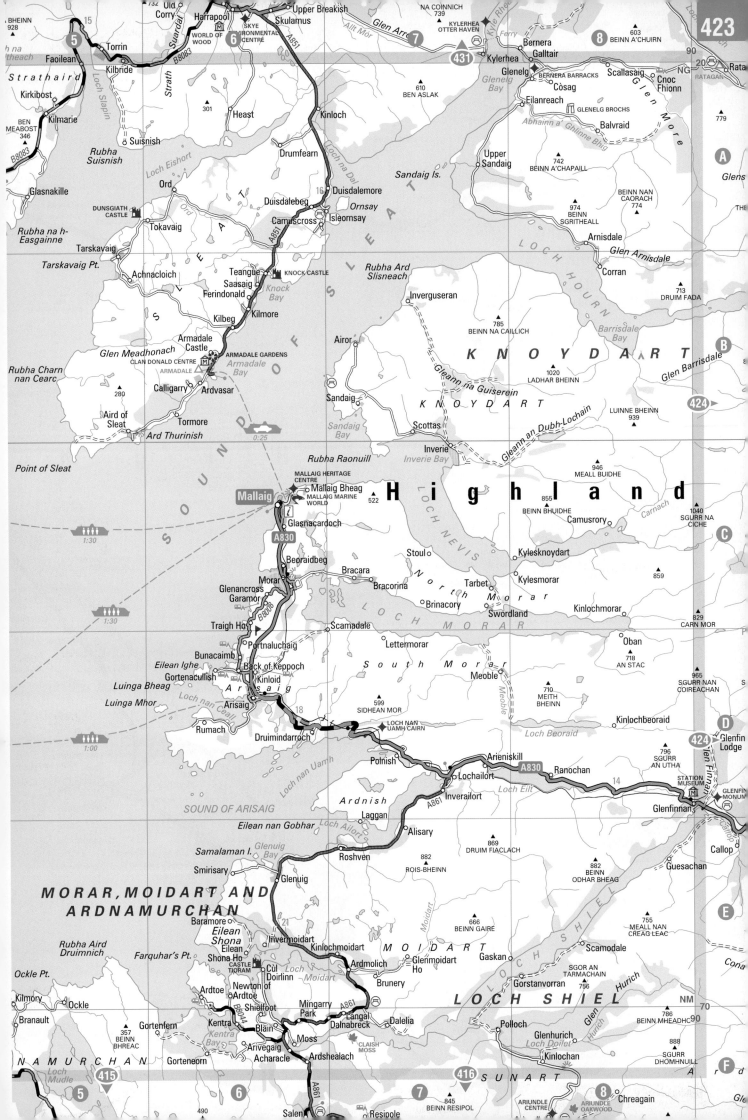

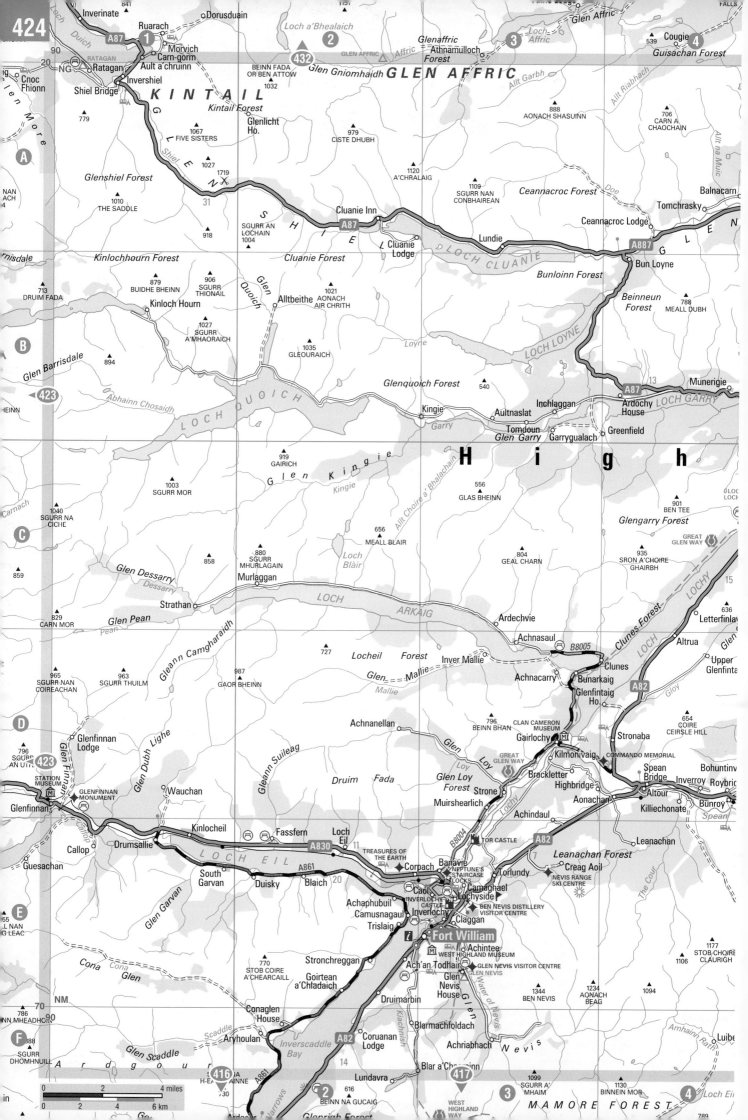

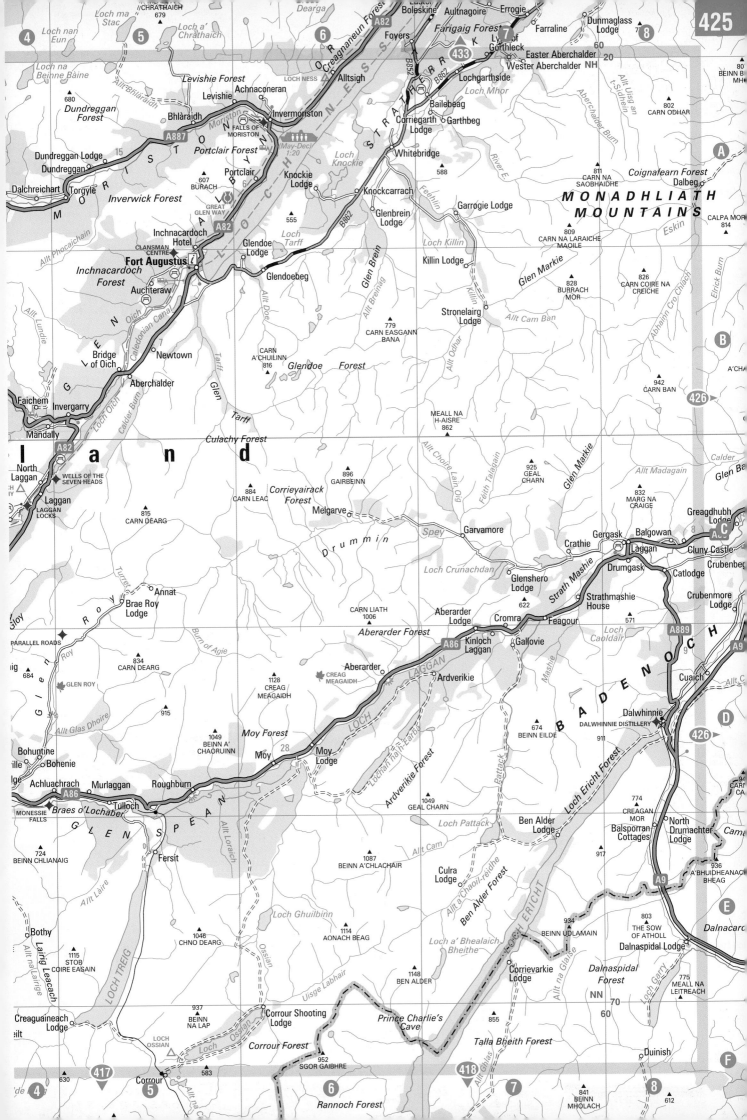

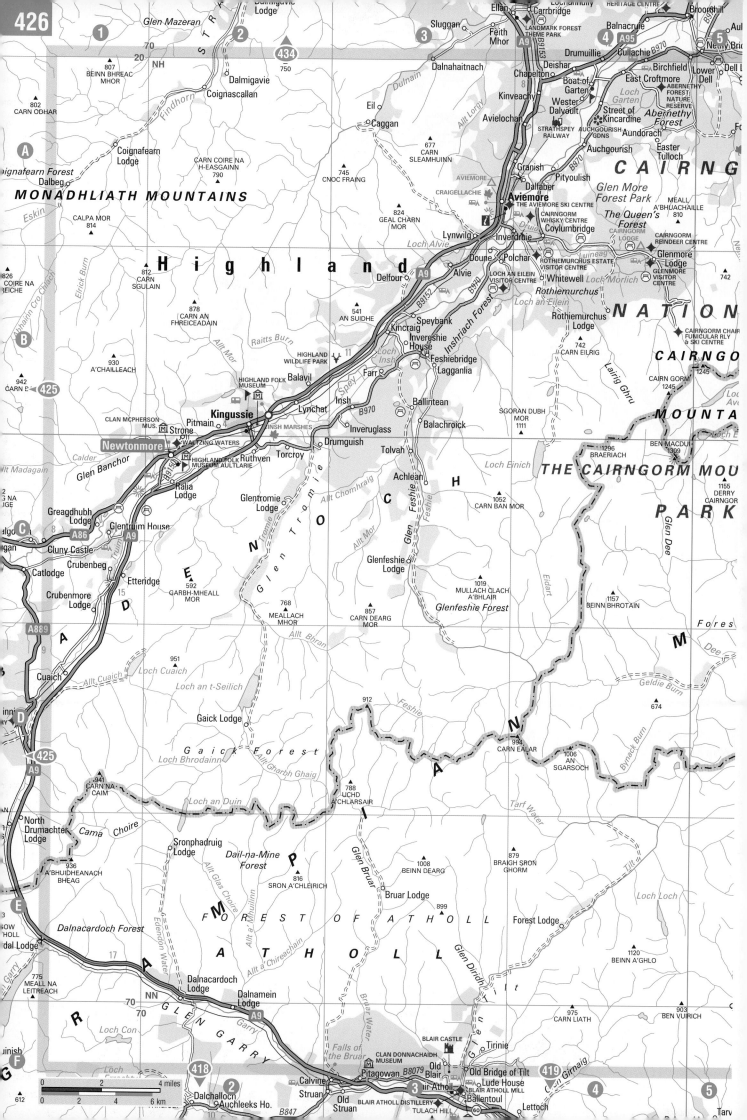

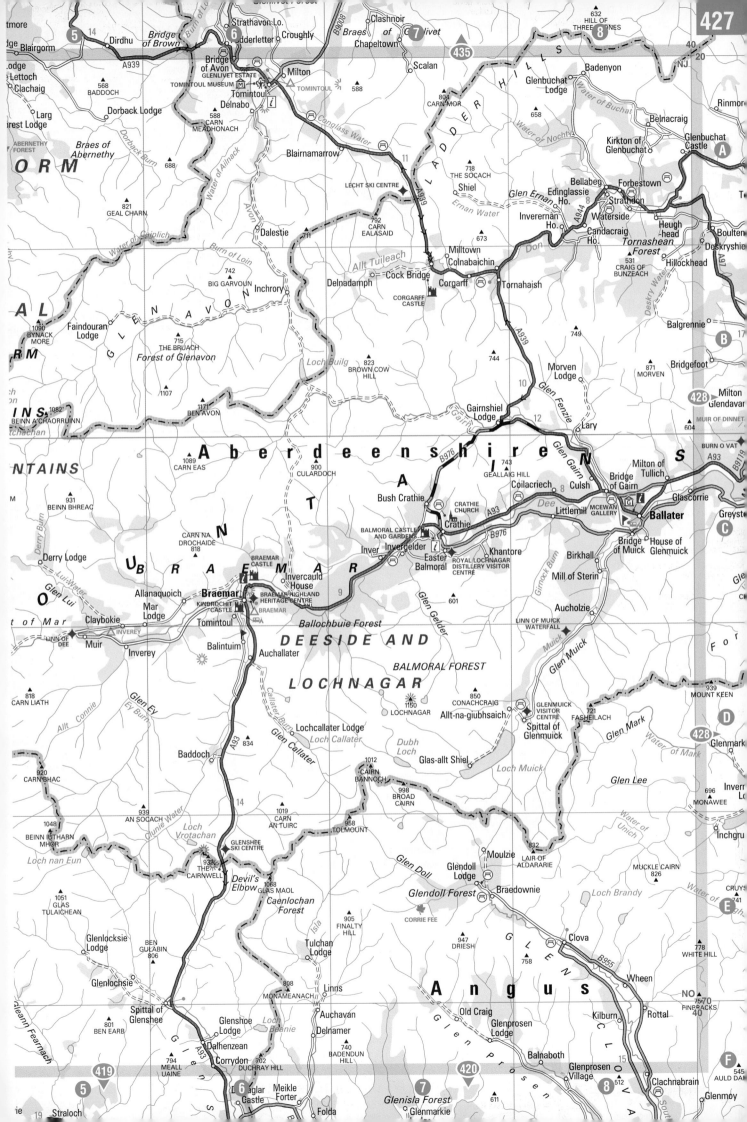

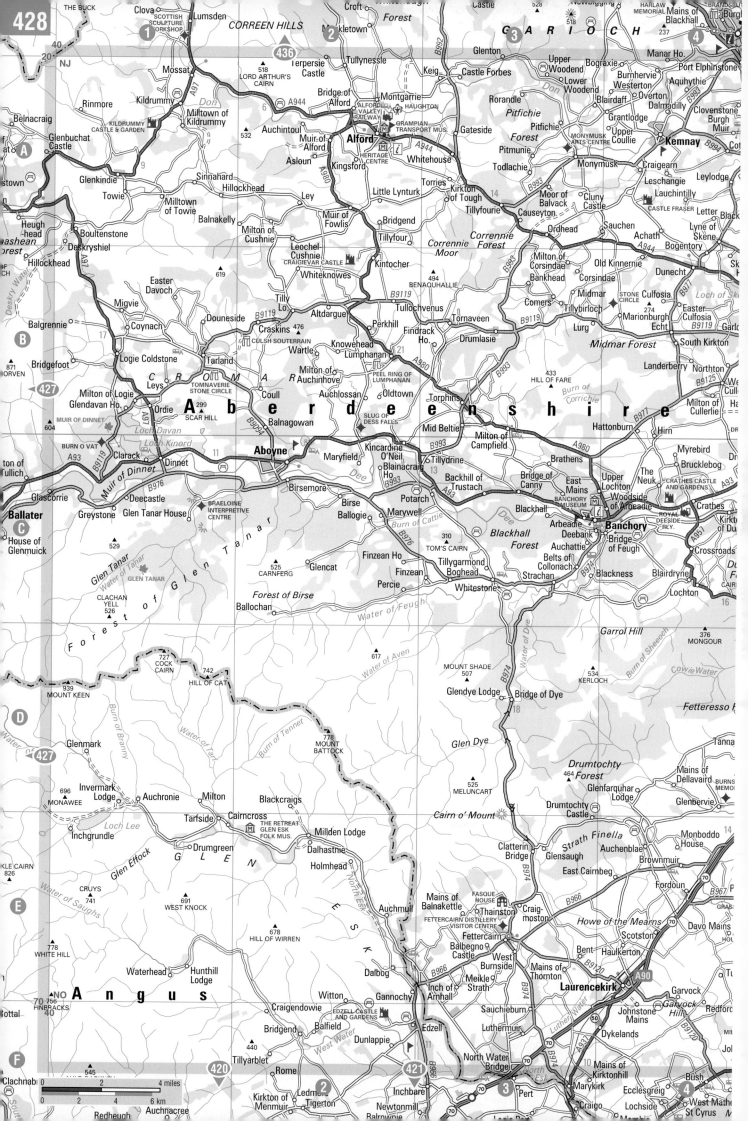

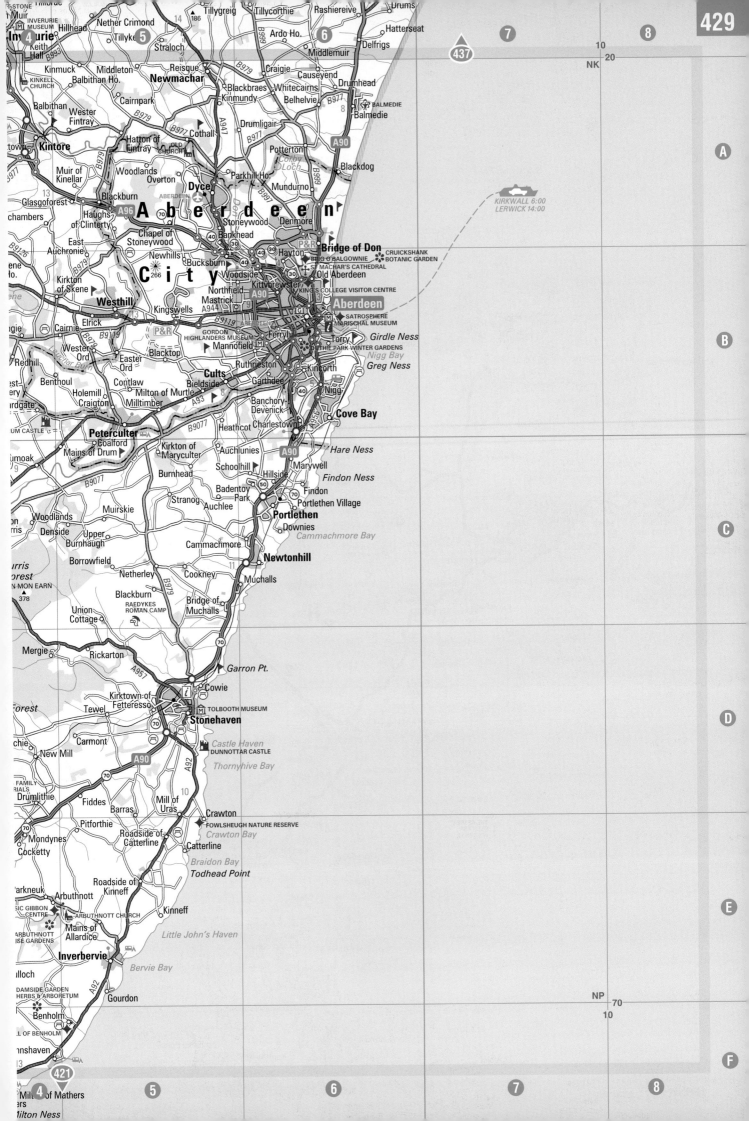

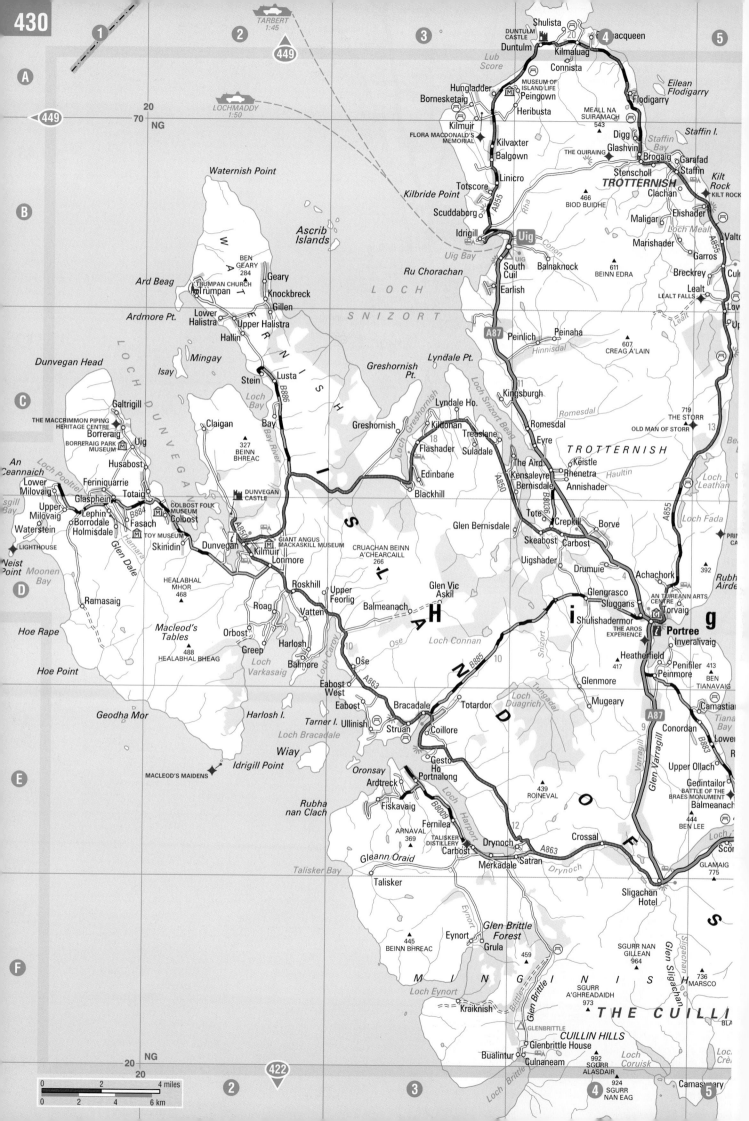

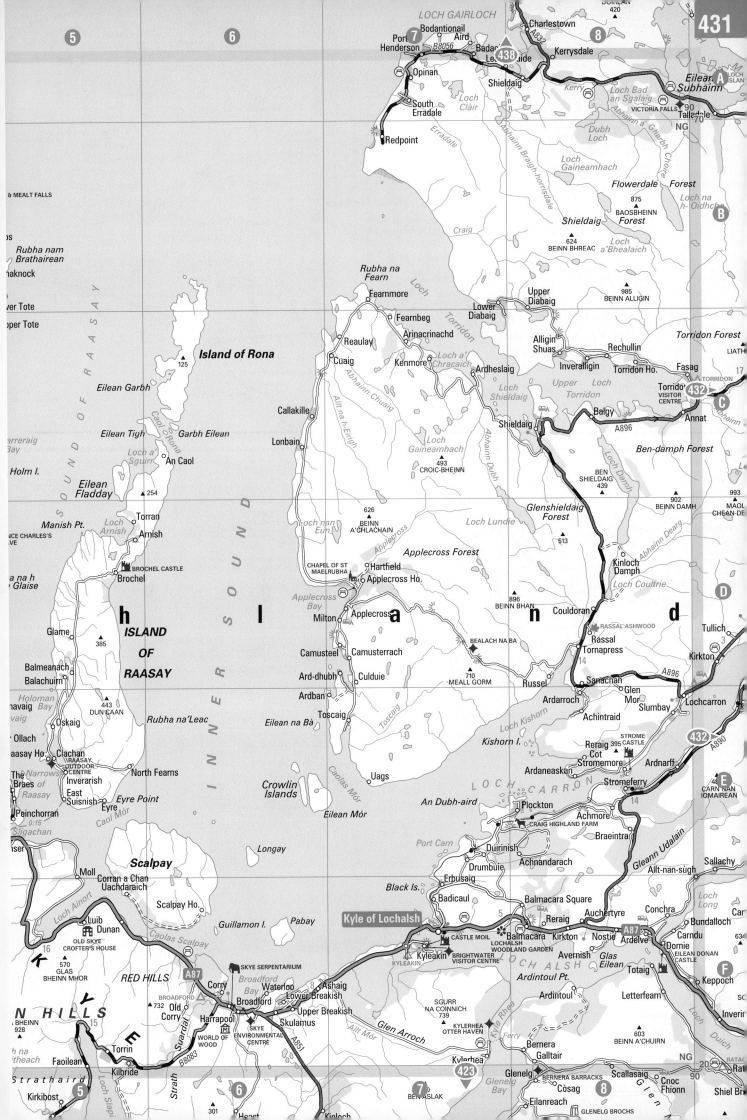

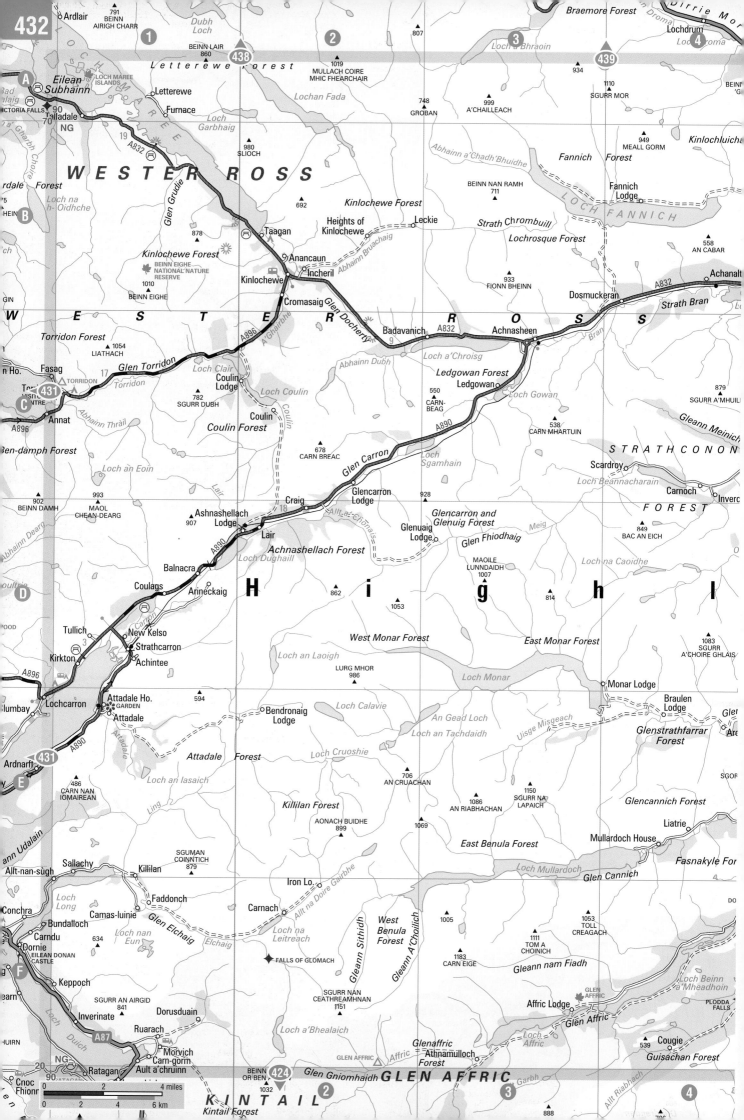

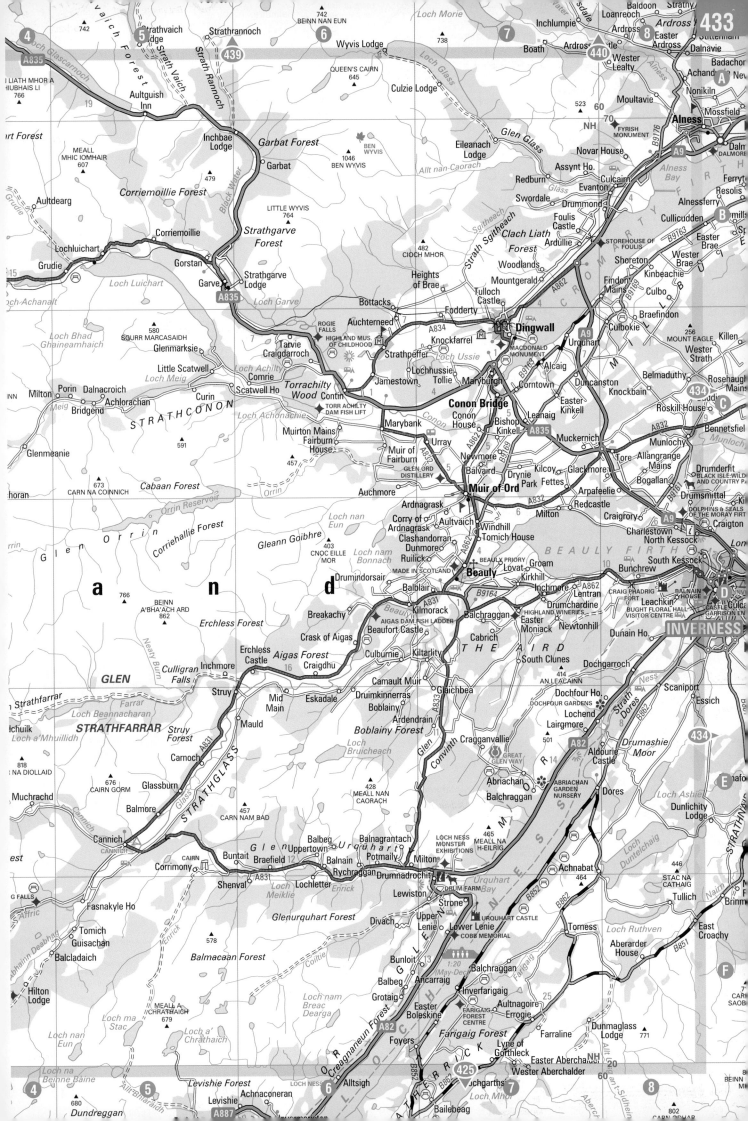

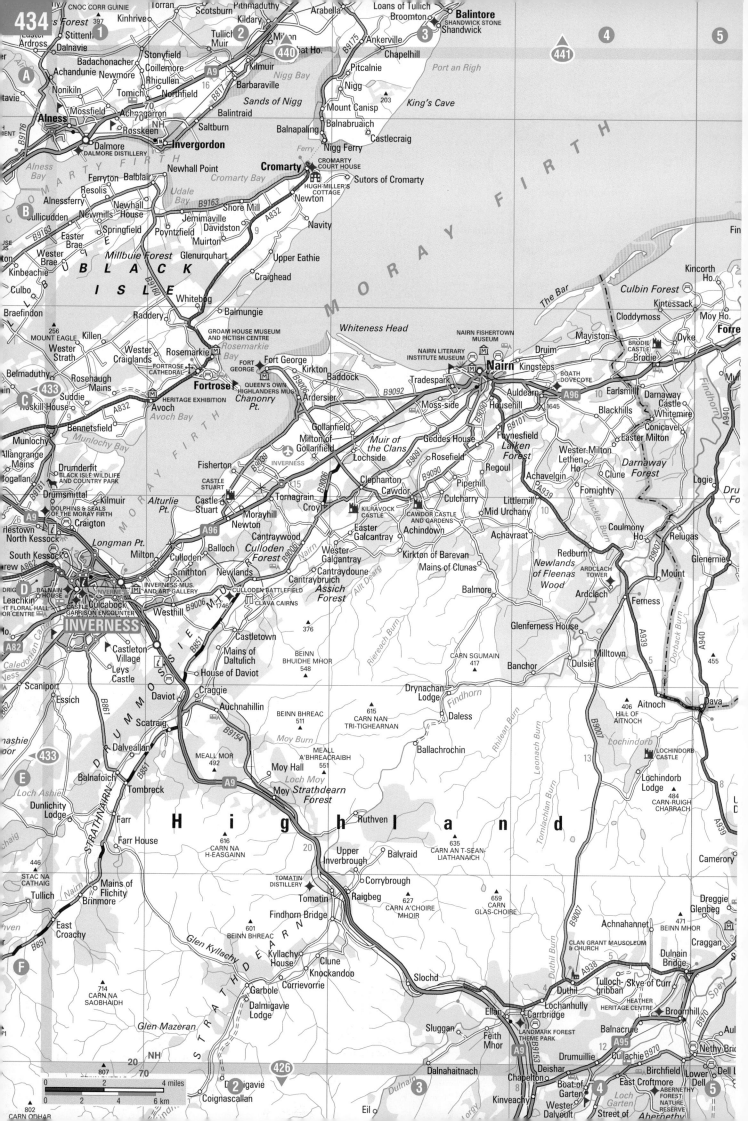

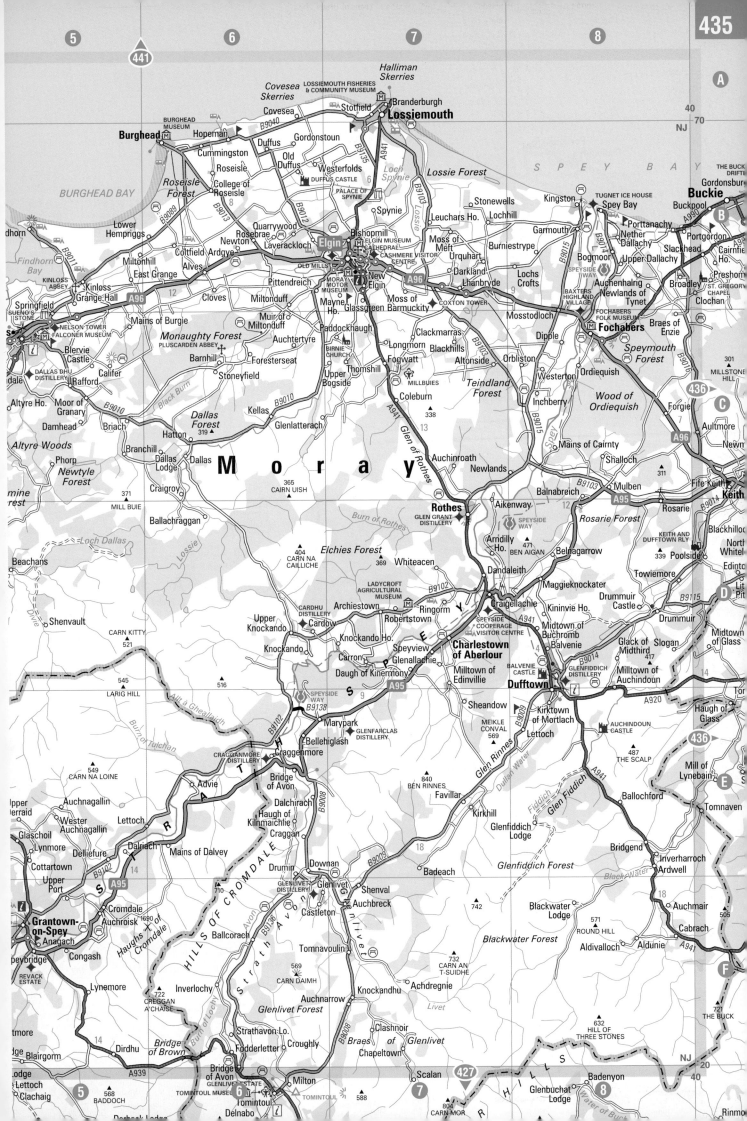

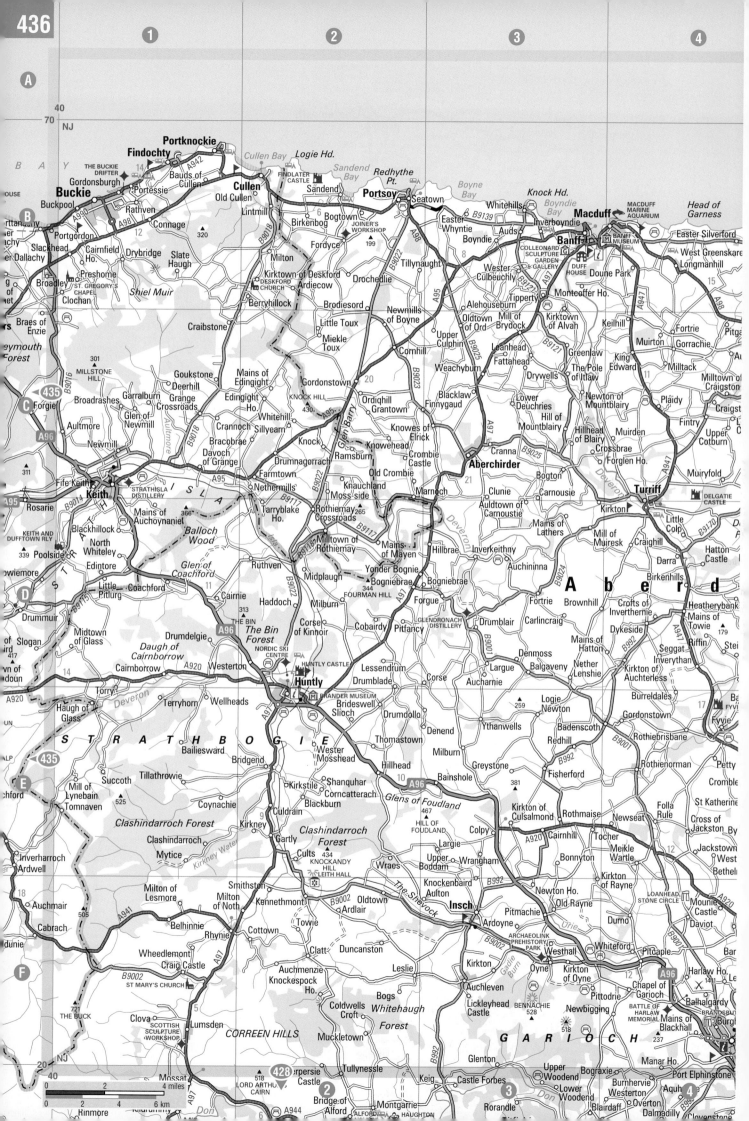

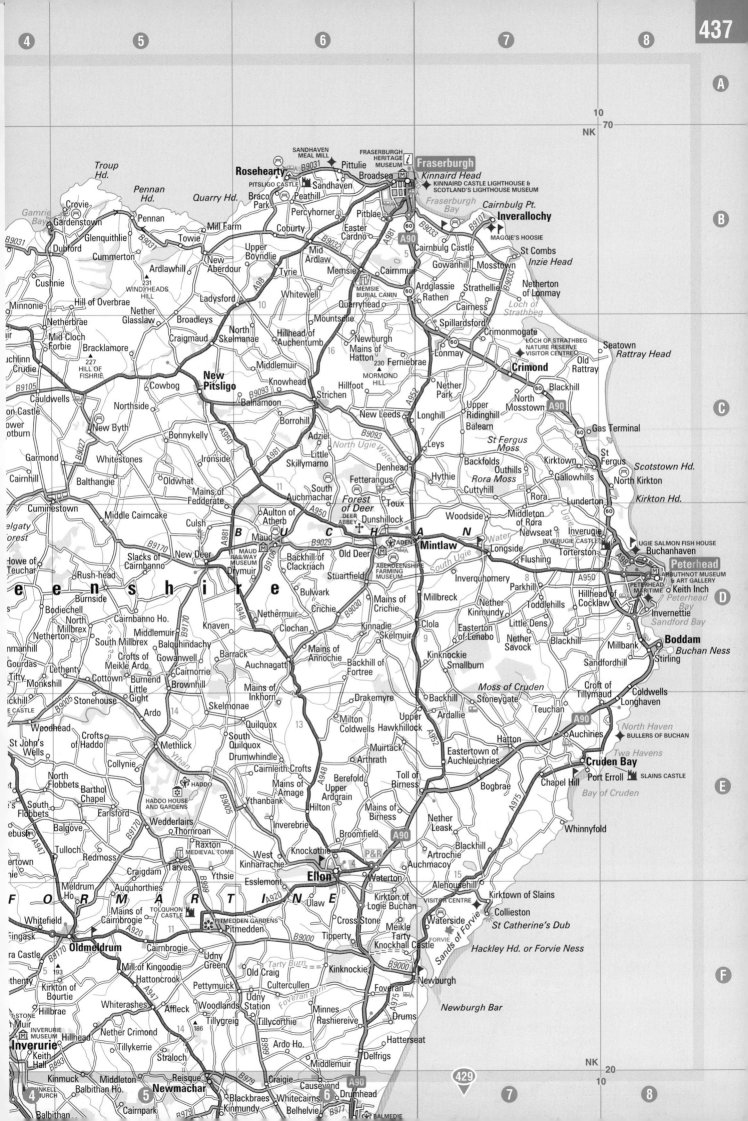

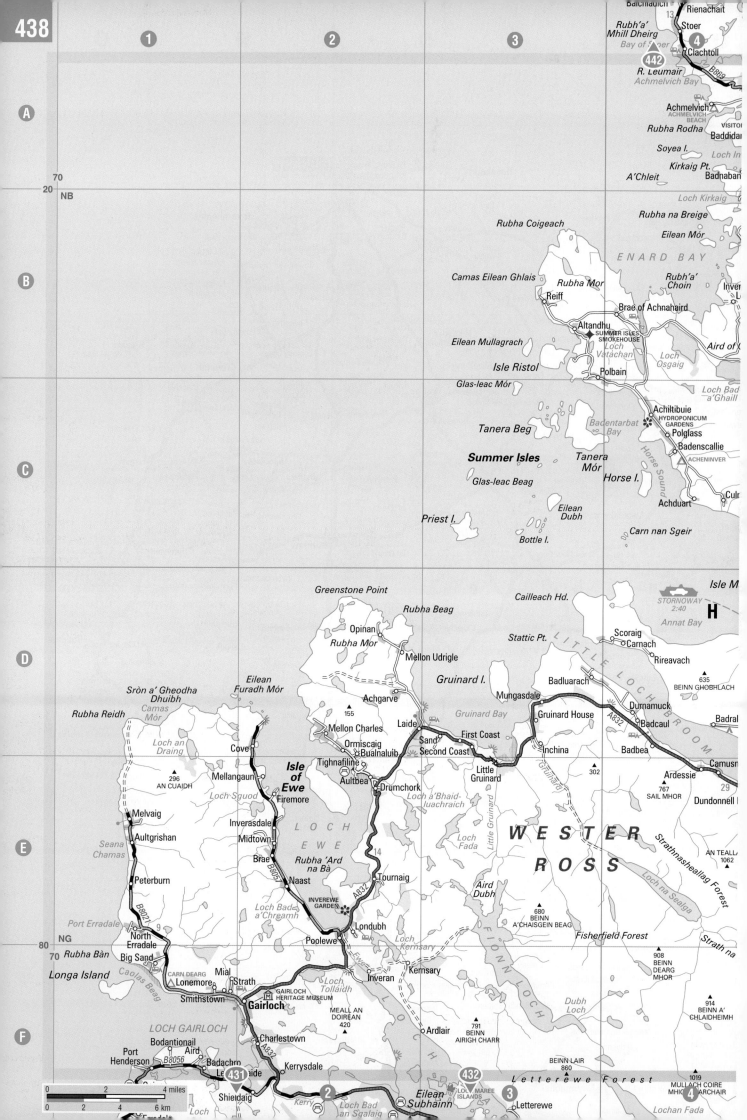

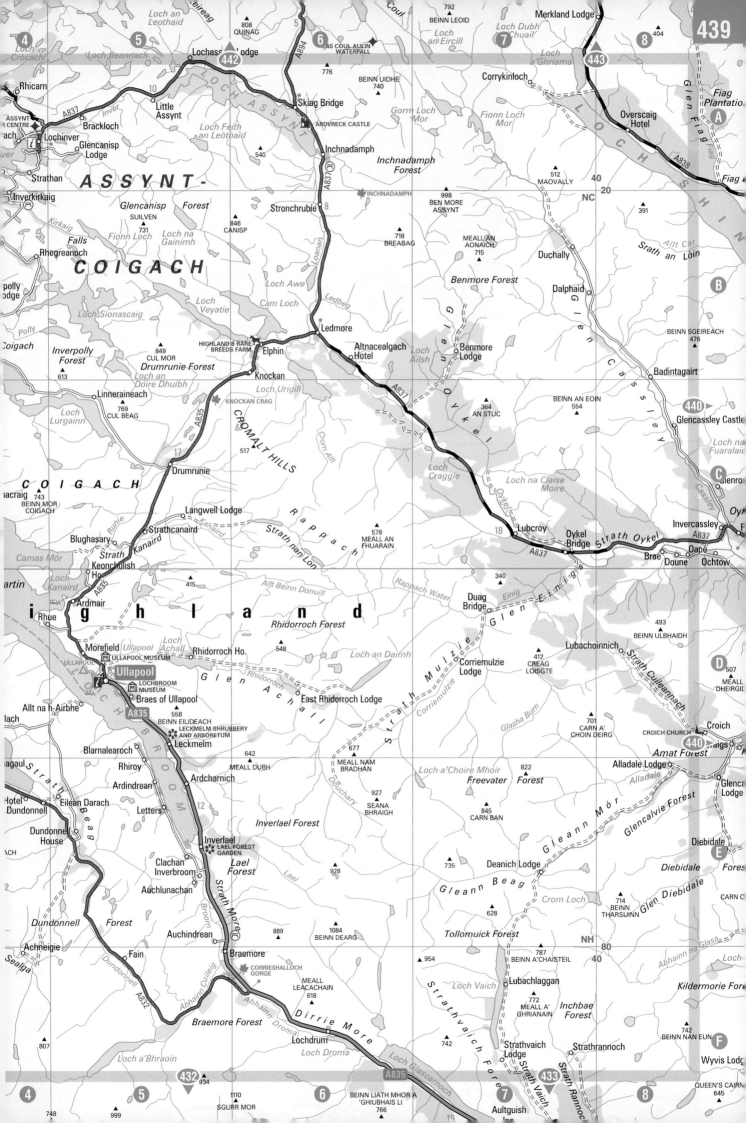

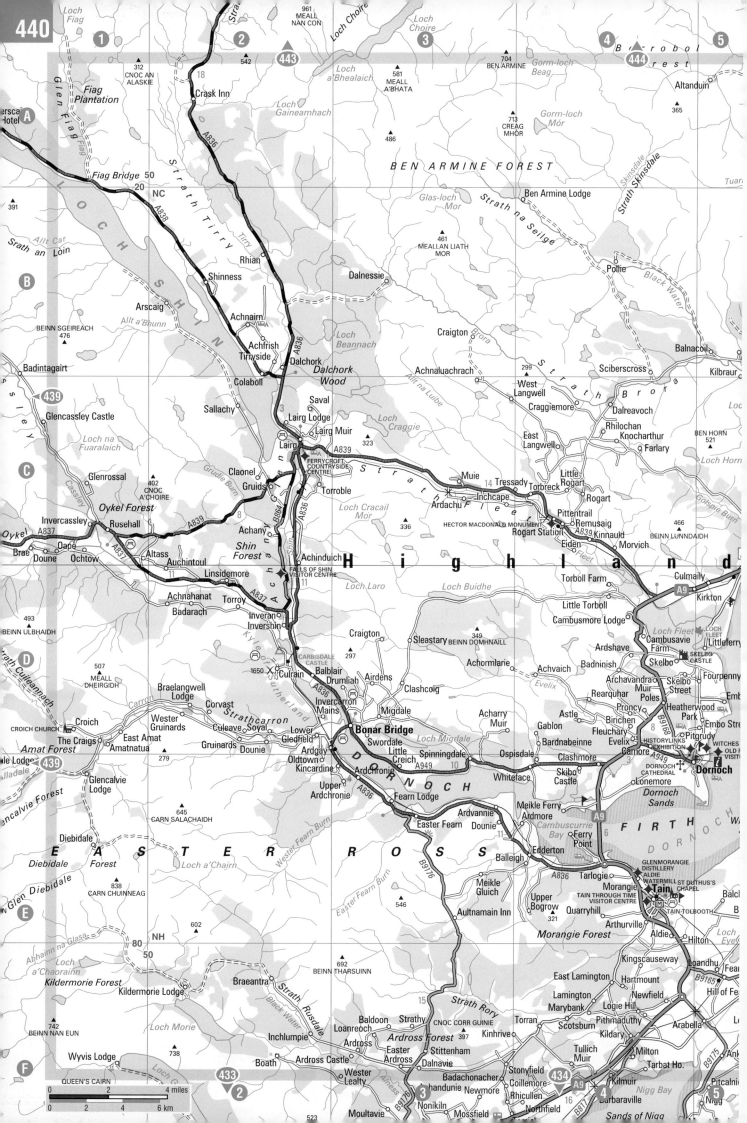

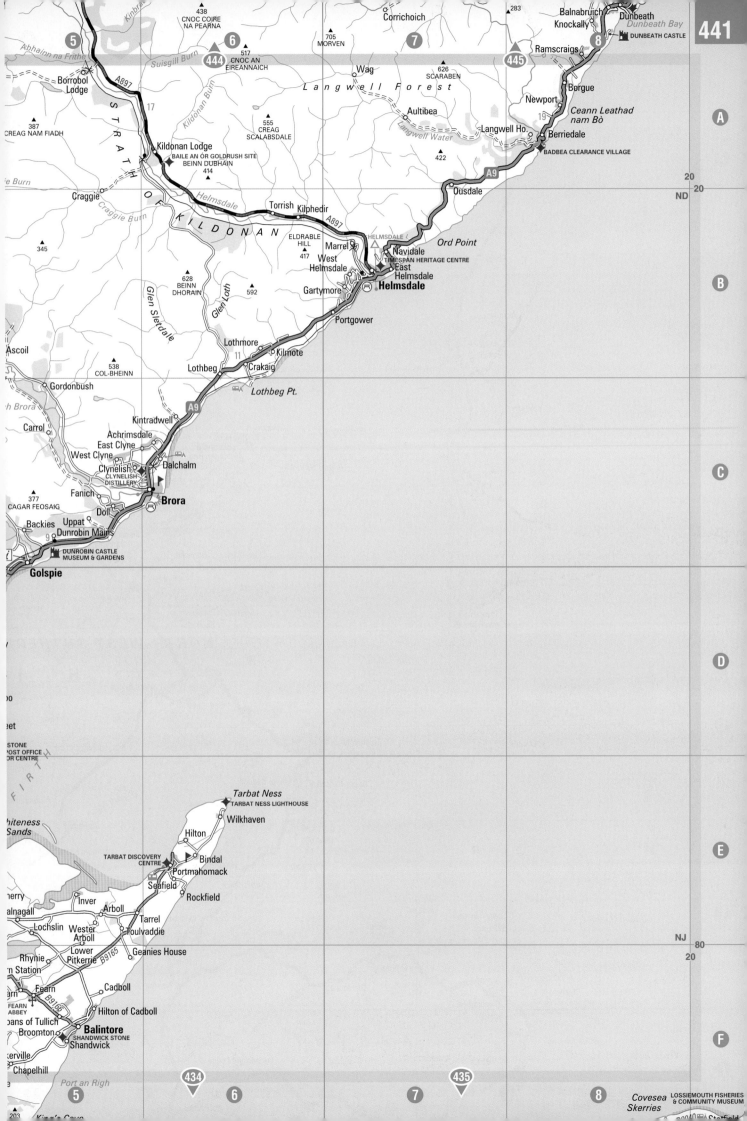

**5** **6** **444** CNOC AN EIREANNAICH **7** **445** **8**

438
CNOC COIRE
NA PEARNA
517
CNOC AN
EIREANNAICH

Balnabruich
Knockally
Dunbeath
Dunbeath Bay
DUNBEATH CASTLE

Corrichoich
283

705
MORVEN

Ramscraigs

Suisgill Burn
A897

Abhainn na Frithe

Borrobol
Lodge

Wag

L a n g w e l l   F o r e s t

Newport
19
Borgue

Ceann Leathad
nam Bò

17

387
CREAG NAM FIADH

Kildonan Burn

626
SCARABEN

Aultibea

Langwell Water

Langwell Ho.

Berriedale

**A**

20
20
ND

Kildonan Lodge
BAILE AN ÒR GOLDRUSH SITE
BEINN DUBHAIN
414

555
CREAG
SCALABSDALE

A9
422

BADBEA CLEARANCE VILLAGE

Craggie

Craggie Burn

Helmsdale

Torrish   Kilphedir
A897

Ousdale

S T R A T H   O F   K I L D O N A N

ELDRABLE
HILL
417

Marrel
West
Helmsdale

HELMSDALE
TIMESPAN HERITAGE CENTRE
Navidale
East
Helmsdale

Ord Point

**B**

345

628
BEINN
DHORAIN

592

Gartymore

**Helmsdale**

Glen Sletdale

Glen Loth

Portgower

Ascoil

538
COL-BHEINN

Lothmore

11

Kilmote

Lothbeg

Crakaig

Gordonbush

h Brora

Lothbeg Pt.

A9

**C**

Carrol

Kintradwell

377
CAGAR FEOSAIG

Achrimsdale
East Clyne
West Clyne
Clynelish
CLYNELISH
DISTILLERY

Dalchalm

Fanich
Doll
**Brora**

Backies
9
Uppat
Dunrobin Mains

DUNROBIN CASTLE
MUSEUM & GARDENS

**Golspie**

**D**

STONE
POST OFFICE
OR CENTRE

eet

F I R T H

Tarbat Ness
TARBAT NESS LIGHTHOUSE

Wilkhaven

hiteness
Sands

Hilton

**E**

TARBAT DISCOVERY
CENTRE

Bindal
Portmahomack
Seafield

Rockfield

herry

Inver

Arboll

lnagall

Lochslin
Wester
Arboll

Tarrel
Toulvaddie

Geanies House

NJ
80
20

Rhynie
n Station

Lower
Pitkerrie
B9165

Fearn

Cadboll

FEARN
ABBEY

B9166

Hilton of Cadboll

ans of Tullich
Broomton

**Balintore**

SHANDWICK STONE

Shandwick

**F**

cerville

Chapelhill

Port an Righ

**5** **434** **6** **7** **435** **8**

Covesea
Skerries

LOSSIEMOUTH FISHERIES
& COMMUNITY MUSEUM

203
King's Cave

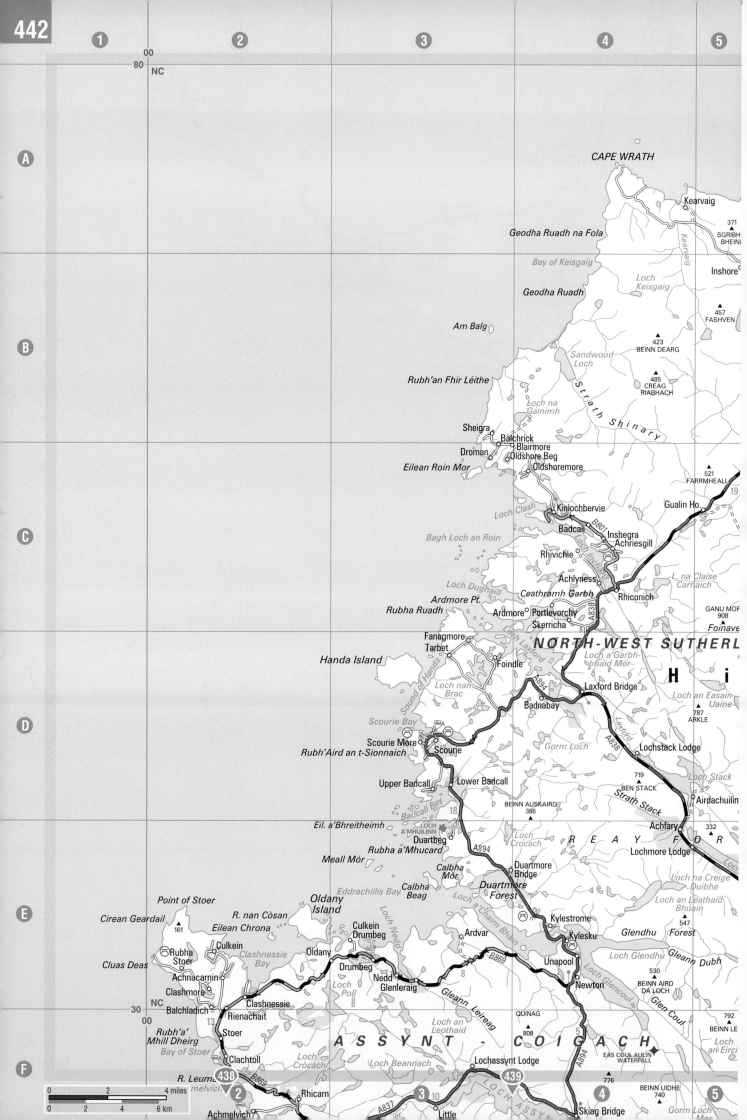

① ② ③ ④ ⑤

00
80 NC

**A**

CAPE WRATH

Kearvaig

371
SGRIBH
BHEINI

Geodha Ruadh na Fola

Bay of Keisgaig

Loch
Keisgaig

Inshore

Geodha Ruadh

457
FASHVEN

**B**

423
BEINN DEARG

Am Balg

485
CREAG
RIABHACH

Rubh'an Fhir Léithe

Loch na
Gáinimh

Sandwood
Loch

Strath Shinary

Sheigra
Balchrick
Blairmore
Droman     Oldshore Beg
Oldshoremore

Eilean Roin Mor

521
FARRMHEALL

**C**

Kinlochbervie          Gualin Ho.        19

Loch Clash     Badcall    Inshegra
                          Achriesgill

Bagh Loch an Roin           Rhivichie

Loch Dughaill           Achlyness          L. na Claise
                                            Carnaich

Ardmore Pt.          Ceathramh Garbh      Rhiconich

Rubha Ruadh     Ardmore  Portlevorchy                 GANU MOR
                        Skerricha                     908
                                                     Foinave

Fanagmore          NORTH-WEST SUTHERL

Tarbet      Loch       Loch a 'Garbh-
            Laxford    bhaid Mór           H  i

Handa Island          Foindle

Loch nam                    Laxford Bridge    Loch an Easain
Brac                A894                      Uaine

Sound of Handa      Badnabay

**D**

Scourie Bay                                 787
                                            ARKLE

Scourie More          Scourie

Rubh'Aird an t-Sionnaich         Gorm Loch    A838   Lochstack Lodge

                                                     Loch Stack

Upper Badcall    Lower Badcall       719
                                     BEN STACK
                              BEINN AUSKAIRD         Strath Stack   Airdachuilin
Badcall Bay            18      386

Eil. a'Breitheimh     LOCH                           R  E  A  Y   F  O R   Achfary   332
                      A'MHUILINN
                    Duartbeg      A894    Loch                Lochmore Lodge
Rubha a'Mhucard              Cro!ach

Meall Mór                    Duartmore        Loch na Creige
                     Calbha    Bridge          Duibhe
                     Mór     Duartmore
            Calbha          Forest            Loch an Léathaid
**E**         Beag      Loch a 'Chairn Bhàin         Bhúain

Point of Stoer                                547
                    R. nan Còsan                GLENDHU
Cirean Geardail    Eilean Chrona   Culkein     Kylestrome   Glendhu  Forest
        161                        Drumbeg
                        Oldany Island  Ardvar  Kylesku   Loch Glendhu  Gleann
Culkein                                                                 Dubh
Rubha       Oldany    Drumbeg   B869   Unapool
Stoer       Clashnessie                        Loch Glencoul  530
Achnacarnin    Bay           Nedd    Newton                  BEINN AIRD
Cluas Deas                   Glenleraig                       DA LOCH
Clashmore                            Gleann Leireag
30                  Clashnessie                    QUINAG  792
NC    Balchladich   Rienachait         Loch an        808   BEINN LE
00                                     Leothaid
         Rubh'a'          Stoer   13      Loch Beannach
**F**    Mhill Dheirg    Clachtoll                               EAS COUL AULIN  776
         Bay of Stoer                                           WATERFALL
                    R. Leuma  ⑤438      Lochassynt Lodge  ⑤439   BEINN UIDHE
                    melvich   ②                                  740
         0    2    4 miles           A837    Little            Skiag Bridge  Gorm Loch
         0  2  4  6 km     Achmelvich  Rhicarn  ③  10          ④  A894  ⑤

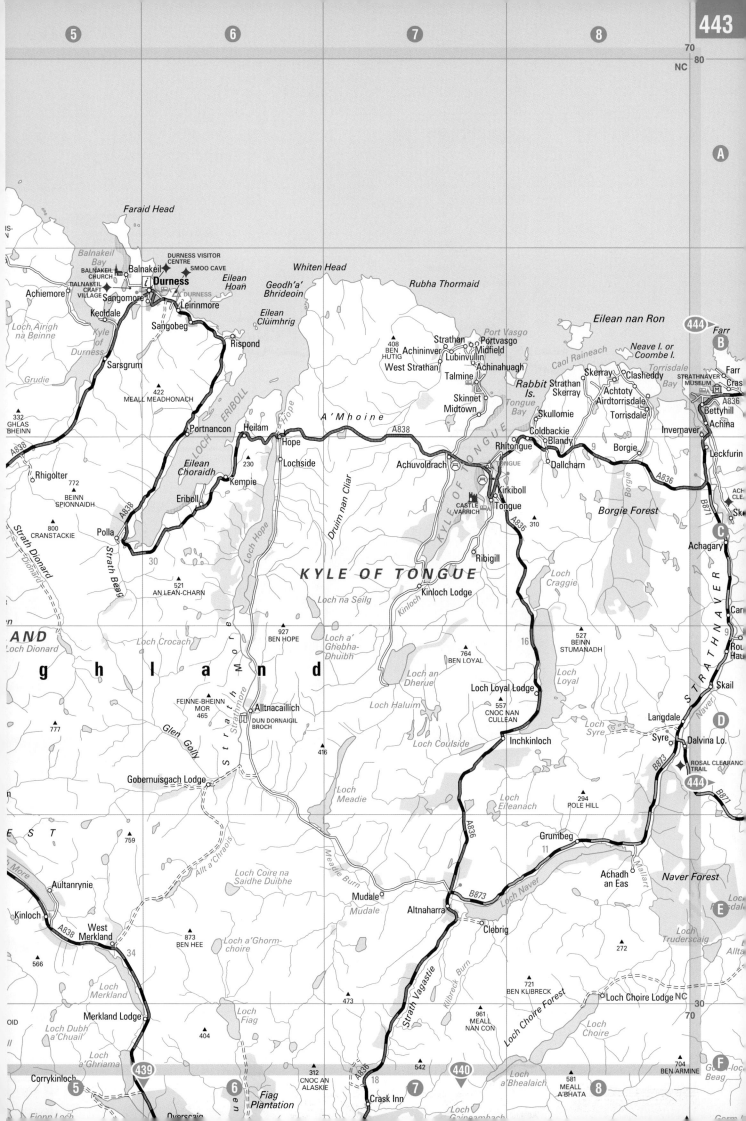

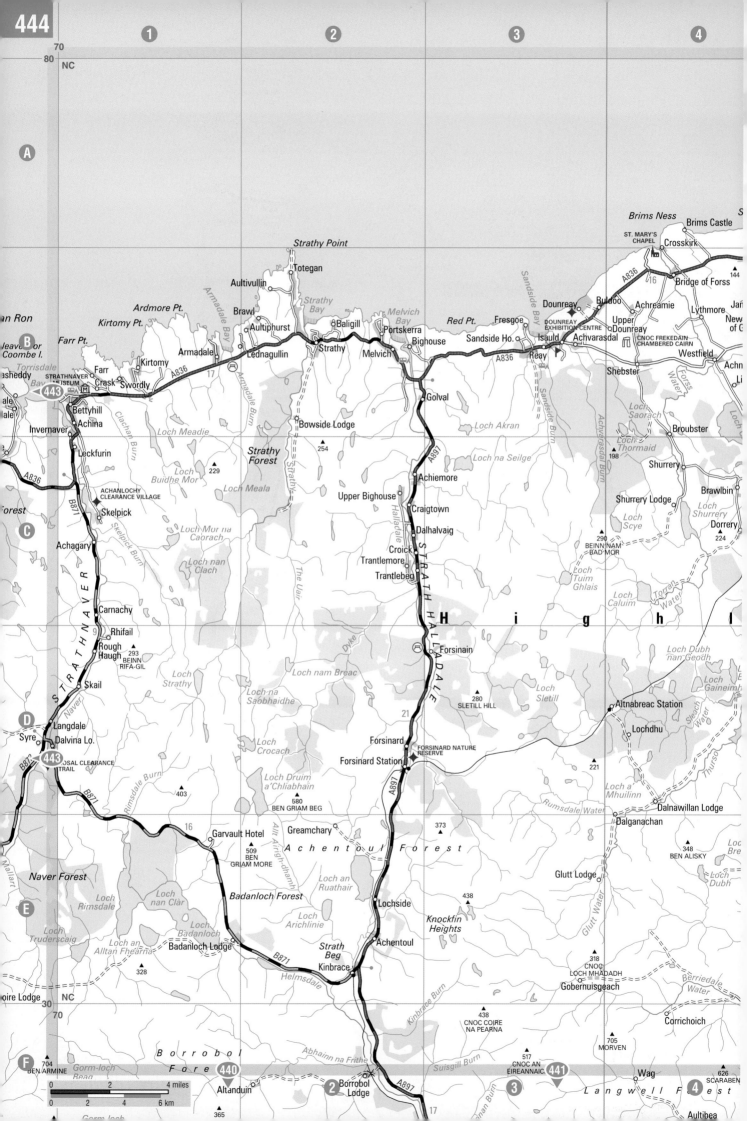

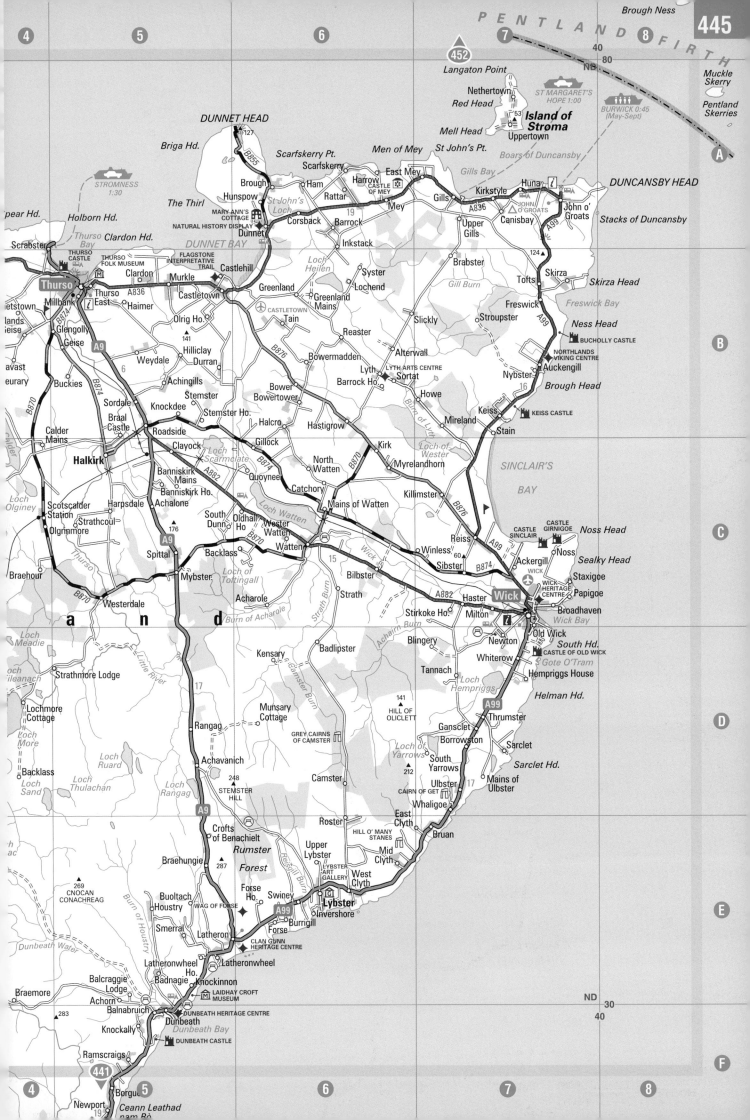

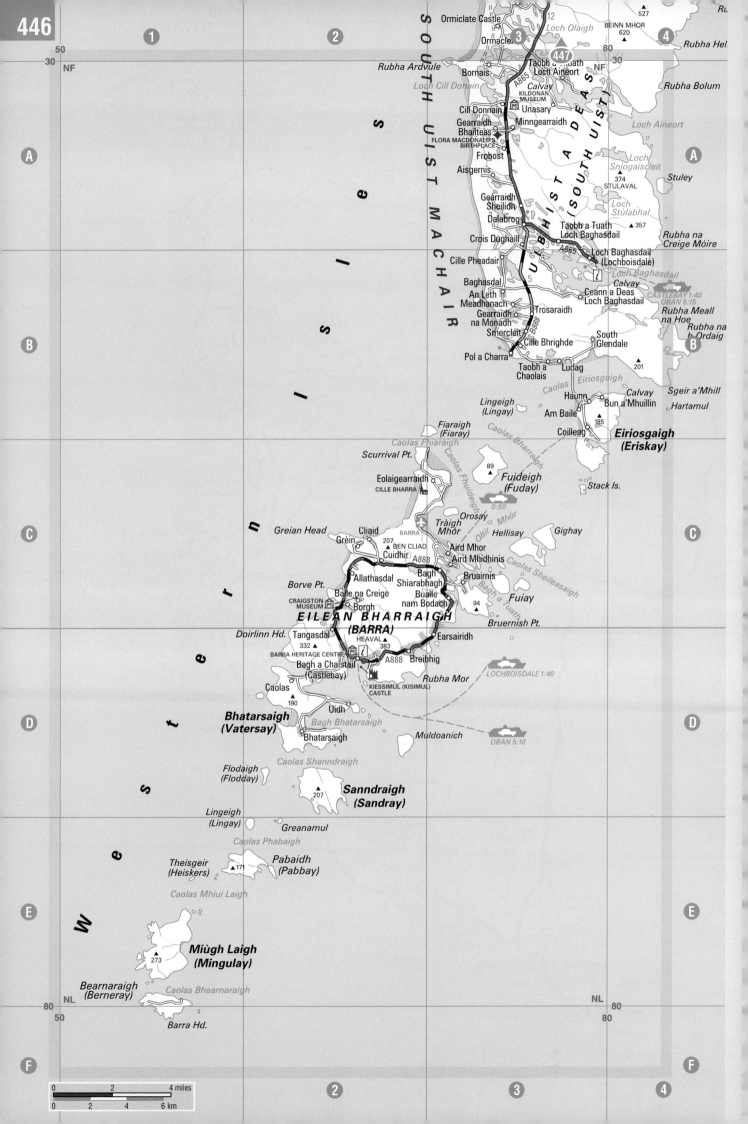

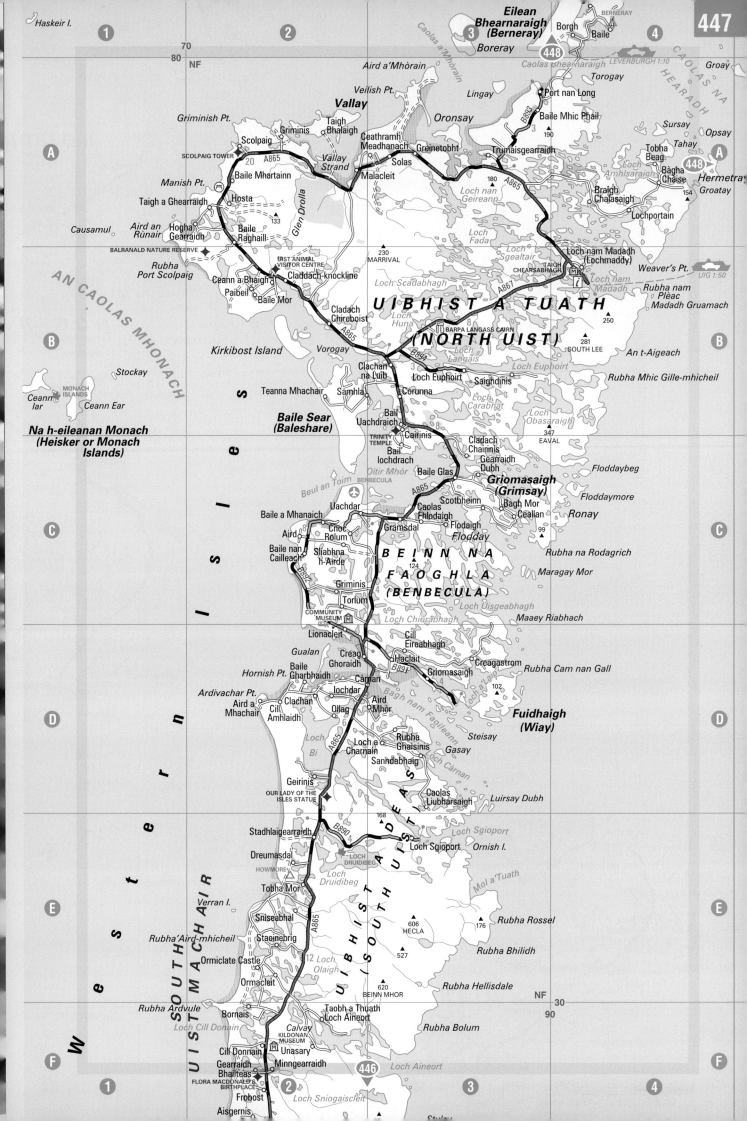

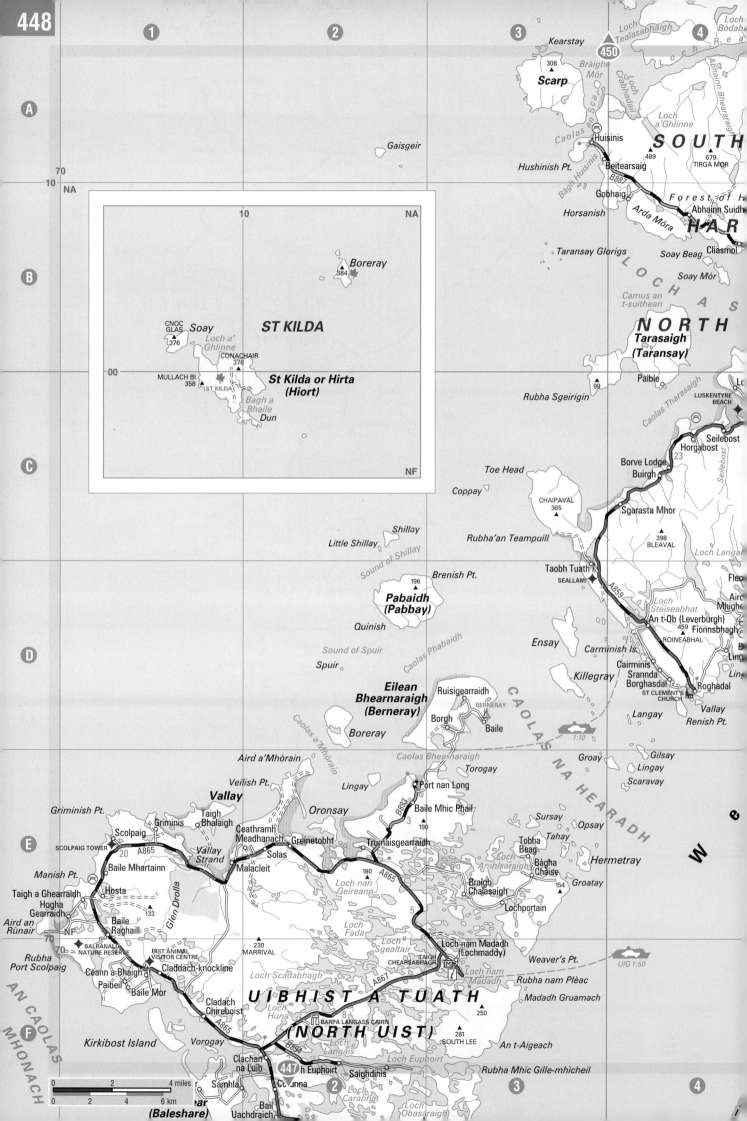

## Map labels

**1** **2** **3** **4**

**A**

Kearstay

450

308

**Scarp**

Bràighe
Mór

Loch
Tealasabhaigh

Loch
Bòdam
Bea

Loch
Crabhadail

Huisinis

Loch
a'Ghlinne

**SOUTH**

Hushinish Pt.

Beitearsaig

489      679
TIRGA MOR

Gobhaig

B887

Forest of

Horsanish

Arda Móra

Abhainn Suidh

**HAR**

Abhainn Suidhe

Caolas an Scarp

Bàgh Huisinis

Soay Beag

Cliasmol

Gaisgeir

Taransay Glorigs

Soay Mór

**B**

Camus an
t-suithean

Boreray

384

**ST KILDA**

**NORTH**

CNOC
GLAS    Soay

376

Loch a'
Ghlinne

Tarasaigh
(Taransay)

CONACHAIR

376

Paible

Rubha Sgeirigin

Caolas Tharasaigh

LUSKENTYRE
BEACH

MULLACH BI

358

ST KILDA

**St Kilda or Hirta
(Hiort)**

Bàgh a
Bhaile
Dun

99

Seilebost

**C**

NF

Toe Head

Horgabost

23

Borve Lodge
Buirgh

Coppay

CHAIPAVAL
365

Sgarasta Mhor

398
BLEAVAL

Loch Langa

Little Shillay

Shillay

Rubha'an Teampuill

Taobh Tuath
SEALLAM!

A859

An t-Ob (Leverburgh)

Loch
Steiseabhat

Sound of Shillay

Brenish Pt.

459
ROINEABHAL

Fionnsbhagh

Fleo

Aird
Mhighe

196

**Pabaidh
(Pabbay)**

Ensay

Carminish Is.

**D**

Sound of Spuir

Quinish

Caolas Phabaidh

Killegray

Cairminish
Srannda
Borghasdal

Roghadal

B
Ling

Spuir

ST CLEMENT'S
CHURCH

Ling

**Eilean
Bhearnaraigh
(Berneray)**

Ruisigearraidh

BERNERAY

Langay

Valley
Renish Pt.

Borgh

Caolas a'Mhòrain

Boreray

Baile

CAOLAS NA HEARADH

1:10

Groay

Gilsay

Aird a'Mhòrain

Caolas Bhearnaraigh

Torogay

Lingay

Scaravay

Veilish Pt.

Lingay

Port nan Long

**Valley**

Oronsay

B893

Baile Mhic Phail

Sursay

Opsay

**E**

Griminish Pt.

Griminis

Taigh
Bhalaigh

Trumaisgearraidh

3

190

Tahay

Tobha
Beag

Hermetray

W

Scolpaig

Ceathramh
Meadhanach

Greinetobht

Bàgha
Chaise

SCOLPAIG TOWER

A865

20

Valley
Strand

Solas

A865

Loch
Amhlsaraigh

Braigh
Chalasaigh

Groatay

e

Baile Mhartainn

Malacleit

180

154

Manish Pt.

Hosta

Lochportain

Taigh a Ghearraidh
Hogha
Gearraidh

133

Glen Drolla

Loch nan
Geireann

Aird an
Rùnair

NF

Baile
Raghaill

70

5

Loch
Fada

Loch nam Madadh
(Lochmaddy)

Weaver's Pt.

UIG 1:50

Rubha
Port Scolpaig

70

BALRANALD
NATURE RESERVE

UIST ANIMAL
VISITOR CENTRE

Claddach-knockline

230
MARRIVAL

Loch
Sgeallair

TAIGH
CHEARSABHAGH

M

i

Loch nam
Madadh

Rubha nam Plèac

**F**

Ceann a'Bhaigh

Cladach
Chirboist

Barpa Langass Cairn

A867

250

Madadh Gruamach

Paibeil

Baile Mor

8

Loch Huna

Loch Scadabhagh

Rubha Mhic Gille-mhìcheil

AN CAOLAS MHONACH

Kirkibost Island

Vorogay

Cladach
na Luib

B894

447

281
SOUTH LEE

An t-Aigeach

**UIBHIST A TUATH
(NORTH UIST)**

Loch
Langais

**2**

Loch
Carabhat

Loch
Obasaraigh

Samhla

Conna

Loch Euphoirt

Saighdinis

Euphoirt

**(Baleshare)**

Bail
Uachdraich

0    2    4 miles
0    2    4    6 km

**2**    **3**    **4**

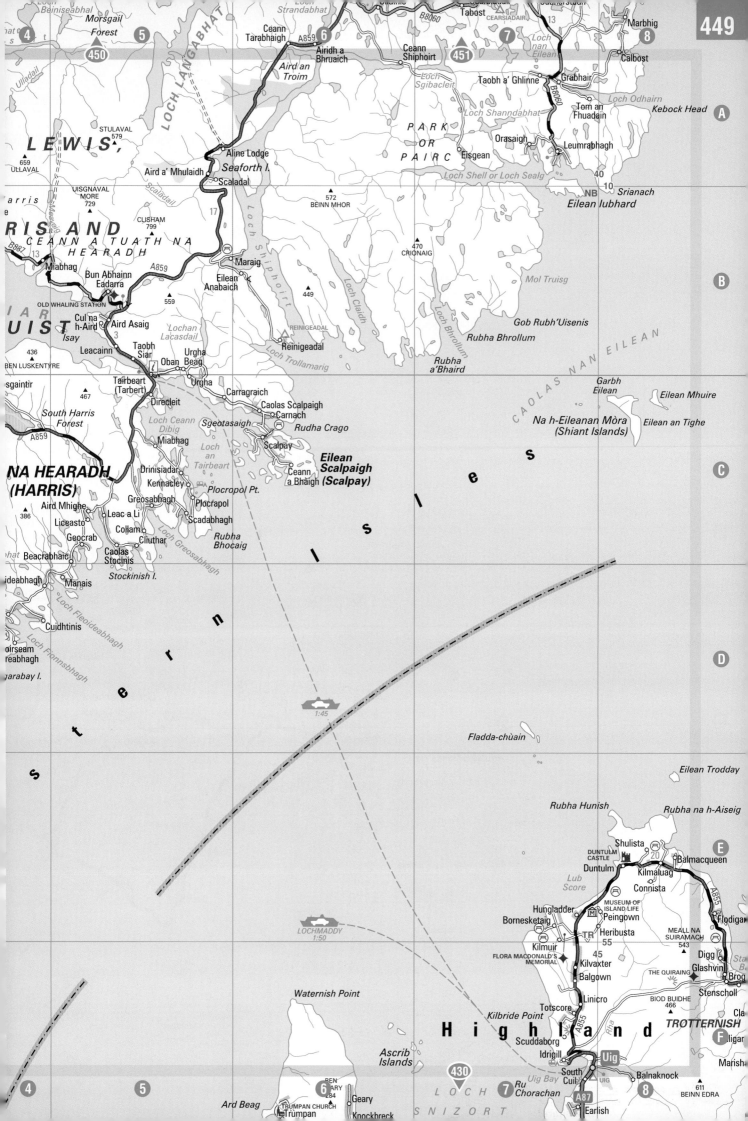

LEWIS

Morsgail Forest

Beiniseabhal

Loch Langabhat

Loch Strandabhat

B8060

Tabost

CEARSIADAIR

13

Marbhig

Calbost

Ceann Tarabhaigh

A859

Ceann Shiphoirt

451

Loch nan Eilean

B8060

Grabhair

Taobh a' Ghlinne

Airidh a Bhruaich

Aird an Troim

Loch Sgibacleit

PARK OR PAIRC

Loch Shanndabhat

Tom an Fhuadain

Loch Odhairn

Kebock Head

A

Orasaigh

Eisgean

Loch Shell or Loch Sealg

Leumrabhagh

40

10

NB

Srianach

Eilean Iubhard

STULAVAL 579

UISGNAVAL MORE 729

Aline Lodge

Seaforth I.

Scaladal

659 ULLAVAL

Ulladail

Harris

HARRIS AND

CEANN A TUATH NA HEARADH

CLISHAM 799

A859

17

Maraig

BEINN MHOR 572

470 CRIONAIG

Mol Truisg

B

B887

13

Miabhag

Bun Abhainn Eadarra

OLD WHALING STATION

Eilean Anabaich

559

449

Loch Claidh

Loch Bhrollum

Gob Rubh'Uisenis

Rubha Bhrollum

UIST

Isay

Cul na h-Aird

Aird Asaig

Leacainn

3

Taobh Siar

Oban Beag

Lochan Lacasdail

Urgha Beag

REINIGEADAL

Reinigeadal

Loch Trollamarig

Rubha a'Bhaird

CAOLAS NAN EILEAN

Garbh Eilean

Eilean Mhuire

436

BEN LUSKENTYRE

Tairbeart (Tarbert)

Urgha

Carragraich

Na h-Eileanan Mòra (Shiant Islands)

Eilean an Tighe

Direcleit

Caolas Scalpaigh

Carnach

Rudha Crago

467

South Harris Forest

A859

Loch Ceann Dibig

Miabhag

Sgeotasaigh

Scalpay

Eilean Scalpaigh (Scalpay)

C

sgaintir

Drinisiadar

Kennacley

Loch an Tairbeart

Ceann a Bhàigh

NA HEARADH (HARRIS)

386

Aird Mhighe

Greosabhagh

Plocrapol Pt.

Liceasto

Leac a Li

Plocrapol

Geocrab

Collam

Scadabhagh

Rubha Bhocaig

Cliuthar

Caolas Stocinis

Loch Greosabhagh

Beacrabhaic

Stockinish I.

hat

Cuidhtinis

Manais

Loch Fleoideabhagh

W e s t e r n   I s l e s

D

oirseam reabhagh

Loch Fionnsbhagh

arabay I.

1:45

Fladda-chùain

Eilean Trodday

Rubha Hunish

Rubha na h-Aiseig

Shulista

DUNTULM CASTLE

20

Balmacqueen

E

Duntulm

Kilmaluag

Connista

A855

Lub Score

Hungladder

MUSEUM OF ISLAND LIFE

Peingown

Bornesketaig

Heribusta

TR

MEALL NA SUIRAMACH 543

Flodigar

Kilmuir

55

FLORA MACDONALD'S MEMORIAL

Kilvaxter

45

THE QUIRAING

Digg

Glashvin

Brog

1:50

LOCHMADDY

Balgown

BIOD BUIDHE 466

Stenscholl

Waternish Point

Linicro

Totscore

TROTTERNISH

F

Kilbride Point

Ascrib Islands

H i g h l a n d

A855

Scuddaborg

Idrigill

Uig

Sta

Cla

igar

Marish

4

5

430

6

BEN ... 284

7

Ru Chorachan

South Cuil

A87

Uig

Balnaknock

8

611 BEINN EDRA

Ard Beag

TRUMPAN CHURCH

Trumpan

Geary

Knockbreck

LOCH SNIZORT

Uig Bay

Earlish

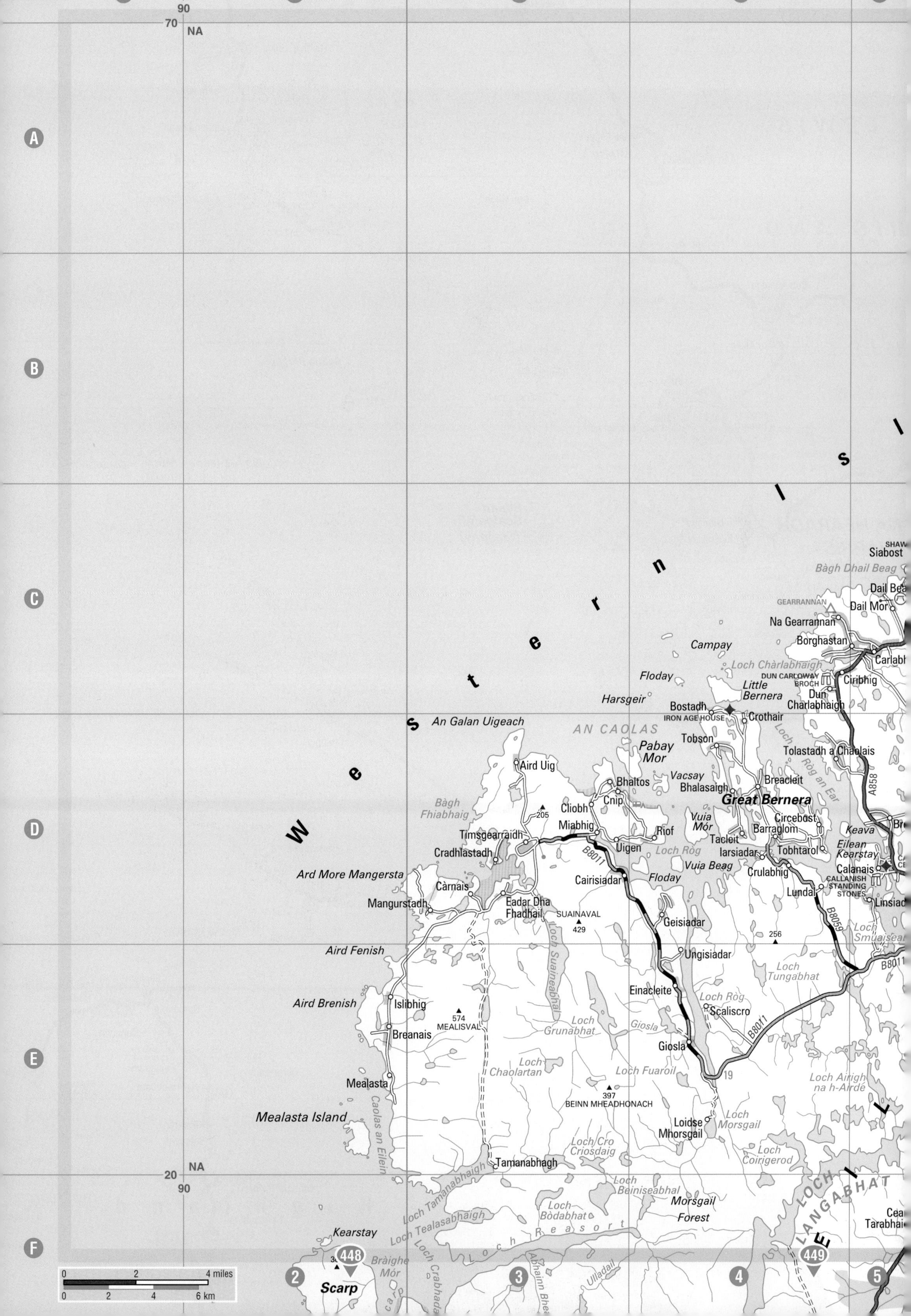

① ② ③ ④ ⑤

90
70
NA

**A**

**B**

SHAW
Siabost
*Bàgh Dhail Beag*
Dail Be
GEARRANNAN
Na Gearrannan
Dail Mòr
Borghastan

**C**

Campay
*Loch Chàrlabhaigh*
Carlabh
Floday
DUN CARLOWAY
BROCH
Cribhig
*Harsgeir*
Little
Bernera
Dun
Charlabhaigh
Bostadh
IRON AGE HOUSE
Crothair
*An Galan Uigeach*
AN CAOLAS
Tobson
Tolastadh a Chaolais
A858

**D**
We
st
er
n
I
s
I

Pabay
Mòr
Aird Uig
Vacsay
Bhaltos
Bhalasaigh
Breacleit
Cnip
**Great Bernera**
Cliobh
*205*
Vuia
Mór
Circebost
Keava
Br
Timsgearraidh
Miabhig
Barraglom
Eilean
Kearstay
Cradhlastadh
Uigen
Riof
Iarsiadar
Tobhtarol
Calanais
*Loch Ròg*
E
*Ard More Mangersta*
Vuia Beag
Crulabhig
CALLANISH
STANDING
STONES
Cairisiadar
Floday
Lundal
Linsiad
Mangurstadh
Càrnais
Eadar Dha
Fhadhail
SUAINAVAL
*429*
Geisiadar
*256*
*Loch
Smuaiseal*
*Aird Fenish*
*Loch Suaineabhal*
Ungisiadar
*Loch
Tungabhat*
B8011

**E**
*Aird Brenish*
Islibhig
MEALISVAL
*574*
Einacleite
*Loch Ròg*
Breanais
Scaliscro
*Loch
Grunabhat*
*Giosla*
*Loch Airigh
na h-Airdé*
Mealasta
*Loch
Chaolartan*
Giosla
*Loch Fuaroil*
19
*Mealasta Island*
*Caolas an Eilein*
BEINN MHEADHONACH
*397*
Loidse
Mhorsgail
*Loch
Morsgail*
*Loch
Coirigerod*
*Loch Cro
Criosdaig*
Tamanabhagh
*Loch
Beiniseabhal*
20
NA
90
Morsgail
Forest
*Loch
Bòdabhat*
LOCH
LANGABHAT

**F**
Kearstay
*Loch Tamanabhaigh*
448
Bràighe
Mór
*Abhainn Bhe*
*Loch Tealasabhaigh*
*Loch Crabhadai*
R e a s o r t
*Ulladail*
449
Cea
Tarabhai

② ③ ④ ⑤

0        2        4 miles
0    2    4    6 km

**Scarp**

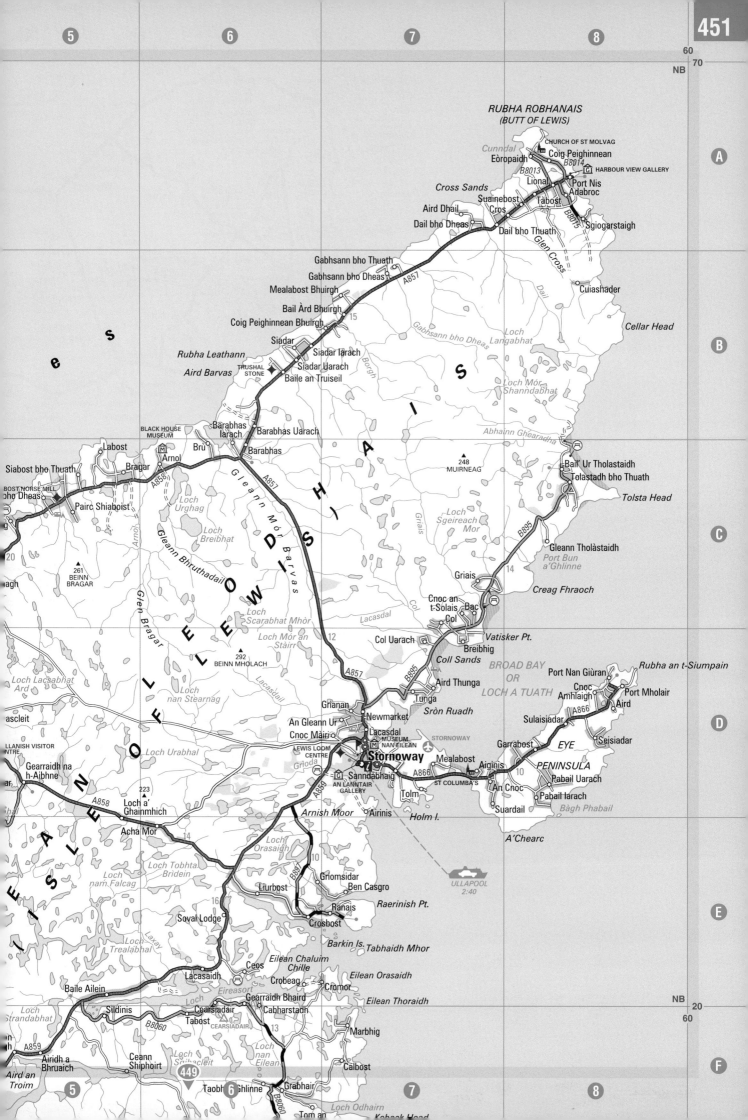

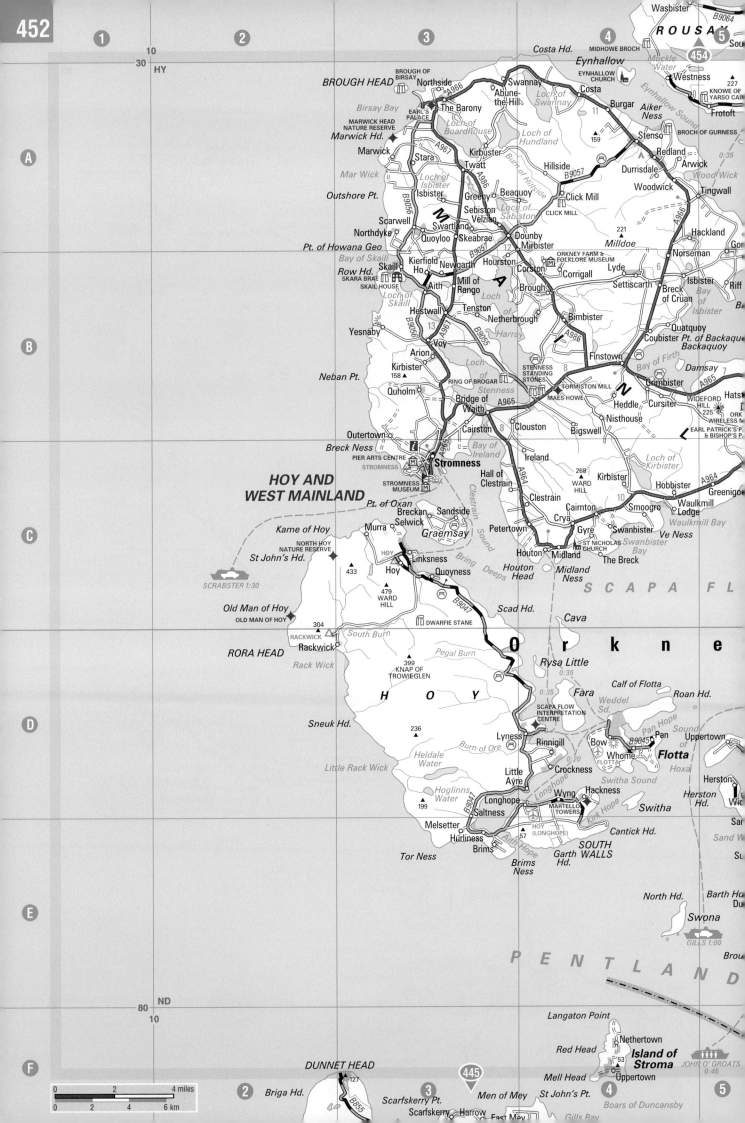

**452**

1  2  3  4  5

10
30
HY

Wasbister
B9064
ROUSAY
454

Costa Hd.
MIDHOWE BROCH
Eynhallow
Muckle
Water

BROUGH OF
BIRSAY
Northside
Swannay
EYNHALLOW
CHURCH
Westness
227
KNOWE OF
YARSO CAIRN

BROUGH HEAD
A966
The Barony
Abune-
the-Hill
Costa
Burgar
11
Aiker
Ness
Stenso
Frotoft

Birsay Bay
EARL'S
PALACE
Loch of
Swannay
BROCH OF GURNESS

MARWICK HEAD
NATURE RESERVE
Marwick Hd.
Loch of
Boardhouse
Loch of
Hundland
159
Redland
Arwick
Wood Wick

Marwick
Stara
Kirbuster
Hillside
Durrisdale
Woodwick

Mar Wick
Twatt
Beaquoy
Click Mill
Tingwall

Outshore Pt.
Isbister
A986
Greeny
Sebiston
Velzian
CLICK MILL
Norseman

Scarwell
Swartland
Dounby
Milldoe
Hackland
Gor

Northdyke
Quoyloo
Skeabrae
Mirbister
221
Isbister
Riff

Pt. of Howana Geo
B9057
ORKNEY FARM &
FOLKLORE MUSEUM
Lyde
6
Breck
of Cruan
Bay
of
Isbister

Bay of Skaill
Kierfield
Ho.
Newgarth
Hourston
Corston
Corrigall
Settiscarth

Row Hd.
SKARA BRAE
Skaill
Mill of
Rango
Brough
Bimbister
Quatquoy
Coubister
Pt. of Backaquoy
Backaquoy

SKAIL HOUSE
Aith
Netherbrough
Finstown
Bay of Firth

Hestwall
Tenston
8
Damsay

Yesnaby
Voy
Loch
of
Harray
Grimbister
A965

Arion
 of
STENNESS
STANDING
STONES
TORMISTON MILL
Heddle
Cursiter
Hats

Kirbister
158
RING OF BROGAR
Stenness
MAES HOWE
Nisthouse
WIDEFORD
HILL
225
ORK
WIRELESS M

Neban Pt.
Quholm
Bridge of
Waith
A965
EARL PATRICK'S P.
& BISHOP'S P.

Outertown
Cairston
8
Clouston
Bigswell
Loch of
Kirkwall

Breck Ness
Bay of
Ireland
Ireland
268
WARD
HILL
Kirbister
Hobbister
A964
Greenigo

i
PIER ARTS CENTRE
STROMNESS
Stromness
Hall of
Clestrain
A964
Clestrain
Cairnton
10
Smoogro
Waulkmill
Lodge

STROMNESS MUSEUM
Crya
Gyre
Swanbister
Ve Ness
Waulkmill Bay

HOY AND
WEST MAINLAND
Pt. of Oxan
Breckan
Selwick
Sandside
Petertown
Houton
ST NICHOLAS
CHURCH
Midland
The Breck
Swanbister
Bay

Kame of Hoy
NORTH HOY
NATURE RESERVE
Murra
Graemsay
Houton
Head
Midland
Ness
SCAPA FL

St John's Hd.
HOY
Linksness
Houton
Midland

SCRABSTER 1:30
433
Hoy
Quoyness
Cava

Old Man of Hoy
479
WARD
HILL
Scad Hd.

OLD MAN OF HOY
304
DWARFIE STANE
Rysa Little
0:35
Calf of Flotta
Roan Hd.

RORA HEAD
RACKWICK
Rackwick
South Burn
KNAP OF
TROWIEGLEN
O r k n e
Fara
0:35
Weddel
Sd.

Rack Wick
399
Pegal Burn
B9047
0:35
SCAPA FLOW
INTERPRETATION
CENTRE
Pan Hope
Pan
Uppertown
Sound
of

H O Y
236
Lyness
Bow
B9045
Flotta
Herston

Sneuk Hd.
Burn of Ore
Rinnigill
Whome
FLOTTA
Hoxal
Herston
Hd.

Heldale
Water
Crockness
0:20
Hackness
Swithe Sound
Wic

Little Rack Wick
Little
Ayre
Wyng
MARTELLO
TOWERS
Switha

Hoglinns
Water
199
Longhope
Saltness
Kirk Hope
Sand W

Melsetter
B9047
HOY
(LONGHOPE)
57
SOUTH
WALLS
Garth
Hd.

Hurliness
Brims
Cantick Hd.
Sar
Su

Tor Ness
Brims
Ness
Brims
Ness

North Hd.
Barth Ho
Du

Swona

GILLS 1:00

P E N T L A N D
Brou

80
ND
10

Langaton Point
Netherton
Island of
Stroma

Red Head
53
JOHN O' GROATS
0:45

DUNNET HEAD
445
Mell Head
Uppertown

0    2    4 miles
0  2  4  6 km

Briga Hd.
Scarfskerry Pt.
Men of Mey
St John's Pt.
Boars of Duncansby

B855
Scarfskerry  Harrow
East Mey
Gills Bay

A
B
C
D
E
F

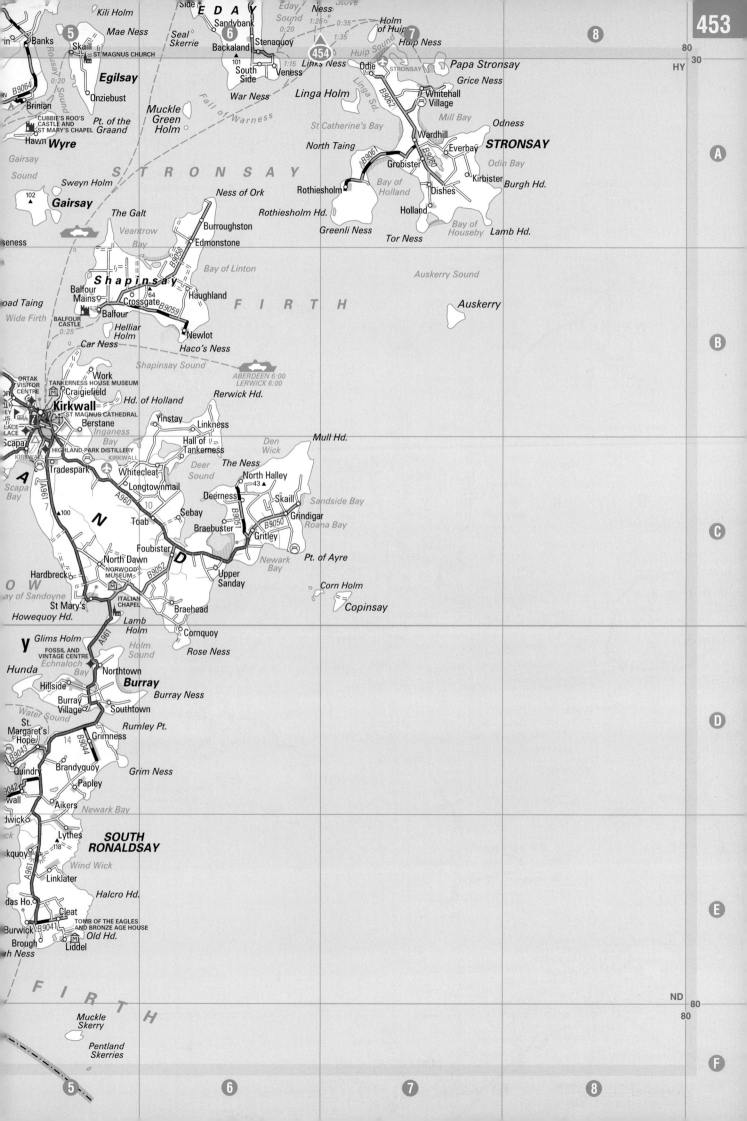

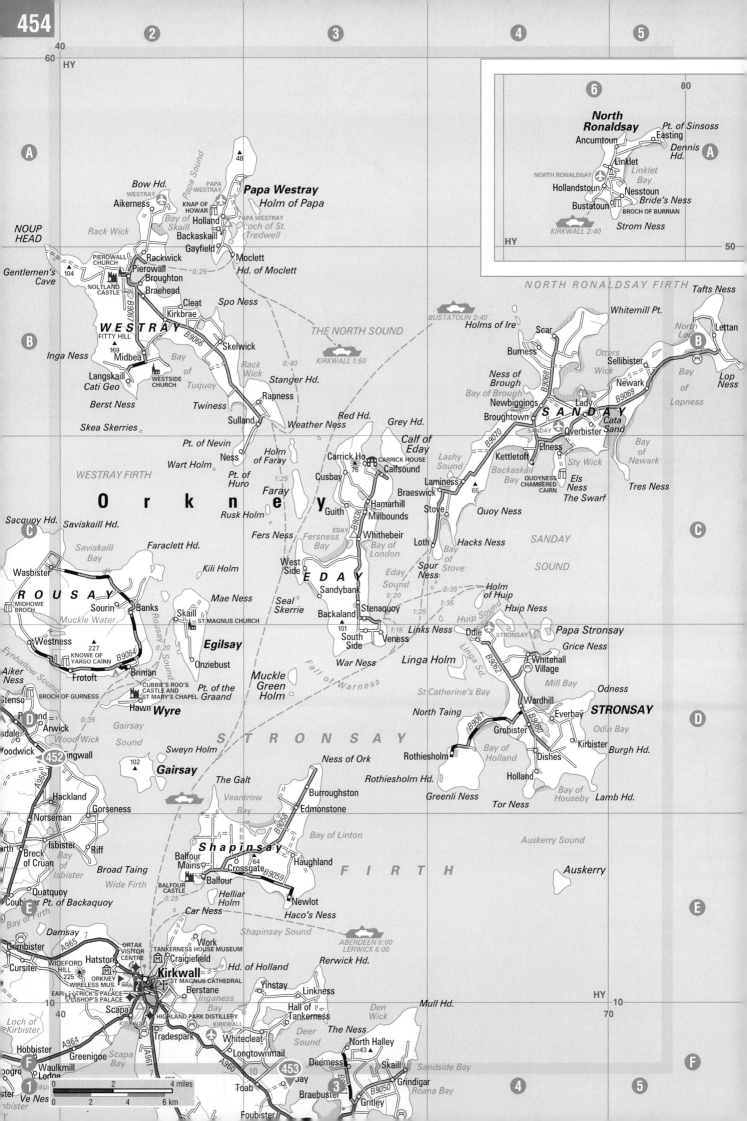

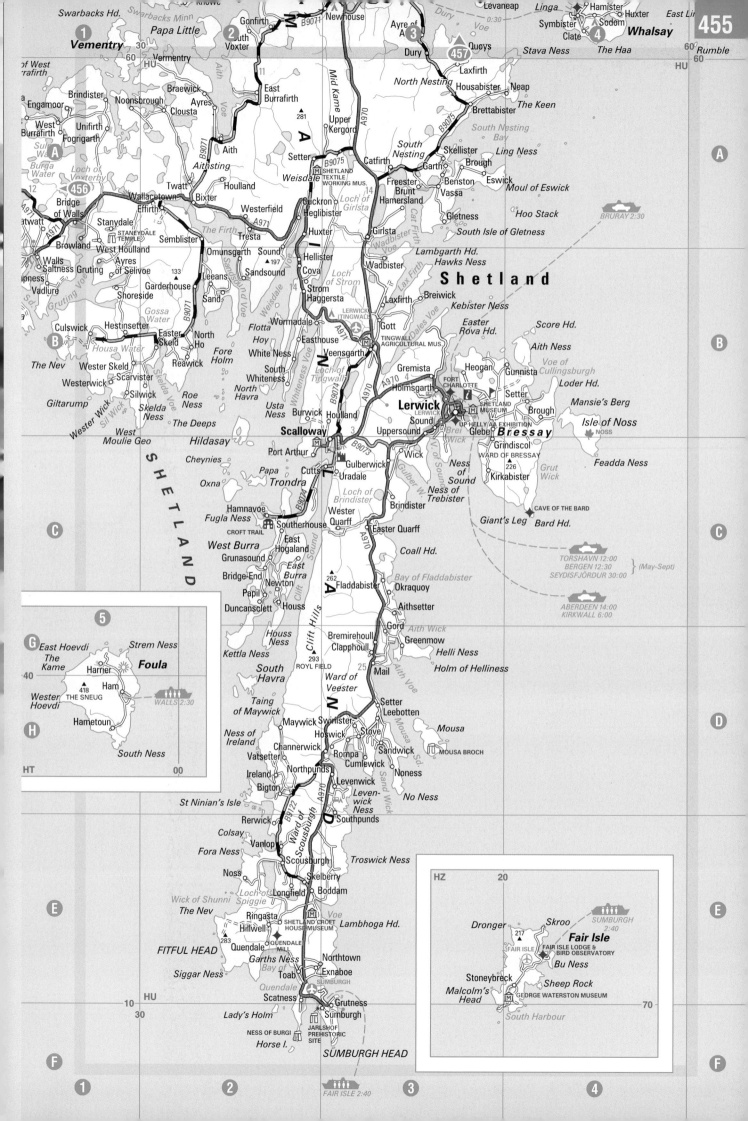

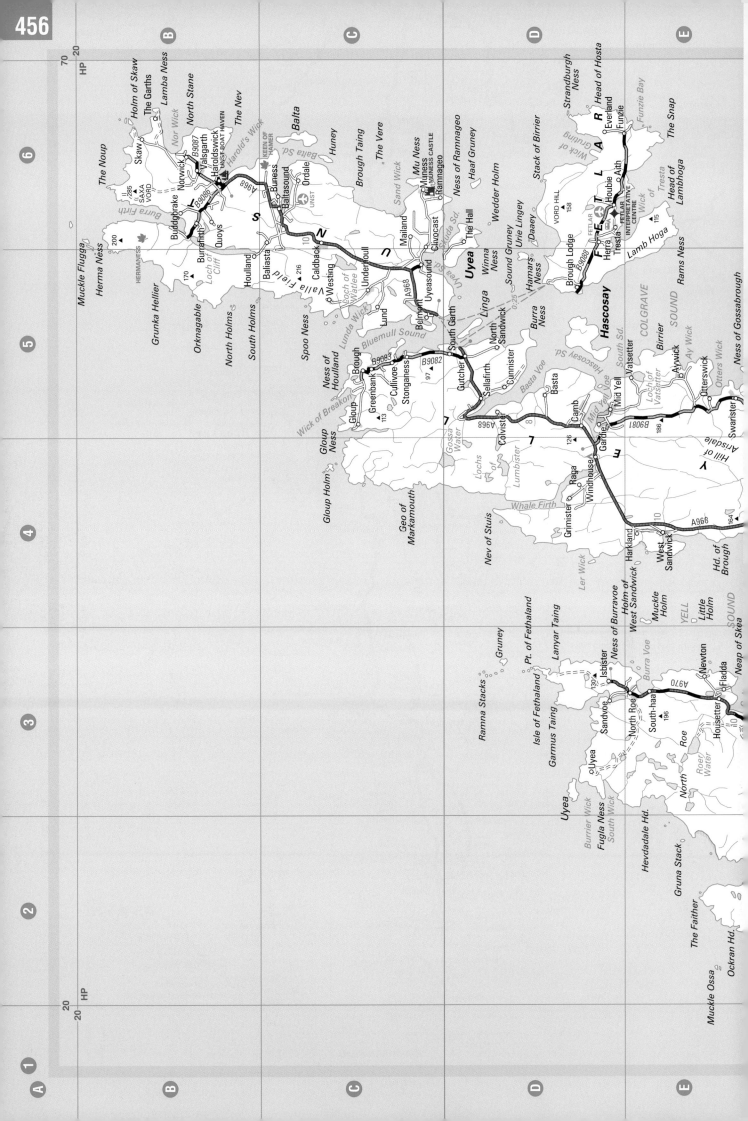

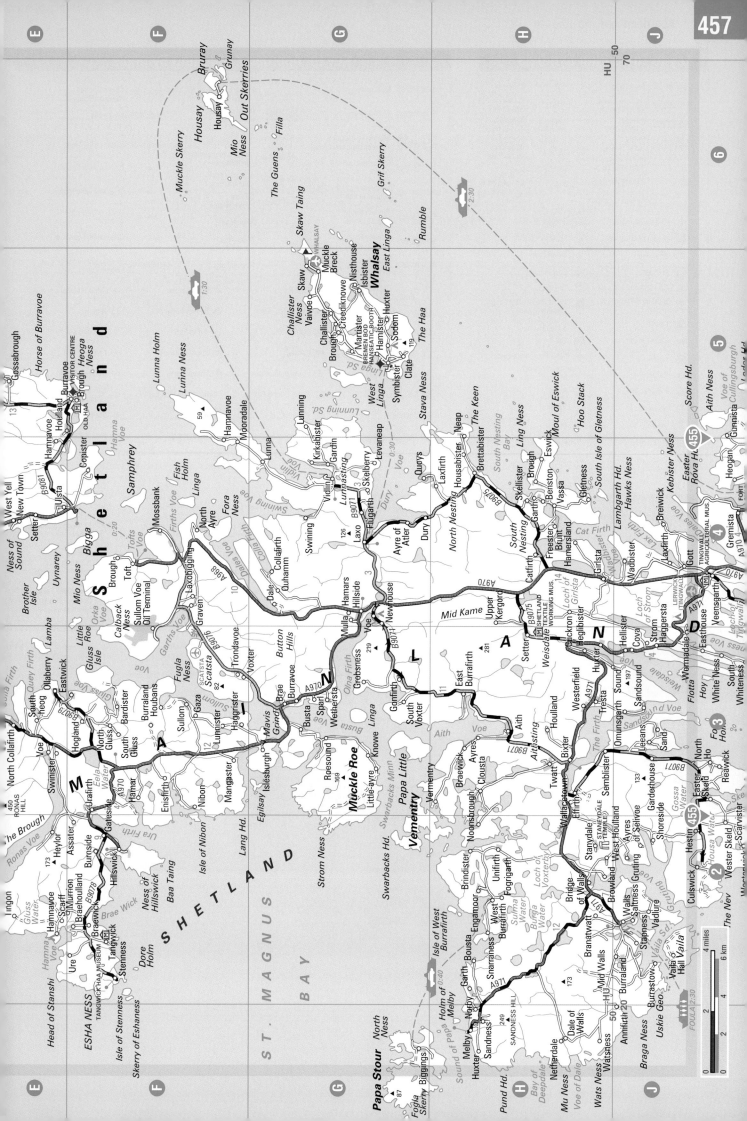

E    F    G    H    J

HU  50
70

Bruray
Grunay
Housay
Out Skerries
Housay
Muckle Skerry
Mio Ness
The Guens
Filla
Skaw Taing
Grif Skerry
WHALSAY
Rumble
2:30
Muckle Breck
Skaw
Nisthouse
Isbister
East Linga
Challister Ness
Vaivoe
Challister
Creediknowe
Whalsay
Brough
BREMEN BÖD
HANSEATIC BOOTH
Marrister
Hamister
Huxter
1:30
Sodom
The Haa
Linga Sd.
Clate
119
West Linga
Symbister
Stava Ness
The Keen
Horse of Burravoe
Gossabrough
Brough Heoga Ness
Lunna Holm
Lunna Ness
Hamnavoe
Mooradale
Lunning
Neap
Hoo Stack
Moul of Eswick
Eswick
South Isle of Gletness
Burravoe
VISITOR CENTRE
Houlland
OLD HAA
Copister
Samphrey
Lunna
Kirkabister
Gardin
Vidlin
Lunna Voe
Skelberry
Levaneap
Quoys
Laxfirth
Housabister
Brettabister
South Nesting Bay
Ling Ness
Brough
Gletness
South Isle of Gletness
Lambgarth Hd.
Hawks Ness
Kebister Ness
Aith Ness
Voe of Cullingsburgh
Score Hd.
Easter Rova Hd.
455
West Yell
New Town
13
B9081
Setter
Ulsta
Ness of Sound
Bigga
Uynarey
Mio Ness
Mossbank
North Ayre
Firths Voe
Fish Holm
Linga
Fora Ness
Swining Voe
Vidlin Voe
Swining
Vidlin
Lumnasting
Fladgarth
B9071
Laxo
126
Dury Voe
Ayre of Atler
Dury
0:30
North Nesting
Skellister
Skellister
B9075
Freester
Hamersland
Brunt
Girlsta
Freester
Cat Firth
Wadbister
Laxfirth
Laxfirth
Loch of Girlsta
Breiwick
Gremista
AGRICULTURAL MUS
4
FORT
Heogan
910
A970
Shetland
Brother Isle
Lamba
Little Roe
Gluss Isle
Calback Ness
Orka Voe
Brough
Toft
Sullom Voe Oil Terminal
Dales Voe
A968
Laxobigging
Garths Voe
0:20
Tofts Voe
Dale
Collafirth
Ouhamm
Graven
3
Mulla
Hamars
Hillside
NewHouse
Voe
B9071
A970
Upper Kergord
Mid Kame
B9075
Cuckron
Heglibister
SHETLAND TEXTILE WORKING MUS.
Weisdale
A
N
D
Hellister
LERWICK
Cova
Strom
Haggersta
Loch of Strom
Wormadale
TINGWALL
A971
A970
Scalloway
Gott
Veensgarth
Easthouse
Shetland Voe
South Whiteness
White Ness
North Collafirth
South Collafirth
Heog
Ollaberry
Eastwick
B9079
North Gluss
South Gluss
Bardister
Burraland
Houbans
Sullom
Gaza
Lunnister
Haggrister
Mavis Grind
Busta
Wethersta
Voe
Sparl
Brae
Burravoe
A970
N
Grobsness
Gonfirth
Linga
South Voxter
Aith Voe
East Burrafirth
Setter
A971
Westerfield
Houlland
Sound
Sandsound
Tresta
The Firth
Sandsound Voe
Flotta
Hoy
Voe
Fo 3
Holm
A970
Gluss Water
Eela Water
Urafirth
Gateside
A970
Hamar
Enisfirth
Nibon
Mangaster
Egilsay
Isleburgh
Islesburgh
Roesound
169
Little-ayre
Papa Little
Vementry
Clousta
Ayres
Braewick
Aithsting
B9071
Aith
Bixter
Twatt
Omunsgarth
Effirth
Wallacetown
Stanydale
133
Gardlehouse
Gossa Water
Reawick
North Ho
Easter Skeld
B9071
ESHA NESS
TANGWICK HAA MUSEUM
Heylor
Assater
Burnside
Braehoulland
B9078
173
The Brough
Ura Firth
RONAS HILL
450
Swinister
M
A
Voe
Ronas Voe
Hillswick
Ness of Hillswick
Baa Taing
Isle of Nibon
Lang Hd.
Swarbacks Minn
Swarbacks Hd.
Strom Ness
Vementry
Vermentry
Brindister
Noonsbrough
Unifirth
Fogrigarth
Loch of Voxterby
Bridge of Walls
Browland
Saltness
Gruting
of Selivoe
West Houlland
STANEYDALE TEMPLE
West Houlland
Shoreside
Hestin
Culswick
2
2
455
Ingon
Gluss Water
Hamnavoe
Scarff
Murrion
Braewick
Tangwick
Dore Holm
Stenness
Isle of Stenness
Sker y of Eshaness
Head of Stanshi
The Nev
Wester Skeld
Vaila Sd.
S  T  .
M  A  G  N  U  S
Isle of West Burrafirth
North Ness
Papa Stour
Melby
Melby
Holm of Melby
0:40
Garth
Bousta
Snarraness
West Burrafirth
Engamoor
Burga Water
Sulma Water
Walls
Stapness
Vadlure
Mid Walls
Burraland
Watsness
Voe of Dale
Netherdale
Sandness
SANDNESS HILL
249
Dale of Walls
A971
Anrifirth 20
12
173
S  H  E  T  L  A  N  D
B  A  Y
Fogla
Skerry
Biggings
87
Papa Stour
Pund Hd.
Mu Ness
Wats Ness
Braga Ness
Bay of Deepdale
Uskie Geo
FOULA 2:30
Annfirth 20
Burrastow
Hall
Vaila
Vaila

0:40
1:30
2:30

4 miles
6 km
0  2  4
0  2  4  6

E    F    G    H    J

## Key to Town Plan Symbols

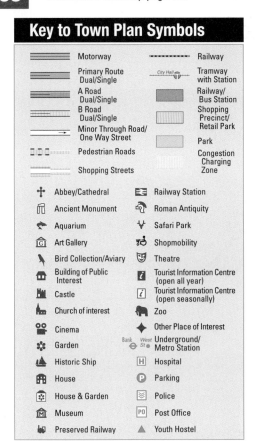

| | | | |
|---|---|---|---|
| Motorway | | Railway | |
| Primary Route Dual/Single | | Tramway with Station | City Hall |
| A Road Dual/Single | | Railway/ Bus Station | |
| B Road Dual/Single | | Shopping Precinct/ Retail Park | |
| Minor Through Road/ One Way Street | | Park | |
| Pedestrian Roads | | Congestion Charging Zone | |
| Shopping Streets | | | |

| | | | |
|---|---|---|---|
| ✝ | Abbey/Cathedral | 🚂 | Railway Station |
| 🏛 | Ancient Monument | | Roman Antiquity |
| 🐠 | Aquarium | | Safari Park |
| 🅖 | Art Gallery | 🕭 | Shopmobility |
| 🦅 | Bird Collection/Aviary | 🎭 | Theatre |
| 🏛 | Building of Public Interest | i | Tourist Information Centre (open all year) |
| 🏰 | Castle | i | Tourist Information Centre (open seasonally) |
| 🏛 | Church of interest | 🐘 | Zoo |
| 🎥 | Cinema | ◆ | Other Place of Interest |
| 🌼 | Garden | Bank West St⊖ | Underground/ Metro Station |
| 🚢 | Historic Ship | H | Hospital |
| 🏠 | House | P | Parking |
| 🏡 | House & Garden | 🛡 | Police |
| 🏛 | Museum | PO | Post Office |
| 🚂 | Preserved Railway | ▲ | Youth Hostel |

## Key to Approach Mapping Symbols

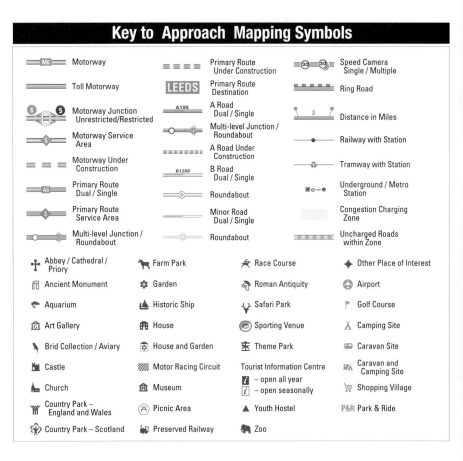

| | | | |
|---|---|---|---|
| M6 | Motorway | 30 30 | Speed Camera Single / Multiple |
| | Toll Motorway | | Ring Road |
| 6 5 | Motorway Junction Unrestricted/Restricted | 3 | Distance in Miles |
| S | Motorway Service Area | | Railway with Station |
| | Motorway Under Construction | | Tramway with Station |
| A6 | Primary Route Dual / Single | Ⓜ⊖● | Underground / Metro Station |
| S | Primary Route Service Area | | Congestion Charging Zone |
| | Multi-level Junction / Roundabout | | Uncharged Roads within Zone |
| | Primary Route Under Construction | | |
| LEEDS | Primary Route Destination | | |
| A195 | A Road Dual / Single | | |
| | Multi-level Junction / Roundabout | | |
| | A Road Under Construction | | |
| B1288 | B Road Dual / Single | | |
| | Roundabout | | |
| | Minor Road Dual / Single | | |
| | Roundabout | | |

| | | | | | | | |
|---|---|---|---|---|---|---|---|
| ✝ | Abbey / Cathedral / Priory | 🐕 | Farm Park | 🐎 | Race Course | ◆ | Other Place of Interest |
| 🏛 | Ancient Monument | 🌸 | Garden | | Roman Antiquity | ✈ | Airport |
| 🐠 | Aquarium | ⛵ | Historic Ship | | Safari Park | ⛳ | Golf Course |
| 🅖 | Art Gallery | 🏠 | House | ◎ | Sporting Venue | ⛺ | Camping Site |
| 🦅 | Brid Collection / Aviary | 🏡 | House and Garden | 🌳 | Theme Park | | Caravan Site |
| 🏰 | Castle | ▦ | Motor Racing Circuit | | Tourist Information Centre | | Caravan and Camping Site |
| 🏛 | Church | 🏛 | Museum | i | – open all year | | Shopping Village |
| 🎋 | Country Park – England and Wales | Ⓐ | Picnic Area | i | – open seasonally | P&R | Park & Ride |
| 🎋 | Country Park – Scotland | 🚂 | Preserved Railway | ▲ | Youth Hostel | | |
| | | | | 🐘 | Zoo | | |

## Aberdeen

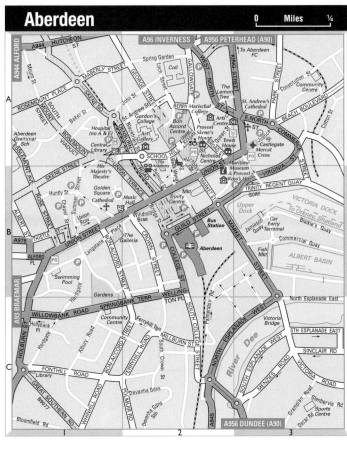

Miles 0 ¼

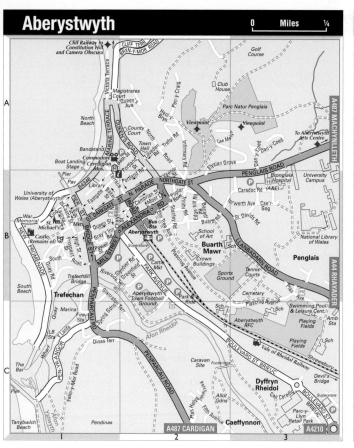

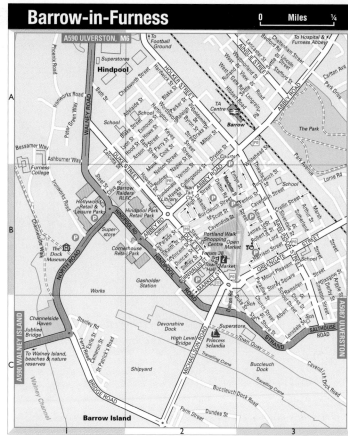

## Aberystwyth

Aberystwyth RFC . . C3
Aberystwyth
  Station ⭆ . . . . . . B2
Aberystwyth Town
  Football Ground . . B2
Alexandra Rd . . . . . B2
Ambulance Station  C3
Baker St . . . . . . . . . B1
Banadl Rd. . . . . . . . B2
Bandstand . . . . . . . A1
Bath St . . . . . . . . . . A2
Boat Landing
  Stage . . . . . . . . . A1
Boulevard
  St. Brieuc . . . . . . . C3
Bridge St . . . . . . . . B1
Bronglais
  Hospital Ⓗ . . . . . . B3
Bryn-y-Mor Rd . . . . A2
Buarth Rd . . . . . . . . B2
Bus Station . . . . . . B2
Cae Ceredig . . . . . . C3
Cae Melyn . . . . . . . A2
Cae'r-Gog . . . . . . . . B3
Cambrian St . . . . . . B2
Caradoc Rd . . . . . . B3
Caravan Site . . . . . . C2
Castle
  (Remains of) ▉ . . . B1
Castle St . . . . . . . . B1
Cattle Market . . . . . B2
Cemetary . . . . . . . . B3
Ceredigion
  Museum ▉ . . . . . . A1

Chalybeate St . . . . . B1
Cliff Terr . . . . . . . . . A2
Club House . . . . . . . A2
Commodore ⚓ . . . . A1
County Court . . . . . A2
Crown Buildings . . . B2
Dan-y-Coed . . . . . . A3
Dinas Terr . . . . . . . C1
Eastgate . . . . . . . . B1
Edge-hill Rd . . . . . . B2
Elm Tree Ave. . . . . . B2
Elysian Gr. . . . . . . . A2
Felin-y-Mor Rd . . . . C1
Fifth Ave . . . . . . . . . C2
Fire Station . . . . . . . C1
Glanrafon Terr. . . . . B1
Glyndwr Rd . . . . . . . B2
Golf Course . . . . . . A3
Gray's Inn Rd . . . . . B1
Great Darkgate St . . B1
Greenfield St . . . . . . B2
Heol-y-Bryn . . . . . . A2
High St . . . . . . . . . . B1
Infirmary Rd . . . . . . A2
Information Ctr Ⓘ . . B1
Iorwerth Ave . . . . . . B3
King St . . . . . . . . . . B1
Lauraplace . . . . . . . B1
Library . . . . . . . . . . B1
Lifeboat Station . . . C1
Llanbadarn Rd. . . . . B3
Loveden Rd . . . . . . A2
Magistrates Court. . A1
Marina. . . . . . . . . . . C1
Marine Terr . . . . . . . A1
Market . . . . . . . . . . B1

Mill St . . . . . . . . . . . B1
Moor La . . . . . . . . . B2
National Library
  of Wales . . . . . . . . B3
New Promenade. . . . B1
New St . . . . . . . . . . B1
North Beach . . . . . . A1
North Parade . . . . . B2
North Rd. . . . . . . . . A2
Northgate St. . . . . . B2
Parc Natur
  Penglais . . . . . . . . A3
Parc-y-Llyn
  Retail Park . . . . . . C3
Park & Ride . . . . . . B2
Park Ave . . . . . . . . . B2
Pavillion . . . . . . . . . B1
Pendinas. . . . . . . . . C1
Penglais Rd . . . . . . B3
Penparcau Rd . . C1/C2
Penrheidol . . . . . . . B2
Pen-y-Craig . . . . . . A2
Pen-yr-angor . . . . . C1
Pier St . . . . . . . . . . B1
Plas Ave . . . . . . . . . B3
Plas Helyg . . . . . . . B2
Plascrug Ave . . B2/C3
Police Station ▣ . . C2
Poplar Row . . . . . . . B1
Portland Rd . . . . . . B2
Portland St . . . . . . . A2
Post Office ⓅⓄ . . B1/B3
Powell St . . . . . . . . B1
Prospect St . . . . . . B1
Quay Rd . . . . . . . . . B1
Queen St . . . . . . . . B1

Queen's Ave . . . . . . A2
Queen's Rd. . . . . . . A2
Riverside Terr . . . . . B1
St. Davids Rd . . . . . B3
St. Michael's ⛴ . . . . B1
School of Art . . . . . . B2
South Beach. . . . . . B1
South Rd . . . . . . . . B1
Sports Ground . . . . B2
Spring Gdns . . . . . . C1
Stanley Rd . . . . . . . B2
Swimming Pool &
  Leisure Centre . . . C3
Tanybwlch Beach . . C1
Tennis Courts . . . . . B2
Terrace Rd . . . . . . . B1
The Bar. . . . . . . . . . C1
Town Hall . . . . . . . . A2
Trefechan Bridge . . B1
Trefor Rd . . . . . . . . A2
Trinity Rd . . . . . . . . B2
University
  Campus . . . . . . . . B3
University of Wales
  (Aberystwyth) . . . . B1
Vaenor St . . . . . . . . B2
Vale of Rheidol
  Railway 🚂 . . . . . . C3
Victoria Terr . . . . . . A1
Viewpoint ✦ . . . . . . A2
Viewpoint ✦ . . . . . . A3
War Memorial . . . . . B1
Y Lanfa . . . . . . . . . . C1

## Barrow-in-Furness

Abbey Rd . . . . . A3/B2
Adelaide St . . . . . . . A2
Ainslie St . . . . . . . . A3
Albert St . . . . . . . . . C3
Allison St . . . . . . . . B3
Anson St . . . . . . . . . A2
Argyle St . . . . . . . . B3
Arthur St . . . . . . . . A3
Ashburner Way. . . . A1
Barrow Raiders
  RLFC . . . . . . . . . . B1
Barrow
  Station ⭆ . . . . . A2
Bath St . . . . . . . A1/B2
Bedford Rd. . . . . . . A3
Bessamer Way . . . . A1
Blake St . . . . . . A1/A2
Bridge Rd . . . . . . . . C1
Buccleuch Dock. . . C3
Buccleuch
  Dock Rd . . . . C2/C3
Buccleuch St . . . . . B2
Byron St . . . . . . . . . A2
Calcutta St . . . . . . . A1
Cameron St . . . . . . C1
Carlton Ave . . . . . . . A3
Cavendish
  Dock Rd . . . . . . . . C3
Cavendish St . . B2/B3
Channelside Walk. . B1
Channelside
  Haven . . . . . . . . . C1
Chatsworth St . . . . A2
Cheltenham St . . . . A3
Church St . . . . . . . . C3
Clifford St . . . . . . . . B2
Clive St . . . . . . . . . . B1
Collingwood St. . . . B2

Cook St . . . . . . . . . A2
Cornernhouse
  Retail Park . . . . . . B2
Cornwallis St . . . . . B2
Courts. . . . . . . . . . . A2
Crellin St . . . . . . . . B3
Cross St . . . . . . . . . C3
Dalkeith St . . . . . . . B2
Dalton Rd . . . . . B2/C2
Derby St . . . . . . . . . B3
Devonshire Dock . . C2
Dock Museum,
  The ▉ . . . . . . . . . B1
Drake St . . . . . . . . . A2
Dryden St . . . . . . . . A2
Duke St . . . . . A1/B2/C3
Duncan St . . . . . . . A2
Dundee St . . . . . . . C2
Dundonald St . . . . . B2
Earle St . . . . . . . . . C1
Emlyn St . . . . . . . . B2
Exmouth St . . . . . . A2
Farm St . . . . . . . . . C2
Fell St . . . . . . . . . . B3
Fenton St . . . . . . . . B3
Ferry Rd . . . . . . . . . C1
Forum 28 ⛭ . . . . . . B2
Furness College . . . B1
Glasgow St . . . . . . B3
Goldsmith St . . . . . A2
Greengate St . . . . . B3
Hardwick St . . . . . . A2
Harrison St . . . . . . . B3
Hartington St . . . . . A2
Hawke St . . . . . . . . A2
Hibbert Rd . . . . . . . A2
High Level Bridge. . C2
High St . . . . . . . . . . B2
Hindpool Park
  Retail Park . . . . . . B2
Hindpool Rd . . . . . . B2
Holker St . . . . . . . . A2

Hollywood Retail &
  Leisure Park . . . . . B1
Hood St . . . . . . . . . A2
Howard St . . . . . . . B2
Howe St . . . . . . . . . A2
Information Ctr Ⓘ . . B2
Ironworks Rd . . A1/B1
James St . . . . . . . . B3
Jubilee Bridge . . . . C1
Keith St . . . . . . . . . B2
Keyes St . . . . . . . . . A2
Lancaster St . . . . . . A2
Lawson St . . . . . . . B2
Library . . . . . . . . . . B2
Lincoln St . . . . . . . . A3
Longreins Rd . . . . . A3
Lonsdale St . . . . . . C3
Lord St . . . . . . . . . . B2
Lorne Rd. . . . . . . . . B3
Lyon St . . . . . . . . . . A2
Manchester St . . . . B2
Market . . . . . . . . . . B2
Market St . . . . . . . . B2
Marsh St . . . . . . . . B3
Michaelson Rd. . . . C2
Milton St . . . . . . . . A2
Monk St . . . . . . . . . B3
Mount Pleasant . . . B3
Nan Tait Centre. . . . B2
Napier St . . . . . . . . B2
Nelson St . . . . . . . . B2
North Rd . . . . . . . . . B1
Open Market . . . . . B2
Parade St . . . . . . . . B2
Paradise St. . . . . . . A3
Park Ave . . . . . . . . . A3
Park Dr . . . . . . . . . . A3
Parker St . . . . . . . . A2
Parry St . . . . . . . . . A2
Peter Green Way . . A1
Phoenix Rd . . . . . . A1
Police Station ▣ . . B2

Portland Walk
  Shopping Centre . B2
Post Office ⓅⓄ
  . . . . . . . . A3/B2/B3
Princess
  Selandia ⛴ . . . . . . C2
Raleigh St. . . . . . . . A2
Ramsden St . . . . . . B3
Rawlinson St . . . . . B3
Robert St . . . . . . . . B3
Rodney St. . . . . . . . B2
Rutland St . . . . . . . A2
St Patrick's Rd . . . . C1
Salthouse Rd . . . . . C3
School St . . . . . . . . B3
Scott St . . . . . . . . . B2
Settle St . . . . . . . . . A3
Shore St . . . . . . . . . C3
Sidney St . . . . . . . . B2
Silverdale St . . . . . . B3
Slater St . . . . . . . . . B2
Smeaton St . . . . . . B3
Stafford St . . . . . . . A3
Stanley Rd . . . . . . . C1
Stark St . . . . . . . . . C3
Steel St . . . . . . . . . B1
Storey Sq . . . . . . . . B3
Strand. . . . . . . . . . . C3
Sutherland St . . . . . B3
TA Centre . . . . . . . . A2
The Park . . . . . . . . . A3
Thwaite St . . . . . . . B3
Town Hall . . . . . . . . B2
Town Quay . . . . . . . C3
Vernon St . . . . . . . . B2
Vincent St. . . . . . . . B2
Walney Rd . . . . . . . A1
West Gate Rd. . . . . A2
West View Rd. . . . . A3
Westmorland St . . . A3
Whitehead St . . . . . A3
Wordsworth St . . . . A2

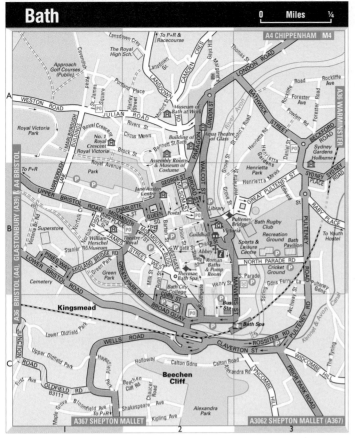

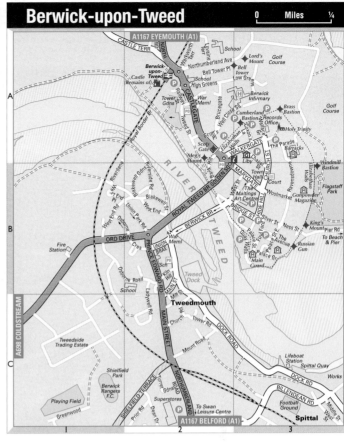

## Bath

Alexandra Park. . . . . C2
Alexandra Rd . . . . . C2
Approach Golf
  Courses (Public) . . A1
Aqua Theatre
  of Glass 🏛 . . . . A2
Archway St. . . . . . . C3
Assembly Rooms
  & Museum of
  Costume 🏛 . . . . . A2
Avon St. . . . . . . . . B2
Barton St . . . . . . . B2
Bath Abbey ✝. . . . . B2
Bath City College . . B2
Bath Pavilion . . . . . B3
Bath Rugby Club . . . B3
Bath Spa
  Station 🚆 . . . . C3
Bathwick St . . . . . . A3
Beechen Cliff Rd . . C2
Bennett St . . . . . . . B2
Bloomfield Ave . . . . C1
Broad Quay . . . . . . C2
Broad St . . . . . . . . B2
Brock St . . . . . . . . A1
Building of Bath
  Museum 🏛 . . . . A2
Bus Station . . . . . . C2
Calton Gdns . . . . . . C2
Calton Rd . . . . . . . C2
Camden Cr . . . . . . A2
Cavendish Rd. . . . . A1
Cemetery . . . . . . . B1
Charlotte St . . . . . . B2
Chaucer Rd . . . . . . C2
Cheap St . . . . . . . . B2
Circus Mews. . . . . . A2
Claverton St . . . . . C2
Corn St. . . . . . . . . C2

Cricket Ground. . . . B3
Daniel St. . . . . . . . A3
Edward St. . . . . . . A3
Ferry La . . . . . . . . B3
First Ave . . . . . . . . C1
Forester Ave . . . . . A3
Forester Rd. . . . . . A3
Gays Hill . . . . . . . . A2
George St . . . . . . . B3
Great Pulteney St. . B3
Green Park . . . . . . B1
Green Park Rd . . . . B2
Grove St. . . . . . . . B2
Guildhall 🏛 . . . . . B2
Harley St. . . . . . . . A2
Hayesfield Park . . . C1
Henrietta Gdns . . . A3
Henrietta Mews . . . B3
Henrietta Park . . . . B3
Henrietta Rd . . . . . A3
Henrietta St . . . . . B3
Henry St . . . . . . . . B2
Holburne
  Museum 🏛 . . . . B3
Holloway. . . . . . . . C2
Information Ctr 🅸 . . B2
James St West . . B1/B2
Jane Austen
  Centre 🏛 . . . . . A2
Julian Rd . . . . . . . A1
Junction Rd . . . . . . C1
Kipling Ave . . . . . . C2
Lansdown Cr . . . . . A1
Lansdown Gr . . . . . A2
Lansdown Rd . . . . . A2
Library . . . . . . . . . B2
London Rd . . . . . . A3
London St. . . . . . . A2
Lower Bristol Rd. . . B1
Lower Oldfield
  Park . . . . . . . . . C1

Lyncombe Hill. . . . . C3
Manvers St. . . . . . . B3
Maple Gr. . . . . . . . C1
Margaret's Hill. . . . A2
Marlborough
  Buildings. . . . . . A1
Marlborough La . . . B1
Midland
  Bridge Rd . . . . . B1
Milk St . . . . . . . . . B2
Milson St . . . . . . . B2
Monmouth St . . . . . B2
Morford St . . . . . . A2
Museum of Bath
  at Work 🏛 . . . . . A2
New King St . . . . . . B1
No. 1 Royal
  Crescent 🏛 . . . . A1
Norfolk Bldgs . . . . A1
Norfolk Cr. . . . . . . B1
North Parade Rd . . B3
Oldfield Rd . . . . . . C1
Paragon . . . . . . . . A2
Pines Way. . . . . . . A1
Police Station 🛆 . . B3
Portland Pl . . . . . . A2
Post Office 🏤
  . . . . . .A1/A3/B2/C2
Postal Museum 🏛 . B2
Powlett Rd . . . . . . A3
Prior Park Rd . . . . . C3
Pulteney Bridge ✦ . B2
Pulteney Gdns . . . . B3
Pulteney Rd . . . . . . B3
Queen Sq . . . . . . . B2
Raby Pl . . . . . . . . . B3
Recreation
  Ground . . . . . . . B3
Rivers St . . . . . . . . A2
Rockliffe Ave . . . . . A3
Rockliffe Rd . . . . . A3

Roman Baths &
  Pump Room 🏛 . . B2
Rossiter Rd. . . . . . . C3
Royal Ave . . . . . . . A1
Royal Cr . . . . . . . . A1
Royal High
  School, The . . . . A2
Royal Victoria Park. A1
St James Sq. . . . . . A1
St John's Rd. . . . . . A3
Shakespeare Ave . . C2
Southgate. . . . . . . B2
South Pde . . . . . . . B3
Sports & Leisure
  Centre. . . . . . . . B3
Spring Gdns . . . . . C3
Stall St . . . . . . . . . B2
Stanier Rd . . . . . . . A1
Sydney Gdns . . . . . A3
Sydney Pl. . . . . . . . B3
Theatre Royal 🎭 . . B2
Thermae
  Bath Spa ✦ . . . . B2
The Tyning . . . . . . C3
Thomas St . . . . . . A3
Union St . . . . . . . . B2
Upper Bristol Rd . . B1
Upper Oldfield
  Park . . . . . . . . . C1
Victoria Art
  Gallery 🏛 . . . . . B2
Victoria Bridge Rd . B1
Walcot St . . . . . . . A2
Wells Rd . . . . . . . . C1
Westgate St . . . . . B2
Weston Rd . . . . . . A1
Widcombe Hill . . . . C3
William Herschel
  Museum 🏛 . . . . . B1

## Berwick-upon-Tweed

Bank Hill . . . . . . . . B2
Barracks 🏛 . . . . . A3
Bell Tower ✦ . . . . A3
Bell Tower Pl. . . . . A2
Berwick Br . . . . . . B2
Berwick
  Infirmary 🏥 . . . A3
Berwick
  Rangers F.C. . . . . C1
Berwick-upon-
  Tweed 🚆 . . . . . A2
Billendean Rd. . . . . C3
Blakewell Gdns . . . B2
Blakewell St . . . . . B2
Brass Bastion ✦ . . A3
Bridge St . . . . . . . B3
Brucegate St . . . . . A2
Castle
  (Remains of) 🏰 . . A2
Castle Terr . . . . . . A2
Castlegate . . . . . . A2
Chapel St . . . . . . . A3
Church Rd . . . . . . . C2
Church St . . . . . . . B3
Coxon's La . . . . . . A3
Cumberland
  Bastion ✦ . . . . . A3
Dean Dr . . . . . . . . C2

Dock Rd . . . . . . C2/C3
Elizabethan
  Walls . . . . . . A2/B3
Fire Station . . . . . . B1
Flagstaff Park . . . . B3
Football Ground . . . C3
Foul Ford . . . . . . . B3
Gallery . . . . . . . . . A3
Golden Sq . . . . . . . B2
Golf Course . . . . . A3
Greenwood. . . . . . C1
Gunpowder
  Magazine 🏛 . . . B3
Hide Hill . . . . . . . . B3
High Greens . . . . . A2
Holy Trinity ⛪ . . . A3
Information Ctr 🅸 . . A2
Kiln Hill . . . . . . . . B3
King's Mount ✦ . . . B3
Ladywell Rd . . . . . C2
Library . . . . . . . . . A3
Lifeboat Station . . . C3
Lord's Mount ✦ . . . A2
Lovaine Terr . . . . . A2
Low Greens . . . . . . A3
Main Guard 🏛 . . . B3
Main St. . . . . . . B2/C2
Maltings Art
  Centre, The . . . . B3
Marygate . . . . . . . B3
Meg's Mount ✦ . . A2
Middle St . . . . . . . C3
Mill St. . . . . . . . . . C2

Mount Rd . . . . . . . C2
Museum 🏛 . . . . . . B3
Ness St. . . . . . . . . B3
North Rd . . . . . . . A2
Northumberland
  Ave . . . . . . . . . A2
Northumberland
  Rd. . . . . . . . . . . C2
Ord Dr. . . . . . . . . B1
Osborne Cr. . . . . . B2
Osborne Rd . . . . . B1
Palace Gr . . . . . . . B3
Palace St. . . . . . . . B3
Palace St East . . . . B3
Pier Rd . . . . . . . . . B3
Playing Field. . . . . C1
Police Station 🛆 . . B3
Post Office 🏤
  . . . . . . . . A2/B2/B2
Prince Edward Rd . B2
Prior Rd . . . . . . . . C2
Quay Walls . . . . . . B3
Railway St . . . . . . A2
Ravensdowne . . . . A3
Records Office . . . . A3
Riverdene . . . . . . . B1
Riverside Rd. . . . . . B2
Royal Border Br . . A2
Royal Tweed Br . . . B2
Russian Gun ✦ . . . B3
Scots Gate ✦ . . . . A2
Scott's Pl . . . . . . . A2
Shielfield Park . . . . C1

Shielfield Terr . . . . C2
Silver St . . . . . . . . B3
Spittal Quay . . . . . C3
Superstores . . . . . C2
The Avenue . . . . . B3
The Parade . . . . . . A3
Tower Gdns . . . . . A2
Tower Rd . . . . . . . C2
Town Hall ✦ . . . . . B3
Turret Gdns. . . . . . C2
Tweed Dock . . . . . B2
Tweed St. . . . . . . . A2
Tweedside Trading
  Estate . . . . . . . . C1
Union Brae . . . . . . A2
Union Park Rd . . . . B2
Walkergate . . . . . . A3
Wallace Gr . . . . . . A2
War Memorial . . . . A2
War Memorial . . . . B2
Warkworth Terr. . . . A2
Well Close Sq . . . . A2
West End . . . . . . . B2
West End Pl . . . . . B1
West End Rd . . . . . B1
West St. . . . . . . . . C3
West St. . . . . . . . . C3
Windmill
  Bastion ✦ . . . . . B3
Woolmarket . . . . . B3
Works. . . . . . . . . . C3

## Birmingham

Abbey St. . . . . . . . A2
Aberdeen St . . . . . A1
Acorn Gr. . . . . . . . A1
Adams St. . . . . . . . A5
Adderley St. . . . . . C5
Albert St . . . . . B4/B5
Albion St. . . . . . . . A2
Alcester St . . . . . . C5

Aldgate Gr . . . . . . A3
Alexandra
  Theatre 🎭 . . . . . C3
All Saints St . . . . . A2
All Saints Rd. . . . . A2
Allcock St. . . . . . . C5
Allesley St. . . . . . . A4
Allison St . . . . . . . C4
Alma Cr . . . . . . . . B6
Alston Rd . . . . . . . C1

Arcadian Centre . . C4
Arthur St. . . . . . . . C6
Assay Office 🏛 . . B3
Aston
  Expressway . . . . A5
Aston Science
  Park . . . . . . . . . B5
Aston St . . . . . . . . B4
Avenue Rd . . . . . . A5
BT Tower ✦ . . . . . B3

Bacchus Rd . . . . . A1
Bagot St . . . . . . . B5
Banbury St . . . . . . B5
Barford Rd . . . . . . B1
Barford St. . . . . . . C4
Barn St . . . . . . . . . C5
Barnwell Rd . . . . . C6
Barr St . . . . . . . . . A3
Barrack St . . . . . . B5
Bartholomew St . . C4

Barwick St . . . . . . B4
Bath Row . . . . . . . C3
Beaufort Rd . . . . . C1
Belmont Row . . . . . B5
Benson Rd . . . . . . A1
Berkley St . . . . . . . C3
Bexhill Gr . . . . . . . C3
Birchall St. . . . . . . C5
Birmingham City F.C.
  (St Andrew's) . . . C6

Birmingham City
  Hospital (A&E) 🏥 . A1
Bishopsgate St. . . . C3
Blews St. . . . . . . . A4
Bloomsbury St . . . . A6
Blucher St. . . . . . . C3
Bordesley St. . . . . C4
Bowyer St. . . . . . . C5
Bradburne Way . . . A5
Bradford St. . . . . . C5

Branston St . . . . . A3
Brearley St . . . . . . A4
Brewery St . . . . . . A4
Bridge St . . . . . . . A3
Bridge St . . . . . . . C3
Bridge St West . . . A4
Brindley Dr . . . . . . B3
Broad St . . . . . . . . C2
Broad St UGC 🎦. . C2
Broadway Plaza ✦ . C2

Bromley St . . . . . . C5
Bromsgrove St . . . . C4
Brookfield Rd . . . . A2
Browning St . . . . . C2
Bryant St . . . . . . . A1
Buckingham St. . . . A4
Bullring . . . . . . . . C4
Bull St. . . . . . . . . . B4
Cambridge St . . . . C3
Camden Dr. . . . . . . B3

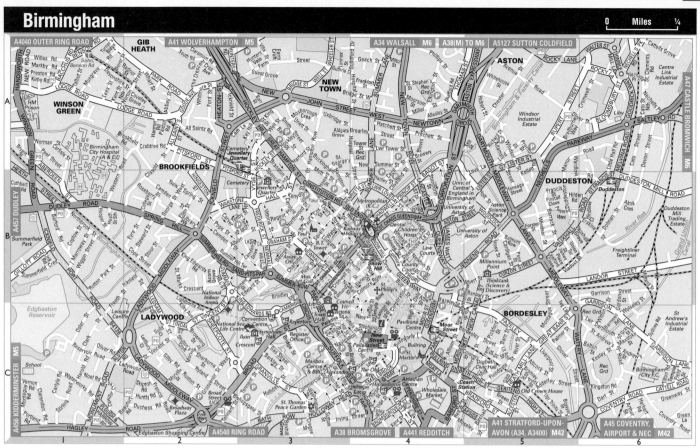

# Birmingham

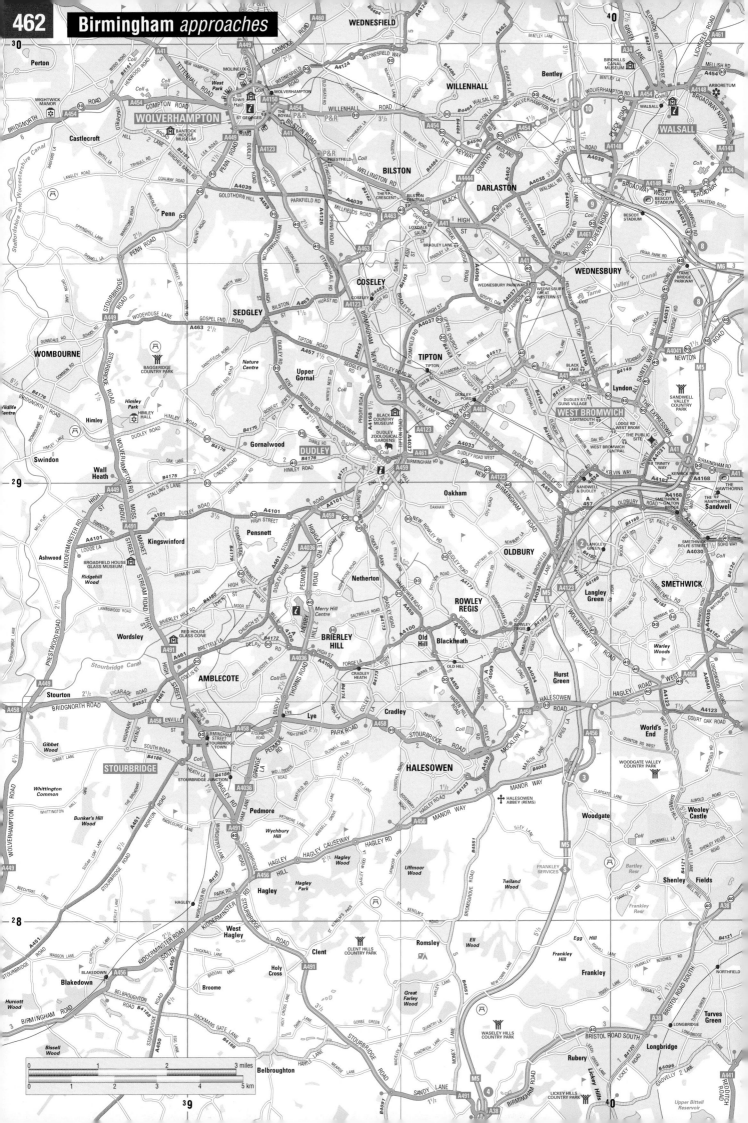

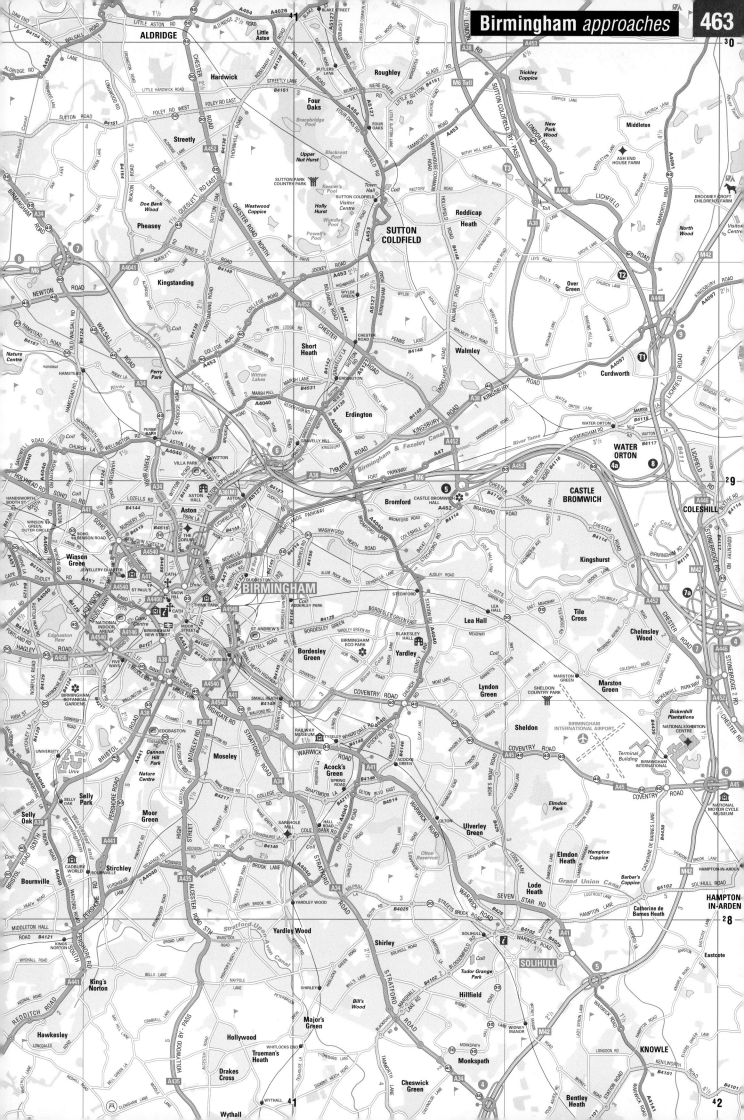

## Blackpool

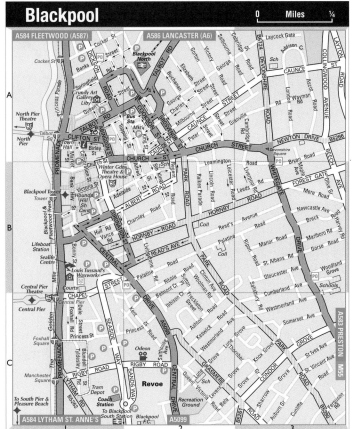

## Bournemouth

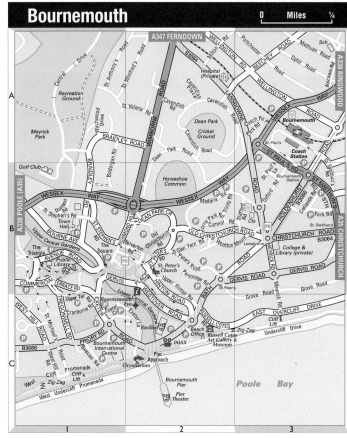

# Bradford

0  Miles  ¼

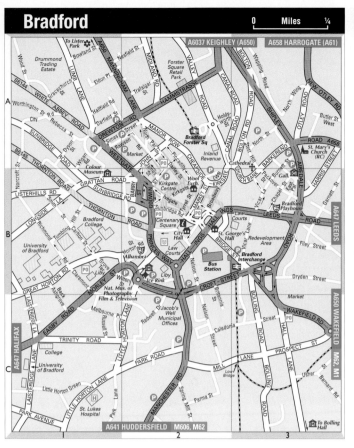

# Brighton

0  Miles  ¼

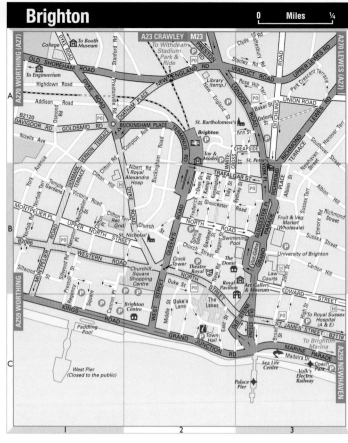

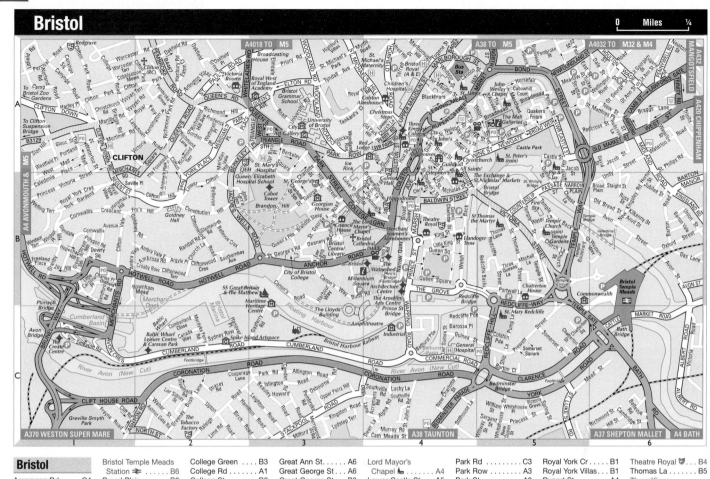

## Bristol

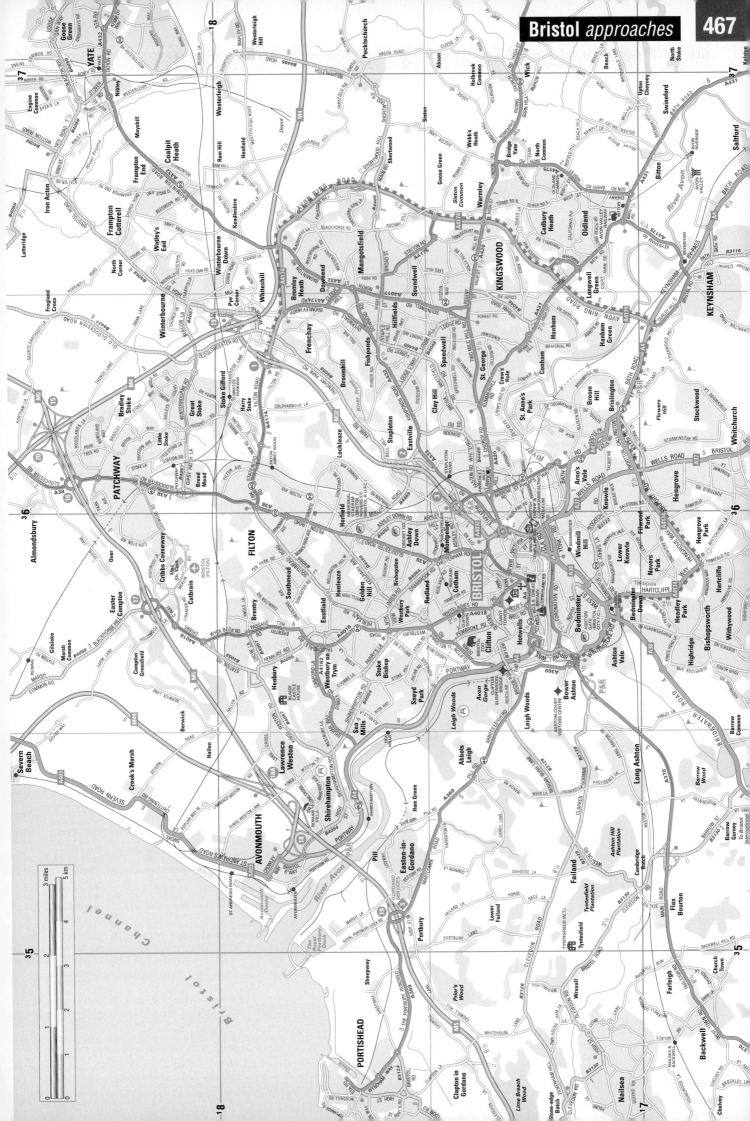

# Cardiff / Caerdydd

0    Miles    ¼

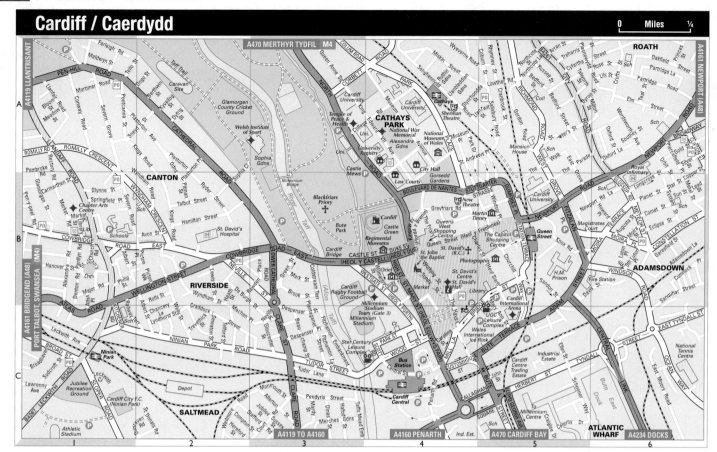

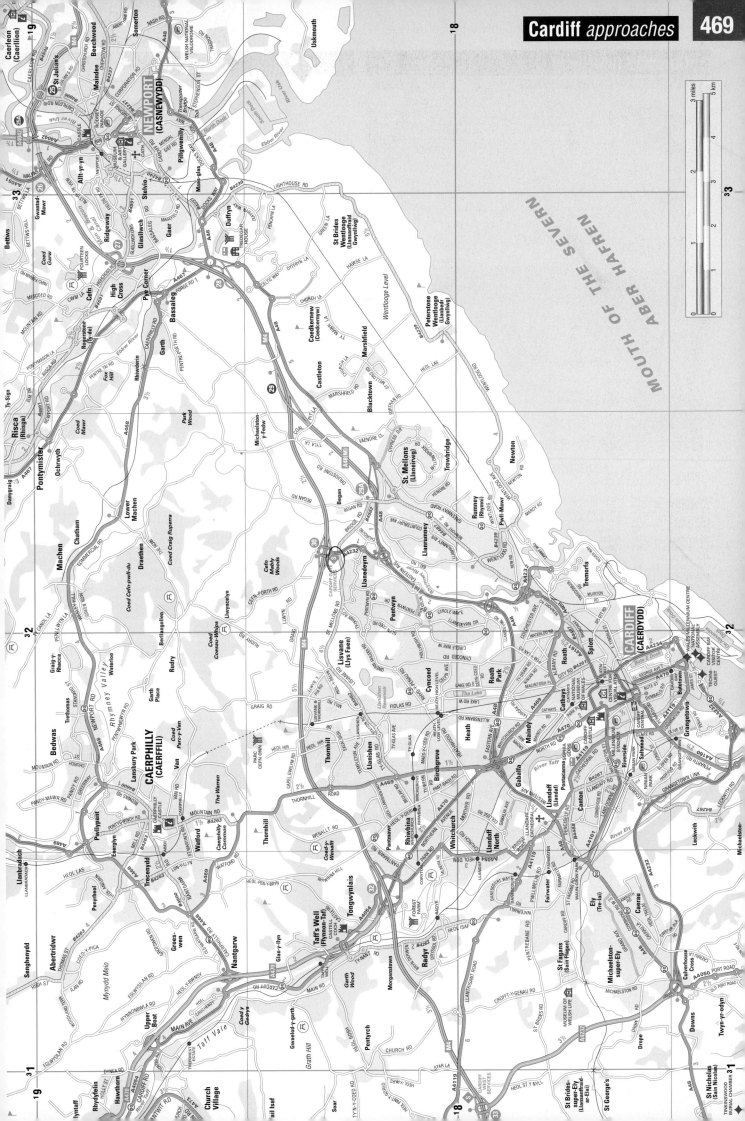

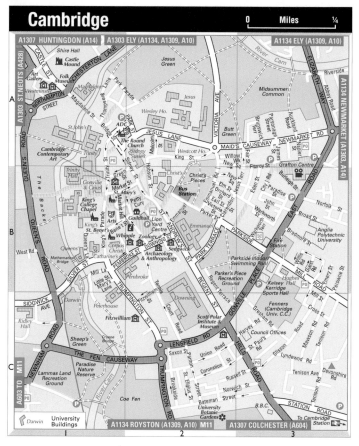

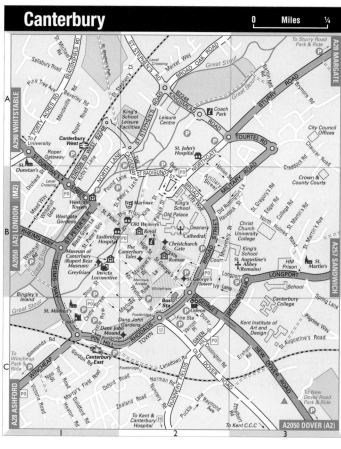

## Cambridge

| | |
|---|---|
| Abbey Rd | A3 |
| ADC 🎭 | A2 |
| Anglia Polytechnic University | B3 |
| Archaeology & Anthropology 🏛 | B2 |
| Art Gallery 🏛 | A1 |
| Arts Theatre 🎭 | B1 |
| Auckland Rd | A3 |
| Bateman St | C2 |
| B.B.C. | C3 |
| Bene't St | B1 |
| Bradmore St | B3 |
| Bridge St | A1 |
| Broad St | B3 |
| Brookside | C2 |
| Brunswick Terr | A3 |
| Burleigh St | B3 |
| Bus Station | B2 |
| Butt Green | A2 |
| Cambridge Contemporary Art Gallery 🏛 | B1 |
| Castle Mound 🏰 | A1 |
| Castle St | A1 |
| Chesterton La | A1 |
| Christ's (Coll) | B2 |
| Christ's Pieces | B2 |
| City Rd | B3 |
| Clare (Coll) | B1 |
| Clarendon St | B2 |
| Coe Fen | C2 |
| Coronation St | C2 |
| Corpus Christi (Coll) | B1 |
| Council Offices | C3 |
| Cross St | C3 |
| Crusoe Bridge | C1 |
| Darwin (Coll) | C1 |
| Devonshire Rd | C3 |
| Downing (Coll) | B2 |
| Downing St | B2 |
| Earl St | B2 |
| East Rd | B3 |
| Eden St | B3 |
| Elizabeth Way | A3 |
| Elm St | B2 |
| Emery St | B3 |
| Emmanuel (Coll) | B2 |
| Emmanuel Rd | B2 |
| Emmanuel St | B2 |
| Fair St | A3 |
| Fenners (Cambridge Univ. C. C.) | C3 |
| Fire Station | B3 |
| Fitzroy St | A3 |
| Fitzwilliam Museum 🏛 | C1 |
| Fitzwilliam (Coll) | A1 |
| Folk Museum 🏛 | A1 |
| Glisson Rd | C3 |
| Gonville & Caius (Coll) | B1 |
| Gonville Place | B3 |
| Grafton Centre | A3 |
| Green St | B1 |
| Gresham Rd | C3 |
| Guest Rd | B3 |
| Guildhall 🏛 | B2 |
| Harvey Rd | C3 |
| Hills Rd | C2 |
| Hobson St | B2 |
| Hughes Hall (Coll) | B3 |
| Information Ctr 🛈 | B2 |
| James St | B3 |
| Jesus (Coll) | A2 |
| Jesus Green | A2 |
| Jesus La | A2 |
| Jesus Terr | B3 |
| John St | B3 |
| Kelsey Kerridge Sports Hall | B3 |
| King St | B2 |
| King's (Coll) | B1 |
| King's College Chapel | B1 |
| King's Parade | B1 |
| Lensfield Rd | C2 |
| Lion Yard Centre | B2 |
| Little St Mary's La | B1 |
| Lyndewod Rd | C3 |
| Magdalene (Coll) | A1 |
| Magdalene St | A1 |
| Maid's Causeway | A3 |
| Malcolm St | A2 |
| Market Hill | B1 |
| Market St | B1 |
| Mathematical Bridge | B1 |
| Mawson Rd | C3 |
| Midsummer Common | A3 |
| Mill La | B1 |
| Mill Rd | B3 |
| Napier St | A3 |
| New Square | A2 |
| Newmarket Rd | A3 |
| Newnham Rd | C1 |
| Norfolk St | B3 |
| Northampton St | A1 |
| Norwich St | C2 |
| Orchard St | B2 |
| Panton St | C2 |
| Paradise Nature Reserve | C1 |
| Paradise St | B3 |
| Park Parade | A1 |
| Park St | A2 |
| Park Terr | B2 |
| Parker St | B2 |
| Parker's Piece | B2 |
| Parkside | B3 |
| Parkside Swimming Pool | B3 |
| Parsonage St | A3 |
| Pembroke (Coll) | B2 |
| Pembroke St | B1 |
| Perowne St | B3 |
| Peterhouse (Coll) | C1 |
| Petty Cury | B2 |
| Police Station 🚓 | B3 |
| Post Office 🏤 | A1/A3/ B2/B3/C1/C2/C3 |
| Queens' (Coll) | B1 |
| Queen's La | B1 |
| Queen's Rd | B1 |
| Regent St | B2 |
| Regent Terr | B2 |
| Ridley Hall (Coll) | C1 |
| Riverside | A3 |
| Round Church, The | A1 |
| Russell St | C2 |
| St Andrew's St | B2 |
| St Benet's 🏛 | B1 |
| St Catharine's (Coll) | B1 |
| St Eligius St | C2 |
| St John's (Coll) | A1 |
| St Mary's 🏛 | B1 |
| St Paul's Rd | C3 |
| Saxon St | C2 |
| Scott Polar Institute & Museum 🏛 | C2 |
| Sedgwick Museum 🏛 | B2 |
| Sheep's Green | C1 |
| Shelly Row | A1 |
| Shire Hall | A1 |
| Sidgwick Ave | A1 |
| Sidney St | A1 |
| Sidney Sussex (Coll) | A2 |
| Silver St | B1 |
| Station Rd | C3 |
| Tenison Ave | C3 |
| Tenison Rd | C3 |
| Tennis Court Rd | B2 |
| The Backs | B1 |
| The Fen Causeway | C1 |
| Thompson's La | A1 |
| Trinity (Coll) | A1 |
| Trinity Hall (Coll) | B1 |
| Trinity St | A2 |
| Trumpington Rd | C2 |
| Trumpington St | C2 |
| Union Rd | C2 |
| University Botanic Gardens 🌼 | C2 |
| Victoria Ave | A2 |
| Victoria St | B2 |
| Warkworth St | B3 |
| Warkworth Terr | B3 |
| Wesley House (Coll) | A2 |
| West Rd | B1 |
| Westcott House (Coll) | A2 |
| Westminster (Coll) | A1 |
| Whipple 🏛 | B2 |
| Willis Rd | B3 |
| Willow Walk | A2 |
| Zoology 🏛 | B2 |

## Canterbury

| | |
|---|---|
| Artillery St | B2 |
| Barton Mill Rd | A3 |
| Beaconsfield Rd | A1 |
| Beverley Rd | A1 |
| Bingley's Island | B1 |
| Black Griffin La | B1 |
| Broad Oak Rd | A2 |
| Broad St | B2 |
| Brymore Rd | A3 |
| Burgate | B2 |
| Bus Station | C2 |
| Canterbury College | C3 |
| Canterbury East 🚉 | C1 |
| Canterbury Tales, The ♦ | B2 |
| Canterbury West 🚉 | A1 |
| Castle | C1 |
| Castle Row | C1 |
| Castle St | C1 |
| Cathedral † | B2 |
| Chaucer Rd | A3 |
| Christ Church University College | B3 |
| Christchurch Gate ♦ | B2 |
| City Council Offices | A3 |
| City Wall | C3 |
| Coach Park | A2 |
| College Rd | B3 |
| Cossington Rd | C2 |
| Court | A2 |
| Craddock Rd | A3 |
| Crown & County Courts | B3 |
| Dane John Gdns | C2 |
| Dane John Mound ♦ | C1 |
| Deanery | B2 |
| Dover St | C2 |
| Duck La | B2 |
| Eastbridge Hospital 🏛 | B1 |
| Edgar Rd | B3 |
| Ersham Rd | C3 |
| Ethelbert Rd | C3 |
| Fire Station | C2 |
| Forty Acres Rd | A1 |
| Gordon Rd | C1 |
| Greyfriars ♦ | B1 |
| Guildford Rd | C1 |
| Havelock St | B2 |
| Heaton Rd | C1 |
| High St | B2 |
| HM Prison | B3 |
| Information Ctr 🛈 | A2/B2 |
| Invicta Locomotive 🚂 | B1 |
| Ivy La | C1 |
| Kent Institute of Art and Design | C3 |
| King St | A2 |
| King's School | B3 |
| Kingsmead Rd | A2 |
| Kirby's La | B1 |
| Lansdown Rd | C2 |
| Leisure Centre | A2 |
| Longport | B3 |
| Lower Chantry La | C3 |
| Mandeville Rd | A1 |
| Market Way | A2 |
| Marlowe Arcade | B2 |
| Marlowe Ave | C2 |
| Marlowe Theatre 🎭 | B2 |
| Martyr's Field Rd | C1 |
| Mead Way | B1 |
| Military Rd | B2 |
| Monastery St | B2 |
| Museum of Canterbury (Rupert Bear Museum) | B1 |
| New Dover Rd | C3 |
| New St | C1 |
| Norman Rd | C2 |
| North Holmes Rd | B3 |
| North La | B1 |
| Northgate | A2 |
| Nunnery Fields | C2 |
| Nunnery Rd | C2 |
| Oaten Hill | C2 |
| Odeon Cinema 🎦 | C2 |
| Old Dover Rd | C2 |
| Old Palace | B2 |
| Old Ruttington La | B2 |
| Old Weavers 🏛 | B2 |
| Orchard St | B1 |
| Oxford Rd | C1 |
| Palace St | B2 |
| Pilgrims Way | C2 |
| Pin Hill | C1 |
| Pine Tree Ave | A1 |
| Police Station 🚓 | A2 |
| Post Office 🏤 | B1/B2/C1/C2 |
| Pound La | B1 |
| Puckle La | C2 |
| Raymond Ave | C2 |
| Rheims Way | B1 |
| Rhodaus Town | C2 |
| Roman Museum 🏛 | B2 |
| Roper Gateway | A1 |
| Roper Rd | A1 |
| Rose La | C2 |
| Royal Museum 🏛 | B2 |
| St Augustine's Abbey (remains) † | B2 |
| St Augustine's Rd | C3 |
| St Dunstan's 🏛 | A1 |
| St Dunstan's St | A1 |
| St George's Pl | C2 |
| St George's St | B2 |
| St George's Tower ♦ | B2 |
| St Gregory's Rd | B3 |
| St John's Hospital 🏛 | A2 |
| St Margaret's St | C2 |
| St Martin's 🏛 | B3 |
| St Martin's Ave | B3 |
| St Martin's Rd | B3 |
| St Michael's Rd | A1 |
| St Mildred's 🏛 | C1 |
| St Peter's Gr | C1 |
| St Peter's La | B2 |
| St Peter's Pl | B1 |
| St Peter's St | B1 |
| St Radigunds St | B2 |
| St Stephen's Ct | A1 |
| St Stephen's Path | A1 |
| St Stephen's Rd | A2 |
| Salisbury Rd | A1 |
| Simmonds La | C1 |
| Spring La | C3 |
| Station Rd West | B1 |
| Stour St | B2 |
| Sturry Rd | A3 |
| The Causeway | A2 |
| The Friars | B2 |
| Tourtel Rd | A3 |
| Union St | B2 |
| Vernon Pl | C2 |
| Victoria Rd | C1 |
| Watling St | B2 |
| Westgate Towers 🏛 | B1 |
| Westgate Gdns | B1 |
| Whitefriars | B1 |
| Whitehall Gdns | B1 |
| Whitehall Rd | B1 |
| Wincheap | C1 |
| York Rd | C1 |
| Zealand Rd | C2 |

# Carlisle

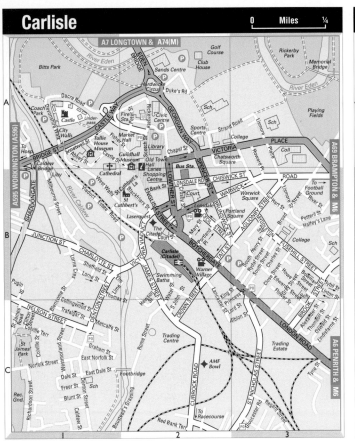

# Cheltenham

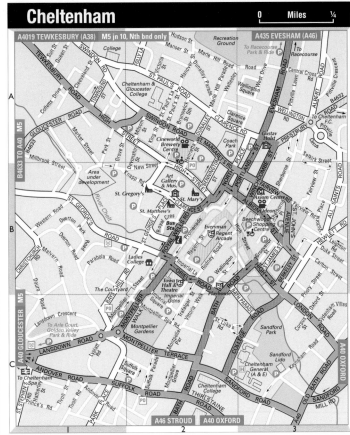

## Chester

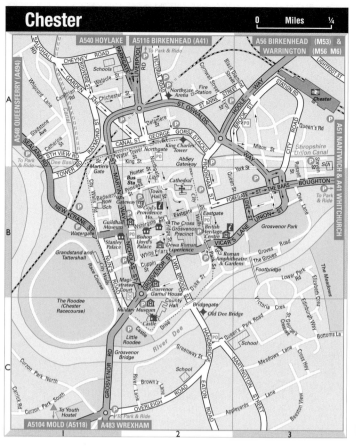

## Colchester

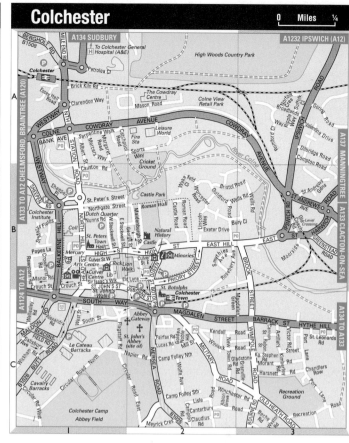

# Coventry

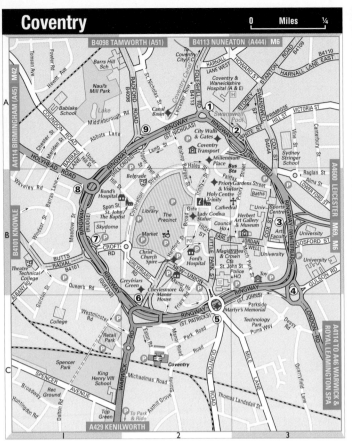

# Derby

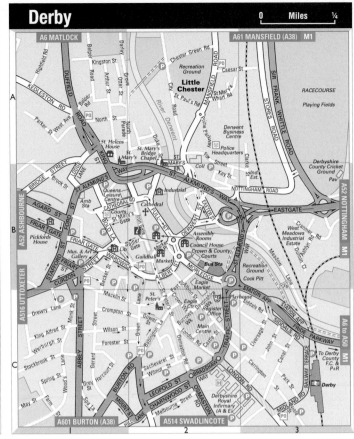

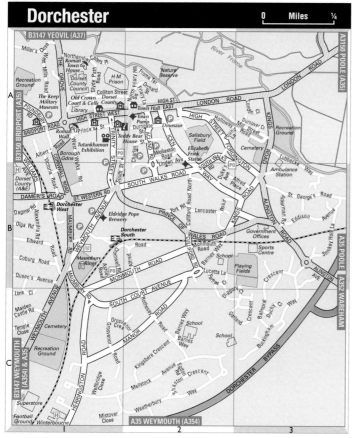

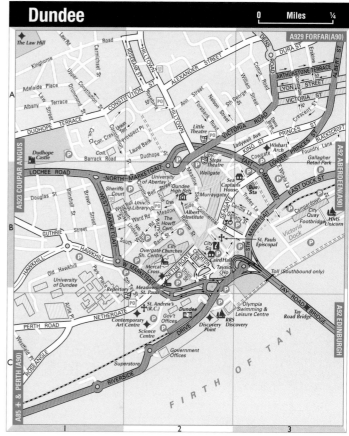

## Dorchester

| | |
|---|---|
| Ackerman Rd . . . . . B3 | |
| Acland Rd . . . . . . . A2 | |
| Albert Rd . . . . . . . A1 | |
| Alexandra Rd . . . . . B1 | |
| Alfred Place . . . . . . B3 | |
| Alfred Rd . . . . . . . A2 | |
| Alington Ave . . . . . B3 | |
| Alington Rd. . . . . . B3 | |
| Ambulance | |
| Station . . . . . . . . . B3 | |
| Ashley Rd . . . . . . . B1 | |
| Balmoral Cres. . . . . C3 | |
| Barnes Way . . . . . B2/C2 | |
| Borough Gdns . . . . A1 | |
| Bridport Rd . . . . . . B1 | |
| Buckingham Way . . C3 | |
| Caters Place . . . . . . A1 | |
| Charles St. . . . . . . A2 | |
| Coburg Rd . . . . . . B1 | |
| Colliton St. . . . . . . A1 | |
| Cornwall Rd . . . . . A1 | |
| Cromwell Rd. . . . . . B1 | |
| Culliford Rd . . . . . . B2 | |
| Culliford Rd North . . B2 | |
| Dagmar Rd . . . . . . B1 | |
| Damer's Rd. . . . . . . B1 | |
| Diggory Cres . . . . . B2 | |
| Dinosaur | |
| Museum 🏛 . . . . . A2 | |
| Dorchester | |
| Bypass . . . . . . . . C3 | |
| Dorchester South | |
| Station ⇌ . . . . . . B1 | |

| | |
|---|---|
| Dorchester West | |
| Station ⇌ . . . . . . B1 | |
| Dorset County | |
| Council Offices . . . A1 | |
| Dorset County | |
| (A+E) 🄷 . . . . . . . B1 | |
| Dorset County | |
| Museum 🏛 . . . . . . A1 | |
| Duchy Close . . . . . C3 | |
| Duke's Ave . . . . . . B2 | |
| Durngate St . . . . . . A2 | |
| Durnover Court. . . . A3 | |
| Eddison Ave . . . . . B3 | |
| Edward Rd . . . . . . B1 | |
| Egdon Rd . . . . . . . C2 | |
| Eldridge Pope | |
| Brewery ♦ . . . . . B1 | |
| Elizabeth Frink | |
| Statue ♦ . . . . . . . B2 | |
| Farfrae Cres . . . . . B3 | |
| Friary Hill . . . . . . . A2 | |
| Friary Lane . . . . . . A2 | |
| Frome Terr . . . . . . A2 | |
| Garland Cres . . . . . C3 | |
| Glyde Path Rd . . . . A1 | |
| Gt. Western Rd. . . . B1 | |
| Grosvenor Cres . . . C1 | |
| Grosvenor Rd. . . . . C1 | |
| H M Prison . . . . . . A1 | |
| Herrington Rd. . . . . C1 | |
| High St East . . . . . A2 | |
| High Street | |
| Fordington . . . . . A2 | |
| High Street West . . A1 | |
| Holloway Rd. . . . . . A2 | |

| | |
|---|---|
| Icen Way. . . . . . . . A2 | |
| Keep Military | |
| Museum, The 🏛. . A1 | |
| Kings Rd . . . . . A3/B3 | |
| Kingsbere Cres. . . . C2 | |
| Lancaster Rd . . . . . B2 | |
| Library . . . . . . . . . A1 | |
| Lime Cl . . . . . . . . . B1 | |
| Linden Ave . . . . . . B2 | |
| London Cl. . . . . . . A3 | |
| London Rd . . . . . . A3 | |
| Lubbecke Way . . . . A3 | |
| Lucetta La . . . . . . . B2 | |
| Maiden Castle Rd. . C1 | |
| Manor Rd . . . . . . . C2 | |
| Maumbury Rd. . . . . B1 | |
| Maumbury | |
| Rings 🏛. . . . . . . B1 | |
| Mellstock Ave . . . . C2 | |
| Mill St . . . . . . . . . A3 | |
| Miller's Cl . . . . . . . A1 | |
| Mistover Cl. . . . . . . C1 | |
| Monmouth Rd . . . . B1 | |
| North Sq . . . . . . . . A2 | |
| Northernhay . . . . . A1 | |
| Old Crown Court | |
| & Cells . . . . . . . A1 | |
| Olga Rd . . . . . . . . B1 | |
| Orchard St . . . . . . A2 | |
| Police Station 🄿 . . B1 | |
| Post Office 🄿 . . . . . | |
| . . . . . . . . . A1/B1/B2 | |
| Pound Lane . . . . . . A2 | |
| Poundbury Rd . . . . A1 | |
| Prince of Wales Rd  B2 | |

| | |
|---|---|
| Prince's St . . . . . . A1 | |
| Queen's Ave . . . . . B1 | |
| Roman Town | |
| House 🏛. . . . . . . A1 | |
| Roman Wall 🏛 . . . A1 | |
| Rothesay Rd. . . . . . C2 | |
| St George's Rd. . . . B3 | |
| Salisbury Field . . . . A2 | |
| Shaston Cres . . . . . C2 | |
| Smokey Hole La. . . B3 | |
| South Court Ave . . . C1 | |
| South St . . . . . . . . A2 | |
| South Walks Rd . . . B2 | |
| Teddy Bear | |
| House 🏛 . . . . . . A1 | |
| Temple Cl . . . . . . . C1 | |
| The Grove. . . . . . . A1 | |
| Town Hall 🏛. . . . . A2 | |
| Town Pump ♦ . . . . A2 | |
| Trinity St . . . . . . . . A1 | |
| Tutankhamun | |
| Exhibition 🏛. . . . A1 | |
| Victoria Rd . . . . . . B1 | |
| Weatherbury Way. . C2 | |
| Wellbridge Cl . . . . . C1 | |
| West Mills Rd. . . . . A1 | |
| West Walks Rd . . . . A1 | |
| Weymouth Ave . . . . C1 | |
| Williams Ave. . . . . . B1 | |
| Winterbourne | |
| Hospital 🄷 . . . . . C1 | |
| Wollaston Rd . . . . . A2 | |
| York Rd. . . . . . . . . B2 | |

## Dundee

| | |
|---|---|
| Adelaide Pl . . . . . . . A1 | |
| Airlie Pl . . . . . . . . . C1 | |
| Albany Terr . . . . . . A1 | |
| Albert Institute 🏛 . . B2 | |
| Albert St . . . . . . . . A3 | |
| Alexander St. . . . . . A2 | |
| Ann St. . . . . . . . . . A2 | |
| Arthurstone Terr . . . A3 | |
| Bank St. . . . . . . . . B2 | |
| Barrack Rd . . . . . . B2 | |
| Barrack St . . . . . . . B2 | |
| Bell St. . . . . . . . . . B2 | |
| Blackscroft . . . . . . A3 | |
| Blinshall St . . . . . . B1 | |
| Brown St. . . . . . . . B1 | |
| Bus Station . . . . . . B3 | |
| Caird Hall . . . . . . . B2 | |
| Camperdown St . . . B3 | |
| Candle La. . . . . . . . A3 | |
| Carmichael St. . . . . A1 | |
| Carnegie St . . . . . . A2 | |
| City Churches 🏛 . . . B2 | |
| City Quay . . . . . . . B3 | |
| City Sq . . . . . . . . . B2 | |
| Commercial St . . . . B2 | |
| Constable St. . . . . . A3 | |
| Constitution Ct . . . . A1 | |
| Constitution Cres . . A1 | |
| Constitution St . A1/B2 | |
| Contemporary | |
| Art Centre ♦ . . . . C2 | |
| Cotton Rd. . . . . . . . A3 | |
| Courthouse Sq . . . . B1 | |
| Cowgate. . . . . . . . A3 | |

| | |
|---|---|
| Crescent St . . . . . . A3 | |
| Crichton St . . . . . . B2 | |
| Dens Brae . . . . . . . A3 | |
| Dens Rd . . . . . . . . A3 | |
| Discovery Point ♦ . . C2 | |
| Douglas St . . . . . . B1 | |
| Drummond St. . . . . A1 | |
| Dudhope Castle 🏰. . A1 | |
| Dudhope St . . . . . . A2 | |
| Dudhope Terr . . . . . A1 | |
| Dundee ⇌ . . . . . . . C2 | |
| Dundee High | |
| School . . . . . . . . B2 | |
| Dura St . . . . . . . . . A3 | |
| East Dock St . . . . . B3 | |
| East Whale La . . . . B3 | |
| East Marketgait . . . B3 | |
| Erskine St . . . . . . . A3 | |
| Euclid Cr. . . . . . . . B2 | |
| Forebank Rd. . . . . . A2 | |
| Foundry La . . . . . . A3 | |
| Gallagher | |
| Retail Park . . . . . B3 | |
| Gellatly St. . . . . . . B3 | |
| Government | |
| Offices . . . . . . . . C2 | |
| Guthrie St. . . . . . . . B1 | |
| Hawkhill . . . . . . . . B1 | |
| Hilltown. . . . . . . . . A2 | |
| HMS Unicorn ♦ . . . B3 | |
| Howff Cemetery, | |
| The . . . . . . . . . . . B2 | |
| Information Ctr 🄸. . . B2 | |
| King St . . . . . . . . . A3 | |
| Kinghorne Rd . . . . . A1 | |
| Ladywell Ave . . . . . A3 | |

| | |
|---|---|
| Laurel Bank . . . . . . A2 | |
| Law Hill, The ♦ . . . A1 | |
| Law Rd . . . . . . . . . A1 | |
| Law St . . . . . . . . . A1 | |
| Library . . . . . . . . . A2 | |
| Little Theatre 🎭 . . . A2 | |
| Lochee Rd . . . . . . . B1 | |
| Lower Princes St . . A3 | |
| Lyon St . . . . . . . . . A3 | |
| Meadow Side . . . . . B2 | |
| Meadowside | |
| St. Pauls 🏛. . . . . B2 | |
| Mercat Cross ♦ . . . B2 | |
| Murraygate . . . . . . B2 | |
| Nelson St . . . . . . . A2 | |
| Nethergate . . . . B2/C1 | |
| North Marketgait . . B2 | |
| North Lindsay St . . B2 | |
| Old Hawkhill . . . . . . B1 | |
| Olympia Swimming | |
| & Leisure Centre. . C3 | |
| Overgate Shopping | |
| Centre. . . . . . . . . B2 | |
| Park Pl . . . . . . . . . B1 | |
| Perth Rd . . . . . . . . C1 | |
| Police | |
| Station 🄿 . . . A2/B1 | |
| Post Office 🄿 . . . . | |
| . . . . . . . . . A2/B2/C2 | |
| Princes St . . . . . . . A3 | |
| Prospect Pl. . . . . . . A2 | |
| Reform St . . . . . . . B2 | |
| Repertory 🎭 . . . . . C1 | |
| Riverside Dr . . . . . . C2 | |
| Roseangle. . . . . . . C1 | |
| Rosebank St. . . . . . A2 | |

| | |
|---|---|
| RRS Discovery ⚓. . C2 | |
| St Andrew's ✝ . . . . C2 | |
| St Pauls | |
| Episcopal ✝ . . . . B3 | |
| Science Centre ♦ . . C2 | |
| Sea Captains | |
| House 🏛 . . . . . . B3 | |
| Sheriffs Court. . . . . B1 | |
| South Ward Rd. . . . B2 | |
| South George St . . . A2 | |
| South Marketgait . . B3 | |
| South Tay St. . . . . . B2 | |
| Steps . . . . . . . . . . A2 | |
| Tay Road Bridge ♦ . C3 | |
| Tayside House . . . . B2 | |
| Trades La . . . . . . . B3 | |
| Union St . . . . . . . . B2 | |
| Union Terr. . . . . . . A1 | |
| University Library . . B2 | |
| University of | |
| Abertay . . . . . . . . B2 | |
| University of | |
| Dundee. . . . . . . . B1 | |
| Upper Constitution | |
| St . . . . . . . . . . . . A1 | |
| Victoria Rd . . . . . . A2 | |
| Victoria St. . . . . . . A3 | |
| West | |
| Marketgait. . . . B1/B2 | |
| Ward Rd . . . . . . . . B1 | |
| Wellgate . . . . . . . . B2 | |
| West Bell St . . . . . B1 | |
| Westfield Pl. . . . . . . C1 | |
| William St . . . . . . . A3 | |
| Wishart Arch ♦ . . . A3 | |

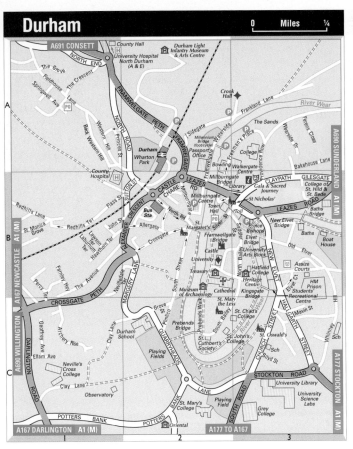

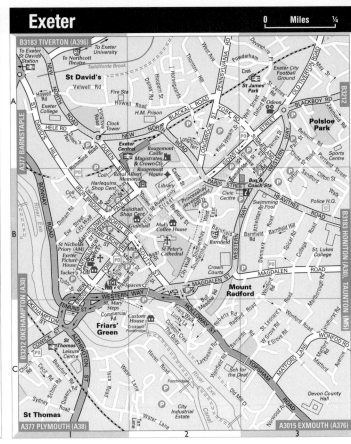

## Durham

| | |
|---|---|
| Alexander Cr | B2 |
| Allergate | B2 |
| Archery Rise | C1 |
| Assize Courts | B3 |
| Back Western Hill | A1 |
| Bakehouse La | A3 |
| Baths Bridge | B3 |
| Boat House | B3 |
| Bowling | A2 |
| Boyd St | C3 |
| Bus Station | B2 |
| Castle 🏰 | B2 |
| Castle Chare | B2 |
| Cathedral † | B2 |
| Church St | C3 |
| Clay La | C1 |
| Claypath | B3 |
| College of St. Hild | |
| & St. Bede | B3 |
| County Hall | A1 |
| County | |
| Hospital 🄷 | B1 |
| Crook Hall ♦ | A3 |
| Crossgate | B2 |
| Crossgate Peth | C1 |
| Darlington Rd | C1 |
| Durham Station ≷ | A2 |
| Durham Light Infantry | |
| Museum & Arts | |
| Centre 🏛 | B3 |
| Durham School | C2 |
| Ellam Ave | C1 |
| Elvet Bridge | B3 |
| Elvet Court | B3 |
| Farnley Hey | B1 |

| | |
|---|---|
| Ferens Cl | A3 |
| Fieldhouse La | A1 |
| Flass St | B1 |
| Framwelgate | A2 |
| Framwelgate | |
| Bridge | B2 |
| Framwelgate Peth | A2 |
| Framwelgate | |
| Waterside | A2 |
| Frankland La | A3 |
| Freeman's Pl | A3 |
| Gala & Sacred | |
| Journey 🎭 | B3 |
| Geoffrey Ave | C1 |
| Gilesgate | B3 |
| Grey College | C3 |
| Grove St | C2 |
| Hallgarth St | C3 |
| Hatfield College | B3 |
| Hawthorn Terr | B1 |
| Heritage | |
| Centre 🏛 | B3 |
| HM Prison | B3 |
| Information Ctr ℹ | B2 |
| John St | B1 |
| Kingsgate Bridge | B3 |
| Laburnum Terr | B1 |
| Lawson Terr | B1 |
| Leazes Rd | B2/B3 |
| Library | B2 |
| Margery La | B2 |
| Mavin St | C3 |
| Millburngate | B2 |
| Millburngate | |
| Bridge | B2 |
| Millburngate | |
| Centre | B2 |

| | |
|---|---|
| Millennium Bridge | |
| (foot/cycle) | A2 |
| Museum of | |
| Archaeology 🏛 | B2 |
| Neville's Cross | |
| College | C1 |
| Nevilledale Terr | B1 |
| New Elvet | B3 |
| New Elvet Bridge | B3 |
| North Bailey | B3 |
| North End | A1 |
| North Rd | A1/B2 |
| Observatory | C1 |
| Old Elvet | B3 |
| Oriental | |
| Museum 🏛 | C2 |
| Passport Office | A2 |
| Percy Terr | B1 |
| Pimlico | C2 |
| Police Station 🄿 | B3 |
| Post Office 🄿 | A1/B2 |
| Potters Bank | C1/C2 |
| Prebends Bridge | C2 |
| Prebends Walk | C2 |
| Prince Bishops | |
| Shopping Centre | B3 |
| Princes St | A1 |
| Providence Row | A3 |
| Quarryheads La | C2 |
| Redhills La | B2 |
| Redhills Terr | B1 |
| Saddler St | B3 |
| St Chad's College | C3 |
| St Cuthbert's | |
| Society | C2 |
| St John's College | C2 |
| St Margaret's ♒ | B2 |

| | |
|---|---|
| St Mary The | |
| Less ♒ | C2 |
| St Mary's College | C2 |
| St Monica Grove | B1 |
| St Nicholas' ♒ | B3 |
| St Oswald's ♒ | C3 |
| Sidegate | A2 |
| Silver St | B2 |
| South Bailey | B3 |
| South Rd | C3 |
| South St | B2 |
| Springwell Ave | A1 |
| Stockton Rd | C3 |
| Students' Rec | |
| Centre | B3 |
| Sutton St | B2 |
| The Avenue | B1 |
| The Crescent | A1 |
| The Grove | A1 |
| The Sands | A3 |
| Town Hall | B2 |
| Treasury | |
| Museum 🏛 | B2 |
| University ♦ | B2 |
| University Arts | |
| Block | B3 |
| University Library | C3 |
| University Science | |
| Labs | C3 |
| Walkergate Centre | A3 |
| Wearside Dr | A3 |
| Western Hill | A1 |
| Wharton Park | A2 |
| Whinney Hill | C3 |

## Exeter

| | |
|---|---|
| Alphington St | C1 |
| Athelstan Rd | B3 |
| Bampfylde St | B2 |
| Barnardo Rd | C3 |
| Barnfield Hill | B3 |
| Barnfield Rd | B2/B3 |
| Barnfield | |
| Theatre 🎭 | B2 |
| Bartholomew St | |
| East | B1 |
| Bartholomew St | |
| West | B1 |
| Bear St | B2 |
| Beaufort Rd | C1 |
| Bedford St | B2 |
| Belgrave Rd | A3 |
| Belmont Rd | A3 |
| Blackall Rd | A2 |
| Blackboy Rd | A3 |
| Bonhay Rd | B1 |
| Bull Meadow Rd | C2 |
| Bus & Coach Sta | B3 |
| Castle St | B2 |
| Cecil Rd | C1 |
| Cheeke St | A3 |
| Church Rd | C1 |
| Chute St | A3 |
| City Industrial | |
| Estate | C2 |
| City Wall | B1/B2 |
| Civic Centre | B2 |
| Clifton Rd | B3 |
| Clifton St | B3 |
| Clock Tower | A1 |
| College Rd | B3 |
| Colleton Cr | C2 |
| Commercial Rd | C1 |
| Coombe St | B2 |
| Cowick St | C1 |
| Crown Courts | B2 |
| Custom House 🏛 | C2 |
| Danes' Rd | A2 |
| Denmark Rd | B3 |
| Devon County Hall | C3 |

| | |
|---|---|
| Devonshire Pl | A3 |
| Dinham Rd | B1 |
| East Grove Rd | C3 |
| Edmund St | C1 |
| Elmgrove Rd | A1 |
| Exe St | B1 |
| Exeter Central | |
| Station ≷ | A1 |
| Exeter City Football | |
| Ground | A3 |
| Exeter College | A1 |
| Exeter Picture | |
| House 🎬 | B1 |
| Fire Station | A1 |
| Fore St | B1 |
| Friars Walk | C2 |
| Guildhall 🏛 | B2 |
| Guildhall Shopping | |
| Centre | B2 |
| Harlequins Shopping | |
| Centre | B1 |
| Haven Rd | C2 |
| Heavitree Rd | A3 |
| Hele Rd | A1 |
| High St | B2 |
| HM Prison | A2 |
| Holloway St | C2 |
| Hoopern St | A2 |
| Horseguards | A2 |
| Howell Rd | A1 |
| Information Ctr ℹ | B3 |
| Iron Bridge | B1 |
| Isca Rd | C1 |
| Jesmond Rd | A3 |
| King William St | A1 |
| King St | B1 |
| Larkbeare Rd | C2 |
| Leisure Centre | C1 |
| Library | B2 |
| Longbrook St | A2 |
| Longbrook Terr | A2 |
| Lucky La | C2 |
| Lower North St | B1 |
| Lyndhurst Rd | C3 |
| Magdalen Rd | B3 |
| Magdalen St | B2 |

| | |
|---|---|
| Magistrates & Crown | |
| Courts | A2 |
| Market | A2 |
| Market St | B2 |
| Marlborough Rd | C3 |
| Mary Arches St | B1 |
| Matford Rd | C3 |
| Matford Ave | C3 |
| Matford La | C3 |
| May St | A3 |
| Mol's Coffee | |
| House | B2 |
| New Bridge St | B1 |
| New North Rd | A1/A2 |
| North St | B1 |
| Northernhay St | B1 |
| Norwood Ave | C3 |
| Odeon 🎬 | A3 |
| Okehampton St | C1 |
| Old Mill Cl | C2 |
| Old Tiverton Rd | A3 |
| Oxford Rd | A3 |
| Paris St | B2 |
| Parr St | A3 |
| Paul St | B1 |
| Pennsylvania Rd | A2 |
| Police H.Q. 🄿 | B3 |
| Post Office 🄿 | A3/B1/B3/C1 |
| Powderham Cr | A3 |
| Preston St | B1 |
| Princesshay | |
| development | B2 |
| Queen St | A1 |
| Queens Rd | C1 |
| Queen's Terr | A1 |
| Radford Rd | C2 |
| Richmond Rd | A1 |
| Roberts Rd | C2 |
| Rougemont | |
| Castle 🏰 | A2 |
| Rougemont | |
| House ♦ | B2 |
| Royal Albert Memorial | |
| Museum 🏛 | B2 |

| | |
|---|---|
| St David's Hill | A1 |
| St James' Park | |
| Station ≷ | A3 |
| St James' Rd | A3 |
| St Leonard's Rd | C3 |
| St Lukes College | B3 |
| St Mary Steps ♒ | C1 |
| St Nicholas | |
| Priory (AM) † | B1 |
| St Peter's | |
| Cathedral † | B2 |
| St Thomas | |
| Station ≷ | C1 |
| Sandford Walk | B3 |
| School for | |
| the Deaf | C2 |
| School Rd | C1 |
| Sidwell St | A2 |
| Smythen St | B1 |
| South St | B2 |
| Southernhay East | B2 |
| Southernhay West | B2 |
| Spacex Gallery 🏛 | B1 |
| Spicer Rd | B3 |
| Sports Centre | A3 |
| Summerland St | A3 |
| Swimming Pool | B3 |
| Sydney Rd | C1 |
| Tan La | C2 |
| The Quay | C2 |
| Thornton Hill | A2 |
| Topsham Rd | C3 |
| Tucker's Hall 🏛 | B1 |
| Tudor St | B1 |
| Velwell Rd | A1 |
| Verney St | A3 |
| Water La | C1/C2 |
| Weirfield Rd | C2 |
| Well St | A3 |
| West Ave | A2 |
| West Grove Rd | C3 |
| Western | |
| Way | A3/B1/B2 |
| Wonford Rd | B3/C3 |
| York Rd | A2 |

# Edinburgh

0     Miles     ¼

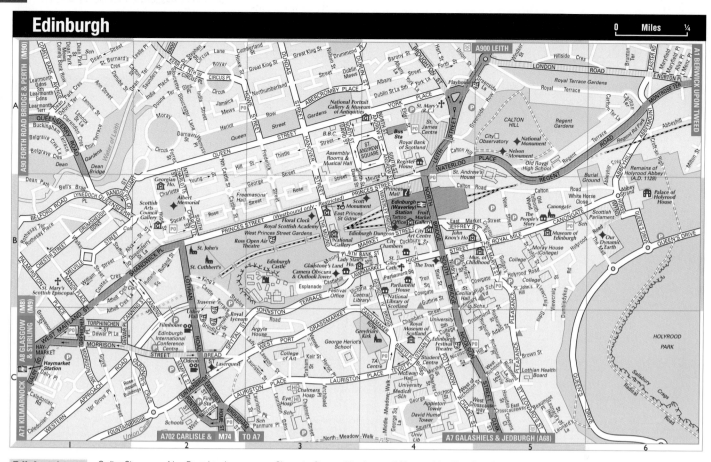

## Edinburgh

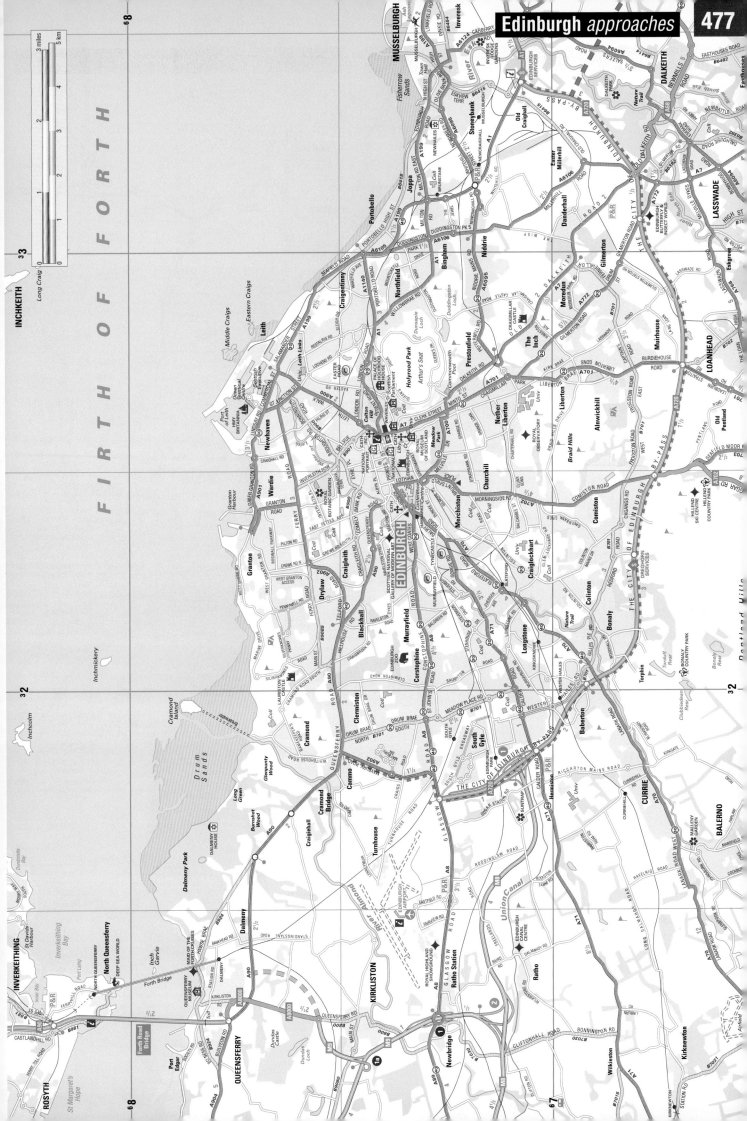

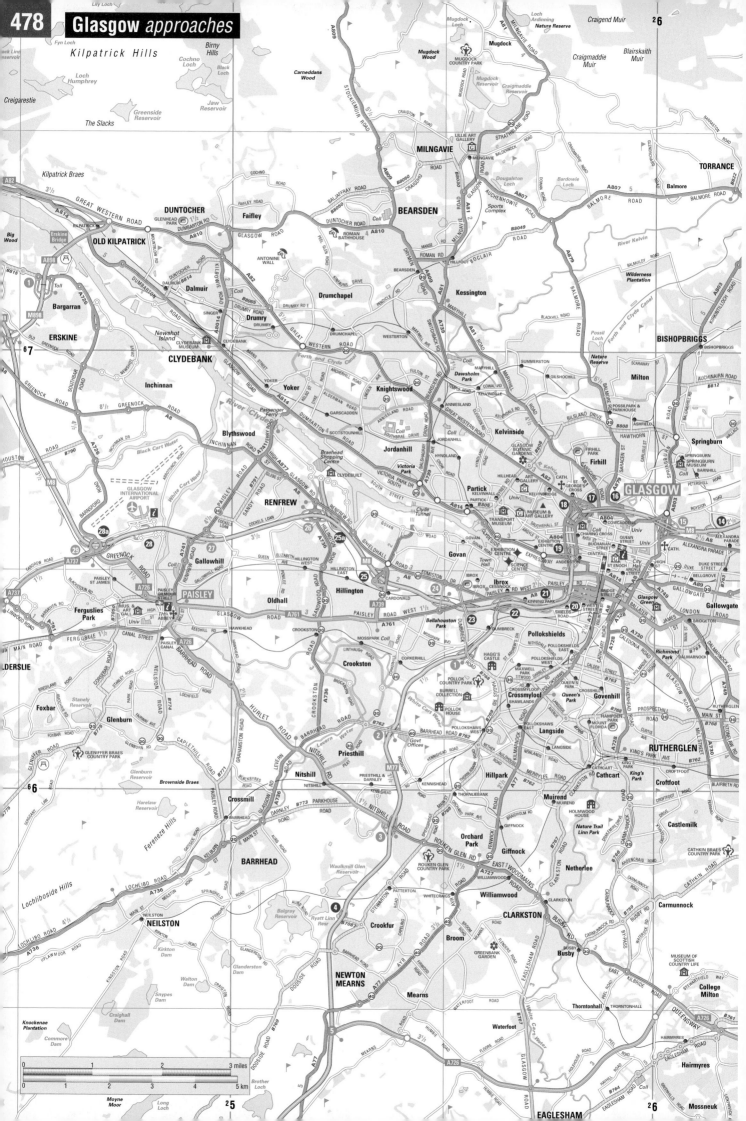

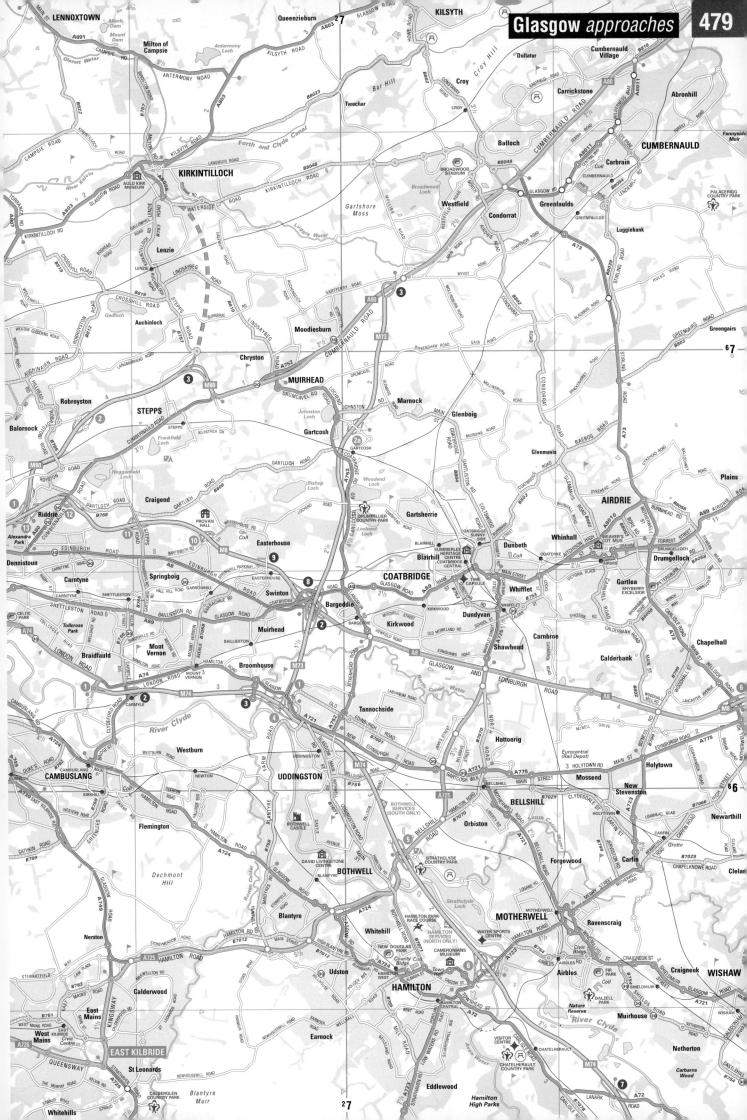

# Glasgow

0 Miles ¼

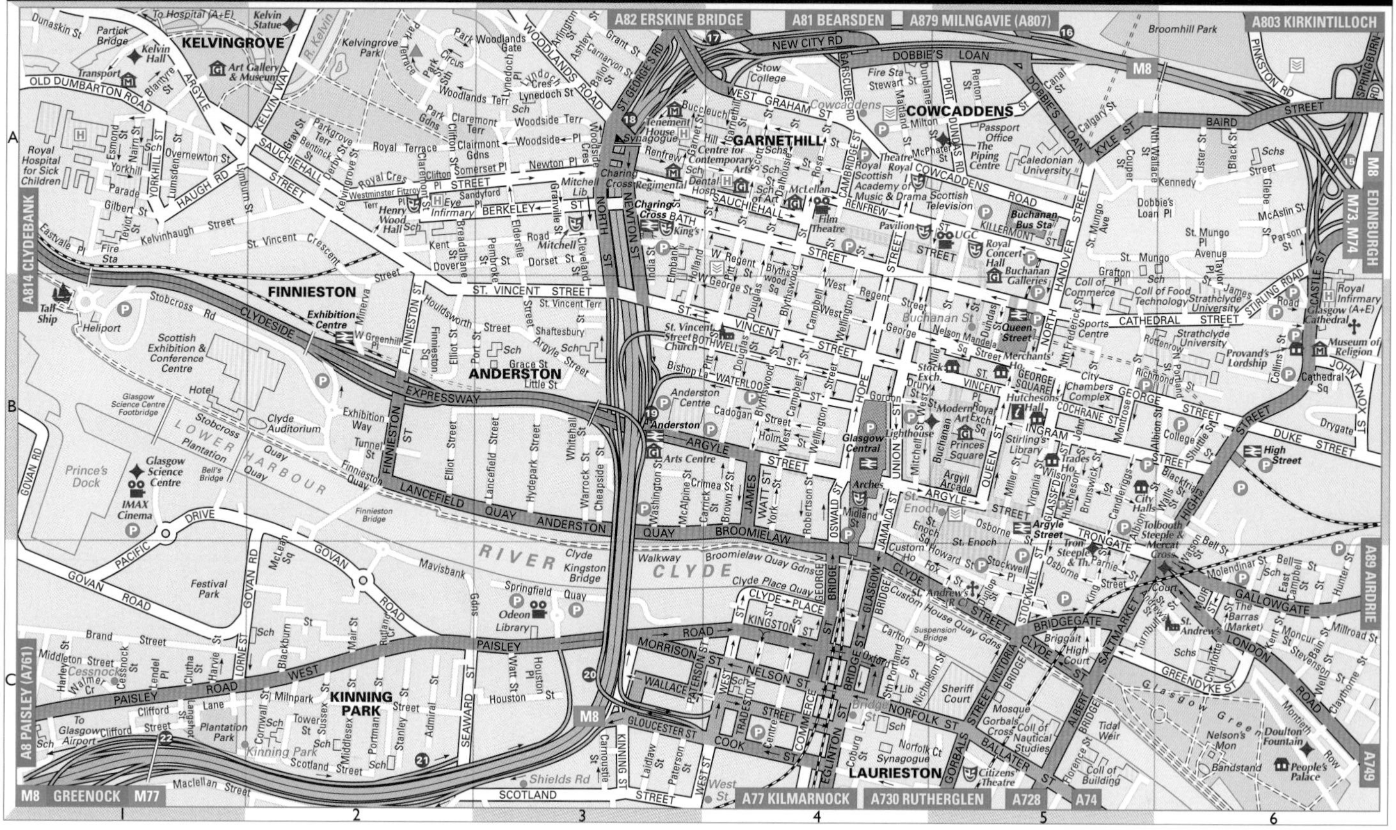
A82 ERSKINE BRIDGE
A81 BEARSDEN
A879 MILNGAVIE (A807)
A803 KIRKINTILLOCH
M8 EDINBURGH
M73, M74
A89 AIRDRIE
A749
A74
A728
A730 RUTHERGLEN
A77 KILMARNOCK
M8 GREENOCK M77
A8 PAISLEY (A761)
A814 CLYDEBANK
KELVINGROVE
COWCADDENS
GARNETHILL
FINNIESTON
ANDERSTON
KINNING PARK
LAURIESTON
RIVER CLYDE
LOWER HARBOUR
Prince's Dock
Kelvingrove Park
Festival Park
Broomhill Park
Glasgow Green
CLYDESIDE EXPRESSWAY
SAUCHIEHALL ST
ST. VINCENT STREET
ARGYLE ST
LANCEFIELD QUAY
ANDERSTON QUAY
BROOMIELAW
PAISLEY ROAD
MORRISON ST
GOVAN ROAD
GALLOWGATE
LONDON ROAD
CATHEDRAL STREET
GEORGE ST
DUKE STREET
HIGH ST
TRONGATE
NEW CITY RD
DOBBIE'S LOAN
BAIRD STREET
SCOTLAND STREET
NORFOLK ST
1
2
3
4
5
6
A
B
C

## Glasgow


Admiral St. . . . C2
Albert Bridge . . . C5
Albion St. . . . B5
Anderston Centre . . B3
Anderston Quay . . . B3
Anderston Station ⇌ . . . B3
Arches 🎭 . . . B4
Argyle St . . . A1/A2/B3/B4/B5
Argyle Street Station ⇌ . . . A3
Argyll Arcade . . . B5
Arlington St. . . . A3
Art Gallery & Museum 🏛 . . . A1
Arts Centre 🏛 . . . B3
Ashley St . . . A3
Bain St . . . C6
Baird St . . . A6
Baliol St . . . A3
Ballater St. . . . C5
Barras, The (Market). . . . C6
Bath St . . . A3
Bell St. . . . C6
Bell's Bridge . . . B1
Bentinck St. . . . A2
Berkeley St. . . . A3
Bishop La. . . . B3
Black St . . . A6
Blackburn St. . . . C2
Blackfriars St . . . B6
Blantyre St . . . A1
Blythswood Sq. . . A4
Blythswood St . . . B4
Bothwell St. . . . B4
Brand St . . . C1
Breadalbane St. . . A2
Bridge St . . . C4
Bridge St (Metro Station) . . . C4
Bridgegate . . . C5
Briggait . . . C5
Broomhill Park . . . A6
Broomielaw. . . . B4
Broomielaw Quay Gdns . . . B3
Brown St. . . . B4
Brunswick St . . . B5
Buccleuch St . . . A3
Buchanan Bus Station . . . A5
Buchanan Galleries 🏛 . . . A5
Buchanan St. . . . B5
Buchanan St (Metro Station) . . . B5
Cadogan St . . . B4
Caledonian University . . . A5
Calgary St. . . . A5
Cambridge St. . . . A4
Campbell St . . . B4
Canal St . . . A5
Candleriggs . . . B5
Carlton Pl . . . C4
Carnarvon St . . . A3
Carnoustie St . . . C3
Carrick St . . . B4
Castle St. . . . B6
Cathedral Sq . . . B6
Cathedral St . . . B5
Centre for Contemporary Arts 🏛 . . . A4
Centre St . . . C4
Cessnock (Metro Station) . . . C1
Cessnock St. . . . C1
Charing Cross Station ⇌ . . . A3
Charlotte St . . . C6
Cheapside St . . . B3
Citizens' Theatre 🎭 . . . C5
City Chambers Complex . . . B5
City Halls 🏛 . . . B5
Clairmont Gdns . . . A2
Claremont St . . . A2
Claremont Terr . . . A2
Claythorne St . . . C6
Cleveland St. . . . A3
Clifford La. . . . C1
Clifford St . . . C1
Clifton Pl. . . . A2
Clifton St . . . A2
Clutha St . . . C1
Clyde Auditorium . . B2
Clyde Pl . . . C4
Clyde Place Quay. . C4
Clyde St . . . C5
Clyde Walkway. . . C3
Clydeside Expressway . . . B2
Coburg St. . . . C4
Cochrane St . . . B5
College of Building C5
College of Commerce . . . B5
College of Food Technology . . . B5
College of Nautical Studies . . . C5
College St. . . . B6
Collins St . . . B6
Commerce St . . . C4
Cook St . . . C4
Cornwall St. . . . C2
Couper St. . . . A5
Cowcaddens (Metro Station) . . . A4
Cowcaddens Rd. . . A4
Crimea St . . . B3
Custom House 🏛 . C4
Custom House Quay Gdns. . . . C4
Dalhousie St. . . . A4
Dental Hospital H . A4
Derby St . . . A2
Dobbie's Loan . . A4/A5
Dobbie's Loan Pl . . A5
Dorset St . . . A3
Douglas St . . . B4
Doulton Fountain ✦ . . . C6
Dover St . . . A2
Drury St . . . B4
Drygate . . . B6
Duke St. . . . B6
Dunaskin St . . . A1
Dunblane St . . . A4
Dundas St. . . . B5
Dunlop St . . . C5
East Campbell St . . C6
Eastvale Pl . . . A1
Eglinton St . . . C4
Elderslie St . . . A3
Elliot St . . . B2
Elmbank St. . . . A3
Esmond St . . . A1
Exhibition Centre Station ⇌ . . . B2
Exhibition Way . . . B2
Eye Infirmary H . . . A2
Festival Park. . . . C1
Film Theatre 🎦 . . . A4
Finnieston Bridge . . B2
Finnieston Quay . . . B2
Finnieston Sq . . . B2
Finnieston St . . . B2
Fitzroy Pl. . . . A2
Florence St . . . C5
Fox St. . . . C5
Gallowgate . . . C6
Garnet St . . . A3
Garnethill St . . . A4
Garscube Rd . . . A4
George Sq . . . B5
George St. . . . B5
George V Bridge. . . C4
Gilbert St . . . A1
Glasgow Bridge . . . C4
Glasgow Cathedral ✝ . . . B6
Glasgow Central Station ⇌ . . . B4
Glasgow Green. . . . C6
Glasgow Science Centre ✦ . . . B1
Glasgow Science Centre Footbridge . . . B1
Glassford St . . . B5
Glebe St . . . A6
Gloucester St . . . C3
Gorbals Cross . . . C5
Gorbals St . . . C5
Gordon St. . . . B4
Govan Rd . . B1/C1/C2
Grace St. . . . B3
Grafton Pl . . . A5
Grant St . . . A3
Granville St. . . . A3
Gray St . . . A2
Greendyke St . . . C6
Harley St. . . . C1
Harvie St. . . . C1
Haugh Rd . . . A1
Heliport. . . . B1
Henry Wood Hall 🎭 . . . A2
High St . . . B6
High Street Station ⇌ . . . B6
Hill St . . . A3
Holland St. . . . A3
Holm St . . . B4
Hope St . . . A5
Houldsworth St . . . B2
Houston Pl . . . C3
Houston St. . . . C3
Howard St . . . C5
Hunter St . . . B6
Hutcheson St . . . B5
Hydepark St . . . B3
Imax Cinema 🎦 . . . B1
India St. . . . A3
Information Ctr ℹ. . B5
Ingram St . . . B5
Jamaica St . . . B4
James Watt St . . . B4
John Knox St . . . B6
John St. . . . B5
Kelvin Hall ✦ . . . A1
Kelvin Statue ✦ . . . A2
Kelvin Way . . . A2
Kelvingrove Park . . A2
Kelvingrove St . . . A2
Kelvinhaugh St. . . . A1
Kennedy St. . . . A6
Kent Rd . . . A2
Killermont St. . . . A5
King St . . . B5
King's 🎭 . . . A3
Kingston Bridge . . . C3
Kingston St. . . . C4
Kinning Park (Metro Station) . . . C2
Kinning St. . . . C3
Kyle St . . . A5
Laidlaw St. . . . C3
Lancefield Quay . . . B2
Lancefield St . . . B3
Langshot St . . . C1
Lendel Pl . . . C1
Lighthouse ✦ . . . B4
Lister St . . . A6
Little St. . . . B3
London Rd . . . C6
Lorne St . . . C1
Lower Harbour . . . B1
Lumsden St . . . A1
Lymburn St. . . . A1
Lyndoch Cr. . . . A3
Lynedoch Pl . . . A3
Lynedoch St . . . A3
Maclellan St . . . C1
Mair St . . . C2
Maitland St . . . A4
Mavisbank Gdns . . C2
Mcalpine St . . . B3
Mcaslin St. . . . A6
McLean Sq. . . . C2
McLellan Gallery 🏛 . . . A4
McPhater St. . . . A4
Merchants' House 🏛 . . . B5
Middlesex St . . . C2
Middleton St. . . . C1
Midland St . . . B4
Miller St . . . B5
Millroad St . . . C6
Milnpark St. . . . C2
Milton St. . . . A4
Minerva St . . . B2
Mitchell Library. . . A3
Mitchell St West . . . B4
Mitchell Theatre 🎭 . A3
Modern Art Gallery 🏛 . . . B5
Moir St . . . C6
Molendinar St. . . . C6
Moncur St. . . . C6
Montieth Row. . . . C6
Montrose St . . . B5
Morrison St. . . . C3
Mosque . . . C5
Museum of Religion 🏛 . . . B6
Nairn St . . . A1
Nelson Mandela Sq. . . . B5
Nelson St . . . C4
Nelson's Monument . . . C6
New City Rd . . . A4
Newton St . . . A3
Newton Pl. . . . A3
Nicholson St. . . . C4
Nile St. . . . A5
Norfolk Court . . . C4
Norfolk St. . . . C4
North Frederick St . B5
North Hanover St . . B5
North Portland St. . B5
North St . . . A3
North Wallace St . . A5
Odeon 🎦 . . . C3
Old Dumbarton Rd. A1
Osborne St. . . . B5/C5
Oswald St. . . . B4
Overnewton St . . . A1
Oxford St . . . C4
Pacific Dr . . . B1
Paisley Rd . . . C3
Paisley Rd West . . . C1
Park Circus. . . . A2
Park Gdns . . . A2
Park St South. . . . A2
Park Terr. . . . A2
Parkgrove Terr . . . A2
Parnie St. . . . C5
Parson St . . . A6
Partick Bridge. . . . A1
Passport Office. . . . A5
Paterson St. . . . C3
Pavilion Theatre 🎭. A4
Pembroke St . . . A3
People's Palace 🏛 C6
Pinkston Rd . . . A6
Piping Centre, The ✦ . . . A5
Pitt St . . . A4/B4
Plantation Park. . . . C1
Plantation Quay . . . B1
Police Station ⊠ . . . A4/A6/B5
Port Dundas Rd . . . A5
Port St . . . B2
Portman St. . . . C2
Prince's Dock . . . B1
Princes Sq . . . B5
Provand's Lordship 🏛 . . . B6
Queen St . . . B5
Queen Street Station ⇌ . . . B5
Regimental Museum 🏛. . . A3
Renfrew St . . . A3/A4
Renton St . . . A5
Richmond St . . . B5
Robertson St . . . B4
Rose St. . . . A4
Rottenrow. . . . B5
Royal Concert Hall 🎭 . . . A5
Royal Cr . . . A2
Royal Exchange Sq B5
Royal Hospital For Sick Children H . . A1
Royal Infirmary H . . B6
Royal Scottish Academy of Music & Drama . . . A4
Royal Terr . . . A2
Rutland Cr . . . C2
St Kent St. . . . C6
St Andrew's (R.C.) ✝. . . C5
St Andrew's ⛪ . . . C6
St Andrew's St . . . C5
St Enoch (Metro Station) . . . B5
St Enoch Shopping Centre. . . . B5
St Enoch Sq . . . B4
St George's Rd. . . A3
St James Rd. . . . B6
St Mungo Ave. . A5/A6
St Mungo Pl . . . A6
St Vincent Cr . . . A2
St Vincent Pl. . . . B5
St Vincent St . . B3/B4
St Vincent Street Church ⛪ . . . B4
St Vincent Terr . . . B3
Saltmarket . . . C5
Sandyford Pl. . . . A3
Sauchiehall St . . A2/A4
School of Art . . . A4
Scotland St. . . C2/C3
Scott St . . . A4
Scottish Exhibition & Conference Centre. . . . B1
Scottish Television . A5
Seaward St. . . . C2
Shaftesbury St . . . B3
Sheriff Court. . . . C5
Shields Rd . . . C3
Shields Rd (Metro Station) . . . C3
Shuttle St . . . B6
Somerset Pl . . . A2
Springburn Rd . . . A6
Springfield Quay. . . C3
Stanley St. . . . C2
Stevenson St . . . C6
Stewart St. . . . A4
Sth Portland St. . . . C4
Stirling Rd. . . . B6
Stirling's Library . . . B5
Stobcross Quay . . . B1
Stobcross Rd . . . B1
Stock Exchange 🏛 . . . B5
Stockwell Pl . . . C5
Stockwell St . . . B5
Stow College . . . A4
Strathclyde University . . . B6
Sussex St . . . C2
Synagogues . . . A3/C4
Tall Ship ⛴ . . . B1
Taylor Pl . . . A6
Tenement House 🏛 . . . A3
Teviot St . . . A1
Theatre Royal 🎭. . . A3
Tolbooth Steeple & Mercat Cross ✦ . . C6
Tower St . . . C2
Trades House 🏛 . . B5
Tradeston St. . . . C4
Transport Museum 🏛. . . A1
Tron Steeple & Theatre 🎭 . . . C5
Trongate . . . B5
Tunnel St . . . B2
Turnbull St . . . C5
UGC 🎦 . . . A5
Union St . . . B4
Victoria Bridge . . . C5
Virginia St. . . . B5
West Greenhill Pl . . B2
West Regent St . . . A4
Wallace St . . . C3
Walls St . . . B6
Walmer Cr . . . C1
Warrock St . . . B3
Washington St . . . B3
Waterloo St. . . . B4
Watson St. . . . B6
Watt St . . . C3
Well St . . . C6
Wellington St . . . B4
West George St . . . B4
West Graham St. . . A4
West Regent St . . . B4
West St. . . . C4
West St (Metro Station) . . . C4
Westminster Terr . . A2
Whitehall St . . . B3
Wilson St . . . B5
Woodlands Gate. . . A3
Woodlands Rd . . . A3
Woodlands Terr . . . A2
Woodside Cr. . . . A3
Woodside Pl. . . . A3
Woodside Terr . . . A3
York St West. . . . B4
Yorkhill Pde. . . . A1
Yorkhill St . . . A1

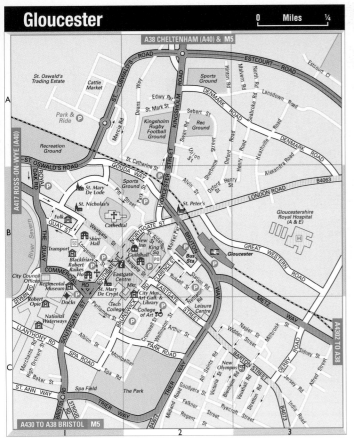

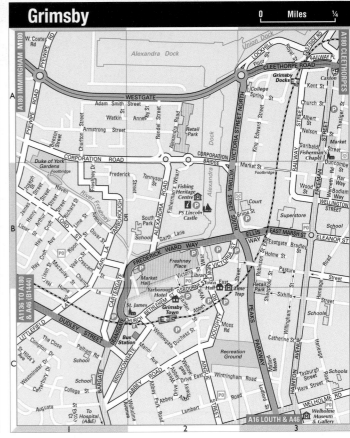

## Gloucester

Albion St . . . . . . . . C1
Alexandra Rd . . . . . B3
Alfred St . . . . . . . . C3
All Saints Rd . . . . . C2
Alvin St . . . . . . . . . B2
Arthur St . . . . . . . . C2
Baker St . . . . . . . . C1
Barton St . . . . . . . C2
Blackfriars † . . . . . . B1
Blenheim Rd . . . . . C2
Bristol Rd . . . . . . . C1
Brunswick Rd . . . . . C2
Bruton Way . . . . . . B2
Bus Station . . . . . . B2
Cattle Market . . . . . A1
City Council
   Offices . . . . . . . . B1
City Mus., Art Gall.
   & Library 🏛 . . . . B2
Clarence St . . . . . . B2
College of Art . . . . . C2
Commercial Rd . . . B1
Cromwell St . . . . . . C2
Deans Way . . . . . . A2
Denmark Rd . . . . . . A3
Derby Rd . . . . . . . . C3
Docks ✦ . . . . . . . . C1
Eastgate Centre . . . B2
Eastgate St . . . . . . B2
Edwy Pde . . . . . . . A2
Estcourt Cl . . . . . . A3
Estcourt Rd . . . . . . A3
Falkner St . . . . . . . C2

Folk Museum 🏛 . . . B1
Gloucester
   Cathedral † . . . . B1
Gloucester
   Station ≧ . . . . . . B2
Gloucestershire
Royal Hospital
   (A & E) 🏥 . . . . . . B3
Goodyere St . . . . . . C2
Gouda Way . . . . . . A1
Great Western Rd . . B3
Guildhall 🏛 . . . . . . B2
Heathville Rd . . . . . A3
Henry Rd . . . . . . . . B3
Henry St . . . . . . . . B2
High Orchard St . . . C1
Hinton Rd . . . . . . . A2
India Rd . . . . . . . . C3
Information Ctr 🛈 . . B1
Jersey Rd . . . . . . . C3
King's Sq . . . . . . . . B2
Kingsholm Rd . . . . . A2
Kingsholm Rugby
   Football Ground . . A2
Lansdown Rd . . . . . A3
Llanthony Rd . . . . . C1
London Rd . . . . . . . B3
Longsmith St . . . . . B1
Malvern Rd . . . . . . A3
Market Pde . . . . . . B2
Merchants Rd . . . . . C1
Mercia Rd . . . . . . . A1
Metz Way . . . . . . . C3
Midland Rd . . . . . . C2

Millbrook St . . . . . . C3
Market . . . . . . . . . B2
Montpellier . . . . . . C1
Napier St . . . . . . . C3
National
   Waterways 🏛 . . . C1
Nettleton Rd . . . . . C2
New Inn 🏛 . . . . . . . B2
New Olympus 🎭 . . . C3
North Rd . . . . . . . . A3
Northgate St . . . . . B2
Oxford Rd . . . . . . . B2
Oxford St . . . . . . . B2
Park & Ride
   Gloucester . . . . . A1
Park Rd . . . . . . . . C2
Park St . . . . . . . . . B2
Parliament St . . . . . C1
Pitt St . . . . . . . . . B1
Police Station 🛃 . . . B1
Post Office 🏤 . . . . . B2
Quay St . . . . . . . . B1
Recreation Gd . A1/A2
Regent St . . . . . . . C2
Regimental 🏛 . . . . . B1
Robert Opie 🏛 . . . . C1
Robert Raikes
   House 🏛 . . . . . . B1
Royal Oak Rd . . . . . B1
Russell St . . . . . . . B2
Ryecroft St . . . . . . C2
St Aldate St . . . . . . B2
St Ann Way . . . . . . C1
St Catherine St . . . . A2
St Mark St . . . . . . . A2

St Mary
   De Crypt 🔺 . . . . . B1
St Mary
   De Lode 🔺 . . . . . B1
St Nicholas's 🔺 . . . B1
St Oswald's Rd . . . . A1
St Oswald's Trading
   Estate . . . . . . . . A1
St Peter's 🔺 . . . . . B2
Seabroke Rd . . . . . A3
Sebert St . . . . . . . A2
Severn Rd . . . . . . . C1
Sherborne St . . . . . B2
Shire Hall 🏛 . . . . . B1
Sidney St . . . . . . . C3
Southgate St . . B1/C1
Spa Field 🏛 . . . . . . C1
Spa Rd . . . . . . . . . C1
Sports Ground . A2/B2
Station Rd . . . . . . . B2
Stratton Rd . . . . . . C3
Stroud Rd . . . . . . . C1
Swan Rd . . . . . . . . A2
Technical College . . C1
The Park . . . . . . . . C2
The Quay . . . . . . . . B1
Transport 🏛 . . . . . . B1
Trier Way . . . . . . C1/C2
Union St . . . . . . . . A1
Vauxhall Rd . . . . . . C3
Victoria St . . . . . . . C2
Wellington St . . . . . C2
Westgate St . . . . . . B1
Widden St . . . . . . . C2
Worcester St . . . . . B2

## Grimsby

Abbey Drive East . . C2
Abbey Drive West . . C2
Abbey Park Rd . . . . C2
Abbey Rd . . . . . . . C2
Abbey Walk . . . . . . C2
Abbotsway . . . . . . C2
Adam Smith St . A1/A2
Ainslie St . . . . . . . C2
Albert St . . . . . . . . A3
Alexandra Rd . . A2/B2
Annesley St . . . . . . A2
Armstrong St . . . . . A1
Arthur St . . . . . . . . B1
Augusta St . . . . . . C1
Bargate . . . . . . . . C1
Beeson St . . . . . . . A1
Bethlehem St . . . . . C2
Bodiam Way . . . . . B3
Bradley St . . . . . . . B3
Brighowgate . . . C1/C2
Bus Station . . . . . . C2
Canterbury Dr . . . . C1
Cartergate . . . . B1/C1
Catherine St . . . . . C3
Caxton 🎭 . . . . . . . A3
Chantry La . . . . . . B1
Charlton St . . . . . . A1
Church La . . . . . . . C2
Church St . . . . . . . A3
Cleethorpe Rd . . . . A3
College . . . . . . . . A3
College St . . . . . . . C1
Compton Dr . . . . . C1
Corporation Bridge . A2
Corporation Rd . . . . A1
Court . . . . . . . . . . B3
Crescent St . . . . . . B1
Deansgate . . . . . . C1
Doughty Rd . . . . . . C2

Dover St . . . . . . . . B1
Duchess St . . . . . . C2
Dudley St . . . . . . . C1
Duke of York
   Gardens . . . . . . B1
Duncombe St . . . . . B3
Earl La . . . . . . . . . B1
East Marsh St . . . . B3
East St . . . . . . . . . B2
Eastgate . . . . . . . . B3
Eastside Rd . . . . . . A3
Eaton Ct . . . . . . . . C2
Eleanor St . . . . . . . B3
Ellis Way . . . . . . . . B3
Fisherman's
   Chapel 🔺 . . . . . A3
Fisherman's Wharf . B2
Fishing Heritage
   Centre 🏛 . . . . . B2
Flour Sq . . . . . . . . A3
Frederick St . . . . . . B1
Frederick
   Ward Way . . . . . B2
Freeman St . . . . A3/B3
Freshney Dr . . . . . . B1
Freshney Pl . . . . . . B2
Garden St . . . . . . . C2
Garibaldi St . . . . . . A3
Garth La . . . . . . . . B2
Grime St . . . . . . . . B3
Grimsby Docks
   Station ≧ . . . . . . A3
Grimsby Town
   Station ≧ . . . . . . C2
Hainton Ave . . . . . . C3
Har Way . . . . . . . . B3
Hare St . . . . . . . . . C3
Harrison St . . . . . . B1
Haven Ave . . . . . . . B1
Hay Croft Ave . . . . . B1
Hay Croft St . . . . . . B1

Heneage Rd . . . B3/C3
Henry St . . . . . . . . B1
Holme St . . . . . . . . B3
Hume St . . . . . . . . C1
Information Ctr 🛈 . . B2
James St . . . . . . . . B2
Joseph St . . . . . . . B1
Kent St . . . . . . . . . A3
King Edward St . . . . A3
Lambert Rd . . . . . . C2
Library . . . . . . . . . B2
Lime St . . . . . . . . . B2
Lister St . . . . . . . . B1
Littlefield La . . . . . . C1
Lockhill . . . . . . . . . A3
Lord St . . . . . . . . . B1
Ludford St . . . . . . . C3
Macaulay St . . . . . . C3
Mallard Mews . . . . . C3
Manor Ave . . . . . . . C2
Market . . . . . . . . . A3
Market Hall . . . . . . B2
Market St . . . . . . . B3
Moss Rd . . . . . . . . C3
Nelson St . . . . . . . A3
New St . . . . . . . . . B2
Osbourne St . . . . . B2
Pasture St . . . . . . . B3
Peaks Parkway . . . . C3
Pelham Rd . . . . . . . C1
Police
   Station 🛃 . . . A3/B2
Post Office 🏤
   . . . B1/B2/B3/C2/C3
PS Lincoln
   Castle 🚢 . . . . . . B2
Pyewipe Rd . . . . . . A1
Railway Pl . . . . . . . A3
Railway St . . . . . . . A3
Rendel St . . . . . . . A2
Retail Park . . . . . . . A2

Retail Park . . . . . . . B3
Richard St . . . . . . . B1
Ripon St . . . . . . . . B1
Robinson St East . . B3
Royal St . . . . . . . . A3
St. Hilda's Ave . . . . C1
St. James 🔺 . . . . . C2
Sheepfold St . . B3/C3
Sixhills St . . . . . . . C3
South Park . . . . . . B2
Spring St . . . . . . . . A3
Superstore . . . . . . B3
Tasburgh St . . . . . . C3
Tennyson St . . . . . . B2
The Close . . . . . . . C1
Thesiger St . . . . . . A3
Time Trap 🏛 . . . . . C2
Town Hall 🏛 . . . . . B2
Veal St . . . . . . . . . B1
Victoria St North . . . A2
Victoria St South . . B2
Victoria St West . . . B2
Watkin St . . . . . . . A1
Welholme Ave . . . . . C2
Welholme Museum
   & Gallery 🏛 . . . . C3
Welholme Rd . . . . . C3
Wellington St . . . . . B3
Wellowgate . . . . . . C2
Werneth Rd . . . . . . B3
West Coates Rd . . . A1
Westgate . . . . . . . . A2
Westminster Dr . . . . C1
Willingham St . . . . . C3
Wintringham Rd . . . C2
Wood St . . . . . . . . B3
Yarborough Dr . . . . B1
Yarborough
   Hotel 🏛 . . . . . . . C2

## Harrogate

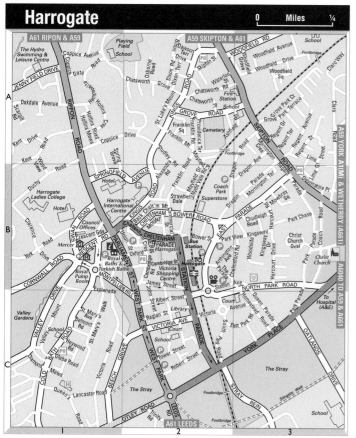

## Hull

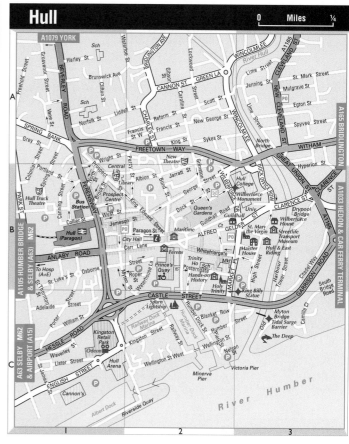

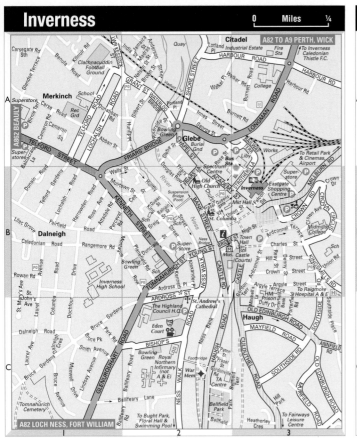

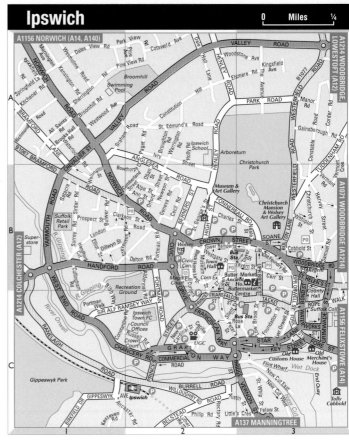

## Inverness

Abban St . . . . . . . . A1
Academy St . . . . . B2
Alexander Pl . . . . . B2
Anderson St . . . . . A2
Annfield Rd . . . . . . C3
Ardconnel St . . . . . B3
Ardconnel Terr . . . . B3
Ardross Pl . . . . . . . B2
Ardross St . . . . . . B2
Argyle St . . . . . . B3
Argyle Terr . . . . . B3
Attadale Rd . . . . . B1
Ballifeary La . . . . . C2
Ballifeary Rd . . . C1/C2
Balnacraig La . . . . A1
Balnain St . . . . . . B2
Bank St . . . . . . . . B2
Bellfield Park . . . . C2
Bellfield Terr . . . . . C3
Benula Rd . . . . . . A1
Birnie Terr . . . . . . . A1
Bishop's Rd . . . . . C2
Bowling Green . . . . A1
Bowling Green . . . . B2
Bowling Green . . . . C2
Bridge St . . . . . . . B2
Brown St . . . . . . . A2
Bruce Ave . . . . . . C1
Bruce Gdns . . . . . C1
Bruce Pk . . . . . . . C1
Burial Ground . . . . A2
Burnett Rd . . . . . . A3
Bus Station . . . . . . B3
Caledonian Rd . . . . B1
Cameron Rd . . . . . A1
Cameron Sq . . . . . A1
Carse Rd . . . . . . . A2
Carsegate Rd South A1
Castle (Courts) . . . . B3
Castle Rd . . . . . . B2
Castle St . . . . . . . B3
Celt St . . . . . . . . . B2
Chapel St . . . . . . . A2
Charles St . . . . . . B3

Church St . . . . . . . B2
Clachnacuddin
  Football Ground . . A1
College . . . . . . . . A3
Columba Rd . . . B1/C1
Crown Ave . . . . . . B3
Crown Circus . . . . B3
Crown Dr . . . . . . . B3
Crown Rd . . . . . . . B3
Crown St . . . . . . . B3
Culduthel Rd . . . . . C3
Dalneigh Cres . . . . C1
Dalneigh Rd . . . . . C1
Denny St . . . . . . . B3
Dochfour Dr . . . B1/C1
Douglas Row . . . . . A2
Duffy Dr . . . . . . . . C3
Dunabban Rd . . . . . A1
Dunain Rd . . . . . . B1
Duncraig St . . . . . B2
Eastgate Shopping
  Centre . . . . . . . . B3
Eden Court ⚕ 🎭 . . C2
Fairfield Rd . . . . . . B1
Falcon Sq . . . . . . . B3
Fire Station . . . . . . A3
Fraser St . . . . . . . B2
Fraser St . . . . . . . C2
Friars' Bridge . . . . A2
Friars' La . . . . . . . B2
Friars' St . . . . . . . A2
George St . . . . . . . A2
Gilbert St . . . . . . . A2
Glebe St . . . . . . . . A2
Glendoe Terr . . . . . A1
Glenurquhart Rd . . . C1
Gordon Terr . . . . . B3
Gordonville Rd . . . . C2
Grant St . . . . . . . . A2
Greig St . . . . . . . . B2
H.M. Prison . . . . . . B3
Harbour Rd . . . . . . A3
Harrowden Rd . . . . B1
Haugh Rd . . . . . . . C2
Heatherley Cres . . . C3
High St . . . . . . . . B3

Highland Council
  H.Q., The . . . . . . C2
Hill Park . . . . . . . C3
Hill St . . . . . . . . . B3
Huntly Pl . . . . . . . A2
Huntly St . . . . . . . B2
India St . . . . . . . . A2
Industrial Estate . . . A3
Information Ctr ⓘ . . B2
Innes St . . . . . . . . A2
Inverness High
  School . . . . . . . . B1
Inverness ≷ . . . . . B3
Jamaica St . . . . . . A2
Kenneth St . . . . . . B1
Kilmuir Rd . . . . . . A1
King St . . . . . . . . B2
Kingsmills Rd . . . . B3
Laurel Ave . . . . B1/C1
Library . . . . . . . . . A3
Lilac Gr . . . . . . . . C1
Lindsay Ave . . . . . C1
Lochalsh Rd . . . A1/B1
Longman Rd . . . . . A3
Lotland Pl . . . . . . . A2
Lower Kessock St . . A1
Madras St . . . . . . B2
Market Hall . . . . . . B3
Maxwell Dr . . . . . . C1
Mayfield Rd . . . . . C3
Midmills College . . . B3
Millburn Rd . . . . . B3
Mitchell's La . . . . . C3
Montague Row . . . . A2
Muirfield Rd . . . . . C3
Muirtown St . . . . . B1
Museum 🏛 . . . . . . B2
Nelson St . . . . . . . A2
Ness Bank . . . . . . C2
Ness Bridge . . . . . B2
Ness Walk . . . . B2/C2
Old Edinburgh Rd . . C3
Old High
  Church ⛪ . . . . . . B2
Park Rd . . . . . . . . C1
Paton St . . . . . . . C2

Perceval Rd . . . . . B1
Planefield Rd . . . . B2
Police Station 🛡 . . A3
Porterfield Bank . . . C3
Porterfield Rd . . . . C3
Portland Pl . . . . . . A2
Post Office 🏤 . . . . .
  . . . . . . A2/B1/B2/B3
Queen St . . . . . . . B2
Queensgate . . . . . B2
Railway Terr . . . . . A3
Rangemore Rd . . . . B1
Reay St . . . . . . . . B3
Riverside St . . . . . A2
Rose St . . . . . . . . A2
Ross Ave . . . . . . . B1
Rowan Rd . . . . . . B1
Royal Northern
  Infirmary 🏥 . . . . C2
St. Andrew's
  Cathedral ✝ . . . . C2
St. Columba ⛪ . . . B2
St. John's Ave . . . . C1
St. Mary's Ave . . . . C1
Shore St . . . . . . . A2
Smith Ave . . . . . . C1
Southside Pl . . . . . C3
Southside Rd . . . . C3
Spectrum Centre . . B2
Strothers La . . . . . B2
TA Centre . . . . . . C2
Telford Gdns . . . . . B1
Telford Rd . . . . . . A1
Telford St . . . . . . . A1
Tomnahurich
  Cemetery . . . . . . C1
Tomnahurich St . . . B2
Town Hall . . . . . . . B3
Union Rd . . . . . . . B3
Union St . . . . . . . B3
Walker Pl . . . . . . . A2
Walker Rd . . . . . . A2
War Memorial ✦ . . . C2
Waterloo Bridge . . . A2
Wells St . . . . . . . . B1
Young St . . . . . . . B2

## Ipswich

Alderman Rd . . . . . B2
All Saints' Rd . . . . A1
Alpe St . . . . . . . . B2
Ancaster Rd . . . . . C1
Ancient House 🏠 . . B3
Anglesea Rd . . . . . B2
Ann St . . . . . . . . . B2
Austin St . . . . . . . C2
Belstead Rd . . . . . C2
Berners St . . . . . . B2
Bibb Way . . . . . . . B2
Birkfield Dr . . . . . . C1
Black Horse La . . . B2
Bolton La . . . . . . . B3
Bond St . . . . . . . . C3
Bowthorpe Cl . . . . B2
Bramford La . . . . . A1
Bramford Rd . . . . . A1
Bridge St . . . . . . . C2
Brookfield Rd . . . . A1
Brooks Hall Rd . . . A1
Broomhill Rd . . . . . A1
Broughton Rd . . . . A2
Bulwer Rd . . . . . . B1
Burrell Rd . . . . . . C2
Bus Station . . . B2/C3
Butter Market . . . . B2
Butter Market
  Centre . . . . . . . . B3
Carr St . . . . . . . . B3
Cecil Rd . . . . . . . . B2
Cecilia St . . . . . . . C2
Chancery Rd . . . . . C2
Charles St . . . . . . C1
Chevallier St . . . . . A1
Christchurch Mansion
  & Wolsey Art
  Gallery 🏛 . . . . . . B3
Christchurch Park . . A3
Christchurch St . . . B3
Civic Centre . . . . . B2
Civic Dr . . . . . . . . B2
Clarkson St . . . . . . B1
Cobbold St . . . . . . B3
Commercial Rd . . . C2
Constable Rd . . . . A3
Constantine Rd . . . C1
Constitution Hill . . . A2

Corder Rd . . . . . . A3
Corn Exchange . . . B2
Cotswold Ave . . . . A3
Council Offices . . . C2
County Hall . . . . . B3
Crown Court . . . . . C2
Crown St . . . . . . . B2
Cullingham Rd . . . . B1
Cumberland St . . . . B2
Curriers La . . . . . . B2
Dale Hall La . . . . . A2
Dales View Rd . . . . A1
Dalton St . . . . . . . B2
Dillwyn St . . . . . . . B1
Elliot St . . . . . . . . B1
Elm St . . . . . . . . . B2
Elsmere Rd . . . . . A3
End Quay . . . . . . . C3
Falcon St . . . . . . . C2
Felaw St . . . . . . . C3
Flint Wharf . . . . . . C3
Fonnereau Rd . . . . B2
Fore St . . . . . . . . C3
Foundation St . . . . C3
Franciscan Way . . . C2
Friars St . . . . . . . . C2
Gainsborough Rd . . A3
Gatacre Rd . . . . . . B1
Geneva Rd . . . . . . B2
Gippeswyk Ave . . . C1
Gippeswyk Park . . . C1
Grafton Way . . . . . C2
Graham Rd . . . . . . A1
Grimwade St . . . . . C3
Great Whip St . . . . C3
Handford Cut . . . . . B2
Handford Rd . . . . . B1
Henley Rd . . . . . . A2
Hervey St . . . . . . . B3
High St . . . . . . . . B2
Holly Rd . . . . . . . . A2
Information Ctr ⓘ . . B3
Ipswich School . . . A2
Ipswich
  Station ≷ . . . . . . C2
Ipswich Town FC
  (Portman Road) . . C2
Ivry St . . . . . . . . . A2
Kensington Rd . . . . A1
Kesteven Rd . . . . . C1

Key St . . . . . . . . . C3
Kingsfield Ave . . . . A3
Kitchener Rd . . . . . A1
Magistrates Court . . B2
Little's Cr . . . . . . . C2
London Rd . . . . . . B1
Low Brook St . . . . B2
Lower Orwell St . . . C3
Luther Rd . . . . . . . C2
Manor Rd . . . . . . . A3
Mornington Ave . . . A1
Museum & Art
  Gallery 🏛 . . . . . . B2
Museum St . . . . . . B2
Neale St . . . . . . . . B3
New Cardinal St . . . C2
New Cut East . . . . C3
New Cut West . . . . C3
Newson St . . . . . . B2
Norwich Rd . . . A1/B1
Oban St . . . . . . . . B2
Old Customs
  House 🏠 . . . . . . C3
Old Foundry Rd . . . B3
Old Merchant's
  House 🏠 . . . . . . C3
Orford St . . . . . . . B3
Paget Rd . . . . . . . A2
Park Rd . . . . . . . . A3
Park View Rd . . . . C2
Peter's St . . . . . . . C2
Philip Rd . . . . . . . C2
Pine Ave . . . . . . . C2
Pine View Rd . . . . A2
Police Station 🛡 . . B2
Portman Rd . . . . . B2
Portman Walk . . . . C1
Post Office 🏤 . . B2/B3
Princes St . . . . . . C2
Prospect St . . . . . B1
Queen St . . . . . . . B2
Ranelagh Rd . . . . . C1
Rectory Rd . . . . . . C2
Regent Theatre 🎭 . B3
Richmond Rd . . . . A1
Rope Walk . . . . . . C2
Rose La . . . . . . . . C2
Russell Rd . . . . . . C1
St Edmund's Rd . . . A2
St George's St . . . . B2

St Helen's St . . . . . B3
Samuel Rd . . . . . . B3
Sherrington Rd . . . . A1
Silent St . . . . . . . . C2
Sir Alf Ramsey
  Way . . . . . . . . . . C1
Sirdar Rd . . . . . . . B1
Soane St . . . . . . . B3
Springfield La . . . . A1
Star La . . . . . . . . C3
Stevenson Rd . . . . B1
Suffolk College . . . C3
Suffolk Retail Park . B1
Superstore . . . . . . B1
Surrey Rd . . . . . . . B1
Swimming Pool . . . A1
Tacket St . . . . . . . C3
Tavern St . . . . . . . B3
The Avenue . . . . . A3
Tolly Cobbold
  Museum . . . . . . . C3
Tower Ramparts . . . B2
Tower St . . . . . . . B3
Town Hall 🏠 . . . . . B2
Tuddenham Rd . . . . A3
UGC 🎭 . . . . . . . . C2
Upper Brook St . . . B3
Upper Orwell St . . . B3
Valley Rd . . . . . . . A2
Vermont Cr . . . . . . B3
Vermont Rd . . . . . B3
Vernon St . . . . . . C3
Warrington Rd . . . . A2
Waterloo Rd . . . . . A1
Waterworks St . . . . C3
Wellington St . . . . B1
West End Rd . . . . . B1
Westerfield Rd . . . . A3
Westgate St . . . . . B2
Westholme Rd . . . . A1
Westwood Ave . . . A1
Willoughby Rd . . . . C2
Withipoll St . . . . . . B3
Wolsey Theatre 🎭 . B2
Woodbridge Rd . . . B3
Woodstone Ave . . . A3
Yarmouth Rd . . . . . B1

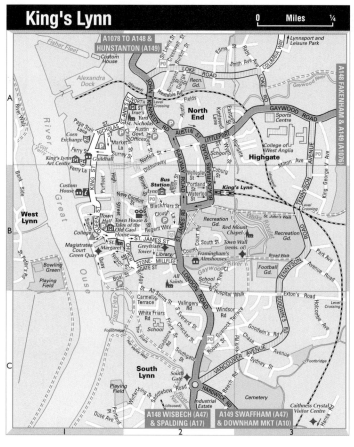

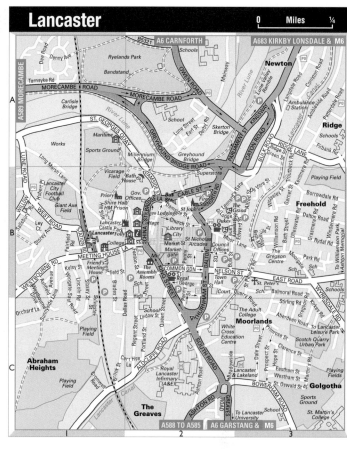

## King's Lynn

| | |
|---|---|
| Albert St . . . . . . . . A2 | Edma St . . . . . . . . A2 |
| Albion St . . . . . . . B2 | Exton's Rd . . . . . . C3 |
| All Saints ⓗ . . . . . B2 | Ferry La . . . . . . . . B1 |
| All Saints St . . . . . B2 | Ferry St . . . . . . . . A1 |
| Austin Fields . . . . . A2 | Framingham's |
| Austin St . . . . . . . A2 | Almshouses ⓗ . . B2 |
| Avenue Rd . . . . . . B3 | Friars St . . . . . . . . B2 |
| Bank Side . . . . . . B1 | Gaywood Rd . . . . . A3 |
| Beech Rd . . . . . . C2 | George St . . . . . . . A2 |
| Birch Tree Cl. . . . . B2 | Gladstone Rd . . . . C2 |
| Birchwood St . . . . . A2 | Goodwin's Rd . . . . C3 |
| Blackfriars Rd. . . . . B2 | Green Quay ◆ . . . . B1 |
| Blackfriars St . . . . . B2 | Greyfriars' |
| Boal St . . . . . . . . B1 | Tower ◆ . . . . . . B2 |
| Bridge St . . . . . . . B2 | Guanock Terr . . . . . C2 |
| Broad St . . . . . . . B2 | Guildhall ⓗ . . . . . A1 |
| Broad Walk . . . . . . B3 | Hansa Rd . . . . . . C3 |
| Burkitt St . . . . . . . A2 | Hardwick Rd. . . . . . C2 |
| Bus Station . . . . . . B2 | Hextable Rd . . . . . A1 |
| Carmelite Terr. . . . . C2 | High St . . . . . . . . B1 |
| Chapel St . . . . . . . A2 | Holcombe Ave . . . . C3 |
| Chase Ave . . . . . . C3 | Hospital Walk . . . . . B3 |
| Checker St . . . . . . C2 | Information Ctr ⓘ . . B1 |
| Church St . . . . . . . B2 | John Kennedy Rd. . . A2 |
| Clough La. . . . . . . B2 | Kettlewell Lane . . . A2 |
| Coburg St . . . . . . . B2 | King George |
| College of West | V Ave . . . . . . . B3 |
| Anglia . . . . . . . A3 | King's Lynn Art |
| Columbia Way . . . . A3 | Centre ⓗ . . . . . A1 |
| Corn Exchange ⓦ . A1 | King's Lynn |
| County Court Rd . . . B2 | Station ⓩ . . . . . B2 |
| Cresswell St . . . . . A2 | King St . . . . . . . . B1 |
| Custom House ⓗ. . . A1 | Library . . . . . . . . B2 |
| Eastgate St . . . . . . A2 | Littleport St. . . . . . B2 |
| | Loke Rd . . . . . . . A2 |
| | London Rd . . . . . . B2 |

| | |
|---|---|
| Lynn Museum . . . . . B2 | St Nicholas St . . . . A1 |
| Majestic ⓦ . . . . . . B2 | St Peter's Rd . . . . . B1 |
| Magistrates Court. . . B1 | Sir Lewis St . . . . . A2 |
| Market La . . . . . . . A1 | Smith Ave . . . . . . A3 |
| Millfleet . . . . . . . . B2 | South Everard St . . . C2 |
| Milton Ave . . . . . . A3 | South Gate ◆ . . . . C2 |
| Nar Valley Walk. . . . C2 | South Quay . . . . . . B1 |
| Nelson St . . . . . . . B1 | South St . . . . . . . B2 |
| New Conduit St . . . . B2 | Southgate St . . . . . C2 |
| Norfolk St . . . . . . . A2 | Stonegate St . . . . . B2 |
| North St . . . . . . . . A2 | Surrey St . . . . . . . A1 |
| Oldsunway . . . . . . B2 | Sydney St . . . . . . . C3 |
| Ouse Ave . . . . . . . C1 | Tennyson Ave . . . . . B3 |
| Page Stair Lane . . . A1 | Tennyson Rd. . . . . . B3 |
| Park Ave . . . . . . . B3 | The Friars . . . . . . . B2 |
| Police Station ⓟ . . . B2 | Tower St . . . . . . . B2 |
| Portland Pl . . . . . . C1 | Town Hall . . . . . . . B1 |
| Portland St . . . . . . B2 | Town House & Tales |
| Post Office ⓟ . . . . . | of The Old Gaol |
| . . . . . . . . A3/B2/C2 | House ⓗ . . . . . . B1 |
| Purfleet . . . . . . . . B1 | Town Wall |
| Queen St . . . . . . . B1 | (Remains) ◆ . . . . B3 |
| Raby Ave . . . . . . . A3 | True's Yard |
| Railway Rd . . . . . . A2 | Museum ⓗ . . . . A2 |
| Red Mount | Valingers Rd . . . . . C2 |
| Chapel ⓗ . . . . . B3 | Vancouver Ave . . . . C2 |
| Regent Way . . . . . . B2 | Waterloo St . . . . . . B2 |
| River Walk . . . . . . A1 | Wellesley St . . . . . B2 |
| Robert St . . . . . . . C2 | White Friars Rd. . . . C2 |
| Saddlebow Rd . . . . C2 | Windsor Rd . . . . . . C2 |
| St Ann's St . . . . . . A1 | Winfarthing St. . . . . C2 |
| St James' Rd . . . . . B2 | Wyatt St . . . . . . . A2 |
| St James St . . . . . B2 | York Rd. . . . . . . . C3 |
| St John's Walk . . . . B3 | |
| St Margaret's ⓗ . . . B1 | |
| St Nicholas ⓗ . . . . A2 | |

## Lancaster

| | |
|---|---|
| Aberdeen Rd . . . . . C3 | Dee Rd . . . . . . . . A1 |
| Adult College, The . C3 | Denny Ave . . . . . . A1 |
| Aldcliffe Rd . . . . . . C2 | Derby Rd . . . . . . . A2 |
| Alfred St . . . . . . . . B3 | Dukes ⓦⓗ . . . . . B2 |
| Ambleside Rd . . . . . A3 | Earl St . . . . . . . . A2 |
| Ambulance Sta . . . . A3 | East Rd. . . . . . . . B3 |
| Ashfield Ave . . . . . B1 | Eastham St . . . . . . C3 |
| Ashton Rd . . . . . . C2 | Edward St . . . . . . . B3 |
| Assembly Rooms, | Fairfield Rd . . . . . . B1 |
| The . . . . . . . . . B2 | Fenton St . . . . . . . B2 |
| Balmoral Rd . . . . . B3 | Firbank Rd . . . . . . A3 |
| Bath House ⓗ . . . . B2 | Fire Station . . . . . . B2 |
| Bath Mill La . . . . . . B3 | Folly Gallery ⓗ . . . B2 |
| Bath St . . . . . . . . B3 | Friend's Meeting |
| Blades St . . . . . . . B1 | House ⓗ . . . . . . B1 |
| Borrowdale Rd . . . . B3 | Garnet St . . . . . . . B3 |
| Bowerham Rd . . . . . C3 | George St . . . . . . . B2 |
| Brewery La . . . . . . B2 | Giant Axe Field . . . . B1 |
| Bridge La . . . . . . . B2 | Gov. Offices . . . . . B2 |
| Brook St . . . . . . . C1 | Grand, The ⓦ . . . . B2 |
| Bulk Rd . . . . . . . . A3 | Grasmere Rd . . . . . B3 |
| Bulk St . . . . . . . . B2 | Greaves Rd . . . . . . C2 |
| Bus Station . . . . . . B2 | Green St . . . . . . . A3 |
| Cable St . . . . . . . B2 | Gregson Centre, |
| Carlisle Bridge . . . . A1 | The . . . . . . . . . B3 |
| Carr House La . . . . C2 | Gregson Rd . . . . . . C3 |
| Castle ⓗ . . . . . . . B1 | Greyhound |
| Castle Park . . . . . . B1 | Bridge Rd . . . . . A2 |
| Caton Rd . . . . . . . A3 | Greyhound Bridge . A2 |
| China St . . . . . . . B2 | High St . . . . . . . . B2 |
| Church St . . . . . . . B2 | Hill Side . . . . . . . B1 |
| City Museum ⓗ . . . B2 | Hope St . . . . . . . C3 |
| Clarence St . . . . . . C3 | Hubert Pl . . . . . . . B2 |
| Common Gdn St . . . B2 | Information Ctr ⓘ . . B2 |
| Coniston Rd . . . . . . A3 | Judges |
| Cottage | Lodgings ⓗ . . . . B2 |
| Museum ⓗ . . . . B2 | Kelsy St . . . . . . . B1 |
| Council Offices . . . . B2 | Kentmere Rd . . . . . B3 |
| Court. . . . . . . . . . B2 | King St . . . . . . . . B2 |
| Cromwell Rd. . . . . . C1 | Kingsway . . . . . . . A3 |
| Dale St . . . . . . . . C3 | Kirkes Rd . . . . . . . C3 |
| Dallas Rd . . . . . . . B1/C1 | Lancaster & |
| Dalton Rd . . . . . . . B3 | Lakeland ⓗ . . . . C3 |
| Dalton Sq . . . . . . . B2 | Lancaster City |
| Damside St . . . . . . B2 | Football Club . . . . B1 |
| De Vitre St . . . . . . B3 | Lancaster |
| | Station ⓩ . . . . . B1 |
| | Langdale Rd . . . . . A3 |

| | |
|---|---|
| Ley Ct . . . . . . . . . B1 | St. John's ⓗ . . . . . B2 |
| Library . . . . . . . . . B2 | St. Leonard's |
| Lincoln Rd . . . . . . B1 | Gate . . . . . . . . B2 |
| Lindow St . . . . . . . C2 | St. Martin's |
| Lodge St . . . . . . . B2 | College . . . . . . . C3 |
| Long Marsh La . . . . B1 | St. Martin's Rd . . . . C3 |
| Lune Rd . . . . . . . . A1 | St. Nicholas Arcades |
| Lune St . . . . . . . . A2 | Shopping Centre . B2 |
| Lune Valley | St. Oswald St . . . . . C3 |
| Maritime | St. Peter's ✝ . . . . . B3 |
| Museum ⓗ . . . . A1 | St. Peter's Rd . . . . . B3 |
| Mainway . . . . . . . A2 | Salisbury Rd . . . . . B1 |
| Maritime | Scotch Quarry |
| Museum ⓗ . . . . A1 | Urban Park . . . . . C3 |
| Market St . . . . . . . B2 | Shire Hall/ |
| Marketgate Shopping | HM Prison. . . . . . B1 |
| Centre. . . . . . . . B2 | Sibsey St . . . . . . . B1 |
| Meadowside . . . . . C2 | Skerton Bridge . . . . A2 |
| Meeting House La . . B1 | South Rd . . . . . . . C2 |
| Millennium Bridge . A2 | Station Rd . . . . . . . B1 |
| Moorgate . . . . . . . B3 | Stirling Rd. . . . . . . C3 |
| Moor La . . . . . . . . B2 | Storey Ave . . . . . . B1 |
| Morecambe Rd. A1/A2 | Storey Gallery ⓗ . . B2 |
| Nelson St . . . . . . . B2 | Sunnyside La . . . . . C1 |
| North Rd. . . . . . . . B2 | Sylvester St . . . . . C3 |
| Orchard La . . . . . . C1 | Tarnsyke Rd . . . . . A1 |
| Owen Rd . . . . . . . A2 | Thurnham St. . . . . . C2 |
| Park Rd . . . . . . . . B3 | Town Hall . . . . . . . B2 |
| Parliament St . . . . . A3 | Troutbeck Rd . . . . . B3 |
| Patterdale Rd . . . . . A3 | Ulleswater Rd . . . . . B3 |
| Penny St. . . . . . . . B2 | Vicarage Field. . . . . B1 |
| Police Station ⓟ . . . B2 | West Rd . . . . . . . . B1 |
| Portland St . . . . . . C2 | Westbourne Dr . . . . C1 |
| Post Office ⓟ . . A2/A3/ | Westbourne Rd . . . . B1 |
| . . . . . . B1/B2/B3/C3 | Westham St . . . . . . C3 |
| Primrose St. . . . . . C3 | Wheatfield St . . . . . B1 |
| Priory ⓗ . . . . . . . B1 | White Cross Education |
| Prospect St . . . . . . C3 | Centre. . . . . . . . C2 |
| Quarry Rd. . . . . . . B3 | Williamson Rd . . . . B3 |
| Queen St . . . . . . . C2 | Willow La . . . . . . . B1 |
| Regal ⓦ . . . . . . . B2 | Windermere Rd . . . . B3 |
| Regent St . . . . . . . C2 | Wingate-Saul Rd . . . B1 |
| Ridge La . . . . . . . A3 | Wolseley St. . . . . . B1 |
| Ridge St . . . . . . . . A3 | Woodville St . . . . . B3 |
| Royal Lancaster | Wyresdale Rd . . . . . C3 |
| Infirmary (A&E) ⓗ . C2 | |
| Rydal Rd. . . . . . . . B3 | |
| Ryelands Park . . . . A1 | |
| St. Georges Quay . . A1 | |

# Leeds

0    Miles    ¼

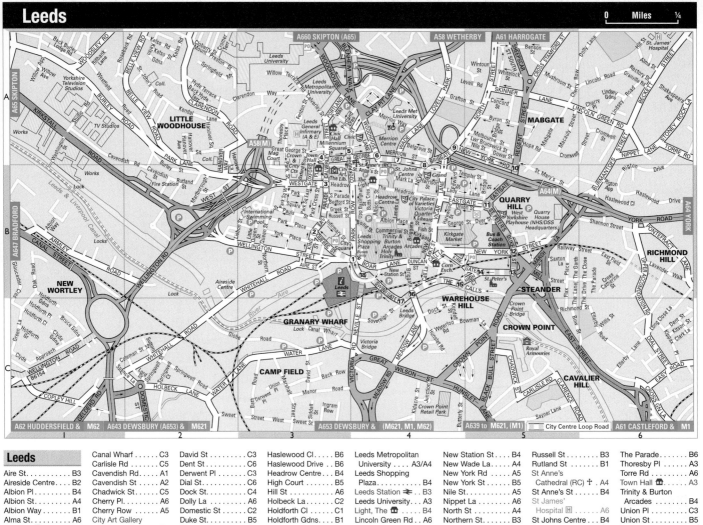

A65 SKIPTON | A62 BRADFORD | A65 SKIPTON (A65) | A58 WETHERBY | A61 HARROGATE | A64(M) | A64 YORK

A62 HUDDERSFIELD & M62 | A643 DEWSBURY (A653) & M621 | A653 DEWSBURY & (M621, M1, M62) | A639 to M621, (M1) | City Centre Loop Road | A61 CASTLEFORD & M1

1 | 2 | 3 | 4 | 5 | 6

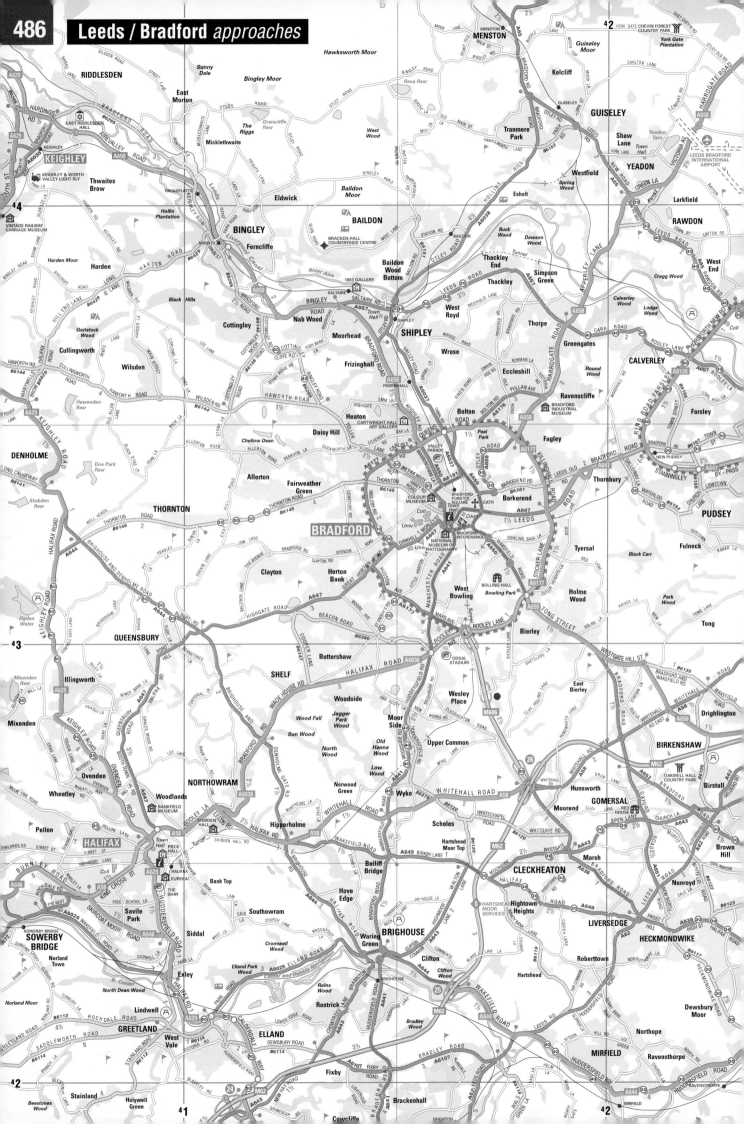

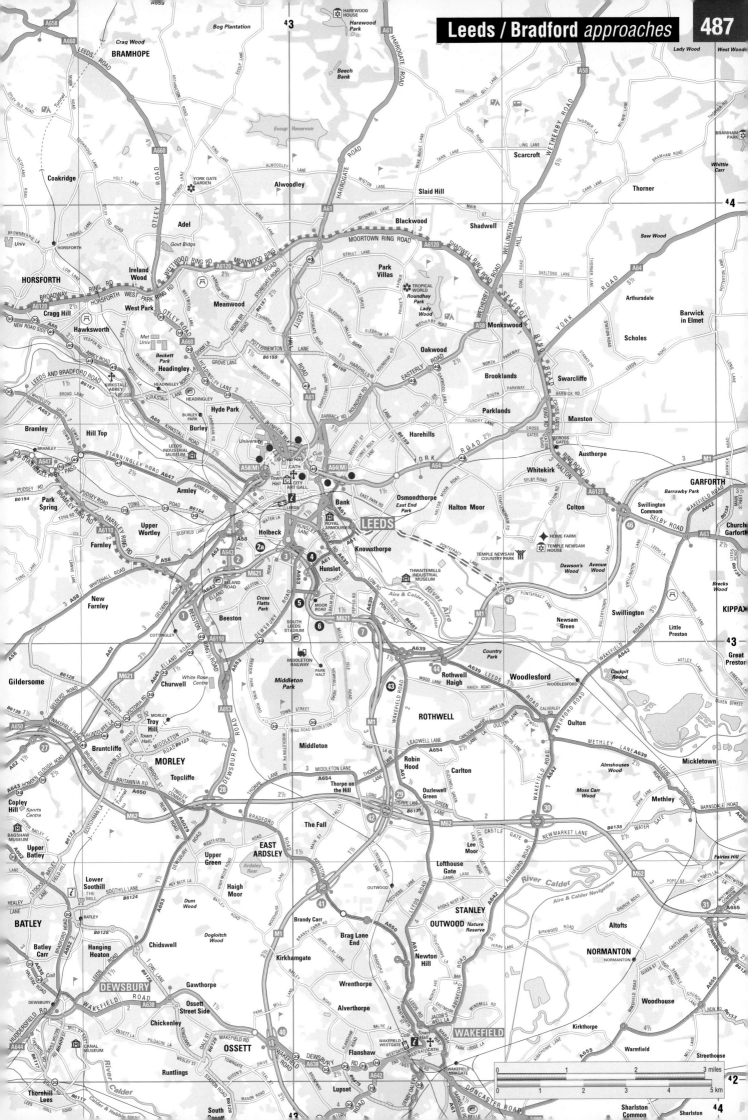

# Liverpool

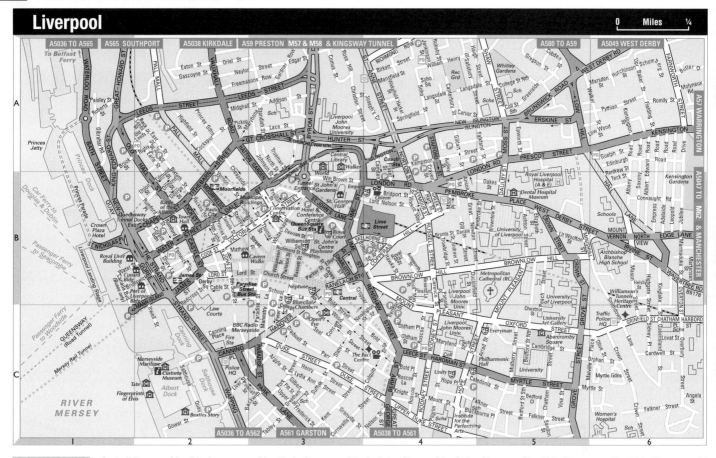

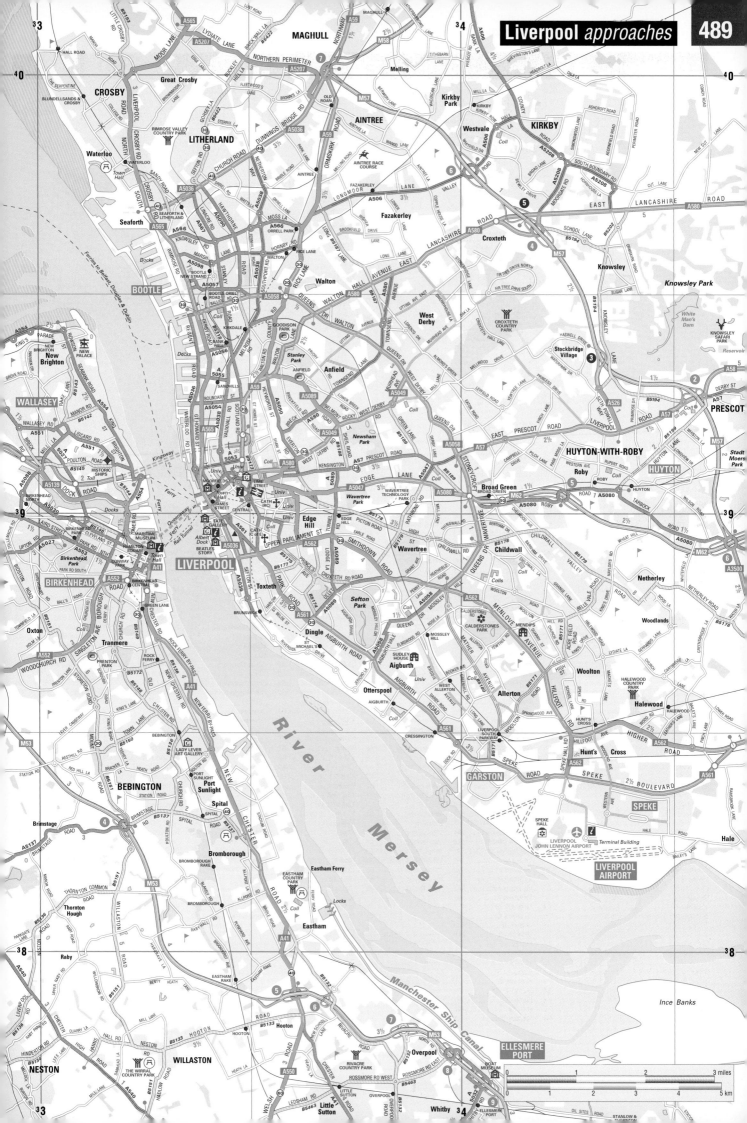

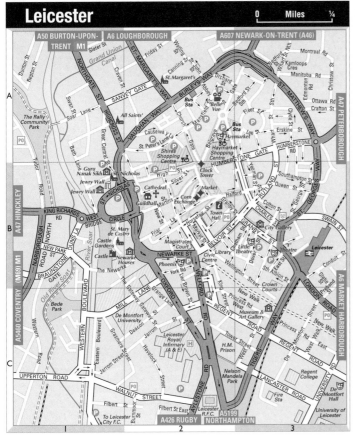

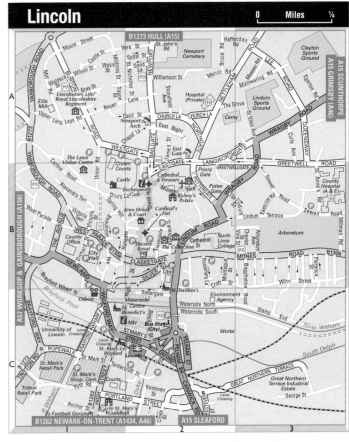

# London

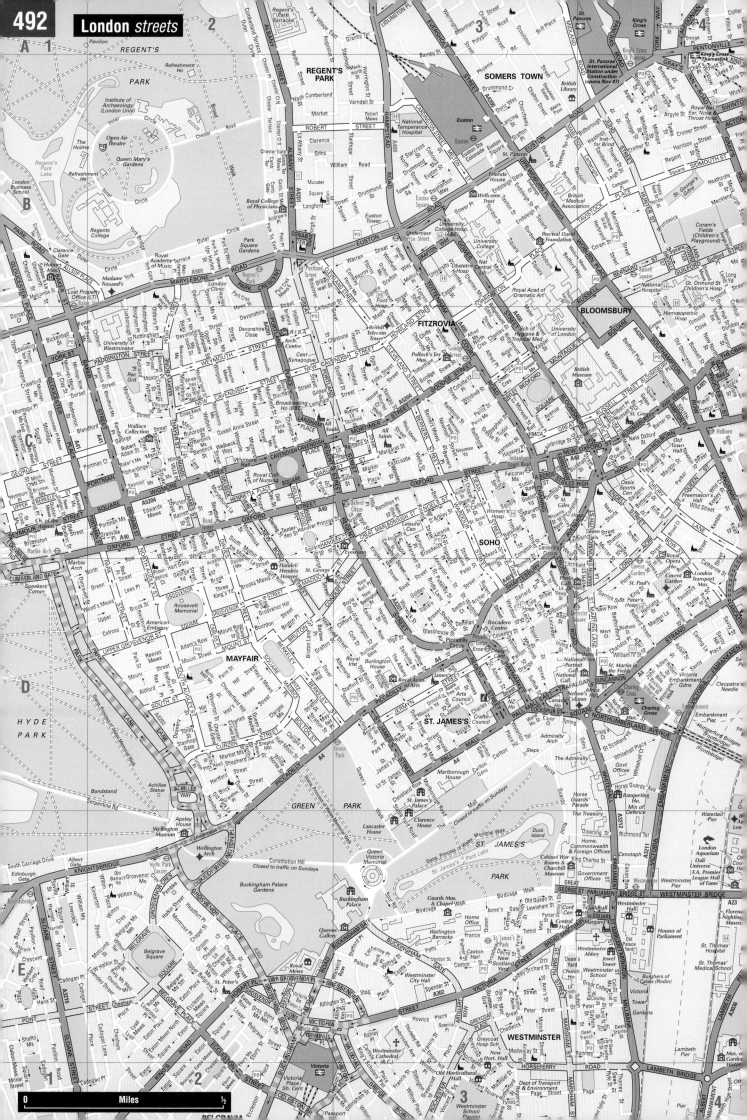

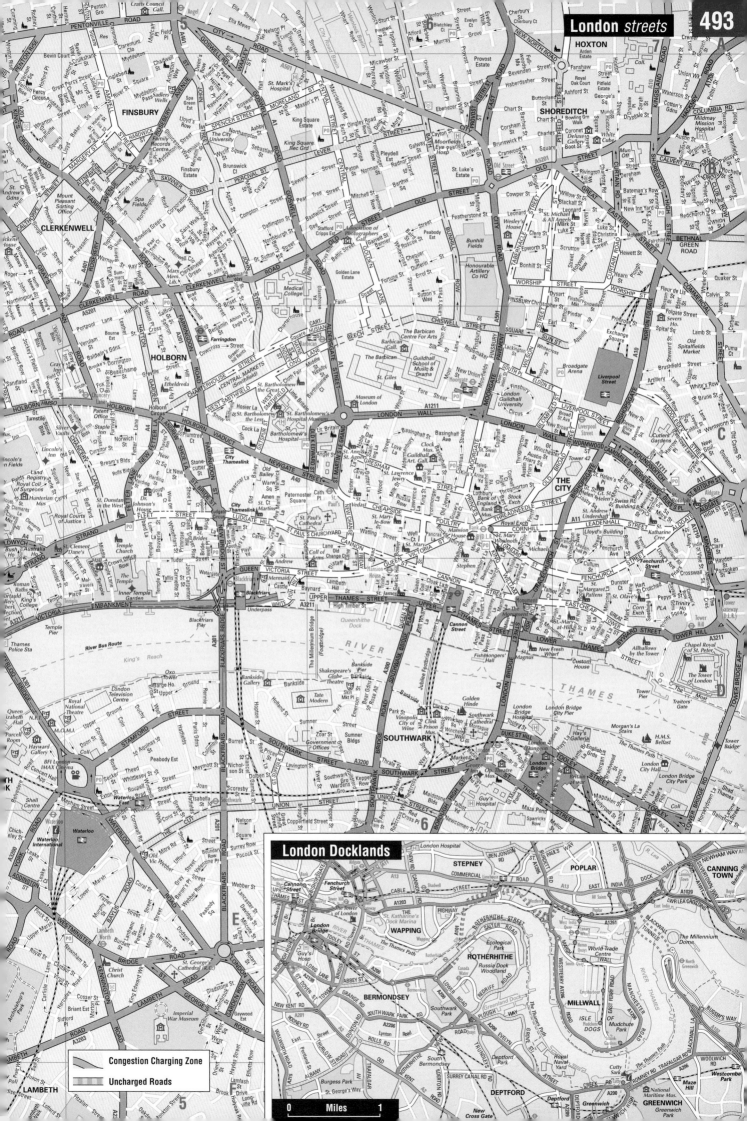

**HOXTON**
**SHOREDITCH**
**COLUMBIA RD**
**BETHNAL GREEN ROAD**

**FINSBURY**

**CLERKENWELL**

**HOLBORN**

**THE CITY**

**RIVER THAMES**

**KING'S REACH**

**THAMES**

**SOUTHWARK**

**London Docklands**

**STEPNEY**
**POPLAR**
**CANNING TOWN**
**WAPPING**
**ROTHERHITHE**
**MILLWALL**
**ISLE OF DOGS**
**BERMONDSEY**

**LAMBETH**

**DEPTFORD**
**GREENWICH**

Congestion Charging Zone
Uncharged Roads

0        Miles        1

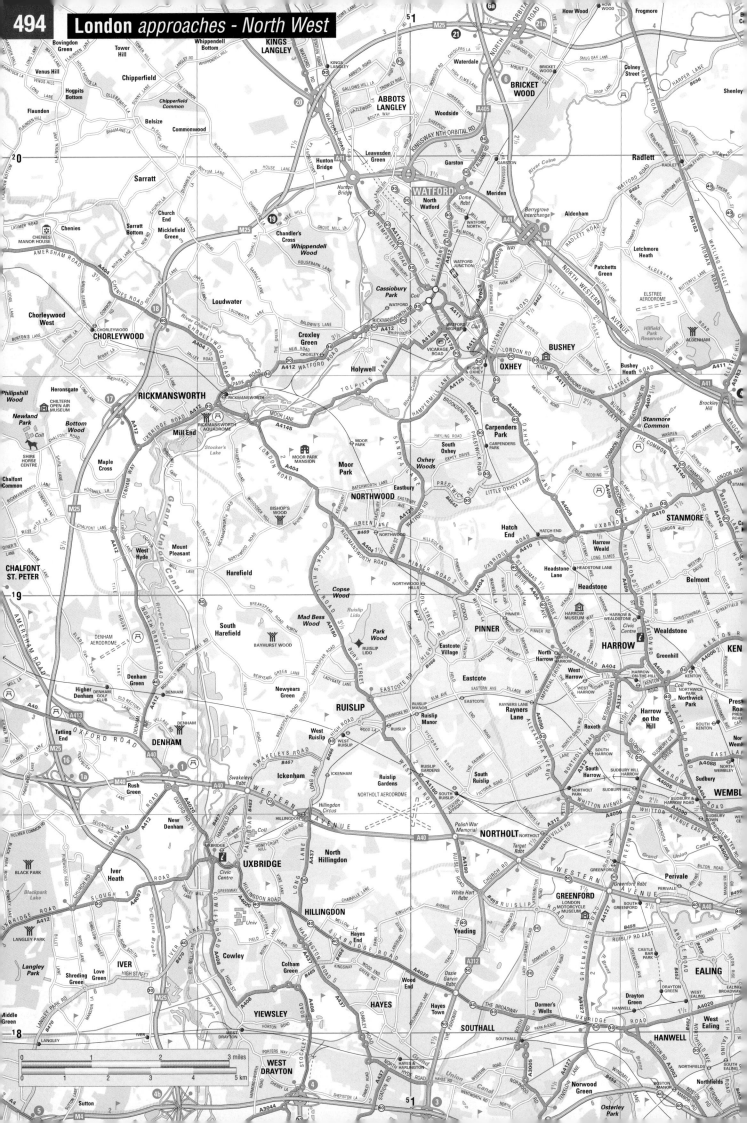

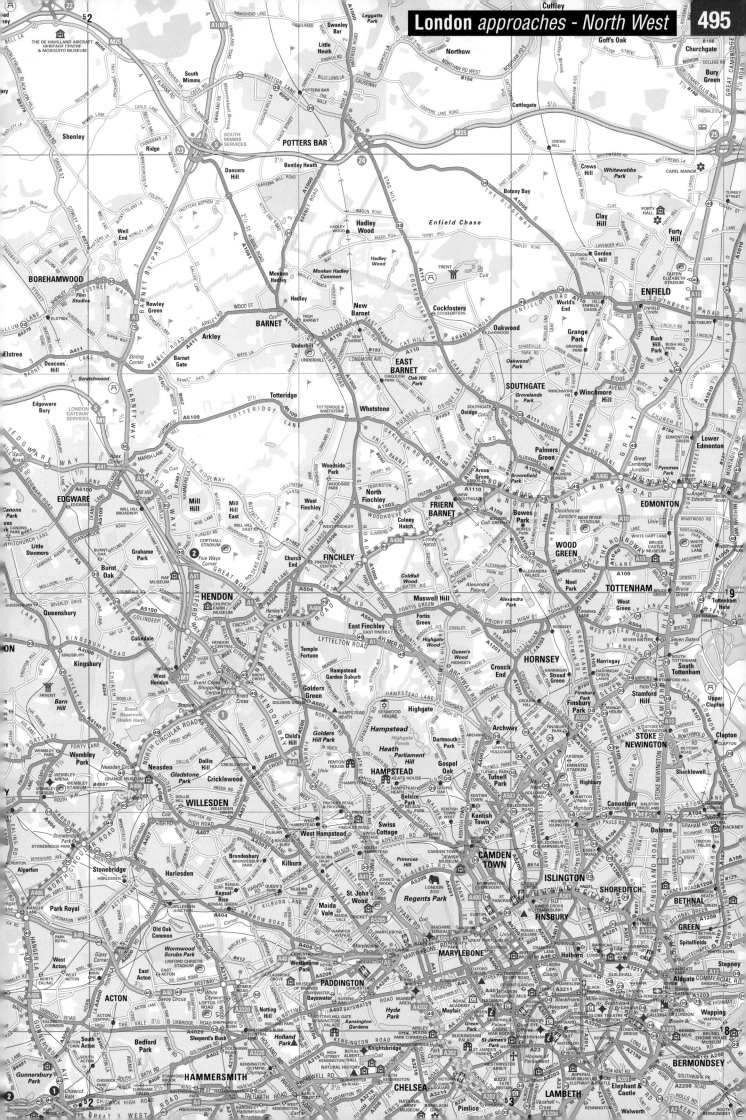

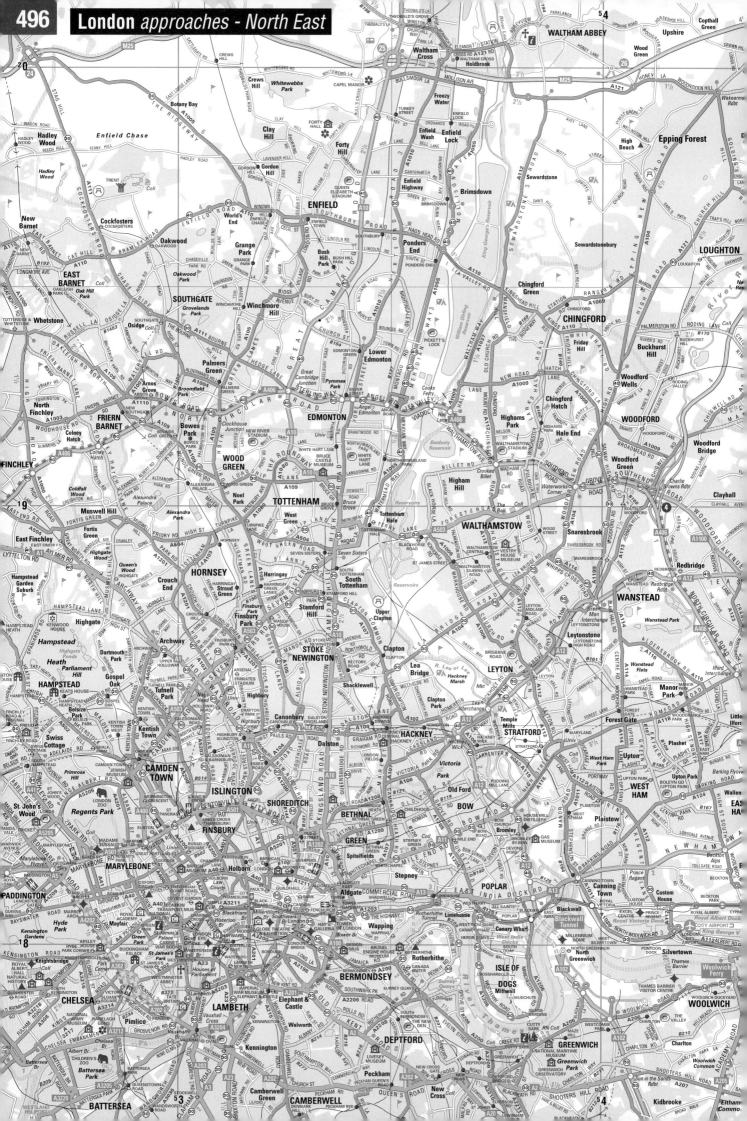

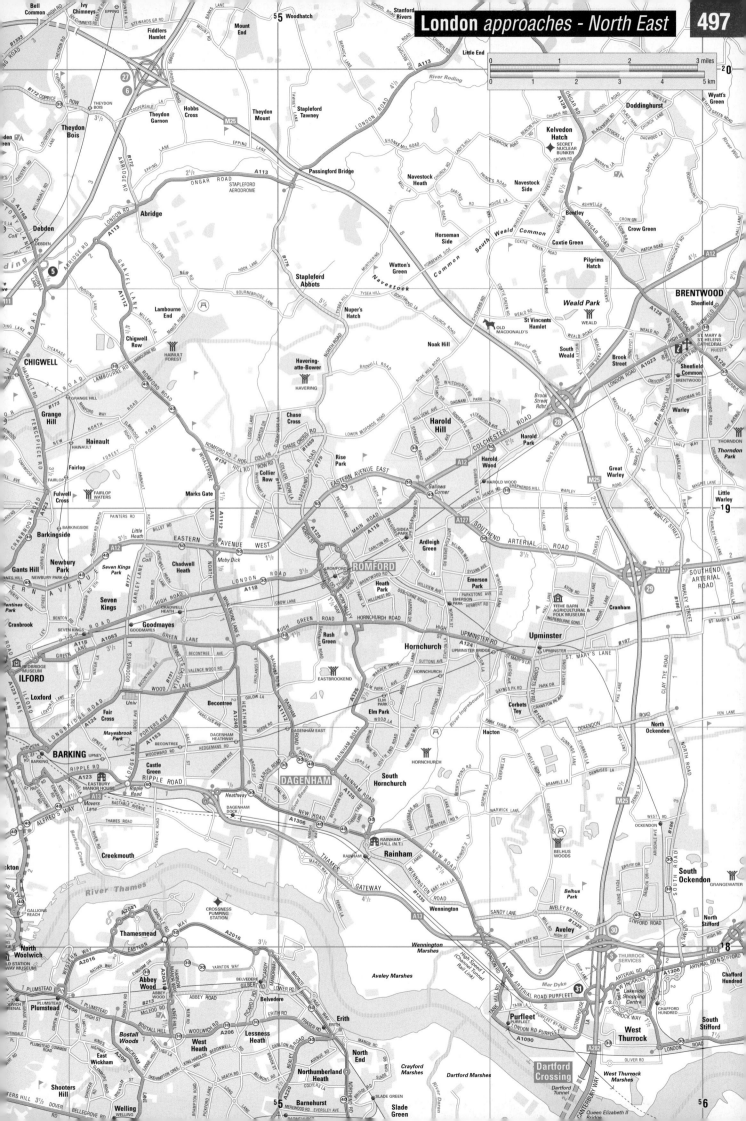

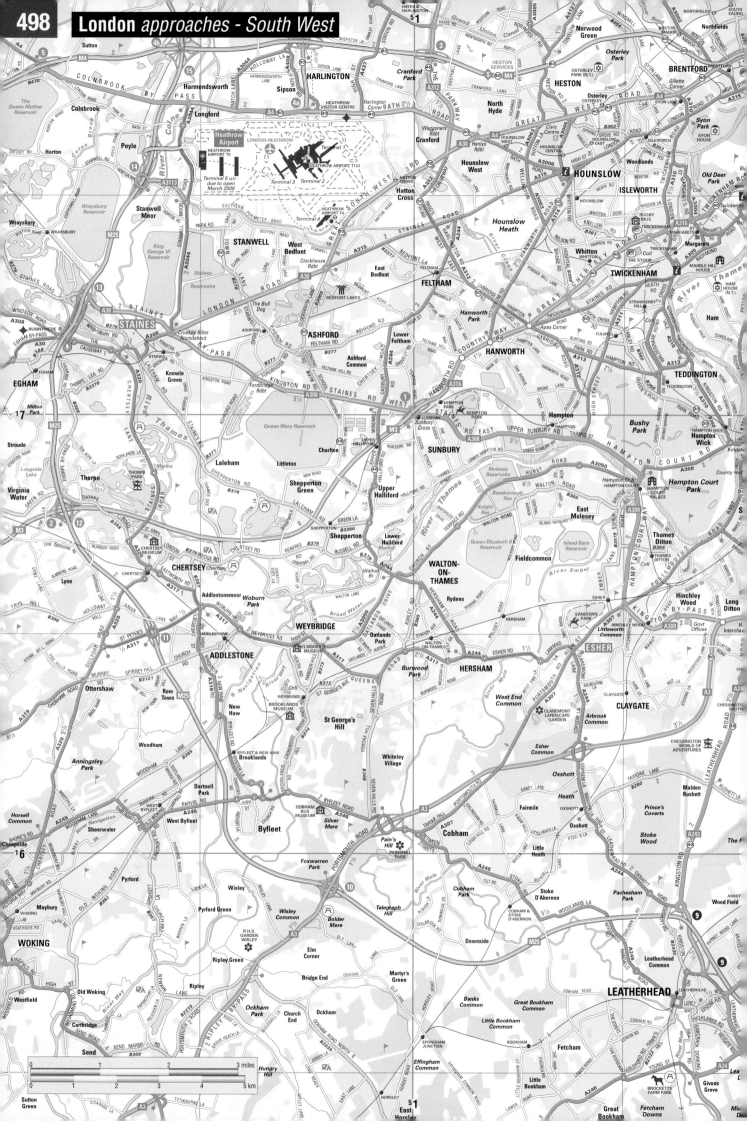

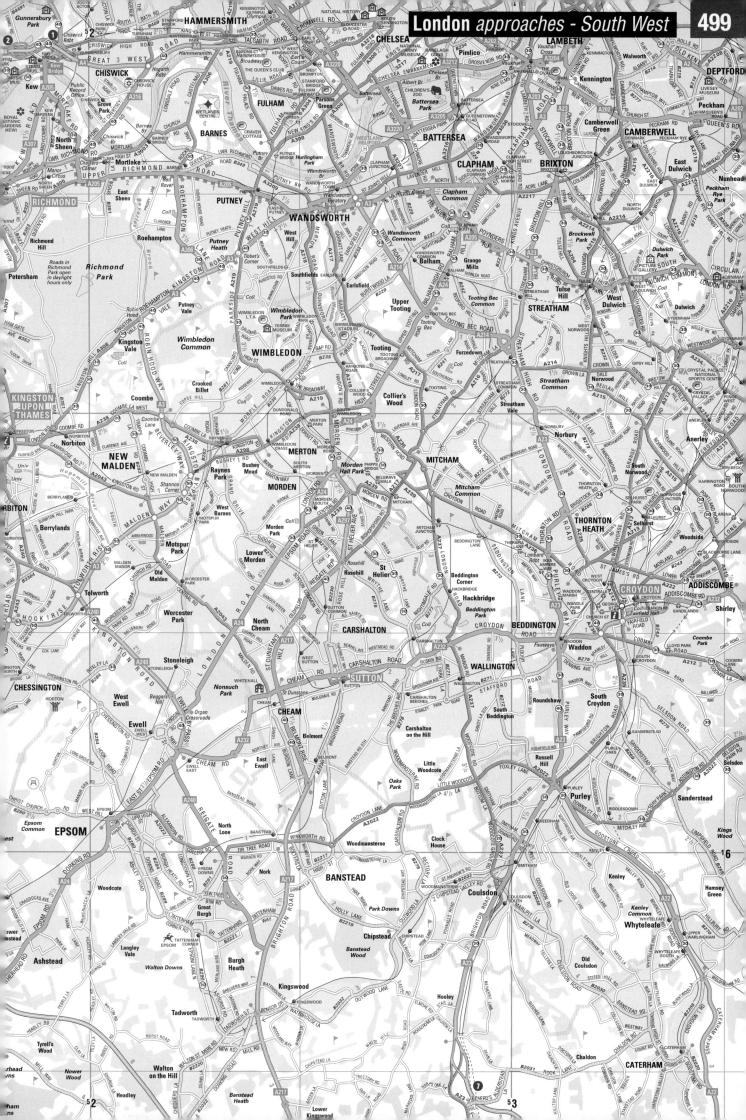

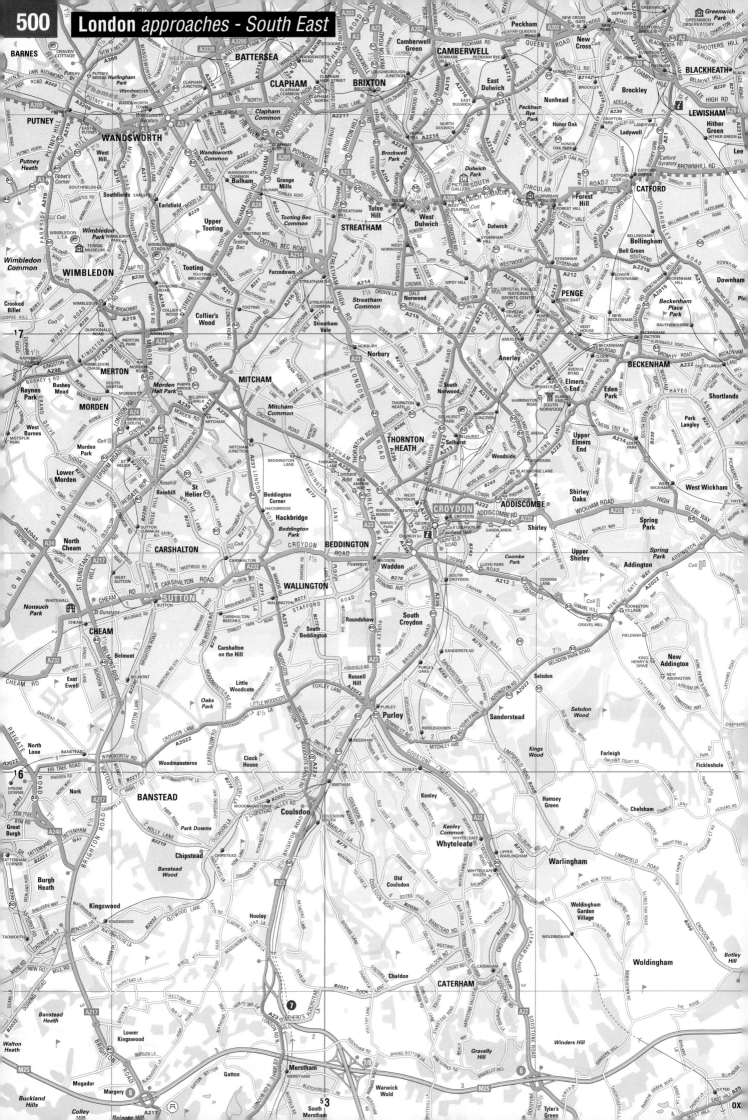

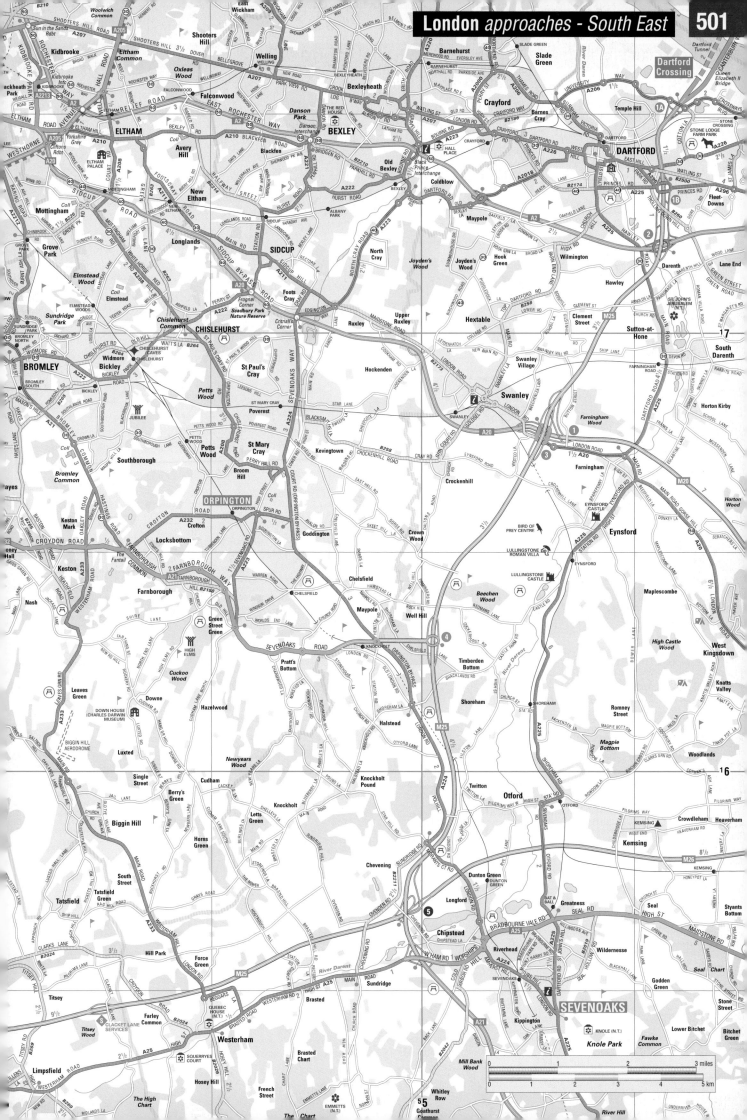

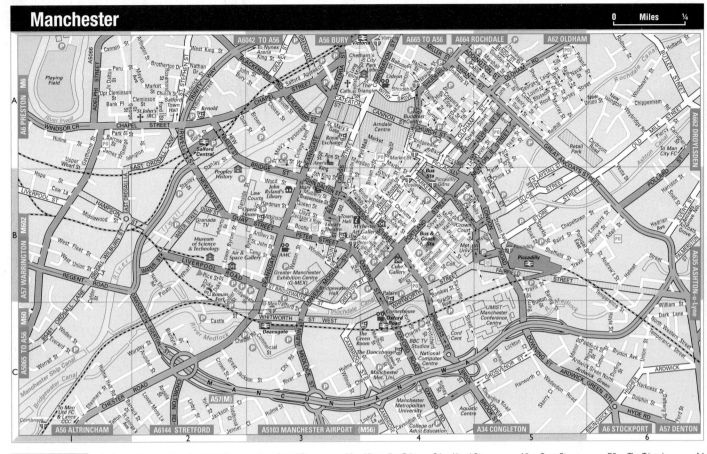

## Manchester

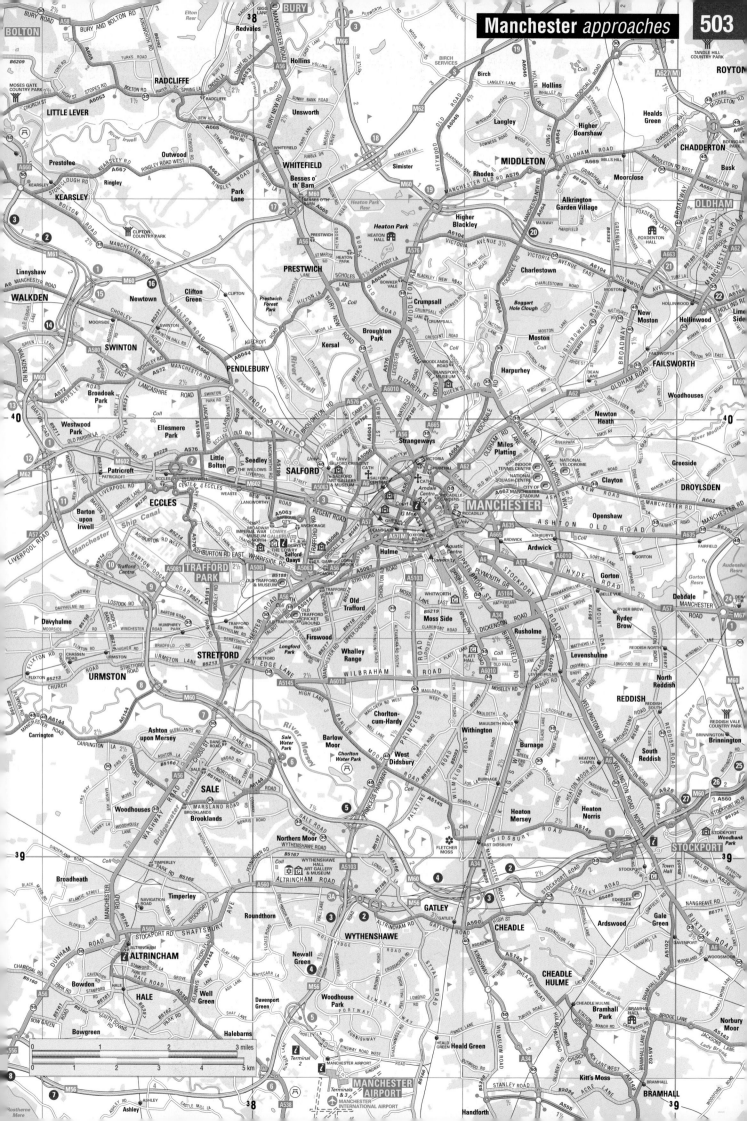

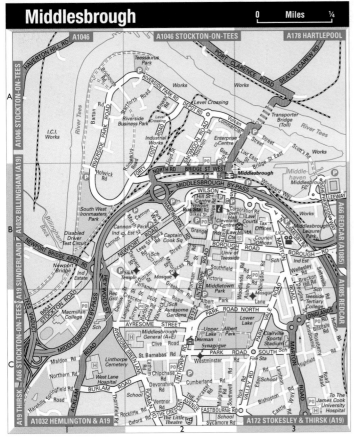

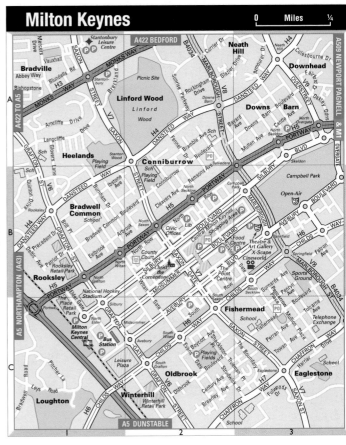

## Middlesbrough

Abingdon Rd . . . . . C3
Acklam Rd . . . . . . C1
Albert Park . . . . . . C2
Albert Rd . . . . . . . B2
Albert Terr. . . . . . . C3
Aubrey St . . . . . . . C3
Ayresome
  Gardens . . . . . . C2
Ayresome
  Green La. . . . . . C1
Ayresome St . . . . . C2
Barton Rd . . . . . . . A1
Bilsdale Rd . . . . . . C3
Bishopton Rd . . . . B2
Borough Rd . . . B2/B3
Bowes Rd . . . . . . . A2
Breckon Hill Rd . . . B3
Bridge St East . . . . B3
Bridge St West . . . B2
Brighouse Rd . . . . A1
Burlam Rd . . . . . . C1
Bus Station . . . . . . B2
Cannon Park . . . . . B2
Cannon Park Way . B2
Cannon St . . . . . . B1
Captain Cook Sq . . B2
Carlow St . . . . . . . B1
Castle Way . . . . . . C3
Chipchase Rd. . . . . C2
Clairville Sports
  Stadium . . . . . . C3
Cleveland Centre . . B2
Clive Rd . . . . . . . . C2
Commercial St . . . . A2
Corporation Rd. . . . B2
Costa St . . . . . . . . C2
Council Offices. . . . B3
Crescent Rd . . . . . C2
Cumberland Rd . . . C2
Depot St . . . . . . . . A2
Derwent St . . . . . . B1
Devonshire Rd . . . . C2
Diamond Rd . . . . . B2

Disabled Driver
  Test Circuit . . . . . B1
Dorman
  Museum 🏛 . . . . C2
Douglas St . . . . . . B3
Eastbourne Rd . . . . C2
Eden Rd . . . . . . . . C3
Enterprise Centre . . A2
Forty Foot Rd . . . . A2
Gilkes St . . . . . . . B2
Gosford St . . . . . . A2
Grange Rd . . . . . . B2
Gresham Rd . . . . . B2
Harehills Rd . . . . . C1
Harford St . . . . . . C2
Hartington Rd . . . . B2
Haverton Hill Rd . . A1
Hey Wood St . . . . B1
Highfield Rd . . . . . C3
Hill St Centre . . . . B2
Holwick Rd . . . . . . B1
Hutton Rd . . . . . . C3
I.C.I. Works . . . . . . A1
Information Ctr 🅉 . B2
Lambton Rd . . . . . C3
Lancaster Rd . . . . . C2
Lansdowne Rd . . . . C3
Latham Rd . . . . . . C2
Law Courts . . . B2/B3
Lees Rd . . . . . . . . B2
Leeway . . . . . . . . B3
Linthorpe
  Cemetery . . . . . C1
Linthorpe Rd. . . . . B2
Little Theatre,
  The . . . . . . . . . C2
Longford St . . . . . C2
Longlands Rd . . . . C3
Lower East St. . . . . A3
Lower Lake. . . . . . C3
Macmillan College . C1
Maldon Rd . . . . . . C1
Manor St. . . . . . . . B2
Marsh St. . . . . . . . B1
Marton Rd . . . . . . B3

Middlehaven . . . . . B3
Middlesbrough
  By-Pass . . . . . B2/C1
Middlesbrough F.C. B3
Middlesbrough
  General (A+E) 🏥 . C2
Middlesbrough
  Leisure Park . . . . B3
Middlesbrough ⇌ . B2
Middletown Park . . C2
MIMA 🏛 . . . . . . . B3
Mosque ✦ . . . . . . B2
Mosque ✦ . . . . . . C3
Mulgrave Rd . . . . . C2
North
  Ormesby Rd . . . . B3
Newport Bridge . . . B1
Newport Bridge
  Approach Rd . . . . B1
Newport Rd . . . . . B2
North Rd . . . . . . . B2
Northern Rd . . . . . C1
Outram St . . . . . . B2
Oxford Rd . . . . . . C2
Park La . . . . . . . . C2
Park Rd North . . . . C2
Park Rd South . . . . C2
Park Vale Rd . . . . . C3
Parliament Rd . . . . B1
Police Station 🏤 . . B2
Port Clarence Rd . . A3
Portman St . . . . . . B2
Post Office 🏤 . . . .
  . . . B2/B3/C1/C2/C3
Princes Rd . . . . . . B2
Riverside Business
  Park . . . . . . . . . A2
Riverside Park Rd. . A1
Rockliffe Rd . . . . . B2
Romaldkirk Rd . . . . B1
Roman Rd . . . . . . C2
Roseberry Rd . . . . B3
St Barnabas' Rd. . . C2
St Paul's Rd . . . . . B2
Saltwells Rd . . . . . B3

Scott's Rd . . . . . . A3
Seaton Carew Rd. . A3
Shepherdson Way . B3
Sikh Temple ✦ . . . B2
Snowdon Rd . . . . . A2
South West
  Ironmasters Park . B1
Southfield Rd . . . . B3
Southwell Rd . . . . C2
Springfield Rd. . . . C1
Startforth Rd. . . . . A2
Stockton Rd . . . . . C1
Stockton St . . . . . C1
Surrey St. . . . . . . C2
Sycamore Rd . . . . C2
Synagogue ✦. . . . B2
Tax Offices . . . . . . B3
Tees Viaduct . . . . . C1
Teessaurus Park. . . A2
Teesside Tertiary
  College . . . . . . . C3
The Avenue . . . . . C2
The Crescent . . . . C2
Thornfield Rd . . . . C1
Town Hall . . . . . . B2
Transporter Bridge
  (Toll) . . . . . . . . A3
UGC 🎦. . . . . . . . B3
Union St . . . . . . . B2
University of
  Teesside . . . . . . B2
Upper Lake. . . . . . C2
Valley Rd . . . . . . . C3
Ventnor Rd . . . . . . C2
Victoria Rd . . . . . . B2
Vulcan St . . . . . . . A2
Warwick St . . . . . . C2
Wellesley Rd. . . . . B3
West Lane
  Hospital 🏥 . . . . C1
Westminster Rd . . . C2
Wilson St . . . . . . . B2
Windward Way . . . B3
Woodlands Rd . . . . B2
York Rd. . . . . . . . C3

## Milton Keynes

Abbey Way . . . . . . A1
Arbrook Ave . . . . . B1
Armourer Dr . . . . . A3
Arncliffe Dr . . . . . . A1
Avebury (r'about) . . C2
Avebury Blvd . . . . . C2
Bankfield (r'about) . B3
Bayard Ave . . . . . . C2
Belvedere
  (r'about) . . . . . . A2
Bishopstone . . . . . A1
Blundells Rd . . . . . A1
Boycott Ave . . . . . C2
Bradwell Common
  Blvd . . . . . . . . . B1
Bradwell Rd . . . . . C1
Bramble Ave . . . . . A2
Brearley Ave . . . . . C2
Breckland . . . . . . . A1
Brill Place . . . . . . . B1
Burnham Dr . . . . . B1
Bus Station . . . . . . C1
Campbell Park
  (r'about) . . . . . . B3
Cantle Ave . . . . . . A3
Central Milton Keynes
  Shopping Area . . B2
Century Ave . . . . . C2
Chaffron Way . . . . C3
Childs Way . . . . . . C1
Christ the
  Cornerstone ⛪ . . B2
Cineworld 🎦. . . . . B2
Civic Offices . . . . . B2
Cleavers Ave . . . . . B2
Colesbourne Dr . . . A3
Conniburrow Blvd . B2
County Court . . . . . B2
Currier Dr . . . . . . . A2

Dansteed
  Way. . . . A2/A3/B1
Deltic Ave . . . . . . B1
Downs Barn
  (r'about) . . . . . . A2
Downs Barn Blvd . . A3
Eaglestone
  (r'about) . . . . . . C3
Eelbrook Ave . . . . . B1
Elder Gate . . . . . . B1
Evans Gate . . . . . . C2
Fairford Cr . . . . . . A3
Falcon Ave . . . . . . B3
Fennel Dr . . . . . . . A2
Fishermead Blvd . . C3
Food Centre . . . . . B3
Fulwoods Dr. . . . . C3
Glazier Dr . . . . . . A2
Glovers La . . . . . . A1
Grafton Gate. . . . . C1
Grafton St. . . . A1/C2
Gurnards Ave . . . . B3
Harrier Dr . . . . . . C3
Ibstone Ave . . . . . B1
Langcliffe Dr . . . . . A1
Leisure Plaza . . . . C1
Leys Rd . . . . . . . . C2
Library . . . . . . . . B2
Linford Wood . . . . A2
Marlborough Gate . B3
Marlborough
  St . . . . . . . . A2/B3
Mercers Dr . . . . . . A1
Midsummer
  (r'about) . . . . . . C2
Midsummer Blvd . . B2
Milton Keynes
  Central ⇌ . . . . . C1
Monks Way. . . . . . A1
Mullen Ave . . . . . . A3
Mullion Pl . . . . . . C3

National Hockey
  Stadium . . . . . . B1
Neath Hill (r'about) . A3
North Elder
  (r'about) . . . . . . C1
North Grafton
  (r'about) . . . . . . B1
North Overgate
  (r'about) . . . . . . A3
North Row . . . . . . B2
North Saxon
  (r'about) . . . . . . B2
North Secklow
  (r'about) . . . . . . B2
North Skeldon
  (r'about) . . . . . . A3
North Witan
  (r'about) . . . . . . B1
Oakley Gdns . . . . . A3
Oldbrook Blvd . . . . C2
Open-Air
  Theatre 🎭 . . . . . B3
Overgate. . . . . . . A3
Overstreet . . . . . . A3
Patriot Dr . . . . . . B1
Pencarrow Pl . . . . . B3
Penryn Ave . . . . . . B3
Perran Ave . . . . . . C3
Pitcher La . . . . . . C1
Place Retail
  Park, The . . . . . . C1
Point Centre, The . . B2
Police Station 🏤 . . B2
Portway (r'about) . . B2
Post Office 🏤 . . . .
  . . . . . . A2/B2/B2
Precedent Dr . . . . . B1
Quinton Dr . . . . . . B1
Ramsons Ave . . . . B2
Rockingham Dr . . . A2
Rooksley (r'about) . B1

Rooksley Retail
  Park . . . . . . . . . C1
Saxon Gate . . . . . B2
Saxon St. . . . . A1/C3
Secklow Gate . . . . B2
Shackleton Pl . . . . C1
Silbury (r'about) . . C1
Silbury Blvd . . . . . B2
Skeldon (r'about) . . A3
South Grafton
  (r'about) . . . . . . C2
South Row . . . . . . C2
South Saxon
  (r'about) . . . . . . C2
South Secklow
  (r'about) . . . . . . B3
South Witan
  (r'about) . . . . . . C2
Springfield
  (r'about) . . . . . . B3
Stanton Wood
  (r'about) . . . . . . A1
Stantonbury
  (r'about) . . . . . . A1
Stantonbury Leisure
  Centre ✦ . . . . . . A1
Strudwick Dr. . . . . C1
Sunrise Parkway. . . A2
Telephone
  Exchange . . . . . . C3
The Boundary. . . . C3
Theatre & Art
  Gallery 🎭 . . . . . B3
Tolcarne Ave . . . . . C3
Towan Ave . . . . . . C3
Trueman Pl . . . . . . C2
Vauxhall . . . . . . . A1
Winterhill Retail
  Park . . . . . . . . . C2
Witan Gate . . . . . . B2
X-Scape . . . . . . . B3

## Newport / Casnewydd
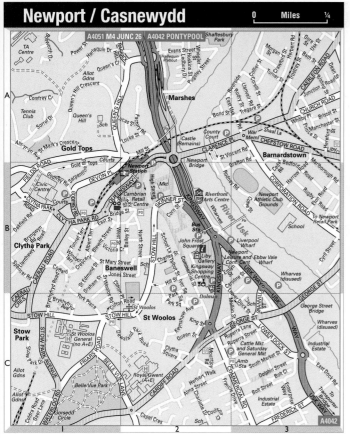

## Northampton
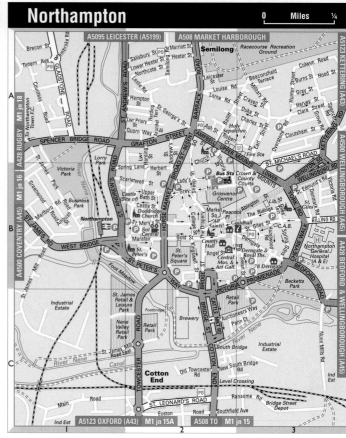

### Newport / Casnewydd

| | | | |
|---|---|---|---|
| Albert Terr. . . . . . . . B1 | Clytha Sq . . . . . . . . C2 | Hill St . . . . . . . . . . B2 | Railway St . . . . . . . B2 |
| Allt-yr-Yn Ave . . . . A1 | Coldra Rd . . . . . . . C1 | Hoskins St . . . . . . . A2 | Riverfront Arts |
| Alma St. . . . . . . . . C2 | Collier St. . . . . . . . A3 | Information Ctr ⓘ . . B2 | Centre ▤ ⓘ . . . . B2 |
| Ambulance | Colne St . . . . . . . . B3 | Ivor Sq . . . . . . . . . B2 | Riverside. . . . . . . . A3 |
| Station . . . . . . . C3 | Comfrey Cl . . . . . . A1 | John Frost Sq. . . . . B2 | Rodney Rd . . . . . . B2 |
| Allt-yr-Yn Ave . . . . A1 | Commercial Rd . . . C3 | Jones St . . . . . . . . B1 | Royal Gwent |
| Alma St. . . . . . . . . C2 | Commercial St . . . . B2 | Junction Rd . . . . . . A3 | (A+E) Ⓗ . . . . . . . C2 |
| Bailey St . . . . . . . . B2 | Corelli St. . . . . . . . A3 | Keynshaw Ave . . . . C2 | Rudry St . . . . . . . . A2 |
| Barrack Hill . . . . . . A2 | Corn St. . . . . . . . . B2 | King St . . . . . . . . . C2 | Rugby Rd . . . . . . . B3 |
| Bath St . . . . . . . . . C2 | Corporation Rd. . . . B3 | Kingsway . . . . . . . B2 | Ruperra La . . . . . . C3 |
| Bedford Rd . . . . . . B3 | Coulson Cl . . . . . . C2 | Kingsway Shopping | Ruperra St . . . . . . C3 |
| Belle Vue La . . . . . C1 | County Court . . . . . A2 | Centre. . . . . . . . B2 | St. Edmund St . . . . B1 |
| Belle Vue Park . . . . C1 | Courts. . . . . . . . . . A1 | Ledbury Dr . . . . . . A2 | St. Mark's Cres. . . . A1 |
| Bishop St . . . . . . . A3 | Courts. . . . . . . . . . B1 | Library . . . . . . . . . A3 | St. Mary St . . . . . . B1 |
| Blewitt St . . . . . . . B1 | Crawford St . . . . . . A3 | Library, Museum & | St. Vincent Rd . . . . B1 |
| Bolt Cl. . . . . . . . . . C3 | Cyril St . . . . . . . . . B3 | Art Gallery ▥ . . . B2 | St. Woolos ✝ . . . . . C2 |
| Bolt St . . . . . . . . . C3 | Dean St. . . . . . . . . A3 | Liverpool Wharf . . . B3 | St. Woolos General |
| Bond St . . . . . . . . A2 | Devon Pl. . . . . . . . B1 | Llanthewy Rd . . . . . B1 | (no A+E) Ⓗ . . . . C1 |
| Bosworth Dr . . . . . A1 | Dewsland Park Rd . . C2 | Llanvair Rd . . . . . . A3 | St. Woolos Rd . . . . B1 |
| Bridge St . . . . . . . B1 | Dolman ▤ . . . . . . . B2 | Locke St . . . . . . . . A2 | School La. . . . . . . . B3 |
| Bristol St . . . . . . . A3 | Dolphin St. . . . . . . C3 | Lower Dock St . . . . C3 | Serpentine Rd . . . . B1 |
| Bryngwyn Rd . . . . . B1 | East Dock Rd . . . . . C3 | Lucas St . . . . . . . . A2 | Shaftesbury Park . . A2 |
| Brynhyfryd Ave . . . . C1 | East St . . . . . . . . . B1 | Manchester St . . . . A3 | Sheaf La . . . . . . . . A3 |
| Brynhyfryd Rd . . . . C1 | East Usk Rd . . . . . . A3 | Market . . . . . . . . . B2 | Skinner St . . . . . . . B2 |
| Bus Station . . . . . . C3 | Ebbw Vale Wharf . . B3 | Marlborough Rd . . . B3 | Sorrel Dr . . . . . . . . A1 |
| Caerau Cres . . . . . C1 | Emlyn St . . . . . . . . B2 | Mellon St . . . . . . . C3 | South Market St . . . C3 |
| Caerau Rd . . . . . . . B1 | Enterprise Way . . . . C3 | Mill St . . . . . . . . . A2 | Spencer Rd . . . . . . B1 |
| Caerleon Rd . . . . . A2 | Eton Rd . . . . . . . . B3 | Morgan St. . . . . . . A3 | Stow Hill . . . B2/C1/C2 |
| Cambrian Retail | Evans St . . . . . . . . A2 | Mountjoy Rd. . . . . . C2 | Stow Park Ave . . . . C1 |
| Centre. . . . . . . . B2 | Factory Rd . . . . . . A2 | Newport Athletic | Stow Park Dr . . . . . C1 |
| Capel Cres . . . . . . C3 | Fields Rd . . . . . . . B1 | Club Grounds . . . . B3 | TA Centre . . . . . . . A1 |
| Cardiff Rd . . . . . . . C2 | Francis Dr . . . . . . . C2 | Newport Bridge . . . B2 | Talbot St . . . . . . . . A2 |
| Caroline St . . . . . . B3 | Frederick St . . . . . . C3 | Newport Leisure and | Tennis Club. . . . . . . A1 |
| Castle (Remains) . . A2 | Friars Rd . . . . . . . . C1 | Conference Ctr. . . B2 | Tregare St . . . . . . . A3 |
| Cattle Market and | Gaer La. . . . . . . . . C1 | Newport | Trostrey St . . . . . . A3 |
| Saturday General | George St. . . . . . . C3 | Station ≷ . . . . . . . B2 | Tunnel Terr . . . . . . B1 |
| Market . . . . . . . C3 | George Street | North St . . . . . . . . B2 | Turner St. . . . . . . . A3 |
| Cedar Rd . . . . . . . B3 | Bridge. . . . . . . . C3 | Oakfield Rd. . . . . . . B1 | Usk St . . . . . . . . . A3 |
| Charles St. . . . . . . B2 | Godfrey Rd. . . . . . . B1 | Park Sq. . . . . . . . . C2 | Usk Way . . . . . . B3/C3 |
| Charlotte Dr . . . . . C2 | Gold Tops. . . . . . . . B1 | Police | Victoria Cr. . . . . . . . B1 |
| Chepstow Rd . . . . . A3 | Gore St. . . . . . . . . A3 | Station ▣ . . . A3/C2 | War Memorial . . . . . A3 |
| Church Rd . . . . . . . A3 | Gorsedd Circle . . . . C1 | Post Office Ⓟ | Waterloo Rd . . . . . . C1 |
| City Cinema ▦ . . . . B1 | Grafton Rd . . . . . . A3 | . . . . . B1/B2/C1/C3 | West St. . . . . . . . . B1 |
| Civic Centre . . . . . B1 | Graham St . . . . . . . B1 | Power St. . . . . . . . A1 | Wharves . . . . . . . . B2 |
| Clarence Pl. . . . . . . A2 | Granville St . . . . . . C3 | Prince St. . . . . . . . A3 | Wheeler St . . . . . . A2 |
| Clifton Pl. . . . . . . . B1 | Harlequin Dr . . . . . A1 | Pugsley St . . . . . . A2 | Whitby Pl . . . . . . . A3 |
| Clifton Rd . . . . . . . C1 | Harrow Rd . . . . . . . B3 | Queen St . . . . . . . C2 | Windsor Terr. . . . . . B1 |
| Clyffard Cres . . . . . B1 | Herbert Rd . . . . . . A3 | Queen's Cl . . . . . . A1 | York Pl . . . . . . . . . C1 |
| Clytha Park Rd. . . . . B1 | Herbert Walk . . . . . C2 | Queen's Hill . . . . . . A1 | |
| | Hereford St. . . . . . . A3 | Queen's Hill Cres . . A1 | |
| | High St . . . . . . . . . B2 | Queensway. . . . . . . B2 | |

### Northampton

| | | | |
|---|---|---|---|
| 78 Derngate ▣ . . . B3 | Crown & County | Lower Harding St . . A2 | St James' Mill |
| Abington Sq . . . . . B3 | Courts. . . . . . . . . B3 | Lower Hester St . . . A2 | Rd East. . . . . . . . C1 |
| Abington St . . . . . . B3 | Denmark Rd . . . . . . B3 | Lower Mounts . . . . B3 | St James Park Rd . B1 |
| All Saints' ▟ . . . . . B2 | Derngate. . . . . . . . B3 | Lower Priory St. . . . A2 | St James Retail |
| Ambush St . . . . . . B1 | Derngate & Royal | Main Rd . . . . . . . . C1 | & Leisure Park . . C1 |
| Angel St . . . . . . . . B2 | Theatres ▣ . . . . B3 | Marefair . . . . . . . . B2 | St James Rd. . . . . B1 |
| Arundel St. . . . . . . A2 | Doddridge | Market Sq. . . . . . . B2 | St Leonard's Rd . . C2 |
| Ash St. . . . . . . . . . A2 | Church ▟ . . . . . . B2 | Marlboro Rd. . . . . . B1 | St Mary's St . . . . . B2 |
| Auctioneers Way . . C2 | Duke St. . . . . . . . . A3 | Marriott St . . . . . . A2 | St Michael's Rd . . A3 |
| Bailiff St . . . . . . . . A2 | Earl St. . . . . . . . . . A3 | Military Rd . . . . . . A3 | St Peter's ▟ . . . . . B2 |
| Barrack Rd . . . . . . A2 | Euston Rd. . . . . . . C2 | Nene Valley | St Peter's Square |
| Beaconsfield Terr . . A3 | Fire Station . . . . . . A3 | Retail Park . . . . . C1 | Shopping |
| Becketts Park. . . . . C3 | Foot Meadow . . . . . B2 | New South | Precinct . . . . . . . B2 |
| Bedford Rd . . . . . . B3 | Gladstone Rd . . . . . A1 | Bridge Rd . . . . . C2 | St Peter's Way . . . B2 |
| Billing Rd . . . . . . . B3 | Gold St. . . . . . . . . B2 | Northampton | Salisbury St . . . . . A2 |
| Brecon St . . . . . . . A1 | Grafton St. . . . . . . A2 | General Hospital | Scarletwell St . . . . B2 |
| Brewery . . . . . . . . C2 | Gray St. . . . . . . . . A3 | (A & E) Ⓗ . . . . B3 | Semilong Rd. . . . . A2 |
| Bridge St . . . . . . . C2 | Greenwood Rd. . . . B1 | Northampton | Sheep St. . . . . . . . B2 |
| Bridge St Depot . . B3 | Greyfriars . . . . . . . B2 | Station ≷ . . . . . . B1 | Sol Central |
| Broad St. . . . . . . . B2 | Grosvenor Centre. . B2 | Northcote St. . . . . . A2 | (Leisure Centre) . . B2 |
| Burns St . . . . . . . . A3 | Grove Rd . . . . . . . A3 | Nunn Mills Rd. . . . . C3 | South Bridge . . . . C2 |
| Bus Station . . . . . . A2 | Guildhall ▣ . . . . . B2 | Old Towcester Rd. . C2 | Southfield Ave . . . . C2 |
| Campbell St . . . . . A2 | Hampton St . . . . . . A3 | Overstone Rd. . . . . A3 | Spencer Bridge Rd. A1 |
| Castle (Site of) . . . B2 | Harding Terr . . . . . A2 | Peacock Pl . . . . . . B2 | Spencer Rd . . . . . A3 |
| Castle St. . . . . . . . B2 | Hazelwood Rd . . . . B3 | Pembroke Rd . . . . . A1 | Spring Gdns . . . . . B3 |
| Cattle Market Rd . . C2 | Herbert St . . . . . . . B2 | Penn Court . . . . . . C2 | Spring La . . . . . . . B2 |
| Central Museum & | Hervey St. . . . . . . . A3 | Police Station ▣ . . B3 | Swan St . . . . . . . . B3 |
| Art Gallery ▥ . . . B2 | Hester St . . . . . . . A2 | Post Office Ⓟ . . . | The Drapery . . . . . B2 |
| Charles St. . . . . . . A3 | Holy Sepulchre ▟ . . A2 | . . . . A1/A2/B3/C2 | The Ridings . . . . . B3 |
| Cheyne Walk . . . . . B3 | Hood St . . . . . . . . A3 | Quorn Way . . . . . . A2 | Tintern Ave . . . . . . A1 |
| Church La. . . . . . . . A2 | Horse Market . . . . . B2 | Ransome Rd. . . . . . C3 | Towcester Rd . . . . C2 |
| Clare St. . . . . . . . . A3 | Hunter St . . . . . . . A2 | Regent Sq . . . . . . A2 | Upper Bath St . . . . B2 |
| Cloutsham St . . . . . A3 | Information Ctr ⓘ . . B1 | Retail Park . . . . . . C2 | Upper Mounts . . . . B2 |
| College St. . . . . . . B2 | Kettering Rd . . . . . A3 | Robert St . . . . . . . A2 | Victoria Park . . . . . A1 |
| Colwyn Rd . . . . . . . A3 | Kingswell St . . . . . B2 | St Andrew's Rd . . . B1 | Victoria |
| Countess Rd . . . . . A1 | Lady's La . . . . . . . B2 | St Andrew's St . . . . A2 | Promenade . . . . B2 |
| County Hall ▣ . . . . B2 | Leicester St . . . . . A2 | St Edmund's Rd . . . B3 | Victoria Rd . . . . . . B3 |
| Court. . . . . . . . . . . A2 | Leslie Rd . . . . . . . A2 | St George's St . . . . A2 | Victoria St . . . . . . A2 |
| Craven St . . . . . . . A3 | Library . . . . . . . . . B3 | St Giles . . . . . . . . B3 | Wellingborough |
| | Lorne Rd. . . . . . . . A2 | St Giles St . . . . . . B3 | Rd. . . . . . . . . . . B3 |
| | Lorry Park . . . . . . . A1 | St Giles' Terr. . . . . B3 | West Bridge . . . . . B1 |
| | Louise Rd . . . . . . . A2 | St James' Mill Rd. . . B1 | York Rd. . . . . . . . . B3 |

# Newcastle upon Tyne

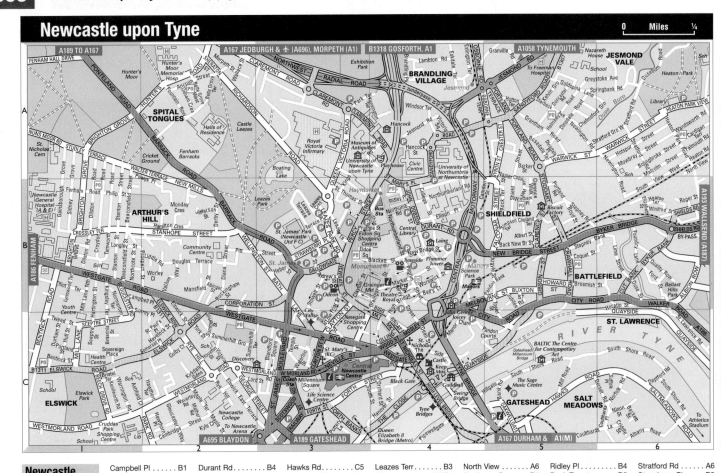

## Newcastle upon Tyne

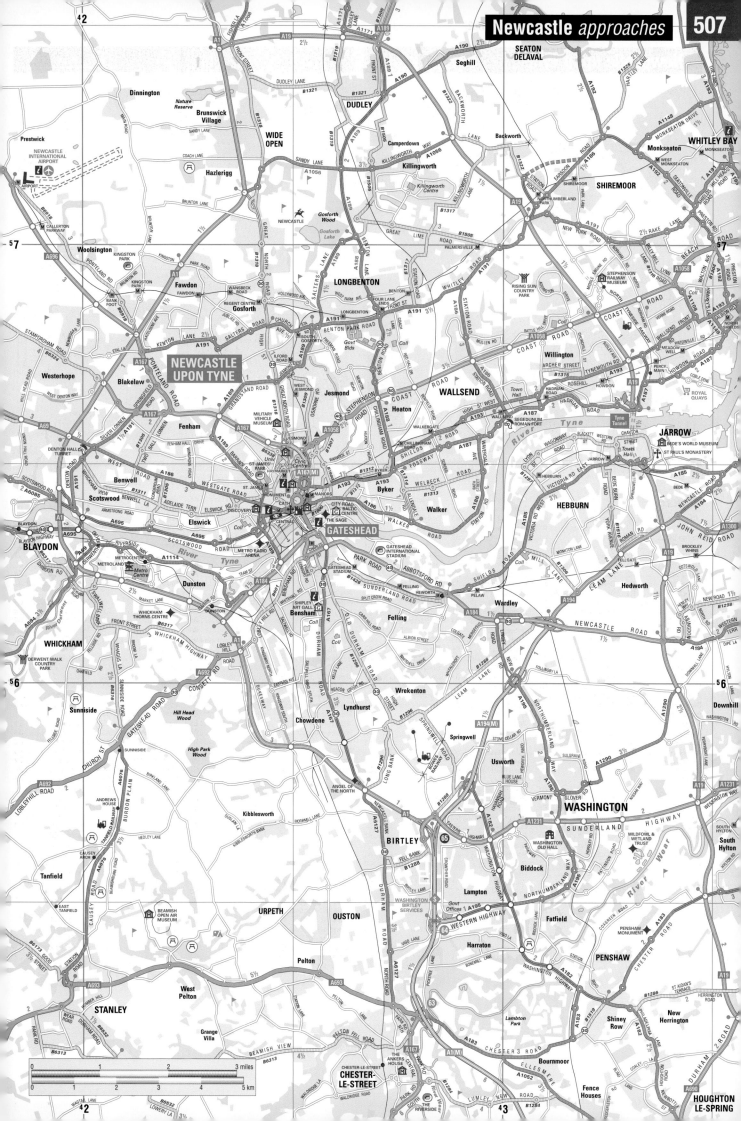

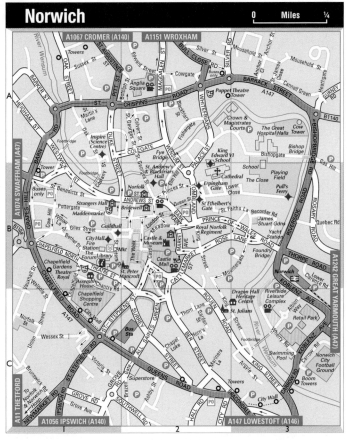

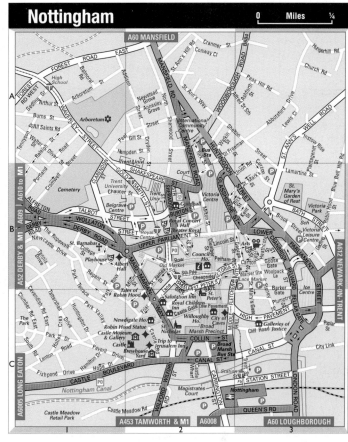

## Norwich

| | | | |
|---|---|---|---|
| Albion Way . . . . . . . C3 | City Rd . . . . . . . . . C2 | Lower | St Augustines St . . . A1 |
| All Saints Green . . . C2 | City Wall . . . . . . C1/C3 | Clarence Rd . . . . . B3 | St Benedicts St . . . . B1 |
| Anchor Cl . . . . . . . A3 | Colegate . . . . . . . . A2 | Lower Cl . . . . . . . . B3 | St Crispins Rd . . . . A1 |
| Anchor . . . . . . . . . A3 | Coslany St . . . . . . B1 | Maddermarket ☷ . . B1 | St Ethelbert's |
| Anglia Sq . . . . . . . B2 | Cow Hill . . . . . . . . B1 | Magdalen St . . . . . A2 | Gate ✦ . . . . . . . B2 |
| Argyle St. . . . . . . . C3 | Cow Tower . . . . . . A3 | Mariners La . . . . . . C2 | St Faiths La . . . . . . B3 |
| Ashby St. . . . . . . . C2 | Cowgate . . . . . . . . A2 | Market . . . . . . . . . B2 | St Georges St. . . . . A2 |
| Assembly | Crown & Magistrats | Market Ave . . . . . . B2 | St Giles St . . . . . . . B1 |
| House ☷ . . . . . . B1 | Courts. . . . . . . . B2 | Mountergate . . . . . B3 | St James Cl . . . . . . A3 |
| Bank Plain . . . . . . B2 | Dragon Hall Heritage | Mousehold St . . . . . A3 | St Julians ⚓ . . . . . C2 |
| Barker St . . . . . . . A1 | Centre ☷ . . . . . . C3 | Newmarket Rd . . . . C1 | St Martin's La . . . . . A1 |
| Barn Rd . . . . . . . . A1 | Duke St. . . . . . . . . A1 | Norfolk Gallery ☷ . . A1 | St Peter |
| Barrack St . . . . . . . A2 | Edward St. . . . . . . A2 | Norfolk St. . . . . . . C1 | Mancroft ⚓ . . . . . B2 |
| Ber St . . . . . . . . . C2 | Elm Hill . . . . . . . . B2 | Norwich City FC . . . C3 | St Peters St . . . . . . B1 |
| Bethel St . . . . . . . B1 | Erpingham | Norwich | St Stephens Rd . . . C1 |
| Bishop Bridge. . . . . A3 | Gate ✦ . . . . . . . B2 | Station ⚐ . . . . . B3 | St Stephens St . . . . C1 |
| Bishopbridge Rd . . A3 | Fire Station . . . . . . B1 | Oak St . . . . . . . . . A1 | Silver Rd. . . . . . . . A2 |
| Bishopgate . . . . . . A3 | Fishergate . . . . . . . A2 | Palace St . . . . . . . A2 | Silver St . . . . . . . . A2 |
| Blackfriars St . . . . . A2 | Foundry Bridge. . . . B3 | Pitt St . . . . . . . . . A1 | Southwell Rd . . . . . C2 |
| Botolph St . . . . . . . A2 | Fye Bridge . . . . . . A2 | Police Station ☷ . . . B1 | Strangers Hall ☷ . . . B1 |
| Bracondale . . . . . . C3 | Garden St . . . . . . . C2 | Post Office ☷ | Superstore . . . . . . C2 |
| Brazen Gate . . . . . C2 | Gas Hill . . . . . . . . B3 | . . . . . . A2/B1/B2/C2 | Surrey St. . . . . . . . C2 |
| Bridewell ☷ . . . . . B2 | Grapes Hill . . . . . . B1 | Pottergate. . . . . . . B1 | Sussex St . . . . . . . A1 |
| Brunswick Rd . . . . . C1 | Great Hospital | Prince of | Swimming Pool . . . B3 |
| Bull Close Rd . . . . . C1 | Halls, The . . . . . . A3 | Wales Rd . . . . . . B2 | The Close . . . . . . . B3 |
| Bus Station. . . . . . C2 | Grove Ave. . . . . . . C1 | Princes St . . . . . . . B2 | The Forum . . . . . . B1 |
| Calvert St . . . . . . . A2 | Grove Rd . . . . . . . C1 | Pull's Ferry ✦ . . . . . B3 | The Walk. . . . . . . . B2 |
| Cannell Green. . . . . A2 | Guildhall ✦ . . . . . . B1 | Puppet Theatre ☷ . . A2 | Theatre Royal ☷ . . . B1 |
| Carrow Rd . . . . . . . C3 | Gurney Rd . . . . . . A3 | Quebec Rd . . . . . . B3 | Theatre St . . . . . . . B1 |
| Castle Mall . . . . . . B2 | Hall Rd . . . . . . . . C2 | Queen St . . . . . . . B2 | Thorn La . . . . . . . . C2 |
| Castle Meadow . . . . B2 | Heathgate . . . . . . A3 | Queens Rd . . . . . . C2 | Thorpe Rd . . . . . . . B3 |
| Castle & | Heigham St. . . . . . A1 | Recorder Rd. . . . . . B3 | Tombland . . . . . . . B2 |
| Museum ☷ . . . . . B1 | Horn's La . . . . . . . C2 | Retail Park . . . . . . C3 | Union St . . . . . . . . C1 |
| Cathedral † . . . . . . B2 | Information Ctr ⓘ . . B1 | Riverside Leisure | Vauxhall St . . . . . . B1 |
| Cattlemarket St . . . B2 | Inspire (Science | Complex . . . . . . B3 | Victoria St. . . . . . . C1 |
| Chantry Rd . . . . . . B1 | Centre) . . . . . . . A1 | Riverside Rd. . . . . . B3 | Walpole St . . . . . . . B1 |
| Chapel Loke . . . . . B2 | Ipswich Rd . . . . . . C1 | Rosary Rd. . . . . . . B3 | Wensum St . . . . . . A2 |
| Chapelfield East . . . B1 | James Stewart | Rose La . . . . . . . . B2 | Wessex St . . . . . . . C1 |
| Chapelfield Gdns . . B1 | Gdns . . . . . . . . . B3 | Rouen Rd . . . . . . . C2 | Westwick St . . . . . . A1 |
| Chapelfield North . . B1 | King Edward VI | Royal Norfolk | Wherry Rd . . . . . . C3 |
| Chapelfield Rd . . . . B1 | School ✦ . . . . . . B2 | Regiment | Whitefriars . . . . . . A2 |
| Chapelfield Shopping | King Edward's . . . . B2 | Museum ☷ . . . . . B2 | Willow La . . . . . . . B1 |
| Centre. . . . . . . . C1 | King St . . . . . . . . C3 | St Andrew's | Yacht Station . . . . . B3 |
| City Hall ✦ . . . . . . B1 | Koblenz Ave . . . . . C3 | & Blackfriars | |
| | Library . . . . . . . . B1 | Hall ✦ . . . . . . . . B2 | |
| | London St. . . . . . . B2 | St Andrews St . . . . B2 | |

## Nottingham

| | | | |
|---|---|---|---|
| Abbotsford Dr. . . . . A3 | Clumber Rd East . . C1 | Long Row. . . . . . . B2 | St Mark's St . . . . . B3 |
| Addison St . . . . . . . A1 | Clumber St . . . . . . B2 | Low Pavement . . . . C2 | St Mary's Garden |
| Albert Hall ✦ . . . . . B1 | College St. . . . . . . B1 | Lower | of Rest . . . . . . . B3 |
| Alfred St South . . . . A1 | Collin St . . . . . . . . C2 | Parliament St . . . . B3 | St Mary's Gate . . . . B3 |
| Alfreton Rd . . . . . . B1 | Conway Cl . . . . . . C2 | Magistrates Court. . C2 | St Nicholas † . . . . . C2 |
| All Saints Rd. . . . . . A1 | Council House ☷ . . B2 | Maid Marian Way . . B2 | St Peter's ⚓ . . . . . B2 |
| Annesley Gr . . . . . . A1 | Court. . . . . . . . . . B2 | Mansfield Rd . . . A2/B2 | St Peter's Gate . . . . B2 |
| Arboretum ❀ . . . . . A1 | Cranbrook St . . . . . B3 | Middle Hill . . . . . . C2 | Salutation Inn ⚓ . . . C2 |
| Arboretum St . . . . . A1 | Cranmer St . . . . . . A2 | Milton St . . . . . . . B2 | Shakespeare St . . . . B2 |
| Arthur St . . . . . . . . A1 | Cromwell St . . . . . . B1 | Mount St. . . . . . . . B2 | Shelton St. . . . . . . A2 |
| Arts Theatre ☷ . . . B3 | Curzon St . . . . . . . B3 | Newcastle Dr . . . . . B1 | South Pde . . . . . . C2 |
| Ashforth St . . . . . . A3 | Derby Rd . . . . . . . B1 | Newdigate | South Rd . . . . . . . C1 |
| Balmoral Rd . . . . . . A1 | Dryden St . . . . . . . A2 | House ☷ . . . . . . C2 | South |
| Barker Gate . . . . . . B3 | Fishpond Dr . . . . . . C1 | Newstead Gr . . . . . A2 | Sherwood St. . . . . B2 |
| Bath St . . . . . . . . . B3 | Fletcher Gate . . . . . B3 | North | Station St . . . . . . . C3 |
| Belgrave Centre . . . B1 | Forest Rd East . . . . A1 | Sherwood St. . . . . A2 | Station Street |
| Bellar Gate . . . . . . B3 | Forest Rd West. . . . A1 | Nottingham | (tram stop) . . . . . C3 |
| Belward St . . . . . . . B3 | Friar La . . . . . . . . C2 | Station ⚐ . . . . . C3 | Stoney St . . . . . . . B3 |
| Blue Bell Hill Rd . . . B3 | Galleries of | Old Market Square | Talbot St . . . . . . . B1 |
| Brewhouse | Justice ☷ . . . . . . C3 | (tram stop) . . . . . B2 | Tales of |
| Yard ☷ . . . . . . . C2 | Gedling Gr . . . . . . A1 | Oliver St . . . . . . . . A1 | Robin Hood ✦ . . . C2 |
| Broad Marsh | Gedling St . . . . . . . B3 | Park Dr . . . . . . . . C1 | Tattershall Dr . . . . . C1 |
| Bus Station. . . . . C2 | George St . . . . . . . B3 | Park Row . . . . . . . C1 | Tennis Dr . . . . . . . C1 |
| Broad Marsh | Gill St . . . . . . . . . A2 | Park Terr. . . . . . . . B1 | Tennyson St . . . . . A1 |
| Precinct . . . . . . . C2 | Glasshouse St . . . . B2 | Park Valley . . . . . . C1 | The Park . . . . . . . C1 |
| Broad St . . . . . . . . B3 | Goldsmith St . . . . . B2 | Peas Hill Rd . . . . . A3 | The Ropewalk . . . . B1 |
| Brook St . . . . . . . . B3 | Goose Gate . . . . . . B3 | Peel St . . . . . . . . . A1 | Theatre Royal ☷ . . . B2 |
| Burns St . . . . . . . . A1 | Great Freeman St . . A2 | Pelham St . . . . . . . B2 | Trent St . . . . . . . . C3 |
| Burton St . . . . . . . B2 | Guildhall ☷ . . . . . B2 | Peveril Dr . . . . . . . C2 | Trent University. . A2/B2 |
| Bus Station . . . . . . A2 | Hamilton Dr . . . . . . C1 | Plantagenet St . . . . A3 | Trent University |
| Canal St . . . . . . . . C2 | Hampden St . . . . . A1 | Playhouse | (tram stop) . . . . . B2 |
| Carlton St . . . . . . . B3 | Heathcote St . . . . . B3 | Theatre ☷ . . . . . B1 | Trip to Jerusalem |
| Carrington St . . . . . C2 | High Pavement . . . C3 | Plumptre St . . . . . . C3 | Inn ✦ . . . . . . . . C2 |
| Castle Blvd . . . . . . C1 | High School | Police Station ☷ . . B2 | Union Rd . . . . . . . B3 |
| Castle ☷ . . . . . . . C2 | (tram stop) . . . . . A1 | Poplar St . . . . . . . C3 | Upper |
| Castle Gate . . . . . . C2 | Holles Cr. . . . . . . . C1 | Portland Rd . . . . . . B1 | Parliament St . . . . B2 |
| Castle Meadow | Hope Dr . . . . . . . . C1 | Post Office ☷ . . B2/C1 | Victoria Centre . . . . B2 |
| Retail Park . . . . . C1 | Hungerhill Rd . . . . . A3 | Queen's Rd . . . . . . C2 | Victoria Leisure |
| Castle | Huntingdon Dr . . . . C1 | Raleigh St . . . . . . . A1 | Centre. . . . . . . . B3 |
| Meadow Rd . . . . . C2 | Huntingdon St . . . . A2 | Regent St . . . . . . . B1 | Victoria Park . . . . . B3 |
| Castle Museum | Ice Centre . . . . . . . C2 | Rick St . . . . . . . . . B3 | Victoria St. . . . . . . B2 |
| & Gallery ☷ . . . . C2 | Information Ctr ⓘ . . B2 | Robin Hood | Walter St. . . . . . . . A1 |
| Castle Rd . . . . . . . C2 | Instow Rise . . . . . . A3 | Statue ✦ . . . . . . C2 | Warser Gate . . . . . B3 |
| Castle Wharf. . . . . . C2 | International | Robin Hood St . . . . B3 | Watkin St . . . . . . . A2 |
| Cavendish Rd East . C1 | Community | Royal Centre | Waverley St . . . . . A1 |
| Cemetery . . . . . . . B1 | Centre. . . . . . . . A2 | (tram stop) . . . . . B2 | Wheeler Gate . . . . B2 |
| Chaucer St . . . . . . B1 | Kent St . . . . . . . . B3 | Royal Children | Wilford Rd . . . . . . . C2 |
| Cheapside . . . . . . . B2 | King St . . . . . . . . B2 | Inn ⚓ . . . . . . . C2 | Wilford St . . . . . . . C2 |
| Church Rd . . . . . . . A3 | Lace Market | Royal Concert | Willoughby |
| City Link . . . . . . . . C3 | (tram stop) . . . . . B3 | Hall ☷ . . . . . . . B2 | House ☷ . . . . . . C2 |
| City of Caves ✦ . . C2 | Lamartine St. . . . . . B3 | St Ann's Hill Rd . . . A2 | Wollaton St. . . . . . B1 |
| Clarendon St . . . . . B1 | Lenton Rd. . . . . . . C1 | St Ann's Way . . . . . A2 | Woodborough Rd. . . A2 |
| Cliff Rd . . . . . . . . . C3 | Lewis Cl . . . . . . . . A3 | St Ann's Well Rd. . . A3 | Woolpack La. . . . . . B3 |
| | Lincoln St . . . . . . . B2 | St Barnabas † . . . . B1 | York St . . . . . . . . . A2 |
| | London Rd . . . . . . C3 | St James' St . . . . . . B2 | |

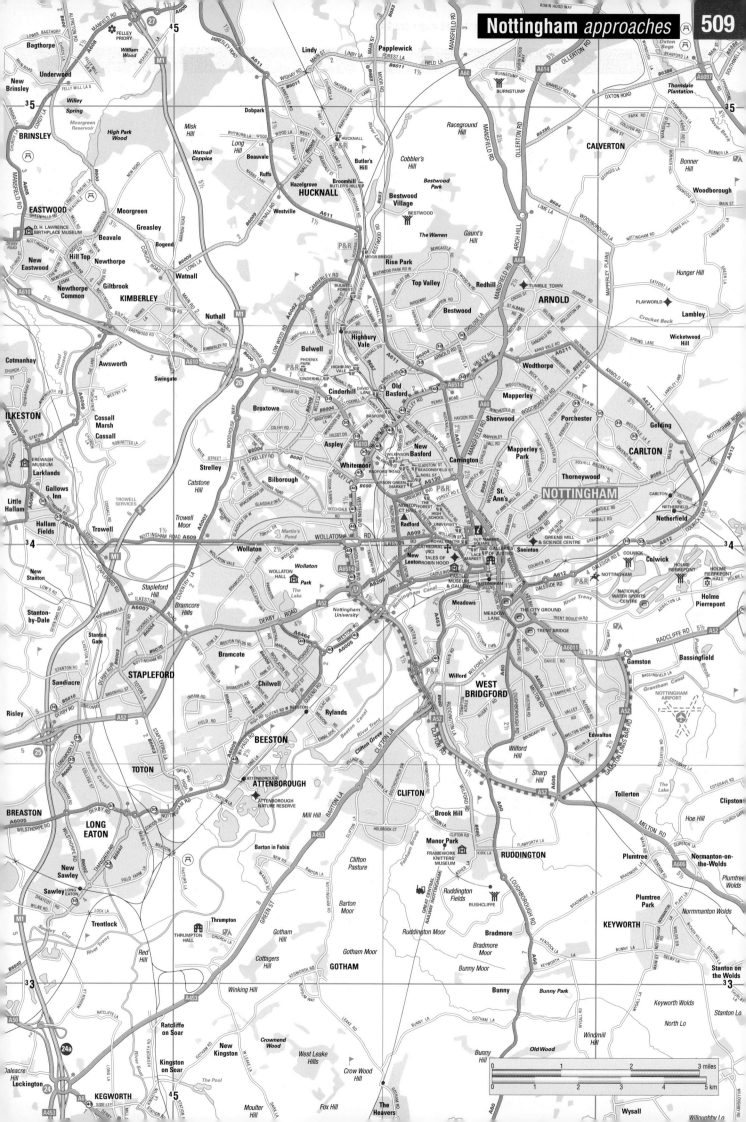

## Oxford

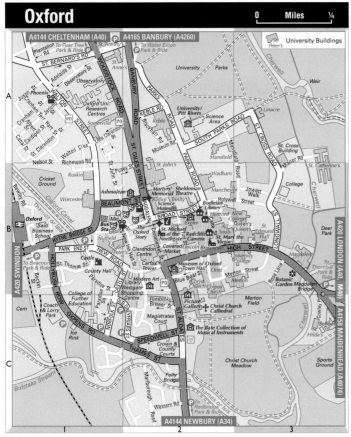

## Peterborough

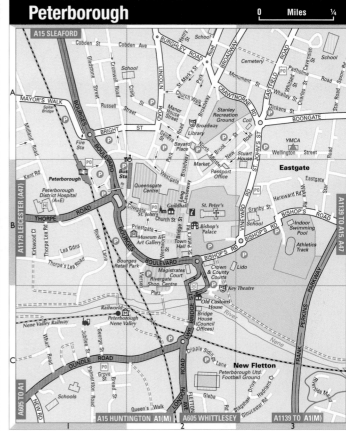

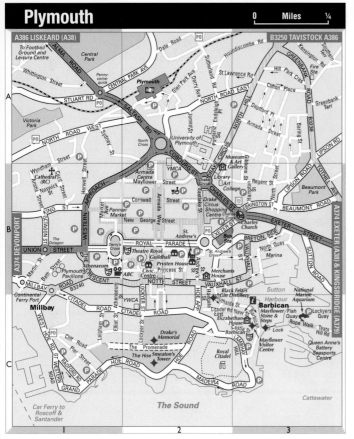

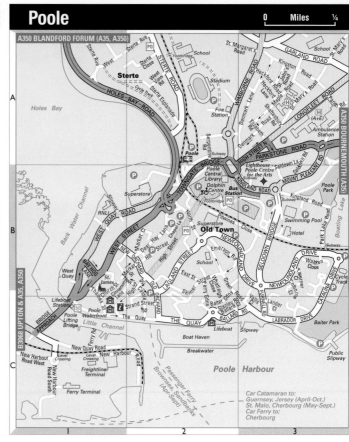

## Plymouth

ABC 🎬 . . . . . . . . . B2
Alma Rd . . . . . . . . A1
Anstis St. . . . . . . . B1
Armada Centre . . . B2
Armada St . . . . . . A3
Armada Way. . . . . B2
Art College . . . . . B2
Athenaeum St. . . . C1
Athenaeum ♨. . . . B1
Barbican . . . . . . . C3
Barbican ♨. . . . . . C3
Baring St . . . . . . . A3
Bath St . . . . . . . . B3
Beaumont Park . . . B3
Beaumont Rd. . . . B3
Black Friars
  Gin Distillery ✦ . . C2
Breton Side . . . . . B3
Bus Station. . . . . . B2
Castle St. . . . . . . . C3
Cathedral (RC) † . . B1
Cecil St. . . . . . . . . B1
Central Park . . . . . A1
Central Park Ave . . A2
Charles Church ⚓ . B3
Charles Cross
  (r'about) . . . . . . . B3
Charles St. . . . . . . B2
Citadel Rd . . . . . . C2
Citadel Rd East . . . C2
Civic Centre 🏛. . . B2
Cliff Rd . . . . . . . . C1
Clifton Pl. . . . . . . A3
Cobourg St. . . . . . A2
Continental
  Ferry Port . . . . . . B1
Cornwall St. . . . . . B2
Dale Rd. . . . . . . . A2
Deptford Pl. . . . . . A3
Derry Ave . . . . . . . A2
Derry's Cross
  (r'about) . . . . . . . B1
Drake Circus. . . . . B2
Drake Circus
  Shopping Centre . B2
Drake's
  Memorial ✦ . . . . C2
Eastlake St. . . . . . B2
Ebrington St . . . . . B3
Elizabethan
  House 🏛 . . . . . . C3
Elliot St. . . . . . . . . C1
Endsleigh Pl . . . . . A2
Exeter St. . . . . . . . B3
Fire Station . . . . . . A3
Fish Quay . . . . . . . C3
Gibbons St. . . . . . A3
Glen Park Ave. . . . A2
Grand Pde . . . . . . C1
Great Western Rd. . C1
Greenbank Rd . . . . A3
Greenbank Terr. . . A3
Guildhall 🏛 . . . . . B2
Hampton St . . . . . B3
Harwell St. . . . . . . B1
Hill Park Cr . . . . . . A3
Hoe Approach . . . . B2
Hoe Rd. . . . . . . . . C2
Hoegate St. . . . . . C2
Houndiscombe Rd . A2
Information Ctr 🅸 . . C3
James St . . . . . . . A2
Kensington Rd . . . . A3
King St . . . . . . . . B1
Lambhay Hill. . . . . C3
Leigham St . . . . . . C1
Library . . . . . . . . . B2
Lipson Rd. . . . . A3/B3
Lockyer St . . . . . . C2
Lockyers Quay . . . . C3
Madeira Rd. . . . . . C2
Marina. . . . . . . . . B3
Market Ave . . . . . . B1
Martin St. . . . . . . . B1
Mayflower St . . . . . B2
Mayflower Stone
  & Steps ✦ . . . . . C3
Mayflower Visitor
  Centre ✦ . . . . . . C3
Merchants
  House 🏛 . . . . . . B2
Millbay Rd. . . . . . . B1
Museum & Art
  Gallery 🏛 . . . . . B2
National Marine
  Aquarium 🐟. . . . C3
Neswick St . . . . . . B1
New George St. . . . B2
New St . . . . . . . . . C3
North Cross
  (r'about) . . . . . . . A2
North Hill . . . . . . . A3
North Quay. . . . . . C2
North Rd East. . . . A2
North Rd West . . . A1
North St . . . . . . . . B3
Notte St . . . . . . . . B2
Octagon St . . . . . . B1
Pannier Market . . . B1
Pennycomequick
  (r'about) . . . . . . . A1
Pier St. . . . . . . . . C1
Plymouth
  Pavilions . . . . . . . B1
Plymouth
  Station 🚄 . . . . . A2
Police Station 🚓. . B3
Portland Sq . . . . . A2
Post Office 📮 . . . .
  . . . . . .A1/A2/B2/C1
Princess St. . . . . . B2
Prysten House 🏠. . B2
Queen Anne's Battery
  Seaports Centre C3
Radford Rd. . . . . . C1
Regent St . . . . . . . B3
Rope Walk . . . . . . C3
Royal Citadel 🏰. . . C2
Royal Pde . . . . . . . B2
St.Andrew's ⚓. . . . B2
St Andrew's Cross
  (r'about) . . . . . . . B2
St Andrew's St . . . B2
St Lawrence Rd . . . A2
Saltash Rd . . . . . . A2
Smeaton's
  Tower ✦ . . . . . . . C2
Southern Terr . . . . A3
Southside St. . . . . C2
Stuart Rd . . . . . . . A1
Sutherland Rd . . . . A2
Sutton Rd. . . . . . . B3
Sydney St. . . . . . . A1
Teats Hill Rd . . . . . C3
The Crescent . . . . B1
The Hoe . . . . . . . . C2
The Octagon
  (r'about) . . . . . . . B1
The Promenade . . . C2
Theatre Royal ♨. . B2
Tothill Ave . . . . . . B3
Union St . . . . . . . . B1
University of
  Plymouth . . . . . . A2
Vauxhall St . . . . B2/3
Victoria Park. . . . . A1
West Hoe Rd . . . . C1
Western Approach . B1
Whittington St . . . . A1
Wyndham St. . . . . B1
YMCA. . . . . . . . . B2
YWCA. . . . . . . . . C2

## Poole

Ambulance Station. A3
Baiater Gdns . . . . C2
Baiter Park . . . . . . C3
Ballard Cl . . . . . . . C2
Ballard Rd. . . . . . . C2
Bay Hog La . . . . . B2
Bridge Approach . . C1
Bus Station. . . . . . B2
Castle St. . . . . . . . B2
Catalina Dr . . . . . . B3
Chapel La. . . . . . . B2
Church St . . . . . . . B1
Cinnamon La . . . . B2
Colborne Cl . . . . . B3
Dear Hay La . . . . . B2
Denmark La . . . . . A3
Denmark Rd. . . . . A3
East St . . . . . . . . . B2
Elizabeth Rd . . . . . B2
Emerson Rd . . . . . B2
Ferry Rd . . . . . . . . C1
Ferry Terminal. . . . C1
Fire Station . . . . . . A2
Freightliner
  Terminal. . . . . . . C1
Furnell Rd. . . . . . . B3
Garland Rd . . . . . . A3
Green Rd . . . . . . . B2
Heckford La . . . . . A3
Heckford Rd. . . . . A3
High St . . . . . . . . B2
High St North . . . . A3
Hill St . . . . . . . . . B2
Holes Bay Rd . . . . A1
Hospital (A+E) 🅷 . . A3
Information Ctr 🅸 . . C2
Kingland Rd . . . . . B3
Kingston Rd . . . . . A3
Labrador Dr . . . . . C3
Lagland St . . . . . . B2
Lander Cl . . . . . . . C3
Lifeboat 🏛 . . . . . . C2
Lighthouse - Poole
  Centre for the
  Arts ✦ . . . . . . . . B3
Longfleet Rd. . . . . A3
Maple Rd . . . . . . . A3
Market Cl . . . . . . . B2
Market St . . . . . . . B2
Mount
  Pleasant Rd . . . . B3
New Harbour Rd . . C1
New Harbour
  Rd South . . . . . . C1
New Harbour
  Rd West . . . . . . . C1
New Orchard . . . . B1
New Quay Rd. . . . C1
New St . . . . . . . . . B2
Newfoundland Dr . . B2
North St . . . . . . . . B2
Old Orchard . . . . . B2
Parish Rd . . . . . . . A3
Park Lake Rd . . . . B3
Parkstone Rd . . . . A3
Perry Gdns . . . . . . B2
Pitwines Cl . . . . . . B2
Police Station 🚓 . . C1
Poole Lifting
  Bridge. . . . . . . . . C1
Poole Central
  Library. . . . . . . . . B2
Poole Park . . . . . . B2
Poole Station 🚄 . . A2
Poole Waterfront
  Museum 🏛. . . . . C1
Post Office 📮 . . A2/B2
RNLI . . . . . . . . . . C1
St John's Rd. . . . . A3
St Margaret's Rd . . A2
St Mary's Rd. . . . . A3
Seldown Bridge . . . B3
Seldown La . . . . . B3
Seldown Rd . . . . . B3
Serpentine Rd . . . . A2
Shaftesbury Rd . . . A3
Skinner St. . . . . . . B2
Slipway. . . . . . . . . B1
Stanley Rd . . . . . . C2
Sterte Ave. . . . . . . A2
Sterte Ave West . . . A1
Sterte Cl . . . . . . . A2
Sterte Esplanade . . A2
Sterte Rd . . . . . . . A2
Strand St . . . . . . . C2
Swimming Pool . . . B3
Taverner Cl . . . . . . B3
Thames St . . . . . . B1
The Quay . . . . . . . C2
Towngate Bridge . . B2
Vallis Cl. . . . . . . . C3
Waldren St . . . . . . B3
West Quay . . . . . . B1
West Quay Rd . . . . B1
West St. . . . . . . . . B1
West View Rd. . . . A2
Whatleigh Cl. . . . . B2
Wimborne Rd. . . . . A3

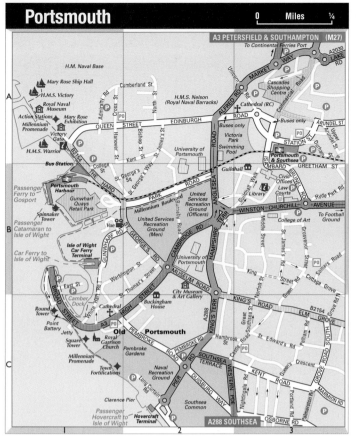

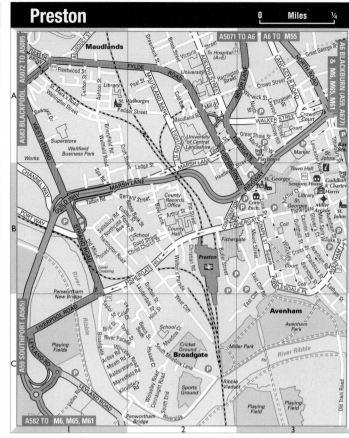

## Portsmouth

| | |
|---|---|
| Action Stations ✦ . C1 | |
| Admiralty Rd . . . . . . A1 | |
| Alfred Rd . . . . . . . A2 | |
| Anglesea Rd . . . . . . B2 | |
| Arundel St . . . . . . . B3 | |
| Bishop St . . . . . . . A2 | |
| Broad St . . . . . . . . C1 | |
| Buckingham | |
| House 🏛 . . . . . . C2 | |
| Burnaby Rd . . . . . . B2 | |
| Bus Station . . . . . . B1 | |
| Camber Dock . . . . . C1 | |
| Cambridge Rd . . . . B2 | |
| Car Ferry to | |
| Isle of Wight . . . . B1 | |
| Cascades Shopping | |
| Centre . . . . . . . . A3 | |
| Castle Rd . . . . . . . C3 | |
| Cathedral † . . . . . . C1 | |
| Cathedral (RC) † . . A3 | |
| City Museum & | |
| Art Gallery 🏛 . . B2 | |
| Civic Offices . . . . . B3 | |
| Clarence Pier . . . . . C2 | |
| College of Art . . . . B3 | |
| College St . . . . . . . B1 | |
| Commercial Rd . . . A3 | |
| Cottage Gr . . . . . . . C3 | |
| Cross St . . . . . . . . A1 | |
| Cumberland St . . . . A2 | |
| Duisburg Way . . . . C2 | |
| Durham St . . . . . . A3 | |
| East St . . . . . . . . . B1 | |
| Edinburgh Rd . . . . A2 | |
| Elm Gr . . . . . . . . . C3 | |
| Great Southsea St . C3 | |
| Green Rd . . . . . . . B3 | |
| Greetham St . . . . . B3 | |
| Grosvenor St . . . . . B3 | |
| Grove Rd North . . . C3 | |
| Grove Rd South . . . C3 | |
| Guildhall 🏛 . . . . . . B3 | |
| Guildhall Walk . . . . B3 | |
| Gunwharf Quays | |
| Retail Park . . . . . B1 | |
| Gunwharf Rd . . . . . B1 | |
| Hambrook St . . . . . C2 | |
| Hampshire Terr . . . . B2 | |
| Hanover St . . . . . . A1 | |
| High St . . . . . . . . . C2 | |
| HM Naval Base . . . A1 | |
| HMS Nelson (Royal | |
| Naval Barracks) . . A2 | |
| HMS Victory ⚓ . . . A1 | |
| HMS Warrior ⚓ . . . A1 | |
| Hovercraft | |
| Terminal . . . . . . C2 | |
| Hyde Park Rd . . . . B3 | |
| Information | |
| Ctr 🅸 . . . . . . A1/B3 | |
| Isambard | |
| Brunel Rd . . . . . . A2 | |
| Isle of Wight Car | |
| Ferry Terminal . . . B1 | |
| Kent Rd . . . . . . . . C3 | |
| Kent St . . . . . . . . . A2 | |
| King St . . . . . . . . . B3 | |
| King's Rd . . . . . . . C3 | |
| King's Terr. . . . . . . C2 | |
| Lake Rd . . . . . . . . A3 | |
| Law Courts . . . . . . B3 | |
| Library . . . . . . . . . B3 | |
| Long Curtain Rd . . . C2 | |
| Market Way . . . . . . A3 | |
| Marmion Rd . . . . . C3 | |
| Mary Rose | |
| Exhibition 🏛 . . . . A1 | |
| Mary Rose | |
| Ship Hall ⚓ . . . . A1 | |
| Middle St . . . . . . . B3 | |
| Millennium Blvd . . B2 | |
| Millennium | |
| Promenade . . A1/C1 | |
| Museum Rd . . . . . . B2 | |
| Naval Recreation | |
| Ground . . . . . . . C2 | |
| Nightingale Rd . . . . C3 | |
| Norfolk St . . . . . . . B3 | |
| North St . . . . . . . . A2 | |
| Osborne Rd . . . . . C3 | |
| Park Rd . . . . . . . . B2 | |
| Passenger Catamaran | |
| to Isle of Wight . . B1 | |
| Passenger Ferry | |
| to Gosport . . . . . B1 | |
| Pelham Rd . . . . . . C3 | |
| Pembroke Gdns . . . C2 | |
| Pembroke Rd . . . . . C2 | |
| Pier Rd . . . . . . . . . C2 | |
| Point Battery . . . . . C1 | |
| Police Station 🄿 . . B3 | |
| Portsmouth & | |
| Southsea 🚉 . . . . A3 | |
| Portsmouth | |
| Harbour 🚉 . . . . . B1 | |
| Post Office 🄿 | |
| . . . . A1/A3/B3/C1/C3 | |
| Queen St . . . . . . . A1 | |
| Queen's Cr . . . . . . C3 | |
| Round Tower ✦ . . . C1 | |
| Royal Garrison | |
| Church ⛪ . . . . . . C1 | |
| Royal Naval | |
| Museum 🏛 . . . . . A1 | |
| St Edward's Rd . . . C3 | |
| St George's Rd . . . B2 | |
| St George's Sq . . . . B1 | |
| St George's Way . . . B1 | |
| St James's Rd . . . . B3 | |
| St James's St . . . . A2 | |
| St Thomas's St . . . . B2 | |
| Somers Rd . . . . . . B3 | |
| Southsea | |
| Common . . . . . . . C2 | |
| Southsea Terr . . . . C2 | |
| Station St . . . . . . . A3 | |
| Spinnaker | |
| Tower ✦ . . . . . . . B1 | |
| Square Tower ✦ . . C1 | |
| Swimming Pool . . . A3 | |
| The Hard . . . . . . . . B1 | |
| Town | |
| Fortifications ✦ . . C1 | |
| Unicorn Rd . . . . . . A2 | |
| United Services | |
| Recreation | |
| Ground . . . . . . . B2 | |
| University of | |
| Portsmouth . . . A2/B2 | |
| Upper Arundel St . . A3 | |
| Victoria Park . . . . . A2 | |
| Victory Gate . . . . . A1 | |
| Vue 🎬 . . . . . . . . . B1 | |
| Warblington St . . . . B1 | |
| Western Pde . . . . . C2 | |
| White Hart Rd . . . . C1 | |
| Winston | |
| Churchill Ave . . . . B3 | |

## Preston

| | |
|---|---|
| Adelphi St . . . . . . A2 | |
| Anchor Ct . . . . . . . B3 | |
| Aqueduct St . . . . . A1 | |
| Ardee Rd . . . . . . . C1 | |
| Arthur St . . . . . . . B2 | |
| Ashton St . . . . . . . A1 | |
| Avenham La . . . . . B3 | |
| Avenham Park . . . . C3 | |
| Avenham Rd . . . . . B3 | |
| Avenham St . . . . . B3 | |
| Bairstow St . . . . . . B3 | |
| Balderstone Rd . . . C1 | |
| Beamont Dr . . . . . . A1 | |
| Beech St South . . . C2 | |
| Bird St . . . . . . . . . C1 | |
| Bow La . . . . . . . . . B2 | |
| Brieryfield Rd . . . . A1 | |
| Broadgate . . . . . . . C1 | |
| Brook St . . . . . . . . A2 | |
| Bus Station . . . . . . A3 | |
| Butler St . . . . . . . B2 | |
| Cannon St . . . . . . B3 | |
| Carlton St . . . . . . . A1 | |
| Chaddock St . . . . . B3 | |
| Channel Way . . . . . B1 | |
| Chapel St . . . . . . . B3 | |
| Christ Church St . . B2 | |
| Christian Rd . . . . . B2 | |
| Cold Bath St . . . . . A2 | |
| Coleman Ct . . . . . . C1 | |
| Connaught Rd . . . . C2 | |
| Corn | |
| Exchange 🏛 . . . . B3 | |
| Corporation St . A2/B2 | |
| County Hall . . . . . . B2 | |
| County Records | |
| Office . . . . . . . . B2 | |
| Court. . . . . . . . . . A3 | |
| Court. . . . . . . . . . B3 | |
| Cricket Ground . . . . C2 | |
| Croft St . . . . . . . . A1 | |
| Cross St . . . . . . . . B3 | |
| Crown Court . . . . . A3 | |
| Crown St . . . . . . . A3 | |
| East Cliff . . . . . . . C3 | |
| East Cliff Rd . . . . . C3 | |
| Edward St . . . . . . . A2 | |
| Elizabeth St . . . . . A2 | |
| Euston St . . . . . . . B1 | |
| Fishergate . . . . . B2/B3 | |
| Fishergate Hill . . . . C2 | |
| Fishergate Shopping | |
| Centre . . . . . . . . B2 | |
| Fitzroy St . . . . . . . A2 | |
| Fleetwood St . . . . . A1 | |
| Friargate . . . . . . . A3 | |
| Fylde Rd . . . . . A1/A2 | |
| Gerrard St . . . . . . A2 | |
| Glover's Ct . . . . . . B3 | |
| Good St . . . . . . . . A2 | |
| Grafton St . . . . . . B3 | |
| Great George St . . . A3 | |
| Great Shaw St . . . . A3 | |
| Greenbank St . . . . A2 | |
| Guild Way . . . . . . . B1 | |
| Guildhall & | |
| Charter 🎭 . . . . . B3 | |
| Guildhall St . . . . . . B3 | |
| Harrington St . . . . A2 | |
| Harris Museum 🏛 . B3 | |
| Hartington Rd . . . . B1 | |
| Hasset Cl . . . . . . . C2 | |
| Heatley St . . . . . . . B2 | |
| Hind St . . . . . . . . . C2 | |
| Information Ctr 🅸 . B3 | |
| Kilruddery Rd . . . . C1 | |
| Lancaster Rd . . . A3/B3 | |
| Latham St . . . . . . . B3 | |
| Lauderdale St . . . . C2 | |
| Lawson St . . . . . . . A3 | |
| Leighton St . . . . . . A2 | |
| Leyland Rd . . . . . . C1 | |
| Library . . . . . . . . . A1 | |
| Library . . . . . . . . . B3 | |
| Liverpool Rd . . . . . C1 | |
| Lodge St . . . . . . . . B2 | |
| Lune St . . . . . . . . . B3 | |
| Main Sprit West . . . B2 | |
| Maresfield Rd . . . . C1 | |
| Market St West . . . A3 | |
| Marsh La . . . . . . B1/B2 | |
| Maudland Bank . . . A2 | |
| Maudland Rd . . . . . A2 | |
| Meadow Ct. . . . . . C2 | |
| Meath Rd . . . . . . . C1 | |
| Mill Hill . . . . . . . . A3 | |
| Miller Arcade ✦ . . B3 | |
| Miller Park . . . . . . C3 | |
| Moor La . . . . . . . . A3 | |
| Mount St . . . . . . . B3 | |
| North Rd . . . . . . . A3 | |
| North St . . . . . . . . A2 | |
| Northcote Rd . . . . . B1 | |
| Old Milestones . . . B1 | |
| Old Tram Rd . . . . . C3 | |
| Pedder St . . . . . A1/A2 | |
| Peel St . . . . . . . . . A2 | |
| Penwortham | |
| Bridge. . . . . . . . C2 | |
| Penwortham | |
| New Bridge. . . . . C1 | |
| Pitt St . . . . . . . . . B2 | |
| Playhouse 🎭 . . . . A3 | |
| Police Station 🄿 . . A3 | |
| Port Way . . . . . . . . B1 | |
| Post Office 🄿 . . . . . | |
| . . . . . . . . A1/B3/C1 | |
| Preston | |
| Station 🚉 . . . . . . B2 | |
| Ribble Bank St . . . . B2 | |
| Ribble Viaduct . . . . C2 | |
| Ribblesdale Pl . . . . B3 | |
| Ringway . . . . . . . . B3 | |
| River Parade. . . . . C1 | |
| Riverside. . . . . . . . C2 | |
| St Georges . . . . . . B3 | |
| St Georges Shopping | |
| Centre. . . . . . . . B3 | |
| St Johns . . . . . . . . B3 | |
| St Johns Shopping | |
| Centre. . . . . . . . A3 | |
| St Mark's Rd . . . . . A1 | |
| St Walburges ⛪ . . A1 | |
| Salisbury Rd . . . . . B1 | |
| Sessions | |
| House 🏛 . . . . . . B3 | |
| Snow Hill . . . . . . . A3 | |
| South End . . . . . . . C2 | |
| South Meadow La . . C2 | |
| Spa Rd . . . . . . . . . B1 | |
| Sports Ground . . . . C2 | |
| Strand Rd . . . . . . . B1 | |
| Syke St . . . . . . . . . B3 | |
| Talbot Rd . . . . . . . B1 | |
| Taylor St . . . . . . . . C1 | |
| Tithebarn St . . . . . A3 | |
| Town Hall . . . . . . . B3 | |
| Tulketh Brow. . . . . A1 | |
| University of Central | |
| Lancashire . . . . . A2 | |
| Valley Rd. . . . . . . . C1 | |
| Victoria St . . . . . . . A2 | |
| Walker St . . . . . . . A3 | |
| Walton's Parade . . . B3 | |
| Warwick St . . . . . . A3 | |
| Wellfield Business | |
| Park . . . . . . . . . A1 | |
| Wellfield Rd . . . . . A1 | |
| Wellington St . . . . . A1 | |
| West Cliff . . . . . . . C2 | |
| West Strand . . . . . A1 | |
| Winckley Rd . . . . . C1 | |
| Winckley Square . . B3 | |
| Wolseley Rd . . . . . C2 | |

# Reading

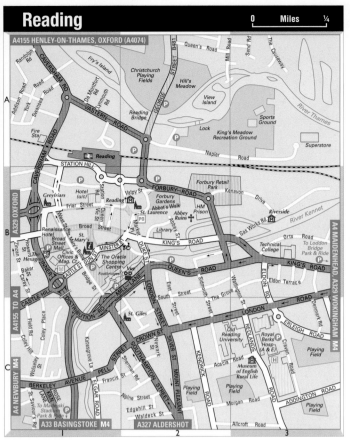

# Salisbury

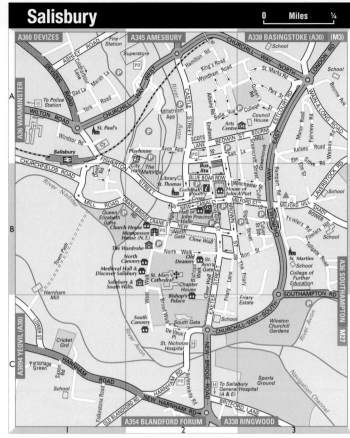

# Sheffield

0 Miles ¼

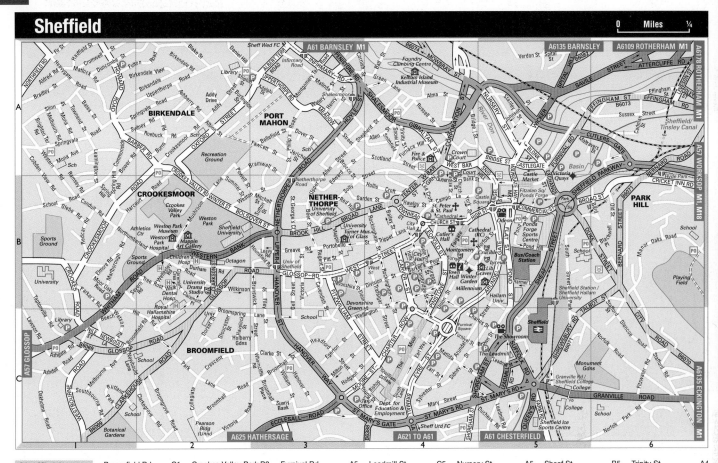

## Sheffield

Addy Dr . . . . . . . . A2
Addy St . . . . . . . . A2
Adelphi St . . . . . . . A3
Albert Terrace Rd . . A3
Albion St . . . . . . . . A4
Aldred Rd . . . . . . . A1
Allen St . . . . . . . . A4
Alma St . . . . . . . . A4
Angel St . . . . . . . . B5
Arundel Gate . . . . . B5
Arundel St . . . . . . . C4
Ashberry Rd . . . . . . A2
Ashdell St . . . . . . . C1
Ashgate Rd . . . . . . C1
Athletics Centre . . . . B2
Attercliffe Rd . . . . . A6
Bailey St . . . . . . . . B4
Ball St . . . . . . . . . A4
Balm Green . . . . . . B4
Bank St . . . . . . . . B4
Barber Rd . . . . . . . A2
Bard St . . . . . . . . B5
Barker's Pool . . . . . B4
Bates St . . . . . . . . A1
Beech Hill Rd . . . . . C1
Beet St . . . . . . . . B3
Bellefield St . . . . . . A3
Bernard Rd . . . . . . A6
Bernard St . . . . . . . B5
Birkendale . . . . . . . A2
Birkendale
  (tram station) . . . . B4
Birkendale View . . . A1
Bishop St . . . . . . . C4
Blackwell Pl . . . . . . B6
Blake St . . . . . . . . A4
Blonk St . . . . . . . . A5
Bolsover St . . . . . . B2
Botanical Gdns . . . . C1
Bower Rd . . . . . . . A1
Bradley St . . . . . . . A1
Bramall La . . . . . . . C4
Bramwell St . . . . . . A3
Bridge St . . . . . A4/A5
Brighton
  Terrace Rd . . . . . A1
Broad La . . . . . . . . B3
Broad St . . . . . . . . B6
Brocco St . . . . . . . A3
Brook Hill . . . . . . . B3

Broomfield Rd . . . . C1
Broomgrove Rd . . . . C2
Broomhall Pl . . . . . . C3
Broomhall Rd . . . . . C2
Broomhall St . . . . . C3
Broomspring La . . . . C2
Brown St . . . . . . . . C5
Brunswick St . . . . . B3
Burgess St . . . . . . . B4
Burlington St . . . . . . A2
Burns Rd . . . . . . . . A2
Bus/Coach
  Station . . . . . . . B5
Cadman St . . . . . . A6
Cambridge St . . . . . B4
Campo La . . . . . . . B4
Carver St . . . . . . . . B4
Castle Market . . . . . B5
Castle Square
  (tram station) . . . . B5
Castlegate . . . . . . . A5
Cathedral (RC) ✝ . . B4
Cathedral
  (tram station) . . . . B4
Cavendish St . . . . . B3
Charles St . . . . . . . C4
Charter Row . . . . . . C4
Children's
  Hospital Ⓗ . . . . . B2
Church St . . . . . . . B4
City Hall . . . . . . . . B4
City Hall
  (tram station) . . . . B4
City Rd . . . . . . . . . C6
Claremont Cr . . . . . B2
Claremont Pl . . . . . . B2
Clarke St . . . . . . . . C3
Clarkegrove Rd . . . . C2
Clarkehouse Rd . . . . C1
Clarkson St . . . . . . B2
Cobden View Rd . . . A1
Collegiate Cr . . . . . . C2
Commercial St . . . . . B5
Commonside . . . . . . A1
Conduit Rd . . . . . . . B1
Cornish St . . . . . . . A3
Corporation St . . . . . A4
Court . . . . . . . . . . A4
Cricket Inn Rd . . . . . B6
Cromwell St . . . . . . A1
Crookes Rd . . . . . . B1

Crookes Valley Park B2
Crookes Valley Rd . B2
Crookesmoor Rd . . . B2
Crown Court . . . . . . A4
Crucible
  Theatre Ⓦ . . . . . B5
Cutlers Gate . . . . . . A6
Cutler's Hall ⌂ . . . . B4
Daniel Hill . . . . . . . A2
Dental Hospital Ⓗ . . B2
Dept for Education &
  Employment . . . . . C3
Devonshire Green . . B3
Devonshire St . . . . . B3
Division St . . . . . . . B4
Dorset St . . . . . . . . C2
Dover St . . . . . . . . A3
Duchess Rd . . . . . . C5
Duke St . . . . . . . . B5
Duncombe St . . . . . A1
Durham Rd . . . . . . . B2
Earl St . . . . . . . . . C4
Earl Way . . . . . . . . C4
Ecclesall Rd . . . . . . C3
Edward St . . . . . . . B3
Effingham Rd . . . . . A6
Effingham St . . . . . . A6
Egerton St . . . . . . . C3
Eldon St . . . . . . . . B3
Elmore Rd . . . . . . . B1
Exchange St . . . . . . B5
Eyre St . . . . . . . . . C4
Fargate . . . . . . . . . B4
Farm Rd . . . . . . . . C5
Fawcett St . . . . . . . A3
Filey St . . . . . . . . . B3
Fire & Police
  Museum ⌂ . . . . . A4
Fir St . . . . . . . . . . A1
Fitzalan Sq/
  Ponds Forge
  (tram station) . . . . B5
Fitzwater Rd . . . . . . C6
Fitzwilliam Gate . . . C4
Fitzwilliam St . . . . . B3
Flat St . . . . . . . . . B5
Foley St . . . . . . . . A6
Foundry Climbing
  Centre . . . . . . . . A4
Fulton Rd . . . . . . . A1
Furnace Hill . . . . . . A4

Furnival Rd . . . . . . A5
Furnival Sq . . . . . . . C4
Furnival St . . . . . . . C4
Garden St . . . . . . . B3
Gell St . . . . . . . . . B3
Gibraltar St . . . . . . . A4
Glebe Rd . . . . . . . . B1
Glencoe Rd . . . . . . C6
Glossop
  Rd . . . . . . B2/B3/C1
Gloucester St . . . . . C2
Granville Rd . . . . . . C5
Granville Rd/
  Sheffield College
  (tram station) . . . . C5
Graves Gallery ⌂ . . B5
Greave Rd . . . . . . . B3
Green La . . . . . . . . A4
Hadfield St . . . . . . . A1
Hallam University . . . B5
Hanover St . . . . . . . C3
Hanover Way . . . . . C3
Harcourt Rd . . . . . . B1
Harmer La . . . . . . . B5
Havelock St . . . . . . C2
Hawley St . . . . . . . B4
Haymarket . . . . . . . B5
Headford St . . . . . . C3
Heavygate Rd . . . . . A1
Henry St . . . . . . . . A3
High St . . . . . . . . . B4
Hodgson St . . . . . . C3
Holberry Gdns . . . . C2
Hollis Croft . . . . . . . B4
Holly St . . . . . . . . . B4
Hounsfield Rd . . . . . B3
Howard Rd . . . . . . . A1
Hoyle St . . . . . . . . A3
Hyde Park
  (tram station) . . . . A6
Infirmary Rd . . . . . . A3
Infirmary Rd
  (tram station) . . . . A3
Information Ctr Ⓘ . . B4
Jericho St . . . . . . . A3
Johnson St . . . . . . . A5
Kelham Island
  Industrial
  Museum ⌂ . . . . . A4
Lawson Rd . . . . . . . C1
Leadmill Rd . . . . . . C5

Leadmill St . . . . . . . C5
Leadmill, The . . . . . C5
Leamington St . . . . . A1
Leavy Rd . . . . . . . . B3
Lee Croft . . . . . . . . B4
Leopold St . . . . . . . B4
Leveson St . . . . . . . A6
Library . . . . . . . . . A2
Library . . . . . . . . . B5
Library . . . . . . . . . C1
Lyceum
  Theatre Ⓦ . . . . . B5
Malinda St . . . . . . . A3
Maltravers St . . . . . A5
Manor Oaks Rd . . . . B6
Mappin Art
  Gallery ⌂ . . . . . . B2
Mappin St . . . . . . . B3
Marlborough Rd . . . . B1
Mary St . . . . . . . . . C4
Matilda St . . . . . . . C4
Matlock Rd . . . . . . . A1
Meadow St . . . . . . . A3
Melbourn Rd . . . . . . A1
Melbourne Ave . . . . C1
Millennium
  Galleries ⌂ . . . . . B5
Milton St . . . . . . . . C3
Mitchell St . . . . . . . B3
Mona Ave . . . . . . . A1
Mona Rd . . . . . . . . A1
Montgomery
  Terrace Rd . . . . . A3
Montgomery
  Theatre Ⓦ . . . . . B4
Monument Gdns . . . C6
Moor Oaks Rd . . . . . B1
Moore St . . . . . . . . C3
Mowbray St . . . . . . A4
Mushroom La . . . . . B2
Netherthorpe Rd . . . B3
Netherthorpe Rd
  (tram station) . . . . B3
Newbould La . . . . . C1
Nile St . . . . . . . . . C1
Norfolk Park Rd . . . C6
Norfolk Rd . . . . . . . C6
Norfolk St . . . . . . . B4
North Church St . . . B4
Northfield Rd . . . . . A1
Northumberland Rd B1

Nursery St . . . . . . . A5
Oakholme Rd . . . . . C1
Octagon . . . . . . . . B2
Odeon ☎ . . . . . . . B5
Old St . . . . . . . . . . B6
Oxford St . . . . . . . A2
Paradise St . . . . . . B4
Park La . . . . . . . . . C2
Park Sq . . . . . . . . . B5
Parker's Rd . . . . . . B1
Pearson Building
  (Univ) . . . . . . . . C2
Penistone Rd . . . . . A3
Pinstone St . . . . . . B4
Pitt St . . . . . . . . . . B3
Police
  Station Ⓟ . . . . A4/B5
Pond Hill . . . . . . . . B5
Pond St . . . . . . . . . B5
Ponds Forge
  Sports Centre . . . . B5
Portobello St . . . . . . B3
Post Office ⊠
  . . . . . . . . A1/A2/
  . . . . . A4/B3/B5/
  . . . . . B6/C1/C3/C4
Powell St . . . . . . . . A2
Queen St . . . . . . . . B4
Queen's Rd . . . . . . C5
Ramsey Rd . . . . . . B1
Red Hill . . . . . . . . . B3
Redcar Rd . . . . . . . B1
Regent St . . . . . . . B3
Rockingham St . . . . B4
Roebuck Rd . . . . . . A2
Royal Hallamshire
  Hospital Ⓗ . . . . . C2
Russell St . . . . . . . A4
Rutland Park . . . . . . C1
St George's Cl . . . . B3
St Mary's Gate . . . . C3
St Mary's Rd . . . C4/C5
St Peter & St Paul
  Cathedral ✝ . . . . B4
St Philip's Rd . . . . . A3
Savile St . . . . . . . . A5
School Rd . . . . . . . B1
Scotland St . . . . . . B4
Severn Rd . . . . . . . B1
Shalesmoor . . . . . . A4
Shalesmoor
  (tram station) . . . . A3

Sheaf St . . . . . . . . B5
Sheffield Ice
  Sports Centre . . . . C5
Sheffield Parkway . . A6
Sheffield
  Station ≊ . . . . . . C5
Sheffield Station/
  Sheffield Hallam
  University
  (tram station) . . . . B5
Sheffield University B2
Shepherd St . . . . . . A3
Shipton St . . . . . . . A2
Shoreham St . . . . . C4
Showroom, The ☎ . . C4
Shrewsbury Rd . . . . C5
Sidney St . . . . . . . C4
Slinn St . . . . . . . . . A1
Smithfield . . . . . . . A4
Snig Hill . . . . . . . . A5
Snow La . . . . . . . . A4
Solly St . . . . . . . . . B3
Southbourne Rd . . . C1
South La . . . . . . . . B4
South Street Park . . B5
Spital Hill . . . . . . . A5
Spital St . . . . . . . . A5
Spring Hill . . . . . . . B1
Spring Hill Rd . . . . . B1
Springvale Rd . . . . . A1
Stafford Rd . . . . . . C6
Stafford St . . . . . . . B6
Stanley St . . . . . . . A5
Suffolk Rd . . . . . . . C5
Summer St . . . . . . . B2
Sunny Bank . . . . . . C3
Surrey St . . . . . . . . B4
Sussex St . . . . . . . A6
Sutton St . . . . . . . . B3
Sydney Rd . . . . . . . A2
Sylvester St . . . . . . C4
Talbot St . . . . . . . . B4
Taptonville Rd . . . . . B1
Tax Office . . . . . . . C4
Tenter St . . . . . . . . B4
The Moor . . . . . . . C4
Town Hall ⌂ . . . . . B4
Townend . . . . . . . . A1
Townend St . . . . . . A1
Townhead St . . . . . B4
Trafalgar St . . . . . . B4
Tree Root Walk . . . . B2

Trinity St . . . . . . . . A4
Trippet La . . . . . . . B4
Turner Museum
  of Glass ⌂ . . . . . B3
Union St . . . . . . . . B4
University Drama
  Studio Ⓦ . . . . . . B2
University of Sheffield
  (tram station) . . . . B3
Upper Allen St . . . . A3
Upper Hanover St . . B3
Upperthorpe Rd A2/A3
Verdon St . . . . . . . A5
Victoria Quays ♦ . . B5
Victoria Rd . . . . . . . C2
Victoria St . . . . . . . B3
Waingate . . . . . . . . B5
Watery St . . . . . . . . A3
Watson Rd . . . . . . . C1
Wellesley Rd . . . . . B2
Wellington St . . . . . B3
West Bar . . . . . . . . A4
West Bar Green . . . . A4
West St . . . . . . . . . B3
West St
  (tram station) . . . . B4
Westbourne Rd . . . . C1
Western Bank . . . . . B2
Western Rd . . . . . . A1
Weston Park . . . . . . B2
Weston Park
  Hospital Ⓗ . . . . . B2
Weston Park
  Museum ⌂ . . . . . B2
Weston St . . . . . . . B2
Wharncliffe Rd . . . . C3
Whitham Rd . . . . . . B1
Wicker . . . . . . . . . A5
Wilkinson St . . . . . . B2
William St . . . . . . . C3
Winter Garden ♦ . . B4
Winter St . . . . . . . . B2
York St . . . . . . . . . B4
Young St . . . . . . . . C4

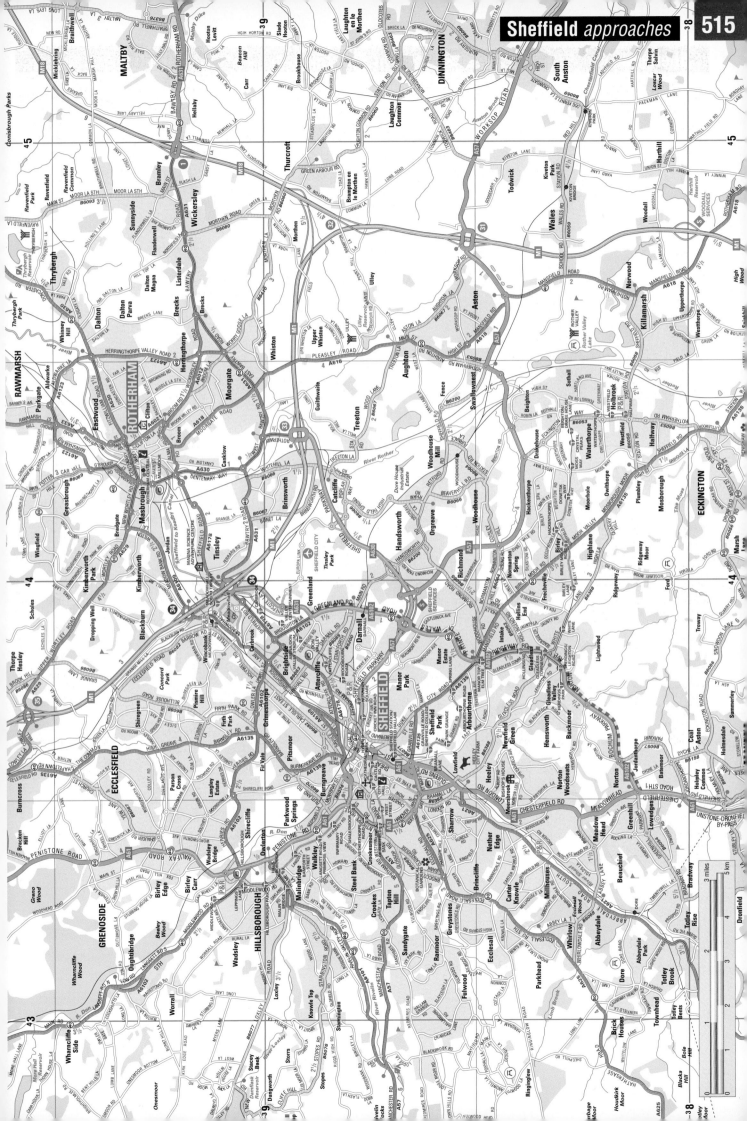

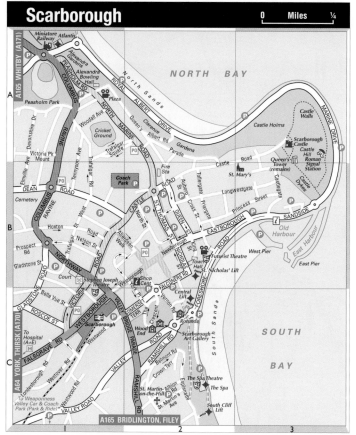

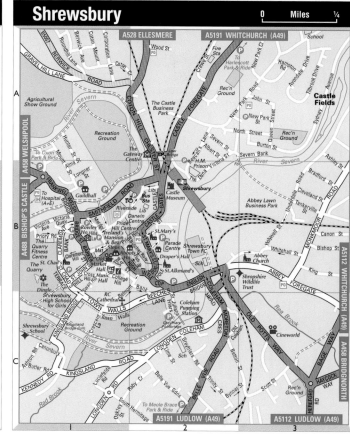

## Scarborough

| | | | |
|---|---|---|---|
| Aberdeen Walk.... B2 | East Harbour ..... B3 | Peasholm Park.... A1 | Scarborough |
| Albert Rd ........ A2 | East Pier......... B3 | Peasholm Rd ..... A1 | Station ≈ ...... C1 |
| Albion Rd ........ C2 | Eastborough....... B2 | Plaza ☎ ......... A1 | Somerset Terr.... C2 |
| Alexandra Bowling | Elmville Ave ...... C1 | Police Station ⊠.. B1 | South Cliff Lift ✦.. C2 |
| Hall .......... A1 | Esplanade........ C2 | Post Office ⊠ .... | Spa, The ✦ ...... C2 |
| Alexandra Gardens. A1 | Falconers Rd ..... B2 | ......A2/B1/B2/C1 | Spa Theatre, |
| Atlantis ✦ ...... A1 | Falsgrave Rd ..... C1 | Princess St....... B3 | The ☎ ......... C2 |
| Auborough St..... B2 | Fire Station ...... B2 | Prospect Rd ...... B1 | Stephen Joseph |
| Belle Vue St ..... C1 | Foreshore Rd ..... B2 | Queen St ........ B2 | Theatre ☎ ☎.... B1 |
| Belmont Rd ...... C2 | Friargate ........ B2 | Queen's Parade ... A2 | Tennyson Ave.... B1 |
| Brunswick Shopping | Futurist | Queen's Tower | The Crescent .... C2 |
| Centre .......... B2 | Theatre ☎ ☎.... B2 | (Remains) ..... A3 | Tollergate ....... B2 |
| Castle Dykes ..... B3 | Gladstone Rd ..... B1 | Ramshill Rd ...... C2 | Town Hall ....... B2 |
| Castlegate ....... B3 | Gladstone St ..... B1 | Roman Signal | Trafalgar Rd ..... B1 |
| Castle Holms ..... A3 | Hoxton Rd ....... B1 | Station ≈ ..... A3 | Trafalgar Square.. A1 |
| Castle Hill ....... B3 | Information | Roscoe St........ C1 | Trafalgar St West . B1 |
| Castle Rd ....... B2 | Ctr 🛈 ...... B2/B3 | Rotunda | Valley Bridge |
| Castle Walls ..... A3 | King St ......... B2 | Museum 🏛...... C2 | Parade ........ C1 |
| Cemetery ....... B1 | Londesborough | Royal Albert Dr ... A2 | Valley Rd........ C1 |
| Central Lift ✦.... C2 | Rd............. C1 | St Martin-on- | Vernon Rd....... C2 |
| Clarence Gardens . A2 | Longwestgate..... B3 | the-Hill ♙...... C2 | Victoria Park |
| Coach Park....... A2 | Marine Dr ....... A3 | St Martin's Ave ... C2 | Mount ......... A1 |
| Columbus Ravine.. A1 | Miniature | St Mary's ♙..... B3 | Victoria Rd...... B1 |
| Court............ B1 | Railway 🚂..... A1 | St Nicholas' | West Pier ....... B3 |
| Cricket Ground.... A1 | Nelson St ....... B1 | Lift ✦......... B2 | Westborough ..... B1 |
| Cross St ........ B2 | Newborough...... B2 | St Thomas St ..... B2 | Westover Rd...... C1 |
| Crown Terr ...... C2 | Nicolas St ....... B2 | Sandside ........ B3 | Westwood........ C1 |
| Dean Rd ........ B1 | North Marine Rd... A1 | Scarborough Art | Woodall Ave ..... A1 |
| Devonshire Dr .... A1 | North St ........ B2 | Gallery 🏛...... C2 | Wood End |
| | Northway ....... B1 | Scarborough | Museum 🏛..... C2 |
| | Old Harbour ..... B3 | Castle 🏰...... A3 | York Pl ......... B2 |

## Shrewsbury

| | | | |
|---|---|---|---|
| Abbey Church ♙.. B3 | Cineworld ☎..... C3 | King St ......... B3 | St.Alkmund's ♙... B2 |
| Abbey Foregate ... B3 | Claremont Bank ... B1 | Kingsland Bridge .. C1 | St Chad's ♙..... B1 |
| Abbey Lawn | Claremont Hill.... B1 | Kingsland Bridge | St Chad's Terr.... B1 |
| Business Park.... B3 | Cleveland St...... B3 | (toll)..........C1 | St John's Hill ... B1 |
| Abbots House 🏛.. B2 | Coleham Head ... B2 | Kingsland Rd ..... C1 | St Julians Friars .. C2 |
| Agricultural Show | Coleham Pumping | Lime St ......... B2 | St Mary's ♙..... B2 |
| Ground ........ A1 | Station 🏛...... C2 | Longden Coleham . C2 | St Mary's St ..... B2 |
| Albert St ........ B1 | College Hill ...... B1 | Longden Rd ...... C1 | Scott St ......... C3 |
| Alma St ........ B1 | Corporation La .... A1 | Longner St ...... B1 | Severn Bank ..... A2 |
| Ashley St ........ A3 | Coton Cres....... A1 | Luciefelde Rd ..... C1 | Severn St ....... A2 |
| Ashton Rd ....... C1 | Coton Hill ....... A2 | Mardol ......... B1 | Shrewsbury ≈.... B2 |
| Avondale Dr ..... A3 | Coton Mount ..... A1 | Market ......... B1 | Shrewsbury High |
| Bage Way....... C3 | Crescent La ...... C1 | Monkmoor Rd .... B3 | School for Girls.. C1 |
| Barker St ....... B2 | Crewe St........ A2 | Moreton Cr....... C2 | Shrewsbury |
| Beacall's La ..... A2 | Cross Hill ....... B1 | Mount St........ A1 | School ✦...... C1 |
| Beeches La ...... C2 | Darwin Centre ... B2 | Music Hall ☎ .... B1 | Shrewsbury |
| Belle Vue Gdns ... C2 | Dingle, The ✿ .... B1 | New Park Cl ..... A3 | Town FC ....... B2 |
| Belle Vue Rd..... C2 | Dogpole ........ B2 | New Park Rd ..... A2 | Shropshire Wildlife |
| Belmont Bank..... C1 | Draper's Hall 🏛 .. B2 | New Park St ..... A3 | Trust ✦....... B3 |
| Berwick Ave ..... A1 | English Bridge .... B2 | North St ........ A2 | Smithfield Rd .... B1 |
| Berwick Rd...... A1 | Fish St ......... B2 | Oakley St ....... C1 | South Hermitage .. C1 |
| Betton St ....... C2 | Frankwell ....... B1 | Old Coleham ..... C2 | Swan Hill ....... B2 |
| Bishop St ....... B1 | Gateway Centre, | Old Market Hall ☎ . B1 | Sydney Ave ...... A3 |
| Bradford St ...... B3 | The .......... A2 | Old Potts Way .... C3 | Tankerville St .... B3 |
| Bridge St ....... B1 | Gravel Hill La .... A1 | Parade Centre ... B2 | The Castle Business |
| Bus Station ...... B2 | Greyfriars Rd ..... C2 | Police Station ⊠.. B1 | Park .......... A2 |
| Butcher Row ..... B2 | Guildhall 🏛..... B1 | Post Office ⊠ .... | The Dana ....... B2 |
| Burton St ....... A3 | Hampton Rd...... A3 | .....A2/B1/B2/B3 | The Quarry ...... B1 |
| Butler Rd ....... C1 | Haycock Way..... C3 | Pride Hill........ B1 | The Square ...... B1 |
| Bynner St ....... C2 | HM Prison ....... B2 | Pride Hill Centre... B1 | Tilbrook Dr ...... A3 |
| Canon St ....... B3 | Hereford Rd ...... C3 | Priory Rd ....... B1 | Town Walls ...... C1 |
| Canonbury ...... C1 | High St ......... B1 | Queen St ........ A3 | Trinity St ........ C2 |
| Castle Foregate ... A2 | Hills La ......... B1 | Raby Cr ........ C2 | Underdale Rd .... B3 |
| Castle Gates...... B2 | Holywell St ...... B3 | Rad Brook ....... C1 | Victoria Ave ..... B1 |
| Castle Museum 🏛.. B2 | Hunter St ....... A1 | Rea Brook ....... C3 | Victoria Quay ..... B1 |
| Castle St........ B2 | Information Ctr 🛈.. B1 | Riverside......... B1 | Victoria St....... B1 |
| Cathedral (RC) ✝.. C1 | Ireland's Mansion | Roundhill La ..... A1 | Welsh Bridge .... B1 |
| Chester St ...... A2 | & Bear Steps 🏛.. B1 | Rowley's | Whitehall St ..... B3 |
| | John St ......... A3 | House 🏛 ...... B1 | Wood St ........ A2 |
| | Kennedy Rd ..... C1 | | Wyle Cop ....... B2 |

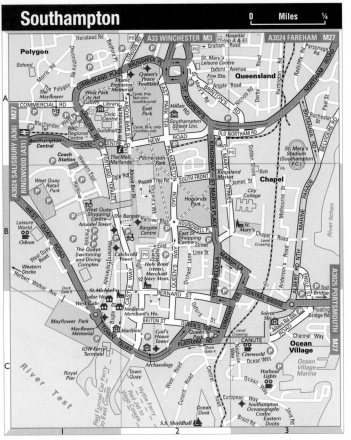

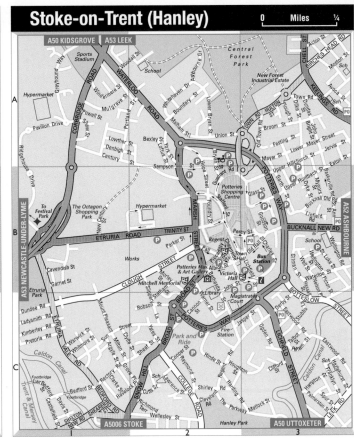

## Southampton

Above Bar St . . . . . A2
Albert Rd North . . B3
Albert Rd South . . . C3
Anderson's Rd . . . B3
Archaeology
  Museum 🏛 . . . . . C2
Argyle Rd . . . . . . A2
Arundel Tower ✦ . . B1
Bargate, The ✦ . . B2
Bargate Centre . . . B2
BBC Regional
  Centre . . . . . . . . . A1
Bedford Pl . . . . . . A1
Belvidere Rd . . . . A3
Bernard St . . . . . C2
Blechynden Terr . . A1
Brazil Rd . . . . . . . C3
Brinton's Rd . . . . . A2
Britannia Rd . . . . A3
Briton St . . . . . . . C2
Brunswick Pl . . . . A2
Bugle St . . . . . . . C1
Canute Rd . . . . . . C3
Castle Way . . . . . C2
Catchcold
  Tower ✦ . . . . . . . B1
Central Bridge . . . . C3
Central Rd . . . . . . C2
Channel Way . . . . C3
Chapel Rd . . . . . . B3
Cineworld 🎬 . . . . C3
City Art Gallery 🏛 . A1
City College . . . . . B3
Civic Centre . . . . . A1
Civic Centre Rd . . . A1
Coach Station . . . . B1
Commercial Rd . . . A1
Cumberland Pl . . . A1
Cunard Rd . . . . . . C2
Derby Rd . . . . . . . A3
Devonshire Rd . . . A1
Dock Gate 4 . . . . . C2

Dock Gate 8 . . . . . B1
East Park . . . . . . . A2
East Park Terr . . . . A2
East St . . . . . . . . B2
East St Shopping
  Centre . . . . . . . . B2
Endle St . . . . . . . B3
European Way . . . . C2
Fire Station . . . . . C2
Floating
  Bridge Rd . . . . . . C3
God's House
  Tower ✦ . . . . . . . C2
Golden Gr . . . . . . A3
Graham Rd . . . . . . A2
Guildhall . . . . . . . A1
Hanover Bldgs . . . . B2
Harbour Lights 🎬 . . B1
Harbour Pde . . . . . B1
Hartington Rd . . . . A3
Havelock Rd . . . . . A1
Henstead Rd . . . . A1
Herbert Walker
  Ave . . . . . . . . . . B1
High St . . . . . . . . B2
Hoglands Park . . . . B2
Holy Rood (Rems),
  Merchant Navy
  Memorial 🏛 . . . . B2
Hospital 🏥 . . . . . A1
Houndwell Pl . . . . B2
Hythe Ferry . . . . . C2
Information Ctr 🅿 . . A1
Isle of Wight
  Ferry Terminal . . . . C1
James St . . . . . . . B3
Java Rd . . . . . . . . C3
Kingsland Market . . B2
Kingsway . . . . . . B1
Leisure World . . . . B1
Library . . . . . . . . A1
Lime St . . . . . . . . B2
London Rd . . . . . . A2
Marine Pde . . . . . B3

Maritime 🏛 . . . . . C1
Marsh La . . . . . . . B2
Mayflower
  Memorial ✦ . . . . . C1
Mayflower Park . . . C1
Mayflower Theatre,
  The 🎭 . . . . . . . . A1
Medieval Merchant's
  House 🏛 . . . . . . C1
Melbourne St . . . . B3
Millais 🏛 . . . . . . A2
Morris Rd . . . . . . A3
Neptune Way . . . . C3
New Rd . . . . . . . . A2
Nichols Rd . . . . . . A3
Northam Rd . . . . . A3
Ocean Dock . . . . . C2
Ocean Village
  Marina . . . . . . . . C3
Ocean Way . . . . . C3
Odeon 🎬 . . . . . . B1
Ogle Rd . . . . . . . B1
Old Northam Rd . . . A2
Orchard La . . . . . . C2
Oxford Ave . . . . . A2
Oxford St . . . . . . C2
Palmerston Park . . . A2
Palmerston Rd . . . . A2
Parsonage Rd . . . . A3
Peel St . . . . . . . . A3
Platform Rd . . . . . C2
Police Station 🚓 . . A1
Portland Terr . . . . . B1
Post Office 🏤
  . . . . . . . . A2/A3/B2
Pound Tree Rd . . . . B2
Quays Swimming
  & Diving
  Complex, The . . . . B1
Queen's Park . . . . C2
Queen's Peace
  Fountain ✦ . . . . . A2
Queen's Terr . . . . . C2
Queen's Way . . . . B2

Radcliffe Rd . . . . . A3
Rochester St . . . . A3
Royal Pier . . . . . . C1
St Andrew's Rd . . . A2
St Mary St . . . . . . A2
St Mary's 🏛 . . . . . B3
St Mary's Leisure
  Centre . . . . . . . . A2
St Mary's Pl . . . . . B2
St Mary's Rd . . . . . A2
St Mary's Stadium
  (Southampton F.C.) A3
St Michael's ✦ . . . . C1
Solent Sky 🏛 . . . . C3
South Front . . . . . B2
Southampton Central
  Station 🚉 . . . . . A1
Southampton Solent
  University . . . . . . A2
Southhampton
  Oceanography
  Centre ✦ . . . . . . C3
SS Shieldhall ⚓ . . . C2
Terminus Terr . . . . C2
The Mall, Marlands . A1
The Polygon . . . . . A1
Threefield La . . . . . B2
Titanic Engineers'
  Memorial ✦ . . . . A2
Town Quay . . . . . C1
Town Walls . . . . . C1
Tudor House 🏛 . . . C1
Vincent's Walk . . . B2
West Gate . . . . . . B1
West Marlands Rd . A1
West Park . . . . . . A1
West Park Rd . . . . A1
West Quay Rd . . . . B1
West Quay
  Retail Park . . . . . B1
West Quay
  Shopping Centre . B1
West Rd . . . . . . . C2
Western Esplanade B1

## Stoke-on-Trent (Hanley)

Acton St . . . . . . . A3
Albion St . . . . . . B2
Argyle St . . . . . . . C1
Ashbourne Gr . . . . A2
Avoca St . . . . . . . A3
Baskerville Rd . . . . B3
Bedford Rd . . . . . C1
Bedford St . . . . . . C1
Bethesda St . . . . . B2
Bexley St . . . . . . A2
Birches Head Rd . . A3
Botteslow St . . . . C3
Boundary St . . . . . A3
Broad St . . . . . . . C2
Broom St . . . . . . A3
Bryan St . . . . . . . A2
Bucknall New Rd . . B3
Bucknall Old Rd . . . B3
Bus Station . . . . . B3
Cannon St . . . . . . C1
Castlefield St . . . . C1
Hanley Park . . . . . C2
Cavendish St . . . . B1
Central Forest
  Park . . . . . . . . . A2
Charles St . . . . . . B3
Cheapside . . . . . . B2
Chell St . . . . . . . A3
Clarke St . . . . . . . C1
Cleveland Rd . . . . C2
Clifford St . . . . . . C3
Clough St . . . . . . B2
Clyde St . . . . . . . C1
College Rd . . . . . . C2
Cooper St . . . . . . C2
Corbridge Rd . . . . A1
Cutts St . . . . . . . C2
Davis St . . . . . . . C1
Denbigh St . . . . . A1
Derby St . . . . . . . C3
Dilke St . . . . . . . A3
Dundas St . . . . . . A3
Dundee Rd . . . . . C1

Dyke St . . . . . . . B3
Eastwood Rd . . . . C3
Eaton St . . . . . . . A3
Etruria Park . . . . . B1
Etruria Rd . . . . . . B1
Etruria Vale Rd . . . C1
Festing St . . . . . . A3
Fire Station . . . . . C2
Foundry St . . . . . A3
Franklyn St . . . . . C3
Garnet St . . . . . . B1
Garth St . . . . . . . B2
George St . . . . . . A3
Gilman St . . . . . . B3
Glass St . . . . . . . B2
Goodson St . . . . . B3
Greyhound Way . . . A1
Grove Pl . . . . . . . C1
Hampton St . . . . . B3
Hanley Park . . . . . C2
Harding Rd . . . . . C2
Hassall St . . . . . . B3
Havelock Pl . . . . . C1
Hazlehurst St . . . . C3
Hinde St . . . . . . . C2
Hope St . . . . . . . B2
Houghton St . . . . C3
Hulton St . . . . . . A3
Hypermarket . . . . A1/B2
Information Ctr 🅿 . B3
Jasper St . . . . . . . A3
Jervis St . . . . . . . A3
John Bright St . . . . A3
John St . . . . . . . . B3
Keelings Rd . . . . . A3
Kimberley Rd . . . . C1
Ladysmith Rd . . . . C1
Lawrence St . . . . . C2
Leek Rd . . . . . . . C2
Library . . . . . . . . C2
Lichfield St . . . . . C3
Linfield Rd . . . . . . A3
Loftus St . . . . . . . A2
Lower Bedford St . . C1
Lower Bryan St . . . A2
Lower Mayer St . . . A3
Lowther St . . . . . A1

Magistrates Court . . C2
Malham St . . . . . . A2
Marsh St . . . . . . . B2
Matlock St . . . . . . C3
Mayer St . . . . . . A3
Milton St . . . . . . C1
Mitchell Memorial
  Theatre 🎭 . . . . . B2
Morley St . . . . . . C2
Moston St . . . . . . A3
Mount Pleasant . . . C1
Mulgrave St . . . . . A1
Mynors St . . . . . . B3
Nelson Pl . . . . . . B3
New Century St . . . B3
New Forest Industrial
  Estate . . . . . . . . . A3
Octagon Shopping
  Park, The . . . . . . B1
Ogden Rd . . . . . . C3
Old Hall St . . . . . . B3
Old Town Rd . . . . A3
Pall Mall . . . . . . . B2
Palmerston St . . . . C3
Park and Ride . . . . C3
Parker St . . . . . . B2
Pavilion Dr . . . . . . A1
Pelham St . . . . . . C3
Percy St . . . . . . . B2
Piccadilly . . . . . . B2
Picton St . . . . . . . C1
Plough St . . . . . . C2
Police Station 🚓 . . C2
Portland St . . . . . A1
Post Office 🏤
  . . . . . . . . A3/B3/C3
Potteries Museum
  & Art Gallery 🏛 . . B2
Potteries Shopping
  Centre . . . . . . . . B2
Potteries Way . . . . C2
Powell St . . . . . . A1
Pretoria Rd . . . . . C1
Quadrant Rd . . . . B2
Ranelagh St . . . . . C2
Raymond St . . . . . C2
Rectory Rd . . . . . C1

Regent Rd . . . . . . C2
Regent Theatre 🎭 . B2
Richmond Terr . . . C2
Ridgehouse Dr . . . . A1
Robson St . . . . . . C2
St Ann St . . . . . . B3
St Luke St . . . . . . B3
Sampson St . . . . . B2
Shaw St . . . . . . . A1
Sheaf St . . . . . . . C2
Shearer St . . . . . . C1
Shelton New Rd . . . C1
Shirley Rd . . . . . . C2
Slippery La . . . . . B2
Snow Hill . . . . . . C2
Sports Stadium . . . A1
Spur St . . . . . . . . C3
Stafford St . . . . . . B2
Statham St . . . . . B2
Stubbs La . . . . . . C3
Sun St . . . . . . . . C1
Talbot St . . . . . . C3
The Parkway . . . . . C2
Town Hall . . . . . . B2
Town Rd . . . . . . . A3
Trinity St . . . . . . . B2
Union St . . . . . . . A2
Upper
  Hillchurch St . . . . A3
Upper
  Huntbach St . . . . B3
Victoria Hall
  Theatre 🎭 . . . . . B3
Warner St . . . . . . C2
Warwick St . . . . . C1
Waterloo Rd . . . . . A1
Waterloo St . . . . . B3
Well St . . . . . . . . B3
Wellesley St . . . . . C2
Wellington Rd . . . . B3
Wellington St . . . . B3
Whitehaven Dr . . . A2
Whitmore St . . . . C1
Windermere St . . . A1
Woodall St . . . . . A1
Yates St . . . . . . . C2
York St . . . . . . . . A2

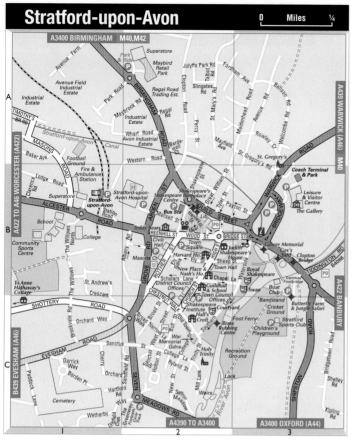

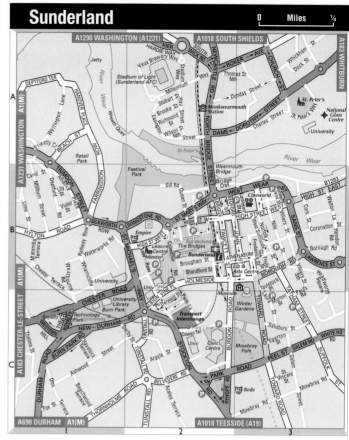

## Stratford-upon-Avon

Albany Rd . . . . . . . B1
Alcester Rd . . . . . . B1
Ambulance Sta . . . . B1
Arden St . . . . . . . . B2
Avenue Farm . . . . . A1
Avenue Field
Industrial Estate . . A1
Avenue Rd . . . . . . A3
Avon Industrial
Estate . . . . . . . . A2
Baker Ave . . . . . . . A1
Bandstand . . . . . . C2
Benson Rd . . . . . . A3
Birmingham Rd . . . B1
Boat Club . . . . . . B3
Borden Pl . . . . . . . C1
Brass Rubbing
Centre ◆ . . . . . . C2
Bridge St . . . . . . . B2
Bridgetown Rd . . . . C3
Bridgeway . . . . . . B3
Broad St . . . . . . . . C2
Broad Walk . . . . . . C2
Brookvale Rd . . . . . C1
Bull St . . . . . . . . . C2
Butterfly Farm &
Jungle Safari ◆ . . C3
Bus Station . . . . . . B2
Cemetery . . . . . . . C1
Chapel La . . . . . . . B2
Cherry Orchard . . . C1
Chestnut Walk . . . . B2
Children's
Playground . . . . . C3
Church St . . . . . . . C2
Civic Hall . . . . . . . B2
Clarence Rd . . . . . B1
Clopton Bridge ◆ . . B3
Clopton Rd . . . . . . A2
Coach Terminal
& Park . . . . . . . . B3

College . . . . . . . . B1
College La . . . . . . C2
College St . . . . . . . C2
Community Sports
Centre . . . . . . . . B1
Council Offices
(District) . . . . . . B2
Council Offices
(Town) . . . . . . . . B2
Courtyard ⛫ . . . . . C2
Cox's Yard ◆ . . . . . B3
Cricket Ground . . . . C3
Ely Gdns . . . . . . . B2
Ely St . . . . . . . . . B2
Evesham Rd . . . . . C1
Fire Station . . . . . . B1
Foot Ferry . . . . . . . C3
Football Ground . . . A1
Fordham Ave . . . . . A2
Gallery, The 🏛 . . . . B3
Garrick Way . . . . . C1
Gower
Memorial ◆ . . . . B3
Great William St . . . B2
Greenhill St . . . . . . B2
Grove Rd . . . . . . . B2
Guild St . . . . . . . . B2
Guildhall &
School . . . . . . . . B2
Hall's Croft 🏛 . . . . C2
Hartford Rd . . . . . . C1
Harvard House 🏛 . . B2
Henley St . . . . . . . B2
High St . . . . . . . . B2
Holton St . . . . . . . C2
Holy Trinity ⛪ . . . . C2
Information Ctr ℹ . . B3
Jolyffe Park Rd . . . . A2
Judith Shakespeare's
House . . . . . . . . B2
Kipling Rd . . . . . . . C3
Leisure & Visitor
Centre . . . . . . . . B3
Library . . . . . . . . . B2
Lodge Rd . . . . . . . B1

Maidenhead Rd . . . A3
Mansell St . . . . . . B2
Masons Court . . . . B2
Masons Rd . . . . . . A1
Maybird Retail
Park . . . . . . . . . A2
Maybrook Rd . . . . A1
Mayfield Ave . . . . . A2
Meer St . . . . . . . . B2
Mill La . . . . . . . . . C2
Moat House Hotel . . B3
Narrow La . . . . . . C2
New Place &
Nash's House 🏛 . . B2
New St . . . . . . . . . C2
Old Town . . . . . . . C2
Orchard Way . . . . . C1
Paddock La . . . . . . C1
Park Rd . . . . . . . . A1
Payton St . . . . . . . B2
Percy St . . . . . . . . A2
Police Station 🏢 . . . B2
Post Office 📮 . . . . .
. . . . . . . . . B2/B3/C2
Recreation
Ground . . . . . . . C2
Regal Road . . . . . . A2
Regal Road Trading
Estate . . . . . . . . A2
Rother St . . . . . . . B2
Rowley Cr . . . . . . . A3
Royal Shakespeare
Theatre ⛫ . . . . . B3
Ryland St . . . . . . . C2
Saffron Meadow . . . C2
St Andrew's Cr . . . . B1
St Gregory's ⛪ . . . . A3
St Gregory's Rd . . . A3
St Mary's Rd . . . . . A2
Sanctus Dr . . . . . . C2
Sanctus St . . . . . . C1
Sandfield Rd . . . . . C2
Scholars La . . . . . . B2
Seven
Meadows Rd . . . . C2

Shakespeare
Centre ◆ . . . . . . B2
Shakespeare
Institute . . . . . . . C2
Shakespeare St . . . B2
Shakespeare's
Birthplace ◆ . . . . B2
Sheep St . . . . . . . B2
Shelley Rd . . . . . . C3
Shipston Rd . . . . . . C3
Shottery Rd . . . . . . C1
Slingates Rd . . . . . A2
Southern La . . . . . C2
Station Rd . . . . . . . B1
Stratford Sports
Club . . . . . . . . . B1
Stratford-upon-Avon
Hospital 🏥 . . . . . B1
Stratford-upon-Avon
Station �排 . . . . . B1
Swan Theatre ⛫ . . . B3
Talbot Rd . . . . . . . A2
Teddy Bears
Museum 🏛 . . . . . B2
The Greenway . . . . C2
The Willows . . . . . B1
The Willows North . B1
Tiddington Rd . . . . B3
Timothy's
Bridge Rd . . . . . . A1
Town Hall . . . . . . . B2
Town Sq . . . . . . . . B2
Tramway Bridge . . . B3
Trinity St . . . . . . . . B2
Tyler St . . . . . . . . B2
War Memorial
Gdns . . . . . . . . . B3
Warwick Rd . . . . . . B3
Waterside . . . . . . . B2
Welcombe Rd . . . . A3
West St . . . . . . . . C2
Western Rd . . . . . . A2
Wharf Rd . . . . . . . A2
Wood St . . . . . . . . B2

## Sunderland

Albion Pl . . . . . . . C2
Alliance Pl . . . . . . B1
Argyle St . . . . . . . C2
Ashwood St . . . . . C1
Athenaeum St . . . . B2
Azalea Terr . . . . . . C2
Beach St . . . . . . . A1
Bede Theatre ⛫ . . . C3
Bedford St . . . . . . B2
Beechwood Terr . . . C1
Belvedere Rd . . . . . B3
Blandford St . . . . . B2
Borough Rd . . . . . . B3
Bridge Cr . . . . . . . B2
Bridge St . . . . . . . B2
Brooke St . . . . . . . A2
Brougham St . . . . . B2
Burdon Rd . . . . . . C2
Burn Park . . . . . . . C1
Burn Park Rd . . . . . C1
Carol St . . . . . . . . B1
Charles St . . . . . . . A3
Chester Rd . . . . . . C1
Chester Terr . . . . . B1
Church St . . . . . . . A3
Cineworld 🎬 . . . . . B2
Civic Centre . . . . . C2
Cork St . . . . . . . . B3
Coronation St . . . . B2
Cowan Terr . . . . . . C2
Crowtree Rd . . . . . B2
Dame Dorothy St . . A2
Deptford Rd . . . . . B1
Deptford Terr . . . . . A1
Derby St . . . . . . . . C2
Derwent St . . . . . . C2
Dock St . . . . . . . . A3
Dundas St . . . . . . A2
Durham Rd . . . . . . C1
Easington St . . . . . A2
Egerton St . . . . . . C3

Empire Theatre ⛫ . . B2
Farringdon Row . . . B1
Fawcett St . . . . . . . B2
Festival Park . . . . . B2
Fox St . . . . . . . . . C1
Foyle St . . . . . . . . B3
Frederick St . . . . . B3
Gill Rd . . . . . . . . . B2
Hanover Pl . . . . . . A1
Havelock Terr . . . . . C1
Hay St . . . . . . . . . A2
Headworth Sq . . . . B3
Hendon Rd . . . . . . B3
High St East . . . . . B3
High St West . . . B2/B3
Holmeside . . . . . . B2
Hylton Rd . . . . . . . B1
Information Ctr ℹ . . B2
John St . . . . . . . . . B3
Kier Hardie Way . . . A2
Lambton St . . . . . . B3
Laura St . . . . . . . . C3
Lawrence St . . . . . B3
Leisure Centre . . . . B2
Library & Arts
Centre . . . . . . . . B3
Lily St . . . . . . . . . B1
Lime St . . . . . . . . B1
Livingstone Rd . . . . B2
Low Row . . . . . . . B2
Matamba Terr . . . . B1
Millburn St . . . . . . B1
Millennium Way . . . A2
Minster ⛪ . . . . . . . B2
Monkwearmouth
Station
Museum 🏛 . . . . . A2
Mowbray Park . . . . C3
Mowbray Rd . . . . . C3
Murton St . . . . . . . C3
Museum 🏛 . . . . . . B3
National Glass
Centre ◆ . . . . . . A3

New Durham Rd . . . C1
Newcastle Rd . . . . . A2
Nile St . . . . . . . . . B3
Norfolk St . . . . . . . B3
North Bridge St . . . A2
Otto Terr . . . . . . . . C1
Park La . . . . . . . . . C2
Park Lane
(metro station) . . . C2
Park Rd . . . . . . . . C2
Paul's Rd . . . . . . . B3
Peel St . . . . . . . . . C2
Police Station 🏢 . . . B2
Post Office 📮 . . . . . B2
Priestly Cr . . . . . . . A1
Queen St . . . . . . . B2
Railway Row . . . . . B1
Retail Park . . . . . . A1
Richmond St . . . . . A2
Roker Ave . . . . . . . A2
Royalty
Theatre ⛫ . . . . . C1
Ryhope Rd . . . . . . C2
St Mary's Way . . . . B2
St Michael's
Way . . . . . . . . . B2
St Peter's ⛪ . . . . . A3
St Peter's
(metro station) . . . A2
St Peter's Way . . . . A3
St Vincent St . . . . . C3
Salem Rd . . . . . . . C3
Salem St . . . . . . . . C3
Salisbury St . . . . . . C3
Sans St . . . . . . . . . B3
Silkworth Row . . . . B1
Southwick Rd . . . . . A2
Stadium of Light
(Sunderland AFC) . A2
Stadium Way . . . . . A2
Stobart St . . . . . . . A2
Stockton Rd . . . . . C2
Suffolk St . . . . . . . C3

Sunderland
(metro station) . . . B2
Sunderland
Station ≏ . . . . . B2
Sunderland St . . . . B3
Tatham St . . . . . . . C3
Tavistock Pl . . . . . . A3
Technology Park . . . C1
The Bridges . . . . . B2
The Royalty . . . . . . C1
Thelma St . . . . . . . C1
Thomas St North . . A2
Thornholme Rd . . . C1
Toward Rd . . . . . . C3
Transport
Interchange . . . . . C2
Trimdon St Way . . . B1
Tunstall Rd . . . . . . C2
University . . A3/B1/C2
University
(metro station) . . . A2
University . . A3/B1/C2
University Library . . C1
Vaux Brewery Way . A2
Villiers St . . . . . . . B3
Villiers St South . . . B3
Vine Pl . . . . . . . . . C2
Violet St . . . . . . . . B3
Walton La . . . . . . . B3
Waterworks Rd . . . . B1
Wearmouth
Bridge . . . . . . . . B2
Wellington La . . . . . A1
West Sunniside . . . . B3
West Wear St . . . . . B3
Westbourne Rd . . . A1
Western Hill . . . . . . C1
Wharncliffe . . . . . . B1
Whickham St . . . . . A3
White House Rd . . . C1
Wilson St North . . . A2
Winter Gdns . . . . . C3
Wreath Quay . . . . . A1

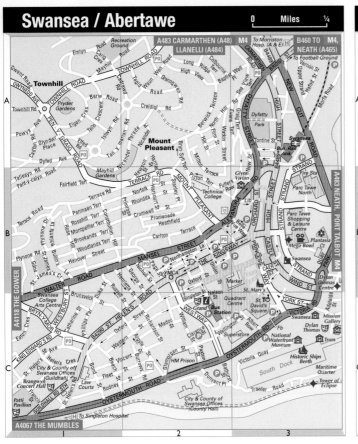

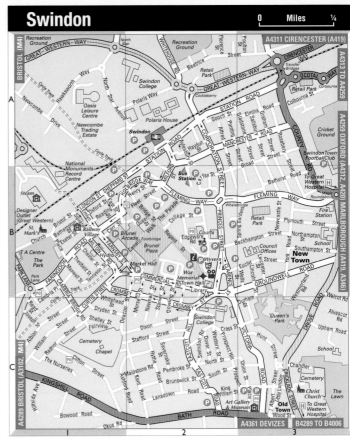

## Swansea/ Abertawe

Adelaide St . . . . . . . C3
Albert Row . . . . . . . A2
Alexandra Rd . . . . . B3
Argyle St . . . . . . . . C1
Baptist Well Pl . . . . A2
Beach St . . . . . . . . C1
Belle Vue Way . . . B3
Berw Rd . . . . . . . . A1
Berwick Terr . . . . . A2
Bond St . . . . . . . . . C1
Brangwyn Concert
  Hall . . . . . . . . . . . B3
Bridge St . . . . . . . . A3
Brookands Terr. . . . B1
Brunswick St . . . . . C1
Bryn-Syfi Terr . . . . . A2
Bryn-y-Mor Rd . . . . C1
Bullins La . . . . . . . . B1
Burrows Rd . . . . . . C1
Bus Station. . . . . . . C2
Cadfan Rd . . . . . . . A1
Cadrawd Rd . . . . . . A1
Caer St . . . . . . . . . B3
Carig Cr . . . . . . . . . A1
Carlton Terr. . . . . . . B2
Carmarthen Rd. . . . A3
Castle St. . . . . . . . . B3
Catherine St . . . . . . C1
City & County of
  Swansea Offices
  (County Hall). . . . . C2
City & County of
  Swansea Offices
  (Guildhall) . . . . . . C1
Clarence St . . . . . . C2
Colbourne Terr . . . . A2
Constitution Hill . . . B1
Court. . . . . . . . . . . . B3
Creidiol Rd . . . . . . . A2
Cromwell St . . . . . . B2
Duke St. . . . . . . . . . B1
Dunvant Pl . . . . . . . C2
Dyfatty Park . . . . . . A3
Dyfatty St . . . . . . . . A3
Dyfed Ave . . . . . . . A1
Dylan Thomas
  Ctr ✦ . . . . . . . . . . B3

Dylan Thomas
  Theatre 🎭 . . . . . . . C3
Eaton Cr. . . . . . . . . C1
Eigen Cr . . . . . . . . . A1
Elfed Rd . . . . . . . . . A1
Emlyn Rd . . . . . . . . A1
Evans Terr. . . . . . . . A3
Fairfield Terr . . . . . . B1
Ffynone Dr . . . . . . . B1
Ffynone Rd . . . . . . . B1
Fire Station . . . . . . . B3
Firm St . . . . . . . . . . C1
Fleet St . . . . . . . . . . C1
Francis St . . . . . . . . C1
Fullers Row. . . . . . . A2
George St . . . . . . . . B2
Glamorgan St. . . . . C2
Glyndwr Pl . . . . . . . A1
Glynn Vivian 🏛. . . . B3
Graig Terr . . . . . . . . A3
Grand Theatre 🎭 . . B2
Granogwen Rd . . . . A2
Guildhall Rd
  South . . . . . . . . . . C1
Gwent Rd . . . . . . . . A1
Gwynedd Ave . . . . . A1
Hafod St . . . . . . . . . A3
Hanover St . . . . . . . B1
Harcourt St . . . . . . . B2
Harries St . . . . . . . . A2
Heathfield . . . . . . . . B2
Henrietta St . . . . . . B1
Hewson St . . . . . . . B2
High St . . . . . . . A3/B3
High View . . . . . . . . A2
Hill St . . . . . . . . . . . A2
Historic Ships
  Berth ⚓ . . . . . . . . C3
HM Prison . . . . . . . C2
Information Ctr ℹ . . . C2
Islwyn Rd . . . . . . . . A1
King Edward's Rd. . . C1
Law Courts . . . . . . . C2
Library . . . . . . . . . . B3
Long Ridge. . . . . . . A2
Madoc St . . . . . . . . B2
Mansel St . . . . . . . . B2
Maritime Quarter . . C3
Market . . . . . . . . . . B3
Mayhill Gdns . . . . . B1
Mayhill Rd. . . . . . . . A1

Mega Bowl ✦ 🎳 . . B3
Milton Terr . . . . . . . A2
Mission Gallery 🏛 . C1
Montpellier Terr . . . B1
Morfa Rd . . . . . . . . A3
Mount Pleasant . . . B2
National Waterfront
  Museum 🏛 . . . . . . C3
Nelson St . . . . . . . . C2
New Cut Rd . . . . . . A3
New St . . . . . . . . . . A3
Nicander Pde . . . . . A2
Nicander Pl. . . . . . . A2
Nicholl St . . . . . . . . B2
Norfolk St . . . . . . . . B1
North Hill Rd. . . . . . A2
Northampton La. . . . B2
Orchard St . . . . . . . B3
Oxford St . . . . . . . . B2
Oystermouth Rd. . . . C1
Page St . . . . . . . . . . B2
Pant-y-Celyn Rd. . . . B1
Parc Tawe North. . . B3
Parc Tawe Shopping
  & Leisure Centre. . B3
Patti Pavilion 🎭 . . . C1
Paxton St . . . . . . . . C2
Penmaen Terr . . . . . B1
Pen-y-Graig Rd . . . . A1
Phillips Pde. . . . . . . C1
Picton Terr . . . . . . . B1
Plantasia 🌿 . . . . . . B3
Police Station 🛡 . . . B2
Post Office 🏤. . A1/A2/
  . . . A3/B2/C1/C2/C3
Powys Ave . . . . . . . A1
Primrose St. . . . . . . B2
Princess Way . . . . . B3
Promenade . . . . . . . B2
Pryder Gdns . . . . . . A1
Quadrant Centre. . . C2
Quay Park. . . . . . . . B3
Rhianfa La . . . . . . . C1
Rhondda St . . . . . . B2
Richardson St. . . . . C2
Rodney St. . . . . . . . C2
Rose Hill . . . . . . . . . B1
Rosehill Terr . . . . . . B1
Russell St . . . . . . . . C1
St David's Sq . . . . . C3
St Helen's Ave . . . . C1

St Helen's Cr . . . . . C1
St Helen's Rd . . . . . C1
St James Gdns . . . . B1
St James's Cr . . . . . B1
St Mary's ♦ . . . . . . B3
Sea View Terr . . . . . A3
Singleton St . . . . . . C2
South Dock . . . . . . . C3
Stanley Pl . . . . . . . . B2
Strand. . . . . . . . . . . B3
Swansea
  Castle 🏰 . . . . . . . B3
Swansea College
  Arts Centre . . . . . . C1
Swansea
  Museum 🏛. . . . . . C3
Swansea
  Station 🚃 . . . . . . A3
Taliesyn Rd . . . . . . . B1
Tan y Marian Rd . . . A1
Technical College . . B2
Tegid Rd . . . . . . . . . A2
Teilo Cr . . . . . . . . . . A1
Terrace Rd . . . . . B1/B2
The Kingsway . . . . . B2
Tontine St . . . . . . . . A3
Tower of
  Eclipse ✦ . . . . . . . C3
Townhill Rd. . . . . . . A1
Tram Museum 🏛 . . . C3
Trawler Rd . . . . . . . C3
Union St . . . . . . . . . B2
Upper Strand . . . . . A3
Vernon St . . . . . . . . A3
Victoria Quay . . . . . C3
Victoria Rd. . . . . . . . B3
Vincent St . . . . . . . . C1
Walter Rd . . . . . . . . B1
Watkin St . . . . . . . . A2
Waun-Wen Rd . . . . . A2
Wellington St . . . . . C2
Westbury St . . . . . . C1
Western St . . . . . . . C1
Westway. . . . . . . . . C2
William St . . . . . . . . C1
Wind St . . . . . . . . . . B3
Woodlands Terr . . . . B1
YMCA. . . . . . . . . . . B2
York St . . . . . . . . . . C3

## Swindon

Albert St . . . . . . . . C3
Albion St. . . . . . . . . C1
Alfred St . . . . . . . . . A2
Alvescot Rd . . . . . . C3
Art Gallery &
  Museum 🏛 . . . . . C3
Ashford Rd . . . . . . . C1
Aylesbury St . . . . . . A2
Bath Rd . . . . . . . . . C2
Bathampton St . . . . B1
Bathurst Rd . . . . . . B3
Beatrice St . . . . . . . A2
Beckhampton St . . B3
Bowood Rd . . . . . . C1
Bristol St . . . . . . . . B1
Broad St . . . . . . . . . A3
Brunel Arcade. . . . . B2
Brunel Plaza . . . . . . B2
Brunswick St . . . . . C2
Bus Station. . . . . . . B2
Cambria
  Bridge Rd . . . . . . . B1
Cambria Place . . . . B1
Canal Walk . . . . . . . B2
Carfax St . . . . . . . . B2
Carr St . . . . . . . . . . B1
Cemetery . . . . . C1/C3
Chandler Cl . . . . . . C1
Chapel . . . . . . . . . . C1
Chester St . . . . . . . B1
Christ Church ♦. . . . C3
Church Place . . . . . B1
Cirencester Way. . . A3
Clarence St. . . . . . . B1
Clifton St . . . . . . . . C1
Cockleberry Rdbt. . A2
Colbourne Rdbt . . . A3
Colbourne St . . . . . A3
College St. . . . . . . . B2
Commercial Rd . . . . B2
Corporation St . . . . A2
Council Offices. . . . B3
County Rd . . . . . . . C2
Courts. . . . . . . . . . . B2
Cricket Ground. . . . C3
Cricklade Street . . . C3
Crombey St . . . . B1/C2

Cross St . . . . . . . . C2
Curtis St. . . . . . . . . B1
Deacon St. . . . . . . . C1
Designer Outlet
  (Great Western). . . B1
Dixon St . . . . . . . . . C2
Dover St . . . . . . . . . C2
Dowling St . . . . . . . C2
Drove Rd . . . . . . . . C3
Dryden St . . . . . . . . C1
Durham St . . . . . . . C2
East St . . . . . . . . . . B1
Eastcott Hill . . . . . . C2
Eastcott Rd . . . . . . C2
Edgeware Rd . . . . . B2
Elmina Rd . . . . . . . A3
Emlyn Square. . . . . B1
Euclid St . . . . . . . . B2
Exeter St. . . . . . . . . B1
Fairview . . . . . . . . . C1
Faringdon Rd . . . . . B1
Farnsby St . . . . . . . B1
Fire Station . . . . . . . B2
Fleet St . . . . . . . . . . B2
Fleming Way . . . B2/B3
Florence St . . . . . . A2
Gladstone St . . . . . A3
Gooch St . . . . . . . . A2
Graham St . . . . . . . A3
Great Western
  Way. . . . . . . . . A1/A2
Groundwell Rd . . . . B3
Hawksworth Way . . A1
Haydon St . . . . . . . A2
Henry St. . . . . . . . . B2
Hillside Ave. . . . . . . C1
Holbrook Way. . . . . B2
Hunt St . . . . . . . . . . C2
Hydro . . . . . . . . . . . B1
Hythe Rd . . . . . . . . C2
Information Ctr ℹ . . B2
Joseph St. . . . . . . . C1
Kent Rd . . . . . . . . . C2
King William St. . . . C2
Kingshill Rd . . . . . . C1
Lansdown Rd . . . . . C2
Leicester St . . . . . . B3
Library . . . . . . . . . . B3
Lincoln St . . . . . . . . B3

Little London . . . . . C3
London St. . . . . . . . B1
Magic Rdbt. . . . . . . B3
Maidstone Rd . . . . . C2
Manchester Rd . . . . A3
Market Hall . . . . . . . B2
Maxwell St . . . . . . . B1
Milford St . . . . . . . . C2
Milton Rd . . . . . . . . B1
Morse St . . . . . . . . C2
National Monuments
  Record Centre . . . B1
Newcastle St . . . . . B3
Newcombe Drive . . A1
Newcombe Trading
  Estate . . . . . . . . . A1
Newhall St . . . . . . . C2
North St . . . . . . . . . C2
North Star Ave . . . . A1
North Star Rdbt . . . A2
Northampton St . . . B3
Oasis Leisure
  Centre. . . . . . . . . . A1
Ocotal Way . . . . . . A3
Okus Rd . . . . . . . . . C1
Old Town . . . . . . . . C3
Oxford St . . . . . . . . B1
Park Lane . . . . . . . . B1
Park Lane Rdbt . . . B1
Pembroke St . . . . . C2
Plymouth St . . . . . . B3
Polaris House . . . . . A2
Polaris Way. . . . . . . A2
Police Station 🛡 . . B2
Ponting St . . . . . . . A2
Post Office 🏤
  . . . B1/B2/C1/C3
Poulton St . . . . . . . A3
Princes St. . . . . . . . B2
Prospect Hill . . . . . C2
Prospect Place . . . . C2
Queen St . . . . . . . . B2
Queen's Park . . . . . C3
Radnor St . . . . . . . . C1
Railway Village 🏛 . . B1
Read St . . . . . . . . . C1
Reading St . . . . . . . B1
Regent St . . . . . . . . B2
Retail Park . A2/A3/B3

Rosebery St . . . . . . A3
St Mark's ♦ . . . . . . B1
Salisbury St . . . . . . A3
Savernake St . . . . . C2
Shelley St . . . . . . . . C1
Sheppard St . . . . . . B1
South St . . . . . . . . . C2
Southampton St . . . B3
Spring Gardens . . . B3
Stafford Street . . . . C2
Stanier St . . . . . . . . C2
Station Road . . . . . . A2
Steam 🏛 . . . . . . . . B1
Swindon
  College . . . . . . A2/C2
Swindon Rd . . . . . . C2
Swindon
  Station 🚃 . . . . . . A2
Swindon Town
  Football Club . . . . A3
T A Centre . . . . . . . B1
Tennyson St . . . . . . B1
The Lawn . . . . . . . . C3
The Nurseries . . . . . C1
The Parade. . . . . . . B2
The Park . . . . . . . . . B1
Theobald St . . . . . . B1
Town Hall . . . . . . . . B2
Transfer Bridges
  Rdbt . . . . . . . . . . A3
Union St . . . . . . . . . C2
Upham Rd . . . . . . . C3
Victoria Rd . . . . . . . C3
Walcot Rd. . . . . . . . B3
War Memorial ✦ . . . B2
Wells St . . . . . . . . . B3
Western St . . . . . . . C2
Westmorland Rd. . . B3
Whalebridge Rdbt . B2
Whitehead St . . . . . C1
Whitehouse Rd. . . . A2
William St . . . . . . . . C3
Wood St . . . . . . . . . C3
Wyvern Theatre &
  Arts Centre 🎭 🎳 . . B2
York Rd. . . . . . . . . . B3

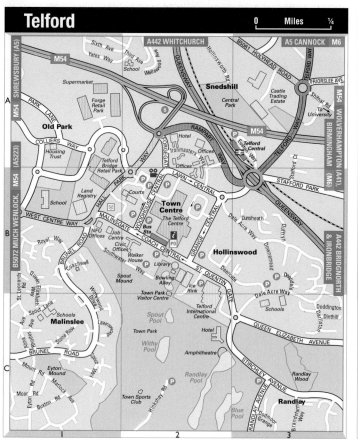

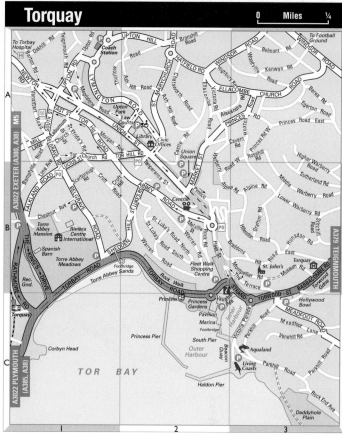

## Telford

Alma Ave . . . . . . . . C1
Amphitheatre . . . . . C2
Bowling Alley . . . . . B2
Brandsfarm Way. . . C3
Brunel Rd . . . . . . . B1
Bus Station. . . . . . . B2
Buxton Rd . . . . . . . C1
Castle Trading
  Estate . . . . . . . . . A3
Central Park . . . . . . B2
Civic Offices . . . . . B2
Coach Central . . . . B2
Coachwell Cl . . . . . B1
Colliers Way . . . . . A1
Courts. . . . . . . . . . . B2
Dale Acre Way . . . . B3
Darliston. . . . . . . . . C3
Deepdale . . . . . . . . B3
Deercote. . . . . . . . . B2
Dinthill. . . . . . . . . . C3
Doddington. . . . . . . C3
Dodmoor Grange . . C3
Downemead . . . . . . B3

Duffryn . . . . . . . . . B3
Dunsheath . . . . . . . B3
Euston Way . . . . . . A3
Eyton Mound . . . . . C1
Eyton Rd. . . . . . . . . C1
Forge Retail Park . . A1
Forgegate . . . . . . . . B2
Grange Central . . . . B2
Hall Park Way. . . . . B1
Hinkshay Rd. . . . . . C2
Hollinsworth Rd. . . A2
Holyhead Rd. . . . . . A3
Housing Trust . . . . A1
Ice Rink . . . . . . . . . B2
Information Ctr 🏛. . B2
Ironmasters Way . . A2
Job Centre . . . . . . . B1
Land Registry . . . . . B1
Lawn Central . . . . . B2
Lawnswood . . . . . . C1
Library . . . . . . . . . . B2
Malinsgate . . . . . . . B2
Matlock Ave . . . . . . C1
Moor Rd . . . . . . . . C1
Mount Rd . . . . . . . . C1

NFU Offices . . . . . . B1
Park Lane . . . . . . . . A1
Police Station 🏛 . . B1
Post Office 🏤 . . . . B2
Priorslee Ave . . . . . A3
Queen Elizabeth
  Ave . . . . . . . . . . . C3
Queen Elizabeth
  Way. . . . . . . . . . . B1
Queensway. . . . A2/B3
Rampart Way . . . . . A2
Randlay Ave . . . . . . C3
Randlay Wood . . . . C3
Rhodes Ave . . . . . . C1
Royal Way . . . . . . . B1
St Leonards Rd . . . . B1
St Quentin Gate . . . B2
Shifnal Rd. . . . . . . . A3
Sixth Ave . . . . . . . . A1
Southwater Way. . . B1
Spout Lane . . . . . . . C1
Spout Mound . . . . . B1
Spout Way . . . . . . . C1
Stafford Court. . . . . B3
Stafford Park . . . . . B3

Stirchley Ave. . . . . . C3
Stone Row . . . . . . . C1
Telford Bridge
  Retail Park . . . . . A1
Telford Central
  Station 🚉 . . . . . . A3
Telford Centre, The B2
Telford International
  Centre. . . . . . . . . C2
Telford Way. . . . . . . A3
Third Ave . . . . . . . . A2
Town Park. . . . . . . . C2
Town Park Visitor
  Centre. . . . . . . . . B2
Town Sports Club. . C2
Walker House . . . . . B1
Wellswood Ave. . . . A2
West Centre Way . . B1
Withywood Drive . . C1
Woodhouse
  Central . . . . . . . . B2
Yates Way. . . . . . . . A1

## Torquay

Abbey Rd . . . . . . . . B2
Alexandra Rd . . . . . A2
Alpine Rd . . . . . . . . B3
Aqualand 🐧 . . . . . . C3
Ash Hill Rd . . . . . . . A2
Babbacombe Rd . . B3
Bampfylde Rd . . . . . B1
Barton Rd . . . . . . . . A1
Beacon Quay . . . . . C2
Belgrave Rd . . . . A1/B1
Belmont Rd . . . . . . . A3
Berea Rd . . . . . . . . A3
Braddons Hill Rd
  East. . . . . . . . . . . B3
Bronshill Rd . . . . . . A2
Castle Rd . . . . . . . . A2
Cavern Rd . . . . . . . A3
Central 🏛 . . . . . . . . B2
Chatsworth Rd. . . . A2
Chestnut Ave . . . . . B1
Church St . . . . . . . . A1
Civic Offices 🏛 . . . A2
Coach Station . . . . A1
Corbyn Head . . . . . C1
Croft Hill . . . . . . . . B1
Croft Rd . . . . . . . . . B1
Daddyhole Plain . . . C3
East St . . . . . . . . . . A1
Egerton Rd . . . . . . . A3
Ellacombe
  Church Rd . . . . . . A3
Ellacombe Rd. . . . . A2
Falkland Rd . . . . . . B1
Fleet St . . . . . . . . . B2
Fleet Walk Shopping
  Centre. . . . . . . . . B2

Grafton Rd . . . . . . . B3
Haldon Pier. . . . . . . C2
Hatfield Rd . . . . . . . A2
Highbury Rd . . . . . . A2
Higher
  Warberry Rd . . . . A3
Hillesdon Rd. . . . . . B3
Hollywood Bowl . . . C3
Hoxton Rd . . . . . . . A3
Hunsdon Rd. . . . . . B3
Information Ctr 🏛. . B2
Inner Harbour . . . . C3
Kenwyn Rd. . . . . . . A3
Laburnum St. . . . . . A1
Law Courts. . . . . . . A2
Library . . . . . . . . . . A2
Lime Ave. . . . . . . . . B1
Living Coasts 🐧 . . . C3
Lower
  Warberry Rd . . . . B3
Lucius St . . . . . . . . B1
Lymington Rd . . . . . A1
Magdalene Rd . . . . A1
Marina. . . . . . . . . . . C2
Market St . . . . . . . . B2
Meadfoot Lane . . . . C3
Meadfoot Rd . . . . . C3
Melville St. . . . . . . . B2
Middle
  Warberry Rd . . . . B3
Mill Lane. . . . . . . . . A1
Montpellier Rd . . . . B3
Morgan Ave . . . . . . A1
Museum Rd . . . . . . A3
Newton Rd . . . . . . . A1
Oakhill Rd. . . . . . . . A1
Outer Harbour . . . . C2
Parkhill Rd . . . . . . . C3

Pavilion. . . . . . . . . . C2
Pimlico . . . . . . . . . . B2
Police Station 🏛 . . A1
Post Office 🏤 . . . . .
  . . . . . . . . . A2/B1/B2
Princes Rd . . . . . . . A3
Princes Rd East . . . A3
Princes Rd West. . . A3
Princess
  Theatre 🎭 . . . . . . C2
Princess Gdns . . . . C2
Princess Pier . . . . . C1
Rathmore Rd . . . . . B1
Recreation Grd . . . . B1
Riviera Centre
  International . . . . . B1
Rock End Ave. . . . . C3
Rock Rd . . . . . . . . . B2
Rock Walk . . . . . . . B2
Rosehill Rd. . . . . . . A3
St Efride's Rd . . . . . A1
St John's ⛪ . . . . . . B3
St Luke's Rd . . . . . . B2
St Luke's Rd
  North. . . . . . . . . . B2
St Luke's Rd
  South . . . . . . . . . B2
St Marychurch Rd . . A2
Scarborough Rd. . . B1
Shedden Hill. . . . . . B2
South Pier. . . . . . . . C2
South St . . . . . . . . . A1
Spanish Barn . . . . . B1
Stitchill Rd. . . . . . . . B3
Strand. . . . . . . . . . . B3
Sutherland Rd . . . . B3
Teignmouth Rd. . . . A1
Temperance St . . . . B2

The King's Drive . . . B1
The Terrace. . . . . . . B3
Thurlow Rd . . . . . . . A1
Tor Bay . . . . . . . . . B1
Tor Church Rd . . . . A1
Tor Hill Rd. . . . . . . . A1
Torbay Rd. . . . . . . . B2
Torquay
  Museum 🏛. . . . . . B3
Torquay
  Station 🚉 . . . . . . C1
Torre Abbey
  Mansion 🏛 . . . . . B1
Torre Abbey
  Meadows . . . . . . B1
Torre Abbey
  Sands. . . . . . . . . B1
Torwood Gdns . . . . B3
Torwood St. . . . . . . C3
Union Square . . . . . A2
Union St . . . . . . . . . A1
Upton Hill . . . . . . . . A2
Upton Park . . . . . . . A1
Upton Rd . . . . . . . . A1
Vanehill Rd . . . . . . . C3
Vansittart Rd. . . . . . A1
Vaughan Parade. . . C3
Victoria Parade. . . . C3
Victoria Rd . . . . . . . A2
Warberry Rd
  West . . . . . . . . . . B2
Warren Rd . . . . . . . B2
Windsor Rd . . . . A2/A3
Woodville Rd . . . . . A3

## Winchester

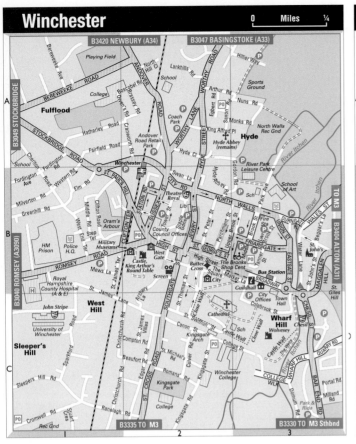

## Windsor

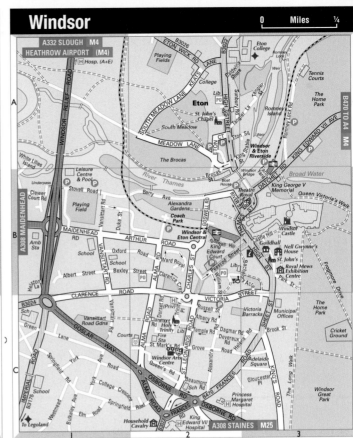

### Winchester

| | |
|---|---|
| Andover Rd . . . . . . A2 | |
| Andover Road | |
| Retail Park . . . . . A2 | |
| Archery La . . . . . . C2 | |
| Arthur Rd . . . . . . . A2 | |
| Bar End Rd . . . . . . C3 | |
| Beaufort Rd . . . . . A1 | |
| Beggar's La . . . . . B3 | |
| Bereweeke Ave. . . . A1 | |
| Bereweeke Rd . . . . A1 | |
| Boscobel Rd. . . . . A2 | |
| Brassey Rd . . . . . . A2 | |
| Broadway . . . . . . . B3 | |
| Brooks Shopping | |
| Centre, The. . . . . B3 | |
| Bus Station. . . . . . B3 | |
| Butter Cross ✦. . . . B2 | |
| Canon St . . . . . . . C2 | |
| Castle Wall . . . . C2/C3 | |
| Castle, King Arthur's | |
| Round Table ▥. . . B2 | |
| Cathedral † . . . . . . C2 | |
| Cheriton Rd . . . . . A1 | |
| Chesil St . . . . . . . . C3 | |
| Chesil Theatre ♖ . . C3 | |
| Christchurch Rd. . . C1 | |
| City Museum ▥ . . . B2 | |
| City Offices. . . . . . C3 | |
| City Rd . . . . . . . . . B2 | |
| Clifton Rd. . . . . . . B2 | |
| Clifton Terr . . . . . . B2 | |
| Close Wall . . . . C2/C3 | |
| Coach Park. . . . . . A2 | |
| Colebrook St . . . . . C3 | |
| College St . . . . . . C2 | |
| College Walk . . . . . C3 | |
| Compton Rd. . . . . . C2 | |
| County Council | |
| Offices . . . . . . . . B2 | |

| | |
|---|---|
| Cranworth Rd . . . . . A2 | |
| Cromwell Rd. . . . . . C1 | |
| Culver Rd . . . . . . . C2 | |
| Domun Rd . . . . . . . C3 | |
| Durngate Pl . . . . . . B3 | |
| Eastgate St. . . . . . B3 | |
| Edgar Rd . . . . . . . C2 | |
| Egbert Rd . . . . . . . A2 | |
| Elm Rd . . . . . . . . . B1 | |
| Fairfield Rd . . . . . . A1 | |
| Fire Station . . . . . . B3 | |
| Fordington Ave. . . . B1 | |
| Fordington Rd . . . . A1 | |
| Friarsgate. . . . . . . B3 | |
| Gordon Rd . . . . . . B3 | |
| Greenhill Rd . . . . . B1 | |
| Guildhall ▥ . . . . . . B3 | |
| HM Prison . . . . . . B1 | |
| Hatherley Rd . . . . . A1 | |
| High St . . . . . . . . . B2 | |
| Hillier Way. . . . . . . A3 | |
| Hyde Abbey | |
| (Remains) † . . . A2 | |
| Hyde Abbey Rd . . . B2 | |
| Hyde Cl. . . . . . . . . A2 | |
| Hyde St . . . . . . . . A2 | |
| Information Ctr ⓘ . . B2 | |
| John Stripe | |
| Theatre ♖ . . . . . . C1 | |
| King Alfred Pl . . . . A2 | |
| Kingsgate Arch. . . . C2 | |
| Kingsgate Park. . . . C2 | |
| Kingsgate Rd . . . . C2 | |
| Kingsgate St . . . . . C2 | |
| Lankhills Rd . . . . . A2 | |
| Library . . . . . . . . . B2 | |
| Lower Brook St . . . B3 | |
| Magdalen Hill . . . . B3 | |
| Market La. . . . . . . B2 | |
| Mews La. . . . . . . . B1 | |

| | |
|---|---|
| Middle Brook St . . . B3 | |
| Middle Rd. . . . . . . B1 | |
| Military | |
| Museums ▥ . . . . . B2 | |
| Milland Rd . . . . . . C3 | |
| Milverton Rd. . . . . . B3 | |
| Monks Rd . . . . . . . A3 | |
| North Hill Cl . . . . . A2 | |
| North Walls . . . . . . B2 | |
| North Walls | |
| Rec Gnd . . . . . . . A3 | |
| Nuns Rd . . . . . . . . A3 | |
| Oram's Arbour . . . . B1 | |
| Owen's Rd . . . . . . A2 | |
| Parchment St . . . . . B2 | |
| Park & Ride . . . . . . C3 | |
| Park Ave. . . . . . . . B2 | |
| Playing Field. . . . . A1 | |
| Police H.Q. ▣ . . . . B1 | |
| Police Station ▣ . . B3 | |
| Portal Rd . . . . . . . C3 | |
| Post Office ▣ . . . . . | |
| . . . A2/B2/B3/C1/C2 | |
| Quarry Rd. . . . . . . C3 | |
| Ranelagh Rd. . . . . . C1 | |
| River Park | |
| Leisure Centre . . . B3 | |
| Romans' Rd . . . . . C2 | |
| Romsey Rd. . . . . . B1 | |
| Royal Hampshire | |
| County Hospital | |
| (A & E) ⊞ . . . . . . B1 | |
| St Cross Rd . . . . . C2 | |
| St George's St . . . . B2 | |
| St Giles Hill. . . . . . C3 | |
| St James' La . . . . . B1 | |
| St James' Terr . . . . B1 | |
| St James Villas. . . . C2 | |
| St John's ♖ . . . . . . B3 | |
| St John's St . . . . . B3 | |
| St Michael's Rd . . . C2 | |

| | |
|---|---|
| St Paul's Hill . . . . . B1 | |
| St Peter St . . . . . . B2 | |
| St Swithun St . . . . . C2 | |
| St Thomas St . . . . C2 | |
| Saxon Rd . . . . . . . A2 | |
| School of Art . . . . . B3 | |
| Screen ▤ . . . . . . . B2 | |
| Sleepers Hill Rd . . . C1 | |
| Southgate St . . . . . B2 | |
| Sparkford Rd . . . . . C1 | |
| Staple Gdns . . . . . B2 | |
| Station Rd . . . . . . B2 | |
| Step Terr. . . . . . . . B1 | |
| Stockbridge Rd . . . A1 | |
| Stuart Cres . . . . . . C1 | |
| Sussex St . . . . . . . B2 | |
| Swan Lane . . . . . . B2 | |
| Tanner St . . . . . . . B3 | |
| The Square. . . . . . B2 | |
| The Weirs . . . . . . . C3 | |
| Theatre Royal ♖ . . B2 | |
| Tower St . . . . . . . . B2 | |
| Town Hall . . . . . . . C3 | |
| Union St . . . . . . . . B3 | |
| University of | |
| Winchester . . . . . C2 | |
| Upper Brook St . . . B2 | |
| Wales St . . . . . . . . B3 | |
| Water Lane . . . . . . B3 | |
| West End Terr . . . . B1 | |
| West Gate ▥ . . . . . B2 | |
| Western Rd . . . . . . B1 | |
| Wharf Hill . . . . . . . C3 | |
| Winchester | |
| College . . . . . . . C2 | |
| Winchester | |
| Station ⊋ . . . A2 | |
| Wolvesey | |
| Castle ▥ . . . . . . C3 | |
| Worthy Lane . . . . . A2 | |
| Worthy Rd . . . . . . A2 | |

### Windsor

| | |
|---|---|
| Adelaide Sq . . . . . . C3 | |
| Albany Rd. . . . . . . C2 | |
| Albert St . . . . . . . B1 | |
| Alexandra Gdns . . . B2 | |
| Alexandra Rd . . . . C2 | |
| Alma Rd . . . . . . . . C2 | |
| Ambulance | |
| Station . . . . . . . . B1 | |
| Arthur Rd . . . . . . . B2 | |
| Bachelors Acre. . . . B3 | |
| Barry Ave . . . . . . . B2 | |
| Beaumont Rd . . . . . C2 | |
| Bexley St . . . . . . . B1 | |
| Boat House . . . . . . B2 | |
| Brocas St . . . . . . . A2 | |
| Brook St . . . . . . . . C3 | |
| Bulkeley Ave. . . . . C1 | |
| Castle Hill . . . . . . B3 | |
| Charles St. . . . . . . B2 | |
| Claremont Rd. . . . . C2 | |
| Clarence Cr . . . . . C2 | |
| Clarence Rd . . . . . B1 | |
| Clewer Court Rd. . . B1 | |
| Coach Park. . . . . . B2 | |
| College Cr . . . . . . C1 | |
| Courts. . . . . . . . . . C2 | |
| Cricket Ground. . . . C3 | |
| Dagmar Rd . . . . . . C2 | |
| Datchet Rd. . . . . . B3 | |
| Devereux Rd. . . . . C2 | |
| Dorset Rd . . . . . . . C2 | |
| Duke St. . . . . . . . . B1 | |
| Elm Rd . . . . . . . . . C1 | |

| | |
|---|---|
| Eton College ✦ . . . A3 | |
| Eton Ct . . . . . . . . . A2 | |
| Eton Sq. . . . . . . . . A2 | |
| Eton Wick Rd . . . . A2 | |
| Fire Station . . . . . . B1 | |
| Farm Yard . . . . . . . B3 | |
| Frances Rd. . . . . . C2 | |
| Frogmore Dr. . . . . B3 | |
| Gloucester Pl . . . . C2 | |
| Goslar Way . . . . . . C1 | |
| Goswell Hill. . . . . . B2 | |
| Goswell Rd. . . . . . B2 | |
| Green La. . . . . . . . C1 | |
| Grove Rd . . . . . . . C2 | |
| Guildhall ▥ . . . . . . B3 | |
| Helena Rd. . . . . . . C2 | |
| Helston La . . . . . . B1 | |
| High St . . . . . . A2/B3 | |
| Holy Trinity ♰ . . . . C2 | |
| Hospital | |
| (Private) ⊞ . . . . . C2 | |
| Household | |
| Cavalry ▥ . . . . . . C2 | |
| Imperial Rd . . . . . . C1 | |
| Information Ctr ⓘ . . B3 | |
| Keats La. . . . . . . . A2 | |
| King Edward Ct . . . B3 | |
| King Edward VII | |
| Ave . . . . . . . . . . . A3 | |
| King Edward VII | |
| Hospital ⊞ . . . . . . C2 | |
| King George V | |
| Memorial. . . . . . . B3 | |
| King's Rd . . . . . . . C3 | |
| King Stable St . . . . A2 | |

| | |
|---|---|
| Leisure Centre | |
| & Pool. . . . . . . . . B1 | |
| Library . . . . . . . . . C2 | |
| Maidenhead Rd . . . B1 | |
| Meadow La. . . . . . A2 | |
| Municipal Offices . . C3 | |
| Nell Gwynne's | |
| House ▥ . . . . . . . B3 | |
| Osborne Rd . . . . . C2 | |
| Oxford Rd. . . . . . . B1 | |
| Park St . . . . . . . . . B3 | |
| Peascod St. . . . . . B2 | |
| Police Station ▣ . . C2 | |
| Post Office ▣ . . . A2/B2 | |
| Princess Margaret | |
| Hospital ⊞ . . . . . C2 | |
| Queen Victoria's | |
| Walk . . . . . . . . . B3 | |
| Queen's Rd. . . . . . C2 | |
| River St. . . . . . . . . B2 | |
| Romney Island . . . . A3 | |
| Romney Lock . . . . A3 | |
| Romney Lock Rd . . A3 | |
| Royal Mews Exhibition | |
| Centre ▥ . . . . . . B3 | |
| Russell St . . . . . . C2 | |
| St John's ♖ . . . . . . B3 | |
| St John's | |
| Chapel ♰ . . . . . . A2 | |
| St Leonards Rd . . . C2 | |
| St Mark's Rd. . . . . C2 | |
| Sheet St. . . . . . . . C3 | |
| South Meadow . . . . A2 | |
| South Meadow La . . A2 | |
| Springfield Rd. . . . . C1 | |

| | |
|---|---|
| Stovell Rd . . . . . . . B1 | |
| Sunbury Rd . . . . . . A2 | |
| Tangier La . . . . . . A2 | |
| Tangier St . . . . . . . A3 | |
| Temple Rd . . . . . . C2 | |
| Thames St . . . . . . B3 | |
| The Brocas. . . . . . A2 | |
| The Home | |
| Park . . . . . . . A3/C3 | |
| The Long Walk . . . . C3 | |
| Theatre Royal ♖ . . B3 | |
| Trinity Pl . . . . . . . . C2 | |
| Vansittart Rd. . . . B1/C1 | |
| Vansittart | |
| Rd Gdns . . . . . . C1 | |
| Victoria Barracks . . C2 | |
| Victoria St. . . . . . . C2 | |
| Ward Royal. . . . . . B2 | |
| Westmead . . . . . . C1 | |
| White Lilies Island . A1 | |
| William St . . . . . . . A2 | |
| Windsor Arts | |
| Centre ♖ . . . . . . C2 | |
| Windsor Castle ▥ . B3 | |
| Windsor & Eton | |
| Central . . . . . . . B2 | |
| Windsor & Eton | |
| Riverside ⊋ . . . . A3 | |
| Windsor Bridge . . . B3 | |
| Windsor Great | |
| Park . . . . . . . . . . C3 | |
| Windsor Relief Rd . . A1 | |
| York Ave . . . . . . . . C1 | |
| York Rd. . . . . . . . . C1 | |

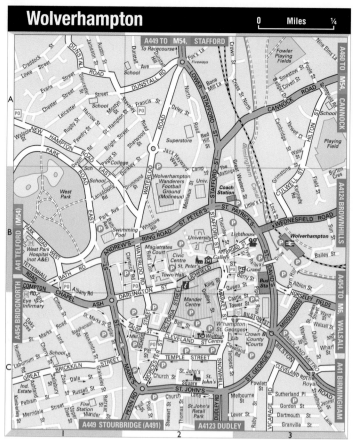

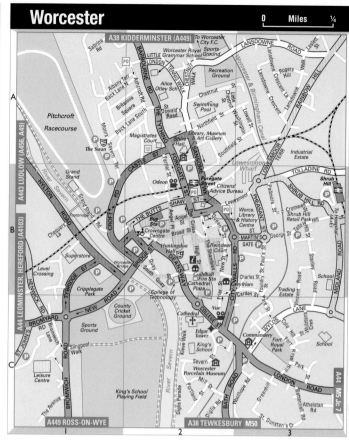

## Wolverhampton

| | |
|---|---|
| Albany Rd. | B1 |
| Albion St. | B3 |
| Alexandra St. | C1 |
| Gallery 🏛 | B2 |
| Ashland St | C1 |
| Austin St. | A1 |
| Badger Dr. | A3 |
| Bailey St. | B3 |
| Bath Ave. | B1 |
| Bath Rd | B1 |
| Bell St. | C2 |
| Berry St | B3 |
| Bilston Rd. | C3 |
| Bilston St | C2 |
| Birmingham Canal . | A3 |
| Bone Mill La. | A2 |
| Bright St | A1 |
| Burton Cres | A2 |
| Bus Station | B3 |
| Cambridge St. | A1 |
| Camp St. | B2 |
| Cannock Rd. | A3 |
| Castle St. | C2 |
| Chapel Ash. | C1 |
| Cherry St. | C1 |
| Chester St | A1 |
| Church La. | C2 |
| Church St. | C2 |
| Civic Centre | B2 |
| Clarence Rd | B2 |
| Cleveland Rd | C2 |
| Cleveland St. | C2 |
| Clifton St | C1 |
| Coach Station | B2 |
| Compton Rd. | B1 |
| Corn Hill | C1 |
| Coven St. | A3 |
| Craddock St. | A1 |
| Cross St North | A2 |
| Crown & County Courts. | C3 |
| Crown St | C2 |
| Culwell St. | B3 |
| Dale St. | C1 |
| Darlington St. | C1 |
| Dartmouth St. | C3 |
| Devon Rd | A1 |
| Drummond St. | B2 |
| Dudley Rd. | C2 |
| Dudley St. | B2 |
| Duke St. | C3 |

| | |
|---|---|
| Dunkley St | B1 |
| Dunstall Ave. | A2 |
| Dunstall Hill | A2 |
| Dunstall Rd. | A1/A2 |
| Evans St. | A1 |
| Eye Infirmary 🏥 | C1 |
| Fawdry St. | A1 |
| Field St. | B3 |
| Fire Station | C1 |
| Fiveways (r'about) | A2 |
| Fowler Playing Fields | A3 |
| Fox's La. | A2 |
| Francis St. | A2 |
| Fryer St. | B3 |
| Gloucester St. | A1 |
| Gordon St. | C3 |
| Graiseley St. | C1 |
| Grand 🎭 | B3 |
| Granville St. | C3 |
| Great Western St | A2 |
| Great Brickkiln St. | C1 |
| Grimstone St. | B3 |
| Gt. Hampton St. | A1 |
| Harrow St. | A1 |
| Hilton St. | A3 |
| Horseley Fields. | C3 |
| Humber Rd. | C1 |
| Jack Hayward Way. | A1 |
| Jameson St. | A1 |
| Jenner St. | C3 |
| Kennedy Rd | B3 |
| Kimberley St. | C1 |
| King St. | B2 |
| Laburnum St. | C1 |
| Lansdowne Rd. | B1 |
| Leicester St. | A1 |
| Lever St | C3 |
| Library | C3 |
| Lichfield St. | B2 |
| Lighthouse 🎬 | B3 |
| Little's La. | B3 |
| Lock St. | B3 |
| Lord St. | C1 |
| Lowe St. | C1 |
| Lower Stafford St. | A2 |
| Magistrates Court. | B2 |
| Mander Centre. | C2 |
| Mander St. | C1 |
| Market St. | B2 |
| Market | C2 |
| Melbourne St. | C3 |
| Merridale St. | C1 |

| | |
|---|---|
| Middlecross | C3 |
| Molineux St. | B2 |
| Mostyn St. | A1 |
| New Hampton Rd East. | A1 |
| Nine Elms La . | A3 |
| North Rd. | A2 |
| Oaks Cres. | C1 |
| Oxley St. | A2 |
| Paget St. | A1 |
| Park Ave. | B1 |
| Park Rd East | A1 |
| Park Road West . | B1 |
| Paul St | C2 |
| Pelham St. | C1 |
| Penn Rd. | C2 |
| Piper's Row | B3 |
| Pitt St. | C2 |
| Police Station 🏢 | C3 |
| Pool St | C2 |
| Poole St | A3 |
| Post Office ⊠ A1/A2/B2/B2/C2 |  |
| Powlett St. | C3 |
| Queen St. | B2 |
| Raby St. | C3 |
| Raglan St. | C1 |
| Railway Dr | B3 |
| Red Lion St | A2 |
| Red Lion St | B2 |
| Retreat St. | C1 |
| Ring Rd | B2 |
| Rugby St. | A1 |
| Russell St. | C1 |
| St. Andrew's. | B1 |
| St. David's. | B3 |
| St. George's. | C3 |
| St. James St. | C3 |
| St. John's. | C2 |
| St. John's 🚉 | C2 |
| St. John's Retail Park | C2 |
| St. John's Square . | C2 |
| St. Mark's. | C1 |
| St. Marks Rd | C1 |
| St. Marks St. | C1 |
| St. Patrick's. | B2 |
| St. Peter's. | B2 |
| St. Peter's 🚉 | B2 |
| Salisbury St. | C1 |
| Salop St . | C2 |
| School St . | C2 |
| Sherwood St . | A2 |

| | |
|---|---|
| Smestow St | A3 |
| Snowhill | C2 |
| Springfield Rd. | A3 |
| Stafford St | B2 |
| Staveley Rd. | A1 |
| Steelhouse La. | C1 |
| Stephenson St. | C1 |
| Stewart St. | C2 |
| Sun St. | B3 |
| Sutherland Pl . | C3 |
| Tempest St. | C2 |
| Temple St. | C2 |
| Tettenhall Rd | B1 |
| The Maltings. | A2 |
| The Royal (Metro) . | C3 |
| Thomas St. | C2 |
| Thornley St. | B2 |
| Tower St . | C2 |
| Town Hall | B2 |
| University | C1 |
| Upper Zoar St | C1 |
| Vicarage Rd | C3 |
| Victoria St. | C2 |
| Walpole St. | A1 |
| Walsall St. | C3 |
| Ward St. | C2 |
| Warwick St. | C3 |
| Water St. | A3 |
| Waterloo Rd. | A1 |
| Wednesfield Rd | B3 |
| West Park (not A&E) 🏥 | B1 |
| West Park Swimming Pool | B1 |
| Wolverhampton St. Georges (Metro) . | C3 |
| Wharf St. | C3 |
| Whitmore Hill . | B2 |
| Wolverhampton Station 🚉 | B3 |
| Wolverhampton Wanderers Football Gnd. (Molineux) . | B2 |
| Worcester St. | C2 |
| Wulfrun Centre . | C2 |
| Yarwell Cl . | A3 |
| York St . | C3 |
| Zoar St | C1 |

## Worcester

| | |
|---|---|
| Albany Terr. | A1 |
| Alice Otley School . | A2 |
| Angel Pl . | B2 |
| Angel St. | B2 |
| Ashcroft Rd . | A2 |
| Athelstan Rd . | C3 |
| Back Lane North . | A1 |
| Back Lane South . | A1 |
| Barbourne Rd. | A2 |
| Bath Rd . | C2 |
| Battenhall Rd. | C3 |
| Bridge St. | B2 |
| Britannia Sq . | A2 |
| Broad St. | B2 |
| Bromwich La . | C1 |
| Bromwich Rd . | C1 |
| Bromyard Rd . | C1 |
| Bus Station . | B2 |
| Carden St. | B2 |
| Castle St. | A2 |
| Cathedral ✝ | C2 |
| Cathedral Plaza . | B2 |
| Charles St. | B3 |
| Chequers La. | B1 |
| Chestnut St . | A2 |
| Chestnut Walk . | A2 |
| Citizens' Advice Bureau . | B2 |
| City Walls Rd . | B2 |
| Cole Hill . | C3 |
| College of Technology . | B2 |
| College St. | C2 |
| Commandery 🏛 . | C2 |
| County Cricket Ground . | C1 |

| | |
|---|---|
| Cripplegate Park . | B1 |
| Croft Rd . | B1 |
| Cromwell St . | B3 |
| Crowngate Centre . | B2 |
| Deansway . | B2 |
| Diglis Pde . | C2 |
| Diglis Rd. | C2 |
| Edgar Tower ✦ . | C2 |
| Farrier St. | A2 |
| Fire Station . | B2 |
| Foregate St. | B2 |
| Foregate Street 🚉 | B2 |
| Fort Royal Hill. | C3 |
| Fort Royal Park . | C3 |
| Foundry St . | B3 |
| Friar St . | C2 |
| George St. | B3 |
| Grand Stand Rd. | B1 |
| Greenhill . | C3 |
| Greyfriars 🏛 . | B2 |
| Guildhall 🏛 . | B2 |
| Henwick Rd . | B1 |
| High St. | B2 |
| Hill St . | B3 |
| Huntingdon Hall 🎭 . | B2 |
| Hylton Rd . | B1 |
| Information Ctr ℹ . | B2 |
| King's School . | C2 |
| King's School Playing Field . | C2 |
| Kleve Walk . | C2 |
| Lansdowne Cr . | A3 |
| Lansdowne Rd . | A3 |
| Lansdowne Walk . | A3 |
| Laslett St . | A3 |
| Leisure Centre . | A3 |

| | |
|---|---|
| Library, Museum & Art Gallery 🏛 . | A2 |
| Little Chestnut St. | A2 |
| Little London . | A2 |
| London Rd . | C3 |
| Lowell St. | C2 |
| Lowesmoor. | B2 |
| Lowesmoor Terr . | A3 |
| Lowesmoor Wharf . | A3 |
| Magistrates Court. | A2 |
| Midland Rd. | B3 |
| Mill St. | C2 |
| Moors Severn Terr. | A1 |
| New Rd . | C1 |
| New St . | B2 |
| Northfield St. | A2 |
| Odeon 🎬 . | B2 |
| Padmore St. | B3 |
| Park St . | C3 |
| Pheasant St . | B3 |
| Pitchcroft Racecourse . | A1 |
| Police Station 🏢 . | A2 |
| Portland St. | C2 |
| Post Office ⊠ A1/A2/B2 |  |
| Quay St . | B2 |
| Queen St . | B2 |
| Rainbow Hill . | A3 |
| Recreation Ground. | A2 |
| Reindeer Court. | B2 |
| Rogers Hill . | A3 |
| Sabrina Rd . | A1 |
| St Dunstan's Cr . | C3 |
| St John's . | C1 |
| St Martin's Gate . | B3 |
| St Oswald's. Rd. | A2 |
| St Paul's St. | B3 |

| | |
|---|---|
| St Wulstans Cr . | C3 |
| Sansome Walk . | A2 |
| Severn St . | C2 |
| Shaw St . | B2 |
| Shire Hall . | A2 |
| Shrub Hill . | B3 |
| Shrub Hill Retail Park . | B3 |
| Shrub Hill Rd . | B3 |
| Slingpool Walk . | C1 |
| South Quay . | B2 |
| Southfield St. | A2 |
| Sports Ground . | A2/C1 |
| Stanley Rd . | B3 |
| Swimming Pool . | A2 |
| Swan, The 🎭 . | A1 |
| Tallow Hill . | B3 |
| Tennis Walk . | A2 |
| The Avenue . | C1 |
| The Butts . | B2 |
| The Cross . | B2 |
| The Shambles . | B2 |
| The Tything . | A2 |
| Tolladine Rd . | B3 |
| Tybridge St. | B1 |
| Vincent Rd . | B3 |
| Vue 🎬 . | C2 |
| Washington St . | A3 |
| Woolhope Rd . | C3 |
| Worcester Bridge . | B2 |
| Worcester Library & History Centre . | B3 |
| Worcester Porcelain Museum 🏛 . | C2 |
| Worcester Royal Grammar School . | A2 |
| Wylds La. | C3 |

## Wrexham / Wrecsam

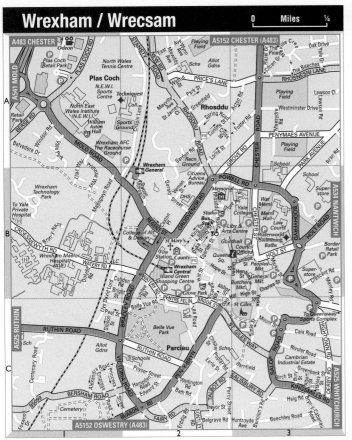

## York

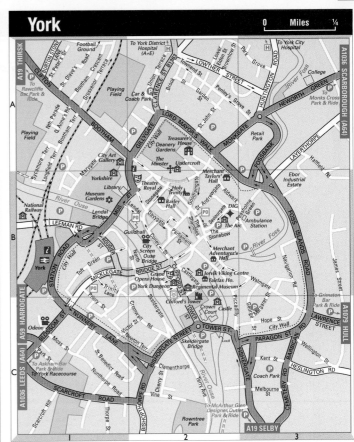

## Heathrow Airport (London)

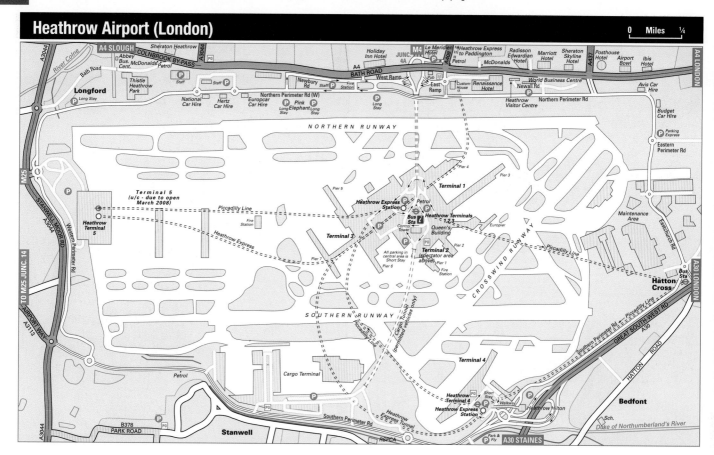

## Gatwick Airport (London)

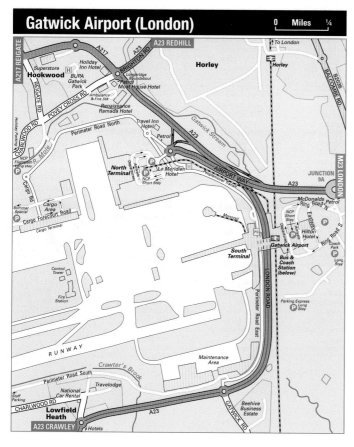

## Manchester Airport

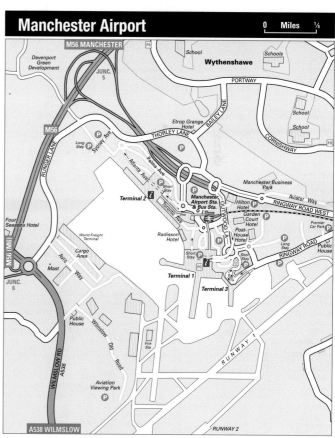

## Port of Dover

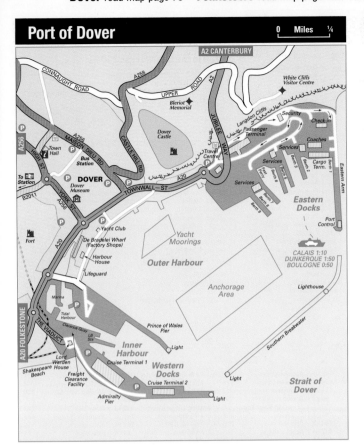

## Port of Felixstowe

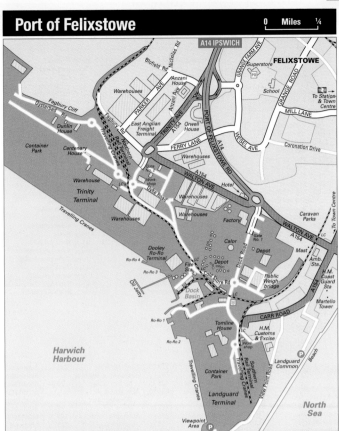

## Portsmouth-Continental Ferry Port

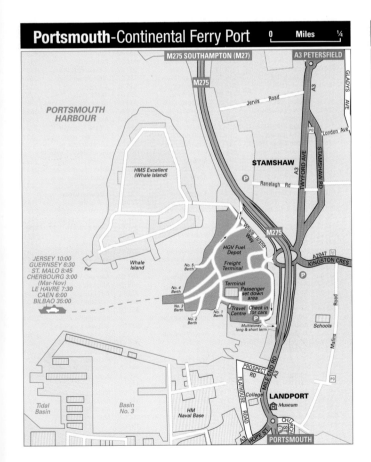

## Port of Southampton

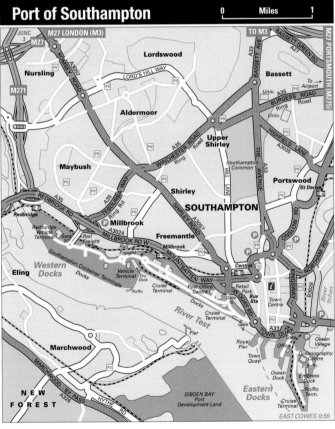

# Index to road maps of Britain

## Abbreviations used in the index

| | |
|---|---|
| Aberdeen | Aberdeen City |
| Aberds | Aberdeenshire |
| Ald | Alderney |
| Anglesey | Isle of Anglesey |
| Angus | Angus |
| Argyll | Argyll and Bute |
| Bath | Bath and North East Somerset |
| Beds | Bedfordshire |
| Bl Gwent | Blaenau Gwent |
| Blkburn | Blackburn with Darwen |
| Blkpool | Blackpool |
| Bmouth | Bournemouth |
| Borders | Scottish Borders |
| Brack | Bracknell |
| Bridgend | Bridgend |
| Brighton | City of Brighton and Hove |
| Bristol | City and County of Bristol |
| Bucks | Buckinghamshire |
| Caerph | Caerphilly |
| Cambs | Cambridgeshire |
| Cardiff | Cardiff |
| Carms | Carmarthenshire |
| Ceredig | Ceredigion |
| Ches | Cheshire |
| Clack | Clackmannanshire |
| Conwy | Conwy |
| Corn | Cornwall |
| Cumb | Cumbria |
| Darl | Darlington |
| Denb | Denbighshire |
| Derby | City of Derby |
| Derbys | Derbyshire |
| Devon | Devon |
| Dorset | Dorset |
| Dumfries | Dumfries and Galloway |
| Dundee | Dundee City |
| Durham | Durham |
| E Ayrs | East Ayrshire |
| E Dunb | East Dunbartonshire |
| E Loth | East Lothian |
| E Renf | East Renfrewshire |
| E Sus | East Sussex |
| E Yorks | East Riding of Yorkshire |
| Edin | City of Edinburgh |
| Essex | Essex |
| Falk | Falkirk |
| Fife | Fife |
| Flint | Flintshire |
| Glasgow | City of Glasgow |
| Glos | Gloucestershire |
| Gtr Man | Greater Manchester |
| Guern | Guernsey |
| Gwyn | Gwynedd |
| Halton | Halton |
| Hants | Hampshire |
| Hereford | Herefordshire |
| Herts | Hertfordshire |
| Highld | Highland |
| Hrtlpl | Hartlepool |
| Hull | Hull |
| I o M | Isle of Man |
| I o W | Isle of Wight |
| Invclyd | Inverclyde |
| Jersey | Jersey |
| Kent | Kent |
| Lancs | Lancashire |
| Leicester | City of Leicester |
| Leics | Leicestershire |
| Lincs | Lincolnshire |
| London | Greater London |
| Luton | Luton |
| M Keynes | Milton Keynes |
| M Tydf | Merthyr Tydfil |
| M'bro | Middlesbrough |
| Medway | Medway |
| Mers | Merseyside |
| Midloth | Midlothian |
| Mon | Monmouthshire |
| Moray | Moray |
| N Ayrs | North Ayrshire |
| N Lincs | North Lincolnshire |
| N Lnrk | North Lanarkshire |
| N Som | North Somerset |
| N Yorks | North Yorkshire |
| NE Lincs | North East Lincolnshire |
| Neath | Neath Port Talbot |
| Newport | City and County of Newport |
| Norf | Norfolk |
| Northants | Northamptonshire |
| Northumb | Northumberland |
| Nottingham | City of Nottingham |
| Notts | Nottinghamshire |
| Orkney | Orkney |
| Oxon | Oxfordshire |
| P'boro | Peterborough |
| Pembs | Pembrokeshire |
| Perth | Perth and Kinross |
| Plym | Plymouth |
| Poole | Poole |
| Powys | Powys |
| Ptsmth | Portsmouth |
| Reading | Reading |
| Redcar | Redcar and Cleveland |
| Renfs | Renfrewshire |
| Rhondda | Rhondda Cynon Taff |
| Rutland | Rutland |
| S Ayrs | South Ayrshire |
| S Glos | South Gloucestershire |
| S Lnrk | South Lanarkshire |
| S Yorks | South Yorkshire |
| Scilly | Scilly |
| Shetland | Shetland |
| Shrops | Shropshire |
| Slough | Slough |
| Som | Somerset |
| Soton | Southampton |
| Staffs | Staffordshire |
| Sthend | Southend-on-Sea |
| Stirl | Stirling |
| Stockton | Stockton-on-Tees |
| Stoke | Stoke-on-Trent |
| Suff | Suffolk |
| Sur | Surrey |
| Swansea | Swansea |
| Swindon | Swindon |
| T & W | Tyne and Wear |
| Telford | Telford and Wrekin |
| Thurrock | Thurrock |
| Torbay | Torbay |
| Torf | Torfaen |
| V Glam | The Vale of Glamorgan |
| W Berks | West Berkshire |
| W Dunb | West Dunbartonshire |
| W Isles | Western Isles |
| W Loth | West Lothian |
| W Mid | West Midlands |
| W Sus | West Sussex |
| W Yorks | West Yorkshire |
| Warks | Warwickshire |
| Warr | Warrington |
| Wilts | Wiltshire |
| Windsor | Windsor and Maidenhead |
| Wokingham | Wokingham |
| Worcs | Worcestershire |
| Wrex | Wrexham |
| York | City of York |

## How to use the index

Example

**Barton in the Beans** Leics **200 B1**

- B1 – grid square
- 200 – page number
- Leics – county or unitary authority

Places of special interest are highlighted in magenta

## A


**Aaron's Town** Cumb 348 D4
**Ab Kettleby** Leics 226 D1
**Abbas Combe** Som'set 40 B4
**Abberley** Worcs 175 E5
**Abberton** Essex 141 D9
**Abberton** Worcs 154 B2
**Abberwick** Northum 376 E4
**Abbess End** Essex 139 E7
**Abbess Roding** Essex 139 E7
**Abbey** Devon 37 D7
**Abbey Dore** Heref'd 127 A8
**Abbey Field** Essex 141 C8
**Abbey Gate** Kent 92 E2
**Abbey Green** Staffs 245 C5
**Abbey Hey** Gtr Man 279 E6
**Abbey Hulton** Stoke 244 E4
**Abbey Mead** Surrey 88 C2
**Abbey St. Bathans** Scot Borders 398 F5
**Abbey Town** Cumb 338 A2
**Abbey Village** Lancs 290 F1
**Abbey Wood** London 90 A4
**Abbey-cwm-hir** Powys 171 D5
**Abbeydale** Glos 130 D3
**Abbeydale** S Yorks 269 C6
**Abbeydale Park** S Yorks 269 C6
**Abbeyhill** C/Edinb 396 D2
**Abbeymead** Glos 130 D3
**Abbeystead** Lancs 302 E3
**Abbots Bickington** Devon 33 D7
**Abbots Bromley** Staffs 222 D3
**Abbots Langley** Herts 110 B3
**Abbots Leigh** N Som'set 80 B2
**Abbots Morton** Worcs 154 A3
**Abbots Ripton** Cambs 182 C4
**Abbot's Salford** Warwick 154 B4
**Abbots Worthy** Hants 65 E6
**Abbotsbury** Dorset 25 C6
**Abbotsbury Sub Tropical Gardens** Dorset 25 C6
**Abbotsford House** Scot Borders 385 F7
**Abbotsham** Devon 33 A8
**Abbotskerswell** Devon 15 B5
**Abbotsleigh** Devon 14 F4
**Abbotsley** Cambs 160 A4
**Abbotstone** Hants 65 E8
**Abbotswood** Surrey 68 A2
**Abbotswood** Worcs 153 C7
**Abbotts Ann** Hants 64 C3
**Abbottswood** Hants 44 B2
**Abcott** Shrops 173 C5
**Abenhall** Glos 129 D7
**Abdon** Shrops 174 A1
**Aber** Ceredig'n 146 C2
**Aber Village** Powys 126 C3
**Aberaeron** Ceredig'n 168 F2
**Aberaman** Rh Cyn Taff 99 B7
**Aberangell** Powys 191 B7
**Aber-Arad** Carms 145 D6
**Aberarder** H'land 425 D6
**Aberarder House** H'land 433 F8
**Aberarder Lodge** H'land 425 D7
**Aberargie** Perth/Kinr 420 F1
**Aberarth** Ceredig'n 168 F2
**Aberavon** Rh Cyn Taff 98 D2
**Aber-banc** Ceredig'n 145 D7
**Aberbargoed** Caerph 100 C3
**Aberbechan** Powys 193 E6
**Aberbeeg** Bl Gwent 100 B4
**Aberbran** Powys 125 B8
**Abercanaid** Merth Tyd 99 B8
**Abercarn** Caerph 100 D4
**Abercastle** Pembs 118 C5
**Abercegir** Powys 191 C7
**Aberchalder** H'land 425 B5
**Aberchirder** Aberds 436 C3
**Aberconwy House, Conwy** Conwy 261 D5
**Abercorn** W Loth 395 C6
**Abercraf** Powys 124 E5
**Abercregan** Denbs 241 F6
**Abercregan** Neath P Talb 98 C3
**Abercrombie** Fife 412 B3
**Abercwmboi** Rh Cyn Taff 99 C7
**Abercych** Pembs 144 D4
**Abercynafon** Powys 126 D2
**Abercynffig = Aberkenfig** Bridg 98 F4
**Abercynon** Rh Cyn Taff 99 C8
**Aber-Cywarch** Gwyn 216 E2
**Aberdâr = Aberdare** Rh Cyn Taff 99 B7
**Aberdalgie** Perth/Kinr 419 E8
**Aberdare = Aberdâr** Rh Cyn Taff 99 B7
**Aberdaron** Gwyn 212 C3
**Aberdaugleddau = Milford Haven** Pembs 116 C4
**Aberdeen** Aberd C 429 B6
**Aberdeen Airport** Aberd C 429 A5
**Aberdesach** Gwyn 236 D4
**Aberdour** Fife 411 D6
**Aberdovey = Aberdyfi** Gwyn 190 D3
**Aberdulais** Rh Cyn Taff 98 C2
**Aberdyfi = Aberdovey** Gwyn 190 D3
**Aberedw** Powys 149 C6
**Abereiddy** Pembs 118 C3
**Abererch** Gwyn 213 A7
**Aberfan** Merth Tyd 99 B8
**Aberfeldy** Perth/Kinr 419 C6
**Aberffraw** Angl 258 F4
**Aberffrwd** Ceredig'n 169 C6
**Aberford** W Yorks 294 C2
**Aberfoyle** Stirl 409 B8
**Abergarw** Bridg 99 F5
**Abergarwed** Neath P Talb 98 B3
**Abergavenny** Monmouths 127 E7
**Abergele** Conwy 262 D9
**Aber-Giâr** Carms 146 D3
**Abergorlech** Carms 146 F4
**Abergwaun = Fishguard** Pembs 119 B7
**Abergwesyn** Powys 148 B2
**Abergwili** Carms 122 C4
**Abergwynfi** Neath P Talb 98 C4
**Abergwyngregyn** Gwyn 260 E3
**Abergynolwyn** Gwyn 190 B4
**Aberhafesp** Powys 192 E5
**Aberhonddu = Brecon** Powys 126 B1
**Aberhosan** Powys 191 D7
**Aberkenfig = Abercynffig** Bridg 98 F4
**Aberlady** E Loth 397 B6
**Aberlemno** Angus 421 B5
**Aberllefenni** Gwyn 191 B6
**Aberllydan = Broad Haven** Pembs 116 B3
**Abermagwr** Ceredig'n 169 D6
**Abermaw = Barmouth** Gwyn 214 E4
**Abermeurig** Ceredig'n 146 A4
**Abermorddu** Flints 241 C7
**Abermule** Powys 193 E7
**Abernant** Carms 122 C2
**Aber-nant** Rh Cyn Taff 99 B7
**Abernethy** Perth/Kinr 420 F1
**Abernyte** Perth/Kinr 420 D2
**Aber-oer** Wrex 241 E6
**Aberogwr = Ogmore-by-Sea** V/Glam 76 B4
**Aberpennar = Mountain Ash** Rh Cyn Taff 99 C7
**Aberporth** Ceredig'n 145 B5
**Abersoch** Gwyn 213 C6
**Abersychan** Torf 100 B5
**Aber-Tafol** Gwyn 190 D3
**Abertawe = Swansea** Swan 97 D8
**Aberteifi = Cardigan** Ceredig'n 144 C3
**Aberthin** V/Glam 77 A7
**Abertillery** Bl Gwent 100 B4
**Abertridwr** Caerph 100 E2
**Abertridwr** Powys 217 E5
**Abertysswg** Caerph 100 A2
**Aberuchill Castle** Perth/Kinr 419 E5
**Aberuthven** Perth/Kinr 419 F7
**Aberyscir** Powys 125 B8
**Aberystwyth** Ceredig'n 168 B4
**Abhainn Suidhe** W Isles 448 B4
**Abingdon** Oxon 107 C6
**Abinger Common** Surrey 68 B4
**Abinger Hammer** Surrey 68 B3
**Abington** Northants 180 F3
**Abington** S Lanarks 370 C3
**Abington Pigotts** Cambs 161 C6
**Abingworth** W Sussex 48 C2
**Ablington** Glos 131 F8
**Ablington** Wilts 63 B8
**Abney** Derby 268 D3
**Aboyne** Aberds 428 C2
**Abraham Heights** Lancs 301 C8
**Abram** Gtr Man 277 D9
**Abriachan** H'land 433 F7
**Abridge** Essex 112 C4
**Abronhill** N Lanarks 393 C7
**Abson** S Glos 81 B6
**Abthorpe** Northants 157 C8
**Abune-the-Hill** Orkney 452 A3
**Aby** Lincs 275 D5
**Acaster Malbis** C/York 295 A5
**Acaster Selby** N Yorks 295 B5
**Accrington** Lancs 290 E4
**Acha** Arg/Bute 416 F2
**Acha** Arg/Bute 414 B4
**Acha Mor** W Isles 451 E6
**Achabraid** Arg/Bute 407 D8
**Achachork** H'land 430 D4
**Achad nan Darach** H'land 417 B5
**Achadh an Eas** H'land 443 E8
**Achadunan** Arg/Bute 408 A4
**Achafolla** Arg/Bute 407 A7
**Achagary** H'land 444 C1
**Achaglass** Arg/Bute 404 B3
**Achahoish** Arg/Bute 407 E7
**Achalader** Perth/Kinr 420 C1
**Achallader** Arg/Bute 417 C8
**Achalone** H'land 445 C5
**Ach'an Todhair** H'land 424 E2
**Achanalt** H'land 432 B4
**Achanamara** Arg/Bute 407 D7
**Achandunie** H'land 433 A8
**Achanelid** Arg/Bute 408 D3
**Achany** H'land 440 C2
**Achaphubuil** H'land 424 E2
**Acharacle** H'land 423 F6
**Acharn** H'land 416 B2
**Acharn** Perth/Kinr 419 C5
**Acharole** H'land 445 C6
**Acharossan** Arg/Bute 408 E2
**Acharry Muir** H'land 440 D3
**Achath** Aberds 428 A4
**Achavanich** H'land 445 D5
**Achavelgin** H'land 434 C4
**Achavraat** H'land 434 D4
**Achddu** Carms 96 B3
**Achdregnie** Moray 435 F7
**Achduart** H'land 438 C4
**Achentoul** H'land 444 E2
**Achfary** H'land 442 E4
**Achfrish** H'land 440 B2
**Achgarve** H'land 438 D2
**Achiemore** H'land 443 B5
**Achiemore** H'land 444 C2
**A'Chill** H'land 422 B2
**Achiltibuie** H'land 438 C4
**Achina** H'land 444 B1
**Achinahuagh** H'land 443 B7
**Achindaul** H'land 424 D3
**Achindown** H'land 434 D3
**Achinduich** H'land 440 C2
**Achinduin** Arg/Bute 416 D3
**Achingills** H'land 445 B5
**Achininver** H'land 443 B7
**Achintee** H'land 424 E3
**Achintee** H'land 432 D1
**Achintraid** H'land 431 E8
**Achlaven** Arg/Bute 416 D4
**Achlean** H'land 426 C3
**Achleck** Arg/Bute 415 C7
**Achlorachan** H'land 433 C5
**Achluachrach** H'land 425 D4
**Achlyness** H'land 442 C4
**Achmelvich** H'land 438 A4
**Achmore** H'land 431 E8
**Achmore** Stirl 418 D3
**Achnaba** Arg/Bute 408 D2
**Achnaba** Arg/Bute 416 D4
**Achnabat** H'land 433 E7
**Achnabreck** Arg/Bute 408 C1
**Achnacarnin** H'land 442 E2
**Achnacarry** H'land 424 D3
**Achnacloich** Arg/Bute 416 D4
**Achnacloich** H'land 423 B5
**Achnaconeran** H'land 425 A6
**Achnacraig** Arg/Bute 415 C7
**Achnacree** Arg/Bute 416 D4
**Achnacree Bay** Arg/Bute 416 D4
**Achnacroish** Arg/Bute 416 C3
**Achnadrish** Arg/Bute 415 B7
**Achnafalnich** Arg/Bute 417 E7
**Achnagarron** H'land 434 B1
**Achnaha** H'land 422 F4
**Achnahanat** H'land 440 D2
**Achnahannet** H'land 434 F4
**Achnahard** Arg/Bute 415 E6
**Achnairn** H'land 440 B2
**Achnaluachrach** H'land 440 C3
**Achnandarach** H'land 431 E8
**Achnanellan** H'land 424 D2
**Achnasaul** H'land 424 D3
**Achnasheen** H'land 432 C3
**Achnashelloch** Arg/Bute 407 C8
**Achnavast** H'land 445 B4
**Achneigie** H'land 439 F4
**Achormlarie** H'land 440 D3
**Achorn** H'land 445 E5
**Achosnich** H'land 422 F4
**Achranich** H'land 416 C2
**Achreamie** H'land 444 B4
**Achriabhach** H'land 424 F3
**Achriesgill** H'land 442 C4
**Achrimsdale** H'land 441 C6
**Achtoty** H'land 443 B8
**Achurch** Northants 181 B8
**Achuvoldrach** H'land 443 C7
**Achvaich** H'land 440 D4
**Achvarasdal** H'land 444 B3
**Ackenthwaite** Cumb 314 D4
**Ackergill** H'land 445 C7
**Acklam** Middlesbro 332 C4
**Acklam** N Yorks 308 C4
**Ackleton** Shrops 196 D4
**Acklington** Northum 365 B6
**Ackton** W Yorks 294 F2
**Ackworth Moor Top** W Yorks 282 A2
**Acle** Norfolk 210 A4
**Acock's Green** W Midlands 176 B5
**Acol** Kent 95 C6
**Acomb** C/York 307 E8
**Acomb** Northum 351 C5
**Aconbury** Heref'd 128 A4
**Acrefair** Wrex 241 F6
**Acton** Ches 243 D5
**Acton** Dorset 27 E6
**Acton** London 111 F6
**Acton** Shrops 172 B4
**Acton** Suffolk 164 D2
**Acton** Staffs 244 F2
**Acton** Worcs 175 E6
**Acton** Wrex 241 D7
**Acton Beauchamp** Heref'd 152 B3
**Acton Bridge** Ches 265 D6
**Acton Burnell** Shrops 195 C6
**Acton Green** Heref'd 152 C3
**Acton Park** Wrex 241 D7
**Acton Pigott** Shrops 195 C6
**Acton Round** Shrops 196 D1
**Acton Scott** Shrops 195 F5
**Acton Trussell** Staffs 221 E8
**Acton Turville** S Glos 103 F8
**Adabroc** W Isles 451 A8
**Adam's Green** Dorset 39 E8
**Adbaston** Staffs 220 C5
**Adber** Dorset 40 B1
**Adderley** Shrops 220 A3
**Adderley Green** Stoke 244 F4
**Adders Moss** Ches 266 D4
**Adderstone** Northum 376 A4
**Addiewell** W Loth 394 F4
**Addingham** W Yorks 305 F5
**Addington** Bucks 135 B5
**Addington** Cornw'l 9 B8
**Addington** Kent 91 E8
**Addington** London 90 D2
**Addinston** Scot Borders 385 B7
**Addiscombe** London 90 C1
**Addlestone** Surrey 88 D2
**Addlestonemoor** Surrey 88 C2
**Addlethorpe** Lincs 275 F7
**Adel** W Yorks 293 B7
**Adeney** Telford 220 E4
**Adeyfield** Herts 136 F5
**Adfa** Powys 192 C5
**Adforton** Heref'd 173 D6
**Adgestone** I/Wight 30 C3
**Adisham** Kent 94 F4
**Adlestrop** Glos 132 B3
**Adlingfleet** ER Yorks 296 F3
**Adlington** Ches 267 C5
**Adlington** Lancs 277 B8
**Admaston** Staffs 222 D3
**Admaston** Telford 195 A8
**Admington** Warwick 155 C7
**Adpar** Ceredig'n 145 D6
**Adsborough** Som'set 58 F5
**Adscombe** Som'set 58 D3
**Adsett** Glos 129 E8
**Adstock** Bucks 135 B5
**Adstone** Northants 157 B6
**Adswood** Gtr Man 266 B4
**Adversane** W Sussex 48 B1
**Advie** H'land 435 E6
**Adwalton** W Yorks 293 E6
**Adwell** Oxon 108 C3
**Adwick le Street** S Yorks 282 C4
**Adziel** Aberds 437 C6
**Ae** Dumf/Gal 358 E3
**Ae Bridgend** Dumf/Gal 358 E4
**Affetside** Gtr Man 278 B4
**Affleck** Aberds 437 F5
**Affpuddle** Dorset 26 B3
**Affric Lodge** H'land 432 F3
**Afon Eltha** Wrex 241 E6
**Afon-wen** Flints 262 E4
**Afton** Devon 14 C4
**Afton** I/Wight 29 C7
**Agar Nook** Leics 224 F3
**Agbrigg** W Yorks 281 A8
**Aggborough** Worcs 175 C6
**Agglethorpe** N Yorks 317 C7
**Aglionby** Cumb 348 E2
**Agneash** I/Man 336 C4
**Aigburth** Mersey 264 B2
**Aiginis** W Isles 451 D7
**Aike** ER Yorks 297 A7
**Aikenway** Moray 435 D7
**Aikerness** Orkney 454 A2
**Aikers** Orkney 453 D5
**Aiketgate** Cumb 339 B8
**Aikhead** Cumb 338 B3
**Aikton** Cumb 338 A4
**Ailey** Heref'd 150 C4
**Ailstone** Warwick 155 B7
**Ailsworth** Peterbro 203 D8
**Aimes Green** Essex 112 B2
**Ainderby Quernhow** N Yorks 319 D5
**Ainderby Steeple** N Yorks 319 B5
**Aingers Green** Essex 142 C3
**Ainsdale** Mersey 276 B3
**Ainsdale-on-Sea** Mersey 276 B2
**Ainstable** Cumb 340 B1
**Ainsworth** Gtr Man 278 C4
**Ainthorpe** N Yorks 333 E9
**Aintree** Mersey 276 E4
**Aintree Racecourse** Mersey 276 E4
**Aird** Arg/Bute 407 B7
**Aird** Dumf/Gal 400 C2
**Aird** H'land 438 F1
**Aird** W Isles 447 C2
**Aird** W Isles 451 D8
**Aird a Mhachair** W Isles 447 D2
**Aird a'Mhulaidh** W Isles 449 A5
**Aird Asaig** W Isles 449 B5
**Aird Dhail** W Isles 451 A7
**Aird Mhidhinis** W Isles 446 C3
**Aird Mhighe** W Isles 449 D4
**Aird Mhighe** W Isles 449 C5
**Aird Mhòr** W Isles 447 D3
**Aird Mhor** W Isles 446 C3
**Aird of Sleat** H'land 423 B5
**Aird Thunga** W Isles 451 D7
**Aird Uig** W Isles 450 D3
**Airdachuilinn** H'land 442 D4
**Airdens** H'land 440 D3
**Airdeny** Arg/Bute 417 E4
**Airdrie** N Lanarks 393 E7
**Airdriehill** N Lanarks 393 E7
**Airds of Kells** Dumf/Gal 401 B8
**Airdtorrisdale** H'land 443 B8
**Aire View** N Yorks 292 A1
**Airedale** W Yorks 294 E2
**Airidh a Bhruaich** W Isles 451 F5
**Airieland** Dumf/Gal 402 D1
**Airinis** W Isles 451 D7
**Airlie** Angus 420 B3
**Airlies** Dumf/Gal 401 D5
**Airmyn** ER Yorks 295 F8
**Airntully** Perth/Kinr 419 D8
**Airor** H'land 423 B7
**Airth** Falk 410 D3
**Airton** N Yorks 304 D1
**Airy Hill** N Yorks 334 D4
**Airyhassen** Dumf/Gal 401 E5
**Airyligg** Dumf/Gal 400 C4
**Aisby** Lincs 272 A2
**Aisby** Lincs 227 A7
**Aisgernis** W Isles 446 A3
**Aish** Devon 14 C1
**Aish** Devon 14 D4
**Aisholt** Som'set 58 D3
**Aiskew** N Yorks 318 C4
**Aislaby** N Yorks 321 C6
**Aislaby** N Yorks 334 E4
**Aislaby** Stockton 332 D3
**Aisthorpe** Lincs 272 C4
**Aith** Orkney 452 B3
**Aith** Shetl'd 456 D6
**Aith** Shetl'd 457 H3
**Aithsetter** Shetl'd 455 C3
**Aitkenhead** S Ayrs 367 F6
**Aitnoch** H'land 434 E4
**Akeld** Northum 375 B9
**Akeley** Bucks 158 E2
**Akenham** Suffolk 165 C7
**Aketon** N Yorks 306 E4
**Albany** Tyne/Wear 352 E4
**Albaston** Cornw'l 10 A4
**Alberbury** Shrops 218 F4
**Albert Dock, Liverpool** Mersey 264 B1
**Albert Town** Pembs 116 B4
**Albert Village** Derby 223 E8
**Albourne** W Sussex 49 C5
**Albourne Green** W Sussex 49 C5
**Albrighton** Shrops 219 E6
**Albrighton** Shrops 196 C5
**Alburgh** Norfolk 209 F9
**Albury** Herts 138 C4
**Albury** Oxon 134 F4
**Albury** Surrey 68 B2
**Albury End** Herts 138 C4
**Albury Heath** Surrey 68 B3
**Alby Hill** Norfolk 233 B8
**Albyfield** Cumb 340 A1
**Alcaig** H'land 433 C7
**Alcaston** Shrops 195 F5
**Alcester** Dorset 41 B7
**Alcester** Warwick 154 A4
**Alcester Lane's End** W Midlands 176 B4
**Alciston** E Sussex 50 E3
**Alcombe** Som'set 57 B6
**Alconbury** Cambs 182 C3
**Alconbury Hill** Cambs 182 C3
**Alconbury Weston** Cambs 182 C3
**Aldbar Castle** Angus 421 B5
**Aldborough** Norfolk 233 B8
**Aldborough** N Yorks 306 B5
**Aldborough Hatch** London 112 E4
**Aldbourne** Wilts 84 A2
**Aldbrough** ER Yorks 298 C3
**Aldbrough St. John** N Yorks 331 D6
**Aldbury** Herts 136 E3
**Aldcliffe** Lancs 301 C8
**Aldclune** Perth/Kinr 419 A7
**Aldeburgh** Suffolk 167 A7
**Aldeby** Norfolk 211 E5
**Aldenham** Herts 110 C4
**Alder Forest** Gtr Man 278 E3
**Alder Moor** Staffs 223 C6
**Alder Row** Som'set 61 C7
**Alderbrook** E Sussex 70 F5
**Alderbury** Wilts 43 A6
**Aldercar** Derby 247 E6
**Alderford** Norfolk 233 E7
**Alderholt** Dorset 42 D5
**Alderley** Glos 103 D7
**Alderley Edge** Ches 266 E3

Belchawell Street Dorset 41 E5
Belchford Lincs 274 D2
Beleybridge Fife 412 A3
Belfield Gtr Man 279 B7
Belford Northum 388 F4
Belgrano Conwy 262 D9
Belgrave Blackb'n 290 F2
Belgrave Leics C 201 B5
Belgrave Staffs 199 C5
Belgravia London 89 A7
Belhaven E Loth 398 C3
Belhelvie Aberds 429 A6
Belhinnie Aberds 436 F1
Bell Bar Herts 111 A6
Bell Busk N Yorks 304 D2
Bell End Worcs 176 C1
Bell Heath Worcs 176 C2
Bell Hill Hants 46 B2
Bell o'th'Hill Ches 242 E3
Bellabeg Aberds 427 A8
Bellahouston Glasg C 392 F3
Bellamore S Ayrs 354 E3
Bellanoch Arg/Bute 407 C7
Bellasize ER Yorks 296 E3
Bellaty Angus 420 B2
Belle Isle W Yorks 293 E8
Belle Vale Mersey 264 B3
Belle Vale W Midlands 176 B2
Belle Vue Cumb 337 E8
Belle Vue Cumb 348 E1
Belle Vue Gtr Man 279 E6
Belle Vue Shrops 195 A5
Belle Vue W Yorks 281 A8
Belleau Lincs 275 D5
Bellehiglash Moray 435 E6
Bellerby N Yorks 317 B8
Bellerby Camp N Yorks 317 B7
Bellever Devon 20 E3
Bellfield E Ayrs 379 E8
Bellfields Surrey 68 A1
Belliehill Angus 421 A5
Bellingham London 90 B2
Bellingham Northum 363 F5
Belloch Arg/Bute 404 C2
Bellochantuy Arg/Bute 404 C2
Bell's Close Tyne/Wear 352 D2
Bell's Corner Suffolk 164 E4
Bell's Cross Suffolk 165 B8
Bells Yew Green E Sussex 71 D7
Bellsbank E Ayrs 355 B8
Bellshill N Lanarks 381 A6
Bellshill Northum 376 A4
Bellside N Lanarks 381 A8
Bellsmyre W Dunb 391 C8
Bellspool Scot Borders 383 E8
Bellsquarry W Loth 395 F6
Belluton Bath/NE Som'set 80 D4
Belmaduthy H'land 433 C8
Belmesthorpe Leics 203 A6
Belmont Blackb'n 278 A2
Belmont Derby 269 E6
Belmont Durham 344 C2
Belmont London 89 D7
Belmont London 111 D5
Belmont Oxon 106 E4
Belmont S Ayrs 367 C6
Belmont Shetl'd 456 C5
Belnacraig Aberds 427 A8
Belnagarrow Moray 435 D8
Belnie Lincs 228 B5
Belowda Cornw'l 8 C2
Belper Derby 247 E5
Belper Lane End Derby 246 E4
Belph Derby 270 D2
Belsay Northum 351 A9
Belsay Hall Northum 351 A8
Belsize Herts 110 B2
Belstead Suffolk 165 D7
Belston S Ayrs 367 C7
Belstone Devon 20 B2
Belstone Corner Devon 20 A2
Belthorn Lancs 290 F3
Beltinge Kent 94 C3
Beltingham Northum 350 D2
Beltoft N Lincs 284 C3
Belton Leics 224 D3
Belton Lincs 227 A5
Belton Norfolk 210 C5
Belton N Lincs 284 C2
Belton House, Grantham Lincs 227 A5
Belton-in-Rutland Rutl'd 202 C2
Beltring Kent 71 B8
Belts of Collonach Aberds 428 C3
Belvedere London 90 A4
Belvedere W Loth 394 E4
Belvoir Leics 226 B3
Belvoir Castle Leics 226 B3
Bembridge I/Wight 31 C5
Bemersyde Scot Borders 386 F1
Bemerton Wilts 63 E7
Bempton ER Yorks 311 B5
Ben Alder Lodge H'land 425 E7
Ben Armine Lodge H'land 440 B4
Ben Casgro W Isles 451 E7
Ben Rhydding W Yorks 305 F6
Benacre Suffolk 189 B8
Benbecula Airport W Isles 447 C2
Benbuie Dumf/Gal 357 C6
Benchill Gtr Man 266 B3
Benderloch Arg/Bute 416 D4
Bendish Herts 137 C7
Bendronaig Lodge H'land 432 E2
Beneknowle Devon 14 D2
Benenden Kent 72 E3
Benfield Dumf/Gal 401 C5
Benfieldside Durham 343 A5
Bengate Norfolk 234 C3
Bengeworth Worcs 154 D3
Benhall Glos 130 C4
Benhall Green Suffolk 189 F5
Benhall Street Suffolk 188 F5
Benham Burslot W Berks 85 B5
Benholm Aberds 429 F5
Beningbrough N Yorks 307 D7
Beningbrough Hall N Yorks 307 D7
Benington Herts 138 C2
Benington Lincs 252 E3
Benington Sea End Lincs 252 E4
Benllech Angl 259 C7
Benmore Arg/Bute 408 D4
Benmore Stirl 418 E2
Benmore Lodge Arg/Bute 415 D8
Benmore Lodge H'land 439 B7
Bennacott Cornw'l 18 B2
Bennah Devon 21 D6
Bennan N Ayrs 405 D5
Bennane Lea S Ayrs 400 A2
Bennetland ER Yorks 296 E3
Bennetsfield H'land 434 C1
Bennett End Bucks 109 C5
Bennetts End Herts 110 A3
Benniworth Lincs 273 C9
Benoak Cornw'l 9 C7
Benover Kent 71 B9
Bensham Tyne/Wear 352 D4
Benslie N Ayrs 379 D6
Benson Oxon 108 D2
Benston Shetl'd 457 H4
Bent Aberds 428 E3
Bent Gate Lancs 290 F4
Benthall Shrops 196 C2
Bentham Glos 130 D4
Benthoul Aberd C 429 B5
Bentilee Stoke 244 E4
Bentlawnt Shrops 194 C2
Bentley Essex 113 C6
Bentley ER Yorks 297 C7
Bentley Hants 67 C5
Bentley Suffolk 165 E7
Bentley S Yorks 283 C5
Bentley Warwick 199 D6
Bentley W Midlands 197 D8
Bentley Common Warwick 199 D6
Bentley Heath Herts 111 C6
Bentley Heath W Midlands 177 C6
Bentley Rise S Yorks 283 D5
Benton Square Tyne/Wear 352 C4
Bentpath Dumf/Gal 360 D3
Bents W Loth 394 F4
Bentwichen Devon 56 E1
Bentworth Hants 66 C3
Benvie Dundee C 420 D3
Benville Lane Dorset 39 F8
Benwell Tyne/Wear 352 D3
Benwick Cambs 205 E5
Beoley Worcs 176 E4
Beoraidbeg H'land 423 C6
Bepton W Sussex 46 C5
Berden Essex 139 C5
Bere Alston Devon 10 B4
Bere Ferrers Devon 10 C5
Bere Regis Dorset 26 A3
Berefold Aberds 437 E6
Berepper Cornw'l 3 F9
Bergh Apton Norfolk 210 C2
Berhill Som'set 59 D8
Berinsfield Oxon 107 C8
Berkeley Glos 103 C5
Berkeley Heath Glos 103 C5
Berkeley Road Glos 103 C6
Berkeley Towers Ches 243 D6
Berkhamsted Herts 136 F4
Berkley Som'set 61 B8
Berkley Marsh Som'set 61 B8
Berkswell W Midlands 177 C7
Bermondsey London 90 A1
Bernards Heath Herts 137 F7
Bernera H'land 431 F8
Berner's Hill E Sussex 71 E9
Berners Roding Essex 139 F8
Bernice Arg/Bute 408 C4
Bernisdale H'land 430 C4
Berrick Prior Oxon 108 D2
Berrick Salome Oxon 108 D2
Berriedale H'land 441 A8
Berrier Cumb 339 F6
Berriew Powys 193 C7
Berrington Northum 388 D2
Berrington Shrops 195 B6
Berrington Worcs 174 E1
Berrington Green Worcs 174 E1
Berriowbridge Cornw'l 18 E2
Berrow Som'set 59 A5
Berrow Worcs 153 F5
Berrow Green Worcs 152 A4
Berry Brow W Yorks 280 B4
Berry Cross Devon 34 D2
Berry Hill Glos 128 E5
Berry Hill Stoke 244 E3
Berry Hill Worcs 175 F7
Berry Pomeroy Devon 14 C4
Berryfield Wilts 82 D2
Berryhillock Moray 436 B2
Berrylands London 89 C5
Berrynarbor Devon 55 B6
Berry's Green London 90 E3
Bersham Wrex 241 E7
Berstane Orkney 453 B5
Berthengam Flints 262 D4
Berthlwyd Swan 97 C6
Berwick E Sussex 50 E3
Berwick Kent 74 D2
Berwick S Glos 102 F3
Berwick Bassett Wilts 83 B6
Berwick Hill Northum 352 A2
Berwick Hills Middlesbro 332 C5
Berwick St. James Wilts 63 D6
Berwick St. John Wilts 42 B1
Berwick St. Leonard Wilts 62 E3
Berwick-upon-Tweed Northum 388 B2
Berwyn Denbs 240 F4
Bescaby Leics 226 C3
Bescar Lancs 276 B4
Bescot W Midlands 197 D9
Besford Worcs 153 D8
Besom Hill Gtr Man 279 C8
Bessacarr S Yorks 283 D6
Bessels Green Kent 90 E5
Bessels Leigh Oxon 107 B6
Besses o'th' Barn Gtr Man 279 C5
Bessingby ER Yorks 310 B5
Bessingham Norfolk 257 E6
Besthorpe Norfolk 208 D5
Besthorpe Notts 249 B7
Bestwood Nott'ham 248 E2
Bestwood Village Notts 248 E2
Beswick ER Yorks 310 F2
Betchworth Surrey 69 B6
Beth Shalom Holocaust Centre, Laxton Notts 271 F6
Bethania Ceredig'n 168 F4
Bethania Gwyn 238 E2
Bethania Gwyn 237 D8
Bethel Cornw'l 8 E3
Bethel Gwyn 216 A4
Bethel Gwyn 237 A6
Bethel Angl 258 E4
Bethel Row Kent 93 F7
Bethelnie Aberds 437 E4
Bethersden Kent 73 C5
Bethesda Gwyn 260 F2
Bethesda Pembs 117 A7
Bethlehem Carms 124 B2
Bethnal Green London 112 F1
Betley Staffs 243 E8
Betsham Kent 91 B7
Betteshanger Kent 75 A6
Bettiscombe Dorset 24 A3
Bettisfield Wrex 219 A6
Betton Shrops 220 A3
Betton Abbots Shrops 195 B6
Betton Strange Shrops 195 B6
Betts-y-crwyn Shrops 172 B2
Bettws Bridg 98 E4
Bettws Monmouths 127 D6
Bettws Newp 101 D5
Bettws Cedewain Powys 193 D6
Bettws Gwerfil Goch Denbs 239 E8
Bettws Newydd Monmouths 101 A7
Bettyhill H'land 444 B1
Betws Carms 124 E1
Betws Bledrws Ceredig'n 146 B4
Betws Garmon Gwyn 237 C6
Betws-Ifan Ceredig'n 145 C6
Betws-y-Coed Conwy 238 C3
Betws-yn-Rhos Conwy 262 E8
Beulah Ceredig'n 145 C5
Beulah Powys 148 B3
Bevendean Brighton/Hove 49 E6
Bevercotes Notts 271 E5
Bevere Worcs 153 A6
Beverley ER Yorks 297 B7
Beverley Minster ER Yorks 297 C7
Beverley Racecourse ER Yorks 297 B7
Beverston Glos 104 D2
Bevington Glos 103 C5
Bewaldeth Cumb 338 E3
Bewbush W Sussex 69 D6
Bewcastle Cumb 349 B5
Bewdley Worcs 175 D5
Bewerley N Yorks 305 C7
Bewholme ER Yorks 310 E5
Bewley Common Wilts 82 C3
Bewsey Warrington 265 B6
Bexfield Norfolk 233 C5
Bexhill E Sussex 51 E7
Bexhill Down E Sussex 51 E7
Bexley London 90 B4
Bexleyheath London 90 A4
Bexleyhill W Sussex 47 A6
Bexwell Norfolk 206 C3
Beyton Suffolk 186 F3
Beyton Green Suffolk 186 F3
Bhalasaigh W Isles 450 D4
Bhaltos W Isles 450 D3
Bhatarsaigh W Isles 446 D2
Bhlàraidh H'land 425 A5
Bibbington Derby 267 D8
Bibstone S Glos 103 D6
Bibury Glos 105 A7
Bicester Oxon 134 C2
Bickenhall Som'set 38 C3
Bickenhill W Midlands 177 B6
Bicker Lincs 228 A4
Bicker Bar Lincs 228 A4
Bicker Friest Lincs 228 A4
Bicker Gauntlet Lincs 228 A4
Bickershaw Gtr Man 278 D1
Bickerstaffe Lancs 277 D5
Bickerton Ches 242 D3
Bickerton Northum 364 B1
Bickerton N Yorks 307 E6
Bickington Devon 14 A3
Bickleigh Devon 11 C7
Bickleigh Devon 36 E3
Bickleton Devon 54 E5
Bickley London 90 C3
Bickley Worcs 174 D2
Bickley Moss Ches 242 E3
Bickley Town Ches 242 E3
Bicklington Devon 55 E5
Bicknacre Essex 114 B2
Bicknoller Som'set 58 D2
Bicknor Kent 92 E4
Bickton Hants 43 D5
Bicton Heref'd 173 F7
Bicton Shrops 172 B3
Bicton Shrops 219 E5
Bicton Heath Shrops 195 A5
Bicton Park Gardens Devon 22 C3
Bidborough Kent 71 C6
Biddenden Kent 72 D3
Biddenden Green Kent 72 C4
Biddenham Beds 159 B8
Biddestone Wilts 82 B2
Biddick Tyne/Wear 353 E5
Biddick Hall Tyne/Wear 353 D6
Biddisham Som'set 79 F7
Biddlesdon Northants 157 D7
Biddulph Staffs 244 C3
Biddulph Moor Staffs 244 C4
Bideford Devon 54 F3
Bidford on Avon Warwick 154 B5
Bidlake Devon 19 C6
Bidston Mersey 263 A7
Bidwell Beds 136 C4
Bielby ER Yorks 296 B2
Bieldside Aberd C 429 B5
Bierley I/Wight 30 E2
Bierley W Yorks 293 D5
Bierton Bucks 135 D7
Big Mancot Flints 263 F8
Big Pit National Mining Museum, Blaenavon Torf 127 F5
Big Sand H'land 438 F1
Bigbury Devon 12 C4
Bigbury-on-Sea Devon 12 D4
Bigby Lincs 285 C8
Bigfrith Windsor 109 F7
Biggar Cumb 300 B2
Biggar S Lanarks 383 E5
Biggar Road N Lanarks 393 F7
Biggin Derby 245 C9
Biggin Derby 246 E3
Biggin N Yorks 294 D4
Biggin Hill London 90 E3
Biggings Shetl'd 457 G1
Biggleswade Beds 160 D3
Bighouse H'land 444 B2
Bighton Hants 66 E2
Biglands Cumb 347 F7
Bignor W Sussex 47 D7
Bigod's Hill Norfolk 210 E3
Bigram Stirl 410 B1
Bigrigg Cumb 324 D5
Bigsby's Corner Suffolk 189 F5
Bigswell Orkney 452 B4
Bigton Shetl'd 455 D2
Bilborough Nott'ham 247 F8
Bilbrook Som'set 57 C7
Bilbrook Staffs 197 C6
Bilbrough N Yorks 294 A4
Bilbster H'land 445 C6
Bilby Notts 270 C4
Bildershaw Durham 331 B5
Bildeston Suffolk 164 C4
Bill Quay Tyne/Wear 352 D4
Billacombe Plym'th 11 E6
Billacott Cornw'l 18 B2
Billericay Essex 113 D8
Billesdon Leics 201 C8
Billesley Warwick 155 A5
Billesley W Midlands 176 B4
Billingborough Lincs 228 B2
Billinge Mersey 277 D7
Billingford Norfolk 187 C8
Billingford Norfolk 232 C5
Billingham Stockton 332 B4
Billinghay Lincs 251 D6
Billingley S Yorks 282 D2
Billingshurst W Sussex 48 A1
Billingsley Shrops 174 A4
Billington Beds 136 C2
Billington Lancs 290 C3
Billockby Norfolk 210 A4
Billown Motor Racing Circuit I/Man 336 E2
Billy Mill Tyne/Wear 353 C5
Billy Row Durham 343 D7
Bilsborrow Lancs 289 C7
Bilsby Lincs 275 D6
Bilsdean E Loth 398 D5
Bilsington Kent 73 E7
Bilson Green Glos 129 E6
Bilsthorpe Notts 248 B3
Bilsthorpe Moor Notts 248 C4
Bilston Midloth 396 F2
Bilston W Midlands 197 D8
Bilstone Leics 199 B8
Bilting Kent 73 B8
Bilton ER Yorks 298 D2
Bilton Northum 377 E6
Bilton N Yorks 306 D3
Bilton Warwick 178 D4
Bilton in Ainsty N Yorks 307 F6
Bimbister Orkney 452 B4
Binbrook Lincs 286 F3
Binchester Blocks Durham 343 E8
Bincombe Dorset 25 D8
Bindal H'land 441 E6
Bindon Som'set 37 B7
Binegar Som'set 60 B4
Bines Green W Sussex 48 C3
Binfield Brackn'l 87 B6
Binfield Heath Oxon 86 A4
Bingfield Northum 351 B6
Bingham C/Edinb 396 D2
Bingham Notts 225 A9
Bingham's Melcombe Dorset 41 F5
Bingley W Yorks 292 C4
Binham Norfolk 256 E2
Binley Hants 65 A5
Binley W Midlands 178 C2
Binley Woods Warwick 178 C2
Binnegar Dorset 26 C4
Binniehill Falk 394 D2
Binsey Oxon 133 F8
Binsoe N Yorks 318 E3
Binstead I/Wight 30 B3
Binsted Hants 67 C5
Binsted W Sussex 47 E7
Binton Warwick 155 B5
Bintree Norfolk 232 C5
Binweston Shrops 194 C2
Birch Essex 141 C8
Birch Gtr Man 279 C6
Birch Cross Staffs 222 B4
Birch Green Essex 141 D7
Birch Green Herts 138 E1
Birch Green Lancs 277 C6
Birch Green Worcs 153 C7
Birch Heath Ches 242 B3
Birch Hill Ches 264 E5
Birch Vale Derby 267 B7
Birch Wood Som'set 38 D2
Birchall Staffs 245 D5
Birchall Corner Essex 142 A1
Bircham Newton Norfolk 231 B7
Bircham Tofts Norfolk 231 B7
Birchanger Essex 139 C6
Birchburn N Ayrs 405 D5
Birchen Coppice Worcs 175 D6
Birchencliffe W Yorks 280 A4
Birchend Heref'd 152 D3
Bircher Heref'd 173 E7
Bircher Common Heref'd 173 E7
Birches Green W Midlands 198 E3
Birchett's Green E Sussex 71 E8
Birchfield H'land 434 F4
Birchfield W Midlands 198 E2
Birchgrove Card 100 F3
Birchgrove Swan 97 C9
Birchgrove W Sussex 70 F2
Birchill Devon 38 F4
Birchington Kent 95 C5
Birchley Heath Warwick 199 E6
Birchmoor Warwick 199 C6
Birchmoor Green Beds 159 F6
Bircholt Forstal Kent 73 C8
Birchover Derby 246 B2
Birchwood Lincs 272 F3
Birchwood Warrington 265 A8
Bircotes Notts 270 A4
Bird Green Essex 162 F2
Bird Street Suffolk 165 B5
Birdbrook Essex 163 D7
Birdfield Arg/Bute 408 C2
Birdham W Sussex 46 F4
Birdholme Derby 269 F7
Birdingbury Warwick 178 E3
Birdland Park, Bourton-on-the-Water Glos 132 C2
Birdlip Glos 130 E4
Birds Edge W Yorks 281 C6
Birds Green Essex 139 F7
Birdsall N Yorks 309 B5
Birdsend Glos 129 C9
Birdsgreen Shrops 175 B5
Birdsmoor Gate Dorset 39 F5
Birdston E Dunb 393 C5
Birdwell S Yorks 281 D8
Birdwood Glos 129 D8
Birdworld and Underwaterworld, Farnham Hants 67 C6
Birgham Scot Borders 387 E5
Birichen H'land 440 D4
Birkacre Lancs 277 B8
Birkby Cumb 337 D4
Birkby N Yorks 331 F8
Birkby W Yorks 280 A4
Birkdale Mersey 276 B3
Birkenbog Aberds 436 B2
Birkenhead Mersey 263 B8
Birkenhills Aberds 436 D4
Birkenshaw S Lanarks 393 F5
Birkenshaw S Lanarks 381 C7
Birkenshaw W Yorks 293 E6
Birkett Mire Cumb 326 B3
Birkhall Aberds 427 C8
Birkhill Angus 420 D3
Birkhill Dumf/Gal 371 D9
Birkholme Lincs 227 D6
Birkin N Yorks 294 E4
Birks W Yorks 293 E7
Birkshaw Northum 350 C2
Birley Heref'd 151 B7
Birley Carr S Yorks 269 A6
Birley Edge S Yorks 269 A6
Birleyhay Derby 269 C7
Birling Kent 91 D8
Birling Northum 365 A7
Birling Gap E Sussex 52 F3
Birlingham Worcs 153 D8
Birmingham W Midlands 176 A3
Birmingham Botanical Gardens W Midlands 176 A3
Birmingham International Airport W Midlands 177 B6
Birmingham Museum and Art Gallery W Midlands 198 F2
Birmingham Museum of Science and Technology W Midlands 198 F2
Birnam Perth/Kinr 419 C8
Birniehill S Lanarks 380 B4
Birse Aberds 428 C2
Birsemore Aberds 428 C2
Birstall Leics 201 B5
Birstall W Yorks 293 E6
Birstall Smithies W Yorks 293 E6
Birstwith N Yorks 306 D1
Birthorpe Lincs 228 B2
Birtle Gtr Man 279 B5
Birtley Heref'd 172 E5
Birtley Northum 350 A4
Birtley Tyne/Wear 352 E4
Birts Street Worcs 153 E5
Birtsmorton Worcs 153 E6
Bisbrooke Rutl'd 202 D3
Biscathorpe Lincs 274 C1
Biscombe Som'set 37 D8
Biscot Luton 137 C5
Biscovey Cornw'l 8 E4
Bish Mill Devon 35 A7
Bisham Windsor 109 F6
Bishampton Worcs 154 B2
Bishop Auckland Durham 343 F7
Bishop Burton ER Yorks 297 B6
Bishop Kinkell H'land 433 C7
Bishop Middleham Durham 344 E2
Bishop Monkton N Yorks 306 B3
Bishop Norton Lincs 272 A4
Bishop Sutton Bath/NE Som'set 80 E3
Bishop Thornton N Yorks 306 C2
Bishop Wilton ER Yorks 309 D5
Bishopbridge Lincs 273 A5
Bishopbriggs E Dunb 392 D4
Bishopdown Wilts 63 E8
Bishopmill Moray 435 B7
Bishops Cannings Wilts 82 D5
Bishop's Castle Shrops 194 F2
Bishop's Caundle Dorset 40 D3
Bishop's Cleeve Glos 131 B5
Bishops Frome Heref'd 152 C3
Bishops Gate Surrey 88 B1
Bishop's Green Essex 139 D8
Bishop's Green Hants 85 D6
Bishop's Hull Som'set 38 B2
Bishop's Itchington Warwick 156 A2
Bishops Lydeard Som'set 58 F3
Bishop's Norton Glos 130 C2
Bishop's Nympton Devon 35 B8
Bishop's Offley Staffs 221 C5
Bishop's Stortford Herts 139 C5
Bishops Sutton Hants 66 E2
Bishop's Tachbrook Warwick 178 F1
Bishop's Tawton Devon 55 F6
Bishop's Waltham Hants 45 C5
Bishop's Wood Staffs 197 B5
Bishopsbourne Kent 74 A3
Bishopsgarth Stockton 332 B3
Bishopsteignton Devon 21 F8
Bishopstoke Hants 44 C4
Bishopston Bristol 80 A3
Bishopston Swan 97 E6
Bishopstone Bucks 135 E7
Bishopstone E Sussex 50 F2
Bishopstone Heref'd 151 D6
Bishopstone Kent 94 C4
Bishopstone Swindon 106 F1
Bishopstone Wilts 42 A4
Bishopstrow Wilts 62 C2
Bishopswood Som'set 38 D3
Bishopsworth Bristol 80 C3
Bishopthorpe C/York 307 F8
Bishopton D'lington 332 B2
Bishopton Dumf/Gal 401 E6
Bishopton N Yorks 306 A2
Bishopton Renf 391 D8
Bishopton Warwick 155 A6
Bishopwearmouth Tyne/Wear 353 E6
Bishpool Newp 101 E6
Bishton Newp 101 E7
Bishton Staffs 222 D2
Bisley Glos 104 A3
Bisley Surrey 87 E9
Bisley Camp Surrey 87 E8
Bispham Blackp'l 288 B3
Bispham Green Lancs 277 B6
Bissoe Cornw'l 4 B3
Bisterne Hants 43 F5
Bisterne Close Hants 43 F7
Bitchet Green Kent 91 F6
Bitchfield Lincs 227 C6
Bittadon Devon 55 C5
Bittaford Devon 14 D1
Bitterley Shrops 174 C1
Bitterne S'thampton 44 D3
Bitterne Park S'thampton 44 D3
Bitterscote Staffs 199 C5
Bitteswell Leics 179 B5
Bittles Green Dorset 41 A7
Bitton S Glos 81 C5
Bix Oxon 108 E4
Bixter Shetl'd 457 H3
Blaby Leics 200 D5
Black Bank Cambs 184 A3
Black Bank Warwick 178 A2
Black Barn Lincs 229 C8
Black Bourton Oxon 106 B2
Black Bridge Pembs 116 C4
Black Callerton Tyne/Wear 352 C2
Black Carr Norfolk 209 D5
Black Clauchrie S Ayrs 400 A4
Black Corner W Sussex 69 C7
Black Corries Lodge H'land 417 B7
Black Crofts Arg/Bute 416 D4
Black Cross Cornw'l 7 C9
Black Dog Devon 35 E9
Black Heddon Northum 351 A8
Black Hill W Yorks 292 B3
Black Lane Gtr Man 278 C4
Black Lane Ends Lancs 291 B7
Black Moor W Yorks 293 C7
Black Mount Arg/Bute 417 C7
Black Notley Essex 140 C4
Black Pill Swan 97 D7
Black Pole Lancs 289 D6
Black Rock Brighton/Hove 49 F6
Black Rock Monmouths 102 E2
Black Street Suffolk 211 F6
Black Tar Pembs 117 C5
Black Torrington Devon 34 E2
Black Vein Caerph 100 D4
Blackacre Dumf/Gal 358 D4
Blackadder West Scot Borders 387 B6
Blackawton Devon 14 E4
Blackbeck Cumb 325 E5
Blackborough Devon 37 F6
Blackborough Norfolk 231 F5
Blackborough End Norfolk 231 F5
Blackboys E Sussex 50 B3
Blackbraes Aberds 429 A5
Blackbraes Falk 394 C3
Blackbrook Derby 246 E4
Blackbrook Derby 267 C8
Blackbrook Mersey 277 E7
Blackbrook Surrey 69 B5
Blackbrook Staffs 220 A5
Blackburn Aberds 429 A5
Blackburn Aberds 429 C5
Blackburn Aberds 436 E2
Blackburn Blackb'n 290 E2
Blackburn S Yorks 269 A7
Blackburn W Loth 394 E4
Blackchambers Aberds 429 A4
Blackcraig Dumf/Gal 357 F6
Blackcraigs Angus 428 D2
Blackden Heath Ches 266 E2
Blackditch Oxon 107 A5
Blackdog Aberds 429 A6
Blackdown Dorset 39 F5
Blackdyke Cumb 338 A1
Blackenhall Ches 243 E7
Blackenhall W Midlands 197 D7
Blacker S Yorks 281 C8
Blacker Hill S Yorks 282 D1
Blackfell Tyne/Wear 352 E4
Blackfen London 90 B4
Blackfield Hants 44 F3
Blackford Cumb 347 D9
Blackford Perth/Kinr 410 B3
Blackford Som'set 59 B8
Blackford Som'set 40 A3
Blackford Bridge Gtr Man 278 C4
Blackfordby Leics 223 E8
Blackgang I/Wight 30 E1
Blackgang Chine Fantasy Park I/Wight 30 E1
Blackgate Angus 421 B4
Blackhall Aberds 428 C3
Blackhall C/Edinb 395 D9
Blackhall Herts 138 A4
Blackhall Renf 392 F1
Blackhall Colliery Durham 344 D4
Blackhall Mill Tyne/Wear 352 E1
Blackhall Rocks Durham 345 D5
Blackham E Sussex 70 D4
Blackhaugh Scot Borders 385 E5
Blackheath Essex 141 C9
Blackheath London 90 A2
Blackheath Suffolk 189 C6
Blackheath W Midlands 176 A2
Blackhill Aberds 437 C7
Blackhill Aberds 437 D7
Blackhill Aberds 437 E7
Blackhill Durham 343 A5
Blackhill H'land 430 C3
Blackhillock Moray 436 D1
Blackhills H'land 434 C4
Blackhills Moray 435 C7
Blackhills Swan 97 D6
Blackhorse Devon 22 B1
Blackhorse S Glos 81 A5
Blackjack Lincs 228 A5
Blackland Som'set 56 D3
Blackland Wilts 82 C5
Blacklaw Aberds 436 C3
Blackleach Lancs 289 D6
Blackley Gtr Man 279 D6
Blackley W Yorks 280 A4
Blacklunans Perth/Kinr 420 A1
Blackmanston Dorset 27 D5
Blackmarstone Heref'd 151 E8
Blackmill Bridg 99 E5
Blackmoor Gtr Man 278 D2
Blackmoor Hants 67 E5
Blackmoor N Som'set 80 D1
Blackmoor Som'set 37 C8
Blackmoorfoot W Yorks 280 B4
Blackmore Essex 113 B7
Blackmore Shrops 194 B2
Blackmore End Essex 140 A3
Blackmore End Herts 137 D7
Blackmore End Worcs 153 D6
Blackness Aberds 428 C3
Blackness E Sussex 70 F5
Blackness Falk 411 D5
Blacknest Hants 67 C5
Blacknest Windsor 87 C9

Blackney Dorset 24 A3
Blacknoll Dorset 26 C3
Blacko Lancs 291 B6
Blackpark Dumf/Gal 401 C5
Blackpole Worcs 153 A7
Blackpool Blackp'l 288 C3
Blackpool Devon 15 F5
Blackpool Devon 21 F6
Blackpool Pembs 117 B7
Blackpool Airport Lancs 288 D3
Blackpool Corner Devon 23 A8
Blackpool Pleasure Beach Blackp'l 288 D3
Blackpool Tower Blackp'l 288 C3
Blackpool Zoo Park Blackp'l 288 C3
Blackridge W Loth 394 E2
Blackrock Arg/Bute 406 F3
Blackrock Monmouths 127 E5
Blackrod Gtr Man 277 B9
Blackshaw Dumf/Gal 346 C3
Blackshaw Head W Yorks 291 F7
Blacksmith's Corner Suffolk 165 D7
Blacksmith's Green Suffolk 187 E7
Blacksnape Blackb'n 290 F3
Blackstone W Sussex 48 C4
Blackthorn Oxon 134 D3
Blackthorpe Suffolk 186 F3
Blacktoft ER Yorks 296 F3
Blacktop Aberd C 429 B5
Blacktown Newp 100 F5
Blackwall London 112 F2
Blackwall Tunnel London 112 F2
Blackwater Cornw'l 4 A2
Blackwater Dorset 28 A2
Blackwater Hants 87 E6
Blackwater I/Wight 30 C2
Blackwater Norfolk 233 D6
Blackwater Som'set 38 C3
Blackwater Lodge Moray 435 F8
Blackwaterfoot N Ayrs 404 D4
Blackwell Cumb 339 A7
Blackwell D'lington 331 D7
Blackwell Derby 247 C6
Blackwell Derby 268 E2
Blackwell Som'set 37 A5
Blackwell Warwick 155 D7
Blackwell Worcs 176 D2
Blackwell W Sussex 70 D2
Blackwell's End Green Glos 130 B1
Blackwood = Coed Duon Caerph 100 C3
Blackwood S Lanarks 381 D7
Blackwood Warrington 265 A7
Blackwood Hill Staffs 244 C4
Blacky Moor Northants 158 A3
Blacon Ches 264 F2
Bladbean Kent 74 B3
Blades N Yorks 317 A5
Bladnoch Dumf/Gal 401 D6
Bladon Oxon 133 E7
Blaen Clydach Rh Cyn Taff 99 D6
Blaenannerch Ceredig'n 144 C4
Blaenau Bl Gwent 100 B4
Blaenau Dolwyddelan Conwy 238 D2
Blaenau Ffestiniog Gwyn 238 E2
Blaenau Uchaf Wrex 241 F6
Blaenavon Torf 127 F6
Blaencaerau Bridg 98 C4
Blaencarno Caerph 126 F2
Blaencelyn Ceredig'n 145 B7
Blaencwm Rh Cyn Taff 99 C5
Blaendulais = Seven Sisters Neath P Talb 124 F5
Blaendyryn Powys 148 E3
Blaenffos Pembs 144 E3
Blaengarw Bridg 99 D5
Blaengavenny Monmouths 127 D7
Blaen-geuffordd Ceredig'n 169 B5
Blaengwawr Rh Cyn Taff 99 B7
Blaengwrach Neath P Talb 98 A4
Blaengwynfi Neath P Talb 98 C4
Blaenllechau Rh Cyn Taff 99 C7
Blaenpennal Ceredig'n 169 F5
Blaenplwyf Ceredig'n 168 C4
Blaenporth Ceredig'n 145 C5
Blaenrhondda Rh Cyn Taff 99 C5
Blaenwaun Carms 121 B8
Blaen-y-Coed Carms 122 B2
Blaen-y-cwm Bl Gwent 126 E3
Blaenycwm Ceredig'n 170 C1
Blaen-y-cwm Torf 100 B4
Blagdon N Som'set 80 E2
Blagdon Torbay 15 C5
Blagdon Hill Som'set 38 C2
Blagill Cumb 341 B5
Blaguegate Lancs 277 C6
Blaich H'land 424 E2
Blain H'land 423 F6
Blaina Bl Gwent 127 F5
Blainacraig Ho Aberds 428 C2
Blair Atholl Perth/Kinr 419 A6
Blair Castle, Blair Atholl Perth/Kinr 419 A6
Blair Drummond Stirl 410 C2
Blair Drummond Safari Park, Dunblane Stirl 410 C2
Blairanbolch Arg/Bute 390 E2
Blairbeg N Ayrs 405 C6
Blairdaff Aberds 428 A3
Blairdryne Aberds 428 C4
Blairgorm H'land 435 F5
Blairgowrie Perth/Kinr 420 C1
Blairhall Fife 411 D5
Blairhill N Lanarks 393 E6
Blairingone Perth/Kinr 411 C4
Blairland N Ayrs 379 C6
Blairlinn N Lanarks 393 D7
Blairlogie Stirl 410 C3
Blairlomond Arg/Bute 408 C4
Blairmore Arg/Bute 408 D4
Blairmore H'land 442 C3
Blairnamarrow Moray 427 A7
Blair's Ferry Arg/Bute 408 F2
Blairskaith E Dunb 392 C3
Blaisdon Glos 129 D8
Blaise Hamlet Bristol 80 A3
Blaize Bailey Glos 129 E7
Blake End Essex 140 C3
Blakebrook Worcs 175 C6
Blakedown Worcs 175 C7
Blakelands M/Keynes 158 D5
Blakelaw Scot Borders 374 A5
Blakelaw Tyne/Wear 352 C3
Blakeley Staffs 197 E6
Blakeley Lane Staffs 245 E5
Blakelow Ches 243 D6
Blakemere Heref'd 150 D5
Blakenall Heath W Midlands 197 C9
Blakeney Glos 129 F7
Blakeney Norfolk 256 D3
Blakeney Hill Glos 129 F7
Blakeney Point NNR Norfolk 256 C3
Blakeshall Worcs 175 B6
Blakesley Northants 157 B7
Blanchland Northum 342 A3
Bland Hill N Yorks 305 E8
Blandford Camp Dorset 41 E8
Blandford Forum Dorset 41 E7
Blandford St. Mary Dorset 41 E7
Blandy H'land 443 C8
Blanefield Stirl 392 C3
Blanerne Scot Borders 387 A6
Blankney Lincs 250 B4
Blantyre S Lanarks 381 A5
Blar a'Chaorainn H'land 424 F3
Blaran Arg/Bute 416 F3
Blarghour Arg/Bute 417 F4
Blarmachfoldach H'land 424 F2
Blarnalearoch H'land 439 D5
Blasford Hill Essex 140 E3
Blashford Hants 43 E5
Blaston Leics 202 D2
Blatherwycke Northants 203 D5
Blawith Cumb 313 D5
Blaxhall Suffolk 166 A5
Blaxton S Yorks 283 D7
Blaydon Tyne/Wear 352 D2
Blaydon Burn Tyne/Wear 352 D2
Blazefield N Yorks 305 B7
Bleach Green Cumb 324 C4
Bleach Green Suffolk 188 C2
Bleadney Som'set 60 B1
Bleadon N Som'set 79 E6
Bleak Hey Nook Gtr Man 280 C2
Bleak Hill Hants 43 D5
Bleak Street Som'set 61 E7
Blean Kent 94 D2
Bleasby Lincs 273 C7
Bleasby Notts 248 E5
Bleasby Moor Lincs 273 C7
Bleasdale Lancs 289 A8
Bleatarn Cumb 328 D4
Blebocraigs Fife 420 F4
Bleddfa Powys 172 E2
Bledington Glos 132 C3
Bledlow Bucks 109 B5
Bledlow Ridge Bucks 109 C5
Bleet Wilts 82 E2
Blegbie E Loth 397 F6
Blencarn Cumb 340 E3
Blencogo Cumb 338 B2
Blendworth Hants 46 D2
Blenheim Palace, Woodstock Oxon 133 D7
Blenheim Park Norfolk 231 B8
Blennerhasset Cumb 338 C2
Blervie Castle Moray 435 C5
Bletchingdon Oxon 133 D9
Bletchingley Surrey 69 A8
Bletchley M/Keynes 158 F5
Bletchley Shrops 220 B2
Bletherston Pembs 120 C5
Bletsoe Beds 159 A8
Blewbury Oxon 107 E7
Blickling Norfolk 233 C8
Blickling Hall, Aylsham Norfolk 233 C8
Blidworth Notts 248 C2
Blidworth Bottoms Notts 248 D2
Blindcrake Cumb 338 E2
Blindley Heath Surrey 70 B2
Blindmore Som'set 38 D3
Blingery H'land 445 D7
Blisland Cornw'l 8 A4
Bliss Gate Worcs 174 D4
Blissford Hants 43 D6
Blisworth Northants 158 B2
Blithbury Staffs 222 D3
Blitterlees Cumb 337 A8
Blo' Norton Norfolk 187 C5
Blockley Glos 155 F6
Blofield Norfolk 210 B2
Blofield Corner Norfolk 210 A2
Blofield Heath Norfolk 210 A2
Bloodman's Corner Suffolk 211 D6
Bloomfield Scot Borders 374 C1
Bloomfield W Midlands 197 E8
Bloomsbury London 111 F8
Blore Staffs 245 E8
Blossomfield W Midlands 177 C5
Blount's Green Staffs 222 B3
Blowick Mersey 276 A4
Bloxham Oxon 156 E3
Bloxholm Lincs 250 D4
Bloxwich W Midlands 197 C8
Bloxworth Dorset 26 B4
Blubberhouses N Yorks 305 D7
Blue Anchor Cornw'l 7 D9
Blue Anchor Som'set 57 C7
Blue Anchor Swan 97 C5
Blue Bank N Yorks 334 E4
Blue Bell Hill Kent 92 D1
Blue Bridge M/Keynes 158 D4
Blue Planet Aquarium Ches 264 E3
Blue Reef Aquarium, Newquay Cornw'l 7 C7
Blue Reef Aquarium, Portsmouth Portsm'th 30 A4
Blue Reef Aquarium, Tynemouth Tyne/Wear 353 B6
Blue Row Essex 142 E1
Blue Town Kent 93 A5
Blue Vein Wilts 81 C8
Bluetown Kent 93 E5
Blughasary H'land 439 C5
Blundell's Hill Mersey 264 A4
Blundellsands Mersey 276 E3
Blundeston Suffolk 211 D6
Blunham Beds 160 B3
Blunsdon St. Andrew Swindon 105 E7
Bluntington Worcs 175 D7
Bluntisham Cambs 183 D7
Blunt's Cornw'l 10 C2
Blunt's Green Warwick 177 E5
Blurton Stoke 244 F3
Blyborough Lincs 285 F5
Blychau Conwy 239 B7
Blyford Suffolk 189 C6
Blymhill Staffs 196 A5
Blymhill Common Staffs 196 A4
Blymhill Lawn Staffs 196 A5
Blyth Notts 270 B4
Blyth Northum 365 F8
Blyth Bridge Scot Borders 383 C7
Blyth End Warwick 199 E5
Blythburgh Suffolk 189 C7
Blythe Scot Borders 385 C8
Blythe Bridge Staffs 244 F5
Blythe Marsh Staffs 244 F5
Blythswood Renf 392 E2
Blyton Lincs 284 F4
Boarhills Fife 421 F5
Boarhunt Hants 45 E7
Boar's Head Gtr Man 277 C8
Boars Hill Oxon 107 B6
Boarshead E Sussex 71 E5
Boarstall Bucks 134 E3
Boasley Cross Devon 19 B7
Boat of Garten H'land 426 A4
Boath H'land 440 F2
Bobbing Kent 92 C4
Bobbington Staffs 196 E5
Bobbingworth Essex 113 A5
Bobby Hill Suffolk 187 D5
Boblainy H'land 433 E6
Bocaddon Cornw'l 9 D6
Bochastle Stirl 410 B1
Bocking Essex 140 C4
Bocking Churchstreet Essex 140 B4
Bockings Elm Essex 142 D4
Bockleton Worcs 174 F1
Bockmer End Bucks 109 E6
Bodantionail H'land 438 F1
Boddam Aberds 437 D8
Boddam Shetl'd 455 E2
Bodden Som'set 60 C4
Boddington Glos 130 C3
Bodedern Angl 258 C3
Bodelwyddan Denbs 262 D2
Bodenham Heref'd 151 B8
Bodenham Arboretum and Earth Centre Worcs 175 B6
Bodenham Bank Heref'd 129 A7
Bodenham Moor Heref'd 151 B8
Bodernham Wilts 43 A6
Bodewryd Angl 258 A4
Bodfari Denbs 262 E3
Bodffordd Angl 259 D5
Bodham Norfolk 257 D5
Bodiam E Sussex 51 A8
Bodiam Castle E Sussex 72 F2
Bodicote Oxon 156 E4
Bodiechell Aberds 437 D4
Bodieve Cornw'l 16 F4
Bodilly Cornw'l 4 D1
Bodiniel Cornw'l 8 B4
Bodinnick Cornw'l 9 E5
Bodle Street Green E Sussex 51 D6
Bodley Devon 55 B8
Bodlith Powys 217 C9
Bodlondeb Conwy 262 E6
Bodmin Cornw'l 8 B4
Bodnant Conwy 262 E6
Bodnant Garden, Colwyn Bay Conwy 261 E5
Bodney Norfolk 207 D7
Bodrane Cornw'l 9 C7
Bodsham Kent 74 B2
Boduan Gwyn 213 A6
Boduel Cornw'l 9 C7
Bodwen Cornw'l 8 C3
Bodymoor Heath Warwick 198 D4
Bofarnel Cornw'l 9 C5
Bogallan H'land 433 C8
Bogbrae Aberds 437 E7
Bogend Notts 247 E7
Bogend S Ayrs 367 A7
Bogentory Aberds 428 B4
Boghall Midloth 396 E1
Boghall W Loth 394 E4
Boghead Aberds 428 C3
Boghead E Dunb 392 D4
Boghead S Lanarks 381 D7
Bogmarsh Heref'd 151 E8
Bogmoor Moray 435 B8
Bogniebrae Aberds 436 D2
Bogniebrae Aberds 436 D3
Bognor Regis W Sussex 31 E8
Bograxie Aberds 428 A4
Bogs Aberds 436 F2
Bogside N Lanarks 381 B8
Bogthorn W Yorks 292 C2
Bogton Aberds 436 C3
Bogtown Aberds 436 B2
Bogtown Devon 19 A6
Bogue Dumf/Gal 356 F4
Bohemia E Sussex 52 E1
Bohemia Wilts 43 C7
Bohenie H'land 425 D4
Bohetherick Cornw'l 10 B4
Boholt Gtr Man 278 B4
Bohortha Cornw'l 5 D5
Bohuntine H'land 425 D4
Bohuntinville H'land 425 D4
Boirseam W Isles 449 D4
Bojewyan Cornw'l 2 D3
Bokiddick Cornw'l 8 C3
Bolam Durham 331 B5
Bolam Northum 364 F3
Bolberry Devon 12 E4
Bold Heath Mersey 265 B5
Boldmere W Midlands 198 E3
Boldon Colliery Tyne/Wear 353 D5
Boldre Hants 29 A6
Boldron Durham 330 D2
Bole Notts 271 B7
Bolehall Staffs 199 C5
Bolehill Derby 246 C3
Bolehill S Yorks 269 C7
Bolenowe Cornw'l 4 C1
Boleside Scot Borders 385 F6
Bolham Devon 36 D4
Bolham Notts 271 C6
Bolham Water Devon 37 D8
Bolingey Cornw'l 7 E6
Bollihope Durham 342 E4
Bollington Ches 267 D5
Bollington Cross Ches 267 D5
Bollow Glos 129 E8
Bolney W Sussex 49 B5
Bolnhurst Beds 160 A1
Bolshan Angus 421 B6
Bolsover Derby 270 E1
Bolster Moor W Yorks 280 A3
Bolsterstone S Yorks 281 E7
Bolstone Heref'd 128 A4
Boltby N Yorks 319 C8
Bolter End Bucks 109 D5
Boltgate N Lincs 284 A3
Bolton Cumb 328 B3
Bolton E Loth 397 D7
Bolton ER Yorks 308 E4
Bolton Gtr Man 278 C3
Bolton Northum 376 E4
Bolton W Yorks 292 C5
Bolton Abbey N Yorks 305 E5
Bolton Abbey, Skipton N Yorks 305 E5
Bolton Bridge N Yorks 305 E5
Bolton by Bowland Lancs 303 F7
Bolton Castle, Leyburn N Yorks 317 B6
Bolton Green Lancs 277 A8
Bolton Low Houses Cumb 338 C3
Bolton New Houses Cumb 338 C3
Bolton Percy N Yorks 294 B4
Bolton Town End Lancs 301 B8
Bolton upon Dearne S Yorks 282 D2
Bolton Wood Lane Cumb 338 C4
Bolton Woods W Yorks 292 C5
Boltonfellend Cumb 348 C3
Boltongate Cumb 338 C3
Bolton-le-Sands Lancs 301 B8
Bolton-on-Swale N Yorks 318 A4
Boltshope Park Durham 342 B2
Bolventor Cornw'l 17 E8
Bomarsund Northum 365 F7
Bombie Dumf/Gal 402 D1
Bomby Cumb 327 C7
Bomere Heath Shrops 219 E6
Bonar Bridge H'land 440 D3
Bonawe Arg/Bute 417 D5
Bonbusk Notts 270 E2
Bonby N Lincs 285 A7
Bonc Wrex 217 A8
Boncath Pembs 144 E4
Bonchester Bridge Scot Borders 374 E1
Bonchurch I/Wight 30 E3
Bond End Staffs 222 E4
Bondend Glos 130 D3
Bondleigh Devon 35 F5
Bonds Lancs 289 A6
Bonehayne Devon 23 B6
Bonehill Devon 20 E4
Bonehill Staffs 198 C4
Bo'ness Falk 411 D4
Boney Hay Staffs 198 A2
Bonhill W Dunb 391 C7
Boningdale Shrops 196 C5
Bonjedward Scot Borders 374 C3
Bonkle N Lanarks 382 A1
Bonnavoulin H'land 415 B8
Bonning Gate Cumb 314 A3
Bonnington C/Edinb 395 E7
Bonnington Kent 73 D8
Bonnybank Fife 412 B1
Bonnybridge Falk 410 D3
Bonnykelly Aberds 437 C5
Bonnyrigg Midloth 396 E3
Bonnyton Aberds 436 E3
Bonnyton Angus 421 B6
Bonnyton Angus 420 D3
Bonnyton E Ayrs 379 E8
Bonsall Derby 246 C3
Bonskeid House Perth/Kinr 419 A6
Bonson Som'set 58 C4
Bont Monmouths 127 D8
Bont Dolgadfan Powys 191 C8
Bont Newydd Gwyn 238 F2
Bontddu Gwyn 215 E5
Bont-goch = Elerch Ceredig'n 169 A6
Bonthorpe Lincs 275 E6
Bont-newydd Conwy 262 E2
Bontnewydd Ceredig'n 168 E5
Bontnewydd Gwyn 237 C5
Bontuchel Denbs 240 C2
Bonvilston V/Glam 77 B8
Bonwm Denbs 240 F3
Bon-y-maen Swan 97 C8
Boode Devon 54 D5
Booker Bucks 109 D6
Boomer Som'set 59 E5
Boon Scot Borders 385 C8
Boon Hill Staffs 244 D2
Boorley Green Hants 45 D5
Boosbeck Redcar/Clevel'd 333 C8
Boose's Green Essex 141 A5
Boot Cumb 325 F8
Boot Street Suffolk 166 C2
Booth W Yorks 292 E2
Booth Bank Ches 266 B1
Booth Green Ches 267 C5
Booth Wood W Yorks 280 A2
Boothby Graffoe Lincs 250 C2
Boothby Pagnell Lincs 227 B6
Boothen Stoke 244 F3
Boothferry ER Yorks 295 E8
Boothroyd W Yorks 293 F6
Booth's Hill Warrington 265 B8
Boothsdale Ches 265 F5
Boothstown Gtr Man 278 D3
Boothtown W Yorks 292 E3
Boothville Northants 180 F3
Bootle Cumb 312 C3
Bootle Mersey 263 A8
Booton Norfolk 233 D7
Boots Green Ches 266 E2
Booze N Yorks 330 F2
Boquhan Stirl 409 D8
Boraston Shrops 174 E2
Borden Kent 92 D4
Borden W Sussex 46 B4
Border Cumb 346 F5
Bordesley Green W Midlands 176 A5
Bordley N Yorks 304 C2
Bordon Hants 67 D6
Bordon Camp Hants 67 D5
Boreham Essex 140 F4
Boreham Wilts 62 C2
Boreham Street E Sussex 51 D6
Borehamwood Herts 111 C5
Boreland Dumf/Gal 401 C5
Boreland Dumf/Gal 359 D7
Boreland Stirl 418 D3
Boreland of Southwick Dumf/Gal 402 C3
Borgh W Isles 448 D3
Borgh W Isles 446 C2
Borghasdal W Isles 448 D4
Borghastan W Isles 450 C5
Borgie H'land 443 C8
Borgue Dumf/Gal 401 E8
Borgue H'land 441 A8
Borley Essex 164 D1
Borley Green Essex 164 D1
Borley Green Herts 138 A4
Borley Green Suffolk 186 F4
Bornais W Isles 446 A3
Bornesketaig H'land 430 A3
Borness Dumf/Gal 401 E8
Borough Green Kent 91 E7
Boroughbridge N Yorks 306 B4
Borras Wrex 241 D7
Borreraig H'land 430 C1
Borrobol Lodge H'land 441 A5
Borrodale H'land 430 D1
Borrohill Aberds 437 C6
Borrowash Derby 224 B3
Borrowby N Yorks 319 C7
Borrowby N Yorks 334 C2
Borrowcop Hill Staffs 198 B3
Borrowfield Aberds 429 C5
Borrowston H'land 445 D7
Borstal Medway 92 C1
Borth = Y Borth Ceredig'n 190 E3
Borthwick Midloth 384 A4
Borthwickbrae Scot Borders 373 E5
Borthwickshiels Scot Borders 373 D5
Borthwnog Gwyn 215 E5
Borth-y-Gest Gwyn 214 A3
Borve H'land 430 D4
Borve Lodge W Isles 448 C4
Borwick Lancs 302 A2
Borwick Rails Cumb 312 E4
Bosavern Cornw'l 2 D3
Bosbury Heref'd 152 D3
Boscarne Cornw'l 8 B3
Boscastle Cornw'l 17 B6
Boscombe Bournem'th 28 B2
Boscombe Wilts 63 D9
Boscomoor Staffs 221 F8
Boscoppa Cornw'l 8 E3
Boscreege Cornw'l 3 D7
Bosham W Sussex 46 F4
Bosherston Pembs 117 F5
Boskenna Cornw'l 2 F4
Bosleake Cornw'l 4 B1
Bosley Ches 244 A4
Bossall N Yorks 308 C3
Bossiney Cornw'l 17 C6
Bossingham Kent 74 B3
Bossington Hants 64 E3
Bossington Kent 94 E4
Bossington Som'set 56 B4
Bostadh W Isles 450 C4
Bostock Green Ches 265 F8
Boston Lincs 252 F2
Boston Long Hedges Lincs 252 E2
Boston Spa W Yorks 294 A2
Boswarthen Cornw'l 2 D4
Boswinger Cornw'l 5 B7
Botallack Cornw'l 2 D3
Botany Bay Bristol 80 A3
Botany Bay London 111 C7
Botany Bay Monmouths 102 B2
Botcherby Cumb 348 E2
Botcheston Leics 200 B3
Botely Oxon 107 A6
Botesdale Suffolk 187 C5
Bothal Northum 365 E6
Bothampstead W Berks 85 A7
Bothamsall Notts 271 E5
Bothel Cumb 338 D2
Bothenhampton Dorset 24 B4
Bothwell S Lanarks 381 A6
Bothy H'land 425 E4
Botley Bucks 110 B1
Botley Hants 45 D5
Botloe's Green Glos 129 B8
Botolph Bridge Peterbro 204 D2
Botolph Claydon Bucks 135 C5
Botolphs W Sussex 48 E3
Botolph's Bridge Kent 74 E2
Bottacks H'land 433 B6
Botternell Cornw'l 18 F2
Bottesford Leics 226 A3
Bottesford N Lincs 284 C5
Bottisham Cambs 184 F3
Bottlesford Wilts 83 E7
Bottom Boat W Yorks 293 F9
Bottom House Staffs 245 D6
Bottom of Hutton Lancs 289 E6
Bottom o'th'Moor Gtr Man 278 B2
Bottomcraig Fife 420 E3
Bottomley W Yorks 291 F7
Bottoms Cornw'l 2 F3
Botton N Yorks 333 F8
Botusfleming Cornw'l 10 C4
Botwnnog Gwyn 212 B5
Bough Beech Kent 70 B4
Boughrood Powys 149 E7
Boughrood Brest Powys 149 E7
Boughspring Glos 102 C3
Boughton Norfolk 207 C5
Boughton Northants 180 E3
Boughton Notts 271 F5
Boughton Aluph Kent 73 B7
Boughton Corner Kent 73 B7
Boughton End Beds 159 E7
Boughton Green Kent 72 A2
Boughton Heath Ches 242 A1
Boughton Hill Kent 93 E8
Boughton Lees Kent 73 B7
Boughton Malherbe Kent 72 B4
Boughton Monchelsea Kent 72 A2
Boughton Street Kent 93 E8
Boulby Redcar/Clevel'd 334 C2
Boulder Clough W Yorks 292 F2
Bouldnor I/Wight 29 C7
Bouldon Shrops 173 A8
Boulge Suffolk 166 B3
Boulmer Northum 377 E7
Boulsdon Glos 129 C8
Boultenstone Aberds 428 A1
Boultham Moor Lincs 272 F4
Boulton Derby C 224 B2
Boundary Derby 224 E1
Boundary Staffs 245 F5
Boundstone Surrey 67 C6
Bourn Cambs 161 A6
Bournbrook W Midlands 176 B3
Bourne Lincs 228 D1
Bourne End Beds 159 D7
Bourne End Beds 110 A2
Bourne End Beds 181 F8
Bourne End Bucks 109 E7
Bournemouth Bournem'th 28 B1
Bournemouth International Airport Dorset 28 A2
Bournes Green Glos 104 B3
Bournes Green Southend 115 E5
Bournheath Worcs 176 D1
Bournmoor Durham 344 A2
Bournside Glos 130 C4
Bournstream Glos 103 D7
Bournville W Midlands 176 B3
Bourton Bucks 135 A5
Bourton Dorset 61 E7
Bourton N Som'set 79 D7
Bourton Oxon 106 E1
Bourton Shrops 195 D7
Bourton Wilts 83 D5
Bourton on Dunsmore Warwick 178 D3
Bourton on the Hill Glos 132 A2
Bourton-on-the-Water Glos 132 C2
Bourtreehill N Ayrs 379 E6
Bousd Arg/Bute 415 A5
Bousta Shetl'd 457 H2
Boustead Hill Cumb 347 E7
Bouth Cumb 313 C7
Bouthwaite N Yorks 305 A6
Bouts Worcs 154 A3
Bovain Stirl 418 D3
Boveney Bucks 87 A8
Boveridge Dorset 42 D4
Boverton V/Glam 77 C6
Bovey Tracey Devon 21 E6
Bovingdon Herts 110 B2
Bovingdon Green Bucks 109 E6
Bovingdon Green Herts 110 B2
Bovinger Essex 112 A5
Bovington Camp Dorset 26 C3
Bow Scot Borders 385 D6
Bow Cumb 347 E8
Bow Devon 35 F7
Bow London 112 F2
Bow Orkney 452 D4
Bow Oxon 106 D3
Bow Brickhill M/Keynes 159 F6
Bow Broom S Yorks 282 E3
Bow of Fife Fife 411 A8
Bow Street Ceredig'n 168 B5
Bow Street Norfolk 208 D4
Bowbank Durham 329 B8
Bowbeck Suffolk 186 C3
Bowbridge Glos 104 B2
Bowbrook Shrops 195 A5
Bowburn Durham 344 D2
Bowcombe I/Wight 30 C1
Bowd Devon 22 B4
Bowden Scot Borders 373 A8
Bowden Devon 14 F4
Bowden Derra Cornw'l 18 D2
Bowden Hill Wilts 82 C3
Bowdon Gtr Man 266 B2
Bower H'land 445 B6
Bower Ashton Bristol 80 B3
Bower Hinton Som'set 39 C7
Bower House Tye Suffolk 164 D4
Bowerchalke Wilts 42 B3
Bowerhill Wilts 82 D3
Bowermadden H'land 445 B6
Bowers Staffs 221 A6
Bowers Gifford Essex 114 E2
Bowershall Fife 411 C5
Bowertower H'land 445 B6
Bowes Durham 330 D1
Bowe's Gate Ches 242 C4
Bowes Park London 111 D8
Bowgreave Lancs 289 B6
Bowgreen Gtr Man 266 B2
Bowhill Scot Borders 373 B5
Bowhouse Dumf/Gal 346 C2
Bowhousebog N Lanarks 382 A2
Bowithick Cornw'l 17 D8
Bowker's Green Lancs 276 D5
Bowland Bridge Cumb 314 C2
Bowlee Gtr Man 279 C5
Bowlees Durham 342 F2
Bowley Heref'd 151 B8
Bowley Town Heref'd 151 B8
Bowlhead Green Surrey 67 D8
Bowling W Dunb 391 D8
Bowling W Yorks 293 D5
Bowling Alley Hants 67 B5
Bowling Bank Wrex 241 E9
Bowling Green Cornw'l 10 A3
Bowling Green Worcs 153 B6
Bowlish Som'set 60 C4
Bowmanstead Cumb 313 A7
Bowmore Arg/Bute 403 A3
Bowness-on-Solway Cumb 347 D6
Bowness-on-Windermere Cumb 314 A2
Bowood House and Gardens, Calne Wilts 82 B4
Bowrie-fauld Angus 421 C5
Bowring Park Mersey 264 B3
Bowscale Cumb 339 E6
Bowsden Northum 388 D1
Bowside Lodge H'land 444 B2
Bowston Cumb 314 A3
Bowthorpe Norfolk 209 B7
Box Glos 104 B2
Box Wilts 81 C8
Box End Beds 159 C8
Box Hill Surrey 69 A5
Box Hill Wilts 81 C8
Boxbush Glos 129 C7
Boxbush Glos 129 E8
Boxford Suffolk 164 D4
Boxford W Berks 85 B5
Boxgrove W Sussex 47 E6
Boxley Kent 92 E2
Boxmoor Herts 110 A2
Box's Shop Cornw'l 32 F4
Boxted Essex 141 A8
Boxted Essex 141 A9
Boxted Suffolk 164 B1
Boxted Cross Essex 141 A9
Boxwell Glos 103 D8

Boxworth Cambs 183 F6
Boxworth End Cambs 183 E7
Boyden End Suffolk 163 A7
Boyden Gate Kent 94 C4
Boyland Common Norfolk 187 B6
Boylestone Derby 223 A5
Boyndie Aberds 436 B3
Boynton ER Yorks 310 B4
Boys Hill Dorset 40 D3
Boys Village V/Glam 77 C7
Boysack Angus 421 C6
Boysack Angus 421 C5
Boythorpe Derby 269 F7
Boyton Cornw'l 18 B3
Boyton Suffolk 167 C5
Boyton Wilts 62 D4
Boyton Cross Essex 140 F2
Boyton End Essex 139 A8
Boyton End Suffolk 163 D7
Bozeat Northants 159 A6
Braaid I/Man 336 D3
Braal Castle H'land 445 B5
Brabling Green Suffolk 188 F3
Brabourne Kent 74 C2
Brabourne Lees Kent 73 C8
Brabster H'land 445 B7
Bracadale H'land 430 E3
Bracara H'land 423 C7
Braceborough Lincs 203 A7
Bracebridge Lincs 272 F4
Bracebridge Heath Lincs 272 F4
Braceby Lincs 227 A7
Bracewell Lancs 303 F9
Bracken Hall W Yorks 280 A5
Bracken Hill W Yorks 293 F5
Bracken Park W Yorks 293 B9
Brackenber Cumb 328 C4
Brackenfield Derby 247 C5
Brackenhill W Yorks 282 A2
Brackenlands Cumb 338 B4
Brackenthwaite Cumb 325 B8
Brackenthwaite Cumb 338 B4
Brackenthwaite N Yorks 306 E2
Bracklamore Aberds 437 C5
Bracklesham W Sussex 31 E6
Brackletter H'land 424 D3
Brackley Arg/Bute 404 B3
Brackley Northants 157 E6
Brackley Hatch Northants 157 D8
Brackloch H'land 439 A5
Bracknell Brackn'l 87 C7
Braco Perth/Kinr 410 B3
Braco Castle Perth/Kinr 410 A3
Braco Park Aberds 437 B6
Bracobrae Moray 436 C2
Bracon N Lincs 284 C2
Bracon Ash Norfolk 209 D7
Bracorina H'land 423 C7
Bradbourne Derby 246 D2
Bradbury Durham 344 F2
Bradda I/Man 336 E1
Bradden Northants 157 C7
Braddock Cornw'l 9 C6
Braddocks Hay Staffs 244 C3
Bradeley Stoke 244 D3
Bradenham Bucks 109 C6
Bradenham Norfolk 208 B2
Bradenstoke Wilts 82 A5
Brades Village W Midlands 197 E8
Bradfield Devon 37 E6
Bradfield Essex 142 A3
Bradfield Norfolk 234 B2
Bradfield W Berks 86 B1
Bradfield Combust Suffolk 164 A2
Bradfield Green Ches 243 C6
Bradfield Heath Essex 142 B3
Bradfield St. Clare Suffolk 164 A3
Bradfield St. George Suffolk 164 A3
Bradford Cornw'l 17 E7
Bradford Devon 33 E8
Bradford Gtr Man 279 E6
Bradford W Yorks 293 D5
Bradford Abbas Dorset 40 D1
Bradford Cathedral W Yorks 292 D5
Bradford Industrial Museum W Yorks 293 C5
Bradford Leigh Wilts 82 D1
Bradford on Avon Wilts 81 D8
Bradford on Tone Som'set 37 B8
Bradford Peverell Dorset 25 B8
Bradgate S Yorks 269 A8
Bradiford Devon 55 E6
Brading I/Wight 30 C4
Bradley Ches 265 D5
Bradley Derby 246 E2
Bradley Glos 103 D6
Bradley Hants 66 C2
Bradley NE Lincs 286 C3
Bradley Staffs 221 E7
Bradley W Midlands 197 D8
Bradley Wrex 241 D7
Bradley W Yorks 292 F5
Bradley Cross Som'set 60 A1
Bradley Fold Gtr Man 278 C4
Bradley Green Ches 242 E3
Bradley Green Som'set 58 D5
Bradley Green Warwick 199 C6
Bradley Green Worcs 176 F2
Bradley in the Moors Staffs 245 F7
Bradley Mills W Yorks 280 A5
Bradley Mount Ches 267 D5
Bradley Stoke S Glos 102 F4
Bradlow Heref'd 152 E4
Bradmore Notts 225 B6
Bradmore W Midlands 197 D6
Bradney Som'set 59 D6
Bradninch Devon 36 F4
Bradnop Staffs 245 C6
Bradpole Dorset 24 B4
Bradshaw Gtr Man 278 B3
Bradshaw W Yorks 280 B3
Bradshaw W Yorks 292 D3
Bradstone Devon 18 D4
Bradville M/Keynes 158 D4
Bradwall Green Ches 243 B8
Bradway S Yorks 269 C6
Bradwell Derby 268 C3
Bradwell Devon 54 C4
Bradwell Essex 140 C5
Bradwell M/Keynes 158 E4
Bradwell Norfolk 211 C6
Bradwell Staffs 244 E2
Bradwell Hills Derby 268 C3
Bradwell on Sea Essex 141 F9
Bradwell Waterside Essex 141 F8
Bradworthy Devon 33 D6
Brae Dumf/Gal 402 B2
Brae H'land 438 E2
Brae H'land 439 C8
Brae Shetl'd 457 G3
Brae of Achnahaird H'land 438 B4
Brae of Boquhapple Stirl 410 B1
Brae Roy Lodge H'land 425 C5
Braeantra H'land 440 F2
Braebuster Orkney 453 C6
Braedownie Angus 427 E7
Braefield H'land 433 E6
Braefindon H'land 433 C8
Braegrum Perth/Kinr 419 E8
Braehead Dumf/Gal 401 D6
Braehead Orkney 454 B2
Braehead Orkney 453 C6
Braehead S Ayrs 367 C6
Braehead S Lanarks 381 F8
Braehead S Lanarks 382 B4
Braehead of Lunan Angus 421 B6
Braehoulland Shetl'd 457 F2
Braehour H'land 445 C4
Braehungie H'land 445 E5
Braeintra H'land 431 E8
Braelangwell Lodge H'land 440 D2
Braemar Aberds 427 C6
Braemore H'land 439 F5
Braemore H'land 445 E4
Braepark C/Edinb 395 C8
Braes of Enzie Moray 435 C8
Braes of Ullapool H'land 439 D5
Braeside Invercl 390 C4
Braeswick Orkney 454 C4
Braevallich Arg/Bute 408 B2
Braewick Shetl'd 457 F2
Braewick Shetl'd 457 H3
Brafferton D'lington 331 B7
Brafferton N Yorks 307 A5
Brafield-on-the-Green Northants 158 A4
Bragar W Isles 451 C5
Bragbury End Herts 138 C1
Bragleenmore Arg/Bute 416 E4
Braichmelyn Gwyn 237 A8
Braid C/Edinb 396 D1
Braidfauld Glasg C 392 F4
Braidley N Yorks 317 E6
Braids Arg/Bute 404 B3
Braidwood S Lanarks 382 C2
Braigh Chalasaigh W Isles 447 A4
Braigo Arg/Bute 406 F2
Brailsford Derby 246 F3
Brailsford Green Derby 246 F2
Braingortan Arg/Bute 408 E3
Brain's Green Glos 129 F7
Braintree Essex 140 C4
Braiseworth Suffolk 187 D7
Braishfield Hants 44 A2
Braithwaite Cumb 326 B1
Braithwaite S Yorks 283 B6
Braithwaite W Yorks 292 B2
Braithwell S Yorks 282 E4
Brakefield Green Norfolk 208 B4
Bramber W Sussex 48 D3
Brambledown Kent 93 B6
Brambridge Hants 44 B4
Bramcote Notts 224 A5
Bramcote Camp Warwick 200 F2
Bramdean Hants 66 F2
Bramelane N Yorks 305 E8
Bramerton Norfolk 210 C1
Bramfield Herts 138 D1
Bramfield Suffolk 189 D6
Bramford Suffolk 165 C7
Bramford W Midlands 197 E7
Bramhall Gtr Man 266 B4
Bramhall Moor Gtr Man 267 B5
Bramhall Park Gtr Man 266 B4
Bramham W Yorks 294 B2
Bramhope W Yorks 293 B7
Bramley Hants 86 E2
Bramley Surrey 68 B2
Bramley S Yorks 270 A1
Bramley W Yorks 293 D6
Bramley Corner Hants 86 E2
Bramley Green Hants 86 E3
Bramley Head N Yorks 305 D6
Bramley Vale Derby 247 A7
Bramling Kent 94 E4
Brampford Speke Devon 21 A8
Brampton Cambs 182 D4
Brampton Cumb 328 B3
Brampton Cumb 348 D4
Brampton Derby 269 D7
Brampton Heref'd 151 E6
Brampton Lincs 272 D1
Brampton Norfolk 234 D1
Brampton Suffolk 189 B6
Brampton S Yorks 282 D2
Brampton Abbotts Heref'd 129 B6
Brampton Ash Northants 202 F1
Brampton Bryan Heref'd 172 D5
Brampton en le Morthen S Yorks 270 B1
Brampton Park Cambs 182 D4
Brampton Park Cambs 182 E4
Brampton Street Suffolk 189 B6
Bramshall Staffs 222 B3
Bramshaw Hants 43 C8
Bramshill Hants 86 D4
Bramshott Hants 67 E6
Bramshott Vale Hants 67 E6
Bramwell Som'set 59 F8
Bran End Essex 140 B2
Branatwatt Shetl'd 457 H2
Branault H'land 423 F5
Branbridges Kent 71 B8
Brancaster Norfolk 255 D5
Brancaster Staithe Norfolk 255 D5
Brancepeth Durham 343 D8
Branch End Northum 351 D8
Branchill Moray 435 C5
Brand End Lincs 252 E3
Brand Green Glos 129 B8
Brand Green Heref'd 153 D5
Branderburgh Moray 435 A7
Brandesburton ER Yorks 310 F4
Brandeston Suffolk 188 F3
Brandhill Shrops 173 C6
Brandingill Cumb 325 A7
Brandis Corner Devon 33 F8
Brandish Street Som'set 57 B5
Brandiston Norfolk 233 D7
Brandon Durham 343 C8
Brandon Lincs 249 E9
Brandon Northum 376 D2
Brandon Suffolk 185 A8
Brandon Warwick 178 C3
Brandon Bank Norfolk 206 F3
Brandon Creek Norfolk 206 E3
Brandon Parva Norfolk 208 B5
Brands Hatch Motor Racing Circuit Kent 91 D6
Brandsby N Yorks 307 A8
Brandwood End W Midlands 176 C4
Brandy Wharf Lincs 285 E7
Brandyquoy Orkney 453 D5
Brane Cornw'l 2 E4
Branksome D'lington 331 C7
Branksome Poole 27 B8
Branksome Park Poole 27 B8
Bransbury Hants 65 C5
Bransby Lincs 272 D2
Branscombe Devon 23 C5
Bransford Worcs 153 B5
Bransgore Hants 28 A3
Branshill Clack 410 C3
Bransholme Kingston/Hull 297 D9
Bransley Shrops 174 C3
Branson's Cross Worcs 176 D4
Branston Leics 226 C3
Branston Lincs 272 F5
Branston Staffs 223 D6
Branston Booths Lincs 273 F6
Branstone I/Wight 30 D3
Bransty Cumb 324 C4
Brant Broughton Lincs 250 D1
Brantham Suffolk 165 F7
Branthwaite Cumb 325 B6
Branthwaite Cumb 338 D4
Branthwaite Edge Cumb 325 B6
Brantingham ER Yorks 297 E5
Branton Northum 376 D2
Branton S Yorks 283 D6
Branton Green N Yorks 307 C5
Branxholm Park Scot Borders 373 E6
Branxholme Scot Borders 373 E6
Branxton Northum 387 E7
Brascote Leics 200 C2
Brassey Green Ches 242 B3
Brasside Durham 344 B1
Brassington Derby 246 D2
Brassknocker Bath/NE Som'set 81 D7
Brasted Kent 90 F4
Brasted Chart Kent 90 F4
Brathens Aberds 428 C3
Bratoft Lincs 252 A5
Bratoft Corner Lincs 253 B5
Brattle Kent 73 E5
Brattleby Lincs 272 C3
Bratton Som'set 57 B5
Bratton Wilts 62 A3
Bratton Clovelly Devon 19 B6
Bratton Fleming Devon 55 D7
Bratton Seymour Som'set 61 F5
Braughing Herts 138 B3
Braughing Friars Herts 138 C4
Braulen Lodge H'land 432 E4
Brauncewell Lincs 250 D3
Braunston Northants 179 E5
Braunstone Town Leics 200 C5
Braunston-in-Rutland Rutl'd 202 B2
Braunton Devon 54 D4
Brawby N Yorks 321 E5
Brawl H'land 444 B2
Brawlbin H'land 444 C4
Bray Windsor 87 A8
Bray Shop Cornw'l 18 F3
Bray Wick Windsor 87 A7
Braybrooke Northants 180 B3
Braydon Side Wilts 104 E5
Brayford Devon 55 E8
Brayfordhill Devon 55 E8
Brays Grove Essex 139 F5
Bray's Hill E Sussex 51 D6
Braystones Cumb 324 E5
Braythorn N Yorks 306 F1
Brayton N Yorks 295 D6
Braytown Dorset 26 C3
Braywoodside Windsor 87 A7
Brazacott Cornw'l 18 B2
Brea Cornw'l 4 B1
Breach Kent 74 B3
Breach Kent 92 C3
Breach W Sussex 46 E3
Breach Hill Bath/NE Som'set 80 E2
Breachacha Castle Arg/Bute 414 B4
Breachwood Green Herts 137 C6
Breacleit W Isles 450 D4
Bread Street Glos 103 A8
Breaden Heath Shrops 219 A5
Breadsall Derby 224 A2
Breadsall Hilltop Derby C 224 A2
Breadstone Glos 103 B6
Breage Cornw'l 3 E8
Breakachy H'land 433 D6
Bream Glos 102 A4
Breamore Hants 43 C6
Bream's Meend Glos 102 A3
Brean Som'set 79 E5
Breanais W Isles 450 E2
Brearley W Yorks 292 E2
Brearton N Yorks 306 C3
Breascleit W Isles 450 D5
Breaston Derby 224 B4
Brechfa Carms 123 A6
Brechin Angus 421 A5
Breck of Cruan Orkney 452 B4
Breckan Orkney 452 C3
Breckles Norfolk 208 E3
Breckrey H'land 430 B5
Brecks S Yorks 269 A9
Brecon = Aberhonddu Powys 126 B1
Brecon Beacons Mountain Centre Powys 125 B8
Bredbury Gtr Man 267 A5
Bredbury Green Gtr Man 267 A5
Brede E Sussex 52 C1
Bredenbury Heref'd 152 A2
Bredfield Suffolk 166 B3
Bredgar Kent 92 D4
Bredhurst Kent 92 D2
Bredicot Worcs 153 B8
Bredon Worcs 153 E8
Bredon's Hardick Worcs 153 E8
Bredon's Norton Worcs 153 E8
Bredwardine Heref'd 150 C4
Breedon on the Hill Leics 224 D3
Breibhig W Isles 446 D2
Breibhig W Isles 451 D7
Breich W Loth 394 F4
Breightmet Gtr Man 278 C3
Breighton ER Yorks 295 D8
Breinton Common Heref'd 151 E7
Breiwick Shetl'd 457 J4
Brelston Green Heref'd 128 C5
Bremhill Wilts 82 B4
Bremhill Wick Wilts 82 B4
Bremirehoull Shetl'd 455 D3
Brenachoile Lodge Stirl 409 B7
Brenchley Kent 71 C8
Brenchoillie Arg/Bute 408 B3
Brendon Devon 33 D7
Brendon Devon 56 B2
Brenkley Tyne/Wear 352 A3
Brent Cross London 111 E6
Brent Eleigh Suffolk 164 C3
Brent Knoll Som'set 59 A6
Brent Mill Devon 14 D1
Brent Pelham Herts 138 A4
Brentford London 89 A5
Brentingby Leics 226 E2
Brentry Bristol 80 A3
Brentwood Essex 113 D7
Brenzett Kent 73 F6
Brenzett Green Kent 73 F7
Brereton Staffs 222 E3
Brereton Cross Staffs 222 E3
Brereton Green Ches 243 B8
Brereton Heath Ches 244 B2
Breretonhill Staffs 222 E3
Bressingham Norfolk 187 B6
Bressingham Common Norfolk 187 B6
Bretby Derby 223 D7
Bretford Warwick 178 C3
Bretforton Worcs 154 D4
Bretherton Lancs 289 F6
Brettabister Shetl'd 457 H4
Brettenham Norfolk 186 B3
Brettenham Suffolk 164 B4
Bretton Derby 268 D4
Bretton Flints 241 B8
Bretton Peterbro 204 C2
Brewer Street Surrey 69 A8
Brewer's End Essex 139 C7
Brewers Green Norfolk 187 B7
Brewlands Bridge Angus 420 A1
Brewood Staffs 197 B6
Briach Moray 435 C5
Briantspuddle Dorset 26 B3
Brick End Essex 139 B7
Brick Houses S Yorks 269 C6
Brickendon Herts 138 F2
Bricket Wood Herts 110 B4
Brickfields Worcs 153 A7
Brickhill Beds 159 B9
Brickkiln Green Essex 140 A3
Bricklehampton Worcs 154 D2
Bride I/Man 336 A4
Bridekirk Cumb 337 E8
Bridell Pembs 144 D3
Bridestowe Devon 19 C7
Brideswell Aberds 436 E2
Bridford Devon 21 C6
Bridfordmills Devon 21 C6
Bridge Cornw'l 4 B1
Bridge Dorset 41 D5
Bridge Kent 94 E3
Bridge End C/Edinb 396 D2
Bridge End Cumb 339 B6
Bridge End Durham 342 D4
Bridge End Devon 14 F1
Bridge End Devon 22 C3
Bridge End Essex 140 A2
Bridge End Flints 241 C7
Bridge End Heref'd 152 C2
Bridge End Lincs 228 A2
Bridge End Northum 351 D5
Bridge End Northum 350 C5
Bridge End Oxon 107 D8
Bridge End Surrey 88 E3
Bridge End Warwick 177 F8
Bridge End Worcs 130 A2
Bridge Green Essex 162 E2
Bridge Green Norfolk 187 B7
Bridge Hewick N Yorks 306 A3
Bridge Ho Arg/Bute 403 A3
Bridge of Alford Aberds 428 A2
Bridge of Allan Stirl 410 C2
Bridge of Avon Moray 435 E6
Bridge of Avon Moray 435 F6
Bridge of Awe Arg/Bute 417 E5
Bridge of Balgie Perth/Kinr 418 C3
Bridge of Cally Perth/Kinr 420 B1
Bridge of Canny Aberds 428 C3
Bridge of Craigisla Angus 420 B2
Bridge of Dee Dumf/Gal 402 D1
Bridge of Don Aberd C 429 A6
Bridge of Dun Angus 421 B6
Bridge of Dye Aberds 428 D3
Bridge of Earn Perth/Kinr 420 F1
Bridge of Ericht Perth/Kinr 418 B3
Bridge of Feugh Aberds 428 C4
Bridge of Forss H'land 444 B4
Bridge of Gairn Aberds 427 C8
Bridge of Gaur Perth/Kinr 418 B3
Bridge of Lyon Perth/Kinr 418 C5
Bridge of Muchalls Aberds 429 C5
Bridge of Muick Aberds 427 C8
Bridge of Oich H'land 425 B5
Bridge of Orchy Arg/Bute 417 D7
Bridge of Waith Orkney 452 B3
Bridge of Walls Shetl'd 457 H2
Bridge of Weir Renf 391 E7
Bridge Reeve Devon 35 D6
Bridge Sollars Heref'd 151 D6
Bridge Street Suffolk 164 C2
Bridge Trafford Ches 264 E4
Bridge-End Shetl'd 455 C2
Bridgefield Derby 280 F2
Bridgefoot Aberds 428 B1
Bridgefoot Angus 420 D3
Bridgefoot Cumb 337 F7
Bridgehampton Som'set 39 B9
Bridgehill Durham 343 A5
Bridgehouse Gate N Yorks 305 B7
Bridgemary Hants 45 F6
Bridgemont Derby 267 C7
Bridgend Aberds 428 A2
Bridgend Aberds 436 E2
Bridgend Angus 428 F2
Bridgend Arg/Bute 404 C3
Bridgend Arg/Bute 406 F3
Bridgend Arg/Bute 408 C1
Bridgend Bridg 77 A5
Bridgend Cumb 327 D5
Bridgend Cornw'l 9 D5
Bridgend Devon 11 F7
Bridgend Fife 412 A1
Bridgend Glos 103 B8
Bridgend H'land 433 C5
Bridgend Invercl 391 C5
Bridgend Moray 435 E8
Bridgend N Lanarks 393 D5
Bridgend Pembs 144 C3
Bridgend W Loth 395 C5
Bridgend of Lintrathen Angus 420 B2
Bridgerule Devon 33 F5
Bridges Cornw'l 8 D3
Bridges Shrops 194 D3
Bridgeton Glasg C 392 F4
Bridgetown Cornw'l 18 C3
Bridgetown Devon 14 C4
Bridgetown Som'set 57 E5
Bridgeyate S Glos 81 B5
Bridgham Norfolk 186 A4
Bridgnorth Shrops 196 E3
Bridgnorth Cliff Railway Shrops 196 E3
Bridgtown Staffs 197 B8
Bridgwater Som'set 59 D5
Bridlington ER Yorks 311 B5
Bridport Dorset 24 B4
Bridstow Heref'd 129 C5
Briercliffe Lancs 291 B5
Brierfield Lancs 291 C6
Brierholme Carr S Yorks 283 B7
Brierley Glos 129 D6
Brierley S Yorks 282 B2
Brierley Gap S Yorks 282 B2
Brierley Hill W Midlands 197 F7
Brierton Hartlep'l 345 F5
Briery Cumb 326 B2
Briery Hill Bl Gwent 126 F4
Briestfield W Yorks 281 A6
Brig o'Turk Stirl 409 B8
Brigg N Lincs 285 C7
Briggate Norfolk 234 C3
Briggsworth N Yorks 334 E4
Brigham Cumb 337 E4
Brigham Cumb 326 B2
Brigham ER Yorks 310 E3
Brighouse W Yorks 292 F4
Brighstone I/Wight 29 D8
Brightgate Derby 246 C3
Brighthampton Oxon 106 B4
Brightholmlee S Yorks 281 F7
Brightley Devon 20 A1
Brightling E Sussex 51 B6
Brightlingsea Essex 142 D2
Brighton Brighton/Hove 49 F6
Brighton Cornw'l 7 E9
Brighton Hill Hants 66 B2
Brighton le Sands Mersey 276 E3
Brighton Museum and Art Gallery Brighton/Hove 49 F6
Brighton Racecourse Brighton/Hove 49 E6
Brighton Sea Life Centre Brighton/Hove 49 F6
Brightons Falk 394 C3
Brightor Cornw'l 10 C3
Brightside S Yorks 269 B7
Brightwalton W Berks 85 A5
Brightwalton Green W Berks 85 A5
Brightwalton Holt W Berks 85 A5
Brightwell Suffolk 166 D2
Brightwell Baldwin Oxon 108 D3
Brightwell-cum-Sotwell Oxon 107 D8
Brigmarston Wilts 63 B8
Brignall Durham 330 D3
Brignam Park N Yorks 321 D7
Brigsley NE Lincs 286 D4
Brigsteer Cumb 314 C3
Brigstock Northants 181 A6
Brill Bucks 134 E4
Brill Cornw'l 4 E2
Brilley Heref'd 150 C3
Brimaston Pembs 120 B2
Brimfield Heref'd 173 E8
Brimington Derby 269 E8
Brimington Common Derby 269 E8
Brimley Devon 21 E5
Brimpsfield Glos 130 E4
Brimpton W Berks 85 D8
Brimpton Common W Berks 85 D8
Brims Orkney 452 E3
Brims Castle H'land 444 A4
Brimscombe Glos 104 B2
Brimsdown London 112 C2
Brimstage Mersey 263 C8
Brinacory H'land 423 C7
Brincliffe S Yorks 269 B6
Brind ER Yorks 296 D1
Brindister Shetl'd 457 H2
Brindister Shetl'd 455 C3
Brindle Lancs 289 F8
Brindle Heath Gtr Man 279 E5
Brindley Ches 242 D4
Brindley Ford Stoke 244 D3
Brineton Staffs 221 F6
Bringhurst Leics 202 E2
Brington Cambs 182 C1
Brinian Orkney 454 D2
Briningham Norfolk 233 B5
Brinkhill Lincs 274 E4
Brinkley Cambs 163 A5
Brinkley Notts 248 D5
Brinkley Hill Heref'd 129 A5
Brinklow M/Keynes 159 E6
Brinklow Warwick 178 C3
Brinkworth Wilts 104 F5
Brinmore H'land 434 F1
Brinnington Gtr Man 267 A5
Brinscall Lancs 290 F1
Brinscombe Som'set 59 A8
Brinsea N Som'set 79 D8
Brinsley Notts 247 E7
Brinsop Heref'd 151 D6
Brinsworth S Yorks 269 B8
Brinton Norfolk 256 E3
Brisco Cumb 339 A7
Brisley Norfolk 232 D4
Brislington Bristol 80 B4
Brissenden Green Kent 73 D5
Brister End Dorset 40 D1
Bristnall Fields W Midlands 197 F8
Bristol Bristol 80 B4
Bristol City Museum and Art Gallery Bristol 80 B3
Bristol International Airport N Som'set 80 D2
Bristol Zoo Bristol 80 B3
Briston Norfolk 233 B6
Briston Common Norfolk 233 B6
Britannia Lancs 291 F6
Britford Wilts 63 F8
Brithdir Caerph 100 B3
Brithdir Ceredig'n 145 C6
Brithdir Denbs 215 E7
Brithem Bottom Devon 37 D5
British Museum London 111 F7
Briton Ferry = Llansawel Rh Cyn Taff 98 D1
Britwell Salome Oxon 108 D3
Brixham Torbay 15 D6
Brixton Devon 11 E7
Brixton London 89 A8
Brixton Deverill Wilts 62 D2
Brixworth Northants 180 D2
Brize Norton Oxon 132 F5
Broad Alley Worcs 175 E7
Broad Blunsdon Swindon 105 D8
Broad Campden Glos 155 E6
Broad Carr W Yorks 280 A3
Broad Chalke Wilts 42 A3
Broad Clough Lancs 291 F6
Broad Colney Herts 111 B5
Broad Ford Kent 71 D9
Broad Green Beds 159 D7
Broad Green Cambs 163 A6
Broad Green Essex 162 E1
Broad Green Essex 141 C6
Broad Green Mersey 264 B3
Broad Green Suffolk 163 A8
Broad Green Suffolk 165 A6
Broad Green Suffolk 187 F7
Broad Green Worcs 153 A5
Broad Green Worcs 176 D2
Broad Haven = Aberllydan Pembs 116 B3
Broad Heath Worcs 174 F3
Broad Hill Cambs 184 C4
Broad Hinton Wilts 83 A7
Broad Laying Hants 85 D5
Broad Marston Worcs 155 C5
Broad Mead S Glos 102 F4
Broad Meadow Staffs 244 E2
Broad Oak Carms 123 C7
Broad Oak Cumb 312 B3
Broad Oak Dorset 41 D5
Broad Oak Dorset 22 B3
Broad Oak E Sussex 52 B1
Broad Oak E Sussex 50 B5
Broad Oak Hants 66 A5
Broad Oak Hants 44 D4
Broad Oak Heref'd 128 C3
Broad Oak Kent 94 D3
Broad Oak Mersey 277 E7
Broad Parkham Devon 33 B7
Broad Street E Sussex 52 C2
Broad Street Kent 74 C2
Broad Street Kent 74 C3
Broad Street Kent 92 E3
Broad Street Medway 92 B2
Broad Street Suffolk 164 D4
Broad Street Wilts 83 E7
Broad Street Green Essex 141 F6
Broad Town Wilts 83 A6
Broadbottom Gtr Man 279 F8
Broadbridge W Sussex 46 E4
Broadbridge Heath W Sussex 68 E4
Broadbush Swindon 105 D8
Broadclyst Devon 22 A1
Broadfield Gtr Man 279 B5
Broadfield Invercl 391 D6
Broadfield Lancs 289 F7
Broadfield Lancs 290 E3
Broadfield Pembs 117 D8
Broadfield W Sussex 69 E7
Broadford H'land 431 F6
Broadford Surrey 68 B1
Broadford Bridge W Sussex 48 B1
Broadgrass Green Suffolk 186 F4
Broadhalgh Gtr Man 279 B6
Broadham Green Surrey 70 A2
Broadhaugh Scot Borders 373 F5
Broadhaven H'land 445 C7
Broadheath Gtr Man 266 B2
Broadhembury Devon 37 F6
Broadhempston Devon 14 B4
Broadholm Derby 247 E5
Broadholme Notts 272 E2
Broadland Row E Sussex 52 C1
Broadlands Devon 14 A4
Broadlane Cornw'l 4 B1
Broadley Carms 122 F3
Broadley Gtr Man 279 A6
Broadley Moray 435 B8
Broadley Common Essex 138 F4
Broadleys Aberds 437 B5
Broadmayne Dorset 26 C1
Broadmeadows Scot Borders 373 A5
Broadmere Hants 66 B2
Broadmoor Glos 129 D6
Broadmoor Pembs 116 B2
Broadmoor Pembs 117 C7
Broadoak Dorset 24 A3
Broadoak Glos 129 E7
Broadoak Kent 93 D5
Broadoak End Herts 138 E2
Broadoak Park Gtr Man 278 D4
Broadrashes Moray 436 C1
Broadrock Glos 102 C2

Bro – Bur 533

Broad's Green Essex 140 E2
Broad's Green Wilts 82 C4
Broadsands Torbay 15 D5
Broadsea Aberds 437 B6
Broadshard Som'set 39 D6
Broadstairs Kent 95 C7
Broadstone Kent 72 B4
Broadstone Monmouths 102 B2
Broadstone N Ayrs 379 B7
Broadstone Poole 27 A7
Broadstone Shrops 195 F6
Broadstreet Common Newp 101 E7
Broadview Gardens, Hadlow Kent 71 B7
Broadwas Worcs 153 A5
Broadwater Herts 137 C9
Broadwater W Sussex 48 F3
Broadwater Down Kent 71 D6
Broadwaters Worcs 175 C6
Broadwath Cumb 348 E3
Broadway Carms 122 E1
Broadway Oxon 107 E6
Broadway Pembs 116 B3
Broadway Suffolk 189 C5
Broadway Som'set 38 C4
Broadway Som'set 60 A4
Broadway Worcs 154 E4
Broadway Pound Som'set 38 C4
Broadwell Glos 132 B3
Broadwell Glos 129 E5
Broadwell Oxon 106 B2
Broadwell Warwick 178 E4
Broadwey Dorset 25 D8
Broadwindsor Dorset 39 F6
Broadwood Kelly Devon 34 E5
Broadwoodwidger Devon 19 C5
Brobury Heref'd 150 D4
Brochel H'land 431 D5
Brochloch Dumf/Gal 356 C2
Brochroy Arg/Bute 417 D5
Brock Lancs 289 B7
Brockamin Worcs 153 B5
Brockbridge Hants 45 C7
Brockdish Norfolk 188 C2
Brockencote Worcs 175 D7
Brockenhurst Hants 43 F9
Brockford Green Suffolk 187 E7
Brockford Street Suffolk 187 E7
Brockhall Northants 179 F7
Brockhall Village Lancs 290 C3
Brockham Surrey 69 B5
Brockham End Bath/NE Som'set 81 C6
Brockhampton Glos 131 B5
Brockhampton Glos 131 C6
Brockhampton Hants 46 E2
Brockhampton Heref'd 152 A3
Brockhampton Heref'd 129 A5
Brockhampton Green Dorset 40 E4
Brockhill Scot Borders 372 C4
Brockhole -National Park Visitor Centre, Windermere Cumb 326 F4
Brockholes W Yorks 280 B4
Brockhollands Glos 102 A4
Brockhurst Derby 246 B4
Brockhurst Portsm'th 45 F7
Brockhurst Warwick 178 B4
Brocklebank Cumb 338 C5
Brocklehirst Dumf/Gal 346 B2
Brocklesby Lincs 286 B1
Brockley London 90 B2
Brockley N Som'set 80 C1
Brockley Suffolk 186 D1
Brockley Green Suffolk 163 C7
Brockley Green Suffolk 164 B1
Brockleymoor Cumb 339 D8
Brockmoor W Midlands 197 F7
Brock's Green Hants 85 D7
Brockscombe Devon 19 B6
Brockton Shrops 172 A4
Brockton Shrops 195 E7
Brockton Shrops 194 C2
Brockton Shrops 196 C3
Brockton Staffs 221 B6
Brockton Telford 220 E4
Brockweir Glos 102 B2
Brockworth Glos 130 D3
Brocton Cornw'l 8 B3
Brocton Staffs 222 E1
Brodick N Ayrs 405 C6
Brodick Castle N Ayrs 405 C6
Brodie Moray 434 C4
Brodiesord Aberds 436 B2
Brodley NE Lincs 286 C3
Brodsworth S Yorks 282 C4
Brogaig H'land 430 B4
Brogborough Beds 159 E7
Broken Cross Ches 265 E8
Broken Cross Ches 266 D4
Brokenborough Wilts 104 E3
Brokerswood Wilts 61 A8
Brokes N Yorks 318 A2
Brombil Neath P Talb 98 E2
Bromborough Mersey 264 C2
Brome Suffolk 187 C7
Brome Street Suffolk 187 C8
Bromeswell Suffolk 166 B4
Bromfield Cumb 338 B2
Bromfield Shrops 173 C7
Bromford W Midlands 198 F3
Bromham Beds 159 B8
Bromham Wilts 82 C4
Bromley Herts 138 C4
Bromley London 90 C3
Bromley London 112 F2
Bromley Shrops 196 D3
Bromley W Midlands 197 F7
Bromley Common London 90 C3
Bromley Cross Essex 142 B2
Bromley Cross Gtr Man 278 B3
Bromley Green Kent 73 D6
Bromley Heath S Glos 81 A5
Bromley Wood Staffs 222 D4
Bromlow Shrops 194 C2
Brompton Medway 92 C2
Brompton N Yorks 319 A6
Brompton N Yorks 322 D2
Brompton Shrops 195 B6
Brompton Ralph Som'set 57 E8
Brompton Regis Som'set 57 E6
Brompton-on-Swale N Yorks 318 A3
Bromsash Heref'd 129 C6
Bromsberrow Glos 152 F4
Bromsberrow Heath Glos 129 A8
Bromsgrove Worcs 176 D2
Bromstead Heath Staffs 221 E5
Bromstone Kent 95 C7
Bromyard Heref'd 152 B3
Bronaber Gwyn 215 B6
Brondesbury London 111 F6
Brondwydd Arms Carms 122 C4
Broneirion Powys 192 F4
Brongest Ceredig'n 145 C6
Brongwyn Ceredig'n 145 D5
Bronington Wrex 219 A6
Bronllys Powys 149 E7
Bronnant Ceredig'n 169 E5
Bronte Parsonage Museum, Keighley W Yorks 292 C2
Bronwydd Ceredig'n 145 D7
Bronydd Powys 150 C2
Bronygarth Shrops 218 A2
Bron-y-main Powys 217 F8
Brook Carms 122 F1
Brook Devon 11 A5
Brook Hants 64 F3
Brook Hants 43 D8
Brook I/Wight 29 D7
Brook Kent 73 C8
Brook Surrey 67 D8
Brook Surrey 68 B3
Brook Wilts 62 A2
Brook Bottom Derby 267 B6
Brook Bottom Gtr Man 279 D8
Brook End Beds 182 F1
Brook End Beds 160 C3
Brook End Cambs 182 D1
Brook End Herts 138 B2
Brook End M/Keynes 159 D6
Brook End Wilts 104 F1
Brook End Worcs 153 C7
Brook Hill Notts 225 B6
Brook Street Essex 113 D6
Brook Street Kent 73 E5
Brook Street Kent 71 B6
Brook Street W Sussex 49 A6
Brookbottoms Gtr Man 278 A4
Brooke Norfolk 210 D1
Brooke Rutl'd 202 B2
Brookeador Devon 15 B5
Brookenby Lincs 286 E3
Brookend Essex 140 F3
Brookend Glos 102 C3
Brookend Oxon 133 C5
Brookend S Glos 103 B5
Brookfield Derby 280 E2
Brookfield Glos 130 C3
Brookfield Lancs 289 D8
Brookfield Middlesbro 332 C4
Brookfield Renf 391 F8
Brookfoot W Yorks 292 F4
Brookgreen I/Wight 29 D7
Brookhampton Oxon 108 C2
Brookhampton Som'set 60 F4
Brookhill Hants 43 D8
Brookhouse Blackb'n 290 E2
Brookhouse Ches 267 D5
Brookhouse Lancs 302 C2
Brookhouse S Yorks 270 B2
Brookhouse Green Ches 244 B2
Brookhouses Derby 267 B7
Brookhouses Staffs 245 F5
Brookhurst Mersey 264 C1
Brookland Kent 52 A4
Brooklands Dumf/Gal 402 B2
Brooklands Gtr Man 266 A2
Brooklands Shrops 242 F3
Brooklands W Yorks 293 C8
Brookmans Park Herts 111 B6
Brooks Powys 193 D6
Brooks End Kent 95 C5
Brooks Green W Sussex 48 A2
Brooksby Leics 225 E8
Brookside Derby 269 E6
Brookside Telford 196 B3
Brookthorpe Glos 130 E2
Brookvale Halton 265 C5
Brookville Norfolk 207 D5
Brookwood Surrey 87 E9
Broom Beds 160 D3
Broom Cumb 328 B3
Broom E Renf 380 A2
Broom Pembs 117 C8
Broom S Yorks 269 A8
Broom Warwick 154 B4
Broom Court Warwick 154 B4
Broom Green Norfolk 232 D4
Broom Hill Bristol 80 B4
Broom Hill Dorset 42 F3
Broom Hill Durham 351 F9
Broom Hill London 90 C4
Broom Hill Medway 92 B2
Broom Hill Tyne/Wear 344 B3
Broom Hill Worcs 175 C8
Broom Street Kent 93 D7
Broome Norfolk 210 E3
Broome Shrops 173 B6
Broome Worcs 175 C8
Broomedge Warrington 265 B9
Broomer's Corner W Sussex 48 B2
Broomershill W Sussex 48 C1
Broomfield Aberds 437 E6
Broomfield Cumb 339 B5
Broomfield Essex 140 E3
Broomfield Kent 94 C4
Broomfield Kent 72 A3
Broomfield Som'set 58 E4
Broomfields Shrops 219 E5
Broomfleet E R Yorks 296 E4
Broomhall Surrey 87 C9
Broomhaugh Northum 351 D7
Broomhill Bristol 80 A4
Broomhill Glasg C 392 E2
Broomhill H'land 434 F4
Broomhill Kent 94 E4
Broomhill Norfolk 206 C3
Broomhill Notts 247 E8
Broomhill Northum 365 B7
Broomhill S Yorks 282 D2
Broomholm Norfolk 234 B3
Broomhouse Glasg C 393 F5
Broomlands N Ayrs 379 E6
Broomley Northum 351 D7
Broompark Durham 343 C8
Broom's Green Heref'd 129 A8
Broomton H'land 441 F5
Broomy Hill Heref'd 151 E8
Brora H'land 441 C6
Broseley Shrops 196 C2
Broseley Wood Shrops 196 C2
Brotherhouse Bar Lincs 228 F5
Brotheridge Green Worcs 153 D6
Brotherlee Durham 342 D3
Brothertoft Lincs 251 E8
Brotherton W Yorks 294 E3
Brothybeck Cumb 339 C6
Brotton Redcar/Clevel'd 333 C8
Broubster H'land 444 B4
Brough Cumb 329 D5
Brough Derby 268 C3
Brough ER Yorks 297 E5
Brough H'land 445 A6
Brough Notts 249 C7
Brough Orkney 452 B4
Brough Orkney 453 E5
Brough Shetl'd 456 C5
Brough Shetl'd 457 F4
Brough Shetl'd 457 F5
Brough Shetl'd 457 G5
Brough Shetl'd 457 H4
Brough Shetl'd 455 B4
Brough Lodge Shetl'd 456 D5
Brough Sowerby Cumb 329 D5
Broughall Shrops 242 F4
Brougham Cumb 340 F1
Broughton Scot Borders 383 E7
Broughton Cambs 183 C5
Broughton Flints 241 B7
Broughton Hants 64 E3
Broughton Lancs 289 C7
Broughton M/Keynes 159 E5
Broughton Northants 180 C4
Broughton N Lincs 285 C6
Broughton N Yorks 304 E2
Broughton N Yorks 308 A4
Broughton Orkney 454 B2
Broughton Oxon 156 E3
Broughton V/Glam 77 B5
Broughton Astley Leics 200 E4
Broughton Beck Cumb 313 D6
Broughton Common Wilts 82 D2
Broughton Cross Cumb 337 E4
Broughton Gifford Wilts 82 D2
Broughton Green Worcs 176 F2
Broughton Hackett Worcs 153 B8
Broughton in Furness Cumb 313 C5
Broughton Mills Cumb 313 B5
Broughton Moor Cumb 337 E4
Broughton Park Gtr Man 279 D5
Broughton Poggs Oxon 106 B1
Broughtown Orkney 454 B4
Broughty Ferry Dundee C 420 D4
Browhouses Dumf/Gal 347 D7
Browland Shetl'd 457 H2
Brown Candover Hants 65 D8
Brown Edge Lancs 276 B4
Brown Edge Mersey 264 A4
Brown Edge Staffs 244 D4
Brown Heath Ches 242 B2
Brown Heath Hants 45 C5
Brown Knowl Ches 242 D2
Brown Lees Staffs 244 C3
Brown Street Suffolk 187 F6
Brownber Cumb 328 E4
Brownbread Street E Sussex 51 C6
Brownheath Shrops 219 C6
Brownhill Aberds 436 D3
Brownhill Aberds 437 D5
Brownhill Blackb'n 290 D2
Brownhill Shrops 219 D5
Brownhills Fife 421 F5
Brownhills W Midlands 198 B1
Brownieside Northum 377 C5
Browninghill Green Hants 85 E8
Brownlow Gtr Man 277 D7
Brownlow Fold Gtr Man 278 B3
Brownmuir Aberds 428 E4
Brown's Bank Ches 243 F5
Brown's Green W Midlands 198 E1
Browns Wood M/Keynes 159 E6
Brownshill Glos 104 B2
Brownshill Green W Midlands 177 B9
Brownside Lancs 291 D6
Brownsover Warwick 179 C5
Brownston Devon 14 E1
Brownstone Devon 35 E8
Browsburn N Lanarks 393 F7
Browston Green Norfolk 210 C5
Broxa N Yorks 322 B3
Broxbourne Herts 138 F3
Broxburn E Loth 398 C3
Broxburn W Loth 395 D6
Broxholme Lincs 272 D3
Broxstowe Nott'ham 247 F8
Broxted Essex 139 B7
Broxton Ches 242 D2
Broyle Side E Sussex 50 D2
Bruairnis W Isles 446 C3
Bruan H'land 445 E7
Bruar Lodge Perth/Kinr 426 E3
Brucehill W Dunb 391 C7
Bruchag Arg/Bute 378 A2
Bruche Warrington 265 B7
Brucklebog Aberds 428 C4
Bruera Ches 242 B1
Brù W Isles 451 C6
Bruichladdich Arg/Bute 406 F2
Bruisyard Suffolk 188 E4
Brumby N Lincs 284 C4
Brundall Norfolk 210 B2
Brundish Norfolk 210 D3
Brundish Suffolk 188 E3
Brundish Street Suffolk 188 D3
Brundon Suffolk 164 D2
Brunery H'land 423 E7
Brune's Purlieu Hants 43 C6
Brunshaw Lancs 291 D6
Brunstock Cumb 348 E2
Brunswick Park London 111 D7
Brunswick Village Tyne/Wear 352 B3
Brunt Hamersland Shetl'd 457 H4
Bruntcliffe W Yorks 293 E6
Brunthwaite W Yorks 292 A3
Bruntingthorpe Leics 201 F6
Brunton Fife 420 E3
Brunton Northum 377 C6
Brunton Wilts 84 E1
Brushes Gtr Man 279 E8
Brushfield Derby 268 E3
Brushford Som'set 35 E6
Brushford Som'set 36 A3
Bruton Som'set 61 E5
Bryan's Green Worcs 175 E7
Bryanston Dorset 41 E7
Bryant's Bottom Bucks 109 C7
Brycethin Bridg 99 F5
Brydekirk Dumf/Gal 347 B5
Brymbo Conwy 262 E6
Brymbo Wrex 241 D6
Brympton D'Evercy Som'set 39 C8
Bryn Caerph 100 C3
Bryn Ches 265 E7
Bryn Gtr Man 277 D8
Bryn Gwyn 260 E1
Bryn Heref'd 127 B7
Bryn Neath P Talb 98 D3
Bryn Rh Cyn Taff 99 A5
Bryn Shrops 172 A3
Bryn Bwbach Gwyn 214 A4
Bryn Du Angl 258 E3
Bryn Eden Gwyn 215 C6
Bryn Eglwys Gwyn 237 A8
Bryn Eisteddfod Conwy 262 D6
Bryn Gates Gtr Man 277 D8
Bryn Golau Rh Cyn Taff 99 E7
Bryn Gwynant Gwyn 237 D8
Bryn Iwan Carms 122 A2
Bryn Mawr Powys 218 E2
Bryn Rhyd-yr-Arian Conwy 262 F8
Bryn Saith Marchon Denbs 240 D2
Brynafan Ceredig'n 169 D7
Brynamman Carms 124 E3
Brynawel Caerph 100 D3
Brynberian Pembs 144 D3
Brynbryddan Rh Cyn Taff 98 D2
Bryncae Rh Cyn Taff 99 F6
Bryn-celyn Flints 263 D5
Bryn-celyn Gwyn 213 C6
Bryncir Gwyn 237 F5
Bryncoch Bridg 99 F5
Bryn-coch Rh Cyn Taff 98 C1
Bryncroes Gwyn 212 B4
Bryncrug Gwyn 190 C3
Bryndrinog Shrops 172 B3
Bryneglwys Denbs 240 E3
Brynford Flints 263 E5
Brynglas Newp 101 D6
Bryngwran Angl 258 D4
Bryngwyn Ceredig'n 169 A5
Bryngwyn Ceredig'n 145 C5
Bryngwyn Monmouths 128 F1
Bryngwyn Powys 150 C1
Bryn-henllan Pembs 119 B8
Brynhoffnant Ceredig'n 145 B6
Bryniau Denbs 262 C3
Bryning Lancs 288 E5
Brynithel Bl Gwent 100 B4
Brynmawr Bl Gwent 126 E4
Bryn-mawr Gwyn 212 B5
Brynmenyn Bridg 98 F4
Brynmill Swan 97 D7
Brynna Rh Cyn Taff 99 F6
Bryn-nantllech Conwy 262 F8
Bryn-newydd Denbs 240 F4
Bryn-Offa Wrex 241 E7
Brynowen Ceredig'n 190 F3
Bryn-penarth Powys 193 C6
Bryn-Pen-y-lan Wrex 241 F7
Bryn-Perthy Powys 218 E2
Brynrefail Gwyn 237 B7
Brynrefail Angl 259 B6
Bryn-rhys Conwy 262 D6
Brynrodyn Ceredig'n 190 F3
Brynsadler Rh Cyn Taff 99 F7
Brynsiencyn Angl 259 F6
Bryn-Tanat Powys 218 D1
Brynteg Ceredig'n 146 D2
Brynteg Angl 259 C6
Brynteg Rh Cyn Taff 99 F8
Brynteg Wrex 241 D7
Bryntirion Bridg 98 F4
Bryn-Vyrnwy Powys 218 D1
Bryn-y-cochin Shrops 218 A4
Brynygwenin Monmouths 127 D7
Bryn-y-gwin Denbs 215 E6
Bryn-y-maen Conwy 262 D6
Buaile nam Bodach W Isles 446 C3
Bualintur H'land 430 F4
Bualnaluib H'land 438 D2
Bubbenhall Warwick 178 D2
Bubnell Derby 268 E4
Bubwith ER Yorks 295 C8
Buccleuch Scot Borders 372 E3
Buchanhaven Aberds 437 D8
Buchanty Perth/Kinr 419 E7
Buchley E Dunb 392 D3
Buchlyvie Stirl 409 C8
Buck Hill Wilts 82 B4
Buckabank Cumb 339 B6
Buckcastle Hill Heref'd 128 B5
Buckden Cambs 182 E3
Buckden N Yorks 316 E4
Buckenham Norfolk 210 B3
Buckerell Devon 37 F7
Buckfast Devon 14 B2
Buckfast Abbey, Buckfastleigh Devon 14 B2
Buckfastleigh Devon 14 B2
Buckhaven Fife 412 C1
Buckholm Scot Borders 385 E6
Buckholt Heref'd 128 D4
Buckhorn Devon 18 A4
Buckhorn Weston Dorset 41 B5
Buckhurst Hill Essex 112 D3
Buckie Moray 436 B1
Buckies H'land 445 B5
Buckingham Bucks 158 F1
Buckingham Palace London 89 A7
Buckland Bucks 135 E8
Buckland Devon 12 D4
Buckland Devon 15 A5
Buckland Glos 154 E4
Buckland Hants 29 A6
Buckland Herts 161 F7
Buckland Kent 75 C6
Buckland Oxon 106 C3
Buckland Surrey 69 A6
Buckland Abbey Devon 11 B5
Buckland Brewer Devon 33 B8
Buckland Common Bucks 136 F2
Buckland Dinham Som'set 61 A7
Buckland End W Midlands 198 F3
Buckland Filleigh Devon 34 E2
Buckland in the Moor Devon 14 A2
Buckland Manachorum Devon 11 B5
Buckland Newton Dorset 40 E3
Buckland Ripers Dorset 25 D7
Buckland St. Mary Som'set 38 D3
Buckland Valley Kent 75 C6
Buckland-tout-Saints Devon 13 C6
Bucklandwharf Bucks 136 E2
Bucklebury W Berks 85 B8
Bucklebury Alley W Berks 85 B7
Bucklegate Lincs 229 A6
Buckleigh Devon 54 F3
Bucklerheads Angus 420 D4
Bucklers Hard Hants 44 F3
Bucklesham Suffolk 166 D3
Buckley = Bwcle Flints 241 B6
Buckley Gtr Man 279 A7
Buckley Green Warwick 177 E6
Buckley Hill Mersey 276 E4
Bucklow Hill Ches 266 C1
Buckminister Leics 226 D4
Bucknall Lincs 273 F8
Bucknall Stoke 244 E4
Bucknell Oxon 134 B2
Bucknell Shrops 172 D5
Buckpool Moray 436 B1
Buckpool W Midlands 197 F6
Buckridge Worcs 174 D4
Buck's Cross Devon 33 B6
Bucks Green W Sussex 68 E3
Bucks Hill Herts 110 B3
Bucks Horn Oak Hants 67 C6
Buck's Mills Devon 33 B7
Bucksburn Aberd C 429 B5
Buckshaw Village Lancs 289 F8
Buckshead Cornw'l 4 A4
Buckskin Hants 66 A2
Buckton ER Yorks 311 A5
Buckton Heref'd 173 D5
Buckton Vale Gtr Man 279 D8
Buckworth Cambs 182 C2
Budbrooke Warwick 177 E8
Budby Notts 270 F4
Buddgbrake Shetl'd 456 B6
Buddileigh Staffs 243 E7
Budds Kent 71 A6
Bude Cornw'l 32 E4
Budge's Shop Cornw'l 10 D2
Budlake Devon 36 F4
Budle Northum 389 E5
Budleigh Salterton Devon 22 D3
Budlett's Common E Sussex 50 B2
Budna Beds 160 C2
Budock Water Cornw'l 4 D3
Budworth Heath Ches 265 D8
Buersil Head Gtr Man 279 B7
Buerton Ches 243 F6
Buffler's Holt Bucks 157 F8
Bugbrooke Northants 157 A8
Bugford Devon 55 C7
Bughtlin C/Edinb 395 D8
Buglawton Ches 244 B3
Bugle Cornw'l 8 D3
Bugley Wilts 62 C2
Bugthorpe ER Yorks 308 D4
Building End Essex 162 E1
Buildwas Shrops 196 C1
Builth Road Powys 149 B5
Builth Wells = Llanfair-ym-Muallt Powys 149 B5
Buirgh W Isles 448 C4
Bulbourne Herts 136 E2
Bulbridge Wilts 63 E6
Bulby Lincs 227 C8
Bulcote Notts 248 F4
Buldoo H'land 444 B3
Bulford Wilts 63 C8
Bulford Camp Wilts 63 C8
Bulkeley Ches 242 D3
Bulkington Warwick 178 A2
Bulkington Wilts 82 E3
Bulkworthy Devon 33 D7
Bull Bay = Porthllechog Angl 259 A5
Bull Farm Notts 247 B8
Bull Hill Hants 29 A6
Bullamoor N Yorks 319 B6
Bullbridge Derby 247 D5
Bullbrook Brackn'l 87 C7
Bullen's Bank Heref'd 150 D3
Bullen's Green Herts 111 A6
Bulley Glos 130 D1
Bullgill Cumb 337 D4
Bullinghope Heref'd 151 E8
Bullingstone Kent 71 C5
Bullington Lincs 273 D6
Bullockstone Kent 94 C3
Bull's Cross London 112 C1
Bull's Green Herts 138 D1
Bull's Green Norfolk 210 E4
Bulls Green Som'set 61 B6
Bullwood Arg/Bute 390 D3
Bullyhole Bottom Monmouths 102 C1
Bulmer Essex 164 D1
Bulmer N Yorks 308 B2
Bulmer Tye Essex 164 E1
Bulmore Newp 101 D7
Bulphan Thurr'k 113 E7
Bulstrode Herts 110 B2
Bulthy Shrops 218 F3
Bulverhythe E Sussex 51 E8
Bulverton Devon 22 C4
Bulwark Aberds 437 D6
Bulwell Nott'ham 247 F8
Bulwick Northants 203 E5
Bulworthy Devon 34 A3
Bumble's Green Essex 112 A3
Bun Abhainn Eadarra W Isles 449 B5
Bun a'Mhuillin W Isles 446 B3
Bun Loyne H'land 424 B4
Bunacaimb H'land 423 D6
Bunarkaig H'land 424 D3
Bunbury Ches 242 C4
Bunbury Heath Ches 242 C4
Bunce Common Surrey 69 B6
Bunchrew H'land 433 D8
Bundalloch H'land 431 F8
Buness Shetl'd 456 C6
Bunessan Arg/Bute 415 E6
Bungay Suffolk 210 F2
Bunker Hill Norfolk 209 B7
Bunker's Hill Cambs 205 B7
Bunkers Hill Gtr Man 267 B5
Bunkers Hill Hants 45 D7
Bunkers Hill Lancs 291 C6
Bunker's Hill Lincs 251 D8
Bunker's Hill Norfolk 211 C6
Bunloit H'land 433 F7
Bunnahabhain Arg/Bute 406 E4
Bunny Notts 225 C6
Bunree H'land 417 A5
Bunroy H'land 424 D4
Buntait H'land 433 E5
Buntingford Herts 138 B3
Bunting's Green Essex 141 A5
Bunwell Norfolk 209 E6
Bunwell Bottom Norfolk 209 D6
Bunwell Hill Norfolk 209 E6
Buoltach H'land 445 E5
Burbage Derby 267 E7
Burbage Leics 200 E2
Burbage Wilts 84 D1
Burchett's Green Windsor 109 F6
Burcombe Wilts 63 E6
Burcot Oxon 107 C8
Burcot Worcs 176 D2
Burcott Bucks 135 D7
Burcott Bucks 135 C8
Burcott Som'set 60 B2
Burdale N Yorks 309 C6
Burdiehouse C/Edinb 396 E2
Burdon Tyne/Wear 344 A3
Burdrop Oxon 156 E2
Bures Suffolk 164 F3
Bures Green Suffolk 164 E3
Burford Ches 243 D5
Burford Devon 33 B6
Burford Oxon 132 E4
Burford Shrops 174 E1
Burford Som'set 60 C3
Burg Arg/Bute 415 C6
Burg Arg/Bute 415 E7
Burgar Orkney 452 A4
Burgate Suffolk 187 C6
Burgates Hants 67 F5
Burge End Herts 137 A6
Burgedin Powys 218 F1
Burgess Hill W Sussex 49 C6
Burgh Suffolk 166 B2
Burgh by Sands Cumb 347 E8
Burgh Castle Norfolk 210 C5
Burgh Heath Surrey 89 E6
Burgh Hill E Sussex 71 F9
Burgh le Marsh Lincs 253 A5
Burgh Muir Aberds 428 A4
Burgh Muir Aberds 436 F4
Burgh next Aylsham Norfolk 234 C1
Burgh on Bain Lincs 274 B1
Burgh St. Margaret = Fleggburgh Norfolk 235 F5
Burgh St. Peter Norfolk 211 E5
Burghclere Hants 85 D6
Burghead Moray 435 B6
Burghfield W Berks 86 C3
Burghfield Common W Berks 86 C2
Burghfield Hill W Berks 86 C3
Burghill Heref'd 151 D7
Burghope Heref'd 151 B8
Burghwallis S Yorks 282 B4
Burham Kent 92 D1
Buriton Hants 46 B2
Burland Ches 243 D5
Burlawn Cornw'l 8 A2
Burleigh Brackn'l 87 B8
Burleigh Glos 104 B2
Burlescombe Devon 37 C6
Burleston Dorset 26 B2
Burlestone Devon 14 F4
Burley Hants 43 F7
Burley Rutl'd 202 A3
Burley W Yorks 293 D7
Burley Gate Heref'd 152 C1
Burley in Wharfdale W Yorks 292 A5
Burley Lawn Hants 43 F7
Burley Street Hants 43 F7
Burley Woodhead W Yorks 292 B5
Burleydam Ches 243 F5
Burlingham Green Norfolk 210 A3
Burlingjobb Powys 150 A3
Burlish Park Worcs 175 D6
Burlow E Sussex 50 C4
Burlton Shrops 219 C6
Burmantofts W Yorks 293 D8
Burmarsh Kent 74 E1
Burmarsh Kent 74 E2
Burmington Warwick 155 E8
Burn N Yorks 295 E5
Burn Bridge N Yorks 306 E2
Burn Naze Lancs 288 B3
Burn of Cambus Stirl 410 B2
Burnage Gtr Man 266 A4
Burnaston Derby 223 B7
Burnbank S Lanarks 381 A6
Burnbanks Cumb 327 C7
Burnbrae N Lanarks 382 A2
Burnby ER Yorks 296 A3
Burncross S Yorks 281 E8
Burndell W Sussex 47 F7
Burnden Gtr Man 278 C3
Burnedge Gtr Man 279 B7
Burnend Aberds 437 D5
Burneside Cumb 314 A4
Burness Orkney 454 B4
Burneston N Yorks 318 D5
Burnett Bath/NE Som'set 81 C5
Burnfoot Scot Borders 373 E5
Burnfoot Scot Borders 373 D7
Burnfoot Dumf/Gal 358 D3
Burnfoot Dumf/Gal 347 B7
Burnfoot E Ayrs 367 F8
Burnfoot N Lanarks 393 E6
Burnfoot Perth/Kinr 411 B4
Burnfoot S Lanarks 381 D8
Burngreave S Yorks 269 B7
Burnham Bucks 109 F8
Burnham N Lincs 285 A8
Burnham Deepdale Norfolk 255 D6
Burnham Green Herts 138 D1
Burnham Market Norfolk 255 D6
Burnham Norton Norfolk 255 D6
Burnham on Sea Som'set 59 B6
Burnham Overy Norfolk 255 D6
Burnham Overy Staithe Norfolk 255 D6
Burnham Thorpe Norfolk 255 D7
Burnham-on-Crouch Essex 115 C6
Burnhead Aberds 429 C5
Burnhead Dumf/Gal 402 A3
Burnhead Dumf/Gal 358 C1
Burnhead S Ayrs 354 B3
Burnhead S Lanarks 381 B7
Burnhervie Aberds 428 A4
Burnhill Green Staffs 196 C4
Burnhope Durham 343 B7

Burnhouse N Ayrs 379 B7
Burnhouse S Lanarks 380 B4
Burniestrype Moray 435 B8
Burniston N Yorks 322 B4
Burnlee W Yorks 280 C4
Burnley Lancs 291 D5
Burnley Lane Lancs 291 D5
Burnley Wood Lancs 291 D5
Burnmouth Scot Borders 399 F9
Burnopfield Durham 352 E2
Burnrigg Cumb 348 E3
Burn's Green Herts 138 C2
Burnsall N Yorks 304 C4
Burnside Aberds 437 D5
Burnside Angus 421 B5
Burnside E Ayrs 368 E3
Burnside Fife 411 B6
Burnside Perth/Kinr 419 E8
Burnside Shetl'd 457 F2
Burnside S Lanarks 392 F4
Burnside Tyne/Wear 344 A2
Burnside W Loth 395 D6
Burnside W Loth 395 C6
Burnside of Duntrune Angus 420 D4
Burnswark Dumf/Gal 347 A5
Burnt Heath Derby 268 D4
Burnt Heath Essex 142 B2
Burnt Hill W Berks 85 B8
Burnt Houses Durham 330 B4
Burnt Oak E Sussex 70 F5
Burnt Oak London 111 D6
Burnt Tree W Midlands 197 E8
Burnt Yates N Yorks 306 C2
Burntcommon Surrey 88 E2
Burntheath Derby 223 B6
Burnthouse Cornw'l 4 C3
Burntisland Fife 411 D7
Burnton E Ayrs 368 F1
Burnturk Fife 411 B8
Burntwood Staffs 198 B2
Burntwood Green Staffs 198 B2
Burnworthy Som'set 38 C1
Burnwynd C/Edinb 395 E7
Burpham Surrey 68 A2
Burpham W Sussex 47 E8
Burradon Northum 363 A8
Burradon Tyne/Wear 352 B4
Burrafirth Shetl'd 456 B6
Burraland Shetl'd 457 F3
Burraland Shetl'd 457 J2
Burras Cornw'l 4 D1
Burrastow Shetl'd 457 J2
Burraton Cornw'l 10 D4
Burraton Coombe Cornw'l 10 D4
Burravoe Shetl'd 457 F5
Burravoe Shetl'd 457 G3
Burray Village Orkney 453 D5
Burreldales Aberds 436 E4
Burrells Cumb 328 C3
Burrelton Perth/Kinr 420 D2
Burridge Devon 35 D7
Burridge Devon 38 E4
Burridge Devon 55 D6
Burridge Hants 45 D5
Burrigill H'land 445 E6
Burrill N Yorks 318 C3
Burringham N Lincs 284 C3
Burrington Devon 35 C5
Burrington Heref'd 173 D6
Burrington N Som'set 80 E1
Burrough End Cambs 162 B5
Burrough Green Cambs 163 A5
Burrough on the Hill Leics 201 A9
Burroughs Grove Bucks 109 E7
Burroughston Orkney 453 A6
Burrow Devon 22 C3
Burrow Devon 22 A1
Burrow Som'set 57 C5
Burrow Som'set 39 B6
Burrow Bridge Som'set 59 F7
Burrowhill Surrey 88 D1
Burrows Cross Surrey 68 B3
Burrs Gtr Man 278 B4
Burrsville Park Essex 142 D4
Burry Swan 96 D4
Burry Green Swan 96 D4
Burry Port = Porth Tywyn Carms 96 B3
Burscough Lancs 277 B5
Burscough Bridge Lancs 277 B5
Bursea ER Yorks 296 D3
Burshill ER Yorks 310 F3
Bursledon Hants 44 E4
Burslem Stoke 244 E3
Burstall Suffolk 165 D6
Burstock Dorset 39 F6
Burston Devon 35 F7
Burston Norfolk 187 B7
Burston Staffs 221 B8
Burstow Surrey 69 C8
Burstwick ER Yorks 298 E3
Burtersett N Yorks 316 C3
Burtholme Cumb 348 D4
Burthorpe Suffolk 185 F8
Burthwaite Cumb 339 B7
Burtle Som'set 59 C8
Burtle Hill Som'set 59 C7
Burtoft Lincs 228 A5
Burton Ches 263 E8
Burton Ches 242 B3
Burton Dorset 25 B8
Burton Dorset 28 B3
Burton Lincs 272 E4
Burton Pembs 117 C5
Burton Som'set 39 D8
Burton Som'set 58 C3
Burton Wilts 61 E8
Burton Wilts 81 A8
Burton Wrex 241 C8
Burton Agnes ER Yorks 310 C4
Burton Bradstock Dorset 24 C4
Burton Constable ER Yorks 298 C2
Burton Corner Lincs 252 E2
Burton Dassett Warwick 156 B2
Burton End Essex 139 C6
Burton Ferry Pembs 117 C5
Burton Fleming ER Yorks 310 A3
Burton Green W Midlands 177 C8
Burton Green Wrex 241 C7
Burton Hastings Warwick 200 F2
Burton in Lonsdale N Yorks 302 A5
Burton Joyce Notts 248 F3
Burton Latimer Northants 181 D6
Burton Lazars Leics 226 E2
Burton Leonard N Yorks 306 C3
Burton on the Wolds Leics 225 D6
Burton Overy Leics 201 D7
Burton Pedwardine Lincs 251 F5
Burton Pidsea ER Yorks 298 D3
Burton Salmon N Yorks 294 E3
Burton Stather N Lincs 284 A4
Burton upon Trent Staffs 223 D7
Burton-in-Kendal Cumb 314 E4
Burton-le-Coggles Lincs 227 C6
Burton's Green Essex 141 B5
Burton-upon-Stather N Lincs 284 A4
Burtonwood Warrington 265 A6
Burtree Ford Durham 341 C8
Burwardsley Ches 242 C3
Burwarton Shrops 174 B2
Burwash E Sussex 51 B6
Burwash Common E Sussex 51 B5
Burwash Weald E Sussex 51 B5
Burwell Cambs 184 E4
Burwell Lincs 274 D4
Burwen Angl 259 A5
Burwick Orkney 453 E5
Burwick Shetl'd 455 B2
Burwood Park Surrey 88 D3
Bury Cambs 183 B5
Bury Gtr Man 278 B4
Bury Som'set 57 F5
Bury W Sussex 47 D8
Bury End Beds 160 E2
Bury End Beds 159 B7
Bury End Worcs 154 E4
Bury Green Herts 112 B1
Bury Green Herts 139 C5
Bury Hill S Glos 103 E6
Bury St. Edmunds Suffolk 186 F2
Burys Bank W Berks 85 C6
Burythorpe N Yorks 308 C4
Busbridge Surrey 68 C1
Busby E Renf 380 A3
Buscot Oxon 106 C1
Buscott Som'set 59 D8
Bush Aberds 421 A7
Bush Cornw'l 32 E4
Bush Som'set 58 D4
Bush Bank Heref'd 151 B6
Bush Crathie Aberds 427 C7
Bush Green Norfolk 208 D4
Bush Green Norfolk 209 F8
Bush Green Suffolk 164 A3
Bush Hill London 111 C8
Bush Hill Park London 111 C8
Bushbury Surrey 69 B5
Bushbury W Midlands 197 C7
Bushby Leics 201 C7
Bushey Dorset 27 D6
Bushey Herts 110 C4
Bushey Heath Herts 111 D5
Bushley Worcs 153 F7
Bushley Green Worcs 153 F7
Bushmead Beds 182 F2
Bushton Wilts 83 A6
Bushy Common Norfolk 232 F4
Bushy Hill Surrey 68 A2
Busk Cumb 340 C3
Busk Gtr Man 279 C7
Buslingthorpe Lincs 273 B6
Bussage Glos 104 B2
Bussex Som'set 59 D7
Buss's Green E Sussex 71 D7
Busta Shetl'd 457 G3
Bustard Green Essex 140 B1
Bustard's Green Norfolk 209 E7
Bustatoun Orkney 454 A6
Busveal Cornw'l 4 B2
Butcher's Common Norfolk 234 D3
Butcher's Cross E Sussex 50 A4
Butcher's Row W Sussex 48 B3
Butcombe N Som'set 80 D2
Bute Town Caerph 126 F3
Butetown Card 78 A3
Butleigh Som'set 60 E2
Butleigh Wootton Som'set 60 E2
Butler's Cross Bucks 135 F7
Butler's Hill Notts 248 E1
Butlers Marston Warwick 156 B1
Butley Suffolk 166 B5
Butley Corner Suffolk 167 C5
Butley Town Ches 267 D5
Butlocks Heath Hants 44 E4
Butt Green Ches 243 D6
Butt Green Glos 130 E3
Butt Lane Staffs 244 D2
Buttercrambe N Yorks 308 D3
Butterfield Green Beds 137 A8
Butterhaugh Northum 362 D1
Butterknowle Durham 330 A4
Butterleigh Devon 36 E4
Butterley Derby 247 D6
Butterley Grange Derby 247 D6
Buttermere Cumb 325 C8
Buttermere Wilts 84 D3
Butterow Glos 104 B2
Butters Green Staffs 244 D2
Buttershaw W Yorks 292 E4
Butterstone Perth/Kinr 419 C8
Butterton Staffs 244 F2
Butterton Staffs 245 C7
Butterwick Cumb 327 C7
Butterwick Durham 344 F3
Butterwick Lincs 252 E3
Butterwick N Yorks 321 E5
Butterwick N Yorks 309 A8
Buttington Powys 193 B9
Button Haugh Green Suffolk 186 E4
Buttonbridge Shrops 174 C4
Buttonoak Shrops 174 C4
Butts Devon 21 C6
Butt's Close Herts 137 B7
Butt's Green Essex 114 B2
Butt's Green Hants 43 A9
Butt's Knap Dorset 41 B7
Buttsash Hants 44 E3
Buttsole Kent 95 F6
Buxhall Suffolk 165 A5
Buxhall Fen Street Suffolk 165 A5
Buxley Scot Borders 387 A6
Buxted E Sussex 50 B2
Buxton Derby 267 E8
Buxton Norfolk 234 D1
Buxworth Derby 267 C7
Bwcle = Buckley Flints 241 B6
Bwlch Powys 126 C3
Bwlch Shrops 218 C2
Bwlch y Garreg Powys 192 D4
Bwlch-derwin Gwyn 236 E5
Bwlchgwyn Wrex 241 D6
Bwlch-Llan Ceredig'n 146 A4
Bwlchnewydd Carms 122 C3
Bwlchtocyn Gwyn 213 C6
Bwlch-y-cibau Powys 217 E8
Bwlchyddar Powys 217 D8
Bwlch-y-fadfa Ceredig'n 145 C8
Bwlch-y-ffridd Powys 192 D5
Bwlch-y-groes Ceredig'n 145 C7
Bwlchygroes Pembs 144 E4
Bwlch-y-haiarn Conwy 238 C3
Bwlchyllyn Gwyn 237 C6
Bwlchymynydd Swan 97 C6
Bwlch-y-sarnau Powys 171 D5
Bybrook Kent 73 C7
Bye Green Bucks 135 E8
Byeastwood Bridg 99 F5
Byebush Aberds 437 E4
Byermoor Tyne/Wear 352 E2
Byers Green Durham 343 E8
Byfield Northants 157 B5
Byfleet Surrey 88 D3
Byford Heref'd 151 D5
Byford Common Heref'd 151 D5
Bygrave Herts 161 E5
Byker Tyne/Wear 352 D4
Byland Abbey N Yorks 320 E1
Byley Ches 266 F1
Bynea Carms 97 C5
Byram N Yorks 294 E3
Byram-cum-Sutton N Yorks 294 F3
Byrness Northum 362 B4
Bystock Devon 22 D2
Bythorn Cambs 181 C9
Byton Heref'd 172 F5
Bywell Northum 351 D7
Byworth W Sussex 47 B7


## C


Cabharstadh W Isles 451 E6
Cablea Perth/Kinr 419 D7
Cabourne Lincs 286 D1
Cabrach Arg/Bute 407 F4
Cabrach Moray 435 F8
Cabrich H'land 433 D7
Cabus Lancs 302 F1
Cackle Hill Lincs 229 C7
Cackle Street E Sussex 50 A2
Cackle Street E Sussex 52 C1
Cad Green Som'set 39 C5
Cadboll H'land 441 F5
Cadbury Devon 36 F3
Cadbury Heath S Glos 81 B5
Cadbury World, Bournville W Midlands 176 B3
Cadder E Dunb 392 D4
Cadderlie Arg/Bute 417 D5
Caddington Beds 136 D5
Caddleton Arg/Bute 416 F2
Caddonfoot Scot Borders 385 E6
Cade Street E Sussex 50 B5
Cadeby Leics 200 C2
Cadeby S Yorks 282 D4
Cadeleigh Devon 36 E3
Cadger Path Angus 421 B4
Cadgwith Cornw'l 5 H2
Cadham Fife 411 B7
Cadishead Gtr Man 265 A9
Cadle Swan 97 C7
Cadley Lancs 289 D7
Cadley Wilts 84 F1
Cadley Wilts 83 C9
Cadmore End Bucks 109 D5
Cadnam Hants 43 D8
Cadney N Lincs 285 D7
Cadole Flints 240 B5
Cadoxton V/Glam 78 C2
Cadoxton-Juxta-Neath Rh Cyn Taff 98 C2
Cadshaw Blackb'n 278 A3
Cadwell Herts 137 A7
Cadwell Park Lincs 274 C2
Cadwell Park Motor Racing Circuit Lincs 274 C2
Cadwin Cornw'l 8 C3
Cadwst Denbs 217 A5
Cadzow S Lanarks 381 B6
Caeathro Gwyn 237 B6
Caehopkin Powys 124 E5
Caenby Lincs 272 B5
Caerau Bridg 98 D4
Caerau Card 78 A2
Cae'r-bont Powys 124 E5
Cae'r-bryn Carms 123 E7
Caerdeon Gwyn 215 E5
Cae'r-dynyn Gwyn 215 D8
Caerfarchell Pembs 118 D3
Caerfyrddin = Carmarthen Carms 122 C4
Caergeiliog Angl 258 D3
Caergwrle Flints 241 C7
Caergybi = Holyhead Angl 258 C2
Caerhendy Rh Cyn Taff 98 D2
Caerhun Gwyn 259 F8
Cae'r-Lan Powys 124 E5
Caerleon Newp 101 D6
Caernarfon Gwyn 237 B5
Caernarfon Castle Gwyn 236 B5
Caerphilly Caerph 100 E3
Caersws Powys 192 E4
Caerwedros Ceredig'n 145 A7
Caerwent Monmouths 102 D1
Caerwent Brook Monmouths 102 E1
Caerwys Flints 262 E4
Caethiwed Conwy 262 D6
Cafn-coed-y-cymmer Merth Tyd 126 F1
Cage Green Kent 71 B6
Caggan H'land 426 A3
Caggle Street Monmouths 127 D8
Càrnais W Isles 450 D3
Càrnan W Isles 447 D2
Cailness Stirl 409 B6
Caim Angl 260 C2
Cainscross Glos 103 B8
Caio Carms 147 E6
Cairinis W Isles 447 B3
Cairisiadar W Isles 450 D3
Cairminis W Isles 448 D4
Cairnbaan Arg/Bute 407 C8
Cairnbanno Ho. Aberds 437 D5
Cairnborrow Aberds 436 D1
Cairnbrogie Aberds 437 F5
Cairnbulg Castle Aberds 437 B7
Cairncross Angus 428 E1
Cairncross Scot Borders 399 F7
Cairnderry Dumf/Gal 401 B5
Cairndow Arg/Bute 408 A4
Cairness Aberds 437 B7
Cairneyhill Fife 411 D5
Cairnfield Ho. Moray 436 B1
Cairngaan Dumf/Gal 400 F3
Cairngarroch Dumf/Gal 400 E2
Cairnhill Aberds 436 E3
Cairnhill Aberds 437 C4
Cairnhill N Lanarks 393 F7
Cairnie Aberds 429 B5
Cairnie Aberds 436 D1
Cairnlea S Ayrs 400 A4
Cairnleith Crofts Aberds 437 E6
Cairnmuir Aberds 437 B6
Cairnorrie Aberds 437 D5
Cairnpark Aberds 429 A5
Cairnryan Dumf/Gal 400 C2
Cairnton Orkney 452 C4
Cairston Orkney 452 B3
Caister-on-Sea Norfolk 211 A6
Caistor Lincs 286 D1
Caistor St. Edmund Norfolk 209 C8
Caitha Bowland Scot Borders 385 D6
Caithness Glass, Perth Perth/Kinr 419 E8
Cakebole Worcs 175 D7
Calais Street Suffolk 164 E4
Calamansack Cornw'l 4 E2
Calanais W Isles 450 D5
Calbost W Isles 451 F7
Calbourne I/Wight 29 C8
Calceby Lincs 274 D4
Calcoed Flints 263 E5
Calcot Glos 131 E7
Calcot W Berks 86 B3
Calcott Kent 94 D3
Calcott Shrops 219 F6
Calcott's Green Glos 130 D1
Calcutt N Yorks 306 D3
Caldback Shetl'd 456 C6
Caldbeck Cumb 339 D5
Caldbergh N Yorks 317 C7
Caldecote Cambs 204 F1
Caldecote Cambs 160 A4
Caldecote Cambs 161 A6
Caldecote Herts 160 E4
Caldecote M/Keynes 159 D5
Caldecote Northants 158 B1
Caldecote Warwick 199 E8
Caldecott Northants 181 E7
Caldecott Oxon 107 C6
Caldecott Rutl'd 202 E3
Caldecotte M/Keynes 159 E5
Calder Cumb 325 F5
Calder Bridge Cumb 325 E5
Calder Grove W Yorks 281 A7
Calder Mains H'land 445 C4
Calder Vale Lancs 289 A7
Calderbank N Lanarks 393 F7
Calderbrook Gtr Man 279 A7
Caldercruix N Lanarks 393 E8
Caldermill S Lanarks 380 D4
Caldermoor Gtr Man 279 A7
Calderstones Mersey 264 B3
Calderwood S Lanarks 380 A4
Caldhame Angus 420 C4
Caldicot Monmouths 102 E1
Caldwell N Yorks 331 D5
Caldwell Staffs 223 E7
Caldy Mersey 263 B6
Calebrack Cumb 338 D5
Calenick Cornw'l 4 B4
Calf Bridge Lincs 228 B3
Calford Green Suffolk 163 C6
Calfsound Orkney 454 C3
Calgary Arg/Bute 415 B6
Caliach Arg/Bute 415 B6
Califer Moray 435 C5
California Cambs 184 B3
California Falk 394 C3
California Norfolk 235 F7
California W Midlands 176 B3
Calke Derby 224 D2
Callakille H'land 431 C6
Callaly Northum 376 F3
Callander Stirl 410 B1
Callandrode Stirl 410 B1
Callands Warrington 265 A6
Callaughton Shrops 195 D8
Callert Ho. H'land 417 A5
Callerton Tyne/Wear 352 C2
Callestick Cornw'l 7 E6
Calligarry H'land 423 B6
Callington Cornw'l 10 B3
Callingwood Staffs 223 D5
Callop H'land 424 E1
Callow Heref'd 151 F7
Callow End Worcs 153 C6
Callow Hill Som'set 79 E8
Callow Hill Surrey 88 C1
Callow Hill Wilts 105 F5
Callow Hill Worcs 176 F3
Callow Hill Worcs 174 D4
Callowell Glos 104 A1
Callow's Grave Worcs 174 E1
Calmore Hants 44 D1
Calmsden Glos 131 F6
Calne Wilts 82 B5
Calne Marsh Wilts 82 B5
Calow Derby 269 E8
Calow Green Derby 269 F8
Calshot Hants 44 F4
Calstock Cornw'l 10 B4
Calstone Wellington Wilts 83 C5
Calthorpe Norfolk 233 B8
Calthorpe Oxon 156 E4
Calthorpe Street Norfolk 235 C5
Calthwaite Cumb 339 C8
Calton N Yorks 304 D2
Calton Staffs 245 D8
Calton Lees Derby 268 F5
Calveley Ches 242 C4
Calver Derby 268 E4
Calver Hill Heref'd 150 C5
Calver Sough Derby 268 E4
Calverhall Shrops 220 A2
Calverleigh Devon 36 D3
Calverley W Yorks 293 C6
Calvert Bucks 134 C4
Calverton M/Keynes 158 E3
Calverton Notts 248 E3
Calvine Perth/Kinr 419 A6
Calvo Cumb 346 F4
Cam Glos 103 C7
Camaghael H'land 424 E3
Camas an Staca Arg/Bute 406 F4
Camas Salach H'land 416 A1
Camas-luinie H'land 432 F1
Camasnacroise H'land 416 B3
Camastianavaig H'land 431 E6
Camasunary H'land 422 A5
Cambaull Muir H'land 433 D7
Camb Shetl'd 456 D5
Camber E Sussex 52 C4
Camberley Surrey 87 D7
Camberwell London 89 A8
Camblesforth N Yorks 295 E7
Cambo Northum 364 E2
Cambois Northum 365 F8
Camborne Cornw'l 3 B9
Cambourne Cambs 161 A6
Cambridge Cambs 162 A2
Cambridge Glos 103 B6
Cambridge W Yorks 293 A6
Cambridge Airport Cambs 162 A2
Cambridge Batch N Som'set 80 B2
Cambridge Town Southend 115 E5
Cambrose Cornw'l 4 A1
Cambus Clack 410 C3
Cambusavie Farm H'land 440 D4
Cambusbarron Stirl 410 C2
Cambuskenneth Stirl 410 C3
Cambuslang S Lanarks 380 A4
Cambusmore Lodge H'land 440 D4
Cambusnethan N Lanarks 381 A8
Camden Town London 111 F7
Camel Hill Som'set 40 A1
Cameley Bath/NE Som'set 80 E4
Camelford Cornw'l 17 D7
Camelot Theme Park, Chorley Lancs 277 A7
Camelsdale W Sussex 67 E7
Camer Kent 91 C8
Camerory H'land 434 E5
Camer's Green Worcs 153 F5
Camerton Bath/NE Som'set 81 E5
Camerton Cumb 337 E3
Camerton ER Yorks 298 E3
Camghouran Perth/Kinr 418 B3
Cammachmore Aberds 429 C6
Cammeringham Lincs 272 C3
Camore H'land 440 D4
Camp Hill N Yorks 318 D5
Camp Hill Warwick 199 E7
Camp Town W Yorks 293 C8
Campbeltown Arg/Bute 404 D3
Campbeltown Airport Arg/Bute 404 D2
Camperdown Tyne/Wear 352 B4
Campion Hills Warwick 178 E1
Campie Dumf/Gal 358 D2
Campmuir Perth/Kinr 420 D2
Camps W Loth 395 E7
Camps End Cambs 162 D5
Camps Heath Suffolk 211 E6
Campsall S Yorks 282 B4
Campsey Ash Suffolk 166 A4
Campsfield Oxon 133 D8
Campton Beds 160 E2
Camptoun E Loth 397 C7
Camptown Scot Borders 374 E3
Camquhart Arg/Bute 408 D2
Camrose Pembs 116 A4
Camserney Perth/Kinr 419 C6
Camster H'land 445 D6
Camuschoirk H'land 416 A2
Camuscross H'land 423 A6
Camusnagaul H'land 424 E2
Camusnagaul H'land 438 E4
Camusrory H'land 423 C8
Camusteel H'land 431 D7
Camusterrach H'land 431 D7
Camusvrachan Perth/Kinr 418 C4
Canada Hants 43 C8
Canada Lincs 286 D1
Canada Common Hants 43 C8
Canadia E Sussex 51 C7
Canal Side S Yorks 283 B7
Canary Wharf London 112 F2
Canaston Bridge Pembs 117 B7
Candacraig Ho. Aberds 427 A8
Candie Falk 394 D3
Candle Street Suffolk 187 D5
Candlesby Lincs 275 F6
Candy Mill S Lanarks 383 D6
Cane End Oxon 86 A3
Canewdon Essex 115 D5
Canfield End Essex 139 C7
Canford Cliffs Dorset 27 C8
Canford Magna Poole 27 A7
Canham's Green Suffolk 187 E6
Canisbay H'land 445 A7
Canklow S Yorks 269 A8
Canley W Midlands 178 C1
Cann Dorset 41 B7
Cann Common Dorset 41 B7
Cannard's Grave Som'set 60 C4
Cannich H'land 433 E5
Canning Town London 112 F2
Cannington Som'set 58 D5
Cannock Staffs 197 B8
Cannock Wood Staffs 198 A1
Cannon Hill London 89 C6
Cannon's Green Essex 113 A6
Cannop Glos 129 E6
Canon Bridge Heref'd 151 C7
Canon Frome Heref'd 152 D3
Canon Pyon Heref'd 151 D6
Canonbie Dumf/Gal 348 A1
Canonbury London 111 F8
Canons Ashby Northants 157 B6
Canons Park London 111 D5
Canonstown Cornw'l 3 C6
Canterbury Kent 94 E3
Canterbury Cathedral Kent 94 E3
Canterbury Tales Kent 94 E2
Cantley Norfolk 210 C3
Cantley S Yorks 283 D6
Cantlop Shrops 195 B6
Canton Card 78 A3
Cantraybruich H'land 434 D2
Cantraydoune H'land 434 D2
Cantraywood H'land 434 D2
Cantsfield Lancs 302 A4
Canvey Island Essex 114 F2
Canwick Lincs 272 F4
Canworthy Cornw'l 18 B1
Canworthy Water Cornw'l 18 B1
Caol H'land 424 E3
Caol Ila Arg/Bute 406 E4
Caolas Arg/Bute 414 C3
Caolas W Isles 446 D2
Caolas Fhlodaigh W Isles 447 C3
Caolas Liubharsaigh W Isles 447 D3
Caolas Scalpaigh W Isles 449 C6
Caolas Stocinis W Isles 449 C5
Caoslasnacon H'land 417 A6
Capel Carms 96 B5
Capel Kent 71 C7
Capel Surrey 69 C5
Capel Bangor Ceredig'n 169 B6
Capel Betws Lleucu Ceredig'n 146 A5
Capel Carmel Gwyn 212 C3
Capel Coch Angl 259 C6
Capel Curig Conwy 238 C2
Capel Cynon Ceredig'n 145 C7
Capel Dewi Carms 123 C5
Capel Dewi Ceredig'n 169 B5
Capel Dewi Ceredig'n 146 D2
Capel Garmon Conwy 238 C4
Capel Green Suffolk 166 C5
Capel Gwyn Carms 123 C5
Capel Gwyn Angl 258 D3
Capel Gwynfe Carms 124 C3
Capel Hendre Carms 123 E7
Capel Isaac Carms 123 B7
Capel Iwan Carms 145 E5
Capel le Ferne Kent 74 D4
Capel Mawr Angl 259 E5
Capel St. Andrew Suffolk 166 C5
Capel St. Mary Suffolk 165 E6
Capel Seion Ceredig'n 169 C5
Capel Tygwydd Ceredig'n 145 D5
Capel Uchaf Gwyn 236 E4
Capelulo Conwy 260 D4
Capel-y-ffin Powys 127 A6
Capel-y-graig Gwyn 259 F7
Capenhurst Ches 264 E2
Capernwray Lancs 302 A2
Capheaton Northum 364 F2
Capon's Green Suffolk 188 E3
Cappercleugh Scot Borders 372 C1
Capplegill Dumf/Gal 371 F7
Caprington E Ayrs 379 E8
Capstone Medway 92 D2
Captain Fold Gtr Man 279 B6
Capton Devon 14 E4
Capton Som'set 57 D8
Caputh Perth/Kinr 419 D8
Car Colston Notts 248 E5
Caradon Town Cornw'l 10 A1
Carbis Cornw'l 8 D3
Carbis Bay Cornw'l 3 C6
Carbost H'land 430 E3
Carbost H'land 430 D4
Carbrain N Lanarks 393 D7
Carbrook S Yorks 269 B7
Carbrooke Norfolk 208 C3
Carburton Notts 270 E4
Carcant Scot Borders 384 B4
Carcary Angus 421 B6
Carclaze Cornw'l 8 E3
Carcroft S Yorks 282 B4
Cardenden Fife 411 C7
Cardeston Shrops 194 A3
Cardewlees Cumb 339 A5
Cardiff Card 78 A3
Cardiff Bay Barrage Card 78 B3
Cardiff Castle Card 78 A3
Cardiff International Airport V/Glam 77 C8
Cardigan = Aberteifi Ceredig'n 144 C3
Cardinal's Green Cambs 162 C5
Cardington Beds 160 C1
Cardington Shrops 195 D6
Cardinham Cornw'l 9 B5
Cardonald Glasg C 392 F2
Cardow Moray 435 D6
Cardrona Scot Borders 384 E3
Cardross Invercl 391 C6
Cardurnock Cumb 347 E5
Careby Lincs 227 E7
Careston Angus 421 A5
Careston Castle Angus 421 B5
Carew Pembs 117 D6
Carew Cheriton Pembs 117 D6
Carew Newton Pembs 117 D6
Carey Heref'd 128 A5
Carey Park Cornw'l 9 E7
Carfin N Lanarks 381 A7
Carfrae E Loth 397 E8
Carfury Cornw'l 2 D4
Cargate Suffolk 164 A3
Cargate Common Norfolk 209 E6
Cargate Green Norfolk 210 A3
Cargenbridge Dumf/Gal 402 B3
Cargill Perth/Kinr 420 D1
Cargo Cumb 348 E1
Cargreen Cornw'l 10 C4
Carham Scot Borders 387 E5
Carhampton Som'set 57 C7
Carharrack Cornw'l 4 B2
Carie Perth/Kinr 418 B4
Carie Perth/Kinr 418 D4
Caring Kent 92 F3
Carisbrooke I/Wight 30 C1
Carisbrooke Castle I/Wight 30 C1
Cark Cumb 313 E8
Carkeel Cornw'l 10 C4
Carlabhagh W Isles 450 C5
Carlbury D'lington 331 C6
Carlby Lincs 227 F7
Carlecotes S Yorks 280 D5
Carleen Cornw'l 3 D8
Carlesmoor N Yorks 318 F2
Carleton Blackp'l 288 C3
Carleton Cumb 324 E5
Carleton Cumb 340 F1
Carleton Cumb 339 A7
Carleton N Yorks 304 F3
Carleton W Yorks 294 F3
Carleton Forehoe Norfolk 209 B5

Carleton Rode Norfolk 209 E6
Carleton St. Peter Norfolk 210 C2
Carley Hill Tyne/Wear 353 E6
Carlidnack Cornw'l 4 E3
Carlin How Redcar/Clevel'd 333 C9
Carlincraig Aberds 436 D3
Carlingcott Bath/NE Som'set 81 E5
Carlisle Cumb 348 E1
Carlisle Airport Cumb 348 D3
Carlisle Cathedral Cumb 348 E1
Carlisle Racecourse Cumb 339 A7
Carloggas Cornw'l 7 B8
Carloonan Arg/Bute 408 A3
Carlops Scot Borders 383 A8
Carlton Beds 159 A7
Carlton Cambs 163 B5
Carlton Leics 200 B1
Carlton Notts 248 F3
Carlton N Yorks 295 F6
Carlton N Yorks 317 D7
Carlton N Yorks 320 C3
Carlton N Yorks 331 D5
Carlton Suffolk 189 F5
Carlton Stockton 332 B2
Carlton S Yorks 282 B1
Carlton W Yorks 293 E8
Carlton Colville Suffolk 211 E6
Carlton Curlieu Leics 201 D7
Carlton Green Cambs 163 B5
Carlton Husthwaite N Yorks 319 E8
Carlton in Cleveland N Yorks 333 F6
Carlton in Lindrick Notts 270 B3
Carlton Miniott N Yorks 319 D7
Carlton Scroop Lincs 250 E1
Carlton-le-Moorland Lincs 249 C9
Carlton-on-Trent Notts 249 B6
Carluke S Lanarks 382 B1
Carmarthen = Caerfyrddin Carms 122 C4
Carmel Carms 123 D7
Carmel Flints 263 D5
Carmel Gwyn 237 C5
Carmel Angl 258 C4
Carmichael S Lanarks 382 E3
Carmont Aberds 429 D5
Carmunnock Glasg C 380 A4
Carmyle Glasg C 392 F4
Carmyllie Angus 421 C5
Carn Brea Cornw'l 4 B1
Carn Towan Cornw'l 2 E3
Carnaby ER Yorks 310 B4
Carnach H'land 432 F2
Carnach H'land 438 D4
Carnach W Isles 449 C6
Carnachy H'land 444 C1
Carnbahn Perth/Kinr 418 C4
Carnbee Fife 412 B3
Carnbo Perth/Kinr 411 B5
Carnbroe N Lanarks 393 F6
Carndu H'land 431 F8
Carnduff S Lanarks 381 C5
Carnduncan Arg/Bute 406 F2
Carne Cornw'l 5 C6
Carne Cornw'l 8 D2
Carnebone Cornw'l 4 D2
Carnetown Rh Cyn Taff 99 D8
Carnforth Lancs 302 A1
Carnglas Swan 97 D7
Carn-gorm H'land 432 F1
Carnhedryn Pembs 118 D4
Carnhell Green Cornw'l 3 C8
Carnhot Cornw'l 4 A2
Carnkie Cornw'l 4 C1
Carnkie Cornw'l 4 D2
Carnkief Cornw'l 7 E6
Carno Powys 192 D3
Carnoch H'land 432 C4
Carnoch H'land 433 E5
Carnock Fife 411 D5
Carnon Downs Cornw'l 4 B3
Carnousie Aberds 436 C3
Carnoustie Angus 421 D5
Carntyne Glasg C 392 E4
Carnwadric Glasg C 380 A2
Carnwath S Lanarks 382 C4
Carnyorth Cornw'l 2 D3
Carol Green W Midlands 177 C8
Carpalla Cornw'l 8 E2
Carperby N Yorks 317 C6
Carr Gtr Man 278 A4
Carr Cross Lancs 276 B4
Carr Gate W Yorks 293 F8
Carr Green Gtr Man 266 B1
Carr Hill Tyne/Wear 352 D4
Carr Houses Mersey 276 D3
Carr Shield Northum 341 B7
Carr Vale Derby 270 F1
Carradale Arg/Bute 404 C4
Carragraich W Isles 449 C5
Carrbridge H'land 434 F4
Carrbrook Gtr Man 280 D1
Carreglefn Angl 258 B4
Carregwen Pembs 144 D4
Carreg-y-Garth Gwyn 237 A7
Carrhouse N Lincs 284 C2
Carrick Arg/Bute 408 D2
Carrick Dumf/Gal 401 D7
Carrick Fife 420 E4
Carrick Castle Arg/Bute 408 C4
Carrick Ho. Orkney 454 C3
Carriden Falk 411 D5
Carrington Nott'ham 248 F2
Carrington Gtr Man 266 A1
Carrington Lincs 252 C2
Carrington Midloth 396 F3
Carrog Conwy 238 E3
Carrog Denbs 240 F3
Carroglen Perth/Kinr 419 E5
Carrol H'land 441 C5
Carron Falk 410 D3
Carron Moray 435 D7
Carron Bridge Stirl 410 D2
Carronbridge Dumf/Gal 358 C1
Carrot Angus 420 C4
Carrow Hill Monmouths 101 D8
Carrutherstown Dumf/Gal 346 B4
Carrville Durham 344 C2
Carry Arg/Bute 408 F2
Carsaig Arg/Bute 407 D7
Carsaig Arg/Bute 415 E8
Carscreugh Dumf/Gal 400 D4
Carse Gray Angus 420 B4
Carse Ho. Arg/Bute 407 F7
Carsegowan Dumf/Gal 401 D6
Carseriggan Dumf/Gal 400 C5
Carsethorn Dumf/Gal 402 D3
Carshalton London 89 C7
Carshalton Beeches London 89 D7
Carshalton on the Hill London 89 D7
Carsington Derby 246 D2
Carskiey Arg/Bute 404 F2
Carsluith Dumf/Gal 401 D6
Carsphairn Dumf/Gal 356 D3
Carstairs S Lanarks 382 C3
Carstairs Junction S Lanarks 382 C4
Cartbridge Surrey 88 E2
Carter Knowle S Yorks 269 C6
Carter's Clay Hants 43 B9
Carter's Green Essex 139 E6
Carterton Oxon 106 A2
Carterway Heads Northum 342 A4
Carthew Cornw'l 8 D3
Carthorpe N Yorks 318 D5
Cartington Northum 364 B2
Cartland S Lanarks 382 C2
Cartledge Derby 269 D6
Cartmel Cumb 313 E8
Cartmel Fell Cumb 314 C2
Cartmel Racecourse Cumb 313 E8
Cartworth W Yorks 280 C4
Carty Port Dumf/Gal 401 C6
Carway Carms 96 A4
Carwinley Cumb 348 B2
Cary Fitzpaine Som'set 60 E2
Cascob Powys 172 E2
Cashes Green Glos 103 A8
Cashlie Perth/Kinr 418 C2
Cashmere Visitor Centre, Elgin Moray 435 B7
Cashmoor Dorset 42 D3
Cassey Compton Glos 131 D6
Cassington Oxon 133 E8
Cassop Durham 344 D2
Casswell's Bridge Lincs 228 C3
Castallack Cornw'l 2 E5
Castell Conwy 260 F5
Castell Coch Card 100 F2
Castell Howell Ceredig'n 146 C1
Castell Newydd Emlyn = Newcastle Emlyn Carms 145 D6
Castell-nedd = Neath Rh Cyn Taff 98 C2
Casterton Cumb 315 E6
Castle Acre Norfolk 231 E8
Castle Ashby Northants 158 A5
Castle Bolton N Yorks 317 B6
Castle Bromwich W Midlands 198 F4
Castle Bytham Lincs 227 E6
Castle Caereinion Powys 193 B7
Castle Camps Cambs 163 D5
Castle Carlton Lincs 274 C4
Castle Carrock Cumb 348 E4
Castle Cary Som'set 60 E4
Castle Combe Wilts 82 A1
Castle Combe Motor Racing Circuit Wilts 82 A2
Castle Donington Leics 224 C3
Castle Douglas Dumf/Gal 402 C1
Castle Drogo, Exeter Devon 20 B4
Castle Eaton Swindon 105 C7
Castle Eden Durham 344 D4
Castle End Peterbro 203 B8
Castle End Warwick 177 D8
Castle Field Som'set 59 D6
Castle Forbes Aberds 428 A3
Castle Frome Heref'd 152 C3
Castle Gate Cornw'l 3 D5
Castle Goring W Sussex 48 E2
Castle Green Surrey 88 D1
Castle Green S Yorks 281 D7
Castle Gresley Derby 223 E7
Castle Heaton Northum 387 D8
Castle Hedingham Essex 163 E8
Castle Hill E Sussex 71 F5
Castle Hill Gtr Man 264 A3
Castle Hill Kent 71 C8
Castle Hill Suffolk 165 C7
Castle Hill Wilts 63 E7
Castle Howard, Malton N Yorks 308 A3
Castle Huntly Perth/Kinr 420 E3
Castle Kennedy Dumf/Gal 400 D3
Castle Mill Wrex 218 A2
Castle O'er Dumf/Gal 360 D1
Castle Park N Yorks 334 D4
Castle Rising Norfolk 231 D5
Castle Shaw Gtr Man 280 C2
Castle Street W Yorks 291 F8
Castle Stuart H'land 434 D2
Castle Toward Arg/Bute 408 F4
Castle Town W Sussex 48 E4
Castle Vale W Midlands 198 E3
Castlebay = Bagh a Chaisteil W Isles 446 D2
Castlebythe Pembs 120 B4
Castlecary Falk 393 C7
Castlecraig H'land 434 B3
Castlecroft W Midlands 197 D6
Castlefairn Dumf/Gal 357 E6
Castlefields Halton 265 C5
Castleford W Yorks 294 E2
Castleford Ings W Yorks 294 E2
Castlehead Renf 392 F1
Castlehill Arg/Bute 403 A3
Castlehill Scot Borders 384 E1
Castlehill H'land 445 B5
Castlehill S Ayrs 367 C7
Castlehill S Lanarks 382 B1
Castlehill W Dunb 391 C7
Castlemaddy Dumf/Gal 356 E3
Castlemartin Pembs 116 E4
Castlemilk Glasg C 380 A4
Castlemilk Dumf/Gal 346 A5
Castlemorris Pembs 119 C6
Castlemorton Worcs 153 E5
Castlerigg Cumb 326 B2
Castleside Durham 343 B5
Castlethorpe M/Keynes 158 D4
Castlethorpe N Lincs 285 C6
Castleton Angus 420 C3
Castleton Arg/Bute 408 D1
Castleton Derby 268 C3
Castleton Gtr Man 279 B6
Castleton Moray 435 F6
Castleton Newp 100 F5
Castleton N Yorks 333 E8
Castletown Ches 242 D1
Castletown Cumb 339 E9
Castletown Dorset 24 D2
Castletown H'land 434 D2
Castletown H'land 445 B5
Castletown I/Man 336 E2
Castletown Staffs 221 D8
Castletown Tyne/Wear 353 E6
Castleweary Scot Borders 360 B5
Castlewigg Dumf/Gal 401 E6
Castley W Yorks 293 A7
Castling's Heath Suffolk 164 D4
Caston Norfolk 208 D3
Castor Peterbro 203 D8
Caswell Swan 97 E6
Cat Bank Cumb 313 A7
Catacol N Ayrs 405 B5
Catbrain S Glos 102 F3
Catbrook Monmouths 102 B2
Catchall Cornw'l 2 E4
Catchems Corner W Midlands 177 C8
Catchems End Worcs 175 C5
Catchgate Durham 343 A7
Catchory H'land 445 C6
Catcleugh Northum 362 B3
Catcliffe S Yorks 269 B8
Catcomb Wilts 82 A5
Catcott Som'set 59 D7
Caterham Surrey 89 F8
Catfield Norfolk 234 D4
Catfirth Shetl'd 457 H4
Catford London 90 B2
Catforth Lancs 289 C6
Cathays Card 78 A3
Cathays Park Card 78 A3
Cathcart Glasg C 392 F3
Cathedine Powys 126 B3
Catherine de Barnes Heath W Midlands 177 B6
Catherine Hill S Glos 102 E3
Catherine Slack W Yorks 292 E3
Catherington Hants 46 D1
Catherston Leweston Dorset 24 B2
Cathiron Warwick 178 C4
Catholes Cumb 315 B7
Cathpair Scot Borders 385 C6
Catisfield Hants 45 E6
Catley Lane Head Gtr Man 279 A6
Catley Southfield Heref'd 152 D3
Catlodge H'land 425 C8
Catlow Lancs 291 C6
Catlowdy Cumb 348 A3
Catmere End Essex 162 E2
Catmore W Berks 107 F5
Caton Devon 14 A3
Caton Lancs 302 B3
Caton Green Lancs 302 B3
Catrine E Ayrs 368 B2
Cat's Ash Newp 101 D7
Catsfield E Sussex 51 D7
Catsfield Stream E Sussex 51 D7
Catsgore Som'set 39 A8
Catsham Som'set 60 E3
Catshill W Midlands 198 C2
Catshill Worcs 176 D2
Cattadale Arg/Bute 406 F3
Cattal N Yorks 307 E6
Cattawade Suffolk 142 A3
Cattedown Plym'th 11 E5
Catterall Lancs 289 B6
Catteralslane Shrops 242 F4
Catterick N Yorks 318 A3
Catterick Bridge N Yorks 318 A3
Catterick Garrison N Yorks 318 A2
Catterick Racecourse N Yorks 318 A3
Catterlen Cumb 339 E8
Catterline Aberds 429 E5
Catterton N Yorks 294 A4
Catteshall Surrey 68 C1
Catthorpe Leics 179 C5
Cattistock Dorset 25 A6
Cattle End Northants 157 D8
Catton Northum 350 E3
Catton N Yorks 319 E6
Catwick ER Yorks 298 A1
Catworth Cambs 182 D1
Caudle Green Glos 130 E4
Caudlesprings Norfolk 208 C2
Caudwell's Mill, Matlock Derby 246 A3
Caudworthy Park Cornw'l 18 B2
Caulcott Beds 159 D8
Caulcott Oxon 133 C9
Cauldcots Angus 421 C6
Cauldham Kent 74 D4
Cauldhame Stirl 410 C1
Cauldmill Scot Borders 373 D7
Cauldon Staffs 245 E7
Cauldon Lowe Staffs 245 E7
Cauldwell Derby 223 E7
Cauldwell Tyne/Wear 353 C6
Cauldwells Aberds 437 C4
Caulkerbush Dumf/Gal 402 D3
Caulside Dumf/Gal 361 F5
Caundle Marsh Dorset 40 D3
Caundle Wake Dorset 40 D3
Caunsall Worcs 175 B7
Caunton Notts 249 B5
Causeway Hants 46 B2
Causeway Hants 45 D8
Causeway End Cumb 314 C3
Causeway End Dumf/Gal 401 C6
Causeway End Essex 140 D2
Causeway Foot W Yorks 281 B5
Causeway Green W Midlands 197 F8
Causewayend S Lanarks 383 E5
Causewayhead Stirl 410 C2
Causey Tyne/Wear 352 E3
Causey Park Bridge Northum 365 D5
Causeyend Aberds 429 A6
Causeyton Aberds 428 A3
Caute Devon 33 D8
Cavendish Suffolk 163 C9
Cavenham Suffolk 185 D8
Caversfield Oxon 134 B2
Caversham Reading 86 B4
Caversham Heights Reading 86 A4
Caverswall Staffs 244 F5
Cavil ER Yorks 296 D2
Cawdor H'land 434 C3
Cawdor Castle and Gardens H'land 434 D3
Cawkeld ER Yorks 310 E1
Cawkwell Lincs 274 D2
Cawood N Yorks 295 C5
Cawsand Cornw'l 10 E4
Cawston Norfolk 233 D7
Cawston Warwick 178 D4
Cawthorne N Yorks 321 C6
Cawthorne S Yorks 281 C7
Cawthorpe Lincs 227 D8
Cawton N Yorks 320 E3
Caxton Cambs 161 A6
Cay Hill Suffolk 187 F6
Caynham Shrops 173 D8
Caythorpe Lincs 250 E1
Caythorpe Notts 248 E4
Cayton N Yorks 322 D5
Ceallan W Isles 447 C3
Ceann a Bhàigh W Isles 449 C6
Ceann a Bhaigh W Isles 447 B2
Ceann a Deas Loch Baghasdail W Isles 446 B3
Ceann Shiphoirt W Isles 451 F5
Ceann Tarabhaigh W Isles 451 F5
Ceannacroc Lodge H'land 424 A4
Cearsiadair W Isles 451 E6
Ceathramh Meadhanach W Isles 447 A3
Cefn Newp 101 E5
Cefn Powys 194 A1
Cefn Berain Conwy 262 F1
Cefn Canol Powys 218 B1
Cefn Coch Powys 192 C4
Cefn Cŏch Powys 217 C7
Cefn Cribwr Bridg 98 F4
Cefn Cross Bridg 98 F4
Cefn Einion Shrops 172 A3
Cefn Fforest Caerph 100 C3
Cefn Glas Bridg 98 F4
Cefn Golau Bl Gwent 126 F3
Cefn Hengoed Caerph 100 C2
Cefn Rhigos Rh Cyn Taff 125 F7
Cefn-brith Conwy 239 D6
Cefn-bryn-brain Carms 123 E8
Cefn-bychan Flints 240 B4
Cefnbychan Swan 97 C5
Cefn-bychan Wrex 241 F6
Cefn-Byrle Powys 125 E5
Cefncaeau Carms 97 C5
Cefn-coch Conwy 262 F7
Cefn-crib Torf 100 C4
Cefn-ddwysarn Gwyn 216 A4
Cefneithin Carms 123 E7
Cefngorwydd Powys 148 C3
Cefn-hengoed Swan 97 C8
Cefn-llwyd Ceredig'n 169 B6
Cefn-mawr Wrex 241 F6
Cefnpennar Rh Cyn Taff 99 B7
Cefn-Rhouniarth Powys 218 F1
Cefn-y-Bedd Flints 241 C7
Cefn-y-garth Swan 97 B9
Cefn-y-pant Carms 121 B7
Cegidfa = Guilsfield Powys 193 A8
Cegidfa Powys 193 A8
Cei-bach Ceredig'n 145 A8
Ceinewydd = New Quay Ceredig'n 145 A7
Cellan Ceredig'n 146 C5
Cellarhead Staffs 244 E5
Celleron Cumb 327 A6
Celyn-Mali Flints 240 A4
Cemaes Angl 258 A4
Cemmaes Powys 191 B7
Cemmaes Road Powys 191 C7
Cenarth Ceredig'n 145 D5
Ceos W Isles 451 E6
Ceres Fife 412 A2
Cerne Abbas Dorset 40 F3
Cerney Wick Glos 105 C6
Cerrigceinwen Angl 259 E5
Cerrigydrudion Conwy 239 E7
Cess Norfolk 235 E5
Cessford Scot Borders 374 C4
Ceunant Gwyn 237 B6
Chaceley Glos 130 A3
Chacewater Cornw'l 4 B2
Chackmore Bucks 157 E8
Chacombe Northants 156 D4
Chad Valley W Midlands 176 A3
Chadderton Gtr Man 279 C7
Chadderton Fold Gtr Man 279 C6
Chaddesden Derby C 224 A2
Chaddesden Common Derby C 224 A2
Chaddesley Corbett Worcs 175 D7
Chaddlehanger Devon 19 E6
Chaddlewood Plym'th 11 D7
Chaddleworth W Berks 85 A5
Chadlington Oxon 133 C5
Chadshunt Warwick 156 B1
Chadstone Northants 158 A4
Chadwell Leics 226 D2
Chadwell Shrops 221 F5
Chadwell End Beds 182 E1
Chadwell Heath London 112 E4
Chadwell St. Mary Thurr'k 91 A7
Chadwick Worcs 175 E6
Chadwick End W Midlands 177 D7
Chadwick Green Mersey 277 E7
Chaffcombe Som'set 38 D5
Chagford Devon 20 C4
Chailey E Sussex 49 C7
Chain Bridge Lincs 252 F2
Chainbridge Cambs 205 D7
Chainhurst Kent 72 B1
Chalbury Dorset 42 E3
Chalbury Common Dorset 42 E3
Chaldon Surrey 89 E8
Chaldon Herring Dorset 26 D2
Chale I/Wight 30 E1
Chale Green I/Wight 30 E1
Chalfont Common Bucks 110 D2
Chalfont St. Giles Bucks 110 D1
Chalfont St. Peter Bucks 110 D2
Chalford Glos 104 B3
Chalford Wilts 62 A2
Chalgrave Beds 136 B4
Chalgrove Oxon 108 C2
Chalk Kent 91 B8
Chalk End Essex 139 E8
Chalk Hill Beds 136 C4
Chalk Hill Glos 131 B8
Chalkhouse Green Oxon 86 A4
Chalkshire Bucks 135 F7
Chalksole Kent 74 C4
Chalkway Som'set 39 E5
Chalkwell Kent 92 D4
Chalkwell Southend 114 E4
Challaborough Devon 12 C3
Challacombe Devon 55 C8
Challister Shetl'd 457 G5
Challoch Dumf/Gal 401 C5
Challock Kent 73 A7
Chalmington Dorset 40 F1
Chalton Beds 136 B4
Chalton Beds 160 B2
Chalton Hants 46 C2
Chalvey Slough 87 A9
Chalvington E Sussex 50 E3
Chambercombe Devon 55 B5
Chamber's Green Kent 73 C5
Chambers Wall Kent 95 C5
Chance Inn Fife 412 A1
Chancery Ceredig'n 168 C4
Chanderhill Derby 269 E6
Chandler's Cross Herts 110 C3
Chandler's Cross Worcs 153 E5
Chandler's Ford Hants 44 B3
Channel's End Beds 160 A2
Channerwick Shetl'd 455 D3
Chantry Suffolk 165 D7
Chantry Som'set 61 B6
Chapel Cumb 338 E3
Chapel Fife 411 C7
Chapel N Lanarks 382 B1
Chapel Allerton Som'set 59 A8
Chapel Allerton W Yorks 293 C7
Chapel Amble Cornw'l 16 E4
Chapel Brampton Northants 180 E2
Chapel Chorlton Staffs 221 A6
Chapel Cleeve Som'set 57 C7
Chapel Cross E Sussex 50 B5
Chapel End Beds 160 C1
Chapel End Beds 159 D9
Chapel End Ches 243 F6
Chapel End Essex 139 B7
Chapel End Northants 203 F8
Chapel End Warwick 199 E7
Chapel Field Gtr Man 278 C4
Chapel Field Norfolk 234 D4
Chapel Fields C/York 307 E8
Chapel Fields W Midlands 177 C9
Chapel Green Herts 161 E6
Chapel Green Warwick 178 F4
Chapel Green Warwick 177 A8
Chapel Green Wokingham 87 C6
Chapel Haddlesey N Yorks 295 E5
Chapel Hill Aberds 437 E7
Chapel Hill Glos 102 B4
Chapel Hill Lincs 251 D7
Chapel Hill Monmouths 102 C2
Chapel Hill N Yorks 283 A5
Chapel Hill N Yorks 293 A8
Chapel House Lancs 277 C6
Chapel Houses Medway 91 D6
Chapel Lawn Shrops 172 C4
Chapel Leigh Som'set 58 F2
Chapel Milton Derby 267 C8
Chapel of Ease Caerph 100 C4
Chapel of Garioch Aberds 436 F4
Chapel of Stoneywood Aberd C 429 A5
Chapel Outon Dumf/Gal 401 E6
Chapel Plaister Wilts 81 C8
Chapel Row E Sussex 51 D5
Chapel Row Essex 114 B2
Chapel Row W Berks 85 C8
Chapel St. Leonards Lincs 275 E8
Chapel Stile Cumb 326 E3
Chapel Town Cornw'l 7 D8
Chapelbridge Cambs 204 E4
Chapel-en-le-Frith Derby 267 C8
Chapelgate Lincs 229 D8
Chapelhall N Lanarks 393 F7
Chapelhill Dumf/Gal 359 D5
Chapelhill H'land 441 F5
Chapelhill N Ayrs 378 D4
Chapelhill Perth/Kinr 419 D8
Chapelhill Perth/Kinr 419 E7
Chapelhill Perth/Kinr 420 E2
Chapelknowe Dumf/Gal 347 B8
Chapel-le-Dale N Yorks 315 E8
Chapels Blackb'n 290 F2
Chapels Cumb 313 D5
Chapelthorpe W Yorks 281 A8
Chapelton Angus 421 C6
Chapelton Devon 34 A4
Chapelton H'land 426 A4
Chapelton S Lanarks 381 C5
Chapelton Row Dumf/Gal 401 E8
Chapeltown Blackb'n 278 A3
Chapeltown Moray 435 F7
Chapeltown S Yorks 281 E9
Chapeltown W Yorks 293 C8
Chapman's Town E Sussex 50 C5
Chapmans Well Devon 18 B4
Chapmanslade Wilts 61 B8
Chapmore End Herts 138 D2
Chappel Essex 141 B6
Charaton Cornw'l 10 B2
Charcott Kent 70 B5
Chard Som'set 38 E4
Chard Junction Dorset 38 F4
Chardleigh Green Som'set 38 D4
Chardstock Devon 38 F4
Charfield S Glos 103 D6
Charford Worcs 176 E2
Chargrove Glos 130 D4
Chargy Hill Glos 130 C2
Charing Kent 73 B6
Charing Cross Dorset 42 D5
Charing Heath Kent 73 B5
Charing Hill Kent 73 A6
Charingworth Glos 155 E7
Charitonbrook S Yorks 281 E8
Charlacott Devon 55 F5
Charlbury Oxon 133 D6
Charlcombe Bath/NE Som'set 81 C7
Charlcutt Wilts 82 A4
Charlecote Warwick 155 A8
Charlecote Park, Wellesbourne Warwick 155 A8
Charles Devon 55 E8
Charles Bottom Devon 55 E8
Charles Manning's Amusement Park, Felixstowe Suffolk 166 F3
Charles Tye Suffolk 165 B5
Charlesfield Dumf/Gal 346 C5
Charleshill Surrey 67 C7
Charleston Angus 420 C3
Charleston Renf 392 F1
Charlestown Aberd C 429 B6
Charlestown Cornw'l 8 E3
Charlestown Derby 267 A7
Charlestown Dorset 25 E8
Charlestown Fife 411 D5
Charlestown Gtr Man 279 E5
Charlestown Gtr Man 279 D6
Charlestown H'land 438 F2
Charlestown H'land 433 D8
Charlestown W Yorks 291 E8
Charlestown W Yorks 292 D4
Charlestown of Aberlour Moray 435 D7
Charlesworth Derby 267 A6
Charlinch Som'set 58 D4
Charlottetown Fife 411 A7
Charlton Hants 64 B4
Charlton Herts 137 B7
Charlton London 90 A3
Charlton Northants 157 E5
Charlton Northum 363 E5
Charlton Oxon 107 E5
Charlton Redcar/Clevel'd 333 C7
Charlton Som'set 38 A3
Charlton Som'set 60 C4
Charlton Som'set 61 A5
Charlton Surrey 88 C3
Charlton Telford 195 A7
Charlton Wilts 41 B8
Charlton Wilts 83 E7
Charlton Wilts 104 E4
Charlton Worcs 154 C3
Charlton Worcs 175 D6
Charlton W Sussex 47 D5
Charlton Abbots Glos 131 C6
Charlton Adam Som'set 60 F2
Charlton All Saints Wilts 43 B6
Charlton Down Dorset 25 B8
Charlton Horethorne Som'set 40 B2
Charlton Kings Glos 131 C5
Charlton Mackrell Som'set 60 F2
Charlton Marshall Dorset 41 F8
Charlton Musgrove Som'set 61 E6
Charlton on Otmoor Oxon 134 D2
Charlton on the Hill Dorset 41 F7
Charlwood E Sussex 70 E2
Charlwood Hants 66 E3
Charlwood Surrey 69 C6
Charminster Bournem'th 28 B2
Charminster Dorset 25 B8
Charmouth Dorset 24 B2
Charndon Bucks 134 C4
Charney Bassett Oxon 106 D4
Charnock Green Lancs 277 A8
Charnock Richard Lancs 277 A8
Charsfield Suffolk 166 A2
Chart Corner Kent 72 A2
Chart Hill Kent 72 B2
Chart Sutton Kent 72 B3
Charter Alley Hants 86 E1
Charterhouse Som'set 80 E2
Chartham Kent 94 F2
Chartham Hatch Kent 94 E2
Chartridge Bucks 109 B8
Chartwell, Westerham Kent 70 A4
Charvil Wokingham 86 A5
Charwelton Northants 157 A5
Chase Cross London 112 D5
Chase End Street Worcs 153 E5
Chase Hill Glos 103 E6
Chase Terrace Staffs 198 B1
Chaselbourne Dorset 26 A2
Chasetown Staffs 198 B2
Chastleton Oxon 132 B3
Chasty Devon 33 F6
Chatburn Lancs 290 B4
Chatcull Staffs 221 B5
Chatham Caerph 100 E4
Chatham Medway 92 C1
Chatham Green Essex 140 D3
Chathill Northum 377 B5
Chatley Worcs 175 F7
Chatsworth, Bakewell Derby 268 E5
Chattenden Medway 92 B2
Chatter End Essex 139 C5
Chatteris Cambs 183 A7
Chattern Hill Surrey 88 B3
Chattisham Suffolk 165 D6
Chatto Scot Borders 374 D5
Chatton Northum 376 B3
Chaul End Beds 136 C5
Chaulden Herts 110 A2
Chavel Shrops 194 A4
Chavenage Green Glos 104 C2
Chavey Down Brackn'l 87 C7
Chawleigh Devon 35 D7
Chawley Oxon 107 B6
Chawson Worcs 175 F7
Chawston Beds 160 A3
Chawton Hants 66 D4
Chaxhill Glos 129 E8
Chazey Heath Oxon 86 A3
Cheadle Gtr Man 266 B4
Cheadle Staffs 245 F6
Cheadle Heath Gtr Man 266 B4
Cheadle Hulme Gtr Man 266 B4
Cheadle Park Staffs 245 F6
Cheam London 89 D6
Cheapside Herts 138 A4
Cheapside Surrey 88 D2
Cheapside Windsor 87 C8
Cheapside Worcs 154 C5
Chearsley Bucks 135 E5
Chebsey Staffs 221 C7
Checkendon Oxon 108 F3
Checkley Heref'd 152 E1
Checkley Staffs 222 A2
Checkleybank Staffs 222 A2
Chedburgh Suffolk 163 A8
Cheddar Som'set 80 F1

Clifford Chambers Warwick 155 B6
Clifford's Mesne Glos 129 C7
Cliffs End Kent 95 D6
Clifftown Southend 114 E4
Clifton Beds 160 E3
Clifton Bristol 80 B3
Clifton Nott'ham 225 B6
Clifton Cumb 340 F1
Clifton C/York 307 E8
Clifton Derby 246 F1
Clifton Devon 55 C7
Clifton Lancs 289 D6
Clifton Northum 365 F6
Clifton N Yorks 305 F7
Clifton Oxon 133 A8
Clifton Stirl 417 D8
Clifton S Yorks 269 A8
Clifton S Yorks 282 E4
Clifton Worcs 153 C6
Clifton W Yorks 292 F5
Clifton Campville Staffs 199 A6
Clifton Dykes Cumb 340 F1
Clifton Green Gtr Man 278 D4
Clifton Hampden Oxon 107 C7
Clifton Hill Worcs 174 F4
Clifton Maybank Dorset 40 D1
Clifton Reynes M/Keynes 159 B6
Clifton upon Dunsmore Warwick 179 D5
Clifton upon Teme Worcs 174 F4
Clifton Wood W Yorks 292 F5
Cliftonville Kent 95 B7
Cliftonville Norfolk 234 A3
Cliftonville N Lanarks 393 E6
Climping W Sussex 47 F8
Climpy S Lanarks 382 A3
Clink Som'set 61 B7
Clinkham Wood Mersey 277 E7
Clint N Yorks 306 D2
Clint Green Norfolk 208 A4
Clintmains Scot Borders 374 A2
Clints N Yorks 330 F4
Cliobh W Isles 450 D3
Clippesby Norfolk 235 F5
Clippings Green Norfolk 208 A4
Clipsham Rutl'd 227 E6
Clipston Northants 180 B2
Clipston Notts 225 B7
Clipstone Notts 248 B2
Clitheroe Lancs 290 B3
Cliuthar W Isles 449 C5
Clive Ches 243 A6
Clive Shrops 219 D7
Clive Vale E Sussex 52 D1
Clivocast Shetl'd 456 C6
Clixby Lincs 285 D9
Cloatley Wilts 104 D4
Cloatley End Wilts 104 D4
Clocaenog Denbs 240 D2
Clochan Aberds 437 D6
Clochan Moray 436 B1
Clock Face Mersey 264 A5
Clockmill Scot Borders 387 B5
Cloddiau Powys 193 B8
Cloddymoss Moray 434 C4
Clodock Heref'd 127 B7
Cloford Som'set 61 C6
Clogwyn Melyn Gwyn 237 D5
Cloigyn Carms 122 E4
Clola Aberds 437 D7
Clophill Beds 160 E1
Clopton Northants 182 B1
Clopton Corner Suffolk 166 B2
Clopton Green Suffolk 166 B2
Clopton Green Suffolk 163 B8
Clopton Green Suffolk 186 F4
Close Clark I/Man 336 D2
Close House Durham 343 F8
Closeburn Dumf/Gal 358 D1
Closworth Som'set 39 D9
Clothall Herts 138 A1
Clotton Ches 242 B3
Clough Gtr Man 279 C7
Clough Gtr Man 279 A7
Clough W Yorks 280 B3
Clough Dene Durham 352 E2
Clough Fold Lancs 291 F5
Clough Foot W Yorks 291 F7
Clough Hall Staffs 244 D2
Clough Head W Yorks 292 F3
Cloughton N Yorks 322 B4
Cloughton Newlands N Yorks 322 A4
Clounlaid H'land 416 B2
Clousta Shetl'd 457 H3
Clouston Orkney 452 B3
Clova Aberds 436 F1
Clova Angus 427 E8
Clovelly Devon 33 B6
Clovelly Village Devon 33 B6
Clovenfords Scot Borders 385 E6
Clovenstone Aberds 428 A4
Cloves Moray 435 B6
Clovullin H'land 417 A5
Clow Bridge Lancs 291 E5
Clown Hills Leics C 201 C6
Clowne Derby 270 D1
Clows Top Worcs 174 D4
Cloy Wrex 241 F8
Cluanie Inn H'land 424 A2
Cluanie Lodge H'land 424 A2
Clubmoor Mersey 264 A2
Cluddley Telford 195 A8
Clun Shrops 172 B4
Clunbury Shrops 172 B5
Clunderwen Pembs 121 D6
Clune H'land 434 C4
Clune H'land 434 F2
Clunes H'land 424 D4
Clungunford Shrops 173 C6
Clunie Aberds 436 C3
Clunie Perth/Kinr 420 C1
Clunton Shrops 172 B4
Cluny Fife 411 C7
Cluny Castle Aberds 428 A3
Cluny Castle H'land 425 C8
Clutton Bath/NE Som'set 80 E4
Clutton Ches 242 D2
Clutton Hill Bath/NE Som'set 80 E4
Clwt-grugoer Conwy 239 B7
Clwt-y-bont Gwyn 237 B7
Clydach Monmouths 127 E5
Clydach Swan 97 B8
Clydach Terrace Bl Gwent 126 E4
Clydach Vale Rh Cyn Taff 99 D6
Clydebank Renf 392 E1
Clydey Pembs 145 E5
Clyffe Pypard Wilts 83 A6
Clynder Arg/Bute 409 D5
Clyne Neath P Talb 98 B3
Clynelish H'land 441 C5
Clyn-mil Merth Tyd 99 B8
Clynnog-fawr Gwyn 236 E4
Clyro Powys 150 D2
Clyst Honiton Devon 22 B1
Clyst Hydon Devon 37 F5
Clyst St. George Devon 22 C1
Clyst St. Lawrence Devon 37 F5
Clyst St. Mary Devon 22 B1
Cnip W Isles 450 D3
Cnoc Amhlaigh W Isles 451 D8
Cnoc an t-Solais W Isles 451 C7
Cnoc Fhionn H'land 423 A8
Cnoc Màiri W Isles 451 D7
Cnoc Rolum W Isles 447 C2
Cnocbreac Arg/Bute 406 E4
Cnwch Coch Ceredig'n 169 D6
Coachford Aberds 436 D1
Coad's Green Cornw'l 18 E2
Coal Aston Derby 269 D7
Coal Pool W Midlands 198 C1
Coalbournbrook W Midlands 175 A7
Coalbrookdale Telford 196 C2
Coalbrookvale Bl Gwent 126 F4
Coalburn S Lanarks 381 F6
Coalburns Tyne/Wear 352 D1
Coalcleugh Northum 341 B7
Coaley Glos 103 B7
Coaley Peak Glos 103 B7
Coalford Aberds 429 C5
Coalhall E Ayrs 367 D8
Coalhill Essex 114 C2
Coalpit Field Warwick 199 F8
Coalpit Heath S Glos 103 F5
Coalpit Hill Staffs 244 D2
Coalport Telford 196 C2
Coalsnaughton Clack 410 C4
Coaltown of Balgonie Fife 411 C7
Coaltown of Wemyss Fife 411 C8
Coalville Leics 200 A2
Coalway Glos 129 E5
Coanwood Northum 349 E7
Coat Som'set 39 B7
Coatbridge N Lanarks 393 F6
Coatdyke N Lanarks 393 F7
Coate Swindon 105 F8
Coate Wilts 83 D5
Coates Cambs 204 D5
Coates Glos 104 B4
Coates Lancs 304 F1
Coates Lincs 272 C3
Coates Notts 271 C8
Coates W Sussex 47 C7
Coatham Redcar/Clevel'd 333 A6
Coatham Mundeville D'lngton 331 B7
Cobairdy Aberds 436 D2
Cobb Dorset 24 B1
Cobbaton Devon 55 F7
Cobbler's Green Norfolk 210 E1
Cobbler's Plain Monmouths 102 B1
Cobbs Warrington 265 B7
Coberley Glos 131 D5
Cobhall Common Heref'd 151 E7
Cobham Kent 91 C8
Cobham Surrey 88 D4
Cobholm Island Norfolk 211 B6
Cobleland Stirl 409 C8
Cobler's Green Essex 140 D2
Cobnash Heref'd 173 F7
Cobridge Stoke 244 E3
Coburg Devon 21 E7
Coburty Aberds 437 B6
Cock Alley Derby 269 F8
Cock and End Suffolk 163 B7
Cock Bank Wrex 241 E8
Cock Bridge Aberds 427 B7
Cock Clarks Essex 114 B3
Cock Gate Heref'd 173 E7
Cock Green Essex 140 D2
Cock Marling E Sussex 52 C2
Cock Street Kent 72 A2
Cockayne N Yorks 320 A3
Cockayne Hatley Beds 161 C5
Cockburnspath Scot Borders 398 D5
Cockden Lancs 291 D6
Cockenzie & Port Seton E Loth 396 C4
Cockerham Lancs 301 E8
Cockermouth Cumb 337 E8
Cockernhoe Herts 137 C6
Cockersdale W Yorks 293 E6
Cockerton D'lngton 331 C7
Cockett Swan 97 D7
Cockett Hill Dorset 27 A5
Cocketty Aberds 429 E4
Cockfield Durham 330 B4
Cockfield Suffolk 164 B3
Cockfosters London 111 C7
Cockhill Som'set 60 E4
Cocking W Sussex 47 C5
Cocking Causeway W Sussex 47 C5
Cockington Torbay 15 C5
Cocklake Som'set 59 B8
Cocklaw Northum 351 B5
Cockley Beck Cumb 326 F1
Cockley Cley Norfolk 207 C6
Cockpole Green Windsor 109 F5
Cocks Cornw'l 7 E6
Cocks Green Suffolk 164 A2
Cockshead Ceredig'n 147 A5
Cockshoot Hill Beds 160 E2
Cockshutford Shrops 174 A1
Cockshutt Shrops 174 B4
Cockshutt Shrops 219 C5
Cockthorpe Norfolk 256 D2
Cockwood Devon 22 D1
Cockwood Som'set 58 C4
Cockyard Derby 267 D7
Cockyard Heref'd 151 F6
Coddenham Suffolk 165 B7
Coddenham Green Suffolk 165 A7
Coddington Ches 242 C2
Coddington Heref'd 152 D4
Coddington Notts 249 D7
Codford St. Mary Wilts 62 D4
Codford St. Peter Wilts 62 C4
Codicote Herts 137 D8
Codmore Hill W Sussex 47 B9
Codnor Derby 247 E6
Codnor Breach Derby 247 E6
Codnor Gate Derby 247 D6
Codrington S Glos 81 A6
Codsall Staffs 197 C6
Codsall Wood Staffs 197 C5
Codsend Som'set 56 D4
Coed Duon = Blackwood Caerph 100 C3
Coed Eva Torf 101 D5
Coed Mawr Gwyn 259 E8
Coed Morgan Monmouths 127 E8
Coed Ystumgwern Gwyn 214 D3
Coedcae Bl Gwent 127 F5
Coedcae Torf 127 F6
Coed-Cwnwr Monmouths 101 C8
Coedely Rh Cyn Taff 99 E7
Coedkernew Newp 100 F5
Coedpoeth Wrex 241 D6
Coed-Talon Flints 241 C6
Coedway Powys 218 F3
Coed-y-bryn Ceredig'n 145 C7
Coed-y-caerau Newp 101 D7
Coed-y-go Shrops 218 C2
Coed-y-maen Powys 217 F8
Coed-y-paen Monmouths 101 C6
Coed-y-parc Gwyn 237 A8
Coed-yr-ynys Powys 126 C4
Coelbren Powys 125 E5
Coffee Hall M/Keynes 158 E5
Coffinswell Devon 15 B5
Cofton Devon 22 D1
Cofton Common W Midlands 176 C3
Cofton Hackett Worcs 176 C3
Cogan V/Glam 78 B3
Cogenhoe Northants 180 F4
Cogges Oxon 133 F6
Coggeshall Essex 141 C6
Coggeshall Hamlet Essex 141 C5
Coggins Mill E Sussex 71 F6
Còsag H'land 423 A8
Coham Devon 34 E2
Coig Peighinnean W Isles 451 A8
Coig Peighinnean Bhuirgh W Isles 451 B7
Coignafearn Lodge H'land 426 A1
Coignascallan H'land 426 A2
Coilacriech Aberds 427 C8
Coilantogle Stirl 409 B8
Coilessan Arg/Bute 409 B5
Coilleag W Isles 446 B3
Coillemore H'land 434 A1
Coillore H'land 430 E3
Coirea-chrombe Stirl 409 B8
Coity Bridg 99 F5
Cokenach Herts 161 E7
Cokhay Green Derby 223 C7
Col W Isles 451 C7
Col Uarach W Isles 451 D7
Colaboll H'land 440 B2
Colan Cornw'l 7 C8
Colaton Raleigh Devon 22 C3
Colbost H'land 430 D2
Colbrooke Devon 35 F8
Colburn N Yorks 318 A3
Colbury Hants 44 D2
Colby Cumb 328 B3
Colby I/Man 336 D2
Colby Norfolk 234 B1
Colchester Essex 141 C9
Colchester Green Suffolk 164 A3
Colchester Zoo Essex 141 C8
Colcot V/Glam 78 C2
Cold Ash W Berks 85 C7
Cold Ashby Northants 179 C8
Cold Ashton S Glos 81 B6
Cold Aston Glos 131 D8
Cold Brayfield M/Keynes 159 B6
Cold Cotes N Yorks 303 A6
Cold Elm Heref'd 152 D3
Cold Hanworth Lincs 273 C5
Cold Harbour Herts 137 D6
Cold Harbour Oxon 86 A2
Cold Harbour Wilts 62 B2
Cold Hatton Telford 220 D2
Cold Hatton Heath Telford 220 D2
Cold Hesledon Durham 344 B4
Cold Hiendley W Yorks 282 B1
Cold Higham Northants 157 B8
Cold Inn Pembs 117 C8
Cold Kirby N Yorks 320 D1
Cold Northcott Cornw'l 17 C9
Cold Norton Essex 114 B3
Cold Overton Leics 202 A2
Cold Row Lancs 288 B4
Coldbackie H'land 443 C8
Coldblow London 90 B5
Coldbrook Powys 149 E8
Coldean Brighton/Hove 49 E6
Coldeast Devon 21 F6
Colden W Yorks 291 E8
Colden Common Hants 44 B4
Coldham Cambs 205 C7
Coldharbour Cornw'l 7 F6
Coldharbour Dorset 25 D7
Coldharbour Devon 37 D6
Coldharbour Glos 102 B3
Coldharbour Kent 71 A6
Coldharbour London 90 A5
Coldingham Scot Borders 399 E8
Coldmeece Staffs 221 B7
Coldpool N Yorks 332 D4
Coldrain Perth/Kinr 411 B5
Coldred Kent 74 B5
Coldridge Devon 35 E6
Coldstream Angus 420 D3
Coldstream Scot Borders 387 E6
Coldvreath Cornw'l 8 D2
Coldwaltham W Sussex 47 C8
Coldwells Aberds 437 D8
Coldwells Croft Aberds 436 F2
Cole Som'set 61 E5
Cole End Essex 162 E4
Cole End Warwick 199 F5
Cole Green Herts 138 E1
Cole Green Herts 138 A4
Cole Henley Hants 65 A6
Colebatch Shrops 194 F2
Colebrook Devon 37 E5
Coleburn Moray 435 C7
Coleby Lincs 250 B2
Coleby N Lincs 284 A4
Coleford Devon 35 F8
Coleford Glos 129 E5
Coleford Som'set 61 B5
Coleford Water Som'set 58 E2
Colegate End Norfolk 209 F7
Colehill Dorset 42 F3
Coleman Green Herts 137 E7
Coleman's Hatch E Sussex 70 E3
Colemere Shrops 219 B5
Colemore Hants 66 E4
Colemore Green Shrops 196 D3
Coleorton Leics 224 E3
Coleorton Moor Leics 224 E3
Colerne Wilts 81 B8
Cole's Common Norfolk 209 F8
Cole's Cross Dorset 39 F5
Coles Green Suffolk 165 D6
Coles Green Worcs 153 B5
Coles Meads Surrey 69 A7
Colesbourne Glos 131 E5
Colesbrook Dorset 61 F8
Colesden Beds 160 A2
Coleshill Bucks 109 C8
Coleshill Oxon 106 D1
Coleshill Warwick 199 F5
Colestocks Devon 37 F6
Coley Bath/NE Som'set 80 E3
Coley Wokingham 86 B4
Colfin Dumf/Gal 400 D2
Colgate W Sussex 69 E6
Colgrain Arg/Bute 409 D6
Colham Green London 110 F3
Colindale London 111 E6
Colinsburgh Fife 412 B2
Colinton C/Edinb 396 E1
Colintraive Arg/Bute 408 E3
Colkirk Norfolk 232 C3
Collace Perth/Kinr 420 D2
Collafirth Shetl'd 457 G4
Collam W Isles 449 C5
Collaton Devon 13 E5
Collaton St. Mary Torbay 15 D5
College Milton S Lanarks 380 A4
College of Roseisle Moray 435 B6
College Town Brackn'l 87 D7
Collennan S Ayrs 367 A6
Collessie Fife 420 F2
Collett's Bridge Norfolk 205 B8
Collett's Green Worcs 153 B6
Collfryn Powys 218 E1
Collier Row London 112 D5
Collier Street Kent 72 B1
Collier's End Herts 138 C3
Collier's Green E Sussex 51 B8
Colliers Green Kent 72 D2
Colliers Hatch Essex 112 B5
Colliery Row Tyne/Wear 344 B2
Collieston Aberds 437 F7
Collin Dumf/Gal 346 A2
Collingbourne Ducis Wilts 84 F1
Collingbourne Kingston Wilts 84 E1
Collingham Notts 249 B7
Collingham W Yorks 294 A1
Collington Heref'd 174 F3
Collingtree Northants 158 A3
Collingwood Northum 352 A4
Collins End Oxon 86 A3
Collins Green Worcs 152 A4
Collins Green Warrington 277 F8
Colliston Angus 421 C6
Collow Lincs 273 C7
Collum Green Bucks 109 E9
Collycroft Warwick 199 F8
Collyhurst Gtr Man 279 D6
Collynie Aberds 437 E5
Collyweston Northants 203 C5
Colmonell S Ayrs 400 A3
Colmworth Beds 160 A2
Coln Rogers Glos 131 F7
Coln St. Aldwyn Glos 105 A7
Coln St. Dennis Glos 131 E7
Colnabaichin Aberds 427 B7
Colnbrook Slough 88 A2
Colne Cambs 183 C7
Colne Lancs 291 B6
Colne Bridge W Yorks 281 A5
Colne Edge Lancs 291 B6
Colne Engaine Essex 141 A6
Colney Norfolk 209 B7
Colney Hatch London 111 D7
Colney Heath Herts 111 A6
Colney Street Herts 111 B5
Cologin Arg/Bute 416 E3
Colpy Aberds 436 E3
Colquhar Scot Borders 384 D3
Colscott Devon 33 D7
Colsesden Beds 160 A2
Colsterdale N Yorks 317 D8
Colsterworth Lincs 227 D5
Colston Pembs 120 B3
Colston Bassett Notts 225 B8
Colt Hill Hants 66 A4
Coltfield Moray 435 B6
Colthouse Cumb 313 A8
Colthrop W Berks 85 C7
Colthurst Lancs 290 B3
Coltishall Norfolk 234 E2
Coltness N Lanarks 381 A7
Colton Cumb 313 C7
Colton Norfolk 209 B6
Colton N Yorks 294 B4
Colton Staffs 222 D3
Colton W Yorks 294 D1
Colt's Green S Glos 103 F6
Colt's Hill Kent 71 C7
Colts Hill Swan 97 E7
Columbia Tyne/Wear 353 E5
Columbjohn Devon 21 A9
Colva Powys 150 B2
Colvend Dumf/Gal 402 D2
Colvister Shetl'd 456 D5
Colwall Heref'd 152 D4
Colwall Green Heref'd 153 D5
Colwall Stone Heref'd 153 D5
Colwell Northum 351 A6
Colwich Staffs 222 D2
Colwick Notts 225 A7
Colwinston V/Glam 77 A5
Colworth W Sussex 47 F6
Colwyn Bay = Bae Colwyn Conwy 262 D7
Colyford Devon 23 B7
Colyton Devon 23 B6
Colzie Fife 420 F2
Combe Devon 11 E6
Combe Devon 14 B2
Combe Heref'd 172 F4
Combe Oxon 133 D7
Combe Som'set 59 F8
Combe W Berks 84 D4
Combe Almer Dorset 27 A5
Combe Common Surrey 67 D9
Combe Down Bath/NE Som'set 81 D7
Combe Fishacre Devon 14 B4
Combe Florey Som'set 58 E2
Combe Hay Bath/NE Som'set 81 E6
Combe Martin Devon 55 B6
Combe Moor Heref'd 172 F5
Combe Pafford Torbay 15 B6
Combe Raleigh Devon 37 F8
Combe St. Nicholas Som'set 38 D4
Combe Throop Som'set 40 B4
Combebow Devon 19 C6
Combeinteignhead Devon 15 A6
Comberbach Ches 265 D7
Comberford Staffs 198 B4
Comberton Cambs 161 A7
Comberton Heref'd 173 E8
Comberton Worcs 175 C6
Combpyne Devon 23 B7
Combridge Staffs 222 A3
Combrook Warwick 155 B9
Combs Derby 267 D7
Combs Suffolk 165 A5
Combs W Yorks 281 A6
Combs Ford Suffolk 165 A5
Combwich Som'set 58 C5
Comely Bank C/Edinb 396 D1
Comers Aberds 428 B3
Come-to-Good Cornw'l 4 B4
Comeytrowe Som'set 38 B2
Comford Cornw'l 4 C2
Comhampton Worcs 175 E6
Comins Coch Ceredig'n 168 B5
Commercial End Cambs 184 F4
Commins Capel Betws Ceredig'n 146 A5
Commins Coch Powys 191 C7
Common Edge Blackp'l 288 D3
Common End Cumb 324 B5
Common End Derby 247 B6
Common End Norfolk 232 C3
Common Gate Dorset 41 D5
Common Hill Heref'd 152 F1
Common Moor Cornw'l 9 B7
Common Platt Wilts 105 E7
Common Side Ches 265 F6
Common Side Derby 247 E6
Common Side Derby 269 D6
Commondale N Yorks 333 D8
Commonside Ches 265 E5
Commonside Derby 246 F2
Commonwood Herts 110 B2
Common-y-Coed Monmouths 101 E8
Comp Kent 91 E7
Compass Som'set 59 E6
Compstall Gtr Man 267 A6
Compton Devon 15 C5
Compton Hants 64 F3
Compton Hants 44 A4
Compton Plym'th 11 D5
Compton Surrey 67 B7
Compton Surrey 67 B9
Compton Staffs 175 B6
Compton W Berks 85 A7
Compton Wilts 63 A7
Compton W Midlands 197 D6
Compton W Sussex 46 D3
Compton W Yorks 294 B1
Compton Abbas Dorset 41 C7
Compton Abdale Glos 131 D7
Compton Acres Poole 27 C8
Compton Bassett Wilts 83 B5
Compton Beauchamp Oxon 106 E2
Compton Bishop Som'set 79 E8
Compton Chamberlayne Wilts 63 F5
Compton Common Bath/NE Som'set 80 D4
Compton Common Surrey 68 B1
Compton Dando Bath/NE Som'set 80 D4
Compton Dundon Som'set 60 E1
Compton Durville Som'set 39 C6
Compton End Hants 44 A4
Compton Green Glos 129 B8
Compton Greenfield S Glos 102 F3
Compton Martin Bath/NE Som'set 80 E2
Compton Pauncefoot Som'set 40 A2
Compton Valance Dorset 25 B6
Compton Verney Warwick 155 B9
Comrie Fife 411 D5
Comrie H'land 433 C6
Comrie Perth/Kinr 419 C5
Comrie Perth/Kinr 419 E5
Conaglen House H'land 424 F2
Conanby S Yorks 282 E4
Conchra Arg/Bute 408 D3
Conchra H'land 431 F8
Concord Tyne/Wear 353 E5
Concraig Perth/Kinr 419 F6
Concraigie Perth/Kinr 420 C1
Conderton Worcs 154 E2
Condicote Glos 132 B1
Condorrat N Lanarks 393 D6
Condover Shrops 195 B5
Coney Garth N Lincs 284 D2
Coney Green Notts 249 B7
Coney Hill Glos 130 D3
Coneygar Hill Dorset 24 B4
Coneyhurst W Sussex 48 B2
Coneysthorpe N Yorks 308 A3
Coneythorpe N Yorks 306 D4
Coney-Weston Suffolk 186 C4
Conford Hants 67 E6
Congash H'land 435 F5
Congdon's Shop Cornw'l 18 E2
Congeith Dumf/Gal 402 C2
Congelow Kent 71 B8
Congerstone Leics 199 B8
Congham Norfolk 231 D6
Congleton Ches 244 B3
Congl-y-wal Gwyn 238 F2
Congresbury N Som'set 79 D8
Conham S Glos 80 B4
Conicavel Moray 434 C4
Coningsby Lincs 251 C7
Coningsby Moor Lincs 251 C7
Conington Cambs 182 A3
Conington Cambs 183 E6
Conisbrough S Yorks 282 E4
Conisby Arg/Bute 406 F2
Conisholme Lincs 287 E6
Coniston Cumb 313 A7
Coniston ER Yorks 298 C2
Coniston Cold N Yorks 304 E2
Conistone N Yorks 304 B3
Conkwell Wilts 81 D7
Connage Moray 436 B1
Connah's Quay Flints 263 F7
Connaught Park Kent 75 C6
Connel Arg/Bute 416 D4
Connel Park E Ayrs 368 E4
Conniburrow M/Keynes 158 E5
Connista H'land 430 A4
Connor Downs Cornw'l 3 C7
Conock Wilts 83 E6
Conon Bridge H'land 433 C7
Conon House H'land 433 C7
Cononish Stirl 417 E8
Cononley N Yorks 304 F3
Cononsyth Angus 421 C5
Conordan H'land 430 E5
Consall Staffs 245 E5
Consett Durham 343 A6
Constable Burton N Yorks 318 B2
Constable Lee Lancs 291 F5
Constantine Cornw'l 4 E2
Constantine Bay Cornw'l 16 F2
Contin H'land 433 C6
Contlaw Aberd C 429 B5
Conwy Conwy 260 D5
Conwy Castle Conwy 261 D5
Conyer Kent 93 D6
Conyers Green Suffolk 186 E2
Cooden E Sussex 51 E7
Cooil I/Man 336 D3
Cookbury Devon 33 E8
Cookbury Wick Devon 33 E7
Cookham Windsor 109 E7
Cookham Dean Windsor 109 F7
Cookham Rise Windsor 109 F7
Cookhill Worcs 154 A4
Cookley Suffolk 188 C4
Cookley Worcs 175 B6
Cookley Green Oxon 108 D4
Cookley Green Suffolk 188 C4
Cookney Aberds 429 C5
Cookridge W Yorks 293 B6
Cook's Green Essex 142 D4
Cook's Green Suffolk 164 B4
Cooksbridge E Sussex 49 D8
Cooksey Green Worcs 175 E8
Cookshill Stoke 244 F4
Cooksmill Green Essex 113 A7
Cooksongreen Ches 265 E6
Coolham W Sussex 48 B2
Cooling Medway 92 A2
Cooling Street Medway 92 B1
Coolinge Kent 74 D4
Coombe Bucks 109 A6
Coombe Cornw'l 32 D4
Coombe Cornw'l 4 B4
Coombe Cornw'l 8 E2
Coombe Devon 21 F8
Coombe Devon 22 B4
Coombe Glos 103 D7
Coombe Hants 45 B8
Coombe Kent 95 E5
Coombe London 89 B6
Coombe Som'set 39 E6
Coombe Wilts 41 B7
Coombe Wilts 63 A7
Coombe Bissett Wilts 42 A5
Coombe End Som'set 57 F7
Coombe Green Wilts 104 E3
Coombe Hill Glos 130 B3
Coombe Keynes Dorset 26 D3
Coombe Street Som'set 61 E7
Coombelake Devon 22 A3
Coombes W Sussex 48 E3
Coombes End S Glos 103 F7
Coombeswood W Midlands 176 A2
Coombs Pembs 116 C4
Cooper Street Kent 95 E6
Cooper Turning Gtr Man 278 C1
Cooper's Corner Kent 70 B4
Cooper's Green E Sussex 50 B2
Cooper's Hill Beds 159 E8
Coopersale Common Essex 112 B4
Coopersale Street Essex 112 B4
Cootham W Sussex 48 D1
Cop Street Kent 95 E5
Copalder Corner Cambs 205 E6
Copdock Suffolk 165 D7
Copford Essex 141 C7
Copford Green Essex 141 C7
Copgrove N Yorks 306 C3
Copister Shetl'd 457 F4
Cople Beds 160 C2
Copley Durham 330 A3
Copley Gtr Man 279 E8
Copley W Yorks 292 F3
Copley Hill W Yorks 293 E6
Coplow Dale Derby 268 D3
Copmanthorpe C/York 307 F8
Copmere End Staffs 221 C6
Copnor Portsm'th 45 F8
Copp Lancs 288 C5
Copp Hill S Glos 103 F6
Coppathorne Cornw'l 32 F4
Coppenhall Staffs 221 E8
Coppenhall Moss Ches 243 C7
Copperhouse Cornw'l 3 C7
Copperhurst Kent 73 D8
Coppice Gtr Man 279 D7
Coppicegate Shrops 174 B4
Coppingford Cambs 182 B3
Coppins Corner Kent 73 B5
Coppleridge Dorset 41 A6
Copplestone Devon 35 F8
Coppull Lancs 277 B8
Coppull Moor Lancs 277 B8
Coppy Durham 352 E3
Copsale W Sussex 48 A3
Copshaw Holm = Newcastleton Scot Borders 361 E6
Copster Green Lancs 290 D2
Copster Hill Gtr Man 279 D7
Copston Magna Warwick 200 F3
Copt Green Warwick 177 E6
Copt Heath W Midlands 177 C6
Copt Hewick N Yorks 306 A3
Copt Oak Leics 200 A3
Copthall Green Essex 112 B3
Copthill Durham 341 C8

Copthorne Ches 243 F5
Copthorne Cornw'l 18 B2
Copthorne Shrops 195 A5
Copthorne W Sussex 69 D8
Copthorne Common W Sussex 69 D8
Copy's Green Norfolk 256 E1
Copythorne Hants 44 D1
Corbets Tey London 113 E6
Corbridge Northum 351 D6
Corby Northants 202 F4
Corby Glen Lincs 227 C6
Corby Hill Cumb 348 E3
Cordon N Ayrs 405 C6
Cordwell Derby 269 D6
Cordwell Norfolk 209 E6
Coreley Shrops 174 D2
Cores End Bucks 109 E8
Corfe Som'set 38 C2
Corfe Castle Dorset 27 D6
Corfe Castle Dorset 27 D6
Corfe Mullen Dorset 27 A6
Corfton Shrops 173 B8
Corgarff Aberds 427 B7
Corhampton Hants 45 B7
Corkickle Cumb 324 C4
Corlae Dumf/Gal 356 C5
Corlannau Rh Cyn Taff 98 D2
Corley Warwick 177 A8
Corley Ash Warwick 177 A8
Corley Moor Warwick 177 A8
Cornaa I/Man 336 C4
Cornabus Arg/Bute 403 B3
Cornaigbeg Arg/Bute 414 C2
Cornaigmore Arg/Bute 415 A5
Cornaigmore Arg/Bute 414 C2
Cornard Tye Suffolk 164 D3
Corncatterach Aberds 436 E2
Corndon Devon 20 C3
Corner Row Lancs 288 C5
Cornets End W Midlands 177 B7
Corney Cumb 312 B3
Cornforth Durham 344 E2
Cornhill Aberds 436 C2
Cornhill Staffs 244 D3
Cornhill on Tweed Northum 387 E7
Cornholme W Yorks 291 E7
Cornish Cyder Farm, Truro Cornw'l 7 E6
Cornish Hall End Essex 163 E6
Cornmeadow Green Worcs 153 A7
Cornquoy Orkney 453 D6
Cornriggs Durham 341 C7
Cornsay Durham 343 C6
Cornsay Colliery Durham 343 C7
Corntown H'land 433 C7
Corntown V/Glam 77 A5
Cornwal Conwy 239 B6
Cornwell Oxon 132 B4
Cornwood Devon 11 D8
Cornworthy Devon 14 D4
Corpach H'land 424 E2
Corpusty Norfolk 233 C7
Corran H'land 417 A5
Corran H'land 423 B8
Corran a Chan Uachdaraich H'land 431 F5
Corranbuie Arg/Bute 407 F8
Corrany I/Man 336 C4
Corrichoich H'land 444 F4
Corrie N Ayrs 405 B6
Corrie Common Dumf/Gal 359 E8
Corriecravie N Ayrs 405 D5
Corriecravie Moor N Ayrs 405 D5
Corriedoo Dumf/Gal 401 A8
Corriegarth Lodge H'land 425 A7
Corriemoillie H'land 433 B5
Corriemulzie Lodge H'land 439 D7
Corrievarkie Lodge Perth/Kinr 425 E7
Corrievorrie H'land 434 F2
Corrigall Orkney 452 B4
Corrimony H'land 433 E5
Corringham Lincs 272 A2
Corringham Thurr'k 113 F9
Corris Gwyn 191 B6
Corris Uchaf Gwyn 191 B5
Corrour H'land 418 A1
Corrour Shooting Lodge H'land 425 F6
Corrow Arg/Bute 408 B4
Corry H'land 431 F6
Corry of Ardnagrask H'land 433 D7
Corrybrough H'land 434 F3
Corrydon Perth/Kinr 427 F6
Corryghoil Arg/Bute 417 E6
Corrykinloch H'land 439 A7
Corrylach Arg/Bute 404 C3
Corrymuckloch Perth/Kinr 419 D6
Corrynachenchy Arg/Bute 416 C1
Corsback H'land 445 A6
Corscombe Dorset 39 E8
Corse Aberds 436 D3
Corse Glos 130 B1
Corse Covert Warrington 265 A8
Corse Lawn Glos 130 A2
Corse of Kinnoir Aberds 436 D2
Corsewall Dumf/Gal 400 C2
Corsey Wilts 61 B8
Corsham Wilts 82 B2
Corsindae Aberds 428 B3
Corsley Heath Wilts 61 B8
Corsock Dumf/Gal 402 B1
Corston Bath/NE Som'set 81 C5
Corston Orkney 452 B4
Corston Wilts 104 F3
Corstopitum Roman Station, Corbridge Northum 351 D6
Corstorphine C/Edinb 395 D8
Cors-y-Gedol Gwyn 214 D4
Cortachy Angus 420 B3
Corton Suffolk 211 D6
Corton Wilts 62 C3
Corton Denham Som'set 40 B2
Coruanan Lodge H'land 424 F2
Corunna W Isles 447 B3
Corvast H'land 440 D2
Corwen Denbs 240 F2
Coryates Dorset 25 C7
Coryton Devon 19 D6
Coryton Thurr'k 114 F1
Cosby Leics 200 D4
Coscote Oxon 107 E7
Coseley W Midlands 197 E8
Cosford Warwick 179 C5
Cosgrove Northants 158 D3
Cosham Portsm'th 45 F8
Cosheston Pembs 117 D6
Coskills N Lincs 285 B8
Cosmeston V/Glam 78 C3
Cossall Notts 247 E7
Cossall Marsh Notts 247 F7
Cosses S Ayrs 400 A3
Cossington Leics 225 F7
Cossington Som'set 59 C7
Costa Orkney 452 A4
Costessey Norfolk 209 A7
Costhorpe Notts 270 B3
Costock Notts 225 C6
Coston Leics 226 D4
Coston Norfolk 208 B5
Cote Oxon 106 B4
Cote Som'set 59 C6
Cote W Sussex 48 E2
Cote Green Gtr Man 267 A6
Cote Holme Lancs 290 E3
Cotebrook Ches 242 A4
Cotehele House Cornw'l 10 B4
Cotehill Cumb 339 A8
Cotes Cumb 314 C3
Cotes Leics 225 D6
Cotes Staffs 221 B6
Cotes Park Derby 247 D6
Cotesbach Leics 179 B5
Cotford Devon 22 B4
Cotford St. Luke Som'set 58 F3
Cotgrave Notts 225 A7
Cothall Aberds 429 A5
Cotham Bristol 80 B3
Cotham Notts 249 E6
Cothelstone Som'set 58 E3
Cotherstone Durham 330 C2
Cothill Oxon 107 C6
Cotland Monmouths 102 B2
Cotleigh Devon 38 F2
Cotleigh Devon 38 F2
Cotmanhay Derby 247 F7
Cotmaton Devon 22 C4
Coton Cambs 161 A8
Coton Northants 179 D8
Coton Shrops 219 B7
Coton Staffs 221 D6
Coton Staffs 198 B4
Coton Staffs 222 B1
Coton Hill Shrops 219 F6
Coton in the Clay Staffs 223 C5
Coton in the Elms Derby 223 E6
Coton Park Derby 223 E7
Cotonwood Shrops 219 A7
Cotonwood Staffs 221 D6
Cotswold Community Glos 105 C5
Cotswold Wild Life Park, Burford Oxon 132 F3
Cott Devon 14 C3
Cottage End Hants 65 C5
Cottagers Plot NE Lincs 286 C3
Cottam ER Yorks 310 C1
Cottam Lancs 289 D7
Cottam Notts 271 C8
Cottartown H'land 435 E5
Cottenham Cambs 184 E2
Cottenham Park London 89 C6
Cotterdale N Yorks 316 B2
Cottered Herts 138 B2
Cotteridge W Midlands 176 B3
Cotterstock Northants 203 E6
Cottesbrooke Northants 180 D2
Cottesmore Rutl'd 227 F5
Cotteylands Devon 36 D3
Cottingham ER Yorks 297 D7
Cottingham Northants 202 E2
Cottingley W Yorks 292 C4
Cottisford Oxon 134 A2
Cotton Suffolk 187 E6
Cotton Staffs 245 E7
Cotton End Beds 160 C1
Cotton End Northants 158 A2
Cotton Tree Lancs 291 C7
Cottonworth Hants 64 D4
Cottown Aberds 428 A4
Cottown Aberds 436 F2
Cottown Aberds 437 D5
Cotwall Telford 220 E2
Cotwalton Staffs 221 B8
Coubister Orkney 452 B4
Couch Green Hants 65 E7
Couch's Mill Cornw'l 9 D5
Coughton Heref'd 129 C5
Coughton Warwick 176 F4
Cougie H'land 432 F4
Coulaghailtro Arg/Bute 407 F7
Coulags H'land 432 D1
Coulby Newham Middlesbro 332 D5
Coulderton Cumb 324 E4
Couldoran H'land 431 D8
Couligartan Stirl 409 B7
Coulin H'land 432 C2
Coulin Lodge H'land 432 C2
Coull Aberds 428 B2
Coull Arg/Bute 406 F2
Coulmony Ho H'land 434 D4
Coulport Arg/Bute 408 D5
Coulsdon London 89 E8
Coulshill Perth/Kinr 411 B4
Coulter S Lanarks 382 F5
Coultings Som'set 58 C4
Coulton N Yorks 320 F3
Coultra Fife 420 E3
Cound Shrops 195 C7
Coundlane Shrops 195 B7
Coundmoor Shrops 195 C7
Coundon Durham 343 F8
Coundon W Midlands 177 B9
Coundon Grange Durham 343 F8
Coundongate Durham 343 F8
Countersett N Yorks 316 C4
Countess Wilts 63 C8
Countess Cross Essex 141 A6
Countess Wear Devon 21 B8
Countesthorpe Leics 201 D5
Countisbury Devon 56 B1
County Oak W Sussex 69 D7
Coup Green Lancs 289 E8
Coupar Angus Perth/Kinr 420 C2
Coupland Cumb 328 C4
Coupland Northum 375 A8
Cour Arg/Bute 404 B4
Courance Dumf/Gal 359 D5
Court Colman Bridg 98 F4
Court Corner Hants 86 E2
Court Henry Carms 123 C7
Court Herbert Rh Cyn Taff 98 C1
Court Hey Merseyside 264 B3
Court House Green W Midlands 178 B2
Court-at-Street Kent 74 D1
Courteenhall Northants 158 B3
Courthill Perth/Kinr 420 C1
Courtsend Essex 115 D7
Courtway Som'set 58 E4
Cousland Midloth 396 E4
Cousley Wood E Sussex 71 E8
Couston Arg/Bute 408 E3
Cova Shetl'd 457 J3
Cove Arg/Bute 408 D5
Cove Scot Borders 398 D5
Cove Devon 36 C4
Cove Hants 87 E6
Cove H'land 438 D2
Cove Bay Aberd C 429 B6
Cove Bottom Suffolk 189 C7
Covehithe Suffolk 189 B8
Coven Staffs 197 B7
Coven Heath Staffs 197 C7
Coveney Cambs 184 B2
Covenham St. Bartholomew Lincs 287 E5
Covenham St. Mary Lincs 287 E5
Coventry W Midlands 178 C2
Coventry Airport Warwick 178 D2
Coventry Cathedral W Midlands 178 C1
Coverack Cornw'l 5 G3
Coverack Bridges Cornw'l 4 D1
Coverham N Yorks 317 C8
Covesea Moray 435 A6
Covingham Swindon 105 F8
Covington Cambs 181 D9
Covington S Lanarks 382 E4
Cow Green Suffolk 187 E6
Cowan Bridge Lancs 315 E6
Cowbar Redcar/Clevel'd 334 C2
Cowbeech E Sussex 50 D5
Cowbeech Hill E Sussex 50 D5
Cowbit Lincs 228 E5
Cowbog Aberds 437 C5
Cowbridge Lincs 252 E2
Cowbridge Som'set 57 C6
Cowbridge V/Glam 77 B6
Cowcliffe W Yorks 280 A4
Cowden Kent 70 C4
Cowden Pound Kent 70 C4
Cowdenbeath Fife 411 C6
Cowdenburn Scot Borders 383 B9
Cowen Head Cumb 314 A3
Cowers Lane Derby 246 E4
Cowes I/Wight 30 A1
Cowesby N Yorks 319 C8
Cowesfield Green Wilts 43 B8
Cowey Green Essex 142 B2
Cowfold W Sussex 48 B4
Cowgate Tyne/Wear 352 C3
Cowgill Cumb 315 C9
Cowgrove Dorset 27 A6
Cowhill Derby 247 E5
Cowhill S Glos 102 D4
Cowie Aberds 429 D5
Cowie Stirl 410 D3
Cowlands Cornw'l 4 B4
Cowley Derby 269 D6
Cowley Devon 21 A8
Cowley Glos 131 E5
Cowley London 110 F3
Cowley Oxon 107 B7
Cowley Staffs 221 E6
Cowley Bar Derby 269 D6
Cowley Peachey London 110 F3
Cowleymoor Devon 36 D4
Cowling Lancs 277 A8
Cowling N Yorks 291 B8
Cowling N Yorks 318 C3
Cowlinge Suffolk 163 B7
Cowlow Derby 268 E1
Cowmes W Yorks 281 A5
Cowpe Lancs 291 F5
Cowpen Northum 365 F7
Cowpen Bewley Stockton 332 B4
Cowplain Hants 46 D1
Cowsden Worcs 154 B1
Cowshill Durham 341 C8
Cowslip Green N Som'set 80 D1
Cowstrandburn Fife 411 C5
Cowthorpe N Yorks 307 E6
Cox Common Suffolk 189 B6
Cox Green Essex 114 C1
Cox Green Surrey 68 E3
Cox Green Tyne/Wear 353 E5
Cox Green Windsor 87 A7
Cox Hill Beds 160 C3
Cox Moor Notts 247 C8
Coxbank Ches 243 F6
Coxbench Derby 247 F5
Coxbridge Som'set 60 D2
Coxford Cornw'l 17 A8
Coxford Norfolk 232 C1
Coxford S'thampton 44 D2
Coxheath Kent 72 A1
Coxhoe Durham 344 D2
Coxley Som'set 60 C2
Coxley Wick Som'set 60 C2
Coxlodge Tyne/Wear 352 C3
Coxpark Cornw'l 10 A4
Coxtie Green Essex 113 C6
Coxwold N Yorks 320 E1
Coychurch Bridg 77 A5
Coylton S Ayrs 367 D8
Coylumbridge H'land 426 A4
Coynach Aberds 428 B1
Coynachie Aberds 436 E1
Coytrahen Bridg 98 E4
Crab Orchard Dorset 42 E4
Crabble Kent 75 C5
Crabbs Cross Worcs 176 F3
Crabgate Norfolk 233 C6
Crabtree Plym'th 11 D6
Crabtree W Sussex 69 F6
Crabtree Green Wrex 241 F7
Crackaig Arg/Bute 407 F5
Crackenedge W Yorks 293 F6
Crackenthorpe Cumb 328 B3
Crackington Haven Cornw'l 17 A7
Crackley Staffs 244 D2
Crackleybank Shrops 196 A4
Crackpot N Yorks 317 A5
Crackstone Glos 104 B2
Cracoe N Yorks 304 D3
Craddock Devon 37 D6
Cradhlastadh W Isles 450 D3
Cradle End Herts 139 C5
Cradley Heref'd 152 C4
Cradley W Midlands 176 B1
Cradley Heath Worcs 176 A1
Cradoc Powys 126 A1
Crafthole Cornw'l 10 E3
Crag Bank Lancs 301 B8
Crag Foot Lancs 314 F3
Cragg Hill W Yorks 293 C6
Craggan H'land 434 F5
Craggan Moray 435 E6
Craggan Stirl 418 E3
Cragganvallie H'land 433 E7
Craggenmore Moray 435 E6
Craggie H'land 434 E2
Craggie H'land 441 B5
Craggiemore H'land 440 C4
Craghead Durham 343 A8
Crai Powys 125 C6
Craibstone Moray 436 C1
Craichie Angus 421 C5
Craig Conwy 262 E6
Craig Dumf/Gal 401 B8
Craig Dumf/Gal 401 C8
Craig H'land 432 D2
Craig Berthlwyd Merth Tyd 100 C1
Craig Castle Aberds 436 F1
Craig Gellinudd Neath P Talb 98 B1
Craig Llangiwg Neath P Talb 98 B1
Craig Lodge Arg/Bute 408 F2
Craig-moston Aberds 428 E3
Craiganor Lodge Perth/Kinr 418 B4
Craig-cefn-parc Swan 97 B8
Craigdallie Perth/Kinr 420 E2
Craigdam Aberds 437 E5
Craigdarroch Dumf/Gal 357 D6
Craigdarroch H'land 433 C6
Craigdhu H'land 433 D6
Craigearn Aberds 428 A4
Craigellachie Moray 435 D7
Craigencallie Ho. Dumf/Gal 401 B7
Craigencross Dumf/Gal 400 C2
Craigend Glasg C 393 E5
Craigend Perth/Kinr 419 F7
Craigend Perth/Kinr 420 E1
Craigend Renf 391 D9
Craigend Stirl 410 D2
Craigend S Lanarks 380 B4
Craigendive Arg/Bute 408 D3
Craigendoran Arg/Bute 409 D6
Craigendowie Angus 428 F2
Craigends Renf 391 E8
Craigens Arg/Bute 406 F2
Craigens E Ayrs 368 D3
Craigentinny C/Edinb 396 D2
Craighall Perth/Kinr 420 C1
Craighat Stirl 409 D7
Craighead Fife 412 B4
Craighead H'land 434 B2
Craighill Aberds 436 D4
Craighlaw Mains Dumf/Gal 400 C5
Craighouse Arg/Bute 407 F5
Craigie Aberds 429 A6
Craigie Dundee C 420 D4
Craigie Perth/Kinr 420 C1
Craigie Perth/Kinr 420 E1
Craigie S Ayrs 367 C6
Craigiefield Orkney 453 B5
Craigiehall C/Edinb 395 C8
Craigielaw E Loth 397 C6
Craigleith C/Edinb 396 D1
Craig-llwyn Shrops 218 C1
Craiglockhart C/Edinb 396 D1
Craigmalloch E Ayrs 355 D8
Craigmaud Aberds 437 C5
Craigmillar C/Edinb 396 D2
Craigmore Arg/Bute 390 E2
Craignant Shrops 218 B2
Craignell Dumf/Gal 401 B7
Craigneuk N Lanarks 393 E7
Craigneuk N Lanarks 381 A7
Craignish Castle Arg/Bute 407 B7
Craignure Arg/Bute 416 D2
Craigo Angus 421 A6
Craigow Perth/Kinr 411 B5
Craigrory H'land 433 D8
Craigrothie Fife 412 A1
Craigroy Moray 435 C6
Craigruie Stirl 418 E2
Craig's End Essex 163 E7
Craigshall Dumf/Gal 402 D2
Craigshill W Loth 395 E6
Craigston Castle Aberds 436 C4
Craigton Aberd C 429 B5
Craigton Angus 420 B3
Craigton Angus 421 D5
Craigton H'land 434 D1
Craigton H'land 440 B3
Craigton H'land 440 D3
Craigtown H'land 444 C2
Craig-y-don Conwy 262 C5
Craig-y-Duke Neath P Talb 98 B1
Craig-y-nos Powys 125 D5
Craig-y-pal Swan 97 B9
Craik Scot Borders 372 F4
Crail Fife 412 B4
Crailing Scot Borders 374 C3
Crailinghall Scot Borders 374 C3
Crakaig H'land 441 B6
Crakehill N Yorks 319 F7
Crakemarsh Staffs 222 A3
Crambe N Yorks 308 C3
Crambeck N Yorks 308 B3
Cramlington Northum 352 A4
Cramond C/Edinb 395 C8
Cramond Bridge C/Edinb 395 C8
Crampmoor Hants 44 B2
Cranage Ches 266 F2
Cranberry Staffs 221 A6
Cranborne Dorset 42 D3
Cranbourne Brackn'l 87 B8
Cranbourne Hants 66 A2
Cranbrook Kent 72 D2
Cranbrook London 112 E3
Cranbrook Common Kent 72 D2
Crane Moor S Yorks 281 D8
Cranes Essex 114 D1
Crane's Corner Norfolk 232 F3
Cranfield Beds 159 D7
Cranford Devon 33 B6
Cranford London 88 A4
Cranford St. Andrew Northants 181 C6
Cranford St. John Northants 181 C6
Cranham Glos 130 E3
Cranham London 113 E6
Cranhill Glasg C 392 E4
Crank Mersey 277 E7
Crankwood Gtr Man 278 D1
Cranleigh Surrey 68 D3
Cranley Suffolk 187 D8
Cranley Gardens London 111 E7
Cranmer Green Suffolk 187 D5
Cranmore I/Wight 29 B7
Cranmore Som'set 61 C5
Cranna Aberds 436 C3
Crannich Arg/Bute 415 C8
Crannoch Moray 436 C1
Cranoe Leics 202 D1
Cransford Suffolk 188 F4
Cranshaws Scot Borders 398 F3
Cranstal I/Man 336 A4
Cranswick ER Yorks 310 E2
Crantock Cornw'l 7 C6
Cranwell Lincs 250 D3
Cranwich Norfolk 207 D6
Cranworth Norfolk 208 C3
Craobh Haven Arg/Bute 407 B7
Crapstone Devon 11 B6
Crarae Arg/Bute 408 C2
Crask H'land 444 B1
Crask Inn H'land 440 A2
Crask of Aigas H'land 433 D6
Craskins Aberds 428 B2
Craster Northum 377 D7
Craswall Heref'd 127 A6
Crateford Staffs 197 B7
Cratfield Suffolk 188 C4
Crathes Aberds 428 C4
Crathes Castle and Gardens Aberds 428 C4
Crathie Aberds 427 C7
Crathie H'land 425 C7
Crathorne N Yorks 332 E3
Craven Arms Shrops 173 B6
Crawcrook Tyne/Wear 352 D1
Crawford Lancs 277 D6
Crawford S Lanarks 370 C4
Crawforddyke S Lanarks 382 B2
Crawfordjohn S Lanarks 370 C2
Crawick Dumf/Gal 369 E7
Crawley Devon 38 E3
Crawley Glos 103 C7
Crawley Hants 65 E5
Crawley Oxon 132 E5
Crawley W Sussex 69 D7
Crawley Down W Sussex 69 D8
Crawley End Essex 162 E1
Crawley Hill Surrey 87 D7
Crawleyside Durham 342 C3
Crawshawbooth Lancs 291 E5
Crawton Aberds 429 E5
Cray N Yorks 316 E4
Cray Perth/Kinr 420 A1
Crayford London 90 A5
Crayke N Yorks 307 A8
Craymere Beck Norfolk 233 B6
Crays Hill Essex 114 D1
Cray's Pond Oxon 108 F2
Crazies Hill Wokingham 109 F5
Creacombe Devon 36 C1
Creag Aoil H'land 424 E3
Creag Ghoraidh W Isles 447 D2
Creagan Arg/Bute 416 C4
Creagan Sithe Arg/Bute 409 B5
Creagastrom W Isles 447 D3
Creaguaineach Lodge H'land 425 F5
Creamore Bank Shrops 219 B7
Creaton Northants 180 D2
Creca Dumf/Gal 347 B6
Credenhill Heref'd 151 D6
Crediton Devon 36 F1
Creebridge Dumf/Gal 401 C6
Creech Dorset 27 D5
Creech Heathfield Som'set 59 F5
Creech St. Michael Som'set 38 A3
Creed Cornw'l 8 F1
Creediknowe Shetl'd 457 G5
Creegbrawse Cornw'l 4 B2
Creekmouth London 112 F4
Creephole Glos 103 E8
Creeting Bottoms Suffolk 165 A7
Creeting St. Mary Suffolk 165 A6
Creeting St. Peter Suffolk 165 A6
Creeton Lincs 227 E7
Creetown Dumf/Gal 401 D6
Creggans Arg/Bute 408 B3
Cregneash I/Man 336 E1
Creg-ny-Baa I/Man 336 C3
Cregrina Powys 149 B7
Creich Fife 420 E3
Creigau Card 99 F8
Creigau Monmouths 102 C1
Creighton Staffs 222 A3
Cremyll Cornw'l 10 E5
Crendell Dorset 42 D4
Crepkill H'land 430 D4
Creslow Bucks 135 C7
Cress Green Glos 103 B7
Cressage Shrops 195 C7
Cressbrook Derby 268 E3
Cresselly Pembs 117 C7
Cressex Bucks 109 D7
Cressing Essex 140 C4
Cresswell Northum 365 D7
Cresswell Staffs 222 A1
Cresswell Quay Pembs 117 C7
Creswell Derby 270 E2
Creswell Staffs 221 D8
Creswell Green Staffs 198 A2
Cretingham Suffolk 188 F2
Cretshengan Arg/Bute 407 F7
Creunant = Crynant Neath P Talb 98 B2
Crewe Ches 242 D1
Crewe Ches 243 C7
Crewgarth Cumb 340 E2
Crewgreen Powys 218 E3
Crewkerne Som'set 39 E6
Crew's Hole Bristol 80 B4
Crewton Derby C 224 B2
Crianlarich Stirl 418 E1
Cribyn Ceredig'n 146 B4
Criccieth Gwyn 214 A2
Crich Derby 247 D5
Crich Carr Derby 246 D4
Crich Common Derby 247 D5
Crich Tramway Village Derby 246 C4
Crichie Aberds 437 D6
Crichmere Surrey 67 E7
Crichton Midloth 396 F4
Crick Monmouths 102 D1
Crick Northants 179 D6
Crickadarn Powys 149 D6
Cricket Malherbie Som'set 38 D5
Cricket St. Thomas Som'set 38 E5
Crickham Som'set 59 A8
Crickheath Shrops 218 D2
Crickhowell Powys 127 D5
Cricklade Wilts 105 D6
Cricklewood London 111 E6
Cricladarn Powys 149 D6
Criddlestyle Hants 43 D6
Cridling Stubbs N Yorks 294 F4
Crieff Perth/Kinr 419 E6
Crieff Visitors' Centre Perth/Kinr 419 E6
Criggan Cornw'l 8 C3
Criggion Powys 218 E2
Crigglestone W Yorks 281 A8
Crimble Gtr Man 279 B6
Crimchard Som'set 38 E4
Crimond Aberds 437 C7
Crimonmogate Aberds 437 C7
Crimp Cornw'l 33 C5
Crimplesham Norfolk 206 C4
Crimscote Warwick 155 C7
Crinan Arg/Bute 407 C7
Crinan Ferry Arg/Bute 407 C7
Crindau Newp 101 E6
Crindledyke N Lanarks 382 A1
Cringleford Norfolk 209 B7
Cringles W Yorks 304 F4
Crinow Pembs 121 E6
Cripple Corner Essex 164 F2
Cripplesease Cornw'l 3 C6
Cripplestyle Dorset 42 D4
Cripp's Corner E Sussex 51 B8
Crispie Arg/Bute 408 E2
Critchell's Green Hants 43 A8
Crizeley Heref'd 128 A2
Croanford Cornw'l 8 A3
Croasdale Cumb 325 C6
Crobeag W Isles 451 E6
Crock Street Som'set 38 D4
Crockenhill Kent 90 C5
Crockernwell Devon 20 B5
Crocker End Oxon 108 E4
Crockerhill Hants 45 E6
Crockerhill W Sussex 47 E6
Crocker's Ash Heref'd 128 D4
Crockerton Wilts 62 C2
Crockerton Green Wilts 62 C2
Crocketford or Ninemile Bar Dumf/Gal 402 B2
Crockett Cornw'l 10 A3
Crockey Hill C/York 295 A6
Crockham Hill Kent 70 A3
Crockhurst Street Kent 71 C7
Crockleford Heath Essex 142 B1
Crockleford Hill Essex 142 B1
Crockness Orkney 452 D4
Croes Hywel Monmouths 127 E7
Croesau Bach Shrops 218 C1
Croeserw Neath P Talb 98 C4
Croes-goch Pembs 118 C4
Croes-lan Ceredig'n 145 D7
Croesor Gwyn 237 F8
Croespenmaen Caerph 100 C3
Croes-wian Flints 262 E4
Croesyceiliog Carms 122 D4
Croesyceiliog Torf 101 C6
Croes-y-mwyalch Torf 101 D6
Croes-y-pant Monmouths 101 B6
Croesywaun Gwyn 237 C6
Croford Som'set 58 F2
Croft Leics 200 D4
Croft Lincs 253 B6
Croft Pembs 144 D3
Croft Warrington 278 F1
Croft End Lincs 253 B5
Croft Motor Racing Circuit N Yorks 331 E7
Croft of Tillymaud Aberds 437 E8
Croft West Cornw'l 4 A3
Croftamie Stirl 409 D7
Croftfoot Glasg C 392 F4
Crofthandy Cornw'l 4 B2
Croftlands Cumb 313 E6
Croftmalloch W Loth 394 F3
Croftmoraig Perth/Kinr 419 C5
Crofton Cumb 338 A5
Crofton London 90 C3
Crofton Wilts 84 D2
Crofton W Yorks 282 A1
Croft-on-Tees N Yorks 331 E7
Crofts Dumf/Gal 402 B1
Crofts Bank Gtr Man 278 E4
Crofts of Benachielt H'land 445 E5
Crofts of Haddo Aberds 437 E5
Crofts of Inverthernie Aberds 436 D4
Crofts of Meikle Ardo Aberds 437 D5
Crofty Swan 96 C5
Crogen Iddon Wrex 218 A2
Croggan Arg/Bute 416 E2
Croglin Cumb 340 B2
Croich H'land 440 D1
Croick H'land 444 C2
Croig Arg/Bute 415 B6
Crois Dughaill W Isles 446 A3
Cromarty H'land 434 B2
Cromasaig H'land 432 B2
Crombie Castle Aberds 436 C2
Cromblet Aberds 437 E4
Cromdale H'land 435 F5
Cromer Herts 138 B1
Cromer Norfolk 257 D7
Cromford Derby 246 C3
Cromhall S Glos 103 D5
Cromhall Common S Glos 103 E5
Cromor W Isles 451 F7
Crompton Fold Gtr Man 279 C8
Cromra H'land 425 C7
Cromwell Notts 249 B6
Cromwell Bottom W Yorks 292 F4
Crondall Hants 67 B5
Cronk-y-Voddy I/Man 336 C3
Cronton Halton 264 B5
Crook Cumb 314 A3
Crook Durham 343 D7
Crook of Devon Perth/Kinr 411 B5
Crookdale Cumb 338 C2
Crooke Gtr Man 277 C7

Crooked End Glos 129 D6
Crooked Soley Wilts 84 B3
Crooked Withies Dorset 42 E4
Crookedholm E Ayrs 379 E9
Crookes S Yorks 269 B6
Crookfur E Renf 380 A2
Crookhall Durham 343 A6
Crookham Northum 387 E8
Crookham W Berks 85 D7
Crookham Eastfield Northum 387 E8
Crookham Village Hants 67 A5
Crookhaugh Scot Borders 371 B7
Crookhill Tyne/Wear 352 D2
Crooklands Cumb 314 D4
Crook's Marsh Bristol 102 F2
Crooksmoor S Yorks 269 B6
Crookston Glasg C 392 F2
Croome Park, Pershore Worcs 153 D7
Cropredy Oxon 156 C4
Cropston Leics 200 A5
Cropthorne Worcs 154 D2
Cropton N Yorks 321 C6
Cropwell Bishop Notts 225 A8
Cropwell Butler Notts 225 A8
Cros W Isles 451 A8
Crosben H'land 416 B2
Crosbost W Isles 451 E6
Crosby Cumb 337 D4
Crosby I/Man 336 D3
Crosby Mersey 276 E3
Crosby N Lincs 284 B4
Crosby Garrett Cumb 328 E4
Crosby Ravensworth Cumb 328 C2
Crosby Villa Cumb 337 D4
Croscombe Som'set 60 C3
Crosemere Shrops 219 C5
Crosland Edge W Yorks 280 B4
Crosland Hill W Yorks 280 B4
Crosland Moor W Yorks 280 A4
Cross Devon 54 D4
Cross Devon 55 E7
Cross Som'set 38 D5
Cross Som'set 79 F8
Cross Ash Monmouths 128 D2
Cross at Hand Kent 72 B2
Cross Bank Worcs 174 D4
Cross Coombe Cornw'l 7 E5
Cross End Beds 159 A9
Cross End Essex 164 F2
Cross End M/Keynes 159 E6
Cross Gates W Yorks 293 D9
Cross Green Suffolk 164 A2
Cross Green Suffolk 164 B1
Cross Green Suffolk 164 B4
Cross Green Staffs 197 B7
Cross Green Warwick 156 A2
Cross Green W Yorks 293 D8
Cross Hands Carms 123 E7
Cross Hands Pembs 117 B7
Cross Heath Staffs 244 E2
Cross Hill Derby 247 E6
Cross Hill ER Yorks 283 A6
Cross Hill Glos 102 C3
Cross Hills N Yorks 292 B2
Cross Houses Shrops 196 E2
Cross Houses Shrops 195 B6
Cross in Hand E Sussex 50 B4
Cross Inn Ceredig'n 168 F3
Cross Inn Ceredig'n 145 A7
Cross Inn Rh Cyn Taff 99 F8
Cross Keys Kent 71 A5
Cross Keys Wilts 82 B2
Cross Lane Powys 193 C7
Cross Lane Head Shrops 196 D3
Cross Lanes Bucks 109 B5
Cross Lanes Cornw'l 4 F1
Cross Lanes Dorset 41 F5
Cross Lanes Durham 330 D3
Cross Lanes N Yorks 307 C7
Cross Lanes Wrex 241 E8
Cross Oak Powys 126 C3
Cross of Jackston Aberds 436 E4
Cross Roads Devon 19 C6
Cross Roads W Yorks 292 C2
Cross Stone Aberds 437 F6
Cross Street Suffolk 187 C8
Cross Town Ches 266 D2
Crossaig Arg/Bute 404 A4
Crossal H'land 430 E4
Crossapol Arg/Bute 414 C2
Crossbarrow Cumb 337 F6
Crossbrae Aberds 436 C3
Crossburn Falk 394 D2
Crossbush W Sussex 47 E8
Crosscanonby Cumb 337 D4
Crosscynon Powys 171 D7
Crossdale Street Norfolk 257 E7
Crossens Mersey 288 F4
Crossflatts W Yorks 292 B4
Crossford Fife 411 D5
Crossford S Lanarks 381 C8
Crossgate Lincs 228 C4
Crossgate Orkney 453 B5
Crossgate Staffs 221 A8
Crossgatehall E Loth 396 E4
Crossgates Cumb 325 B6
Crossgates Fife 411 D6
Crossgates Powys 171 F6
Crossgill Cumb 341 C8
Crossgill Lancs 302 C3
Crossgreen Shrops 219 E6
Crosshands Carms 121 C7
Crosshill Glasg C 393 F5
Crosshill E Ayrs 368 C1
Crosshill Fife 411 C6
Crosshill S Ayrs 355 A5
Crosshill S Lanarks 380 B4
Crosshouse E Ayrs 379 E7
Crosskeys Caerph 100 D4
Crosskirk H'land 444 A4
Crosslands Cumb 313 C7
Crosslands Park Cumb 300 A3
Crosslanes Shrops 218 E3
Crosslee Scot Borders 372 D3
Crosslee Renf 391 E8
Crosslees E Renf 380 B3
Crossley W Yorks 293 F6
Crossley Hall W Yorks 292 D4
Crossmichael Dumf/Gal 402 C1
Crossmill E Renf 380 A2
Crossmoor Lancs 289 C5
Crossmount Perth/Kinr 418 B5
Crossmyloof Glasg C 392 F3
Crossport W Sussex 49 B5
Crossroads Aberds 428 C4
Crossroads E Ayrs 380 F1
Crosston Angus 421 B5
Crosstown Cornw'l 32 D4
Crosstown V/Glam 77 B7
Crossway Heref'd 129 A6
Crossway Monmouths 128 D2
Crossway Powys 149 A5
Crossway Green Monmouths 102 D2
Crossway Green Worcs 175 E6
Crossways Dorset 26 C2
Crossways Glos 128 E5
Crossways S Glos 103 D5
Crosswell Pembs 144 E2
Crosswood Ceredig'n 169 D6
Crosthwaite Cumb 314 B2
Croston Lancs 277 A6
Crostwick Norfolk 234 E2
Crostwright Norfolk 234 C3
Crothair W Isles 450 D4
Crouch Kent 91 E7
Crouch Kent 93 E7
Crouch End London 111 E7
Crouch Green Herts 137 C8
Crouch Hill Dorset 40 D4
Croucheston Wilts 42 A4
Croughly Moray 435 F6
Croughton Northants 157 F5
Crovie Aberds 437 B5
Crow Hants 43 F6
Crow Edge S Yorks 281 D5
Crow Green Essex 113 C6
Crow Hill Heref'd 129 B6
Crow Nest W Yorks 292 C4
Crow Wood Halton 265 B5
Crowan Cornw'l 3 D8
Crowborough E Sussex 70 E5
Crowborough Warren E Sussex 70 E5
Crowcombe Som'set 58 D2
Crowdecote Derby 245 A8
Crowden Derby 280 E3
Crowden Devon 19 A6
Crowdhill Hants 44 C4
Crowdhole Devon 36 C1
Crowdleham Kent 91 E6
Crowdon N Yorks 322 A3
Crowell Oxon 108 C4
Crowfield Northants 157 D7
Crowfield Suffolk 165 A7
Crowgate Street Norfolk 234 D3
Crowhill Gtr Man 279 E7
Crowhurst E Sussex 51 D8
Crowhurst Surrey 70 B2
Crowhurst Lane End Surrey 70 B2
Crowland Lincs 204 A3
Crowlas Cornw'l 3 D6
Crowle N Lincs 284 B2
Crowle Worcs 153 A8
Crowle Green Worcs 153 A8
Crowmarsh Gifford Oxon 108 E2
Crown Corner Suffolk 188 D3
Crownfield Bucks 109 C6
Crownhill M/Keynes 158 E4
Crownhill Plym'th 11 D5
Crownland Suffolk 187 D5
Crownpits Surrey 68 C1
Crownthorpe Norfolk 209 C5
Crowntown Cornw'l 3 D8
Crow's Green Essex 140 B2
Crow's Nest Cornw'l 9 B8
Crows-an-wra Cornw'l 2 E3
Crowshill Norfolk 208 B2
Crowsnest Shrops 194 C3
Crowther's Pool Powys 150 C2
Crowthorne Wokingham 87 D6
Crowton Ches 265 E6
Croxall Staffs 223 F5
Croxby Lincs 286 E2
Croxdale Durham 344 D1
Croxden Staffs 222 A3
Croxley Green Herts 110 C3
Croxteth Mersey 276 E5
Croxton Cambs 160 A4
Croxton Norfolk 207 F8
Croxton Norfolk 232 B4
Croxton N Lincs 285 B8
Croxton Staffs 221 B5
Croxton Green Ches 242 D4
Croxton Kerrial Leics 226 C3
Croxtonbank Staffs 221 B5
Croy H'land 434 D2
Croy N Lanarks 393 C6
Croyde Devon 54 D3
Croyde Bay Devon 54 D3
Croydon Cambs 161 C6
Croydon London 89 D8
Crozen Heref'd 152 C1
Crubenbeg H'land 426 C1
Crubenmore Lodge H'land 426 C1
Cruckmeole Shrops 194 B4
Cruckton Shrops 194 A4
Cruden Bay Aberds 437 E7
Crudgington Telford 220 E2
Crudie Aberds 437 C4
Crudwell Wilts 104 D4
Crugmeer Cornw'l 16 E3
Crugybar Carms 147 E6
Crûg Powys 172 D1
Crulabhig W Isles 450 D4
Crumlin Caerph 100 C4
Crumplehorn Cornw'l 9 E7
Crumpsall Gtr Man 279 D5
Crundale Kent 73 B8
Crundale Pembs 117 A5
Crungoed Powys 172 D1
Crunwere Pembs 121 E7
Cruse Heref'd 128 D5
Cruwys Morchard Devon 36 D2
Crux Easton Hants 85 E5
Cruxton Dorset 25 A6
Crwbin Carms 123 E5
Crya Orkney 452 C4
Cryers Hill Bucks 109 C7
Crymych Pembs 144 F3
Crynant = Creunant Neath P Talb 98 B2
Crynfryn Ceredig'n 168 F4
Crystal Palace National Sports Centre London 89 B8
Cuaich H'land 426 D1
Cuaig H'land 431 C7
Cuan Arg/Bute 416 F2
Cubbington Warwick 178 E1
Cubeck N Yorks 317 C5
Cubert Cornw'l 7 D6
Cubitt Town London 90 A2
Cubley S Yorks 281 D6
Cublington Bucks 135 C7
Cublington Heref'd 151 E6
Cuck Hill Som'set 79 E8
Cuckfield W Sussex 49 A6
Cucklington Som'set 61 F7
Cuckney Notts 270 E3
Cuckold's Green Suffolk 189 B7
Cuckold's Green Wilts 82 E4
Cuckoo Bridge Lincs 228 D4
Cuckoo Green Suffolk 211 D6
Cuckoo's Corner Hants 66 C4
Cuckoo's Corner Wilts 83 E5
Cuckron Shetl'd 457 H4
Cuddesdon Oxon 107 B8
Cuddington Bucks 135 E5
Cuddington Ches 265 E6
Cuddington Heath Ches 242 E2
Cuddra Cornw'l 8 E4
Cuddy Hill Lancs 289 C6
Cudham London 90 E3
Cudliptown Devon 19 E7
Cudworth Som'set 39 D5
Cudworth Surrey 69 C6
Cudworth S Yorks 282 C1
Cuerdley Cross Warrington 265 B5
Cufaude Hants 86 E2
Cuffern Pembs 119 E5
Cuffley Herts 111 B8
Cùl Doirlinn H'land 423 E6
Cuiashader W Isles 451 B8
Cuidhir W Isles 446 C2
Cuidhtinis W Isles 449 D4
Cuiken Midloth 396 F1
Cuilcheanna Ho. H'land 417 A5
Cuin Arg/Bute 415 B7
Cul na h-Aird W Isles 449 B5
Culbo H'land 433 B8
Culbokie H'land 433 C8
Culburnie H'land 433 D6
Culcabock H'land 434 D1
Culcairn H'land 433 B8
Culcharry H'land 434 C3
Culcheth Warrington 278 E2
Culcronchie Dumf/Gal 401 C7
Culdrain Aberds 436 E2
Culduie H'land 431 D7
Culeave H'land 440 D2
Culford Suffolk 186 D1
Culfordheath Suffolk 186 C2
Culfosia Aberds 428 B4
Culgaith Cumb 340 F3
Culham Oxon 107 C7
Culkein H'land 442 E2
Culkein Drumbeg H'land 442 E3
Culkerton Glos 104 C3
Cullachie H'land 434 F4
Cullen Moray 436 B2
Cullercoats Tyne/Wear 353 B6
Cullicudden H'land 434 B1
Cullingworth W Yorks 292 C3
Cullipool Arg/Bute 407 A7
Cullivoe Shetl'd 456 C5
Culloch Perth/Kinr 419 F5
Culloden H'land 434 D2
Culloden Battlefield, Inverness H'land 434 D2
Cullompton Devon 37 E5
Culm Davy Devon 37 D7
Culmaily H'land 440 D5
Culmazie Dumf/Gal 401 D5
Culmer Surrey 67 D9
Culmers Kent 93 D8
Culmington Shrops 173 B7
Culmstock Devon 37 D6
Culnacraig H'land 438 C4
Culnaightrie Dumf/Gal 402 D1
Culnaknock H'land 430 B5
Culnaneam H'land 430 F4
Culpho Suffolk 166 C2
Culra Lodge H'land 425 E7
Culrain H'land 440 D2
Culross Fife 411 D4
Culroy S Ayrs 367 E6
Culscadden Dumf/Gal 401 E6
Culsh Aberds 427 C8
Culsh Aberds 437 D5
Culshabbin Dumf/Gal 400 D5
Culswick Shetl'd 457 J2
Cultercullen Aberds 437 F6
Cults Aberds 436 E2
Cults Aberd C 429 B5
Cults Dumf/Gal 401 E6
Cults Fife 412 B1
Culverhouse Cross Card 78 B2
Culverlane Devon 14 C2
Culverstone Green Kent 91 D7
Culverthorpe Lincs 250 F3
Culworth Northants 157 C5
Culzean Castle, Maybole S Ayrs 366 E4
Culzie Lodge H'land 433 A7
Cumberlow Green Herts 138 A2
Cumbernauld N Lanarks 393 D7
Cumbernauld Village N Lanarks 393 C7
Cumber's Bank Wrex 219 A5
Cumberworth Lincs 275 E7
Cumdivock Cumb 339 B5
Cumeragh Village Lancs 289 C8
Cuminestown Aberds 437 C5
Cumlewick Shetl'd 455 D3
Cumlodden Arg/Bute 408 C3
Cumloden Dumf/Gal 401 C6
Cummersdale Cumb 339 A6
Cummerton Aberds 437 B5
Cummertrees Dumf/Gal 346 C4
Cummingston Moray 435 B6
Cumnock E Ayrs 368 D3
Cumnor Oxon 107 B6
Cumrew Cumb 340 A1
Cumrue Dumf/Gal 359 E5
Cumwhinton Cumb 339 A7
Cumwhitton Cumb 339 A9
Cundall N Yorks 306 A5
Cundy Cross S Yorks 282 C1
Cunning Park S Ayrs 367 D6
Cunninghamhead N Ayrs 379 D7
Cunnister Shetl'd 456 D5
Cupar Fife 420 F3
Cupar Muir Fife 420 F3
Cupernham Hants 44 B2
Cupid Green Herts 136 F5
Curbar Derby 268 E5
Curbidge Oxon 133 F5
Curborough Staffs 198 A3
Curbridge Hants 45 D5
Curdleigh Devon 38 C2
Curdridge Hants 45 D5
Curdworth Warwick 198 E4
Curgurrel Cornw'l 5 C5
Curin H'land 433 C5
Curland Som'set 38 C3
Curlew Green Suffolk 189 E5
Curling Tye Green Essex 140 F5
Curlott Hill Som'set 39 E6
Currarie S Ayrs 354 D2
Currian Vale Cornw'l 8 D2
Curridge W Berks 85 B6
Currie C/Edinb 395 E8
Currock Cumb 348 F2
Curry Mallet Som'set 38 B4
Curry Rivel Som'set 39 A5
Cursiter Orkney 452 B4
Curteis Corner Kent 72 D3
Curtisden Green Kent 72 C1
Curtisknowle Devon 14 E2
Curtismill Green Essex 112 C5
Cury Cornw'l 4 F1
Cusbay Orkney 454 C3
Cusgarne Cornw'l 4 B3
Cushnie Aberds 437 B4
Cushuish Som'set 58 E3
Cusop Heref'd 150 D2
Custards Hants 43 E9
Custom House London 112 F3
Cusworth S Yorks 282 D4
Cutcloy Dumf/Gal 401 F6
Cutcombe Som'set 57 D5
Cutgate Gtr Man 279 B6
Cuthill E Loth 396 D4
Cutiau Gwyn 214 E4
Cutlers Green Essex 139 A7
Cutler's Green Som'set 60 A3
Cutmadoc Cornw'l 8 C4
Cutmere Cornw'l 10 C2
Cutnall Green Worcs 175 E7
Cutsdean Glos 131 A7
Cutsyke W Yorks 281 A2
Cutthorpe Green Derby 269 E6
Cuttivett Cornw'l 10 C3
Cutts Shetl'd 455 C3
Cutts End Oxon 107 B6
Cutty Sark, Greenwich London 90 A2
Cuttybridge Pembs 116 A4
Cuttyhill Aberds 437 C7
Cuxham Oxon 108 C3
Cuxton Medway 91 C9
Cuxwold Lincs 286 D2
Cwm Bl Gwent 100 A3
Cwm Denbs 262 D3
Cwm Swan 97 C8
Cwm Capel Carms 96 B4
Cwm Collo Shrops 172 C2
Cwm Dulais Swan 97 B7
Cwm Gelli Caerph 100 C3
Cwm Penmachno Conwy 238 E3
Cwm Plysgog Pembs 144 D3
Cwmafan Rh Cyn Taff 98 D2
Cwmaman Rh Cyn Taff 99 C7
Cwmann Carms 146 D4
Cwmavon Torf 100 A5
Cwmbach Carms 96 B4
Cwmbach Carms 121 B9
Cwmbach Powys 149 B5
Cwmbach Powys 149 E8
Cwmbach Rh Cyn Taff 99 B7
Cwmbelan Powys 170 B3
Cwm-brain Shrops 172 C2
Cwmbran Torf 101 C5
Cwmbrwyno Ceredig'n 169 B7
Cwmcarn Caerph 100 D4
Cwmcarvan Monmouths 128 F3
Cwm-celyn Bl Gwent 127 F5
Cwm-Cewydd Gwyn 191 A8
Cwm-cou Ceredig'n 145 D5
Cwmcrawnon Powys 126 D3
Cwmcych Pembs 145 E5
Cwm-cynnar Swan 97 D5
Cwmdare Rh Cyn Taff 99 B6
Cwm-dows Caerph 100 C4
Cwmdu Carms 123 A8
Cwmdu Powys 126 C4
Cwmdu Swan 97 D7
Cwmduad Carms 122 A3
Cwmdwr Carms 124 A3
Cwmerfyn Ceredig'n 169 B6
Cwmfelin Boeth Carms 121 D7
Cwmfelin Mynach Carms 121 C8
Cwmfelinfach Caerph 100 D3
Cwmffrwd Carms 122 D4
Cwm-Ffrwd-oer Torf 100 B5
Cwm-Fields Torf 101 B5
Cwmgiedd Powys 124 E4
Cwmgors Neath P Talb 124 E3
Cwmgwili Carms 123 E7
Cwmgwrach Neath P Talb 98 B4
Cwmheyope Powys 172 D2
Cwmhiraeth Carms 145 E6
Cwm-hwnt Rh Cyn Taff 99 A5
Cwmifor Carms 124 B2
Cwmisfael Carms 123 D5
Cwm-Llinau Powys 191 B7
Cwmllyfri Carms 122 E2
Cwmllynfell Neath P Talb 124 E3
Cwmmawr Carms 123 E6
Cwmmiles Carms 121 C7
Cwmnantyrodyn Caerph 100 C3
Cwmorgan Carms 145 F5
Cwmparc Rh Cyn Taff 99 C5
Cwmpennar Rh Cyn Taff 99 B7
Cwmpengraig Carms 145 E6
Cwmrhos Powys 126 C4
Cwmrhydyceirw Swan 97 C8
Cwmsychbant Ceredig'n 146 C2
Cwmsyfiog Caerph 100 B3
Cwmsymlog Ceredig'n 169 B7
Cwmtillery Bl Gwent 100 A4
Cwmtwrch-isaf Neath P Talb 124 E4
Cwmtwrch-uchaf Powys 124 E4
Cwmwysg Powys 125 B6
Cwm-y-gaist Powys 171 D8
Cwm-y-glo Carms 123 E7
Cwm-y-glo Gwyn 237 B7
Cwmynyscoy Torf 101 C5
Cwmyoy Monmouths 127 C7
Cwm-yr-Eglwys Pembs 119 B8
Cwmystwyth Ceredig'n 169 D8
Cwrt Gwyn 190 C4
Cwrt-newydd Ceredig'n 146 C2
Cwrt-y-Cadno Carms 147 D6
Cwrt-y-carne Swan 97 B6
Cwrt-y-gollen Monmouths 127 D5
Cydweli = Kidwelly Carms 122 F4
Cyffordd Llandudno = Llandudno Junction Conwy 262 D6
Cyffylliog Denbs 240 C2
Cyfronydd Powys 193 B6
Cymau Flints 241 C6
Cymbyr Carms 123 A8
Cymdda Bridg 99 F5
Cymer Neath P Talb 98 C4
Cymfelin Bridg 98 E4
Cymfelin Merth Tyd 100 B1
Cymmer Rh Cyn Taff 99 D7
Cyncoed Card 100 F3
Cynghordy Carms 147 E9
Cynheidre Carms 123 F5
Cynonville Neath P Talb 98 C3
Cyntwell Card 78 A2
Cynwyd Denbs 240 F2
Cynwyl Elfed Carms 122 B3
Cywarch Gwyn 216 E2


## D


Daccombe Devon 15 B6
Dacre Cumb 327 A6
Dacre N Yorks 305 C7
Dacre Banks N Yorks 305 C7
Daddry Shield Durham 342 D1
Dadford Bucks 157 E8
Dadlington Leics 200 D2
Dafen Carms 97 B5
Daffy Green Norfolk 208 B3
Dagdale Staffs 222 B3
Dagenham London 112 F4
Daggons Dorset 42 D5
Daglingworth Glos 104 A4
Dagnall Bucks 136 D3
Dagtail End Worcs 176 F3
Dagworth Suffolk 187 F5
Dail Beag W Isles 451 C5
Dail bho Dheas W Isles 451 A7
Dail bho Thuath W Isles 451 A7
Dail Mor W Isles 450 C5
Daill Arg/Bute 406 F3
Dailly S Ayrs 354 B4
Dainton Devon 15 B5
Dairsie or Osnaburgh Fife 420 F4
Daisy Bank W Midlands 198 D1
Daisy Green Essex 141 B7
Daisy Green Suffolk 187 E5
Daisy Green Suffolk 187 E6
Daisy Hill Gtr Man 278 D2
Daisy Hill W Yorks 292 D4
Daisy Hill W Yorks 293 E7
Daisy Nook Gtr Man 279 D7
Dalabrog W Isles 446 A3
Dalavich Arg/Bute 408 A2
Dalbeattie Dumf/Gal 402 C2
Dalbeg H'land 426 A1
Dalblair E Ayrs 368 D4
Dalbog Angus 428 E2
Dalbrack Stirl 410 B2
Dalbury Derby 223 B7
Dalby I/Man 336 D2
Dalby Lincs 275 E5
Dalby N Yorks 308 A1
Dalchalloch Perth/Kinr 419 A5
Dalchalm H'land 441 C6
Dalchenna Arg/Bute 408 B3
Dalchirach Moray 435 E6
Dalchonzie Perth/Kinr 419 E5
Dalchork H'land 440 B2
Dalchreichart H'land 425 A4
Dalchruin Perth/Kinr 418 F5
Dalderby Lincs 251 A8
Dale Cumb 340 C1
Dale Gtr Man 279 C8
Dale Pembs 116 C2
Dale Shetl'd 457 G4
Dale Abbey Derby 224 A3
Dale Bottom Cumb 326 B2
Dale End Derby 246 B2
Dale End Derby 268 C3
Dale End N Yorks 291 A8
Dale Hill E Sussex 71 E9
Dale Moor Derby 224 A3
Dale of Walls Shetl'd 457 H1
Dalehouse N Yorks 334 C2
Dalelia H'land 423 F7
Dalemain Cumb 339 F8
Dales Brow Gtr Man 278 D4
Daless H'land 434 E3
Dalestie Moray 427 A6
Dalfaber H'land 426 A4
Dalganachan H'land 444 D4
Dalgarven N Ayrs 379 C5
Dalgety Bay Fife 411 D6
Dalginross Perth/Kinr 419 E5
Dalguise Perth/Kinr 419 C7
Dalhalvaig H'land 444 C2
Dalham Suffolk 185 F7
Dalhastnie Angus 428 E2
Dalhenzean Perth/Kinr 427 F6
Dalinlongart Arg/Bute 408 D4
Dalkeith Midloth 396 E3
Dallam Warrington 265 A6
Dallam Tower Cumb 314 D3
Dallas Moray 435 C6
Dallas Lodge Moray 435 C6
Dallcharn H'land 443 C8
Dalleagles E Ayrs 368 E3
Dallinghoo Suffolk 166 A3
Dallington E Sussex 51 C6
Dallington Northants 180 F2
Dallow N Yorks 305 A7
Dalmadilly Aberds 428 A4
Dalmahoy C/Edinb 395 E7
Dalmally Arg/Bute 417 E6
Dalmarnock Glasg C 392 F4
Dalmarnock Perth/Kinr 419 C7
Dalmary Stirl 409 C8
Dalmellington E Ayrs 355 A8
Dalmeny C/Edinb 395 C7
Dalmigavie H'land 426 A2
Dalmigavie Lodge H'land 434 F2
Dalmilling S Ayrs 367 C7
Dalmore H'land 434 B1
Dalmuir W Dunb 392 D1
Dalnabreck H'land 423 F6
Dalnacardoch Lodge Perth/Kinr 426 E2
Dalnacroich H'land 433 C5
Dalnaglar Castle Perth/Kinr 420 A1
Dalnahaitnach H'land 434 F3
Dalnamein Lodge Perth/Kinr 426 F2
Dalnarrow Arg/Bute 416 D2
Dalnaspidal Lodge Perth/Kinr 425 E8
Dalnavaid Perth/Kinr 419 A8
Dalnavie H'land 440 F3
Dalnaw Dumf/Gal 400 B5
Dalnawillan Lodge H'land 444 D4
Dalness H'land 417 B6
Dalnessie H'land 440 B3
Dalphaid H'land 439 B7
Dalqueich Perth/Kinr 411 B5
Dalrannoch Arg/Bute 416 C4
Dalreavoch H'land 440 C4
Dalriach H'land 435 E5
Dalrigh Stirl 417 E8
Dalry C/Edinb 396 D1
Dalry N Ayrs 379 C5
Dalrymple E Ayrs 367 E7
Dalscote Northants 157 B8
Dalserf S Lanarks 381 B7
Dalshannon N Lanarks 393 D6
Dalston Cumb 339 A6
Dalston London 112 F1
Dalswinton Dumf/Gal 358 E2
Dalton Cumb 314 E4
Dalton Dumf/Gal 346 B4
Dalton Lancs 277 C6
Dalton Northum 350 E5
Dalton Northum 351 B9
Dalton N Yorks 319 E7
Dalton N Yorks 330 E4
Dalton S Lanarks 381 A5
Dalton S Yorks 282 F3
Dalton W Yorks 280 A5
Dalton Gates N Yorks 331 E7
Dalton Magna S Yorks 270 A1
Dalton Parva S Yorks 282 F3
Dalton Piercy Hartlep'l 345 E5
Dalton-in-Furness Cumb 313 F5
Dalton-le-Dale Durham 344 B4
Dalton-on-Tees N Yorks 331 E7
Dalveallan H'land 434 E1
Dalveich Stirl 418 E4
Dalvina Lo. H'land 443 D8
Dalwhinnie H'land 425 D8
Dalwood Devon 38 F2
Dalwyne S Ayrs 355 C5
Dam Green Norfolk 187 A6
Dam Head W Yorks 292 E4
Dam Mill Staffs 197 C6
Dam of Quoiggs Perth/Kinr 410 B3
Dam Side Lancs 301 F7
Damask Green Herts 137 B9
Damerham Hants 42 C5
Damery Glos 103 D6
Damgate Norfolk 210 B4
Damgate Norfolk 235 E6
Damhead Moray 435 C5
Damhead Holdings Midloth 396 E2
Damnaglaur Dumf/Gal 400 F3
Damsbrook Derby 270 E1
Damside Scot Borders 383 C8
Dan Caerlan Rh Cyn Taff 99 F7
Danaway Kent 92 D4
Danbury Essex 114 A1
Danby N Yorks 333 E9
Danby Botton N Yorks 333 F8
Danby Wiske N Yorks 319 A5
Dancers Hill Herts 111 C6
Dancing Green Heref'd 129 C6
Dandaleith Moray 435 D7
Danderhall Midloth 396 E3
Dane Bank Gtr Man 279 E7
Dane Chantry Kent 74 B2
Dane End Herts 138 C2
Dane End Herts 161 E6
Dane Hills Leics C 200 C5
Dane in Shaw Ches 244 B3
Dane Street Kent 73 A8
Danebank Ches 267 C6
Danebridge Ches 244 A5
Danehill E Sussex 70 F3
Danemoor Green Norfolk 208 B5
Danesbury Herts 137 D8
Daneshill Hants 86 F3
Danesmoor Derby 247 B6
Daneway Glos 104 B3
Dangerous Corner Gtr Man 278 D2
Dangerous Corner Lancs 277 B7
Daniel's Water Kent 73 C6
Danna na Cloiche Arg/Bute 407 E6
Danskine E Loth 397 E8
Danthorpe ER Yorks 298 D3
Danygraig Torf 100 D4
Danzey Green Warwick 176 E5
Darby End Worcs 197 F8
Darby Green Hants 87 D6
Darbys Green Worcs 152 A4
Darby's Hill W Midlands 197 F8
Darcy Lever Gtr Man 278 C3
Dardy Powys 127 D5
Darenth Kent 91 B6
Darenthdale Kent 90 D5
Daresbury Halton 265 C6
Darfield S Yorks 282 D2
Dargate Kent 93 D8
Dargate Common Kent 93 D8
Darite Cornw'l 9 B8
Dark Hill Glos 129 F5
Darkland Moray 435 B7
Darland Medway 92 C2
Darlaston Staffs 221 A7
Darlaston W Midlands 197 D8
Darlaston Green W Midlands 197 D8
Darley N Yorks 305 D8
Darley Abbey Derby C 224 A2
Darley Bridge Derby 246 B3
Darley Dale Derby 246 B3
Darley Green Warwick 177 D6
Darley Head N Yorks 305 D7
Darley Hillside Derby 246 B3
Darley Moor Motor Racing Circuit Derby 246 F1
Darleyford Cornw'l 9 A8
Darleyhall Herts 137 C6
Darlingscott Warwick 155 D7
Darlington D'lington 331 D7
Darliston Shrops 219 B8
Darlton Notts 271 E7
Darmsden Suffolk 165 B6
Darn Hill Gtr Man 279 B5
Darnall S Yorks 269 B7
Darnaway Castle Moray 434 C4
Darnick Scot Borders 385 F7
Darowen Powys 191 C7
Darra Aberds 436 D4
Darracott Devon 32 C4
Darracott Devon 54 D4
Darras Hall Northum 352 B2
Darren Powys 127 D5
Darrington W Yorks 282 A3
Darrow Green Norfolk 209 F9
Darsham Suffolk 189 E6
Darshill Som'set 60 C4
Dartford Kent 91 B5
Dartford Crossing Kent 91 A6

**Dartington** Devon 14 C3
Dartington Cider Press Centre Devon 14 C3
Dartington Crystal Devon 34 C2
**Dartmeet** Devon 20 F3
**Dartmouth** Devon 15 E5
**Darton** S Yorks 281 B8
**Darvel** E Ayrs 380 E3
**Darvillshill** Bucks 109 C6
**Darwell Hole** E Sussex 51 C6
**Darwen** Blackb'n 290 F2
**Dassels** Herts 138 B3
**Datchet** Windsor 88 A1
**Datchet Common** Windsor 88 A2
**Datchworth** Herts 138 D1
**Datchworth Green** Herts 138 D1
**Daubhill** Gtr Man 278 C3
**Daugh of Kinermony** Moray 435 D7
**Dauntsey** Wilts 104 F4
**Dauntsey Green** Wilts 104 F4
**Dauntsey Lock** Wilts 104 F4
**Dava** Moray 434 E5
**Davenham** Ches 265 E8
**Davenport** Gtr Man 266 B4
**Davenport Green** Ches 266 E3
**Davenport Green** Gtr Man 266 B3
**Daventry** Northants 179 F6
**David Street** Kent 91 D7
**David's Well** Powys 171 C6
**Davidson's Mains** C/Edinb 395 C9
**Davidston** H'land 434 B2
**Davidstow** Cornw'l 17 C8
**Davington** Dumf/Gal 359 B8
**Davington** Kent 93 D7
**Daviot** Aberds 436 F4
**Daviot** H'land 434 E2
**Davis's Town** E Sussex 50 C3
**Davo Mains** Aberds 428 E4
**Davoch of Grange** Moray 436 C1
**Davyhulme** Gtr Man 278 E4
**Daw Cross** N Yorks 306 E2
**Daw End** W Midlands 198 C1
**Dawdon** Durham 344 B4
**Dawesgreen** Surrey 69 B6
**Dawley** Telford 196 B2
**Dawley Bank** Telford 196 B2
**Dawlish** Devon 22 E1
**Dawlish Warren** Devon 22 E1
**Dawn** Conwy 262 E7
**Dawney's Hill** Surrey 87 E9
**Daw's Green** Som'set 38 B1
**Daws Heath** Essex 114 E3
**Daw's House** Cornw'l 18 D3
**Dawshill** Worcs 153 B6
**Dawsmere** Lincs 229 B8
**Dayhills** Staffs 221 B9
**Dayhouse Bank** Worcs 176 C2
**Daylesford** Glos 132 B3
**Ddôl-Cownwy** Powys 216 E5
**Ddol** Wrex 241 E7
**Deacons Hill** London 111 C5
**Dead Maids** Wilts 61 B8
**Deadman's Cross** Beds 160 D2
**Deadman's Green** Staffs 222 A2
**Deadwater** Hants 67 D6
**Deadwater** Northum 361 C9
**Deaf Hill** Durham 344 D3
**Deal** Kent 75 A7
**Dean** Cumb 325 A6
**Dean** Dorset 42 C2
**Dean** Devon 14 C2
**Dean** Devon 55 B7
**Dean** Devon 55 B9
**Dean** Devon 55 B7
**Dean** Hants 65 E5
**Dean** Hants 45 C6
**Dean** Lancs 291 F5
**Dean** Oxon 133 C5
**Dean** Som'set 61 C5
**Dean Bank** Durham 344 E1
**Dean Court** Oxon 107 A6
**Dean Head** S Yorks 281 D7
**Dean Park** Renf 392 E2
**Dean Prior** Devon 14 C2
**Dean Row** Ches 266 C4
**Dean Street** Kent 72 A1
**Deanburnhaugh** Scot Borders 372 E4
**Deane** Gtr Man 278 C2
**Deane** Hants 65 A7
**Deanend** Dorset 42 C2
**Deanich Lodge** H'land 439 E7
**Deanland** Dorset 42 C2
**Deanlane End** W Sussex 46 D2
**Deans** W Loth 395 E5
**Deans Bottom** Kent 92 E4
**Deans Hill** Kent 92 D4
**Deanscales** Cumb 325 A6
**Deansgreen** Ches 265 B8
**Deanshanger** Northants 158 E3
**Deanston** Stirl 410 B2
**Dearham** Cumb 337 D4
**Dearnley** Gtr Man 279 A7
**Debach** Suffolk 166 B2
**Debdale** Gtr Man 279 E6
**Debden** Essex 112 C3
**Debden** Essex 162 F4
**Debden Green** Essex 112 C3
**Debden Green** Essex 139 A7
**Debenham** Suffolk 187 F8
**Deblin's Green** Worcs 153 C6
**Dechmont** W Loth 395 D5
**Deckham** Tyne/Wear 352 D4
**Deddington** Oxon 133 A8
**Dedham** Essex 142 A2
**Dedham Heath** Essex 142 A2
**Dedridge** W Loth 395 E6
**Dedworth** Windsor 87 A8
**Deebank** Aberds 428 C3
**Deecastle** Aberds 428 C1
**Deene** Northants 202 D4
**Deenethorpe** Northants 203 E5
Deep Sea World, North Queensferry Fife 411 D6
**Deepcar** S Yorks 281 E7
**Deepcut** Surrey 87 E8
**Deepdale** Beds 160 D4
**Deepdale** N Yorks 316 E3
**Deepdene** Surrey 69 B5
**Deeping Gate** Lincs 204 B1
**Deeping St. James** Lincs 204 B2
**Deeping St. Nicholas** Lincs 228 E4
**Deepweir** Monmouths 102 E1
**Deerhill** Moray 436 C1
**Deerhurst** Glos 130 B3
**Deerhurst Walton** Glos 130 B3
**Deerness** Orkney 453 C6
**Deer's Green** Essex 139 A5
**Deerton Street** Kent 93 D6
**Defford** Worcs 153 D8
**Defynnog** Powys 125 B7
**Deganwy** Conwy 262 D5
**Deighton** C/York 295 B6
**Deighton** N Yorks 332 F2
**Deighton** W Yorks 280 A5
**Deiniolen** Gwyn 237 B7
**Deishar** H'land 426 A4
**Delabole** Cornw'l 17 D6
**Delamere** Ches 265 F6
**Delfour** H'land 426 B3
**Delfrigs** Aberds 437 F6
**Dell Lodge** H'land 426 A5
**Dell Quay** W Sussex 46 F4
**Delliefure** H'land 435 E5
**Dellingham** Cambs 163 B5
**Delly End** Oxon 133 E6
**Delnabo** Moray 427 A6
**Delnadamph** Aberds 427 B7
**Delnamer** Angus 427 F6
**Delph** Gtr Man 279 C8
**Delves** Durham 343 B6
**Delvin End** Essex 163 E8
**Delvine** Perth/Kinr 420 C1
**Dembleby** Lincs 227 A7
**Demelza** Cornw'l 8 C2
**Den Bank** S Yorks 269 B6
**Denaby Main** S Yorks 282 E3
**Denbigh = Dinbych** Denbs 240 A1
**Denbury** Devon 14 B4
**Denby** Derby 247 E5
**Denby Bottles** Derby 247 E5
**Denby Common** Derby 247 E6
**Denby Dale** W Yorks 281 C6
**Denchworth** Oxon 106 D4
**Dendron** Cumb 300 A4
**Denend** Aberds 436 E3
**Deneside** Durham 344 B4
**Denford** Northants 181 C7
**Dengie** Essex 115 B6
**Denham** Bucks 110 E2
**Denham** Suffolk 188 D1
**Denham** Suffolk 185 F8
**Denham End** Suffolk 185 F8
**Denham Green** Bucks 110 E2
**Denham Street** Suffolk 187 D8
**Denhead** Aberds 437 C6
**Denhead** Fife 420 F4
**Denhead of Arbilot** Angus 421 C5
**Denhead of Gray** Dundee C 420 D3
**Denholm** Scot Borders 373 D8
**Denholme** W Yorks 292 D3
**Denholme Clough** W Yorks 292 D3
**Denholme Gate** W Yorks 292 D3
**Denio** Gwyn 213 A7
**Denmead** Hants 45 D8
**Denmore** Aberd C 429 A6
**Denmoss** Aberds 436 D3
**Dennel Hill** Glos 102 C3
**Dennington** Suffolk 188 E3
**Dennistoun** Glasg C 392 E4
**Denny** Falk 410 D3
**Denny Bottom** Kent 71 D6
**Denny End** Cambs 184 E2
**Dennyloanhead** Falk 393 C8
**Dennystown** W Dunb 391 C7
**Denshaw** Gtr Man 279 B8
**Denside** Aberds 429 C5
**Densole** Kent 74 C4
**Denston** Suffolk 163 B8
**Denstone** Staffs 245 F7
**Denstroude** Kent 94 D2
**Dent** Cumb 315 C8
**Dent Bank** Durham 329 A8
**Denton** Cambs 204 F1
**Denton** D'lington 331 C6
**Denton** E Sussex 50 F2
**Denton** Gtr Man 279 E7
**Denton** Kent 74 B4
**Denton** Kent 91 B8
**Denton** Lincs 226 B4
**Denton** Norfolk 210 F1
**Denton** Northants 158 A4
**Denton** N Yorks 305 F6
**Denton** Oxon 108 B1
**Denton Burn** Tyne/Wear 352 C2
**Denton Holme** Cumb 348 E1
**Denton's Green** Mersey 277 E6
**Denver** Norfolk 206 C3
**Denver Sluice** Norfolk 206 C2
**Denvilles** Hants 46 E2
**Denwick** Northum 377 E6
**Deopham** Norfolk 208 C5
**Deopham Green** Norfolk 208 D4
**Depden** Suffolk 163 A8
**Depden Green** Suffolk 163 A8
**Deppers Hill** Warwick 156 A2
**Deptford** London 90 A2
**Deptford** Wilts 62 D5
**Derby** Derby C 224 A2
**Derby** Devon 55 E6
**Derbyhaven** I/Man 336 E2
**Derbyshire Hill** Mersey 277 E7
**Dereham** Norfolk 208 A3
**Dergoals** Dumf/Gal 400 D4
**Deri** Caerph 100 B2
**Derndale** Heref'd 151 C7
**Derriford** Plym'th 11 D5
**Derril** Devon 33 F6
**Derringstone** Kent 74 B4
**Derrington** Staffs 221 D7
**Derriton** Devon 33 F6
**Derry** Stirl 418 E4
**Derry Hill** Wilts 82 B4
**Derry Lodge** Aberds 427 C5
**Derrydaroch** Stirl 417 E8
**Derryguaig** Arg/Bute 415 D7
**Derrythorpe** N Lincs 284 C3
**Dersingham** Norfolk 231 B5
**Dervaig** Arg/Bute 415 B7
**Derwen** Bridg 99 F5
**Derwen** Denbs 240 D2
**Derwenlas** Powys 191 D5
**Derwent Haugh** Tyne/Wear 352 D3
**Derwydd** Carms 123 D8
**Desborough** Northants 180 B4
**Desford** Leics 200 C3
**Deskryshiel** Aberds 428 A1
**Detchant** Northum 388 E3
**Dethick** Derby 246 C4
**Detling** Kent 92 E2
**Deuchar** Angus 420 A4
**Deuddwr** Powys 218 E1
**Devauden** Monmouths 102 C1
**Devil's Bridge = Pontarfynach** Ceredig'n 169 C7
**Devitts Green** Warwick 199 E6
**Devizes** Wilts 82 D5
**Devol** Invercl 391 D6
Devon & Exeter Racecourse Devon 21 D7
**Devonport** Plym'th 10 D5
**Devonside** Clack 410 C4
**Devoran** Cornw'l 4 C3
**Dewar** Scot Borders 384 C3
**Dewlish** Dorset 26 A2
**Dewsbury** W Yorks 293 F6
**Dewsbury Moor** W Yorks 293 F6
**Dhoon** I/Man 336 C4
**Dhoor** I/Man 336 B4
**Dhowin** I/Man 336 A4
**Dial Green** W Sussex 67 F8
**Dial Post** W Sussex 48 C3
**Diamond End** Herts 137 C6
**Dibberford** Dorset 39 F7
**Dibden** Hants 44 E3
**Dibden Purlieu** Hants 44 E3
**Dicken's Heath** W Midlands 176 C5
**Dickleburgh** Norfolk 187 B8
**Dickleburgh Moor** Norfolk 187 B8
**Dickon Hills** Lincs 252 C4
**Didbrook** Glos 131 A7
**Didcot** Oxon 107 D7
**Diddington** Cambs 182 E3
**Diddlebury** Shrops 173 A8
**Diddywell** Devon 54 F4
**Didley** Heref'd 128 A3
**Didling** W Sussex 46 C4
**Didmarton** Glos 103 E8
**Didsbury** Gtr Man 266 A3
**Didworthy** Devon 14 C1
**Diebidale** H'land 440 E1
**Digby** Lincs 250 D4
**Digg** H'land 430 B4
Diggerland, Cullompton Devon 37 E5
Diggerland, Langley Park Durham 343 B8
**Diggle** Gtr Man 280 C2
**Digmoor** Lancs 277 D6
**Digswell** Herts 137 D9
**Digswell Park** Herts 137 D8
**Digswell Water** Herts 137 D9
**Dihewyd** Ceredig'n 146 A2
**Dilham** Norfolk 234 C3
**Dilhorne** Staffs 245 F5
**Dill Hall** Lancs 290 E3
**Dillarburn** S Lanarks 381 D8
**Dillington** Cambs 182 E2
**Dillington** Som'set 38 C5
**Dilston** Northum 351 D6
**Dilton Marsh** Wilts 62 A1
**Dilwyn** Heref'd 151 B6
**Dimmer** Som'set 60 E4
**Dimple** Derby 246 B3
**Dimple** Gtr Man 278 A3
**Dimsdale** Staffs 244 E2
**Dimson** Cornw'l 10 A4
**Dinas** Carms 122 A1
**Dinas** Gwyn 212 A5
**Dinas** Rh Cyn Taff 99 D7
**Dinas Cross** Pembs 119 B8
**Dinas Dinlle** Gwyn 236 C4
**Dinas Mawddwy** Gwyn 216 F2
**Dinas Powys** V/Glam 78 B3
**Dinbych = Denbigh** Denbs 240 A1
**Dinbych-y-Pysgod = Tenby** Pembs 117 D8
**Dinckley** Lancs 290 C2
**Dinder** Som'set 60 C3
**Dinedor** Heref'd 151 E8
**Dinedor Cross** Heref'd 151 E8
**Dines Green** Worcs 153 A6
**Dingestow** Monmouths 128 E3
**Dinghurst** N Som'set 79 E8
**Dingle** Mersey 264 B2
**Dingleden** Kent 72 E3
**Dingleton** Scot Borders 385 F7
**Dingley** Northants 202 F1
**Dingwall** H'land 433 C7
**Dinlabyre** Scot Borders 361 D7
**Dinmael** Conwy 239 F8
**Dinnet** Aberds 428 C1
**Dinnington** Som'set 39 D6
**Dinnington** S Yorks 270 B2
**Dinnington** Tyne/Wear 352 B3
**Dinorwig** Gwyn 237 B7
**Dinsdale** D'lington 332 D1
**Dinton** Wilts 62 E5
**Dinwoodie Mains** Dumf/Gal 359 D6
**Dinworthy** Devon 33 C6
**Dipford** Som'set 38 B2
**Dipley** Hants 86 E4
**Dippen** N Ayrs 405 D6
**Dippenhall** Surrey 67 B6
**Dippertown** Devon 19 D5
**Dipple** Moray 435 C8
**Dipple** S Ayrs 354 B3
**Diptford** Devon 14 D2
**Dipton** Durham 352 F2
**Diptonmill** Northum 351 D5
**Dirdhu** H'land 435 F5
**Direcleit** W Isles 449 C5
**Dirleton** E Loth 397 B7
**Dirt Pot** Northum 341 B8
**Discoed** Powys 172 F3
Discovery Museum, Newcastle Tyne/Wear 352 D3
Discovery Point Dundee C 420 E4
**Diseworth** Leics 224 D4
**Dishes** Orkney 454 D4
**Dishforth** N Yorks 306 A4
**Disley** Ches 267 C6
**Diss** Norfolk 187 B7
**Disserth** Powys 149 A5
**Distington** Cumb 324 B5
**Ditchampton** Wilts 63 E6
**Ditcheat** Som'set 60 D4
**Ditchfield** Bucks 109 D6
**Ditchingham** Norfolk 210 E2
**Ditchling** E Sussex 49 C6
**Ditherington** Shrops 219 F7
**Ditteridge** Wilts 81 C8
**Dittisham** Devon 15 E5
**Ditton** Halton 264 B4
**Ditton** Kent 92 E1
**Ditton Green** Cambs 163 A6
**Ditton Priors** Shrops 195 F8
**Dittons** E Sussex 50 F5
**Divach** H'land 433 F6
**Dixton** Glos 131 A5
**Dixton** Monmouths 128 E4
**Dizzard** Cornw'l 17 A8
**Dobcross** Gtr Man 280 C1
**Dobpark** Notts 247 E8
**Dobson's Bridge** Shrops 219 B6
**Dobwalls** Cornw'l 9 B7
**Doc Penfro = Pembroke Dock** Pembs 117 D5
**Doccombe** Devon 21 C5
**Dochfour Ho.** H'land 433 E8
**Dochgarroch** H'land 433 D8
**Dockenfield** Surrey 67 C6
**Docker** Lancs 314 F5
**Docking** Norfolk 255 E5
**Docklow** Heref'd 151 A9
**Dockray** Cumb 326 B4
**Dockray** Cumb 338 B4
**Dockroyd** W Yorks 292 C2
**Dodbrooke** Devon 13 D5
**Dodburn** Scot Borders 373 F6
**Doddinghurst** Essex 113 C6
**Doddington** Cambs 205 E6
**Doddington** Kent 93 E5
**Doddington** Lincs 272 E3
**Doddington** Northum 376 A1
**Doddington** Shrops 174 C2
**Doddiscombsleigh** Devon 21 C7
**Doddshill** Norfolk 231 C5
**Doddycross** Cornw'l 10 C2
**Dodford** Northants 179 F7
**Dodford** Worcs 175 D8
**Dodington** S Glos 103 F6
**Dodington** Som'set 58 C3
**Dodington Ash** S Glos 81 A7
**Dodleston** Ches 241 B8
**Dodmarsh** Heref'd 152 D1
**Dods Leigh** Staffs 222 B2
**Dodworth** S Yorks 281 C8
**Dodworth Bottom** S Yorks 281 D8
**Dodworth Green** S Yorks 281 D8
**Doe Bank** W Midlands 198 D3
**Doe Green** Warrington 265 B6
**Doe Lea** Derby 247 A7
**Doffcocker** Gtr Man 278 B2
**Dog & Gun** Mersey 276 E5
**Dog Hill** Gtr Man 279 C8
**Dog Village** Devon 22 A1
**Dogdyke** Lincs 251 C7
**Dogmersfield** Hants 67 A5
**Dogridge** Wilts 105 E6
**Dogsthorpe** Peterbro 204 C2
**Doirlinn** H'land 416 B1
**Dolanog** Powys 192 A5
**Dolarddyn** Powys 193 B7
**Dolau** Powys 171 E7
**Dolau** Rh Cyn Taff 99 F7
**Dolau-gwyrddon** Ceredig'n 146 C4
**Dolbenmaen** Gwyn 237 F6
**Dole** Ceredig'n 169 A5
**Dolemeads** Bath/NE Som'set 81 D7
**Doley** Staffs 220 C4
**Dolfach** Powys 192 C2
**Dol-for** Powys 191 B7
**Dolfor** Powys 193 F6
**Dolgadfan** Powys 191 C8
**Dolgarrog** Conwy 260 F5
**Dolgellau** Gwyn 215 E6
**Dolgoch** Gwyn 190 C4
**Dolgran** Carms 145 F8
**Dolhelfa** Powys 170 D3
**Dolhendre** Gwyn 216 B2
**Doll** H'land 441 C5
**Dollar** Clack 410 C4
**Dolley Green** Powys 172 E3
**Dollis Hill** London 111 E6
**Dollwen** Ceredig'n 169 B6
**Dolphin** Flints 263 E5
**Dolphingstone** E Loth 396 D4
**Dolphinholme** Lancs 302 E2
**Dolphinton** S Lanarks 383 C7
**Dol-rhyd** Denbs 215 E6
**Dolserau** Gwyn 215 E7
**Dolton** Devon 34 D4
**Dolwen** Conwy 262 E7
**Dolwen** Powys 192 B3
**Dolwyd** Conwy 262 D6
**Dolwyddelan** Conwy 238 D2
**Dol-y-Bont** Ceredig'n 190 F3
**Dol-y-cannau** Powys 150 C2
**Dolydd** Gwyn 237 C5
**Dolyfelin** Powys 172 D2
**Dolyhir** Powys 150 A2
**Dolypandy** Ceredig'n 169 C6
**Dolywern** Wrex 218 A1
**Domewood** Surrey 70 C1
**Domgay** Powys 218 E2
**Dominion Estate** Leics C 200 C4
**Donaldson's Lodge** Northum 387 D7
**Doncaster** S Yorks 283 D5
Doncaster Racecourse S Yorks 283 D6
**Dones Green** Ches 265 D7
**Donhead St. Andrew** Wilts 41 B8
**Donhead St. Mary** Wilts 41 B8
**Doniford** Som'set 58 C1
**Donington** Lincs 228 A4
**Donington** Shrops 196 C5
**Donington Eaudike** Lincs 228 A4
**Donington le Heath** Leics 200 A2
Donington Park Motor Racing Circuit Leics 224 C3
**Donington South Ing** Lincs 228 B4
**Donisthorpe** Leics 223 F8
**Donkey Street** Kent 74 E2
**Donkey Town** Surrey 87 D8
**Donna Nook** Lincs 287 E7
**Donnington** Glos 132 B2
**Donnington** Shrops 195 B7
**Donnington** Telford 220 F4
**Donnington** W Berks 85 C6
**Donnington** W Sussex 47 F5
**Donnington Holt** W Berks 85 C6
**Donnington Wood** Telford 196 A3
**Donnington-on-Bain** Lincs 274 C1
**Donwell** Tyne/Wear 352 E4
**Donyatt** Som'set 38 D4
**Doomsday Green** W Sussex 69 E5
**Doonfoot** S Ayrs 367 D6
**Dora's Green** Hants 67 B6
**Dorback Lodge** H'land 427 A5
**Dorcan** Swindon 105 F8
**Dorchester** Dorset 25 B8
**Dorchester** Oxon 107 D8
Dorchester Abbey, Wallingford Oxon 107 D8
**Dordon** Warwick 199 C6
**Dore** S Yorks 269 C6
**Dores** H'land 433 E7
**Dorking** Surrey 69 B5
**Dorking Tye** Suffolk 164 E3
**Dorley's Corner** Suffolk 189 E5
**Dormans Park** Surrey 70 C2
**Dormansland** Surrey 70 C3
**Dormanston** Redcar/Clevel'd 333 B6
**Dormer's Wells** London 110 F4
**Dormington** Heref'd 152 D1
**Dormston** Worcs 154 A2
**Dornal** S Ayrs 400 B4
**Dorney** Bucks 87 A8
**Dorney Reach** Bucks 87 A8
**Dornie** H'land 431 F8
**Dornoch** H'land 440 E4
**Dornock** Dumf/Gal 347 C6
**Dorrery** H'land 444 C4
**Dorridge** W Midlands 177 C6
**Dorrington** Lincs 250 D4
**Dorrington** Shrops 195 C5
**Dorsington** Warwick 155 C5
**Dorstone** Heref'd 150 D4
**Dorton** Bucks 134 E4
**Dorusduain** H'land 432 F1
**Doseley** Telford 196 B2
**Dosmuckeran** H'land 432 B4
**Dosthill** Staffs 199 C5
**Dothan** Angl 258 E4
**Dothill** Telford 196 A1
**Dotland** Northum 350 E5
**Dottery** Dorset 24 A4
**Doublebois** Cornw'l 9 B6
**Dougarie** N Ayrs 404 C4
**Doughton** Glos 104 D2
**Douglas & Angus** Dundee C 420 D4
**Douglas** I/Man 336 D3
**Douglas** S Lanarks 370 A1
**Douglas Water** S Lanarks 382 E2
**Douglas West** S Lanarks 369 A8
**Douglastown** Angus 420 C4
**Douievale** Dumf/Gal 346 A2
**Doularg** S Ayrs 354 D4
**Doulting** Som'set 60 C4
**Dounby** Orkney 452 A3
**Doune** H'land 426 B3
**Doune** H'land 439 C8
**Doune** Stirl 410 B2
**Doune Park** Aberds 436 B4
**Douneside** Aberds 428 B1
**Dounie** Arg/Bute 407 C7
**Dounie** H'land 440 D2
**Dounie** H'land 440 E3
**Dounreay** H'land 444 B3
**Doura** N Ayrs 379 D6
**Dousland** Devon 11 B6
**Dovaston** Shrops 218 D3
Dove Cottage and Wordsworth Museum Cumb 326 E3
**Dove Green** Notts 247 D7
**Dove Holes** Derby 267 D8
**Dovecot** Mersey 264 A3
**Dovecothall** E Renf 380 A2
**Dovenby** Cumb 337 E4
**Dovendale** Lincs 274 C3
**Dover** Gtr Man 277 D9
**Dover** Kent 75 C6
Dover Castle Kent 75 C6
**Dovercourt** Essex 143 A6
**Doverdale** Worcs 175 E7
**Doverhay** Som'set 56 B4
**Doveridge** Derby 222 B4
**Doversgreen** Surrey 69 B7
**Dowally** Perth/Kinr 419 C8
**Dowanhill** Glasg C 392 E3
**Dowbridge** Lancs 289 D5
**Dowdeswell** Glos 131 D6
**Dowlais** Merth Tyd 126 F2
**Dowland** Devon 34 D4
**Dowlesgreen** Wokingham 87 C6
**Dowlish Ford** Som'set 38 D5
**Dowlish Wake** Som'set 39 D5
**Down Ampney** Glos 105 C6
**Down End** Som'set 59 C6
**Down Hall** Cumb 347 F7
**Down Hatherley** Glos 130 C3
**Down St. Mary** Devon 35 F7
**Down Street** E Sussex 50 B1
**Down Thomas** Devon 11 E6
**Downall Green** Mersey 277 D8
**Downan** Moray 435 E6
**Downan** S Ayrs 400 A2
**Downcraig Ferry** N Ayrs 378 A3
**Downderry** Cornw'l 8 E2
**Downderry** Cornw'l 10 E2
**Downe** London 90 D3
**Downend** Glos 104 C1
**Downend** I/Wight 30 C2
**Downend** S Glos 80 A4
**Downend** W Berks 85 A6
**Downfield** Cambs 184 D5
**Downfield** Dundee C 420 D3
**Downgate** Cornw'l 9 A8
**Downgate** Cornw'l 10 A3
**Downham** Essex 114 C1
**Downham** Lancs 290 B4
**Downham** London 90 B2
**Downham Green** Lancs 290 B4
**Downham Hythe** Cambs 184 B2
**Downham Market** Norfolk 206 C3
**Downhead** Som'set 40 A1
**Downhead** Som'set 61 B5
**Downhead Park** M/Keynes 158 D5
**Downhill** Perth/Kinr 419 D8
**Downhill** Tyne/Wear 353 E6
**Downholland Cross** Lancs 276 C4
**Downholme** N Yorks 317 A8
**Downies** Aberds 429 C6
**Downing** Flints 263 D5
**Downington** Glos 105 C9
**Downley** Bucks 109 C7
**Downs** V/Glam 78 B2
**Downside** Som'set 60 C4
**Downside** Som'set 60 A4
**Downside** Surrey 88 E4
**Downton** Hants 28 B5
**Downton** Powys 172 F2
**Downton** Wilts 43 B6
**Downton on the Rock** Heref'd 173 D6
**Dowsby** Lincs 228 C2
**Dowsdale** Lincs 204 A4
**Dowslands** Som'set 38 B2
**Doxey** Staffs 221 D8
**Doxford** Northum 377 C5
**Doxford Park** Tyne/Wear 344 A3
**Doynton** S Glos 81 B6
**Drabblegate** Norfolk 233 C9
**Draethen** Caerph 100 E4
**Draffan** S Lanarks 381 C7
**Dragley Beck** Cumb 313 E6
**Dragonby** N Lincs 284 B5
**Dragons Green** W Sussex 48 B2
**Drakehouse** S Yorks 269 C8
**Drakelow** Worcs 175 B6
**Drakemyre** Aberds 437 E6
**Drakemyre** N Ayrs 379 B5
**Drakes Broughton** Worcs 153 C8
**Drakes Cross** Worcs 176 C4
**Drakestone Green** Suffolk 164 C4
**Drakewalls** Cornw'l 10 A4
**Draughton** Northants 180 C3
**Draughton** N Yorks 304 E4
**Drax** N Yorks 295 E7
**Draycot** Oxon 108 A2
**Draycot Cerne** Wilts 82 A3
**Draycot Foliat** Swindon 83 A8
**Draycote** Warwick 178 D3
**Draycott** Derby 224 B3
**Draycott** Glos 155 E6
**Draycott** Shrops 196 E5
**Draycott** Som'set 39 B8
**Draycott** Som'set 60 A1
**Draycott** Worcs 153 C7
**Draycott Cross** Staffs 245 F5
**Draycott in the Clay** Staffs 223 C5
**Draycott in the Moors** Staffs 245 F5
**Drayford** Devon 35 D8
**Draynes** Cornw'l 9 B7
**Drayton** Leics 202 E2
**Drayton** Lincs 228 A4
**Drayton** Norfolk 233 F8
**Drayton** Oxon 156 D3
**Drayton** Oxon 107 D6
**Drayton** Portsm'th 45 E8
**Drayton** Som'set 39 B6
**Drayton** Worcs 175 C8
**Drayton Bassett** Staffs 198 C4
**Drayton Beauchamp** Herts 136 E2
Drayton Manor Park, Tamworth Staffs 198 C4
**Drayton Parslow** Bucks 135 B7
**Drayton St. Leonard** Oxon 108 C1
**Draytons** Som'set 39 C6
Dreamland Theme Park, Margate Kent 95 B7
**Drebley** N Yorks 305 D5
**Dreemskerry** I/Man 336 B4
**Dreenhill** Pembs 117 A5
**Dre-fach** Carms 124 D2
**Drefach** Carms 145 E7
**Drefach** Carms 123 E6
**Dre-fach** Ceredig'n 146 C3
**Drefâch** Ceredig'n 146 C3
**Drefelin** Carms 145 E7
**Dreggie** H'land 434 F5
**Dreghorn** N Ayrs 379 E7
**Dreghorn Mains** C/Edinb 396 E1
**Drellingonre** Kent 74 C4
**Drem** E Loth 397 C7
**Dresden** Stoke 244 F4
**Dreumasdal** W Isles 447 E2
**Drewsteington** Devon 20 B4
**Drewston** Devon 20 C4
**Driby** Lincs 274 E4
**Driby Top** Lincs 275 E5
**Driffield** ER Yorks 310 D2
**Driffield** Glos 105 C6
**Drigg** Cumb 312 A2
**Drighlington** W Yorks 293 E6
**Drimnin** H'land 415 B8
**Drimnin Ho** H'land 415 B8
**Drimpton** Dorset 39 E6
**Drimsynie** Arg/Bute 408 B4
**Dringhoe** ER Yorks 310 D5
**Dringhouses** C/York 307 F8
**Drinisiadar** W Isles 449 C5
**Drinkers End** Worcs 130 A2
**Drinkfield** D'lington 331 C7
**Drinkstone** Suffolk 186 F4
**Drinkstone Green** Suffolk 186 F4
**Drishaig** Arg/Bute 408 A4
**Drissaig** Arg/Bute 416 F4
**Drive End** Dorset 40 E1
**Driver's Heath** Herts 137 D8
**Drochedlie** Aberds 436 B2
**Drochil** Scot Borders 383 D8
**Drointon** Staffs 222 C2
**Droitwich Spa** Worcs 175 F7
**Droman** H'land 442 C3
**Dromore** Dumf/Gal 401 C7
**Dron** Perth/Kinr 420 F1
**Dronfield** Derby 269 D7
**Dronfield Woodhouse** Derby 269 D6
**Drongan** E Ayrs 367 D8
**Dronley** Angus 420 D3
**Droop** Dorset 41 E5
**Drope** V/Glam 78 A2
**Dropmore** Bucks 109 E8
**Dropping Well** S Yorks 282 F1
**Droughduil** Dumf/Gal 400 D3
**Droxford** Hants 45 C7
**Droylsden** Gtr Man 279 E6
**Drub** W Yorks 293 E5
**Druggers End** Worcs 153 E5
**Druid** Denbs 240 F1
**Druidston** Pembs 116 A3
**Druim** H'land 434 C4
**Druimarbin** H'land 424 E2
**Druimavuic** Arg/Bute 417 C5
**Druimdrishaig** Arg/Bute 407 E7
**Druimindarroch** H'land 423 D6
**Druimkinnerras** H'land 433 E6
**Druimnacroish** Arg/Bute 415 C7
**Druimsornaig** Arg/Bute 416 D2
**Druimyeon More** Arg/Bute 404 A2
**Drum** Arg/Bute 408 E2
**Drum** Perth/Kinr 411 B5
**Drumardoch** Stirl 410 A1
**Drumbeg** H'land 442 E3
**Drumblade** Aberds 436 D2
**Drumblair** Aberds 436 D3
**Drumbuie** Dumf/Gal 356 F3

Drumbuie H'land 431 E7
Drumburgh Cumb 347 E7
Drumburn Dumf/Gal 402 C3
Drumchapel Glasg C 392 D2
Drumchardine H'land 433 D7
Drumchork H'land 438 E2
Drumclog S Lanarks 380 E4
Drumdelgie Aberds 436 D1
Drumderfit H'land 434 C1
Drumdollo Aberds 436 E3
Drumeldrie Fife 412 B2
Drumelzier Scot Borders 383 F7
Drumfearn H'land 423 A6
Drumgask H'land 425 C8
Drumgelloch N Lanarks 393 E7
Drumgley Angus 420 B4
Drumgreen Angus 428 E1
Drumguish H'land 426 C2
Drumhead Aberds 429 A6
Drumin Moray 435 E6
Drumindorsair H'land 433 D6
Drumlasie Aberds 428 B3
Drumlean Stirl 409 B7
Drumlemble Arg/Bute 404 E2
Drumliah H'land 440 D3
Drumligair Aberds 429 A6
Drumlithie Aberds 429 D4
Drumloist Stirl 410 B1
Drummick Perth/Kinr 419 E7
Drummoddie Dumf/Gal 401 E5
Drummond H'land 433 B8
Drummore Dumf/Gal 400 F3
Drummuir Moray 435 D8
Drummuir Castle Moray 435 D8
Drumnadrochit H'land 433 F7
Drumnagorrach Moray 436 C2
Drumness Perth/Kinr 419 F6
Drumoak Aberds 429 C4
Drumore Arg/Bute 404 D3
Drumoyne Glasg C 392 E2
Drumpark Dumf/Gal 402 A2
Drumpellier N Lanarks 393 E6
Drumphail Dumf/Gal 400 C4
Drumrash Dumf/Gal 401 B8
Drumrunie H'land 439 C5
Drumry W Dunb 392 D2
Drums Aberds 437 F6
Drumsallie H'land 424 E1
Drumsmittal H'land 434 D1
Drumstinchall Dumf/Gal 402 D2
Drumsturdy Angus 421 D4
Drumtochty Castle Aberds 428 E3
Drumtroddan Dumf/Gal 401 E5
Drumuie H'land 430 D4
Drumuillie H'land 434 F4
Drumvaich Stirl 410 B1
Drumwalt Dumf/Gal 400 D5
Drumwhindle Aberds 437 E6
Drunkendub Angus 421 C6
Druridge Northum 365 C7
Drury Flints 241 B6
Drury Square Norfolk 232 F3
Drusillas Park, Polegate E Sussex 50 F3
Dry Doddington Lincs 249 E8
Dry Drayton Cambs 183 F7
Dry Sandford Oxon 107 B6
Dry Street Essex 113 E8
Drybeck Cumb 328 C3
Drybridge Moray 436 B1
Drybridge S Ayrs 379 E7
Drybrook Glos 129 D6
Drybrook Heref'd 129 D5
Dryburgh Scot Borders 374 A1
Dryhill Kent 90 F4
Dryhope Scot Borders 372 C2
Drylaw C/Edinb 396 C1
Drym Cornw'l 3 D8
Drymen Stirl 409 D7
Drymuir Aberds 437 D6
Drynachan Lodge H'land 434 E3
Drynham Wilts 82 E2
Drynie Park H'land 433 C7
Drynoch H'land 430 E4
Dryslwyn Carms 123 C7
Dryton Shrops 195 B7
Drywells Aberds 436 C3
Duag Bridge H'land 439 D7
Duartbeg H'land 442 E3
Duartmore Bridge H'land 442 E3
Dubford Aberds 437 B5
Dubhchladach Arg/Bute 407 F8
Dublin Suffolk 187 E8
Dubton Angus 421 B5
Dubwath Cumb 338 E2
Duchally H'land 439 B7
Duchrae Dumf/Gal 401 A8
Duck Corner Suffolk 166 D5
Duck End Beds 159 D9
Duck End Beds 159 B7
Duck End Bucks 135 B6
Duck End Cambs 182 F4
Duck End Essex 140 B2
Duck End Essex 140 A2
Duck Street Hants 64 B3
Duckend Green Essex 140 C3
Duckington Ches 242 D2
Ducklington Oxon 133 F6
Duckmanton Derby 269 E8
Duck's Cross Beds 160 A2
Ducks Island London 111 C6
Duckworth Hall Lancs 290 E3
Dudbridge Glos 103 B8
Duddenhoe End Essex 162 E2
Duddingston C/Edinb 396 D2
Duddington Northants 203 C5
Duddlestone Som'set 38 B2
Duddleswell E Sussex 70 F4
Duddo Northum 387 D8
Duddon Ches 242 B3
Duddon Bridge Cumb 312 C4
Duddon Heath Ches 242 A3
Dudleston Shrops 218 A3
Dudleston Grove Shrops 218 A4
Dudleston Heath Shrops 218 A4
Dudley Tyne/Wear 352 B4
Dudley W Midlands 197 D8
Dudley Hill W Yorks 293 D5
Dudley Port W Midlands 197 E8
Dudley Wood W Midlands 197 F7
Dudley Zoological Gardens W Midlands 197 E7
Dudlow's Green Warrington 265 C7
Dudsbury Dorset 27 A8
Dudswell Herts 136 F3
Dudwells Pembs 120 C2
Duffield Derby 246 F4
Duffryn Neath P Talb 98 C3
Duffryn Newp 101 E5
Duffryn Shrops 172 B2
Dufftown Moray 435 E8
Duffus Moray 435 B6
Dufton Cumb 328 A3
Duggleby N Yorks 309 B6
Duich Arg/Bute 403 A3
Duiletter Arg/Bute 417 D6
Duinish Perth/Kinr 425 F8
Duirinish H'land 431 E7
Duisdalebeg H'land 423 A6
Duisdalemore H'land 423 A7
Duisky H'land 424 E2
Duke End Warwick 199 F5
Duke Street Suffolk 165 D6
Dukesfield Northum 351 E5
Dukestown Bl Gwent 126 E3
Dukinfield Gtr Man 279 E7
Dulas Angl 259 B6
Dulcote Som'set 60 C3
Dulford Devon 37 F6
Dull Perth/Kinr 419 C6
Dullatur N Lanarks 393 C6
Dullingham Cambs 163 A5
Dullingham Ley Cambs 163 A5
Dulnain Bridge H'land 434 F4
Duloe Beds 182 F3
Duloe Cornw'l 9 D7
Dulsie H'land 434 D4
Dulverton Som'set 57 F5
Dulwich Village London 89 B8
Dumbarton W Dunb 391 C7
Dumbleton Glos 154 E3
Dumbreck Glasg C 392 E3
Dumcrieff Dumf/Gal 359 B6
Dumfries Dumf/Gal 402 B3
Dumgoyne Stirl 409 D8
Dummer Hants 66 B1
Dumpford W Sussex 46 B4
Dumpling Green Norfolk 208 A4
Dumplington Gtr Man 278 E4
Dumpton Kent 95 C7
Dun Angus 421 B6
Dun Charlabhaigh W Isles 450 C4
Dunach Arg/Bute 416 E3
Dunadd Arg/Bute 407 C8
Dunain Ho. H'land 433 D8
Dunalastair Perth/Kinr 418 B5
Dunan H'land 431 F5
Dunans Arg/Bute 408 C3
Dunans Arg/Bute 407 C8
Dunball Som'set 59 C6
Dunbar E Loth 398 C3
Dunbeath H'land 445 F5
Dunbeg Arg/Bute 416 D3
Dunblane Stirl 410 B2
Dunbog Fife 420 F2
Dunbridge Hants 44 A1
Dunburgh Norfolk 210 E4
Duncan Down Kent 94 C2
Duncanclett Shetl'd 455 C2
Duncanston Aberds 436 F2
Duncanston H'land 433 C7
Dunchurch Warwick 178 D4
Duncote Northants 157 B8
Duncow Dumf/Gal 358 F3
Duncraggan Stirl 409 B8
Duncrievie Perth/Kinr 411 B6
Duncroisk Stirl 418 D3
Duncton W Sussex 47 C7
Dundas Ho. Orkney 453 E5
Dundee Dundee C 420 D4
Dundee Airport Dundee C 420 E3
Dundeugh Dumf/Gal 356 E4
Dundon Som'set 60 E1
Dundon Hayes Som'set 60 E1
Dundonald S Ayrs 379 F7
Dundonald Camp N Ayrs 379 F6
Dundonnell H'land 439 E4
Dundonnell Hotel H'land 439 E4
Dundonnell House H'land 439 E5
Dundraw Cumb 338 B3
Dundreggan H'land 425 A5
Dundreggan Lodge H'land 425 A5
Dundrennan Dumf/Gal 402 E1
Dundridge Hants 45 C6
Dundry N Som'set 80 C3
Dundurn Perth/Kinr 418 E5
Dundyvan N Lanarks 393 F6
Dunecht Aberds 428 B4
Dunfermline Fife 411 D5
Dunfield Glos 105 C7
Dungate Kent 93 E5
Dunge Wilts 82 F2
Dungeness Kent 53 C6
Dungworth S Yorks 269 B5
Dunham Massey Gtr Man 266 B1
Dunham on Trent Notts 271 E8
Dunham Town Gtr Man 266 B1
Dunham Woodhouses Gtr Man 266 B1
Dunham-on-the-Hill Ches 264 E4
Dunhampton Worcs 175 E7
Dunholme Lincs 273 D5
Dunino Fife 412 A3
Dunipace Falk 410 D3
Dunira Perth/Kinr 419 E5
Dunkeld Perth/Kinr 419 C8
Dunkerton Bath/NE Som'set 81 E6
Dunkeswell Devon 37 E7
Dunkeswick W Yorks 306 F3
Dunkirk Cambs 184 A3
Dunkirk Ches 264 E2
Dunkirk Kent 93 E8
Dunkirk Norfolk 233 C9
Dunkirk S Glos 103 E7
Dunkirk Wilts 82 D4
Dunk's Green Kent 71 A7
Dunlappie Angus 428 F2
Dunley Hants 85 F6
Dunley Worcs 175 E5
Dunlichity Lodge H'land 434 E1
Dunlop E Ayrs 379 C8
Dunmaglass Lodge H'land 433 F7
Dunmere Cornw'l 8 B3
Dunmore Arg/Bute 407 F7
Dunmore Falk 410 D3
Dunmore H'land 433 D7
Dunn Street Kent 73 B6
Dunn Street Kent 92 D2
Dunnet H'land 445 A6
Dunnichen Angus 421 C5
Dunninald Angus 421 B7
Dunning Perth/Kinr 419 F8
Dunnington C/York 308 E2
Dunnington ER Yorks 310 E5
Dunnington Warwick 154 B4
Dunningwell Cumb 312 D4
Dunnockshaw Lancs 291 E5
Dunollie Arg/Bute 416 D3
Dunoon Arg/Bute 390 C3
Dunragit Dumf/Gal 400 D3
Dunrobin Castle Museum & Gardens H'land 441 C5
Dunrobin Mains H'land 441 C5
Dunrostan Arg/Bute 407 D7
Duns Scot Borders 387 B5
Duns Tew Oxon 133 B8
Dunsby Lincs 228 C2
Dunscar Gtr Man 278 B3
Dunscore Dumf/Gal 358 F1
Dunscroft S Yorks 283 C7
Dunsdale Redcar/Clevel'd 333 C7
Dunsden Green Oxon 86 A4
Dunsfold Surrey 68 D2
Dunsfold Green Surrey 68 D2
Dunsford Devon 21 C6
Dunshalt Fife 411 A7
Dunshill Notts 247 B7
Dunshill Worcs 130 A2
Dunshillock Aberds 437 D6
Dunsinnan Perth/Kinr 420 D1
Dunskey Ho. Dumf/Gal 400 D2
Dunsley N Yorks 334 D4
Dunsley Staffs 175 B7
Dunsmore Bucks 109 A7
Dunsop Bridge Lancs 302 E5
Dunstable Beds 136 C4
Dunstall Staffs 223 D5
Dunstall Green Suffolk 185 F7
Dunstall Hill W Midlands 197 D7
Dunstall Hill W Midlands 197 C7
Dunstan Northum 377 D6
Dunstan Staffs 221 E8
Dunster Som'set 57 C6
Dunster Beach Som'set 57 C7
Dunster Castle, Minehead Som'set 57 C6
Dunston Derby 269 E7
Dunston Lincs 250 B4
Dunston Norfolk 209 C8
Dunston Tyne/Wear 352 D3
Dunston Hill Tyne/Wear 352 D3
Dunstone Devon 11 E7
Dunstone Devon 20 E4
Dunsville S Yorks 283 C6
Dunswell ER Yorks 297 C8
Dunsyre S Lanarks 383 C6
Dunterton Devon 18 E4
Dunthrop Oxon 133 B6
Duntisbourne Abbots Glos 131 F5
Duntisbourne Leer Glos 131 F5
Duntisbourne Rouse Glos 104 A4
Duntish Dorset 40 E3
Duntocher W Dunb 392 D1
Dunton Beds 160 D4
Dunton Bucks 135 C7
Dunton Norfolk 232 B2
Dunton Bassett Leics 200 E4
Dunton Green Kent 90 E5
Dunton Patch Norfolk 232 B2
Dunton Wayletts Essex 113 D8
Duntrune Castle Arg/Bute 407 C7
Duntulm H'land 430 A4
Dunure S Ayrs 366 D5
Dunvant = Dynfant Swan 97 D6
Dunvegan H'land 430 D2
Dunvegan Castle H'land 430 D2
Dunwear Som'set 59 D6
Dunwich Suffolk 189 D7
Duporth Cornw'l 8 E3
Dupplin Castle Perth/Kinr 419 F8
Durdar Cumb 339 A7
Durgan Cornw'l 4 E3
Durgates E Sussex 71 E7
Durham Durham 344 C1
Durham Cathedral Durham 344 C1
Durham Tees Valley Airport Stockton 332 D2
Durisdeer Dumf/Gal 358 B1
Durisdeermill Dumf/Gal 358 B1
Durkar W Yorks 281 A8
Durleigh Som'set 59 D5
Durley Hants 45 C5
Durley Wilts 84 D1
Durley Hill Bath/NE Som'set 80 C4
Durlock Kent 95 D6
Durlock Kent 95 E5
Durlow Common Heref'd 152 E2
Durn Gtr Man 279 A7
Durnamuck H'land 438 D4
Durness H'land 443 B6
Durno Aberds 436 F4
Durns Town Hants 29 A5
Durns Town Hants 29 A5
Duror H'land 417 B4
Durran Arg/Bute 408 B2
Durran H'land 445 B5
Durrant Green Kent 72 D4
Durrants Hants 46 E2
Durrington Wilts 63 C8
Durrington W Sussex 48 F2
Durrisdale Orkney 452 A4
Dursley Glos 103 C7
Dursley Cross Glos 129 D7
Durston Som'set 59 F5
Durweston Dorset 41 E7
Dury Shetl'd 457 G4
Duston Northants 180 F2
Duthil H'land 434 F4
Dutlas Powys 172 C2
Duton Hill Essex 139 B8
Dutson Cornw'l 18 C3
Dutton Warrington 265 D6
Dutwoods Derby 223 D6
Duxford Cambs 162 C2
Duxford Oxon 106 C4
Duxford Airfield (Imperial War Museum), Sawston Cambs 162 C2
Duxmoor Shrops 173 C6
Dwygyfylchi Conwy 260 D4
Dwyran Angl 236 A4
Dyce Aberd C 429 A5
Dye House Northum 351 E5
Dyer's Common S Glos 102 F3
Dyfatty Carms 96 B4
Dyffryn Bridg 98 D4
Dyffryn Carms 122 C2
Dyffryn Pembs 119 B6
Dyffryn Powys 193 A6
Dyffryn Powys 127 C6
Dyffryn V/Glam 78 B1
Dyffryn Ardudwy Gwyn 214 D3
Dyffryn Castell Ceredig'n 169 B8
Dyffryn Cellwen Neath P Talb 125 F6
Dyke Devon 33 B6
Dyke Lincs 228 D2
Dyke Moray 434 C4
Dykehead Angus 420 A3
Dykehead N Lanarks 382 A2
Dykehead Stirl 409 C8
Dykelands Aberds 428 F4
Dykends Angus 420 B2
Dykesfield Cumb 347 E8
Dykeside Aberds 436 D4
Dykesmains N Ayrs 378 D4
Dylife Powys 191 E8
Dymchurch Kent 74 F2
Dymock Glos 129 A7
Dynfant = Dunvant Swan 97 D6
Dyrham S Glos 81 A6
Dyrham Park S Glos 81 A6
Dysart Fife 411 C8
Dyserth Denbs 262 D3

# E

Eabost H'land 430 E3
Eabost West H'land 430 D3
Each End Kent 95 E6
Eachway Worcs 176 C2
Eachwick Northum 352 B1
Eadar Dha Fhadhail W Isles 450 D3
Eagland Hill Lancs 289 A5
Eagle Lincs 272 F2
Eagle Barnsdale Lincs 249 A8
Eagle Hall Lincs 249 A8
Eagle Moor Lincs 272 F2
Eaglescliffe Stockton 332 C3
Eaglesfield Cumb 337 F7
Eaglesfield Dumf/Gal 347 B6
Eaglesham E Renf 380 B3
Eaglestone M/Keynes 158 E5
Eaglethorpe Northants 203 E7
Eagley Gtr Man 278 B3
Eairy I/Man 336 D2
Eakley M/Keynes 158 B4
Eakring Notts 248 B4
Ealand N Lincs 284 B2
Ealing London 111 F5
Ealing Common London 111 F5
Eals Northum 349 E7
Eamont Bridge Cumb 340 F1
Earby Lancs 291 A7
Earcroft Blackb'n 290 F2
Eardington Shrops 196 E3
Eardisland Heref'd 151 A6
Eardisley Heref'd 150 C4
Eardiston Shrops 218 D4
Eardiston Worcs 174 E3
Earith Cambs 183 C7
Earl Shilton Leics 200 D3
Earl Soham Suffolk 188 F2
Earl Sterndale Derby 268 F1
Earl Stonham Suffolk 165 A7
Earle Northum 376 B1
Earlesfield Lincs 226 A4
Earlestown Mersey 277 E8
Earley Wokingham 86 B5
Earlham Norfolk 209 B7
Earlish H'land 430 B3
Earls Barton Northants 180 F5
Earls Colne Essex 141 B6
Earl's Common Worcs 154 A2
Earl's Court London 89 A7
Earl's Croome Worcs 153 D7
Earl's Down E Sussex 51 C6
Earl's Green Suffolk 187 E5
Earlsdon W Midlands 178 C1
Earlsferry Fife 412 C2
Earlsfield London 89 B7
Earlsford Aberds 437 E5
Earlsheaton W Yorks 293 F7
Earlsmill Moray 434 C4
Earlston Scot Borders 385 E8
Earlston E Ayrs 379 E8
Earlstoun Dumf/Gal 401 A8
Earlswood Monmouths 101 C9
Earlswood Surrey 69 B7
Earlswood Warwick 176 D5
Earnley W Sussex 31 E6
Earnock S Lanarks 381 B5
Earnshaw Bridge Lancs 289 F7
Earsairidh W Isles 446 D3
Earsdon Northum 365 D6
Earsdon Tyne/Wear 353 B5
Earsham Norfolk 210 F2
Earsham Street Suffolk 188 C2
Earswick C/York 308 D1
Eartham W Sussex 47 E6
Earthcott Green S Glos 102 E4
Easby N Yorks 331 F5
Easby N Yorks 333 E6
Easdale Arg/Bute 416 F2
Easebourne W Sussex 47 B5
Easenhall Warwick 178 C4
Eashing Surrey 67 C8
Easington Bucks 134 E4
Easington Durham 344 C4
Easington ER Yorks 287 A6
Easington Northum 388 F4
Easington Oxon 108 C3
Easington Oxon 156 E4
Easington Redcar/Clevel'd 334 C1
Easington Colliery Durham 344 C4
Easington Lane Tyne/Wear 344 B3
Easingwold N Yorks 307 B7
Easole Street Kent 74 A5
Eassie Angus 420 C3
East Aberthaw V/Glam 77 C7
East Acton London 111 F6
East Adderbury Oxon 156 E4
East Allington Devon 14 F3
East Amat H'land 440 D1
East Anstey Devon 36 A2
East Anton Hants 64 B4
East Appleton N Yorks 318 A3
East Ardsley W Yorks 293 E7
East Ashling W Sussex 46 E4
East Ashton Hants 65 B5
East Auchronie Aberds 429 B5
East Ayton N Yorks 322 C3
East Bank Bl Gwent 100 A4
East Barkwith Lincs 273 C8
East Barming Kent 92 F1
East Barnby N Yorks 334 D3
East Barnet London 112 D1
East Barns E Loth 398 C4
East Barsham Norfolk 232 B3
East Barton Suffolk 186 E3
East Beach W Sussex 31 F7
East Beckham Norfolk 257 D6
East Bedfont London 88 B3
East Bergholt Suffolk 165 E6
East Bierley W Yorks 293 E5
East Bilney Norfolk 232 E4
East Blackdene Durham 341 D8
East Blackdene Durham 341 D8
East Blatchington E Sussex 50 F2
East Bloxworth Dorset 26 B4
East Boldon Tyne/Wear 353 D6
East Boldre Hants 44 F2
East Bonhard Perth/Kinr 420 E1
East Bower Som'set 59 D6
East Brent Som'set 59 A6
East Bridgeford Notts 248 F4
East Briscoe Durham 330 C1
East Buckland Devon 55 E8
East Budleigh Devon 22 D3
East Burnham Bucks 109 F9
East Burrafirth Shetl'd 457 H3
East Burton Dorset 26 C3
East Butsfield Durham 343 B6
East Butterleigh Devon 36 E4
East Butterwick N Lincs 284 C3
East Cairnbeg Aberds 429 E4
East Calder W Loth 395 E6
East Carleton Norfolk 209 C7
East Carlton Northants 202 F2
East Carlton W Yorks 293 B6
East Chaldon Dorset 26 D2
East Challow Oxon 106 E4
East Charleton Devon 13 D6
East Chelborough Dorset 39 E9
East Chiltington E Sussex 49 D7
East Chinnock Som'set 39 D7
East Chisenbury Wilts 63 A7
East Cholderton Hants 64 B2
East Clandon Surrey 68 A3
East Claydon Bucks 135 B5
East Clevedon N Som'set 79 B8
East Clyne H'land 441 C6
East Clyth H'land 445 E7
East Coker Som'set 39 D8
East Combe Som'set 58 E3
East Common N Yorks 295 D6
East Compton Dorset 41 C7
East Compton Som'set 60 C4
East Cornworthy Devon 14 D4
East Cottingwith ER Yorks 295 B8
East Coulston Wilts 82 F4
East Cowes I/Wight 30 A2
East Cowick ER Yorks 295 F7
East Cowton N Yorks 331 F8
East Cramlington Northum 352 A4
East Cranmore Som'set 61 C5
East Creech Dorset 27 D5
East Croachy H'land 434 F1
East Croftmore H'land 426 A4
East Curthwaite Cumb 339 B5
East Dean E Sussex 52 F3
East Dean Glos 129 C7
East Dean Hants 43 A8
East Dean W Sussex 47 D6
East Dene S Yorks 269 A8
East Denton Tyne/Wear 352 C3
East Didsbury Gtr Man 266 B4
East Down Devon 55 C7
East Drayton Notts 271 D7
East Dulwich London 90 B1
East Dundry N Som'set 80 C3
East Ella Kingston/Hull 297 E8
East End Beds 159 D7
East End Beds 160 A2
East End Bucks 135 D7
East End Cambs 185 D6
East End Dorset 27 A6
East End Essex 141 F9
East End ER Yorks 298 E4
East End ER Yorks 298 D2
East End ER Yorks 310 D5
East End Glos 105 B8
East End Hants 45 B8
East End Hants 85 D5
East End Hants 29 A7
East End Herts 139 C5
East End Kent 72 D3
East End Kent 93 B6
East End M/Keynes 159 D6
East End N Som'set 80 B1
East End Oxon 133 E6
East End Oxon 133 A6
East End Oxon 133 D7
East End Oxon 156 E4
East End Suffolk 165 F6
East End Suffolk 165 A8
East End S Glos 81 B7
East End Som'set 61 B5
East End Som'set 60 A3
East End Green Herts 138 E1
East Everleigh Wilts 83 F9
East Ewell Surrey 89 D6
East Farleigh Kent 72 A1
East Farndon Northants 180 A2
East Ferry Lincs 284 E3
East Finchley London 111 E7
East Flexford Surrey 67 B8
East Fortune E Loth 397 C7
East Garforth W Yorks 294 D2
East Garston W Berks 84 A4
East Garston Woodlands W Berks 84 B4
East Gateshead Tyne/Wear 352 D4
East Gillibrands Lancs 277 C6
East Ginge Oxon 107 E5
East Gores Essex 141 C6
East Goscote Leics 225 F7
East Grafton Wilts 84 D2
East Grange Moray 435 B5
East Green Hants 67 C6
East Green Suffolk 189 E6
East Green Suffolk 163 B6
East Grimstead Wilts 64 F1
East Grinstead W Sussex 70 D2
East Guldeford E Sussex 73 F5
East Haddon Northants 179 E8
East Hagbourne Oxon 107 E7
East Halton N Lincs 286 A1
East Ham London 112 F3
East Hampnett W Sussex 47 E6
East Hanney Oxon 107 D5
East Hanningfield Essex 114 B2
East Hardwick W Yorks 282 A3
East Harling Norfolk 186 A4
East Harlsey N Yorks 319 A7
East Harnham Wilts 63 F7
East Harptree Bath/NE Som'set 80 E3
East Hartford Northum 352 A4
East Harting W Sussex 46 C3
East Hatch Wilts 62 F3
East Hatley Cambs 161 B5
East Hauxwell N Yorks 318 B2
East Haven Angus 421 D5
East Heckington Lincs 251 F6
East Hedleyhope Durham 343 C7
East Helmsdale H'land 441 B7
East Hendred Oxon 107 E6
East Herringthorpe S Yorks 282 F3
East Herrington Tyne/Wear 353 F6
East Heslerton N Yorks 322 E2
East Hewish N Som'set 79 D7
East Hill Hants 67 F5
East Hill Kent 91 D6
East Hoathly E Sussex 50 C3
East Hogaland Shetl'd 455 C2
East Holme Dorset 26 C4
East Holywell Northum 353 B5
East Horrington Som'set 60 B3
East Horsley Surrey 68 A3
East Horton Northum 376 A2
East Howdon Tyne/Wear 353 C5
East Howe Bournem'th 27 A8
East Huntspill Som'set 59 C6
East Hyde Beds 137 D6
East Ilsley W Berks 107 F6
East Keal Lincs 252 B3
East Kennett Wilts 83 C7
East Keswick W Yorks 293 B8
East Ketton D'lington 331 B8
East Kilbride S Lanarks 380 B4
East Kingston W Sussex 48 F1
East Kirkby Lincs 252 B2
East Knapton N Yorks 321 E8
East Knighton Dorset 26 C3
East Knowstone Devon 36 B1
East Knoyle Wilts 62 E2
East Kyloe Northum 388 E3
East Kyo Durham 343 A7
East Lambrook Som'set 39 C6
East Lamington H'land 440 F4
East Langdon Kent 75 B6
East Langton Leics 201 E8
East Langwell H'land 440 C4
East Lavant W Sussex 46 E5
East Lavington W Sussex 47 C6
East Law Durham 351 F8
East Layton N Yorks 331 E5
East Leake Notts 225 C6
East Learmouth Northum 387 E7
East Leigh Devon 14 E1
East Leigh Devon 35 E6
East Lenham Kent 73 A5
East Lexham Norfolk 232 E2
East Lilburn Northum 376 C2
East Linton E Loth 398 C1
East Liss Hants 67 F5
East Lockinge Oxon 107 E5
East Loftus Redcar/Clevel'd 334 C1
East Looe Cornw'l 9 E8
East Lound N Lincs 284 E2
East Lulworth Dorset 26 D4
East Lutton N Yorks 309 B7
East Lydford Som'set 60 E3
East Lynch Som'set 57 B5
East Lyng Som'set 59 F6
East Mains Aberds 428 C3
East Mains S Lanarks 380 B4
East Malling Kent 91 E9
East Malling Heath Kent 91 E8
East March Angus 420 D4
East Marden W Sussex 46 D4
East Markham Notts 271 E6
East Marsh NE Lincs 286 C4
East Martin Hants 42 C4
East Marton N Yorks 304 E2
East Meon Hants 45 B8
East Mere Devon 36 C4
East Mersea Essex 142 E2
East Mey H'land 445 A7
East Molesey Surrey 88 C4
East Moor W Yorks 293 F8
East Morden Dorset 27 B5
East Morton W Yorks 292 B4
East Ness N Yorks 320 E4
East Newton ER Yorks 298 C4
East Newton N Yorks 320 E3
East Norton Leics 202 C1
East Nynehead Som'set 37 B8
East Oakley Hants 65 B8
East Ogwell Devon 14 A4
East Orchard Dorset 41 C6
East Ord Northum 388 B1
East Parley Dorset 28 A2
East Peckham Kent 71 B8
East Pennard Som'set 60 D3
East Perry Cambs 182 E3
East Portlemouth Devon 13 E5
East Prawle Devon 13 E6
East Preston W Sussex 48 F1
East Pulham Dorset 40 E4
East Putford Devon 33 C7
East Quantoxhead Som'set 58 C2
East Rainton Tyne/Wear 344 B2
East Ravendale NE Lincs 286 E3
East Raynham Norfolk 232 C2
East Rhidorroch Lodge H'land 439 D6
East Rigton W Yorks 294 B1
East Rolstone N Som'set 79 D7
East Rounton N Yorks 332 F3
East Row N Yorks 334 D4
East Rudham Norfolk 231 C8
East Runton Norfolk 257 D6
East Ruston Norfolk 234 C3
East Saltoun E Loth 397 E6
East Scrafton N Yorks 317 D7
East Sheen London 89 A5
East Shefford W Berks 84 A4
East Sleekburn Northum 365 F7
East Somerton Norfolk 235 E6
East Stanley Durham 352 F3

East Stockwith Lincs 284 F2
East Stoke Dorset 26 C4
East Stoke Notts 249 E6
East Stoke Som'set 39 C7
East Stour Dorset 41 B5
East Stourmouth Kent 94 D5
East Stowford Devon 35 A5
East Stratton Hants 65 D7
East Street Kent 95 E6
East Street Som'set 60 D2
East Studdal Kent 75 B6
East Suisnish H'land 431 E5
East Taphouse Cornw'l 9 C6
East Third Scot Borders 386 E2
East Thirston Northum 365 C5
East Tilbury Thurr'k 91 A8
East Tisted Hants 66 E4
East Torrington Lincs 273 C7
East Town Som'set 58 E2
East Town Som'set 60 C4
East Tuddenham Norfolk 209 A5
East Tytherley Hants 64 F2
East Tytherton Wilts 82 A4
East Village Devon 36 E1
East Village V/Glam 77 B6
East Wall Shrops 195 E6
East Walton Norfolk 231 E6
East Water Som'set 60 A2
East Week Devon 20 B3
East Wellow Hants 43 B9
East Wemyss Fife 411 C8
East Whitburn W Loth 394 E4
East Wickham London 90 A4
East Williamston Pembs 117 D7
East Winch Norfolk 231 E5
East Winterslow Wilts 64 E1
East Wittering W Sussex 31 E6
East Witton N Yorks 318 C1
East Woodburn Northum 363 E7
East Woodhay Hants 85 D5
East Woodlands Som'set 61 C7
East Worldham Hants 66 D4
East Worlington Devon 35 D8
East Worthing W Sussex 48 F3
Eastacombe Devon 55 F5
Eastbourne D'lington 331 D8
Eastbourne E Sussex 52 F4
Eastbridge Suffolk 189 E6
Eastbrook Som'set 38 B2
Eastbrook V/Glam 78 B3
Eastburn ER Yorks 310 D1
Eastburn W Yorks 292 B2
Eastbury Herts 110 D3
Eastbury W Berks 84 A3
Eastby N Yorks 304 E4
Eastchurch Kent 93 B6
Eastcombe Glos 104 B2
Eastcote London 110 E4
Eastcote Northants 157 B8
Eastcote W Midlands 177 C6
Eastcote Village London 110 E4
Eastcott Cornw'l 33 C5
Eastcott Devon 19 D6
Eastcott Wilts 83 E5
Eastcotts Beds 160 C1
Eastcourt Wilts 84 D1
Eastcourt Wilts 104 D4
Eastend Essex 138 E4
Eastend Green Essex 142 D2
Easter Aberchalder H'land 425 A7
Easter Ardross H'land 440 F3
Easter Balgedie Perth/Kinr 411 B6
Easter Balmoral Aberds 427 C7
Easter Boleskine H'land 433 F7
Easter Brackland Stirl 410 B1
Easter Brae H'land 434 B1
Easter Bush Midloth 396 F2
Easter Carbeth Stirl 392 C2
Easter Cardno Aberds 437 B6
Easter Compton S Glos 102 F3
Easter Cringate Stirl 410 D2
Easter Culfosia Aberds 428 B4
Easter Davoch Aberds 428 B1
Easter Earshaig Dumf/Gal 358 B4
Easter Ellister Arg/Bute 403 A2
Easter Fearn H'land 440 E3
Easter Galcantray H'land 434 D3
Easter Howgate Midloth 396 F1
Easter Kinkell H'land 433 C7
Easter Knox Angus 421 D5
Easter Lednathie Angus 420 A3
Easter Milton H'land 434 C4
Easter Moniack H'land 433 D7
Easter Ord Aberds 429 B5
Easter Quarff Shetl'd 455 C3
Easter Rhynd Perth/Kinr 420 F1
Easter Row Stirl 410 C2
Easter Silverford Aberds 436 B4
Easter Skeld Shetl'd 455 B2
Easter Tulloch H'land 426 C4
Easter Whyntie Aberds 436 B3
Eastergate W Sussex 47 E7
Easterhouse Glasg C 393 E5
Easterside Middlesbro 332 C5
Easterton Wilts 82 E5
Easterton of Lenabo Aberds 437 D7
Easterton Sands Wilts 82 E5
Eastertown Som'set 79 F6
Eastertown of Auchleuchries Aberds 437 E7
Eastfield Bristol 80 A3
Eastfield N Lanarks 394 F2
Eastfield N Lanarks 393 C6
Eastfield Northum 352 A4
Eastfield N Yorks 322 D4
Eastfield Peterbro 204 D3
Eastfield S Lanarks 392 F4
Eastfield S Yorks 281 D7
Eastfield S Yorks 283 F5
Eastgate Durham 342 D3
Eastgate Norfolk 233 D7
Easthall Herts 137 C8
Eastham Mersey 264 C2
Eastham Worcs 174 E3
Eastham Ferry Mersey 264 C2
Easthampstead Brackn'l 87 C7
Easthampton Heref'd 173 F6
Easthaugh Norfolk 233 E6
Eastheath Wokingham 87 C6
Easthope Shrops 195 D7
Easthorpe Essex 141 C8
Easthorpe Leics 226 A3
Easthorpe Notts 248 D5
Easthouse Shetl'd 455 B2
Easthouses Midloth 396 E3
Easting Orkney 454 A6
Eastington Devon 35 E7
Eastington Glos 103 A7
Eastington Glos 131 E8
Eastleach Martin Glos 105 A9
Eastleach Turville Glos 105 A8
Eastleaze Swindon 105 F7
Eastleigh Devon 54 F4
Eastleigh Hants 44 C4
Eastling Kent 93 E6
Eastly End Surrey 88 C2
Eastmoor Derby 269 E6
Eastmoor Norfolk 207 C5
Eastney Portsm'th 31 A5
Eastnor Heref'd 152 E4
Eastoft N Lincs 284 A3
Eastoke Hants 31 A6
Easton Cambs 182 D2
Easton Cumb 347 E7
Easton Cumb 348 B2
Easton Dorset 24 D2
Easton Devon 20 C4
Easton Hants 65 E7
Easton I/Wight 29 C6
Easton Lincs 227 C5
Easton Norfolk 209 A6
Easton Suffolk 166 A3
Easton Som'set 60 B2
Easton W Berks 85 B5
Easton Wilts 82 B2
Easton Grey Wilts 104 E2
Easton Maudit Northants 159 A5
Easton on the Hill Northants 203 B6
Easton Royal Wilts 83 D9
Easton Town Som'set 60 E4
Easton Town Wilts 104 E2
Easton-in-Gordano N Som'set 80 A2
Eastrea Cambs 204 D4
Eastriggs Dumf/Gal 347 C7
Eastrington ER Yorks 296 E2
Eastrip Wilts 81 B8
Eastrop Wilts 105 D9
Eastry Kent 95 F6
East-the-Water Devon 34 A2
Eastville Bristol 80 A4
Eastville Lincs 252 C4
Eastwell Leics 226 C2
Eastwick Herts 138 E4
Eastwick Shetl'd 457 F3
Eastwood Notts 247 E7
Eastwood Southend 114 E4
Eastwood S Yorks 282 F2
Eastwood End Cambs 205 E7
Eastwood Park S Glos 103 D5
Eathorpe Warwick 178 E2
Eaton Ches 242 B4
Eaton Ches 244 A3
Eaton Heref'd 151 A8
Eaton Leics 226 C2
Eaton Norfolk 209 B8
Eaton Norfolk 254 E3
Eaton Notts 271 D6
Eaton Oxon 107 B5
Eaton Shrops 194 F3
Eaton Bishop Heref'd 151 E6
Eaton Bray Beds 136 C3
Eaton Constantine Shrops 195 B7
Eaton Green Beds 136 C3
Eaton Hastings Oxon 106 C2
Eaton Socon Cambs 160 A3
Eaton upon Tern Shrops 220 D3
Eau Brink Norfolk 230 E3
Eau Well Lincs 228 D2
Eau Withington Heref'd 151 D8
Eaves Green W Midlands 177 B8
Eaves Hall Lancs 290 B3
Eavestone N Yorks 306 B1
Ebberston N Yorks 322 D1
Ebbesbourne Wake Wilts 42 B2
Ebblake Dorset 42 E5
Ebbw Vale = Glyn Ebwy Bl Gwent 126 F4
Ebchester Durham 351 E9
Ebdon N Som'set 79 D7
Ebford Devon 22 C1
Ebley Glos 103 B8
Ebnal Ches 242 E2
Ebreywood Shrops 219 E7
Ebrington Glos 155 D6
Ecchinswell Hants 85 E7
Ecclefechan Dumf/Gal 347 B5
Eccles Scot Borders 386 D5
Eccles Gtr Man 278 E4
Eccles Kent 92 D1
Eccles Green Heref'd 151 C5
Eccles on Sea Norfolk 235 C5
Eccles Road Norfolk 208 E4
Ecclesall S Yorks 269 C6
Ecclesfield S Yorks 281 F9
Ecclesgreig Aberds 421 A7
Eccleshall Staffs 221 C6
Eccleshill W Yorks 292 C5
Ecclesmachan W Loth 395 D6
Eccleston Ches 241 B9
Eccleston Lancs 277 A7
Eccleston Mersey 277 E6
Eccleston Park Mersey 264 A4
Eccliffe Dorset 41 A6
Eccup W Yorks 293 B7
Echt Aberds 428 B4
Eckford Scot Borders 374 B4
Eckington Derby 269 D8
Eckington Worcs 153 D8
Ecton Northants 180 F4
Ecton Brook Northants 180 F4
Edale Derby 268 B2
Edbrook Som'set 58 C4
Edbrooke Som'set 57 E5
Edburton W Sussex 48 D4
Edderside Cumb 337 B8
Edderthorpe S Yorks 282 C2
Edderton H'land 440 E4
Eddington Kent 94 C3
Eddington W Berks 84 C3
Eddleston Scot Borders 384 C1
Eddlewood S Lanarks 381 B6
Eden Camp, Malton N Yorks 321 F6
Eden Mount Cumb 314 E2
Eden Vale Durham 344 D4
Eden Vale Wilts 62 A2
Edenbridge Kent 70 B3
Edenfield Lancs 279 A5
Edenhall Cumb 340 E2
Edenham Lincs 227 D8
Edensor Derby 268 E4
Edenthorpe S Yorks 283 C6
Edentown Cumb 348 E1
Ederline Arg/Bute 408 B1
Edern Gwyn 213 A5
Edford Som'set 61 B5
Edgarley Som'set 60 D2
Edgbaston W Midlands 176 B4
Edgcote Northants 157 C5
Edgcott Bucks 134 C4
Edgcott Som'set 56 D3
Edgcumbe Cornw'l 4 D2
Edge Glos 130 F2
Edge Shrops 194 B3
Edge End Glos 129 E5
Edge End Lancs 290 D3
Edge Fold Blackb'n 278 A3
Edge Fold Gtr Man 278 C2
Edge Green Norfolk 187 B5
Edge Green Warrington 277 E9
Edge Hill Mersey 264 B2
Edge Hill Warwick 199 D5
Edgebolton Shrops 219 D8
Edgefield Norfolk 233 B6
Edgefield S Yorks 268 A5
Edgefield Street Norfolk 233 B6
Edgehill Derby 247 F5
Edgeley Gtr Man 266 B4
Edgerston Scot Borders 374 E3
Edgerton W Yorks 280 A4
Edgeside Lancs 291 F5
Edgeworth Glos 104 A3
Edginswell Devon 15 B5
Edgiock Worcs 176 F3
Edgmond Telford 220 E4
Edgmond Marsh Telford 220 D4
Edgton Shrops 173 B5
Edgware London 111 D5
Edgworth Blackb'n 278 A3
Edinample Stirl 418 E3
Edinbane H'land 430 C3
Edinburgh C/Edinb 396 D1
Edinburgh Airport C/Edinb 395 D7
Edinburgh Castle C/Edinb 396 D2
Edinburgh Crystal Visitor Centre, Penicuik Midloth 396 F1
Edinburgh Hill Kent 75 C6
Edinburgh Zoo C/Edinb 395 D9
Edinchip Stirl 418 E3
Edingale Staffs 199 A5
Edingight Ho. Moray 436 C2
Edinglassie Ho. Aberds 427 A8
Edingley Notts 248 C4
Edingthorpe Norfolk 234 B3
Edingthorpe Green Norfolk 234 B3
Edington Som'set 59 D7
Edington Wilts 62 A3
Edingworth Som'set 79 F7
Edintore Moray 436 D1
Edistone Devon 32 B4
Edith Weston Rutl'd 202 B4
Edithmead Som'set 59 B6
Edlaston Derby 246 F1
Edlesborough Bucks 136 D3
Edlingham Northum 376 F4
Edlington Lincs 274 E1
Edmondsham Dorset 42 D4
Edmondsley Durham 343 B8
Edmondstown Rh Cyn Taff 99 D7
Edmondthorpe Leics 226 E4
Edmonstone C/Edinb 396 D3
Edmonstone Orkney 453 A6
Edmonstown Rh Cyn Taff 99 D7
Edmonton Cornw'l 8 A2
Edmonton London 112 D1
Edmund Hill Som'set 60 D2
Edmundbyers Durham 342 B4
Ednam Scot Borders 386 E4
Ednaston Derby 246 F2
Edney Common Essex 113 B8
Edradynate Perth/Kinr 419 B6
Edrom Scot Borders 387 A6
Edstaston Shrops 219 B7
Edvin Loach Heref'd 152 A3
Edwalton Notts 225 A6
Edwardstone Suffolk 164 D3
Edwardsville Merth Tyd 100 C1
Edwinstowe Notts 270 F4
Edworth Beds 160 D4
Edwyn Ralph Heref'd 152 A2
Edzell Angus 428 F2
Efail Isaf Rh Cyn Taff 99 F8
Efail-fach Rh Cyn Taff 98 C2
Efailnewydd Gwyn 213 A7
Efail-rhyd Powys 217 C8
Efailwen Carms 121 B6
Efenechtyd Denbs 240 C3
Effingham Surrey 68 A4
Effirth Shetl'd 457 H3
Efflinch Staffs 223 E5
Efford Plym'th 11 D6
Egbury Hants 65 A5
Egde Green Ches 242 D2
Egdean W Sussex 47 B7
Egdon Worcs 153 B8
Egerton Gtr Man 278 B3
Egerton Kent 73 B5
Egerton Forstal Kent 72 B4
Egerton Green Ches 242 D3
Eggborough N Yorks 295 F5
Eggbuckland Plym'th 11 D5
Eggington Beds 136 C3
Egginton Derby 223 C7
Egglesburn Durham 330 B1
Egglescliffe Stockton 332 D3
Eggleston Durham 330 B2
Egham Surrey 88 B2
Egham Wick Surrey 88 B1
Egleton Rutl'd 202 B3
Eglingham Northum 376 D4
Egloshayle Cornw'l 8 A3
Egloskerry Cornw'l 18 C2
Eglwys Cross Wrex 242 F2
Eglwys Fach Ceredig'n 190 D4
Eglwysbach Conwy 262 E6
Eglwys-Brewis V/Glam 77 C7
Eglwyswen Pembs 144 E3
Eglwyswrw Pembs 144 E2
Egmanton Notts 271 F6
Egremont Cumb 324 D5
Egremont Mersey 263 A8
Egton N Yorks 334 E3
Egton Bridge N Yorks 334 E3
Egypt Hants 65 D6
Eiden H'land 440 C4
Eight Ash Green Essex 141 B7
Eighton Banks Tyne/Wear 352 E4
Eign Hill Heref'd 151 E8
Eignaig H'land 416 C2
Eil H'land 426 A3
Eilanreach H'land 423 A8
Eildon Scot Borders 373 A8
Eilean Anabaich W Isles 449 B6
Eilean Darach H'land 439 E5
Eilean Shona Ho H'land 423 E6
Eileanach Lodge H'land 433 B7
Einacleite W Isles 450 E4
Eisgean W Isles 449 A7
Eisingrug Gwyn 214 B4
Elan Village Powys 170 E3
Eland Green Northum 352 B2
Elberton S Glos 102 E4
Elborough N Som'set 79 E7
Elburton Plym'th 11 E6
Elcho Perth/Kinr 420 E1
Elcombe Glos 103 C7
Elcombe Swindon 105 F7
Elcot W Berks 84 C4
Eldene Swindon 105 F8
Elder Street Essex 162 F4
Eldernell Cambs 204 D5
Eldersfield Worcs 130 A2
Elderslie Renf 391 F8
Eldon Durham 343 F8
Eldon Lane Durham 343 F8
Eldroth N Yorks 303 B7
Eldwick W Yorks 292 B4
Elemore Vale Tyne/Wear 344 B3
Elerch = Bont-goch Ceredig'n 169 A6
Elerch Ceredig'n 169 A6
Elfhowe Cumb 314 A3
Elford Northum 377 A5
Elford Staffs 198 A4
Elford Closes Cambs 184 D3
Elgin Moray 435 B7
Elgol H'land 422 A5
Elham Kent 74 C3
Eliburn W Loth 395 E5
Elie Fife 412 B2
Elim Angl 258 C4
Eling Hants 44 D2
Eling W Berks 85 A7
Elishader H'land 430 B5
Elishaw Northum 363 C6
Elizafield Dumf/Gal 346 B2
Elkesley Notts 271 D5
Elkington Northants 179 C7
Elkins Green Essex 113 B7
Elkstone Glos 131 E5
Ellacombe Torbay 15 C6
Ellan H'land 434 F3
Ellanbrook Gtr Man 278 D3
Elland W Yorks 292 F4
Elland Lower Edge W Yorks 292 F4
Elland Upper Edge W Yorks 292 F4
Ellary Arg/Bute 407 E7
Ellastone Staffs 245 F8
Ellbridge Cornw'l 10 C4
Ellel Lancs 301 D8
Ellenborough Cumb 337 D3
Ellenbrook Herts 137 F8
Ellenbrook I/Man 336 D3
Ellenglaze Cornw'l 7 D6
Ellenhall Staffs 221 C6
Ellen's Green Surrey 68 D3
Ellerbeck N Yorks 319 A7
Ellerburn N Yorks 321 D7
Ellerby N Yorks 334 D2
Ellerdine Telford 220 D2
Ellerdine Heath Telford 220 D2
Ellergreen Cumb 314 A4
Ellerhayes Devon 36 F4
Elleric Arg/Bute 417 C5
Ellerker ER Yorks 296 E5
Ellers N Yorks 292 B2
Ellerton ER Yorks 295 C8
Ellerton N Yorks 318 A4
Ellesborough Bucks 109 A6
Ellesmere Shrops 218 B4
Ellesmere Park Gtr Man 278 E4
Ellesmere Port Ches 264 D3
Ellicombe Som'set 57 C6
Ellinge Kent 74 C4
Ellingham Hants 43 E5
Ellingham Norfolk 210 E3
Ellingham Northum 377 B5
Ellingstring N Yorks 318 D2
Ellington Cambs 182 D3
Ellington Northum 365 D7
Ellington Thorpe Cambs 182 D3
Elliot Angus 421 D6
Elliots Green Som'set 61 B7
Ellisfield Hants 66 B2
Ellistown Leics 200 A2
Ellon Aberds 437 E6
Ellonby Cumb 339 D7
Ellough Suffolk 189 A6
Ellough Moor Suffolk 210 F4
Elloughton ER Yorks 297 E5
Ellwood Glos 129 F5
Elm Cambs 205 B8
Elm Corner Surrey 88 E3
Elm Park London 112 E5
Elmbridge Glos 130 D3
Elmbridge Worcs 175 E8
Elmdon Essex 162 E2
Elmdon W Midlands 177 B6
Elmdon Heath W Midlands 177 B6
Elmer W Sussex 47 F7
Elmers End London 90 C2
Elmer's Green Lancs 277 C7
Elmesthorpe Leics 200 D3
Elmfield I/Wight 30 B4
Elmhurst Bucks 135 D7
Elmhurst Staffs 198 A3
Elmley Castle Worcs 154 D2
Elmley Lovett Worcs 175 E7
Elmore Glos 130 D1
Elmore Back Glos 130 D1
Elms Farm Beds 160 B1
Elmscott Devon 32 B4
Elmsett Suffolk 165 C6
Elmslack Lancs 314 E3
Elmstead Essex 142 B2
Elmstead Kent 74 B2
Elmstead London 90 B3
Elmstead Heath Essex 142 C2
Elmstead Market Essex 142 C2
Elmstone Kent 94 D5
Elmstone Hardwicke Glos 130 B4
Elmswell ER Yorks 310 D1
Elmswell Suffolk 186 F4
Elmton Derby 270 E2
Elmton Park Derby 270 E1
Elness Orkney 454 C4
Elphin H'land 439 B6
Elphinstone E Loth 396 D4
Elrick Aberds 429 B5
Elrig Dumf/Gal 400 E5
Elrigbeag Arg/Bute 417 F6
Elrington Northum 350 D4
Elsdon Heref'd 150 B4
Elsdon Northum 363 D7
Elsecar S Yorks 282 D1
Elsenham Essex 139 B6
Elsfield Oxon 134 F1
Elsham N Lincs 285 B7
Elsing Norfolk 233 E6
Elslack N Yorks 304 F2
Elson Portsm'th 45 F7
Elson Shrops 218 A4
Elsrickle S Lanarks 383 D6
Elstead Surrey 67 C8
Elsted W Sussex 46 C4
Elsted Marsh W Sussex 46 B4
Elsthorpe Lincs 227 D8
Elstob Durham 332 B1
Elston Lancs 289 D9
Elston Notts 249 E6
Elston Wilts 63 C6
Elstone Devon 35 C6
Elstow Beds 159 C9
Elstree Herts 111 C5
Elstronwick ER Yorks 298 D3
Elswick Lancs 288 C5
Elswick Tyne/Wear 352 D3
Elsworth Cambs 183 F6
Elterwater Cumb 326 F3
Eltham London 90 B3
Eltisley Cambs 161 A5
Elton Cambs 203 E7
Elton Ches 264 D4
Elton Derby 246 B2
Elton Glos 129 E7
Elton Gtr Man 278 B4
Elton Heref'd 173 D7
Elton Notts 226 A2
Elton Stockton 332 C3
Elton Green Ches 264 E4
Elton's Marsh Heref'd 151 D7
Eltringham Northum 351 D8
Elvanfoot S Lanarks 370 D3
Elvaston Derby 224 B3
Elveden Suffolk 186 B1
Elverland Kent 93 E6
Elvingston E Loth 397 D6
Elvington C/York 308 F2
Elvington Kent 75 A5
Elwell Dorset 25 C8
Elwick Hartlep'l 345 E5
Elwick Northum 388 E4
Elworth Ches 243 B7
Elworthy Som'set 57 E8
Ely Cambs 184 B3
Ely Card 78 A2
Ely Cathedral and Museum Cambs 184 B3
Emberton M/Keynes 159 C5
Embleton Cumb 338 E2
Embleton Durham 344 F4
Embleton Northum 377 C6
Embo H'land 440 D5
Embo Street H'land 440 D5
Emborough Som'set 60 A4
Embsay N Yorks 304 E4
Emerson Park London 113 E5
Emery Down Hants 43 E8
Emley W Yorks 281 B6
Emmbrook Wokingham 87 C6
Emmer Green Wokingham 86 A4
Emmets Nest Brackn'l 87 B6
Emmett Carr Derby 269 D9
Emmington Oxon 108 B4
Emneth Norfolk 205 B8
Emneth Hungate Norfolk 206 B1
Emorsgate Norfolk 230 D2
Empingham Rutl'd 203 B5
Empshott Hants 66 E5
Empshott Green Hants 66 E4
Emstrey Shrops 195 A6
Emsworth Hants 46 E2
Enborne W Berks 85 C5
Enborne Row W Berks 85 D5
Enchmarsh Shrops 195 D6
Enderby Leics 200 D4
Endmoor Cumb 314 D4
Endon Staffs 244 D4
Endon Bank Staffs 244 D4
Energlyn Caerph 100 E3
Enfield London 112 C1
Enfield Worcs 176 E3
Enfield Highway London 112 C2
Enfield Island Village Essex 112 C2
Enfield Lock London 112 C2
Enfield Town London 111 C8
Enfield Wash London 112 C2
Enford Wilts 63 A7
Engamoor Shetl'd 457 H2
Engedi Angl 258 D4
Engine Common S Glos 103 F5
Englefield W Berks 86 B2
Englefield Green Surrey 88 B1
Englemere Brackn'l 87 C8
Engleseabrook Ches 243 D8
English Bicknor Glos 129 D5
English Frankton Shrops 219 C6
Englishcombe Bath/NE Som'set 81 D6
Engollen Cornw'l 7 B8
Enham-Alamein Hants 64 B4
Enisfirth Shetl'd 457 F3
Enmore Som'set 58 D4
Enmore Green Dorset 41 B7
Ennerdale Bridge Cumb 325 C6
Enniscaven Cornw'l 8 D2
Enoch Dumf/Gal 358 B1
Enochdhu Perth/Kinr 419 A8
Ensay Arg/Bute 415 C6
Ensbury Bournem'th 27 A8
Ensbury Park Dorset 27 B8
Ensdon Shrops 219 E5
Enslow Oxon 133 D8
Enson Staffs 221 C8
Enstone Oxon 133 C6
Enterkinfoot Dumf/Gal 357 B9
Enterpen N Yorks 332 E4
Enton Green Surrey 67 C9
Enville Staffs 197 F5
Eòropaidh W Isles 451 A8
Eolaigearraidh W Isles 446 C3
Eorabus Arg/Bute 415 E6
Epney Glos 130 E1
Eppelby N Yorks 331 D5
Epperstone Notts 248 E4
Epping Essex 112 B4
Epping Green Essex 112 A3
Epping Green Herts 138 F1
Epping Upland Essex 112 B3
Eppleworth ER Yorks 297 D7
Epsom Surrey 89 D6
Epsom Racecourse Surrey 89 E6
Epwell Oxon 156 D2
Epworth N Lincs 284 D2
Epworth Turbary N Lincs 284 D2
Erbistock Wrex 241 F8
Erbusaig H'land 431 F7
Erchless Castle H'land 433 D6
Erddig Wrex 241 E7
Erdington W Midlands 198 E3
Eredine Arg/Bute 408 B2
Eriboll H'land 443 C6
Ericstane Dumf/Gal 371 E6
Eridge Green E Sussex 71 D6
Erines Arg/Bute 408 E1
Eriswell Suffolk 185 C7
Erith London 90 A5
Erlestoke Wilts 82 F4
Ermine Lincs 272 E4
Ermington Devon 11 E8
Ernesettle Plym'th 10 D4
Erpingham Norfolk 233 B8
Erriottwood Kent 93 E5
Errogie H'land 433 F7
Errol Perth/Kinr 420 E2
Errol Station Perth/Kinr 420 E2
Erskine Renf 391 D9
Erskine Bridge Renf 391 D9
Ervie Dumf/Gal 400 C2
Erwarton Suffolk 166 F2
Erwood Powys 149 D6
Eryholme N Yorks 331 E8
Eryrys Denbs 240 C5
Escalls Cornw'l 2 E3
Escomb Durham 343 E7
Escott Som'set 58 D1
Escrick N Yorks 295 B6
Esgair Carms 122 B3
Esgairgeiliog Powys 191 B6
Esgyryn Conwy 262 D6
Esh Durham 343 C7
Esh Winning Durham 343 C7
Esher Surrey 88 D4
Esholt W Yorks 293 B5
Eshott Northum 365 C6
Eshton N Yorks 304 D2
Esk Valley N Yorks 334 F3
Eskadale H'land 433 E6
Eskbank Midloth 396 E3
Eskdale Green Cumb 325 F7
Eskdalemuir Dumf/Gal 360 C2
Eskeleth N Yorks 330 F1
Eskett Cumb 325 C6
Eskham Lincs 287 E6
Eskholme S Yorks 283 A6
Esknish Arg/Bute 406 F3
Esperley Lane Ends Durham 330 B4
Esprick Lancs 288 C5
Essendine Rutl'd 203 A6
Essendon Herts 138 F1
Essich H'land 434 E1
Essington Staffs 197 C8
Esslemont Aberds 437 F6
Eston Redcar/Clevel'd 333 C6
Estover Plym'th 11 D6
Eswick Shetl'd 457 H4
Etal Northum 387 E8
Etchilhampton Wilts 83 D5
Etchingham E Sussex 51 A7
Etchinghill Kent 74 D3
Etchinghill Staffs 222 E2
Etchingwood E Sussex 50 B3
Etherley Dene Durham 343 F7
Etherley Grange Durham 343 F7
Ethie Castle Angus 421 C6
Ethie Mains Angus 421 C6
Etling Green Norfolk 232 F5
Etloe Glos 103 A5
Eton Windsor 87 A9
Eton Wick Windsor 87 A8
Etrop Green Gtr Man 266 B3
Etruria Stoke 244 E3
Etterby Cumb 348 E1
Etteridge H'land 426 C1
Ettersgill Durham 341 F8
Ettiley Heath Ches 243 B7
Ettingshall W Midlands 197 D7
Ettingshall Park W Midlands 197 D7
Ettington Warwick 155 C8
Etton ER Yorks 297 B6
Etton Peterbro 204 B1
Ettrick Scot Borders 372 E2
Ettrickbridge Scot Borders 372 C4
Ettrickdale Arg/Bute 408 F3
Ettrickhill Scot Borders 372 E2
Etwall Derby 223 B7
Eudon George Shrops 196 F2
Eureka!, Halifax W Yorks 292 F3
Euston Suffolk 186 C2
Euximoor Drove Cambs 205 D8
Euxton Lancs 277 A8
Evancoyd Powys 172 F3
Evanstown Bridg 99 E6
Evanton H'land 433 B8
Eve Hill W Midlands 197 E7
Evedon Lincs 250 E4
Evelix H'land 440 D4
Even Swindon Swindon 105 E7
Evendine Heref'd 153 D5
Evenjobb Powys 172 F3
Evenley Northants 157 E6
Evenlode Glos 132 B3
Evenwood Durham 331 A5
Evenwood Gate Durham 331 B5
Ever Green Suffolk 163 B6
Everbay Orkney 454 D4
Evercreech Som'set 60 E4
Everdon Northants 157 A6
Everingham ER Yorks 296 B3
Everland Shetl'd 456 D6
Everleigh Wilts 83 F9
Eversholt Beds 136 A3
Evershot Dorset 40 F1
Eversley Hants 87 D5
Eversley Cross Hants 87 D5
Everthorpe ER Yorks 296 D5
Everton Beds 160 B4
Everton Hants 29 B5
Everton Mersey 264 A2
Everton Notts 271 A5
Evertown Dumf/Gal 347 A9
Eves Corner Essex 114 A1
Eves Corner Essex 115 C5
Evesbatch Heref'd 152 C3
Evesham Worcs 154 D3
Evington Leics C 201 C6
Ewanrigg Cumb 337 D3

**Ewden Village** S Yorks 281 E7
**Ewell** Surrey 89 D6
**Ewell Minnis** Kent 74 C5
**Ewelme** Oxon 108 D2
**Ewen** Glos 104 C5
**Ewenny** V/Glam 77 A5
**Ewerby** Lincs 251 E5
**Ewerby thorpe** Lincs 251 E5
**Ewes** Dumf/Gal 360 D4
**Ewhurst** Surrey 68 C3
**Ewhurst Green** E Sussex 51 B8
**Ewhurst Green** Surrey 68 D3
**Ewloe** Flints 241 A7
**Ewloe Green** Flints 241 B6
**Ewood** Blackb'n 290 E2
**Ewood Bridge** Lancs 290 F4
**Eworthy** Devon 19 A5
**Ewshot** Hants 67 B6
**Ewyas Harold** Heref'd 128 B1
**Exbourne** Devon 34 F5
**Exbury** Hants 44 F3
**Exbury Gardens, Fawley** Hants 44 F3
**Exebridge** Som'set 36 B3
**Exelby** N Yorks 318 C4
**Exeter** Devon 21 B8
**Exeter Cathedral** Devon 21 B8
**Exeter International Airport** Devon 22 B2
**Exford** Som'set 56 D4
**Exfords Green** Shrops 195 B5
**Exhall** Warwick 154 A5
**Exhall** Warwick 178 A1
**Exlade Street** Oxon 108 F3
**Exley** W Yorks 292 F3
**Exley Head** W Yorks 292 B2
**Exminster** Devon 21 C8
**Exmouth** Devon 22 D2
**Exnaboe** Shetl'd 455 E2
**Exning** Suffolk 184 E5
**Explosion, Gosport** Hants 45 F7
**Exted** Kent 74 C3
**Exton** Devon 22 C1
**Exton** Hants 45 B7
**Exton** Rutl'd 202 A4
**Exton** Som'set 57 E5
**Exwick** Devon 21 B8
**Eyam** Derby 268 D4
**Eydon** Northants 157 B5
**Eye** Heref'd 173 F7
**Eye** Peterbro 204 C3
**Eye** Suffolk 187 D7
**Eye Green** Peterbro 204 C3
**Eye Kettleby** Leics 226 E1
**Eyemouth** Scot Borders 399 F8
**Eyeworth** Beds 161 C5
**Eyhorne Street** Kent 92 F3
**Eyke** Suffolk 166 B4
**Eynesbury** Cambs 160 A2
**Eynort** H'land 430 F3
**Eynsford** Kent 91 C5
**Eynsham** Oxon 133 F7
**Eype** Dorset 24 B4
**Eyre** H'land 431 E5
**Eyre** H'land 430 C4
**Eyres Monsell** Leics 200 D5
**Eythorne** Kent 75 B5
**Eyton** Heref'd 173 F7
**Eyton** Shrops 194 F3
**Eyton** Shrops 218 F4
**Eyton** Wrex 221 A6
**Eyton on Severn** Shrops 195 B7
**Eyton upon the Weald Moors** Telford 220 F3

## F

**Faberstown** Hants 64 A2
**Faccombe** Hants 84 E4
**Faceby** N Yorks 332 F4
**Fachwen** Gwyn 237 B7
**Facit** Lancs 279 A6
**Faddiley** Ches 242 D4
**Faddonch** H'land 432 F1
**Fadmoor** N Yorks 320 C4
**Faerdre** Swan 97 B8
**Fagley** W Yorks 293 C5
**Fagwyr** Swan 97 B8
**Faichem** H'land 425 B4
**Faifley** W Dunb 392 D2
**Fail** S Ayrs 367 B8
**Failand** N Som'set 80 B2
**Failford** S Ayrs 367 B9
**Failsworth** Gtr Man 279 D7
**Fain** H'land 439 F5
**Faindouran Lodge** Moray 427 B5
**Fair Cross** W Berks 86 D3
**Fair Green** Norfolk 231 E5
**Fair Hill** Cumb 340 E1
**Fair Moor** Northum 365 E5
**Fair Oak** Hants 85 D8
**Fair Oak** Hants 44 C4
**Fair Oak** Lancs 290 A2
**Fair Oak Green** Hants 86 D3
**Fairbourne** Gwyn 190 A3
**Fairbourne Heath** Kent 72 A4
**Fairburn** N Yorks 294 E3
**Fairburn House** H'land 433 C6
**Fairfield** Derby 267 E8
**Fairfield** Gtr Man 279 B5
**Fairfield** Gtr Man 279 E7
**Fairfield** Kent 52 A4
**Fairfield** Mersey 264 A2
**Fairfield** Stockton 332 C3
**Fairfield** Worcs 154 D3
**Fairfield** Worcs 175 C6
**Fairfield** Worcs 176 C2
**Fairfield Park** Bath/NE Som'set 81 C7
**Fairford** Glos 105 B8
**Fairhaven** Lancs 288 E3
**Fairhaven** N Ayrs 405 B5
**Fairhill** S Lanarks 381 B6
**Fairlands** Surrey 67 A9
**Fairlie** N Ayrs 378 A4
**Fairlight** E Sussex 52 D2
**Fairlight Cove** E Sussex 52 D2
**Fairlop** London 112 D4
**Fairmile** Devon 22 A3
**Fairmile** Surrey 88 D4
**Fairmile Common** Surrey 88 D4
**Fairmilehead** C/Edinb 396 E1
**Fairoak** Caerph 100 C3
**Fairoak** Staffs 220 B5
**Fairseat** Kent 91 D7
**Fairstead** Essex 140 D4
**Fairstead** Norfolk 230 E4
**Fairwarp** E Sussex 50 A2
**Fairwater** Card 78 A2
**Fairwater** Torf 101 D5
**Fairy Cottage** I/Man 336 C4
**Fairy Cross** Cornw'l 9 C5
**Fairy Cross** Devon 33 B8
**Fakenham** Norfolk 232 B3
**Fakenham Magna** Suffolk 186 C3
**Fakenham Racecourse** Norfolk 232 C3
**Fala** Midloth 397 F5
**Fala Dam** Midloth 397 F5
**Falahill** Scot Borders 384 A4
**Falcon** Heref'd 129 A6
**Falcon Lodge** W Midlands 198 D3
**Falconwood** London 90 A3
**Faldingworth** Lincs 273 C6
**Falfield** Fife 412 B2
**Falfield** S Glos 103 D5
**Falkenham** Suffolk 166 E3
**Falkirk** Falk 394 C2
**Falkland** Fife 411 B7
**Falkland Palace** Fife 411 B7
**Fallin** Stirl 410 C3
**Fallings Heath** W Midlands 197 D8
**Fallowfield** Gtr Man 279 F6
**Fallowfield** Northum 351 C5
**Fallside** N Lanarks 393 F6
**Falmer** E Sussex 49 E7
**Falmouth** Cornw'l 4 D4
**Falnash** Scot Borders 360 A4
**Falsgrave** N Yorks 322 C4
**Falside** W Loth 394 E4
**Falstone** Northum 362 E3
**Fanagmore** H'land 442 D3
**Fancott** Beds 136 B4
**Fangdale Beck** N Yorks 320 B2
**Fangfoss** ER Yorks 308 E4
**Fanich** H'land 441 C5
**Fankerton** Falk 410 D2
**Fanmore** Arg/Bute 415 C7
**Fanner's Green** Essex 140 E2
**Fannich Lodge** H'land 432 B4
**Fans** Scot Borders 386 D2
**Fanshawe** Ches 266 D4
**Fant** Kent 92 F1
**Faoilean** H'land 431 F5
**Far Bletchley** M/Keynes 158 F4
**Far Cotton** Northants 158 A2
**Far End** Cumb 313 A7
**Far End** Derby 268 E5
**Far Forest** Worcs 174 C4
**Far Green** Glos 103 B7
**Far Hoarcross** Staffs 222 D4
**Far Moor** Gtr Man 277 D7
**Far Oakridge** Glos 104 B3
**Far Royds** W Yorks 293 D7
**Far Sawrey** Cumb 313 A8
**Farcet** Cambs 204 E3
**Farden** Shrops 174 C1
**Fareham** Hants 45 E6
**Farewell** Staffs 198 A2
**Farforth** Lincs 274 D3
**Faringdon** Oxon 106 C2
**Farington** Lancs 289 F8
**Farlam** Cumb 349 E5
**Farlands Booth** Derby 267 B8
**Farlary** H'land 440 C4
**Farleigh** N Som'set 80 C1
**Farleigh** Surrey 90 D2
**Farleigh Green** Kent 72 A1
**Farleigh Hungerford** Som'set 81 E8
**Farleigh Wallop** Hants 66 B2
**Farleigh Wick** Wilts 81 D8
**Farlesthorpe** Lincs 275 E6
**Farleton** Cumb 314 D4
**Farleton** Lancs 302 B3
**Farley** N Som'set 79 B8
**Farley** Shrops 194 B3
**Farley** Staffs 245 F7
**Farley** Wilts 64 F1
**Farley Common** Kent 90 F3
**Farley Green** Suffolk 163 B7
**Farley Green** Surrey 68 B3
**Farley Hill** Luton 137 C5
**Farley Hill** Wokingham 86 D5
**Farlington** N Yorks 308 B1
**Farlington** Portsm'th 45 E8
**Farlow** Shrops 174 B2
**Farm Town** Leics 224 E2
**Farmborough** Bath/NE Som'set 81 D5
**Farmbridge End** Essex 139 E8
**Farmcote** Glos 131 B7
**Farmington** Glos 131 D8
**Farmoor** Oxon 133 F8
**Farms Common** Cornw'l 4 D1
**Farmtown** Moray 436 C2
**Farnborough** Hants 87 F7
**Farnborough** London 90 D3
**Farnborough** Warwick 156 C3
**Farnborough** W Berks 107 F5
**Farnborough Green** Herts 87 E7
**Farnborough Park** Hants 87 E7
**Farncombe** Surrey 67 B9
**Farndish** Beds 181 F6
**Farndon** Ches 242 D1
**Farndon** Notts 249 D6
**Farnell** Angus 421 B6
**Farneyside** Northum 341 A6
**Farnham** Dorset 42 C2
**Farnham** Essex 139 C5
**Farnham** N Yorks 306 C3
**Farnham** Suffolk 188 F5
**Farnham** Surrey 67 B6
**Farnham Common** Bucks 110 E1
**Farnham Green** Essex 139 C5
**Farnham Royal** Bucks 110 F1
**Farnhill** N Yorks 292 A2
**Farningham** Kent 91 C5
**Farnley** N Yorks 305 F8
**Farnley** W Yorks 293 D7
**Farnley Tyas** W Yorks 280 B5
**Farnsfield** Notts 248 C4
**Farnworth** Gtr Man 278 C3
**Farnworth** Halton 264 B5
**Farr** H'land 426 B3
**Farr** H'land 434 E1
**Farr** H'land 444 B1
**Farr House** H'land 434 E1
**Farraline** H'land 433 F7
**Farringdon** Devon 22 B2
**Farringdon** Tyne/Wear 353 F6
**Farringdon Cross** Devon 22 B2
**Farrington Gurney** Bath/NE Som'set 80 E4
**Farsley** W Yorks 293 C6
**Farsley Beck Bottom** W Yorks 293 C6
**Farther Howegreen** Essex 114 B3
**Farthing Common** Kent 74 C2
**Farthing Corner** Medway 92 D3
**Farthing Green** Kent 72 B3
**Farthinghoe** Northants 157 E5
**Farthingloe** Kent 75 C5
**Farthingstone** Northants 157 B7
**Fartown** W Yorks 280 A4
**Farway** Devon 23 A5
**Fasach** H'land 430 D1
**Fasag** H'land 431 C8
**Fascadale** H'land 422 E5
**Faslane Port** Arg/Bute 409 D5
**Fasnacloich** Arg/Bute 417 C5
**Fasnakyle Ho** H'land 433 F5
**Fassfern** H'land 424 E2
**Fatfield** Tyne/Wear 353 F5
**Fattahead** Aberds 436 C3
**Faucheldean** W Loth 395 D6
**Faugh** Cumb 348 E4
**Fauld** Staffs 223 C5
**Fauldhouse** W Loth 394 F3
**Fauldiehill** Angus 421 D5
**Faulkbourn** Essex 140 D4
**Faulkland** Som'set 81 F6
**Fauls** Shrops 220 B1
**Faulston** Wilts 42 A4
**Faverdale** D'lington 331 C7
**Faversham** Kent 93 D7
**Favillar** Moray 435 E7
**Fawdington** N Yorks 307 A5
**Fawdon** Northum 376 D2
**Fawdon** Tyne/Wear 352 C3
**Fawfieldhead** Staffs 245 B7
**Fawkham** Kent 91 C6
**Fawler** Oxon 106 E3
**Fawler** Oxon 133 D6
**Fawley** Bucks 108 E5
**Fawley** Hants 44 F4
**Fawley** W Berks 106 F4
**Fawley Bottom** Bucks 108 E4
**Fawley Chapel** Heref'd 129 B5
**Fawton** Cornw'l 9 B6
**Faxfleet** ER Yorks 296 F4
**Faxton** Northants 180 C3
**Faygate** W Sussex 69 E6
**Fazakerley** Mersey 276 E4
**Fazeley** Staffs 199 C5
**Feagour** H'land 425 C7
**Fearby** N Yorks 318 D2
**Fearn** H'land 441 F5
**Fearn Lodge** H'land 440 E3
**Fearn Station** H'land 440 F5
**Fearnan** Perth/Kinr 418 C5
**Fearnbeg** H'land 431 C7
**Fearnhead** Warrington 265 A7
**Fearnmore** H'land 431 B7
**Featherstone** Staffs 197 C7
**Featherstone** W Yorks 294 F2
**Feckenham** Worcs 176 F3
**Fedw** Monmouths 102 C2
**Feering** Essex 141 C6
**Feetham** N Yorks 317 A5
**Fegg Hayes** Stoke 244 D3
**Fèith Mhor** H'land 434 F3
**Feizor** N Yorks 303 B7
**Felbridge** Surrey 70 D2
**Felbrigg** Norfolk 257 E7
**Felcourt** Surrey 70 C2
**Felday** Surrey 68 C4
**Felden** Herts 110 B2
**Felderland** Kent 95 E6
**Felhampton** Shrops 194 F4
**Felin-Crai** Powys 125 C6
**Felindre** Bridg 99 F6
**Felindre** Carms 123 C7
**Felindre** Carms 145 E6
**Felindre** Carms 124 A2
**Felindre** Carms 124 B3
**Felindre** Ceredig'n 146 A4
**Felindre** Powys 193 C7
**Felindre** Powys 171 B8
**Felindre** Powys 126 C4
**Felindre** Swan 97 B7
**Felindre Farchog** Pembs 144 E2
**Felinfach** Ceredig'n 146 A3
**Felinfach** Powys 126 A2
**Felinfoel** Carms 96 B5
**Felingwmisaf** Carms 123 C6
**Felingwmuchaf** Carms 123 C6
**Felin-Wnda** Ceredig'n 145 C6
**Felinwynt** Ceredig'n 144 B4
**Felixkirk** N Yorks 319 D8
**Felixstowe** Suffolk 166 F3
**Felixstowe Ferry** Suffolk 166 E4
**Felkington** Northum 387 D8
**Felkirk** W Yorks 282 B1
**Fell Beck** N Yorks 306 B1
**Fell Lane** W Yorks 292 B2
**Fell Side** Cumb 338 D5
**Felldyke** Cumb 325 C6
**Fellgate** Tyne/Wear 353 D5
**Felling** Tyne/Wear 352 D4
**Felling Shore** Tyne/Wear 352 D4
**Fellside** Tyne/Wear 352 D2
**Felmersham** Beds 159 A7
**Felmingham** Norfolk 234 C1
**Felpham** W Sussex 47 G7
**Felsham** Suffolk 164 A3
**Felsted** Essex 140 C2
**Feltham** London 88 B4
**Feltham** Som'set 38 C2
**Felthamhill** London 88 B4
**Felthorpe** Norfolk 233 E8
**Felton** Heref'd 152 C1
**Felton** N Som'set 80 C2
**Felton** Northum 365 B5
**Felton Butler** Shrops 218 E4
**Feltwell** Norfolk 207 E5
**Fen Ditton** Cambs 184 F2
**Fen Drayton** Cambs 183 E6
**Fen End** Lincs 228 D4
**Fen End** W Midlands 177 C7
**Fen Side** Cambs 184 D4
**Fen Side** Lincs 252 C2
**Fen Street** Norfolk 187 B6
**Fen Street** Suffolk 186 C4
**Fen Street** Suffolk 187 C6
**Fenay Bridge** W Yorks 281 A5
**Fence** Lancs 291 C5
**Fence** S Yorks 269 B8
**Fence Houses** Tyne/Wear 344 A2
**Fencott** Oxon 134 D2
**Fengate** Norfolk 207 F6
**Fengate** Norfolk 233 D8
**Fengate** Peterbro 204 D3
**Fenham** Tyne/Wear 352 C3
**Fenhouses** Lincs 251 F8
**Feniscliffe** Blackb'n 290 E2
**Feniscowles** Blackb'n 290 E2
**Feniton** Devon 22 A3
**Fenlake** Beds 160 C1
**Fenn Green** Shrops 175 B5
**Fenn Street** Medway 92 A3
**Fennifach** Powys 126 B1
**Fennington** Som'set 58 F3
**Fenny Bentley** Derby 246 D1
**Fenny Bridges** Devon 22 A4
**Fenny Compton** Warwick 156 B3
**Fenny Drayton** Leics 199 D7
**Fenny Stratford** M/Keynes 159 F5
**Fenrother** Northum 365 D5
**Fenstanton** Cambs 183 E6
**Fenstead End** Suffolk 163 B9
**Fenton** Cambs 183 C6
**Fenton** Cumb 348 E4
**Fenton** Lincs 249 D8
**Fenton** Lincs 272 D1
**Fenton** Notts 271 C7
**Fenton** Northum 388 F1
**Fenton** Stoke 244 F4
**Fenton Barns** E Loth 397 B7
**Fenwick** E Ayrs 380 D1
**Fenwick** Northum 351 B8
**Fenwick** Northum 388 D3
**Fenwick** S Yorks 283 A5
**Feochaig** Arg/Bute 404 E3
**Feock** Cornw'l 4 C4
**Feolin Ferry** Arg/Bute 406 F4
**Ferens Art Gallery, Hull** Kingston/Hull 297 E8
**Ferguslie Park** Renf 392 F1
**Ferindonald** H'land 423 B6
**Feriniquarrie** H'land 430 C1
**Ferlochan** Arg/Bute 416 C4
**Fern** Angus 421 A4
**Fern Bank** Gtr Man 279 E8
**Fern Gore** Lancs 290 E4
**Ferndale** Rh Cyn Taff 99 C6
**Ferndown** Dorset 42 F4
**Ferness** H'land 434 D4
**Ferney Green** Cumb 314 A2
**Fernham** Oxon 106 D2
**Fernhill** Gtr Man 279 B5
**Fernhill** S Lanarks 380 A4
**Fernhill** W Sussex 69 C8
**Fernhill Gate** Gtr Man 278 C2
**Fernhill Heath** Worcs 153 A7
**Fernhurst** W Sussex 67 F7
**Fernie** Fife 420 F3
**Ferniebrae** Aberds 437 C6
**Ferniegair** S Lanarks 381 B6
**Fernilea** H'land 430 E3
**Fernilee** Derby 267 D7
**Fernsplatt** Cornw'l 4 B3
**Ferrensby** N Yorks 306 C4
**Ferriby Sluice** N Lincs 297 F6
**Ferring** W Sussex 48 F1
**Ferry Hill** Cambs 183 B7
**Ferry Point** H'land 440 E4
**Ferrybridge** W Yorks 294 F3
**Ferryden** Angus 421 B7
**Ferryhill** Aberd C 429 B6
**Ferryhill** Durham 344 E1
**Ferryhill Station** Durham 344 E2
**Ferryside = Glan-y-Fferi** Carms 122 F3
**Ferryton** H'land 434 B1
**Fersfield** Norfolk 187 B6
**Fersfield Common** Norfolk 187 B6
**Fersit** H'land 425 E5
**Ferwig** Ceredig'n 144 C3
**Feshiebridge** H'land 426 B3
**Festival Park Visitor Centre, Ebbw Vale** Bl Gwent 126 F4
**Fetcham** Surrey 88 E4
**Fetlar Airport** Shetl'd 456 D6
**Fetterangus** Aberds 437 C6
**Fettercairn** Aberds 428 E3
**Fetterdale** Fife 420 E4
**Fettes** H'land 433 C7
**Fewcott** Oxon 134 B1
**Fewston** N Yorks 305 E7
**Ffair Rhos** Ceredig'n 169 E7
**Ffairfach** Carms 123 C8
**Ffaldy-brenin** Carms 147 C5
**Ffarmers** Carms 147 D6
**Ffawyddog** Powys 127 D5
**Ffestiniog Railway, Porthmadog** Gwyn 214 A3
**Ffinnant** Powys 217 D9
**Ffordd las** Denbs 240 B3
**Fforddlas** Powys 150 E2
**Fforest** Carms 97 B6
**Fforest Gôch** Neath P Talb 98 B1
**Fforest-fach** Swan 97 C7
**Ffos y frân** Merth Tyd 99 A8
**Ffostrasol** Ceredig'n 145 C7
**Ffos-y-ffin** Ceredig'n 168 F2
**Ffridd** Powys 193 D7
**Ffrith** Flints 241 C6
**Ffrwd** Gwyn 236 C5
**Ffynnon Gynydd** Powys 149 D8
**Ffynnongroyw** Flints 262 C4
**Ffynnon-oer** Ceredig'n 146 B3
**Ffynone** Pembs 144 E4
**Fickleshole** Surrey 90 D2
**Fidden** Arg/Bute 415 E6
**Fidder's Green** Norfolk 231 E8
**Fiddes** Aberds 429 D5
**Fiddington** Glos 130 A4
**Fiddington** Som'set 58 C4
**Fiddington Sands** Wilts 62 B3
**Fiddleford** Dorset 41 D6
**Fiddler's Ferry** Warrington 265 B6
**Fiddler's Green** Cornw'l 7 E7
**Fiddler's Green** Glos 130 C4
**Fiddler's Green** Heref'd 152 E1
**Fiddler's Green** Norfolk 208 D4
**Fiddlers Hamlet** Essex 112 B3
**Field** Som'set 60 C4
**Field** Staffs 222 B2
**Field Assarts** Oxon 132 E5
**Field Broughton** Cumb 314 D1
**Field Common** Surrey 88 C4
**Field Dalling** Norfolk 256 E3
**Field Green** Kent 72 F2
**Field Head** Leics 200 B3
**Fieldhead** Cumb 339 D8
**Fields End** Herts 136 F4
**Fife Keith** Moray 436 C1
**Fifehead Magdalen** Dorset 41 B5
**Fifehead Neville** Dorset 41 D5
**Fifehead St. Quintin** Dorset 41 D5
**Fifield** Oxon 132 D3
**Fifield** Wilts 63 A7
**Fifield** Windsor 87 A8
**Fifield Bavant** Wilts 42 A3
**Figheldean** Wilts 63 B8
**Filands** Wilts 104 E3
**Filby** Norfolk 211 A5
**Filey** N Yorks 323 D6
**Filford** Dorset 24 A3
**Filgrave** M/Keynes 158 C5
**Filham** Devon 11 D9
**Filkins** Oxon 106 B1
**Filleigh** Devon 55 F8
**Fillingham** Lincs 272 B3
**Fillongley** Warwick 199 F6
**Filmore Hill** Hants 66 F3
**Filton** S Glos 80 A3
**Filwood Park** Bristol 80 C3
**Fimber** ER Yorks 309 C6
**Finavon** Angus 421 B4
**Fincastle Ho.** Perth/Kinr 419 A6
**Finchairn** Arg/Bute 408 B2
**Fincham** Mersey 264 A3
**Fincham** Norfolk 206 B4
**Finchampstead** Wokingham 87 D6
**Finchdean** Hants 46 D2
**Finchingfield** Essex 140 A2
**Finchley** London 111 D7
**Findern** Derby 223 B8
**Findhorn** Moray 435 B5
**Findhorn Bridge** H'land 434 F3
**Findo Gask** Perth/Kinr 419 E8
**Findochty** Moray 436 B1
**Findon** Aberds 429 C6
**Findon** W Sussex 48 E2
**Findon Mains** H'land 433 B8
**Findon Valley** W Sussex 48 E2
**Findrack Ho.** Aberds 428 B3
**Finedon** Northants 181 D6
**Fineglen** Arg/Bute 416 F4
**Fingal Street** Suffolk 188 E2
**Fingask** Aberds 437 F4
**Fingerpost** Worcs 174 D4
**Fingest** Bucks 109 D5
**Finghall** N Yorks 318 C2
**Fingland** Cumb 347 E7
**Fingland** Dumf/Gal 369 D7
**Finglesham** Kent 95 F6
**Fingringhoe** Essex 142 C1
**Finham** W Midlands 178 C1
**Finkle Green** Essex 163 D7
**Finkle Street** S Yorks 281 E8
**Finlarig** Stirl 418 D3
**Finmere** Oxon 134 A3
**Finnart** Perth/Kinr 418 B3
**Finney Green** Ches 266 C4
**Finney Hill** Lincs 224 E4
**Finningham** Suffolk 187 E6
**Finningley** S Yorks 283 E7
**Finnygaud** Aberds 436 C2
**Finsbury** London 111 F8
**Finstall** Worcs 176 D2
**Finsthwaite** Cumb 313 C8
**Finstock** Oxon 133 D6
**Finstown** Orkney 452 B4
**Fintry** Aberds 436 C4
**Fintry** Dundee C 420 D4
**Fintry** Stirl 410 D1
**Finwood** Warwick 177 E6
**Finzean** Aberds 428 C3
**Finzean Ho** Aberds 428 C2
**Fionnphort** Arg/Bute 415 E6
**Fionnsbhagh** W Isles 448 D4
**Fir Tree** Durham 343 E6
**Fir Vale** S Yorks 269 A7
**Firbank** Cumb 315 B6
**Firbeck** S Yorks 270 B3
**Firby** N Yorks 308 B3
**Firby** N Yorks 318 C4
**Firemore** H'land 438 E2
**Firepool** Som'set 38 A2
**Firgrove** Gtr Man 279 B7
**Firkin** Arg/Bute 409 B6
**Firs Lane** Gtr Man 278 D1
**Firs Road** Wilts 63 E9
**Firsby** Lincs 252 B5
**Firsby** S Yorks 282 E3
**First Coast** H'land 438 D3
**Firswood** Gtr Man 279 E5
**Firth Moor** D'lington 331 D8
**Firth Park** S Yorks 269 A7
**Fishbourne** I/Wight 30 B3
**Fishbourne** W Sussex 46 F4
**Fishbourne Palace** W Sussex 46 F4
**Fishburn** Durham 344 E3
**Fishcross** Clack 410 C3
**Fisher** W Sussex 47 F5
**Fisher Place** Cumb 326 C3
**Fisherford** Aberds 436 E3
**Fishermead** M/Keynes 158 E5
**Fisherrow** E Loth 396 D3
**Fishers Green** Essex 112 B2
**Fisher's Green** Herts 137 B8
**Fisher's Pond** Hants 44 B4
**Fishersgate** W Sussex 48 E4
**Fisherstreet** W Sussex 67 E9
**Fisherton** H'land 434 C2
**Fisherton** S Ayrs 366 D5
**Fisherton de la Mere** Wilts 62 D5
**Fishery Estate** Windsor 109 F7
**Fishguard = Abergwaun** Pembs 119 B7
**Fishlake** S Yorks 283 B7
**Fishley** Norfolk 210 A4
**Fishmere End** Lincs 229 A5
**Fishpond Bottom** Dorset 24 A2
**Fishponds** Bristol 80 A4
**Fishpool** Gtr Man 279 C5
**Fishpool** Heref'd 129 B7
**Fishtoft** Lincs 252 F3
**Fishtoft Drove** Lincs 252 E2
**Fishtown of Usan** Angus 421 B7
**Fishwick** Scot Borders 387 B8
**Fishwick** Lancs 289 E8
**Fiskavaig** H'land 430 E3
**Fiskerton** Lincs 273 E6
**Fiskerton** Notts 249 D5
**Fitling** ER Yorks 298 D4
**Fittleton** Wilts 63 B7
**Fittleworth** W Sussex 47 C8
**Fitton End** Cambs 205 A7
**Fitton Hill** Gtr Man 279 D7
**Fitz** Shrops 219 E5
**Fitzhead** Som'set 58 F2
**Fitzroy** Som'set 58 F3
**Fitzwilliam** W Yorks 282 A2
**Fitzwilliam Museum, Cambridge** Cambs 162 A1
**Fiunary** H'land 416 C1
**Five Acres** Glos 129 E5
**Five Ash Down** E Sussex 50 B2
**Five Ashes** E Sussex 50 A4
**Five Bells** Som'set 57 C8
**Five Bridges** Heref'd 152 C3
**Five Chimneys** E Sussex 50 B3
**Five Houses** I/Wight 29 C8
**Five Lanes** Monmouths 101 D8
**Five Oak Green** Kent 71 C7
**Five Oaks** W Sussex 68 F3
**Five Roads** Carms 96 A4
**Five Ways** Warwick 177 D7
**Five Wents** Kent 72 A3
**Fivecrosses** Ches 265 D5
**Fivehead** Som'set 38 B5
**Fivelanes** Cornw'l 18 D1
**Flackley Ash** E Sussex 52 B2
**Flack's Green** Essex 140 E4
**Flackwell Heath** Bucks 109 D7
**Fladbury** Worcs 154 C2
**Fladbury Cross** Worcs 154 C2
**Fladda** Shetl'd 456 E3
**Fladdabister** Shetl'd 455 C3
**Flagg** Derby 268 F2
**Flakebridge** Cumb 328 B4
**Flambards Experience, Helston** Cornw'l 4 E1
**Flamborough** ER Yorks 311 A6
**Flamingo Land, Pickering** N Yorks 321 E6
**Flamstead** Herts 137 E5
**Flamstead End** Herts 112 B1
**Flanders Green** Herts 138 B2
**Flanderwell** S Yorks 282 E3
**Flansham** W Sussex 47 F7
**Flanshaw** W Yorks 293 F8
**Flappit Spring** W Yorks 292 C3
**Flasby** N Yorks 304 D2
**Flash** Staffs 267 F7
**Flashader** H'land 430 C3
**Flaunden** Herts 110 B2
**Flawborough** Notts 249 F6
**Flawith** N Yorks 307 B6
**Flax Bourton** N Som'set 80 C2
**Flax Moss** Lancs 290 F4
**Flaxby** N Yorks 306 D4
**Flaxholme** Derby 246 F4
**Flaxlands** Norfolk 209 E6
**Flaxley** Glos 129 D7
**Flaxpool** Som'set 58 D2
**Flaxton** N Yorks 308 C2
**Fleckney** Leics 201 E6
**Flecknoe** Warwick 179 F5
**Fledborough** Notts 271 E8
**Fleet** Dorset 25 D7
**Fleet** Hants 46 F2
**Fleet** Hants 67 A6
**Fleet** Lincs 229 D7
**Fleet Air Arm Museum, Yeovil** Som'set 39 B9
**Fleet Hargate** Lincs 229 C7
**Fleetend** Hants 45 E5
**Fleetlands** Hants 45 F6
**Fleetville** Herts 137 F7
**Fleetwood** Lancs 301 F5
**Fleggburgh = Burgh St. Margaret** Norfolk 235 F5
**Flemings** Kent 95 E5
**Flemingston** V/Glam 77 B7
**Flemington** S Lanarks 381 A5
**Flemington** S Lanarks 381 C6
**Flempton** Suffolk 185 E9
**Fleoideabhagh** W Isles 449 D4
**Fletcher's Green** Kent 71 B5
**Fletchersbridge** Cornw'l 9 B5
**Fletchertown** Cumb 338 C3
**Fletching** E Sussex 49 B8
**Fleuchary** H'land 440 D4
**Fleuchlang** Dumf/Gal 401 D8
**Fleur-de-lis** Caerph 100 C3
**Flexbury** Cornw'l 32 E4
**Flexford** Hants 44 B3
**Flexford** Surrey 67 B8
**Flimby** Cumb 337 E3
**Flimwell** E Sussex 72 E1
**Flint = Y Fflint** Flints 263 E6
**Flint Cross** Cambs 161 D8
**Flint Hill** Durham 352 F2
**Flint Mountain** Flints 263 E6
**Flintham** Notts 249 E5
**Flinton** ER Yorks 298 C3
**Flint's Green** W Midlands 177 B8
**Flishinghurst** Kent 72 D2
**Flitcham** Norfolk 231 C6
**Flitholme** Cumb 328 D5
**Flitton** Beds 159 E9
**Flitwick** Beds 159 F8
**Flixborough** N Lincs 284 A4
**Flixborough Stather** N Lincs 284 B4
**Flixton** Gtr Man 278 F3
**Flixton** N Yorks 322 E4
**Flixton** Suffolk 188 A4
**Flockton** W Yorks 281 A6
**Flockton Green** W Yorks 281 A7
**Flodaigh** W Isles 447 C3
**Flodigarry** H'land 430 A4
**Flood Street** Hants 43 C5
**Flood's Ferry** Cambs 205 E6
**Flookburgh** Cumb 313 E8
**Flordon** Norfolk 209 D7
**Flore** Northants 157 A7
**Florence** Stoke 244 F4
**Flouch Inn** S Yorks 281 D5
**Flowers Bottom** Bucks 109 C6
**Flowers Green** E Sussex 51 D5
**Flowery Field** Gtr Man 279 E7
**Flowton** Suffolk 165 C6
**Fluchter** E Dunb 392 D3
**Fluder** Devon 15 B5
**Flugarth** Shetl'd 457 G4
**Flush House** W Yorks 280 C4
**Flushdyke** W Yorks 293 F7
**Flushing** Aberds 437 D7
**Flushing** Cornw'l 4 E3
**Flushing** Cornw'l 4 D4
**Fluxton** Devon 22 B3
**Flyford Flavell** Worcs 154 B2
**Foals Green** Suffolk 188 D3
**Fobbing** Thurr'k 114 F1
**Fochabers** Moray 435 C8
**Fochriw** Bl Gwent 100 A2
**Fockerby** N Lincs 284 A3
**Fodderletter** Moray 435 F6
**Fodderty** H'land 433 C7
**Foddington** Som'set 60 F3
**Foel** Powys 192 A3
**Foelgastell** Carms 123 E6
**Foffarty** Angus 420 C4
**Foggathorpe** ER Yorks 296 C2
**Foggbrook** Gtr Man 267 B5
**Fogo** Scot Borders 386 C5
**Fogrigarth** Shetl'd 457 H2
**Fogwatt** Moray 435 C7
**Foindle** H'land 442 D3
**Fold Head** Lancs 279 A6
**Fold Hill** Lincs 252 D5
**Folda** Angus 420 A1
**Fole** Staffs 222 A2
**Foleshill** W Midlands 178 B2
**Foley Park** Worcs 175 C6

Folke Dorset 40 D3
Folkestone Kent 74 D4
Folkestone Racecourse Kent 74 D2
Folkingham Lincs 227 B8
Folkington E Sussex 50 F4
Folksworth Cambs 203 F8
Folkton N Yorks 322 E5
Folla Rule Aberds 436 E4
Follifoot N Yorks 306 E3
Follingsby Tyne/Wear 353 D5
Folly Pembs 120 C2
Folly Gate Devon 19 A8
Fonmon V/Glam 77 C7
Fonston Cornw'l 17 B9
Fonthill Bishop Wilts 62 E3
Fonthill Gifford Wilts 62 E3
Fontmell Magna Dorset 41 C7
Fontmell Parva Dorset 41 D6
Fontwell W Sussex 47 E7
Fontwell Park Racecourse W Sussex 47 E6
Font-y-gary V/Glam 77 C8
Foodieash Fife 420 F3
Foolow Derby 268 D3
Footbridge Glos 131 B6
Footherley Staffs 198 C3
Foots Cray London 90 B4
Forbestown Aberds 427 A8
Force Forge Cumb 313 B7
Force Green Kent 90 E4
Force Mills Cumb 313 B8
Forcett N Yorks 331 D5
Ford Arg/Bute 408 B1
Ford Bucks 135 F6
Ford Derby 269 C8
Ford Devon 11 E8
Ford Devon 13 D6
Ford Devon 38 F2
Ford Devon 33 B5
Ford Devon 33 B8
Ford Glos 131 B7
Ford Kent 94 C4
Ford Mersey 276 E3
Ford Northum 387 E8
Ford Pembs 120 B3
Ford Plym'th 10 D5
Ford Shrops 219 F5
Ford Som'set 58 F1
Ford Som'set 80 F3
Ford Tyne/Wear 353 E6
Ford Wilts 82 A1
Ford W Sussex 47 F7
Ford End Essex 139 A5
Ford End Essex 140 D2
Ford Green Lancs 301 F8
Ford Heath Shrops 194 A4
Ford Street Som'set 37 C8
Forda Devon 19 B7
Forda Devon 54 D4
Fordbridge W Midlands 198 F4
Fordcombe Kent 71 C5
Fordell Fife 411 D6
Forden Powys 193 C8
Forder Cornw'l 10 D4
Forder Green Devon 14 B3
Fordgate Som'set 59 E6
Fordham Cambs 185 D5
Fordham Essex 141 B7
Fordham Norfolk 206 D3
Fordham Heath Essex 141 B7
Fordhill Northum 387 E9
Fordhouses W Midlands 197 C7
Fordingbridge Hants 43 D5
Fordon ER Yorks 322 E5
Fordoun Aberds 428 E4
Ford's Green E Sussex 70 F3
Ford's Green Suffolk 187 E6
Ford's Water Kent 73 C8
Fordstreet Essex 141 B7
Fordton Mill Devon 21 A6
Fordwells Oxon 132 E5
Fordwich Kent 94 E3
Fordyce Aberds 436 B2
Forebridge Staffs 221 D8
Foredale N Yorks 303 B8
Forehill S Ayrs 367 C6
Foreland Ho Arg/Bute 406 F2
Foremark Derby 223 C8
Forest N Yorks 331 F7
Forest Becks Lancs 303 E7
Forest Coal Pit Monmouths 127 C6
Forest Gate London 112 E3
Forest Green Glos 104 B1
Forest Green Surrey 68 C4
Forest Hall Tyne/Wear 352 C4
Forest Head Cumb 349 E5
Forest Hill London 90 B2
Forest Hill Oxon 134 F2
Forest Hill Wilts 84 C1
Forest Holme Lancs 291 E5
Forest Lane N Yorks 306 D3
Forest Lodge Arg/Bute 417 C7
Forest Lodge Dumf/Gal 356 E3
Forest Lodge H'land 426 A5
Forest Lodge Perth/Kinr 426 E4
Forest Mill Clack 410 C4
Forest Row E Sussex 70 D3
Forest Side I/Wight 30 C1
Forest Town Notts 248 B2
Forestburn Gate Northum 364 C3
Foresterseat Moray 435 C6
Forest-in-Teesdale Durham 341 F8
Forestside W Sussex 46 D3
Forfar Angus 420 B4
Forgandenny Perth/Kinr 419 F8
Forge Powys 191 D6
Forge Hammer Torf 101 C5
Forge Side Torf 127 F5
Forgewood N Lanarks 381 A6
Forgie Moray 435 C8
Forglen Ho. Aberds 436 C3
Forgue Aberds 436 D3
Formby Mersey 276 C2
Forncett End Norfolk 209 E6
Forncett St. Mary Norfolk 209 E7
Forncett St. Peter Norfolk 209 E7
Forneth Perth/Kinr 419 C8
Fornham All Saints Suffolk 186 E1
Fornham St. Martin Suffolk 186 E1
Fornighty H'land 434 C4
Forres Moray 435 C5
Forrestfield N Lanarks 394 E2
Forry's Green Essex 140 A4
Forsbrook Staffs 244 F5
Forse H'land 445 E6
Forse Ho. H'land 445 E6
Forsinain H'land 444 D3
Forsinard H'land 444 D2
Forsinard Station H'land 444 D2
Forstal Kent 92 E1
Forston Dorset 25 A8
Fort Augustus H'land 425 B5
Fort George H'land 434 C2
Fort Green Suffolk 167 A7
Fort Victoria Country Park & Marine Aquarium I/Wight 29 C6
Fort William H'land 424 E3
Fortescue Devon 22 C4
Forteviot Perth/Kinr 419 F8
Forth S Lanarks 382 B3
Forth Road Bridge Fife 411 D6
Forthampton Glos 130 A3
Forthay Glos 103 C6
Fortingall Perth/Kinr 419 C5
Fortis Green London 111 E7
Forton Hants 65 C5
Forton Lancs 302 E1
Forton Shrops 219 E5
Forton Som'set 38 E4
Forton Staffs 220 D5
Fortrie Aberds 436 D3
Fortrie Aberds 436 C4
Fortrose H'land 434 C2
Fortune Green London 111 E6
Fortuneswell Dorset 24 D2
Forty Foot Bridge Norfolk 206 B1
Forty Green Bucks 109 D8
Forty Green Oxon 108 B5
Forty Hill London 111 C8
Forward Green Suffolk 165 A6
Forwood Glos 104 B2
Foryd Denbs 262 C1
Fosbury Wilts 84 E3
Foscot Glos 132 C3
Foscote Bucks 158 E2
Foscote Wilts 82 A2
Fosdyke Lincs 229 B6
Fosdyke Bridge Lincs 229 B6
Foss Perth/Kinr 419 B5
Foss Cross Glos 131 F7
Fossebridge Glos 131 E7
Fostall Kent 93 D8
Fosten Green Kent 72 D3
Foster Street Essex 139 F5
Fosters Green Lancs 277 C6
Foston Derby 223 B5
Foston Leics 201 E6
Foston Lincs 249 F8
Foston N Yorks 308 B2
Foston on the Wolds ER Yorks 310 D4
Fotherby Lincs 274 A3
Fothergill Cumb 337 E3
Fotheringhay Northants 203 E7
Foubister Orkney 453 C6
Foul Anchor Cambs 229 E9
Foul End Warwick 199 D5
Foul Green N Yorks 333 D8
Foul Mile E Sussex 51 C5
Foulbridge Cumb 339 B7
Foulby W Yorks 282 A2
Foulden Scot Borders 387 A8
Foulden Norfolk 207 D6
Foulis Castle H'land 433 B7
Foulrice N Yorks 308 A1
Foulridge Lancs 291 B6
Foulsham Norfolk 233 C5
Foulstone Cumb 314 D5
Fountainhall Scot Borders 385 C5
Fountains Abbey, Ripon N Yorks 306 B2
Four Ashes Suffolk 187 D5
Four Crosses Powys 218 E2
Four Crosses Staffs 197 B7
Four Crosses Wrex 241 D6
Four Elms Devon 38 E3
Four Elms Kent 70 B4
Four Foot Som'set 60 E3
Four Forks Som'set 58 D4
Four Gates Gtr Man 278 C2
Four Gotes Cambs 229 E8
Four Lane End S Yorks 281 D7
Four Lane Ends Blackb'n 290 E2
Four Lane Ends Ches 242 B4
Four Lane Ends C/York 308 E2
Four Lane Ends Gtr Man 278 B4
Four Lane Ends S Yorks 269 C7
Four Lane Ends W Yorks 292 D4
Four Lanes Cornw'l 4 C1
Four Lanes End Hants 86 F3
Four Marks Hants 66 E3
Four Mile Bridge Angl 258 D2
Four Mile Elm Glos 130 E2
Four Oaks E Sussex 52 B2
Four Oaks Glos 129 B7
Four Oaks W Midlands 198 D3
Four Oaks W Midlands 177 B7
Four Oaks Park W Midlands 198 D3
Four Points W Berks 85 A8
Four Pools Worcs 154 D3
Four Roads Carms 122 F4
Four Roads I/Man 336 E2
Four Sisters Suffolk 165 E6
Four Throws Kent 72 F2
Four Wents Kent 71 A7
Fourlane Ends Derby 247 C5
Fourlanes End Ches 244 C2
Fourpenny H'land 440 D5
Fourstones Northum 350 C4
Fovant Wilts 62 F5
Foveran Aberds 437 F6
Fowey Cornw'l 9 E5
Fowler's Plot Som'set 59 D6
Fowley Common Warrington 278 E2
Fowlis Angus 420 D3
Fowlis Wester Perth/Kinr 419 E7
Fowlmere Cambs 161 C8
Fownhope Heref'd 152 F1
Fox Corner Surrey 88 F1
Fox Hatch Essex 113 C6
Fox Hill Bath/NE Som'set 81 D7
Fox Lane Hants 87 E7
Fox Royal W Yorks 281 A6
Fox Street Essex 142 B1
Foxash Estate Essex 142 A2
Foxbar Renf 391 F9
Foxcombe Hill Oxon 107 B6
Foxcote Glos 131 D6
Foxcote Som'set 81 E6
Foxcotte Hants 64 B3
Foxdale I/Man 336 D2
Foxearth Essex 164 D1
Foxendown Kent 91 C8
Foxfield Cumb 313 C5
Foxford W Midlands 178 B2
Foxham Wilts 82 A4
Foxhills Hants 44 D1
Foxhole Cornw'l 8 E2
Foxhole Norfolk 209 D8
Foxholes N Yorks 310 A2
Foxholt Kent 74 C4
Foxhunt Green E Sussex 50 C3
Foxley Norfolk 233 D5
Foxley Wilts 104 E2
Foxlydiate Worcs 176 E3
Fox's Cross Kent 94 D1
Foxt Staffs 245 E6
Foxton Cambs 161 C8
Foxton Durham 332 B2
Foxton Leics 201 E8
Foxton N Yorks 319 A7
Foxton Canal Locks Leics 201 F7
Foxup N Yorks 316 E3
Foxwist Green Ches 265 F7
Foxwood Shrops 174 C2
Foy Heref'd 129 B6
Foyers H'land 433 F6
Foynesfield H'land 434 C3
Fraddam Cornw'l 3 D7
Fraddon Cornw'l 7 D9
Fradley Staffs 223 F5
Fradley South Staffs 198 A4
Fradswell Staffs 222 B1
Fraisthorpe ER Yorks 310 C5
Framfield E Sussex 50 B2
Framingham Earl Norfolk 210 C1
Framingham Pigot Norfolk 210 C1
Framlingham Suffolk 188 F3
Framlingham Castle Suffolk 188 F3
Frampton Dorset 25 A7
Frampton Lincs 229 A6
Frampton Cotterell S Glos 103 F5
Frampton End S Glos 103 F5
Frampton Mansell Glos 104 B3
Frampton on Severn Glos 129 F8
Frampton West End Lincs 252 F2
Framsden Suffolk 166 A1
Framwellgate Moor Durham 344 C1
France Lynch Glos 104 B3
Franche Worcs 175 C6
Frandley Ches 265 D7
Frankby Mersey 263 B6
Frankfort Norfolk 234 D3
Frankley Worcs 176 C2
Frankley Worcs 176 B2
Frank's Bridge Powys 149 A7
Frankton Warwick 178 D3
Frankwell Shrops 219 F6
Frant E Sussex 71 D6
Fraserburgh Aberds 437 B6
Frating Essex 142 C2
Frating Green Essex 142 C2
Fratton Portsm'th 45 F8
Freasley Warwick 199 D5
Freathy Cornw'l 10 E3
Frecheville S Yorks 269 C7
Freckenham Suffolk 185 D6
Freckleton Lancs 288 E5
Free Piece Hants 67 D5
Free Town Gtr Man 279 B5
Freeby Leics 226 D3
Freefolk Priors Hants 65 B6
Freehay Staffs 245 F6
Freeland Oxon 133 E7
Freeland Renf 392 E1
Freemantle S'thampton 44 D3
Freeport W Yorks 294 F2
Freeport Hornsea Outlet Village ER Yorks 311 F5
Freester Shetl'd 457 H4
Freethorpe Norfolk 210 B4
Freezing Hill S Glos 81 B6
Freezy Water London 112 C2
Freiston Lincs 252 F3
Freiston Shore Lincs 252 F3
Fremington Devon 54 E5
French Street Kent 70 A4
Frenchay S Glos 80 A4
Frenchbeer Devon 20 C3
Frenches Green Essex 140 C3
Frenchwood Lancs 289 E7
Frenich Stirl 409 B7
Frensham Surrey 67 C6
Frenze Norfolk 187 B7
Fresgoe H'land 444 B3
Freshbrook Swindon 105 F7
Freshfield Mersey 276 C2
Freshford Bath/NE Som'set 81 D7
Freshwater I/Wight 29 C6
Freshwater Bay I/Wight 29 C6
Freshwater East Pembs 117 E6
Fressingfield Suffolk 188 C3
Freston Suffolk 165 E8
Freswick H'land 445 B7
Fretherne Glos 129 F8
Frettenham Norfolk 234 E1
Freuchie Fife 411 B7
Freuchies Angus 420 A2
Freystrop Pembs 117 B5
Friar Park W Midlands 197 E9
Friar Waddon Dorset 25 C7
Friars Gate E Sussex 70 E4
Friarton Perth/Kinr 420 E1
Friday Bridge Cambs 205 C8
Friday Hill London 112 D2
Friday Street E Sussex 50 F5
Friday Street Suffolk 188 F5
Friday Street Suffolk 166 A2
Friday Street Suffolk 166 B4
Friday Street Surrey 68 B4
Fridaythorpe ER Yorks 309 D6
Friendly W Yorks 292 F3
Friern Barnet London 111 D7
Friesland Arg/Bute 414 B4
Friesthorpe Lincs 273 C6
Frieston Lincs 250 E1
Frieth Bucks 109 D5
Frieze Hill Som'set 38 A2
Friezeland Notts 247 D7
Frilford Oxon 107 C5
Frilsham W Berks 85 B7
Frimley Surrey 87 E7
Frimley Green Surrey 87 E7
Frimley Ridge Surrey 87 E7
Frindsbury Medway 92 C1
Fring Norfolk 231 B6
Fringford Oxon 134 B3
Friningham Kent 92 E3
Frinsted Kent 92 E4
Frinton-on-Sea Essex 143 D5
Friockheim Angus 421 C5
Friog Gwyn 190 A3
Frisby on the Wreake Leics 225 E8
Friskney Lincs 252 C5
Friskney Eaudyke Lincs 252 C5
Friskney Tofts Lincs 252 D5
Friston E Sussex 52 F2
Friston Suffolk 189 F6
Fritchley Derby 247 D5
Frith Bank Lincs 252 E2
Frith Common Worcs 174 E3
Fritham Hants 43 D7
Frithelstock Devon 34 C2
Frithelstock Stone Devon 34 C2
Frithend Hants 67 D6
Frithsden Herts 136 F4
Frithvile Lincs 252 D2
Frittenden Kent 72 C3
Frittiscombe Devon 13 D7
Fritton Norfolk 209 E8
Fritton Norfolk 210 C5
Fritton Norfolk 235 E5
Fritwell Oxon 134 B1
Frizinghall W Yorks 292 C4
Frizington Cumb 325 C5
Frizzeler's Green Suffolk 185 F8
Frobost W Isles 446 A3
Frocester Glos 103 B7
Frochas Powys 193 B7
Frodesley Shrops 195 C6
Frodingham N Lincs 284 B4
Frodsham Ches 265 D5
Frog End Cambs 161 B8
Frog End Cambs 162 A3
Frog Pool Worcs 175 E6
Frog Street Som'set 38 C4
Froggatt Derby 268 D4
Froghall Staffs 245 E6
Frogham Hants 43 D6
Frogham Kent 74 A5
Froghole Kent 70 A4
Frogholt Kent 74 D3
Frogland Cross S Glos 102 F4
Frogmore Devon 13 D6
Frogmore Hants 87 E6
Frogmore Herts 111 B5
Frognall Kent 94 E4
Frognall Lincs 204 A2
Frogpool Cornw'l 4 C3
Frogs Green Essex 162 E4
Frogshall Norfolk 257 E7
Frogwell Cornw'l 10 B2
Frogwell Devon 36 D3
Frogwell Wilts 82 B3
Frolesworth Leics 200 E4
Frome Som'set 61 B7
Frome St. Quintin Dorset 40 F1
Frome Whitfield Dorset 25 B8
Fromefield Som'set 61 B7
Fromes Hill Heref'd 152 C3
Fron Denbs 240 A2
Fron Flints 263 E5
Fron Gwyn 237 D6
Fron Powys 171 E6
Fron Powys 193 D7
Fron Powys 193 C8
Fron Powys 193 B8
Fron Isaf Wrex 241 F6
Fron Uchaf Wrex 241 F6
Froncysyllte Wrex 241 F6
Frongoch Gwyn 216 A3
Fron-las Powys 193 A7
Frost Devon 35 E8
Frost Row Norfolk 208 C4
Frost Street Som'set 38 C3
Frostenden Suffolk 189 B7
Frostenden Bottom Suffolk 189 B7
Frostenden Corner Suffolk 189 B7
Frosterley Durham 342 D4
Frotoft Orkney 454 D2
Froxfield Beds 159 F7
Froxfield Wilts 84 C2
Froxfield Green Hants 46 A2
Fryern Hill Hants 44 B3
Fryerning Essex 113 B7
Fryerns Essex 114 E1
Fryton N Yorks 320 E4
Fugglestone St. Peter Wilts 63 E7
Fulbeck Lincs 250 D1
Fulbeck Northum 365 E5
Fulbourn Cambs 162 A3
Fulbrook Oxon 132 E4
Fulflood Hants 65 F6
Fulford C/York 308 F1
Fulford Som'set 58 F4
Fulford Staffs 221 A9
Fulham London 89 A6
Fulking W Sussex 48 D4
Full Sutton ER Yorks 308 D3
Fullaford Devon 55 D8
Fullarton Glasg C 392 F4
Fullarton N Ayrs 379 E6
Fuller Street Essex 140 D3
Fuller's End Essex 139 B6
Fuller's Moor Ches 242 D2
Fullers Slade M/Keynes 158 E3
Fullerton Hants 64 D4
Fulletby Lincs 274 E2
Fullready Warwick 155 C8
Fullwood E Ayrs 379 B8
Fullwood Gtr Man 279 C7
Fulmer Bucks 110 E2
Fulmodestone Norfolk 232 B4
Fulneck W Yorks 293 D6
Fulnetby Lincs 273 D6
Fulney Lincs 228 D5
Fulshaw Park Ches 266 E3
Fulstone W Yorks 280 C5
Fulstow Lincs 287 E5
Fulwell Oxon 133 C6
Fulwell Tyne/Wear 353 E6
Fulwood Lancs 289 D7
Fulwood Notts 247 C7
Fulwood Som'set 38 B2
Fulwood S Yorks 269 B6
Fulwood Row Lancs 289 C8
Fundenhall Norfolk 209 D6
Fundenhall Street Norfolk 209 D6
Funtington W Sussex 46 E3
Funtley Hants 45 E6
Funtullich Perth/Kinr 419 E5
Funzie Shetl'd 456 D6
Furley Devon 38 F3
Furnace Arg/Bute 408 B3
Furnace Carms 96 B5
Furnace Ceredig'n 190 D4
Furnace H'land 432 A1
Furnace End Warwick 199 E5
Furnace Green W Sussex 69 D7
Furneaux Pelham Herts 138 B4
Furner's Green E Sussex 49 A8
Furness Vale Derby 267 C7
Furnham Som'set 38 E4
Further Ford End Essex 138 A4
Further Quarter Kent 72 D4
Furze Green Norfolk 188 B2
Furze Platt Windsor 109 F7
Furzebrook Dorset 27 D5
Furzehill Dorset 42 F3
Furzeley Corner Hants 45 D8
Furzley Hants 43 C8
Furzton M/Keynes 158 E4
Futho Northants 158 D3
Fyfett Som'set 38 D2
Fyfield Essex 139 F7
Fyfield Hants 64 B2
Fyfield Oxon 107 C5
Fyfield Wilts 83 D8
Fyfield Wick Oxon 107 C5
Fyling Park N Yorks 335 F5
Fylingthorpe N Yorks 335 F5
Fyning W Sussex 46 B4
Fyvie Aberds 436 E4


## G


Gabalfa Card 78 A3
Gabhsann bho Dheas W Isles 451 B7
Gabhsann bho Thuath W Isles 451 B7
Gable Head Hants 31 A6
Gablon H'land 440 D4
Gabroc Hill E Ayrs 379 B9
Gadbrook Surrey 69 B6
Gaddesby Leics 201 A7
Gadebridge Herts 136 F4
Gadfa Angl 259 B6
Gadlas Shrops 218 A4
Gadlys Rh Cyn Taff 99 B6
Gadshill Kent 92 B1
Gaer Newp 101 E5
Gaer Powys 126 C4
Gaer-fawr Monmouths 101 C8
Gaerllwyd Monmouths 101 C8
Gaerwen Angl 259 E6
Gagingwell Oxon 133 B7
Gaick Lodge H'land 426 D2
Gailey Staffs 197 A7
Gain Hill Kent 71 B9
Gainford Durham 331 C5
Gainsborough Lincs 271 A8
Gainsborough Suffolk 165 D8
Gainsford End Essex 163 E7
Gairloch H'land 438 F2
Gairlochy H'land 424 D3
Gairney Bank Perth/Kinr 411 C6
Gairnshiel Lodge Aberds 427 B7
Gaisgill Cumb 328 E2
Gaitsgill Cumb 339 B6
Galashiels Scot Borders 385 E6
Gale Gtr Man 279 A7
Gale Green Gtr Man 266 B4
Galgate Lancs 301 D8
Galhampton Som'set 60 F4
Gallaberry Dumf/Gal 358 F3
Gallachoille Arg/Bute 407 D7
Gallanach Arg/Bute 414 A5
Gallanach Arg/Bute 416 E3
Gallanach H'land 422 D4
Gallantry Bank Ches 242 D3
Gallatown Fife 411 C7
Galley Common Warwick 199 E7
Galley Hill Cambs 183 E6
Galley Hill Lincs 250 E4
Galleyend Essex 114 B1
Galleywood Essex 113 B9
Galligill Cumb 341 C6
Gallin Perth/Kinr 418 C3
Gallovie H'land 425 D7
Gallowfauld Angus 420 C4
Gallowhill Glasg C 380 A4
Gallowhill Renf 392 E1
Gallowhills Aberds 437 C7
Gallows Green Essex 139 B8
Gallows Green Essex 141 B7
Gallows Green Staffs 245 F7
Gallows Inn Derby 247 F7
Gallowsgreen Torf 127 F6
Gallowstree Common Oxon 108 F3
Gallt Melyd = Meliden Denbs 262 C3
Galltair H'land 431 F8
Galltegfa Denbs 240 C3
Gallt-y-foel Gwyn 237 B7
Gallypot Street E Sussex 70 D4
Galmington Som'set 38 B2
Galmisdale H'land 422 D4
Galmpton Devon 12 D4
Galmpton Torbay 15 D5
Galmpton Warborough Torbay 15 D5
Galon Uchaf Merth Tyd 125 F8
Galphay N Yorks 306 A2
Galston E Ayrs 380 E2
Galton Dorset 26 C2
Galtrigill H'land 430 C1
Gamble Hill W Yorks 293 D7
Gamble's Green Essex 140 E4
Gamblesby Cumb 340 D3
Gamelsby Cumb 347 F7
Gamesley Derby 280 F2
Gamlingay Cambs 160 B4
Gamlingay Cinques Cambs 160 B4
Gamlingay Great Heath Cambs 160 B4
Gammersgill N Yorks 317 D7
Gamston Notts 225 A7
Gamston Notts 271 D6
Ganavan Arg/Bute 416 D3
Ganborough Glos 132 B2
Gandale N Yorks 318 B2
Gang Cornw'l 10 B2
Ganllwyd Gwyn 215 D6
Gannochy Angus 428 E2
Gannochy Perth/Kinr 420 E1
Gannow Hill Shrops 218 B4
Gansclet H'land 445 D7
Ganstead ER Yorks 298 D2
Ganthorpe N Yorks 308 A2
Ganton N Yorks 322 E3
Gants Hill London 112 E3
Ganwick Corner Herts 111 C7
Gaodhail Arg/Bute 416 D1
Gappah Devon 21 E7
Garafad H'land 430 B4
Garamor H'land 423 C6
Garaway Hill Heref'd 128 B2
Garazim Conwy 260 D3
Garbat H'land 433 B6
Garbhallt Arg/Bute 408 C3
Garboldisham Norfolk 187 B5
Garbole H'land 434 F2
Garden City Bl Gwent 126 E4
Garden City Flints 263 F8
Garden Village S Yorks 281 E7
Garden Village Swan 97 C6
Garden Village Wrex 241 D7
Garden Village W Yorks 294 D2
Gardener's Green Wokingham 87 C6
Gardenstown Aberds 437 B4
Garderhouse Shetl'd 457 J3
Gardham ER Yorks 297 B6
Gardie Shetl'd 456 D5
Gardin Shetl'd 457 G4
Gare Hill Som'set 61 C7
Garelochhead Arg/Bute 409 C5
Garford Oxon 107 C5
Garforth W Yorks 294 D2
Gargrave N Yorks 304 E2
Gargunnock Stirl 410 C2
Garker Cornw'l 8 E3
Garlandhayes Devon 37 C8
Garlands Cumb 348 F2
Garleffin S Ayrs 400 A2
Garlic Street Norfolk 188 B2
Garlieston Dumf/Gal 401 E6
Garlinge Kent 95 C6
Garlinge Green Kent 74 A2
Garlogie Aberds 429 B4
Garmond Aberds 437 C5
Garmondsway Durham 344 E2
Garmony Arg/Bute 416 C1
Garmouth Moray 435 B8
Garmston Shrops 195 B8
Garnant Carms 124 E2
Garndiffaith Torf 100 B5
Garndolbenmaen Gwyn 237 F5
Garnett Bridge Cumb 314 A4
Garnfadryn Gwyn 213 B5
Garnkirk N Lanarks 393 E5
Garnlydan Bl Gwent 126 E4
Garnsgate Lincs 229 D8
Garnswilt Swan 123 F8
Garn-yr-erw Torf 127 E5
Garra Ellabus Arg/Bute 406 E2
Garrabost W Isles 451 D8
Garrachra Arg/Bute 408 D3
Garralburn Moray 436 C1
Garraron Arg/Bute 407 B8
Garras Cornw'l 4 F2
Garreg Gwyn 237 F8
Garrett's Green W Midlands 177 A5
Garrick Perth/Kinr 410 A3
Garrigill Cumb 341 C5
Garrison Stirl 409 B6
Garriston N Yorks 318 B2
Garroch Dumf/Gal 356 F3
Garrogie Lodge H'land 425 A7
Garros H'land 430 B4
Garrow Perth/Kinr 419 C6
Garrowhill Glasg C 393 F5
Garrygualach H'land 424 B3
Garryhorn Dumf/Gal 356 D2
Garsdale Cumb 315 C8
Garsdale Head Cumb 316 B1
Garsdon Wilts 104 E4
Garshall Green Staffs 222 B1
Garsington Oxon 107 B8
Garstang Lancs 289 A6
Garston Herts 110 B4
Garston Mersey 264 C3
Garswood Mersey 277 E7
Gartbreck Arg/Bute 403 A2
Gartcosh N Lanarks 393 E5
Garth Bridg 98 D4
Garth Ceredig'n 169 B5
Garth Gwyn 259 E8
Garth Monmouths 101 D6
Garth Perth/Kinr 419 B5
Garth Powys 191 C6
Garth Powys 148 C4
Garth Powys 172 D3
Garth Shetl'd 457 H2
Garth Shetl'd 457 H4
Garth Wrex 241 F6
Garth Owen Powys 193 E6
Garth Place Caerph 100 E3
Garth Row Cumb 314 A4
Garth Trevor Wrex 241 F6
Garthamlock Glasg C 393 E5
Garthbeg H'land 425 A7
Garthbrengy Powys 149 F5
Garthdee Aberd C 429 B6
Garthell Ceredig'n 146 A4
Garthmyl Powys 193 D7
Garthmyn Conwy 238 C4
Garthocharn W Dunb 409 D7
Garthorpe Leics 226 D3
Garthorpe N Lincs 284 A3
Gartlea N Lanarks 393 F7
Gartly Aberds 436 E2
Gartmore Stirl 409 C8
Gartmore Ho. Stirl 409 C8
Gartnagrenach Arg/Bute 404 A3
Gartness N Lanarks 393 F7
Gartness Stirl 409 D8
Garton ER Yorks 298 C4
Garton-on-the-Wolds ER Yorks 309 D8
Gartsherrie N Lanarks 393 E6
Gartur Stirl 409 C8
Gartymore H'land 441 B7
Garvald Scot Borders 383 C7
Garvald E Loth 398 D1
Garvamore H'land 425 C7
Garvard Arg/Bute 406 C3
Garvault Hotel H'land 444 E1
Garve H'land 433 B5
Garvestone Norfolk 208 B4
Garvock Aberds 428 E4
Garway Heref'd 128 C3
Garway Common Heref'd 128 C3
Garwick Lincs 251 F6
Gas Terminal Aberds 437 C7
Gascote W Midlands 198 C1
Gaskan H'land 423 E7
Gasper Wilts 61 E7
Gastard Wilts 82 C2
Gasthorpe Norfolk 186 B4
Gaston Green Essex 139 D5
Gatcombe I/Wight 30 D1
Gate Burton Lincs 272 C1
Gate Helmsley N Yorks 308 D2
Gateacre Mersey 264 B3
Gatebeck Cumb 314 C4

Gateford Common Notts 270 C3
Gateforth N Yorks 295 E5
Gatehead E Ayrs 379 E7
Gatehouse of Fleet Dumf/Gal 401 D8
Gatelawbridge Dumf/Gal 358 C2
Gateley Norfolk 232 D4
Gatenby N Yorks 318 C5
Gateshead Tyne/Wear 352 D4
Gateshead International Stadium Tyne/Wear 352 D4
Gatesheath Ches 242 B2
Gateside Aberds 428 A3
Gateside Angus 420 C4
Gateside E Renf 380 A1
Gateside Fife 411 B6
Gateside N Ayrs 379 B7
Gateside Shetl'd 457 F2
Gathurst Gtr Man 277 C7
Gatley Gtr Man 266 B3
Gatley End Cambs 161 D5
Gattonside Scot Borders 385 E7
Gatwick Glos 129 E8
Gatwick Airport W Sussex 69 C7
Gaufron Powys 170 E4
Gaulby Leics 201 C7
Gauldry Fife 420 E3
Gauntons Bank Ches 242 E4
Gaunt's Common Dorset 42 E3
Gaunt's Earthcott S Glos 102 F4
Gaunt's End Essex 139 B6
Gautby Lincs 273 E8
Gavinton Scot Borders 386 B5
Gawber S Yorks 281 C8
Gawcott Bucks 134 A4
Gawsworth Ches 266 F4
Gawthorpe W Yorks 281 A5
Gawthorpe W Yorks 281 B5
Gawthrop Cumb 315 C7
Gawthwaite Cumb 313 D6
Gay Bowers Essex 114 B2
Gay Street W Sussex 48 B1
Gaydon Warwick 156 B2
Gayfield Orkney 454 A2
Gayhurst M/Keynes 158 C4
Gayle N Yorks 316 C3
Gayles N Yorks 330 E4
Gayton Mersey 263 C7
Gayton Norfolk 231 E6
Gayton Northants 158 B2
Gayton Staffs 222 C1
Gayton Engine Lincs 275 B6
Gayton le Marsh Lincs 275 C5
Gayton le Wold Lincs 274 B1
Gayton Thorpe Norfolk 231 E6
Gayton Top Lincs 275 C5
Gaywood Norfolk 230 D4
Gaza Shetl'd 457 F3
Gazeley Suffolk 185 F7
Geàrraidh Sheilidh W Isles 446 A3
Geanies House H'land 441 F5
Gear Sands Cornw'l 7 D6
Gearraidh Bhailteas W Isles 446 A3
Gearraidh Bhaird W Isles 451 E6
Gearraidh Dubh W Isles 447 C3
Gearraidh na h-Aibhne W Isles 451 D5
Gearraidh na Monadh W Isles 446 B3
Geary H'land 430 B2
Geddes House H'land 434 C3
Gedding Suffolk 164 A3
Geddington Northants 181 A5
Gedintailor H'land 430 E5
Gedling Notts 248 F3
Gedney Lincs 229 D8
Gedney Broadgate Lincs 229 D8
Gedney Drove End Lincs 230 C1
Gedney Dyke Lincs 229 C8
Gedney Hill Lincs 205 A5
Gee Cross Gtr Man 267 A6
Geenmoor Hill Oxon 108 F2
Geeston Rutl'd 203 C5
Gefnan Gwyn 237 A8
Geilston Invercl 391 C6
Geirinis W Isles 447 D2
Geise H'land 445 B5
Geisiadar W Isles 450 D4
Geldeston Norfolk 210 E3
Gell Conwy 262 F7
Gelli Pembs 117 A7
Gelli Rh Cyn Taff 99 D6
Gellideg Merth Tyd 126 F1
Gellifor Denbs 240 B3
Gelligaer Caerph 100 C2
Gelligroes Caerph 100 C3
Gelli-haf Caerph 100 C3
Gellilydan Gwyn 215 A5
Gellinudd Neath P Talb 98 B1
Gellyburn Perth/Kinr 419 D8
Gellywen Carms 122 C1
Gelston Dumf/Gal 402 D1
Gelston Lincs 250 E1
Gembling ER Yorks 310 D4
Gendros Swan 97 C7
Genesis Green Suffolk 163 A8
Geneva Ceredig'n 146 A2
Gentleshaw Staffs 198 A2
Geocrab W Isles 449 C5
George Green Bucks 110 F2
George Nympton Devon 35 B7
Georgefield Dumf/Gal 360 D2
Georgeham Devon 54 D4
Georgetown Bl Gwent 126 F3
Gergask H'land 425 C8
Gerlan Gwyn 260 F2
Germansweek Devon 19 B5
Germiston Glasg C 392 E4
Germoe Cornw'l 3 E7
Gerrans Cornw'l 5 C5
Gerrard's Cross Bucks 110 E1
Gerrick Redcar/Clevel'd 333 D9
Gestingthorpe Essex 164 E1
Gesto Ho H'land 430 E3
Geuffordd Powys 218 F1
Gib Heath W Midlands 198 F2
Gibb Hill Ches 265 D7
Gibbet Hill Som'set 61 B7
Gibbshill Dumf/Gal 402 B1
Gibraltar Beds 159 C8
Gibraltar Bucks 135 E6
Gibraltar Kent 74 D4
Gibraltar Oxon 133 D8
Gibraltar Suffolk 166 B1
Gibshill Invercl 391 D6
Giddeahall Wilts 82 B2
Giddy Green Dorset 26 C3
Gidea Park London 112 D5
Gidleigh Devon 20 C3
Giffnock E Renf 380 A3
Gifford E Loth 397 E7
Giffordland N Ayrs 378 C5
Giffordtown Fife 411 A7
Gigg Gtr Man 279 C5
Giggleswick N Yorks 303 C8
Giggshill Surrey 89 C5
Gignog Pembs 119 E5
Gilbent Gtr Man 266 C4
Gilberdyke ER Yorks 296 E3
Gilbert Street Hants 66 E3
Gilbert's Coombe Cornw'l 4 B1
Gilbert's End Worcs 153 D6
Gilbert's Green Warwick 176 D5
Gilbertstone W Midlands 177 B5
Gilchriston E Loth 397 E6
Gilcrux Cumb 337 D8
Gildersome W Yorks 293 E6
Gildersome Street W Yorks 293 E6
Gildingwells S Yorks 270 B3
Gilesgate Durham 344 C1
Gilesgate Moor Durham 344 C1
Gileston V/Glam 77 C7
Gilfach Caerph 100 C3
Gilfach Goch Rh Cyn Taff 99 E6
Gilfachrheda Ceredig'n 145 A8
Gilgarran Cumb 325 B5
Gill N Yorks 291 B8
Gillamoor N Yorks 320 C4
Gillan Cornw'l 4 E3
Gillar's Green Mersey 277 F6
Gillbank Cumb 313 A8
Gillen H'land 430 C2
Gillesbie Dumf/Gal 359 D7
Gillham Kent 72 C4
Gilling East N Yorks 320 E3
Gilling West N Yorks 331 E5
Gillingham Dorset 61 F8
Gillingham Medway 92 C2
Gillingham Norfolk 210 E4
Gillmoss Mersey 276 E5
Gillock H'land 445 C6
Gillow Heath Staffs 244 C3
Gills H'land 445 A7
Gill's Green Kent 72 E2
Gilmanscleuch Scot Borders 372 C3
Gilmerton C/Edinb 396 E2
Gilmerton Perth/Kinr 419 E6
Gilmonby Durham 330 D1
Gilmorton Leics 200 F5
Gilmourton S Lanarks 380 E3
Gilnow Gtr Man 278 C3
Gilridge Kent 70 C4
Gilroyd S Yorks 281 D8
Gilslake S Glos 102 F3
Gilsland Cumb 349 C6
Gilson Warwick 198 E4
Gilstead W Yorks 292 C4
Gilston Scot Borders 385 A5
Gilston Herts 139 E5
Giltbrook Notts 247 E7
Gilver's Lane Worcs 153 D6
Gilwern Monmouths 127 E5
Gimingham Norfolk 257 E8
Gin Pit Gtr Man 278 D2
Ginclough Ches 267 D6
Ginger's Green E Sussex 50 D5
Giosla W Isles 450 E4
Gippeswyk Park Suffolk 165 D7
Gipping Suffolk 187 F6
Gipsey Bridge Lincs 251 E8
Gipsy Row Suffolk 165 E6
Gipsyville Kingston/Hull 297 E8
Gipton W Yorks 293 C8
Girdle Toll N Ayrs 379 D6
Girlington W Yorks 292 D4
Girlsta Shetl'd 457 H4
Girsby N Yorks 332 E2
Girtford Beds 160 B2
Girthon Dumf/Gal 401 D8
Girton Cambs 183 F8
Girton Notts 249 A7
Girvan S Ayrs 354 C2
Gisburn Lancs 303 F8
Gisburn Cotes Lancs 303 F8
Gisleham Suffolk 211 F6
Gislingham Suffolk 187 D6
Gissing Norfolk 187 A7
Gissing Common Norfolk 209 F7
Gittisham Devon 22 A4
Givons Grove Surrey 69 A5
Glachavoil Arg/Bute 408 E3
Glack of Midthird Moray 435 D8
Glackmore H'land 433 C8
Gladestry Powys 150 A2
Gladsmuir E Loth 397 D6
Glaichbea H'land 433 E7
Glais Swan 97 B9
Glaisdale N Yorks 334 E2
Glaisdale Side N Yorks 334 F2
Glame H'land 431 D5
Glamis Angus 420 C3
Glamis Castle Angus 420 C3
Glan Duar Carms 146 D3
Glan Dwyfach Gwyn 237 F5
Glan yr afon Gwyn 214 A2
Glanaber Angl 259 D6
Glanaber Terrace Conwy 238 E3
Glan-Adda Gwyn 259 E8
Glanafon Pembs 117 A5
Glanaman Carms 124 E2
Glandford Norfolk 256 D3
Glandwr Bl Gwent 100 B4
Glandwr Pembs 121 B7
Glandy Cross Carms 121 B6
Glaneirw Ceredig'n 145 C5
Glangrwyney Monmouths 127 D5
Glanllynfi Bridg 98 D4
Glanmule Powys 193 E7
Glanpwllafon Pembs 144 D3
Glanrafon Ceredig'n 168 B5
Glan-rhyd Gwyn 236 C5
Glanrhyd Pembs 144 D2
Glan-rhyd Powys 124 F4
Glanton Northum 376 E3
Glanvilles Wootton Dorset 40 E3
Glanwern Ceredig'n 190 F3
Glan-wr-afon Denbs 239 F8
Glanwydden Conwy 262 C6
Glan-y-don Flints 263 D5
Glan-y-Fferi = Ferryside Carms 122 F3
Glan-y-llyn Rh Cyn Taff 100 F2
Glan-y-nant Caerph 100 C2
Glan-y-nant Powys 170 B3
Glan-yr-afon Gwyn 239 F6
Glan-yr-afon Angl 258 D4
Glan-yr-afon Angl 260 C2
Glanyrafon Powys 217 C9
Glan-y-wern Gwyn 214 B4
Glapthorn Northants 203 E6
Glapwell Derby 247 A7
Glas-allt Shiel Aberds 427 D7
Glasbury Powys 149 E8
Glaschoil H'land 435 E5
Glascoed Denbs 262 E1
Glascoed Monmouths 101 B6
Glascoed Powys 193 B6
Glascoed Powys 193 A6
Glascoed Wrex 241 D6
Glascorrie Aberds 427 C8
Glascorrie Perth/Kinr 419 E6
Glascote Staffs 199 C5
Glascote Heath Staffs 199 C5
Glascwm Powys 149 B8
Glasdrum Arg/Bute 417 C5
Glasfryn Conwy 239 D6
Glasgoforest Aberds 429 A5
Glasgow Glasg C 392 E3
Glasgow Airport Renf 392 E1
Glasgow Art Gallery & Museum Glasg C 392 E3
Glasgow Botanic Gardens Glasg C 392 E3
Glasgow Bridge E Dunb 392 D4
Glasgow Cathedral Glasg C 392 E4
Glasgow Prestwick International Airport S Ayrs 367 B7
Glashvin H'land 430 B4
Glasinfryn Gwyn 259 F8
Glasllwch Newp 101 E5
Glasnacardoch H'land 423 C6
Glasnakille H'land 423 A5
Glasphein H'land 430 D1
Glaspwll Powys 191 D5
Glass Houghton W Yorks 294 F2
Glassburn H'land 433 E5
Glassenbury Kent 72 D2
Glasserton Dumf/Gal 401 F6
Glassford S Lanarks 381 C6
Glassgreen Moray 435 B7
Glasshouse Glos 129 C8
Glasshouse Hill Glos 129 C8
Glasshouses N Yorks 305 C7
Glasslie Fife 411 B7
Glasson Cumb 347 D7
Glasson Lancs 301 D7
Glassonby Cumb 340 D2
Glasterlaw Angus 421 B5
Glaston Rutl'd 202 C3
Glastonbury Som'set 60 D2
Glastonbury Abbey Som'set 60 D2
Glatton Cambs 182 A3
Glazebrook Warrington 265 A8
Glazebury Warrington 278 E2
Glazeley Shrops 196 F3
Gleadless S Yorks 269 C7
Gleadless Valley S Yorks 269 C7
Gleadsmoss Ches 266 F3
Gleanhead Dumf/Gal 401 A6
Gleann Tholàstaidh W Isles 451 C8
Gleaston Cumb 300 A4
Glebe Shetl'd 455 B3
Glebe Tyne/Wear 353 E5
Glebe Cliff Cornw'l 17 C6
Glebe Farm W Midlands 198 F3
Glecknabae Arg/Bute 408 F3
Gledhow W Yorks 293 C8
Gleiniant Powys 192 E3
Glemsford Suffolk 164 C1
Glen Dumf/Gal 402 B2
Glen Dumf/Gal 401 D7
Glen Auldyn I/Man 336 B4
Glen Bernisdale H'land 430 D4
Glen Ho Scot Borders 372 A2
Glen Mona I/Man 336 C4
Glen Mor H'land 431 E8
Glen Nevis House H'land 424 E3
Glen of Newmill Moray 436 C1
Glen Parva Leics C 200 D5
Glen Sluain Arg/Bute 408 C3
Glen Tanar House Aberds 428 C1
Glen Trool Lodge Dumf/Gal 401 A6
Glen Vic Askil H'land 430 D3
Glen Village Falk 394 C2
Glen Vine I/Man 336 D3
Glenallachie Moray 435 D7
Glenalmond College Perth/Kinr 419 E7
Glenalmond Ho. Perth/Kinr 419 E7
Glenamachrie Arg/Bute 416 E4
Glenample Stirl 418 E3
Glenancross H'land 423 C6
Glenapp Castle S Ayrs 400 A2
Glenaros Ho Arg/Bute 415 C8
Glenbarr Arg/Bute 404 C2
Glenbeg H'land 415 A8
Glenbeg H'land 434 F5
Glenbervie Aberds 428 D4
Glenboig N Lanarks 393 E6
Glenborrodale H'land 416 A1
Glenbranter Arg/Bute 408 C4
Glenbreck Scot Borders 371 C6
Glenbrein Lodge H'land 425 A6
Glenbrittle House H'land 430 F4
Glenbuchat Castle Aberds 427 A8
Glenbuchat Lodge Aberds 427 A8
Glenbuck E Ayrs 369 B7
Glenburn Renf 392 F1
Glenbyre Arg/Bute 415 E8
Glencalvie Lodge H'land 440 E1
Glencanisp Lodge H'land 439 A5
Glencaple Dumf/Gal 402 C3
Glencarron Lodge H'land 432 C2
Glencarse Perth/Kinr 420 E1
Glencassley Castle H'land 439 C8
Glencat Aberds 428 C2
Glenceitlein H'land 417 C6
Glencoe H'land 417 B5
Glencraig Fife 411 C6
Glencripesdale H'land 416 B1
Glencrosh Dumf/Gal 357 E7
Glendavan Ho. Aberds 428 B1
Glendevon Perth/Kinr 411 B4
Glendoe Lodge H'land 425 B6
Glendoebeg H'land 425 B6
Glendoick Perth/Kinr 420 E2
Glendoll Lodge Angus 427 E7
Glendon Hall Northants 180 B4
Glendoune S Ayrs 354 C2
Glenduckie Fife 420 F2
Glendye Lodge Aberds 428 D3
Gleneagles Hotel Perth/Kinr 410 A4
Gleneagles House Perth/Kinr 410 B4
Glenearn Perth/Kinr 420 F1
Glenegedale Arg/Bute 403 A3
Glenelg H'land 423 A8
Glenernie Moray 434 D5
Glenfarg Perth/Kinr 411 A6
Glenfarquhar Lodge Aberds 428 D4
Glenferness House H'land 434 D4
Glenfeshie Lodge H'land 426 C3
Glenfiddich Distillery, Dufftown Moray 435 D8
Glenfiddich Lodge Moray 435 E8
Glenfield Leics 200 B4
Glenfinnan H'land 423 D8
Glenfinnan Lodge H'land 424 D1
Glenfintaig Ho. H'land 424 D4
Glenfoot Perth/Kinr 420 F1
Glenfyne Lodge Arg/Bute 417 F7
Glengap Dumf/Gal 401 D8
Glengarnock N Ayrs 379 B6
Glengolly H'land 445 B5
Glengorm Castle Arg/Bute 415 B7
Glengoulandie Perth/Kinr 419 B5
Glengrasco H'land 430 D4
Glenhead Farm Angus 420 A2
Glenholt Plym'th 11 C6
Glenhoul Dumf/Gal 356 E4
Glenhurich H'land 423 F8
Glenkerry Scot Borders 372 E2
Glenkiln Dumf/Gal 402 B2
Glenkindie Aberds 428 A1
Glenlair Dumf/Gal 402 B1
Glenlatterach Moray 435 C6
Glenlee Dumf/Gal 356 F4
Glenleraig H'land 442 E3
Glenlichorn Perth/Kinr 410 A2
Glenlicht Ho. H'land 424 A2
Glenlivet Moray 435 F6
Glenlochar Dumf/Gal 402 C1
Glenlochsie Perth/Kinr 427 E5
Glenlocksie Lodge Perth/Kinr 427 E5
Glenloig N Ayrs 405 C5
Glenlomond Perth/Kinr 411 B6
Glenluce Dumf/Gal 400 D4
Glenlussa Ho Arg/Bute 404 D3
Glenmallan Arg/Bute 409 C5
Glenmark Angus 428 D1
Glenmarkie Lodge Angus 420 A2
Glenmarksie H'land 433 C5
Glenmassan Arg/Bute 408 D4
Glenmavis N Lanarks 393 E7
Glenmavis W Loth 394 E4
Glenmaye I/Man 336 D2
Glenmeanie H'land 433 C4
Glenmidge Dumf/Gal 358 E1
Glenmoidart Ho H'land 423 E7
Glenmore Arg/Bute 407 A8
Glenmore Arg/Bute 408 E3
Glenmore H'land 430 D4
Glenmore Lodge H'land 426 B4
Glenmoy Angus 420 A4
Glennoe Arg/Bute 417 D5
Glenogil Angus 420 A4
Glenprosen Lodge Angus 427 F7
Glenprosen Village Angus 420 A3
Glenquaich Lodge Perth/Kinr 419 D6
Glenquiech Angus 420 A4
Glenquithlie Aberds 437 B5
Glenrazie Dumf/Gal 401 C5
Glenreasdell Mains Arg/Bute 404 A4
Glenree N Ayrs 405 D5
Glenridding Cumb 326 C4
Glenrosa N Ayrs 405 C5
Glenrossal H'land 440 C1
Glenrothes Fife 411 B7
Glensanda H'land 416 C3
Glensaugh Aberds 428 E3
Glenshero Lodge H'land 425 C7
Glenshoe Lodge Perth/Kinr 427 F6
Glenstockadale Dumf/Gal 400 C2
Glenstriven Arg/Bute 408 E3
Glentaggart S Lanarks 369 B8
Glentarkie Perth/Kinr 411 A6
Glentham Lincs 272 A5
Glentirranmuir Stirl 410 C1
Glenton Aberds 436 F3
Glentress Scot Borders 384 E2
Glentromie Lodge H'land 426 C2
Glentrool Village Dumf/Gal 401 B5
Glentruan I/Man 336 A4
Glentruim House H'land 426 C1
Glenturret Distillery, Crieff Perth/Kinr 419 E6
Glentworth Lincs 272 B3
Glenuaig Lodge H'land 432 D3
Glenuig H'land 423 E6
Glenure Arg/Bute 417 C5
Glenurquhart H'land 434 B2
Glenview Arg/Bute 417 E6
Glespin S Lanarks 369 B8
Gletness Shetl'd 457 H4
Glewstone Heref'd 128 C5
Glinton Peterbro 204 B2
Glodwick Gtr Man 279 D7
Glogue Pembs 121 A8
Glooston Leics 201 D9
Glossop Derby 280 F2
Gloucester Glos 130 D2
Gloucester Cathedral Glos 130 D2
Gloucestershire Airport Glos 130 C3
Gloup Shetl'd 456 C5
Glover's Hawes Kent 70 C4
Gloweth Cornw'l 4 B3
Glusburn N Yorks 292 A2
Glutt Lodge H'land 444 E3
Glutton Bridge Derby 245 A7
Gluvian Cornw'l 8 C1
Glympton Oxon 133 C7
Glyn Ceiriog Wrex 217 A9
Glyn Ebwy = Ebbw Vale Bl Gwent 126 F4
Glynarthen Ceredig'n 145 C6
Glynbrochan Powys 170 B3
Glyncoch Rh Cyn Taff 99 D8
Glyncorrwg Neath P Talb 98 C4
Glynde E Sussex 50 E2
Glyndebourne E Sussex 50 D2
Glyndyfrdwy Denbs 240 F3
Glynedd = Glyn-neath Neath P Talb 125 F6
Glynmorlas Shrops 218 A3
Glyn-neath = Glynedd Neath P Talb 125 F6
Glynogwr Bridg 99 E6
Glyntaff Rh Cyn Taff 100 E1
Glyntawe Powys 125 D5
Gnosall Staffs 221 D6
Gnosall Heath Staffs 221 D6
Goadby Leics 201 D9
Goadby Marwood Leics 226 C2
Goadsbarrow Cumb 300 B4
Goat Lees Kent 73 B7
Goatacre Wilts 82 A5
Goatham Green E Sussex 52 C1
Goathill Dorset 40 C3
Goathland N Yorks 334 F3
Goathurst Som'set 58 E5
Goathurst Common Kent 70 A4
Gobernuisgach Lodge H'land 443 D6
Gobernuisgeach H'land 444 E3
Gobhaig W Isles 448 B4
Gobowen Shrops 218 B3
Godalming Surrey 68 C1
Goddard's Corner Suffolk 188 E3
Goddard's Green Kent 72 D2
Goddard's Green Kent 72 E3
Goddard's Green W Berks 86 C3
Goddard's Green W Sussex 49 B5
Godden Green Kent 91 E6
Goddington London 90 C4
Godford Cross Devon 37 F7
Godington Oxon 134 B3
Godley Gtr Man 279 E8
Godmanchester Cambs 183 D5
Godmanstone Dorset 25 A8
Godmersham Kent 73 A8
Godney Som'set 60 C1
Godolphin Cross Cornw'l 3 D8
Godre'r-graig Neath P Talb 124 F3
Godshill Hants 43 D6
Godshill I/Wight 30 D2
Godstone Surrey 70 A1
Godstone Staffs 222 B2
Godstone Farm Surrey 70 A2
Godsworthy Devon 19 E7
Godwell Devon 11 D8
Godwinscroft Hants 28 A3
Goetre Monmouths 101 A6
Goff's Oak Herts 111 B8
Gogar C/Edinb 395 D8
Gogarth Conwy 260 C5
Goginan Ceredig'n 169 B6
Goirtean a'Chladaich H'land 424 E2
Golan Gwyn 237 F6
Golant Cornw'l 9 D5
Golberdon Cornw'l 10 A2
Golborne Gtr Man 277 E9
Golcar W Yorks 280 A3
Gold Hill Cambs 206 E1
Gold Hill Dorset 41 D6
Goldcliff Newp 101 F7
Golden Cross E Sussex 50 D3
Golden Green Kent 71 B7
Golden Grove Carms 123 D7
Golden Hill Bristol 80 A3
Golden Hill Hants 28 A5
Golden Hill Pembs 117 D5
Golden Hill Pembs 119 E7
Golden Pot Hants 66 C4
Golden Square Devon 38 F2
Golden Valley Derby 247 D6
Golden Valley Glos 130 C4
Golden Valley Heref'd 152 C3
Golden Valley S Glos 81 B5
Goldenhill Stoke 244 D2
Golders Green London 111 E6
Goldfinch Bottom W Berks 85 D7
Goldhanger Essex 141 F7
Goldington Beds 160 B1
Golds Green W Midlands 197 E8
Goldsborough N Yorks 306 D4
Goldsborough N Yorks 334 D3
Goldsithney Cornw'l 3 D6
Goldstone Shrops 220 C4
Goldsworth Park Surrey 88 E1
Goldthorn Park W Midlands 197 D7
Goldthorpe S Yorks 282 D3
Goldwick Glos 103 C6
Goldworthy Devon 33 B7
Golfa Powys 217 C8
Golford Kent 72 D3
Golftyn Flints 263 F7
Golgotha Kent 74 B5
Gollanfield H'land 434 C3
Gollawater Cornw'l 7 E6
Gollinglith Foot N Yorks 318 D1
Golly Wrex 241 C7
Golsoncott Som'set 57 D7
Golspie H'land 441 C5
Golval H'land 444 B2
Golynus Torf 100 B5
Gomeldon Wilts 63 D8
Gomersal W Yorks 293 E6
Gometra Ho Arg/Bute 415 C6
Gomshall Surrey 68 B3
Gonalston Notts 248 E4
Gonamena Cornw'l 9 A8
Gonerby Hill Foot Lincs 227 A5
Gonfirth Shetl'd 457 G3
Good Easter Essex 139 E8
Gooderstone Norfolk 207 C6
Goodleigh Devon 55 E6
Goodmanham ER Yorks 296 B4
Goodmayes London 112 E4
Goodnestone Kent 94 F5
Goodnestone Kent 93 D7
Goodrich Heref'd 128 D5
Goodrington Torbay 15 D5
Goodshaw Lancs 291 E5
Goodshaw Chapel Lancs 291 E5
Goodshaw Fold Lancs 291 E5
Goodstone Devon 14 A3
Goodwick = Wdig Pembs 119 B6
Goodwood Racecourse W Sussex 47 D5
Goodworth Clatford Hants 64 C4
Goodyers End Warwick 178 A1
Goodyhills Cumb 337 B8
Goole ER Yorks 296 F1
Goole Fields ER Yorks 296 F2
Goonabarn Cornw'l 8 E2
Goonbell Cornw'l 7 F5
Goonhavern Cornw'l 7 E6
Goonown Cornw'l 7 E5
Goonpiper Cornw'l 4 C4
Goonvrea Cornw'l 6 F5
Goose Eye W Yorks 292 B2
Goose Green Essex 142 B3
Goose Green Gtr Man 277 D8
Goose Green Hants 43 E9
Goose Green Herts 138 F3
Goose Green Kent 72 D3
Goose Green Kent 71 A7
Goose Green Norfolk 209 F6
Goose Green S Glos 81 B5
Goose Green S Glos 103 F6
Goose Green W Sussex 48 C2
Goose Pool Heref'd 151 E7
Gooseberry Green Essex 113 C8
Gooseham Cornw'l 32 C4
Goosehill W Yorks 294 F1
Goosemoor Devon 22 C3
Goosemoor Green Staffs 198 A2
Goosenford Som'set 58 F4
Goosewell Plym'th 11 E6
Goosey Oxon 106 D4
Goosnargh Lancs 289 D8
Goostrey Ches 266 E2
Gorbals Glasg C 392 F3
Gorcott Hill Worcs 176 E4
Gord Shetl'd 455 D3
Gorddinog Conwy 260 E3
Gordon Scot Borders 386 D2
Gordonbush H'land 441 C5
Gordonsburgh Moray 436 B1
Gordonstoun Moray 435 B6
Gordonstown Aberds 436 C2
Gordonstown Aberds 436 E4
Gore Kent 95 E6
Gore End Hants 85 D5
Gore Houses Mersey 276 D4
Gore Pit Essex 141 D6
Gore Street Kent 95 C5
Gorebridge Midloth 396 F3
Gorefield Cambs 205 A7
Gores Wilts 83 E7
Gorgie C/Edinb 396 D1
Goring Oxon 108 F2
Goring Heath Oxon 86 A3
Goring-by-Sea W Sussex 48 F2
Gorleston-on-Sea Norfolk 211 C6
Gornalwood W Midlands 197 E7
Gorrachie Aberds 436 C4
Gorran Churchtown Cornw'l 5 B7
Gorran Haven Cornw'l 5 B8
Gorran High Lanes Cornw'l 5 B7
Gorrenberry Scot Borders 361 C6
Gors Ceredig'n 169 C5
Gorse Covert Warrington 265 A8
Gorse Hill Gtr Man 279 E5
Gorse Hill Swindon 105 E8
Gorsedd Flints 263 D5
Gorseinon Swan 97 C6
Gorseness Orkney 452 B5
Gorsey Bank Shrops 196 A4
Gorseybank Derby 246 D3
Gorsgoch Ceredig'n 146 B2
Gorslas Carms 123 E7
Gorsley Glos 129 B7
Gorsley Common Heref'd 129 B7
Gorstage Ches 265 E7
Gorstan H'land 433 B5
Gorstanvorran H'land 423 E8
Gorstella Ches 241 B8
Gorsty Hill Staffs 222 C4
Gortan Arg/Bute 406 F2
Gortantaoid Arg/Bute 406 E3
Gortenacullish H'land 423 D6
Gorteneorn H'land 423 F6
Gortenfern H'land 423 F6
Gortinanane Arg/Bute 404 B3
Gortleigh Devon 34 E2
Gorton Gtr Man 279 E6
Gosbeck Suffolk 165 A8
Gosberton Lincs 228 B4
Gosberton Cheal Lincs 228 C4
Gosberton Clough Lincs 228 C3
Gosfield Essex 140 B4
Gosford Devon 22 A3
Gosford Heref'd 173 E8
Gosford Oxon 133 E9
Gosford Green W Midlands 178 C1
Gosforth Cumb 325 F6
Gosforth Tyne/Wear 352 C3
Gosforth Valley Derby 269 D6
Gosland Green Ches 242 C4
Gosland Green Suffolk 163 B8
Gosling Green Suffolk 164 D4
Gosmore Herts 137 B7
Gospel End Staffs 197 E6
Gospel Oak London 111 E7
Gosport Hants 44 B2
Gosport Hants 30 A4
Gossabrough Shetl'd 457 E5
Gossard's Green Beds 159 D7
Gossington Glos 103 B6
Goss Green W Sussex 69 D6
Goswick Northum 388 C3
Gotham Dorset 42 D4
Gotham E Sussex 51 E7
Gotham Notts 225 B5
Gothelney Green Som'set 58 D5

Gotherington Glos 131 B5
Gothers Cornw'l 8 D2
Gott Arg/Bute 414 C3
Gott Shetl'd 457 J4
Gotton Som'set 58 F4
Goudhurst Kent 72 D1
Goukstone Moray 436 C1
Goulceby Lincs 274 D2
Goulton N Yorks 332 F4
Gourdas Aberds 437 D4
Gourdon Aberds 429 E5
Gourock Invercl 390 C4
Govan Glasg C 392 E3
Govanhill Glasg C 392 F3
Gover Valley Cornw'l 8 E2
Goverton Notts 248 D5
Goveton Devon 13 C6
Govilon Monmouths 127 E6
Gowanhill Aberds 437 B7
Gowanwell Aberds 437 D5
Gowdall ER Yorks 295 F6
Gowerton = Tre-Gwyr Swan 97 C6
Gowkhall Fife 411 D5
Gowkthrapple N Lanarks 381 B7
Gowthorpe ER Yorks 308 E4
Goxhill ER Yorks 298 B2
Goxhill N Lincs 297 F9
Goxhill Haven N Lincs 298 E1
Goytre Neath P Talb 98 E2
Gozzard's Ford Oxon 107 C6
Grabhair W Isles 449 A7
Graby Lincs 228 C1
Gracca Cornw'l 8 D3
Grade Cornw'l 5 H2
Gradeley Green Ches 242 D4
Graffham W Sussex 47 C6
Grafham Cambs 182 E3
Grafham Surrey 68 C2
Grafton Bucks 135 E8
Grafton Heref'd 151 E7
Grafton N Yorks 306 C5
Grafton Oxon 106 B2
Grafton Shrops 219 E5
Grafton Worcs 154 E2
Grafton Flyford Worcs 154 A2
Grafton Regis Northants 158 C3
Grafton Underwood Northants 181 B6
Grafty Green Kent 72 B4
Graianrhyd Denbs 240 C5
Graig Carms 96 B3
Graig Conwy 262 E6
Graig Denbs 262 E3
Graig Rh Cyn Taff 99 E8
Graig Shrops 172 C3
Graig Felen Swan 97 B8
Graig Penllyn V/Glam 77 A6
Graig Trewyddfa Swan 97 C8
Graig-Fawr Swan 97 B7
Graig-fechan Denbs 240 D3
Grain Medway 92 A4
Grains Bar Gtr Man 279 C8
Grainsby Lincs 286 E4
Grainthorpe Lincs 287 E6
Graizelound N Lincs 284 E2
Grampound Cornw'l 8 F1
Grampound Road Cornw'l 8 E1
Gramsdal W Isles 447 C3
Granborough Bucks 135 B6
Granby Notts 226 A2
Grandborough Warwick 178 E4
Grandpont Oxon 107 A7
Grandtully Perth/Kinr 419 B7
Grange Cumb 326 C2
Grange Dorset 42 F3
Grange E Ayrs 379 E8
Grange Fife 412 B2
Grange Halton 264 C5
Grange Lancs 288 C4
Grange Lancs 289 D8
Grange Mersey 263 B6
Grange Medway 92 C2
Grange NE Lincs 286 C4
Grange N Yorks 316 B4
Grange N Yorks 320 A2
Grange Perth/Kinr 420 E2
Grange Warrington 265 A7
Grange Crossroads Moray 436 C1
Grange Estate Dorset 42 F5
Grange Hall Moray 435 B5
Grange Hill Durham 343 F8
Grange Hill Essex 112 D3
Grange Moor W Yorks 281 A6
Grange of Cree Dumf/Gal 401 D6
Grange of Lindores Fife 420 F2
Grange Park London 111 C8
Grange Park Mersey 277 F6
Grange Park Swindon 105 F7
Grange Villa Durham 343 A8
Grangemill Derby 246 C2
Grangemouth Falk 410 D4
Grangemuir Fife 412 B3
Grange-over-Sands Cumb 314 E2
Grangepans Falk 411 D5
Grangetown Card 78 B3
Grangetown Redcar/Clevel'd 333 B6
Grangetown Tyne/Wear 353 F7
Granish H'land 426 A4
Gransmoor ER Yorks 310 D4
Gransmore Green Essex 140 C2
Granston = Treopert Pembs 119 C5
Grant Thorold NE Lincs 286 C4
Grantchester Cambs 161 A8
Grantham Lincs 227 A5
Granthouse Scot Borders 399 E6
Grantley N Yorks 306 B1
Grantlodge Aberds 428 A4
Granton C/Edinb 396 C1
Grantown Aberds 436 C2
Grantown-on-Spey H'land 435 F5
Graplin Dumf/Gal 401 E8
Grappenhall Warrington 265 B7
Grasby Lincs 285 D8
Grasmere Cumb 326 E3
Grass Green Essex 163 E7
Grasscroft Gtr Man 279 D8
Grassendale Mersey 264 B2
Grassgarth Cumb 314 A2
Grassgarth Cumb 339 C5
Grasshill Derby 269 F8
Grassington N Yorks 304 C4
Grassmoor Derby 269 F8
Grassthorpe Notts 271 F7
Grasswell Tyne/Wear 344 A2
Grateley Hants 64 C2
Gratton Devon 33 D7
Gratwich Staffs 222 B2
Gravel Castle Kent 74 B4
Gravel Hill Bucks 110 D2
Gravel Hole Gtr Man 279 C7
Graveley Cambs 183 F5
Graveley Herts 137 B8
Gravelly Hill W Midlands 198 E3
Gravelsbank Shrops 194 C2
Graven Shetl'd 457 F4
Graveney Kent 93 D8
Graveney Hill Kent 93 D8
Gravesend Herts 138 B4
Gravesend Kent 91 B7
Grayingham Lincs 285 E5
Grayrigg Cumb 315 A5
Grays Thurr'k 91 A7
Grayshott Hants 67 D7
Grayson Green Cumb 324 A4
Grayswood Surrey 67 E8
Graythorp Hartlep'l 345 F6
Graze Hill Beds 159 B9
Grazeley Wokingham 86 C3
Greagdhubh Lodge H'land 426 C1
Greamchary H'land 444 E2
Greasbrough S Yorks 282 E2
Greasby Mersey 263 B7
Greasley Notts 247 E7
Great Abington Cambs 162 C3
Great Addington Northants 181 C7
Great Alne Warwick 154 A5
Great Altcar Lancs 276 C3
Great Amwell Herts 138 E3
Great Asby Cumb 328 D3
Great Ashfield Suffolk 186 E4
Great Ayton N Yorks 333 D6
Great Baddow Essex 114 B1
Great Bardfield Essex 140 A2
Great Barford Beds 160 B2
Great Barr W Midlands 198 D1
Great Barrington Glos 132 E3
Great Barrow Ches 264 F4
Great Barton Suffolk 186 E2
Great Barugh N Yorks 321 E5
Great Bavington Northum 363 F8
Great Bealings Suffolk 166 C2
Great Bedwyn Wilts 84 D2
Great Bentley Essex 142 C3
Great Billing Northants 180 F4
Great Bircham Norfolk 231 B7
Great Blakenham Suffolk 165 B7
Great Blencow Cumb 339 E8
Great Bolas Telford 220 D3
Great Bookham Surrey 88 F4
Great Bourton Oxon 156 C4
Great Bowden Leics 201 F8
Great Bradley Suffolk 163 B6
Great Braxted Essex 141 E6
Great Bricett Suffolk 165 B5
Great Brickhill Bucks 136 A2
Great Bridge W Midlands 197 E8
Great Bridgeford Staffs 221 C7
Great Brington Northants 179 E8
Great Bromley Essex 142 B2
Great Broughton Cumb 337 E4
Great Broughton N Yorks 333 E6
Great Buckland Kent 91 D8
Great Budworth Ches 265 D8
Great Burdon D'lington 331 C8
Great Burgh Surrey 89 E6
Great Burstead Essex 113 D8
Great Busby N Yorks 332 E5
Great Cambourne Cambs 161 A6
Great Canfield Essex 139 D7
Great Carlton Lincs 275 B5
Great Casterton Rutl'd 203 B6
Great Chart Kent 73 C6
Great Chatfield Wilts 82 D2
Great Chatwell Staffs 221 F5
Great Chell Staffs 244 D3
Great Chesterford Essex 162 D3
Great Cheveney Kent 72 C1
Great Cheverell Wilts 82 F4
Great Chilton Durham 344 E1
Great Chishill Cambs 161 E8
Great Clacton Essex 142 D4
Great Cliff W Yorks 281 A8
Great Clifton Cumb 337 F6
Great Coates NE Lincs 286 B3
Great Comberton Worcs 154 D2
Great Common Suffolk 210 F3
Great Corby Cumb 339 A8
Great Cornard Suffolk 164 D2
Great Cowden ER Yorks 298 B3
Great Coxwell Oxon 106 D2
Great Crakehall N Yorks 318 C4
Great Cransley Northants 180 C4
Great Cressingham Norfolk 207 C8
Great Crosby Mersey 276 E3
Great Crosthwaite Cumb 326 B2
Great Cubley Derby 223 A5
Great Dalby Leics 226 F1
Great Doddington Northants 181 F5
Great Doward Heref'd 128 D5
Great Dunham Norfolk 232 F2
Great Dunmow Essex 139 C8
Great Durnford Wilts 63 D7
Great Easton Essex 139 B8
Great Easton Leics 202 E2
Great Eccleston Lancs 289 B5
Great Edstone N Yorks 321 D5
Great Ellingham Norfolk 208 D4
Great Elm Som'set 61 B6
Great Eppleton Tyne/Wear 344 B3
Great Eversden Cambs 161 B7
Great Fen Cambs 184 C4
Great Fencote N Yorks 318 B4
Great Finborough Suffolk 165 A5
Great Fransham Norfolk 208 A1
Great Gaddesden Herts 136 E4
Great Gidding Cambs 182 B2
Great Givendale ER Yorks 309 E5
Great Glemham Suffolk 188 F4
Great Glen Leics 201 D7
Great Gonerby Lincs 226 A4
Great Gransden Cambs 161 A5
Great Green Cambs 161 D5
Great Green Norfolk 210 F1
Great Green Suffolk 187 C6
Great Green Suffolk 187 C7
Great Green Suffolk 164 A3
Great Green Suffolk 186 E3
Great Habton N Yorks 321 E6
Great Hale Lincs 251 F5
Great Hallingbury Essex 139 D6
Great Hampden Bucks 109 B7
Great Harrowden Northants 181 D5
Great Harwood Lancs 290 D3
Great Haseley Oxon 108 B2
Great Hatfield ER Yorks 298 B2
Great Haywood Staffs 222 D1
Great Heath W Midlands 178 B1
Great Heck N Yorks 295 F5
Great Henny Essex 164 E2
Great Hinton Wilts 82 E3
Great Hivings Bucks 109 B9
Great Hockham Norfolk 208 E3
Great Holland Essex 143 D5
Great Hollands Brackn'l 87 C7
Great Holm M/Keynes 158 E4
Great Horkesley Essex 141 A8
Great Hormead Herts 138 A4
Great Horton W Yorks 292 D4
Great Horwood Bucks 135 A6
Great Houghton Northants 158 A3
Great Houghton S Yorks 282 C2
Great Howarth Gtr Man 279 A7
Great Hucklow Derby 268 D3
Great Job's Cross Kent 72 F3
Great Kelk ER Yorks 310 D4
Great Kimble Bucks 109 A6
Great Kingshill Bucks 109 C7
Great Langdale Cumb 326 E3
Great Langton N Yorks 318 A4
Great Lea Common Wokingham 86 C4
Great Leighs Essex 140 D3
Great Leighs Racecourse Essex 140 D3
Great Lever Gtr Man 278 C3
Great Limber Lincs 286 C1
Great Linford M/Keynes 158 D5
Great Livermere Suffolk 186 D2
Great Longstone Derby 268 E4
Great Lumley Durham 344 B1
Great Malvern Worcs 153 C5
Great Maplestead Essex 163 F9
Great Marton Blackp'l 288 C3
Great Marton Moss Lancs 288 D4
Great Massingham Norfolk 231 D7
Great Melton Norfolk 209 B6
Great Milton Oxon 108 B2
Great Missenden Bucks 109 B7
Great Mitton Lancs 290 C3
Great Mongeham Kent 75 A6
Great Moor Gtr Man 267 B5
Great Moulton Norfolk 209 E7
Great Munden Herts 138 C3
Great Musgrave Cumb 328 D5
Great Ness Shrops 218 E4
Great Norman Street Kent 70 A4
Great Notley Essex 140 C3
Great Oak Monmouths 127 F8
Great Oakley Essex 142 B4
Great Oakley Northants 180 A5
Great Offley Herts 137 B6
Great Orme Tramway, Llandudno Conwy 260 C5
Great Ormside Cumb 328 C3
Great Orton Cumb 347 F8
Great Ouseburn N Yorks 307 C5
Great Oxendon Northants 180 B2
Great Oxney Green Essex 113 A8
Great Parndon Essex 138 F4
Great Pattenden Kent 72 B1
Great Paxton Cambs 182 F4
Great Plumpton Lancs 288 D4
Great Plumstead Norfolk 210 A2
Great Ponton Lincs 227 B5
Great Preston W Yorks 294 E2
Great Purston Northants 157 E5
Great Raveley Cambs 183 B5
Great Rissington Glos 132 D2
Great Rollright Oxon 132 A5
Great Ryburgh Norfolk 232 C4
Great Ryle Northum 376 E2
Great Ryton Shrops 195 C5
Great Saling Essex 140 B3
Great Salkeld Cumb 340 D1
Great Sampford Essex 163 E5
Great Sankey Warrington 265 B6
Great Saredon Staffs 197 B8
Great Saxham Suffolk 185 F8
Great Shefford W Berks 84 A4
Great Shelford Cambs 162 B2
Great Smeaton N Yorks 332 F2
Great Snoring Norfolk 232 B3
Great Somerford Wilts 104 F4
Great Stainton D'lington 331 B8
Great Stambridge Essex 115 D5
Great Staughton Cambs 182 F2
Great Steeping Lincs 252 B4
Great Stoke S Glos 102 F4
Great Stonar Kent 95 E6
Great Strickland Cumb 327 B8
Great Stukeley Cambs 182 D4
Great Sturton Lincs 274 D1
Great Sutton Ches 264 D2
Great Sutton Shrops 173 B8
Great Swinburne Northum 351 A5
Great Tew Oxon 133 B6
Great Tey Essex 141 B6
Great Thorness I/Wight 29 B9
Great Thurlow Suffolk 163 B6
Great Torrington Devon 34 C2
Great Tosson Northum 364 B2
Great Totham Essex 141 E6
Great Tows Lincs 274 A1
Great Tree Cornw'l 9 D8
Great Urswick Cumb 313 F6
Great Wakering Essex 115 E5
Great Waldingfield Suffolk 164 D3
Great Walsingham Norfolk 256 E1
Great Waltham Essex 140 E2
Great Warley Essex 113 D6
Great Washbourne Glos 154 F2
Great Watersend Kent 74 C5
Great Weeke Devon 20 C4
Great Welnetham Suffolk 164 A2
Great Wenham Suffolk 165 E6
Great Whittington Northum 351 B7
Great Wigborough Essex 141 E8
Great Wilbraham Cambs 162 A3
Great Wilne Derby 224 B4
Great Wishford Wilts 63 D6
Great Witchingham Norfolk 233 E7
Great Witcombe Glos 130 E4
Great Witley Worcs 175 E5
Great Wolford Warwick 155 F8
Great Wratting Suffolk 163 C6
Great Wymondley Herts 137 B8
Great Wyrley Staffs 197 B8
Great Wytheford Shrops 219 E8
Great Yarmouth Norfolk 211 B6
Great Yarmouth Sea Life Centre Norfolk 211 B6
Great Yeldham Essex 163 E8
Greatfield Wilts 105 E6
Greatford Lincs 203 A7
Greatgap Bucks 136 D2
Greatgate Staffs 245 F7
Greatham Hants 67 E5
Greatham Hartlep'l 345 F5
Greatham W Sussex 47 C8
Greatness Kent 91 E5
Greatstone-on-Sea Kent 53 B6
Greatworth Northants 157 D6
Greave Gtr Man 267 A5
Greave Lancs 291 F6
Grebby Lincs 275 F5
Greeba I/Man 336 C3
Green Denbs 262 F3
Green Bottom Cornw'l 4 A3
Green Bottom Glos 129 D7
Green Cross Surrey 67 D7
Green End Beds 159 C8
Green End Beds 182 F1
Green End Beds 160 B2
Green End Beds 182 F2
Green End Bucks 136 A2
Green End Cambs 182 D4
Green End Cambs 184 E2
Green End Cambs 161 A7
Green End Herts 138 A1
Green End Herts 138 C2
Green End Herts 161 F6
Green End Lancs 291 A7
Green End N Yorks 334 F3
Green End Warwick 177 A8
Green Gate Devon 37 C5
Green Hailey Bucks 109 B6
Green Hammerton N Yorks 307 D6
Green Haworth Lancs 290 E4
Green Head Cumb 339 B6
Green Heath Staffs 197 A8
Green Hill Lincs 227 A5
Green Hill Wilts 105 E6
Green Hill Worcs 154 C3
Green Lane Devon 21 E5
Green Lane Heref'd 152 C2
Green Lane Powys 193 D7
Green Lane Worcs 176 F4
Green Moor S Yorks 281 E7
Green Ore Som'set 60 A3
Green Quarter Cumb 327 F6
Green Street E Sussex 51 D8
Green Street Essex 113 C7
Green Street Glos 103 B7
Green Street Glos 130 D3
Green Street Herts 139 C5
Green Street Worcs 153 C7
Green Street W Sussex 48 B2
Green Street Green Kent 91 B6
Green Street Green London 90 D4
Green Tye Herts 138 D4
Greenacres Gtr Man 279 C7
Greenan Arg/Bute 408 F3
Greenbank Shetl'd 456 C5
Greenburn W Loth 394 F3
Greencroft Durham 343 A7
Greencroft Norfolk 256 D3
Greendown Som'set 80 F3
Greendykes Northum 358 C1
Greenend Oxon 132 C5
Greenfaulds N Lanarks 393 D7
Greenfield Beds 159 F9
Greenfield Flints 263 D5
Greenfield Gtr Man 280 D1
Greenfield H'land 417 B4
Greenfield H'land 424 B4
Greenfield Oxon 108 D4
Greenfoot N Lanarks 393 E6
Greenford London 110 F4
Greengairs N Lanarks 393 D7
Greengate Gtr Man 279 A7
Greengate Norfolk 232 E5
Greengates W Yorks 293 C5
Greenhalgh Lancs 288 C5
Greenham Dorset 39 E6
Greenham Som'set 37 B6
Greenham W Berks 85 C6
Greenhaugh Northum 362 E4
Greenhead Dumf/Gal 358 F3
Greenhead N Lanarks 381 A8
Greenhead Northum 349 C7
Greenheyes Gtr Man 278 D3
Greenhill Dumf/Gal 359 F6
Greenhill Durham 344 B3
Greenhill Falk 393 C8
Greenhill Heref'd 152 C4
Greenhill Kent 94 C3
Greenhill Leics 224 E3
Greenhill London 111 E5
Greenhill S Glos 102 E4
Greenhill S Yorks 269 C6
Greenhill Worcs 175 C6
Greenhillocks Derby 247 E6
Greenhills N Ayrs 379 B7
Greenhithe Kent 91 A6
Greenholm E Ayrs 380 E2
Greenholme Cumb 328 E1
Greenhouse Scot Borders 373 C8
Greenhow Hill N Yorks 305 C6
Greenigoe Orkney 452 C5
Greenland H'land 445 B6
Greenland S Yorks 269 B7
Greenland Mains H'land 445 B6
Greenlands Worcs 176 E4
Greenlaw Aberds 436 C3
Greenlaw Scot Borders 386 C4
Greenlea Dumf/Gal 346 A2
Greenleys M/Keynes 158 D4
Greenloaning Perth/Kinr 410 B3
Greenmeadow Swindon 105 E7
Greenmeadow Torf 101 C5
Greenmeadow Community Farm, Pontnewydd Torf 101 C5
Greenmount Gtr Man 278 B4
Greenmow Shetl'd 455 D3
Greenoak ER Yorks 296 E3
Greenock Invercl 391 C5
Greenock West Invercl 390 C5
Greenodd Cumb 313 D7
Greenrigg W Loth 394 F3
Greenrow Cumb 337 A8
Greens Norton Northants 157 C8
Greensforge Staffs 197 F6
Greenshills S Lanarks 380 B4
Greenside Cumb 328 F4
Greenside Derby 269 D7
Greenside Tyne/Wear 352 D1
Greenside W Yorks 280 A5
Greenstead Essex 142 B1
Greenstead Green Essex 141 B5
Greensted Essex 113 B5
Greensted Green Essex 113 B5
Greensted Log Church, Chipping Ongar Essex 113 B5
Greenstreet Green Suffolk 165 B5
Greenway Glos 129 A8
Greenway Som'set 38 B4
Greenway V/Glam 77 B8
Greenway Worcs 174 D4
Greenways Som'set 58 F3
Greenwell Cumb 348 E4
Greenwich London 90 A2
Greenwich Wilts 62 E3
Greenwith Common Cornw'l 4 B3
Greeny Orkney 452 A3
Greep H'land 430 D2
Greet Glos 131 A6
Greete Shrops 174 D1
Greetham Lincs 274 E3
Greetham Rutl'd 227 F5
Greetland W Yorks 292 F3
Greetland Wall Nook W Yorks 292 F3
Greetwell N Lincs 285 D5
Grèin W Isles 446 C2
Gregson Lane Lancs 289 E8
Gregynog Powys 193 D5
Greinetobht W Isles 447 A3
Greinton Som'set 59 D8
Gremista Shetl'd 455 B3
Grenaby I/Man 336 D2
Grendon Northants 181 F5
Grendon Warwick 199 C6
Grendon Bishop Heref'd 152 A1
Grendon Common Warwick 199 D6
Grendon Underwood Bucks 134 C4
Grenend N Lanarks 393 F6
Grenofen Devon 10 A5
Grenoside S Yorks 281 F8
Greosabhagh W Isles 449 C5
Gresford Wrex 241 D8
Gresham Norfolk 257 E6
Greshornish H'land 430 C3
Gressenhall Norfolk 232 E4
Gressingham Lancs 302 B3
Greta Bridge Durham 330 D3
Gretna Dumf/Gal 347 C8
Gretna Green Dumf/Gal 347 C8
Gretton Glos 131 A6
Gretton Northants 202 E3
Gretton Shrops 195 D6
Gretton Field Glos 131 A6
Grewelthorpe N Yorks 318 E3
Grey Green N Lincs 284 C2
Greyfriars Surrey 68 B2
Greygarth N Yorks 305 A7
Greylake Som'set 59 E7
Greylake Fosse Som'set 59 D8
Greynor Carms 123 F7
Greyrigg Dumf/Gal 359 E5
Greys Green Oxon 108 F4
Greysouthern Cumb 337 F7
Greystoke Cumb 339 E7
Greystoke Gill Cumb 339 F7
Greystone Aberds 428 C1
Greystone Aberds 436 E3
Greystone Angus 421 C5
Greystone Dumf/Gal 402 B3
Greystones S Yorks 269 B6
Greytree Heref'd 129 B5
Greywell Hants 66 A4
Griais W Isles 451 C7
Grianan W Isles 451 D7
Grianllyn Conwy 262 D6
Gribb Dorset 38 F5
Gribbleford Bridge Devon 34 F3
Gribthorpe ER Yorks 296 C2
Griff Warwick 199 F8
Griff Hollow Warwick 199 F8
Griffithstown Torf 101 C5
Griffydam Leics 224 E3
Griggs Green Hants 67 E6
Grimbister Orkney 452 B4
Grimblethorpe Lincs 274 B1
Grimeford Village Lancs 278 B1
Grimesthorpe S Yorks 269 A7
Grimethorpe S Yorks 282 C2
Griminis W Isles 447 A2
Griminis W Isles 447 C2
Grimister Shetl'd 456 D4
Grimley Worcs 175 F6
Grimness Orkney 453 D5
Grimoldby Lincs 274 B4
Grimpo Shrops 218 C4
Grimsargh Lancs 289 D8
Grimsbury Oxon 156 D4
Grimsby NE Lincs 286 B4
Grimscote Northants 157 B7
Grimscott Cornw'l 33 E5
Grimshaw Blackb'n 290 F3
Grimshaw Green Lancs 277 B6
Grimsthorpe Lincs 227 D7
Grimston C/York 308 E1
Grimston ER Yorks 298 C4
Grimston Leics 225 D8
Grimston Norfolk 231 D6
Grimstone Dorset 25 B7
Grimstone End Suffolk 186 E3
Grindale ER Yorks 310 A4
Grindigar Orkney 453 C6
Grindiscol Shetl'd 455 C3
Grindle Shrops 196 C4
Grindleford Derby 268 D4
Grindleton Lancs 290 A4
Grindley Staffs 222 C2
Grindley Brook Shrops 242 F3
Grindlow Derby 268 D3
Grindon Northum 387 D8
Grindon Stockton 332 A2
Grindon Staffs 245 D7
Grindon Tyne/Wear 353 E6
Grindsbrook Booth Derby 268 B2
Gringley on the Hill Notts 271 A6
Grinnacombe Moor Devon 19 B5
Grinshill Shrops 219 D7
Grinton N Yorks 317 A6
Griomasaigh W Isles 447 D3
Griomsidar W Isles 451 E6
Grisdale Cumb 316 B1
Grishipoll Arg/Bute 414 B4
Grisling Common E Sussex 49 B8
Gristhorpe N Yorks 323 D5
Griston Norfolk 208 D2
Gritley Orkney 453 C6
Grittenham Wilts 105 F5
Grittlesend Heref'd 152 C4
Grittleton Wilts 104 F2
Grizebeck Cumb 313 C5
Grizedale Cumb 313 B7
Groam H'land 433 D7
Grobister Orkney 454 D4
Grobsness Shetl'd 457 G3
Groby Leics 200 B4
Groes Conwy 239 B8
Groes Neath P Talb 98 E2
Groes Efa Denbs 240 A3
Groesfaen Rh Cyn Taff 99 F8
Groesffordd Conwy 260 D5
Groesffordd Gwyn 212 A5
Groeslon Gwyn 237 B6
Groeslon Gwyn 237 C5
Groes-lwyd Powys 193 A8
Groespluan Powys 193 B8
Groes-wen Caerph 100 E2
Grogoth Wallas Cornw'l 5 B6
Grogport Arg/Bute 404 B4
Gronant Flints 262 C3
Groombridge E Sussex 71 D5
Groomford Suffolk 167 A5
Grosmont Monmouths 128 C2
Grosmont N Yorks 334 E3
Grosvenor Museum, Chester Ches 241 A9
Grotaig H'land 433 F6
Groton Suffolk 164 D4
Grotton Gtr Man 279 D8
Groudle Glen Railway I/Man 336 D4
Grougfoot Falk 394 C5
Grove Dorset 24 D2
Grove Kent 94 D4
Grove Notts 271 D6
Grove Oxon 107 D5
Grove Pembs 117 D5
Grove End Bucks 135 F5
Grove End Warwick 198 D4
Grove Green Kent 92 E2
Grove Park London 90 B3
Grove Town W Yorks 294 F3
Grove Vale W Midlands 198 E1
Grovehill ER Yorks 297 C7
Grovehill Herts 136 F5
Grovehurst Kent 72 C1
Groves Kent 94 E5
Grovesend S Glos 103 E5
Grovesend Swan 97 B6
Grub Street Kent 91 C6
Grudie H'land 433 B5
Gruids H'land 440 C2
Gruinard House H'land 438 D3
Gruinards H'land 440 D2
Grula H'land 430 F3
Gruline Arg/Bute 415 C8
Gruline Ho Arg/Bute 415 D8
Grumbeg H'land 443 E8
Grumbla Cornw'l 2 E4
Grunasound Shetl'd 455 C2
Grundisburgh Suffolk 166 B2
Gruting Shetl'd 457 J2
Grutness Shetl'd 455 F3
Gualachulain H'land 417 C6
Gualin Ho. H'land 443 C5
Guard House W Yorks 292 B2
Guardbridge Fife 420 F4
Guarlford Worcs 153 C6
Guay Perth/Kinr 419 C8
Gubbions Green Essex 140 D3
Gubblacote Herts 136 D2
Guesachan H'land 423 E8
Guestling Green E Sussex 52 D1
Guestling Thorn E Sussex 52 C2
Guestwick Norfolk 233 C6
Guestwick Green Norfolk 233 C6
Guide Blackb'n 290 E3
Guide Bridge Gtr Man 279 E7
Guide Post Northum 365 E7
Guilden Morden Cambs 161 D5
Guilden Sutton Ches 264 F4
Guildford Surrey 68 B2
Guildford Park Surrey 68 B1
Guildiehaugh W Loth 394 E4
Guildtown Perth/Kinr 420 D1
Guilford Pembs 117 C5
Guilsborough Northants 179 D8
Guilsfield = Cegidfa Powys 193 A8
Guilthwaite S Yorks 269 B8
Guilton Kent 95 E5
Guineaford Devon 55 D6
Guisachan H'land 433 F5
Guisborough Redcar/Clevel'd 333 C7
Guiseley W Yorks 293 B5
Guist Norfolk 232 C4
Guith Orkney 454 C3
Guiting Power Glos 131 C7
Gulberwick Shetl'd 455 C3
Gullane E Loth 397 B6
Guller's End Worcs 153 E7

Gulling Green Suffolk 164 A1
Gully W Yorks 280 C4
Gulpher Suffolk 166 E4
Gulval Cornw'l 3 D5
Gulworthy Devon 10 A5
Gumfreston Pembs 117 D8
Gumley Leics 201 E7
Gummow's Shop Cornw'l 7 D8
Gun Green Kent 72 E2
Gun Hill E Sussex 50 D4
Gun Hill Warwick 199 F6
Gunby Lincs 275 F6
Gunby Lincs 227 D5
Gundleton Hants 66 E2
Gunn Devon 55 E7
Gunnerby NE Lincs 286 E3
Gunnersbury London 113 F6
Gunnerside N Yorks 316 A4
Gunnerton Northum 350 A5
Gunness N Lincs 284 B3
Gunnislake Cornw'l 10 A4
Gunnista Shetl'd 455 B4
Guns Village W Midlands 197 E8
Gunthorpe Norfolk 232 B5
Gunthorpe N Lincs 284 E3
Gunthorpe Notts 248 F4
Gunthorpe Peterbro 204 C2
Gunthorpe Rutl'd 202 B3
Gunton Suffolk 211 D6
Gunville I/Wight 30 C1
Gunwalloe Cornw'l 3 F9
Gunwalloe Fishing Cove Cornw'l 3 F9
Gupworthy Som'set 57 E6
Gurnard I/Wight 29 A9
Gurnett Ches 267 E5
Gurney Slade Som'set 60 B4
Gurney Street Som'set 58 D5
Gurnos Merth Tyd 126 F1
Gurnos Powys 124 F4
Gushmere Kent 93 E8
Gussage All Saints Dorset 42 D3
Gussage St. Andrew Dorset 42 D2
Gussage St. Michael Dorset 42 D2
Guston Kent 75 C6
Gutcher Shetl'd 456 D5
Guthram Gowt Lincs 228 D3
Guthrie Angus 421 B5
Guyhirn Cambs 205 C7
Guyhirn Gull Cambs 205 C6
Guy's Marsh Dorset 41 B6
Guyzance Northum 365 B6
Gwaelod-y-garth Rh Cyn Taff 100 F2
Gwaenysgor Flints 262 C3
Gwaithla Powys 150 A2
Gwalchmai Angl 258 D4
Gwar-cwm Ceredig'n 190 E4
Gwarn-Leisian Neath P Talb 124 E3
Gwarthlow Shrops 193 D8
Gwastad Pembs 119 E8
Gwastadgoed Gwyn 190 A3
Gwastadnant Gwyn 237 C8
Gwaun Leisian Carms 124 E3
Gwaun Meisgyn Rh Cyn Taff 99 F8
Gwaun-Cae-Gurwen Neath P Talb 124 E3
Gwbert Ceredig'n 144 C3
Gweek Cornw'l 4 E2
Gwehelog Monmouths 101 B7
Gweithdy Angl 259 D7
Gwenddwr Powys 149 D6
Gwennap Cornw'l 4 B2
Gwent Bl Gwent 100 B4
Gwenter Cornw'l 5 G2
Gwernaffel Powys 172 D3
Gwernaffield Flints 240 B5
Gwernau Caerph 100 D3
Gwerneirin Powys 192 F4
Gwerneirin Powys 171 B8
Gwernesney Monmouths 101 B8
Gwern-Estyn Flints 241 C7
Gwernogle Carms 146 F3
Gwernymynydd Flints 240 B5
Gwern-y-Steeple V/Glam 77 A8
Gwersyllt Wrex 241 D7
Gwespyr Flints 262 C4
Gwindra Cornw'l 8 E2
Gwinear Cornw'l 3 C7
Gwithian Cornw'l 3 B7
Gwredog Angl 259 B5
Gwrhay Caerph 100 C3
Gwrhyd Mawr Pembs 118 D3
Gwyddelwern Denbs 240 E2
Gwyddgrug Carms 146 E2
Gwydir Gwyn 236 E3
Gwynfryn Wrex 241 D6
Gwystre Powys 171 E6
Gwytherin Conwy 239 B5
Gyfelia Wrex 241 E7
Gyffin Conwy 262 D5
Gylen Park Arg/Bute 416 E3
Gyre Orkney 452 C4
Gyrn Goch Gwyn 236 E4

## H

Habberley Shrops 194 C4
Habberley Worcs 175 C6
Habergham Lancs 291 D5
Habertoft Lincs 275 F7
Habin W Sussex 46 B4
Habrough NE Lincs 286 B1
Haccombe Devon 15 A5
Hacconby Lincs 228 C2
Haceby Lincs 227 A7
Hacheston Suffolk 166 A4
Hackbridge London 89 C7
Hackenthorpe S Yorks 269 C8
Hackford Norfolk 208 C5
Hackforth N Yorks 318 B3
Hackland Orkney 452 A4
Hackleton Northants 158 A4
Hacklinge Kent 95 F6
Hackman's Gate Worcs 175 C7
Hackness N Yorks 322 B3
Hackness Orkney 452 D4
Hackness Som'set 59 B6
Hackney London 112 F1
Hackney Wick London 112 F2
Hackthorn Lincs 272 C4
Hackthorpe Cumb 327 B7
Hackwood Northum 351 D5
Haclait W Isles 447 D3
Hacton London 113 F6
Hadden Scot Borders 387 E5
Haddenham Bucks 135 F5
Haddenham Cambs 184 C2
Haddington E Loth 397 D7
Haddington Lincs 249 B9
Haddiscoe Norfolk 210 D4
Haddoch Aberds 436 D2
Haddon Cambs 204 E1
Haddon Hall Derby 246 A2
Hademore Staffs 198 B4
Haden Cross W Midlands 176 A2
Hadfield Derby 280 E2
Hadham Cross Herts 138 D4
Hadham Ford Herts 138 C4
Hadleigh Essex 114 E3
Hadleigh Suffolk 165 D5
Hadleigh Heath Suffolk 165 D5
Hadley London 111 C6
Hadley Telford 196 A2
Hadley Worcs 175 F7
Hadley Castle Telford 196 A2
Hadley End Staffs 222 D4
Hadley Wood London 111 C7
Hadlow Kent 71 B7
Hadlow Down E Sussex 50 B3
Hadlow Stair Kent 71 B7
Hadnall Shrops 219 D7
Hadspen Som'set 61 E5
Hadstock Essex 162 D4
Hadston Northum 365 C7
Hady Derby 269 E7
Hadzor Worcs 175 F8
Haffenden Quarter Kent 72 C4
Hafod Swan 97 D8
Hafod Dinbych Conwy 239 D5
Hafodrisclawdd Caerph 100 B3
Hafodyrynys Torf 100 C4
Hag Fold Gtr Man 278 D2
Hagg Hill Derby 247 A6
Haggate Gtr Man 279 C7
Haggate Lancs 291 C6
Haggbeck Cumb 348 B3
Haggersta Shetl'd 457 J3
Haggerston London 112 F1
Haggerston Northum 388 D2
Hagget End Cumb 324 D5
Haggington Hill Devon 55 B6
Haggrister Shetl'd 457 F3
Haggs Falk 393 C7
Hagley Heref'd 151 D9
Hagley Worcs 175 B8
Hagmore Green Suffolk 164 E3
Hagnaby Lincs 252 B2
Hagnaby Lincs 275 D6
Hague Bar Derby 267 B6
Hagworthingham Lincs 274 F3
Haigh Gtr Man 277 C9
Haigh S Yorks 281 B7
Haigh Moor W Yorks 293 F7
Haighton Green Lancs 289 D8
Hail Weston Cambs 182 F3
Haile Cumb 325 E5
Hailey Herts 138 E3
Hailey Oxon 108 E2
Hailey Oxon 133 E6
Hailsham E Sussex 50 E4
Haimer H'land 445 B5
Hainault London 112 D4
Haine Kent 95 C7
Haines Hill Som'set 38 B2
Hainford Norfolk 234 E1
Hainton Lincs 273 C8
Hainworth W Yorks 292 C3
Hairmyres S Lanarks 380 B4
Haisthorpe ER Yorks 310 C4
Hakin Pembs 116 C3
Halabezack Cornw'l 4 D2
Halam Notts 248 D4
Halamanning Cornw'l 3 D7
Halbeath Fife 411 D6
Halberton Devon 37 D5
Halcon Som'set 38 A2
Halcro H'land 445 B6
Haldens Herts 137 E8
Hale Cumb 314 E4
Hale Gtr Man 266 B2
Hale Hants 43 C6
Hale Halton 264 C4
Hale Kent 95 C5
Hale Medway 92 C2
Hale Som'set 61 F7
Hale Surrey 67 B6
Hale Bank Halton 264 C4
Hale End London 112 D2
Hale Green E Sussex 50 D4
Hale Mills Cornw'l 4 B3
Hale Nook Lancs 288 B4
Hale Street Kent 71 B8
Halebarns Gtr Man 266 B2
Halehird Cumb 327 F5
Hales Norfolk 210 D3
Hales Staffs 220 B4
Hales Green Derby 246 F1
Hales Park Worcs 175 C5
Hales Place Kent 94 E2
Hales Street Norfolk 209 F7
Halesfield Telford 196 C3
Halesgate Lincs 229 C6
Halesowen W Midlands 176 B2
Halesworth Suffolk 189 C5
Halewood Halton 264 B4
Halford Devon 21 F6
Halford Shrops 173 B6
Halford Warwick 155 C8
Halfpenny Furze Carms 122 E1
Halfpenny Green Staffs 197 E6
Halfway Carms 96 B5
Halfway Carms 123 A8
Halfway Carms 125 A5
Halfway S Yorks 269 C8
Halfway W Berks 85 C5
Halfway Bridge W Sussex 47 B6
Halfway House Shrops 194 A2
Halfway Houses Kent 93 B5
Halfway Houses Lincs 249 B8
Halfway Street Kent 74 B5
Halgabron Cornw'l 17 C6
Halifax W Yorks 292 F3
Halket E Ayrs 379 B8
Halkirk H'land 445 C5
Halkyn Flints 263 E6
Hall E Renf 379 A8
Hall Suffolk 165 B6
Hall Bower W Yorks 280 B4
Hall Common Norfolk 234 E4
Hall Cross Lancs 289 D5
Hall Dunnerdale Cumb 313 A5
Hall End Beds 160 E1
Hall End Beds 159 C7
Hall End Lincs 252 D4
Hall End S Glos 103 E6
Hall End Warwick 199 C6
Hall Green Ches 244 C2
Hall Green Essex 163 E8
Hall Green Lancs 289 F6
Hall Green Lancs 277 C7
Hall Green Norfolk 232 E3
Hall Green S Yorks 281 B8
Hall Green W Midlands 176 B5
Hall Green W Midlands 178 B2
Hall Green Wrex 242 F3
Hall Grove Herts 137 E9
Hall of Clestrain Orkney 452 C3
Hall of Tankerness Orkney 453 C6
Hall Stanton Cumb 325 F7
Hall Waberthwaite Cumb 312 A2
Hallam Fields Derby 247 F6
Halland E Sussex 50 C3
Hallaton Leics 202 D1
Hallatrow Bath/NE Som'set 80 E4
Hallbankgate Cumb 349 E5
Hallbeck Cumb 315 C6
Hallen S Glos 102 F2
Hallew Cornw'l 8 D3
Hallfield Gate Derby 247 C5
Hallgarth Durham 344 C2
Hallglen Falk 394 C2
Hallin H'land 430 C2
Halling Medway 92 D1
Hallingbury Street Essex 139 D6
Hallington Lincs 274 B3
Hallington Northum 351 A6
Halliwell Gtr Man 278 B3
Halloughton Notts 248 D4
Hallow Worcs 153 A6
Hallow Heath Worcs 153 A6
Hallowes Derby 269 D7
Hallrule Scot Borders 374 E1
Halls E Loth 398 D3
Halls Green Essex 138 F4
Hall's Green Herts 138 B1
Hall's Green Kent 71 B5
Hallsands Devon 13 E7
Hallside S Lanarks 393 F5
Hallspill Devon 34 B2
Hallthwaites Cumb 312 C4
Hallwood Green Heref'd 152 F3
Hallwood Park Halton 265 C5
Hallworthy Cornw'l 17 C8
Hallyburton House Perth/Kinr 420 D2
Hallyne Scot Borders 383 D8
Halmer End Staffs 244 E1
Halmond's Frome Heref'd 152 C3
Halmore S Glos 103 B5
Halmyre Mains Scot Borders 383 C8
Halnaker W Sussex 47 E6
Halpenny Cumb 314 C4
Halsall Lancs 276 B4
Halse Northants 157 D6
Halse Som'set 58 F2
Halsetown Cornw'l 3 C6
Halsfordwood Devon 21 B7
Halsham ER Yorks 298 E4
Halstead Essex 140 A5
Halstead Kent 90 D4
Halstead Leics 201 B9
Halstock Dorset 39 E8
Halsway Som'set 58 D2
Haltcliff Bridge Cumb 339 D6
Halterworth Hants 44 B2
Haltham Lincs 251 B7
Haltoft End Lincs 252 E3
Halton Bucks 135 E8
Halton Halton 264 B4
Halton Lancs 302 C2
Halton Northum 351 C6
Halton Wrex 218 A3
Halton W Yorks 293 D8
Halton Brook Halton 265 C5
Halton East N Yorks 304 E4
Halton Fenside Lincs 252 B4
Halton Gill N Yorks 316 E3
Halton Green Lancs 302 B2
Halton Holegate Lincs 252 A4
Halton Moor W Yorks 293 D8
Halton Park Lancs 302 B2
Halton Shields Northum 351 C7
Halton View Halton 264 B5
Halton West N Yorks 303 E8
Halton-Lea-Gate Northum 349 E7
Haltwhistle Northum 349 D8
Halvergate Norfolk 210 B4
Halwell Devon 14 E3
Halwill Devon 19 A5
Halwill Junction Devon 19 A5
Ham Devon 38 F2
Ham Glos 103 C5
Ham Glos 131 C5
Ham H'land 445 A6
Ham Kent 95 F6
Ham London 89 B5
Ham Plym'th 10 D5
Ham Shetl'd 455 H5
Ham Som'set 38 D3
Ham Som'set 37 B8
Ham Som'set 38 A3
Ham Som'set 61 B5
Ham Som'set 59 A6
Ham Wilts 84 D3
Ham Common Dorset 41 A6
Ham Green Bristol 80 A2
Ham Green Hants 65 E5
Ham Green Kent 52 A2
Ham Green Kent 92 C3
Ham Green Worcs 176 F3
Ham Hill Medway 91 D9
Ham Street Som'set 60 E3
Hamar Shetl'd 457 F3
Hamarhill Orkney 454 C3
Hamars Shetl'd 457 G4
Hambleden Bucks 109 E5
Hambledon Hants 45 C7
Hambledon Surrey 68 D1
Hamble-le-Rice Hants 44 E4
Hambleton Lancs 288 B4
Hambleton N Yorks 295 D5
Hambleton Moss Side Lancs 288 B4
Hambridge Som'set 39 B5
Hambrook S Glos 80 A4
Hambrook W Sussex 46 E3
Hameringham Lincs 274 F3
Hamerton Cambs 182 C2
Hametoun Shetl'd 455 H5
Hamilton Leics C 201 B6
Hamilton S Lanarks 381 A6
Hamilton Park Racecourse S Lanarks 381 A6
Hamister Shetl'd 457 G5
Hamlet Dorset 40 E1
Hamlet of Shell Ness Kent 93 C8
Hammer W Sussex 67 E7
Hammer Bottom Hants 67 E7
Hammerpot W Sussex 48 E1
Hammersmith Derby 247 D5
Hammersmith London 89 A6
Hammerwich Staffs 198 B2
Hammerwood E Sussex 70 D3
Hammill Kent 95 E5
Hammond Street Herts 111 B8
Hammond's Green Hants 44 D1
Hammoon Dorset 41 D6
Hamnavoe Shetl'd 457 E2
Hamnavoe Shetl'd 457 E4
Hamnavoe Shetl'd 457 F4
Hamnavoe Shetl'd 455 C2
Hamnish Clifford Heref'd 151 A8
Hamp Som'set 59 D6
Hampden National Stadium Glasg C 392 F3
Hampden Park E Sussex 50 F5
Hamperden End Essex 139 A7
Hampnett Glos 131 D8
Hampole S Yorks 282 B4
Hampreston Dorset 27 A8
Hampsfield Cumb 314 D2
Hampson Green Lancs 302 E1
Hampstead London 111 E7
Hampstead Garden Suburb London 111 E7
Hampstead Norreys W Berks 85 A7
Hampsthwaite N Yorks 306 D2
Hampt Cornw'l 18 F4
Hampton Devon 23 A7
Hampton Kent 94 C3
Hampton London 88 B4
Hampton Shrops 174 A4
Hampton Swindon 105 D8
Hampton Worcs 154 D3
Hampton Bishop Heref'd 151 E9
Hampton Court Palace, Teddington London 89 C5
Hampton Fields Glos 104 C2
Hampton Gay Oxon 133 D8
Hampton Green Ches 242 E3
Hampton Heath Ches 242 E3
Hampton Hill London 88 B4
Hampton in Arden W Midlands 177 B7
Hampton Loade Shrops 196 F4
Hampton Lovett Worcs 175 E7
Hampton Lucy Warwick 155 A8
Hampton Magna Warwick 177 E8
Hampton on the Hill Warwick 177 F8
Hampton Park S'thampton 44 C3
Hampton Park Wilts 63 E8
Hampton Poyle Oxon 133 D9
Hampton Wick London 89 C5
Hamptons Kent 71 A7
Hamptworth Wilts 43 C7
Hamrow Norfolk 232 D3
Hams Som'set 39 C6
Hamsey E Sussex 49 D8
Hamsey Green Surrey 90 E2
Hamshill Glos 103 B7
Hamstall Ridware Staffs 222 E4
Hamstead W Midlands 198 E1
Hamstead Marshall W Berks 85 C5
Hamsterley Durham 343 E6
Hamsterley Durham 352 E1
Hamsterley Mill Durham 352 E1
Hamstreet Kent 73 E7
Hamwood N Som'set 79 E7
Hamworthy Poole 27 B6
Hanbury Staffs 223 C5
Hanbury Worcs 176 F2
Hanbury Woodend Staffs 223 C5
Hanby Lincs 227 B7
Hanchet End Suffolk 163 C6
Hanchurch Staffs 244 F2
Hand and Pen Devon 22 A2
Hand Green Ches 242 B3
Handale Redcar/Clevel'd 334 C1
Handbridge Ches 241 A9
Handcross W Sussex 69 F7
Handforth Ches 266 C4
Handley Ches 242 C2
Handley Derby 247 B5
Handley Green Essex 113 B8
Handsacre Staffs 222 E3
Handside Herts 137 E8
Handsworth S Yorks 269 B8
Handsworth W Midlands 198 E1
Handy Cross Bucks 109 D6
Handy Cross Devon 33 A8
Hanford Dorset 41 D6
Hanford Stoke 244 E3
Hangersley Hants 43 E6
Hanging Bank Kent 70 A4
Hanging Heaton W Yorks 293 F7
Hanging Houghton Northants 180 D3
Hanging Langford Wilts 63 D5
Hangleton Brighton/Hove 49 E5
Hangleton W Sussex 48 F1
Hanham S Glos 80 B4
Hanham Green S Glos 80 B4
Hankelow Ches 243 E6
Hankerton Wilts 104 D4
Hankham E Sussex 50 E5
Hanley Stoke 244 E3
Hanley Castle Worcs 153 D6
Hanley Child Worcs 174 E3
Hanley Swan Worcs 153 D6
Hanley William Worcs 174 E3
Hanlith N Yorks 304 C2
Hanmer Wrex 219 A6
Hannaford Devon 55 F7
Hannafore Cornw'l 9 E8
Hannah Lincs 275 D7
Hanningfields Green Suffolk 164 B2
Hannington Hants 85 E7
Hannington Northants 180 D4
Hannington Swindon 105 D8
Hannington Wick Swindon 105 C8
Hanscombe End Beds 160 F2
Hansel Village S Ayrs 367 A7
Hanslope M/Keynes 158 C4
Hanthorpe Lincs 227 D8
Hanwell London 111 F5
Hanwell Oxon 156 D3
Hanwood Shrops 194 B4
Hanwood Bank Shrops 195 A5
Hanworth London 88 B4
Hanworth Norfolk 257 E6
Happendon S Lanarks 381 E7
Happisburgh Norfolk 234 B4
Happisburgh Common Norfolk 234 C4
Hapsford Ches 264 E4
Hapton Lancs 290 D4
Hapton Norfolk 209 D7
Harberton Devon 14 D3
Harbertonford Devon 14 D3
Harbledown Kent 94 E2
Harborne W Midlands 176 B3
Harborough Magna Warwick 178 C4
Harborough Parva Warwick 178 C4
Harbottle Northum 363 B7
Harbour Park, Littlehampton W Sussex 47 F8
Harbourland Kent 92 E2
Harbourneford Devon 14 C2
Harbours Hill Worcs 176 E2
Harbridge Hants 43 D5
Harbridge Green Hants 43 D5
Harburn W Loth 395 F5
Harbury Warwick 156 A2
Harby Leics 226 B1
Harby Notts 272 E2
Harcombe Devon 23 D7
Harcombe Devon 23 B5
Harcombe Bottom Devon 23 A8
Harcourt Cornw'l 4 C4
Hardbreck Orkney 453 C5
Harden W Midlands 197 C9
Harden W Yorks 292 C3
Harden Park Ches 266 E3
Hardendale Cumb 327 D8
Hardengreen Midloth 396 E3
Hardenhuish Wilts 82 B3
Hardgate Aberds 429 B4
Hardgate Dumf/Gal 402 C2
Hardgate N Yorks 306 C2
Hardgate W Dunb 392 D2
Hardham W Sussex 47 C8
Hardhorn Lancs 288 C4
Hardingham Norfolk 208 C4
Hardings Booth Staffs 245 B7
Hardings Wood Ches 244 D2
Hardingstone Northants 158 A3
Hardington Som'set 61 A6
Hardington Mandeville Som'set 39 D8
Hardington Marsh Som'set 39 E8
Hardington Moor Som'set 39 D8
Hardley Hants 44 F3
Hardley Street Norfolk 210 C3
Hardmead M/Keynes 159 C6
Hardraw N Yorks 316 B3
Hardstoft Derby 247 B6
Hardstoft Common Derby 247 B6
Hardway Portsm'th 45 F7
Hardway Som'set 61 E6
Hardwick Bucks 135 D7
Hardwick Cambs 161 A7
Hardwick Cambs 182 E3
Hardwick Lincs 272 D2
Hardwick Norfolk 209 E8
Hardwick Norfolk 230 E4
Hardwick Northants 180 E5
Hardwick Oxon 106 B4
Hardwick Oxon 156 D3
Hardwick Oxon 134 B2
Hardwick Stockton 332 B3
Hardwick S Yorks 270 B1
Hardwick W Midlands 198 D2
Hardwick Green Worcs 130 A2
Hardwick Hall Derby 247 B7
Hardwick Village Notts 270 E4
Hardwicke Glos 130 E1
Hardwicke Glos 130 B4
Hardwicke Heref'd 150 D3
Hardy's Green Essex 141 C8
Hare Green Essex 142 C2
Hare Hatch Wokingham 87 A6
Hare Street Essex 138 F4
Hare Street Herts 138 B3
Hareby Lincs 252 A2
Harecroft W Yorks 292 C3
Harefield London 110 D3
Harefield S'thampton 44 D4
Haregate Staffs 245 C5
Harehill Derby 223 A5
Harehills W Yorks 293 D8
Harelaw Durham 343 A7
Hareleeshill S Lanarks 381 B7
Hareplain Kent 72 D3
Hare's Down Devon 21 B7
Haresceugh Cumb 340 C3
Harescombe Glos 130 E2
Haresfield Glos 130 E2
Haresfinch Mersey 277 E7
Hareshaw N Lanarks 393 F8
Harestanes E Dunb 393 D5
Harestock Hants 65 E6
Harewood Windsor 87 C9
Harewood W Yorks 293 B8
Harewood End Heref'd 128 B4
Harewood House, Wetherby W Yorks 293 B8
Harford Carms 147 D5
Harford Devon 11 D8
Hargate Norfolk 209 E6
Hargatewall Derby 268 D2
Hargrave Ches 242 B2
Hargrave Northants 181 D8
Hargrave Suffolk 163 A8
Harker Cumb 347 D9
Harker Marsh Cumb 337 E4
Harkland Shetl'd 456 E4
Harknett's Gate Essex 112 A3
Harkstead Suffolk 165 F8
Harlaston Staffs 199 A5
Harlaw Ho. Aberds 436 F4
Harlaxton Lincs 226 B4
Harle Syke Lancs 291 C6
Harlech Gwyn 214 B3
Harlech Castle Gwyn 214 B3
Harlequin Notts 225 A8
Harlescott Shrops 219 E7
Harlesden London 111 F6
Harlesthorpe Derby 270 D1
Harleston Devon 13 C6
Harleston Norfolk 188 B2
Harleston Suffolk 187 F5
Harleston Common Norfolk 188 B2
Harlestone Northants 180 F2
Harley Shrops 195 C7
Harley S Yorks 282 E1
Harley Shute E Sussex 51 E8
Harleywood Glos 104 C1
Harling Road Norfolk 208 F3
Harlington Beds 136 A4
Harlington London 88 A3
Harlington S Yorks 282 D3
Harlington Woodend Beds 136 A4
Harlosh H'land 430 D2
Harlow Essex 139 E5
Harlow Carr RHS Garden, Harrogate N Yorks 306 E2
Harlow Green Tyne/Wear 352 E4
Harlow Hill Northum 351 C8
Harlow Hill N Yorks 306 E2
Harlthorpe ER Yorks 296 C1
Harlton Cambs 161 B7
Harlyn Cornw'l 16 E2
Harman's Corner Kent 92 D4
Harman's Cross Dorset 27 D6
Harmans Water Brackn'l 87 C7
Harmby N Yorks 317 C8
Harmer Green Herts 137 D9
Harmer Hill Shrops 219 D6
Harmondsworth London 88 A3
Harmston Lincs 250 B2
Harnage Shrops 195 C7
Harnham Northum 364 F3
Harnham Wilts 63 F7
Harnhill Glos 105 B6
Harold Hill London 113 D5
Harold Park London 113 D6
Harold Wood London 113 D6
Haroldston West Pembs 116 A3
Haroldswick Shetl'd 456 B6
Harome N Yorks 320 D3
Harpenden Herts 137 E6
Harper Green Gtr Man 278 C3
Harperley Durham 343 A7
Harper's Hill Devon 14 C3
Harpford Devon 22 B3
Harpham ER Yorks 310 C3
Harpley Norfolk 231 C7
Harpley Worcs 174 F3
Harpole Northants 180 F1
Harpsdale H'land 445 C5
Harpsden Oxon 108 F5
Harpsden Bottom Oxon 108 F4
Harpswell Lincs 272 B3
Harpur Hill Derby 267 E8
Harpurhey Gtr Man 279 D6
Harraby Cumb 348 F2
Harracott Devon 55 F6
Harrapool H'land 431 F6
Harras Cumb 324 C4
Harraton Tyne/Wear 352 F4
Harrier Shetl'd 455 G5
Harrietfield Perth/Kinr 419 E7
Harrietsham Kent 72 A4
Harringay London 111 E8
Harrington Cumb 324 A4
Harrington Lincs 274 E4
Harrington Northants 180 C3
Harringworth Northants 202 D4
Harris H'land 422 C3
Harris Green Norfolk 209 F8
Harris Museum, Preston Lancs 289 E7
Harriseahead Staffs 244 C3
Harriston Cumb 338 C2
Harrogate N Yorks 306 D3
Harrold Beds 159 A6
Harrop Dale Gtr Man 280 C2
Harrow H'land 445 A6
Harrow London 110 E4
Harrow Green Suffolk 164 B2
Harrow Hill Glos 129 D6
Harrow on the Hill London 111 E5
Harrow Weald London 110 D4
Harrowbarrow Cornw'l 10 B3
Harrowbeer Devon 11 B6
Harrowden Beds 160 C1
Harrowgate Hill D'lington 331 C7
Harrowgate Village D'lington 331 C7
Harry Stoke S Glos 80 A4
Harsley Castle N Yorks 319 A7
Harston Cambs 161 B8
Harston Leics 226 B3
Harswell ER Yorks 296 B3
Hart Hartlep'l 345 E5
Hart Common Gtr Man 278 D1
Hart Hill Luton 137 C6
Hart Station Hartlep'l 345 D5
Hartbarrow Cumb 314 B2
Hartbarrow Cumb 314 B2
Hartburn Northum 364 E3
Hartburn Stockton 332 C3
Hartcliffe Bristol 80 C3
Hartest Suffolk 164 B1
Hartest Hill Suffolk 164 B1
Hartfield E Sussex 70 D4
Hartfield H'land 431 D7
Hartford Cambs 182 D4
Hartford Ches 265 E7
Hartford Som'set 57 F6
Hartford End Essex 140 D2
Hartfordbeach Ches 265 E7
Hartfordbridge Hants 87 E5
Hartforth N Yorks 331 E5
Hartgrove Dorset 41 C6
Harthill Ches 242 C3
Harthill Derby 267 B7
Harthill N Lanarks 394 F3
Harthill S Yorks 270 C1
Hartington Derby 245 B8
Hartland Devon 33 B5
Hartland Quay Devon 32 B4
Hartlands Hill Glos 129 D9
Hartle Worcs 175 C8
Hartlebury Worcs 175 D6
Hartlepool Hartlep'l 345 E6
Hartlepool's Maritime Experience Hartlep'l 345 E6
Hartley Cumb 329 E5
Hartley Kent 72 E2
Hartley Kent 91 C7
Hartley Northum 353 A5
Hartley Plym'th 11 D5
Hartley W Yorks 291 E7
Hartley Green Kent 91 C6
Hartley Green Staffs 222 C1
Hartley Mauditt Hants 66 D4
Hartley Wespall Hants 86 E4
Hartley Wintney Hants 86 E5
Hartlington N Yorks 304 C4
Hartlip Kent 92 D3
Hartlip Hill Kent 92 D3
Hartmount H'land 440 F4
Hartoft End N Yorks 321 B5

Harton N Yorks 308 C3
Harton Shrops 195 F5
Harton Tyne/Wear 353 D6
Hartpury Glos 130 C2
Hart's Green Suffolk 164 A2
Hartshead W Yorks 293 F5
Hartshead Green Gtr Man 279 D8
Hartshill Warwick 199 E7
Hartsholme Lincs 272 F3
Hartshorne Derby 223 D8
Hartsop Cumb 327 D5
Hartswell Som'set 57 F8
Hartwell Northants 158 B3
Hartwith N Yorks 305 C8
Hartwood Lancs 277 A8
Hartwood N Lanarks 382 A2
Harvel Kent 91 D7
Harvieston Stirl 409 D8
Harvington Worcs 154 C4
Harvington Worcs 175 D7
Harwell Notts 283 E6
Harwell Oxon 107 E6
Harwich Essex 143 A6
Harwood Durham 341 E7
Harwood Gtr Man 278 B3
Harwood Northum 364 D1
Harwood Dale N Yorks 322 A3
Harwood Lee Gtr Man 278 B3
Harworth Notts 283 E6
Hasbury W Midlands 176 B2
Hascombe Surrey 68 C1
Haselbech Northants 180 C2
Haselbury Plucknett Som'set 39 D7
Haseley Warwick 177 E7
Haseley Green Warwick 177 E7
Haseley Knob Warwick 177 D7
Haselor Warwick 154 A5
Hasendean Scot Borders 373 C7
Hasfield Glos 130 B2
Hasguard Pembs 116 C3
Hasguard Cross Pembs 116 B2
Haskayne Lancs 276 C4
Hasketon Suffolk 166 B3
Hasland Derby 269 F7
Hasland Green Derby 269 F7
Haslemere Surrey 67 E7
Hasleston Suffolk 187 F5
Haslingden Lancs 290 F4
Haslingden Grane Lancs 290 F4
Haslingfield Cambs 161 B8
Haslington Ches 243 C7
Hasluck's Green W Midlands 176 C5
Hassal Ches 243 C8
Hassal Green Ches 243 C8
Hassell Street Kent 74 B1
Hassingham Norfolk 210 B3
Hassocks W Sussex 49 C6
Hassop Derby 268 E4
Haster H'land 445 C7
Hasthorpe Lincs 275 F6
Hastigrow H'land 445 B6
Hasting Hill Tyne/Wear 353 F6
Hastingleigh Kent 74 C1
Hastings E Sussex 52 E1
Hastings Som'set 38 C4
Hastings Castle E Sussex 52 E1
Hastings Sea Life Centre E Sussex 52 E1
Hastingwood Essex 139 F5
Hastoe Herts 136 F2
Haswell Durham 344 C3
Haswell Moor Durham 344 C3
Haswell Plough Durham 344 C3
Hatch Beds 160 C3
Hatch Hants 66 A3
Hatch Beauchamp Som'set 38 B4
Hatch Bottom Hants 44 C4
Hatch End Beds 182 F1
Hatch End London 110 D4
Hatch Green Som'set 38 C4
Hatch Warren Hants 66 B2
Hatchet Gate Hants 44 F2
Hatchet Green Hants 43 C6
Hatching Green Herts 137 E6
Hatchmere Ches 265 E6
Hatcliffe NE Lincs 286 D3
Hatfield Heref'd 152 A1
Hatfield Herts 137 F8
Hatfield S Yorks 283 B7
Hatfield Worcs 153 B7
Hatfield Broad Oak Essex 139 D6
Hatfield Garden Village Herts 137 F8
Hatfield Heath Essex 139 E6
Hatfield House Herts 137 F8
Hatfield Hyde Herts 137 E8
Hatfield Peverel Essex 140 E4
Hatfield Woodhouse S Yorks 283 C7
Hatford Oxon 106 D3
Hatherden Hants 64 A3
Hatherleigh Devon 34 F3
Hatherley Glos 130 B4
Hathern Leics 224 D5
Hatherop Glos 105 A8
Hathersage Derby 268 C4
Hathersage Booths S Yorks 268 C4
Hathershaw Gtr Man 279 D7
Hatherton Ches 243 E6
Hatherton Staffs 197 A8
Hatley St. George Cambs 161 B5
Hatston Orkney 453 B5
Hatt Cornw'l 10 C3
Hatt Hill Hants 44 A1
Hatterseat Aberds 437 F6
Hattersley Gtr Man 279 F8
Hattingley Hants 66 D2
Hatton Aberds 437 E7
Hatton Angus 421 D5
Hatton Derby 223 B6
Hatton Lincs 273 D8
Hatton London 88 A4
Hatton Moray 435 C6
Hatton Shrops 195 E5
Hatton Warwick 177 E7
Hatton Warrington 265 C6
Hatton Castle Aberds 436 D4
Hatton Country World Warwick 177 E7
Hatton Heath Ches 242 B2
Hatton of Fintray Aberds 429 A5
Hattonburn Aberds 428 B4
Hattoncrook Aberds 437 F5
Hattonrig N Lanarks 393 F6
Haugh E Ayrs 368 B1
Haugh Gtr Man 279 B7
Haugh Lincs 275 D5
Haugh Head Northum 376 B2
Haugh of Glass Moray 436 E1
Haugh of Kilnmaichlie Moray 435 E6
Haugh of Urr Dumf/Gal 402 C2
Haugham Lincs 274 C3
Haughhead E Dunb 392 C4
Haughland Orkney 453 B6
Haughley Suffolk 187 F5
Haughley Green Suffolk 187 F5
Haughley New Street Suffolk 187 F5
Haughs of Clinterty Aberd C 429 A5
Haughton Notts 271 E5
Haughton Powys 218 E3
Haughton Shrops 218 C4
Haughton Shrops 219 E8
Haughton Shrops 196 B3
Haughton Staffs 221 D7
Haughton Green Gtr Man 279 F7
Haughton Le Skerne D'lington 331 C8
Haughton Moss Ches 242 C4
Haulkerton Aberds 428 E4
Haultwick Herts 138 C2
Haunn Arg/Bute 415 C6
Haunn W Isles 446 B3
Haunton Staffs 199 A5
Hauxton Cambs 162 A1
Havannah Ches 244 B3
Havant Hants 46 E2
Haven Heref'd 151 B6
Haven Bank Lincs 251 D7
Havenside ER Yorks 298 E2
Havenstreet I/Wight 30 B3
Haverbrack Cumb 314 D3
Havercroft N Yorks 282 B1
Haverfordwest = Hwlffordd Pembs 116 A4
Haverhill Suffolk 163 C6
Haverholme Priory Lincs 251 E5
Haverigg Cumb 312 E4
Havering-atte-Bower London 112 D5
Haversham M/Keynes 158 D4
Haverthwaite Cumb 313 D7
Haverton Hill Stockton 332 B4
Haviker Street Kent 72 B1
Havyatt Som'set 60 D2
Havyatt Green N Som'set 80 D1
Hawarden = Penarlâg Flints 241 A7
Hawbridge Worcs 153 C8
Hawbush Green Essex 140 C4
Hawcoat Cumb 300 A3
Hawen Ceredig'n 145 C6
Hawes N Yorks 316 C3
Hawe's Green Norfolk 209 D8
Hawes Side Blackp'l 288 D3
Hawford Worcs 175 F6
Hawick Scot Borders 373 E7
Hawk Green Gtr Man 267 B6
Hawkchurch Devon 38 F4
Hawkcombe Som'set 56 B4
Hawkedon Suffolk 163 B9
Hawkenbury Kent 72 C3
Hawkenbury Kent 71 D7
Hawkeridge Wilts 82 F2
Hawkerland Devon 22 C3
Hawkes End W Midlands 177 B8
Hawkesbury S Glos 103 E7
Hawkesbury Warwick 178 B2
Hawkesbury Common S Glos 103 E7
Hawkesbury Upton S Glos 103 E7
Hawkhill N Ayrs 379 D5
Hawkhill Northum 377 E6
Hawkhurst Kent 72 E2
Hawkinge Kent 74 C4
Hawkley Gtr Man 277 D8
Hawkley Hants 66 F4
Hawkridge Som'set 56 E4
Hawks Green Staffs 197 A8
Hawks Hill Bucks 109 E8
Hawksdale Cumb 339 B6
Hawkshaw Gtr Man 278 B4
Hawkshead Cumb 313 A7
Hawkshead Hill Cumb 313 A7
Hawkshill Down Kent 75 B7
Hawksland S Lanarks 382 D1
Hawkspur Green Essex 140 A2
Hawkswick N Yorks 304 A3
Hawkswick Cote N Yorks 304 A2
Hawksworth Notts 249 F6
Hawksworth W Yorks 292 B5
Hawksworth W Yorks 293 C7
Hawkwell Essex 114 D4
Hawkwell Northum 351 B8
Hawley Hants 87 E7
Hawley Kent 91 B5
Hawley's Corner London 90 E3
Hawling Glos 131 C7
Hawn Orkney 454 D2
Hawnby N Yorks 320 C1
Haworth W Yorks 292 C2
Haws Bank Cumb 313 A7
Hawsker Bottoms N Yorks 335 E5
Hawstead Suffolk 164 A2
Hawstead Green Suffolk 164 A2
Hawthorn Durham 344 B4
Hawthorn Hants 66 E3
Hawthorn Rh Cyn Taff 100 E1
Hawthorn Wilts 82 C1
Hawthorn Corner Kent 94 C4
Hawthorn Hill Brackn'l 87 B7
Hawthorn Hill Lincs 251 C7
Hawthorpe Lincs 227 C7
Hawton Notts 249 D6
Haxby C/York 307 D9
Haxby Gates C/York 307 D9
Haxey N Lincs 284 E2
Haxey Turbany N Lincs 284 D2
Haxted Surrey 70 B3
Haxton Wilts 63 B7
Hay Green Essex 113 B7
Hay Green Herts 161 E6
Hay Green Norfolk 230 E2
Hay Mills W Midlands 176 B5
Hay on Wye = Y Gelli Gandryll Powys 150 D2
Hay Street Herts 138 B3
Haybridge Shrops 174 D2
Haybridge Som'set 60 B2
Haybridge Telford 196 A2
Hayden Glos 130 C4
Haydock Mersey 277 E8
Haydock Park Racecourse Mersey 277 E8
Haydon Bath/NE Som'set 81 F5
Haydon Dorset 40 C3
Haydon Devon 36 C3
Haydon Som'set 38 B3
Haydon Swindon 105 E7
Haydon Bridge Northum 350 D3
Haydon Wick Swindon 105 E7
Haye Cornw'l 10 A2
Hayes London 90 C3
Hayes London 110 F3
Hayes End London 110 F3
Hayes End Som'set 39 C6
Hayes Green Warwick 178 A1
Hayes Town London 110 F4
Hayfield Derby 267 B7
Hayfield Fife 411 C7
Haygate Telford 195 A8
Hayhill E Ayrs 367 D9
Hayhillock Angus 421 C5
Haylands I/Wight 30 B3
Hayle Cornw'l 3 C7
Hayley Green W Midlands 176 B2
Haymoor Bottom Poole 27 B7
Haymoor End Som'set 38 A4
Hayne Devon 36 E2
Hayne Devon 36 C4
Hayne Som'set 38 C2
Haynes Beds 160 D1
Haynes Church End Beds 160 D1
Haynes West End Beds 160 D1
Hayscastle Pembs 119 D5
Hayscastle Cross Pembs 120 B2
Haysden Kent 71 B6
Haysford Pembs 120 C2
Hayshead Angus 421 C6
Hayston E Dunb 392 D4
Haythorn Dorset 42 E3
Hayton Aberd C 429 B6
Hayton Cumb 337 C8
Hayton Cumb 348 E4
Hayton ER Yorks 296 A3
Hayton Notts 271 C6
Hayton's Bent Shrops 173 B8
Haytor Vale Devon 20 E5
Haytown Devon 33 D7
Haywards Heath W Sussex 49 B6
Haywood S Lanarks 382 B4
Haywood S Yorks 281 E7
Haywood S Yorks 283 B5
Hazard's Green E Sussex 51 D6
Hazel Grove Gtr Man 267 B5
Hazel Head Cumb 312 B4
Hazel Street Kent 71 D8
Hazel Stub Suffolk 163 C6
Hazelbank S Lanarks 382 C1
Hazelbeach Pembs 116 D4
Hazelbury Bryan Dorset 40 E4
Hazeleigh Essex 114 B3
Hazeley Hants 86 E4
Hazeley Heath Hants 86 E5
Hazelford Ferry Notts 248 E5
Hazelgrove Notts 247 E8
Hazelhead S Yorks 281 D5
Hazelhurst Gtr Man 278 D4
Hazelhurst Gtr Man 278 A4
Hazelhurst Gtr Man 279 D8
Hazelmere Bucks 109 D7
Hazelslack Cumb 314 E3
Hazelslade Staffs 198 A1
Hazelton Walls Fife 420 E3
Hazelwood Derby 246 E4
Hazelwood Devon 14 E2
Hazelwood London 90 D3
Hazler Shrops 195 E5
Hazlerigg Tyne/Wear 352 B3
Hazleton Glos 131 D7
Hazlewood N Yorks 305 E5
Heacham Norfolk 254 E3
Headbourne Worthy Hants 65 E6
Headcorn Kent 72 C3
Headham Durham 331 C5
Headingley W Yorks 293 C7
Headington Oxon 134 F1
Headington Hill Oxon 134 F1
Headless Cross Worcs 176 E3
Headley Hants 67 D6
Headley Hants 85 D7
Headley Surrey 89 F6
Headley Down Hants 67 D6
Headley Heath Worcs 176 C4
Headley Park Bristol 80 C3
Headon Devon 33 F7
Headon Notts 271 D6
Heads S Lanarks 381 C6
Heads Nook Cumb 348 E3
Headstone London 110 E4
Heady Hill Gtr Man 279 B5
Heage Derby 247 D5
Healaugh N Yorks 307 F6
Healaugh N Yorks 317 A6
Heald Green Gtr Man 266 B4
Healds Green Gtr Man 279 C6
Heale Devon 55 B7
Heale Som'set 39 A5
Heale Som'set 61 C5
Healey Lancs 279 A6
Healey Northum 351 E8
Healey N Yorks 318 D2
Healey W Yorks 281 A7
Healey W Yorks 293 F6
Healeyfield Durham 342 B5
Healing NE Lincs 286 B3
Heamoor Cornw'l 2 D5
Heaning Cumb 314 A2
Heanish Arg/Bute 414 C3
Heanor Derby 247 E6
Heanor Gate Derby 247 E6
Heap Bridge Gtr Man 279 B5
Heapham Lincs 272 B2
Hearn Hants 67 D6
Hearnden Green Kent 72 B3
Hearthstane Scot Borders 371 B7
Hearts Delight Kent 92 D4
Heasley Mill Devon 56 E1
Heast H'land 423 A6
Heath Card 78 A3
Heath Derby 269 F8
Heath W Yorks 293 F9
Heath and Reach Beds 136 B2
Heath Charnock Lancs 277 B8
Heath Common Devon 38 F3
Heath Common W Sussex 48 D2
Heath Cross Devon 20 A4
Heath End Bucks 109 C7
Heath End Bucks 136 F3
Heath End Hants 85 D5
Heath End Hants 85 D8
Heath End Leics 224 D2
Heath End S Glos 103 E5
Heath End Surrey 67 B6
Heath End Warwick 177 F7
Heath End W Midlands 198 C1
Heath End W Sussex 47 C7
Heath Green Hants 66 D2
Heath Green Worcs 176 D4
Heath Hayes Staffs 198 A1
Heath Hill Shrops 220 F5
Heath House Som'set 59 B8
Heath Park London 112 E5
Heath Town W Midlands 197 D7
Heathbrook Shrops 220 C2
Heathcot Aberds 429 B5
Heathcote Derby 245 B8
Heathcote Warwick 177 F9
Heathencote Northants 158 C2
Heather Leics 199 A8
Heather Row Hants 86 F4
Heatherfield H'land 430 D4
Heatherside Surrey 87 E8
Heatherwood Park H'land 440 D5
Heatherybanks Aberds 436 D4
Heathfield Devon 21 E6
Heathfield E Sussex 50 B4
Heathfield N Yorks 305 B6
Heathfield S Ayrs 367 C7
Heathfield Som'set 37 A8
Heathhall Dumf/Gal 402 B3
Heathlands Wokingham 87 C6
Heathrow Airport London 88 A3
Heathstock Devon 38 F2
Heathton Shrops 196 E5
Heathtop Derby 223 B6
Heathwaite Cumb 314 A2
Heathy Brow E Sussex 49 F8
Heatley Ches 265 B9
Heatley Staffs 222 C3
Heaton Gtr Man 278 C3
Heaton Lancs 301 C7
Heaton Staffs 244 B5
Heaton Tyne/Wear 352 C4
Heaton W Yorks 292 C4
Heaton Chapel Gtr Man 266 A4
Heaton Mersey Gtr Man 266 A4
Heaton Moor Gtr Man 266 A4
Heaton Norris Gtr Man 266 A4
Heaton Punchardon Devon 54 D5
Heaton's Bridge Lancs 276 B5
Heaverham Kent 91 E6
Heaviley Gtr Man 267 B5
Heavitree Devon 21 B8
Hebburn Tyne/Wear 353 D5
Hebburn Colliery Tyne/Wear 353 C5
Hebburn Hall Ponds Tyne/Wear 353 D5
Hebburn New Town Tyne/Wear 353 D5
Hebden N Yorks 304 C4
Hebden Bridge W Yorks 292 E1
Hebden Green Ches 243 A5
Hebing End Herts 138 C2
Hebron Carms 121 B7
Hebron Angl 259 C6
Hebron Northum 365 E5
Heck Dumf/Gal 359 F5
Heckdyke Notts 284 E2
Heckfield Hants 86 D4
Heckfield Green Suffolk 188 C1
Heckfordbridge Essex 141 C7
Heckingham Norfolk 210 D3
Heckington Lincs 251 F5
Heckmondwike W Yorks 293 F6
Heddington Wilts 82 C5
Heddington Wick Wilts 82 C4
Heddle Orkney 452 B4
Heddon Devon 55 F8
Heddon Oak Som'set 58 D2
Heddon-on-the-Wall Northum 352 C1
Hedenham Norfolk 210 E2
Hedge End Hants 44 D4
Hedgefield Tyne/Wear 352 D2
Hedgerley Bucks 110 E1
Hedgerley Green Bucks 110 E1
Hedging Som'set 59 F6
Hedley on the Hill Northum 351 E8
Hednesford Staffs 197 A8
Hedon ER Yorks 298 E2
Hedsor Bucks 109 E8
Hedworth Tyne/Wear 353 D5
Heelands M/Keynes 158 E4
Heeley S Yorks 269 C7
Heeley City Farm, Sheffield S Yorks 269 B7
Heggle Lane Cumb 339 D6
Heglibister Shetl'd 457 H3
Heighington D'lington 331 B6
Heighington Lincs 273 F5
Height End Lancs 290 F4
Heightington Worcs 175 D5
Heights of Brae H'land 433 B7
Heights of Kinlochewe H'land 432 B2
Heilam H'land 443 B6
Heiton Scot Borders 374 A4
Helbeck Cumb 329 C5
Hele Devon 14 A2
Hele Devon 18 B3
Hele Devon 36 F4
Hele Devon 55 B5
Hele Som'set 37 B8
Hele Torbay 15 B6
Hele Lane Devon 35 D8
Helebridge Cornw'l 32 F4
Helensburgh Arg/Bute 409 D6
Helentongate S Ayrs 367 A7
Helford Cornw'l 4 E3
Helford Passage Cornw'l 4 E3
Helham Green Herts 138 D4
Helhoughton Norfolk 232 C2
Helions Bumpstead Essex 163 D6
Hell Corner W Berks 84 D4
Hellaby S Yorks 270 A3
Helland Cornw'l 8 A4
Helland Som'set 38 B4
Hellandbridge Cornw'l 8 A4
Hellescott Cornw'l 18 C2
Hellesdon Norfolk 209 A8
Hellesveor Cornw'l 3 B6
Hellgill Cumb 316 A1
Hellidon Northants 157 A5
Hellifield N Yorks 303 D9
Hellifield Green N Yorks 303 D9
Hellingly E Sussex 50 D4
Hellington Norfolk 210 C2
Hellington Corner Norfolk 210 C2
Hellister Shetl'd 457 J3
Helm Northum 365 C5
Helmdon Northants 157 D6
Helme W Yorks 280 B3
Helmingham Suffolk 165 A8
Helmington Row Durham 343 D7
Helmsdale H'land 441 B7
Helmshore Lancs 290 F4
Helmsley N Yorks 320 D3
Helperby N Yorks 307 B5
Helperthorpe N Yorks 309 A8
Helpringham Lincs 251 F5
Helpston Peterbro 203 B8
Helsby Ches 264 D4
Helsey Lincs 275 E7
Helston Cornw'l 4 E1
Helston Water Cornw'l 4 B3
Helstone Cornw'l 17 D6
Helton Cumb 327 B7
Helwith N Yorks 330 F3
Helwith Bridge N Yorks 303 B8
Hem Powys 193 C8
Hem Heath Stoke 244 F3
Hemble Hill Redcar/Clevel'd 333 C6
Hemblington Norfolk 210 A2
Hemblington Corner Norfolk 210 A2
Hemel Hempstead Herts 110 A3
Hemerdon Devon 11 D7
Hemingbrough N Yorks 295 D7
Hemingby Lincs 274 D1
Hemingfield S Yorks 282 D1
Hemingford Abbots Cambs 183 D5
Hemingford Grey Cambs 183 D5
Hemingstone Suffolk 165 B7
Hemington Leics 224 C4
Hemington Northants 182 A1
Hemington Som'set 61 A6
Hemley Suffolk 166 D3
Hemlington Middlesbro 332 D5
Hemp Green Suffolk 189 E5
Hempholme ER Yorks 310 E3
Hempnall Norfolk 209 E8
Hempnall Green Norfolk 209 E8
Hempriggs House H'land 445 D7
Hemp's Green Essex 141 B7
Hempstead Essex 163 E5
Hempstead Medway 92 D2
Hempstead Norfolk 256 E5
Hempstead Norfolk 235 C5
Hempsted Glos 130 D2
Hempton Norfolk 232 C3
Hempton Oxon 133 A7
Hempton Wainhill Bucks 108 B5
Hemsby Norfolk 235 E6
Hemsted Kent 74 C2
Hemswell Lincs 272 A3
Hemswell Cliff Lincs 272 B4
Hemsworth Dorset 42 E2
Hemsworth S Yorks 269 C7
Hemsworth W Yorks 282 B2
Hemyock Devon 37 D7
Hen Bentref Llandagfan Angl 259 D8
Henbrook Worcs 175 E8
Henbury Bristol 80 A3
Henbury Ches 266 D4
Henbury Kent 74 C3
Hendomen Powys 193 D8
Hendon London 111 E6
Hendon Tyne/Wear 353 E7
Hendra Cornw'l 17 D5
Hendra Cornw'l 4 C2
Hendra Cornw'l 8 D2
Hendra Croft Cornw'l 7 D6
Hendrabridge Cornw'l 9 B8
Hendre Bridg 99 F5
Hendre Flints 263 F5
Hendre Heref'd 128 C4
Hendre-ddu Conwy 239 A5
Hendreforgan Rh Cyn Taff 99 E6
Hendre-hen Powys 193 A8
Hendy Carms 97 B6
Hendy-Gwyn = Whitland Carms 121 D7
Heneglwys Angl 259 D5
Henfield S Glos 81 A5
Henfield W Sussex 48 C4
Henford Devon 18 B4
Henfords Marsh Wilts 62 C2
Henghurst Kent 73 D6
Hengoed Caerph 100 C3
Hengoed Shrops 218 B2
Hengrave Suffolk 186 E1
Hengrove Bristol 80 C4
Hengrove Park Bristol 80 C3
Henham Essex 139 B6
Heniarth Powys 193 B6
Henlade Som'set 38 B3
Henley Dorset 40 F3
Henley Glos 130 D4
Henley Shrops 195 F5
Henley Suffolk 165 B8
Henley Som'set 39 E6
Henley Som'set 59 E8
Henley Wilts 81 C8
Henley W Sussex 47 A5
Henley Green W Midlands 178 B2
Henley in Arden Warwick 177 E5
Henley Park Surrey 67 A8
Henley Street Kent 91 C8
Henley-on-Thames Oxon 108 F5
Henley's Down E Sussex 51 D7
Henllan Ceredig'n 145 D7
Henllan Denbs 262 F2
Henllan Amgoed Carms 121 D7
Henllys Torf 100 D5
Henllys Vale Torf 101 D5
Henlow Beds 160 E3
Hennock Devon 21 D6
Henny Street Essex 164 E2
Henryd Conwy 260 E5
Henry's Moat Pembs 120 B4
Hensall N Yorks 295 F5
Henshaw Northum 350 D2
Henshaw W Yorks 293 B5
Hensingham Cumb 324 C4
Hensington Oxon 133 D8
Henstead Suffolk 189 A7
Hensting Hants 44 B4
Henstridge Som'set 40 C4
Henstridge Ash Som'set 40 B4
Henstridge Bowden Som'set 40 B3
Henstridge Marsh Som'set 40 B4
Henton Oxon 108 B5
Henton Som'set 60 B1
Henwood Cornw'l 9 A8
Henwood Oxon 107 B6
Henwood Green Kent 71 C7
Henzleaze Bristol 80 A3
Heogan Shetl'd 455 B3
Heol Senni Powys 125 C7
Heolgerrig Merth Tyd 99 A7
Heol-laethog Bridg 99 F5
Heol-las Bridg 99 F5
Heol-y-Cyw Bridg 99 F5
Hepburn Northum 376 C3
Hepple Northum 363 B8
Hepscott Northum 365 F6
Hepthorne Lane Derby 247 B6
Heptonstall W Yorks 291 E8
Hepworth Suffolk 186 D4
Hepworth W Yorks 280 C5
Herbrandston Pembs 116 C3
Hereford Heref'd 151 E8
Hereford Cathedral Heref'd 151 E8
Hereford Racecourse Heref'd 151 D8
Heribusta H'land 430 A4
Heriot Scot Borders 384 B4
Heritage Motor Centre, Gaydon Warwick 156 B2
Hermiston C/Edinb 395 D8
Hermit Hill S Yorks 281 D8
Hermitage Scot Borders 361 C7
Hermitage Dorset 40 E2
Hermitage W Berks 85 B7
Hermitage W Sussex 46 E3
Hermitage Green Warrington 277 F9
Hermon Carms 122 A3
Hermon Carms 124 B2
Hermon Angl 258 F4
Hermon Pembs 121 A8
Herne Kent 94 C3
Herne Bay Kent 94 C3
Herne Common Kent 94 D3
Herne Hill London 89 B8
Herne Pound Kent 91 F8
Hernhill Kent 93 D8
Hernston V/Glam 77 A5
Herodsfoot Cornw'l 9 C7
Heronden Kent 95 F5
Herongate Essex 113 D7
Heron's Ghyll E Sussex 70 F4
Heronsford S Ayrs 400 A3
Heronsgate Herts 110 D2
Herra Shetl'd 456 D6
Herriard Hants 66 B3
Herringfleet Suffolk 211 D5
Herring's Green Beds 160 D1
Herringswell Suffolk 185 E7
Herringthorpe S Yorks 269 A9
Hersden Kent 94 D4
Hersham Cornw'l 33 E5
Hersham Surrey 88 D4
Herstmonceux E Sussex 51 D5
Herston Dorset 27 E7
Herston Orkney 452 D5
Hertford Herts 138 E2
Hertford Heath Herts 138 E2
Hertingfordbury Herts 138 E2
Hesket Newmarket Cumb 339 D5
Hesketh Bank Lancs 289 F5
Hesketh Lane Lancs 290 B1
Heskin Green Lancs 277 A7
Hesleden Durham 344 D4
Heslington C/York 308 E1
Hessay C/York 307 E7
Hessenford Cornw'l 10 D2
Hessett Suffolk 186 F3
Hessilhead N Ayrs 379 B7
Hessle ER Yorks 297 E7
Hessle W Yorks 282 A2
Hest Bank Lancs 301 B8
Hester's Way Glos 130 C4
Hestinsetter Shetl'd 455 B1
Hestley Green Suffolk 187 E8
Heston London 88 A4
Hestwall Orkney 452 B3
Heswall Mersey 263 C7
Hethe Oxon 134 B2
Hethel Norfolk 209 C7
Hethelpit Cross Glos 130 B1
Hethersett Norfolk 209 C6
Hethersgill Cumb 348 C3
Hetherside Cumb 348 C2
Hetherson Green Ches 242 E3
Hethpool Northum 375 B7
Hett Durham 344 D1
Hetton N Yorks 304 D3
Hetton Downs Tyne/Wear 344 B3
Hetton le Hill Tyne/Wear 344 C3
Hetton-le-Hole Tyne/Wear 344 B3
Heugh Northum 351 B8
Heugh-head Aberds 427 A8
Heveningham Suffolk 188 D4
Hever Kent 70 C4
Hever Castle and Gardens Kent 70 B4
Heversham Cumb 314 D3
Hevingham Norfolk 233 D8
Hewas Cornw'l 7 E9
Hewas Water Cornw'l 8 F2
Hewelsfield Glos 102 B3
Hewelsfield Common Glos 102 B2
Hewer Hill Cumb 339 D6
Hewish Som'set 39 E6
Hewood Dorset 38 F5
Heworth C/York 308 E1
Heworth Tyne/Wear 352 D4
Hexham Northum 351 D5
Hexham Abbey Northum 351 D5
Hexham Racecourse Northum 350 D5
Hextable Kent 90 B5
Hexthorpe S Yorks 283 D5
Hexton Herts 137 A6
Hexworthy Devon 11 A9
Hey Gtr Man 279 D8
Hey Lancs 291 B6
Hey Green W Yorks 280 B2
Hey Houses Lancs 288 E3
Heybridge Essex 113 C7
Heybridge Essex 141 F6

Hey – Hol 549

Heybridge Basin Essex 141 F6
Heybrook Bay Devon 11 F5
Heydon Cambs 161 E8
Heydon Norfolk 233 C7
Heydour Lincs 227 A7
Heyhead Gtr Man 266 B3
Heyheads Gtr Man 279 D8
Heyhouses Lancs 290 C4
Heylipol Arg/Bute 414 C2
Heylor Shetl'd 457 E2
Heyop Powys 172 D2
Heyrod Gtr Man 279 E8
Heysham Lancs 301 C7
Heyshaw N Yorks 305 C7
Heyshott W Sussex 47 C5
Heyshott Green W Sussex 47 C5
Heyside Gtr Man 279 C7
Heytesbury Wilts 62 C3
Heythrop Oxon 133 B6
Heywood Gtr Man 279 C6
Heywood Wilts 82 F2
Hibaldstow N Lincs 285 D6
Hibb's Green Suffolk 164 B2
Hickford Hill Essex 163 D8
Hickleton S Yorks 282 C3
Hickling Norfolk 235 D5
Hickling Notts 225 C8
Hickling Green Norfolk 235 D5
Hickling Heath Norfolk 235 D5
Hickmans Green Kent 93 E8
Hicks Forstal Kent 94 D3
Hick's Mill Cornw'l 4 B3
Hickstead W Sussex 49 B5
Hidcote Bartrim Glos 155 D6
Hidcote Boyce Glos 155 D6
Hidcote Manor Garden, Moreton-in-Marsh Glos 155 D6
Higford Shrops 196 C4
Higginshaw Gtr Man 279 C7
High Ackworth W Yorks 282 A2
High Angerton Northum 364 E3
High Bankhill Cumb 340 C2
High Barnes Tyne/Wear 354 D4
High Barnet London 111 C6
High Beach Essex 112 C3
High Beechburn Durham 343 E7
High Bentham N Yorks 302 B5
High Bickington Devon 34 B4
High Biggins Cumb 315 E6
High Blantyre S Lanarks 381 A5
High Bonnybridge Falk 393 C8
High Borrans Cumb 327 F5
High Bradfield S Yorks 268 A5
High Bradley N Yorks 304 F4
High Bray Devon 55 E8
High Brooms Kent 71 C6
High Bullen Devon 34 B3
High Buston Northum 377 F6
High Callerton Northum 352 B2
High Casterton Cumb 315 E6
High Catton ER Yorks 308 E3
High Church Northum 365 E5
High Clarence Stockton 332 B4
High Close N Yorks 331 C5
High Cogges Oxon 133 F6
High Common Norfolk 208 B3
High Common Norfolk 187 B8
High Common Suffolk 210 F3
High Condurrow Cornw'l 3 C9
High Coniscliffe D'lington 331 C6
High Crompton Gtr Man 279 C7
High Crosby Cumb 348 E3
High Cross Cornw'l 4 E2
High Cross Hants 46 A2
High Cross Herts 110 C4
High Cross Herts 138 D3
High Cross Lancs 288 C3
High Cross Leics 200 F3
High Cross Newp 101 E5
High Cross Warwick 177 E6
High Cross W Sussex 49 C5
High Cross Bank Derby 223 F6
High Crosshill S Lanarks 392 F4
High Dubmire Tyne/Wear 344 B2
High Dyke Cumb 339 E8
High Dyke Durham 329 A9
High Easter Essex 139 E8
High Eldrig Dumf/Gal 400 C4
High Ellington N Yorks 318 D2
High Entercommon N Yorks 331 E8
High Ercall Telford 220 E1
High Etherley Durham 343 F7
High Ferry Lincs 252 E2
High Flatts W Yorks 281 C6
High Fremington N Yorks 317 A6
High Friarside Durham 352 E2
High Gallowhill E Dunb 393 D5
High Garrett Essex 140 B4
High Grange Durham 343 E7
High Green Cumb 327 F5
High Green Norfolk 208 B2
High Green Norfolk 209 B6
High Green Shrops 174 B4
High Green Suffolk 186 F2
High Green S Yorks 281 E8
High Green Worcs 153 C7
High Green W Yorks 281 B5
High Halden Kent 72 D4
High Halstow Medway 92 B2
High Ham Som'set 59 B8
High Harrington Cumb 324 A5
High Harrogate N Yorks 306 D3
High Haswell Durham 344 C3
High Hatton Shrops 220 D2
High Hauxley Northum 365 B7
High Hawsker N Yorks 335 E5
High Heath Shrops 220 C3
High Heath W Midlands 198 C1
High Hesket Cumb 339 C8
High Hesleden Durham 345 D5
High Hoyland S Yorks 281 B7
High Hunsley ER Yorks 297 C6
High Hurstwood E Sussex 50 A2
High Hutton N Yorks 308 B4
High Ireby Cumb 338 D3
High Kelling Norfolk 256 D5
High Kilburn N Yorks 320 E1
High Knipe Cumb 327 C7
High Lands Durham 330 A4
High Lane Derby 247 F6
High Lane Gtr Man 267 B6
High Lane Heref'd 174 F3
High Lanes Cornw'l 3 C7
High Laver Essex 139 F6
High Leas Lincs 274 C4
High Legh Ches 265 C9
High Leven Stockton 332 D4
High Littleton Bath/NE Som'set 80 E4
High Longthwaite Cumb 338 B4
High Lorton Cumb 325 A8
High Marishes N Yorks 321 E7
High Marnham Notts 271 E8
High Melton S Yorks 282 D4
High Melwood N Lincs 284 D2
High Mickley Northum 351 D8
High Mindork Dumf/Gal 400 D5
High Moor C/York 307 E7
High Moor Lancs 277 B7
High Moorland Visitor Centre, Princetown Devon 20 F1
High Moorsley Tyne/Wear 344 C2
High Nash Glos 129 E5
High Newport Tyne/Wear 353 F6
High Newton Cumb 314 D3
High Newton-by-the-Sea Northum 377 B6
High Nibthwaite Cumb 313 D5
High Offley Staffs 221 C5
High Ongar Essex 113 B6
High Onn Staffs 221 E6
High Orchard Glos 130 D2
High Park Mersey 276 A4
High Risby N Lincs 284 B5
High Rocks Kent 71 D5
High Roding Essex 139 D8
High Rougham Suffolk 186 F3
High Row Cumb 326 B4
High Row Cumb 339 D6
High Salvington W Sussex 48 E2
High Scales Cumb 338 B2
High Sellafield Cumb 324 F5
High Shaw N Yorks 316 B3
High Shields Tyne/Wear 353 C6
High Shincliffe Durham 344 D2
High Side Cumb 338 E3
High Southwick Tyne/Wear 353 E6
High Spen Tyne/Wear 352 E1
High Stakesby N Yorks 334 D4
High Stittenham N Yorks 308 B2
High Street Cornw'l 8 E2
High Street Kent 72 E1
High Street Suffolk 189 D6
High Street Suffolk 188 B5
High Street Suffolk 167 A6
High Street Suffolk 164 C2
High Street Green Suffolk 165 A5
High Throston Hartlep'l 345 E5
High Tirfergus Arg/Bute 404 E2
High Town Staffs 197 A8
High Toynton Lincs 274 F2
High Urpeth Durham 352 F3
High Valleyfield Fife 411 D5
High Westwood Durham 352 E1
High Whinnow Cumb 338 A5
High Woolaston Glos 102 C3
High Worsall N Yorks 332 E2
High Wray Cumb 326 F4
High Wych Herts 139 E5
High Wycombe Bucks 109 D7
High Yarridge Northum 350 D5
Higham Derby 247 C5
Higham Fife 420 F2
Higham Kent 91 B9
Higham Lancs 291 C5
Higham Suffolk 165 E5
Higham Suffolk 185 E7
Higham S Yorks 281 C8
Higham Common S Yorks 281 C8
Higham Cross M/Keynes 158 C3
Higham Ferrers Northants 181 E7
Higham Gobion Beds 137 A6
Higham Hill London 112 D2
Higham on the Hill Leics 199 D8
Higham Park Northants 181 F7
Higham Wood Kent 71 B7
Highams Park London 112 D2
Highbridge Cumb 339 C6
Highbridge Hants 44 B4
Highbridge H'land 424 D3
Highbridge Som'set 59 B6
Highbrook W Sussex 70 E2
Highburton W Yorks 281 B5
Highbury London 111 E8
Highbury Som'set 61 B5
Highbury Vale Nott'ham 248 F1
Highclere Hants 85 D5
Highcliffe Dorset 28 B4
Highcliffe Northum 388 B2
Higher Alham Som'set 61 C5
Higher Ansty Dorset 41 F5
Higher Ashton Devon 21 D7
Higher Audley Blackb'n 290 E2
Higher Bal Cornw'l 6 E5
Higher Ballam Lancs 288 D4
Higher Bartle Lancs 289 D7
Higher Bebington Mersey 263 B8
Higher Berry End Beds 159 F7
Higher Blackley Gtr Man 279 D5
Higher Boarshaw Gtr Man 279 C6
Higher Bockhampton Dorset 26 B1
Higher Boscaswell Cornw'l 2 D3
Higher Broughton Gtr Man 279 D5
Higher Burrow Som'set 39 B6
Higher Burwardsley Ches 242 C3
Higher Change Lancs 291 F6
Higher Cheriton Devon 37 F7
Higher Chiswick Derby 267 A6
Higher Crackington Cornw'l 17 A8
Higher Croft Blackb'n 290 E2
Higher Denham Bucks 110 E2
Higher Dinting Derby 280 F2
Higher Disley Ches 267 C6
Higher Downs Cornw'l 3 D7
Higher End Gtr Man 277 D7
Higher Folds Gtr Man 278 D2
Higher Gabwell Devon 15 B6
Higher Green Gtr Man 278 D3
Higher Halstock Leigh Dorset 39 E8
Higher Heysham Lancs 301 C7
Higher Holnest Dorset 40 E2
Higher Holton Som'set 61 F5
Higher Hurdsfield Ches 267 E5
Higher Kingcombe Dorset 39 F8
Higher Kinnerton Flints 241 B7
Higher Marsh Som'set 40 B4
Higher Marston Ches 265 D8
Higher Melcombe Dorset 40 F4
Higher Metcombe Devon 22 B3
Higher Muddiford Devon 55 D6
Higher Northcott Devon 18 B3
Higher Nyland Dorset 40 B4
Higher Penwortham Lancs 289 E7
Higher Porthpean Cornw'l 8 E3
Higher Poynton Ches 267 C5
Higher Priestacott Devon 18 A4
Higher Rocombe Barton Devon 15 B6
Higher Row Dorset 42 F3
Higher Runcorn Halton 264 C5
Higher Sandford Dorset 40 B2
Higher Shotton Flints 263 F8
Higher Shurlach Ches 265 E8
Higher Slade Devon 54 B5
Higher Stanbear Cornw'l 9 A8
Higher Street Som'set 58 C2
Higher Tale Devon 37 F6
Higher Town Cornw'l 8 C3
Higher Town I/Scilly 6 A3
Higher Town Som'set 57 B6
Higher Tremarcoombe Cornw'l 9 B8
Higher Vexford Som'set 58 D4
Higher Walton Lancs 289 E8
Higher Walton Warrington 265 B6
Higher Wambrook Som'set 38 E3
Higher Warcombe Devon 54 B4
Higher Waterston Dorset 26 A1
Higher Whatcombe Dorset 41 F6
Higher Wheelton Lancs 289 F9
Higher Whitley Ches 265 C6
Higher Wincham Ches 265 D8
Higher Woodhill Gtr Man 278 B4
Higher Wraxall Dorset 40 F1
Higher Wych Ches 242 F2
Higherfence Ches 267 E5
Higherford Lancs 291 B6
Highertown Cornw'l 17 D7
Highertown Cornw'l 4 B4
Highfield ER Yorks 295 C8
Highfield Gtr Man 278 C3
Highfield Gtr Man 277 D8
Highfield Herts 136 F5
Highfield N Ayrs 379 B6
Highfield Oxon 134 C2
Highfield S'thampton 44 D3
Highfield Stockton 332 D3
Highfield S Yorks 269 B7
Highfield Tyne/Wear 352 E2
Highfields Cambs 161 A7
Highfields Derby 247 A6
Highfields Northum 388 B1
Highfields Staffs 221 D8
Highfields S Yorks 282 C4
Highgate E Sussex 70 E3
Highgate Kent 72 E2
Highgate London 111 E7
Highgate N Ayrs 379 B7
Highgate N Yorks 283 A5
Highgate Powys 193 D6
Highgate S Yorks 282 D3
Highhampton Devon 34 F2
Highland Folk Museum, Aultlarie H'land 426 C2
Highland Folk Museum, Kingussie H'land 426 B2
Highlane Ches 266 F4
Highlane Derby 269 C8
Highlaws Cumb 338 B1
Highleadon Glos 130 C1
Highleigh W Sussex 31 E6
Highley Shrops 174 B4
Highmoor Cumb 338 B4
Highmoor Oxon 108 E3
Highmoor Cross Oxon 108 F4
Highmoor Hill Monmouths 102 E1
Highnam Glos 130 D1
Highnam Green Glos 130 C1
Highridge Bristol 80 C3
Highstead Kent 94 C4
Highsted Kent 93 D5
Highstreet Kent 93 D8
Highstreet Green Essex 163 F8
Highstreet Green Surrey 68 D1
Hightae Dumf/Gal 346 A3
Highters Heath W Midlands 176 C4
Hightown Ches 244 B3
Hightown Hants 43 F6
Hightown Mersey 276 D3
Hightown S'thampton 44 D4
Hightown Wrex 241 E7
Hightown W Yorks 293 F5
Hightown Green Suffolk 164 A4
Hightown Heights W Yorks 293 F5
Highway Cornw'l 4 B2
Highway Cornw'l 9 E5
Highway Heref'd 151 C7
Highway Wilts 83 B5
Highweek Devon 14 A4
Highwood Dorset 26 C4
Highwood Hants 43 E6
Highwood Staffs 222 B3
Highwood Worcs 174 E3
Highwood Hill London 111 D6
Highworth Swindon 105 D8
Hilborough Norfolk 207 C7
Hilcote Derby 247 C7
Hilcott Wilts 83 E7
Hilden Park Kent 71 B6
Hildenborough Kent 71 B6
Hildersham Cambs 162 C3
Hildersley Heref'd 129 C6
Hilderstone Staffs 221 B8
Hilderthorpe ER Yorks 311 B5
Hilgay Norfolk 206 D3
Hill Devon 55 F8
Hill S Glos 102 C4
Hill Warwick 178 E4
Hill Worcs 154 C2
Hill Bottom Oxon 86 A2
Hill Brow W Sussex 67 F5
Hill Chorlton Staffs 221 A5
Hill Common Norfolk 235 D5
Hill Cottages N Yorks 321 A5
Hill Crest Worcs 175 C6
Hill Croome Worcs 153 D7
Hill Dale Lancs 277 B6
Hill Deverill Wilts 62 C2
Hill End Durham 342 D4
Hill End Fife 411 C5
Hill End Glos 153 E8
Hill End London 110 D3
Hill End N Yorks 305 E5
Hill End Shrops 195 E6
Hill End Worcs 175 F8
Hill Gate Heref'd 128 B3
Hill Green Essex 139 A5
Hill Green Kent 92 D3
Hill Head Hants 45 F5
Hill Heath Kent 70 C4
Hill Houses Derby 269 F7
Hill Houses Shrops 174 C2
Hill Mountain Pembs 117 C5
Hill of Beath Fife 411 C6
Hill of Fearn H'land 441 F5
Hill of Keillor Angus 420 C2
Hill of Mountblairy Aberds 436 C3
Hill of Overbrae Aberds 437 B5
Hill Park Kent 90 E3
Hill Ridware Staffs 222 E3
Hill Side Hants 67 F5
Hill Side Hants 66 A5
Hill Side S Yorks 281 D6
Hill Side W Yorks 281 A5
Hill Somersal Derby 222 B4
Hill Street Dorset 40 D4
Hill Street Kent 74 B2
Hill Top Derby 269 D7
Hill Top Durham 330 B1
Hill Top Durham 352 F2
Hill Top Durham 343 C8
Hill Top Gtr Man 278 D3
Hill Top Hants 44 F3
Hill Top Notts 247 E7
Hill Top S Yorks 281 C7
Hill Top S Yorks 269 B5
Hill Top W Midlands 197 E8
Hill Top W Yorks 280 B3
Hill Top W Yorks 281 A8
Hill Top W Yorks 292 D3
Hill Top W Yorks 293 D7
Hill Top, Sawrey Cumb 313 A8
Hill View Dorset 27 A6
Hill Wootton Warwick 177 E9
Hillam N Yorks 294 E4
Hillborough Kent 94 C4
Hillbourne Dorset 27 B7
Hillbrae Aberds 436 D3
Hillbrae Aberds 437 F4
Hillbutts Dorset 42 F2
Hillcliffe Warrington 265 B7
Hillcommon Som'set 37 A7
Hillcross Derby C 223 B8
Hilldyke Lincs 252 E2
Hillend Fife 411 D6
Hillend N Lanarks 393 E8
Hillend N Som'set 79 E7
Hillend Green Glos 129 B8
Hillersland Glos 128 E5
Hillerton Devon 20 A4
Hillesden Bucks 134 B4
Hillesley Glos 103 E7
Hillfarrance Som'set 37 B8
Hillfield Dorset 40 E2
Hillfield Devon 14 E4
Hillfields Bristol 80 A4
Hillfields W Berks 86 C3
Hillfoot Aberds 437 C6
Hillfoot W Yorks 293 D6
Hillfoot End Beds 160 F2
Hillgreen W Berks 85 A6
Hillgrove W Sussex 67 F8
Hillhampton Heref'd 152 C1
Hillhead Aberds 436 E2
Hillhead Aberds 437 F5
Hillhead Cornw'l 8 C4
Hillhead Devon 15 E6
Hillhead E Ayrs 379 E8
Hillhead S Ayrs 367 D8
Hillhead of Auchentumb Aberds 437 C6
Hillhead of Blairy Aberds 436 C3
Hillhead of Cocklaw Aberds 437 D7
Hillhouse Scot Borders 385 A7
Hilliard's Cross Staffs 198 A3
Hilliclay H'land 445 B5
Hillier Gardens and Arboretum Hants 44 B2
Hillingdon London 110 F3
Hillingdon Heath London 110 F3
Hillington Glasg C 392 F2
Hillington Norfolk 231 C6
Hillington Industrial Estate Glasg C 392 E2
Hillis Corner I/Wight 30 B1
Hillmorton Warwick 179 D5
Hillock Vale Lancs 290 E4
Hillockhead Aberds 428 A1
Hillockhead Aberds 427 B8
Hillpool Worcs 175 C7
Hill's End Beds 136 A3
Hills Town Derby 270 F1
Hillsborough S Yorks 269 A6
Hillside Aberds 429 C6
Hillside Angus 421 A7
Hillside Devon 14 C2
Hillside Orkney 452 A4
Hillside Orkney 453 D5
Hillside Shetl'd 457 G4
Hillside Wilts 105 D6
Hillside Worcs 175 F5
Hillstreet Hants 44 C1
Hillswick Shetl'd 457 F2
Hillview Tyne/Wear 353 E6
Hillway I/Wight 30 C4
Hillwell Shetl'd 455 E2
Hilmarton Wilts 82 A5
Hilperton Wilts 82 E2
Hilperton Marsh Wilts 82 D2
Hilsea Portsm'th 45 F8
Hilston ER Yorks 298 D4
Hiltingbury Hants 44 B3
Hilton Aberds 437 E6
Hilton Cambs 183 E5
Hilton Cumb 328 B4
Hilton Derby 223 B6
Hilton Dorset 41 F5
Hilton Durham 331 B5
Hilton H'land 440 E4
Hilton H'land 441 E6
Hilton Shrops 196 D4
Hilton Stockton 332 D4
Hilton Staffs 198 B2
Hilton House Gtr Man 278 C1
Hilton Lodge H'land 433 F4
Hilton of Cadboll H'land 441 F5
Hilton Park Gtr Man 279 D5
Himbleton Worcs 154 A1
Himley Staffs 197 D6
Hincaster Cumb 314 D4
Hinchley Wood Surrey 89 D5
Hinchwick Glos 132 A1
Hinckley Leics 200 E2
Hinderclay Suffolk 187 C5
Hinderton Ches 263 D8
Hinderwell N Yorks 334 C2
Hindford Shrops 218 B3
Hindhead Surrey 67 D7
Hindle Fold Lancs 290 D3
Hindley Gtr Man 278 D1
Hindley Northum 351 E8
Hindley Green Gtr Man 278 D1
Hindolveston Norfolk 233 C5
Hindon Wilts 62 E3
Hindringham Norfolk 256 E2
Hindsford Gtr Man 278 D2
Hingham Norfolk 208 C4
Hinlip Worcs 153 A7
Hinstock Shrops 220 C3
Hintlesham Suffolk 165 D6
Hinton Glos 103 B5
Hinton Hants 28 A4
Hinton Heref'd 150 E4
Hinton Northants 157 B5
Hinton Shrops 194 B4
Hinton S Glos 81 A6
Hinton Som'set 40 B1
Hinton Ampner Hants 66 F1
Hinton Blewett Bath/NE Som'set 80 E3
Hinton Charterhouse Bath/NE Som'set 81 E7
Hinton Green Worcs 154 D3
Hinton Martell Dorset 42 E3
Hinton on the Green Worcs 154 E3
Hinton Parva Dorset 42 F2
Hinton Parva Swindon 106 F1
Hinton St. George Som'set 39 D6
Hinton St. Mary Dorset 41 C5
Hinton Waldrist Oxon 106 C4
Hinton-in-the-Hedges Northants 157 E6
Hints Staffs 198 C4
Hinwick Beds 181 F6
Hinxhill Kent 73 C8
Hinxton Cambs 162 C2
Hinxworth Herts 160 D4
Hipperholme W Yorks 292 E4
Hipsburn Northum 377 E6
Hipswell N Yorks 318 A2
Hirael Gwyn 259 E8
Hiraeth Carms 121 C7
Hirn Aberds 428 B4
Hirnant Powys 217 D5
Hirst N Lanarks 394 F2
Hirst Northum 365 E7
Hirst Courtney N Yorks 295 F6
Hirwaen Denbs 240 B3
Hirwaun Rh Cyn Taff 99 A6
Hiscott Devon 34 A3
Histon Cambs 183 F8
Historic Royal Dockyard Portsm'th 45 F7
Hitcham Suffolk 164 B4
Hitcham Causeway Suffolk 164 B4
Hitchill Dumf/Gal 346 C4
Hitchin Herts 137 B7
Hither Green London 90 B2
Hittisleigh Devon 20 B4
Hive ER Yorks 296 D3
Hixon Staffs 222 C2
HMS Victory Portsm'th 45 F7
HMY Britannia C/Edinb 396 C2
Hoaden Kent 94 E5
Hoar Cross Staffs 222 D4
Hoarwithy Heref'd 128 B4
Hoath Kent 94 D4
Hoath Corner Kent 70 C4
Hobarris Shrops 172 C4
Hobbister Orkney 452 C4
Hobbles Green Suffolk 163 B7
Hobbs Cross Essex 112 C4
Hobbs Cross Essex 139 F5
Hobbs Point Pembs 117 D5
Hobkirk Scot Borders 373 E8
Hobroyd Derby 267 A7
Hobson Durham 352 E2
Hoby Leics 225 E8
Hoccombe Som'set 58 F2
Hockenden London 90 C4
Hockerill Herts 139 C5
Hockering Norfolk 209 A5
Hockering Heath Norfolk 233 F6
Hockerton Notts 248 C5
Hockholler Som'set 37 B8
Hockleton Shrops 194 C1
Hockley Ches 267 C5
Hockley Derby 269 F7
Hockley Essex 114 D3
Hockley Kent 93 E6
Hockley Staffs 199 C5
Hockley W Midlands 177 C8
Hockley Heath W Midlands 177 D6
Hockliffe Beds 136 B3
Hockwold cum Wilton Norfolk 207 F5
Hockworthy Devon 37 C5
Hoddesdon Herts 138 F3
Hoddlesden Blackb'n 290 F3
Hoddom Mains Dumf/Gal 346 B5
Hodgehill Ches 266 F3
Hodgehill W Midlands 198 F3
Hodgeston Pembs 117 E6
Hodley Powys 193 E7
Hodnet Shrops 220 C2
Hodnetheath Shrops 220 C2
Hodsall Street Kent 91 D7
Hodsock Notts 270 C4
Hodson Swindon 105 F8
Hodthorpe Derby 270 D3
Hoe Hants 45 C6
Hoe Norfolk 232 E4
Hoe Benham W Berks 85 B5
Hoe Gate Hants 45 D7
Hoel-ddu Swan 97 C8
Hoff Cumb 328 C3
Hog Hatch Surrey 67 B6
Hog Hill E Sussex 52 C2
Hogbarn Kent 92 E4
Hogben's Hill Kent 93 E7
Hogganfield Glasg C 392 E4
Hoggard's Green Suffolk 164 A2
Hoggeston Bucks 135 B7
Hoggrill's End Warwick 199 E5
Hogha Gearraidh W Isles 447 A2
Hoghton Lancs 289 E9
Hoghton Bottoms Lancs 290 E1
Hogland Shetl'd 457 F3
Hogley Green W Yorks 280 C4
Hognaston Derby 246 D2
Hogspit Bottom Herts 110 B2
Hogsthorpe Lincs 275 E7
Holbeach Lincs 229 D7
Holbeach Bank Lincs 229 C7
Holbeach Clough Lincs 229 C6
Holbeach Drove Lincs 205 A5
Holbeach Hurn Lincs 229 C7
Holbeach St. Johns Lincs 229 E6
Holbeach St. Marks Lincs 229 B7
Holbeach St. Matthew Lincs 229 B8
Holbeache Worcs 175 C5
Holbeck Notts 270 E2
Holbeck W Yorks 293 D7
Holbeck Woodhouse Notts 270 E2
Holberrow Green Worcs 154 A3
Holbeton Devon 11 E8
Holborn London 111 F8
Holborough Kent 91 D8
Holbrook Derby 247 E5
Holbrook Suffolk 165 E8
Holbrook S Yorks 269 C8
Holbrook Common S Glos 81 B5
Holbrooks W Midlands 178 B1
Holburn Northum 388 E2
Holbury Hants 44 F3
Holbury Purlieu Hants 44 F3
Holcombe Devon 22 F1
Holcombe Devon 23 B8
Holcombe Gtr Man 278 A4
Holcombe Som'set 61 B5
Holcombe Brook Gtr Man 278 A4
Holcombe Burnell Barton Devon 21 B7
Holcombe Rogus Devon 37 C6
Holcot Northants 180 E3
Holden Lancs 303 F7
Holden Fold Gtr Man 279 C7
Holdenby Northants 180 E1
Holdenhurst Bournem'th 28 A2
Holder's Green Essex 139 B8
Holders Hill London 111 D6
Holdgate Shrops 195 F7
Holdingham Lincs 250 E4
Holditch Dorset 38 F4
Holdsworth W Yorks 292 E3
Hole Devon 37 D8
Hole Bottom W Yorks 291 F7
Hole in the Wall Heref'd 129 B6
Hole Street W Sussex 48 D2
Holefield Scot Borders 387 F6
Holehills N Lanarks 393 E7
Holehouse Derby 267 A6
Holehouse E Renf 380 A1
Holemill Aberd C 429 B5
Holemoor Devon 33 E8
Holestane Dumf/Gal 358 C1
Holford Som'set 58 C3
Holgate C/York 307 E8
Holincote Som'set 57 B5
Holker Cumb 313 E8
Holkham Norfolk 255 D7
Hollacombe Devon 33 F7
Holland Orkney 454 A2
Holland Orkney 454 D4
Holland Surrey 70 A3
Holland Fen Lincs 251 E7
Holland Lees Lancs 277 C7
Holland Moor Lancs 277 D7
Holland Park W Midlands 198 B1
Holland-on-Sea Essex 143 D5
Hollandstoun Orkney 454 A6
Hollee Dumf/Gal 347 C7
Hollesley Suffolk 166 D4
Hollicombe Torbay 15 C5
Hollin Green Ches 242 D4
Hollin Hall Lancs 291 C7
Hollinfare Warrington 265 A8
Hollingbourne Kent 92 E3
Hollingbury Brighton/Hove 49 E6
Hollingdon Bucks 135 B8
Hollingove E Sussex 51 B6
Hollington Derby 223 A6
Hollington E Sussex 51 D8
Hollington Hants 85 D5
Hollington Staffs 222 A3
Hollington Grove Derby 223 A6
Hollingwood Derby 269 E8
Hollingworth Gtr Man 280 E2
Hollins Cumb 315 B7
Hollins Derby 269 E6
Hollins Gtr Man 278 C3
Hollins Gtr Man 279 C6
Hollins Gtr Man 279 C5
Hollins Staffs 244 D2
Hollins End S Yorks 269 C7
Hollins Green Warrington 265 A8
Hollins Lane Lancs 302 E1
Hollinsclough Staffs 245 A7
Hollinswood Telford 196 B3
Hollinthorpe W Yorks 294 D1
Hollinwood Gtr Man 279 D7
Hollinwood Shrops 219 A7
Hollis Head Devon 36 F4
Hollocombe Devon 35 D5
Hollocombe Town Devon 35 D5
Hollow Oak Dorset 26 B3
Hollow Street Kent 94 D4
Holloway Derby 246 C4
Holloway Wilts 62 E2
Holloway Windsor 109 F6
Holloway End W Midlands 175 B7
Holloway Hill Surrey 68 C1
Hollowell Northants 180 D1
Hollows Dumf/Gal 348 A1
Hollowsgate Ches 264 F5

Hyde End Wokingham 86 C4
Hyde Heath Bucks 109 B8
Hyde Lea Staffs 221 D8
Hyde Park S Yorks 283 D5
Hydestile Surrey 68 C1
Hylton Castle Tyne/Wear 353 E6
Hylton Red House Tyne/Wear 353 E6
Hyndburn Bridge Lancs 290 D4
Hyndford Bridge S Lanarks 382 D3
Hynish Arg/Bute 414 D2
Hyssington Powys 194 E2
Hystfield Glos 103 C5
Hythe Hants 44 E3
Hythe Kent 74 E3
Hythe Som'set 59 A9
Hythe Surrey 88 B2
Hythe End Bucks 88 B2
Hythie Aberds 437 C7
Hyton Cumb 312 C2

## I

Iarsiadar W Isles 450 D4
Ibberton Dorset 41 E5
Ible Derby 246 C3
Ibrox Glasg C 392 F3
Ibsley Hants 43 E6
Ibstock Leics 200 A2
Ibstone Bucks 108 D5
Ibthorpe Hants 84 F4
Iburndale N Yorks 334 E4
Ibworth Hants 86 F1
Icelton N Som'set 79 C7
Ichrachan Arg/Bute 417 D5
Ickburgh Norfolk 207 D7
Ickenham London 110 E3
Ickenthwaite Cumb 313 C7
Ickford Bucks 134 F3
Ickham Kent 94 E4
Ickleford Herts 137 A7
Ickles S Yorks 269 A8
Icklesham E Sussex 52 C2
Ickleton Cambs 162 D2
Icklingham Suffolk 185 D8
Ickornshaw N Yorks 291 B8
Ickwell Beds 160 C3
Ickwell Green Beds 160 C3
Ickworth House Suffolk 186 F1
Icomb Glos 132 C3
Icy Park Devon 14 F1
Idbury Oxon 132 D3
Iddesleigh Devon 34 E4
Ide Devon 21 B7
Ide Hill Kent 70 A4
Ideford Devon 21 E7
Iden E Sussex 73 F5
Iden Green Kent 72 E3
Idle W Yorks 293 C5
Idle Moor W Yorks 292 C5
Idless Cornw'l 7 F7
Idlicote Warwick 155 D8
Idmiston Wilts 63 D8
Idole Carms 122 D4
Idridgehay Derby 246 E3
Idrigill H'land 430 B3
Idstone Oxon 106 F2
Idvies Angus 421 C5
Iet-y-bwlch Carms 121 B7
Iffley Oxon 107 B7
Ifield W Sussex 69 D7
Ifieldwood W Sussex 69 D6
Ifold W Sussex 68 E2
Iford Bournem'th 28 B2
Iford E Sussex 49 E8
Ifton Monmouths 102 E1
Ifton Heath Shrops 218 A3
Ightfield Shrops 220 A1
Ightfield Heath Shrops 220 A1
Ightham Kent 91 E6
Ightham Common Kent 91 E6
Ightham Mote, Sevenoaks Kent 91 F6
Iken Suffolk 167 A7
Ilam Staffs 245 D8
Ilchester Som'set 39 B8
Ilderton Northum 376 C2
Ilford London 112 E3
Ilford Som'set 38 C5
Ilfracombe Devon 54 B5
Ilkeston Derby 247 F7
Ilketshall St. Andrew Suffolk 210 F3
Ilketshall St. Lawrence Suffolk 189 B5
Ilketshall St. Margaret Suffolk 188 A5
Ilkley W Yorks 305 F6
Illand Cornw'l 18 E2
Illey W Midlands 176 B2
Illington Norfolk 208 F2
Illingworth W Yorks 292 E3
Illogan Cornw'l 4 B1
Illogan Highway Cornw'l 4 B1
Ilmer Bucks 108 A5
Ilmington Warwick 155 D7
Ilminster Som'set 38 C5
Ilshaw Heath W Midlands 177 D5
Ilsington Devon 21 E5
Ilston Swan 97 D6
Ilston on the Hill Leics 201 D8
Ilton N Yorks 318 E2
Ilton Som'set 38 C4
Imachar N Ayrs 404 B4
Imber Wilts 62 B4
Imeraval Arg/Bute 403 B3
Immervoulin Stirl 418 F3
Immingham NE Lincs 286 B2
Immingham Dock NE Lincs 286 A3
Imperial War Museum London 89 A8
Imperial War Museum North Gtr Man 279 E5
Impington Cambs 184 F1
Ince Ches 264 D3
Ince Blundell Mersey 276 D3
Ince-in-Makerfield Gtr Man 277 D8
Inch of Arnhall Aberds 428 E3
Inchbae Lodge H'land 433 B6
Inchbare Angus 421 A6
Inchberry Moray 435 C8
Inchbraoch Angus 421 B7
Inchbrook Glos 104 B1
Inchcape H'land 440 C3
Incheril H'land 432 B2
Inchgrundle Angus 428 E1
Inchina H'land 438 D3
Inchinnan Renf 392 E1
Inchkinloch H'land 443 D7
Inchlaggan H'land 424 B3
Inchlumpie H'land 440 F2
Inchmore H'land 433 D5
Inchmore H'land 433 D7
Inchnacardoch Hotel H'land 425 A5
Inchnadamph H'land 439 A6
Inchock Angus 421 C6
Inchree H'land 417 A5
Inchrory Moray 427 B6
Inchture Perth/Kinr 420 E2
Inchyra Perth/Kinr 420 E1
Indian Queens Cornw'l 8 D1
Inerval Arg/Bute 403 B3
Ingatestone Essex 113 C8
Ingbirchworth S Yorks 281 C6
Ingerthorpe N Yorks 306 B2
Ingestre Staffs 222 D1
Ingham Lincs 272 C3
Ingham Norfolk 234 C4
Ingham Suffolk 186 D2
Ingham Corner Norfolk 234 C4
Ingleborough Norfolk 230 E1
Ingleby Derby 224 C1
Ingleby Lincs 272 D2
Ingleby Arncliffe N Yorks 332 F4
Ingleby Barwick Stockton 332 D3
Ingleby Cross N Yorks 332 F4
Ingleby Greenhow N Yorks 333 E6
Ingleigh Green Devon 34 E5
Inglemire Kingston/Hull 297 D8
Inglesbatch Bath/NE Som'set 81 D6
Inglesham Swindon 105 C9
Inglestone Common S Glos 103 E7
Ingleton Durham 331 B5
Ingleton N Yorks 303 A5
Inglewhite Lancs 289 C7
Ingliston C/Edinb 395 D7
Ingoe Northum 351 B7
Ingol Lancs 289 D7
Ingoldmells Lincs 275 F8
Ingoldsby Lincs 227 B7
Ingoldsthorpe Norfolk 231 B5
Ingon Warwick 155 A7
Ingram Northum 376 D2
Ingrave Essex 113 D7
Ingrow W Yorks 292 C2
Ings Cumb 314 A2
Ingst S Glos 102 E3
Ingthorpe Rutl'd 203 B5
Ingworth Norfolk 233 C8
Inham's End Cambs 204 D4
Inhurst Hants 85 D8
Inkberrow Worcs 154 A3
Inkerman Durham 343 D6
Inkersall Derby 269 E8
Inkersall Green Derby 269 E8
Inkford Worcs 176 D4
Inkpen W Berks 84 D4
Inkstack H'land 445 A6
Inlands W Sussex 46 E3
Inmarsh Wilts 82 D3
Innellan Arg/Bute 390 D2
Inner Hope Devon 12 E4
Innerleithen Scot Borders 384 E3
Innerleven Fife 412 B1
Innermessan Dumf/Gal 400 C2
Innerwick E Loth 398 D4
Innerwick Perth/Kinr 418 C3
Innie Arg/Bute 416 F3
Inninbeg H'land 416 C1
Innis Chonain Arg/Bute 417 E6
Innistrynich Arg/Bute 417 E6
Innox Hill Som'set 61 B7
Innsworth Glos 130 C3
Insch Aberds 436 F3
Insh H'land 426 B3
Inshegra H'land 442 C4
Inshore H'land 442 B5
Inskip Lancs 289 C6
Inskip Moss Side Lancs 289 C6
Instoneville S Yorks 283 B5
Instow Devon 54 E4
Insworke Cornw'l 10 E4
Intack Blackb'n 290 E3
Intake S Yorks 283 D6
Intake S Yorks 269 C7
Inver Aberds 427 C7
Inver H'land 441 E5
Inver Perth/Kinr 419 C8
Inver Mallie H'land 424 D3
Inverailort H'land 423 D7
Inveraldie Angus 420 D4
Inveralivaig H'land 430 D4
Inveralligin H'land 431 C8
Inverallochy Aberds 437 B7
Inveran H'land 438 F2
Inveran H'land 440 D2
Inveraray Arg/Bute 408 B3
Inveraray Jail Arg/Bute 408 B3
Inverarish H'land 431 E5
Inverarity Angus 420 C4
Inverarnan Stirl 417 F8
Inverasdale H'land 438 E2
Inverawe Ho. Arg/Bute 417 D5
Inverbeg Arg/Bute 409 C6
Inverbervie Aberds 429 E5
Inverboyndie Aberds 436 B3
Inverbroom H'land 439 E5
Invercarron Mains H'land 440 D2
Invercassley H'land 440 C1
Invercauld House Aberds 427 C6
Inverchaolain Arg/Bute 408 E3
Invercharnan H'land 417 C6
Inverchoran H'land 432 C4
Invercreran Arg/Bute 417 C5
Inverdruie H'land 426 A4
Inverebrie Aberds 437 E6
Invereck Arg/Bute 408 D4
Inverernan Ho. Aberds 427 A8
Invereshie House H'land 426 B3
Inveresk E Loth 396 D3
Inverewe Garden, Gairloch H'land 438 E2
Inverey Aberds 427 D5
Inverfarigaig H'land 433 F7
Invergarry H'land 425 B5
Invergelder Aberds 427 C7
Invergeldie Perth/Kinr 419 E5
Invergordon H'land 434 B2
Invergowrie Perth/Kinr 420 D3
Inverguseran H'land 423 B7
Inverhadden Perth/Kinr 418 B4
Inverhaggernie Stirl 418 E1
Inverharroch Moray 435 E8
Inverherive Stirl 418 E1
Inverie H'land 423 C7
Inverinan Arg/Bute 417 F4
Inverinate H'land 432 F1
Inverkeilor Angus 421 C6
Inverkeithing Fife 411 D6
Inverkeithny Aberds 436 D3
Inverkip Invercl 390 D4
Inverkirkaig H'land 439 B4
Inverlael H'land 439 E5
Inverleith C/Edinb 396 C1
Inverliever Lodge Arg/Bute 408 B1
Inverliver Arg/Bute 417 D5
Inverlochlarig Stirl 418 F2
Inverlochy Arg/Bute 417 E6
Inverlochy H'land 424 E3
Inverlochy Moray 435 F6
Inverlounin Arg/Bute 408 C5
Inverlussa Arg/Bute 407 D6
Invermark Lodge Angus 428 D1
Invermoidart H'land 423 E6
Invermoriston H'land 425 A6
Invernaver H'land 444 B1
Inverneill Arg/Bute 407 D8
Inverness H'land 434 D1
Inverness Airport H'land 434 C2
Invernettie Aberds 437 D8
Invernoaden Arg/Bute 408 C4
Inveronich Arg/Bute 408 B5
Inveroran Hotel Arg/Bute 417 C7
Inverpolly Lodge H'land 438 B4
Inverquharity Angus 420 B4
Inverquhomery Aberds 437 D7
Inverroy H'land 424 D4
Inversanda H'land 416 B4
Invershiel H'land 424 A1
Invershin H'land 440 D2
Invershore H'land 445 E6
Inversnaid Hotel Stirl 409 B6
Invertrossachs Stirl 409 B8
Inverugie Aberds 437 D8
Inveruglas Arg/Bute 409 B6
Inveruglass H'land 426 B3
Inverurie Aberds 437 F4
Invervar Perth/Kinr 418 C4
Inverythan Aberds 436 D4
Inwardleigh Devon 19 A8
Inworth Essex 141 D6
Iochdar W Isles 447 D2
Iolyn Park Conwy 262 D5
Iona Abbey and Cathedral Arg/Bute 415 E5
Iping W Sussex 46 B5
Ipplepen Devon 14 B4
Ipsden Oxon 108 E2
Ipstones Staffs 245 E6
Ipswich Suffolk 165 D8
Ir Wyddgrug = Mold Flints 241 B5
Irby Mersey 263 C7
Irby Hill Mersey 263 B7
Irby in the Marsh Lincs 252 B5
Irby upon Humber NE Lincs 286 D2
Irchester Northants 181 E6
Ireby Cumb 338 D3
Ireby Lancs 315 E7
Ireland Beds 160 D2
Ireland Orkney 452 C4
Ireland Shetl'd 455 D2
Ireland Wood W Yorks 293 C7
Ireland's Cross Shrops 243 F7
Ireleth Cumb 313 E5
Ireshopeburn Durham 341 D8
Ireton Wood Derby 246 E3
Irlam Gtr Man 278 F3
Irlams o' th' Height Gtr Man 278 E4
Irnham Lincs 227 C7
Iron Acton S Glos 103 F5
Iron Bridge Cambs 205 D8
Iron Cross Warwick 154 B4
Iron Lo. H'land 432 F2
Ironbridge Telford 196 C2
Ironbridge Gorge Museum, Telford Shrops 196 C2
Ironmacannie Dumf/Gal 401 B8
Irons Bottom Surrey 69 B7
Ironside Aberds 437 C5
Ironville Derby 247 D6
Irstead Norfolk 234 D4
Irstead Street Norfolk 234 E4
Irthington Cumb 348 D3
Irthlingborough Northants 181 D6
Irton N Yorks 322 D4
Irvine N Ayrs 379 E6
Irwell Vale Lancs 290 F4
Isabella Northum 365 F8
Isauld H'land 444 B3
Isbister Orkney 452 A3
Isbister Orkney 452 B4
Isbister Shetl'd 456 D3
Isbister Shetl'd 457 G5
Isel Cumb 338 E2
Isfield E Sussex 50 C1
Isham Northants 181 D5
Ishriff Arg/Bute 416 D1
Isington Hants 66 C5
Island Carr N Lincs 285 C6
Islawr-dref Gwyn 215 E5
Islay Airport Arg/Bute 403 A3
Islay Ho Arg/Bute 406 F3
Isle Abbotts Som'set 38 B5
Isle Brewers Som'set 38 B5
Isle of Man Dumf/Gal 346 A2
Isle of Man Airport I/Man 336 E2
Isle of Man Steam Railway I/Man 336 D3
Isle of Whithorn Dumf/Gal 401 F6
Isleham Cambs 185 D5
Isleornsay H'land 423 A7
Islesburgh Shetl'd 457 G3
Islesteps Dumf/Gal 402 B3
Isleworth London 89 A5
Isley Walton Leics 224 C3
Islibhig W Isles 450 E2
Islington London 111 E8
Islip Northants 181 C7
Islip Oxon 134 E1
Istead Rise Kent 91 B7
Itchen S'thampton 44 D3
Itchen Abbas Hants 65 E7
Itchen Stoke Hants 65 E8
Itchingfield W Sussex 68 F4
Itchington S Glos 103 E5
Itteringham Norfolk 233 B7
Itteringham Common Norfolk 233 C8
Itton Common Monmouths 102 C1
Ivegill Cumb 339 C7
Ivelet N Yorks 316 A4
Iver Bucks 110 F2
Iver Heath Bucks 110 F2
Iveston Durham 343 A6
Ivetsy Bank Staffs 197 A5
Ivinghoe Bucks 136 D2
Ivinghoe Aston Bucks 136 D2
Ivington Heref'd 151 A7
Ivington Green Heref'd 151 A7
Ivy Chimneys Essex 112 B4
Ivy Cross Dorset 41 B7
Ivy Hatch Kent 91 F6
Ivy Todd Norfolk 208 B1
Ivybridge Devon 11 D8
Ivychurch Kent 73 F7
Iwade Kent 93 C5
Iwerne Courtney Dorset 41 D6
Iwerne Minster Dorset 41 D7
Iwood N Som'set 79 D9
Ixhill Bucks 134 E4
Ixworth Suffolk 186 D3
Ixworth Thorpe Suffolk 186 D3

## J

Jack Bridge W Yorks 291 E8
Jack Hill N Yorks 305 E8
Jackfield Shrops 196 C2
Jack-in-the-Green Devon 22 A2
Jack's Green Essex 139 C7
Jack's Green Glos 130 F3
Jack's Hatch Essex 112 A3
Jacksdale Notts 247 D6
Jackson Bridge W Yorks 280 C5
Jackstown Aberds 436 E4
Jackton E Renf 380 B3
Jacobs Well Surrey 68 A2
Jacobstow Cornw'l 17 A8
Jacobstowe Devon 34 F4
Jagger Green W Yorks 280 A3
Jameston Pembs 117 E7
Jamestown Dumf/Gal 360 C2
Jamestown H'land 433 C6
Jamestown W Dunb 409 D6
Janetstown H'land 445 B4
Janke's Green Essex 141 B7
Jarlshof Prehistoric Site Shetl'd 455 F2
Jarman Park Herts 110 A3
Jarrow Tyne/Wear 353 C5
Jarvis Brook E Sussex 71 F5
Jasper's Green Essex 140 B3
Java Arg/Bute 416 D2
Jaw Hill W Yorks 293 F7
Jawcraig Falk 394 C1
Jaywick Essex 142 E3
Jealott's Hill Brackn'l 87 B7
Jedburgh Scot Borders 374 C3
Jeffreyston Pembs 117 C7
Jellyhill E Dunb 392 D4
Jemimaville H'land 434 B2
Jennett's Hill W Berks 85 B8
Jericho Gtr Man 279 B5
Jersey Marine Neath P Talb 97 C9
Jesmond Tyne/Wear 352 C4
Jevington E Sussex 50 F4
Jewell's Cross Devon 33 F5
Jingle Street Monmouths 128 E3
Jockey End Herts 136 E4
Jodrell Bank Ches 266 D3
Jodrell Bank Visitor Centre, Holmes Chapel Ches 266 E2
John o'Gaunt Leics 201 B8
John O'Gaunts W Yorks 293 E9
John o'Groats H'land 445 A7
Johnby Cumb 339 E7
John's Cross E Sussex 51 B8
Johnshaven Aberds 429 F4
Johnson Fold Gtr Man 278 B2
Johnson Street Norfolk 234 E4
Johnston Pembs 116 B4
Johnstone Renf 391 F8
Johnstone Mains Aberds 428 E4
Johnstonebridge Dumf/Gal 359 D6
Johnstown Carms 122 D3
Johnstown Wrex 241 E7
Joppa C/Edinb 396 D3
Joppa S Ayrs 367 D8
Jordan Green Norfolk 233 D6
Jordanhill Glasg C 392 E2
Jordans Bucks 110 D1
Jordanston Pembs 119 C6
Jordanthorpe S Yorks 269 C7
Jordon S Yorks 269 A8
Jorvik Viking Centre C/York 307 E9
Joyden's Wood Kent 90 B5
Joyford Glos 129 E5
Joy's Green Glos 129 D6
Jubilee Gtr Man 279 B7
Judges Lodging, Presteigne Powys 172 F4
Jugbank Staffs 220 A5
Jump S Yorks 282 D1
Jumper's Common Dorset 28 B2
Jumper's Town E Sussex 70 E4
Juniper Green C/Edinb 395 E9
Jurby East I/Man 336 B3
Jurby South Motor Racing Circuit I/Man 336 B3
Jurby West I/Man 336 B3

## K

Kaber Cumb 329 D5
Kaimend S Lanarks 382 C4
Kaimes C/Edinb 396 E2
Kame Fife 412 B1
Kames Arg/Bute 407 A8
Kames Arg/Bute 408 E2
Kames E Ayrs 369 B5
Kea Cornw'l 4 B4
Keadby N Lincs 284 B3
Keal Cotes Lincs 252 B3
Kearsley Gtr Man 278 D4
Kearsney Kent 75 C5
Kearstwick Cumb 315 E6
Kearton N Yorks 317 A5
Kearvaig H'land 442 A4
Keasden N Yorks 303 B6
Keason Cornw'l 10 B2
Keaton Devon 11 E8
Kebroyd W Yorks 292 F2
Keckwick Halton 265 C6
Keddington Lincs 274 B3
Keddington Corner Lincs 274 B4
Kedington Suffolk 163 C7
Kedleston Derby 246 F3
Kedleston Hall Derby 246 F4
Keekle Cumb 324 C5
Keelars Tye Essex 142 C2
Keelby Lincs 286 C2
Keele Staffs 244 E2
Keeley Green Beds 159 C8
Keelham W Yorks 292 D3
Keeres Green Essex 139 E7
Keeston Pembs 116 A4
Keevil Wilts 82 E3
Kegworth Leics 224 C4
Kehelland Cornw'l 3 B8
Keig Aberds 428 A3
Keighley W Yorks 292 B3
Keighley and Worth Valley Railway W Yorks 292 C3
Keil H'land 416 B4
Keilarsbrae Clack 410 C3
Keilhill Aberds 436 C4
Keillmore Arg/Bute 407 D6
Keillor Perth/Kinr 420 C2
Keillour Perth/Kinr 419 E7
Keills Arg/Bute 406 F4
Keils Arg/Bute 407 F5
Keinton Mandeville Som'set 60 E3
Keir Mill Dumf/Gal 357 D9
Keirsleywell Row Northum 341 A6
Keisby Lincs 227 C7
Keisley Cumb 328 B4
Keiss H'land 445 B7
Keistle H'land 430 C4
Keith Moray 436 C1
Keith Hall Aberds 437 F4
Keith Inch Aberds 437 D8
Keithock Angus 421 A6
Kelbrook Lancs 291 B7
Kelburn Invercl 391 D6
Kelby Lincs 250 F3
Kelcliffe W Yorks 293 B5
Keld Cumb 327 D8
Keld N Yorks 329 F7
Keld Head N Yorks 321 D6
Keldholme N Yorks 321 C5
Kelfield N Lincs 284 D3
Kelfield N Yorks 295 C5
Kelham Notts 249 C6
Kellacott Devon 19 C5
Kellan Arg/Bute 415 C8
Kellas Angus 420 D4
Kellas Moray 435 C6
Kellaton Devon 13 E7
Kellaways Wilts 82 A4
Kelleth Cumb 328 E3
Kelling Norfolk 256 D4
Kellingley N Yorks 294 F4
Kellington N Yorks 295 F5
Kelloe Durham 344 D2
Kelloholm Dumf/Gal 369 E6
Kells Cumb 324 C4
Kelly Devon 18 D4
Kelly Bray Cornw'l 10 A3
Kelmarsh Northants 180 C2
Kelmscott Oxon 106 C2
Kelsale Suffolk 189 F5
Kelsall Ches 264 F5
Kelsall Hill Ches 265 F5
Kelsay Arg/Bute 403 A1
Kelshall Herts 161 E6
Kelsick Cumb 338 A2
Kelso Scot Borders 386 F4
Kelso Racecourse Scot Borders 386 E4
Kelstedge Derby 246 B4
Kelstern Lincs 274 A2
Kelsterton Flints 263 E7
Kelston Bath/NE Som'set 81 C6
Keltneyburn Perth/Kinr 419 C5
Kelton Dumf/Gal 402 B3
Kelton Durham 329 B8
Kelty Fife 411 C6
Kelvedon Essex 141 D6
Kelvedon Hatch Essex 113 C6
Kelvin S Lanarks 380 B4
Kelvindale Glasg C 392 E3
Kelvinside Glasg C 392 E3
Kelynack Cornw'l 2 D3
Kemacott Devon 55 B8
Kemback Fife 420 F4
Kemberton Shrops 196 C3
Kemble Glos 104 C4
Kemerton Worcs 154 E1
Kemeys Commander Monmouths 101 B7
Kemeys Inferior Monmouths 101 D7
Kemnay Aberds 428 A4
Kemp Town Brighton/Hove 49 F6
Kempe's Corner Kent 73 B7
Kempie H'land 443 C6
Kempley Glos 129 B7
Kempley Green Glos 129 B7
Kemp's Green Warwick 177 D5
Kempsey Worcs 153 C7
Kempsford Glos 105 C8
Kempshott Hants 66 B2
Kempston Beds 159 C8
Kempston Church End Beds 159 C8
Kempston Hardwick Beds 159 D8
Kempston West End Beds 159 C8
Kempton Shrops 172 B5
Kempton Park Racecourse Surrey 88 B4
Kemsing Kent 91 E5
Kemsley Kent 93 C5
Kemsley Street Kent 92 D3
Kenardington Kent 73 E6
Kenchester Heref'd 151 D6
Kencot Oxon 106 B2
Kendal Cumb 314 B4
Kendal End Worcs 176 D3
Kendleshire S Glos 81 A5
Kendoon Dumf/Gal 356 E4
Kendray S Yorks 281 D9
Kenfig Bridg 98 F3
Kenfig Bridg 98 F3
Kenfig Hill Bridg 98 F3
Kengharair Arg/Bute 415 C7
Kenilworth Warwick 177 D8
Kenilworth Castle Warwick 177 D8
Kenknock Stirl 418 D2
Kenley London 89 E8
Kenley Shrops 195 C7
Kenmore Arg/Bute 408 B3
Kenmore H'land 431 C7
Kenmore Perth/Kinr 419 C5
Kenmure Dumf/Gal 401 B8
Kenn Devon 21 C8
Kenn N Som'set 79 C8
Kennacley W Isles 449 C5
Kennacraig Arg/Bute 407 F8
Kennards House Cornw'l 18 D2
Kenneggy Cornw'l 3 E7
Kenneggy Downs Cornw'l 3 E7
Kennerleigh Devon 36 E1
Kennet Clack 410 C4
Kennet End Cambs 185 E6
Kennethmont Aberds 436 F2
Kennett Cambs 185 E6
Kennford Devon 21 C8
Kenninghall Norfolk 187 A5
Kenninghall Heath Norfolk 187 B5
Kennington Kent 73 C7
Kennington London 89 A8
Kennington Oxon 107 B7
Kennishead Glasg C 392 F2
Kennoway Fife 411 B8
Kenny Som'set 38 C4
Kennyhill Suffolk 185 B6
Kennythorpe N Yorks 308 B4
Kenovay Arg/Bute 414 C2
Kensal Green London 111 F6
Kensal Rise London 111 F6
Kensal Town London 111 F6
Kensaleyre H'land 430 C4
Kensary H'land 445 D6
Kensington London 89 A7
Kenson V/Glam 77 C8
Kenstone Shrops 220 C1
Kensworth Beds 136 D4
Kent End Wilts 105 D6
Kent Hatch Kent 70 A3
Kent International Airport Kent 95 C6
Kent Street E Sussex 51 C8
Kent Street Kent 91 F8
Kent Street W Sussex 48 B4
Kentallen H'land 417 B5
Kentchurch Heref'd 128 B2
Kentford Suffolk 185 E7
Kentisbeare Devon 37 F6
Kentisbury Devon 55 C7
Kentisbury Ford Devon 55 C7
Kentish Town London 111 F7
Kentmere Cumb 327 F6
Kenton Devon 22 D1
Kenton London 111 E5
Kenton Suffolk 188 E1
Kenton Tyne/Wear 352 C3
Kenton Bankfoot Tyne/Wear 352 C3
Kenton Bar Tyne/Wear 352 C3
Kenton Corner Suffolk 188 E2
Kenton Green Glos 130 E1
Kentra H'land 423 F6
Kentrigg Cumb 314 B4
Kents Bank Cumb 314 E1
Kent's Green Glos 129 C8
Kents Hill M/Keynes 159 E5
Kent's Oak Hants 44 B1
Kenwick Shrops 219 B5
Kenwyn Cornw'l 4 A4
Kenyon Warrington 278 E1
Keoldale H'land 443 B5
Keonchulish Ho H'land 439 D5
Kepnal Wilts 83 D8
Keppanach H'land 417 A5
Keppoch H'land 432 F1
Keprigan Arg/Bute 404 E2
Kepwick N Yorks 319 B8
Kerchesters Scot Borders 387 E5
Kerdiston Norfolk 233 D6
Keresley W Midlands 178 B1
Keresley Newlands Warwick 178 B1
Kerley Downs Cornw'l 4 B3
Kernborough Devon 13 D6
Kerne Bridge Heref'd 129 D5
Kerrsary H'land 438 F2
Kerridge Ches 267 D5
Kerridge-end Ches 267 E5
Kerris Cornw'l 2 E4
Kerry Powys 193 F7
Kerrycroy Arg/Bute 390 F2
Kerrylamont Arg/Bute 378 A2
Kerry's Gate Heref'd 128 A1
Kerrysdale H'land 438 F2
Kerrytonlia Arg/Bute 378 A2
Kersal Gtr Man 279 D5
Kersall Notts 248 B5
Kersbrook Devon 22 D3
Kerscott Devon 55 F7
Kersey Suffolk 164 D4
Kersey Tye Suffolk 164 D4
Kersey Upland Suffolk 164 D4
Kershopefoot Cumb 361 F6
Kerswell Devon 37 F6
Kerswell Green Worcs 153 C7
Kerthen Wood Cornw'l 3 D7
Kesgrave Suffolk 166 C2
Kessingland Suffolk 189 A8
Kessingland Beach Suffolk 189 A8
Kestle Cornw'l 4 E3
Kestle Cornw'l 5 A7
Kestle Mill Cornw'l 7 D7
Keston London 90 D3
Keston Mark London 90 D3
Keswick Cumb 326 B2
Keswick Norfolk 209 C8
Keswick Norfolk 234 B4
Ketley Telford 196 A2
Ketley Bank Telford 196 A2
Ketsby Lincs 274 D4
Kettering Northants 181 C5
Ketteringham Norfolk 209 C7
Kettins Perth/Kinr 420 D2
Kettle Corner Kent 92 F1
Kettle Green Herts 138 D4
Kettlebaston Suffolk 164 B4
Kettlebridge Fife 411 B8
Kettlebrook Staffs 199 C5
Kettleburgh Suffolk 188 F3
Kettlehill Fife 411 B8
Kettleholm Dumf/Gal 346 A4
Kettleness N Yorks 334 C3
Kettleshulme Ches 267 D6
Kettlesing N Yorks 305 D8
Kettlesing Bottom N Yorks 305 D8
Kettlestone Norfolk 232 B4
Kettlethorpe Lincs 272 D1
Kettletoft Orkney 454 C4
Kettlewell N Yorks 304 A3
Ketton Rutl'd 203 C5
Kevingtown London 90 C4
Kew London 89 A5
Keward Som'set 60 C2

KewRoyal Botanic Gardens London 89 A5
Kewstoke N Som'set 79 D6
Kexbrough S Yorks 281 C8
Kexby C/York 308 E3
Kexby Lincs 272 B2
Key Green Ches 244 B3
Key Green N Yorks 334 F3
Key Street Kent 92 D4
Keycol Kent 92 D4
Keyford Som'set 61 B7
Keyham Leics 201 B7
Keyhaven Hants 29 B6
Keyingham ER Yorks 298 E3
Keymer W Sussex 49 D6
Keynsham Bath/NE Som'set 81 C5
Key's Green Kent 71 D8
Keysers Estate Essex 112 A2
Keysoe Beds 182 F1
Keysoe Row Beds 182 F1
Keyston Cambs 181 C8
Keyworth Notts 225 B7
Khantore Aberds 427 C7
Kibblesworth Tyne/Wear 352 E3
Kibworth Beauchamp Leics 201 E7
Kibworth Harcourt Leics 201 E7
Kidbrooke London 90 A3
Kiddal Lane End W Yorks 294 C2
Kiddemore Green Staffs 197 B6
Kidderminster Worcs 175 C6
Kiddington Oxon 133 C7
Kidland Devon 35 B9
Kidlington Oxon 133 E8
Kidmore End Oxon 86 A3
Kidnal Ches 242 E2
Kidsdale Dumf/Gal 401 F6
Kidsgrove Staffs 244 D2
Kidstones N Yorks 317 D5
Kidwelly = Cydweli Carms 122 F4
Kiel Crofts Arg/Bute 416 D4
Kielder Northum 362 D1
Kielder Castle Visitor Centre Northum 362 D1
Kierfiold Ho Orkney 452 B3
Kilbagie Clack 410 C4
Kilbarchan Renf 391 F8
Kilbeg H'land 423 B6
Kilberry Arg/Bute 407 F7
Kilbirnie N Ayrs 379 B6
Kilbowie W Dunb 392 D2
Kilbraur H'land 440 B5
Kilbride Arg/Bute 403 B3
Kilbride Arg/Bute 408 C1
Kilbride Arg/Bute 416 E3
Kilbride Arg/Bute 416 E4
Kilbride H'land 431 F7
Kilbridemore Arg/Bute 408 C3
Kilbryde Castle Stirl 410 B2
Kilburn Angus 427 F8
Kilburn Derby 247 E5
Kilburn London 111 F6
Kilburn N Yorks 319 E9
Kilby Leics 201 D6
Kilchamaig Arg/Bute 407 F8
Kilchattan Arg/Bute 406 C3
Kilchattan Bay Arg/Bute 378 A2
Kilchenzie Arg/Bute 404 D2
Kilcheran Arg/Bute 416 D3
Kilchiaran Arg/Bute 406 F2
Kilchoan Arg/Bute 416 F2
Kilchoan H'land 415 A7
Kilchoman Arg/Bute 406 F2
Kilchrenan Arg/Bute 417 E5
Kilconquhar Fife 412 B2
Kilcot Glos 129 B7
Kilcoy H'land 433 C7
Kilcreggan Arg/Bute 409 D5
Kildale N Yorks 333 E7
Kildalloig Arg/Bute 404 E3
Kildary H'land 440 F4
Kildaton Ho Arg/Bute 403 B4
Kildavanan Arg/Bute 408 F3
Kildermorie Lodge H'land 440 F2
Kildonan Dumf/Gal 400 D2
Kildonan H'land 430 C3
Kildonan N Ayrs 405 D6
Kildonan Lodge H'land 441 A6
Kildonnan H'land 422 D4
Kildrum N Lanarks 393 C7
Kildrummy Aberds 428 A1
Kildwick W Yorks 292 A2
Kilfinan Arg/Bute 408 E2
Kilfinnan H'land 425 C4
Kilgetty Pembs 117 C8
Kilgour Fife 411 B7
Kilgrammie S Ayrs 354 B3
Kilgwrrwg Common Monmouths 102 C1
Kilhallon Cornw'l 8 E4
Kilham ER Yorks 310 C3
Kilham Northum 375 A7
Kilkeddan Arg/Bute 404 D3
Kilkenneth Arg/Bute 414 C2
Kilkerran Arg/Bute 404 E3
Kilkhampton Cornw'l 33 D5
Killamarsh Derby 270 C1
Killay Swan 97 D7
Killbeg Arg/Bute 416 C1
Killean Arg/Bute 404 B2
Killearn Stirl 409 D8
Killegruer Arg/Bute 404 C2
Killellan Arg/Bute 390 E2
Killen H'land 434 C1
Killerby D'lington 331 C5
Killerton House, Exeter Devon 36 F4
Killichonan Perth/Kinr 418 B3
Killiechoinich Arg/Bute 416 E3
Killiechonate H'land 424 D4
Killiechronan Arg/Bute 415 C8
Killiecrankie Perth/Kinr 419 A7
Killiemor Arg/Bute 415 D7
Killiemore House Arg/Bute 415 E7
Killigorrick Cornw'l 9 C7
Killilan H'land 432 E1
Killimster H'land 445 C7
Killin Stirl 418 D3
Killin Lodge H'land 425 B7
Killinallan Arg/Bute 406 E3
Killinghall N Yorks 306 D2
Killington Cumb 315 C6
Killington Devon 55 B8
Killingworth Tyne/Wear 352 B4
Killingworth Moor Tyne/Wear 352 B4
Killingworth Village Tyne/Wear 352 B4
Killmahumaig Arg/Bute 407 C7
Killochyett Scot Borders 385 C6
Killocraw Arg/Bute 404 C2
Killundine H'land 415 C8
Killylung Dumf/Gal 402 A3
Kilmacolm Invercl 391 E7
Kilmaha Arg/Bute 408 B2
Kilmahog Stirl 410 B1
Kilmalcolm Invercl 391 D7
Kilmalieu H'land 416 B3
Kilmaluag H'land 430 A4
Kilmany Fife 420 E3
Kilmarie H'land 423 A5
Kilmarnock E Ayrs 379 E8
Kilmaron Castle Fife 420 F3
Kilmartin Arg/Bute 407 C8
Kilmaurs E Ayrs 379 D8
Kilmelford Arg/Bute 407 A8
Kilmeny Arg/Bute 406 F3
Kilmersdon Som'set 61 A5
Kilmeston Hants 45 A6
Kilmichael Arg/Bute 404 D2
Kilmichael Arg/Bute 408 E2
Kilmichael Glassary Arg/Bute 408 C1
Kilmichael of Inverlussa Arg/Bute 407 D7
Kilmington Devon 23 A7
Kilmington Wilts 61 D7
Kilmington Common Wilts 61 D7
Kilmington Street Wilts 61 D7
Kilmoluaig Arg/Bute 414 C2
Kilmonivaig H'land 424 D3
Kilmorack H'land 433 D6
Kilmore Arg/Bute 416 E3
Kilmore H'land 423 B6
Kilmory Arg/Bute 407 E7
Kilmory H'land 423 E5
Kilmory H'land 422 B3
Kilmory N Ayrs 405 D5
Kilmory Lodge Arg/Bute 407 B7
Kilmote H'land 441 B6
Kilmuir H'land 430 A3
Kilmuir H'land 430 D2
Kilmuir H'land 434 D1
Kilmuir H'land 434 A2
Kilmun Arg/Bute 416 F4
Kilmun Arg/Bute 416 F4
Kilmun Arg/Bute 408 D4
Kiln Farm M/Keynes 158 E4
Kiln Green Heref'd 129 D6
Kiln Green Wokingham 87 A6
Kiln Pit Hill Northum 351 E7
Kilnave Arg/Bute 406 E2
Kilncadzow S Lanarks 382 C2
Kilndown Kent 71 D9
Kilnhill Cumb 338 E3
Kilnhurst S Yorks 282 E3
Kilninian Arg/Bute 415 C6
Kilninver Arg/Bute 416 E3
Kilnsea ER Yorks 287 A7
Kilnsey N Yorks 304 B3
Kilnwick ER Yorks 310 F1
Kilnwick Percy ER Yorks 309 E5
Kiloran Arg/Bute 406 C3
Kilpatrick N Ayrs 405 D5
Kilpeck Heref'd 128 A2
Kilphedir H'land 441 B6
Kilpin ER Yorks 296 E2
Kilpin Pike ER Yorks 296 E2
Kilrenny Fife 412 B3
Kilsby Northants 179 D6
Kilspindie Perth/Kinr 420 E2
Kilsyth N Lanarks 393 C6
Kiltarlity H'land 433 D7
Kilton Notts 270 B3
Kilton Redcar/Clevel'd 333 C8
Kilton Som'set 58 C3
Kilton Thorpe Redcar/Clevel'd 333 C8
Kiltyrie Perth/Kinr 418 D4
Kilvaxter H'land 430 B3
Kilve Som'set 58 C2
Kilvington Notts 249 F7
Kilwinning N Ayrs 379 D6
Kimberley Notts 247 F7
Kimberley Street Norfolk 208 C5
Kimberworth S Yorks 282 F2
Kimberworth Park S Yorks 282 F2
Kimble Wick Bucks 135 F7
Kimblesworth Durham 343 B9
Kimbolton Cambs 182 E2
Kimbolton Heref'd 173 F8
Kimbridge Hants 44 A1
Kimcote Leics 179 A6
Kimmeridge Dorset 27 E5
Kimmerston Northum 387 E9
Kimpton Hants 64 B2
Kimpton Herts 137 D7
Kimworthy Devon 33 D6
Kinabus Arg/Bute 403 B2
Kinbeachie H'land 433 B8
Kinbrace H'land 444 E2
Kinbuck Stirl 410 B2
Kincaidston S Ayrs 367 D6
Kincaple Fife 420 F4
Kincardine Fife 410 D4
Kincardine H'land 440 E3
Kincardine Bridge Fife 410 D4
Kincardine O'Neil Aberds 428 C2
Kinclaven Perth/Kinr 420 D1
Kincorth Aberd C 429 B6
Kincorth Ho. Moray 434 B5
Kincraig H'land 426 B3
Kincraigie Perth/Kinr 419 C7
Kindallachan Perth/Kinr 419 C7
Kinderland, Scarborough N Yorks 322 B4
Kineton Glos 131 B7
Kineton Warwick 156 B1
Kineton Green W Midlands 177 B5
Kinfauns Perth/Kinr 420 E1
King Edward Aberds 436 C4
King Sterndale Derby 268 E1
King Street Essex 113 B6
Kingairloch H'land 416 B3
Kingarth Arg/Bute 405 A6
Kingarth Arg/Bute 378 A2
Kingates I/Wight 30 E2
Kingcoed Monmouths 101 A8
Kingdown N Som'set 80 D2
Kingerby Lincs 273 A6
Kingfield Surrey 88 E2
Kingford Devon 33 E5
Kingham Oxon 132 C4
Kingholm Quay Dumf/Gal 402 B3
Kinghorn Fife 411 D7
Kingie H'land 424 B3
Kinglassie Fife 411 C7
Kingoodie Perth/Kinr 420 E3
King's Acre Heref'd 151 D7
King's Bank E Sussex 52 B2
King's Bromley Staffs 222 E4
King's Broom Warwick 154 B4
King's Caple Heref'd 128 B5
King's Cliffe Northants 203 D6
King's Coughton Warwick 154 A4
King's End Oxon 134 C2
Kings Farm Kent 91 B8
Kings Furlong Hants 66 A2
King's Green Glos 153 F5
King's Heath Northants 180 F2
King's Heath W Midlands 176 B4
Kings Hedges Cambs 184 F1
King's Hill Kent 91 E8
King's Hill W Midlands 197 D8
Kings Langley Herts 110 B3
King's Lynn Norfolk 230 D4
King's Meaburn Ches 328 B2
King's Mills Wrex 241 E7
King's Moss Gtr Man 277 D7
Kings Muir Scot Borders 384 E2
Kings Newnham Warwick 178 C4
Kings Newton Derby 224 C2
Kings Norton Leics 201 C7
Kings Norton W Midlands 176 C4
King's Nympton Devon 35 C6
King's Park Glasg C 392 F3
King's Pyon Heref'd 151 B6
Kings Ripton Cambs 183 C5
King's Somborne Hants 64 E4
King's Stag Dorset 40 D4
King's Stanley Glos 103 B8
King's Sutton Oxon 156 E4
King's Tamerton Plym'th 10 D5
King's Thorne Heref'd 128 A4
King's Walden Herts 137 C7
Kings Worthy Hants 65 E6
Kingsand Cornw'l 10 E4
Kingsash Bucks 109 A7
Kingsbarns Fife 412 A3
Kingsbridge Devon 13 D5
Kingsbridge Som'set 57 D6
Kingsburgh H'land 430 C3
Kingsbury London 111 E5
Kingsbury Warwick 199 D5
Kingsbury Episcopi Som'set 39 B6
Kingsbury Regis Wilts 40 C3
Kingscauseway H'land 440 F4
Kingscavil W Loth 395 C5
Kingsclere Hants 85 E7
Kingscote Glos 103 C8
Kingscote Wokingham 87 B6
Kingscott Devon 34 C3
Kingscourt Glos 104 B1
Kingscross N Ayrs 405 D6
Kingsditch Glos 130 C4
Kingsdon Som'set 39 A8
Kingsdown Kent 75 B7
Kingsdown Swindon 105 E8
Kingsdown Wilts 81 C8
Kingseat Fife 411 C6
Kingsey Bucks 108 A4
Kingsfold Lancs 289 E7
Kingsfold W Sussex 69 D5
Kingsford Aberds 428 A2
Kingsford E Ayrs 379 C8
Kingsford Worcs 175 B6
Kingsgate Kent 95 B7
Kingshall Green Suffolk 186 F3
Kingshall Street Suffolk 186 F3
Kingsheanton Devon 55 D6
Kingshill Glos 103 C6
Kingsholm Glos 130 D2
Kingshouse Hotel H'land 417 B7
Kingshurst W Midlands 198 F4
Kingside Hill Cumb 338 A2
Kingskerswell Devon 15 B5
Kingskettle Fife 411 B8
Kingsland Dorset 24 A4
Kingsland Heref'd 173 F7
Kingsland Angl 258 C1
Kingsland Shrops 195 A5
Kingsley Ches 265 E6
Kingsley Hants 67 D5
Kingsley Staffs 245 E6
Kingsley Green W Sussex 67 E7
Kingsley Holt Staffs 245 E6
Kingsley Park Northants 180 F3
Kingsmead Ches 265 E8
Kingsmead Hants 45 D6
Kingsmoor Essex 138 F4
Kingsmuir Angus 421 C4
Kingsmuir Fife 412 B3
Kingsnorth Kent 73 D7
Kingstanding W Midlands 198 E2
Kingsteignton Devon 15 A5
Kingsteps H'land 434 C4
Kingsthorpe Northants 180 F3
Kingsthorpe Hollow Northants 180 F2
Kingston Cambs 161 A6
Kingston Cornw'l 18 E4
Kingston Dorset 27 E6
Kingston Dorset 41 E5
Kingston Devon 11 F8
Kingston E Loth 397 B7
Kingston Gtr Man 279 E7
Kingston Hants 43 F6
Kingston I/Wight 30 D1
Kingston Kent 74 A3
Kingston Moray 435 B8
Kingston W Sussex 48 F1
Kingston Bagpuize Oxon 107 C5
Kingston Blount Oxon 108 C4
Kingston by Sea W Sussex 48 E4
Kingston Deverill Wilts 62 D1
Kingston Gorse W Sussex 48 F1
Kingston Lacy, Wimborne Minster Dorset 42 F2
Kingston Lisle Oxon 106 E3
Kingston Maurward Dorset 26 B1
Kingston near Lewes E Sussex 49 E7
Kingston on Soar Notts 224 C5
Kingston Park Tyne/Wear 352 C3
Kingston Russell Dorset 25 B6
Kingston St. Mary Som'set 58 F4
Kingston Seymour N Som'set 79 C8
Kingston Stert Oxon 108 B4
Kingston upon Hull Kingston/Hull 297 E9
Kingston upon Thames London 89 C5
Kingston Vale London 89 B6
Kingstone Heref'd 151 E6
Kingstone Heref'd 129 C6
Kingstone Som'set 39 D5
Kingstone Staffs 222 C3
Kingstone S Yorks 281 C8
Kingstone Winslow Oxon 106 E2
Kingstonia N Yorks 306 B3
Kingstonridge E Sussex 49 E7
Kingstown Cumb 348 E1
Kingstreet Gtr Man 266 C4
Kingsway Halton 264 B5
Kingswear Devon 15 E5
Kingswells Aberd C 429 B5
Kingswinford W Midlands 197 F6
Kingswood Bucks 134 D4
Kingswood Ches 264 E5
Kingswood Glos 103 D6
Kingswood Heref'd 150 B3
Kingswood Herts 110 B4
Kingswood Kent 72 A3
Kingswood Powys 193 C8
Kingswood S Glos 81 B5
Kingswood Som'set 58 D2
Kingswood Surrey 89 E6
Kingswood Warwick 177 D6
Kingswood Warrington 265 A6
Kingswood Warren Surrey 89 E6
Kingthorpe Lincs 273 D7
Kington Heref'd 150 A3
Kington S Glos 102 D4
Kington Worcs 154 A2
Kington Langley Wilts 82 A3
Kington Magna Dorset 41 B5
Kington St. Michael Wilts 82 A3
Kingussie H'land 426 B2
Kingweston Som'set 60 E2
Kinhrive H'land 440 F4
Kininvie Ho. Moray 435 D8
Kinkell Bridge Perth/Kinr 419 F7
Kinknockie Aberds 437 D7
Kinknockie Aberds 437 F6
Kinkry Hill Cumb 349 A5
Kinlet Shrops 174 B4
Kinloch Fife 411 A7
Kinloch H'land 416 B1
Kinloch H'land 422 C3
Kinloch H'land 423 A6
Kinloch H'land 443 E5
Kinloch Perth/Kinr 420 C1
Kinloch Perth/Kinr 420 C2
Kinloch Damph H'land 431 D8
Kinloch Hourn H'land 424 B1
Kinloch Laggan H'land 425 D7
Kinloch Lodge H'land 443 C7
Kinloch Rannoch Perth/Kinr 418 B4
Kinlochan H'land 423 F8
Kinlochard Stirl 409 B7
Kinlochbeoraid H'land 423 D8
Kinlochbervie H'land 442 C4
Kinlocheil H'land 424 E1
Kinlochewe H'land 432 B2
Kinlochleven H'land 417 A6
Kinlochmoidart H'land 423 E7
Kinlochmorar H'land 423 C8
Kinlochmore H'land 417 A6
Kinlochspelve Arg/Bute 416 E1
Kinloid H'land 423 D6
Kinloss Moray 435 B5
Kinmel Bay = Bae Cinmel Conwy 262 C1
Kinmuck Aberds 429 A5
Kinmundy Aberds 429 A5
Kinnadie Aberds 437 D6
Kinnaird Perth/Kinr 419 B7
Kinnaird Perth/Kinr 420 E2
Kinnaird Castle Angus 421 B6
Kinnauld H'land 440 C4
Kinneff Aberds 429 E5
Kinnelhead Dumf/Gal 358 B4
Kinnell Angus 421 B6
Kinnerley Shrops 218 D3
Kinnersley Heref'd 150 C4
Kinnersley Worcs 153 D7
Kinnerton Powys 172 F2
Kinnesswood Perth/Kinr 411 B6
Kinninvie Durham 330 B3
Kinnordy Angus 420 B3
Kinoulton Notts 225 B8
Kinross Perth/Kinr 411 B6
Kinrossie Perth/Kinr 420 D1
Kinsbourne Green Herts 137 D6
Kinsey Heath Ches 243 F6
Kinsham Worcs 153 E8
Kinsley W Yorks 282 B2
Kinson Bournem'th 27 A8
Kintallan Arg/Bute 407 D7
Kintbury W Berks 84 C4
Kintbury Cross Ways W Berks 84 C4
Kintessack Moray 434 B4
Kintillo Perth/Kinr 420 F1
Kintocher Aberds 428 B2
Kinton Heref'd 173 D6
Kinton Shrops 218 E4
Kintore Aberds 429 A4
Kintour Arg/Bute 403 A4
Kintra Arg/Bute 403 B3
Kintra Arg/Bute 415 E6
Kintradwell H'land 441 C6
Kintraw Arg/Bute 407 B8
Kinuachdrachd Arg/Bute 407 C7
Kinveachy H'land 426 A4
Kinver Staffs 175 B6
Kinwarton Warwick 154 A5
Kip Hill Durham 352 F3
Kiplin N Yorks 318 A4
Kippax W Yorks 294 E2
Kippen Stirl 410 C1
Kippford or Scaur Dumf/Gal 402 D2
Kipping's Cross Kent 71 D7
Kippington Kent 90 F5
Kirbister Orkney 454 D4
Kirbister Orkney 452 B3
Kirbister Orkney 452 C4
Kirbuster Orkney 452 A3
Kirby Bedon Norfolk 210 B1
Kirby Bellars Leics 226 E1
Kirby Cane Norfolk 210 E3
Kirby Corner W Midlands 177 C8
Kirby Cross Essex 143 C5
Kirby Fields Leics 200 C4
Kirby Grindalythe N Yorks 309 B7
Kirby Hill N Yorks 306 B4
Kirby Hill N Yorks 330 E4
Kirby Knowle N Yorks 319 C8
Kirby Misperton N Yorks 321 E6
Kirby Muxloe Leics 200 C4
Kirby Row Norfolk 210 E3
Kirby Sigston N Yorks 319 B7
Kirby Underdale ER Yorks 309 D5
Kirby Wiske N Yorks 319 D6
Kirby-le-Soken Essex 143 C5
Kirdford W Sussex 68 F2
Kirk H'land 445 C6
Kirk Bramwith S Yorks 283 B6
Kirk Deighton N Yorks 306 E4
Kirk Ella ER Yorks 297 E7
Kirk Hallam Derby 247 F7
Kirk Hammerton N Yorks 307 D6
Kirk Ireton Derby 246 D3
Kirk Langley Derby 223 A7
Kirk Merrington Durham 344 E1
Kirk Michael I/Man 336 B3
Kirk of Shotts N Lanarks 394 F1
Kirk Sandall S Yorks 283 C6
Kirk Smeaton N Yorks 282 A4
Kirk Yetholm Scot Borders 375 B6
Kirkabister Shetl'd 457 G4
Kirkabister Shetl'd 455 C3
Kirkandrews Dumf/Gal 401 E8
Kirkandrews-on-Eden Cumb 347 E9
Kirkapol Arg/Bute 414 C3
Kirkbampton Cumb 347 E8
Kirkbean Dumf/Gal 402 D3
Kirkbride Orkney 454 B2
Kirkbride Cumb 347 E6
Kirkbridge N Yorks 318 B4
Kirkbuddo Angus 421 C5
Kirkburn Scot Borders 384 E2
Kirkburn ER Yorks 309 D8
Kirkburton W Yorks 281 B6
Kirkby Lincs 273 A6
Kirkby Mersey 276 E5
Kirkby N Yorks 333 E5
Kirkby W Yorks 281 B6
Kirkby Fenside Lincs 252 B2
Kirkby Fleetham N Yorks 318 B4
Kirkby Green Lincs 250 C4
Kirkby in Ashfield Notts 247 C7
Kirkby la Thorpe Lincs 250 E4
Kirkby Lonsdale Cumb 315 E6
Kirkby Malham N Yorks 304 C1
Kirkby Mallory Leics 200 C3
Kirkby Malzeard N Yorks 318 F3
Kirkby Mills N Yorks 321 C5
Kirkby on Bain Lincs 251 B7
Kirkby Overblow N Yorks 306 F3
Kirkby Park Mersey 276 E5
Kirkby Stephen Cumb 328 E5
Kirkby Thore Cumb 328 A2
Kirkby Underwood Lincs 227 C8
Kirkby Village Leics 201 D6
Kirkby Wharfe N Yorks 294 B4
Kirkby Woodhouse Notts 247 D7
Kirkby-in-Furness Cumb 313 D5
Kirkbymoorside N Yorks 320 C4
Kirkcaldy Fife 411 C7
Kirkcambeck Cumb 348 C4
Kirkcarswell Dumf/Gal 402 E1
Kirkcolm Dumf/Gal 400 C2
Kirkconnel Dumf/Gal 369 E6
Kirkconnell Dumf/Gal 402 C3
Kirkcowan Dumf/Gal 401 C5
Kirkcudbright Dumf/Gal 401 D8
Kirkdale Mersey 276 F3
Kirkfieldbank S Lanarks 382 D2
Kirkforthar Feus Fife 411 B7
Kirkgunzeon Dumf/Gal 402 C2
Kirkham Lancs 288 D5
Kirkham N Yorks 308 B3
Kirkhamgate W Yorks 293 F7
Kirkhams Gtr Man 279 D5
Kirkharle Northum 364 F2
Kirkheaton Northum 351 A7
Kirkheaton W Yorks 281 A5
Kirkhill Angus 421 A6
Kirkhill E Renf 380 A3
Kirkhill H'land 433 D7
Kirkhill Midloth 396 F1
Kirkhill Moray 435 E7
Kirkholt Gtr Man 279 B6
Kirkhope Scot Borders 372 C4
Kirkhouse Scot Borders 384 F3
Kirkhouse Cumb 349 E5
Kirkhouse Green S Yorks 283 A6
Kirkiboll H'land 443 C7
Kirkibost H'land 423 A5
Kirkinch Angus 420 C3
Kirkinner Dumf/Gal 401 D6
Kirkintilloch E Dunb 393 D5
Kirkland Cumb 325 C6
Kirkland Cumb 340 E3
Kirkland Cumb 338 B4
Kirkland Dumf/Gal 357 D8
Kirkland Dumf/Gal 369 E6
Kirkland Guards Cumb 338 C2
Kirkleatham Redcar/Clevel'd 333 B6
Kirklees Gtr Man 278 B4
Kirklevington Stockton 332 E3
Kirkley Suffolk 211 E6
Kirklington Notts 248 D3
Kirklington N Yorks 318 D5
Kirklinton Cumb 348 C2
Kirkliston C/Edinb 395 D8
Kirkmaiden Dumf/Gal 400 F3
Kirkmichael Perth/Kinr 419 B8
Kirkmichael S Ayrs 367 F6
Kirkmuirhill S Lanarks 381 D7
Kirknewton Northum 375 A8
Kirknewton W Loth 395 E7
Kirkney Aberds 436 E2
Kirkoswald Cumb 340 C2
Kirkoswald S Ayrs 366 F4
Kirkpatrick Dumf/Gal 358 D2
Kirkpatrick Durham Dumf/Gal 402 B1
Kirkpatrick-Fleming Dumf/Gal 347 B7
Kirksanton Cumb 312 D3
Kirkshaw N Lanarks 393 F6
Kirkstall W Yorks 293 C7
Kirkstile Aberds 436 E2
Kirkstyle H'land 445 A7
Kirkthorpe W Yorks 294 F1
Kirkton Aberds 436 D3
Kirkton Aberds 436 F3
Kirkton Angus 420 C2
Kirkton Angus 420 C4
Kirkton Angus 420 D4
Kirkton Arg/Bute 407 B7
Kirkton Scot Borders 373 E7
Kirkton Dumf/Gal 358 F3
Kirkton Fife 420 E3
Kirkton H'land 431 F8
Kirkton H'land 432 D1
Kirkton H'land 434 C2
Kirkton H'land 440 D4
Kirkton N Ayrs 378 A3
Kirkton Perth/Kinr 419 F7
Kirkton Stirl 409 B8
Kirkton S Lanarks 370 C3
Kirkton W Loth 395 E5
Kirkton Manor Scot Borders 384 E1
Kirkton of Airlie Angus 420 B3
Kirkton of Auchterhouse Angus 420 D3
Kirkton of Auchterless Aberds 436 D4
Kirkton of Barevan H'land 434 D3
Kirkton of Bourtie Aberds 437 F5
Kirkton of Collace Perth/Kinr 420 D1
Kirkton of Craig Angus 421 B7
Kirkton of Culsalmond Aberds 436 E3
Kirkton of Durris Aberds 428 C4
Kirkton of Glenbuchat Aberds 427 A8
Kirkton of Glenisla Angus 420 A2
Kirkton of Kingoldrum Angus 420 B3
Kirkton of Largo Fife 412 B2
Kirkton of Lethendy Perth/Kinr 420 C1
Kirkton of Logie Buchan Aberds 437 F6
Kirkton of Maryculter Aberds 429 C5
Kirkton of Menmuir Angus 421 A5
Kirkton of Monikie Angus 421 D5
Kirkton of Oyne Aberds 436 F3
Kirkton of Rayne Aberds 436 F3
Kirkton of Skene Aberds 429 B5
Kirkton of Tough Aberds 428 A3
Kirktonhill Scot Borders 385 B6
Kirktonhill W Dunb 391 D7
Kirktoun E Ayrs 379 D8
Kirktown Aberds 437 C7
Kirktown of Alvah Aberds 436 B3
Kirktown of Deskford Moray 436 B2
Kirktown of Fetteresso Aberds 429 D5
Kirktown of Mortlach Moray 435 E8
Kirktown of Slains Aberds 437 F7
Kirkud Scot Borders 383 D7
Kirkwall Orkney 453 B5
Kirkwall Airport Orkney 453 C5
Kirkwhelpington Northum 364 F1
Kirkwood Dumf/Gal 346 A4
Kirkwood N Lanarks 393 F6
Kirmington N Lincs 285 B9
Kirmond le Mire Lincs 273 A8
Kirn Arg/Bute 390 C3
Kirriemuir Angus 420 B3
Kirstead Green Norfolk 210 D1
Kirtlebridge Dumf/Gal 347 B6
Kirtleton Dumf/Gal 360 F2
Kirtling Cambs 163 A6
Kirtling Green Cambs 163 A6
Kirtlington Oxon 133 D8
Kirtomy H'land 444 B1
Kirton Lincs 229 A6
Kirton Notts 271 F5
Kirton Suffolk 166 E3
Kirton End Lincs 229 A5
Kirton Holme Lincs 251 F8
Kirton in Lindsey N Lincs 285 E5
Kiskin Cumb 312 C2
Kislingbury Northants 158 A2
Kitchenroyd W Yorks 281 C6
Kites Hardwick Warwick 178 E4
Kit's Coty Kent 92 D1
Kitt Green Gtr Man 277 C8
Kittisford Som'set 37 B6
Kittisford Barton Som'set 37 B6
Kittle Swan 97 E6
Kitt's End Herts 111 C6
Kitt's Green W Midlands 198 F4
Kitt's Moss Gtr Man 266 C4
Kittwhistle Dorset 39 F5
Kittybrewster Aberd C 429 B6
Kitwood Hants 66 E3
Kivernoll Heref'd 128 A3
Kiveton Park S Yorks 270 C1
Knackers Hole Dorset 41 D5
Knaith Lincs 271 C8
Knaith Park Lincs 272 B1
Knap Corner Dorset 41 B6
Knaphill Surrey 88 E1
Knapp Hants 44 B3
Knapp Perth/Kinr 420 D2
Knapp Som'set 38 A3
Knapthorpe Notts 249 C5
Knapton C/York 307 E8
Knapton Norfolk 234 B3
Knapton Green Heref'd 151 B6
Knapwell Cambs 183 F6
Knaresborough N Yorks 306 D4
Knarsdale Northum 349 F7
Knatts Valley Kent 91 D6

Knauchland Moray 436 C2
Knaven Aberds 437 D5
Knave's Ash Kent 94 D4
Knaves Green Suffolk 187 E7
Knavesmire C/York 307 F8
Knayton N Yorks 319 C7
Knebworth Herts 137 C9
Knebworth House, Stevenage Herts 137 C8
Knedlington ER Yorks 295 E8
Kneesall Notts 248 B5
Kneesworth Cambs 161 C6
Kneeton Notts 248 E5
Knelston Swan 96 E4
Knenhall Staffs 221 A8
Knettishall Suffolk 186 B4
Knightacott Devon 55 D7
Knightcote Warwick 156 B2
Knightcott N Som'set 79 E7
Knightley Staffs 221 C6
Knightley Dale Staffs 221 D6
Knighton Dorset 40 D2
Knighton Devon 11 F6
Knighton Leics C 201 C6
Knighton Oxon 106 E2
Knighton Poole 27 A8
Knighton Som'set 58 C3
Knighton Staffs 220 C4
Knighton Staffs 243 F7
Knighton = Tref-y-Clawdd Powys 172 D3
Knighton Wilts 84 B2
Knighton Worcs 154 A3
Knighton Fields Leics C 201 C5
Knighton on Teme Worcs 174 D2
Knight's End Cambs 205 E7
Knights Enham Hants 64 B4
Knight's Green Glos 129 A8
Knightshayes Court Devon 36 C4
Knightsridge W Loth 395 E5
Knightswood Glasg C 392 E2
Knill Heref'd 172 F3
Knipoch Arg/Bute 416 E3
Knipton Leics 226 B3
Knitsley Durham 343 B6
Kniveton Derby 246 D2
Knocharthur H'land 440 C4
Knock Arg/Bute 415 D8
Knock Cumb 340 F4
Knock Moray 436 C2
Knockally H'land 445 F5
Knockan H'land 439 B6
Knockandhu Moray 435 F7
Knockando Moray 435 D6
Knockando Ho. Moray 435 D7
Knockandoo H'land 434 F2
Knockbain H'land 433 C8
Knockbreck H'land 430 B2
Knockbrex Dumf/Gal 401 E7
Knockcarrach H'land 440 F4
Knockdee H'land 445 B5
Knockdolian S Ayrs 400 A3
Knockdow Arg/Bute 390 D2
Knockdown Wilts 104 E1
Knockenbaird Aberds 436 F3
Knockenkelly N Ayrs 405 D6
Knockentiber E Ayrs 379 E7
Knockespock Ho. Aberds 436 F2
Knockfarrel H'land 433 C7
Knockglass Dumf/Gal 400 D2
Knockhall Kent 91 B6
Knockhall Castle Aberds 437 F6
Knockhill Motor Racing Circuit Fife 411 C5
Knockholt London 90 E4
Knockholt Pound London 90 E4
Knockie Lodge H'land 425 A6
Knockin Shrops 218 D3
Knockinlaw E Ayrs 379 E8
Knockinnon H'land 445 E5
Knocklearn Dumf/Gal 402 B1
Knocklearoch Arg/Bute 406 F3
Knockmill Kent 91 D6
Knocknaha Arg/Bute 404 E2
Knocknain Dumf/Gal 400 C1
Knockothie Aberds 437 E6
Knockrome Arg/Bute 407 E5
Knocksharry I/Man 336 C2
Knockstapplemore Arg/Bute 404 E2
Knockvologan Arg/Bute 415 F6
Knodishall Suffolk 189 F6
Knokan Arg/Bute 415 E7
Knole Som'set 39 A7
Knole House & Gardens Kent 91 F5
Knoll Green Som'set 58 D4
Knollbury Monmouths 101 E8
Knolls Green Ches 266 D3
Knolton Wrex 218 A4
Knolton Bryn Wrex 218 A4
Knook Wilts 62 C3
Knossington Rutl'd 202 B2
Knotbury Staffs 267 F7
Knotlow Derby 268 F2
Knott End-on-Sea Lancs 301 F6
Knott Lanes Gtr Man 279 D7
Knott Side N Yorks 305 B7
Knotting Beds 181 F8
Knotting Green Beds 181 F8
Knottingley W Yorks 294 F4
Knotts Cumb 327 B5
Knotty Ash Mersey 264 A3
Knotty Green Bucks 109 D8
Knowbury Shrops 174 D1
Knowe Dumf/Gal 400 B5
Knowe Shetl'd 457 G3
Knowefield Cumb 348 E2
Knowehead Aberds 436 C2
Knowehead Aberds 428 B2
Knowehead Dumf/Gal 356 D4
Knowes of Elrick Aberds 436 C3
Knowesgate Northum 364 E1
Knoweton N Lanarks 381 A7
Knowhead Aberds 437 C6
Knowl Green Essex 163 D8
Knowl Hill Flints 241 B6
Knowl Hill Windsor 87 A6
Knowl Wood W Yorks 291 F7
Knowle Bristol 80 B4
Knowle Devon 37 E5
Knowle Devon 22 D3
Knowle Devon 35 F8
Knowle Devon 54 D4
Knowle Shrops 174 D1
Knowle Som'set 57 C6
Knowle Som'set 59 D6
Knowle Wilts 83 D8
Knowle W Midlands 177 C6
Knowle Cross Devon 22 A2
Knowle Green Lancs 290 C1
Knowle Green Surrey 88 B2
Knowle Hill Surrey 88 C1
Knowle Park W Yorks 292 B3
Knowle St. Giles Som'set 38 D4
Knowle Top S Yorks 269 B6
Knowle Village Hants 45 E6
Knowles Hill Devon 15 A5
Knowlton Kent 95 F5
Knowsley Mersey 277 E5
Knowsley Industrial Estate Mersey 277 E5
Knowsley Safari Park Mersey 277 F6
Knowsthorpe W Yorks 293 D8
Knowstone Devon 36 B1
Knox N Yorks 306 D2
Knox Bridge Kent 72 C2
Knucklas Powys 172 D3
Knuston Northants 181 E6
Knutsford Ches 266 D2
Knutton Staffs 244 E2
Knuzden Brook Lancs 290 E3
Knypersley Staffs 244 C3
Kraiknish H'land 430 F3
Krumlin W Yorks 280 B2
Kuggar Cornw'l 5 G2
Kyle of Lochalsh H'land 431 F7
Kyleakin H'land 431 F7
Kylepark S Lanarks 393 F5
Kylerhea H'land 431 F7
Kylesknoydart H'land 423 C8
Kylesku H'land 442 E4
Kylesmorar H'land 423 C8
Kylestrome H'land 442 E4
Kyllachy House H'land 434 F2
Kymin Monmouths 128 E4
Kynaston Heref'd 128 B4
Kynaston Heref'd 152 E2
Kynaston Shrops 218 D4
Kynnersley Telford 220 E3
Kyre Green Worcs 174 F2
Kyrewood Worcs 174 E2
Kyrle Som'set 37 B6


## L


Labost W Isles 451 C5
Lacasaidh W Isles 451 E6
Lacasdal W Isles 451 D7
Laceby NE Lincs 286 C3
Lacey Green Bucks 109 B6
Lacey Green Ches 266 C3
Lach Dennis Ches 265 E9
Lache Ches 241 B8
Lackenby Redcar/Clevel'd 333 C6
Lackford Suffolk 185 D8
Lacock Wilts 82 C3
Ladbroke Warwick 156 A3
Laddingford Kent 71 B8
Lade Bank Lincs 252 D3
Ladock Cornw'l 7 E8
Ladwood Kent 74 C4
Lady Orkney 454 B4
Lady Balk W Yorks 294 F3
Lady Green Mersey 276 D3
Lady Hall Cumb 312 C4
Lady House Gtr Man 279 B7
Ladybank Fife 411 A8
Ladybrook Notts 247 B8
Ladyburn Inverci 391 C6
Ladycross Cornw'l 18 C3
Ladykirk Scot Borders 387 C7
Ladyridge Heref'd 129 A5
Lady's Green Suffolk 163 A8
Ladysford Aberds 437 B6
Ladywell London 90 B2
Ladywell W Loth 395 E5
Ladywood W Midlands 176 A4
Ladywood Worcs 175 F7
Laga H'land 416 A1
Lagafater Lodge Dumf/Gal 400 B3
Lagalochan Arg/Bute 408 A1
Lagavulin Arg/Bute 403 B4
Lagg Arg/Bute 407 E5
Lagg N Ayrs 405 D5
Laggan Arg/Bute 403 A2
Laggan H'land 423 E7
Laggan H'land 425 C4
Laggan H'land 425 C8
Laggan Lodge Arg/Bute 416 E1
Lagganlia H'land 426 B3
Lagganmullan Dumf/Gal 401 D7
Lagganulva Arg/Bute 415 C7
Lagness W Sussex 47 F5
Laide H'land 438 D2
Laig H'land 422 D4
Laigh Fenwick E Ayrs 380 D1
Laigh-Glengall S Ayrs 367 D6
Laighmuir E Ayrs 380 C1
Laighstonehall S Lanarks 381 B6
Laindon Essex 113 E8
Lair H'land 432 D2
Lair Perth/Kinr 420 A1
Laira Plym'th 11 D6
Lairg H'land 440 C2
Lairg Lodge H'land 440 C2
Lairg Muir H'land 440 C2
Lairgmore H'land 433 E7
Laisterdyke W Yorks 293 D5
Laithes Cumb 339 E8
Laithkirk Durham 329 B9
Laity Moor Cornw'l 4 C3
Lake Devon 55 E6
Lake I/Wight 30 D3
Lake Poole 27 B6
Lake Wilts 63 D7
Lake End Windsor 87 A8
Lakenham Norfolk 209 B8
Lakenheath Suffolk 185 B7
Lakesend Norfolk 206 D1
Lakeside Cumb 313 C8
Lakeside Worcs 176 E4
Lakeside and Haverthwaite Railway Cumb 313 C7
Laleham Surrey 88 C3
Laleston Bridg 76 A4
Lamarsh Essex 164 E2
Lamas Norfolk 234 D1
Lamb Corner Essex 142 A1
Lamb Roe Lancs 290 C3
Lambden Scot Borders 386 D4
Lamberhead Green Gtr Man 277 D7
Lamberhurst Kent 71 D8
Lamberhurst Quarter Kent 71 D8
Lamberton Scot Borders 388 A1
Lambert's End W Midlands 197 E8
Lambeth London 89 A8
Lambfair Green Suffolk 163 B7
Lambfoot Cumb 338 E2
Lambhill Glasg C 392 E3
Lambley Notts 248 F3
Lambley Northum 349 E7
Lambourn W Berks 84 A3
Lambourn Woodlands W Berks 84 A3
Lambourne Cornw'l 7 E6
Lambourne End Essex 112 D4
Lambridge Bath/NE Som'set 81 C7
Lamb's Green Dorset 27 A6
Lambs Green W Sussex 69 D6
Lambston Pembs 116 A4
Lambton Tyne/Wear 352 F4
Lamellion Cornw'l 9 C7
Lamerton Devon 19 E6
Lamesley Tyne/Wear 352 E4
Laminess Orkney 454 C4
Lamington H'land 440 F4
Lamington S Lanarks 382 F4
Lamlash N Ayrs 405 C6
Lamledra Cornw'l 5 B8
Lamloch Dumf/Gal 356 C2
Lamonby Cumb 339 D7
Lamorick Cornw'l 8 C3
Lamorna Cornw'l 2 F4
Lamorran Cornw'l 5 B5
Lampardbrook Suffolk 188 F3
Lampen Cornw'l 9 B6
Lampeter = Llanbedr Pont Steffan Ceredig'n 146 C4
Lampeter Velfrey Pembs 121 E7
Lamphey Pembs 117 D6
Lamplugh Cumb 325 B6
Lamport Northants 180 D3
Lampton London 88 A4
Lamyatt Som'set 61 D5
Lana Devon 18 A3
Lana Devon 33 E6
Lanark S Lanarks 382 D2
Lancaster Lancs 301 C8
Lancaster Leisure Park Lancs 301 C8
Lanchester Durham 343 B7
Lancing W Sussex 48 E3
Land Gate Gtr Man 277 D8
Land Side Gtr Man 278 E2
Landbeach Cambs 184 E2
Landcross Devon 34 B2
Landerberry Aberds 428 B4
Landford Wilts 43 C8
Landford Common Wilts 43 C8
Landfordwood Wilts 43 B8
Landican Mersey 263 B7
Landimore Swan 96 D4
Landkey Devon 55 E6
Landkey Newland Devon 55 E6
Landore Swan 97 C8
Landport E Sussex 49 D8
Landport Portsm'th 45 F7
Landrake Cornw'l 10 C3
Land's End Cornw'l 2 E2
Land's End Airport Cornw'l 2 E3
Landscove Devon 14 B3
Landshipping Pembs 117 B6
Landulph Cornw'l 10 C4
Landwade Cambs 185 E5
Landywood Staffs 197 B8
Lane Cornw'l 7 C7
Lane Bottom Lancs 291 C6
Lane End Bucks 109 D6
Lane End Cumb 312 B3
Lane End Derby 247 B6
Lane End Dorset 26 B4
Lane End Flints 241 B6
Lane End Gtr Man 266 A4
Lane End Gtr Man 279 C6
Lane End Hants 45 A6
Lane End Heref'd 129 D6
Lane End I/Wight 31 C5
Lane End Kent 91 B6
Lane End Lancs 304 F1
Lane End N Yorks 319 A7
Lane End Surrey 67 C6
Lane End Wilts 61 B8
Lane End W Yorks 292 C2
Lane Ends Ches 267 C6
Lane Ends Derby 223 B6
Lane Ends Derby 247 D5
Lane Ends Gtr Man 267 A6
Lane Ends Lancs 290 D1
Lane Ends Lancs 290 D4
Lane Ends Lancs 303 E6
Lane Ends Lancs 278 A1
Lane Ends N Yorks 291 B8
Lane Ends W Yorks 293 C6
Lane Green Staffs 197 C6
Lane Head Derby 268 D3
Lane Head Durham 330 A3
Lane Head Durham 330 D4
Lane Head Gtr Man 278 E1
Lane Head W Midlands 197 C8
Lane Head W Yorks 281 B5
Lane Head W Yorks 281 C5
Lane Heads Lancs 289 C5
Lane Side Lancs 290 F4
Lane Side Lancs 290 F4
Laneast Cornw'l 18 D1
Lane-end Cornw'l 8 B3
Laneham Notts 271 D8
Lanehead Durham 341 C7
Lanehead Northum 362 E4
Lanercost Cumb 349 D5
Lanescot Cornw'l 8 D4
Lanesend Pembs 117 C7
Lanesfield W Midlands 197 D7
Laneshaw Bridge Lancs 291 B7
Laney Green Staffs 197 B8
Langaford Devon 19 A5
Langal H'land 423 F7
Langaller Som'set 58 F5
Langar Notts 226 B1
Langbank Renf 391 D7
Langbar N Yorks 305 E5
Langbaurgh N Yorks 333 D6
Langbridge I/Wight 30 C3
Langburnshiels Scot Borders 361 B7
Langcliffe N Yorks 303 C8
Langdale H'land 443 D8
Langdon Cornw'l 18 C3
Langdon Beck Durham 341 E8
Langdon Hills Essex 113 E8
Langdown Hants 44 E3
Langdyke Fife 411 B8
Langeitho Ceredig'n 146 A5
Langenhoe Essex 142 D1
Langford Beds 160 D3
Langford Devon 37 F5
Langford Essex 141 F5
Langford Notts 249 C7
Langford Oxon 106 B1
Langford Som'set 58 F4
Langford Budville Som'set 37 B7
Langford Green N Som'set 80 E1
Langham Dorset 41 A5
Langham Essex 142 A1
Langham Norfolk 256 D3
Langham Rutl'd 202 A2
Langham Suffolk 186 E3
Langhaugh Scot Borders 371 A9
Langho Lancs 290 D3
Langholm Dumf/Gal 360 F4
Langley Ches 267 E5
Langley Derby 247 E6
Langley Essex 162 E1
Langley Glos 131 B6
Langley Gtr Man 279 C6
Langley Hants 44 F3
Langley Herts 137 C8
Langley Kent 72 A2
Langley Northum 350 D3
Langley Slough 88 A2
Langley Som'set 57 F8
Langley Warwick 177 F6
Langley W Midlands 197 F8
Langley Burrell Wilts 82 A3
Langley Common Derby 223 A7
Langley Common Wokingham 86 C5
Langley Corner Bucks 110 E2
Langley Green Derby 223 A7
Langley Green Essex 141 C6
Langley Green Norfolk 210 C3
Langley Green W Sussex 69 D7
Langley Heath Kent 72 A3
Langley Marsh Som'set 57 F8
Langley Mill Derby 247 E6
Langley Moor Durham 343 C8
Langley Park Durham 343 C9
Langley Street Norfolk 210 C3
Langley Vale Surrey 89 E6
Langleyfield Telford 196 B2
Langloan N Lanarks 393 F6
Langmere Norfolk 188 B1
Langney E Sussex 51 F5
Langold Notts 270 B3
Langore Cornw'l 18 C2
Langport Som'set 59 F8
Langrick Lincs 251 E8
Langridge Bath/NE Som'set 81 C6
Langridgeford Devon 34 B4
Langrigg Cumb 328 D5
Langrigg Cumb 338 B2
Langrish Hants 46 B2
Langsett S Yorks 281 D6
Langshaw Scot Borders 385 E7
Langside Glasg C 392 F3
Langside Perth/Kinr 419 F5
Langskaill Orkney 454 B2
Langstone Hants 46 E2
Langstone Newp 101 E7
Langthorne N Yorks 318 B4
Langthorpe N Yorks 306 B4
Langthwaite N Yorks 330 F2
Langtoft ER Yorks 310 B2
Langtoft Lincs 203 A8
Langton Durham 331 C5
Langton Lincs 274 F1
Langton Lincs 274 E4
Langton N Yorks 308 B4
Langton by Wragby Lincs 273 D7
Langton Green Kent 71 D5
Langton Green Suffolk 187 D7
Langton Herring Dorset 25 D7
Langton Long Blandford Dorset 41 E7
Langton Matravers Dorset 27 E6
Langtree Devon 34 C2
Langtree Week Devon 34 C2
Langwathby Cumb 340 E2
Langwell Ho. H'land 441 A8
Langwell Lodge H'land 439 C5
Langwith Derby 270 F2
Langwith Junction Derby 270 F2
Langworth Lincs 273 D6
Lanham Green Essex 140 C4
Lanhydrock House, Bodmin Cornw'l 8 C4
Lanivet Cornw'l 8 C3
Lanjeth Cornw'l 8 E2
Lank Cornw'l 17 E6
Lanlivery Cornw'l 8 D4
Lanmack Blackb'n 290 E2
Lanner Cornw'l 4 C2
Lanoy Cornw'l 18 E2
Lanreath Cornw'l 9 D6
Lanrick Stirl 410 B1
Lansallos Cornw'l 9 E6
Lansbury Park Caerph 100 E3
Lansdown Bath/NE Som'set 81 C6
Lansdown Glos 130 C4
Lansdown Glos 132 C2
Lanstephan Cornw'l 18 C3
Lanteglos Cornw'l 17 D6
Lanton Scot Borders 374 C2
Lanton Northum 375 A8
Lanvean Cornw'l 7 B8
Lapal W Midlands 176 B2
Lapford Devon 35 E7
Laphroaig Arg/Bute 403 B3
Lapley Staffs 197 A6
Lapworth Warwick 177 D6
Larachbeg H'land 416 C1
Larbert Falk 410 D3
Larbreck Lancs 288 B5
Larches Lancs 289 D7
Larden Green Ches 242 D4
Larg H'land 427 A5
Largie Aberds 436 E3
Largiebaan Arg/Bute 404 E2
Largiemore Arg/Bute 408 D2
Largoward Fife 412 B2
Largs N Ayrs 378 A4
Largue Aberds 436 D3
Largybeg N Ayrs 405 D6
Largymeanoch N Ayrs 405 D6
Largymore N Ayrs 405 D6
Larkbeare Devon 22 A3
Larkfield Inverci 390 C4
Larkfield Kent 91 E9
Larkhall Bath/NE Som'set 81 C7
Larkhall S Lanarks 381 B7
Larkhill Wilts 63 C7
Larkhill Worcs 175 C6
Larklands Derby 247 F7
Larling Norfolk 208 F3
Larport Heref'd 152 E1
Larrick Cornw'l 18 E3
Larriston Scot Borders 361 D7
Lartington Durham 330 C2
Lary Aberds 427 B8
Lasborough Glos 103 D8
Lasham Hants 66 C3
Lashenden Kent 72 C4
Laskill N Yorks 320 B2
Lassington Glos 130 C1
Lasswade Midloth 396 E3
Lastingham N Yorks 321 B5
Latcham Som'set 59 B8
Latchford Herts 138 C3
Latchford Oxon 108 B3
Latchford Warrington 265 B7
Latchingdon Essex 114 B4
Latchley Cornw'l 19 F5
Latchmore Bank Essex 139 D5
Latchmore Green Hants 86 E2
Lately Common Warrington 278 E2
Lathallan Mill Fife 412 B2
Lathbury Durham 330 C2
Lathbury M/Keynes 158 C5
Latheron H'land 445 E5
Latheronwheel H'land 445 E5
Latheronwheel Ho. H'land 445 E5
Lathones Fife 412 B2
Latimer Bucks 110 C1
Latteridge S Glos 103 F5
Lattersey Hill Cambs 204 D4
Lattiford Som'set 40 A3
Latton Wilts 105 C6
Latton Bush Essex 139 F5
Lauchintilly Aberds 428 A4
Laudale Ho H'land 416 B2
Lauder Scot Borders 385 C7
Laugharne = Talacharn Carms 122 E2
Laughterton Lincs 272 D1
Laughton E Sussex 50 D2
Laughton Leics 201 F7
Laughton Lincs 227 B8
Laughton Lincs 284 E3
Laughton Common E Sussex 50 D2
Laughton Common S Yorks 270 B3
Laughton en le Morthen S Yorks 270 B3
Launcells Cornw'l 32 E4
Launceston Cornw'l 18 D3
Launcherley Som'set 60 C3
Laund Lancs 291 F5
Laund Lancs 291 C6
Launton Oxon 134 C3
Laurel Street Som'set 60 D2
Laurencekirk Aberds 428 E4
Laurieston Dumf/Gal 401 C8
Laurieston Falk 394 C3
Lavendon M/Keynes 159 B6
Lavenham Suffolk 164 C3
Laverackloch Moray 435 B6
Laverhay Dumf/Gal 359 C6
Laversdale Cumb 348 D3
Laverstock Wilts 63 E8
Laverstoke Hants 65 B6
Laverton Glos 154 E4
Laverton N Yorks 318 F3
Laverton Som'set 61 A7
Lavister Wrex 241 C8
Law S Lanarks 381 B8
Law Hill S Lanarks 381 B8
Lawers Perth/Kinr 418 D4
Lawers Perth/Kinr 419 E5
Lawford Essex 142 A2
Lawford Som'set 58 D2
Lawhill Perth/Kinr 419 F7
Lawhitton Cornw'l 18 D4
Lawkland N Yorks 303 B7
Lawkland Green N Yorks 303 B7
Lawley Telford 196 B2
Lawn Swindon 105 F8
Lawnhead Staffs 221 C6
Lawnswood W Yorks 293 C7
Lawrence Weston Bristol 80 A2
Lawrenny Pembs 117 C6
Lawshall Suffolk 164 B2
Lawshall Green Suffolk 164 B2
Lawson Street Kent 93 D6
Lawton Heath End Ches 244 C1
Lawtongate Ches 244 C2
Laxey I/Man 336 C4
Laxey Wheel and Mines I/Man 336 C4
Laxfield Suffolk 188 D3
Laxfirth Shetl'd 457 H4
Laxfirth Shetl'd 457 J4
Laxford Bridge H'land 442 D4
Laxo Shetl'd 457 G4
Laxobigging Shetl'd 457 F4
Laxton ER Yorks 296 E2
Laxton Northants 203 D5
Laxton Notts 271 B8
Laycock W Yorks 292 B2
Layer Breton Essex 141 D7
Layer Breton Heath Essex 141 D7
Layer de la Haye Essex 141 D8
Layer Marney Essex 141 D7
Layerthorpe C/York 308 E1
Layham Suffolk 165 D5
Laymore Dorset 39 F5
Layter's Green Bucks 110 D1
Laytham ER Yorks 296 C1
Layton Blackp'l 288 C3
Lazenby Redcar/Clevel'd 333 C6
Lazonby Cumb 340 D2
Lea Derby 246 C4
Lea Devon 23 A6
Lea Heref'd 129 C7
Lea Lancs 289 D6
Lea Lincs 271 B8
Lea Shrops 194 F3
Lea Shrops 194 B4
Lea Warwick 199 E5
Lea Wilts 104 E4
Lea Bridge London 112 E2
Lea Brook S Yorks 282 E2
Lea End Worcs 176 C3
Lea Green Mersey 264 A5
Lea Hall Derby 246 C4
Lea Hall W Midlands 198 F3
Lea Heath Staffs 222 C2
Lea Marston Warwick 198 E4
Lea Town Lancs 289 D6
Lea Yeat Cumb 315 C9
Leabrooks Derby 247 D6
Leac a Li W Isles 449 C5
Leacainn W Isles 449 B5
Leachkin H'land 433 D8
Leacnasaide H'land 431 A7
Leadburn Midloth 384 A1
Leaden Roding Essex 139 E7
Leadenham Lincs 250 D1
Leaderfoot Scot Borders 385 F8
Leadgate Cumb 341 C5
Leadgate Durham 343 A6
Leadgate Northum 351 E9
Leadhills S Lanarks 370 D2
Leadingcross Green Kent 72 A4
Leadmill Flints 240 B5
Leadmill S Yorks 268 C4
Leafield Oxon 132 D5
Leafield Wilts 82 C2
Leagrave Luton 136 C4
Leake N Yorks 319 B7
Leake Commonside Lincs 252 D3
Leake Fold Hill Lincs 252 D4
Leake Gride Lincs 252 D3
Leake Hurn's End Lincs 252 E4
Lealholm N Yorks 334 E2
Lealholm Side N Yorks 334 E2
Lealt Arg/Bute 407 C6
Lealt H'land 430 B5
Leam Derby 268 D4
Leam Lane Tyne/Wear 352 D4
Leamington Hastings Warwick 178 E3
Leamonsley Staffs 198 B3
Leamoor Common Shrops 194 F4
Leamore W Midlands 197 C8
Leamside Durham 344 C2
Leanach Arg/Bute 408 C3
Leanachan H'land 424 E4
Leanaig H'land 433 C7
Leargybreck Arg/Bute 407 E5
Lease Rigg N Yorks 334 F3
Leasgill Cumb 314 D3
Leasingham Lincs 250 E4
Leasingthorne Durham 343 F9
Leasowe Mersey 263 A7
Leatherhead Surrey 89 E5
Leatherhead Common Surrey 89 E5
Leathern Bottle Glos 103 B6
Leathley N Yorks 305 F8
Leaths Dumf/Gal 402 C1
Leaton Shrops 219 E6
Leaton Telford 195 A8
Leaveland Kent 93 F7
Leavenheath Suffolk 164 E4
Leavening N Yorks 308 C4
Leaves Green London 90 D3
Leavesden Green Herts 110 B3
Leazes Durham 352 E2
Leazes Northum 350 D5
Lebberston N Yorks 323 D5
Lechlade-on-Thames Glos 106 C1
Leck Lancs 315 E6
Leckford Hants 64 D4
Leckfurin H'land 444 C1
Leckgruinart Arg/Bute 406 F2
Leckhampstead Bucks 158 E2
Leckhampstead W Berks 85 A5
Leckhampstead Street W Berks 85 A5
Leckhampstead Thicket W Berks 85 A5
Leckhampton Glos 130 D4
Leckie H'land 432 B2
Leckmelm H'land 439 D5
Leckuary Arg/Bute 408 C1
Leckwith V/Glam 78 B3
Leconfield ER Yorks 297 B7
Ledaig Arg/Bute 416 D4
Ledburn Bucks 136 C2
Ledbury Heref'd 152 E4
Ledcharrie Stirl 418 E3
Ledgemoor Heref'd 151 B6
Ledgowan H'land 432 C3
Ledicot Heref'd 173 F6
Ledmore Angus 421 A5
Ledmore H'land 439 B6
Lednagullin H'land 444 B1
Ledsham Ches 264 E2
Ledsham W Yorks 294 E3
Ledston W Yorks 294 E2
Ledstone Devon 13 C5
Ledwell Oxon 133 B7
Lee Arg/Bute 415 E7
Lee Devon 54 B4
Lee Devon 55 B6
Lee Devon 56 F3
Lee Hants 44 C2
Lee Lancs 302 D3
Lee London 90 B2
Lee Northum 351 E5
Lee Shrops 219 B5
Lee Brockhurst Shrops 219 C7
Lee Chapel Essex 113 E8
Lee Clump Bucks 109 B8
Lee Green Medway 92 B1
Lee Ground Hants 45 E5
Lee Head Derby 267 A7
Lee Mill Devon 11 D7
Lee Moor Devon 11 C7
Leeans Shetl'd 457 J3
Leebotten Shetl'd 455 D3
Leebotwood Shrops 195 D5
Leece Cumb 300 B3
Leech Pool Pembs 117 A5
Leechpool Monmouths 102 E2
Leedon Beds 136 B2
Leeds Kent 72 A3
Leeds W Yorks 293 C8
Leeds Bradford International Airport W Yorks 293 B6
Leeds Castle Kent 92 F3
Leeds City Art Gallery W Yorks 293 D8
Leedstown Cornw'l 3 D8
Leeford Devon 56 B2
Leegomery Telford 196 A2
Leeholme Durham 343 E8
Leek Staffs 245 C5
Leek Wootton Warwick 177 E8
Leekbrook Staffs 245 D5
Leeming N Yorks 318 C4
Leeming W Yorks 292 D2
Leeming Bar N Yorks 318 B4
Lee-on-the-Solent Hants 45 F6
Lee-over-Sands Essex 142 E3
Lees Derby 223 A7
Lees Gtr Man 279 D8
Lees W Yorks 292 C2
Lees Hill Cumb 349 C5
Leesthorpe Leics 226 F2

Little Turnberry S Ayrs 366 F4
Little Twycross Leics 199 B7
Little Urswick Cumb 313 F6
Little Wakering Essex 115 E5
Little Walden Essex 162 D3
Little Waldingfield Suffolk 164 C3
Little Walsingham Norfolk 255 E8
Little Waltham Essex 140 E3
Little Warley Essex 113 D7
Little Washbourne Glos 131 A5
Little Watersend Kent 74 C5
Little Weighton ER Yorks 297 D5
Little Welland Worcs 153 E6
Little Welnetham Suffolk 186 F2
Little Welton Lincs 274 B3
Little Wenham Suffolk 165 E6
Little Wenlock Telford 196 B1
Little Weston Som'set 40 A2
Little Whittingham Green Suffolk 188 C3
Little Wilbraham Cambs 162 A3
Little Wishford Wilts 63 D6
Little Witcombe Glos 130 D4
Little Witley Worcs 175 F5
Little Wittenham Oxon 107 D8
Little Wolford Warwick 155 E8
Little Woodcote London 89 D7
Little Woolgarston Dorset 27 D6
Little Wratting Suffolk 163 C6
Little Wymington Beds 181 E7
Little Wymondley Herts 137 B8
Little Wyrley Staffs 197 B9
Little Yeldham Essex 163 E8
Little-ayre Shetl'd 457 G3
Littleborough Devon 36 D1
Littleborough Gtr Man 279 A7
Littleborough Notts 271 C8
Littlebourne Kent 94 E3
Littlebredy Dorset 25 C6
Littlebury Essex 162 E3
Littlebury Green Essex 162 E2
Littlecott Wilts 83 A5
Littlecott Wilts 63 A7
Littledean Glos 129 E7
Littledown Bournem'th 28 B2
Littleferry H'land 440 D5
Littlefield NE Lincs 286 C4
Littlefield Green Windsor 87 A7
Littleham Devon 22 D2
Littleham Devon 33 B8
Littlehampton W Sussex 47 F8
Littlehempston Devon 14 C4
Littlehoughton Northum 377 D6
Littlemill Aberds 427 C8
Littlemill E Ayrs 367 D9
Littlemill H'land 434 C4
Littlemoor Derby 247 B5
Littlemoor Dorset 25 D8
Littlemore Oxon 107 B7
Littleover Derby C 223 B8
Littleport Cambs 206 F2
Littleport Norfolk 254 E4
Littler Ches 243 A5
Littlestead Green Oxon 86 A4
Littlestone-on-Sea Kent 53 B6
Littlethorpe Leics 200 D4
Littlethorpe N Yorks 306 B3
Littleton Bath/NE Som'set 80 D3
Littleton Ches 242 A1
Littleton Dorset 41 F7
Littleton Hants 65 E6
Littleton Perth/Kinr 420 D2
Littleton Som'set 60 E1
Littleton Surrey 67 B9
Littleton Surrey 88 C3
Littleton Wilts 82 D3
Littleton Drew Wilts 103 F8
Littleton on Severn S Glos 102 E3
Littleton Pannell Wilts 82 F4
Littletown Durham 344 C2
Littletown Devon 37 F8
Littletown I/Wight 30 B2
Littletown W Yorks 293 F6
Littlewick Green Windsor 87 A6
Littlewindsor Dorset 39 F6
Littlewood Staffs 197 B8
Littlewood Green Warwick 176 F4
Littleworth Beds 160 D1
Littleworth Glos 104 B2
Littleworth Glos 155 E5
Littleworth Oxon 106 C3
Littleworth Oxon 108 A1
Littleworth Oxon 108 D2
Littleworth Staffs 221 D8
Littleworth Staffs 198 A1
Littleworth S Yorks 283 E6
Littleworth Worcs 153 B7
Littleworth Worcs 176 F2
Littleworth W Sussex 48 B3
Littleworth Cross Surrey 67 B7
Littley Green Essex 140 D2
Litton Derby 268 D3
Litton N Yorks 316 F4
Litton Som'set 80 F3
Litton Cheney Dorset 25 B6
Liurbost W Isles 451 E6
Livermead Torbay 15 C6
Liverpool Mersey 264 A1
Liverpool Airport Mersey 264 C3
Liverpool Cathedral (C of E) Mersey 264 B2
Liverpool Cathedral (RC) Mersey 264 A2
Liverpool John Lennon Airport Mersey 264 C3
Liversedge W Yorks 293 F5
Liverton Devon 21 E6
Liverton Redcar/Clevel'd 334 C1
Liverton Mines Redcar/Clevel'd 334 C1
Liverton Street Kent 72 A4
Livesey Street Kent 91 F9
Livingston W Loth 395 E5
Livingston Village W Loth 395 E5
Lix Toll Stirl 418 D3
Lixwm Flints 263 E5
Lizard Cornw'l 5 H2
Llaingarreglwyd Ceredig'n 145 A8
Llaingoch Angl 258 C1
Llaithddu Powys 171 B6
Llampha V/Glam 77 A5
Llan Powys 191 C8
Llan Rh Cyn Taff 99 E7
Llan Ffestiniog Gwyn 238 F2
Llanaber Gwyn 214 E4
Llanaelhaearn Gwyn 236 F3
Llanaeron Ceredig'n 168 F2
Llanafan Ceredig'n 169 D6
Llanafan-fawr Powys 148 A4
Llanallgo Angl 259 B7
Llanandras = Presteigne Powys 172 F4
Llananno Powys 171 D6
Llanarmon Gwyn 213 A8
Llanarmon Dyffryn Ceiriog Wrex 217 B8
Llanarmon Mynydd-Mawr Powys 217 C7
Llanarmon-yn-Ial Denbs 240 C4
Llanarth Ceredig'n 145 A8
Llanarth Monmouths 127 E8
Llanarthne Carms 123 C6
Llanasa Flints 262 C4
Llanbabo Angl 258 B4
Llanbad Bridg 99 F6
Llanbadarn Fawr Ceredig'n 168 B5
Llanbadarn Fynydd Powys 171 C6
Llanbadarn-y-garreg Powys 149 C7
Llanbadoc Monmouths 101 B7
Llanbadrig Angl 258 A4
Llanbeder Newp 101 D7
Llanbedr Gwyn 214 C3
Llanbedr Powys 149 C7
Llanbedr Powys 127 C5
Llanbedr Pont Steffan = Lampeter Ceredig'n 146 C4
Llanbedr-Dyffryn-Clwyd Denbs 240 C3
Llanbedrgoch Angl 259 C7
Llanbedrog Gwyn 213 B6
Llanbedr-y-cennin Conwy 260 F5
Llanberis Gwyn 237 B7
Llanbethery V/Glam 77 C7
Llanbister Powys 171 D7
Llanblethian V/Glam 77 B6
Llanboidy Carms 121 C8
Llanbradach Caerph 100 D2
Llanbrynmair Powys 192 C1
Llancadle V/Glam 77 C7
Llancaiach Merth Tyd 100 C2
Llancarfan V/Glam 77 B8
Llancayo Monmouths 101 B7
Llancloudy Heref'd 128 C3
Llancoch Powys 172 D2
Llancynfelyn Ceredig'n 190 E3
Llan-dafal Bl Gwent 100 B3
Llandaff Card 78 A3
Llandaff North Card 78 A3
Llandanwg Gwyn 214 C3
Llandarcy Rh Cyn Taff 98 C1
Llandawke Carms 122 E1
Llanddaniel Fab Angl 259 E6
Llanddarog Carms 123 D6
Llanddeiniol Ceredig'n 168 D4
Llanddeiniolen Gwyn 237 A6
Llandderfel Gwyn 216 A4
Llanddeusant Carms 124 C4
Llanddeusant Angl 258 B3
Llanddew Powys 126 A2
Llanddewi Swan 96 E4
Llanddewi Brefi Ceredig'n 147 A6
Llanddewi Rhydderch Monmouths 127 E7
Llanddewi Velfrey Pembs 121 D6
Llanddewi Ystradenni Powys 171 E7
Llanddewi'r-Cwm Powys 149 C5
Llanddoged Conwy 238 B4
Llanddona Angl 259 D8
Llanddowror Carms 121 E9
Llanddulas Conwy 262 D8
Llanddwywe Gwyn 214 D3
Llanddygfael Hir Angl 258 A4
Llandecwyn Gwyn 214 A4
Llandefaelog Powys 126 A1
Llandefaelogtre'r-graig Powys 126 B3
Llandefalle Powys 149 E7
Llandegfan Angl 259 E8
Llandegla Denbs 240 D4
Llandegley Powys 171 F7
Llandegveth Monmouths 101 C6
Llandegwning Gwyn 212 C5
Llandeilo'r-Fan Powys 148 F2
Llandeilo Carms 123 C8
Llandeilo Graban Powys 149 D6
Llandeloy Pembs 118 D5
Llandenny Monmouths 101 B8
Llandevaud Newp 101 D8
Llandevenny Monmouths 101 E8
Llandilo Carms 121 B6
Llandinabo Heref'd 128 B4
Llandinam Powys 192 F4
Llandissilio Pembs 121 C6
Llandogo Cleddon Monmouths 102 B2
Llandough V/Glam 77 B6
Llandough V/Glam 78 B3
Llandovery = Llanymddyfri Carms 147 F8
Llandow V/Glam 77 B5
Llandre Carms 147 D6
Llandre Ceredig'n 190 F3
Llandrillo Denbs 217 A5
Llandrillo-yn-Rhôs Conwy 262 C6
Llandrindod = Llandrindod Wells Powys 171 F6
Llandrindod Wells = Llandrindod Powys 171 F6
Llandrinio Powys 218 E2
Llandudno Conwy 260 C5
Llandudno Junction = Cyffordd Llandudno Conwy 262 D6
Llandudoch = St. Dogmaels Pembs 144 C3
Llandwrog Gwyn 236 C5
Llandybie = Llandybïe Carms 123 D8
Llandybïe = Llandybie Carms 123 D8
Llandyfaelog Carms 122 E4
Llandyfan Carms 124 D1
Llandyfriog Ceredig'n 145 D6
Llandyfrydog Angl 259 B5
Llandygai Gwyn 260 E1
Llandygwydd Ceredig'n 144 D4
Llandynan Denbs 240 F4
Llandyrnog Denbs 240 A3
Llandyry Carms 96 A3
Llandysilio Powys 218 E2
Llandyssil Powys 193 D7
Llandysul Ceredig'n 145 D8
Llanedeyrn Card 100 F4
Llanedi Carms 123 F7
Llaneglwys Powys 149 E6
Llanegryn Gwyn 190 B2
Llanegwad Carms 123 C6
Llaneilian Angl 259 A6
Llanelian-yn-Rhos Conwy 262 D7
Llanelidan Denbs 240 D3
Llanelieu Powys 149 F8
Llanellen Monmouths 127 E7
Llanelli Carms 96 B5
Llanelltyd Gwyn 215 E6
Llanelly Monmouths 127 E5
Llanelly Hill Monmouths 127 E5
Llanelwedd Powys 149 B6
Llanelwy = St. Asaph Denbs 262 E2
Llanenddwyn Gwyn 214 D3
Llanengan Gwyn 213 C5
Llanerch Emrys Powys 218 D1
Llanerchymedd Angl 259 C5
Llanerch-y-môr Flints 263 D5
Llanerfyl Powys 192 B4
Llaneuddog Angl 259 B6
Llan-eurgain = Northop Flints 263 F6
Llanfach Caerph 100 C4
Llanfachraeth Angl 258 C3
Llanfachreth Gwyn 215 D7
Llanfaelog Angl 258 E3
Llanfaelrhys Gwyn 212 C4
Llanfaenor Monmouths 128 D2
Llanfaes Angl 260 D2
Llanfaes Powys 126 B1
Llanfaethlu Angl 258 B3
Llanfaglan Gwyn 236 B5
Llanfair Gwyn 214 C3
Llanfair Caereinion Powys 193 B6
Llanfair Clydogau Ceredig'n 146 B5
Llanfair Dyffryn Clwyd Denbs 240 C3
Llanfair Kilgeddin Monmouths 127 F7
Llanfair Talhaiarn Conwy 262 E8
Llanfair Waterdine Shrops 172 C2
Llanfairfechan Conwy 260 D3
Llanfair-Nant-Gwyn Pembs 144 E3
Llanfairpwllgwyngyll Angl 259 E7
Llanfair-ym-Muallt = Builth Wells Powys 149 B5
Llanfairyneubwll Angl 258 D3
Llanfairynghornwy Angl 258 A3
Llanfallteg Carms 121 D7
Llanfaredd Powys 149 B6
Llanfarian Ceredig'n 168 C4
Llanfechain Powys 217 D8
Llanfechan Powys 148 B4
Llanfechell Angl 258 A4
Llanfendigaid Gwyn 190 C2
Llanferres Denbs 240 B4
Llanfflewyn Angl 258 B4
Llanfihangel Crucorney Monmouths 127 C7
Llanfihangel Glyn Myfyr Conwy 239 E7
Llanfihangel Nant Bran Powys 148 F3
Llanfihangel Rhydithon Powys 171 E8
Llanfihangel Tal-y-llyn Powys 126 B3
Llanfihangel yn Nhowyn Angl 258 D3
Llanfihangel-ar-arth Carms 146 E2
Llanfihangel-helygen Powys 171 F5
Llanfihangel-nant-Melan Powys 149 A8
Llanfihangel-y-Creuddyn Ceredig'n 169 C6
Llanfihangel-yng-Ngwnfa Powys 217 E6
Llanfihangel-y-pennant Gwyn 190 B4
Llanfihangel-y-pennant Gwyn 237 F6
Llanfilo Powys 126 A3
Llanfoist Monmouths 127 E6
Llanfor Gwyn 216 A3
Llanfrechfa Torf 101 D6
Llanfrothen Gwyn 237 F8
Llanfrynach Powys 126 B2
Llanfwrog Denbs 240 C3
Llanfwrog Angl 258 C3
Llanfyllin Powys 217 E7
Llanfynydd Carms 123 B7
Llanfynydd Flints 241 C6
Llanfyrnach Pembs 121 A8
Llangadfan Powys 192 A4
Llangadog Carms 122 F4
Llangadog Carms 124 B3
Llangadwaladr Angl 258 F4
Llangadwaladr Powys 217 B8
Llangaffo Angl 259 F5
Llangain Carms 122 D3
Llangammarch Wells Powys 148 C3
Llangan V/Glam 77 A6
Llangarron Heref'd 128 C4
Llangasty-Talyllyn Powys 126 B3
Llangathen Carms 123 C7
Llangattock Powys 127 D5
Llangattock Lingoed Monmouths 127 C8
Llangedwyn Powys 217 D8
Llangefni Angl 259 D6
Llangeinor Bridg 99 E5
Llangeler Carms 145 E7
Llangelynnin Gwyn 190 B2
Llangendeirne Carms 123 E5
Llangennech Carms 97 B6
Llangennith Carms 96 D3
Llangenny Powys 127 D5
Llangernyw Conwy 262 F7
Llangeview Monmouths 101 B8
Llangian Gwyn 213 C5
Llangiwg Neath P Talb 98 A1
Llangloffan Pembs 119 C6
Llanglydwen Carms 121 B7
Llangoed Angl 260 D2
Llangoedmor Ceredig'n 144 C4
Llangollen Denbs 240 F5
Llangolman Pembs 121 B6
Llangors Powys 126 B3
Llangorwen Ceredig'n 168 B5
Llangovan Monmouths 101 A9
Llangower Gwyn 216 B3
Llangrannog Ceredig'n 145 B6
Llangristiolus Angl 259 E5
Llangrove Heref'd 128 D4
Llangua Monmouths 128 B1
Llangunllo Powys 172 D2
Llangunnor Carms 122 C4
Llangurig Powys 170 B3
Llangwm Conwy 239 F7
Llangwm Monmouths 101 C8
Llangwm Pembs 117 C5
Llangwnnadl Gwyn 212 B4
Llangwyfan Denbs 240 A3
Llangwyllog Angl 259 D5
Llangwyryfon Ceredig'n 168 D5
Llangybi Ceredig'n 146 B5
Llangybi Gwyn 236 F4
Llangybi Monmouths 101 C7
Llangyfelach Swan 97 C7
Llangynhafal Denbs 240 B3
Llangynidr Powys 126 D4
Llangynin Carms 121 D9
Llangynllo Ceredig'n 145 D7
Llangynog Carms 122 D2
Llangynog Powys 217 C6
Llangynwyd Bridg 98 E4
Llanhamfach Powys 126 B2
Llanharan Rh Cyn Taff 99 F7
Llanharry Rh Cyn Taff 99 F7
Llanhennock Monmouths 101 D7
Llanhilleth Bl Gwent 100 B4
Llanidloes Powys 170 B4
Llaniestyn Gwyn 212 B5
Llanifihangel-uwch-Gwili Carms 123 C5
Llanifyny Powys 170 B2
Llanigon Powys 150 D2
Llanilar Ceredig'n 169 C5
Llanilid Rh Cyn Taff 99 F6
Llanion Pembs 117 D5
Llanishen Card 100 F3
Llanishen Monmouths 102 B1
Llanllawddog Carms 122 B5
Llanllechid Gwyn 260 F2
Llanllowell = Llanllywell Monmouths 101 C7
Llanllugan Powys 192 C5
Llanllwch Carms 122 D3
Llanllwchaiarn Powys 193 E6
Llanllwni Carms 146 E2
Llanllyfni Gwyn 236 D5
Llanllywell = Llanllowell Monmouths 101 C7
Llanmadoc Carms 96 D3
Llanmaes V/Glam 77 C6
Llanmartin Newp 101 E7
Llanmihangel V/Glam 77 B6
Llan-mill Pembs 121 E6
Llanmiloe Carms 121 F9
Llanmorlais Swan 97 D5
Llannant Swan 97 B6
Llannefydd Conwy 262 E1
Llannon Carms 123 F6
Llan-non = Llanon Ceredig'n 168 E3
Llannor Gwyn 213 A7
Llanon = Llan-non Ceredig'n 168 E3
Llanover Monmouths 127 F7
Llanpumpsaint Carms 122 B4
Llanreath Pembs 117 D5
Llanreithan Pembs 118 D5
Llanrhaeadr Denbs 240 B2
Llanrhaeadr-ym-Mochnant Powys 217 C7
Llanrhian Pembs 118 C4
Llanrhidian Swan 96 D4
Llanrhos Conwy 262 C5
Llanrhyddlad Angl 258 B3
Llanrhystud Ceredig'n 168 E3
Llanrosser Heref'd 150 E3
Llanrothal Heref'd 128 D3
Llanrug Gwyn 237 B6
Llanrumney Card 100 F4
Llanrwst Conwy 238 B4
Llansadurnen Carms 122 E1
Llansadwrn Carms 124 A2
Llansadwrn Angl 259 D8
Llansaint Carms 122 F3
Llansanffraid Glan Conwy Conwy 262 D6
Llansannan Conwy 239 A6
Llansannor V/Glam 77 A6
Llansantffraed Ceredig'n 168 E3
Llansantffraed Powys 126 C3
Llansantffraed-Cwmdeuddwr Powys 170 E4
Llansantffraed-in-Elwel Powys 149 B6
Llansantffraid-ym-Mechain Powys 218 D1
Llansawel = Briton Ferry Rh Cyn Taff 98 D1
Llansawel Carms 146 E5
Llansilin Powys 217 C9
Llansoy Monmouths 101 B8
Llanspyddid Powys 126 B1
Llanstadwell Pembs 117 C5
Llansteffan Carms 122 E3
Llanstephan Powys 149 D7
Llantarnam Torf 101 D6
Llanteg Pembs 121 E7
Llanteglos Pembs 121 F7
Llanthony Monmouths 127 B6
Llantilio Crossenny Monmouths 128 E1
Llantilio Pertholey Monmouths 127 D7
Llantood Pembs 144 D3
Llantrisant Angl 258 C4
Llantrisant Monmouths 101 C7
Llantrisant Rh Cyn Taff 99 F7
Llantrithyd V/Glam 77 B7
Llantwit Fardre Rh Cyn Taff 99 F8
Llantwit Major V/Glam 77 C6
Llanuwchllyn Gwyn 216 B2
Llanvaches Newp 101 D8
Llanvair Discoed Monmouths 101 D8
Llanvapley Monmouths 127 E8
Llanvetherine Monmouths 127 D8
Llanveynoe Heref'd 127 A7
Llanvihangel Gobion Monmouths 127 F7
Llanvihangel Pontymoel Torf 101 B6
Llanvihangel-Ystern-Llewern Monmouths 128 E2
Llanwarne Heref'd 128 B4
Llanwddyn Powys 216 E5
Llanwenarth Monmouths 127 E6
Llanwenog Ceredig'n 146 C2
Llanwern Newp 101 E7
Llanwinio Carms 122 B1
Llanwnda Gwyn 236 C5
Llanwnda Pembs 119 B6
Llanwnnen Ceredig'n 146 C3
Llanwnog Powys 192 E4
Llanwonno Rh Cyn Taff 99 C7
Llanwrda Carms 124 A3
Llanwrin Powys 191 C6
Llanwrthwl Powys 170 F4
Llanwrtud = Llanwrtyd Wells Powys 148 C2
Llanwrtyd Powys 148 C2
Llanwrtyd Wells = Llanwrtud Powys 148 C2
Llanwryglyn Powys 192 E2
Llanwyddelan Powys 193 C5
Llanyblodwel Shrops 218 D1
Llanybri Carms 122 E2
Llanybydder Carms 146 D3
Llanycefn Pembs 121 C5
Llanychaer Pembs 119 B7
Llanycil Gwyn 216 B3
Llanycrwys Carms 147 C5
Llanymawddwy Gwyn 216 E3
Llanymddyfri = Llandovery Carms 147 F8
Llanymynech Shrops 218 D2
Llanynghenedl Angl 258 C3
Llanynys Denbs 240 B3
Llan-y-pwll Wrex 241 D8
Llanyrafon Torf 101 C6
Llanyre Powys 171 F5
Llanystumdwy Gwyn 214 A1
Llanywern Powys 126 B3
Llawhaden Pembs 117 A7
Llawndy Flints 262 C4
Llawnt Shrops 218 B2
Llay Wrex 241 C7
Llechcynfarwy Angl 258 C4
Llecheiddior Gwyn 237 F5
Llechfaen Powys 126 B2
Llechfraith Gwyn 215 E5
Llechryd Caerph 126 F3
Llechryd Ceredig'n 144 D4
Llechwedd Conwy 260 D5
Llechwedd Slate Caverns, Blaenau Ffestiniog Gwyn 238 E2
Lledrod Ceredig'n 169 D5
Llenmerewig Powys 193 E7
Llethrid Swan 97 D5
Lletty Brongu Bridg 98 E4
Llidiadnenog Carms 146 E3
Llidiardau Gwyn 216 A2
Llidiart-y-Parc Denbs 240 F3
Llidiartywaen Powys 171 B5
Llingattock-Vibon-Avel Monmouths 128 D3
Llithfaen Gwyn 236 F3
Lloc Flints 262 D4
Llong Flints 241 B6
Llowes Powys 150 D1
Lloyney Powys 172 C2
Llugwy Gwyn 191 C5
Llundain-fach Ceredig'n 146 A4
Llwydcoed Rh Cyn Taff 99 B6
Llwyn Gwyn 215 A5
Llwyncelyn Ceredig'n 146 A1
Llwyndafydd Ceredig'n 145 A7
Llwynderw Powys 193 C8
Llwyndrain Carms 145 F5
Llwyn-du Monmouths 127 D6
Llwyn-du Swan 97 B9
Llwyndyrys Gwyn 236 F3
Llwyneinion Wrex 241 E6
Llwyngwril Gwyn 190 B2
Llwynhendy Carms 97 B5
Llwynmawr Wrex 218 A1
Llwyn-on-village Merth Tyd 126 E1
Llwyn-y-brain Carms 121 D7
Llwyn-y-Groes Ceredig'n 146 A4
Llwynymaen Shrops 218 C2
Llwynypia Rh Cyn Taff 99 D6
Llynclys Shrops 218 D2
Llynfaes Angl 259 D5
Llyn-y-Pandy Flints 240 A5
Llysdinam Powys 149 A5
Llysfaen Conwy 262 D7
Llysnewydd Carms 145 E7
Llyswen Powys 149 E7
Llysworney V/Glam 77 B6
Llys-y-Fran Pembs 119 E8
Llywel Powys 125 A6
Llywernog Ceredig'n 169 B7
Loan Falk 394 C4
Loandhu H'land 440 F5
Loanhead Aberds 436 C3
Loanhead Midloth 396 E2
Loanhead Perth/Kinr 420 D1
Loanreoch H'land 440 F3
Loans S Ayrs 367 A6
Loans of Tullich H'land 441 F5
Loansdean Northum 365 F5
Lobb Devon 54 D4
Lobhillcross Devon 19 C6
Lobley Hill Tyne/Wear 352 D3
Lobthorpe Lincs 227 D6
Loch a Charnain W Isles 447 D3
Loch a'Ghainmhich W Isles 451 E5
Loch Baghasdail = Lochboisdale W Isles 446 B3
Loch Choire Lodge H'land 443 E8
Loch Eil H'land 424 E2
Loch Euphoirt W Isles 447 B3
Loch Head Dumf/Gal 401 E5
Loch Loyal Lodge H'land 443 D8
Loch nam Madadh = Lochmaddy W Isles 447 B4
Loch Ness Monster Exhibition, Drumnadrochit H'land 433 E7
Loch Sgioport W Isles 447 E3
Lochailort H'land 423 D7
Lochaline H'land 416 C1
Lochanhully H'land 434 F4
Lochans Dumf/Gal 400 D2
Locharbriggs Dumf/Gal 358 F3
Lochassynt Lodge H'land 442 F3
Lochavich Ho Arg/Bute 416 F4
Lochawe Arg/Bute 417 E6
Lochboisdale = Loch Baghasdail W Isles 446 B3
Lochbuie Arg/Bute 416 E1
Lochbuie Ho Arg/Bute 416 E1
Lochcallater Lodge Aberds 427 D6
Lochcarron H'land 431 E8
Lochdhu H'land 444 D4
Lochdochart House Stirl 418 E2
Lochdon Arg/Bute 416 D2
Lochdrum H'land 439 F6
Lochead Arg/Bute 408 D3
Lochead Arg/Bute 407 E7
Lochearnhead Stirl 418 E3
Lochee Dundee C 420 D3
Lochend H'land 433 E7
Lochend H'land 445 B6
Lochend Ho. Stirl 409 C8
Lochetive Ho. H'land 417 C6
Lochfoot Dumf/Gal 402 B2
Lochgair Arg/Bute 408 C2
Lochgarthside H'land 425 A7
Lochgelly Fife 411 C6
Lochgilphead Arg/Bute 408 D1
Lochgoilhead Arg/Bute 408 B5
Lochhill Moray 435 B7
Lochhussie H'land 433 C6
Lochinch Castle Dumf/Gal 400 C3
Lochindorb Lodge H'land 434 E4
Lochinver H'land 439 A4
Lochlane Perth/Kinr 419 E6
Lochletter H'land 433 F6
Lochluichart H'land 433 B5
Lochmaben Dumf/Gal 359 F5
Lochmaddy = Loch nam Madadh W Isles 447 B4
Lochmore Cottage H'land 445 D4
Lochmore Lodge H'land 442 E4
Lochnell Ho Arg/Bute 416 D3
Lochore Fife 411 C6
Lochorodale Arg/Bute 404 E2
Lochportain W Isles 447 A4
Lochranza N Ayrs 405 A5
Lochs Crofts Moray 435 B8
Lochside Aberds 421 A7
Lochside H'land 434 C3
Lochside H'land 443 C6
Lochside H'land 444 E2
Lochslin H'land 441 E5
Lochstack Lodge H'land 442 D4
Lochton Aberds 428 C4
Lochton Scot Borders 386 E5
Lochty Angus 421 A5
Lochty Fife 412 B3
Lochty Perth/Kinr 419 E8
Lochuisge H'land 416 B2
Lochurr Dumf/Gal 357 E7
Lochwinnoch Renf 379 A7
Lochwood Glasg C 393 E5
Lochwood Dumf/Gal 359 C5
Lochyside H'land 424 E3
Lockengate Cornw'l 8 C3
Lockerbie Dumf/Gal 359 F6
Lockeridge Wilts 83 C7
Lockerley Hants 43 A8
Lockhills Cumb 340 B1
Locking N Som'set 79 E7
Locking Stumps Warrington 265 A7
Lockington ER Yorks 310 F1
Lockington Leics 224 C4
Lockleaze Bristol 80 A4
Lockleywood Shrops 220 C3
Locks Heath Hants 45 E5
Locksbottom London 90 D3
Locksbrook Bath/NE Som'set 81 C6
Locksgreen I/Wight 29 B8
Lockton N Yorks 321 C7
Lockwood W Yorks 280 A4
Lockwood W Yorks 280 A4
Locomotion Museum, Shildon Durham 331 A6
Loddington Leics 202 C1
Loddington Northants 180 C4
Loddiswell Devon 14 F2
Loddon Norfolk 210 D3
Lode Cambs 184 F3
Lode Heath W Midlands 177 B6
Loders Dorset 24 B4
Lodge Green W Midlands 177 B8
Lodge Hill Cornw'l 9 C7
Lodge Hill W Midlands 176 B3
Lodge Lees Kent 74 B4
Lodsworth W Sussex 47 B6
Lodway N Som'set 80 A2
Lofthouse N Yorks 317 F8
Lofthouse W Yorks 293 E8
Lofthouse Gate W Yorks 293 F8
Loftus Redcar/Clevel'd 334 C1
Logan E Ayrs 368 C3
Logan Mains Dumf/Gal 400 E2
Loganlea W Loth 394 F4
Logaston Heref'd 150 B4
Loggerheads Staffs 220 A4
Logie Angus 421 A6
Logie Fife 420 E4
Logie Moray 434 C5
Logie Coldstone Aberds 428 B1
Logie Hill H'land 440 F4
Logie Newton Aberds 436 E3
Logie Pert Angus 421 A6
Logiealmond Lodge Perth/Kinr 419 D7
Logierait Perth/Kinr 419 B7
Login Carms 121 C7
Loidse Mhorsgail W Isles 450 E4
Lolworth Cambs 183 F7
Lonbain H'land 431 C6
Londesborough ER Yorks 296 A4
London Apprentice Cornw'l 8 E3
London Beach Kent 72 D4
London City Airport London 112 F3
London Colney Herts 111 B5

London Fields W Midlands 197 E7
London Gatwick Airport W Sussex 69 C7
London Heathrow Airport London 88 A3
London Luton Airport Luton 137 C6
London Minstead Hants 43 D8
London Stansted Airport Essex 139 C6
London Zoo London 111 F7
Londonderry N Yorks 318 C5
Londonderry W Midlands 197 F9
Londonthorpe Lincs 227 A6
Londubh H'land 438 E2
Lonemore H'land 438 F1
Lonemore H'land 440 E4
Long Ashton N Som'set 80 B2
Long Bank Worcs 175 D5
Long Bennington Lincs 249 F7
Long Bredy Dorset 25 B6
Long Buckby Northants 179 E7
Long Buckby Wharf Northants 179 E7
Long Clawson Leics 226 C1
Long Common Hants 45 D5
Long Compton Staffs 221 D7
Long Compton Warwick 132 A4
Long Crendon Bucks 134 F4
Long Crichel Dorset 42 D2
Long Cross N Som'set 80 C2
Long Cross Wilts 61 E7
Long Dean Wilts 82 A2
Long Ditton Surrey 89 C5
Long Drax N Yorks 295 E7
Long Duckmanton Derby 269 E8
Long Eaton Derby 224 B4
Long Gardens Essex 164 E1
Long Green Ches 264 E4
Long Green Worcs 153 F6
Long Hanborough Oxon 133 E7
Long Honeyborough Pembs 117 C5
Long Itchington Warwick 178 E3
Long John's Hill Norfolk 209 B8
Long Lane Telford 220 E2
Long Lawford Warwick 178 C4
Long Load Som'set 39 B7
Long Marston Herts 136 D1
Long Marston N Yorks 307 E7
Long Marston Warwick 155 C6
Long Marton Cumb 328 B3
Long Meadow Cambs 184 F3
Long Meadowend Shrops 173 B6
Long Melford Suffolk 164 C2
Long Moor Wokingham 87 D5
Long Newnton Glos 104 D3
Long Newton E Loth 397 F7
Long Park Hants 65 E5
Long Preston N Yorks 303 D8
Long Riston ER Yorks 298 B1
Long Sandall S Yorks 283 C6
Long Sight Gtr Man 279 C7
Long Stratton Norfolk 209 E7
Long Street M/Keynes 158 C3
Long Sutton Hants 66 B4
Long Sutton Lincs 229 D8
Long Sutton Som'set 39 A7
Long Thurlow Suffolk 187 E5
Long Whatton Leics 224 D4
Long Wittenham Oxon 107 D7
Longbar N Ayrs 379 B6
Longbenton Tyne/Wear 352 C4
Longborough Glos 132 B2
Longbridge Plym'th 11 D6
Longbridge Staffs 221 E8
Longbridge Warwick 177 F8
Longbridge W Midlands 176 C3
Longbridge Deverill Wilts 62 C2
Longburgh Cumb 347 E8
Longburton Dorset 40 D2
Longcause Devon 14 C3
Longcliffe Derby 246 C2
Longcombe Devon 14 D4
Longcot Oxon 106 D2
Longcroft Cumb 347 E6
Longcroft Falk 393 C7
Longcross Surrey 88 C1
Longdale Cumb 328 E2
Longdales Cumb 340 C1
Longden Shrops 194 B4
Longden Common Shrops 194 C4
Longdenwood Shrops 195 B5
Longdon Staffs 222 F3
Longdon Worcs 153 E6
Longdon Green Staffs 198 A2
Longdon Heath Worcs 153 E6
Longdon-on-Tern Telford 220 E2
Longdown Devon 21 B7
Longdowns Cornw'l 4 D2
Longdrum Angus 420 A2
Longfield Kent 91 C7
Longfield Shetl'd 455 E2
Longfield Wilts 82 E2
Longfield Hill Kent 91 C7
Longfleet Poole 27 B7
Longford Derby 223 A6
Longford Glos 130 C2
Longford Kent 90 E5
Longford London 88 A3
Longford Shrops 220 B2
Longford Telford 220 E4
Longford W Midlands 178 B2
Longford Warrington 265 A7
Longforgan Perth/Kinr 420 E3
Longformacus Scot Borders 386 A3
Longframlington Northum 364 B4
Longham Dorset 27 A8
Longham Norfolk 232 E3
Longhaven Aberds 437 E8
Longhedge Wilts 61 C8
Longhill Aberds 437 C6
Longhill S Ayrs 367 D6
Longhirst Northum 365 E6
Longhope Glos 129 D7
Longhope Orkney 452 D4
Longhorsley Northum 365 D5
Longhoughton Northum 377 D6
Longlands Cumb 338 D4
Longlands Lincs 275 C6
Longlands London 90 B4
Longlane Derby 223 A7
Longlane W Berks 85 B7
Longleat House Wilts 61 C8
Longlevens Glos 130 C3
Longley W Yorks 280 C4
Longley W Yorks 292 F2
Longley Estate S Yorks 269 A7
Longley Green Worcs 152 B4
Longleys Perth/Kinr 420 C2
Longmanhill Aberds 436 B4
Longmoor Camp Hants 67 E5
Longmorn Moray 435 C7
Longmoss Ches 266 E4
Longnewton Scot Borders 374 B1
Longnewton Stockton 332 C2
Longney Glos 130 E1
Longniddry E Loth 397 C5
Longnor Shrops 195 C5
Longnor Staffs 245 B7
Longparish Hants 65 C5
Longpark Cumb 348 D2
Longpark E Ayrs 379 E8
Longport Stoke 244 E3
Longridge Glos 130 F3
Longridge Lancs 289 C9
Longridge W Loth 394 F3
Longridge End Glos 130 C2
Longrigg N Lanarks 393 D8
Longriggend N Lanarks 393 D8
Longrock Cornw'l 3 D5
Longsdon Staffs 244 D5
Longshaw Gtr Man 277 D7
Longside Aberds 437 D7
Longsight Gtr Man 279 F6
Longslow Shrops 220 A3
Longsowerby Cumb 348 F1
Longstanton Cambs 183 E7
Longstock Hants 64 D4
Longstone C/Edinb 395 D9
Longstone Cornw'l 8 A4
Longstone Cornw'l 3 C6
Longstone Pembs 117 C8
Longstowe Cambs 161 B6
Longstreet Wilts 63 A7
Longthorpe Peterbro 204 D2
Longton Lancs 289 E6
Longton Stoke 244 F4
Longton Hill End Worcs 153 E6
Longtown Cumb 348 C1
Longtown Heref'd 127 B7
Longtownmail Orkney 453 C5
Longview Mersey 264 A3
Longville in the Dale Shrops 195 E6
Longwell Green S Glos 81 B5
Longwick Bucks 109 A5
Longwitton Northum 364 E3
Longwood W Yorks 280 A4
Longwood Edge W Yorks 280 A4
Longworth Oxon 106 C4
Longyester E Loth 397 E7
Lon-las Rh Cyn Taff 98 C1
Lonmay Aberds 437 C7
Lonmore H'land 430 D2
Looe Cornw'l 9 E8
Looe Mills Cornw'l 9 C7
Loose Kent 72 A2
Loosebeare Devon 35 E7
Loosegate Lincs 229 C6
Loosley Row Bucks 109 B6
Lopcombe Corner Wilts 64 D2
Lopen Som'set 39 D6
Loppington Shrops 219 C6
Lopwell Devon 11 B5
Lordington W Sussex 46 E3
Lord's Cricket Ground London 111 F7
Lord's Hill S'thampton 44 C2
Lords Wood Medway 92 D2
Lordsbridge Norfolk 206 A2
Lornty Perth/Kinr 420 C1
Loscoe Derby 247 E6
Loscombe Dorset 24 A5
Losgaintir W Isles 448 C4
Lossiemouth Moray 435 A7
Lossit Arg/Bute 403 A1
Lossit Lodge Arg/Bute 406 F4
Lostock Gralam Ches 265 D8
Lostock Green Ches 265 E8
Lostock Hall Lancs 289 E7
Lostock Junction Gtr Man 278 C2
Lostwithiel Cornw'l 9 D5
Loth Orkney 454 C4
Lothbeg H'land 441 B6
Lothersdale N Yorks 291 A8
Lothianbridge Midloth 396 E3
Lothmore H'land 441 B6
Lottisham Som'set 60 E3
Loudwater Bucks 109 D8
Loudwater Herts 110 C3
Loughborough Leics 225 E5
Loughor Swan 97 C6
Loughton Essex 112 C3
Loughton Lincs 228 B1
Loughton M/Keynes 158 E4
Loughton Shrops 174 B2
Louis Tussaud's Waxworks Blackp'l 288 C3
Lound Lincs 227 E8
Lound Notts 271 B5
Lound Suffolk 211 D6
Lount Leics 224 E2
Lour Angus 420 C4
Louth Lincs 274 B3
Lovat H'land 433 D7
Love Clough Lancs 291 E5
Love Green Bucks 110 F2
Lovedean Hants 46 D1
Lover Wilts 43 B7
Loversall S Yorks 283 E5
Loves Green Essex 113 B7
Loveston Pembs 117 C7
Lovington Som'set 60 E3
Low Ackworth W Yorks 282 A3
Low Angerton Northum 364 F3
Low Bentham N Yorks 302 B5
Low Biggins Cumb 315 E6
Low Blantyre S Lanarks 381 A5
Low Bolton N Yorks 317 A6
Low Borrowbridge Cumb 328 F2
Low Bradfield S Yorks 268 A5
Low Bradley N Yorks 304 F4
Low Braithwaite Cumb 339 C7
Low Brunton Northum 351 C5
Low Burnham N Lincs 284 D2
Low Catton ER Yorks 308 E3
Low Clanyard Dumf/Gal 400 F3
Low Common Norfolk 187 B6
Low Common Norfolk 209 E6
Low Common Norfolk 234 B1
Low Compton Gtr Man 279 C7
Low Coniscliffe N Yorks 331 D7
Low Cotehill Cumb 339 A8
Low Coylton S Ayrs 367 D8
Low Crosby Cumb 348 E2
Low Dalby N Yorks 321 C8
Low Dinsdale D'lington 332 D1
Low Dyke Cumb 339 E8
Low Eighton Tyne/Wear 352 E4
Low Ellington N Yorks 318 D3
Low Entercommon N Yorks 331 E8
Low Etherley Durham 343 F7
Low Fell Tyne/Wear 352 D4
Low Fold W Yorks 293 C6
Low Fremington N Yorks 317 A6
Low Fulney Lincs 228 D5
Low Garth N Yorks 334 E1
Low Gate Northum 350 D5
Low Gate N Yorks 306 B2
Low Gatherley N Yorks 331 F6
Low Geltbridge Cumb 348 E4
Low Grantley N Yorks 306 A1
Low Green N Yorks 305 D8
Low Green Suffolk 186 F2
Low Green W Yorks 293 C6
Low Greenfield Durham 343 F7
Low Greenside Tyne/Wear 352 D1
Low Habberley Worcs 175 C6
Low Ham Som'set 59 F8
Low Hameringham Lincs 252 A2
Low Harker Cumb 347 D9
Low Hauxley Northum 365 B7
Low Hawkser N Yorks 335 E5
Low Hesket Cumb 339 B8
Low Hutton N Yorks 308 B4
Low Knipe Cumb 327 B7
Low Laithe N Yorks 305 C7
Low Laithes S Yorks 282 D1
Low Lands Durham 343 E6
Low Langton Lincs 273 D8
Low Leighton Derby 267 B7
Low Lorton Cumb 325 A8
Low Marishes N Yorks 321 E7
Low Marnham Notts 271 F8
Low Mill N Yorks 320 A4
Low Moor Lancs 290 B3
Low Moor W Yorks 292 E5
Low Moorsley Tyne/Wear 344 B2
Low Moresby Cumb 324 B4
Low Newbiggin Tyne/Wear 352 C2
Low Newton Cumb 314 D3
Low Newton-by-the-Sea Northum 377 C6
Low Prudhoe Northum 351 D9
Low Risby N Lincs 285 A5
Low Row Cumb 338 C2
Low Row Cumb 349 D5
Low Row N Yorks 317 A5
Low Salchrie Dumf/Gal 400 C2
Low Smerby Arg/Bute 404 D3
Low Street Norfolk 208 B4
Low Street Thurr'k 91 A8
Low Tharston Norfolk 209 D7
Low Torry Fife 411 D5
Low Town Northum 364 B4
Low Town N Yorks 332 D2
Low Toynton Lincs 274 E2
Low Valley S Yorks 282 D2
Low Walworth D'lington 331 C6
Low Waters S Lanarks 381 B6
Low Westwood Durham 351 E9
Low Whinnow Cumb 338 A5
Low Whita N Yorks 317 A6
Low Wood Cumb 313 D7
Low Worsall N Yorks 332 E2
Lowbands Glos 130 A1
Lowca Cumb 324 B4
Lowcote Gate Derby 247 F6
Lowcross Hill Ches 242 D2
Lowden Wilts 82 B3
Lowdham Notts 248 F3
Lowdham Grange Notts 248 F3
Lowe Shrops 219 B7
Lowedges S Yorks 269 C6
Lower Achachenna Arg/Bute 417 E5
Lower Airsholt Som'set 58 D4
Lower Altofts W Yorks 294 F1
Lower Ansty Dorset 41 F5
Lower Apperley Glos 130 B3
Lower Ardtun Arg/Bute 415 E6
Lower Arncott Oxon 134 D3
Lower Ashtead Surrey 89 E5
Lower Ashton Devon 21 D6
Lower Assendon Oxon 108 F4
Lower Badcall H'land 442 D3
Lower Ballam Lancs 288 D4
Lower Bartle Lancs 289 D6
Lower Basildon W Berks 86 A2
Lower Bassingthorpe Lincs 227 C6
Lower Bearwood Heref'd 151 A5
Lower Bebington Mersey 263 C8
Lower Beeding W Sussex 69 F6
Lower Benefield Northants 203 F5
Lower Bentley Worcs 176 E2
Lower Berry Hill Glos 128 E5
Lower Bevendean Brighton/Hove 49 E6
Lower Bitchet Kent 91 F6
Lower Black Moss Lancs 291 B5
Lower Blandford St. Mary Dorset 41 E7
Lower Bobbingworth Green Essex 113 A5
Lower Boddington Northants 156 B4
Lower Bodham Norfolk 256 E5
Lower Bordean Hants 45 A8
Lower Boscaswell Cornw'l 2 D3
Lower Bourne Surrey 67 C6
Lower Brailes Warwick 156 E1
Lower Breakish H'land 431 F6
Lower Bredbury Gtr Man 267 A5
Lower Breinton Heref'd 151 E7
Lower Broadheath Worcs 153 A6
Lower Broughton Gtr Man 279 E5
Lower Broxwood Heref'd 150 B5
Lower Brynamman Neath P Talb 124 E3
Lower Buckland Hants 29 A6
Lower Bullingham Heref'd 151 E8
Lower Bunbury Ches 242 C4
Lower Burgate Hants 43 C5
Lower Burrow Som'set 39 B6
Lower Cadsden Bucks 109 B6
Lower Caldecote Beds 160 C3
Lower Cam Glos 103 B7
Lower Cambourne Cambs 161 A6
Lower Canada N Som'set 79 E7
Lower Catesby Northants 157 A5
Lower Chapel Powys 149 E5
Lower Cheriton Devon 37 F7
Lower Chicksgrove Wilts 62 E4
Lower Chute Wilts 64 A3
Lower Clapton London 112 E2
Lower Clent Worcs 175 C8
Lower Cokeham W Sussex 48 F3
Lower Common Hants 66 C2
Lower Common Hants 86 D5
Lower Cotburn Aberds 436 C4
Lower Cox Street Kent 92 D3
Lower Cragabus Arg/Bute 403 B3
Lower Crossings Derby 267 C7
Lower Cumberworth W Yorks 281 C6
Lower Darwen Blackb'n 290 E2
Lower Dean Beds 181 E9
Lower Dell H'land 426 A5
Lower Denby W Yorks 281 C6
Lower Deuchries Aberds 436 C3
Lower Diabaig H'land 431 B7
Lower Dicker E Sussex 50 D4
Lower Drift Cornw'l 2 E4
Lower Dunsforth N Yorks 307 C5
Lower Earley Wokingham 86 B5
Lower Edmonton London 112 D1
Lower Egleton Heref'd 152 C2
Lower Elkstone Staffs 245 C7
Lower Ellastone Staffs 245 F8
Lower Elsted W Sussex 46 B4
Lower End Beds 159 E6
Lower End Beds 136 C3
Lower End Bucks 134 F4
Lower End Bucks 158 F2
Lower End Devon 37 D6
Lower End Glos 104 B4
Lower End Northants 158 A4
Lower End Northants 181 F5
Lower Ensden Kent 93 E8
Lower Everleigh Wilts 83 F8
Lower Exbury Hants 29 A8
Lower Eythorne Kent 74 B5
Lower Failand N Som'set 80 B2
Lower Faintree Shrops 196 F2
Lower Falkenham Suffolk 166 E3
Lower Farringdon Hants 66 D4
Lower Feltham London 88 B4
Lower Fittleworth W Sussex 47 C8
Lower Ford Lancs 290 E4
Lower Foxdale I/Man 336 D2
Lower Freystrop Pembs 117 B5
Lower Froyle Hants 66 C5
Lower Gabwell Devon 15 B6
Lower Gledfield H'land 440 D2
Lower Godney Som'set 60 C1
Lower Goldstone Kent 95 D5
Lower Gornal W Midlands 197 E7
Lower Grange W Yorks 292 D4
Lower Gravenhurst Beds 160 F2
Lower Green Essex 161 F8
Lower Green Essex 113 B9
Lower Green Essex 140 A3
Lower Green Gtr Man 278 E3
Lower Green Herts 137 A7
Lower Green Herts 138 A4
Lower Green Kent 71 C6
Lower Green Kent 71 C7
Lower Green Norfolk 210 B4
Lower Green Norfolk 256 E2
Lower Green Suffolk 185 F7
Lower Green Suffolk 164 A3
Lower Green Surrey 88 C4
Lower Green Staffs 197 B7
Lower Green Warwick 178 E4
Lower Green W Berks 84 D4
Lower Grove Common Heref'd 128 B5
Lower Hacheston Suffolk 166 A4
Lower Halistra H'land 430 C2
Lower Halliford Surrey 88 C3
Lower Halstock Leigh Dorset 39 E8
Lower Halstow Kent 92 C4
Lower Hamswell S Glos 81 B6
Lower Hamworthy Poole 27 B7
Lower Hardres Kent 74 A3
Lower Harpton Heref'd 172 F3
Lower Hartlip Kent 92 D3
Lower Hartwell Bucks 135 E6
Lower Hawthwaite Cumb 313 C5
Lower Hayne Som'set 38 C2
Lower Hayton Shrops 173 B8
Lower Hazel S Glos 102 E4
Lower Heath Ches 244 B3
Lower Hempriggs Moray 435 B6
Lower Heppington Kent 74 A3
Lower Hergest Heref'd 150 A3
Lower Herne Kent 94 C3
Lower Heyford Oxon 133 C8
Lower Heysham Lancs 301 C7
Lower Higham Kent 91 B9
Lower Holbrook Suffolk 165 E8
Lower Holloway London 111 E8
Lower Hook Worcs 153 D6
Lower Hopton W Yorks 281 A5
Lower Hordley Shrops 218 C4
Lower Horncroft W Sussex 47 C8
Lower Horsebridge E Sussex 50 D4
Lower Houses W Yorks 280 A5
Lower Howsell Worcs 153 C5
Lower Illey W Midlands 176 B2
Lower Island Kent 94 C2
Lower Kersal Gtr Man 279 D5
Lower Kilcott Glos 103 E7
Lower Killeyan Arg/Bute 403 B2
Lower Kingcombe Dorset 25 A6
Lower Kingswood Surrey 89 F7
Lower Kinnerton Ches 241 B7
Lower Kinsham Heref'd 172 F5
Lower Knapp Som'set 38 A4
Lower Knowle Bristol 80 B3
Lower Langford N Som'set 80 D1
Lower Largo Fife 412 B2
Lower Leigh Staffs 222 A2
Lower Leighton Powys 193 B8
Lower Lemington Glos 155 F7
Lower Lenie H'land 433 F7
Lower Ley Glos 129 D8
Lower Lovacott Devon 54 F5
Lower Loxhore Devon 55 D7
Lower Luggy Powys 193 C8
Lower Lydbrook Glos 129 D5
Lower Lye Heref'd 173 E6
Lower Machen Newp 100 E4
Lower Maes-coed Heref'd 127 A7
Lower Mannington Dorset 42 E4
Lower Marston Som'set 61 C7
Lower Mayland Essex 115 B5
Lower Meend Glos 102 B3
Lower Merridge Som'set 58 E4
Lower Middleton Cheney Northants 157 D5
Lower Midway Derby 223 D8
Lower Milovaig H'land 430 C1
Lower Milton Som'set 60 B2
Lower Moor Worcs 154 C2
Lower Morton S Glos 102 D4
Lower Mountain Flints 241 C7
Lower Nash Pembs 117 D6
Lower Nazeing Essex 112 A2
Lower Nobut Staffs 222 B2
Lower North Dean Bucks 109 C7
Lower Noverton Glos 131 C5
Lower Nyland Dorset 40 B4
Lower Oddington Glos 132 B3
Lower Ollach H'land 430 E5
Lower Penarth V/Glam 78 B3
Lower Penn Staffs 197 D6
Lower Pennington Hants 29 B6
Lower Penwortham Lancs 289 E7
Lower Peover Ches 266 E1
Lower Pexhill Ches 266 E4
Lower Pitkerrie H'land 441 E5
Lower Place Gtr Man 279 B7
Lower Porthpean Cornw'l 8 E3
Lower Porthkerry V/Glam 77 C8
Lower Quinton Warwick 155 C6
Lower Race Torf 101 B5
Lower Rainham Medway 92 C3
Lower Ratley Hants 44 B1
Lower Raydon Suffolk 165 E5
Lower Redbrook Glos 128 F4
Lower Roadwater Som'set 57 D7
Lower Row Dorset 42 F3
Lower Sapey Worcs 174 F3
Lower Seagry Wilts 104 F4
Lower Sheering Essex 139 E5
Lower Shelton Beds 159 D7
Lower Shiplake Oxon 86 A5
Lower Shuckburgh Warwick 178 F4
Lower Slackstead Hants 44 A2
Lower Slade Devon 54 B5
Lower Slaughter Glos 132 C2
Lower Soothill W Yorks 293 F7
Lower Soudley Glos 129 E7
Lower Spoad Shrops 172 B3
Lower Stanton St. Quintin Wilts 104 F3
Lower Stoke Medway 92 A3
Lower Stondon Beds 160 E3
Lower Stone Glos 103 D5
Lower Stonnal Staffs 198 C2
Lower Stow Bedon Norfolk 208 E3
Lower Stratton Swindon 105 E8
Lower Street Dorset 26 A3
Lower Street E Sussex 51 D7
Lower Street Norfolk 234 E3
Lower Street Norfolk 233 B8
Lower Street Norfolk 257 E8
Lower Street Suffolk 165 F8
Lower Strensham Worcs 153 D8
Lower Stretton Warrington 265 C7
Lower Strode Dorset 24 A4
Lower Strode N Som'set 80 D2
Lower Studley Wilts 82 E2
Lower Sundon Beds 136 B5
Lower Swainswick Bath/NE Som'set 81 C7
Lower Swanwick Hants 44 E4
Lower Swell Glos 132 B2
Lower Sydenham London 90 B2
Lower Tadmarton Oxon 156 E3
Lower Tale Devon 37 F6
Lower Tasburgh Norfolk 209 D7
Lower Tean Staffs 222 A2
Lower Thorpe Northants 157 C5
Lower Thurlton Norfolk 210 D4
Lower Thurnham Lancs 301 D8
Lower Thurvaston Derby 223 A6
Lower Tote H'land 430 B5
Lower Town Devon 14 A2
Lower Town Devon 37 D5
Lower Town Heref'd 152 D2
Lower Town Pembs 119 B7
Lower Town Som'set 39 C7
Lower Town W Yorks 292 D2
Lower Trebullett Cornw'l 18 E3
Lower Tuffley Glos 130 E2
Lower Turmer Hants 43 E5
Lower Twydall Medway 92 C3
Lower Tysoe Warwick 156 D1
Lower Upham Hants 45 C5
Lower Upnor Medway 92 B2
Lower Vexford Som'set 58 D2
Lower Walton Warrington 265 B7
Lower Wanborough Swindon 106 F1
Lower Waterhay Wilts 105 D6
Lower Waterston Dorset 26 B1
Lower Weald M/Keynes 158 E3
Lower Wear Devon 21 C8
Lower Weare Som'set 79 F8
Lower Welson Heref'd 150 B3
Lower Westmancote Worcs 154 E1
Lower Whatcombe Dorset 41 F6
Lower Whatley Som'set 61 B6
Lower Whitley Ches 265 D7
Lower Wick Glos 103 C6
Lower Wield Hants 66 C2
Lower Willingdon E Sussex 50 F4
Lower Winchendon Bucks 135 E5
Lower Woodend Aberds 428 A3
Lower Woodend Bucks 109 E6
Lower Woodford Wilts 63 D7
Lower Woon Cornw'l 8 C3
Lower Wraxall Dorset 40 F1
Lower Wraxall Som'set 60 D4
Lower Wych Ches 242 F2
Lower Wyche Worcs 153 D5
Lower Wyke W Yorks 292 E5
Lowerford Lancs 291 C6
Lowerhouse Ches 267 E5
Lowerhouse Lancs 291 D5
Lowertown Cornw'l 3 E9
Lowes Barn Durham 343 C9
Lowesby Leics 201 B8
Lowestoft Suffolk 211 E6
Loweswater Cumb 325 B7
Lowfield S Yorks 269 B7
Lowfield Heath W Sussex 69 D7
Lowford Hants 44 D4
Lowgill Cumb 315 A6
Lowgill Lancs 302 C5
Lowick Cumb 313 C6
Lowick Northants 181 B7
Lowick Northum 388 E2
Lowick Bridge Cumb 313 C6
Lowick Green Cumb 313 C6
Lowlands Torf 101 C5
Lowna N Yorks 320 B4
Lownie Moor Angus 421 C4
Lowood Scot Borders 385 E7
Lowsonford Warwick 177 E6
Lowther Cumb 327 B7
Lowther Town Dumf/Gal 347 C6
Lowthorpe ER Yorks 310 C3
Lowthwaite Cumb 327 B5
Lowton Devon 35 F6
Lowton Gtr Man 278 E1
Lowton Som'set 38 C1
Lowton Common Gtr Man 278 E1
Lowton Heath Warrington 277 E9
Lowton St. Mary's Gtr Man 278 E1
Loxbeare Devon 36 C3
Loxford London 112 E3
Loxhill Surrey 68 D2
Loxhore Devon 55 D7
Loxhore Cott Devon 55 D7
Loxley S Yorks 269 B6
Loxley Warwick 155 B8
Loxley Green Staffs 222 B3
Loxton N Som'set 79 E7
Loxwood W Sussex 68 E2
Loyter's Green Essex 139 E6
Lozells W Midlands 198 F2
Lubachlaggan H'land 439 F7
Lubachoinnich H'land 439 D8
Lubcroy H'land 439 C7
Lubenham Leics 201 F7
Lubinvullin H'land 443 B7
Lucas End Herts 111 B8
Luccombe Som'set 57 C5
Luccombe Village I/Wight 30 E3
Lucker Northum 377 A5
Luckett Cornw'l 18 F4
Lucking Street Essex 164 F1
Luckington Wilts 103 F8
Lucklawhill Fife 420 E4
Luck's Bridge Lincs 228 E4
Luckwell Bridge Som'set 57 D5
Lucton Heref'd 173 F6
Ludag W Isles 446 B3
Ludborough Lincs 286 E4
Ludbrook Devon 11 E9
Ludchurch Pembs 121 E6
Luddenden W Yorks 292 E2
Luddenden Foot W Yorks 292 F2
Ludderburn Cumb 314 B2
Luddesdown Kent 91 C8
Luddington N Lincs 284 A3
Luddington Warwick 155 B6
Luddington in the Brook Northants 182 B2
Lude House Perth/Kinr 419 A6
Ludford Lincs 273 B7
Ludford Shrops 173 D8
Ludgershall Bucks 134 D4
Ludgershall Wilts 64 A2
Ludgvan Cornw'l 3 D6
Ludham Norfolk 234 E4
Ludlow Shrops 173 D8
Ludlow Racecourse Shrops 173 C7
Ludney Lincs 287 E6
Ludney Som'set 39 D5
Ludsden Oxon 135 F5
Ludstock Heref'd 152 E3
Ludwell Wilts 41 B8
Ludworth Durham 344 C3
Luffenhall Herts 138 B1
Luffincott Devon 18 B3
Lufton Som'set 39 C8
Lugate Scot Borders 385 D5
Lugg Green Heref'd 173 F7
Luggate Burn E Loth 398 D1
Luggiebank N Lanarks 393 D7
Lugsdale Halton 264 B5
Lugton E Ayrs 379 B8
Lugwardine Heref'd 151 D8
Luib H'land 431 F5
Luibeilt H'land 424 F4
Lulham Heref'd 151 D6
Lullington Derby 199 A6
Lullington Som'set 61 A7
Lulsgate Bottom N Som'set 80 C1
Lulsley Worcs 152 A4
Lulworth Camp Dorset 26 D3
Lulworth Castle Dorset 26 D4
Lumb Lancs 278 A4
Lumb Lancs 291 F5
Lumb W Yorks 292 F2
Lumbutts W Yorks 291 F7
Lumby N Yorks 294 D3
Lumley W Sussex 46 E3
Lumloch E Dunb 392 E4
Lumphanan Aberds 428 B2
Lumphinnans Fife 411 C6
Lumsden Aberds 436 F1

Lunan Angus 421 B6
Lunanhead Angus 420 B4
Luncarty Perth/Kinr 419 E8
Lund ER Yorks 309 F8
Lund N Yorks 295 D7
Lund Shetl'd 456 C5
Lundal W Isles 450 D4
Lundavra H'land 417 A5
Lunderton Aberds 437 D8
Lundie Angus 420 D2
Lundie H'land 424 A3
Lundin Links Fife 412 B2
Lundwood S Yorks 282 C1
Lundy Green Norfolk 209 E8
Lunga Arg/Bute 407 B7
Lunna Shetl'd 457 G4
Lunning Shetl'd 457 G5
Lunnister Shetl'd 457 F3
Lunnon Swan 97 E5
Lunsford Kent 91 E9
Lunsford's Cross E Sussex 51 D7
Lunt Mersey 276 D3
Lunts Heath Halton 264 B5
Lupbridge Devon 14 E2
Luppitt Devon 37 E8
Lupset W Yorks 281 A8
Lupton Cumb 314 D5
Lurg Aberds 428 B3
Lurgashall W Sussex 67 F8
Lurignich Arg/Bute 416 B4
Lurley Devon 36 D3
Lusby Lincs 274 F3
Luscombe Devon 14 D3
Luson Devon 11 E8
Luss Arg/Bute 409 C6
Lussagiven Arg/Bute 407 D6
Lusta H'land 430 C2
Lustleigh Devon 21 D5
Luston Heref'd 173 F7
Lusty Som'set 61 E5
Luthermuir Aberds 428 F3
Luthrie Fife 420 F3
Luton Devon 21 E8
Luton Devon 37 F6
Luton Luton 136 C5
Luton Medway 92 C2
Luton Airport Luton 137 C6
Lutsford Devon 33 C5
Lutterworth Leics 179 B5
Lutton Dorset 27 D5
Lutton Devon 11 D7
Lutton Devon 14 C1
Lutton Lincs 229 C8
Lutton Northants 203 F8
Luxborough Som'set 57 D6
Luxted London 90 D3
Luxton Devon 38 D2
Luxulyan Cornw'l 8 D3
Luzley Gtr Man 279 D8
Luzley Brook Gtr Man 279 C7
Lybster H'land 445 E6
Lydbury North Shrops 172 A5
Lydcott Devon 55 D8
Lydd Kent 53 B5
Lydden Kent 95 C7
Lydden Kent 74 B5
Lydden Motor Racing Circuit Kent 74 B4
Lyddington Rutl'd 202 D3
Lydd-on-Sea Kent 53 C6
Lyde Orkney 452 B4
Lyde Cross Heref'd 151 D8
Lyde Green Hants 86 E4
Lyde Green S Glos 81 A5
Lydeard St. Lawrence Som'set 58 E2
Lydford Devon 19 D7
Lydford Fair Place Som'set 60 E3
Lydford-on-Fosse Som'set 60 E3
Lydgate Gtr Man 279 D8
Lydgate Gtr Man 279 A8
Lydgate W Yorks 291 E7
Lydham Shrops 194 E2
Lydiard Green Wilts 105 E6
Lydiard Millicent Wilts 105 E6
Lydiard Tregoze Swindon 105 F7
Lydiate Mersey 276 D4
Lydiate Ash Worcs 176 C2
Lydlinch Dorset 40 D4
Lydmarsh Som'set 38 E5
Lydney Glos 102 B4
Lydstep Pembs 117 E7
Lye W Midlands 175 B8
Lye Green Bucks 110 B1
Lye Green E Sussex 70 E5
Lye Green Warwick 177 E6
Lye Head Worcs 175 D5
Lye Hole N Som'set 80 D2
Lye's Green Wilts 61 B8
Lyford Oxon 106 D4
Lymbridge Green Kent 74 C2
Lyme Park, Disley Ches 267 C6
Lyme Regis Dorset 24 B1
Lyminge Kent 74 C3
Lymington Hants 29 A6
Lyminster W Sussex 47 F8
Lymm Warrington 265 B8
Lymore Hants 29 B5
Lympne Kent 74 D2
Lympsham Som'set 79 F6
Lympstone Devon 22 D1
Lynbridge Devon 56 B1
Lynch Hants 65 B7
Lynch Som'set 57 B5
Lynchat H'land 426 B2
Lyncombe Som'set 56 D4
Lyndale Ho. H'land 430 C3
Lyndhurst Hants 43 E9
Lyndon Rutl'd 202 C4
Lyndon Green W Midlands 177 A5
Lyne Scot Borders 383 D9
Lyne Surrey 88 C2
Lyne Down Heref'd 129 A6
Lyne of Gorthleck H'land 433 F7
Lyne of Skene Aberds 428 A4
Lyneal Shrops 219 B5
Lyneham Oxon 132 C4
Lyneham Wilts 83 A5
Lynemore H'land 435 F5
Lynemouth Northum 365 D7
Lynesack Durham 330 A3
Lyness Orkney 452 D4
Lynford Norfolk 207 E7
Lyng Norfolk 233 E6
Lyng Som'set 59 F6
Lyngate Norfolk 234 B2
Lyngate Norfolk 234 C3
Lyngford Som'set 38 A2
Lynmore H'land 435 E5
Lynmouth Devon 56 B1
Lynn Staffs 198 C2
Lynsore Bottom Kent 74 B3
Lynsted Kent 93 D5
Lynstone Cornw'l 32 E4
Lynton Devon 56 B1
Lynton & Lynmouth Cliff Railway Devon 56 B1
Lynwilg H'land 426 A3
Lynworth Glos 131 C5
Lyons Tyne/Wear 344 B3
Lyon's Gate Dorset 40 E3
Lyon's Green Norfolk 208 A2
Lyonshall Heref'd 150 A4
Lyrabus Arg/Bute 406 F2
Lytchett Matravers Dorset 27 A5
Lytchett Minster Dorset 27 B6
Lyth H'land 445 B6
Lytham Lancs 288 E4
Lytham St. Anne's Lancs 288 E3
Lythbank Shrops 195 B5
Lythe N Yorks 334 D3
Lythes Orkney 453 E5
Lythmore H'land 444 B4


## M


Maam Arg/Bute 408 A4
Mabe Burnthouse Cornw'l 4 D3
Mabie Dumf/Gal 402 B3
Mablethorpe Lincs 275 B7
Macclesfield Ches 267 E5
Macduff Aberds 436 B4
Mace Green Suffolk 165 D7
Machan S Lanarks 381 B7
Macharioch Arg/Bute 404 F3
Machen Caerph 100 E4
Machrie N Ayrs 404 C4
Machrie Hotel Arg/Bute 403 B3
Machrihanish Arg/Bute 404 D2
Machroes Gwyn 213 C6
Machynlleth Powys 191 C5
Machynys Carms 96 C5
Mackerel's Common W Sussex 68 F2
Mackerye End Herts 137 D7
Mackney Oxon 107 E8
Mackworth Derby 223 A8
Macmerry E Loth 397 D5
Madame Tussaud's London 111 F7
Madderty Perth/Kinr 419 E7
Maddington Wilts 63 C6
Maddiston Falk 394 C3
Maddox Moor Pembs 117 B5
Madehurst W Sussex 47 D7
Madeley Staffs 243 F8
Madeley Telford 196 C3
Madeley Heath Staffs 244 E1
Madeley Heath Worcs 176 C1
Madeleywood Telford 196 C2
Maders Cornw'l 10 A2
Madford Devon 37 D8
Madingley Cambs 183 F7
Madley Heref'd 151 E6
Madresfield Worcs 153 C6
Madron Cornw'l 2 D5
Maen Porth Cornw'l 4 E3
Maenaddwyn Angl 259 C6
Maenclochog Pembs 121 B5
Maendy Card 78 A3
Maendy V/Glam 77 A7
Maenorbŷr = Manorbier Pembs 117 E7
Maentwrog Gwyn 238 F1
Maen-y-groes Ceredig'n 145 A7
Maer Staffs 221 A5
Maerdy Conwy 239 F8
Maerdy Monmouths 101 B8
Maerdy Monmouths 127 C8
Maerdy Rh Cyn Taff 99 C6
Maes Pennant Flints 263 D5
Maes Treylow Powys 172 E3
Maesbrook Shrops 218 D3
Maesbury Shrops 218 C3
Maesbury Marsh Shrops 218 C3
Maesgeichen Gwyn 259 E8
Maes-glas Newp 101 E6
Maesgwn-Isaf Powys 217 F8
Maesgwyn Ganol Powys 193 A7
Maeshafn Denbs 240 B5
Maesllyn Ceredig'n 145 D7
Maesmawr Powys 192 E5
Maesmynis Powys 149 C5
Maesteg Bridg 98 D4
Maesybont Carms 123 D7
Maesycrugiau Carms 146 D2
Maes-y-cwmmer Caerph 100 D3
Maesydd Powys 218 F2
Maes-y-facrell Conwy 260 C5
Maesygwartha Monmouths 127 E5
Maesyrhandir Powys 193 E5
Magdalen Laver Essex 139 F6
Maggieknockater Moray 435 D8
Maggots End Essex 139 C5
Magham Down E Sussex 50 D5
Maghull Mersey 276 D4
Magna Science Adventure Centre, Rotherham S Yorks 269 A8
Magor Monmouths 101 E8
Magpie Green Suffolk 187 C6
Mahaar Dumf/Gal 400 B2
Maida Vale London 111 F7
Maiden Bradley Wilts 61 D8
Maiden Head N Som'set 80 C3
Maiden Law Durham 343 B7
Maiden Newton Dorset 25 A6
Maiden Wells Pembs 117 E5
Maidencombe Torbay 15 B6
Maidenhall Suffolk 165 D8
Maidenhayne Devon 23 A7
Maidenhead Windsor 109 F7
Maidenmarsh W Sussex 46 B3
Maidens S Ayrs 366 F4
Maiden's Green Bracknell 87 B7
Maidensgrave Suffolk 166 C3
Maidenwell Lincs 274 D3
Maidford Northants 157 B7
Maidford Wilts 104 F2
Maids Moreton Bucks 158 E2
Maidstone Kent 92 E2
Maidwell Northants 180 C2
Mail Shetl'd 455 D3
Mailand Shetl'd 456 C6
Main Powys 217 E8
Maindee Newp 101 E6
Mainholm S Ayrs 367 C7
Mains of Airies Dumf/Gal 400 C1
Mains of Allardice Aberds 429 E5
Mains of Annochie Aberds 437 D6
Mains of Ardestie Angus 421 D5
Mains of Arnage Aberds 437 E6
Mains of Auchoynanie Moray 436 D1
Mains of Baldoon Dumf/Gal 401 D6
Mains of Balhall Angus 421 A5
Mains of Ballindarg Angus 420 B4
Mains of Balnakettle Aberds 428 E3
Mains of Birness Aberds 437 E6
Mains of Blackhall Aberds 436 F4
Mains of Burgie Moray 435 C5
Mains of Cairnbrogie Aberds 437 F5
Mains of Cairnty Moray 435 C8
Mains of Clunas H'land 434 D3
Mains of Crichie Aberds 437 D6
Mains of Daltulich H'land 434 D2
Mains of Dalvey H'land 435 E6
Mains of Dellavaird Aberds 428 D4
Mains of Drum Aberds 429 C5
Mains of Edingight Moray 436 C2
Mains of Fedderate Aberds 437 D5
Mains of Flichity H'land 434 F1
Mains of Hatton Aberds 437 C6
Mains of Hatton Aberds 436 D4
Mains of Inkhorn Aberds 437 E6
Mains of Innerpeffray Perth/Kinr 419 F7
Mains of Kirktonhill Aberds 421 A6
Mains of Lathers Aberds 436 D3
Mains of Mayen Moray 436 D2
Mains of Melgund Angus 421 B5
Mains of Taymouth Perth/Kinr 419 C5
Mains of Thornton Aberds 428 E3
Mains of Towie Aberds 436 D4
Mains of Ulbster H'land 445 D7
Mains of Watten H'land 445 C6
Mainsforth Durham 344 E2
Mainsriddle Dumf/Gal 402 D3
Mainstone Plym'th 11 D6
Mainstone Shrops 194 F1
Maisemore Glos 130 C2
Major's Green Worcs 176 C4
Makeney Derby 247 F5
Makerstoun Scot Borders 374 A3
Malacleit W Isles 447 A2
Malborough Devon 13 E5
Malborough Lincs 250 B1
Malcoff Derby 267 C8
Malden Rushett London 89 D5
Maldensgrove Oxon 108 E4
Maldon Essex 141 F6
Malham N Yorks 304 C2
Maligar H'land 430 B4
Malinbridge S Yorks 269 B6
Malins Lee Telford 196 B2
Mallaig H'land 423 C6
Mallaig Bheag H'land 423 C6
Malleny Mills C/Edinb 395 E8
Malling Stirl 409 B8
Mallory Park Motor Racing Circuit Leics 200 C2
Mallows Green Essex 139 C5
Malltraeth Angl 259 F5
Mallwyd Gwyn 191 A8
Malmesbury Wilts 104 E3
Malmsmead Devon 56 B2
Malpas Ches 242 E2
Malpas Cornw'l 4 B4
Malpas Newp 101 D6
Malswick Glos 129 B8
Maltby Stockton 332 D4
Maltby S Yorks 282 E4
Maltby le Marsh Lincs 275 C6
Malting End Suffolk 163 B7
Maltings Angus 421 A7
Maltman's Hill Kent 73 C5
Malton N Yorks 308 A4
Malvern Common Worcs 153 D5
Malvern Link Worcs 153 C5
Malvern Wells Worcs 153 D5
Mamble Worcs 174 D3
Mamhilad Monmouths 101 B6
Manaccan Cornw'l 4 E3
Manadon Plym'th 11 D5
Manafon Powys 193 C6
Manais W Isles 449 D5
Manar Ho. Aberds 436 F4
Manaton Devon 20 D5
Manby Lincs 274 B4
Mancetter Warwick 199 D7
Manchester Gtr Man 279 E6
Manchester Airport Gtr Man 266 C3
Manchester Airport Gtr Man 266 C3
Manchester National Velodrome Gtr Man 279 E6
Mancot Royal Flints 263 F8
Mandally H'land 425 B4
Manea Cambs 205 F8
Maney W Midlands 198 D3
Manfield N Yorks 331 D6
Mangaster Shetl'd 457 F3
Mangerton Dorset 24 A4
Mangotsfield S Glos 81 A5
Mangrove Green Herts 137 C6
Mangurstadh W Isles 450 D3
Mankinholes W Yorks 291 F8
Manley Ches 264 E5
Manley Devon 36 D4
Manmoel Caerph 100 B3
Mannal Arg/Bute 414 C2
Mannamead Plym'th 11 D5
Mannerston W Loth 395 C5
Manningford Abbots Wilts 83 E7
Manningford Bohune Wilts 83 E7
Manningford Bruce Wilts 83 E7
Manningham W Yorks 292 D5
Manning's Common Devon 38 D2
Mannings Heath W Sussex 69 F6
Mannington Dorset 42 E4
Manningtree Essex 142 A3
Mannofield Aberd C 429 B6
Manor Bourne Devon 11 F5
Manor Estate S Yorks 269 B7
Manor Park Bucks 135 E7
Manor Park Ches 243 A6
Manor Park Halton 265 C5
Manor Park London 112 E3
Manor Park Notts 225 B6
Manor Park Slough 110 F1
Manor Park S Yorks 269 B7
Manor Parsley Cornw'l 6 F5
Manorbier = Maenorbŷr Pembs 117 E7
Manorbier Newton Pembs 117 E6
Manordeifi Pembs 144 D4
Manordeilo Carms 124 B2
Manselfield Swan 97 E6
Mansell Gamage Heref'd 151 D5
Mansell Lucy Heref'd 151 C6
Manselton Swan 97 C8
Mansergh Cumb 315 D6
Mansewood Glasg C 392 F3
Mansfield E Ayrs 368 E4
Mansfield Notts 247 B8
Mansfield Woodhouse Notts 247 B8
Manson Green Norfolk 208 C4
Mansriggs Cumb 313 D6
Manston Dorset 41 C6
Manston Kent 95 C7
Manston W Yorks 294 C1
Manswood Dorset 42 E2
Manthorpe Lincs 227 E8
Mantles Green Bucks 109 C9
Manton Notts 270 E4
Manton Rutl'd 202 C3
Manton Wilts 83 C8
Manuden Essex 139 C5
Manwood Green Essex 139 E6
Manx Electric Railway I/Man 336 B4
Maperton Som'set 40 A3
Maple Cross Herts 110 D2
Maple End Essex 162 E4
Maplebeck Notts 248 B5
Mapledurham Oxon 86 A3
Mapledurwell Hants 66 A3
Maplehurst W Sussex 48 B3
Maplescombe Kent 91 D5
Mapleton Derby 246 E1
Mapleton Kent 70 B4
Mapperley Nott'ham 248 F2
Mapperley Derby 247 F6
Mapperley Park Nott'ham 248 F2
Mapperton Dorset 24 A5
Mapperton Dorset 27 A5
Mappleborough Green Warwick 176 E4
Mappleton ER Yorks 298 B3
Mapplewell S Yorks 281 C8
Mappowder Dorset 40 E4
Mar Lodge Aberds 427 C5
Maraig W Isles 449 B5
Marazanvose Cornw'l 7 E7
Marazion Cornw'l 3 D7
Marbhig W Isles 451 F7
Marbury Ches 242 E4
March Cambs 205 D7
March S Lanarks 370 E4
Marcham Oxon 107 C6
Marchamley Shrops 220 C1
Marchamley Wood Shrops 220 B1
Marchington Staffs 222 B4
Marchington Woodlands Staffs 222 C4
Marchwiel Wrex 241 E8
Marchwood Hants 44 D2
Marcle Hill Heref'd 129 A6
Marcross V/Glam 77 C5
Marden Heref'd 151 C8
Marden Kent 72 C1
Marden Tyne/Wear 353 B6
Marden Wilts 83 E6
Marden Ash Essex 113 B6
Marden Beech Kent 72 C1
Marden Thorn Kent 72 C2
Marden's Hill E Sussex 70 E5
Mardleybury Herts 137 D9
Mardon Northum 387 E8
Mardu Shrops 172 B3
Mardy Monmouths 127 D7
Marefield Bucks 109 E6
Marefield Leics 201 B8
Mareham Gate Lincs 251 C8
Mareham le Fen Lincs 251 B8
Mareham on the Hill Lincs 274 F2
Marehay Derby 247 E5
Marehill W Sussex 48 C1
Maresfield E Sussex 50 B2
Marfleet Kingston/Hull 298 E1
Marford Wrex 241 C8
Margam Neath P Talb 98 E2
Margaret Marsh Dorset 41 C6
Margaret Roding Essex 139 E7
Margaretta Norfolk 230 E3
Margaretting Essex 113 B8
Margaretting Tye Essex 113 B8
Margate Kent 95 B7
Margery Surrey 69 A7
Margnaheglish N Ayrs 405 C6
Margreig Dumf/Gal 402 B2
Margrove Park Redcar/Clevel'd 333 C8
Marham Norfolk 207 B5
Marhamchurch Cornw'l 32 F4
Marholm Peterbro 204 C1
Marian Denbs 262 D3
Marian Cwm Denbs 262 D3
Marian Ffrith Denbs 262 D3
Marianglas Angl 259 C7
Mariansleigh Devon 35 B7
Marian-y-de Gwyn 213 B7
Marian-y-mor Gwyn 213 B7
Marine Town Kent 93 B5
Marionburgh Aberds 428 B4
Marishader H'land 430 B4
Marjoriebanks Dumf/Gal 359 F5
Mark Dumf/Gal 400 D3
Mark Dumf/Gal 401 C7
Mark S Ayrs 400 B2
Mark Som'set 59 B7
Mark Causeway Som'set 59 B7
Mark Cross E Sussex 50 D2
Mark Cross E Sussex 71 E6
Mark Hall North Essex 139 E5
Mark Hall South Essex 139 E5
Markbeech Kent 70 C4
Markby Lincs 275 D6
Markeaton Derby C 223 A8
Market Bosworth Leics 200 C2
Market Deeping Lincs 204 A1
Market Drayton Shrops 220 B3
Market End Warwick 199 F7
Market Harborough Leics 201 F8
Market Lavington Wilts 82 F5
Market Overton Rutl'd 226 E4
Market Rasen Lincs 273 B7
Market Rasen Racecourse Lincs 273 B7
Market Stainton Lincs 274 D1
Market Warsop Notts 270 F3
Market Weighton ER Yorks 296 B4
Market Weston Suffolk 186 C4
Markethill Perth/Kinr 420 D2
Markfield Leics 200 A3
Markham Caerph 100 B3
Markham Moor Notts 271 E6
Markinch Fife 411 B7
Markington N Yorks 306 C2
Markland Hill Gtr Man 278 C2
Marks Gate London 112 D4
Marks Tey Essex 141 C7
Marksbury Bath/NE Som'set 81 D5
Markyate Herts 136 D5
Marl Bank Worcs 153 D5
Marland Gtr Man 279 B6
Marlas Heref'd 128 B2
Marlborough Wilts 83 C8
Marlbrook Heref'd 151 B8
Marlbrook Worcs 176 D2
Marlcliff Warwick 154 B4
Marldon Devon 15 C5
Marle Green E Sussex 50 C4
Marle Hill Glos 130 C4
Marlesford Suffolk 166 A4
Marley Kent 74 A3
Marley Kent 75 A6
Marley Green Ches 242 E4
Marley Hill Tyne/Wear 352 E3
Marlingford Norfolk 209 B6
Marloes Pembs 116 C1
Marlow Bucks 109 E7
Marlow Heref'd 173 C6
Marlow Bottom Bucks 109 E6
Marlpit Hill Kent 70 B3
Marlpits E Sussex 51 D7
Marlpits E Sussex 70 F4
Marlpool Derby 247 E6
Marnhull Dorset 41 C5
Marnoch Aberds 436 C2
Marnock N Lanarks 393 E6
Marple Gtr Man 267 B6
Marple Bridge Gtr Man 267 B6
Marpleridge Gtr Man 267 B6
Marr S Yorks 282 C4
Marrel H'land 441 B7
Marrick N Yorks 317 A7
Marridge Hill Wilts 84 B2
Marrister Shetl'd 457 G5
Marros Carms 121 F8
Marsden Tyne/Wear 353 D6
Marsden W Yorks 280 B2
Marsden Hall Lancs 291 C6
Marsden Height Lancs 291 C6
Marsett N Yorks 316 C4
Marsh Bucks 135 F7
Marsh Devon 38 D3
Marsh W Yorks 280 A4
Marsh W Yorks 292 C2
Marsh W Yorks 293 E5
Marsh Baldon Oxon 107 C8
Marsh Benham W Berks 85 C5
Marsh End Worcs 153 E6
Marsh Gibbon Bucks 134 C3
Marsh Green Ches 264 D5
Marsh Green Devon 22 B2
Marsh Green Gtr Man 277 C8
Marsh Green Kent 70 C3
Marsh Green Staffs 244 C3
Marsh Green Telford 220 F2
Marsh Lane Derby 269 D8
Marsh Lane Glos 129 F5
Marsh Leys Beds 159 C8
Marsh Street Som'set 57 C6
Marshall's Cross Mersey 264 A5
Marshall's Elm Som'set 60 E1
Marshall's Heath Herts 137 E7
Marshalswick Herts 137 F7
Marsham Norfolk 233 D8
Marshaw Lancs 302 E3
Marshborough Kent 95 E6
Marshbrook Shrops 194 F4
Marshchapel Lincs 287 E6
Marshfield Newp 100 F5
Marshfield S Glos 81 B7
Marshgate Cornw'l 17 B8
Marshland St. James Norfolk 206 B1
Marshside Kent 94 C4
Marshside Mersey 276 A4
Marshwood Dorset 24 A2
Marske N Yorks 330 F4
Marske-by-the-Sea Redcar/Clevel'd 333 B7
Marsland Green Gtr Man 278 E2
Marston Ches 265 D8
Marston Heref'd 150 A5
Marston Lincs 249 F8
Marston Oxon 134 F1
Marston Staffs 221 F6
Marston Staffs 221 C8
Marston Warwick 199 E5
Marston Wilts 82 E4
Marston Bigot Som'set 61 C7
Marston Doles Warwick 156 A4
Marston Green W Midlands 177 A6
Marston Hill Glos 105 C7
Marston Jabbett Warwick 199 F8
Marston Junction Warwick 199 F8
Marston Magna Som'set 40 B1
Marston Meysey Wilts 105 C7
Marston Montgomery Derby 222 A4
Marston Moretaine Beds 159 D7
Marston on Dove Derby 223 C6
Marston St. Lawrence Northants 157 D5
Marston Trussell Northants 180 A1
Marstow Heref'd 128 D5
Marsworth Bucks 136 E2
Marten Wilts 84 D2
Marthall Ches 266 D3
Martham Norfolk 235 E6
Marthwaite Cumb 315 B6
Martin Hants 42 C4
Martin Kent 75 B6
Martin Lincs 274 F1
Martin Lincs 251 B5
Martin Drove End Hants 42 B4
Martin Hussingtree Worcs 153 A7
Martin Mill Kent 75 B6
Martindale Cumb 327 C5
Martinhoe Devon 55 B8
Martinscroft Warrington 265 B7
Martinslade Wilts 82 D4
Martinstown Dorset 25 C7
Martlesham Suffolk 166 C3
Martlesham Heath Suffolk 166 C3
Martletwy Pembs 117 B6
Martley Worcs 153 A5
Martock Som'set 39 C7
Marton Ches 266 F4
Marton Cumb 313 E5
Marton ER Yorks 298 C2
Marton Lincs 272 C1
Marton Middlesbro 332 C5
Marton N Yorks 306 C5
Marton N Yorks 321 D5
Marton Shrops 194 C1
Marton Shrops 219 D5
Marton Warwick 178 E3
Marton Grove Middlesbro 332 C4
Marton Moss Side Blackp'l 288 D3
Marton-in-the-Forest N Yorks 307 B9
Marton-le Moor N Yorks 306 A4
Martyr Worthy Hants 65 E7
Martyr's Green Surrey 88 E3
Marus Bridge Gtr Man 277 D8
Marwell Zoo, Bishop's Waltham Hants 45 B5
Marwick Orkney 452 A3
Marwood Devon 55 D5
Mary Arden's House, Wilmcote Warwick 155 A6
Mary Rose Portsm'th 45 F7
Mary Tavy Devon 19 E7
Marybank H'land 433 C6
Marybank H'land 440 F4
Maryburgh H'land 433 C7
Maryfield Aberds 428 C2
Maryfield Cornw'l 10 D4
Maryhill Glasg C 392 E3
Marykirk Aberds 421 A6
Maryland Monmouths 102 A2
Marylebone Gtr Man 277 C8
Marylebone London 111 F7
Marypark Moray 435 E6
Maryport Cumb 337 D3
Maryport Dumf/Gal 400 F3
Marystow Devon 19 D5
Maryton Angus 421 B6
Maryton Angus 420 B3
Marywell Aberds 429 C6
Marywell Aberds 428 C2
Marywell Angus 421 C6
Masbrough S Yorks 282 F2
Masham N Yorks 318 D3
Mashbury Essex 140 E2
Mason Tyne/Wear 352 B3
Masongill N Yorks 315 E6
Masonhill S Ayrs 367 C7
Mastin Moor Derby 269 D9
Mastrick Aberd C 429 B5
Matchborough Worcs 176 E4
Matching Essex 139 E6
Matching Green Essex 139 E6
Matching Tye Essex 139 E6
Matfen Northum 351 B7
Matfield Kent 71 C8
Mathern Monmouths 102 D2
Mathon Heref'd 152 C4
Mathrafal Powys 193 A6
Mathry Pembs 119 C5
Matlaske Norfolk 233 B8
Matlock Derby 246 B4
Matlock Bank Derby 246 B3
Matlock Bath Derby 246 C3
Matlock Bridge Derby 246 C3
Matlock Dale Derby 246 C3
Matlock Moor Derby 246 B4
Matravers Dorset 24 B5
Matshead Lancs 289 B7
Matson Glos 130 D2
Matterdale End Cumb 326 B4
Mattersey Notts 271 B5
Mattersey Thorpe Notts 271 A5
Matthewsgreen Wokingham 87 C6
Mattingley Hants 86 E4
Mattishall Norfolk 208 A4
Mattishall Burgh Norfolk 208 A5
Mauchline E Ayrs 368 B2
Maud Aberds 437 D6
Maudlin Cornw'l 8 C4
Maudlin W Sussex 47 E5
Maugersbury Glos 132 B3
Maughold I/Man 336 B4
Mauld H'land 433 E6
Maulden Beds 159 E9
Maulds Meaburn Cumb 328 C2
Maunby N Yorks 319 C6
Maund Bryan Heref'd 151 B9
Maundown Som'set 57 F7
Mautby Norfolk 211 A5
Mavesyn Ridware Staffs 222 E3
Mavis Enderby Lincs 252 A3
Maviston H'land 434 C4
Maw Green Ches 243 C7
Mawbray Cumb 337 B4
Mawdesley Lancs 277 B6
Mawdlam Bridg 98 F3
Mawgan Cornw'l 4 F2
Mawgan Porth Cornw'l 7 B7
Mawla Cornw'l 4 A2
Mawnan Cornw'l 4 E3
Mawnan Smith Cornw'l 4 E3
Mawsley Northants 180 C4
Mawthorpe Lincs 275 E6
Maxey Peterbro 203 B8
Maxstoke Warwick 199 F5

Maxted Street Kent 74 C2
Maxton Scot Borders 374 A2
Maxton Kent 75 C6
Maxwellheugh Scot Borders 374 A4
Maxwelltown Dumf/Gal 402 B3
Maxworthy Cornw'l 18 B2
May Bank Staffs 244 E3
May Hill Monmouths 128 E4
Mayals Swan 97 D7
Maybole S Ayrs 367 F6
Maybury Surrey 88 E2
Maybush S'thampton 44 D2
Mayes Green Surrey 68 D4
Mayeston Pembs 117 D6
Mayfair London 111 F7
Mayfield E Sussex 71 F6
Mayfield Midloth 396 F4
Mayfield N Ayrs 378 D5
Mayfield Northum 352 A4
Mayfield Staffs 245 E9
Mayfield W Loth 394 E3
Mayford Surrey 88 E1
Mayhill Swan 97 D7
Mayland Essex 115 B5
Maylandsea Essex 115 B5
Maynard's Green E Sussex 50 C4
Mayne Ho. Moray 435 B7
Mayon Cornw'l 2 E3
Maypole Kent 94 D3
Maypole Kent 90 B5
Maypole London 90 D4
Maypole Monmouths 128 D3
Maypole W Midlands 176 C4
Maypole Green Essex 141 C8
Maypole Green Norfolk 210 D4
Maypole Green Suffolk 188 E3
Maypole Green Suffolk 164 A3
May's Green N Som'set 79 D7
Mays Green Oxon 86 A4
Mayshill S Glos 103 F5
Maythorn S Yorks 281 C5
Maywick Shetl'd 455 D2
Mead Devon 14 A3
Mead Devon 32 C4
Mead End Hants 28 A5
Mead End Hants 45 D8
Mead End Wilts 42 B3
Mead Vale Surrey 69 B7
Meadgate Bath/NE Som'set 81 E5
Meadle Bucks 109 A6
Meadow Derby 268 E2
Meadow Green Heref'd 152 A4
Meadow Head S Yorks 269 C6
Meadowbank Ches 265 F7
Meadowfield Durham 343 D8
Meadowfoot N Ayrs 378 C4
Meadowmill E Loth 397 D5
Meadows Nott'ham 225 A6
Meadowtown Shrops 194 C2
Meads E Sussex 52 F4
Meadside Oxon 107 D8
Meadwell Devon 19 D5
Meal Bank Cumb 314 A4
Mealabost W Isles 451 D7
Mealabost Bhuirgh W Isles 451 B7
Mealasta W Isles 450 E2
Mealrigg Cumb 337 B8
Mealsgate Cumb 338 C3
Mean Ham Glos 130 D2
Meanwood W Yorks 293 C7
Mearbeck N Yorks 303 C8
Meare Som'set 59 C9
Meare Green Som'set 38 B3
Meare Green Som'set 59 F6
Mearns E Renf 380 A2
Mears Ashby Northants 180 E4
Measborough Dike S Yorks 282 C1
Measham Leics 199 A7
Meath Green Surrey 69 C7
Meathop Cumb 314 D3
Meaux ER Yorks 297 C8
Meavy Devon 11 B6
Medbourne Leics 202 E1
Medburn Northum 352 B1
Meddon Devon 33 C5
Meden Vale Notts 270 F3
Medlam Lincs 252 C2
Medlar Lancs 288 C5
Medlock Vale Gtr Man 279 E7
Medlyn Cornw'l 4 D2
Medmenham Bucks 109 F6
Medomsley Durham 352 F1
Medstead Hants 66 D3
Meer Common Heref'd 150 B5
Meer End W Midlands 177 D7
Meerbrook Staffs 245 B5
Meers Bank Lincs 275 B6
Meers Bridge Lincs 275 B6
Meersbrook S Yorks 269 C6
Meesden Herts 138 A4
Meeth Devon 34 E3
Meethe Devon 35 B6
Meeting Green Suffolk 163 A7
Meeting House Hill Norfolk 234 C3
Meggernie Castle Perth/Kinr 418 C3
Meggethead Scot Borders 371 C8
Meidrim Carms 122 C1
Meifod Powys 193 A7
Meigle Perth/Kinr 420 C2
Meikle Earnock S Lanarks 381 B6
Meikle Ferry H'land 440 E4
Meikle Forter Angus 420 A1
Meikle Gluich H'land 440 E3
Meikle Obney Perth/Kinr 419 D8
Meikle Pinkerton E Loth 398 C4
Meikle Strath Aberds 428 E3
Meikle Tarty Aberds 437 F6
Meikle Wartle Aberds 436 E4
Meikleour Perth/Kinr 420 D1
Meinciau Carms 123 E5
Meir Stoke 244 F4
Meir Heath Staffs 244 F4
Melbourn Cambs 161 D7
Melbourne Derby 224 C2
Melbourne ER Yorks 296 B1
Melbourne S Lanarks 383 D6
Melbury Abbas Dorset 41 B7
Melbury Bubb Dorset 40 E1
Melbury Osmond Dorset 40 E1
Melbury Sampford Dorset 40 E1
Melby Shetl'd 457 H1
Melchbourne Beds 181 E8
Melcombe Som'set 59 E5
Melcombe Bingham Dorset 41 F5
Melcombe Regis Dorset 25 D8
Meldon Devon 19 B8
Meldon Northum 364 F4
Meldreth Cambs 161 C7
Meldrum Ho. Aberds 437 F5
Meledor Cornw'l 8 E1
Melfort Arg/Bute 416 F3
Melgarve H'land 425 C6
Meliden = Gallt Melyd Denbs 262 C3
Melin Meredydd Denbs 240 C3
Melinbyrhedyn Powys 191 D7
Melincourt Neath P Talb 98 B3
Melincryddan Rh Cyn Taff 98 C1
Melin-y-coed Conwy 238 B4
Melin-y-ddôl Powys 193 B5
Melin-y-Grogue Shrops 172 C2
Melin-y-wig Denbs 239 E8
Melkinthorpe Cumb 327 A8
Melkridge Northum 349 D8
Melksham Wilts 82 D3
Melksham Forest Wilts 82 D3
Mell Green W Berks 85 A6
Mellangaun H'land 438 E2
Melldalloch Arg/Bute 408 E2
Mellguards Cumb 339 B7
Melling Lancs 302 A3
Melling Mersey 276 D4
Melling Mount Mersey 276 D5
Mellis Suffolk 187 D7
Mellon Charles H'land 438 D2
Mellon Udrigle H'land 438 D2
Mellor Gtr Man 267 B6
Mellor Lancs 290 D2
Mellor Brook Lancs 290 D1
Mells Som'set 61 B6
Mells Green Som'set 61 B6
Melmerby Cumb 340 D3
Melmerby N Yorks 319 E5
Melmerby N Yorks 317 C7
Melon Green Suffolk 164 A1
Melplash Dorset 24 A4
Melrose Scot Borders 385 F7
Melsetter Orkney 452 E3
Melsonby N Yorks 331 E5
Meltham W Yorks 280 B3
Meltham Mills W Yorks 280 B4
Melton ER Yorks 297 E6
Melton Suffolk 166 B3
Melton Constable Norfolk 233 B5
Melton Mowbray Leics 226 E2
Melton Ross N Lincs 285 B8
Meltonby ER Yorks 308 E4
Melvaig H'land 438 E1
Melverley Shrops 218 E3
Melverley Green Shrops 218 E3
Melvich H'land 444 B2
Membland Devon 11 F7
Membury Devon 38 F3
Memsie Aberds 437 B6
Memus Angus 420 B4
Menabilly Cornw'l 9 E5
Menagissey Cornw'l 6 F5
Menai Bridge = Porthaethwy Angl 259 E8
Mendham Suffolk 188 B3
Mendlesham Suffolk 187 E7
Mendlesham Green Suffolk 187 F6
Menethorpe N Yorks 308 B4
Mengham Hants 31 A6
Menheniot Cornw'l 9 C8
Menherion Cornw'l 4 C2
Menithwood Worcs 174 E4
Menna Cornw'l 8 E1
Mennock Dumf/Gal 369 F8
Menston W Yorks 292 B5
Menstrie Clack 410 C3
Mentmore Bucks 136 D2
Meoble H'land 423 D7
Meole Brace Shrops 195 A5
Meols Mersey 263 A6
Meonstoke Hants 45 C7
Meopham Kent 91 C7
Meopham Green Kent 91 C7
Meopham Station Kent 91 C7
Mepal Cambs 184 B1
Meppershall Beds 160 E2
Merbach Heref'd 150 C4
Merchiston C/Edinb 396 D1
Mere Ches 266 C1
Mere Wilts 61 E8
Mere Brow Lancs 276 A5
Mere Green W Midlands 198 D3
Mere Green Worcs 176 F1
Mere Heath Ches 265 E8
Mereclough Lancs 291 D6
Merefield Northants 158 A2
Meresborough Medway 92 D3
Mereside Blackp'l 288 D3
Mereworth Kent 91 F8
Mergie Aberds 429 D4
Meriden W Midlands 177 B7
Merkadale H'land 430 E3
Merkland Dumf/Gal 402 B1
Merkland N Ayrs 405 C6
Merkland S Ayrs 354 D3
Merkland Lodge H'land 443 F6
Merley Poole 27 A7
Merlin Haven Glos 103 D6
Merlin's Bridge Pembs 116 B4
Merlins Cross Pembs 117 D5
Merridge Som'set 58 E4
Merrifield Devon 14 F4
Merrifield Devon 33 F5
Merrington Shrops 219 D6
Merrion Pembs 116 E4
Merriott Som'set 39 D6
Merriottsford Som'set 39 D6
Merritown Dorset 28 A2
Merrivale Devon 19 E7
Merrivale Heref'd 129 C6
Merrow Surrey 68 A2
Merry Field Corner Som'set 61 B5
Merry Field Hill Dorset 42 F3
Merry Hill Herts 110 D4
Merry Hill Staffs 197 D6
Merrybent Durham 331 D6
Merryhill Green Wokingham 87 B5
Merrylee E Renf 380 A3
Merrymeet Cornw'l 9 B8
Mersham Kent 73 D8
Merstham Surrey 69 A7
Merston W Sussex 47 F5
Merstone I/Wight 30 C2
Merther Cornw'l 5 B5
Merther Lane Cornw'l 5 B5
Merthyr Carms 122 C3
Merthyr Cynog Powys 148 E4
Merthyr Dyfan V/Glam 78 C2
Merthyr Mawr Bridg 76 A4
Merthyr Tudful = Merthyr Tydfil Merth Tyd 126 F2
Merthyr Tydfil = Merthyr Tudful Merth Tyd 126 F2
Merton Devon 34 D3
Merton London 89 C6
Merton Norfolk 208 D2
Merton Oxon 134 D2
Merton Park London 89 C6
Meshaw Devon 35 C8
Messing Essex 141 D6
Messingham N Lincs 284 D4
Mesty Croft W Midlands 197 D8
Metcombe Devon 22 B3
Metfield Suffolk 188 B3
Metfield Common Suffolk 188 C3
Metherell Cornw'l 10 B4
Metheringham Lincs 250 B4
Methersgate Suffolk 166 C3
Methil Fife 412 C1
Methley W Yorks 294 E1
Methley Junction W Yorks 294 E1
Methlick Aberds 437 E5
Methven Perth/Kinr 419 E8
Methwold Norfolk 207 E5
Methwold Hythe Norfolk 207 D5
Metroland, Gateshead Tyne/Wear 352 D3
Mettingham Suffolk 210 F3
Metton Norfolk 257 E7
Mevagissey Cornw'l 5 B8
Mewith Head N Yorks 303 B6
Mexborough S Yorks 282 D3
Mey H'land 445 A6
Meyllteyrn Gwyn 212 B4
Meysey Hampton Glos 105 C7
Miabhag W Isles 449 B4
Miabhag W Isles 449 C5
Miabhig W Isles 450 D3
Mial H'land 438 F1
Michaelchurch Heref'd 128 B4
Michaelchurch Escley Heref'd 150 F4
Michaelchurch-on-Arrow Powys 150 B2
Michaelston-le-pit V/Glam 78 B2
Michaelston-super-Ely Card 78 A2
Michaelston-y-Fedw Newp 100 F4
Michaelstow Cornw'l 17 E6
Michel Troy Monmouths 128 E3
Michelcombe Devon 14 B1
Micheldever Hants 65 D7
Micheldever Station Hants 65 C7
Michelmersh Hants 44 A2
Mickfield Suffolk 187 F7
Mickle Trafford Ches 264 F3
Micklebring S Yorks 282 E4
Mickleby N Yorks 334 D3
Micklefield Bucks 109 D7
Micklefield Green Herts 110 C3
Mickleham Surrey 69 A5
Micklehurst Gtr Man 279 D8
Mickleover Derby C 223 B8
Micklethwaite Cumb 347 F7
Micklethwaite W Yorks 292 B4
Mickleton Durham 330 B1
Mickleton Glos 155 D6
Mickletown W Yorks 294 E1
Mickley Derby 269 D6
Mickley N Yorks 318 E4
Mickley Green Suffolk 164 A1
Mickley Square Northum 351 D8
Mid Ardlaw Aberds 437 B6
Mid Auchinlek Invercl 391 D6
Mid Beltie Aberds 428 B3
Mid Calder W Loth 395 E6
Mid Cloch Forbie Aberds 437 C4
Mid Clyth H'land 445 E6
Mid Garrary Dumf/Gal 401 B7
Mid Lavant W Sussex 46 E5
Mid Letter Arg/Bute 408 B3
Mid Main H'land 433 E6
Mid Urchany H'land 434 D3
Mid Walls Shetl'd 457 H2
Mid Yell Shetl'd 456 D5
Midanbury S'thampton 44 D4
Midbea Orkney 454 B2
Middle Assendon Oxon 108 E4
Middle Aston Oxon 133 B8
Middle Balnald Perth/Kinr 419 B8
Middle Barton Oxon 133 B7
Middle Bickenhill W Midlands 177 B7
Middle Bockhampton Dorset 28 A3
Middle Bridge N Som'set 80 A1
Middle Burnham Som'set 59 A6
Middle Cairncake Aberds 437 D5
Middle Chinnock Som'set 39 D7
Middle Claydon Bucks 135 B5
Middle Drums Angus 421 B5
Middle Duntisbourne Glos 104 A4
Middle Green Suffolk 185 F7
Middle Green Slough 110 F1
Middle Green Som'set 37 C7
Middle Handley Derby 269 D8
Middle Harling Norfolk 186 A4
Middle Herrington Tyne/Wear 353 F6
Middle Hill Pembs 117 B5
Middle Kames Arg/Bute 408 D2
Middle Lambrook Som'set 39 C6
Middle Littleton Worcs 154 C4
Middle Maes-coed Heref'd 127 A7
Middle Marwood Devon 55 D5
Middle Mayfield Staffs 245 F8
Middle Mill Pembs 118 D4
Middle Quarter Kent 72 D4
Middle Rainton Tyne/Wear 344 C2
Middle Rasen Lincs 273 B6
Middle Rigg Perth/Kinr 411 B5
Middle Rocombe Devon 15 B6
Middle Stoford Som'set 37 B8
Middle Stoke Medway 92 A3
Middle Stoke W Midlands 178 C2
Middle Stoughton Som'set 59 B8
Middle Street Glos 103 B7
Middle Street Norfolk 257 E8
Middle Taphouse Cornw'l 9 C6
Middle Town I/Scilly 6 A3
Middle Town Warwick 176 F4
Middle Tysoe Warwick 156 D1
Middle Wallop Hants 64 D2
Middle Weald M/Keynes 158 E3
Middle Wick Glos 103 C6
Middle Winterslow Wilts 64 E1
Middle Woodford Wilts 63 D7
Middlebie Dumf/Gal 347 A6
Middlecave N Yorks 308 A4
Middlecliffe S Yorks 282 C2
Middlecott Devon 20 C4
Middlecroft Derby 269 E8
Middlefield Leics 200 E2
Middleforth Green Lancs 289 E7
Middleham N Yorks 317 C8
Middlehill Cornw'l 10 B1
Middlehill Wilts 81 C8
Middlehope Shrops 195 F5
Middlemarsh Dorset 40 E3
Middlemore Devon 11 A5
Middlemuir Aberds 437 C6
Middlemuir Aberds 437 D5
Middlemuir Aberds 437 F6
Middleport Stoke 244 E3
Middlesbrough Middlesbro 332 C5
Middlesceugh Cumb 339 C6
Middleshaw Cumb 314 C5
Middleshaw Dumf/Gal 346 A4
Middlesmoor N Yorks 317 F7
Middlestone Durham 343 E9
Middlestone Moor Durham 343 E8
Middlestown W Yorks 281 A7
Middlethorpe C/York 307 F8
Middleton Aberds 429 A5
Middleton Arg/Bute 414 C2
Middleton Cumb 315 C6
Middleton Derby 246 C3
Middleton Derby 246 B1
Middleton Essex 164 E2
Middleton Gtr Man 279 C6
Middleton Hants 65 C5
Middleton Heref'd 173 E8
Middleton Hartlep'l 345 E6
Middleton I/Wight 29 C6
Middleton Lancs 301 D7
Middleton Midloth 384 A4
Middleton Norfolk 231 E5
Middleton Northants 202 E2
Middleton Northum 364 E3
Middleton Northum 388 E4
Middleton N Yorks 291 B8
Middleton N Yorks 305 F6
Middleton N Yorks 321 D6
Middleton Perth/Kinr 420 C1
Middleton Perth/Kinr 419 F6
Middleton Perth/Kinr 411 B6
Middleton Shrops 173 C8
Middleton Shrops 218 C3
Middleton Suffolk 189 E6
Middleton Swan 96 E3
Middleton Warwick 198 D4
Middleton W Yorks 293 E8
Middleton Cheney Northants 157 D5
Middleton Green Staffs 222 A1
Middleton Hall Northum 376 B1
Middleton Junction Gtr Man 279 D6
Middleton Moor Suffolk 189 E6
Middleton of Rora Aberds 437 D7
Middleton on the Hill Heref'd 173 F8
Middleton One Row D'lington 332 D2
Middleton Place Cumb 312 B2
Middleton Quernhow N Yorks 319 E5
Middleton Railway, Hunslet W Yorks 293 D8
Middleton St. George D'lington 332 D2
Middleton Scriven Shrops 196 F2
Middleton Stoney Oxon 134 C1
Middleton Tyas N Yorks 331 E6
Middleton-in-Teesdale Durham 329 A9
Middleton-on-Leven N Yorks 332 E4
Middleton-on-Sea W Sussex 47 G7
Middleton-on-the-Wolds ER Yorks 309 F7
Middletown Cumb 324 E4
Middletown N Som'set 79 B8
Middletown Powys 194 A2
Middlewich Ches 243 A7
Middlewood Ches 267 C5
Middlewood Cornw'l 18 E2
Middlewood Heref'd 150 D3
Middlewood S Yorks 269 A6
Middlewood Green Suffolk 187 F6
Middleyard Glos 103 B8
Middlezoy Som'set 59 E7
Midridge Durham 331 A7
Midfield H'land 443 B7
Midford Bath/NE Som'set 81 D7
Midge Hall Lancs 289 F7
Midgehole W Yorks 292 E1
Midgeholme Cumb 349 E6
Midgham W Berks 85 C8
Midgham Green W Berks 85 C8
Midgley W Yorks 281 B7
Midgley W Yorks 292 E2
Mid-Hants Railway (Watercress Line), New Alresford Hants 66 E1
Midhopestones S Yorks 281 E6
Midhurst W Sussex 47 B5
Midland Orkney 452 C4
Midlem Scot Borders 373 B7
Midmar Aberds 428 B3
Midmuir Arg/Bute 416 E4
Midney Som'set 60 F1
Midpark Arg/Bute 405 A6
Midplaugh Aberds 436 D2
Midsomer Norton Bath/NE Som'set 81 F5
Midton Invercl 390 C4
Midtown H'land 438 E2
Midtown H'land 443 B7
Midtown of Buchromb Moray 435 D8
Midtown of Glass Aberds 436 D1
Midville Lincs 252 C3
Midway Ches 267 C5
Miekle Toux Aberds 436 C2
Migdale H'land 440 D3
Migdale Invercl 391 D7
Migvie Aberds 428 B1
Milber Devon 15 A5
Milborne Port Wilts 40 C3
Milborne St. Andrew Dorset 26 A3
Milborne Wick Som'set 40 B3
Milbourne Northum 352 A1
Milbourne Wilts 104 E3
Milburn Aberds 436 D2
Milburn Aberds 436 E3
Milburn Cumb 340 F4
Milbury Heath S Glos 103 D5
Milby Cambs 204 E3
Milby N Yorks 306 B5
Milcombe Oxon 156 F3
Milden Suffolk 164 C4
Mildenhall Suffolk 185 D7
Mildenhall Wilts 84 C1
Mile Cross Norfolk 209 A8
Mile Elm Wilts 82 C4
Mile End Cambs 184 B5
Mile End Devon 14 A4
Mile End Essex 141 B8
Mile End Glos 129 E5
Mile End London 112 F2
Mile End Suffolk 164 B1
Mile Oak Brighton/Hove 48 E4
Mile Oak Kent 71 C8
Mile Town Kent 93 B5
Milebrook Powys 172 D4
Milebush Kent 72 B2
Mileham Norfolk 232 E3
Miles Cross Dorset 24 B3
Miles Green Staffs 244 E2
Mile's Green W Berks 85 C7
Miles Hope Heref'd 174 F1
Miles Platting Gtr Man 279 E6
Milesmark Fife 411 D5
Milestones, Basingstoke Hants 66 A2
Milfield Northum 387 F8
Milford Derby 247 E5
Milford Devon 32 B4
Milford Powys 193 E5
Milford Surrey 67 C8
Milford Staffs 222 D1
Milford Wilts 63 F8
Milford Haven = Aberdaugleddau Pembs 116 C4
Milford Heath Surrey 67 C8
Milford on Sea Hants 29 B5
Milking Nook Peterbro 204 B2
Milkwall Glos 129 F5
Milkwell Wilts 41 B8
Mill Bank W Yorks 292 F2
Mill Brow Gtr Man 267 B6
Mill Common Norfolk 210 C2
Mill Common Suffolk 189 B6
Mill Corner E Sussex 52 B1
Mill End Bucks 109 E5
Mill End Cambs 163 A6
Mill End Glos 131 E8
Mill End Herts 110 D2
Mill End Herts 138 A2
Mill End Worcs 153 E8
Mill End Green Essex 139 B8
Mill Farm Aberds 437 B5
Mill Green Cambs 162 C5
Mill Green Essex 113 B7
Mill Green Hants 85 D7
Mill Green Lincs 228 D4
Mill Green Norfolk 187 B7
Mill Green Shrops 220 C3
Mill Green Suffolk 188 F4
Mill Green Suffolk 164 D3
Mill Green Suffolk 164 A4
Mill Green Suffolk 187 F7
Mill Green W Midlands 198 C2
Mill Hall Dumf/Gal 401 E8
Mill Hill Blackb'n 290 E2
Mill Hill Cambs 160 B4
Mill Hill E Sussex 51 E6
Mill Hill Glos 102 B2
Mill Hill Glos 102 A4
Mill Hill Gtr Man 278 C3
Mill Hill Kent 75 A7
Mill Hill Lincs 253 A6
Mill Hill London 111 D6
Mill Lane Hants 67 A5
Mill of Brydock Aberds 436 C3
Mill of Chon Stirl 409 B7
Mill of Kingoodie Aberds 437 F5
Mill of Lynebain Aberds 436 E1
Mill of Muiresk Aberds 436 D3
Mill of Rango Orkney 452 B3
Mill of Sterin Aberds 427 C8
Mill of Uras Aberds 429 D5
Mill Park Arg/Bute 404 F3
Mill Place N Lincs 285 C6
Mill Shaw W Yorks 293 D7
Mill Side Cumb 314 D3
Mill Street Kent 91 E8
Mill Street Suffolk 164 E4
Mill Throop Bournem'th 28 A2
Milland W Sussex 67 F6
Millarston Renf 392 F1
Millbank Aberds 437 D8
Millbank H'land 445 B5
Millbank Kent 94 C4
Millbeck Cumb 326 A2
Millbounds Orkney 454 C3
Millbreck Aberds 437 D7
Millbridge Surrey 67 C7
Millbrook Beds 159 E8
Millbrook Cornw'l 10 E4
Millbrook Devon 23 A8
Millbrook Gtr Man 279 E8
Millbrook S'thampton 44 D2
Millburn S Ayrs 367 B8
Millcombe Devon 14 F4
Milldale Staffs 245 D8
Millden Lodge Angus 428 E2
Milldens Angus 421 B5
Millend Glos 128 F5
Millend Glos 103 C7
Millend Oxon 133 C5
Millennium Stadium Card 78 A3
Miller Fold Lancs 290 E4
Millerhill Midloth 396 E3
Miller's Dale Derby 268 E2
Millers Green Derby 246 D3
Miller's Green Essex 139 F7
Millersneuk E Dunb 393 D5
Millerston Glasg C 393 E5
Millfield Peterbro 204 C2
Millfield Tyne/Wear 353 E6
Millgate Lancs 279 A6
Millgate Norfolk 233 C8
Millgillhead Cumb 325 B6
Millhalf Heref'd 150 C3
Millhall E Renf 380 B3
Millhall Kent 92 E1
Millhayes Devon 38 F2
Millhayes Devon 36 E3
Millhayes Devon 37 D7
Millhead Lancs 302 A1
Millheugh S Lanarks 381 B7
Millholme Cumb 314 B5
Millhouse Arg/Bute 408 E2
Millhouse Cumb 339 D6
Millhouse Green S Yorks 281 D6
Millhousebridge Dumf/Gal 359 E6
Millhouses S Yorks 282 D2
Millhouses S Yorks 269 C6
Millikenpark Renf 391 F8
Millin Cross Pembs 117 B5
Millington ER Yorks 309 E5
Millington Green Derby 246 E3
Millmeece Staffs 221 B6
Millmoor Devon 37 D7
Millness Cumb 314 D4
Millom Cumb 312 D4
Millook Cornw'l 17 A8
Millow Beds 160 D4
Millpool Cornw'l 9 A5
Millport N Ayrs 378 B3
Millquarter Dumf/Gal 401 A8
Milltack Aberds 436 C4
Millthorpe Derby 269 D6
Millthorpe Lincs 228 B2
Millthrop Cumb 315 B7
Milltimber Aberd C 429 B5
Milltown Aberds 427 B7
Milltown Cornw'l 9 D5
Milltown Dumf/Gal 347 A8
Milltown Devon 55 D6
Milltown H'land 434 D4
Milltown of Aberdalgie Perth/Kinr 419 E8
Milltown of Auchindoun Moray 435 D8
Milltown of Craigston Aberds 436 C4
Milltown of Edinvillie Moray 435 D7
Milltown of Kildrummy Aberds 428 A1
Milltown of Rothiemay Moray 436 D2
Milltown of Towie Aberds 428 A1
Millwall London 90 A2
Millwey Rise Devon 23 A8
Milnathort Perth/Kinr 411 B6
Milngate Dumf/Gal 359 E5
Milngavie E Dunb 392 D3
Milnquarter Falk 393 C8
Milnrow Gtr Man 279 B7
Milnsbridge W Yorks 280 A4
Milnshaw Lancs 290 E4
Milnthorpe Cumb 314 D4
Milnthorpe W Yorks 281 A8
Milo Carms 123 D7
Milson Shrops 174 D2
Milstead Kent 92 E4
Milston Wilts 63 B8
Milthorpe Northants 157 C7
Milton Angus 420 C3
Milton Angus 428 D1
Milton Cambs 184 F2
Milton Glasg C 392 E3
Milton Cumb 314 D4
Milton Cumb 349 D5
Milton Derby 223 C8
Milton Dumf/Gal 400 D4
Milton Dumf/Gal 402 B2
Milton Dumf/Gal 357 F8
Milton Fife 420 E4
Milton H'land 431 D7
Milton H'land 433 C5
Milton H'land 433 D7
Milton H'land 433 E6
Milton H'land 440 F4
Milton H'land 434 D2
Milton H'land 445 C7
Milton Kent 91 B8
Milton Moray 427 A6
Milton Moray 436 B2
Milton N Som'set 79 D6
Milton Notts 271 E6
Milton Oxon 107 D6
Milton Oxon 156 E3
Milton Pembs 117 D6
Milton Perth/Kinr 410 A4
Milton Portsm'th 31 A5
Milton Stirl 409 B8
Milton Stoke 244 D4
Milton Som'set 39 B7
Milton S Yorks 282 D1
Milton W Dunb 391 D8
Milton Wilts 62 E2
Milton Abbas Dorset 41 F6
Milton Abbot Devon 19 E5
Milton Bridge Midloth 396 F1
Milton Bryan Beds 136 A3
Milton Clevedon Som'set 61 D5
Milton Coldwells Aberds 437 E6
Milton Combe Devon 11 B5
Milton Common Oxon 108 B3
Milton Damerel Devon 33 D7
Milton End Glos 105 B7
Milton End Glos 129 E8
Milton Ernest Beds 159 A8
Milton Green Ches 242 C2
Milton Green Devon 19 E5
Milton Heights Oxon 107 D6
Milton Hill Oxon 107 D6
Milton Keynes M/Keynes 159 E5
Milton Keynes Village M/Keynes 159 E5
Milton Libourne Wilts 83 D8
Milton Malsor Northants 158 A2
Milton Morenish Perth/Kinr 418 D4
Milton of Auchinhove Aberds 428 B2
Milton of Balgonie Fife 411 B8
Milton of Buchanan Stirl 409 C7
Milton of Campfield Aberds 428 B3

Milton of Campsie E Dunb 393 C5
Milton of Corsindae Aberds 428 B3
Milton of Cullerlie Aberds 428 B4
Milton of Cultoquhey Perth/Kinr 419 E6
Milton of Cushnie Aberds 428 A2
Milton of Dalcapon Perth/Kinr 419 B7
Milton of Drimmie Perth/Kinr 420 B1
Milton of Edradour Perth/Kinr 419 B7
Milton of Gollanfield H'land 434 C2
Milton of Lesmore Aberds 436 F1
Milton of Logie Aberds 428 B1
Milton of Machany Perth/Kinr 419 F7
Milton of Mathers Aberds 421 A7
Milton of Murtle Aberd C 429 B5
Milton of Noth Aberds 436 F2
Milton of Tullich Aberds 427 C8
Milton on Stour Dorset 61 F8
Milton Regis Kent 92 C4
Milton Street E Sussex 50 F3
Milton under Wychwood Oxon 132 D4
Miltonduff Moray 435 B6
Miltonhill Moray 435 B5
Miltonise Dumf/Gal 400 B3
Milverton Som'set 37 A7
Milverton Warwick 177 E9
Milwich Staffs 222 B1
Milwr Flints 263 E5
Mimbridge Surrey 88 D1
Minard Arg/Bute 408 C2
Minard Castle Arg/Bute 408 C2
Minchington Dorset 42 D2
Minchinhampton Glos 104 B2
Mindrum Northum 375 A6
Minehead Som'set 57 B6
Minera Wrex 241 D6
Miners Heath Ches 242 B2
Minesmere RSPB Nature Reserve Suffolk 189 E7
Minety Wilts 105 D5
Minety Lower Moor Wilts 104 D5
Minffordd Gwyn 214 A3
Minffordd Gwyn 259 E8
Mingarry Park H'land 423 F6
Mingoose Cornw'l 6 F5
Miningsby Lincs 252 B2
Minions Cornw'l 9 A8
Minishant S Ayrs 367 E6
Minllyn Gwyn 216 F2
Minnes Aberds 437 F6
Minngearraidh W Isles 446 A3
Minnigaff Dumf/Gal 401 C6
Minnonie Aberds 437 B4
Minnow End Essex 140 E3
Minnygap Dumf/Gal 358 C4
Minskip N Yorks 306 C4
Minson's Hill Devon 38 E2
Minstead Hants 43 D8
Minsted W Sussex 46 B5
Minster Kent 95 D6
Minster Kent 93 B6
Minster Lovell Oxon 132 E5
Minsterley Shrops 194 B3
Minsterworth Glos 130 D1
Minsthorpe W Yorks 282 B3
Minterne Magna Dorset 40 F3
Minterne Parva Dorset 40 F3
Minting Lincs 273 E8
Mintlaw Aberds 437 D7
Minto Scot Borders 373 C8
Minton Shrops 194 E4
Mintsfeet Cumb 314 B4
Minwear Pembs 117 B7
Minworth W Midlands 198 E4
Mirbister Orkney 452 A4
Mirehouse Cumb 324 C4
Mireland H'land 445 B7
Mirfield W Yorks 281 A5
Miserden Glos 130 F4
Misery Corner Norfolk 210 E1
Miskin Rh Cyn Taff 99 F7
Miskin Rh Cyn Taff 99 C7
Misselfore Wilts 42 B3
Misson Notts 283 F7
Misterton Leics 179 B6
Misterton Notts 284 F2
Misterton Som'set 39 E7
Misterton Soss Notts 284 E2
Mistley Essex 142 A3
Mistley Heath Essex 142 A3
Mitcham London 89 C7
Mitcheldean Glos 129 D7
Mitchell Cornw'l 7 E8
Mitcheltroy Common Monmouths 128 F3
Mitford Northum 365 E5
Mithian Cornw'l 7 E5
Mithian Downs Cornw'l 7 F5
Mitton Staffs 221 E7
Mitton Worcs 153 F8
Mixbury Oxon 157 F7
Mixenden W Yorks 292 E3
Moat Cumb 348 B2
Moats Tye Suffolk 165 A5
Mobberley Ches 266 D2
Mobberley Staffs 245 F6
Mobley Glos 103 C5
Mobwell Bucks 109 B7
Moccas Heref'd 150 D5
Mochdre Conwy 262 D6
Mochdre Powys 192 F5
Mochrum Dumf/Gal 401 E5
Mockbeggar Hants 43 E6
Mockbeggar Kent 72 B1
Mockbeggar Kent 74 C2
Mockbeggar Medway 92 B1
Mockerkin Cumb 325 B6
Moclett Orkney 454 B2
Modbury Devon 11 E9
Moddershall Staffs 221 A8
Mode Hill Ches 267 D5
Model Village Derby 270 E2
Model Village, Babbacombe Devon 15 B6
Modest Corner Kent 71 C6
Moel Sychbant Bridg 98 E3
Moel Tryfan Gwyn 237 C6
Moelfre Angl 259 B7
Moelfre Powys 217 C8
Moel-y-crio Flints 263 F5
Moffat Dumf/Gal 359 A5
Moffat Mills N Lanarks 393 F7
Mogador Surrey 69 A6
Moggerhanger Beds 160 C2
Mogworthy Devon 36 C2
Moira Leics 223 E8
Molash Kent 73 A7
Mol-chlach H'land 422 A4
Mold = Ir Wyddgrug Flints 241 B5
Moldgreen W Yorks 280 A5
Molehill Green Essex 139 C7
Molehill Green Essex 140 C3
Molescroft ER Yorks 297 B7
Molesden Northum 364 F4
Molesworth Cambs 182 C1
Molinnis Cornw'l 8 D3
Moll H'land 431 E5
Molland Devon 56 F3
Mollington Ches 264 E2
Mollington Oxon 156 C3
Mollinsburn N Lanarks 393 D6
Monachylemore Stirl 418 F2
Monar Lodge H'land 432 D4
Monaughty Powys 172 E2
Monboddo House Aberds 428 E4
Mondynes Aberds 429 E4
Monemore Stirl 418 D3
Monevechadan Arg/Bute 408 B4
Monewden Suffolk 166 A2
Moneyacres E Ayrs 379 B8
Moneydie Perth/Kinr 419 E8
Moneyrow Green Windsor 87 A7
Mongleath Cornw'l 4 D3
Moniaive Dumf/Gal 357 D7
Monifieth Angus 421 D4
Monikie Angus 421 D4
Monimail Fife 420 F2
Monington Pembs 144 D2
Monk Bretton S Yorks 282 C1
Monk End N Yorks 312 D4
Monk Fryston N Yorks 294 E4
Monk Hesleden Durham 345 D5
Monk Sherborne Hants 86 E2
Monk Soham Suffolk 188 E2
Monk Soham Green Suffolk 188 E2
Monk Street Essex 139 B8
Monken Hadley London 111 C6
Monkerton Devon 21 B9
Monkey Island Windsor 87 A8
Monkhide Heref'd 152 D2
Monkhill Cumb 347 E8
Monkhopton Shrops 195 E8
Monkland Heref'd 151 A7
Monkleigh Devon 34 B2
Monknash V/Glam 77 B5
Monkokehampton Devon 34 E4
Monkroyd Lancs 291 B7
Monk's Eleigh Suffolk 164 C4
Monk's Gate W Sussex 69 F6
Monks Heath Ches 266 E3
Monk's Hill Kent 72 C4
Monks Kirby Warwick 178 B4
Monks Risborough Bucks 109 B6
Monkscross Cornw'l 10 A3
Monkseaton Tyne/Wear 353 B5
Monkshill Aberds 437 D4
Monksilver Som'set 57 D8
Monkspath W Midlands 177 C5
Monksthorpe Lincs 252 A4
Monkston M/Keynes 159 E5
Monkswood Monmouths 101 B6
Monkton Devon 38 F1
Monkton Kent 95 C5
Monkton Pembs 117 D5
Monkton S Ayrs 367 B7
Monkton Tyne/Wear 353 D5
Monkton V/Glam 77 B5
Monkton Combe Bath/NE Som'set 81 D7
Monkton Deverill Wilts 62 D2
Monkton Farleigh Wilts 81 C8
Monkton Heathfield Som'set 58 F4
Monkton Up Wimborne Dorset 42 D3
Monkton Wyld Dorset 23 A8
Monkton Wyld Cross Dorset 23 A8
Monktonhall E Loth 396 D3
Monkwearmouth Tyne/Wear 353 E6
Monkwood Hants 66 E3
Monkwood Green Worcs 175 F6
Monmore Green W Midlands 197 D7
Monmouth Monmouths 128 E4
Monmouth Cap Monmouths 128 B1
Monnington on Wye Heref'd 150 D5
Monreith Dumf/Gal 401 E5
Monreith Mains Dumf/Gal 401 E5
Montacute Som'set 39 C7
Montacute House Som'set 39 C7
Montcliffe Gtr Man 278 B2
Montcoffer Ho. Aberds 436 B3
Montford Arg/Bute 390 F2
Montford Shrops 219 F5
Montford Bridge Shrops 219 E5
Montgarrie Aberds 428 A2
Montgomery = Trefaldwyn Powys 193 D8
Monton Gtr Man 278 E4
Montpelier Bristol 80 B3
Montrave Fife 412 B1
Montrose Angus 421 B7
Monxton Hants 64 C3
Monyash Derby 245 A9
Monymusk Aberds 428 A3
Monzie Perth/Kinr 419 E6
Monzie Castle Perth/Kinr 419 E6
Moodiesburn N Lanarks 393 D5
Moon's Moat Worcs 176 E4
Moonzie Fife 420 F3
Moor Allerton W Yorks 293 C8
Moor Crichel Dorset 42 E2
Moor Cross Devon 11 D8
Moor Edge W Yorks 292 C3
Moor End Beds 159 A8
Moor End Beds 136 C3
Moor End Bucks 109 D6
Moor End Cambs 161 C7
Moor End C/York 308 D2
Moor End Durham 344 C2
Moor End ER Yorks 296 C3
Moor End Lancs 288 B4
Moor End Northants 158 D3
Moor End N Yorks 295 C5
Moor End W Yorks 292 E3
Moor End W Yorks 294 A2
Moor Green Herts 138 B2
Moor Green Staffs 244 F5
Moor Green Wilts 82 C2
Moor Green W Midlands 176 B4
Moor Hall W Midlands 198 D3
Moor Head W Yorks 293 E6
Moor Monkton N Yorks 307 D7
Moor of Balvack Aberds 428 A3
Moor of Granary Moray 435 C5
Moor of Ravenstone Dumf/Gal 401 E5
Moor Park Heref'd 151 D7
Moor Row Cumb 324 D5
Moor Row Cumb 338 B3
Moor Row Durham 331 C5
Moor Side Lancs 289 D5
Moor Side Lincs 251 C8
Moor Side W Yorks 292 E5
Moor Side W Yorks 293 B6
Moor Street Medway 92 C3
Moor Top W Yorks 293 F5
Mooradale Shetl'd 457 F4
Mooray Wilts 62 E4
Moorbath Dorset 24 A3
Moorby Lincs 252 B1
Moorclose Cumb 337 F6
Moorclose Gtr Man 279 C6
Moordown Bournem'th 28 B1
Moore Halton 265 C6
Moorend Cumb 338 A5
Moorend Dumf/Gal 347 B7
Moorend Glos 103 B6
Moorend Glos 130 E3
Moorend Gtr Man 267 B6
Moorend S Glos 81 A5
Moorends S Yorks 283 A7
Moorfield Derby 267 A7
Moorgate Norfolk 233 C8
Moorgate S Yorks 269 A8
Moorgreen Hants 44 C4
Moorgreen Notts 247 E7
Moorhaigh Notts 247 B8
Moorhall Derby 269 E6
Moorhampton Heref'd 151 C5
Moorhead W Yorks 292 C4
Moorhey Gtr Man 279 D7
Moorhouse Cumb 347 F7
Moorhouse Cumb 347 E8
Moorhouse Notts 271 F7
Moorhouse S Yorks 282 B3
Moorhouses Lincs 251 C8
Moorland Beds 159 C8
Moorland Som'set 59 E6
Moorledge Bath/NE Som'set 80 D3
Moorlinch Som'set 59 D7
Moorsholm Redcar/Clevel'd 333 D8
Moorside Cumb 325 F6
Moorside Derby 246 C3
Moorside Dorset 41 C5
Moorside Durham 343 B5
Moorside Gtr Man 278 D4
Moorside Gtr Man 279 C8
Moorside W Yorks 293 E6
Moorside W Yorks 293 C6
Moorstock Kent 74 D2
Moorswater Cornw'l 9 C7
Moorthorpe W Yorks 282 B3
Moortown Devon 19 F7
Moortown Devon 34 B3
Moortown Hants 43 F6
Moortown I/Wight 29 D8
Moortown Lincs 285 E8
Moortown W Yorks 293 C7
Moortown W Yorks 293 C8
Mop End Bucks 109 C8
Morangie H'land 440 E4
Morar H'land 423 C6
Morayhill H'land 434 D2
Morborne Cambs 203 E8
Morchard Bishop Devon 35 E8
Morcombelake Dorset 24 B2
Morcott Rutl'd 202 C4
Morda Shrops 218 C2
Morden Dorset 27 A5
Morden London 89 C6
Morden Green Cambs 161 D5
Morden Park London 89 C6
Mordiford Heref'd 152 E1
Mordon Durham 331 A8
More Shrops 194 E2
Morebath Som'set 36 B4
Morebattle Scot Borders 374 C5
Morecambe Lancs 301 C7
Moredon Swindon 105 E7
Moredun C/Edinb 396 E2
Morefield H'land 439 D5
Morehall Kent 74 D4
Morelaggan Arg/Bute 409 B5
Moreleigh Devon 14 E3
Morenish Perth/Kinr 418 D3
Moresby Cumb 324 B4
Moresby Parks Cumb 324 C4
Morestead Hants 45 A5
Moreton Dorset 26 C3
Moreton Essex 139 F6
Moreton Mersey 263 A7
Moreton Oxon 107 B5
Moreton Oxon 108 B3
Moreton Staffs 221 E5
Moreton Staffs 223 C5
Moreton Corbet Shrops 219 D8
Moreton Jeffries Heref'd 152 C2
Moreton on Lugg Heref'd 151 C8
Moreton Pinkney Northants 157 C6
Moreton Say Shrops 220 B2
Moreton Valence Glos 130 F1
Moretonhampstead Devon 20 C5
Moreton-in-Marsh Glos 132 A3
Morfa Carms 96 C5
Morfa Carms 123 E7
Morfa Ceredig'n 145 B6
Morfa Gwyn 212 B3
Morfa Pembs 119 C5
Morfa Bach Carms 122 E3
Morfa Bychan Gwyn 214 A2
Morfa Dinlle Gwyn 236 C4
Morfa Glas Neath P Talb 98 A4
Morfa Nefyn Gwyn 236 F1
Morgan's Vale Wilts 43 B6
Morganstown Card 100 F2
Moriah Ceredig'n 168 C5
Mork Glos 102 A3
Morland Cumb 328 B2
Morley Ches 266 C3
Morley Derby 247 F5
Morley Durham 343 F6
Morley W Yorks 293 E7
Morley Green Ches 266 C3
Morley St. Botolph Norfolk 208 C5
Morley Smithy Derby 247 F5
Morleymoor Derby 247 F5
Mornick Cornw'l 10 A2
Morningside C/Edinb 396 D1
Morningside N Lanarks 381 A8
Morningthorpe Norfolk 209 E8
Morpeth Northum 365 E6
Morphie Aberds 421 A7
Morrey Staffs 222 E4
Morrillow Heath Staffs 222 A1
Morris Green Essex 140 A3
Morriston = Treforys Swan 97 C8
Morristown V/Glam 78 B3
Morston Norfolk 256 D3
Mortehoe Devon 54 B4
Morthen S Yorks 270 B1
Mortimer W Berks 86 D3
Mortimer West End Hants 86 D2
Mortimer's Cross Heref'd 173 F6
Mortlake London 89 A6
Mortomley S Yorks 281 E8
Morton Cumb 339 D7
Morton Cumb 348 F1
Morton Derby 247 B6
Morton I/Wight 30 C4
Morton Lincs 271 A8
Morton Lincs 228 D1
Morton Lincs 249 B8
Morton Norfolk 233 E7
Morton Notts 248 D5
Morton Shrops 218 D2
Morton S Glos 102 D4
Morton Bagot Warwick 176 F5
Morton Grange Notts 271 D5
Morton Mill Shrops 219 D8
Morton Morrell Warwick 155 A9
Morton Tinmouth Durham 331 B5
Morton-on-Swale N Yorks 319 B5
Morvah Cornw'l 2 C4
Morval Cornw'l 9 D8
Morven Lodge Aberds 427 B8
Morvich H'land 432 F1
Morvich H'land 440 C4
Morville Shrops 196 E2
Morwellham Devon 10 B4
Morwenstow Cornw'l 32 C4
Mosborough S Yorks 269 C8
Moscow E Ayrs 380 D1
Mosedale Cumb 339 E6
Moselden Height W Yorks 280 A2
Moseley W Midlands 197 D7
Moseley W Midlands 176 B4
Moseley Worcs 153 A6
Moseley Green Glos 129 F6
Moses Gate Gtr Man 278 C3
Mosley Common Gtr Man 278 D3
Mosquito Aircraft Museum, London Colney Herts 111 B5
Moss Arg/Bute 414 C2
Moss H'land 423 F6
Moss S Yorks 283 B5
Moss Wrex 241 D7
Moss Bank Halton 265 B5
Moss Bank Mersey 277 E7
Moss Edge Lancs 301 F7
Moss End Brackn'l 87 B7
Moss End Ches 265 D8
Moss Houses Ches 266 E4
Moss Lane Ches 267 E5
Moss Nook Gtr Man 266 B3
Moss Nook Mersey 277 F7
Moss of Barmuckity Moray 435 B7
Moss of Meft Moray 435 B7
Moss Pitt Staffs 221 D8
Moss Side Cumb 338 A2
Moss Side Gtr Man 279 E5
Moss Side Lancs 288 D4
Moss Side Lancs 289 F7
Moss Side Mersey 276 D4
Mossat Aberds 428 A1
Mossbank Shetl'd 457 F4
Mossbay Cumb 337 F5
Mossblown S Ayrs 367 C8
Mossbrow Gtr Man 266 B1
Mossburnford Scot Borders 374 D3
Mossdale Dumf/Gal 401 B8
Mossedge Cumb 348 C3
Mossend Midloth 396 F4
Mossend N Lanarks 393 F6
Mosser Cumb 325 B7
Mosser Mains Cumb 325 A7
Mosseygreen Telford 196 B2
Mossfield H'land 434 A1
Mossgate Staffs 221 A9
Mossgiel E Ayrs 368 B1
Mosside Angus 420 B4
Mossley Ches 244 B3
Mossley Gtr Man 279 D8
Mossley Staffs 222 E3
Mossley Brow Gtr Man 279 D8
Mossley Hill Mersey 264 B2
Mossneuk S Lanarks 380 B4
Mosspark Glasg C 392 F2
Moss-side H'land 434 C3
Moss-side Moray 436 C2
Mosstodloch Moray 435 C8
Mosston Angus 421 C5
Mosstown Aberds 437 B7
Mossy Lea Lancs 277 B7
Mosterton Dorset 39 E7
Moston Gtr Man 279 D6
Moston Shrops 219 C8
Moston Green Ches 244 B3
Mostyn Flints 263 C5
Mostyn Quay Flints 263 C5
Motcombe Dorset 41 A6
Mothecombe Devon 11 F8
Motherby Cumb 339 F8
Motherwell N Lanarks 381 A6
Motspur Park London 89 C6
Mottingham London 90 B3
Mottisfont Hants 44 A1
Mottisfont Abbey Garden Hants 64 F3
Mottistone I/Wight 29 D8
Mottram in Longdendale Gtr Man 279 E8
Mottram Rise Gtr Man 279 E8
Mottram St. Andrew Ches 266 D4
Mott's Green Essex 139 D6
Mott's Mill E Sussex 71 D5
Mouldsworth Ches 264 E5
Moulin Perth/Kinr 419 B7
Moulsecoomb Brighton/Hove 49 E6
Moulsford Oxon 107 F8
Moulsham Essex 113 A9
Moulsoe M/Keynes 159 D6
Moultavie H'land 433 A8
Moulton Ches 265 F8
Moulton Lincs 229 D6
Moulton Northants 180 E3
Moulton N Yorks 331 F6
Moulton Suffolk 185 F6
Moulton V/Glam 77 B8
Moulton Chapel Lincs 229 E5
Moulton Eaugate Lincs 229 E6
Moulton St. Mary Norfolk 210 B3
Moulton Seas End Lincs 229 C6
Moulzie Angus 427 E7
Mounie Castle Aberds 436 F4
Mount Cornw'l 9 B5
Mount H'land 434 D4
Mount Kent 74 C3
Mount W Yorks 280 A3
Mount Ambrose Cornw'l 4 B2
Mount Ararat Kent 75 C5
Mount Bures Essex 141 A7
Mount Canisp H'land 434 A2
Mount Charles Cornw'l 8 E3
Mount End Essex 112 B4
Mount Ephraim E Sussex 50 C2
Mount Farm M/Keynes 158 E5
Mount Florida Glasg C 392 F3
Mount Gould Plym'th 11 D5
Mount Hawke Cornw'l 6 F5
Mount Hill S Glos 81 B5
Mount Pleasant Brackn'l 87 B7
Mount Pleasant Ches 244 C2
Mount Pleasant Cornw'l 8 C3
Mount Pleasant Derby 223 E7
Mount Pleasant Derby 246 E4
Mount Pleasant Durham 344 E1
Mount Pleasant Devon 38 F1
Mount Pleasant E Sussex 49 C8
Mount Pleasant E Sussex 50 F2
Mount Pleasant Flints 263 E6
Mount Pleasant Hants 29 A6
Mount Pleasant Kent 95 C6
Mount Pleasant Merth Tyd 99 C8
Mount Pleasant Neath P Talb 98 C2
Mount Pleasant Norfolk 208 E3
Mount Pleasant Pembs 117 C6
Mount Pleasant Shrops 219 F6
Mount Pleasant Suffolk 163 C7
Mount Pleasant Stoke 244 F3
Mount Pleasant Stockton 332 B4
Mount Pleasant Tyne/Wear 352 D4
Mount Pleasant Tyne/Wear 353 D5
Mount Pleasant W Midlands 197 F6
Mount Pleasant W Yorks 293 F6
Mount Sion Wrex 241 D6
Mount Skippitt Oxon 133 D6
Mount Sorrel Wilts 42 B3
Mount Tabor W Yorks 292 E3
Mount Vernon Glasg C 393 F5
Mount Wise Plym'th 10 E5
Mountain Angl 258 C1
Mountain W Yorks 292 D3
Mountain Air Bl Gwent 126 F3
Mountain Ash = Aberpennar Rh Cyn Taf 99 C7
Mountain Cross Scot Borders 383 C7
Mountain Street Kent 73 A8
Mountbenger Scot Borders 372 B3
Mountblow W Dunb 392 D1
Mountcharles S Ayrs 367 D6
Mountfield E Sussex 51 B7
Mountgerald H'land 433 B7
Mountjoy Cornw'l 7 C8
Mountnessing Essex 113 C7
Mounton Monmouths 102 D2
Mountsolie Aberds 437 C6
Mountsorrel Leics 225 F6
Mountstuart Arg/Bute 378 A2
Mousehill Surrey 67 C8
Mousehold Heath Norfolk 209 A8
Mousehole Cornw'l 2 E5
Mouswald Dumf/Gal 346 B3
Mow Cop Ches 244 C3
Mowden D'lington 331 D7
Mowden Essex 140 F4
Mowhaugh Scot Borders 375 C6
Mowmacre Hill Leics C 200 B5
Mowshurst Kent 70 B4
Mowsley Leics 201 F6
Moxley W Midlands 197 D8
Moy Arg/Bute 404 D3
Moy H'land 425 D6
Moy H'land 434 E2
Moy Hall H'land 434 E2
Moy Ho. Moray 434 B5
Moy Lodge H'land 425 D6
Moylgrove Pembs 144 D2
Muasdale Arg/Bute 404 B2
Much Birch Heref'd 128 A4
Much Cowarne Heref'd 152 C2
Much Dewchurch Heref'd 128 A3
Much Hadham Herts 138 D4
Much Hoole Lancs 289 F6
Much Marcle Heref'd 129 A7
Much Wenlock Shrops 195 D8
Muchalls Aberds 429 C6
Muchelney Som'set 39 B6
Muchelney Ham Som'set 39 B6
Muchlarnick Cornw'l 9 D7
Muchrachd H'land 433 E4
Muckairn Arg/Bute 417 D4
Muckernich H'land 433 C7
Mucking Thurr'k 113 F8
Muckingford Thurr'k 91 A8
Muckle Breck Shetl'd 457 G5
Muckleford Dorset 25 B7
Mucklestone Staffs 220 A4
Muckleton Norfolk 255 E6
Muckleton Shrops 220 D1
Muckletown Aberds 436 F2
Muckley Shrops 196 D1
Muckley Green Staffs 198 B2
Muckton Lincs 274 C4
Muckwell Devon 13 E7
Mudale H'land 443 E7
Mudd Gtr Man 280 F1
Muddiford Devon 55 D6
Muddlebridge Devon 55 E5
Muddles Green E Sussex 50 D3
Mudeford Dorset 28 B3
Mudford Som'set 40 C1
Mudford Sock Som'set 39 C9
Mudgley Som'set 59 B8
Mugdock Stirl 392 C3
Mugeary H'land 430 E4
Mugginton Derby 246 F3
Muggintonlane End Derby 246 F3
Muggleswick Durham 342 B4
Muie H'land 440 C3
Muir Aberds 427 D5
Muir of Alford Aberds 428 A2
Muir of Fairburn H'land 433 C6
Muir of Fowlis Aberds 428 A2
Muir of Kinellar Aberds 429 A5
Muir of Miltonduff Moray 435 C6
Muir of Ord H'land 433 C7
Muir of Pert Angus 420 D4
Muirden Aberds 436 C4
Muirdrum Angus 421 D5
Muirend Glasg C 392 F3
Muirhead Angus 420 D3
Muirhead Glasg C 393 F5
Muirhead Fife 411 B7
Muirhead Fife 420 F4
Muirhead N Lanarks 393 E5
Muirhead S Ayrs 367 A6
Muirhouse C/Edinb 396 C1
Muirhouse N Lanarks 381 B7
Muirhouses Falk 411 D5
Muirkirk E Ayrs 369 B5
Muirmill Stirl 410 D2
Muirshearlich H'land 424 D3
Muirskie Aberds 429 C5
Muirtack Aberds 437 E6
Muirton Aberds 436 C4
Muirton H'land 434 B2
Muirton Perth/Kinr 420 E1
Muirton Perth/Kinr 410 A4
Muirton Mains H'land 433 C6
Muirton of Ardblair Perth/Kinr 420 C1
Muirton of Ballochy Angus 421 A6
Muiryfold Aberds 436 C4
Muker N Yorks 316 A4
Mulbarton Norfolk 209 C7
Mulben Moray 435 C8
Mulgrave Castle N Yorks 334 D3
Mulindry Arg/Bute 403 A3
Mulla Shetl'd 457 G4
Mullardoch House H'land 432 E4
Mullion Cornw'l 5 G1
Mullion Cove Cornw'l 5 G1
Mumby Lincs 275 E7
Mumps Gtr Man 279 C7
Muncaster Owl Trust World HQ Cumb 312 A2
Mundale Moray 434 C5
Munday Bois Kent 73 B5
Munderfield Row Heref'd 152 B3
Munderfield Stocks Heref'd 152 B3
Mundesley Norfolk 234 A3
Mundford Norfolk 207 E7
Mundham Norfolk 210 D2
Mundon Essex 114 B4
Mundurno Aberd C 429 A6
Munerigie H'land 424 B4
Muness Shetl'd 456 C6
Mungasdale H'land 438 D3
Mungrisdale Cumb 339 E6
Munlochy H'land 433 C8
Munsary Cottage H'land 445 D6
Munsley Heref'd 152 D3
Munslow Shrops 195 F6
Munstead Heath Surrey 68 C1
Munstone Heref'd 151 D8
Murch V/Glam 78 B3
Murchington Devon 20 C3
Murcot Worcs 154 D4
Murcott Oxon 134 D2
Murcott Wilts 104 D4
Murdishaw Wood Halton 265 C6
Murieston W Loth 395 F6
Murkle H'land 445 B5
Murlaggan H'land 424 C2
Murlaggan H'land 425 D5
Murra Orkney 452 C3
Murrayfield C/Edinb 396 D1
Murrayfield Stadium C/Edinb 396 D1
Murrays Motorcycle Museum I/Man 336 C3
Murrayshall Perth/Kinr 420 E1
Murraythwaite Dumf/Gal 346 B4
Murrell Green Hants 86 E4
Murrion Shetl'd 457 F2
Murrow Cambs 205 B6
Mursley Bucks 135 B7
Murston Kent 93 D5
Murthill Angus 420 B4
Murthly Perth/Kinr 419 D8
Murton Cumb 328 B4
Murton C/York 308 E2
Murton Durham 344 B3
Murton Swan 97 E6
Murton Tyne/Wear 353 B5
Musbury Devon 23 B7
Muscliff Bournem'th 28 A1
Muscoates N Yorks 320 D4
Muscott Northants 179 F7
Musdale Arg/Bute 416 E4
Museum of the Broads, Sutton Norfolk 234 D4
Musselburgh E Loth 396 D3
Musselburgh Racecourse E Loth 396 D3
Mustard Hyrn Norfolk 235 E5
Muston Leics 226 A3
Muston N Yorks 323 E5
Mustow Green Worcs 175 D7
Muswell Hill London 111 E7
Mutehill Dumf/Gal 401 E8
Mutford Suffolk 211 F5

Newhaven Derby 246 C1
Newhaven E Sussex 50 F1
Newhey Gtr Man 279 B7
Newhill Fife 420 F2
Newhill Perth/Kinr 411 B6
Newhill S Yorks 282 E2
Newhills Aberd C 429 B5
Newholm N Yorks 334 D4
Newhouse N Lanarks 393 F7
Newhouse Shetl'd 457 G4
Newick E Sussex 49 B8
Newingreen Kent 74 D2
Newington C/Edinb 396 D2
Newington Kent 95 C7
Newington Kent 74 D3
Newington Kent 92 D4
Newington Notts 283 F7
Newington Oxon 108 C2
Newington Shrops 173 B6
Newington Bagpath Glos 103 D8
Newland Cumb 313 E6
Newland ER Yorks 296 E3
Newland Glos 128 F5
Newland Kingston/Hull 297 D8
Newland N Yorks 295 F7
Newland Oxon 133 F6
Newland Som'set 56 D3
Newland Worcs 153 C5
Newland Green Kent 73 B5
Newlandrig Midloth 397 E6
Newlands Scot Borders 361 D7
Newlands Glasg C 392 F3
Newlands Cumb 326 B1
Newlands Cumb 339 D5
Newlands Derby 247 E6
Newlands Essex 114 F3
Newlands Heref'd 151 A7
Newlands H'land 434 D2
Newlands Moray 435 C8
Newlands Notts 248 B2
Newlands Northum 351 E8
Newland's Corner Surrey 68 B2
Newlands of Geise H'land 445 B4
Newlands of Tynet Moray 435 B8
Newlands Park Angl 258 C2
Newlandsmuir S Lanarks 380 B4
Newlay W Yorks 293 C6
Newliston C/Edinb 395 D8
Newlot Orkney 453 B6
Newlyn Cornw'l 2 E5
Newlyn East Cornw'l 7 D7
Newmachar Aberds 429 A5
Newmains N Lanarks 381 A8
Newman Street Som'set 61 C5
Newman's End Essex 139 E6
Newman's Green Suffolk 164 D2
Newmarket Glos 104 C1
Newmarket Suffolk 185 F5
Newmarket W Isles 451 D7
Newmarket Racecourse Suffolk 185 F5
Newmill Scot Borders 373 E6
Newmill Moray 436 C1
Newmill of Inshewan Angus 420 A4
Newmillerdam W Yorks 281 A8
Newmills H'land 434 B1
Newmills of Boyne Aberds 436 C2
Newmiln Perth/Kinr 420 D1
Newmilns E Ayrs 380 E2
Newmore H'land 434 A1
Newmore H'land 433 C7
Newney Green Essex 140 F2
Newnham Cambs 162 A1
Newnham Glos 129 E7
Newnham Hants 86 F4
Newnham Herts 160 E4
Newnham Kent 93 E6
Newnham Northants 157 A6
Newnham Warwick 177 F6
Newnham Bridge Worcs 174 E2
Newnham Murren Oxon 108 E2
Newpark Fife 421 F4
Newpool Staffs 244 C3
Newport Cornw'l 18 C3
Newport Dorset 26 A4
Newport Essex 162 F3
Newport ER Yorks 296 E4
Newport Glos 103 C5
Newport H'land 441 A8
Newport I/Wight 30 C2
Newport Norfolk 235 E7
Newport Newp 101 E6
Newport Som'set 38 B4
Newport Telford 220 E4
Newport = Trefdraeth Pembs 119 B9
Newport Museum & Art Gallery Newp 101 E6
Newport Pagnell M/Keynes 158 D5
Newport Sands Pembs 119 B9
Newport-on-Tay Fife 420 E4
Newpound Common W Sussex 68 F3
Newquay Cornw'l 7 C7
Newquay Airport Cornw'l 7 C8
Newsam Green W Yorks 294 D1
Newsbank Ches 244 A2
Newseat Aberds 437 D7
Newseat Aberds 436 E4
Newsells Herts 161 E7
Newsham Lancs 289 C7
Newsham Northum 365 F7
Newsham Northum 353 A5
Newsham N Yorks 330 E4
Newsham N Yorks 319 D6
Newsholme ER Yorks 295 E8
Newsholme Lancs 303 E8
Newsholme W Yorks 292 C2
Newsome W Yorks 280 B4
Newstead Scot Borders 385 F8
Newstead Notts 247 D8
Newstead Stoke 244 F3
Newstead W Yorks 282 B1
Newstead Abbey, Kirkby in Ashfield Notts 248 D1
Newstreet Lane Shrops 220 A2
Newthorpe Notts 247 E7
Newthorpe N Yorks 294 D3
Newthorpe Common Notts 247 E7
Newtoft Lincs 273 B5
Newton Arg/Bute 408 C3
Newton Beds 160 D4
Newton Bridg 76 A3
Newton Cambs 229 F8
Newton Cambs 162 C1
Newton Card 78 A4
Newton Ches 242 C3
Newton Ches 264 F3
Newton Ches 265 D5
Newton Cumb 300 A3
Newton Derby 247 C6
Newton Dumf/Gal 347 B7
Newton Dumf/Gal 359 C6
Newton Dorset 41 D5
Newton Gtr Man 279 E8
Newton Heref'd 151 B8
Newton Heref'd 127 A7
Newton H'land 434 B2
Newton H'land 434 D2
Newton H'land 442 E4
Newton H'land 445 D7
Newton Lancs 288 C3
Newton Lancs 315 F5
Newton Lancs 303 E5
Newton Lincs 227 A7
Newton Mersey 263 B6
Newton Moray 435 B6
Newton Norfolk 231 E8
Newton Northants 181 A5
Newton Notts 248 F4
Newton Northum 351 D7
Newton Northum 364 B2
Newton Perth/Kinr 419 D6
Newton Suffolk 164 D3
Newton Shetl'd 456 E3
Newton Shetl'd 455 C2
Newton S Glos 102 D4
Newton Som'set 58 D2
Newton S Lanarks 370 A3
Newton S Lanarks 393 F5
Newton Staffs 222 C2
Newton S Yorks 283 D5
Newton Swan 97 E7
Newton Warwick 179 C5
Newton Wilts 43 B7
Newton W Midlands 198 E1
Newton W Loth 395 C6
Newton W Yorks 294 E2
Newton Abbot Devon 15 A5
Newton Abbot Racecourse Devon 15 A5
Newton Arlosh Cumb 347 E5
Newton Aycliffe Durham 331 B7
Newton Bewley Hartlep'l 345 F5
Newton Blossomville M/Keynes 159 B6
Newton Bromswold Northants 181 E7
Newton Burgoland Leics 199 B8
Newton by Toft Lincs 273 B5
Newton Court Monmouths 128 E4
Newton Cross Pembs 119 D5
Newton Farm Heref'd 151 E7
Newton Ferrers Devon 11 F6
Newton Flotman Norfolk 209 D8
Newton Green Monmouths 102 D2
Newton Hall Durham 344 C1
Newton Hall Northum 351 C7
Newton Harcourt Leics 201 D6
Newton Heath Gtr Man 279 D6
Newton Hill W Yorks 293 F8
Newton Ho. Aberds 436 F3
Newton Ketton D'lington 331 B8
Newton Kyme N Yorks 294 A3
Newton Longville Bucks 135 A8
Newton Mearns E Renf 380 A2
Newton Morrell N Yorks 331 E6
Newton Mulgrave N Yorks 334 C2
Newton Noyes Pembs 116 C4
Newton of Ardtoe H'land 423 E6
Newton of Balcanquhal Perth/Kinr 411 A6
Newton of Balcormo Fife 412 B3
Newton of Falkland Fife 411 B7
Newton of Mountblairy Aberds 436 C3
Newton of Pitcairns Perth/Kinr 419 F8
Newton on Ayr S Ayrs 367 C6
Newton on the Hill Shrops 219 D6
Newton on Trent Lincs 271 E8
Newton Park Mersey 277 F8
Newton Peveril Dorset 27 A5
Newton Poppleford Devon 22 C3
Newton Purcell Oxon 134 A3
Newton Regis Warwick 199 B6
Newton Reigny Cumb 339 E8
Newton St. Boswells Scot Borders 373 A8
Newton St. Cyres Devon 21 A7
Newton St. Faith Norfolk 234 E1
Newton St. Loe Bath/NE Som'set 81 D6
Newton St. Petrock Devon 33 D8
Newton Solney Derby 223 C7
Newton Stacey Hants 65 C5
Newton Stewart Dumf/Gal 401 C6
Newton Toney Wilts 64 C1
Newton Tracey Devon 34 A3
Newton under Roseberry Redcar/Clevel'd 333 D6
Newton Underwood Northum 365 E5
Newton upon Derwent ER Yorks 308 F3
Newton Valence Hants 66 E4
Newton Wood Gtr Man 279 E7
Newtonairds Dumf/Gal 358 F1
Newtongrange Midloth 396 F3
Newtongrange Midloth 396 F3
Newtonhill Aberds 429 C6
Newtonhill H'land 433 D7
Newtonia Ches 243 A6
Newton-in-St. Martin Cornw'l 4 F2
Newton-le-Willows Mersey 277 E8
Newton-le-Willows N Yorks 318 C3
Newtonmill Angus 421 A6
Newtonmore H'land 426 C2
Newton-on-Ouse N Yorks 307 D7
Newton-on-Rawcliffe W Yorks 321 B7
Newton-on-the-Moor Northum 365 A5
Newton-with-Scales Lancs 289 D5
Newtown Arg/Bute 408 B3
Newtown Bl Gwent 126 F4
Newtown Bridg 99 F5
Newtown Bucks 110 B1
Newtown Cambs 182 D4
Newtown Cambs 182 E1
Newtown Caerph 100 D4
Newtown Ches 243 E5
Newtown Ches 264 D5
Newtown Ches 267 C5
Newtown Cumb 337 B4
Newtown Cumb 348 E1
Newtown Cumb 327 B7
Newtown Cumb 348 D4
Newtown Cornw'l 18 E2
Newtown Cornw'l 3 E7
Newtown Cornw'l 9 E5
Newtown Derby 267 C6
Newtown Dorset 39 F7
Newtown Devon 22 A3
Newtown Devon 35 A8
Newtown Glos 103 B5
Newtown Gtr Man 278 D4
Newtown Gtr Man 277 C8
Newtown Hants 43 B9
Newtown Hants 67 E6
Newtown Hants 85 D6
Newtown Hants 63 D8
Newtown Hants 45 C5
Newtown Hants 44 E4
Newtown Hants 45 D7
Newtown Heref'd 151 A7
Newtown Heref'd 152 D2
Newtown Heref'd 128 A4
Newtown H'land 425 B5
Newtown I/Man 336 D3
Newtown I/Wight 29 B8
Newtown Mersey 277 E6
Newtown Norfolk 211 B6
Newtown Northum 376 B2
Newtown Northum 376 A1
Newtown Oxon 108 F5
Newtown Poole 27 B7
Newtown Rh Cyn Taff 99 C8
Newtown Shrops 219 D5
Newtown Shrops 219 B6
Newtown Som'set 38 D3
Newtown Som'set 59 D5
Newtown Som'set 59 B6
Newtown Som'set 59 F8
Newtown S'thampton 44 D4
Newtown Staffs 197 C8
Newtown Staffs 245 B7
Newtown Warwick 199 F6
Newtown Wilts 84 D3
Newtown Wilts 62 F3
Newtown Worcs 153 A7
Newtown Worcs 153 A5
Newtown Worcs 175 F7
Newtown = Y Drenewydd Powys 193 E6
Newtown Common Hants 85 D6
Newtown Linford Leics 200 A4
Newtown Unthank Leics 200 C3
Newtyle Angus 420 C2
Newyears Green London 110 E3
Nextend Heref'd 150 A4
Neyland Pembs 117 D5
Niarbyl I/Man 336 D2
Nib Heath Shrops 219 E5
Nibley Glos 103 A5
Nibley S Glos 103 F5
Nibley Green Glos 103 C6
Nibon Shetl'd 457 F3
Nicholashayne Devon 37 C7
Nicholaston Swan 97 E5
Nidd N Yorks 306 C3
Niddrie C/Edinb 396 D3
Nigg Aberd C 429 B6
Nigg H'land 434 A3
Nigg Ferry H'land 434 B2
Nimble Nook Gtr Man 279 D7
Nimmer Som'set 38 D4
Nine Ashes Essex 113 B6
Nine Elms London 89 A7
Nine Elms Swindon 105 E7
Nine Mile Burn Scot Borders 383 A8
Nine Wells Pembs 118 E3
Ninebanks Northum 341 A6
Nineveh N Yorks 307 A7
Nineveh Worcs 174 F2
Ninewells Glos 129 E5
Ninfield E Sussex 51 D7
Ningwood I/Wight 29 C8
Ningwood Common I/Wight 29 C7
Ninnes Bridge Cornw'l 3 C6
Ninnis Cornw'l 4 B2
Nisbet Scot Borders 374 B3
Nisbet E Loth 397 E6
Nisthouse Orkney 452 B4
Nisthouse Shetl'd 457 G5
Niton I/Wight 30 E2
Nitshill Glasg C 392 F2
Niwbwrch = Newborough Angl 236 A4
No Man's Green Shrops 175 B5
No Man's Heath Ches 242 E3
No Man's Heath Warwick 199 B6
No Man's Land Hants 65 F7
Noah's Green Worcs 176 F3
Noak Hill London 113 D5
Nob End Gtr Man 278 C4
Nobland Green Herts 138 D4
Noblethorpe S Yorks 281 D7
Nobold Shrops 195 A5
Nobottle Northants 179 F8
Nobs Crook Hants 44 B4
Nocton Lincs 250 B4
Noctorum Mersey 263 B7
Noel Park London 111 D8
Nog Tow Lancs 289 D7
Nogdam End Norfolk 210 C4
Noke Oxon 134 E1
Noke Street Medway 92 B1
Nolton Pembs 116 A3
Nolton Haven Pembs 116 A3
Nomansland Devon 36 D1
Nomansland Herts 137 E7
Nomansland Wilts 43 C8
Noneley Shrops 219 C6
Noness Shetl'd 455 D3
Nonikiln H'land 434 A1
Nonington Kent 74 A5
Nook Cumb 314 D4
Nook Lancs 289 B6
Noon Nick W Yorks 292 C4
Noonsbrough Shetl'd 457 H2
Noranside Angus 420 A4
Norbiton London 89 C5
Norbiton Common London 89 C5
Norbreck Blackp'l 288 B3
Norbridge Heref'd 152 C4
Norbury Ches 242 E4
Norbury Derby 245 F8
Norbury London 89 C8
Norbury Shrops 194 E3
Norbury Staffs 221 D5
Norbury Common Ches 242 E4
Norbury Junction Staffs 221 D5
Norbury Moor Gtr Man 267 B5
Norby N Yorks 319 D7
Norby Shetl'd 457 H1
Norchard Worcs 175 E6
Norcott Brook Ches 265 C7
Norcross Blackp'l 288 B3
Nordelph Norfolk 206 C2
Norden Dorset 27 D5
Norden Gtr Man 279 B6
Nordley Shrops 196 D2
Nore Marsh Wilts 105 F6
Norham Northum 387 C8
Nork Surrey 89 E6
Norland Town W Yorks 292 F3
Norley Ches 265 E6
Norley Devon 34 F2
Norley Gtr Man 277 C7
Norleywood Hants 29 A7
Norlington E Sussex 50 D1
Normacot Stoke 244 F4
Norman Corner NE Lincs 286 D4
Norman Cross Cambs 204 E2
Normanby N Lincs 284 A4
Normanby N Yorks 321 D5
Normanby Redcar/Clevel'd 333 C6
Normanby by Stow Lincs 272 C2
Normanby le Wold Lincs 286 E1
Normanby-by-Spital Lincs 272 B5
Normandy Surrey 67 A8
Norman's Bay E Sussex 51 E6
Norman's Green Devon 37 F6
Normanston Suffolk 211 E6
Normanton Derby C 224 B1
Normanton Leics 249 F7
Normanton Lincs 250 E1
Normanton Notts 248 D5
Normanton Wilts 63 C7
Normanton W Yorks 294 F1
Normanton le Heath Leics 199 A8
Normanton on Soar Notts 224 D5
Normanton on the Wolds Notts 225 B7
Normanton on Trent Notts 271 F7
Normanton Spring S Yorks 269 C8
Normos Blackp'l 288 C3
Nornay Notts 271 B5
Norney Surrey 67 C8
Norridge Common Wilts 62 B1
Norrington Common Wilts 82 D2
Norris Green Cornw'l 10 B4
Norris Green Mersey 276 F4
Norris Hill Leics 223 E8
Norris's Green Wokingham 86 B5
Norristhorpe W Yorks 293 F6
Norseman Orkney 452 B4
North America ER Yorks 296 D3
North Anston S Yorks 270 C2
North Aston Oxon 133 B8
North Ayre Shetl'd 457 F4
North Baddesley Hants 44 C2
North Baddesley Hants 44 C2
North Ballachulish H'land 417 A5
North Barrow Som'set 60 F4
North Barsham Norfolk 232 B3
North Beach Suffolk 211 E7
North Benfleet Essex 114 E2
North Bersted W Sussex 47 F6
North Berwick E Loth 397 A8
North Bitchburn Durham 343 E7
North Blyth Northum 365 F8
North Boarhunt Hants 45 D7
North Bockhampton Dorset 28 A3
North Bovey Devon 20 D4
North Bowood Dorset 24 A3
North Bradley Wilts 82 F2
North Brentor Devon 19 D6
North Brewham Som'set 61 D6
North Brook End Cambs 161 D5
North Buckland Devon 54 C4
North Burlingham Norfolk 210 A3
North Cadbury Som'set 60 F4
North Cairn Dumf/Gal 400 B1
North Carlton Lincs 272 D3
North Carlton Notts 270 C3
North Carrine Arg/Bute 404 F2
North Cave ER Yorks 296 D4
North Cerney Glos 131 F6
North Chailey E Sussex 49 B7
North Charford Hants 43 C6
North Charlton Northum 377 C5
North Cheam London 89 C6
North Cheriton Som'set 40 A3
North Chideock Dorset 24 B3
North Choppingham Northum 365 E6
North Cliffe ER Yorks 296 C4
North Clifton Notts 271 E8
North Close Durham 344 E1
North Cockerington Lincs 274 A4
North Coker Som'set 39 D8
North Collafirth Shetl'd 457 E3
North Common Suffolk 186 C4
North Common S Glos 81 B5
North Connel Arg/Bute 416 D4
North Cornelly Bridg 98 F3
North Corner S Glos 103 F5
North Corriegills N Ayrs 405 C6
North Corry H'land 416 B3
North Cotes Lincs 287 D5
North Country Cornw'l 4 B1
North Cove Suffolk 211 F5
North Cowton N Yorks 331 F7
North Craigo Angus 421 A6
North Crawley M/Keynes 159 D6
North Cray London 90 B4
North Creake Norfolk 255 E7
North Curry Som'set 38 A4
North Dalton ER Yorks 309 E7
North Darley Cornw'l 18 F2
North Dawn Orkney 453 C5
North Deighton N Yorks 306 E4
North Denes Norfolk 211 A6
North Dronley Angus 420 D3
North Drumachter Lodge H'land 425 E8
North Duffield N Yorks 295 C7
North Elham Kent 74 C3
North Elkington Lincs 274 A2
North Elmham Norfolk 232 D4
North Elmsall W Yorks 282 B3
North End Beds 159 C7
North End Bath/NE Som'set 80 D4
North End Bucks 134 B4
North End Bucks 135 B7
North End Cumb 347 E8
North End Dorset 62 F1
North End Durham 343 C9
North End E Sussex 49 D8
North End Essex 162 E3
North End Essex 140 D2
North End Essex 163 E8
North End ER Yorks 298 D4
North End ER Yorks 310 E5
North End ER Yorks 298 B2
North End Hants 65 F8
North End Hants 42 C5
North End Hants 85 D5
North End Leics 225 E6
North End Lincs 251 F7
North End Lincs 275 B5
North End Lincs 285 E7
North End Lincs 287 D5
North End Lincs 274 A4
North End London 90 A5
North End London 111 E7
North End Mersey 276 D3
North End Norfolk 208 E4
North End N Lincs 297 F9
North End N Som'set 79 C8
North End Northum 364 B4
North End Portsm'th 45 F8
North End Som'set 38 A3
North End Wilts 105 D5
North End W Sussex 47 F7
North End W Sussex 48 E2
North End W Sussex 70 D2
North Erradale H'land 438 E1
North Evington Leics C 201 C6
North Fambridge Essex 114 C4
North Fearns H'land 431 E5
North Featherstone W Yorks 294 F2
North Feorline N Ayrs 405 D5
North Ferriby ER Yorks 297 E6
North Finchley London 111 D7
North Flobbets Aberds 437 E4
North Frodingham ER Yorks 310 E3
North Gluss Shetl'd 457 F3
North Gorley Hants 43 D6
North Green Norfolk 208 B4
North Green Norfolk 209 F8
North Green Suffolk 188 C4
North Green Suffolk 188 F4
North Green Suffolk 189 E5
North Greetwell Lincs 272 E5
North Grimston N Yorks 309 B5
North Gyle C/Edinb 395 D8
North Halley Orkney 453 C6
North Halling Medway 91 C9
North Harby Notts 272 E2
North Hayling Hants 46 F2
North Hazelrigg Northum 388 F3
North Heasley Devon 56 E1
North Heath W Berks 85 B6
North Heath W Sussex 48 B1
North Hill Cornw'l 18 E2
North Hill Dorset 25 B7
North Hillingdon London 110 F3
North Hinksey Oxon 107 A6
North Holmwood Surrey 69 B5
North Houghton Hants 64 E3
North Ho Shetl'd 455 B2
North Huish Devon 14 D2
North Hykeham Lincs 250 A1
North Hylton Tyne/Wear 353 E6
North Johnston Pembs 116 B4
North Kelsey Lincs 285 D7
North Kelsey Moor Lincs 285 D8
North Kessock H'land 434 D1
North Killingholme N Lincs 286 A1
North Kilvington N Yorks 319 C7
North Kilworth Leics 179 B7
North Kingston Hants 43 F6
North Kirkton Aberds 437 C8
North Kiscadale N Ayrs 405 D6
North Kyme Lincs 251 D6
North Laggan H'land 425 C4
North Lancing W Sussex 48 E3
North Landing ER Yorks 311 A6
North Leazes Durham 343 F7
North Lee Bucks 135 F7
North Lees N Yorks 318 F4
North Leigh Kent 74 B2
North Leigh Oxon 133 E6
North Leverton with Habblesthorpe Notts 271 C7
North Littleton Worcs 154 C4
North Lobb Devon 54 D4
North Looe Surrey 89 D6
North Lopham Norfolk 187 B5
North Luffenham Rutl'd 202 C4
North Marden W Sussex 46 C4
North Marston Bucks 135 C6
North Middleton Midloth 384 A4
North Middleton Northum 376 C2
North Millbrex Aberds 437 D5
North Molton Devon 56 F1
North Moreton Oxon 107 E8
North Morte Devon 54 B4
North Mosstown Aberds 437 C7
North Motherwell N Lanarks 381 A6
North Moulsecoomb Brighton/Hove 49 E6
North Mundham W Sussex 47 F5
North Muskham Notts 249 C6
North Newbald ER Yorks 296 C5
North Newington Oxon 156 E3
North Newnton Wilts 83 E7
North Newton Som'set 59 E5
North Nibley Glos 103 C6
North Norfolk Railway, Sheringham Norfolk 256 D5
North Oakley Hants 85 F7
North Ockendon London 113 F6
North Ormesby Middlesbro 332 C5
North Ormsby Lincs 274 A2
North Otterington N Yorks 319 C6
North Owersby Lincs 285 F8
North Perrott Som'set 39 E7
North Petherton Som'set 59 E5
North Petherwin Cornw'l 18 C2
North Pickenham Norfolk 207 B8
North Piddle Worcs 154 B2
North Pool Devon 13 D6
North Poorton Dorset 24 A5
North Port Arg/Bute 417 E5
North Poulner Hants 43 E6
North Quarme Som'set 57 D5
North Queensferry Fife 411 D6
North Radworthy Devon 56 E2
North Rauceby Lincs 250 E3
North Reddish Gtr Man 279 F6
North Reston Lincs 274 C4
North Riddingwood Dumf/Gal 358 E3
North Rigton N Yorks 306 F2
North Ripley Hants 28 A3
North Rode Ches 244 A3
North Roe Shetl'd 456 E3
North Ronaldsay Airport Orkney 454 A6
North Row Cumb 338 E3
North Runcton Norfolk 230 E4
North Saltwick Northum 365 F5
North Sandwick Shetl'd 456 D5
North Scale Cumb 300 B2
North Scarle Lincs 272 F2
North Seaton Northum 365 E7
North Sheen London 89 A5
North Shian Arg/Bute 416 C4
North Shields Tyne/Wear 353 C6
North Shoebury Southend 115 E5
North Shore Blackp'l 288 C3
North Side Cumb 337 F6
North Side Peterbro 204 D4
North Skelmanae Aberds 437 C6
North Skelton Redcar/Clevel'd 333 C8
North Somercoates Lincs 287 E7
North Stainley N Yorks 318 E4
North Stainmore Cumb 329 C6
North Stifford Thurr'k 113 F7
North Stoke Bath/NE Som'set 81 C6
North Stoke Oxon 108 E2
North Stoke W Sussex 47 D8
North Street Hants 66 E2
North Street Hants 43 C6
North Street Kent 93 E7
North Street Medway 92 B3
North Street W Berks 86 B2
North Sunderland Northum 377 A6
North Tamerton Cornw'l 18 A3
North Tawton Devon 35 F6
North Thoresby Lincs 286 E4
North Tidworth Wilts 64 B1
North Togston Northum 365 B6
North Town Devon 34 E3
North Town Som'set 60 C3
North Town Som'set 60 F4
North Town Surrey 67 A7
North Town Windsor 109 F7
North Tuddenham Norfolk 233 F5
North Walbottle Tyne/Wear 352 C2
North Walsham Norfolk 234 C2
North Waltham Hants 65 B8
North Warnborough Hants 66 A4
North Water Bridge Angus 421 A6
North Watten H'land 445 C6
North Weald Bassett Essex 112 B5
North Weirs Hants 43 F8
North Wembley London 111 E5
North Weston N Som'set 80 A1
North Wheatley Notts 271 B7
North Whilborough Devon 15 B5
North Whiteley Moray 436 D1
North Wick Bath/NE Som'set 80 C3
North Widcombe Bath/NE Som'set 80 E3
North Willingham Lincs 273 B7
North Wingfield Derby 247 B6
North Witham Lincs 227 D5
North Woods S Glos 102 F4
North Wootton Dorset 40 D3
North Wootton Norfolk 230 D4
North Wootton Som'set 60 C3
North Wraxall Wilts 81 A8
North Wroughton Swindon 105 F7
North Yorkshire Moors Railway, Pickering N Yorks 321 C7
Northacre Norfolk 208 D3
Northall Beds 136 C3
Northall Green Norfolk 232 F4
Northallerton N Yorks 319 B6
Northam Devon 54 F3
Northam S'thampton 44 D3
Northampton Northants 180 F3
Northaw Herts 111 B7
Northay Som'set 38 D3

## O

Penruddock Cumb 339 F7
Penryn Cornw'l 4 D3
Pensarn Carms 122 D4
Pensarn Conwy 262 D9
Pen-sarn Gwyn 214 C3
Pensax Worcs 174 E4
Pensby Mersey 263 C7
Penselwood Som'set 61 E7
Pensford Bath/NE Som'set 80 D4
Pensham Worcs 154 D1
Penshaw Tyne/Wear 353 F5
Penshurst Kent 71 C5
Pensilva Cornw'l 10 B1
Pensnett W Midlands 197 F7
Penston E Loth 397 D5
Penstone Devon 35 F8
Penstraze Cornw'l 4 A3
Penstrowed Powys 192 E5
Pentewan Cornw'l 8 F3
Penthryn Fechan Powys 218 E1
Pentir Gwyn 259 F8
Pentire Cornw'l 7 C6
Pentlepoir Pembs 117 C8
Pentlow Essex 164 D1
Pentney Norfolk 231 F6
Penton Grafton Hants 64 B3
Penton Mewsey Hants 64 B3
Pentonville London 111 F8
Pentraeth Angl 259 D7
Pentrapeod Caerph 100 B3
Pentre Flints 263 F8
Pentre Monmouths 127 E7
Pentre Pembs 144 D4
Pentre Powys 217 F8
Pentre Powys 150 A2
Pentre Powys 171 A6
Pentre Powys 194 E1
Pentre Rh Cyn Taff 99 C6
Pentre Shrops 218 E4
Pentre Wrex 217 B7
Pentre Wrex 241 F6
Pentre Berw Angl 259 E6
Pentre Cilgwyn Wrex 218 A1
Pentre Dolau-Honddu Powys 148 D4
Pentre Ffwrndan Flints 263 E7
Pentre Gwenlais Carms 123 D8
Pentre Gwynfryn Gwyn 214 C3
Pentre Halkyn Flints 263 E5
Pentre Llanrhaeadr Denbs 240 B2
Pentre Llifior Powys 193 D6
Pentre llwyn-llwyd Powys 148 B4
Pentre llyn Ceredig'n 168 C5
Pentre Meyrick V/Glam 77 A6
Pentre Saron Denbs 239 B8
Pentrebach Carms 148 F1
Pentrebach Ceredig'n 146 C4
Pentre-bach Gwyn 236 F3
Pentrebach Merth Tyd 99 B8
Pentre-bach Powys 125 A7
Pentrebach Rh Cyn Taff 99 E8
Pentrebach Swan 97 A7
Pentre-bont Conwy 238 D2
Pentre-cagal Carms 145 D6
Pentre-cefn Shrops 218 C1
Pentre-celyn Denbs 240 D4
Pentre-chwyth Swan 97 C8
Pentre-cwrt Carms 145 E7
Pentre-du Conwy 238 C3
Pentredwr Denbs 240 E4
Pentre-dwr Swan 97 C8
Pentrefelin Carms 123 C7
Pentrefelin Conwy 262 E6
Pentrefelin Ceredig'n 146 C5
Pentrefelin Denbs 240 F5
Pentrefelin Gwyn 214 A2
Pentrefelin Angl 259 A5
Pentrefelin Powys 217 D8
Pentrefoelas Conwy 239 D5
Pentre-Galar Pembs 121 A7
Pentregat Ceredig'n 145 B7
Pentreheyling Shrops 193 E8
Pentre-Isaf Conwy 262 F7
Pentre-llyn-cymmer Conwy 239 D7
Pentre-newydd Shrops 218 A2
Pentre-Poeth Carms 96 B5
Pentre-poeth Newp 100 E5
Pentre-Poid Torf 100 B5
Pentre'r beirdd Powys 217 F8
Pentre'r Felin Conwy 262 F6
Pentre'r-felin Powys 125 A7
Pentre'r-gof Powys 193 A7
Pentre-rhew Ceredig'n 147 B6
Pentre-ty-gwyn Carms 148 E1
Pentre-uchaf Gwyn 213 A7
Pentrich Derby 247 D5
Pentridge Dorset 42 C3
Pentwyn Carms 123 E7
Pen-twyn Caerph 100 B4
Pentwyn Caerph 100 B2
Pen-twyn Monmouths 128 F4
Pentwyn = Pendine Carms 121 F8
Pen-twyn Torf 100 B5
Pentwyn Berthlwyd Merth Tyd 100 C2
Pentwyn-mawr Caerph 100 C3
Pentyrch Card 100 F2
Pen-Ucha'r Plwyf Flints 263 E5
Penuwch Ceredig'n 168 F4
Penwartha Cornw'l 7 E6
Penwartha Coombe Cornw'l 7 E6
Penweathers Cornw'l 4 B3
Penwithick Cornw'l 8 D3
Penwood Hants 85 D5
Penwortham Lane Lancs 289 E7
Penwyllt Powys 125 D6
Pen-y-banc Carms 123 E8
Pen-y-banc Carms 123 C8
Pen-y-Bont Bl Gwent 100 A4
Pen-y-bont Carms 122 B2
Penybont Ceredig'n 190 F3
Penybont Powys 171 F7
Pen-y-bont Llanerch Emrys Powys 218 D1
Penybontfawr Powys 217 D6
Penybryn Caerph 100 C2
Pen-y-bryn Gwyn 215 E5
Pen-y-bryn Pembs 144 D3
Pen-y-bryn Wrex 241 F6
Pen-y-cae Bridg 99 F5
Pen-y-cae Powys 125 E5
Penycae Wrex 241 E6
Pen-y-cae-mawr Monmouths 101 C8
Penycaerau Gwyn 212 C3
Pen-y-cefn Flints 262 D4
Pen-y-clawdd Monmouths 128 F3
Penycoed Caerph 100 C3
Pen-y-coed Gwyn 215 E6
Pen-y-coed Powys 218 E1
Pen-y-coed Shrops 218 D2
Pen-y-coedcae Rh Cyn Taff 99 E8
Penycwm Pembs 118 E5
Pen-y-darren Merth Tyd 126 F2
Penydre Swan 97 B8
Pen-y-fai Bridg 98 F4
Pen-y-Fan Carms 96 C5
Pen-y-fan Monmouths 102 A2
Penyfeidr Pembs 119 D5
Pen-y-felin Flints 263 F5
Pen-y-ffordd Flints 262 C4
Penyffordd Flints 241 B7
Penyffridd Gwyn 237 C6
Pen-y-Garn Carms 123 A7
Pen-y-garn Ceredig'n 169 A5
Penygarn Torf 101 B5
Pen-y-garnedd Angl 259 D7
Penygarnedd Powys 217 D7
Pen-y-graig Gwyn 212 B4
Penygraig Rh Cyn Taff 99 D6
Pen-y-groes Card 100 F4
Penygroes Carms 123 E7
Penygroes Gwyn 236 D5
Penygroes Pembs 144 E3
Pen-y-groeslon Gwyn 212 B4
Pen-y-lan Card 78 A3
Pen-y-lan Newp 100 E5
Pen-y-lan V/Glam 77 A6
Pen-y-maes Flints 263 D5
Pen-y-Parc Flints 241 C6
Penyraber Pembs 119 B7
Pen-yr-englyn Rh Cyn Taff 99 C5
Pen-yr-heol Bridg 99 F6
Penyrheol Caerph 100 E2
Pen-yr-heol Monmouths 128 E2
Penyrheol Swan 97 C6
Penyrheol Swan 97 D6
Penyrheol Torf 101 C5
Penysarn Angl 259 A6
Pen-y-stryt Denbs 240 D4
Penywaun Rh Cyn Taff 99 B6
Penzance Cornw'l 3 D5
Penzance Heliport Cornw'l 2 D5
People's Palace Glasg C 392 F4
Peopleton Worcs 154 B1
Peover Ches 266 E2
Peover Heath Ches 266 E2
Peper Harow Surrey 67 C8
Pepperly Hill Notts 271 D5
Pepper's Green Essex 139 E8
Peppershill Bucks 134 F4
Pepperstock Beds 137 D5
Perceton N Ayrs 379 D7
Percie Aberds 428 C2
Percy Main Tyne/Wear 353 C5
Percyhorner Aberds 437 B6
Perham Downs Wilts 64 B2
Periton Som'set 57 B6
Perivale London 111 F5
Perkhill Aberds 428 B2
Perkin's Village Devon 22 B2
Perkinsville Durham 352 F4
Perlethorpe Notts 271 E5
Perran Downs Cornw'l 3 D7
Perran Wharf Cornw'l 4 C3
Perranarworthal Cornw'l 4 C3
Perrancoombe Cornw'l 7 E6
Perranporth Cornw'l 7 E6
Perranuthnoe Cornw'l 3 E6
Perranwell Cornw'l 4 C3
Perranwell Cornw'l 7 E6
Perranwell Station Cornw'l 4 C3
Perranzabuloe Cornw'l 7 E6
Perry Kent 94 E5
Perry Som'set 58 C2
Perry Barr W Midlands 198 E2
Perry Beeches W Midlands 198 E2
Perry Common W Midlands 198 E2
Perry Crofts Staffs 199 B5
Perry Green Devon 36 E2
Perry Green Essex 140 C5
Perry Green Herts 138 D4
Perry Green Som'set 59 D5
Perry Green Wilts 104 E4
Perry Street Kent 91 B7
Perry Street Som'set 38 E4
Perryfoot Derby 268 C2
Perrymead Bath/NE Som'set 81 D6
Perrywood Kent 93 E7
Pershall Staffs 221 C6
Pershore Worcs 154 C1
Pert Angus 421 A6
Pertenhall Beds 182 E1
Perth Perth/Kinr 420 E1
Perth Racecourse Perth/Kinr 420 E1
Perthcelyn Rh Cyn Taff 99 C8
Perthy Shrops 218 B4
Perton Heref'd 152 D1
Perton Staffs 197 D6
Pertwood Wilts 62 D2
Pested Kent 73 A7
Peter Tavy Devon 19 E7
Peterborough Peterbro 204 D2
Peterborough Cathedral Peterbro 204 D2
Peterburn H'land 438 E1
Peterchurch Heref'd 150 E4
Peterculter Aberd C 429 B5
Peterhead Aberds 437 D8
Peterlee Durham 344 C4
Peters Green Herts 137 D6
Peters Marland Devon 34 D2
Petersburn N Lanarks 393 F7
Petersfield Hants 46 B2
Petersfinger Wilts 63 F8
Petersham London 89 B5
Petershill Glasg C 392 E4
Peterstone Wentlooge Newp 100 F5
Peterston-super-Ely V/Glam 77 A8
Peterstow Heref'd 128 C5
Petertown Orkney 452 C4
Peterville Cornw'l 7 E5
Petham Kent 74 A2
Petherwin Gate Cornw'l 18 C2
Petre Bank Ches 267 C5
Petrockstowe Devon 34 E3
Petsoe End M/Keynes 159 C5
Pett E Sussex 52 D2
Pett Bottom Kent 74 C2
Pett Street Kent 73 B8
Pettaugh Suffolk 165 A8
Petteridge Kent 71 C8
Pettinain S Lanarks 382 D4
Pettistree Suffolk 166 B3
Petton Devon 37 B5
Petton Shrops 219 C5
Petts Wood London 90 C3
Petty Aberds 436 E4
Petty France S Glos 103 E7
Pettycur Fife 411 D7
Pettymuick Aberds 437 F6
Petworth W Sussex 47 B7
Petworth House W Sussex 47 B7
Pevensey E Sussex 51 F6
Pevensey Bay E Sussex 51 F6
Peverell Plym'th 11 D5
Pew Hill Wilts 82 B3
Pewsey Wilts 83 D8
Pewterspear Warrington 265 C7
Pheasants Bucks 109 E5
Pheasant's Hill Bucks 109 E5
Pheasey W Midlands 198 D2
Philadelphia Tyne/Wear 344 A2
Philiphaugh Scot Borders 373 B5
Philipstoun W Loth 395 C5
Phillack Cornw'l 3 C7
Philleigh Cornw'l 5 C5
Phillip's Town Caerph 100 B2
Phocle Green Heref'd 129 B6
Phoenix Green Hants 86 E5
Phorp Moray 435 C5
Pibsbury Som'set 39 A6
Pibwrlwyd Carms 122 D4
Pica Cumb 324 B5
Piccadilly Corner Norfolk 188 A3
Piccott's End Herts 136 F4
Pickburn S Yorks 282 C4
Picken End Worcs 153 D6
Pickering N Yorks 321 D7
Pickering Nook Durham 352 E2
Picket Hill Hants 43 E6
Picket Piece Hants 64 B4
Pickford W Midlands 177 B8
Pickhill N Yorks 319 D5
Pickle Fen Cambs 183 B7
Picklenash Glos 129 B8
Picklescott Shrops 194 D4
Pickletillem Fife 420 E4
Pickley Green Gtr Man 278 D2
Pickmere Ches 265 D8
Pickney Som'set 58 F3
Pickstock Telford 220 D4
Pickup Bank Blackb'n 290 F3
Pickwell Devon 54 C4
Pickwell Leics 201 A9
Pickwood Scar W Yorks 292 F3
Pickworth Lincs 227 B7
Pickworth Rutl'd 227 F6
Picton Ches 264 E3
Picton Flints 262 C4
Picton N Yorks 332 E3
Pict's Cross Heref'd 128 B5
Picts Hill Som'set 59 F8
Piddinghoe E Sussex 49 F8
Piddington Bucks 109 D6
Piddington Northants 158 B4
Piddington Oxon 134 D3
Piddlehinton Dorset 26 A1
Piddletrenthide Dorset 25 A9
Pidley Cambs 183 C6
Pidney Dorset 40 E4
Piece Cornw'l 4 C1
Piece Hall Art Gallery, Halifax W Yorks 292 E3
Pield Heath London 110 F3
Piercebridge D'lington 331 C6
Pierowall Orkney 454 B2
Pierremont D'lington 331 D7
Piff's Elm Glos 130 B4
Pig Oak Dorset 42 F3
Pig Street Heref'd 150 C5
Pigdon Northum 365 E5
Pightley Som'set 58 D4
Pike Hill Lancs 291 D6
Pikehall Derby 246 C1
Pikeshill Hants 43 E8
Pilford Dorset 42 F3
Pilgrim Oak Notts 248 D2
Pilgrims Hatch Essex 113 C6
Pilham Lincs 284 F4
Pill N Som'set 80 A2
Pill Pembs 116 C4
Pillaton Cornw'l 10 C3
Pillatonmill Cornw'l 10 C3
Pillerton Hersey Warwick 155 C9
Pillerton Priors Warwick 155 C8
Pilleth Powys 172 E3
Pilley Glos 131 D5
Pilley Hants 29 A6
Pilley S Yorks 281 D8
Pillgwenlly Newp 101 E6
Pillhead Devon 54 F4
Pilling Lancs 301 F7
Pilling Lane Lancs 301 F6
Pillowell Glos 102 A4
Pillows Green Glos 130 B2
Pillwell Dorset 41 C5
Pilning S Glos 102 E3
Pilsden Dorset 24 A3
Pilsgate Peterbro 203 B7
Pilsley Derby 268 E4
Pilsley Derby 247 B6
Pilsley Green Derby 247 B6
Pilson Green Norfolk 234 F4
Piltdown E Sussex 50 B1
Pilton C/Edinb 396 C1
Pilton Devon 55 E6
Pilton Northants 181 B8
Pilton Rutl'd 202 C4
Pilton Som'set 60 C3
Pilton Swan 96 E3
Pilton Green Swan 96 E3
Piltown Som'set 60 D3
Pimbo Lancs 277 D6
Pimhole Gtr Man 279 B5
Pimlico Herts 110 A3
Pimlico Lancs 290 B3
Pimlico London 89 A7
Pimperne Dorset 41 E8
Pin Green Herts 137 B9
Pin Mill Suffolk 166 E2
Pinchbeck Lincs 228 C4
Pinchbeck West Lincs 228 D4
Pincheon Green S Yorks 283 A7
Pincock Lancs 277 A8
Pineham Kent 75 B6
Pineham M/Keynes 159 D5
Pinehurst Swindon 105 E8
Pinfarthings Glos 104 B2
Pinfold Lancs 276 B4
Pinford End Suffolk 164 A2
Pinged Carms 96 B3
Pinhoe Devon 22 B1
Pinkett's Booth W Midlands 177 B8
Pinkney Wilts 104 E2
Pinkneys Green Windsor 109 F7
Pinley W Midlands 178 C2
Pinley Green Warwick 177 E7
Pinminnoch Dumf/Gal 400 D2
Pinminnoch S Ayrs 354 D2
Pinmore S Ayrs 354 D3
Pinmore Mains S Ayrs 354 E3
Pinn Devon 22 C3
Pinnacles Essex 138 F4
Pinner London 110 D4
Pinner Green London 110 D4
Pinnerwood Park London 110 D4
Pin's Green Worcs 153 C6
Pinsley Green Ches 242 E4
Pinvin Worcs 154 D2
Pinwall Leics 199 D7
Pinwherry S Ayrs 400 A3
Pinxton Derby 247 C7
Pipe and Lyde Heref'd 151 D8
Pipe Gate Shrops 243 F7
Pipe Ridware Staffs 222 E3
Pipehill Staffs 198 B2
Piperhall Arg/Bute 405 A7
Piperhill H'land 434 C3
Piper's Ash Ches 264 F3
Piper's Corner Bucks 109 C7
Piper's End Worcs 153 E6
Piper's Hill Worcs 176 E2
Pipers Pool Cornw'l 18 D2
Pipewell Northants 180 A4
Pipsden Kent 72 E2
Pipton Powys 149 E8
Pirbright Surrey 87 E8
Pirbright Camp Surrey 87 E8
Pirnmill N Ayrs 404 B4
Pirton Herts 137 A7
Pirton Worcs 153 C7
Pisgah Ceredig'n 169 C6
Pisgah Stirl 410 B2
Pishill Oxon 108 D4
Pismire Hill S Yorks 269 A7
Pistyll Gwyn 236 F2
Pit Monmouths 127 F8
Pitagowan Perth/Kinr 419 A6
Pitblae Aberds 437 B6
Pitbrook Glos 103 B5
Pitcairngreen Perth/Kinr 419 E8
Pitcalnie H'land 434 A3
Pitcaple Aberds 436 F4
Pitch Green Bucks 109 B5
Pitch Place Surrey 67 D7
Pitch Place Surrey 68 A1
Pitchcombe Glos 130 F3
Pitchcott Bucks 135 C6
Pitcher's Green Suffolk 164 A3
Pitchford Shrops 195 C6
Pitcombe Som'set 61 E5
Pitcorthie Fife 412 B3
Pitcot V/Glam 76 B4
Pitcox E Loth 398 C2
Pitcur Perth/Kinr 420 D2
Pitfancy Aberds 436 D2
Pitfichie Aberds 428 A3
Pitforthie Aberds 429 E5
Pitgair Aberds 436 C4
Pitgrudy H'land 440 D4
Pithmaduthy H'land 440 F4
Pitkennedy Angus 421 B5
Pitkevy Fife 411 B7
Pitkierie Fife 412 B3
Pitlessie Fife 411 B8
Pitlochry Perth/Kinr 419 B7
Pitmachie Aberds 436 F3
Pitmain H'land 426 B2
Pitman's Corner Suffolk 187 E7
Pitmedden Aberds 437 F5
Pitminster Som'set 38 C2
Pitmuies Angus 421 C5
Pitmunie Aberds 428 A3
Pitney Som'set 59 F9
Pitrocknie Perth/Kinr 420 C2
Pitscottie Fife 412 A2
Pitsea Essex 114 E1
Pitses Gtr Man 279 D7
Pitsford Northants 180 E3
Pitsford Hill Som'set 58 E2
Pitsmoor S Yorks 269 B7
Pitstone Bucks 136 E2
Pitstone Green Bucks 136 E2
Pitt Devon 37 C5
Pitt Court Glos 103 C7
Pitt Rivers Museum (See University Museum) Oxon 107 A7
Pittachar Perth/Kinr 419 E6
Pittendreich Moray 435 B6
Pittentrail H'land 440 C4
Pittenweem Fife 412 B3
Pittington Durham 344 C2
Pittodrie Aberds 436 F3
Pitton Swan 96 E3
Pitton Wilts 63 E9
Pitts Hill Stoke 244 D3
Pittswood Kent 71 B7
Pittulie Aberds 437 B6
Pittville Glos 130 C4
Pitway Som'set 39 C6
Pity Me Durham 344 B1
Pityme Cornw'l 16 E3
Pityoulish H'land 426 A4
Pixey Green Suffolk 188 C2
Pixham Surrey 69 A5
Pixley Heref'd 152 E3
Pizien Well Kent 71 A8
Place Newton N Yorks 309 A6
Plâs Berwyn Denbs 240 F4
Plaidy Aberds 436 C4
Plaidy Cornw'l 9 E8
Plain Dealings Pembs 117 A7
Plain-an-Gwarry Cornw'l 4 B1
Plains N Lanarks 393 E7
Plains Farm Tyne/Wear 353 F6
Plaish Shrops 195 D6
Plaistow Derby 247 C5
Plaistow London 112 F2
Plaistow London 112 F3
Plaistow W Sussex 68 E2
Plaistow Green Essex 140 B5
Plaitford Hants 43 C8
Plaitford Green Hants 43 B8
Plantation Hill Hants 85 E7
Plantationfoot Dumf/Gal 359 D6
Plas Powys 217 E7
Plas Canol Gwyn 214 E4
Plas Gogerddan Ceredig'n 169 B5
Plas Madoc Wrex 241 F6
Plas Mawr, Conwy Conwy 261 D5
Plas Nantyr Wrex 217 A8
Plashet London 112 F3
Plashett Carms 122 F1
Plasiolyn Powys 193 C5
Plasnewydd Gwyn 212 C4
Plaster's Green N Som'set 80 D2
Plastow Green Hants 85 D7
Plas-yn-y-pentre Denbs 241 F6
Platt Kent 91 E7
Platt Bridge Gtr Man 277 D9
Platt Lane Shrops 219 A7
Platts Common S Yorks 282 D1
Platt's Heath Kent 72 A4
Plawsworth Durham 344 B1
Plaxtol Kent 91 F7
Play Hatch Oxon 86 A4
Playden E Sussex 73 F5
Playford Suffolk 166 C2
Playing Place Cornw'l 4 B4
Playley Green Glos 130 A1
Plealey Shrops 194 B4
Plean Stirl 410 D3
Pleasant Valley Pembs 121 F7
Pleasington Blackb'n 290 E1
Pleasley Derby 247 B7
Pleasleyhill Derby 247 B7
Pleasure Island Theme Park NE Lincs 287 C5
Pleck Dorset 40 D4
Pleck W Midlands 197 D8
Pleckgate Blackb'n 290 D2
Pledwick W Yorks 281 A8
Plegdon Green Essex 139 B7
Plenmeller Northum 349 D8
Pleshey Essex 140 E2
Plockton H'land 431 E8
Plocrapol W Isles 449 C5
Plot Gate Som'set 60 E2
Plot Street Som'set 60 D2
Plough Hill Warwick 199 E7
Ploxgreen Shrops 194 C3
Pluckley Kent 73 B5
Pluckley Thorne Kent 73 C5
Plucks Gutter Kent 94 D5
Plumbland Cumb 338 D2
Plumbley S Yorks 269 C8
Plumgarths Cumb 314 B3
Plumley Ches 266 D1
Plump Hill Glos 129 D7
Plumpton Cumb 339 D8
Plumpton E Sussex 49 D7
Plumpton Northants 157 C7
Plumpton End Northants 158 D2
Plumpton Green E Sussex 49 C7
Plumpton Head Cumb 339 E9
Plumpton Racecourse E Sussex 49 C7
Plumptonfoot Cumb 339 D8
Plumstead London 90 A4
Plumstead Norfolk 257 F5
Plumstead Green Norfolk 256 F5
Plumstead Green Norfolk 210 A1
Plumtree Notts 225 B7
Plumtree Green Kent 72 B3
Plumtree Park Notts 225 B7
Plungar Leics 226 B2
Plush Dorset 40 F4
Plusha Cornw'l 18 D2
Plushabridge Cornw'l 10 A2
Plusterwine Glos 102 C3
Plwmp Ceredig'n 145 B7
Plymouth Devon 10 E5
Plymouth City Airport Plym'th 11 C6
Plympton Plym'th 11 D6
Plympton St. Maurice Plym'th 11 D6
Plymstock Plym'th 11 E6
Plymtree Devon 37 F6
Pobgreen Gtr Man 280 C2
Pockley N Yorks 320 C3
Pocklington ER Yorks 309 F5
Pockthorpe Norfolk 233 D5
Pockthorpe Norfolk 208 D2
Pockthorpe Norfolk 233 E6
Pode Hole Lincs 228 D4
Podimore Som'set 39 B8
Podington Beds 181 F6
Podsmead Glos 130 D2
Poffley End Oxon 133 E6
Pogmoor S Yorks 281 C8
Point Cornw'l 4 C4
Point Clear Essex 142 D2
Pointon Lincs 228 B2
Pokesdown Bournem'th 28 B2
Pol a Charra W Isles 446 B3
Polbae Dumf/Gal 400 B4
Polbain H'land 438 B3
Polbathic Cornw'l 10 D2
Polbeth W Loth 395 F5
Polborder Cornw'l 10 C3
Polbrock Cornw'l 8 B3
Polchar H'land 426 B3
Pole Elm Worcs 153 C6
Polebrook Northants 203 F7
Polegate E Sussex 50 E4
Poles H'land 440 D4
Polesden Lacey, Dorking Surrey 68 A4
Poleshill Som'set 37 B6
Polesworth Warwick 199 C6
Polgigga Cornw'l 2 F3
Polglass H'land 438 C4
Polgooth Cornw'l 8 E2
Poling W Sussex 47 F8
Poling Corner W Sussex 47 E8
Polkerris Cornw'l 8 E4
Poll Hill Mersey 263 C7
Polla H'land 443 C5
Polladras Cornw'l 3 D8
Pollard Street Norfolk 234 B3
Pollhill Kent 72 A4
Pollie H'land 440 B4
Pollington ER Yorks 283 A6
Polliwilline Arg/Bute 404 F3
Polloch H'land 423 F7
Pollok Glasg C 392 F3
Pollok House Glasg C 392 F3
Pollokshaws Glasg C 392 F3
Pollokshields Glasg C 392 F3
Pollyfield Kent 92 D2
Polmadie Glasg C 392 F3
Polmarth Cornw'l 4 C2
Polmassick Cornw'l 5 A7
Polmear Cornw'l 8 E4
Polmont Falk 394 C3
Polmont Station Falk 394 C3
Polnessan E Ayrs 367 E8
Polnish H'land 423 D7
Polopit Northants 181 C8
Polperro Cornw'l 9 E7
Polruan Cornw'l 9 E5
Polscoe Cornw'l 9 C5
Polsham Som'set 60 C2
Polsloe Park Devon 21 B8
Polsloe Priory Devon 21 B8
Polstead Suffolk 164 E4
Polstead Heath Suffolk 164 D4
Poltalloch Arg/Bute 407 C8
Poltesco Cornw'l 5 G2
Poltimore Devon 22 A1
Polton Midloth 396 F2
Poltonhall Midloth 396 F3
Polwarth Scot Borders 386 B4
Polyphant Cornw'l 18 D2
Polzeath Cornw'l 16 E3
Pomphlett Plym'th 11 E6
Pond Street Essex 162 E2
Ponde Powys 149 E7
Ponders End London 112 C2
Pondersbridge Cambs 204 E4
Pondtail Hants 87 F6
Pondwell I/Wight 30 B4
Ponjeravah Cornw'l 4 E2
Ponsanooth Cornw'l 4 C3
Ponsford Devon 36 E4
Ponsonby Cumb 325 E6
Ponsongath Cornw'l 5 G3
Ponsworthy Devon 20 F4
Pont Cornw'l 9 E5
Pont Aber-Geirw Gwyn 215 C7
Pont ar Hydfer Powys 125 B6
Pont Cyfyng Conwy 238 C2
Pont Cysyllte Wrex 241 F6
Pont Hwfa Angl 258 C1
Pont Llogel Powys 217 E5
Pont Rhydgaled Powys 170 B1
Pont Rhyd-y-berry Powys 148 E4
Pont Rhyd-y-cyff Bridg 98 E4
Pont Senni = Sennybridge Powys 125 B7
Pont Sion Norton Rh Cyn Taff 99 D8
Pont Walby Neath P Talb 98 A4
Pontamman Carms 124 E1
Pontantwn Carms 122 E4
Pontardawe Neath P Talb 98 B1
Pontarddulais Swan 97 B6
Pontarfynach = Devil's Bridge Ceredig'n 169 C7
Pont-ar-gothi Carms 123 C6
Pont-ar-llechau Carms 124 C3
Pontarsais Carms 122 B4
Pontblyddyn Flints 241 B6
Pontbren Araeth Carms 124 C2
Pontbren Llwyd Rh Cyn Taff 125 F7
Pontcanna Card 78 A3
Pontdolgoch Powys 192 E4
Pontefract W Yorks 294 F3
Pontefract Racecourse W Yorks 294 F2
Ponteland Northum 352 B2
Ponterwyd Ceredig'n 169 B7
Pontesbury Shrops 194 B4
Pontesbury Hill Shrops 194 B3
Pontesford Shrops 194 B4
Pontfadog Wrex 218 A1
Pontfaen Pembs 119 C8
Pont-faen Powys 148 F4
Pont-Faen Shrops 218 A2
Pontgarreg Ceredig'n 145 B6
Pont-Henri Carms 123 F5
Ponthir Torf 101 D6
Ponthirwaun Ceredig'n 145 C5
Pontiago Pembs 119 B6
Pont-iets = Pontyates Carms 123 F5
Pontllanfraith Caerph 100 C3
Pontlliw Swan 97 B7
Pontllyfni Gwyn 236 D4
Pontlottyn Caerph 100 A2
Pontneddfechan Neath P Talb 125 F6
Pont-newydd Carms 122 F4
Pontnewydd Torf 101 C5
Pontnewynydd Torf 101 B5
Pantperthog Powys 191 C5
Pontrhydfendigaid Ceredig'n 169 E7
Pontrhydyfen Rh Cyn Taff 98 D2
Pont-rhyd-y-groes Ceredig'n 169 D7
Pontrhydyrun Torf 101 C5
Pont-Rhys-Powell Monmouths 127 C7
Pont-Rhythallt Gwyn 237 B6
Pontrilas Heref'd 128 B2
Pontrobert Powys 193 A6
Pont-rug Gwyn 237 B6
Ponts Green E Sussex 51 C6
Pontshill Heref'd 129 C6
Pont-Sian Ceredig'n 145 C8
Pontsticill Merth Tyd 126 E2
Pontyates = Pont-iets Carms 123 F5
Pontyberem Carms 123 E6
Pont-y-bodkin Flints 241 C6
Pontyclun Rh Cyn Taff 99 E6
Pontycymer Bridg 99 D5
Pontyglasier Pembs 144 E2
Pont-y-gwaith Rh Cyn Taff 99 D7
Pontymister Caerph 100 E4
Pontymoel Torf 101 B5
Pont-y-pant Conwy 238 D2
Pontypool Torf 101 B6
Pontypool Park Torf 101 B5
Pontypridd Rh Cyn Taff 99 E7
Pont-yr-Hafod Pembs 120 B2
Pont-y-rhyl Bridg 99 E5
Pontywaun Caerph 100 D4
Pooksgreen Hants 44 D2
Pool Cornw'l 4 B1
Pool I/Scilly 6 B2
Pool W Yorks 293 B6
Pool Green W Midlands 198 C2
Pool o'Muckhart Clack 411 B5
Pool Quay Powys 193 A9
Pool Town Som'set 57 D6
Poolbrook Heref'd 153 D5
Poole N Yorks 294 E3
Poole Poole 27 B7

Poole Som'set 37 B7
Poole Keynes Glos 104 C5
Poolend Staffs 244 C5
Poolewe H'land 438 E2
Pooley Bridge Cumb 327 B6
Pooley Street Norfolk 187 B6
Poolford Staffs 244 C3
Poolhill Glos 129 B8
Poolmill Heref'd 129 C5
Poolsbrook Derby 269 E8
Poolside Moray 436 D1
Poolstock Gtr Man 277 D8
Pootings Kent 70 B4
Popeswood Brackn'l 87 C6
Popham Hants 65 C8
Poplar London 112 F2
Popley Hants 86 F2
Porchester Notts 248 F2
Porchfield I/Wight 29 B8
Porin H'land 433 C5
Poringland Norfolk 210 C1
Porkellis Cornw'l 4 D1
Porlock Som'set 56 B4
Porlock Weir Som'set 56 B4
Porlockford Som'set 56 B4
Port Allen Perth/Kinr 420 E2
Port Ann Arg/Bute 408 D2
Port Appin Arg/Bute 416 C4
Port Askaig Arg/Bute 406 F4
Port Bannatyne Arg/Bute 408 F3
Port Carlisle Cumb 347 D6
Port Charlotte Arg/Bute 403 A2
Port Clarence Stockton 332 B4
Port Dinorwic = Y Felinheli Gwyn 259 F7
Port Driseach Arg/Bute 408 E2
Port e Vullen I/Man 336 B4
Port Edgar C/Edinb 395 C7
Port Eliot Cornw'l 10 D3
Port Ellen Arg/Bute 403 B3
Port Elphinstone Aberds 429 A4
Port Erin I/Man 336 E1
Port Erroll Aberds 437 E7
Port Eynon Swan 96 E4
Port Glasgow Invercl 391 D6
Port Ham Glos 130 D2
Port Henderson H'land 438 F1
Port Hill Oxon 108 E3
Port Isaac Cornw'l 16 D4
Port Lamont Arg/Bute 408 E3
Port Lion Pembs 117 C5
Port Logan Dumf/Gal 400 E2
Port Lympne Kent 74 E2
Port Mead Swan 97 C7
Port Mholair W Isles 451 D8
Port Mor H'land 422 E4
Port Mulgrave N Yorks 334 C2
Port Nan Giùran W Isles 451 D8
Port nan Long W Isles 447 A3
Port Nis W Isles 451 A8
Port of Menteith Stirl 409 B8
Port Ramsay Arg/Bute 416 C3
Port St. Mary I/Man 336 E2
Port Sunlight Mersey 264 C1
Port Talbot Neath P Talb 98 E2
Port Tennant Swan 97 D8
Port Wemyss Arg/Bute 403 A1
Port William Dumf/Gal 401 E5
Portachoillan Arg/Bute 404 A3
Portavadie Arg/Bute 408 F2
Portbury N Som'set 80 A2
Portchester Hants 45 F7
Portclair H'land 425 A6
Portencalzie Dumf/Gal 400 B2
Portencross N Ayrs 378 C3
Portesham Dorset 25 C6
Portessie Moray 436 B1
Portfield Arg/Bute 416 E2
Portfield W Sussex 47 F5
Portfield Gate Pembs 116 A4
Portgate Devon 19 C5
Portgaverne Cornw'l 16 D5
Portgordon Moray 435 B8
Portgower H'land 441 B7
Porth Cornw'l 7 C7
Porth Rh Cyn Taff 99 D7
Porth Colmon Gwyn 212 B3
Porth Dinllaen Gwyn 236 F1
Porth Kea Cornw'l 4 B4
Porth Navas Cornw'l 4 E3
Porth Tocyn Gwyn 213 C6
Porth Tywyn = Burry Port Carms 96 B3
Porthaethwy = Menai Bridge Angl 259 E8
Porthallow Cornw'l 4 F3
Porthallow Cornw'l 9 E7
Porthcawl Bridg 76 A3
Porthcothan Cornw'l 7 A8
Porthcurno Cornw'l 2 F3
Porthgain Pembs 118 C4
Porthgwarra Cornw'l 2 F3
Porthill Shrops 195 A5
Porthill Staffs 244 E3
Porthkerry V/Glam 77 C8
Porthleven Cornw'l 3 E8
Porthllechog = Bull Bay Angl 259 A5
Porthloo I/Scilly 6 B3
Porthmadog Gwyn 214 A3
Porth-mawr Pembs 118 D2
Porthmeor Cornw'l 2 C4
Portholland Cornw'l 5 B7
Porthoustock Cornw'l 4 F4
Porthtowan Cornw'l 6 F4
Porthwgan Wrex 241 E8
Porth-y-felin Angl 258 C1
Porthyrhyd Carms 123 D6
Porthyrhyd Carms 147 E7
Porth-y-waen Shrops 218 C2
Portico Mersey 264 A4
Portincaple Arg/Bute 409 C5
Portington Devon 19 E5
Portington ER Yorks 296 D2
Portinnisherrich Arg/Bute 408 A2
Portinscale Cumb 326 B1
Portishead N Som'set 80 A1
Portkil Arg/Bute 409 D5
Portknockie Moray 436 B1
Portland Som'set 60 D1
Portlethen Aberds 429 C6
Portlethen Village Aberds 429 C6
Portlevorchy H'land 442 C4
Portling Dumf/Gal 402 D2
Portloe Cornw'l 5 C6
Portlooe Cornw'l 9 E7
Portmahomack H'land 441 E6
Portmeirion Village Gwyn 214 A3
Portmellon Cornw'l 5 B8
Portmore Hants 29 A6
Portnacroish Arg/Bute 416 C4
Portnahaven Arg/Bute 403 A1
Portnalong H'land 430 E3
Portnaluchaig H'land 423 D6
Portnancon H'land 443 B6
Portnellan Stirl 418 E2
Portnellan Stirl 409 A7
Portobello C/Edinb 396 D3
Portobello Tyne/Wear 352 E4
Portobello W Midlands 197 D8
Portobello W Yorks 281 A8
Porton Wilts 63 D8
Portpatrick Dumf/Gal 400 D2
Portquin Cornw'l 16 D4
Portrack Stockton 332 C4
Portreath Cornw'l 3 A9
Portree H'land 430 D4
Portscatho Cornw'l 5 C5
Portsea Portsm'th 45 F7
Portskerra H'land 444 B2
Portskewett Monmouths 102 E1
Portslade Brighton/Hove 49 E5
Portslade-by-Sea Brighton/Hove 49 F5
Portsmouth Portsm'th 45 F7
Portsmouth W Yorks 291 E7
Portsonachan Arg/Bute 417 E5
Portsoy Aberds 436 B2
Portswood S'thampton 44 D3
Porttanachy Moray 435 B8
Portuairk H'land 422 F4
Portvasgo H'land 443 B7
Portway Heref'd 151 C7
Portway Heref'd 151 E7
Portway Som'set 60 D1
Portway Warwick 176 D4
Portway W Midlands 197 F8
Portwrinkle Cornw'l 10 E3
Posenhall Shrops 196 C2
Poslingford Suffolk 163 C8
Possil Park Glasg C 392 E3
Post Green Dorset 27 B6
Postbridge Devon 20 E3
Postcombe Oxon 108 C4
Postling Kent 74 D2
Postlip Glos 131 B6
Postwick Norfolk 210 B1
Pot Common Surrey 67 C8
Potarch Aberds 428 C3
Potbridge Hants 86 F5
Potholm Dumf/Gal 360 E4
Potmaily H'land 433 E6
Potsgrove Beds 136 A3
Pott Row Norfolk 231 D6
Pott Shrigley Ches 267 D5
Potten End Herts 136 F4
Potten Street Kent 94 C5
Potter Brompton N Yorks 322 E3
Potter Heigham Norfolk 235 E5
Potter Hill S Yorks 281 E8
Potter Somersal Derby 222 A4
Potter Street Essex 139 F5
Pottergate Street Norfolk 209 E7
Potterhanworth Lincs 250 A4
Potterhanworth Booths Lincs 273 F6
Potteries Museum & Art Gallery, Stoke-on-Trent Stoke 244 E3
Potterne Wilts 82 E4
Potterne Wick Wilts 82 E4
Potternewton W Yorks 293 C8
Potters Bar Herts 111 B6
Potters Brook Lancs 301 E8
Potter's Corner Kent 73 C6
Potter's Cross Durham 330 A3
Potter's Cross Staffs 175 B6
Potters Crouch Herts 110 A4
Potter's End Beds 136 B3
Potter's Forstal Kent 72 B4
Potter's Green E Sussex 50 B3
Potter's Green Herts 138 C3
Potter's Green W Midlands 178 B2
Potters Marston Leics 200 D4
Pottersheath Herts 137 D8
Potterspury Northants 158 D3
Potterton Aberds 429 A6
Potterton W Yorks 294 C2
Potthorpe Norfolk 232 D3
Pottington Devon 55 E6
Pottle Street Wilts 62 B2
Pottlelake Devon 23 A6
Potto N Yorks 332 F4
Potton Beds 160 C4
Pott's Green Essex 141 C7
Pouchen End Herts 136 F4
Poughill Cornw'l 32 E4
Poughill Devon 36 E2
Poulner Hants 43 E6
Poulshot Wilts 82 E4
Poulton Ches 241 C8
Poulton Glos 105 B7
Poulton Mersey 263 A7
Poulton-le-Fylde Lancs 288 C4
Pound Bank Worcs 153 C5
Pound Gate Shrops 171 B8
Pound Green E Sussex 50 B3
Pound Green Hants 85 E8
Pound Green I/Wight 29 C6
Pound Green Suffolk 163 B7
Pound Green Worcs 175 C5
Pound Hill W Sussex 69 D7
Pound Street Hants 85 D6
Poundffald Swan 97 D6
Poundfield E Sussex 71 E5
Poundgate E Sussex 70 F4
Poundgreen Wokingham 86 C3
Poundland S Ayrs 400 A3
Poundon Bucks 134 B3
Poundsbridge Kent 71 C5
Poundsgate Devon 14 A2
Poundstock Cornw'l 17 A9
Pounsley E Sussex 50 B3
Powburn Northum 376 D3
Powder Mills Kent 71 B6
Powderham Devon 22 D1
Powderham Castle Devon 22 D1
Powers Hall End Essex 140 D5
Powerstock Dorset 24 A5
Powfoot Dumf/Gal 346 C4
Powhill Cumb 347 E6
Powick Worcs 153 B6
Powis Castle, Welshpool Powys 193 B8
Powler's Piece Devon 33 C7
Powmill Perth/Kinr 411 C5
Pownall Park Ches 266 C3
Powntley Copse Hants 66 C4
Poxwell Dorset 26 D1
Poyle Surrey 88 A2
Poynders End Herts 137 C7
Poynings W Sussex 49 D5
Poyntington Dorset 40 B2
Poynton Ches 267 C5
Poynton Telford 219 E8
Poynton Green Telford 219 E8
Poyntzfield H'land 434 B2
Poyston Pembs 117 A5
Poystreet Green Suffolk 164 A4
Praa Sands Cornw'l 3 E7
Pratling Street Kent 92 E1
Pratthall Derby 269 E6
Pratt's Bottom London 90 D4
Praze-an-Beeble Cornw'l 3 C8
Prees Shrops 219 B8
Prees Green Shrops 219 B8
Prees Heath Shrops 219 A8
Prees Higher Heath Shrops 219 A8
Prees Lower Heath Shrops 219 B8
Prees Wood Shrops 219 B8
Preesall Lancs 301 F6
Preesall Moss Side Lancs 301 F6
Preesall Park Lancs 288 A4
Preesgweene Shrops 218 A2
Prendergast Pembs 117 A5
Prenderguest Scot Borders 387 A8
Pren-gwyn Ceredig'n 145 D8
Prenteg Gwyn 237 F7
Prenton Mersey 263 B8
Prescot Mersey 264 A4
Prescott Devon 37 D6
Prescott Shrops 219 D5
Preshome Moray 436 B1
Preshute Wilts 83 C8
Pressen Northum 387 E6
Prestatyn Denbs 262 C3
Prestbury Ches 267 D5
Prestbury Glos 131 C5
Presteigne = Llanandras Powys 172 F4
Presthope Shrops 195 D7
Prestleigh Som'set 60 C4
Prestolee Gtr Man 278 C4
Preston Brighton/Hove 49 E6
Preston Scot Borders 387 A5
Preston Dorset 25 D9
Preston Devon 21 F7
Preston E Loth 396 D4
Preston E Loth 398 C1
Preston ER Yorks 298 D2
Preston Glos 105 B5
Preston Glos 152 F3
Preston Herts 137 C7
Preston Kent 94 D5
Preston Kent 93 D7
Preston Lancs 289 E7
Preston London 111 E5
Preston Northum 377 B5
Preston Rutl'd 202 C3
Preston Shrops 195 A6
Preston Som'set 58 D1
Preston Torbay 15 C5
Preston Tyne/Wear 353 C6
Preston Wilts 84 B2
Preston Wilts 83 A5
Preston Bagot Warwick 177 E6
Preston Bissett Bucks 134 B4
Preston Bowyer Som'set 37 A7
Preston Brockhurst Shrops 219 D7
Preston Brook Halton 265 C6
Preston Candover Hants 66 C2
Preston Capes Northants 157 B6
Preston Crowmarsh Oxon 108 D2
Preston Deanery Northants 158 A3
Preston Grange Tyne/Wear 353 B5
Preston Green Warwick 177 E6
Preston Gubbals Shrops 219 E6
Preston Hall Museum, Stockton-on-Tees Stockton 332 C3
Preston Marsh Heref'd 152 C1
Preston on Stour Warwick 155 C7
Preston on the Hill Halton 265 C6
Preston on Wye Heref'd 151 D5
Preston Plucknett Som'set 39 C8
Preston St. Mary Suffolk 164 B3
Preston Street Kent 94 D4
Preston upon the Weald Moors Telford 220 E3
Preston Wynne Heref'd 151 C9
Prestonfield C/Edinb 396 D2
Preston-le-Skerne Durham 331 B8
Prestonmill Dumf/Gal 402 D3
Preston-on-Tees Stockton 332 C3
Prestonpans E Loth 396 D4
Preston-under-Scar N Yorks 317 B7
Prestwich Gtr Man 279 D5
Prestwick Northum 352 B2
Prestwick S Ayrs 367 B6
Prestwold Leics 225 D6
Prestwood Bucks 109 B7
Prestwood Staffs 245 F8
Price Town Bridg 99 D5
Prickwillow Cambs 184 B4
Priddy Som'set 60 A2
Priest Hutton Lancs 314 F4
Priest Weston Shrops 194 D1
Priestacott Devon 33 E8
Priestcliffe Derby 268 E2
Priestend Oxon 134 F4
Priestfield W Midlands 197 D7
Priestfield Worcs 153 D6
Priesthaugh Scot Borders 361 B6
Priesthill Glasg C 392 F2
Priesthorpe W Yorks 292 C4
Priesthorpe W Yorks 293 C6
Priestland E Ayrs 380 E3
Priestley Green W Yorks 292 E4
Priestside Dumf/Gal 346 C4
Priestwood Brackn'l 87 C7
Priestwood Kent 91 D8
Priestwood Green Kent 91 D8
Primethorpe Leics 200 E4
Primrose Tyne/Wear 353 D5
Primrose Green Norfolk 233 E6
Primrose Hill Bath/NE Som'set 81 C6
Primrose Hill Bucks 109 C7
Primrose Hill Glos 102 B4
Primrose Hill Lancs 276 C4
Primrose Valley N Yorks 323 E6
Primrosehill W Midlands 197 E8
Prince Royd W Yorks 280 A4
Princes Gate Pembs 121 E6
Princes Park Mersey 264 B2
Princes Park Medway 92 D2
Princes Risborough Bucks 109 B6
Princethorpe Warwick 178 D3
Princetown Caerph 126 F3
Princetown Devon 20 F1
Prinknash Abbey, Gloucester Glos 130 E3
Prinsted W Sussex 46 E3
Printstile Kent 71 C5
Prion Denbs 240 B2
Prior Muir Fife 421 F5
Prior Park Northum 388 B1
Prior Rigg Cumb 348 C3
Prior's Frome Heref'd 152 E1
Priors Halton Shrops 173 C7
Priors Hardwick Warwick 156 A4
Priors Marston Warwick 156 A4
Prior's Norton Glos 130 C3
Priors Park Glos 130 A3
Priorslee Telford 196 B3
Priorswood Som'set 38 A2
Priory Pembs 116 C4
Priory Church, Lancaster Lancs 301 C8
Priory Green Suffolk 164 D3
Priory Heath Suffolk 166 D1
Priory Wood Heref'd 150 C3
Prisk V/Glam 77 A7
Priston Bath/NE Som'set 81 D5
Pristow Green Norfolk 209 F6
Prittlewell Southend 114 E4
Privett Hants 66 F3
Privett Hants 30 A3
Prixford Devon 55 D5
Probus Cornw'l 7 F8
Proncy H'land 440 D4
Prospect Cumb 337 C8
Prospect Village Staffs 198 A1
Prospidnick Cornw'l 3 D8
Provanmill Glasg C 392 E4
Providence Bristol 80 B2
Prudhoe Northum 351 D9
Ptarmigan Lodge Stirl 409 B6
Pubil Perth/Kinr 418 C2
Publow Bath/NE Som'set 80 D4
Puckeridge Herts 138 C3
Puckington Som'set 39 C5
Pucklechurch S Glos 81 A5
Pucknall Hants 44 B2
Puckrup Glos 153 E7
Puckshole Glos 103 A8
Puddaven Devon 14 C3
Puddinglake Ches 266 F1
Puddington Ches 263 E8
Puddington Devon 36 D1
Puddlebrook Glos 129 D6
Puddledock Kent 70 A4
Puddledock Norfolk 208 E5
Puddletown Dorset 26 B1
Puddock Bridge Cambs 205 F6
Pudds Cross Herts 110 B2
Pudleigh Som'set 38 D4
Pudleston Heref'd 152 A1
Pudsey W Yorks 291 E7
Pudsey W Yorks 293 D6
Pulborough W Sussex 47 C9
Pulcree Dumf/Gal 401 D7
Pulford Ches 241 D5
Pulham Dorset 40 E4
Pulham Market Norfolk 188 A1
Pulham St. Mary Norfolk 188 A2
Pullens Green S Glos 102 D4
Pulley Shrops 195 B5
Pulloxhill Beds 159 F9
Pulverbatch Shrops 194 C4
Pumpherston W Loth 395 E6
Pumsaint Carms 147 D6
Puncheston Pembs 120 B4
Puncknowle Dorset 25 C5
Punnett's Town E Sussex 50 B5
Purbrook Hants 45 E8
Purewell Dorset 28 B3
Purfleet Thurr'k 91 A6
Puriton Som'set 59 C6
Purleigh Essex 114 B3
Purley London 89 D8
Purley on Thames W Berks 86 A3
Purlpit Wilts 82 C2
Purls Bridge Cambs 205 F8
Purse Caundle Dorset 40 C3
Purslow Shrops 172 B5
Purston Jaglin W Yorks 282 A2
Purtington Som'set 39 E5
Purton Glos 103 B5
Purton Glos 103 B5
Purton Wilts 105 E6
Purton Stoke Wilts 105 D6
Purving Row Som'set 79 F6
Pury End Northants 158 C2
Pusey Oxon 106 C4
Putley Heref'd 152 E2
Putley Common Heref'd 152 E2
Putley Green Heref'd 152 E3
Putloe Glos 130 F1
Putney London 89 B6
Putney Vale London 89 B6
Putnoe Beds 160 B1
Putsborough Devon 54 C3
Putson Heref'd 151 E8
Puttenham Herts 135 E8
Puttenham Surrey 67 B8
Puttock's End Essex 139 D7
Putton Dorset 25 D8
Puxton N Som'set 79 D8
Pwll Carms 96 B4
Pwllcrochan Pembs 116 D4
Pwlldefaid Gwyn 212 C3
Pwll-du Monmouths 127 E5
Pwll-glas Denbs 240 D3
Pwllgloyw Powys 149 F5
Pwllheli Gwyn 213 A7
Pwll-Mawr Card 78 A4
Pwllmeyric Monmouths 102 D2
Pwll-y-glaw Rh Cyn Taff 98 D2
Pwll-y-pant Caerph 100 E3
Pwltrap Carms 122 D1
Pydew Conwy 262 D6
Pye Corner Kent 72 B4
Pye Corner Newp 101 E5
Pye Corner Powys 172 D2
Pye Corner S Glos 80 A4
Pye Corner Som'set 39 D8
Pye Green Staffs 222 F1
Pye Hill Notts 247 D6
Pyecombe W Sussex 49 D5
Pyewipe NE Lincs 286 B4
Pyle Swan 97 E6
Pyle = Y Pîl Bridg 98 F3
Pylle Som'set 60 E4
Pymoor Cambs 184 A2
Pymore Dorset 24 B4
Pyott's Hill Hants 86 F3
Pyrford Surrey 88 E2
Pyrford Common Surrey 88 E2
Pyrford Green Surrey 88 E2
Pyrland Som'set 58 F4
Pyrton Oxon 108 C3
Pysgodlyn Monmouths 127 D6
Pytchley Northants 180 D5
Pyworthy Devon 33 F6


## Q


Quabbs Shrops 172 B2
Quabrook E Sussex 70 E3
Quadring Lincs 228 B4
Quadring Eaudike Lincs 228 B4
Quainton Bucks 135 C5
Quaker's Yard Merth Tyd 100 C1
Quaking Houses Durham 343 A7
Quality Corner Cumb 324 B4
Quants Som'set 38 C1
Quarley Hants 64 C2
Quarmby W Yorks 280 A4
Quarndon Derby 246 F4
Quarndon Common Derby 246 F4
Quarr Dorset 41 A5
Quarr Hill I/Wight 30 B3
Quarrelton Renf 391 F8
Quarrelwood Dumf/Gal 358 F3
Quarrendon Bucks 135 D7
Quarrier's Village Invercl 391 E7
Quarrington Lincs 250 F4
Quarrington Hill Durham 344 D2
Quarry Bank W Midlands 175 A8
Quarry Bank Mill, Wilmslow Ches 266 C3
Quarry Hill Staffs 199 C5
Quarrybank Ches 242 A4
Quarryford E Loth 397 E8
Quarryhead Aberds 437 B6
Quarryhill H'land 440 E4
Quarrywood Moray 435 B6
Quarter S Lanarks 381 B6
Quatford Shrops 196 E3
Quatquoy Orkney 452 B4
Quatt Shrops 196 F4
Quebb Heref'd 150 B4
Quebec Durham 343 C7
Quedgeley Glos 130 E2
Queen Adelaide Cambs 184 B4
Queen Camel Som'set 40 B1
Queen Charlton Bath/NE Som'set 80 C4
Queen Dart Devon 36 C1
Queen Oak Dorset 61 E7
Queen Street Kent 71 B8
Queen Street Wilts 105 E5
Queenborough Kent 93 B5
Queenhill Worcs 153 E7
Queen's Bower I/Wight 30 D3
Queen's Head Shrops 218 C3
Queen's Park Blackb'n 290 E2
Queen's Park Beds 159 C8
Queens Park Ches 242 A1
Queens Park Essex 113 C8
Queen's Park Northants 180 F3
Queen's View Centre, Loch Tummel Perth/Kinr 419 B6
Queensbury London 111 E5
Queensbury W Yorks 292 D3
Queensferry C/Edinb 395 C7
Queensferry Flints 263 F8
Queenstown Blackp'l 288 C3
Queensville Staffs 221 D8
Queenzieburn N Lanarks 393 C5
Quemerford Wilts 82 B5
Quenchwell Cornw'l 4 B3
Quendale Shetl'd 455 E2
Quendon Essex 139 A6
Queniborough Leics 201 A6
Quenington Glos 105 B7
Quernmore Lancs 302 D2
Queslett W Midlands 198 E2
Quethiock Cornw'l 10 C2
Quhamm Shetl'd 457 G4
Quholm Orkney 452 B3
Quick Gtr Man 279 D8
Quick Edge Gtr Man 279 D8
Quick's Green W Berks 85 A8
Quidenham Norfolk 208 F4
Quidhampton Hants 65 A7
Quidhampton Wilts 63 E7
Quilquox Aberds 437 E6
Quina Brook Shrops 219 B7
Quindry Orkney 453 D5
Quinton Northants 158 B3
Quinton W Midlands 176 B2
Quinton Green Northants 158 B3
Quintrell Downs Cornw'l 7 D8
Quixhill Staffs 245 F8
Quoditch Devon 19 A5
Quoig Perth/Kinr 419 E6
Quorndon Leics 225 E6
Quothquan S Lanarks 382 E4
Quoyloo Orkney 452 A3
Quoynee H'land 445 C6
Quoyness Orkney 452 C3
Quoys Shetl'd 456 B6
Quoys Shetl'd 457 G4


## R


Raasay Ho. H'land 431 E5
Rabbit's Cross Kent 72 B3
Rableyheath Herts 137 D8
Raby Cumb 338 A2
Raby Mersey 263 D8
Racecourse Suffolk 165 D8
Rachan Mill Scot Borders 383 F7
Rachub Gwyn 260 F2
Rack End Oxon 107 B5
Rackenford Devon 36 C2
Rackham W Sussex 47 D9
Rackheath Norfolk 234 F2
Rackley Som'set 79 F7
Racks Dumf/Gal 346 B2
Rackwick Orkney 454 B2
Rackwick Orkney 452 D3
Radbourne Derby 223 A7
Radcliffe Gtr Man 278 C4
Radcliffe Northum 365 B7
Radcliffe on Trent Notts 225 A7
Radclive Bucks 157 F8
Radcot Oxon 106 C2
Raddery H'land 434 C2
Raddington Som'set 37 A5
Radernie Fife 412 B2
Radfall Kent 94 D2
Radford Blackb'n 290 F2
Radford Bath/NE Som'set 81 E5
Radford Notts 248 F2
Radford Oxon 133 C7
Radford W Midlands 178 B1
Radford Worcs 154 A3
Radford Semele Warwick 178 F1
Radipole Dorset 25 D8
Radlet Som'set 58 D4
Radlett Herts 111 B5
Radley Oxon 107 C7
Radley Green Essex 113 A7
Radmanthwaite Notts 247 B8
Radmoor Shrops 220 D2
Radmore Green Ches 242 D4
Radmore Wood Staffs 222 C3
Radnage Bucks 109 C5
Radnor Park W Dunb 392 D1
Radstock Bath/NE Som'set 81 E5
Radstone Northants 157 D6
Radway Warwick 156 C2
Radwell Beds 159 A8
Radwell Herts 160 E4
Radwinter Essex 162 E5
Radwinter End Essex 162 E5
Radyr Card 100 F2
Raera Arg/Bute 416 E3
RAF Museum, Cosford Shrops 196 C4
RAF Museum, Hendon London 111 D6
Rafford Moray 435 C5
Raftra Cornw'l 2 F3
Raga Shetl'd 456 D4
Ragdale Leics 225 E8
Ragged Appleshaw Hants 64 B3
Raginnis Cornw'l 2 E5
Raglan Monmouths 128 F2
Ragley Hall Warwick 154 A4
Ragmere Norfolk 208 E5
Ragnall Notts 271 E8
Rahoy H'land 416 B1
Raigbeg H'land 434 F3
Rain Shore Gtr Man 279 A6
Rainbow Hill Worcs 153 A7
Rainford Mersey 277 D6
Rainford Junction Mersey 277 D6
Rainham London 113 F5
Rainham Medway 92 C3
Rainhill Mersey 264 A4
Rainhill Stoops Mersey 264 A5
Rainow Ches 267 D6
Rainowlow Ches 267 D6
Rainsough Gtr Man 279 D5
Rainton Dumf/Gal 401 D8
Rainton N Yorks 319 E6
Rainton Bridge Tyne/Wear 344 C2
Rainworth Notts 248 D2
Raisbeck Cumb 328 E2
Raise Cumb 341 B5
Rait Perth/Kinr 420 E2
Raithby Lincs 274 F4
Raithby Lincs 274 C3
Raithwaite N Yorks 334 D4
Rake W Sussex 67 F6
Rake End Staffs 222 E3
Rake Head Lancs 291 F5
Rakes Dale Staffs 245 F7
Rakeway Staffs 245 F6
Rakewood Gtr Man 279 B7
Ralia Lodge H'land 426 C2
Rallt Swan 96 D5
Ram Carms 146 C4
Ram Alley Wilts 84 D1
Ram Hill S Glos 81 A5
Ram Lane Kent 73 B6
Ramasaig H'land 430 D1
Rame Cornw'l 4 D2
Rame Cornw'l 10 F4
Rameldry Mill Bank Fife 411 B8
Ramley Hants 29 A5
Ramnageo Shetl'd 456 C6
Rampisham Dorset 39 F9
Rampside Cumb 300 B3
Rampton Cambs 183 E8
Rampton Notts 271 D7
Ramsbottom Gtr Man 279 A5
Ramsburn Moray 436 C2
Ramsbury Wilts 84 B2
Ramscraigs H'land 445 F5
Ramsdean Hants 46 B2
Ramsdell Hants 85 E8
Ramsden London 90 C4
Ramsden Oxon 133 D6
Ramsden Bellhouse Essex 114 D1
Ramsden Heath Essex 114 C1
Ramsey Cambs 183 A5
Ramsey Essex 143 A5
Ramsey I/Man 336 B4
Ramsey Forty Foot Cambs 204 F5
Ramsey Heights Cambs 183 A5
Ramsey Island Essex 115 A5
Ramsey Mereside Cambs 204 F4
Ramsey St. Mary's Cambs 204 F4
Ramseycleuch Scot Borders 372 E2
Ramsgate Kent 95 D7
Ramsgill N Yorks 305 A6
Ramshaw Durham 342 B3
Ramsholt Suffolk 166 D4
Ramshorn Staffs 245 E7
Ramsley Devon 20 B2
Ramslye Kent 71 D6
Ranais W Isles 451 E7
Ranby Lincs 274 D1
Ranby Notts 271 C5

Rand Lincs 273 D7
Randlay Telford 196 B3
Randwick Glos 103 A8
Ranfurly Renf 391 F7
Rangag H'land 445 D5
Rangemore Staffs 223 D5
Rangeworthy S Glos 103 E5
Rankinston E Ayrs 367 E9
Rank's Green Essex 140 D3
Ranmoor S Yorks 269 B6
Ranmore Common Surrey 68 A4
Rannerdale Cumb 325 C8
Rannoch Lodge Perth/Kinr 418 B3
Rannoch Station Perth/Kinr 418 B2
Ranochan H'land 423 D8
Ranscombe Som'set 57 C5
Ranskill Notts 271 C5
Ranton Staffs 221 D7
Ranton Green Staffs 221 D6
Ranworth Norfolk 234 F4
Raploch Stirl 410 C2
Rapness Orkney 454 B3
Rapps Som'set 38 C4
Rascal Moor ER Yorks 296 C3
Rascarrel Dumf/Gal 402 E1
Rashielee Renf 392 D1
Rashiereive Aberds 437 F6
Rashwood Worcs 175 E8
Raskelf N Yorks 307 A6
Rassal H'land 431 D8
Rassau Bl Gwent 126 E4
Rastrick W Yorks 292 F4
Ratagan H'land 424 A1
Ratby Leics 200 B4
Ratcliffe Culey Leics 199 D7
Ratcliffe on Soar Notts 224 C4
Ratcliffe on the Wreake Leics 225 F7
Ratford Wilts 82 B4
Ratfyn Wilts 63 C8
Rathen Aberds 437 B7
Rathillet Fife 420 E3
Rathmell N Yorks 303 D8
Ratho C/Edinb 395 D7
Ratho Byres C/Edinb 395 D7
Ratho Station C/Edinb 395 D7
Rathven Moray 436 B1
Ratlake Hants 44 B3
Ratley Warwick 156 C2
Ratling Kent 74 A4
Ratlinghope Shrops 194 D4
Ratsloe Devon 21 A9
Rattar H'land 445 A6
Ratten Row Cumb 338 C5
Ratten Row Cumb 339 B6
Ratten Row Lancs 289 B5
Ratten Row Norfolk 230 F2
Rattery Devon 14 C2
Rattlesden Suffolk 164 A4
Ratton Village E Sussex 50 F4
Rattray Perth/Kinr 420 C1
Raughton Cumb 339 B6
Raughton Head Cumb 339 B6
Raunds Northants 181 D7
Ravelston C/Edinb 395 D9
Ravenfield S Yorks 282 E3
Ravenglass Cumb 312 A2
Ravenglass and Eskdale Railway & Museum Cumb 312 A2
Ravenhead Mersey 277 F8
Raveningham Norfolk 210 D3
Raven's Green Essex 142 C3
Ravenscar N Yorks 335 F6
Ravenscliffe W Yorks 293 C5
Ravenscraig Invercl 390 D4
Ravensdale I/Man 336 B3
Ravensden Beds 160 B1
Ravenseat N Yorks 329 F7
Ravenshead Notts 248 D2
Ravenshills Green Worcs 152 B4
Ravensmoor Ches 243 D5
Ravensthorpe Northants 179 D8
Ravensthorpe Peterbro 204 C2
Ravensthorpe W Yorks 293 F6
Ravenstone Leics 224 F3
Ravenstone M/Keynes 158 B4
Ravenstonedale Cumb 328 F4
Ravenstown Cumb 313 E8
Ravenstruther S Lanarks 382 C3
Ravenswick N Yorks 320 C4
Ravensworth N Yorks 330 E4
Raw N Yorks 335 E5
Rawcliffe C/York 307 E8
Rawcliffe ER Yorks 295 F7
Rawcliffe Br ER Yorks 295 F7
Rawdon W Yorks 293 C6
Rawgreen Northum 350 E5
Rawmarsh S Yorks 282 E2
Rawnsley Staffs 198 A1
Rawreth Essex 114 D2
Rawridge Devon 38 E2
Rawson Green Derby 247 E5
Rawtenstall Lancs 291 A5
Rawthorpe W Yorks 280 A5
Raxton Aberds 437 E5
Raydon Suffolk 165 E5
Raylees Northum 363 D7
Rayleigh Essex 114 D3
Rayne Essex 140 C3
Rayners Lane London 110 E4
Raynes Park London 89 C6
Rea Glos 130 D2
Rea Hill Torbay 15 D6
Reach Cambs 184 E4
Read Lancs 290 D4
Reader's Corner Essex 114 B1
Reading Reading 86 B4
Reading Green Suffolk 188 D2
Reading Street Kent 95 C7
Reading Street Kent 73 E5
Readings Glos 129 D6
Readymoney Cornw'l 9 E5
Reagill Cumb 328 C2
Rearquhar H'land 440 D4
Rearsby Leics 225 F8
Reasby Lincs 273 D6
Reaster H'land 445 B6
Reaulay H'land 431 C7
Reawick Shetl'd 455 B2
Reawla Cornw'l 3 C8
Reay H'land 444 B3
Rechullin H'land 431 C8
Reculver Kent 94 C4
Red Ball Devon 37 C6
Red Bull Ches 244 C2
Red Bull Staffs 220 A4
Red Dial Cumb 338 B4
Red Hill Bournem'th 28 A1
Red Hill Hants 46 D2
Red Hill Heref'd 151 E8
Red Hill W Berks 85 D5
Red Hill W Midlands 176 C3
Red Hill W Yorks 294 E2
Red House Glass Cone, Wordsley W Midlands 197 F6
Red Lake Telford 196 A2
Red Lodge Suffolk 185 D7
Red Lumb Gtr Man 279 A5
Red Pits Norfolk 233 C6
Red Post Bath/NE Som'set 81 E6
Red Rail Heref'd 128 B4
Red Rock Gtr Man 277 C8
Red Roses Carms 121 E8
Red Row Northum 365 C7
Red Scar Lancs 289 D8
Red Street Staffs 244 D2
Red Wharf Bay Angl 259 C7
Redberth Pembs 117 D7
Redbourn Herts 137 E6
Redbournbury Herts 137 E6
Redbourne N Lincs 285 D6
Redbridge Dorset 26 C2
Redbridge London 112 E3
Redbridge S'thampton 44 D2
Redbrook Glos 128 E4
Redbrook S Yorks 281 C8
Redbrook Wrex 242 F3
Redburn H'land 433 B7
Redburn H'land 434 D4
Redburn Northum 350 D2
Redcar Redcar/Clevel'd 333 A7
Redcar Racecourse Redcar/Clevel'd 333 B7
Redcastle Angus 421 B6
Redcastle H'land 433 D7
Redcliff Bay N Som'set 79 A8
Redcroft Dumf/Gal 402 B1
Redden Scot Borders 387 E5
Reddicap Heath W Midlands 198 D3
Redding Falk 394 C3
Reddingmuirhead Falk 394 C3
Reddish Gtr Man 266 A4
Redditch Worcs 176 E4
Rede Suffolk 164 A1
Redenhall Norfolk 188 B3
Redenham Hants 64 B3
Redesdale Camp Northum 363 C5
Redesmouth Northum 363 F6
Redford Aberds 428 E4
Redford Angus 421 C5
Redfordgreen Scot Borders 372 D4
Redgate Cornw'l 9 B7
Redgorton Perth/Kinr 419 E8
Redgrave Suffolk 187 C5
Redheugh Angus 420 A4
Redhill Aberds 429 B4
Redhill Aberds 436 E3
Redhill Herts 138 A2
Redhill N Som'set 80 D2
Redhill Notts 248 F2
Redhill Surrey 69 A7
Redhills Cumb 339 F9
Redhills Devon 21 B8
Redhouse Arg/Bute 407 F8
Redhouses Arg/Bute 406 F3
Redisham Suffolk 189 B6
Redland Bristol 80 B3
Redland Orkney 452 A4
Redland End Bucks 109 B6
Redlingfield Suffolk 188 D1
Redlynch Som'set 61 E6
Redlynch Wilts 43 B7
Redmain Cumb 338 E1
Redmarley Worcs 175 E5
Redmarley D'Abitot Glos 129 A9
Redmarshall Stockton 332 B2
Redmile Leics 226 A2
Redmire N Yorks 317 B6
Redmoor Cornw'l 8 C4
Redmoss Aberds 437 E5
Rednal Shrops 218 C4
Rednal W Midlands 176 C3
Redpath Scot Borders 385 E8
Redpoint H'land 431 B7
Redruth Cornw'l 4 B2
Redstocks Wilts 82 D3
Redtye Cornw'l 8 C3
Redvales Gtr Man 278 C4
Redwick Newp 101 F8
Redwick S Glos 102 E2
Redworth D'lington 331 B6
Reed Herts 161 E7
Reed End Herts 161 E6
Reed Point Lincs 229 A5
Reedham Lincs 251 C7
Reedham Norfolk 210 C4
Reedley Lancs 291 C6
Reedness ER Yorks 296 F2
Reeds Beck Lincs 251 A7
Reeds Holme Lancs 291 F5
Reedy Devon 21 C6
Reen Sands Cornw'l 7 E6
Reepham Lincs 273 E5
Reepham Norfolk 233 D6
Reeth N Yorks 317 A6
Reeves Green W Midlands 177 C8
Refail Powys 193 C7
Regaby I/Man 336 B4
Regoul H'land 434 C3
Reiff H'land 438 B3
Reigate Surrey 69 B6
Reighton N Yorks 323 E6
Reinigeadal W Isles 449 B6
Reisque Aberds 429 A5
Reiss H'land 445 C7
Rejerrah Cornw'l 7 D6
Releath Cornw'l 3 D9
Relubbus Cornw'l 3 D7
Relugas Moray 434 D4
Remenham Wokingham 108 F5
Remenham Hill Wokingham 109 F5
Remony Perth/Kinr 419 C5
Rempstone Notts 225 D6
Remusaig H'land 440 C4
Rendcomb Glos 131 F6
Rendham Suffolk 188 F4
Rendlesham Suffolk 166 B4
Renfrew Renf 392 E2
Renhold Beds 160 B1
Renishaw Derby 269 D8
Renmure Angus 421 B6
Rennington Northum 377 D6
Renton W Dunb 391 C7
Renville Kent 94 F3
Renwick Cumb 340 C2
Repps Norfolk 235 E5
Repton Derby 223 C8
Reraig H'land 431 F8
Reraig Cot H'land 431 E8
Rerwick Shetl'd 455 E2
Rescassa Cornw'l 5 B7
Rescobie Angus 421 B5
Rescoria Cornw'l 8 D3
Resipole H'land 416 A2
Reskadinnick Cornw'l 3 B8
Resolfen = Resolven Neath P Talb 98 B3
Resolis H'land 434 B1
Resolven = Resolfen Neath P Talb 98 B3
Restalrig C/Edinb 396 D2
Reston Scot Borders 399 F7
Reston Cumb 314 A3
Restrop Wilts 105 E6
Resugga Green Cornw'l 8 D3
Reswallie Angus 421 B5
Retford Notts 271 C6
Retire Cornw'l 8 C3
Rettendon Essex 114 C2
Revesby Lincs 252 B2
Revesby Bridge Lincs 252 B2
Revidge Blackb'n 290 E2
Rew Street I/Wight 29 B9
Rewe Devon 21 A8
Rexon Devon 19 C5
Reybridge Wilts 82 C3
Reydon Suffolk 189 C7
Reydon Smear Suffolk 189 C7
Reymerston Norfolk 208 B4
Reynalton Pembs 117 C7
Reynoldston Swan 96 E4
Rezare Cornw'l 18 E4
Rhadyr Monmouths 101 B7
Rhaeadr Gwy = Rhayader Powys 170 E4
Rhandirmwyn Carms 147 D8
Rhayader = Rhaeadr Gwy Powys 170 E4
Rhegreanoch H'land 439 B4
Rhemore H'land 415 B8
Rhencullen I/Man 336 B3
Rhenetra H'land 430 C4
Rhes-y-cae Flints 263 E5
Rhewl Denbs 240 B3
Rhewl Denbs 240 E4
Rhewl Shrops 218 B3
Rhewl-Mostyn Flints 263 C5
Rhian H'land 440 B2
Rhicarn H'land 439 A4
Rhiconich H'land 442 C4
Rhicullen H'land 434 A1
Rhidorroch Ho. H'land 439 D5
Rhifail H'land 444 D1
Rhigolter H'land 443 C5
Rhigos Rh Cyn Taff 99 A5
Rhilochan H'land 440 C4
Rhiroy H'land 439 E5
Rhiston Shrops 193 E9
Rhitongue H'land 443 C8
Rhivichie H'land 442 C4
Rhiw Gwyn 212 C4
Rhiwabon = Ruabon Wrex 241 F7
Rhiwbina Card 100 F3
Rhiwbryfdir Gwyn 238 E1
Rhiwceiliog Bridg 99 F6
Rhiwderin Newp 100 E5
Rhiwen Gwyn 237 B7
Rhiwinder Rh Cyn Taff 99 E7
Rhiwlas Gwyn 216 A3
Rhiwlas Gwyn 237 A7
Rhiwlas Powys 217 B8
Rhiwnachor Powys 217 E6
Rhiwsaeson Rh Cyn Taff 99 F8
Rhode Som'set 59 E5
Rhode Common Kent 93 E8
Rhodes Gtr Man 279 C5
Rhodes Minnis Kent 74 C2
Rhodesia Notts 270 C3
Rhodiad-y-Brenin Pembs 118 D3
Rhodmad Ceredig'n 168 D4
Rhôs Common Powys 218 E2
Rhôs Lligwy Angl 259 B6
Rhôs on Sea Conwy 262 C6
Rhôs-y-llan Gwyn 212 A4
Rhonadale Arg/Bute 404 C3
Rhondda Rh Cyn Taff 99 C6
Rhonehouse or Kelton Hill Dumf/Gal 402 D1
Rhoose V/Glam 77 C8
Rhos Carms 145 E7
Rhos Neath P Talb 98 B1
Rhos Powys 218 E2
Rhos Powys 126 A4
Rhos Shrops 218 A2
Rhos Hamminiog Ceredig'n 168 F3
Rhosaman Carms 124 E3
Rhosbeirio Angl 258 A4
Rhoscefnhir Angl 259 D7
Rhoscolyn Angl 258 D2
Rhoscrowther Pembs 116 D4
Rhos-ddu Wrex 241 D7
Rhos-ddû Gwyn 212 A5
Rhosdylluan Gwyn 216 C2
Rhosesmor Flints 263 F6
Rhosfach Pembs 121 B6
Rhos-fawr Gwyn 213 A7
Rhosgadfan Gwyn 237 C6
Rhosgoch Angl 259 B5
Rhos-goch Powys 149 C8
Rhosgyll Gwyn 236 F5
Rhos-hill Pembs 144 D3
Rhoshirwaun Gwyn 212 C3
Rhoslan Bl Gwent 126 E3
Rhoslan Gwyn 237 F5
Rhoslefain Gwyn 190 B2
Rhosllanerchrugog Wrex 241 E7
Rhosmaen Carms 124 C1
Rhosmeirch Angl 259 D6
Rhosneigr Angl 258 E3
Rhosnesni Wrex 241 D7
Rhosrobin Wrex 241 D7
Rhossili Swan 96 E3
Rhosson Pembs 118 D2
Rhostrehwfa Angl 259 E5
Rhostryfan Gwyn 237 C5
Rhostyllen Wrex 241 E7
Rhosweil Shrops 218 A2
Rhosybol Angl 259 B5
Rhos-y-brithdir Powys 217 D7
Rhos-y-brwyner Flints 241 B6
Rhos-y-garth Ceredig'n 169 D5
Rhos-y-gwaliau Gwyn 216 B3
Rhos-y-madoc Wrex 241 F7
Rhosymedre Wrex 241 F6
Rhos-y-meirch Powys 172 E3
RHS Garden, Wisley Surrey 88 E3
Rhu Arg/Bute 407 F8
Rhu Arg/Bute 409 D5
Rhuallt Denbs 262 E3
Rhubodach Arg/Bute 408 E3
Rhuddall Heath Ches 242 B4
Rhuddlan Ceredig'n 146 D2
Rhuddlan Denbs 262 D2
Rhue H'land 439 D4
Rhulen Powys 149 C7
Rhunahaorine Arg/Bute 404 B3
Rhyd Ceredig'n 145 D5
Rhyd Gwyn 237 F8
Rhyd y golau Flints 241 A5
Rhydaman = Ammanford Carms 123 E8
Rhydargaeau Carms 122 B4
Rhydcymerau Carms 146 E4
Rhydd Worcs 153 C6
Rhydd Green Worcs 153 D6
Rhyd-Ddu Gwyn 237 D7
Rhydding Rh Cyn Taff 98 C2
Rhydgaled Conwy 239 B7
Rhydleos Powys 217 B9
Rhydlewis Ceredig'n 145 C6
Rhydlios Gwyn 212 B3
Rhyd-Lydan Conwy 239 D5
Rhydlydan Powys 192 E5
Rhyd-meirionydd Ceredig'n 168 A5
Rhydowen Carms 121 B7
Rhydowen Ceredig'n 146 C1
Rhyd-Rosser Ceredig'n 168 E4
Rhydspence Heref'd 150 C2
Rhydtalog Flints 241 D5
Rhyd-uchaf Gwyn 216 A2
Rhydwyn Angl 258 B3
Rhyd-y-clafdy Gwyn 213 B6
Rhydycroesau Shrops 218 B1
Rhyd-y-cwm Shrops 171 B8
Rhydyfelin Ceredig'n 168 C4
Rhydyfelin Rh Cyn Taff 100 E1
Rhyd-y-foel Conwy 262 D8
Rhyd-y-fro Neath P Talb 98 A1
Rhydygele Pembs 118 E5
Rhyd-y-groes Gwyn 259 F8
Rhyd-y-groes Gwyn 193 C8
Rhyd-y-gwin Swan 97 B8
Rhyd-y-gwystl Gwyn 213 A8
Rhydymain Gwyn 215 D8
Rhyd-y-meirch Monmouths 127 F7
Rhydymwyn Flints 263 F6
Rhyd-y-pandy Swan 97 B8
Rhyd-yr-onen Gwyn 190 C3
Rhyd-y-Sarn Gwyn 238 F2
Rhydywrach Carms 121 D7
Rhŷd-y-meudwy Denbs 240 D3
Rhyl = Y Rhyl Denbs 262 C2
Rhymney = Rhymni Caerph 126 F3
Rhymni = Rhymney Caerph 126 F3
Rhynd Fife 420 E4
Rhynd Perth/Kinr 420 E1
Rhynie Aberds 436 F1
Rhynie H'land 441 F5
Ribbesford Worcs 175 D5
Ribblehead N Yorks 316 E1
Ribbleton Lancs 289 D8
Ribby Lancs 288 D5
Ribchester Lancs 290 C1
Ribigill H'land 443 C7
Riby Lincs 286 C2
Riby Cross Roads Lincs 286 C2
Riccall N Yorks 295 C6
Riccarton E Ayrs 379 E8
Richard's Castle Heref'd 173 E7
Richborough Port Kent 95 D6
Richings Park Bucks 88 A2
Richmond London 89 B5
Richmond N Yorks 331 F5
Richmond S Yorks 269 B8
Richmond Hill S Yorks 283 D5
Richmond's Green Essex 139 B8
Rich's Holford Som'set 58 E2
Rickard's Down Devon 54 F3
Rickarton Aberds 429 D5
Rickerby Cumb 348 E2
Rickerscote Staffs 221 D8
Rickford N Som'set 80 E1
Rickinghall Suffolk 187 C5
Rickleton Durham 352 F4
Rickling Essex 139 A5
Rickling Green Essex 139 B6
Rickmansworth Herts 110 D2
Riddings Derby 247 D6
Riddlecombe Devon 34 D5
Riddlesden W Yorks 292 B3
Riddrie Glasg C 392 E4
Ridgacre W Midlands 176 B3
Ridge Dorset 27 C5
Ridge Devon 38 E3
Ridge Hants 44 C1
Ridge Herts 111 B6
Ridge Lancs 289 A8
Ridge Lancs 301 C8
Ridge Wilts 62 E4
Ridge Common Hants 66 F4
Ridge Green Surrey 69 B8
Ridge Hill Gtr Man 279 E8
Ridge Lane Warwick 199 E6
Ridge Row Kent 74 C4
Ridgehill N Som'set 80 D2
Ridgeway Derby 247 D5
Ridgeway Derby 269 C7
Ridgeway Newp 101 E5
Ridgeway Pembs 117 C8
Ridgeway Stoke 244 D3
Ridgeway Som'set 61 C7
Ridgeway Cross Heref'd 152 C4
Ridgeway Moor Derby 269 C8
Ridgewell Essex 163 D7
Ridgewood E Sussex 50 C2
Ridgmont Beds 159 E7
Ridgway Surrey 88 E2
Riding Gate Som'set 61 F6
Riding Mill Northum 351 D7
Ridley Kent 91 D7
Ridley Northum 350 D2
Ridley Green Ches 242 D4
Ridlington Norfolk 234 B3
Ridlington Rutl'd 202 C2
Ridlington Street Norfolk 234 B3
Ridsdale Northum 363 F7
Riechip Perth/Kinr 419 C8
Riemore Perth/Kinr 419 C8
Rienachait H'land 442 E2
Rievaulx N Yorks 320 C2
Rievaulx Abbey N Yorks 320 D2
Riff Orkney 452 B5
Riffin Aberds 436 D4
Rifle Green Torf 127 F6
Rift House Hartlep'l 345 E5
Rifton Devon 36 C2
Rigg Dumf/Gal 347 C7
Riggend N Lanarks 393 D7
Rigsby Lincs 275 D5
Rigside S Lanarks 382 F2
Rigton Hill W Yorks 294 B1
Riley Green Lancs 290 E1
Rileyhill Staffs 222 E4
Rilla Mill Cornw'l 10 A1
Rillaton Cornw'l 18 F2
Rillington N Yorks 321 F8
Rimington Lancs 291 A5
Rimpton Som'set 40 B2
Rimswell ER Yorks 299 E5
Ring o'Bells Lancs 277 B6
Ringasta Shetl'd 455 E2
Ringford Dumf/Gal 401 D8
Ringinglow S Yorks 269 C5
Ringland Norfolk 233 F7
Ringland Newp 101 E7
Ringles Cross E Sussex 50 B2
Ringlestone Kent 92 E4
Ringley Gtr Man 278 D4
Ringmer E Sussex 50 D2
Ringmore Devon 12 C4
Ringmore Devon 15 A6
Ringorm Moray 435 D7
Ring's End Cambs 205 C6
Ringsfield Suffolk 210 F4
Ringsfield Corner Suffolk 210 F4
Ringshall Herts 136 E3
Ringshall Suffolk 165 B5
Ringshall Stocks Suffolk 165 B6
Ringstead Norfolk 254 D4
Ringstead Northants 181 C7
Ringtail Green Essex 140 D2
Ringwood Hants 43 E6
Ringwould Kent 75 B7
Rinmore Aberds 428 A1
Rinnigill Orkney 452 D4
Rinsey Cornw'l 3 E7
Rinsey Croft Cornw'l 3 E8
Riof W Isles 450 D4
Ripe E Sussex 50 D3
Ripley Derby 247 D6
Ripley Hants 28 A3
Ripley N Yorks 306 C2
Ripley Surrey 88 E2
Ripley Green Surrey 88 E3
Riplingham ER Yorks 297 D5
Ripon N Yorks 306 A3
Ripon Cathedral N Yorks 306 A3
Ripon Racecourse N Yorks 306 B3
Rippingale Lincs 228 C2
Ripple Kent 75 A6
Ripple Worcs 153 E7
Ripponden W Yorks 280 A2
Rireavach H'land 438 D4
Risabus Arg/Bute 403 B3
Risbury Heref'd 151 A8
Risby ER Yorks 297 D7
Risby Lincs 273 A8
Risby Suffolk 185 E9
Risca Caerph 100 D4
Rise ER Yorks 298 B2
Rise Carr D'lington 331 C7
Rise End Derby 246 C3
Rise Park Notts 248 F2
Riseden E Sussex 71 E7
Riseden Kent 71 D9
Risegate Lincs 228 C4
Riseholme Lincs 272 D4
Risehow Cumb 337 E3
Riseley Beds 181 F8
Riseley Wokingham 86 D4
Rishangles Suffolk 187 E8
Rishton Lancs 290 D3
Rishworth W Yorks 280 A2
Rising Bridge Lancs 290 E4
Rising Sun Cornw'l 10 A3
Risinghurst Oxon 134 F2
Risley Derby 224 A4
Risley Warrington 265 A8
Risplith N Yorks 306 B1
Rispond H'land 443 B6
Rivar Wilts 84 D3
Rivenhall Essex 141 D5
Rivenhall End Essex 141 D5
River Kent 75 C5
River W Sussex 47 B6
River Bank Cambs 184 E3
River Hall Herts 137 D5
Riverhead Kent 90 E5
River's Corner Dorset 41 D5
Riverside Card 78 A3
Riverside Plym'th 10 D4
Riverview Park Kent 91 B8
Rivington Lancs 278 B1
Rixton Warrington 265 A8
Roa Island Cumb 300 B3
Roach Bridge Lancs 289 E8
Roaches Gtr Man 279 D8
Roachill Devon 36 B1
Road Green Devon 23 B6
Road Green Norfolk 209 E9
Road Weedon Northants 157 A7
Roade Northants 158 B3
Roadhead Cumb 348 B4
Roadmeetings S Lanarks 382 B2
Roadside H'land 445 B5
Roadside of Catterline Aberds 429 E5
Roadside of Kinneff Aberds 429 E5
Roadwater Som'set 57 D7
Roag H'land 430 D2
Roast Green Essex 139 A5
Roath Card 78 A4
Rob Roy and Trossachs Visitor Centre, Callander Stirl 410 B1
Rob Roy's House Arg/Bute 417 F6
Robert Burns Centre, Dumfries Dumf/Gal 402 B3
Roberton Scot Borders 373 E5
Roberton S Lanarks 370 B3
Robertsbridge E Sussex 51 B7
Robertstown Moray 435 D7
Robertstown Rh Cyn Taff 99 B7
Roberttown W Yorks 293 F5
Robeston Back Pembs 117 A7
Robeston Wathen Pembs 117 A7
Robeston West Pembs 116 C3
Robin Hood Derby 269 E5
Robin Hood Lancs 277 B7
Robin Hood W Yorks 293 E8
Robin Hood Doncaster Sheffield Airport S Yorks 283 E7
Robin Hood's Bay N Yorks 335 E6
Robinhood End Essex 163 E7
Robinson's End Warwick 199 E7
Roborough Devon 11 C6
Roborough Devon 34 C4
Robroyston Glasg C 392 E4
Roby Mersey 264 A3
Roby Mill Lancs 277 C7
Rocester Staffs 222 A4
Roch Pembs 118 E5
Rochdale Gtr Man 279 B6
Roche Cornw'l 8 C2
Rochester Medway 92 C1
Rochester Northum 363 C5
Rochester Castle Medway 92 C1
Rochester Cathedral Medway 92 C1
Rochford Essex 114 D4
Rochford Worcs 174 E2
Rock Caerph 100 C3
Rock Cornw'l 16 E3
Rock Devon 38 F3
Rock Northum 377 C6
Rock Worcs 174 D4
Rock W Sussex 48 D2
Rock Ferry Mersey 264 B1
Rock Hall Dumf/Gal 346 A3
Rockbeare Devon 22 A2
Rockbourne Hants 42 C5
Rockcliffe Cumb 347 D9
Rockcliffe Dumf/Gal 402 D2
Rockcliffe Cross Cumb 347 D8
Rockfield H'land 441 E6
Rockfield Monmouths 128 E3
Rockford Hants 43 E6
Rockgreen Shrops 173 C8
Rockhampton S Glos 103 D5
Rockhead Cornw'l 17 D6
Rockhill Shrops 172 C3
Rockingham Northants 202 E3
Rockingham Motor Speedway Northants 202 E4
Rockland All Saints Norfolk 208 D3
Rockland St. Mary Norfolk 210 C2
Rockland St. Peter Norfolk 208 D3
Rockley Notts 271 E6
Rockley Wilts 83 B8
Rockliffe Lancs 291 F6
Rockness Glos 104 C1
Rockrobin E Sussex 71 E7
Rocks Park E Sussex 50 B2
Rocksley M/Keynes 158 E4
Rockstowes Glos 103 C7
Rockwell Cornw'l 18 C3
Rockwell End Bucks 109 E5
Rockwell Green Som'set 37 A7
Rodborough Glos 104 B1
Rodbourne Swindon 105 E7
Rodbourne Wilts 104 F3
Rodbourne Cheney Swindon 105 E7
Rodbridge Corner Suffolk 164 D2
Roddam Northum 376 C2
Rodden Dorset 25 D7
Roddymoor Durham 343 D7
Rode Som'set 81 F8
Rode Heath Ches 244 C2
Rode Hill Som'set 81 F8
Rodeheath Ches 266 F4
Roden Telford 219 E8
Rodford S Glos 103 F6
Rodhuish Som'set 57 D7
Rodington Telford 219 F8
Rodington Heath Telford 219 F8
Rodley Glos 129 E8
Rodley W Yorks 293 C6
Rodmarton Glos 104 C3
Rodmell E Sussex 49 E8
Rodmersham Kent 93 D5
Rodmersham Green Kent 93 D5
Rodney Stoke Som'set 60 A1
Rodsley Derby 246 F2
Rodway Som'set 58 C5
Rodwell Dorset 25 E8
Roe Cross Gtr Man 280 E1
Roe End Herts 136 D4
Roe Green Gtr Man 278 D4
Roe Green Herts 137 F8
Roe Green Herts 161 F6
Roe Lee Blackb'n 290 D2
Roebuck Low Gtr Man 279 C8
Roecliffe N Yorks 306 B4
Roedean Brighton/Hove 49 F6
Roehampton London 89 B6
Roesound Shetl'd 457 G3
Roestock Herts 111 A6
Roffey W Sussex 69 E5
Rogart H'land 440 C4
Rogart Station H'land 440 C4
Rogate W Sussex 46 B4
Roger Ground Cumb 313 A8
Rogerstone Newp 100 E5
Rogerton S Lanarks 380 A4
Roghadal W Isles 448 D4
Rogiet Monmouths 102 E1
Rogues Alley Cambs 205 B6
Roke Oxon 108 D2
Rokemarsh Oxon 108 D2
Roker Tyne/Wear 353 E7
Rollesby Norfolk 235 E5
Rolleston Leics 201 C8
Rolleston Notts 249 D5
Rolleston on Dove Staffs 223 C6
Rolleston Wilts 63 C6
Rolls Park Essex 112 D3
Rolston ER Yorks 298 A3
Rolstone N Som'set 79 D7
Rolvenden Kent 72 E3
Rolvenden Layne Kent 72 F4
Romaldkirk Durham 330 B1
Roman Bank Shrops 195 E6
Roman Baths & Pump Room, Bath Bath/NE Som'set 81 C7
Roman Hill Suffolk 211 E6
Romanby N Yorks 319 B6
Romannobridge Scot Borders 383 C8
Romansleigh Devon 35 B7
Rome Angus 421 A5
Romesdal H'land 430 C4
Romford Dorset 42 E4
Romford Kent 71 C7

Romford London 112 E5
Romiley Gtr Man 267 A5
Romney, Hythe and Dymchurch Light Railway Kent 74 E2
Romney Street Kent 91 D5
Rompa Shetl'd 455 D3
Romsey Hants 44 B1
Romsey Town Cambs 162 A2
Romsley Shrops 175 B5
Romsley Worcs 176 C2
Ronachan Ho Arg/Bute 404 A3
Ronague I/Man 336 D2
Ronkswood Worcs 153 A7
Rood Ashton Wilts 82 E2
Rood End W Midlands 197 F9
Rook Devon 11 C8
Rook End Essex 139 A7
Rookhope Durham 342 C2
Rooking Cumb 327 C5
Rookley I/Wight 30 D2
Rookley Green I/Wight 30 D2
Rooks Bridge Som'set 59 A7
Rook's Nest Som'set 57 E8
Rook's Street Wilts 61 E8
Rooksmoor Glos 104 B1
Rookwith N Yorks 318 C3
Rookwood W Sussex 31 E5
Roos ER Yorks 298 D4
Roose Cumb 300 B3
Roosebeck Cumb 300 B4
Roosecote Cumb 300 B3
Roost End Essex 163 D7
Rootham's Green Beds 160 B2
Rooting Street Kent 73 B6
Rootpark S Lanarks 382 B4
Ropley Hants 66 E2
Ropley Dean Hants 66 E2
Ropley Stoke Hants 66 E3
Ropsley Lincs 227 B6
Rora Aberds 437 C7
Rorandle Aberds 428 A3
Rorrington Shrops 194 C2
Rosarie Moray 435 D8
Roscroggan Cornw'l 3 B8
Rose Cornw'l 7 E6
Rose Ash Devon 35 B8
Rose Green Essex 141 B7
Rose Green Suffolk 164 D4
Rose Green Suffolk 164 E3
Rose Green W Sussex 31 E8
Rose Grove Lancs 291 D5
Rose Hill Derby C 224 A2
Rose Hill E Sussex 50 C2
Rose Hill Gtr Man 278 C3
Rose Hill Lancs 291 D5
Rose Hill Oxon 107 B7
Rose Hill Suffolk 165 D8
Rose Hill Surrey 69 B5
Rose Hill Stockton 332 D3
Roseacre Kent 92 E2
Roseacre Lancs 289 C5
Rose-an-Grouse Cornw'l 3 C6
Rosebank E Dunb 393 D5
Rosebank S Lanarks 381 C8
Rosebrae Moray 435 B6
Rosebush Pembs 120 B5
Rosecare Cornw'l 17 A8
Rosedale Abbey N Yorks 321 A5
Roseden Northum 376 C2
Rosedinnick Cornw'l 8 B1
Rosedown Devon 33 B5
Rosefield H'land 434 C3
Rosehall H'land 440 C1
Rosehall N Lanarks 393 F6
Rosehaugh Mains H'land 434 C1
Rosehearty Aberds 437 B6
Rosehill Blackb'n 290 F3
Rosehill Cornw'l 7 E6
Rosehill London 89 C7
Rosehill Shrops 219 E6
Rosehill Tyne/Wear 353 C5
Roseisle Moray 435 B6
Roseland Cornw'l 9 C8
Roselands E Sussex 50 F5
Rosemarket Pembs 117 C5
Rosemarkie H'land 434 C2
Rosemary Lane Devon 37 D8
Rosemount Perth/Kinr 420 C1
Rosenannon Cornw'l 8 B2
Rosenithon Cornw'l 4 F4
Roser's Cross E Sussex 50 B4
Rosevean Cornw'l 8 D3
Rosevidney Cornw'l 3 D6
Roseville W Midlands 197 E7
Rosevine Cornw'l 5 C5
Rosewarne Cornw'l 3 B8
Rosewarne Cornw'l 3 C8
Rosewell Midloth 396 F2
Roseworth Stockton 332 B3
Roseworthy Cornw'l 7 F6
Roseworthy Cornw'l 3 C8
Rosgill Cumb 327 C7
Roshven H'land 423 E7
Roskhill H'land 430 D2
Roskill House H'land 434 C1
Roskorwell Cornw'l 4 F3
Rosley Cumb 338 B5
Roslin Midloth 396 F2
Rosliston Derby 223 E6
Rosneath Arg/Bute 409 D5
Ross Dumf/Gal 401 E8
Ross Northum 388 E4
Ross Perth/Kinr 419 E5
Ross Green Worcs 175 F5
Ross on Wye Heref'd 129 C6
Rossett Wrex 241 C8
Rossett Green N Yorks 306 E3
Rossie Ochill Perth/Kinr 411 A5
Rossie Priory Perth/Kinr 420 D2
Rossington S Yorks 283 E7
Rosskeen H'land 434 B1
Rossland Renf 391 D8
Rossmore Poole 27 B8
Roster H'land 445 E6
Rostherne Ches 266 C1
Rostholme S Yorks 283 C5
Rosthwaite Cumb 313 C5
Rosthwaite Cumb 326 D2
Roston Derby 245 F8
Rosudgeon Cornw'l 3 E7
Rosyth Fife 411 D6
Rotcombe Bath/NE Som'set 81 E5
Rothbury Northum 364 B3
Rotherby Leics 225 E8
Rotherfield E Sussex 71 F6
Rotherfield Greys Oxon 108 F4
Rotherfield Peppard Oxon 108 F4
Rotherham S Yorks 269 A8
Rotherhithe London 90 A2
Rothersthorpe Northants 158 A2
Rotherwas Heref'd 151 E8
Rotherwick Hants 86 E4
Rothes Moray 435 D7
Rothesay Arg/Bute 408 F3
Rothiebrisbane Aberds 436 E4
Rothiemay Crossroads Moray 436 D2
Rothiemurchus Estate Visitor Centre H'land 426 B4
Rothiemurchus Lodge H'land 426 B4
Rothienorman Aberds 436 E4
Rothiesholm Orkney 454 D4
Rothley Leics 201 A5
Rothley Northum 364 E2
Rothmaise Aberds 436 E3
Rothwell Lincs 286 E2
Rothwell Northants 180 B4
Rothwell W Yorks 293 E8
Rothwell Haigh W Yorks 293 E8
Rotsea ER Yorks 310 E3
Rottal Angus 427 F8
Rotten End Suffolk 188 E5
Rotten Green Hants 87 E5
Rotten Row Norfolk 209 A5
Rottingdean Brighton/Hove 49 F7
Rottington Cumb 324 D4
Rotton Row W Berks 85 B8
Rotton Row W Midlands 177 C6
Rotunda, Folkestone Kent 74 D4
Roud I/Wight 30 D2
Rough Close Staffs 221 A8
Rough Common Kent 94 E2
Rough Haugh H'land 444 D1
Rough Hay Staffs 223 D6
Rougham Norfolk 231 D8
Rougham Suffolk 186 F3
Rougham Green Suffolk 186 F3
Roughbirchworth S Yorks 281 D7
Roughburn H'land 425 D5
Roughlee Lancs 291 B5
Roughley W Midlands 198 D3
Roughrigg N Lanarks 393 D8
Roughsike Cumb 348 A4
Roughton Lincs 251 B7
Roughton Norfolk 257 E7
Roughton Shrops 196 E4
Roughway Kent 71 A7
Round Bush Herts 111 C5
Round Maple Suffolk 164 D4
Round Oak Shrops 173 B5
Round Oak W Berks 86 C2
Round Oak W Midlands 197 F7
Round Spinney Northants 180 E3
Round Street Kent 91 C8
Roundbush Essex 114 B4
Roundbush Glos 130 B1
Roundbush Green Essex 139 E7
Roundham Som'set 39 E6
Roundhay W Yorks 293 C8
Roundstonefoot Dumf/Gal 371 F7
Roundstreet Common W Sussex 68 F3
Roundswell Devon 55 E5
Roundthorn Gtr Man 266 B3
Roundthwaite Cumb 328 F2
Roundway Wilts 82 D5
Roundyhill Angus 420 B3
Rous Lench Worcs 154 B3
Rousdon Devon 23 B7
Rousham Oxon 133 C8
Routenburn N Ayrs 390 F3
Routh ER Yorks 297 B8
Rout's Green Bucks 109 C5
Row Cumb 325 F6
Row Cumb 314 C3
Row Cumb 340 E3
Row Cornw'l 17 E6
Row Ash Hants 45 D5
Row Brow Cumb 337 D4
Row Green Essex 140 C3
Row Heath Essex 142 D3
Row Town Surrey 88 D2
Rowanburn Dumf/Gal 348 A2
Rowanfield Glos 130 C4
Rowardennan Stirl 409 C6
Rowarth Derby 267 B7
Rowbarns Surrey 68 A4
Rowbarton Som'set 38 A2
Rowberrow Som'set 79 E9
Rowde Wilts 82 D4
Rowden N Yorks 306 D2
Rowden Down Wilts 82 D3
Rowell Cumb 314 D4
Rowen Conwy 260 E5
Rowfoot Northum 349 D7
Rowford Som'set 58 F4
Rowhedge Essex 142 C1
Rowhill Surrey 88 D2
Rowhook W Sussex 68 E4
Rowington Warwick 177 E7
Rowington Green Warwick 177 D7
Rowland Derby 268 E4
Rowlands Castle W Sussex 46 D2
Rowlands Gill Tyne/Wear 352 E2
Rowledge Surrey 67 C6
Rowlestone Heref'd 127 B8
Rowley Durham 343 B5
Rowley ER Yorks 297 D6
Rowley Shrops 194 B2
Rowley Hill W Yorks 281 B5
Rowley Park Staffs 221 D8
Rowley Regis W Midlands 197 F8
Rowley's Green Warwick 178 B1
Rowly Surrey 68 C2
Rowner Hants 45 F6
Rowney Green Worcs 176 D3
Rownhams Hants 44 C2
Row-of-Trees Ches 266 D3
Rowrah Cumb 325 C6
Rowsham Bucks 135 D8
Rowsley Derby 246 A3
Rowstock Oxon 107 E6
Rowston Lincs 250 C4
Rowthorn Derby 247 B7
Rowton Ches 242 B1
Rowton Shrops 194 A3
Rowton Telford 220 E2
Roxburgh Scot Borders 374 A3
Roxby N Lincs 284 A5
Roxby N Yorks 334 C2
Roxeth London 110 E4
Roxton Beds 160 B3
Roxwell Essex 140 F1
Royal Botanic Gardens C/Edinb 396 C1
Royal British Legion Village Kent 92 E1
Royal Leamington Spa Warwick 178 E1
Royal Museum of Scotland C/Edinb 396 D2
Royal Oak Durham 331 B6
Royal Oak Lancs 276 D5
Royal Oak N Yorks 323 E6
Royal Pavilion, Brighton Brighton/Hove 49 F6
Royal Tunbridge Wells = Tunbridge Wells Kent 71 D6
Royal Welch Fusiliers Regimental Museum (See Caernarfon Castle) Gwyn 236 B5
Royal Worcester Porcelain, Worcester Worcs 153 B7
Royal's Green Ches 243 F5
Roybridge H'land 424 D4
Roydhouse W Yorks 281 B6
Roydon Essex 138 E4
Roydon Norfolk 187 B6
Roydon Norfolk 231 D6
Roydon Hamlet Essex 138 F4
Royston Herts 161 D7
Royston S Yorks 282 B1
Royston Water Som'set 38 D2
Royton Gtr Man 279 C7
Ruabon = Rhiwabon Wrex 241 F7
Ruaig Arg/Bute 414 C3
Ruan High Lanes Cornw'l 5 C6
Ruan Lanihorne Cornw'l 5 B5
Ruan Major Cornw'l 5 G2
Ruan Minor Cornw'l 5 G2
Ruarach H'land 432 F1
Ruardean Glos 129 D6
Ruardean Hill Glos 129 D6
Ruardean Woodside Glos 129 D6
Rubery Worcs 176 C2
Rubha Ghaisinis W Isles 447 D3
Rubha Stoer H'land 442 E2
Ruchazie Glasg C 393 E5
Ruchill Glasg C 392 E3
Ruckcroft Cumb 340 C1
Ruckhall Heref'd 151 E6
Ruckinge Kent 73 E7
Ruckland Lincs 274 D3
Rucklers Green Herts 110 B3
Rudbaxton Pembs 119 E7
Rudby N Yorks 332 E4
Rudddle Glos 129 E7
Ruddington Notts 225 B6
Ruddlemoor Cornw'l 8 D3
Rudford Glos 130 C1
Rudge Shrops 196 D5
Rudge Som'set 61 A8
Rudgeway S Glos 102 E4
Rudgwick W Sussex 68 E3
Rudhall Heref'd 129 B6
Rudheath Ches 265 E8
Rudhja Garbh Arg/Bute 416 C4
Rudley Green Essex 114 B3
Rudloe Wilts 82 B1
Rudry Caerph 100 E3
Rudston ER Yorks 310 B3
Rudyard Staffs 244 C4
Ruffets Monmouths 102 E2
Rufford Lancs 277 A6
Rufforth C/York 307 E7
Ruffs Notts 247 E8
Ruffside Durham 342 A3
Rugby Warwick 179 D5
Rugeley Staffs 222 E3
Ruggin Som'set 37 C8
Ruglen S Ayrs 354 B4
Ruilick H'land 433 D7
Ruishton Som'set 38 B3
Ruisigearraidh W Isles 448 D3
Ruislip London 110 E3
Ruislip Common London 110 E3
Ruislip Gardens London 110 E3
Ruislip Manor London 110 E4
Ruiton W Midlands 197 E7
Rumach H'land 423 D6
Rumbling Bridge Perth/Kinr 411 C5
Rumburgh Suffolk 188 B4
Rumer Hill Staffs 197 B8
Rumford Cornw'l 7 A8
Rumford Falk 394 C3
Rumney Card 78 A4
Rumsam Devon 55 E6
Rumwell Som'set 38 B1
Runcorn Halton 264 C5
Runcton W Sussex 47 F5
Runcton Bottom Norfolk 206 B3
Runcton Holme Norfolk 206 B3
Rundlestone Devon 19 E8
Runfold Surrey 67 B7
Runhall Norfolk 208 B5
Runham Norfolk 211 B6
Runham Norfolk 211 A5
Running Waters Durham 344 C2
Runnington Som'set 37 B7
Runsell Green Essex 114 B2
Runshaw Moor Lancs 277 A7
Runswick Bay N Yorks 334 C3
Runwell Essex 114 D2
Ruscombe Glos 130 F2
Ruscombe Wokingham 87 A6
Ruscote Oxon 156 D3
Rush Green Essex 142 D4
Rush Green Herts 137 C8
Rush Green Herts 138 B2
Rush Green London 112 E5
Rush Green Norfolk 208 B5
Rush Hill Bath/NE Som'set 81 D6
Rushall Heref'd 152 F2
Rushall Norfolk 188 B1
Rushall Wilts 83 E7
Rushall W Midlands 198 C1
Rushbrooke Suffolk 186 F2
Rushbury Shrops 195 E6
Rushden Herts 138 A2
Rushden Northants 181 E7
Rushenden Kent 93 B5
Rusher's Cross E Sussex 71 F7
Rushey Mead Leics C 201 B6
Rushford Devon 19 E5
Rushford Norfolk 186 B3
Rushgreen Warrington 265 B8
Rush-head Aberds 437 D5
Rushington Hants 44 D2
Rushlake Green E Sussex 51 C5
Rushley Green Essex 163 E8
Rushmere Beds 136 B2
Rushmere Suffolk 211 F5
Rushmere St. Andrew Suffolk 166 C1
Rushmere Street Suffolk 166 C2
Rushmoor Surrey 67 C7
Rushock Worcs 175 D7
Rusholme Gtr Man 279 E6
Rushton Northants 180 B4
Rushton Shrops 195 B8
Rushton Spencer Staffs 244 A4
Rushwick Worcs 153 B6
Rushy Green E Sussex 50 D2
Rushyford Durham 343 F9
Ruskie Stirl 410 B1
Ruskington Lincs 250 D4
Rusland Cumb 313 C7
Rusper W Sussex 69 D6
Ruspidge Glos 129 E7
Russ Hill Surrey 69 C6
Russel H'land 431 D8
Russell's Green E Sussex 51 D7
Russell's Hall W Midlands 197 F7
Russell's Water Oxon 108 E4
Russel's Green Suffolk 188 D3
Rusthall Kent 71 D6
Rustington W Sussex 47 F9
Ruston N Yorks 322 D3
Ruston Parva ER Yorks 310 C3
Ruswarp N Yorks 334 E4
Rutherglen Glasg C 392 F4
Ruthernbridge Cornw'l 8 B3
Ruthin Denbs 240 C3
Ruthin V/Glam 77 A6
Ruthin Craft Centre Denbs 240 C3
Ruthrieston Aberd C 429 B6
Ruthven Aberds 436 D2
Ruthven Angus 420 C2
Ruthven H'land 426 C2
Ruthven H'land 434 E3
Ruthven House Angus 420 C3
Ruthvoes Cornw'l 8 C1
Ruthwaite Cumb 338 D3
Ruthwell Dumf/Gal 346 C4
Ruxley London 90 B4
Ruxton Green Heref'd 128 D4
Ruyton-XI-Towns Shrops 218 D4
Ryal Northum 351 B7
Ryall Worcs 153 D7
Ryarsh Kent 91 D8
Rychraggan H'land 433 E6
Rydal Cumb 326 E4
Ryde I/Wight 30 B3
Rye E Sussex 73 F5
Rye Foreign E Sussex 73 F5
Rye Harbour E Sussex 52 C3
Rye Hill Essex 139 F5
Rye Park Herts 138 F3
Rye Street Worcs 153 E5
Ryebank Shrops 219 B7
Ryecroft W Yorks 292 C3
Ryeford Glos 103 B8
Ryeford Heref'd 129 C6
Ryehill ER Yorks 298 E3
Ryeish Green Wokingham 86 C4
Ryeworth Glos 131 C5
Ryhall Rutl'd 203 A6
Ryhill W Yorks 282 B1
Ryhope Tyne/Wear 344 A4
Ryhope Colliery Tyne/Wear 353 F7
Rylah Derby 270 F1
Rylands Notts 225 A5
Rylstone N Yorks 304 D3
Ryme Intrinseca Dorset 40 D1
Ryther N Yorks 295 C5
Ryton Glos 129 A8
Ryton N Yorks 321 E6
Ryton Shrops 196 C4
Ryton Tyne/Wear 352 D2
Ryton Warwick 200 F1
Ryton on Dunsmore Warwick 178 D2
Ryton Woodside Tyne/Wear 352 D1

## S

Saasaig H'land 423 B6
Sabden Lancs 290 C4
Sabine's Green Essex 113 C5
Sackers Green Suffolk 164 E3
Sacombe Herts 138 D2
Sacombe Green Herts 138 D2
Sacriston Durham 343 B8
Sadberge D'lington 332 C1
Saddell Arg/Bute 404 C3
Saddell Ho Arg/Bute 404 C3
Saddington Leics 201 E7
Saddle Bow Norfolk 230 E4
Saddlescombe W Sussex 49 D5
Sadgill Cumb 327 E6
Saffron Walden Essex 162 E3
Sageston Pembs 117 D7
Saham Grove Norfolk 208 B2
Saham Hill Norfolk 208 C2
Saham Toney Norfolk 208 C2
Saighdinis W Isles 447 B3
Saighton Ches 242 B1
St. Abbs Scot Borders 399 E8
St. Abb's Haven Scot Borders 399 E8
St. Agnes Cornw'l 6 E5
St. Albans Herts 110 A4
St Alban's Abbey Herts 137 F6
St. Allen Cornw'l 7 E7
St. Andrews Fife 421 F5
St. Andrew's Major V/Glam 78 B2
St. Andrew's Well Dorset 24 B4
St. Anne's Lancs 288 E3
St. Anne's Park Bristol 80 B4
St. Ann's Nott'ham 248 F2
St. Ann's Dumf/Gal 359 D5
St. Ann's Chapel Cornw'l 10 A4
St. Ann's Chapel Devon 14 F1
St. Anthony Cornw'l 5 D5
St. Anthony-in-Meneage Cornw'l 4 E3
St. Anthony's Tyne/Wear 352 D4
St. Anthony's Hill E Sussex 51 F5
St. Arvans Monmouths 102 C2
St. Asaph = Llanelwy Denbs 262 E2
St. Athan V/Glam 77 C7
St. Austell Cornw'l 8 E3
St. Bartholomew's Hill Wilts 41 A7
St. Bees Cumb 324 D4
St. Blazey Cornw'l 8 E4
St. Blazey Gte Cornw'l 8 E4
St. Boswells Scot Borders 374 A1
St. Breock Cornw'l 8 A2
St. Breward Cornw'l 17 E6
St. Briavels Glos 102 B3
St. Briavels Common Glos 102 B2
St. Brides Pembs 116 B1
St. Bride's Major = Saint-y-Brid V/Glam 76 B4
St. Bride's Netherwent Monmouths 101 E8
St. Bride's Wentlooge Newp 101 F5
St. Bride's-super-Ely V/Glam 78 A1
St. Budeaux Plym'th 10 D4
St. Buryan Cornw'l 2 E4
St. Catherine Bath/NE Som'set 81 B7
St. Catherine's Arg/Bute 408 B4
St. Chloe Glos 104 B1
St. Clears = Sanclêr Carms 122 D1
St. Cleer Cornw'l 9 B7
St. Clement Cornw'l 4 B4
St Clement's Caves, Hastings E Sussex 52 E1
St. Clether Cornw'l 17 D9
St. Colmac Arg/Bute 408 F3
St. Columb Major Cornw'l 8 C1
St. Columb Minor Cornw'l 7 C7
St. Columb Road Cornw'l 7 D9
St. Combs Aberds 437 B7
St. Cross Hants 65 F6
St. Cross South Elmham Suffolk 188 B4
St. Cyrus Aberds 421 A7
St. David's Perth/Kinr 419 E7
St. David's = Tyddewi Pembs 118 D3
St. Day Cornw'l 4 B2
St. Decumans Som'set 57 C8
St. Dennis Cornw'l 8 D2
St. Denys S'thampton 44 D3
St. Dials Torf 101 D5
St. Dogmaels = Llandudoch Pembs 144 C3
St. Dominick Cornw'l 10 B4
St. Donats V/Glam 77 C5
St. Edith's Marsh Wilts 82 D4
St. Endellion Cornw'l 16 E4
St. Enoder Cornw'l 7 D8
St. Erme Cornw'l 7 F7
St. Erney Cornw'l 10 D3
St. Erth Cornw'l 3 C7
St. Erth Praze Cornw'l 3 C7
St. Ervan Cornw'l 7 A8
St. Eval Cornw'l 7 B8
St. Ewe Cornw'l 5 A7
St. Fagans Card 78 A2
St Fagans Museum of Welsh Life Card 78 A2
St. Fergus Aberds 437 C7
St. Fillans Perth/Kinr 418 E4
St. Florence Pembs 117 D7
St. Gennys Cornw'l 17 A7
St. George Bristol 80 B4
St. George Conwy 262 D1
St. George's N Som'set 79 D7
St. George's Telford 196 A3
St. George's V/Glam 78 A1
St. George's Hill Surrey 88 D3
St. Germans Cornw'l 10 D3
St. Giles Lincs 272 E4
St Giles Cathedral C/Edinb 396 D2
St. Giles in the Wood Devon 34 C3
St. Giles on the Heath Devon 18 B4
St. Giles's Hill Hants 65 F6
St. Gluvias Cornw'l 4 D3
St. Harmon Powys 170 D4
St. Helen Auckland Durham 343 F7
St. Helena Warwick 199 C6
St. Helens Cumb 337 E3
St. Helen's E Sussex 52 D1
St. Helen's I/Wight 30 C4
St. Helens Mersey 277 F8
St. Helen's S Yorks 282 C1
St. Helen's Wood E Sussex 51 D9
St. Helier London 89 C7
St. Hilary Cornw'l 3 D7
St. Hilary V/Glam 77 B7
St. Hill Devon 37 F6
St. Ibbs Herts 137 B7
St. Illtyd Bl Gwent 100 B4
St. Ippollitts Herts 137 B8
St. Ishmael Carms 122 F3
St. Ishmael's Pembs 116 C2
St. Issey Cornw'l 8 A1
St. Ive Cornw'l 10 B2
St. Ive Cross Cornw'l 10 B2
St. Ives Cambs 183 D6
St. Ives Cornw'l 3 B6
St. Ives Dorset 42 F5
St. James Dorset 41 B7
St. James Norfolk 234 D2
St. James South Elmham Suffolk 188 B4
St. James's End Northants 180 F2
St. James's Park Notts 225 A8
St. Jidgey Cornw'l 8 B1
St. John Cornw'l 10 E4
St. John's E Sussex 70 E5
St. John's I/Man 336 C2
St. John's Kent 91 E5
St. John's London 90 A2
St. John's Suffolk 166 D1
St. John's Surrey 88 E1
St. John's W Yorks 294 C2
St. John's Chapel Durham 341 D8
St. John's Fen End Norfolk 206 A1
St. John's Highway Norfolk 206 A1
St. John's Town of Dalry Dumf/Gal 356 F4
St. John's Wells Aberds 437 E4
St. John's Wood London 111 F7
St. Judes I/Man 336 B3
St. Julians Herts 110 A4
St. Julian's Newp 101 E6
St. Just Cornw'l 2 D3
St. Just in Roseland Cornw'l 5 C5
St Just In Roseland Cornw'l 5 C5
St. Katherine's Aberds 437 E4
St. Keverne Cornw'l 4 F3
St. Kew Cornw'l 16 E5
St. Kew Highway Cornw'l 17 E5
St. Keyne Cornw'l 9 C7
St. Lawrence Essex 115 B6
St. Lawrence I/Wight 30 E2
St. Lawrence Kent 95 C7
St. Leonards Bucks 136 F2
St. Leonards Dorset 42 F5
St. Leonards E Sussex 51 E9
St. Leonards S Lanarks 380 B4
St. Leonard's Street Kent 91 E8
St. Levan Cornw'l 2 F3
St. Loy Cornw'l 2 F4
St. Lukes Derby C 223 A8
St. Lythans Card 78 B2
St. Mabyn Cornw'l 8 A3
St. Madoes Perth/Kinr 420 E1
St. Margaret South Elmham Suffolk 188 B4
St. Margaret's Heref'd 150 F5
St. Margarets Herts 138 E3
St. Margaret's Wilts 83 C8
St. Margaret's at Cliffe Kent 75 C7
St. Margaret's Hope Orkney 453 D5
St. Mark's Glos 130 C4
St. Mark's I/Man 336 D2
St. Martin Cornw'l 9 D8
St. Martin Cornw'l 4 F2
St. Martins Perth/Kinr 420 D1
St. Martin's Shrops 218 A3
St. Martin's Wilts 83 C8
St. Martin's Moor Shrops 218 A3
St. Martin's Plain Kent 74 D3
St. Mary Bourne Hants 65 A5
St. Mary Church V/Glam 77 B7
St. Mary Cray London 90 C4
St. Mary Hill V/Glam 77 A6
St. Mary Hoo Medway 92 A3
St. Mary in the Marsh Kent 73 F8
St. Marychurch Torbay 15 B6
St. Mary's Orkney 453 C5
St. Mary's Bay Kent 74 F1
St Mary's Church Warwick 177 E8
St. Mary's Grove N Som'set 80 C1
St. Maughans Monmouths 128 D3
St. Maughans Green Monmouths 128 D3
St. Mawes Cornw'l 4 D4
St. Mawgan Cornw'l 7 B8
St. Mellion Cornw'l 10 B3
St. Mellons Card 100 F4
St. Merryn Cornw'l 16 F2
St. Mewan Cornw'l 8 E2
St. Michael Caerhays Cornw'l 5 B7
St. Michael Church Som'set 59 E6
St. Michael Penkevil Cornw'l 5 B5
St. Michael South Elmham Suffolk 188 B4
St. Michaels Kent 72 D4
St. Michael's Torbay 15 C5
St. Michael's Worcs 174 E1
St. Michael's Hamlet Mersey 264 B2
St. Michael's Mead Herts 139 D5
St Michael's Mount, Penzance Cornw'l 3 E6
St. Michael's-on-Wyre Lancs 289 B6
St. Minver Cornw'l 16 E4
St. Monans Fife 412 B3
St. Neot Cornw'l 9 B6
St. Neots Cambs 160 A2
St. Nicholas Pembs 119 B6
St. Nicholas V/Glam 78 B1
St. Nicholas at Wade Kent 94 C5
St. Nicholas South Elmham Suffolk 188 B4
St. Nicolas Park Warwick 199 E8
St. Ninians Stirl 410 C3
St. Olaves Norfolk 211 D5
St. Osyth Essex 142 D3
St. Osyth Heath Essex 142 D3
St. Owen's Cross Heref'd 128 C4
St Paul's Cathedral London 111 F8
St. Paul's Cray London 90 C4
St. Paul's Walden Herts 137 C8
St. Peter South Elmham Suffolk 188 B4
St. Peter The Great Worcs 153 B7
St. Peters Glos 130 C4
St. Peters Kent 95 C7
St. Peter's Tyne/Wear 352 D4
St. Petrox Pembs 117 E5
St. Pinnock Cornw'l 9 C7
St. Quivox S Ayrs 367 C7
St. Ruan Cornw'l 5 G2
St. Stephen Cornw'l 8 E1
St. Stephens Cornw'l 18 C3
St. Stephens Cornw'l 10 D4
St. Stephen's Herts 110 A4
St. Teath Cornw'l 17 D6
St. Thomas Devon 21 B8
St. Tudy Cornw'l 17 E6
St. Twynnells Pembs 117 E5
St. Veep Cornw'l 9 D5
St. Vigeans Angus 421 C6
St. Vincent's Hamlet Essex 113 D6
St. Wenn Cornw'l 8 C2
St. Weonards Heref'd 128 C3
St. Winnow Cornw'l 9 D5
Saintbridge Glos 130 D3
Saintbury Glos 154 E5
Saint-y-Brid = St. Bride's Major V/Glam 76 B4
Saith Ffynnon Flints 263 D5
Salcombe Devon 13 E5
Salcombe Regis Devon 22 C4

Shaw Green N Yorks 306 E2
Shaw Heath Ches 266 D2
Shaw Heath Gtr Man 266 B4
Shaw Lands S Yorks 281 C8
Shaw Mills N Yorks 306 C2
Shaw Side Gtr Man 279 C7
Shawbirtch Telford 220 F2
Shawbury Shrops 219 D8
Shawclough Gtr Man 279 B6
Shawell Leics 179 B5
Shawfield Gtr Man 279 B6
Shawfield Head N Yorks 306 E2
Shawford Hants 44 B4
Shawforth Lancs 291 F6
Shawhead Dumf/Gal 402 B2
Shawhead N Lanarks 393 F6
Shawhill Dumf/Gal 347 C6
Shawlands Glasg C 392 F3
Shawsburn S Lanarks 381 B7
Shawton S Lanarks 381 C5
Shawtonhill S Lanarks 381 C5
Sheandow Moray 435 E7
Shear Cross Wilts 62 C2
Shearington Dumf/Gal 346 C2
Shearsby Leics 201 E6
Shearston Som'set 59 E5
Shebbear Devon 34 E1
Shebdon Staffs 220 C5
Shebster H'land 444 B4
Sheddens E Renf 380 A3
Shedfield Hants 45 D6
Sheen Staffs 245 B8
Sheep Hill Durham 352 E2
Sheepbridge Derby 269 E7
Sheepcote Close N Yorks 319 A6
Sheeplane Beds 136 A2
Sheepridge W Yorks 280 A4
Sheepscar W Yorks 293 D8
Sheepscombe Glos 130 E3
Sheepstor Devon 11 B6
Sheeptick End Beds 159 E7
Sheepwash Devon 34 E2
Sheepwash Northum 365 E7
Sheepway N Som'set 80 A1
Sheepy Magna Leics 199 C7
Sheepy Parva Leics 199 C7
Sheering Essex 139 E6
Sheerness Kent 93 A5
Sheerwater Kent 94 D5
Sheerwater Surrey 88 D2
Sheet Hants 46 B3
Sheet Shrops 173 D8
Sheets Heath Surrey 87 E9
Sheffield Cornw'l 2 E5
Sheffield S Yorks 269 B7
Sheffield Bottom W Berks 86 C3
Sheffield Common Essex 113 D6
Sheffield Green E Sussex 49 A8
Sheffield Park S Yorks 269 B7
Sheffield Park, Uckfield E Sussex 49 B8
Shefford Beds 160 E2
Shefford Woodlands W Berks 84 B4
Sheigra H'land 442 B3
Sheinton Shrops 195 C8
Shelderton Shrops 173 C6
Sheldon Derby 268 F3
Sheldon Devon 37 E7
Sheldon W Midlands 177 B6
Sheldwich Kent 93 E7
Sheldwich Lees Kent 93 E7
Shelf Bridg 99 F5
Shelf W Yorks 292 E4
Shelfanger Norfolk 187 B7
Shelfield Warwick 177 F5
Shelfield W Midlands 198 C1
Shelfield Green Warwick 176 F5
Shelfleys Northants 158 A2
Shelford Notts 248 F4
Shelford Warwick 200 F2
Shell Green Halton 265 B5
Shelley Essex 113 A6
Shelley Suffolk 165 E5
Shelley W Yorks 281 B6
Shellingford Oxon 106 D3
Shellow Bowells Essex 139 F8
Shellthorn Som'set 58 E4
Shelly Green W Midlands 177 C5
Shelsley Beauchamp Worcs 174 F4
Shelsley Walsh Worcs 174 F4
Shelthorpe Leics 225 E5
Shelton Beds 181 E8
Shelton Norfolk 209 E8
Shelton Notts 249 F6
Shelton Shrops 219 F6
Shelton Common Norfolk 209 E8
Shelton Green Norfolk 209 E8
Shelton Lock Derby C 224 B2
Shelton under Harley Staffs 221 A6
Shelve Shrops 194 D2
Shelvingford Kent 94 C4
Shelwick Heref'd 151 D8
Shelwick Green Heref'd 151 D8
Shenfield Essex 113 D6
Shenington Oxon 156 D2
Shenley Herts 111 B5
Shenley Brook End M/Keynes 158 F4
Shenley Church End M/Keynes 158 E4
Shenley Fields W Midlands 176 B3
Shenley Lodge M/Keynes 158 E4
Shenleybury Herts 111 B5
Shenmore Heref'd 151 E5
Shennanton Dumf/Gal 401 C5
Shennanton Ho. Dumf/Gal 401 C5
Shenstone Staffs 198 C3
Shenstone Worcs 175 D7
Shenstone Woodend Staffs 198 C3
Shenton Leics 199 C8
Shenval H'land 433 F6
Shenval Moray 435 F7
Shenvault Moray 435 D5
Shepard Hill N Yorks 332 F4
Shepard Hill W Yorks 293 F7
Shepeau Stow Lincs 204 A5
Shephall Herts 137 C9
Shepherds Cornw'l 7 E7
Shepherd's Bush London 111 F6
Shepherd's Gate Norfolk 230 E3
Shepherd's Green Oxon 108 F4
Shepherd's Patch Glos 103 B6
Shepherd's Port Norfolk 231 B5
Shepherdswell or Sibertswold Kent 74 B5
Shepley W Yorks 281 C5
Shepperdine S Glos 102 C4
Shepperton Surrey 88 C3
Shepperton Green Surrey 88 C3
Shepreth Cambs 161 C7
Shepshed Leics 224 E4
Shepton Beauchamp Som'set 39 C6
Shepton Mallet Som'set 60 C4
Shepton Montague Som'set 61 E5
Shepway Kent 92 F2
Sheraton Durham 344 D4
Sherborne Dorset 40 C2
Sherborne Glos 132 E2
Sherborne Causeway Dorset 41 B6
Sherborne St. John Hants 86 E2
Sherborne Street Suffolk 164 D4
Sherbourne Warwick 177 F8
Sherburn Durham 344 C2
Sherburn N Yorks 322 E3
Sherburn Hill Durham 344 C2
Sherburn in Elmet N Yorks 294 D3
Shere Surrey 68 B3
Shereford Norfolk 232 C2
Sherfield English Hants 43 B8
Sherfield Hill Hants 86 E3
Sherfield on Loddon Hants 86 E3
Sherfin Lancs 290 E4
Sherford Devon 13 D6
Sherford Som'set 38 B2
Sheriff Hill Tyne/Wear 352 D4
Sheriff Hutton N Yorks 308 B2
Sheriffhales Shrops 196 A4
Sheringham Norfolk 257 D6
Sherington M/Keynes 159 C5
Sheringwood Norfolk 257 D6
Shernal Green Worcs 175 F8
Shernborne Norfolk 231 B6
Sherrard's Green Worcs 153 C6
Sherrardspark Herts 137 E8
Sherrington Wilts 62 D4
Sherston Wilts 104 E2
Sherston Parva Wilts 104 E2
Sherwood Nott'ham 248 F2
Sherwood Lancs 289 D7
Sherwood Park Kent 71 C7
Shettleston Glasg C 392 F4
Shevington Gtr Man 277 C7
Shevington Moor Gtr Man 277 B7
Shevington Vale Gtr Man 277 C7
Sheviock Cornw'l 10 D3
Shewalton N Ayrs 379 E6
Shibden Head W Yorks 292 E3
Shide I/Wight 30 C1
Shiel Aberds 427 A7
Shiel Bridge H'land 424 A1
Shield Row Durham 352 F3
Shieldaig H'land 431 A8
Shieldaig H'land 431 C8
Shieldhall Glasg C 392 E2
Shieldhall Falk 394 C2
Shieldhill Dumf/Gal 358 E4
Shieldhill S Lanarks 382 D5
Shieldmuir N Lanarks 381 A7
Shielfoot H'land 423 F6
Shielhill Angus 420 B4
Shifford Oxon 106 B4
Shifnal Shrops 196 B4
Shilbottle Northum 377 F5
Shilbottle Grange Northum 377 F6
Shildon Durham 331 A6
Shillford E Renf 379 A8
Shillingford Devon 36 B4
Shillingford Oxon 108 D1
Shillingford Abbot Devon 21 C8
Shillingford St. George Devon 21 C8
Shillingstone Dorset 41 D6
Shillington Beds 160 F2
Shillmoor Northum 375 F7
Shilton Oxon 132 F4
Shilton Warwick 178 B3
Shilvinghampton Dorset 25 D7
Shilvington Northum 365 F5
Shimpling Norfolk 187 B8
Shimpling Suffolk 164 B2
Shimpling Street Suffolk 164 B2
Shincliffe Durham 344 C1
Shiney Row Tyne/Wear 344 A2
Shinfield Wokingham 86 C4
Shingay Cambs 161 C6
Shingham Norfolk 207 B6
Shingle Street Suffolk 166 D5
Shinner's Bridge Devon 14 C3
Shinness H'land 440 B2
Shipbourne Kent 71 A6
Shipbrookhill Ches 265 E8
Shipdham Norfolk 208 B3
Shipham Som'set 79 E8
Shiphay Torbay 15 B5
Shiplake Oxon 86 A5
Shiplake Bottom Oxon 108 F4
Shiplake Row Oxon 86 A5
Shiplate N Som'set 79 E7
Shipley Northum 376 D4
Shipley Shrops 196 D5
Shipley W Sussex 48 B2
Shipley W Yorks 292 C4
Shipley Bridge Surrey 69 C8
Shipley Common Derby 247 F7
Shipmeadow Suffolk 210 F3
Shipmeadow Common Suffolk 210 F3
Shippon Oxon 107 C6
Shipston on Stour Warwick 155 D8
Shipton Bucks 135 B6
Shipton Glos 131 D6
Shipton N Yorks 307 D8
Shipton Shrops 195 E7
Shipton Bellinger Hants 64 B1
Shipton Gorge Dorset 24 B4
Shipton Green W Sussex 31 E5
Shipton Moyne Glos 104 E2
Shipton Oliffe Glos 131 D6
Shipton on Cherwell Oxon 133 D8
Shipton Solers Glos 131 D6
Shipton under Wychwood Oxon 132 D4
Shiptonthorpe ER Yorks 296 B4
Shirburn Oxon 108 C4
Shirdley Hill Lancs 276 B4
Shire Cumb 340 D3
Shire Horse Centre, Stratford-upon-Avon Warwick 155 B7
Shire Oak W Midlands 198 C2
Shirebrook Derby 270 F2
Shirecliffe S Yorks 269 A6
Shiregreen S Yorks 269 A7
Shirehampton Bristol 80 A2
Shiremoor Tyne/Wear 353 B5
Shirenewton Monmouths 102 D1
Shireoaks Notts 270 C3
Shirkoak Kent 73 D5
Shirl Heath Heref'd 151 A6
Shirland Derby 247 C5
Shirlett Shrops 196 D2
Shirley Derby 246 F2
Shirley Hants 28 A3
Shirley S'thampton 44 D3
Shirley W Midlands 176 C5
Shirley Heath W Midlands 176 C5
Shirley Warren S'thampton 44 D3
Shirrell Heath Hants 45 D6
Shirwell Devon 55 D6
Shirwell Cross Devon 55 D6
Shiskine N Ayrs 405 D5
Shittlehope Durham 342 D4
Shobdon Heref'd 173 F5
Shobley Hants 43 E6
Shobnall Staffs 223 D6
Shobrooke Devon 36 F2
Shoby Leics 225 D8
Shocklach Ches 242 E1
Shocklach Green Ches 242 E1
Shoeburyness Southend 115 F5
Sholden Kent 75 A7
Sholing S'thampton 44 D4
Sholing Common S'thampton 44 D4
Sholver Gtr Man 279 C7
Shoot Hill Shrops 194 A4
Shootash Hants 44 B1
Shooter's Hill London 90 A3
Shootersway Herts 136 F3
Shop Cornw'l 16 F2
Shop Cornw'l 32 D4
Shop Devon 33 D7
Shop Corner Suffolk 166 F3
Shopford Cumb 349 E5
Shopnoller Som'set 58 E3
Shore Gtr Man 279 A7
Shore W Yorks 291 E7
Shore Mill H'land 434 B2
Shoreditch London 111 F8
Shoreditch Som'set 38 B2
Shoregill Cumb 329 F5
Shoreham Kent 90 D5
Shoreham Airport W Sussex 48 E4
Shoreham Beach W Sussex 48 F4
Shoreham-by-Sea W Sussex 48 F4
Shoresdean Northum 387 C9
Shoreside Shetl'd 457 J2
Shoreswood Northum 387 C8
Shoreton H'land 433 B8
Shorley Hants 45 A6
Shorncote Glos 105 C5
Shorne Kent 91 B8
Shorne Ridgeway Kent 91 B8
Short Cross W Midlands 176 B2
Short Heath Leics 223 F8
Short Heath W Midlands 198 E2
Short Street Wilts 61 B8
Shorta Cross Cornw'l 10 D1
Shortacombe Devon 19 C7
Shortbridge E Sussex 50 B1
Shortfield Common Surrey 67 C6
Shortgate E Sussex 50 C2
Shorthampton Oxon 133 C5
Shortheath Hants 66 D5
Shortheath Surrey 67 C6
Shortlands London 90 C2
Shortlanesend Cornw'l 7 F7
Shortlees E Ayrs 379 E8
Shorton Torbay 15 C5
Shortroods Renf 392 E1
Short's Corner Lincs 252 D2
Shortstanding Glos 128 E5
Shortstown Beds 160 C1
Shortwood Glos 104 C1
Shortwood S Glos 81 A5
Shorwell I/Wight 29 D9
Shoscombe Bath/NE Som'set 81 E6
Shoscombe Vale Bath/NE Som'set 81 E6
Shotesham Norfolk 209 D9
Shotford Heath Suffolk 188 B2
Shotgate Essex 114 D2
Shotley Northants 202 D4
Shotley Suffolk 166 F2
Shotley Bridge Northum 343 A5
Shotley Gate Suffolk 166 F2
Shotleyfield Northum 342 A5
Shottenden Kent 93 F7
Shottermill Surrey 67 E7
Shottery Warwick 155 A6
Shotteswell Warwick 156 C3
Shottisham Suffolk 166 D4
Shottle Derby 246 E4
Shottlegate Derby 246 E4
Shotton Durham 344 D4
Shotton Durham 332 A2
Shotton Flints 263 F8
Shotton Northum 352 A3
Shotton Northum 375 A6
Shotton Colliery Durham 344 C3
Shotts N Lanarks 394 F2
Shotwick Ches 263 E8
Shouldham Norfolk 206 B4
Shouldham Thorpe Norfolk 206 B4
Shoulton Worcs 153 A6
Shover's Green E Sussex 71 E7
Shraleybrook Staffs 243 E8
Shrawardine Shrops 219 E5
Shrawley Worcs 175 E6
Shreding Green Bucks 110 F2
Shrewley Warwick 177 E7
Shrewsbury Shrops 195 A6
Shrewton Wilts 63 C6
Shripney W Sussex 47 F6
Shrivenham Oxon 106 E1
Shropham Norfolk 208 E3
Shroton Dorset 41 D6
Shrub End Essex 141 C8
Shrubs Hill Surrey 88 C1
Shuart Kent 94 C5
Shucknall Heref'd 152 D1
Shudy Camps Cambs 162 D5
Shulishadermor H'land 430 D4
Shulista H'land 430 A4
Shuna Ho Arg/Bute 407 B7
Shurdington Glos 130 D4
Shurlock Row Windsor 87 B6
Shurnock Worcs 176 F3
Shurrery H'land 444 C4
Shurrery Lodge H'land 444 C4
Shurton Som'set 58 C4
Shustoke Warwick 199 E5
Shute Devon 23 A7
Shute Devon 36 F2
Shute End Wilts 63 F8
Shutford Oxon 156 D2
Shutheath Staffs 221 D7
Shuthonger Glos 153 E7
Shutlanger Northants 158 C2
Shutta Cornw'l 9 E8
Shuttington Warwick 199 B6
Shuttlesfield Kent 74 C3
Shuttlewood Derby 270 E1
Shuttleworth Lancs 279 A5
Shwt Bridg 98 E4
Siabost bho Dheas W Isles 451 C5
Siabost bho Thuath W Isles 451 C5
Siadar W Isles 451 B6
Siadar Iarach W Isles 451 B6
Siadar Uarach W Isles 451 B6
Sibbaldbie Dumf/Gal 359 E6
Sibbertoft Northants 179 B8
Sibdon Carwood Shrops 173 B6
Sibford Ferris Oxon 156 E2
Sibford Gower Oxon 156 E2
Sible Hedingham Essex 163 F8
Sibley's Green Essex 139 B8
Sibsey Lincs 252 D3
Sibsey Fen Side Lincs 252 D2
Sibson Cambs 203 D7
Sibson Leics 199 C8
Sibster H'land 445 C7
Sibthorpe Notts 249 E6
Sibthorpe Notts 271 E6
Sibton Suffolk 188 E5
Sibton Green Suffolk 188 D5
Sicklesmere Suffolk 186 F2
Sicklinghall N Yorks 306 F4
Sid Devon 22 C4
Sidbrook Som'set 58 F5
Sidbury Devon 22 B4
Sidbury Shrops 174 A3
Sidcot N Som'set 79 E8
Sidcup London 90 B4
Siddal W Yorks 292 F4
Siddick Cumb 337 E3
Siddington Ches 266 E3
Siddington Glos 105 C5
Side of the Moor Gtr Man 278 B3
Sidemoor Worcs 176 D1
Sidestrand Norfolk 257 E8
Sideway Stoke 244 F3
Sidford Devon 22 B4
Sidlesham W Sussex 31 E7
Sidley E Sussex 51 E7
Sidlow Surrey 69 B7
Sidmouth Devon 22 C4
Siefton Shrops 173 B7
Sigford Devon 21 F5
Sigglesthorne ER Yorks 298 A2
Sighthill C/Edinb 395 D8
Sigingstone V/Glam 77 B6
Signet Oxon 132 E3
Silchester Hants 86 D2
Sildinis W Isles 451 F5
Sileby Leics 225 E7
Silecroft Cumb 312 D3
Silfield Norfolk 209 D6
Silford Devon 54 F3
Silian Ceredig'n 146 B4
Silk Willoughby Lincs 250 F4
Silkstead Hants 44 B3
Silkstone S Yorks 281 C7
Silkstone Common S Yorks 281 D7
Sill Field Cumb 314 C5
Sillaton Cornw'l 10 C3
Silloth Cumb 346 F4
Sillyearn Moray 436 C2
Siloh Carms 147 E7
Silpho N Yorks 322 B3
Silsden W Yorks 304 F4
Silsoe Beds 160 E1
Silver End Essex 140 D5
Silver Green Norfolk 209 E9
Silver Hill E Sussex 51 A7
Silver Street Glos 103 B7
Silver Street Kent 92 D4
Silver Street Som'set 37 B8
Silver Street Som'set 60 E2
Silver Street Worcs 176 C4
Silverburn Midloth 395 F9
Silverdale Lancs 314 E3
Silverdale Staffs 244 E2
Silverdale Green Lancs 314 F3
Silvergate Norfolk 233 C8
Silverhill E Sussex 51 D9
Silverhill Park E Sussex 52 D1
Silverknowes C/Edinb 395 C9
Silverlace Green Suffolk 188 F4
Silverley's Green Suffolk 188 C3
Silverstone Northants 157 D8
Silverstone Motor Racing Circuit Northants 157 D8
Silverton Devon 36 F4
Silverton W Dunb 391 C8
Silvertonhill S Lanarks 381 B6
Silvertown London 112 F3
Silverwell Cornw'l 7 F5
Silvington Shrops 174 C2
Silwick Shetl'd 455 B1
Simister Gtr Man 279 C5
Simmondley Derby 267 A7
Simm's Cross Halton 264 B5
Simm's Lane End Mersey 277 D7
Simonburn Northum 350 B4
Simonsbath Som'set 56 D2
Simonside Tyne/Wear 353 D5
Simonstone Lancs 290 D4
Simonstone N Yorks 316 B3
Simprim Scot Borders 387 C7
Simpson M/Keynes 159 E5
Simpson Pembs 116 A3
Simpson Cross Pembs 116 A3
Simpson Green W Yorks 293 C5
Sinclair's Hill Scot Borders 387 B6
Sinclairston E Ayrs 368 D1
Sinderby N Yorks 319 D5
Sinderhope Northum 341 A7
Sinderland Green Gtr Man 266 A1
Sindlesham Wokingham 86 C5
Sinfin Derby C 224 B1
Singdean Scot Borders 361 B8
Singleborough Bucks 135 A6
Singledge Kent 75 B5
Singleton Lancs 288 D3
Singleton W Sussex 47 D5
Singlewell Kent 91 B8
Singret Wrex 241 C7
Sinkhurst Green Kent 72 C3
Sinnahard Aberds 428 A1
Sinnington N Yorks 321 C5
Sinton Worcs 175 F6
Sinton Green Worcs 175 F6
Sion Hill Bath/NE Som'set 81 C6
Sion Hill N Yorks 319 D6
Sipson London 88 A3
Sirhowy Bl Gwent 126 F3
Sisland Norfolk 210 D2
Sissinghurst Kent 72 D2
Sissinghurst Castle Garden Kent 72 D3
Siston S Glos 81 A5
Sithney Cornw'l 3 E8
Sithney Green Cornw'l 3 E8
Sitterton Dorset 26 B3
Sittingbourne Kent 93 D5
Sitwell Grange Derby 247 B6
Six Ashes Staffs 196 F4
Six Bells Bl Gwent 100 B4
Six Mile Bottom Cambs 162 A3
Sixhills Lincs 273 B7
Sixmile Kent 74 C2
Sixpenny Handley Dorset 42 C2
Sizewell Suffolk 189 F7
Skail H'land 444 D1
Skaill Orkney 454 C2
Skaill Orkney 452 B3
Skaill Orkney 453 C6
Skara Brae Orkney 452 B3
Skares E Ayrs 368 D2
Skateraw E Loth 398 C4
Skaw Shetl'd 456 B6
Skaw Shetl'd 457 G5
Skeabost H'land 430 D4
Skeabrae Orkney 452 A3
Skeeby N Yorks 331 F6
Skeete Kent 74 C2
Skeffington Leics 201 C8
Skeffling ER Yorks 287 A6
Skegby Notts 247 B8
Skegness Lincs 253 B7
Skelberry Shetl'd 457 G4
Skelberry Shetl'd 455 E2
Skelbo H'land 440 D4
Skelbo Street H'land 440 D4
Skelbrooke S Yorks 282 B4
Skeldyke Lincs 229 A6
Skelfhill Scot Borders 361 B6
Skellingthorpe Lincs 272 E3
Skellister Shetl'd 457 H4
Skellorn Green Ches 267 C5
Skellow S Yorks 282 B4
Skelmanthorpe W Yorks 281 B6
Skelmersdale Lancs 277 C6
Skelmonae Aberds 437 E5
Skelmorlie N Ayrs 390 E3
Skelmuir Aberds 437 D6
Skelpick H'land 444 C1
Skelton Cumb 339 D7
Skelton C/York 307 D8
Skelton ER Yorks 296 E2
Skelton N Yorks 306 B4
Skelton N Yorks 330 F3
Skelton Redcar/Clevel'd 333 C8
Skelton Green Redcar/Clevel'd 333 C8
Skelton Wood End Cumb 339 D7
Skelwick Orkney 454 B2
Skelwith Bridge Cumb 326 F3
Skendleby Lincs 275 F5
Skendleby Psalter Lincs 275 E5
Skene Ho. Aberds 428 B4
Skenfrith Monmouths 128 C3
Skerne ER Yorks 310 D2
Skeroblingarry Arg/Bute 404 D3
Skerray H'land 443 B8
Skerricha H'land 442 C4
Skerton Lancs 301 C8
Sketchley Leics 200 E2
Sketchley Hill Leics 200 E2
Sketty Swan 97 D7
Skewen Rh Cyn Taff 98 C1
Skewsby N Yorks 308 A1
Skeyton Norfolk 234 C1
Skeyton Corner Norfolk 234 C2
Skiag Bridge H'land 439 A6
Skibo Castle H'land 440 E4
Skidbrooke Lincs 275 A5
Skidbrooke North End Lincs 287 E7
Skidby ER Yorks 297 D7
Skilgate Som'set 57 F6
Skillington Lincs 226 D4
Skinburness Cumb 346 E4
Skinflats Falk 410 D4
Skinidin H'land 430 D2
Skinnand Lincs 250 C1
Skinner's Bottom Cornw'l 4 A2
Skinners Green W Berks 85 C6
Skinnet H'land 443 B7
Skinningrove Redcar/Clevel'd 334 C1
Skipness Arg/Bute 404 A4
Skippool Lancs 288 B3
Skiprigg Cumb 339 B6
Skipsea ER Yorks 310 E5
Skipsea Brough ER Yorks 310 E5
Skipton N Yorks 304 E3
Skipton-on-Swale N Yorks 319 E6
Skipwith N Yorks 295 C7
Skirbeck Lincs 252 F2
Skirbeck Quarter Lincs 252 F2
Skireholme N Yorks 305 C5
Skirethorns N Yorks 304 C3
Skirlaugh ER Yorks 298 C1
Skirling Scot Borders 383 E6
Skirmett Bucks 109 E5
Skirpenbeck ER Yorks 308 D3
Skirwith N Yorks 315 F8
Skirwith Cumb 340 E3
Skirza H'land 445 B7
Skitby Cumb 348 C3
Skitham Lancs 289 B5
Skittle Green Bucks 108 B5
Skrinkle Pembs 117 E7
Skulamus H'land 431 F6
Skullomie H'land 443 B8
Skyborry Green Shrops 172 D3
Skye Green Essex 141 C6
Skye of Curr H'land 434 F4
Skyfog Pembs 118 D4
Slack W Yorks 291 E8
Slack Head Cumb 314 E3
Slackcote Gtr Man 279 C8
Slackhall Derby 267 C8
Slackhead Moray 436 B1
Slackholme End Lincs 275 E7
Slacks of Cairnbanno Aberds 437 D5
Slad Glos 130 F3
Slade Kent 93 F5
Slade Pembs 116 A4
Slade Swan 96 E4
Slade End Oxon 108 D1
Slade Green London 91 A5
Slade Heath Staffs 197 B7
Slade Hooton S Yorks 270 C3
Slades Green Worcs 153 F7
Sladesbridge Cornw'l 8 A3
Slaggyford Northum 340 A4
Slaid Hill W Yorks 293 B8
Slaidburn Lancs 303 E6
Slaithwaite W Yorks 280 B3
Slaley Derby 246 C3
Slaley Northum 351 E6
Slamannan Falk 394 D2
Slapeworth Redcar/Clevel'd 333 C7
Slapton Bucks 136 C2
Slapton Devon 13 C7
Slapton Northants 157 C7
Slate Haugh Moray 436 B1
Slatepit Dale Derby 269 F6
Slattocks Gtr Man 279 C6
Slaugham W Sussex 69 F7
Slaughterford Wilts 82 B1
Slawston Leics 202 E1
Slay Pits S Yorks 283 C7
Slea View Lincs 250 E4
Sleaford Hants 67 D6
Sleaford Lincs 250 E4
Sleagill Cumb 328 C1
Sleap Shrops 219 C6
Sleapford Telford 220 E2
Sleapshyde Herts 137 F8
Sleastary H'land 440 D3
Sledge Green Worcs 153 F6
Sledmere ER Yorks 309 C7
Sleeches Cross E Sussex 71 E6
Sleet Moor Derby 247 D6
Sleight Dorset 27 A6
Sleights N Yorks 334 E4
Slepe Dorset 27 B5
Slerra Devon 33 B6
Sliabhna h-Airde W Isles 447 C2
Slickly H'land 445 B6
Sliddery N Ayrs 405 D5
Sligachan Hotel H'land 430 F4
Sligneach Arg/Bute 415 E5
Slimbridge Glos 103 B6
Slimbridge Wildfowl & Wetlands Centre, Frampton on Severn Glos 103 B6
Slindon Staffs 221 B6
Slindon W Sussex 47 E7
Slindon Common W Sussex 47 E7
Slinfold W Sussex 68 E4
Sling Glos 129 F5
Sling Gwyn 260 F2
Slingsby N Yorks 321 E5
Slioch Aberds 436 E2
Slip End Beds 137 D5
Slip End Herts 161 E5
Slipperhill Cornw'l 18 E2
Slipton Northants 181 C7
Slitting Mill Staffs 222 E2
Sloadlane Derby 269 C7
Slochd H'land 434 F3
Slockavullin Arg/Bute 407 C8
Slogan Moray 435 D8
Sloley Norfolk 234 D2
Sloncombe Devon 20 C4
Sloothby Lincs 275 E6
Slough Windsor 110 F1
Slough Green Som'set 38 B3
Slough Green W Sussex 49 A5
Sluggan H'land 434 F3
Sluggans H'land 430 D4
Slumbay H'land 431 E8
Slyfield Surrey 68 A1
Slyne Lancs 301 B8
Smailholm Scot Borders 386 E2
Small Dole W Sussex 48 D4
Small End Lincs 252 C4
Small Heath W Midlands 198 F2
Small Hythe Kent 72 E4
Small Way Som'set 60 E4
Smallbridge Gtr Man 279 B7
Smallbrook Devon 21 A7
Smallbrook Glos 102 B3
Smallburgh Norfolk 234 D3
Smallburn Aberds 437 D7
Smallburn E Ayrs 369 B5
Smalldale Derby 268 D1
Smalldale Derby 268 C3
Smalley Derby 247 F6
Smalley Common Derby 247 F6
Smalley Green Derby 247 F6
Smallfield Surrey 69 C8
Smallford Herts 137 F7
Smallholm Dumf/Gal 346 A3
Smallridge Devon 38 F3
Smallshaw Gtr Man 279 D7
Smallwood Worcs 176 E3
Smallwood Green Suffolk 164 A3
Smallwood Hey Lancs 301 F6
Smallworth Norfolk 187 B5
Smannell Hants 64 B4
Smardale Cumb 328 E4
Smarden Kent 72 C4
Smarden Bell Kent 72 C4
Smart's Hill Kent 70 C5
Smaull Arg/Bute 406 F2

570 Sme – Sta


Smeatharpe Devon 38 D1
Smeeth Kent 73 D8
Smeeton Westerby Leics 201 E7
Smelthouses N Yorks 305 C7
Smercleit W Isles 446 B3
Smerral H'land 445 E5
Smestow Staffs 197 E6
Smethcott Shrops 194 D4
Smethwick W Midlands 198 F1
Smirisary H'land 423 E6
Smisby Derby 224 E2
Smith End Green Worcs 153 B5
Smith Green Lancs 302 D1
Smithaleigh Devon 11 D7
Smithbrook W Sussex 47 B6
Smithfield Cumb 348 C2
Smithies S Yorks 281 C9
Smithincott Devon 37 D6
Smithley S Yorks 282 D1
Smith's End Herts 161 E7
Smith's Green Essex 139 C7
Smith's Green Essex 163 D6
Smithston Aberds 436 F2
Smithstown H'land 438 F1
Smithton H'land 434 D2
Smithwood Green Suffolk 164 B3
Smithy Bridge Gtr Man 279 A7
Smithy Gate Flints 263 D5
Smithy Green Ches 266 E1
Smithy Green Cumb 313 D7
Smithy Green Gtr Man 266 B4
Smithy Hill Derby 268 C3
Smithy Lane Ends Lancs 276 B5
Smockington Leics 200 F2
Smoky Row Bucks 109 A6
Smoogro Orkney 452 C4
Smyrton S Ayrs 400 A3
Smythe's Green Essex 141 D7
Snaefell Mountain Railway I/Man 336 C4
Snaigow House Perth/Kinr 419 C8
Snailbeach Shrops 194 C3
Snailswell Herts 137 A7
Snailwell Cambs 185 E5
Snainton N Yorks 322 D2
Snaisgill Durham 342 F3
Snaith ER Yorks 295 F6
Snape N Yorks 318 D4
Snape Suffolk 167 A5
Snape Green Lancs 276 B4
Snape Hill Derby 269 D7
Snape Hill S Yorks 282 D2
Snape Watering Suffolk 167 A5
Snapper Devon 55 E7
Snaresbrook London 112 E2
Snarestone Leics 199 B7
Snarford Lincs 273 C6
Snargate Kent 73 F6
Snarraness Shetl'd 457 H2
Snatchwood Torf 100 B5
Snave Kent 73 F7
Sneachill Worcs 153 B8
Snead Common Heref'd 174 E4
Sneath Common Norfolk 209 F7
Sneaton N Yorks 334 E4
Sneatonthorpe N Yorks 335 E5
Sneedham's Green Glos 130 E2
Sneinton Nott'ham 225 A6
Snelland Lincs 273 C6
Snelston Derby 245 F9
Snetterton Norfolk 208 E3
Snetterton Motor Racing Circuit Norfolk 208 F4
Snettisham Norfolk 231 B5
Sneyd Green Stoke 244 E3
Sneyd Park Bristol 80 A3
Snibston Discovery Park, Coalville Leics 224 F3
Snig's End Glos 130 B1
Snipeshill Kent 93 D5
Sniseabhal W Isles 447 E2
Snitter Northum 364 B2
Snitterby Lincs 285 F6
Snitterfield Warwick 155 A7
Snittlegarth Cumb 338 D3
Snodhill Heref'd 150 D4
Snodland Kent 91 D8
Snods Edge Northum 342 A5
Snow End Herts 138 A4
Snow Hill W Yorks 293 F8
Snow Lea W Yorks 280 A3
Snow Street Norfolk 187 B6
Snowden Hill S Yorks 281 D7
Snowdon Mountain Railway, Llanberis Gwyn 237 C7
Snowdown Kent 74 A4
Snowhill Telford 196 A3
Snowshill Glos 154 F4
Snowshill Manor Glos 154 F4
Snydale W Yorks 294 F2
Soake Hants 45 D8
Soar Card 100 F1
Soar Carms 123 B8
Soar Gwyn 214 A4
Soar Angl 258 E4
Soar Powys 125 A8
Soar-y-Mynydd Ceredig'n 147 B8
Soberton Hants 45 C7
Soberton Heath Hants 45 D7
Sockbridge Cumb 339 F8
Sockburn N Yorks 332 E1
Sodom Shetl'd 457 G5
Sodom Wilts 104 F5
Soham Cambs 184 D4
Soham Cotes Cambs 184 C4
Soho London 111 F7
Soho Som'set 61 B5
Solas W Isles 447 A3
Soldon Cross Devon 33 D6
Soldridge Hants 66 E3
Sole Street Kent 74 B1
Sole Street Kent 91 C8
Solent Breezes Hants 45 F5
Solfach = Solva Pembs 118 E3
Solihull W Midlands 177 C5
Solihull Lodge W Midlands 176 C4
Sollers Dilwyn Heref'd 151 A6
Sollers Hope Heref'd 129 A6
Sollom Lancs 277 A6
Solva = Solfach Pembs 118 E3
Somerby Leics 201 A9
Somerby Lincs 285 C8
Somercotes Derby 247 D6
Somerford Dorset 28 B3
Somerford Keynes Glos 104 C5
Somerley W Sussex 31 E6
Somerleyton Suffolk 211 D5
Somersal Herbert Derby 222 A4
Somersby Lincs 274 E3
Somersham Cambs 183 C7
Somersham Suffolk 165 C6
Somerton Newp 101 E6
Somerton Oxon 133 B8
Somerton Suffolk 163 B9
Somerton Som'set 60 F1
Somerwood Shrops 219 F8
Sompting W Sussex 48 F3
Sompting Abbots W Sussex 48 E3
Sonning Wokingham 86 A5
Sonning Common Oxon 108 F4
Sonning Eye Oxon 86 A5
Sookholme Notts 248 A1
Sopley Hants 28 A3
Sopwell Herts 111 A5
Sopworth Wilts 103 E8
Sorbie Dumf/Gal 401 E6
Sordale H'land 445 B5
Sorisdale Arg/Bute 415 A5
Sorley Devon 13 C5
Sorn E Ayrs 368 B3
Sornhill E Ayrs 380 E2
Sortat H'land 445 B6
Sotby Lincs 273 D9
Sothell S Yorks 269 C8
Sots Hole Lincs 251 B5
Sotterley Suffolk 189 B7
Soudley Shrops 220 C4
Soughton = Sychdyn Flints 241 A5
Soulbury Bucks 135 B8
Soulby Cumb 327 A6
Soulby Cumb 328 D4
Souldern Oxon 134 A1
Souldrop Beds 181 F7
Sound Shetl'd 457 H3
Sound Shetl'd 455 B3
Sound Heath Ches 243 E5
Soundwell S Glos 81 A5
Sourhope Scot Borders 375 C6
Sourin Orkney 454 C2
Sourton Devon 19 B7
Soutergate Cumb 313 D5
South Acre Norfolk 231 F8
South Acton London 89 A6
South Alkham Kent 74 C5
South Allington Devon 13 E6
South Alloa Falk 410 C3
South Ambersham W Sussex 47 B6
South Anston S Yorks 270 C3
South Ascot Windsor 87 C8
South Ashford Kent 73 C7
South Auchmachar Aberds 437 D6
South Baddesley Hants 29 A7
South Ballachulish H'land 417 B5
South Balloch S Ayrs 355 C5
South Bank C/York 307 E8
South Bank Redcar/Clevel'd 333 B5
South Barham Kent 74 B3
South Barrow Som'set 60 F4
South Beddington London 89 D8
South Benfleet Essex 114 E2
South Bents Tyne/Wear 353 D7
South Bersted W Sussex 47 F6
South Bockhampton Dorset 28 A3
South Bowood Dorset 24 A3
South Bramwith S Yorks 283 B6
South Brent Devon 14 C1
South Brewham Som'set 61 D6
South Broomhill Northum 365 C6
South Burlingham Norfolk 210 B3
South Cadbury Som'set 40 A2
South Cairn Dumf/Gal 400 C1
South Carlton Lincs 272 D4
South Carlton Notts 270 C3
South Cave ER Yorks 297 D5
South Cerney Glos 105 C5
South Chailey E Sussex 49 C7
South Chard Som'set 38 E4
South Charlton Northum 377 C5
South Cheriton Som'set 40 B3
South Church Durham 343 F8
South Cleatlam Durham 330 C4
South Cliffe ER Yorks 296 C4
South Clifton Notts 271 E8
South Clunes H'land 433 D7
South Cockerington Lincs 274 B4
South Common Devon 38 F4
South Cornelly Bridg 98 F3
South Corriegills N Ayrs 405 C6
South Cove Suffolk 189 B7
South Creagan Arg/Bute 417 C4
South Creake Norfolk 255 E7
South Crosland W Yorks 280 B4
South Croxton Leics 201 A7
South Croydon London 89 D8
South Cuil H'land 430 B3
South Dalton ER Yorks 297 A6
South Darenth Kent 91 C6
South Devon Railway Devon 14 C3
South Duffield N Yorks 295 D7
South Dunn H'land 445 C5
South Elkington Lincs 274 B2
South Ella ER Yorks 297 E7
South Elmsall W Yorks 282 B3
South End Beds 159 C8
South End Bucks 135 B8
South End ER Yorks 287 A6
South End ER Yorks 298 B2
South End Hants 42 D5
South End Leics 225 F6
South End Norfolk 208 E3
South End N Lincs 297 F9
South End W Berks 86 B1
South Erradale H'land 431 A7
South Fambridge Essex 114 C4
South Fawley W Berks 106 F4
South Ferribly N Lincs 297 F6
South Field ER Yorks 297 E7
South Flobbets Aberds 437 E4
South Garth Shetl'd 456 D5
South Garvan H'land 424 E1
South Glendale W Isles 446 B3
South Gluss Shetl'd 457 F3
South Godstone Surrey 70 B2
South Gorley Hants 43 D6
South Gosforth Tyne/Wear 352 C3
South Green Essex 113 D8
South Green Essex 142 D1
South Green Kent 92 D3
South Green Norfolk 230 E2
South Green Norfolk 188 B2
South Green Norfolk 208 A5
South Green Norfolk 208 A3
South Green Suffolk 187 D8
South Ham Hants 66 A2
South Hanningfield Essex 114 C1
South Harefield London 110 E3
South Harrow London 110 E4
South Harting W Sussex 46 C3
South Hatfield Herts 111 A6
South Hayling Hants 31 A6
South Hazelrigg Northum 376 A3
South Heath Bucks 109 B8
South Heighton E Sussex 50 F2
South Hetton Durham 344 B3
South Hiendley W Yorks 282 B1
South Hill Cornw'l 10 A2
South Hill Som'set 60 F1
South Hinksey Oxon 107 B7
South Hole Devon 32 C4
South Holme N Yorks 321 E5
South Holmwood Surrey 69 B5
South Hornchurch London 112 F5
South Huish Devon 12 D4
South Hykeham Lincs 250 B1
South Hylton Tyne/Wear 353 E6
South Kelsey Lincs 285 E7
South Kensington London 89 A7
South Kessock H'land 434 D1
South Killingholme N Lincs 286 A1
South Kilvington N Yorks 319 D7
South Kilworth Leics 179 B7
South Kirkby W Yorks 282 B3
South Kirkton Aberds 428 B4
South Kiscadale N Ayrs 405 D6
South Knighton Devon 14 A4
South Knighton Leics C 201 C6
South Kyme Lincs 251 E6
South Lambeth London 89 A8
South Lancing W Sussex 48 F3
South Lane S Yorks 281 C7
South Leigh Oxon 133 F6
South Leverton Notts 271 C7
South Littleton Worcs 154 C4
South Loftus Redcar/Clevel'd 334 C1
South Lopham Norfolk 187 B5
South Luffenham Rutl'd 202 C4
South Malling E Sussex 49 D8
South Marston Swindon 105 E8
South Merstham Surrey 69 A7
South Middleton Northum 376 C1
South Milford N Yorks 294 D3
South Millbrex Aberds 437 D5
South Milton Devon 12 D4
South Mimms Herts 111 B6
South Molton Devon 35 A7
South Moor Durham 343 A7
South Moor N Yorks 317 B8
South Moreton Oxon 107 E8
South Mundham W Sussex 47 F5
South Muskham Notts 249 C6
South Newbald ER Yorks 296 C5
South Newbarns Cumb 300 B3
South Newington Oxon 133 A7
South Newsham Northum 353 A5
South Newton Wilts 63 E6
South Normanton Derby 247 C6
South Norwood London 90 C1
South Nutfield Surrey 69 B8
South Ockendon Thurr'k 113 F6
South of Gyle C/Edinb 395 D8
South Ormsby Lincs 274 D4
South Ossett W Yorks 281 A7
South Otterington N Yorks 319 C6
South Owersby Lincs 285 F8
South Oxhey Herts 110 D4
South Park Surrey 69 B6
South Pelaw Durham 344 A1
South Perrot Dorset 39 E7
South Petherton Som'set 39 C6
South Petherwin Cornw'l 18 D3
South Pickenham Norfolk 207 C8
South Pill Cornw'l 10 D4
South Pool Devon 13 D6
South Poorton Dorset 24 A5
South Port Arg/Bute 417 E5
South Quilquox Aberds 437 E5
South Radworthy Devon 56 E1
South Rauceby Lincs 250 E3
South Raynham Norfolk 232 D2
South Reddish Gtr Man 266 A4
South Reston Lincs 275 C5
South Row Oxon 107 E6
South Ruislip London 110 E4
South Runcton Norfolk 206 B3
South Scarle Notts 249 B7
South Shian Arg/Bute 416 C4
South Shields Tyne/Wear 353 D5
South Shields Museum Tyne/Wear 353 C6
South Shore Blackp'l 288 D3
South Side Durham 330 A4
South Side Orkney 454 D3
South Somercotes Lincs 287 E7
South Stainley N Yorks 306 C3
South Stainmore Cumb 329 D6
South Stanley Durham 343 A7
South Stifford Thurr'k 91 A6
South Stoke Bath/NE Som'set 81 D6
South Stoke Oxon 108 F2
South Stoke W Sussex 47 E8
South Stour Kent 73 D7
South Street E Sussex 49 C7
South Street Kent 93 E8
South Street Kent 91 D7
South Street Kent 92 D3
South Street Kent 94 C2
South Street London 90 E3
South Tawton Devon 20 B3
South Tehidy Cornw'l 3 B9
South Thoresby Lincs 275 D5
South Tidworth Hants 64 B1
South Town Devon 22 D1
South Town Hants 66 D3
South Twerton Bath/NE Som'set 81 D6
South View Hants 66 A2
South Voxter Shetl'd 457 G3
South Walsham Norfolk 210 A3
South Warnborough Hants 66 B4
South Weald Essex 113 D6
South Weirs Hants 43 F8
South Weston Oxon 108 C4
South Wheatley Cornw'l 18 B1
South Wheatley Notts 271 B7
South Whiteness Shetl'd 455 B2
South Widcombe Bath/NE Som'set 80 E3
South Wigston Leics 201 D5
South Willesborough Kent 73 C7
South Willingham Lincs 273 C8
South Wimbledon London 89 B7
South Wingate Durham 344 D4
South Wingfield Derby 247 D5
South Witham Lincs 227 E5
South Wonford Devon 33 E7
South Wonston Hants 65 D6
South Woodford London 112 E3
South Woodham Ferrers Essex 114 C3
South Wootton Norfolk 230 D4
South Wraxall Wilts 81 D8
South Yardley W Midlands 176 B5
South Yarrows H'land 445 D7
South Zeal Devon 20 B3
Southall London 110 F4
Southam Glos 131 B5
Southam Warwick 178 F3
Southampton S'thampton 44 D3
Southampton International Airport Hants 44 C4
Southborough Kent 71 C6
Southborough London 89 C5
Southborough London 90 C3
Southbourne Bournem'th 28 B2
Southbourne W Sussex 46 E3
Southbrook Dorset 26 B3
Southbrook Wilts 61 E8
Southburgh Norfolk 208 C3
Southburn ER Yorks 310 E1
Southchurch Southend 115 E5
Southcote Reading 86 B3
Southcott Beds 136 C2
Southcott Devon 34 C1
Southcott Devon 54 F4
Southcott Wilts 83 E8
Southcourt Bucks 135 E7
Southcrest Worcs 176 E3
Southdean Scot Borders 374 F2
Southdene Mersey 276 E5
Southdown Bath/NE Som'set 81 D6
Southease E Sussex 49 E8
Southend Arg/Bute 404 F2
Southend Bucks 108 E5
Southend Glos 103 C6
South-end Herts 138 D4
Southend London 90 B2
Southend Oxon 107 B8
Southend Wilts 83 B8
Southend Airport Essex 114 E4
Southend Sea Life Centre Essex 114 F4
Southend-on-Sea Southend 114 E4
Southerhouse Shetl'd 455 C2
Southern Green Herts 138 A2
Southernby Cumb 339 D6
Southernden Kent 72 B4
Southerndown V/Glam 76 B4
Southerness Dumf/Gal 402 D3
Southerton Devon 22 B3
Southery Norfolk 206 E3
Southey Green Essex 140 A4
Southfield Northum 352 A4
Southfield Thurr'k 113 F8
Southfields London 89 B7
Southfleet Kent 91 B7
Southgate Ceredig'n 168 C4
Southgate London 111 D8
Southgate Norfolk 231 B5
Southgate Norfolk 255 E7
Southgate Norfolk 233 D7
Southgate Swan 97 E6
Southgate W Sussex 69 D7
South-haa Shetl'd 456 E3
South-heog Shetl'd 457 E3
Southill Beds 160 D3
Southington Hants 65 B7
Southleigh Devon 23 B6
Southmarsh Som'set 61 E6
Southmead Bristol 80 A3
Southminster Essex 115 C6
Southmoor Oxon 106 C4
Southoe Cambs 182 F3
Southolt Suffolk 188 E1
Southorpe Peterbro 203 C7
Southover Dorset 24 C4
Southover Dorset 25 B7
Southover E Sussex 71 F8
Southowram W Yorks 292 F4
Southport Mersey 276 A3
Southpunds Shetl'd 455 D3
Southrepps Norfolk 257 E8
Southrey Lincs 273 F7
Southrop Glos 105 A9
Southrope Hants 66 C3
Southsea Portsm'th 31 A5
Southsea Wrex 241 D7
Southtown Norfolk 211 B6
Southtown Orkney 453 D5
Southtown Som'set 38 C4
Southtown Som'set 60 D3
Southwaite Cumb 339 C8
Southwark London 89 A8
Southwater W Sussex 48 A3
Southwater Street W Sussex 69 F5
Southway Plym'th 11 C5
Southway Som'set 60 C2
Southwell Dorset 24 D2
Southwell Notts 248 D4
Southwell Minster Notts 248 D5
Southwell Racecourse Notts 249 D5
Southwick Hants 45 E7
Southwick Northants 203 E6
Southwick Som'set 59 B7
Southwick Tyne/Wear 353 E6
Southwick Wilts 82 E1
Southwick W Sussex 48 E4
Southwold Suffolk 189 C8
Southwood Hants 87 E6
Southwood Norfolk 210 B3
Southwood Som'set 60 E3
Soval Lodge W Isles 451 E6
Sowden Devon 22 D1
Sower Carr Lancs 288 B4
Sowerby N Yorks 319 D7
Sowerby W Yorks 292 F2
Sowerby Bridge W Yorks 292 F3
Sowerby Grange N Yorks 319 B7
Sowerby Row Cumb 339 C6
Sowley Green Suffolk 163 B7
Sowood W Yorks 280 A3
Sowood Green W Yorks 280 A3
Sowton Devon 22 B1
Soyal H'land 440 D2
Soyland Town W Yorks 279 A8
Spa Common Norfolk 234 B2
Spacey Houses N Yorks 306 E3
Spalding Lincs 228 D4
Spaldington ER Yorks 296 D2
Spaldwick Cambs 182 D2
Spalford Notts 272 F1
Spanby Lincs 228 A1
Spanish Green Hants 86 E3
Sparham Norfolk 233 E6
Sparhamhill Norfolk 233 E6
Spark Bridge Cumb 313 D7
Sparket Cumb 327 A5
Sparkford Som'set 40 A2
Sparkhill W Midlands 176 B4
Sparkwell Devon 11 D7
Sparl Shetl'd 457 G3
Sparnon Gate Cornw'l 4 B1
Sparrow Green Norfolk 232 F4
Sparrowpit Derby 267 C8
Sparrow's Green E Sussex 71 E7
Sparsholt Hants 65 E5
Sparsholt Oxon 106 E3
Spartylea Northum 341 B8
Spath Staffs 222 A3
Spaunton N Yorks 321 C5
Spaxton Som'set 58 D4
Spean Bridge H'land 424 D4
Spear Hill W Sussex 48 C2
Spearywell Hants 64 F3
Speedwell Bristol 80 B4
Speen Bucks 109 C6
Speen W Berks 85 C6
Speen Hill W Berks 85 C6
Speeton N Yorks 323 F7
Speke Mersey 264 C3
Speke Hall Mersey 264 C3
Speldhurst Kent 71 C6
Spellbrook Herts 139 D5
Spelsbury Oxon 133 C6
Spelter Bridg 98 D4
Spen W Yorks 293 E6
Spen Green Ches 244 B2
Spencer's Wood Wokingham 86 C4
Spennells Worcs 175 D6
Spennithorne N Yorks 317 C8
Spennymoor Durham 343 E8
Spernall Warwick 176 F4
Spetchley Worcs 153 B7
Spetisbury Dorset 41 F8
Spexhall Suffolk 189 B5
Spey Bay Moray 435 B8
Speybank H'land 426 B3
Speybridge H'land 435 F5
Speyview Moray 435 D7
Spillardsford Aberds 437 C7
Spilsby Lincs 252 A4
Spinkhill Derby 269 D9
Spinney Hill Northants 180 F3
Spinney Hills Leics C 201 C6
Spinningdale H'land 440 E3
Spion Kop Notts 270 F3
Spirit of the West, St Columb Major Cornw'l 8 B1
Spirthill Wilts 82 A4
Spital Mersey 264 C1
Spital Windsor 87 A9
Spital in the Street Lincs 272 A4
Spital Tongues Tyne/Wear 352 C3
Spitfire and Hurricane Memorial, Manston Kent 95 C6
Spithurst E Sussex 49 C8
Spittal Dumf/Gal 401 D5
Spittal E Loth 397 C6
Spittal ER Yorks 308 E4
Spittal H'land 445 C5
Spittal Northum 388 B2
Spittal Pembs 119 E7
Spittal of Glenmuick Aberds 427 D8
Spittal of Glenshee Perth/Kinr 427 E6
Spittalfield Perth/Kinr 420 C1
Spittlegate Lincs 227 A5
Spixworth Norfolk 234 E1
Splatt Cornw'l 18 C1
Splatt Cornw'l 16 E3
Splatt Som'set 58 D4
Splayne's Green E Sussex 49 B8
Splottlands Card 78 A3
Spodegreen Ches 266 B1
Spofforth N Yorks 306 E4
Spon End W Midlands 178 C1
Spon Green Flints 241 B6
Spondon Derby C 224 A3
Spooner Row Norfolk 209 D5
Sporle Norfolk 207 A7
Spotland Bridge Gtr Man 279 B6
Spott E Loth 398 C3
Spratton Northants 180 D2
Spreakley Surrey 67 C6
Spreyton Devon 20 A4
Spriddlestone Devon 11 E6
Spridlington Lincs 272 C5
Spring Bank Gtr Man 277 C8
Spring Bank W Midlands 197 D8
Spring Gardens Durham 331 A5
Spring Gardens Shrops 219 F7
Spring Grove London 89 A5
Spring Head Kent 91 B7
Spring Hill Gtr Man 279 C7
Spring Hill Lancs 290 E3
Spring Hill Staffs 198 B2
Spring Hill W Midlands 197 D6
Spring Park London 90 C2
Spring Vale I/Wight 30 B4
Spring Vale S Yorks 281 D7
Spring Valley I/Man 336 D3
Springbank Glos 130 C4
Springboig Glasg C 393 F5
Springburn Glasg C 392 E4
Springfield Arg/Bute 408 E3
Springfield Caerph 100 C3
Springfield Dumf/Gal 347 C8
Springfield Essex 140 F3
Springfield Fife 411 A8
Springfield Gtr Man 277 C8
Springfield H'land 434 B1
Springfield M/Keynes 158 E5
Springfield Moray 435 C5
Springfield W Midlands 197 F8
Springfield W Midlands 176 B4
Springhill E Renf 380 A2
Springhill N Lanarks 382 A2
Springhill Shrops 172 B3
Springhill Staffs 197 C8
Springhill Staffs 198 B2
Springholm Dumf/Gal 402 C2
Springkell Dumf/Gal 347 A7
Springside N Ayrs 379 E7
Springthorpe Lincs 272 B2
Springwell Tyne/Wear 353 E6
Springwell Tyne/Wear 352 E4
Sproatley ER Yorks 298 D2
Sproston Green Ches 266 F1
Sprotbrough S Yorks 282 D4
Sproughton Suffolk 165 D7
Sprouston Scot Borders 386 E5
Sprowston Norfolk 209 A9
Sproxton Leics 226 D4
Sproxton N Yorks 320 D3
Sprunston Cumb 339 B6
Sprytown Devon 19 C5
Spurlands End Bucks 109 C7
Spurstow Ches 242 C4
Spynie Moray 435 B7
Squires Gate Blackp'l 288 D3
Sraid Ruadh Arg/Bute 414 C2
Srannda W Isles 448 D4
Sronphadruig Lodge Perth/Kinr 426 E2
SS Great Britain Bristol 80 B3
Stable Green Devon 35 D5
Stableford Shrops 196 D4
Stacey Bank S Yorks 269 A5
Stackhouse N Yorks 303 B8
Stackpole Pembs 117 E5
Stackpole Elidor Pembs 117 E5
Stacksford Norfolk 208 E5
Stacksteads Lancs 291 F6
Stackyard Green Suffolk 164 C4
Staddiscombe Devon 11 E6
Staddlethorpe ER Yorks 296 E3
Staden Derby 267 E8
Stadhampton Oxon 108 C2
Stadhlaigearraidh W Isles 447 E2
Staffield Cumb 340 C1
Staffin H'land 430 B4
Stafford Staffs 221 D8
Stafford Park Telford 196 B3
Staffordlake Surrey 87 E8
Stafford's Green Dorset 40 B2
Stagden Cross Essex 139 E8
Stag's Head Devon 55 F8
Stag's Holt Cambs 205 C7
Stagsden Beds 159 C7
Stagsden West End Beds 159 C7
Stain H'land 445 B7
Stainburn Cumb 337 F6
Stainburn N Yorks 306 F1
Stainby Lincs 227 D5
Staincliffe W Yorks 293 F6
Staincross S Yorks 281 B8
Staindrop Durham 330 B4
Staines Surrey 88 B3
Staines Green Herts 138 E2
Stainfield Lincs 227 C8
Stainfield Lincs 273 E7
Stainforth N Yorks 303 B8
Stainforth S Yorks 283 B6
Staining Lancs 288 C4
Stainland W Yorks 280 A3
Stainsacre N Yorks 335 E5
Stainsby Derby 247 A6
Stainton Cumb 314 C4
Stainton Cumb 339 F8
Stainton Cumb 348 E1
Stainton Durham 330 C3
Stainton Middlesbro 332 D4
Stainton N Yorks 317 A8
Stainton S Yorks 283 F5
Stainton by Langworth Lincs 273 D6
Stainton le Vale Lincs 286 F2
Stainton with Adgarley Cumb 300 A3
Staintondale N Yorks 322 A3
Stair Cumb 326 B1
Stair E Ayrs 367 C8
Stairfoot S Yorks 282 D1
Stairhaven Dumf/Gal 400 D4
Staithe Norfolk 211 E5
Staithes N Yorks 334 C2
Stake Hill Gtr Man 279 C6
Stake Pool Lancs 301 F7
Stakeford Northum 365 E7
Stakes Portsm'th 45 E8
Stalbridge Dorset 40 C4
Stalbridge Weston Dorset 40 C4
Stalham Norfolk 234 C4
Stalham Green Norfolk 234 D4
Stalisfield Green Kent 73 A5
Stalland Common Norfolk 208 D4
Stallen Dorset 40 C2
Stalling Busk N Yorks 316 C4
Stallingborough NE Lincs 286 B3
Stalmine Lancs 288 A4
Stalmine Moss Side Lancs 288 A4
Stalybridge Gtr Man 279 E8
Stambermill W Midlands 175 B8
Stambourne Essex 163 E7
Stambourne Green Essex 163 E7
Stamford Lincs 203 B6

Stamford Northum 377 D6
Stamford Bridge Ches 264 F4
Stamford Bridge ER Yorks 308 D3
Stamford Hill London 112 E1
Stamfordham Northum 351 B8
Stamperland E Renf 380 A3
Stamshaw Portsm'th 45 F8
Stanah Lancs 288 B4
Stanborough Herts 137 E8
Stanbridge Beds 136 C3
Stanbridge Dorset 42 F3
Stanbrook Essex 139 B8
Stanbrook Worcs 153 C6
Stanbury W Yorks 292 C2
Stand Gtr Man 278 C4
Stand N Lanarks 393 E7
Standburn Falk 394 D3
Standeford Staffs 197 B7
Standen Kent 72 C4
Standen, East Grinstead W Sussex 70 D2
Standen Manor W Berks 84 C3
Standen Street Kent 72 E3
Standerwick Som'set 61 A8
Standford Hants 67 E6
Standingstone Cumb 338 B4
Standish Glos 130 F2
Standish Gtr Man 277 B8
Standish Lower Ground Gtr Man 277 C8
Standish Moreton Glos 130 F1
Standlake Oxon 106 B4
Standon Hants 65 F5
Standon Herts 138 C3
Standon Staffs 221 B6
Standon Green End Herts 138 D3
Stane N Lanarks 382 A2
Stanecastle N Ayrs 379 D6
Stanfield Norfolk 232 D3
Stanfield Stoke 244 D3
Stanford Beds 160 D3
Stanford Kent 74 D2
Stanford Bishop Heref'd 152 B3
Stanford Bridge Worcs 174 E4
Stanford Dingley W Berks 85 B8
Stanford End Wokingham 86 D4
Stanford in the Vale Oxon 106 D3
Stanford on Avon Northants 179 C6
Stanford on Soar Notts 225 D5
Stanford Rivers Essex 113 B5
Stanford-le-Hope Thurr'k 113 F8
Stanfree Derby 270 E1
Stanghow Redcar/Clevel'd 333 C8
Stanground Peterbro 204 D3
Stanhill Lancs 290 E3
Stanhoe Norfolk 255 E6
Stanhope Scot Borders 371 B7
Stanhope Durham 342 D3
Stanion Northants 202 F4
Stanley Derby 247 F6
Stanley Durham 343 A7
Stanley Lancs 277 C6
Stanley Notts 247 B7
Stanley Perth/Kinr 420 D1
Stanley Shrops 175 B5
Stanley Staffs 244 D4
Stanley Wilts 82 B4
Stanley W Yorks 293 F8
Stanley Common Derby 247 F6
Stanley Crook Durham 343 D7
Stanley Downton Glos 103 B8
Stanley Gate Lancs 277 D5
Stanley Green Gtr Man 266 C4
Stanley Green Poole 27 B7
Stanley Green Shrops 219 A7
Stanley Hill Heref'd 152 D3
Stanley Pontlarge Glos 131 A5
Stanleytown Rh Cyn Taff 99 D7
Stanlow Ches 264 D3
Stanmer Brighton/Hove 49 E6
Stanmore Hants 65 F6
Stanmore London 111 D5
Stanmore W Berks 85 A6
Stanner Powys 150 A3
Stannergate Dundee C 420 D4
Stannersburn Northum 362 E3
Stanningfield Suffolk 164 A2
Stanningley W Yorks 293 D6
Stannington Northum 352 A3
Stannington S Yorks 269 B5
Stanpit Dorset 28 B3
Stansbatch Heref'd 172 F4
Stansfield Suffolk 163 B8
Stanshope Staffs 245 D8
Stanstead Suffolk 164 C1
Stanstead Abbotts Herts 138 E3
Stanstead Street Suffolk 164 C1
Stansted Kent 91 D7
Stansted Airport Essex 139 C6
Stansted Mountfichet Essex 139 C6
Stanton Derby 223 E7
Stanton Glos 154 F4
Stanton Monmouths 127 C7
Stanton Northum 364 D4
Stanton Suffolk 186 D4
Stanton Staffs 245 E8
Stanton by Bridge Derby 224 C2
Stanton Chare Suffolk 186 D4
Stanton Drew Bath/NE Som'set 80 D3
Stanton Fitzwarren Swindon 105 D8
Stanton Gate Notts 224 A4
Stanton Harcourt Oxon 107 A5
Stanton Hill Notts 247 B7
Stanton in Peak Derby 246 B2
Stanton Lacy Shrops 173 C7
Stanton Lees Derby 246 B3
Stanton Long Shrops 195 E7
Stanton on the Wolds Notts 225 B7
Stanton Prior Bath/NE Som'set 81 D5
Stanton St. Bernard Wilts 83 D6
Stanton St. John Oxon 134 F2
Stanton St. Quintin Wilts 82 A3
Stanton Street Suffolk 186 E4
Stanton under Bardon Leics 200 A3
Stanton upon Hine Heath Shrops 219 D8
Stanton Wick Bath/NE Som'set 80 D4
Stantonbury M/Keynes 158 D4
Stanton-by-Dale Derby 224 A4
Stantway Glos 129 E8
Stanwardine in the Fields Shrops 219 D5
Stanwardine in the Wood Shrops 219 C5
Stanway Essex 141 C7
Stanway Glos 131 A7
Stanway Green Essex 141 C8
Stanway Green Suffolk 188 D2
Stanwell Surrey 88 B3
Stanwell Moor Surrey 88 B2
Stanwick Northants 181 D7
Stanwick-St.-John N Yorks 331 D5
Stanwix Cumb 348 E1
Stanycliffe Gtr Man 279 C6
Stanydale Shetl'd 457 H2
Staoinebrig W Isles 447 E2
Stape N Yorks 321 B6
Stapehill Dorset 42 F4
Stapeley Ches 243 E6
Stapeley Water Gardens, Nantwich Ches 243 D6
Stapenhill Staffs 223 D7
Stapford on Teme Worcs 174 E4
Staple Kent 94 E5
Staple Som'set 58 C2
Staple Cross Devon 37 B5
Staple Fitzpaine Som'set 38 C3
Staple Hill S Glos 81 A5
Staple Hill Worcs 176 D2
Staplecross E Sussex 51 B8
Staplefield W Sussex 69 F7
Stapleford Cambs 162 A2
Stapleford Herts 138 D2
Stapleford Leics 226 E3
Stapleford Lincs 249 C8
Stapleford Notts 224 A4
Stapleford Wilts 63 D6
Stapleford Abbots Essex 112 D5
Stapleford Tawney Essex 112 C5
Staplegrove Som'set 38 A2
Staplehay Som'set 38 B2
Staplehurst Kent 72 C2
Staplers I/Wight 30 C2
Staples Hill W Sussex 68 F2
Staplestreet Kent 93 D8
Stapleton Bristol 80 A4
Stapleton Cumb 348 B4
Stapleton Heref'd 172 E4
Stapleton Leics 200 D2
Stapleton N Yorks 331 D6
Stapleton N Yorks 282 A4
Stapleton Shrops 195 C5
Stapleton Som'set 39 B7
Stapley Som'set 37 D7
Staploe Beds 182 F2
Staplow Heref'd 152 D3
Stapness Shetl'd 457 J2
Star Fife 411 B8
Star Angl 259 E7
Star Pembs 144 E4
Star Som'set 79 E8
Stara Orkney 452 A3
Starbeck N Yorks 306 D3
Starbotton N Yorks 317 F5
Starcross Devon 22 D1
Stareton Warwick 178 D1
Stargate Tyne/Wear 352 D2
Starkholmes Derby 246 C4
Starling Gtr Man 278 B4
Starling's Green Essex 139 A5
Starr's Green E Sussex 51 D8
Starston Norfolk 188 B2
Start Devon 13 C7
Startforth Durham 330 C2
Startley Wilts 104 F4
Startop's End Bucks 136 E2
Start's Green Staffs 175 B6
Starve Acre Hants 87 E6
Statenborough Kent 95 E6
Statham Warrington 265 B8
Stathe Som'set 59 F7
Stathern Leics 226 B2
Station Hill Cumb 338 B4
Station Town Durham 344 D4
Staughton Green Cambs 182 E2
Staughton Highway Cambs 182 F2
Staughton Moor Cambs 182 F2
Staunton Glos 128 E4
Staunton Glos 130 B1
Staunton Green Heref'd 172 F5
Staunton in the Vale Notts 249 F7
Staunton on Arrow Heref'd 172 F5
Staunton on Wye Heref'd 150 C5
Staupes N Yorks 305 D8
Staveley Cumb 314 A3
Staveley Derby 269 E8
Staveley N Yorks 306 C4
Staveley-in-Cartmel Cumb 313 C8
Staverton Devon 14 C3
Staverton Glos 130 C3
Staverton Northants 179 F5
Staverton Wilts 82 D2
Staverton Bridge Glos 130 C3
Stawell Som'set 59 D7
Stawley Som'set 37 B6
Staxigoe H'land 445 C7
Staxton N Yorks 322 E4
Staylittle Powys 191 E8
Staynall Lancs 288 B4
Staythorpe Notts 249 D6
Stead W Yorks 292 A4
Stean N Yorks 317 F7
Steanbow Som'set 60 D3
Steane Northants 157 E6
Stearsby N Yorks 307 A9
Steart Som'set 58 C5
Stebbing Essex 140 C2
Stebbing Green Essex 140 C2
Stebbing Park Essex 140 C2
Stechford W Midlands 198 F3
Stede Quarter Kent 72 D4
Stedham W Sussex 46 B5
Steel Northum 351 E5
Steel Bank S Yorks 269 B6
Steel Cross E Sussex 71 E5
Steel Green Cumb 312 E4
Steel Heath Shrops 219 A7
Steel Lane Head W Yorks 280 A3
Steele Road Scot Borders 361 D7
Steen's Bridge Heref'd 151 A8
Steep Hants 46 A2
Steep Lane W Yorks 292 F2
Steep Marsh Hants 46 A3
Steephill I/Wight 30 E3
Steeple Dorset 27 D5
Steeple Essex 115 B5
Steeple Ashton Wilts 82 E3
Steeple Aston Oxon 133 B8
Steeple Barton Oxon 133 B7
Steeple Bumpstead Essex 163 D6
Steeple Claydon Bucks 135 B5
Steeple Gidding Cambs 182 B2
Steeple Longford Wilts 63 D5
Steeple Morden Cambs 161 D5
Steeplechase Suffolk 163 C7
Steeton W Yorks 292 B2
Stein H'land 430 C2
Steinmanhill Aberds 436 D4
Stella Tyne/Wear 352 D2
Stelling Minnis Kent 74 B2
Stelvio Newp 101 E6
Stembridge Som'set 39 B6
Stemster H'land 445 B5
Stemster Ho. H'land 445 B5
Stenalees Cornw'l 8 D3
Stenaquoy Orkney 454 C3
Stenhill Devon 37 D6
Stenhouse C/Edinb 395 D9
Stenhousemuir Falk 410 D3
Stenigot Lincs 274 C2
Stennack Cornw'l 3 C6
Stenness Shetl'd 457 F2
Stenscholl H'land 430 B4
Stenso Orkney 452 A4
Stenson Staffs 223 C8
Stenton E Loth 398 C2
Stenton Fife 411 C7
Stenwith Lincs 226 A3
Stepaside Cornw'l 8 E1
Stepaside Pembs 121 F6
Stepaside Powys 193 F5
Stepney London 112 F2
Stepping Hill Gtr Man 267 B5
Steppingley Beds 159 E8
Stepps N Lanarks 393 E5
Sterndale Moor Derby 268 F2
Sternfield Suffolk 189 F5
Sterridge Devon 55 B6
Stert Wilts 83 E5
Sterte Poole 27 B7
Stetchworth Cambs 163 A5
Stetchworth Ley Cambs 163 A5
Stevenage Herts 137 C8
Stevenston N Ayrs 378 D5
Steventon Hants 65 B7
Steventon Oxon 107 D6
Steventon End Essex 162 D4
Stevington Beds 159 B7
Stewards Essex 139 F5
Stewartby Beds 159 D8
Stewarton Arg/Bute 404 E2
Stewarton E Ayrs 379 C8
Stewkley Bucks 135 B8
Stewley Som'set 38 C4
Stewton Lincs 274 B4
Steyne Cross I/Wight 30 C4
Steyning W Sussex 48 D3
Steynton Pembs 116 C4
Stibb Cornw'l 32 D4
Stibb Cross Devon 33 D8
Stibb Green Wilts 84 D1
Stibbard Norfolk 232 C4
Stibbington Cambs 203 D7
Stichill Scot Borders 386 E4
Stick Hill Kent 70 C4
Sticker Cornw'l 8 E2
Stickford Lincs 252 C3
Sticklepath Devon 20 B2
Sticklepath Devon 55 E6
Sticklepath Som'set 57 D7
Sticklinch Som'set 60 D3
Stickling Green Essex 139 A5
Stickney Lincs 252 C2
Stiff Street Kent 92 D4
Stiffkey Norfolk 256 D2
Stifford's Bridge Heref'd 152 C4
Stileway Som'set 60 C1
Stillingfleet N Yorks 295 B5
Stillington N Yorks 307 B8
Stillington Stockton 332 B2
Stilton Cambs 204 F2
Stinchcombe Glos 103 C6
Stinsford Dorset 26 B1
Stiperstones Shrops 194 C3
Stirchley Telford 196 B3
Stirchley W Midlands 176 B4
Stirkoke Ho. H'land 445 C7
Stirling Aberds 437 D8
Stirling Stirl 410 C3
Stirling Castle Stirl 410 C2
Stirtloe Cambs 182 E3
Stirton N Yorks 304 E3
Stisted Essex 140 C5
Stitchcombe Wilts 84 C1
Stithians Cornw'l 4 C2
Stittenham H'land 440 F3
Stivichall W Midlands 178 C1
Stixwould Lincs 251 A6
Stoak Ches 264 E3
Stobhill Northum 365 E6
Stobhill Gate Northum 365 E6
Stobieside S Lanarks 380 E4
Stobo Scot Borders 383 E8
Stoborough Dorset 27 C5
Stoborough Green Dorset 27 C5
Stobs Castle Scot Borders 373 F7
Stobshiel E Loth 397 F6
Stobswood Northum 365 D6
Stock Essex 113 C8
Stock Lancs 304 F1
Stock N Som'set 79 D9
Stock Green Worcs 154 A2
Stock Wood Worcs 154 A3
Stockbridge Hants 64 D4
Stockbridge W Sussex 46 F5
Stockbridge W Yorks 292 B3
Stockbridge Village Mersey 276 F5
Stockbury Kent 92 D3
Stockcross W Berks 85 C5
Stockdalewath Cumb 339 C6
Stocken Hall Rutl'd 227 E6
Stocker's Head Kent 73 A6
Stockerston Leics 202 D2
Stockham Oxon 106 E4
Stockheath Hants 46 E2
Stockholes Turbary N Lincs 284 C2
Stockiemuir Stirl 409 D7
Stocking Heref'd 129 A6
Stocking Farm Leics C 201 B5
Stocking Green Essex 162 E4
Stocking Green M/Keynes 158 C4
Stocking Pelham Herts 138 B4
Stockingford Warwick 199 E7
Stockland Card 78 A2
Stockland Devon 38 F2
Stockland Bristol Som'set 58 C4
Stockland Green Kent 71 C6
Stockleigh English Devon 36 E1
Stockleigh Pomeroy Devon 36 F2
Stockley Wilts 82 C5
Stocklinch Som'set 39 C5
Stocklinch Ottersey Som'set 39 C5
Stockport Gtr Man 267 A5
Stocks Green Kent 71 B6
Stocksbridge S Yorks 281 E7
Stocksfield Northum 351 D7
Stocksmoor W Yorks 281 B5
Stockton Heref'd 173 F8
Stockton Norfolk 210 E3
Stockton Shrops 196 D3
Stockton Shrops 194 C1
Stockton Warwick 178 F3
Stockton Wilts 62 D4
Stockton Heath Warrington 265 B7
Stockton on Tees Stockton 332 C3
Stockton on Teme Worcs 174 E4
Stockton on the Forest C/York 308 D2
Stockwell London 89 A8
Stockwell End W Midlands 197 C6
Stockwell Heath Staffs 222 D3
Stockwitch Cross Som'set 39 B8
Stockwood Bristol 80 C4
Stockwood Dorset 40 E1
Stockwood Craft Museum Luton 137 D5
Stockwood Vale Bath/NE Som'set 80 C4
Stodday Lancs 301 D8
Stodmarsh Kent 94 D4
Stody Norfolk 256 E4
Stoer H'land 442 F2
Stoford Som'set 40 D1
Stoford Wilts 63 D6
Stogumber Som'set 58 D1
Stogursey Som'set 58 C4
Stoke Devon 14 A1
Stoke Devon 32 B4
Stoke Hants 46 F2
Stoke Hants 65 A5
Stoke Medway 92 A3
Stoke Plym'th 10 D5
Stoke Suffolk 165 D8
Stoke W Midlands 178 C2
Stoke Abbott Dorset 39 F7
Stoke Albany Northants 202 F2
Stoke Aldermoor W Midlands 178 C2
Stoke Ash Suffolk 187 D7
Stoke Bardolph Notts 248 F4
Stoke Bishop Bristol 80 A3
Stoke Bliss Worcs 174 F3
Stoke Bruerne Northants 158 B2
Stoke by Clare Suffolk 163 D7
Stoke Cannon Devon 21 A8
Stoke Charity Hants 65 D6
Stoke Climsland Cornw'l 18 F4
Stoke Common Hants 44 B4
Stoke Cross Heref'd 152 B2
Stoke D'Abernon Surrey 88 E4
Stoke Doyle Northants 181 A8
Stoke Dry Rutl'd 202 D3
Stoke Edith Heref'd 152 D2
Stoke Farthing Wilts 42 A4
Stoke Ferry Norfolk 207 C5
Stoke Fleming Devon 15 F5
Stoke Gabriel Devon 14 D4
Stoke Gifford S Glos 102 F4
Stoke Golding Leics 200 D2
Stoke Goldington M/Keynes 158 C4
Stoke Green Bucks 110 F1
Stoke Hammond Bucks 135 B8
Stoke Heath Shrops 220 C3
Stoke Heath W Midlands 178 B2
Stoke Heath Worcs 176 E1
Stoke Hill Devon 21 B8
Stoke Holy Cross Norfolk 209 C8
Stoke Lacy Heref'd 152 C2
Stoke Lyne Oxon 134 B2
Stoke Mandeville Bucks 135 E7
Stoke Newington London 112 E1
Stoke on Tern Shrops 220 C2
Stoke Orchard Glos 130 B4
Stoke Park Suffolk 165 D7
Stoke Poges Bucks 110 F1
Stoke Pound Worcs 176 E2
Stoke Prior Heref'd 151 A8
Stoke Prior Worcs 176 E2
Stoke Rivers Devon 55 E7
Stoke Rochford Lincs 227 C5
Stoke Row Oxon 108 F3
Stoke St. Gregory Som'set 59 F6
Stoke St. Mary Som'set 38 B3
Stoke St. Michael Som'set 61 B5
Stoke St. Milborough Shrops 174 B1
Stoke sub Hamdon Som'set 39 C7
Stoke Talmage Oxon 108 C3
Stoke Trister Som'set 61 F6
Stoke Villice Bath/NE Som'set 80 D3
Stoke Wake Dorset 41 E5
Stoke-by-Nayland Suffolk 164 E4
Stokeford Dorset 26 C4
Stokeham Notts 271 D7
Stokeinteignhead Devon 15 A6
Stokenchurch Bucks 108 C5
Stokenham Devon 13 D7
Stoke-on-Trent Stoke 244 E3
Stokesay Shrops 173 B6
Stokesby Norfolk 210 A4
Stokesley N Yorks 332 E5
Stolford Som'set 58 B4
Ston Easton Som'set 80 F4
Stondon Massey Essex 113 B6
Stone Bucks 135 E6
Stone Glos 103 C5
Stone Kent 91 B6
Stone Som'set 60 E3
Stone Staffs 221 B8
Stone Worcs 175 D7
Stone Allerton Som'set 59 A8
Stone Bridge Corner Peterbro 204 C4
Stone Chair W Yorks 292 E4
Stone Common Suffolk 166 A5
Stone Cross E Sussex 50 F5
Stone Cross E Sussex 70 F5
Stone Cross E Sussex 71 E7
Stone Cross Kent 95 E6
Stone Cross Kent 73 D7
Stone Cross Kent 70 D5
Stone Cross W Midlands 198 E1
Stone End Glos 130 D1
Stone Fold Lancs 290 E4
Stone Head N Yorks 291 B7
Stone Hill Kent 74 D1
Stone Hill S Glos 80 B4
Stone Hill S Yorks 283 C7
Stone Hill S Yorks 270 C1
Stone House Cumb 316 C1
Stone in Oxney Kent 73 F5
Stone Street Kent 91 F6
Stone Street Suffolk 189 B5
Stone Street Suffolk 164 E4
Stonea Cambs 205 E8
Stonebridge Essex 115 E5
Stonebridge London 111 F6
Stonebridge M/Keynes 158 D4
Stonebridge N Som'set 79 E7
Stonebridge Surrey 69 B5
Stonebridge Warwick 177 B7
Stonebridge Green Kent 73 B5
Stonebroom Derby 247 C6
Stoneclough Gtr Man 278 C4
Stonecross Green Suffolk 164 A1
Stone-edge-Batch N Som'set 80 B1
Stoneferry Kingston/Hull 297 D9
Stonefield Arg/Bute 416 D4
Stonefield S Lanarks 381 A5
Stonefield Staffs 221 B7
Stonefield Castle Hotel Arg/Bute 408 E1
Stonegate E Sussex 71 F8
Stonegate N Yorks 334 E2
Stonegrave N Yorks 320 E4
Stonegravels Derby 269 E7
Stonehall Worcs 153 C7
Stonehaugh Northum 350 A2
Stonehaven Aberds 429 D5
Stonehenge, Amesbury Wilts 63 C7
Stonehill Surrey 88 D2
Stonehill Green Kent 90 B5
Stonehouse Aberds 437 E5
Stonehouse Glos 103 A8
Stonehouse Northum 349 E7
Stonehouse Plym'th 10 E5
Stonehouse S Lanarks 381 C7
Stoneleigh Surrey 89 D6
Stoneleigh Warwick 178 D1
Stoneless Kent 95 D6
Stonely Cambs 182 E2
Stonequarry W Sussex 70 D2
Stoner Hill Hants 46 A2
Stones Green Essex 142 B4
Stonesby Leics 226 D3
Stonesfield Oxon 133 D6
Stonestreet Green Kent 73 D8
Stonethwaite Cumb 326 D2
Stonewells Moray 435 B7
Stonewood Kent 91 B6
Stoney Cross Hants 43 D8
Stoney Middleton Derby 268 D4
Stoney Pound Shrops 172 B2
Stoney Royd W Yorks 292 F4
Stoney Stanton Leics 200 E3
Stoney Stoke Som'set 61 E6
Stoney Stratton Som'set 61 D5
Stoney Stretton Shrops 194 B3
Stoneyard Green Heref'd 152 D4
Stoneybank E Loth 396 D3
Stoneybreck Shetl'd 455 E4
Stoneyburn W Loth 394 F4
Stoneycroft Mersey 264 A2
Stoneydelph Staffs 199 C5
Stoneyfield Gtr Man 279 B6
Stoneyfield Moray 435 C6
Stoneyford Derby 247 E6
Stoneyford Devon 22 C3
Stoneygate Aberds 437 E7
Stoneygate Leics C 201 C6
Stoneyholme Lancs 291 D5
Stoneykirk Dumf/Gal 400 D2
Stoneywood Aberd C 429 A5
Stoneywood Falk 410 D2
Stonganess Shetl'd 456 C5
Stonham Aspal Suffolk 165 A7
Stonor Oxon 108 E4
Stonton Wyville Leics 201 D8
Stony Cross Devon 34 A3
Stony Cross Heref'd 152 C4
Stony Dale Notts 249 F5
Stony Gate Tyne/Wear 344 A3
Stony Green Bucks 109 C7
Stony Houghton Derby 247 A7
Stony Knaps Dorset 38 F5
Stony Lea Staffs 197 A8
Stony Stratford M/Keynes 158 D3
Stonyfield H'land 440 F3
Stonyford Hants 44 C1
Stoodham Som'set 39 C6
Stoodleigh Devon 36 C3
Stopes S Yorks 269 B5
Stopham W Sussex 47 C8
Stopper Lane Lancs 291 A5
Stopsley Luton 137 C5
Stoptide Cornw'l 16 E3
Stores Corner Suffolk 166 C5
Storeton Mersey 263 C8
Storiths N Yorks 305 E5
Stormontfield Perth/Kinr 420 E1
Stormore Wilts 62 B1
Stormsdown Devon 14 A3
Stornoway W Isles 451 D7
Stornoway Airport W Isles 451 D7
Storridge Heref'd 153 C5
Storrington W Sussex 48 D1
Storrs Cumb 314 B1
Storrs S Yorks 269 B5
Stortford Park Herts 139 C5
Storth Cumb 314 E3
Storwood ER Yorks 295 B8
Stotfield Moray 435 A7
Stotfold Beds 160 E4
Stottesdon Shrops 174 B3
Stoughton Leics 201 C6
Stoughton Surrey 68 A1
Stoughton W Sussex 46 D4
Stoughton Cross Som'set 59 B8
Stoul H'land 423 C7
Stoulton Worcs 153 C8
Stour Provost Dorset 41 B5
Stour Row Dorset 41 B6
Stourbridge W Midlands 175 B7
Stourhead Garden Wilts 61 E7
Stourpaine Dorset 41 E7
Stourport on Severn Worcs 175 D6
Stourton Staffs 175 B7
Stourton Warwick 155 E8
Stourton Wilts 61 E7
Stourton W Yorks 293 D8
Stourton Caundle Dorset 40 C4
Stout Som'set 59 E8
Stove Orkney 454 C4
Stove Shetl'd 455 D3
Stoven Suffolk 189 B6
Stover S Glos 103 F5
Stow Scot Borders 385 D6
Stow Lincs 228 B1
Stow Lincs 272 C2
Stow Bardolph Norfolk 206 B3
Stow Bedon Norfolk 208 D3
Stow Cum Quy Cambs 184 F3
Stow Lawn W Midlands 197 D7
Stow Longa Cambs 182 D2
Stow Maries Essex 114 C3
Stow Park Lincs 272 C2
Stow Pasture Lincs 272 C2
Stowbridge Norfolk 206 B2
Stowe Glos 102 A3
Stowe Heref'd 150 C3
Stowe Shrops 172 D4
Stowe Staffs 198 A3
Stowe Green Glos 128 F5
Stowe House and Gardens, Buckingham Bucks 157 E8
Stowe-by-Chartley Staffs 222 C2
Stowehill Northants 157 A7
Stowell Som'set 40 B3
Stowey Bath/NE Som'set 80 E4
Stowfield Glos 129 D5
Stowford Devon 19 C5
Stowford Devon 22 C4
Stowford Devon 55 F7
Stowford Devon 55 C8
Stowlangtoft Suffolk 186 E4
Stowmarket Suffolk 165 A5
Stow-on-the-Wold Glos 132 B2
Stowting Kent 74 C2
Stowting Common Kent 74 C2
Stowting Hill Kent 74 C2
Stowupland Suffolk 165 A6
Straad Arg/Bute 408 F3
Strachan Aberds 428 C3
Strachurmore Arg/Bute 408 B4
Stradbroke Suffolk 188 D2
Stradbrook Wilts 62 A3
Stradishall Suffolk 163 B7
Stradey Castle Carms 96 B4
Stradsett Norfolk 206 B4
Stragglethorpe Lincs 249 D9
Stragglethorpe Notts 225 A8
Straid S Ayrs 354 D1
Straight Soley Wilts 84 B3
Straith Dumf/Gal 357 E8
Straiton C/Edinb 396 E2
Straiton S Ayrs 355 B6
Straloch Aberds 437 F5
Straloch Perth/Kinr 419 A8
Stramshall Staffs 222 A3
Strand Glos 129 E8
Strands Cumb 312 D4
Strang I/Man 336 D3
Strangeways Gtr Man 279 E5
Strangford Heref'd 129 B5
Strangways Wilts 63 C7
Stranog Aberds 429 C5
Stranraer Dumf/Gal 400 C2
Strata Florida Ceredig'n 169 E7
Stratfield Mortimer W Berks 86 D3
Stratfield Saye Hants 86 D3
Stratfield Turgis Hants 86 E3
Stratford Beds 160 C3
Stratford London 112 F2
Stratford Worcs 153 E7
Stratford Castle Wilts 63 E7
Stratford Racecourse Warwick 155 B6
Stratford St. Andrew Suffolk 188 F5
Stratford St. Mary Suffolk 165 F5
Stratford Tony Wilts 42 A4
Stratford-upon-Avon Warwick 155 A7
Strath H'land 438 F1
Strath H'land 445 C6
Strathallan Castle Perth/Kinr 419 F7
Strathan H'land 424 C1
Strathan H'land 439 A4
Strathan H'land 443 B7
Strathan Skerray H'land 443 B8
Strathaven S Lanarks 381 D6
Strathavon Lo. Moray 435 F6
Strathblane Stirl 392 C3
Strathbungo Glasg C 392 F3
Strathcanaird H'land 439 C5
Strathcarron H'land 432 D1
Strathcoil Arg/Bute 416 D1
Strathcoul H'land 445 C5
Strathdon Aberds 427 A8
Strathellie Aberds 437 B7
Strathgarve Lodge H'land 433 B6
Strathkinness Fife 420 F4
Strathmashie House H'land 425 C7
Strathmiglo Fife 411 A7
Strathmore Lodge H'land 445 D5
Strathpeffer H'land 433 C6
Strathrannoch H'land 439 F7
Strathtay Perth/Kinr 419 B7
Strathvaich Lodge H'land 439 F7
Strathwhillan N Ayrs 405 C6

Thunder Bridge W Yorks 281 B5
Thundergay N Ayrs 404 B4
Thundersley Essex 114 E2
Thundridge Herts 138 D3
Thurcaston Leics 200 A5
Thurcroft S Yorks 270 C1
Thurdon Cornw'l 33 D5
Thurgarton Notts 248 F4
Thurgaton Norfolk 233 B8
Thurgoland S Yorks 281 D7
Thurlaston Leics 200 D4
Thurlaston Warwick 178 D4
Thurlbear Som'set 38 B3
Thurlby Lincs 275 D6
Thurlby Lincs 228 E1
Thurlby Lincs 249 B9
Thurleigh Beds 159 A9
Thurlestone Devon 12 D4
Thurloxton Som'set 58 E5
Thurlstone S Yorks 281 D6
Thurlton Norfolk 210 D4
Thurlwood Ches 244 C3
Thurmaston Leics 201 B6
Thurnby Leics 201 C6
Thurne Norfolk 235 E5
Thurnham Kent 92 E3
Thurning Norfolk 233 C6
Thurning Northants 182 A1
Thurnscoe S Yorks 282 C3
Thurnscoe East S Yorks 282 C3
Thursby Cumb 339 A5
Thursden Lancs 291 C7
Thursford Norfolk 232 B4
Thursford Collection, Fakenham Norfolk 232 B4
Thursford Green Norfolk 232 B4
Thursley Hants 67 D8
Thurso H'land 445 B5
Thurso East H'land 445 B5
Thurstaston Mersey 263 C6
Thurston Pembs 117 C5
Thurston Suffolk 186 E3
Thurston Clough Gtr Man 279 C8
Thurston End Suffolk 163 B8
Thurston Planche Suffolk 186 F3
Thurstonfield Cumb 347 E8
Thurstonland W Yorks 280 B5
Thurton Norfolk 210 C2
Thurvaston Derby 223 A6
Thuxton Norfolk 208 B4
Thwaite Durham 330 D2
Thwaite N Yorks 316 A3
Thwaite Suffolk 187 E7
Thwaite Head Cumb 313 B7
Thwaite St. Mary Norfolk 210 D2
Thwaites W Yorks 292 B3
Thwaites Brow W Yorks 292 B3
Thwing ER Yorks 310 A3
Tibbermore Perth/Kinr 419 E8
Tibberton Glos 129 C9
Tibberton Telford 220 D3
Tibberton Worcs 153 A8
Tibenham Norfolk 209 F6
Tibshelf Derby 247 B6
Tibthorpe ER Yorks 309 D8
Ticehurst E Sussex 71 E8
Tichborne Hants 65 E8
Tickencote Rutl'd 203 B5
Tickenham N Som'set 79 B9
Tickenhurst Kent 95 F5
Tickford End M/Keynes 159 D5
Tickhill S Yorks 283 E5
Ticklerton Shrops 195 E5
Tickmorend Glos 104 C1
Ticknall Derby 224 D2
Tickton ER Yorks 297 B8
Tidbury Green W Midlands 176 C5
Tidcombe Wilts 84 E2
Tiddington Oxon 108 B3
Tiddington Warwick 155 A7
Tiddleywink Wilts 82 A2
Tidebrook E Sussex 71 F7
Tideford Cornw'l 10 D2
Tideford Cross Cornw'l 10 C2
Tidenham Glos 102 C3
Tideswell Derby 268 D3
Tidmarsh W Berks 86 B2
Tidmington Warwick 155 E8
Tidnor Heref'd 152 E1
Tidpit Hants 42 C4
Tidworth Wilts 64 B1
Tiers Cross Pembs 116 B4
Tiffield Northants 158 B1
Tifty Aberds 437 D4
Tigerton Angus 421 A5
Tigh-na-Blair Perth/Kinr 419 F5
Tighnabruaich Arg/Bute 408 E2
Tighnacachla Arg/Bute 406 F2
Tighnafiline H'land 438 E2
Tighness Arg/Bute 409 B5
Tigley Devon 14 C3
Tilbrook Cambs 182 E1
Tilbrook M/Keynes 159 F6
Tilbrook Grange Cambs 182 D1
Tilbury Thurr'k 91 A7
Tilbury Green Essex 163 D7
Tile Cross W Midlands 198 F4
Tile Hill W Midlands 177 C8
Tilegate Green Essex 139 F6
Tilehouse Green W Midlands 177 C6
Tilehurst Reading 86 B3
Tilekiln Essex 140 A3
Tilekiln Green Essex 139 C6
Tilford Surrey 67 C7
Tilgate W Sussex 69 E7
Tilgate Forest Row W Sussex 69 E7
Tilkey Essex 141 C5
Tilland Cornw'l 10 C2
Tillathrowie Aberds 436 E1
Tillicoultry Clack 410 C4
Tillers Green Glos 129 A7
Tilley Shrops 219 C7
Tilley Green Shrops 219 C7
Tillingham Essex 115 B6
Tillington Heref'd 151 C7
Tillington Staffs 221 D8
Tillington W Sussex 47 B7
Tillington Common Heref'd 151 C7
Tilly Lo. Aberds 428 B2
Tillyarblet Angus 428 F2
Tillybirloch Aberds 428 B3
Tillycorthie Aberds 437 F6
Tillydrine Aberds 428 C3
Tillyfour Aberds 428 A2
Tillyfourie Aberds 428 A3
Tillygarmond Aberds 428 C3
Tillygreig Aberds 437 F5
Tillykerrie Aberds 437 F5
Tillynaught Aberds 436 B2
Tilmanstone Kent 75 A6
Tiln Notts 271 C6
Tilney All Saints Norfolk 230 E3
Tilney Cum Islington Norfolk 230 F3
Tilney Fen End Norfolk 206 A1
Tilney High End Norfolk 230 E3
Tilney St. Lawrence Norfolk 230 F2
Tilsdown Glos 103 C7
Tilshead Wilts 63 B5
Tilsmore E Sussex 50 B4
Tilstock Shrops 219 A7
Tilston Ches 242 D2
Tilstone Bank Ches 242 C4
Tilstone Fearnall Ches 242 B4
Tilsworth Beds 136 C3
Tilton on the Hill Leics 201 B8
Tiltups End Glos 104 C1
Tilty Essex 139 B7
Timbercombe Som'set 58 E4
Timberden Bottom Kent 90 D5
Timberland Lincs 251 C5
Timbersbrook Ches 244 B3
Timberscombe Som'set 57 C6
Timble N Yorks 305 E7
Timperley Gtr Man 266 B2
Timsbury Bath/NE Som'set 81 E5
Timsbury Hants 44 B1
Timsgearraidh W Isles 450 D3
Timworth Suffolk 186 E2
Timworth Green Suffolk 186 E2
Tincleton Dorset 26 B2
Tindale Cumb 349 E6
Tindale Crescent Durham 343 F7
Tingewick Bucks 134 A4
Tingley W Yorks 293 E7
Tingon Shetl'd 457 E2
Tingrith Beds 136 A4
Tingwall Orkney 452 A4
Tinhay Devon 18 C4
Tinkers End Bucks 135 B6
Tinkers Hill Hants 64 B4
Tinshill W Yorks 293 C7
Tinsley S Yorks 269 A8
Tinsley Green W Sussex 69 D7
Tintagel Cornw'l 17 C6
Tintagel Castle Cornw'l 17 C6
Tintern Abbey Monmouths 102 B2
Tintern Parva Monmouths 102 B2
Tintinhull Som'set 39 C7
Tintwistle Derby 280 E2
Tinwald Dumf/Gal 358 F4
Tinwell Rutl'd 203 B6
Tipperty Aberds 436 B3
Tipperty Aberds 437 F6
Tip's Cross Essex 113 B6
Tips End Norfolk 205 E9
Tiptoe Hants 28 A5
Tipton W Midlands 197 E7
Tipton Cross Devon 22 B3
Tipton Green W Midlands 197 E8
Tipton St. John Devon 22 B3
Tiptree Essex 141 D6
Tiptree Heath Essex 141 E6
Tirabad Powys 148 D2
Tiraghoil Arg/Bute 415 E6
Tircanol Swan 97 C8
Tirdeunaw Swan 97 C7
Tiree Airport Arg/Bute 414 C2
Tirinie Perth/Kinr 426 F3
Tirley Glos 130 B2
Tiroran Arg/Bute 415 E7
Tirphil Caerph 100 B2
Tirril Cumb 339 F9
Tirryside H'land 440 B2
Tir-y-dail Carms 123 E8
Tir-y-fron Flints 241 C6
Tisbury Wilts 62 F3
Tisman's Common W Sussex 68 E3
Tissington Derby 246 D1
Titchberry Devon 32 A4
Titchfield Hants 45 E5
Titchfield Common Hants 45 E5
Titchmarsh Northants 181 C8
Titchwell Norfolk 255 D5
Titcomb W Berks 84 C4
Tithby Notts 225 A8
Tithe Barn Hillock Mersey 277 E8
Tithebarn Staffs 245 F7
Tithill Som'set 58 F3
Titley Heref'd 150 A4
Titmore Green Herts 137 B8
Titsey Surrey 90 F3
Titson Cornw'l 32 F4
Tittenhurst Windsor 87 C8
Tittensor Staffs 221 A7
Tittleshall Norfolk 232 D2
Titton Worcs 175 E6
Tiverton Ches 242 B4
Tiverton Devon 36 D4
Tivetshall Norfolk 187 A8
Tivetshall St. Margaret Norfolk 209 F7
Tividale W Midlands 197 E8
Tivington Som'set 57 B5
Tivoli Cumb 324 C4
Tixall Staffs 222 D1
Tixover Rutl'd 203 C5
Toab Orkney 453 C6
Toab Shetl'd 455 E2
Toad Row Suffolk 189 A8
Toadmoor Derby 247 D5
Tobermory Arg/Bute 415 B8
Toberonochy Arg/Bute 407 B7
Tobha Beag W Isles 447 A4
Tobha Mor W Isles 447 E2
Tobhtarol W Isles 450 D4
Tobson W Isles 450 D4
Toby's Hill Lincs 287 F8
Tocher Aberds 436 E3
Tockenham Wilts 82 A5
Tockenham Wick Wilts 105 F5
Tockholes Blackb'n 290 F2
Tockington S Glos 102 E4
Tockwith N Yorks 307 E6
Todber Dorset 41 B5
Todding Heref'd 173 C6
Toddington Beds 136 B4
Toddington Glos 131 A6
Toddington W Sussex 47 F8
Toddlehills Aberds 437 D7
Todd's Green Herts 137 B8
Todenham Glos 155 E7
Todhill Angus 420 D4
Todhills Cumb 347 D9
Todhills Durham 343 E8
Todlachie Aberds 428 A3
Todmorden W Yorks 291 F7
Todrig Scot Borders 373 D5
Todwick S Yorks 270 C1
Toft Cambs 161 A7
Toft Lincs 227 E8
Toft Shetl'd 457 F4
Toft Warwick 178 D4
Toft Hill Durham 343 F7
Toft Hill Lincs 251 B7
Toft Monks Norfolk 210 E4
Toft next Newton Lincs 273 B5
Toftrees Norfolk 232 C2
Tofts H'land 445 B7
Tofts Northum 350 C3
Toftwood Norfolk 208 A3
Tog Hill S Glos 81 B6
Togston Northum 365 B6
Tokavaig H'land 423 A6
Tokers Green Oxon 86 A4
Tolastadh a Chaolais W Isles 450 D4
Tolastadh bho Thuath W Isles 451 C8
Tolborough Cornw'l 17 E8
Toldish Cornw'l 8 D1
Tolgus Mount Cornw'l 4 B1
Tolhurst E Sussex 71 E8
Toll Bar Mersey 277 F6
Toll Bar S Yorks 283 C5
Toll End W Midlands 197 E8
Toll of Birness Aberds 437 E7
Tolladine Worcs 153 A7
Tolland Som'set 58 E2
Tollard Farnham Dorset 42 C2
Tollard Royal Wilts 42 C1
Tollbar End W Midlands 178 C2
Toller Fratrum Dorset 25 A6
Toller Porcorum Dorset 25 A6
Toller Whelme Dorset 39 F8
Tollerford Dorset 25 A6
Tollerton Notts 225 B7
Tollerton N Yorks 307 C7
Tollesbury Essex 141 E8
Tollesby Middlesbro 332 C5
Tolleshunt D'Arcy Essex 141 E7
Tolleshunt Knights Essex 141 D7
Tolleshunt Major Essex 141 E7
Tollie H'land 433 C7
Tollingham ER Yorks 296 C3
Tolm W Isles 451 D7
Tolpuddle Dorset 26 B2
Tolvah H'land 426 C3
Tolworth London 89 C5
Tom an Fhuadain W Isles 449 A7
Tomaknock Perth/Kinr 419 E6
Tomatin H'land 434 F3
Tombreck H'land 434 E1
Tombui Perth/Kinr 419 B6
Tomchrasky H'land 424 A4
Tomdoun H'land 424 B3
Tomich H'land 434 A1
Tomich H'land 433 F5
Tomich House H'land 433 D7
Tomintoul Aberds 427 C6
Tomintoul Moray 427 A6
Tomlow Warwick 178 F4
Tomnaven Moray 436 E1
Tomnavoulin Moray 435 F7
Tomsleibhe Arg/Bute 416 D1
Ton Monmouths 101 C7
Tonbridge Kent 71 B6
Tonderghie Dumf/Gal 401 F6
Tondu Bridg 98 F4
Tone Som'set 37 B7
Tone Green Som'set 37 B8
Tonedale Som'set 37 B7
Tonfanau Gwyn 190 C2
Tong Kent 72 B3
Tong Shrops 196 B4
Tong W Yorks 293 D6
Tong End Lancs 279 A6
Tong Green Kent 93 F6
Tong Norton Shrops 196 B4
Tong Park W Yorks 292 C5
Tong Street W Yorks 293 D5
Tongdean Brighton/Hove 49 E5
Tonge Leics 224 D3
Tonge Fold Gtr Man 278 C3
Tonge Moor Gtr Man 278 B3
Tongham Surrey 67 B7
Tongland Dumf/Gal 401 D8
Tongue H'land 443 C7
Tongue End Lincs 228 E3
Tongwell M/Keynes 158 D5
Tongwynlais Card 100 F2
Tonmawr Rh Cyn Taff 98 C3
Tonna = Tonnau Rh Cyn Taff 98 C2
Tonnau = Tonna Rh Cyn Taff 98 C2
Ton-Pentre Rh Cyn Taff 99 C6
Ton-teg Rh Cyn Taff 100 E1
Tontine Lancs 277 D7
Ton-ty'r-bel Caerph 100 C4
Tonwell Herts 138 D2
Tonypandy Rh Cyn Taff 99 D6
Ton-y-pistyll Caerph 100 C3
Tonyrefail Rh Cyn Taff 99 E7
Toot Baldon Oxon 107 B8
Toot Hill Essex 112 B5
Toothill Hants 44 C2
Toothill Swindon 105 F7
Toothill W Yorks 292 F4
Tooting Graveney London 89 B7
Top End Beds 181 F8
Top Green Notts 249 E6
Top Lock Gtr Man 277 C9
Top of Hebers Gtr Man 279 C6
Top o'th'Lane Lancs 289 F8
Top Valley Nott'ham 248 F2
Topcliffe N Yorks 319 E7
Topcliffe W Yorks 293 E7
Topcroft Norfolk 210 E1
Topcroft Street Norfolk 210 E1
Topham S Yorks 283 A6
Toppesfield Essex 163 E7
Toppings Gtr Man 278 B3
Toprow Norfolk 209 D7
Topsham Devon 22 C1
Top-y-rhos Flints 241 C6
Torbay Torbay 15 C6
Torbeg N Ayrs 404 D4
Torboll Farm H'land 440 D4
Torbothie N Lanarks 382 A2
Torbreck H'land 440 C4
Torbrex Stirl 410 C2
Torbryan Devon 14 B4
Torbush N Lanarks 381 A8
Torcross Devon 13 D7
Torcroy H'land 426 C2
Tore H'land 433 C8
Torfrey Cornw'l 9 E5
Torgyle H'land 425 A5
Torinturk Arg/Bute 407 F8
Torkington Gtr Man 267 B5
Torksey Lincs 272 D1
Torlum W Isles 447 C2
Torlundy H'land 424 E3
Tormarton S Glos 81 A7
Tormisdale Arg/Bute 403 A1
Tormitchell S Ayrs 354 D3
Tormore H'land 423 B6
Tormore N Ayrs 404 C4
Tornagrain H'land 434 D2
Tornahaish Aberds 427 B7
Tornapress H'land 431 D8
Tornaveen Aberds 428 B3
Torness H'land 433 F7
Toronto Durham 343 E7
Torpenhow Cumb 338 D3
Torphichen W Loth 394 D4
Torphin Midloth 395 E9
Torphins Aberds 428 B3
Torpoint Cornw'l 10 D4
Torquay Torbay 15 C6
Torquhan Scot Borders 385 C5
Torr Devon 11 E7
Torr Devon 11 C8
Torra Arg/Bute 403 A3
Torran Arg/Bute 408 B1
Torran H'land 431 D5
Torran H'land 440 F4
Torrance E Dunb 392 D4
Torrans Arg/Bute 415 E7
Torranyard N Ayrs 379 D7
Torre Som'set 57 C7
Torre Torbay 15 B6
Torridon H'land 432 C1
Torridon Ho. H'land 431 C8
Torries Aberds 428 A3
Torrin H'land 431 F5
Torrisdale H'land 443 B8
Torrisdale Castle Arg/Bute 404 C3
Torrisdale-Square Arg/Bute 404 C3
Torrish H'land 441 B6
Torrisholme Lancs 301 C8
Torroble H'land 440 C2
Torroy H'land 440 D2
Torry Aberds 436 E1
Torry Aberd C 429 B6
Torryburn Fife 411 D5
Torterston Aberds 437 D7
Torthorwald Dumf/Gal 346 A2
Tortington W Sussex 47 E7
Torton Worcs 175 D6
Tortworth S Glos 103 D6
Torvaig H'land 430 D4
Torver Cumb 313 B6
Torwood Falk 410 D3
Torworth Notts 271 C5
Tosberry Devon 33 B5
Toscaig H'land 431 E7
Toseland Cambs 182 F4
Tosside N Yorks 303 D7
Tostock Suffolk 186 F4
Totaig H'land 431 F8
Totaig H'land 430 C2
Totardor H'land 430 E3
Tote H'land 430 D4
Totegan H'land 444 B2
Totford Hants 65 D8
Totgarrick Cornw'l 8 E1
Totham Hill Essex 141 E6
Totham Plains Essex 141 E6
Tothill Lincs 275 C5
Totland I/Wight 29 C6
Totley Bents S Yorks 269 C6
Totley Brook S Yorks 269 C6
Totley Rise S Yorks 269 C6
Totnell Dorset 40 E2
Totnes Devon 14 C4
Toton Notts 224 B5
Totronald Arg/Bute 414 B4
Totscore H'land 430 B3
Tottenham London 111 D8
Tottenhill Norfolk 206 A3
Tottenhill Row Norfolk 206 A3
Totteridge Bucks 109 D7
Totteridge Park London 111 D6
Totternhoe Beds 136 C3
Totties W Yorks 280 C5
Tottington Gtr Man 278 B4
Tottlebank Cumb 313 D7
Totton Hants 44 D2
Touchen-end Windsor 87 A7
Touches Som'set 38 E4
Toulton Som'set 58 E3
Toulvaddie H'land 441 E5
Tournaig H'land 438 E2
Toux Aberds 437 C6
Tovil Kent 92 F1
Tow House Northum 350 D2
Tow Law Durham 343 D6
Towan Cornw'l 16 F2
Towan Cross Cornw'l 6 F5
Toward Arg/Bute 390 E2
Towcester Northants 158 C1
Towcester Racecourse Northants 158 C2
Towednack Cornw'l 3 C5
Tower End Norfolk 231 E5
Tower Hamlets Kent 75 C6
Tower Hill Ches 267 D5
Tower Hill Essex 143 A6
Tower Hill Herts 110 B2
Tower Hill Mersey 276 D5
Tower Hill W Midlands 198 E2
Tower Hill W Sussex 69 F5
Tower Knowe Visitor Centre, Kielder Water Northum 362 E2
Tower of London London 111 F8
Towerhead N Som'set 79 E8
Towersey Oxon 108 A4
Towie Aberds 428 A1
Towie Aberds 436 F2
Towie Aberds 437 B5
Towiemore Moray 435 D8
Town Bent Lancs 290 E3
Town End Bucks 109 C5
Town End Cambs 205 D7
Town End Cumb 313 C8
Town End Cumb 313 A8
Town End Cumb 326 E3
Town End Cumb 314 D2
Town End Cumb 327 F5
Town End Cumb 315 D6
Town End Cumb 327 A7
Town End Cumb 328 A2
Town End Derby 268 D3
Town End Lincs 250 F2
Town End Mersey 264 B4
Town End W Yorks 280 A3
Town End Farm Tyne/Wear 353 E5
Town Fields Ches 243 A5
Town Green Gtr Man 277 E8
Town Green Lancs 276 C5
Town Green Norfolk 233 B9
Town Green Norfolk 210 A3
Town-head Arg/Bute 408 F3
Town Head Cumb 328 D3
Town Head Cumb 326 E3
Town Head Cumb 327 F5
Town Head Cumb 327 A8
Town Head Cumb 328 D2
Town Head Cumb 328 A2
Town Head Derby 268 D3
Town Head N Yorks 303 B7
Town Head N Yorks 303 D8
Town Hill N Yorks 304 C4
Town Kelloe Durham 344 D3
Town Lane Gtr Man 278 D2
Town Littleworth E Sussex 49 C8
Town of Lowton Gtr Man 277 E9
Town Park Telford 196 B3
Town Row E Sussex 71 E6
Town Street Glos 130 B2
Town Yetholm Scot Borders 375 B6
Townend Derby 267 C8
Townend W Dunb 391 C7
Townend W Dunb 391 C8
Townfield Durham 342 B3
Towngate Cumb 340 B1
Towngate Lincs 203 A8
Townhead Arg/Bute 408 F3
Townhead Cumb 337 D4
Townhead Cumb 340 D1
Townhead Cumb 340 E3
Townhead Dumf/Gal 401 E8
Townhead Lancs 303 E6
Townhead N Lanarks 393 E6
Townhead S Ayrs 354 B3
Townhead S Yorks 280 D5
Townhead S Yorks 269 C6
Townhead of Greenlaw Dumf/Gal 402 C1
Townhill Fife 411 D6
Townhill Swan 97 D7
Townhill Park Hants 44 D4
Townlake Devon 19 E5
Townland Green Kent 73 E5
Town's End Bucks 135 F5
Town's End Bucks 134 C3
Town's End Dorset 26 A4
Town's End Dorset 27 D6
Town's End Dorset 40 E1
Towns End Hants 85 E8
Town's End Som'set 58 C2
Town's End Som'set 61 B5
Towns End Som'set 40 C4
Townsend Bath/NE Som'set 80 E3
Townsend Herts 137 F6
Townsend Oxon 106 E4
Townsend S Glos 102 F3
Townsend Stoke 244 E4
Townsend Som'set 60 A2
Townsend Som'set 38 D5
Townsend Som'set 59 E7
Townsend Wilts 82 E4
Townsend Fold Lancs 291 F5
Townshend Cornw'l 3 D7
Townwell S Glos 103 D5
Towthorpe C/York 308 D1
Towthorpe ER Yorks 309 C7
Towton N Yorks 294 C3
Towyn Conwy 262 D1
Toxteth Mersey 264 B2
Toynton All Saints Lincs 252 B3
Toynton Fen Side Lincs 252 B3
Toynton Ings Lincs 252 B4
Toynton St. Peter Lincs 252 B4
Toy's Hill Kent 70 A4
Trabboch E Ayrs 367 C8
Traboe Cornw'l 4 F2
Tracebridge Som'set 37 B6
Tradespark H'land 434 C3
Tradespark Orkney 453 C5
Trafford Park Gtr Man 278 E4
Trago Mills, Newton Abbot Devon 21 F6
Traigh Ho H'land 423 C6
Trallong Powys 125 B8
Trallwn Swan 97 C8
Tram Inn Heref'd 151 F7
Tranch Torf 100 B5
Tranent E Loth 397 D5
Tranmere Mersey 263 B8
Trantlebeg H'land 444 C2
Trantlemore H'land 444 C2
Tranwell Northum 365 F5
Trapp Carms 124 D2
Traprain E Loth 398 C1
Trap's Green Warwick 176 E5
Trapshill W Berks 84 D4
Traquair Scot Borders 384 F3
Trash Green W Berks 86 C3
Travellers Rest Carms 122 D3
Travelmond Cornw'l 9 C7
Trawden Lancs 291 C7
Trawscoed Powys 149 F6
Trawsfynydd Gwyn 215 A6
Trawsmawr Carms 122 C3
Trawsnant Ceredig'n 168 E4
Tre Taliesin = Taliesin Ceredig'n 190 E4
Treaddow Heref'd 128 C4
Trealaw Rh Cyn Taff 99 D7
Treales Lancs 289 D5
Treamble Cornw'l 7 D6
Trearddur Angl 258 D2
Treaslane H'land 430 C3
Treator Cornw'l 16 E3
Tre-Aubrey V/Glam 77 B7
Trebah Garden, Mawnan Smith Cornw'l 4 E3
Trebahwartha Cornw'l 4 E3
Trebanog Rh Cyn Taff 125 F7
Trebanog Rh Cyn Taff 99 D7
Trebanos Neath P Talb 97 B9
Trebarber Cornw'l 7 C8
Trebartha Cornw'l 18 E2
Trebarvah Cornw'l 3 E6
Trebarvah Cornw'l 4 D2
Trebarwith Cornw'l 17 C6
Trebeath Cornw'l 18 C2
Tre-Beferad V/Glam 77 C6
Trebehor Cornw'l 2 F3
Trebetherick Cornw'l 16 E3
Treble's Holford Som'set 58 E2
Tre-boeth Swan 97 C8
Treborough Som'set 57 D7
Trebudannon Cornw'l 7 C8
Trebullett Cornw'l 18 E3
Treburley Cornw'l 18 E3
Treburrick Cornw'l 7 A8
Trebyan Cornw'l 8 C4
Trecastle Powys 125 B6
Trecenydd Caerph 100 E2
Trecrogo Cornw'l 18 D3
Trecwn Pembs 119 C7
Trecynon Rh Cyn Taff 99 B6
Tredarrup Cornw'l 17 B8
Tredaule Cornw'l 18 D1
Tredavoe Cornw'l 2 E5
Tredegar Bl Gwent 126 F3
Tredegar Newydd = New Tredegar Caerph 100 B2
Trederwen Powys 218 E2
Tredington Glos 130 B4
Tredington Warwick 155 D8
Tredinnick Cornw'l 2 D4
Tredinnick Cornw'l 9 B6
Tredinnick Cornw'l 9 D7
Tredogan V/Glam 77 C8
Tredomen Powys 126 A3
Tredrizzick Cornw'l 16 E4
Tredunnock Monmouths 101 D7
Tredustan Powys 126 A3
Tredworth Glos 130 D2
Treen Cornw'l 2 F3
Treen Cornw'l 2 C4
Treesmill Cornw'l 8 D4
Tre-Essey Heref'd 128 C4
Treeton S Yorks 269 B8
Trefaes Gwyn 212 B5
Trefaldwyn = Montgomery Powys 193 D8
Trefasser Pembs 119 B5
Trefdraeth Angl 259 E5
Trefdraeth = Newport Pembs 119 B9
Trefeca Powys 126 A3
Trefechan Ceredig'n 168 B4
Trefechan Merth Tyd 126 F1
Trefeglwys Powys 192 E3
Trefeitha Powys 126 A3
Trefelyn Pembs 118 C5
Trefenter Ceredig'n 168 E5
Treffanney Powys 217 E9
Treffany Hill Cornw'l 9 D7
Treffgarne Pembs 119 E7
Treffynnon Pembs 118 D4
Treffynnon = Holywell Flints 263 D5
Trefgarn Owen Pembs 118 D5
Trefil Bl Gwent 126 E3
Trefilan Ceredig'n 146 A3
Trefin = Trevine Pembs 118 C4
Treflach Shrops 218 C2
Trefnant Denbs 262 E2
Trefonen Shrops 218 C2
Trefor Gwyn 236 E3
Trefor Angl 258 C4
Trefor Angl 259 D7
Treforest Rh Cyn Taff 99 E8
Tre-Forgan Neath P Talb 98 A2
Treforys = Morriston Swan 97 C8
Trefriw Conwy 238 B3
Tref-y-Clawdd = Knighton Powys 172 D3
Tref-y-nant Wrex 241 F6
Tregada Cornw'l 18 D3
Tregadillet Cornw'l 18 D2
Tre-gagle Monmouths 128 F4
Tregaian Angl 259 D6
Tregajorran Cornw'l 4 B1
Tregare Monmouths 128 E2
Tregarland Cornw'l 9 D8
Tregarne Cornw'l 4 F3
Tregaron Ceredig'n 169 F6
Tregarth Gwyn 260 F2
Tregaswith Cornw'l 7 C8
Tregatta Cornw'l 17 C6
Tregavarras Cornw'l 5 B7
Tregear Cornw'l 7 E8
Tregeare Cornw'l 18 C1
Tregeiriog Wrex 217 B8
Tregele Angl 258 A4
Tregellist Cornw'l 16 E5
Tregenna Cornw'l 17 F6
Tregeseal Cornw'l 2 D3
Tre-Gibbon Rh Cyn Taff 99 A6
Tregonce Cornw'l 16 F3
Tregonetha Cornw'l 8 C2
Tregonhawke Cornw'l 10 E4
Tregonna Cornw'l 8 A1
Tregony Cornw'l 5 B6
Tregoodwell Cornw'l 17 D7
Tregorrick Cornw'l 8 E3
Tregoss Cornw'l 8 C2
Tregowris Cornw'l 4 F3
Tregoyd Powys 150 E1
Tregoyd Mill Powys 150 E1
Tregrehan Mills Cornw'l 8 E3
Tregroes Ceredig'n 145 D8
Tregullon Cornw'l 8 C4
Tregunna Cornw'l 16 F4
Tregunnon Cornw'l 18 D1
Tregurrian Cornw'l 7 B8
Tre-Gwyr = Gowerton Swan 97 C6
Tregynon Powys 193 D5
Tre-gynwr Carms 122 D4
Trehafod Rh Cyn Taff 99 D7
Trehan Cornw'l 10 D4
Treharris Merth Tyd 100 C1
Trehemborne Cornw'l 7 A8
Treherbert Rh Cyn Taff 99 C5
Treheveras Cornw'l 7 F7
Trehill V/Glam 77 B8
Trehilyn Pembs 119 B6
Trehunist Cornw'l 10 C2
Tre-Ifon Rh Cyn Taff 99 A6
Trekeivesteps Cornw'l 9 B7
Trekelland Cornw'l 18 E2
Trekelland Cornw'l 18 D3
Trekenner Cornw'l 18 E3
Treknow Cornw'l 17 C6
Trelan Cornw'l 5 G2
Tre-lan Flints 240 A4
Trelash Cornw'l 17 B8
Trelassick Cornw'l 7 E8
Trelawnyd Flints 262 D3
Trelech Carms 122 A1
Trelech-a'r-Bettws Carms 122 B2
Treleddyd fawr Pembs 118 D3

Treleigh Cornw'l 4 B2
Treletert = Letterston Pembs 120 B2
Trelewis Merthyr Tyd 100 C2
Treligga Cornw'l 17 D6
Trelights Cornw'l 16 E4
Trelill Cornw'l 17 E5
Trelinnoe Cornw'l 18 D3
Trelion Cornw'l 8 E1
Trelissick Cornw'l 4 C4
Trelissick Garden, Feock Cornw'l 4 C4
Trellech Monmouths 102 A2
Trelleck Cross Monmouths 102 B2
Trelleck Grange Monmouths 102 B1
Trelogan Flints 262 C4
Trelonk Cornw'l 5 B5
Trelowia Cornw'l 10 D1
Trelowth Cornw'l 8 E2
Trelowthas Cornw'l 7 F8
Treluggan Cornw'l 5 C5
Trelydan Powys 193 A8
Tremadog Gwyn 237 F7
Tremail Cornw'l 17 C8
Tremain Ceredig'n 144 C4
Tremaine Cornw'l 18 C1
Tremar Cornw'l 9 B8
Trematon Cornw'l 10 D3
Trembraze Cornw'l 9 B8
Tremeirchion Denbs 262 E3
Tremollett Cornw'l 18 E2
Tremore Cornw'l 8 C3
Tremorfa Card 78 A4
Tre-Mostyn Flints 262 D4
Trenale Cornw'l 17 C6
Trenance Cornw'l 8 A1
Trenance Cornw'l 7 C7
Trenant Cornw'l 9 B7
Trenarren Cornw'l 8 F3
Trenarrett Cornw'l 18 D1
Trenault Cornw'l 18 D2
Trench Telford 196 A2
Trench Green Oxon 86 A3
Trench Wood Kent 71 B6
Trencreek Cornw'l 7 C7
Trendeal Cornw'l 7 E8
Trendrean Cornw'l 7 D7
Treneague Cornw'l 8 A2
Trenear Cornw'l 4 D1
Treneglos Cornw'l 17 C9
Trenewan Cornw'l 9 E6
Trengune Cornw'l 17 B8
Trenhorne Cornw'l 18 E2
Treninnick Cornw'l 7 C7
Trenode Cornw'l 9 D8
Trenoweth Cornw'l 4 D3
Trent Dorset 40 C1
Trent Vale Stoke 244 F3
Trentham Staffs 244 F3
Trentham Gardens, Newcastle-under-Lyme Staffs 244 F3
Trentishoe Devon 55 B7
Trentlock Derby 224 B4
Trenwheal Cornw'l 3 D8
Treoes V/Glam 77 A5
Treopert = Granston Pembs 119 C5
Treorchy = Treorci Rh Cyn Taff 99 C6
Treorci = Treorchy Rh Cyn Taff 99 C6
Treowen Caerph 100 C4
Treowen Powys 193 E6
Trequite Cornw'l 17 E5
Trerank Moor Cornw'l 8 D2
Tre'r-ddol Ceredig'n 190 E4
Trerhyngyll V/Glam 77 A7
Trerose Cornw'l 4 E3
Trerulefoot Cornw'l 10 D2
Tresaith Ceredig'n 145 B5
Tresawle Cornw'l 5 A5
Tresawsen Cornw'l 7 F6
Trescott Staffs 197 D5
Trescowe Cornw'l 3 D7
Tresean Cornw'l 7 D6
Tresevern Croft Cornw'l 4 C2
Tresham S Glos 103 D7
Tresillian Cornw'l 5 A5
Treskillard Cornw'l 4 C1
Treskinnick Cross Cornw'l 17 A9
Tresmeer Cornw'l 18 C1
Tresowes Green Cornw'l 3 E7
Tresoweshill Cornw'l 3 E7
Tresparrett Cornw'l 17 B7
Tresparrett Posts Cornw'l 17 B7
Trespeane Cornw'l 18 D1
Tressady H'land 440 C4
Tressait Perth/Kinr 419 A6
Tressinney Cornw'l 17 D7
Tresta Shetl'd 456 D6
Tresta Shetl'd 457 H3
Treswell Notts 271 D7
Treswithian Cornw'l 3 B8
Treswithian Downs Cornw'l 3 B8
Trethevy Cornw'l 17 C6
Trethewey Cornw'l 2 F3
Trethomas Caerph 100 E3
Trethosa Cornw'l 8 E1
Trethowel Cornw'l 8 E3
Trethurgy Cornw'l 8 D3
Tretio Pembs 118 D3
Tretire Heref'd 128 C4
Tretower Powys 126 C4
Treuddyn Flints 241 C6
Trevadlock Cornw'l 18 E2
Trevalga Cornw'l 17 B6
Trevalyn Wrex 241 C8
Trevance Cornw'l 8 A1
Trevanger Cornw'l 16 E4
Trevanson Cornw'l 8 A2
Trevarrack Cornw'l 3 D5
Trevarren Cornw'l 8 C1
Trevarrian Cornw'l 7 B8
Trevarrick Cornw'l 5 B7
Trevarth Cornw'l 4 B2
Trevaughan Carms 121 D7
Trevaughan Carms 122 C4
Treveal Cornw'l 7 D6
Treveddw Monmouths 127 C7
Treveighan Cornw'l 17 E6
Trevellas Cornw'l 7 E5
Trevemper Cornw'l 7 D7
Treverbyn Cornw'l 8 D3
Treverbyn Cornw'l 9 B7
Treverva Cornw'l 4 D3
Trevescan Cornw'l 2 F3
Trevethan Cornw'l 4 B2
Trevethin Torf 101 B5
Trevia Cornw'l 17 D6
Trevigro Cornw'l 10 A2
Trevilla Cornw'l 4 C4
Trevillian Cornw'l 17 B8
Trevilson Cornw'l 7 D7
Trevine = Trefin Pembs 118 C4
Treviscoe Cornw'l 8 D1
Treviscoe Barton Cornw'l 8 D1
Trevithal Cornw'l 2 E5
Trevivian Cornw'l 17 C8
Trevoll Cornw'l 7 D7
Trevone Cornw'l 16 E2
Trevor Wrex 241 F6
Trevor Gardens E Sussex 50 E2
Trevor Uchaf Denbs 241 F5
Trevowah Cornw'l 7 D6
Trew Cornw'l 3 E8
Trewalder Cornw'l 17 D6
Trewarlett Cornw'l 18 D3
Trewarmett Cornw'l 17 C6
Trewassa Cornw'l 17 C7
Treween Cornw'l 18 D1
Trewellard Cornw'l 2 D3
Trewen Cornw'l 18 D2
Trewennack Cornw'l 4 E1
Tre-wern Powys 217 C7
Trewern Powys 150 A2
Trewern Powys 194 A1
Trewetha Cornw'l 16 D5
Trewethern Cornw'l 16 E5
Trewidland Cornw'l 9 D8
Trewint Cornw'l 17 A8
Trewint Cornw'l 18 D1
Trewint Cornw'l 10 C1
Trewithian Cornw'l 5 C5
Trewoodloe Cornw'l 10 A2
Trewoofe Cornw'l 2 E4
Trewoon Cornw'l 8 E2
Treworga Cornw'l 5 B5
Treworlas Cornw'l 5 C5
Treworthal Cornw'l 5 C5
Tre-wyn Monmouths 127 C7
Treyarnon Cornw'l 16 F2
Treyford W Sussex 46 C4
Triangle Staffs 198 B1
Triangle W Yorks 292 F2
Trickett's Cross Dorset 42 F4
Tricombe Devon 23 A6
Trill Devon 23 A7
Trimdon Durham 344 E3
Trimdon Colliery Durham 344 D3
Trimdon Grange Durham 344 D3
Trimingham Norfolk 257 E8
Trimley Lower Street Suffolk 166 E3
Trimley St. Martin Suffolk 166 E3
Trimley St. Mary Suffolk 166 E3
Trimpley Worcs 175 C5
Trims Green Herts 139 D5
Trimsaran Carms 96 B4
Trimstone Devon 54 C4
Trinafour Perth/Kinr 418 A5
Trinant Caerph 100 C4
Tring Herts 136 E2
Tring Wharf Herts 136 E2
Tringford Herts 136 E2
Trinity Angus 421 A6
Trinity C/Edinb 396 C1
Trinity Devon 36 E4
Trinity Fields Staffs 221 C8
Trisant Ceredig'n 169 C7
Triscombe Som'set 58 D3
Trislaig H'land 424 E2
Trispen Cornw'l 7 E7
Tritlington Northum 365 D6
Troan Cornw'l 7 D8
Trochry Perth/Kinr 419 C7
Trodigal Arg/Bute 404 D2
Troedrhiwdalar Powys 148 B4
Troedrhiwfuwch Caerph 100 B2
Troedrhiwgwair Bl Gwent 126 F4
Troedyraur Ceredig'n 145 C6
Troed-y-rhiw Ceredig'n 146 B3
Troedyrhiw Merth Tyd 99 B8
Trofarth Conwy 262 E7
Trolway Heref'd 128 C3
Tromode I/Man 336 D3
Trondavoe Shetl'd 457 F3
Troon Cornw'l 3 C9
Troon S Ayrs 367 A6
Trosaraidh W Isles 446 B3
Trossachs Hotel Stirl 409 B8
Troston Suffolk 186 D3
Trostre Carms 97 C5
Trostrey Common Monmouths 101 B7
Troswell Cornw'l 18 B2
Trotten Marsh W Sussex 46 A4
Trottiscliffe Kent 91 D7
Trotton W Sussex 46 B4
Trough Gate Lancs 291 F6
Troutbeck Cumb 327 F5
Troutbeck Cumb 326 A4
Troutbeck Bridge Cumb 326 F4
Trow Devon 23 C5
Trow Green Glos 129 F5
Troway Derby 269 D7
Trowbridge Card 100 F4
Trowbridge Wilts 82 E1
Trowell Notts 224 A4
Trowle Common Wilts 82 E1
Trowley Bottom Herts 137 E5
Trowse Newton Norfolk 209 B8
Troy W Yorks 293 C6
Troy Town Kent 70 B3
Troydale W Yorks 293 D6
Trub Gtr Man 279 C6
Trubshaw Staffs 244 C3
Trudoxhill Som'set 61 C7
True Streek Devon 14 C4
Trueman's Heath Worcs 176 C4
Trull Som'set 38 B2
Trumaisgearraidh W Isles 447 A3
Trumfleet S Yorks 283 B6
Trumpan H'land 430 B2
Trumpet Heref'd 152 E3
Trumpington Cambs 162 A1
Trumps Green Surrey 88 C2
Trunch Norfolk 234 B2
Trunnah Lancs 288 B3
Truro Cornw'l 4 B4
Truro Cathedral Cornw'l 4 A4
Truscott Cornw'l 18 C3
Trusham Devon 21 D7
Trusley Derby 223 A7
Trusthorpe Lincs 275 C7
Truthwall Cornw'l 3 D6
Tryfil Angl 259 C5
Trysull Staffs 197 E6
Trythogga Cornw'l 2 D5
Tubney Oxon 107 C5
Tuckenhay Devon 14 D4
Tuckermarsh Devon 10 B4
Tuckhill Staffs 196 F4
Tuckingmill Cornw'l 18 B1
Tuckingmill Cornw'l 3 B9
Tuckingmill Wilts 62 F3
Tuckton Bournem'th 28 B2
Tuddenham Suffolk 185 D7
Tuddenham St. Martin Suffolk 166 C1
Tudeley Kent 71 B7
Tudeley Hale Kent 71 B7
Tudhoe Durham 344 D1
Tudhoe Grange Durham 343 E9
Tudor Hill W Midlands 198 D3
Tudorville Heref'd 129 C5
Tudweiliog Gwyn 212 A4
Tuebrook Mersey 264 A2
Tuffley Glos 130 D2
Tufnell Park London 111 E7
Tufton Hants 65 B6
Tufton Pembs 120 B4
Tugby Leics 202 C1
Tugford Shrops 195 F7
Tughall Northum 377 B6
Tulchan Lodge Angus 427 E6
Tullibardine Perth/Kinr 419 F7
Tullibody Clack 410 C3
Tullich Arg/Bute 417 F5
Tullich H'land 432 D1
Tullich H'land 433 F8
Tullich Muir H'land 440 F4
Tullie House Museum, Carlisle Cumb 348 E1
Tulliemet Perth/Kinr 419 B7
Tulloch Aberds 428 E4
Tulloch Aberds 437 E5
Tulloch H'land 425 D5
Tulloch Perth/Kinr 419 E8
Tulloch Castle H'land 433 B7
Tulloch-gribban H'land 434 F4
Tullochgorm Arg/Bute 408 C2
Tullochroisk Perth/Kinr 418 B5
Tullochvenus Aberds 428 B2
Tulloes Angus 421 C5
Tullybannocher Perth/Kinr 419 E5
Tullybelton Perth/Kinr 419 D8
Tullyfergus Perth/Kinr 420 C2
Tullymurdoch Perth/Kinr 420 B1
Tullynessle Aberds 428 A2
Tulse Hill London 89 B8
Tumble = Y Tymbl Carms 123 E6
Tumblers Green Essex 140 B5
Tumby Lincs 251 B7
Tumby Woodside Lincs 251 C8
Tummel Bridge Perth/Kinr 419 B5
Tumpy Green Glos 103 B6
Tunbridge Wells Kent 71 D6
Tunbridge Wells = Royal Tunbridge Wells Kent 71 D6
Tunga W Isles 451 D7
Tungate Norfolk 234 C2
Tunley Bath/NE Som'set 81 E5
Tunnel End W Yorks 280 B2
Tunnel Hill Worcs 153 D6
Tunshill Gtr Man 279 B7
Tunstall ER Yorks 299 D5
Tunstall Kent 93 D5
Tunstall Lancs 315 F6
Tunstall Norfolk 210 B4
Tunstall N Yorks 318 A3
Tunstall N Yorks 333 D5
Tunstall Suffolk 166 A5
Tunstall Stoke 244 D3
Tunstall Tyne/Wear 353 F6
Tunstall Hills Tyne/Wear 353 F6
Tunstead Gtr Man 280 D2
Tunstead Norfolk 234 D2
Tunstead Milton Derby 267 C7
Tunworth Hants 66 B3
Tupsley Heref'd 151 D8
Tupton Derby 247 A5
Tur Langton Leics 201 E8
Turf Hill Gtr Man 279 B7
Turfdown Cornw'l 8 B4
Turfholm S Lanarks 381 E8
Turfmoor Devon 38 F3
Turgis Green Hants 86 E4
Turin Angus 421 B5
Turkdean Glos 131 D8
Turkey Island Hants 45 D6
Turkey Island W Sussex 46 C3
Turleigh Wilts 81 D8
Turleygreen Shrops 175 A5
Turlin Moor Poole 27 B6
Turmer Hants 43 E5
Turn Lancs 279 A5
Turnalt Arg/Bute 407 B8
Turnant Heref'd 127 B7
Turnastone Heref'd 150 E5
Turnberry S Ayrs 354 A3
Turnchapel Plym'th 11 E5
Turnditch Derby 246 E3
Turner Green Lancs 290 D1
Turnerheath Ches 267 D5
Turner's Green E Sussex 51 C5
Turner's Green Warwick 177 E6
Turner's Green W Berks 85 C7
Turners Hill W Sussex 69 D8
Turners Puddle Dorset 26 B3
Turner's Tump Glos 129 D6
Turnford Herts 112 B2
Turnhouse C/Edinb 395 D8
Turnhurst Stoke 244 D3
Turnworth Dorset 41 E6
Turrerich Perth/Kinr 419 D6
Turriff Aberds 436 C4
Tursdale Durham 344 D2
Turton Bottoms Blackb'n 278 A3
Turves Green W Midlands 176 C3
Turvey Beds 159 B6
Turville Bucks 108 D5
Turweston Bucks 157 E7
Tushielaw Scot Borders 372 D3
Tutbury Staffs 223 C6
Tutnall Worcs 176 D2
Tutnalls Glos 102 B4
Tutshill Glos 102 C2
Tutt Hill Kent 73 B6
Tuttington Norfolk 234 C1
Tutts Clump W Berks 85 B8
Tutwell Cornw'l 18 E4
Tuxford Notts 271 E6
Twatt Orkney 452 A3
Twatt Shetl'd 457 H3
Twechar E Dunb 393 C6
Tweedmouth Northum 388 B1
Tweedsmuir Scot Borders 371 C6
Tweenaways Torbay 15 D5
Twelve Oaks E Sussex 51 B6
Twelveheads Cornw'l 4 B3
Twemlow Green Ches 266 F2
Twenty Lincs 228 D3
Twerton Bath/NE Som'set 81 D6
Twickenham London 88 B4
Twickenham Stadium London 89 B5
Twig Side Bucks 108 D5
Twigworth Glos 130 C2
Twineham W Sussex 49 C5
Twineham Green W Sussex 49 B5
Twinhoe Bath/NE Som'set 81 E6
Twinstead Essex 164 E2
Twinstead Green Essex 164 E2
Twiss Green Warrington 278 E2
Twiston Lancs 291 B5
Twitchen Devon 56 E2
Twitchen Shrops 172 C5
Twitham Kent 94 E5
Twitton Kent 90 E5
Two Bridges Devon 20 E2
Two Burrows Cornw'l 7 F5
Two Dales Derby 246 B3
Two Gates Staffs 199 C5
Two Mile Ash M/Keynes 158 E4
Two Mile Oak Cross Devon 14 B4
Two Mills Ches 264 E2
Two Waters Herts 110 A3
Twycross Leics 199 C7
Twycross Zoo, Ashby-de-la-Zouch Leics 199 B7
Twydall Medway 92 C2
Twyford Bucks 134 B4
Twyford Dorset 41 C7
Twyford Hants 44 B4
Twyford Leics 201 A8
Twyford Lincs 227 D5
Twyford Norfolk 232 D5
Twyford Oxon 156 E4
Twyford Staffs 223 C8
Twyford Wokingham 87 A5
Twyford Common Heref'd 151 E8
Twyn Allws Monmouths 127 E6
Twyn Shon-Ifan Caerph 100 D3
Twynersh Surrey 88 C2
Twyn-gwyn Torf 101 B5
Twynholm Dumf/Gal 401 D8
Twyning Glos 153 E7
Twyning Green Glos 153 E8
Twynllanan Carms 124 C4
Twynmynydd Carms 124 E2
Twynrodyn Merth Tyd 99 A8
Twyn-yr-odyn V/Glam 78 B2
Twyn-y-Sheriff Monmouths 101 A8
Twywell Northants 181 C7
Tyberton Heref'd 151 E5
Tyburn W Midlands 198 E3
Tyby Norfolk 233 C6
Ty-coch Torf 101 D5
Tycroes Carms 123 E8
Tycrwyn Powys 217 E7
Tydd Gote Lincs 229 E9
Tydd St. Giles Cambs 229 E8
Tydd St. Mary Lincs 229 E8
Tyddewi = St. David's Pembs 118 D3
Tyddyn Powys 192 F3
Tyddyn Dai Angl 259 A5
Tyddyn Llewely Gwyn 213 F6
Tyddyn Sieffre Gwyn 214 F4
Tye Hants 46 F2
Tye Common Essex 113 D8
Tye Green Essex 139 F5
Tye Green Essex 139 C6
Tye Green Essex 162 E4
Tye Green Essex 139 E8
Tye Green Essex 140 C4
Tyes Cross E Sussex 70 E2
Ty-hen Carms 122 C2
Tŷ-gwyn Powys 218 D2
Tyldesley Gtr Man 278 D2
Tyler Hill Kent 94 D2
Tylers Causeway Herts 111 A7
Tyler's Green Bucks 109 D8
Tyler's Green Essex 112 A5
Tyler's Green Surrey 70 A1
Tyllwyd Ceredig'n 145 C5
Tylorstown Rh Cyn Taff 99 C7
Tylwch Powys 170 B4
Ty-Mawr Carms 146 D3
Ty-mawr Denbs 262 D1
Ty-mawr Angl 259 B6
Ty'n Coed Angl 259 D6
Ty-nant Conwy 239 F7
Ty-nant Denbs 240 E2
Tynant Rh Cyn Taff 99 E8
Tyndrum Stirl 417 D8
Tyne Dock Tyne/Wear 353 C6
Tyne Tunnel Tyne/Wear 353 C5
Tyneham Dorset 26 D4
Tynehead Midloth 384 A4
Tynemouth Tyne/Wear 353 C6
Tynewydd Rh Cyn Taff 99 C5
Tyning Bath/NE Som'set 81 E5
Tyninghame E Loth 398 C2
Tyn-lôn Gwyn 236 C5
Tynron Dumf/Gal 357 D8
Tyntesfield N Som'set 80 B2
Tyntetown Rh Cyn Taff 99 C8
Ty'n-y-bryn Rh Cyn Taff 99 E7
Tyn-y-ffridd Powys 217 B7
Ty'n-y-garn Bridg 98 F4
Tynygongl Angl 259 C7
Tynygraig Ceredig'n 169 E6
Tyn-y-graig Powys 149 C5
Ty'n-y-groes Conwy 262 E5
Ty'n-y-maes Gwyn 237 B8
Tyn-y-maes Powys 217 C7
Tyn-y-Pistyll Conwy 239 E7
Ty'n-yr-eithin Ceredig'n 169 F6
Tyn-y-Rhos Shrops 218 A2
Tynywain Powys 171 E8
Tyrie Aberds 437 B6
Tyringham M/Keynes 158 C5
Tyrrell's Wood Surrey 89 E5
Tyseley W Midlands 176 B5
Ty-Sign Caerph 100 D4
Tythe Luton 136 C4
Tythecott Devon 33 C8
Tythegston Bridg 76 A4
Tytherington Ches 267 D5
Tytherington S Glos 103 E5
Tytherington Som'set 61 B7
Tytherington Wilts 62 C3
Tytherleigh Devon 38 F4
Tyttenhanger Herts 111 A5
Tywardreath Cornw'l 8 E4
Tywardreath Highway Cornw'l 8 D4
Tywyn Conwy 262 D5
Tywyn Gwyn 190 C2


## U


Uachdar W Isles 447 C2
Uags H'land 431 E7
Ubberley Stoke 244 E4
Ubbeston Green Suffolk 188 D4
Ubley Bath/NE Som'set 80 E2
Uckerby N Yorks 331 F6
Uckfield E Sussex 50 B2
Uckinghall Worcs 153 E7
Uckington Glos 130 B4
Uddingston S Lanarks 393 F5
Uddington S Lanarks 382 F2
Udimore E Sussex 52 C2
Udley N Som'set 80 D3
Udny Green Aberds 437 F5
Udny Station Aberds 437 F6
Udston S Lanarks 381 A5
Udstonhead S Lanarks 381 C6
Uffcott Wilts 83 A7
Uffculme Devon 37 D6
Uffington Lincs 203 B7
Uffington Oxon 106 E3
Uffington Shrops 219 F7
Ufford Peterbro 203 C7
Ufford Suffolk 166 B3
Ufton Warwick 178 F2
Ufton Green W Berks 86 C2
Ufton Nervet W Berks 86 C2
Ugadale Arg/Bute 404 D3
Ugborough Devon 14 D1
Ugford Wilts 63 E6
Uggeshall Suffolk 189 B6
Ugglebarnby N Yorks 334 E4
Ughill S Yorks 268 A5
Ugley Essex 139 B6
Ugley Green Essex 139 B6
Ugthorpe N Yorks 334 D2
Uidh W Isles 446 D2
Uig Arg/Bute 414 B4
Uig Arg/Bute 408 D4
Uig H'land 430 C1
Uig H'land 430 B3
Uigen W Isles 450 D3
Uigshader H'land 430 D4
Uisken Arg/Bute 415 F6
Ulaw Aberds 437 F6
Ulbster H'land 445 D7
Ulcat Row Cumb 327 B5
Ulceby Lincs 275 E5
Ulceby N Lincs 285 B9
Ulceby Skitter N Lincs 286 A1
Ulcombe Kent 72 B3
Uldale Cumb 338 D3
Uley Glos 103 C7
Ulgham Northum 365 D6
Ullapool H'land 439 D5
Ullcombe Devon 38 E2
Ullenhall Warwick 176 E5
Ullenwood Glos 130 D4
Ulleskelf N Yorks 294 C4
Ullesthorpe Leics 179 B5
Ulley S Yorks 270 B1
Ullingswick Heref'd 152 C1
Ullinish H'land 430 E3
Ullock Cumb 325 B6
Ullock Cumb 326 B1
Ulnes Walton Lancs 277 A7
Ulpha Cumb 312 B4
Ulrome ER Yorks 310 D5
Ulsta Shetl'd 457 E4
Ulting Essex 140 F5
Ulva House Arg/Bute 415 D7
Ulverley Green W Midlands 177 B5
Ulverston Cumb 313 E6
Ulwell Dorset 27 D7
Umberleigh Devon 34 B5
Unapool H'land 442 E4
Unasary W Isles 446 A3
Uncleby ER Yorks 309 D5
Under Tofts S Yorks 269 B6
Underbarrow Cumb 314 B3
Undercliffe W Yorks 292 D5
Underdale Shrops 219 F7
Underdown Devon 20 B4
Underhill London 111 C7
Underhoull Shetl'd 456 C5
Underling Green Kent 72 B2
Underriver Kent 71 A6
Underwood Newp 101 E7
Underwood Notts 247 D7
Underwood Plym'th 11 D6
Undley Suffolk 185 B6
Undy Monmouths 101 E8
Ungisiadar W Isles 450 E4
Unifirth Shetl'd 457 H2
Union Cottage Aberds 429 C5
Union Mills I/Man 336 D3
Union Street E Sussex 71 E9
University Museum, Oxford Oxon 107 A7
Unst Airport Shetl'd 456 C6
Unstone Derby 269 D7
Unstone Green Derby 269 D7
Unsworth Gtr Man 279 C5
Unthank Cumb 339 D7
Unthank Cumb 339 B6
Unthank Cumb 340 C3
Unthank Derby 269 D6
Unthank End Cumb 339 D8
Up Cerne Dorset 40 F3
Up End M/Keynes 159 C6
Up Exe Devon 36 F3
Up Exe Devon 36 F3
Up Green Hants 87 D5
Up Hatherley Glos 130 C4
Up Holland Lancs 277 D7
Up Marden W Sussex 46 D3
Up Mudford Som'set 40 C1
Up Nately Hants 66 A3
Up Somborne Hants 64 E4
Up Sydling Dorset 40 F2
Upavon Wilts 83 F8
Upchurch Kent 92 C3
Upcott Devon 34 E4
Upcott Heref'd 150 B4
Upcott Som'set 36 A3
Upcott Som'set 38 B1
Upend Cambs 163 A6
Upgate Norfolk 233 E7
Upgate Street Norfolk 209 E5
Upgate Street Norfolk 210 E1
Uphall Dorset 39 F9
Uphall W Loth 395 D6
Uphall Station W Loth 395 D6
Upham Devon 36 E2
Upham Hants 45 B5
Uphampton Heref'd 173 F6
Uphampton Worcs 175 F6
Uphempston Devon 14 C4
Uphill N Som'set 79 E6
Uplands Glos 104 A2
Uplands Swan 97 D7
Uplawmoor E Renf 379 A8
Upleadon Glos 129 B9
Upleatham Redcar/Clevel'd 333 C7
Uplees Kent 93 D6
Uploders Dorset 24 A5
Uplowman Devon 37 C5
Uplyms Devon 23 B8
Upminster London 113 E6
Upottery Devon 38 E2
Uppark, Petersfield Hants 46 C3
Uppat H'land 441 C5
Upper Affcot Shrops 173 A6
Upper Ardchronie H'land 440 E3
Upper Ardgrain Aberds 437 E6
Upper Ardroscadale Arg/Bute 408 F3
Upper Arley Worcs 175 B5
Upper Armley W Yorks 293 D7
Upper Arncott Oxon 134 D3
Upper Astley Shrops 219 E7
Upper Astrop Northants 157 E5
Upper Badcall H'land 442 D3
Upper Bangor Gwyn 259 E8
Upper Basildon W Berks 86 A1
Upper Batley W Yorks 293 E6
Upper Battlefield Shrops 219 E7
Upper Beeding W Sussex 48 D3
Upper Benefield Northants 203 F5
Upper Bentley Worcs 176 E2
Upper Bighouse H'land 444 C2
Upper Birchwood Derby 247 D6
Upper Boat Rh Cyn Taff 100 E2
Upper Boddam Aberds 436 E3
Upper Boddington Northants 156 B4
Upper Bogrow H'land 440 E4
Upper Bogside Moray 435 C7
Upper Borth Ceredig'n 190 F3
Upper Boyndlie Aberds 437 B6
Upper Brailes Warwick 155 E9
Upper Breakish H'land 431 F6
Upper Breinton Heref'd 151 D7
Upper Broadheath Worcs 153 A6
Upper Broughton Notts 225 C8
Upper Broxwood Heref'd 150 B5
Upper Brynamman Carms 124 E3
Upper Buckenhill Heref'd 129 A5
Upper Bucklebury W Berks 85 C7
Upper Burgate Hants 43 C5
Upper Burnhaugh Aberds 429 C5
Upper Caldecote Beds 160 C3
Upper Canada N Som'set 79 E7
Upper Canterton Hants 43 D8
Upper Catesby Northants 157 A5
Upper Catshill Worcs 176 D2
Upper Chapel Powys 149 D5
Upper Cheddon Som'set 58 F4
Upper Chicksgrove Wilts 62 F4
Upper Church Village Rh Cyn Taff 99 E8
Upper Chute Wilts 84 F2
Upper Clapton London 112 E1
Upper Clatford Hants 64 C4
Upper Coberley Glos 131 D5
Upper Cokeham W Sussex 48 E3
Upper Colwall Heref'd 153 D5
Upper Common Hants 66 B2
Upper Cotburn Aberds 436 C4
Upper Cotton Staffs 245 E7
Upper Coullie Aberds 428 A4
Upper Cound Shrops 195 C6
Upper Cudworth S Yorks 282 D1
Upper Culphin Aberds 436 C3
Upper Cumberworth W Yorks 281 C6
Upper Cwmbran Torf 101 C5
Upper Dallachy Moray 435 B8
Upper Deal Kent 75 A6
Upper Dean Beds 181 E8
Upper Denby W Yorks 281 C6
Upper Denton Cumb 349 C6
Upper Derraid H'land 435 E5
Upper Diabaig H'land 431 B8
Upper Dicker E Sussex 50 D4
Upper Dounreay H'land 444 B4
Upper Dovercourt Essex 143 A5
Upper Druimfin Arg/Bute 415 B8
Upper Dunsforth N Yorks 307 C5
Upper Eashing Surrey 67 C9
Upper Eastwood W Yorks 291 E8
Upper Eathie H'land 434 B2
Upper Edmonton London 112 D1
Upper Egleton Heref'd 152 C2
Upper Elkstone Staffs 245 C7
Upper Ellastone Staffs 245 F8
Upper Elmers End London 90 C2
Upper End Derby 267 D8
Upper End Glos 131 E8
Upper End Leics 226 F1
Upper Enham Hants 64 A4
Upper Farringdon Hants 66 D4
Upper Feorlig H'land 430 D2
Upper Fivehead Som'set 38 B4
Upper Framilode Glos 129 E8
Upper Froyle Hants 66 C5
Upper Gills H'land 445 A7
Upper Glenfintaig H'land 424 D4
Upper Godney Som'set 60 C1
Upper Goldstone Kent 95 D5
Upper Gornal W Midlands 197 E7
Upper Gravenhurst Beds 160 E2

Upper Green Essex 162 F1
Upper Green Monmouths 128 D1
Upper Green Suffolk 185 F7
Upper Green W Berks 84 D4
Upper Green W Yorks 293 E7
Upper Grove Common Heref'd 128 B5
Upper Guist Norfolk 232 C5
Upper Hackney Derby 246 B3
Upper Hale Surrey 67 B6
Upper Halistra H'land 430 C2
Upper Halliford Surrey 88 C3
Upper Halling Medway 91 D8
Upper Ham Worcs 153 E7
Upper Ham Worcs 153 C7
Upper Hambleton Rutl'd 202 B4
Upper Harbledown Kent 94 E2
Upper Hartfield E Sussex 70 E4
Upper Hartshay Derby 247 D5
Upper Haugh S Yorks 282 F2
Upper Hawkhillock Aberds 437 E7
Upper Haysden Kent 71 C6
Upper Hayton Shrops 173 B8
Upper Heaton W Yorks 281 A5
Upper Hellesdon Norfolk 209 A8
Upper Helmsley N Yorks 308 D2
Upper Hengoed Shrops 218 B2
Upper Hergest Heref'd 150 B3
Upper Heyford Northants 157 A8
Upper Heyford Oxon 133 B8
Upper Hiendley W Yorks 282 B1
Upper Hill Heref'd 151 B7
Upper Hill S Glos 103 C5
Upper Holloway London 111 E7
Upper Holton Suffolk 189 C6
Upper Hopton W Yorks 281 A5
Upper Horsebridge E Sussex 50 D4
Upper Howsell Worcs 153 C5
Upper Hoyland S Yorks 281 D8
Upper Hulme Staffs 245 B6
Upper Ifield Kent 91 B8
Upper Ifold Surrey 68 E2
Upper Inglesham Swindon 105 C9
Upper Inverbrough H'land 434 E3
Upper Kergord Shetl'd 457 H4
Upper Kilcott Glos 103 E7
Upper Killay Swan 97 D6
Upper Killeyan Arg/Bute 403 B2
Upper Kinsham Heref'd 172 E5
Upper Kirton N Ayrs 378 A3
Upper Knockando Moray 435 D6
Upper Lambourn W Berks 106 F3
Upper Landywood Staffs 197 B8
Upper Langford N Som'set 80 E1
Upper Leigh Staffs 222 A2
Upper Lenie H'land 433 F7
Upper Ley Glos 129 D8
Upper Littleton N Som'set 80 D3
Upper Llanover Monmouths 127 F7
Upper Lochton Aberds 428 C3
Upper Longdon Staffs 222 F3
Upper Longwood Shrops 195 B8
Upper Lybster H'land 445 E6
Upper Lydbrook Glos 129 D6
Upper Maes-coed Heref'd 150 F4
Upper Marsh W Yorks 292 C2
Upper Midhope S Yorks 281 E6
Upper Midway Derby 223 D7
Upper Milovaig H'land 430 D1
Upper Milton Oxon 132 D4
Upper Milton Som'set 60 B2
Upper Minety Wilts 104 D5
Upper Moor Worcs 154 C2
Upper Moor Side W Yorks 293 D6
Upper Morton S Glos 103 D5
Upper Nash Pembs 117 D6
Upper Newbold Derby 269 E7
Upper Nobut Staffs 222 A2
Upper North Dean Bucks 109 C7
Upper Norwood London 89 B8
Upper Norwood W Sussex 47 C6
Upper Obney Perth/Kinr 419 D8
Upper Oddington Glos 132 B3
Upper Ollach H'land 430 E5
Upper Outwoods Staffs 223 C6
Upper Padley Derby 268 D4
Upper Pennington Hants 29 A6
Upper Pollicott Bucks 135 E5
Upper Poppleton C/York 307 E8
Upper Port H'land 435 F5
Upper Quinton Warwick 155 C6
Upper Race Torf 100 C5
Upper Ratley Hants 44 B1
Upper Ridinghill Aberds 437 C7
Upper Rochford Worcs 174 E2
Upper Sandaig H'land 423 A7
Upper Sanday Orkney 453 C6
Upper Sapey Heref'd 174 F3
Upper Saxondale Notts 225 A8
Upper Seagry Wilts 104 F3
Upper Shelton Beds 159 D7
Upper Sheringham Norfolk 257 D5
Upper Shirley London 90 C2
Upper Shirley S'thampton 44 D3
Upper Shuckburgh Warwick 178 F4
Upper Siddington Glos 105 C5
Upper Skelmorlie N Ayrs 390 E3
Upper Slackstead Hants 44 A2
Upper Slaughter Glos 132 C2
Upper Soudley Glos 129 E7
Upper Spond Heref'd 150 B4
Upper Stanton Drew Bath/NE Som'set 80 D4
Upper Stoke Norfolk 209 C8
Upper Stoke W Midlands 178 C2
Upper Stondon Beds 160 E3
Upper Stonnall Staffs 198 C2
Upper Stowe Northants 157 A7
Upper Stratton Swindon 105 E8
Upper Street Hants 43 C5
Upper Street Norfolk 187 C8
Upper Street Norfolk 234 D4
Upper Street Norfolk 234 E3
Upper Street Norfolk 234 E4
Upper Street Suffolk 165 E7
Upper Street Suffolk 163 B8
Upper Street Suffolk 165 A7
Upper Strensham Worcs 153 E8
Upper Studley Wilts 82 E1
Upper Sundon Beds 136 B4
Upper Swell Glos 132 B2
Upper Sydenham London 90 B1
Upper Tean Staffs 222 A2
Upper Threapwood Ches 242 E1
Upper Thurnham Lancs 301 E8
Upper Tillyrie Perth/Kinr 411 B6
Upper Tooting London 89 B7
Upper Tote H'land 430 C5
Upper Town Derby 246 D2
Upper Town Durham 342 D5
Upper Town Heref'd 152 C1
Upper Town N Som'set 80 C2
Upper Town Suffolk 186 E3
Upper Town Wilts 82 A4
Upper Town W Yorks 292 D2
Upper Treverward Shrops 172 C3
Upper Tysoe Warwick 156 D1
Upper Upham Wilts 84 A1
Upper Upnor Medway 92 B2
Upper Vobster Som'set 61 B6
Upper Walthamstow London 112 E2
Upper Wardington Oxon 156 C4
Upper Waterhay Wilts 105 D6
Upper Weald M/Keynes 158 E3
Upper Weedon Northants 157 A7
Upper Welland Worcs 153 D5
Upper Wellingham E Sussex 49 D8
Upper Welson Heref'd 150 B3
Upper Weston Bath/NE Som'set 81 C6
Upper Weybread Suffolk 188 C2
Upper Whiston S Yorks 269 B9
Upper Wick Glos 103 C6
Upper Wick Worcs 153 B6
Upper Wield Hants 66 D2
Upper Wilcove Cornw'l 10 D4
Upper Winchendon Bucks 135 E5
Upper Witton W Midlands 198 E2
Upper Wolvercote Oxon 133 E8
Upper Woodend Aberds 428 A3
Upper Woodford Wilts 63 D7
Upper Woolhampton W Berks 85 C8
Upper Wootton Hants 86 F1
Upper Wraxhall S Glos 81 B8
Upper Wyche Worcs 153 D5
Upperby Cumb 348 F2
Uppermill Gtr Man 280 C1
Uppersound Shetl'd 455 B3
Upperthong W Yorks 280 C4
Upperthorpe Derby 270 C1
Upperthorpe N Lincs 284 D2
Upperton E Sussex 50 F5
Upperton W Sussex 47 B7
Uppertown Derby 246 A4
Uppertown H'land 433 E6
Uppertown H'land 445 A7
Uppertown Northum 350 B4
Uppertown Orkney 452 D5
Uppincott Devon 36 F2
Uppingham Rutl'd 202 D3
Uppington Dorset 42 E3
Uppington Shrops 195 B7
Upsall N Yorks 319 C8
Upsettlington Scot Borders 387 C7
Upsher Green Suffolk 164 D3
Upshire Essex 112 B3
Upstreet Kent 94 D4
Upthorpe Glos 103 B7
Upthorpe Suffolk 186 D4
Upton Cambs 182 C3
Upton Ches 264 F3
Upton Cumb 338 D5
Upton Cornw'l 9 A8
Upton Cornw'l 32 F4
Upton Dorset 26 D1
Upton Dorset 27 B6
Upton Devon 13 D5
Upton Devon 37 F6
Upton ER Yorks 310 E4
Upton Hants 84 E4
Upton Hants 44 C2
Upton Halton 264 B4
Upton Kent 95 C7
Upton Leics 199 D8
Upton Lincs 272 C2
Upton London 112 F3
Upton Mersey 263 B7
Upton Norfolk 210 A3
Upton Northants 180 F2
Upton Notts 249 D5
Upton Notts 271 D6
Upton Oxon 107 E7
Upton Oxon 132 E3
Upton Peterbro 203 C8
Upton Pembs 117 C6
Upton Redcar/Clevel'd 334 C1
Upton Slough 88 A1
Upton Som'set 57 F6
Upton Som'set 59 F9
Upton Warwick 154 A5
Upton Wilts 62 E2
Upton W Yorks 282 B3
Upton Bishop Heref'd 129 B7
Upton Cheyney S Glos 81 C5
Upton Cressett Shrops 196 E2
Upton Crews Heref'd 129 B6
Upton Cross Cornw'l 9 A8
Upton Dinton Bucks 135 E6
Upton End Beds 160 F2
Upton Field Notts 248 D5
Upton Green Norfolk 210 A3
Upton Grey Hants 66 B3
Upton Heath Ches 264 F3
Upton Hellions Devon 36 E1
Upton House Warwick 156 C2
Upton Lovell Wilts 62 C3
Upton Magna Shrops 195 A7
Upton Noble Som'set 61 D6
Upton Park London 112 F3
Upton Pyne Devon 21 A8
Upton Rocks Halton 264 B5
Upton St. Leonards Glos 130 E3
Upton Scudamore Wilts 62 B2
Upton Snodsbury Worcs 154 B1
Upton upon Severn Worcs 153 D7
Upton Warren Worcs 175 E8
Upton Wood Kent 74 B5
Upwaltham W Sussex 47 D6
Upware Cambs 184 D3
Upwell Norfolk 205 C8
Upwey Dorset 25 C8
Upwick Green Herts 139 C5
Upwood Cambs 183 B5
Uradale Shetl'd 455 C3
Urafirth Shetl'd 457 F3
Uragaig Arg/Bute 406 C3
Urchfont Wilts 83 E5
Ure Shetl'd 457 F2
Ure Bank N Yorks 306 A3
Urgha W Isles 449 C5
Urgha Beag W Isles 449 B5
Urlar Perth/Kinr 419 C6
Urlay Nook Stockton 332 D3
Urmston Gtr Man 278 F4
Urpeth Durham 352 F4
Urquhart H'land 433 C7
Urquhart Moray 435 B7
Urquhart Castle, Drumnadrochit H'land 433 F7
Urra N Yorks 333 F6
Urray H'land 433 C7
Ushaw Moor Durham 343 C8
Usk Monmouths 101 B7
Uskmouth Newp 101 F6
Usselby Lincs 285 F8
Usworth Tyne/Wear 353 E5
Utkinton Ches 242 B3
Utley W Yorks 292 B3
Uton Devon 21 A6
Utterby Lincs 274 A3
Uttoxeter Staffs 222 B3
Uttoxeter Racecourse Staffs 222 B4
Uwchmynydd Gwyn 212 C2
Uxbridge London 110 F3
Uyea Shetl'd 456 D3
Uyeasound Shetl'd 456 C5
Uzmaston Pembs 117 B5

## V

V & A Museum of Childhood London 111 F8
Vachelich Pembs 118 D3
Vadlure Shetl'd 457 J2
Vaila Hall Shetl'd 457 J2
Vaivoe Shetl'd 457 G5
Vale W Yorks 291 E7
Valeswood Shrops 218 D4
Valley = Y Fali Angl 258 D2
Valley End Surrey 87 D9
Valley Truckle Cornw'l 17 D6
Valleyfield Dumf/Gal 401 D8
Valsgarth Shetl'd 456 B6
Valtos H'land 430 B5
Van Caerph 100 E3
Vange Essex 114 E1
Vanlop Shetl'd 455 E2
Varteg Torf 100 A5
Vassa Shetl'd 457 H4
Vatsetter Shetl'd 456 E5
Vatsetter Shetl'd 455 D2
Vatten H'land 430 D2
Vaul Arg/Bute 414 C3
Vauxhall London 89 A8
Vauxhall W Midlands 198 F2
Vaynor Merth Tyd 126 E2
Vaynor Merth Tyd 126 E1
Veensgarth Shetl'd 455 B3
Velindre Powys 149 E8
Vellanoweth Cornw'l 3 D6
Vellow Som'set 58 D1
Velly Devon 33 B5
Veness Orkney 454 D3
Venn Devon 14 F3
Venn Devon 33 B6
Venn Green Devon 33 D7
Venn Ottery Devon 22 B3
Vennington Shrops 194 B2
Venny Tedburn Devon 21 A6
Venterdon Cornw'l 18 F4
Ventnor I/Wight 30 E3
Ventnor Botanic Garden I/Wight 30 E2
Venton Devon 11 D7
Venton Devon 20 B3
Ventongimps Mill Cornw'l 7 E6
Venus Hill Herts 110 B2
Vermentry Shetl'd 457 H3
Verney Junction Bucks 135 B5
Vernham Dean Hants 84 E3
Vernham Row Hants 84 E3
Vernham Street Hants 84 E4
Vernolds Common Shrops 173 B7
Vertington Som'set 61 F6
Verwood Dorset 42 E4
Veryan Cornw'l 5 C6
Veryan Green Cornw'l 5 B6
Vickerstown Cumb 300 B2
Victoria Cornw'l 8 C2
Victoria S Yorks 281 C5
Victoria and Albert Museum London 89 A7
Victoria Park Bucks 135 E7
Victoria Park Dorset 25 C8
Victoria Park Gtr Man 279 E6
Victory Gardens Renf 392 E2
Vidlin Shetl'd 457 G4
Viewpark N Lanarks 393 F6
Vigo Tyne/Wear 352 F4
Vigo W Midlands 198 C1
Vigo Village Kent 91 D7
Vinegar Hill Monmouths 101 E8
Vinehall Street E Sussex 51 B8
Vines Cross E Sussex 50 C4
Viney Hill Glos 103 A5
Vinny Green S Glos 81 A5
Virginia Water Surrey 88 C1
Virginstow Devon 18 B4
Virley Essex 141 E7
Viscar Cornw'l 4 D2
Vivod Denbs 240 F4
Vobster Som'set 61 B6
Voe Shetl'd 457 E3
Voe Shetl'd 457 G4
Vole Som'set 59 A7
Vowchurch Heref'd 150 E5
Vowchurch Common Heref'd 150 E5
Voxter Shetl'd 457 F3
Voy Orkney 452 B3
Vron Gate Shrops 194 B2
Vulcan Village Mersey 277 F8

## W

Waberthwaite Cumb 312 B3
Wackerfield Durham 331 B5
Wacton Norfolk 209 E7
Wacton Common Norfolk 209 E7
Wadbister Shetl'd 457 J4
Wadborough Worcs 153 C8
Waddesdon Bucks 135 D5
Waddesdon Manor, Aylesbury Bucks 135 D5
Waddeton Devon 15 D5
Waddicar Mersey 276 E4
Waddicombe Devon 56 F4
Waddingham Lincs 285 E6
Waddington Lancs 290 B3
Waddington Lincs 250 B2
Waddingworth Lincs 273 E8
Waddon Dorset 25 C7
Waddon Devon 21 E7
Wade Hall Lancs 289 F7
Wadebridge Cornw'l 8 A2
Wadeford Som'set 38 D4
Wadenhoe Northants 181 B8
Wadesmill Herts 138 D3
Wadhurst E Sussex 71 E7
Wadhurst Park E Sussex 71 F7
Wadshelf Derby 269 E6
Wadsley S Yorks 269 A6
Wadsley Bridge S Yorks 269 A7
Wadswick Wilts 82 C1
Wadwick Hants 65 A5
Wadworth S Yorks 283 E5
Waen Denbs 239 B7
Waen Denbs 240 A3
Waen Flints 263 E5
Waen Powys 218 E1
Waen Aberwheeler Denbs 262 F3
Waen Fach Powys 217 E9
Waen Goleugoed Denbs 262 E3
Waen-dymarch Flints 263 E5
Waen-pentir Gwyn 237 A7
Waen-wen Gwyn 259 F8
Wag H'land 441 A7
Wagbeach Shrops 194 B3
Wagg Som'set 59 F8
Waggersley Staffs 221 A7
Waggs Plot Devon 38 F4
Wainfelin Torf 101 B5
Wainfleet All Saints Lincs 253 C5
Wainfleet Bank Lincs 252 C5
Wainfleet St. Mary Lincs 253 C6
Wainfleet Tofts Lincs 253 C5
Wainford Norfolk 210 E2
Waingroves Derby 247 E6
Wainhouse Corner Cornw'l 17 A8
Wainscott Medway 92 B1
Wainstalls W Yorks 292 E2
Waitby Cumb 328 E5
Waithe NE Lincs 286 D4
Wake Green W Midlands 176 B4
Wakefield W Yorks 293 F8
Wakeham Devon 14 F1
Wakehurst Place Garden, Crawley W Sussex 70 E1
Wakerley Northants 203 D5
Wakes Colne Essex 141 B6
Wakes Colne Green Essex 141 A6
Walberswick Suffolk 189 D7
Walberton W Sussex 47 E7
Walbottle Tyne/Wear 352 C2
Walby Cumb 348 D2
Walcombe Som'set 60 B3
Walcot Lincs 227 A8
Walcot N Lincs 296 F4
Walcot Shrops 194 D1
Walcot Swindon 105 F8
Walcot Telford 195 A7
Walcot Warwick 155 A5
Walcot Green Norfolk 187 B7
Walcot West Swindon 105 F8
Walcote Leics 179 B6
Walcott Lincs 251 C5
Walcott Norfolk 234 B4
Walden N Yorks 317 D6
Walden Head N Yorks 317 D5
Walden Stubbs N Yorks 283 A5
Walderslade Medway 92 D2
Walderslade Bottom Medway 92 D2
Walderton W Sussex 46 D3
Walditch Dorset 24 B4
Waldley Derby 222 A4
Waldridge Durham 343 A9
Waldringfield Suffolk 166 D3
Waldringfield Heath Suffolk 166 D3
Waldron E Sussex 50 C4
Wales Som'set 40 A1
Wales S Yorks 270 C1
Wales Bar S Yorks 270 C1
Wales End Suffolk 163 C8
Walesby Lincs 273 A7
Walesby Notts 271 E5
Walford Heref'd 173 D5
Walford Heref'd 129 C5
Walford Shrops 219 D5
Walford Heath Shrops 219 E5
Walgherton Ches 243 E6
Walgrave Northants 180 D4
Walham Glos 130 C2
Walham Green London 89 A7
Walhampton Hants 29 A6
Walk Mill Lancs 291 D6
Walkden Gtr Man 278 D3
Walker Tyne/Wear 352 C4
Walker Art Gallery Mersey 264 A2
Walker Fold Lancs 290 B2
Walkerburn Scot Borders 384 E4
Walkergate Tyne/Wear 352 C4
Walkeringham Notts 271 A7
Walkerith Lincs 271 A7
Walkern Herts 138 B1
Walker's Green Heref'd 151 C8
Walker's Heath W Midlands 176 C4
Walkerville N Yorks 318 A3
Walkford Dorset 28 B4
Walkhampton Devon 11 B6
Walkington ER Yorks 297 C6
Walkley S Yorks 269 B6
Walkley Clogs, Hebden Bridge W Yorks 292 E2
Walkwood Worcs 176 F3
Wall Cornw'l 3 C8
Wall Northum 350 C5
Wall Staffs 198 B3
Wall Bank Shrops 195 E6
Wall End Cumb 313 D5
Wall End Kent 94 D4
Wall Heath W Midlands 197 F6
Wall Hill Gtr Man 279 C8
Wall Houses Northum 351 C7
Wall Mead Bath/NE Som'set 81 E5
Wall Nook Durham 343 B8
Wall under Heywood Shrops 195 E6
Wallacestone Falk 394 C3
Wallaceton Dumf/Gal 357 E8
Wallacetown S Ayrs 354 B4
Wallacetown S Ayrs 367 C6
Wallacetown Shetl'd 457 H3
Wallands Park E Sussex 49 D8
Wallasey Mersey 263 A7
Wallbank Lancs 279 A6
Wallbrook W Midlands 197 E7
Wallcrouch E Sussex 71 E8
Wallend London 112 F3
Waller's Green Heref'd 152 E3
Wallingford Oxon 108 E2
Wallingswells Notts 270 C3
Wallington Hants 45 E6
Wallington Herts 161 F5
Wallington London 89 D7
Wallington Bury Herts 161 F5
Wallington Heath W Midlands 197 C8
Wallington House, Ponteland Northum 364 F2
Wallis Pembs 120 B4
Wallisdown Poole 27 B8
Walliswood Surrey 68 D4
Wallow Green Glos 103 C8
Walls Shetl'd 457 J2
Wall's Green Essex 113 A7
Wallsend Tyne/Wear 352 C4
Wallston V/Glam 78 B2
Wallsuches Gtr Man 278 B2
Wallsworth Glos 130 C2
Wallyford E Loth 396 D4
Walman's Green Herts 138 C2
Walmer Kent 75 A7
Walmer Bridge Lancs 289 F6
Walmersley Gtr Man 278 B4
Walmestone Kent 94 E5
Walmley W Midlands 198 E3
Walmley Ash W Midlands 198 E3
Walmsgate Lincs 274 D4
Walney Island Airport, Barrow Cumb 300 A2
Walnut Grove Perth/Kinr 420 E1
Walnut Tree M/Keynes 159 E5
Walpole Suffolk 188 D5
Walpole Som'set 59 C6
Walpole Cross Keys Norfolk 230 D2
Walpole Highway Norfolk 230 F2
Walpole Marsh Norfolk 230 E1
Walpole St. Andrew Norfolk 230 E2
Walpole St. Peter Norfolk 230 E1
Walrow Som'set 59 B6
Walsall W Midlands 198 D1
Walsall Arboretum W Midlands 198 D1
Walsall Wood W Midlands 198 C1
Walsden W Yorks 291 F7
Walsgrave on Sowe W Midlands 178 B2
Walsham le Willows Suffolk 187 D5
Walshaw Gtr Man 278 B4
Walshford N Yorks 306 E5
Walsoken Norfolk 205 A7
Walston S Lanarks 383 C6
Walsworth Herts 137 A8
Walter's Ash Bucks 109 C6
Walterston V/Glam 77 B8
Walterstone Heref'd 127 B7
Walterstone Common Heref'd 127 B7
Waltham Kent 74 B2
Waltham NE Lincs 286 D4
Waltham Abbey Essex 112 B2
Waltham Chase Hants 45 C6
Waltham Cross Herts 112 B2
Waltham on the Wolds Leics 226 C3
Waltham St. Lawrence Windsor 87 A6
Waltham's Cross Essex 140 A2
Walthamstow London 112 E2
Walton Bucks 135 E7
Walton Cumb 348 D4
Walton Derby 269 F7
Walton Derby 269 F7
Walton Leics 201 F5
Walton Mersey 276 E4
Walton M/Keynes 159 E5
Walton Peterbro 204 C2
Walton Powys 150 A3
Walton Shrops 173 C7
Walton Suffolk 166 E3
Walton Som'set 60 D1
Walton Staffs 221 B7
Walton Telford 220 E1
Walton Warwick 155 B8
Walton W Yorks 281 A9
Walton W Yorks 307 F5
Walton Cardiff Glos 130 A4
Walton Court Bucks 135 E7
Walton East Pembs 119 E8
Walton Elm Dorset 41 C5
Walton Hall Warrington 265 C6
Walton Highway Norfolk 205 A7
Walton on Thames Surrey 88 C4
Walton on the Hill Surrey 89 F6
Walton on the Hill Staffs 221 D9
Walton on the Wolds Leics 225 E6
Walton on Trent Derby 223 E6
Walton Park N Som'set 79 B8
Walton St. Mary N Som'set 79 B8
Walton Summit Lancs 289 E8
Walton Warren Norfolk 231 E6
Walton West Pembs 116 B3
Walton-in-Gordano N Som'set 79 B8
Walton-le-Dale Lancs 289 E8
Walton-on-the-Naze Essex 143 C6
Walwen Flints 262 D4
Walwen Flints 263 D6
Walwick Northum 350 B5
Walworth D'lington 331 C6
Walworth London 89 A8
Walworth Gate D'lington 331 B6
Walwyn's Castle Pembs 116 B3
Wambrook Som'set 38 E3
Wampool Cumb 347 F6
Wanborough Surrey 67 B8
Wanborough Swindon 105 F9
Wanderwell Dorset 24 B4
Wandon End Herts 137 C6
Wandsworth London 89 B7
Wandylaw Northum 376 B4
Wangford Suffolk 189 C7
Wangford Suffolk 185 B8
Wanlip Leics 201 A5
Wanlockhead Dumf/Gal 370 E2
Wannock E Sussex 50 F4
Wansford ER Yorks 310 D3
Wansford Peterbro 203 D7
Wanshurst Green Kent 72 B2
Wanson Cornw'l 32 F3
Wanstead London 112 E3
Wanstrow Som'set 61 C6
Wanswell Glos 103 B5
Wantage Oxon 107 E5
Wapley S Glos 81 A6
Wappenbury Warwick 178 E2
Wappenham Northants 157 C7
Wapping London 112 F1
Warbleton E Sussex 50 C5
Warblington Hants 46 E2
Warborough Oxon 108 D1
Warboys Cambs 183 B6
Warbreck Blackp'l 288 C3
Warbstow Cornw'l 17 B9
Warbstow Cross Cornw'l 17 B9
Warburton Ches 265 B8
Warburton Green Gtr Man 266 B2
Warburton Park Gtr Man 265 A9
Warcop Cumb 328 C4
Ward End W Midlands 198 F3
Ward Green Suffolk 187 F5
Ward Green S Yorks 281 D8
Ward Green Cross Lancs 290 C1
Warden Kent 93 B7
Warden Northum 350 C5
Warden Hill Beds 160 B2
Warden Hill Glos 130 C4
Warden Street Beds 160 D2
Wardhedges Beds 160 E1
Wardhill Orkney 454 D4
Wardington Oxon 156 C4
Wardlaw Scot Borders 372 D2
Wardle Ches 243 C5
Wardle Gtr Man 279 A7
Wardley Gtr Man 278 D4
Wardley Rutl'd 202 C2
Wardley Tyne/Wear 352 D4
Wardley W Sussex 67 F6
Wardlow Derby 268 E3
Wardpark N Lanarks 393 C7
Wardsend Ches 267 C5
Wardy Hill Cambs 184 B2
Ware Devon 23 B8
Ware Herts 138 E3
Ware Kent 95 D5
Ware Street Kent 92 E2
Wareham Dorset 27 C5
Warehorne Kent 73 E6
Warenford Northum 376 B4
Warenton Northum 376 A4
Wareside Herts 138 D3
Waresley Cambs 161 B5
Waresley Worcs 175 D6
Warfield Brackn'l 87 B7
Warfleet Devon 15 E5
Wargate Lincs 228 B4
Wargrave Mersey 277 F8
Wargrave Wokingham 87 A5
Warham Heref'd 151 E7
Warham Norfolk 256 D1
Warhill Gtr Man 280 E1
Waring's Green W Midlands 177 D5
Wark Northum 350 A4
Wark Northum 387 E6
Warkleigh Devon 35 B5
Warkton Northants 181 A5
Warkworth Northants 156 D4
Warkworth Northum 365 A6
Warlaby N Yorks 319 B5
Warland W Yorks 291 F7
Warleggan Cornw'l 9 B6
Warleigh Bath/NE Som'set 81 D7
Warley Essex 113 D6
Warley W Midlands 197 F9
Warley Town W Yorks 292 E3
Warley Woods W Midlands 176 A3
Warlingham Surrey 90 E2
Warmbrook Derby 246 D3
Warmfield W Yorks 294 F1
Warmingham Ches 243 B7
Warminghurst W Sussex 48 C2
Warmington Northants 203 E7
Warmington Warwick 156 C3
Warminster Wilts 62 C2
Warminster Common Wilts 62 C2
Warmlake Kent 72 A3
Warmley S Glos 81 B5
Warmley Hill S Glos 81 B5
Warmonds Hill Northants 181 E7
Warmsworth S Yorks 282 D4
Warmwell Dorset 26 C2
Warndon Worcs 153 A7
Warners End Herts 136 F4
Warnford Hants 45 B7
Warnham W Sussex 69 E5
Warningcamp W Sussex 47 E8
Warninglid W Sussex 49 A5
Warren Ches 266 E4
Warren Pembs 116 E4
Warren S Yorks 281 E9
Warren Corner Hants 66 F4

West Parley Dorset 27 A8
West Peckham Kent 71 A7
West Pelton Durham 343 A8
West Pennard Som'set 60 D2
West Pentire Cornw'l 7 C6
West Perry Cambs 182 E2
West Poringland Norfolk 210 C1
West Porlock Som'set 56 B4
West Pulham Dorset 40 E4
West Putford Devon 33 C7
West Quantoxhead Som'set 58 C2
West Rainton Durham 344 B2
West Rasen Lincs 273 B6
West Ravendale NE Lincs 286 E3
West Raynham Norfolk 232 C2
West Retford Notts 271 C5
West Rounton N Yorks 332 F3
West Row Suffolk 185 C6
West Royd W Yorks 292 C5
West Rudham Norfolk 231 C8
West Ruislip London 110 E3
West Runton Norfolk 257 D6
West Saltoun E Loth 397 E6
West Sandford Devon 35 F9
West Sandwick Shetl'd 456 E4
West Scholes W Yorks 292 D3
West Scrafton N Yorks 317 D7
West Shepton Som'set 60 C4
West Side Orkney 454 C3
West Skelston Dumf/Gal 402 A2
West Sleekburn Northum 365 E7
West Somerset Railway, Minehead Som'set 57 C7
West Somerton Norfolk 235 E6
West Stafford Dorset 26 C1
West Stockwith Notts 284 E2
West Stoke Som'set 39 C7
West Stoke W Sussex 46 E4
West Stonesdale N Yorks 329 F7
West Stoughton Som'set 59 B8
West Stour Dorset 41 B5
West Stourmouth Kent 94 D5
West Stow Suffolk 186 D1
West Stowell Wilts 83 D7
West Strathan H'land 443 B7
West Stratton Hants 65 C7
West Street Kent 95 E6
West Street Kent 93 F5
West Street Medway 92 A1
West Street Suffolk 186 D4
West Street Suffolk 187 D5
West Tanfield N Yorks 318 E4
West Taphouse Cornw'l 9 C6
West Tarbert Arg/Bute 407 F8
West Tarring W Sussex 48 F2
West Third Scot Borders 386 E2
West Thirston Northum 365 C5
West Thorney W Sussex 46 F3
West Thurrock Thurr'k 91 A6
West Tilbury Thurr'k 91 A8
West Tisted Hants 66 F2
West Tofts Norfolk 207 E7
West Tofts Perth/Kinr 420 D1
West Tolgus Cornw'l 4 B1
West Torrington Lincs 273 C7
West Town Bath/NE Som'set 80 D2
West Town Bucks 109 F8
West Town Devon 21 A7
West Town Devon 33 B6
West Town Hants 31 A6
West Town Heref'd 173 F6
West Town N Som'set 80 C1
West Town Som'set 60 D2
West Town W Sussex 49 C5
West Tytherley Hants 64 F2
West Tytherton Wilts 82 B4
West Vale W Yorks 292 F3
West View Hartlep'l 345 D5
West Village V/Glam 77 C6
West Walton Norfolk 230 F1
West Wellow Hants 43 C8
West Wembury Devon 11 F6
West Wemyss Fife 411 C8
West Wick N Som'set 79 D7
West Wickham Cambs 162 C5
West Wickham London 90 C2
West Williamston Pembs 117 C6
West Willoughby Lincs 250 F2
West Winch Norfolk 230 E4
West Winterslow Wilts 64 E1
West Wittering W Sussex 31 E5
West Witton N Yorks 317 C7
West Woodburn Northum 363 E6
West Woodhay W Berks 84 D4
West Woodlands Som'set 61 C7
West Worldham Hants 66 D4
West Worlington Devon 35 D8
West Worthing W Sussex 48 F2
West Wratting Cambs 162 B5
West Wycombe Bucks 109 D6
West Wylam Northum 351 D9
West Yatton Wilts 82 A2
West Yell Shetl'd 457 E4
West Yeo Som'set 59 E6
Westbere Kent 94 D3
Westborough Lincs 249 F8
Westbourne Bournem'th 27 B8
Westbourne Suffolk 165 C7
Westbourne W Sussex 46 E3
Westbrook Heref'd 150 D3
Westbrook Kent 95 C7
Westbrook Surrey 68 C1
Westbrook W Berks 85 B5
Westbrook Wilts 82 C4
Westbrook Warrington 265 A6
Westbrook Green Norfolk 187 B7
Westburn S Lanarks 393 F5
Westbury Bucks 157 E7
Westbury Shrops 194 B3
Westbury Wilts 62 A2
Westbury Leigh Wilts 62 A2
Westbury on Trym Bristol 80 A3
Westbury Park Bristol 80 A3
Westbury-on-Severn Glos 129 E8
Westbury-sub-Mendip Som'set 60 B2
Westby Lancs 288 D4
Westby Lincs 227 C6
Westcliff I/Wight 30 E2
Westcliff-on-Sea Southend 114 E4
Westcombe Som'set 60 F1
Westcombe Som'set 61 D5
Westcot Oxon 106 E3
Westcote Glos 132 C3
Westcott Bucks 135 D5
Westcott Devon 21 C5
Westcott Devon 37 F5
Westcott Surrey 68 B4
Westcott Barton Oxon 133 B7
Westcourt Wilts 84 D1
Westcraigs W Loth 394 E3
Westcroft M/Keynes 158 F4
Westdean E Sussex 52 F2
Westdene Brighton/Hove 49 E5
Westdowns Cornw'l 17 D6
Westend Glos 130 F1
Westend Oxon 133 C5
Westend S Glos 102 D4
Westend Town Northum 350 C2
Westend Town S Glos 81 B7
West-end-Town V/Glam 77 C6
Westenhanger Kent 74 D2
Wester Aberchalder H'land 433 F7
Wester Arboll H'land 441 E5
Wester Auchinloch N Lanarks 393 D5
Wester Auchnagallin H'land 435 E5
Wester Balgedie Perth/Kinr 411 B6
Wester Brae H'land 434 B1
Wester Craiglands H'land 434 C2
Wester Culbeuchly Aberds 436 B3
Wester Dalvoult H'land 426 A4
Wester Dechmont W Loth 394 D5
Wester Denoon Angus 420 C3
Wester Ellister Arg/Bute 403 A1
Wester Essendy Perth/Kinr 420 C1
Wester Feddal Perth/Kinr 410 B3
Wester Fintray Aberds 429 A5
Wester Galgantray H'land 434 D3
Wester Gospetry Fife 411 B6
Wester Gruinards H'land 440 D2
Wester Hailes C/Edinb 395 E9
Wester Lealty H'land 433 A8
Wester Lix Stirl 418 E3
Wester Milton H'land 434 C4
Wester Mosshead Aberds 436 E2
Wester Newburn Fife 412 B2
Wester Ord Aberds 429 B5
Wester Quarff Shetl'd 455 C3
Wester Skeld Shetl'd 455 B1
Wester Strath H'land 434 C1
Wester Watten H'land 445 C6
Westerdale H'land 445 C5
Westerdale N Yorks 333 E8
Westerfield Suffolk 165 C8
Westerfield Shetl'd 457 H3
Westerfolds Moray 435 B6
Westergate W Sussex 47 E6
Westerham Kent 70 C3
Westerhope Tyne/Wear 352 C2
Westerleigh S Glos 81 A6
Westerleigh Common S Glos 103 F6
Westerleigh Hill S Glos 81 A6
Western Bank Cumb 338 B3
Western Downs Staffs 221 D8
Western Heights Kent 75 C6
Western Hill Durham 344 C1
Western Point Halton 264 C4
Westerton Aberds 428 A4
Westerton Aberds 436 D2
Westerton Angus 421 B6
Westerton Durham 343 E8
Westerton Moray 435 C8
Westerton W Sussex 47 E5
Westertown Aberds 436 E4
Westerwick Shetl'd 455 B1
Westfield Bath/NE Som'set 81 F5
Westfield Cumb 337 F5
Westfield E Sussex 52 C1
Westfield Hants 31 A6
Westfield Heref'd 152 C4
Westfield H'land 444 B4
Westfield Norfolk 208 B3
Westfield N Lanarks 393 D6
Westfield N Lincs 286 A1
Westfield Redcar/Clevel'd 333 B6
Westfield Surrey 88 E2
Westfield S Yorks 269 C8
Westfield W Loth 394 D3
Westfield W Yorks 293 B5
Westfield W Yorks 293 F6
Westfield Sole Kent 92 D2
Westfields Dorset 40 E4
Westfields Heref'd 151 D8
Westfields of Rattray Perth/Kinr 420 C1
Westford Som'set 37 B7
Westgate Durham 342 D2
Westgate Norfolk 256 D2
Westgate N Lincs 284 C2
Westgate Hill W Yorks 293 E6
Westgate on Sea Kent 95 B6
Westgate Street Norfolk 233 D8
Westhall Aberds 436 F3
Westhall Suffolk 189 B6
Westhall Hill Oxon 132 E3
Westham Dorset 25 E8
Westham E Sussex 51 F5
Westham Som'set 59 B8
Westhampnett W Sussex 47 E5
Westhay Som'set 59 C8
Westhead Lancs 277 C5
Westhide Heref'd 152 D1
Westhill Aberds 429 B5
Westhill H'land 434 D2
Westholme Som'set 60 C3
Westhope Heref'd 151 B7
Westhope Shrops 173 A7
Westhorp Northants 157 B5
Westhorpe Derby 269 D9
Westhorpe Lincs 228 B4
Westhorpe Suffolk 187 E5
Westhoughton Gtr Man 278 C2
Westhouse N Yorks 315 F7
Westhouses Derby 247 C6
Westhumble Surrey 69 A5
Westing Shetl'd 456 C5
Westlake Devon 11 E8
Westland Arg/Bute 408 F3
Westland Green Herts 138 C4
Westlands Cambs 206 F1
Westlands Staffs 244 F2
Westlands Worcs 175 F7
Westlea Swindon 105 F7
Westleigh Devon 37 C6
Westleigh Devon 54 F4
Westleigh Gtr Man 278 D2
Westleigh Gtr Man 278 D1
Westleton Suffolk 189 E6
Westley Shrops 194 B3
Westley Suffolk 186 F1
Westley Heights Essex 113 E8
Westley Waterless Cambs 162 B5
Westlington Bucks 135 E6
Westlinton Cumb 347 D9
Westmancote Worcs 154 E1
Westmarsh Kent 95 D5
Westmeston E Sussex 49 D6
Westmill Herts 138 B3
Westminster London 89 A7
Westminster Cathedral London 89 A7
Westmoor End Cumb 337 D8
Westmuir Angus 420 B3
Westness Orkney 454 D1
Westnewton Cumb 337 C8
Westnewton Northum 375 A8
Westoe Tyne/Wear 353 C6
Weston Bath/NE Som'set 81 C6
Weston Ches 243 D7
Weston Ches 266 E4
Weston Dorset 24 D2
Weston Devon 23 C5
Weston Devon 37 F7
Weston Hants 46 B2
Weston Heref'd 150 A5
Weston Halton 264 C5
Weston Herts 138 A1
Weston Lincs 229 C5
Weston Northants 157 C6
Weston Notts 271 F7
Weston N Yorks 305 F7
Weston Shrops 172 D4
Weston Shrops 195 E7
Weston Shrops 219 C8
Weston S Lanarks 383 C5
Weston S'thampton 44 D3
Weston Staffs 222 C1
Weston W Berks 84 B4
Weston Bampfylde Som'set 40 A2
Weston Beggard Heref'd 152 D1
Weston by Welland Northants 202 E1
Weston Colley Hants 65 D7
Weston Colville Cambs 162 B5
Weston Corbett Hants 66 B3
Weston Coyney Stoke 244 F4
Weston Ditch Suffolk 185 C6
Weston Favell Northants 180 F3
Weston Green Cambs 163 B5
Weston Green Norfolk 233 F7
Weston Green Surrey 89 C5
Weston Heath Shrops 219 C8
Weston Heath Shrops 221 F5
Weston Hills Lincs 229 D5
Weston in Arden Warwick 199 F8
Weston Jones Staffs 220 D5
Weston Longville Norfolk 233 E7
Weston Lullingfields Shrops 219 D5
Weston Mill Plym'th 10 D5
Weston on the Green Oxon 134 D1
Weston on Trent Derby 224 C3
Weston Park Bath/NE Som'set 81 C6
Weston Park Staffs 196 A5
Weston Patrick Hants 66 B3
Weston Point Halton 264 C4
Weston Rhyn Shrops 218 A2
Weston Subedge Glos 155 D5
Weston Town Som'set 61 C6
Weston Turville Bucks 135 E8
Weston under Lizard Staffs 196 A5
Weston under Penyard Heref'd 129 C6
Weston under Wetherley Warwick 178 E2
Weston Underwood Derby 246 F3
Weston Underwood M/Keynes 158 B5
Westonbirt Glos 104 E2
Westonbirt Arboretum, Tetbury Glos 104 E2
Westoning Beds 136 A4
Weston-in-Gordano N Som'set 79 B8
Weston-on-Avon Warwick 155 B6
Weston-super-Mare N Som'set 79 D6
Westonzoyland Som'set 59 D7
Westover Hants 64 C4
Westow N Yorks 308 B4
Westowe Som'set 58 E2
Westown Devon 37 D7
Westown Perth/Kinr 420 E2
Westport Arg/Bute 404 D2
Westport Som'set 39 B5
Westquarter Falk 394 C3
Westra V/Glam 78 B2
Westray Airport Orkney 454 A2
Westridge Green W Berks 85 A8
Westrigg W Loth 394 E3
Westrip Glos 103 A8
Westrop Swindon 105 D9
Westrop Wilts 82 B2
Westruther Scot Borders 386 C2
Westry Cambs 205 D7
Westvale Mersey 276 E5
Westville Notts 247 E8
Westward Cumb 338 B4
Westward Ho! Devon 54 F3
Westwell Kent 73 B6
Westwell Oxon 132 E3
Westwell Leacon Kent 73 B6
Westwells Wilts 82 C2
Westwick Cambs 183 E8
Westwick Durham 330 C3
Westwick Norfolk 234 C2
Westwood Devon 36 F1
Westwood Devon 22 A2
Westwood Kent 95 C6
Westwood Kent 91 B6
Westwood Notts 247 D7
Westwood Peterbro 204 D2
Westwood S Lanarks 380 B4
Westwood Wilts 81 E8
Westwood Wilts 63 E7
Westwood Heath W Midlands 177 C8
Westwood Park Gtr Man 278 E4
Westwoodside N Lincs 284 E1
Westy Warrington 265 B7
Wetham Green Kent 92 C3
Wetheral Cumb 339 A8
Wetheral Plain Cumb 348 E3
Wetherby W Yorks 306 F5
Wetherby Racecourse W Yorks 306 F5
Wetherden Suffolk 187 F5
Wetheringsett Suffolk 187 E7
Wethersfield Essex 140 A3
Wethersta Shetl'd 457 G3
Wetherup Street Suffolk 187 F7
Wetley Rocks Staffs 244 E5
Wetmore Staffs 223 D7
Wetreins Green Ches 242 D1
Wettenhall Ches 243 B5
Wetton Staffs 245 C8
Wetwang ER Yorks 309 D7
Wetwood Staffs 221 B5
Wexcombe Wilts 84 E2
Wexham Street Bucks 110 F1
Weybourne Norfolk 256 D5
Weybourne Surrey 67 B7
Weybread Suffolk 188 B2
Weybridge Surrey 88 D3
Weycroft Devon 38 F4
Weydale H'land 445 B5
Weyhill Hants 64 B3
Weymouth Dorset 25 E8
Weymouth Sea Life Park Dorset 25 D8
Weythel Powys 150 A2
Whaddon Bucks 158 F4
Whaddon Cambs 161 C6
Whaddon Glos 130 E2
Whaddon Glos 131 C5
Whaddon Wilts 43 A6
Whaddon Wilts 82 D2
Whaddon Gap Cambs 161 C6
Whale Cumb 327 B7
Whalecombe Pembs 117 C6
Whaley Derby 270 E2
Whaley Bridge Derby 267 C7
Whaley Thorns Derby 270 E2
Whaligoe H'land 445 D7
Whalley Lancs 290 C3
Whalley Banks Lancs 290 C3
Whalley Range Gtr Man 279 F5
Whalleys Mersey 277 C6
Whalsay Airport Shetl'd 457 G5
Whalton Northum 364 F4
Whaplode Lincs 229 D6
Whaplode Drove Lincs 229 F6
Whaplode St. Catherine Lincs 229 D6
Wharf Warwick 156 B3
Wharfe N Yorks 303 B7
Wharles Lancs 289 C5
Wharley End Beds 159 D6
Wharmley Northum 350 C4
Wharncliffe Side S Yorks 281 F7
Wharram le Street N Yorks 309 B6
Wharton Ches 265 F8
Wharton Lincs 272 A1
Wharton Green Ches 265 F8
Whashton N Yorks 331 E5
Whashton Green N Yorks 330 E4
Whasset Cumb 314 D4
Whatcote Warwick 155 D9
Whateley Warwick 199 D5
Whatfield Suffolk 165 C5
Whatley Som'set 38 E5
Whatley Som'set 61 B6
Whatlington E Sussex 51 C8
Whatsole Street Kent 74 C2
Whatstandwell Derby 246 D4
Whatton Notts 226 A1
Whauphill Dumf/Gal 401 E6
Whaw N Yorks 330 F1
Wheal Baddon Cornw'l 4 B3
Wheal Busy Cornw'l 4 B2
Wheal Frances Cornw'l 7 E6
Wheal Rose Cornw'l 4 B2
Wheal Vor Cornw'l 3 D8
Wheatacre Norfolk 211 E5
Wheatcroft Derby 247 C5
Wheatenhurst Glos 130 F1
Wheatfield Oxon 108 C3
Wheathampstead Herts 137 E7
Wheathill Shrops 174 B2
Wheathill Som'set 60 E3
Wheatley Devon 21 B8
Wheatley Hants 67 C5
Wheatley Oxon 107 A8
Wheatley S Yorks 283 D5
Wheatley W Yorks 292 E3
Wheatley Hill Durham 344 D3
Wheatley Hill W Yorks 281 C7
Wheatley Hills S Yorks 283 C6
Wheatley Lane Lancs 291 C5
Wheatley Park S Yorks 283 D5
Wheaton Aston Staffs 197 A5
Wheatridge Glos 130 D3
Wheddon Cross Som'set 57 D5
Wheedlemont Aberds 436 F1
Wheelbarrow Town Kent 74 B2
Wheelerend Common Bucks 109 D6
Wheelerstreet Surrey 67 C8
Wheelock Ches 243 C8
Wheelock Heath Ches 243 C8
Wheelton Lancs 289 F9
Wheen Angus 427 E8
Wheldale W Yorks 294 E3
Wheldrake C/York 295 A7
Whelford Glos 105 C8
Whelley Gtr Man 277 C8
Whelp Street Suffolk 164 C3
Whelpley Hill Bucks 110 B1
Whelpo Cumb 338 D5
Whelprigg Cumb 315 D6
Whelston Flints 263 D6
Whenby N Yorks 308 B1
Whepstead Suffolk 164 A1
Wherry Town Cornw'l 2 E5
Wherstead Suffolk 165 D8
Wherwell Hants 64 C4
Wheston Derby 268 D2
Whetley Cross Dorset 39 F7
Whetsted Kent 71 B8
Whetstone Leics 200 D5
Whetstone London 111 D7
Whicham Cumb 312 D3
Whichford Warwick 156 F1
Whickham Tyne/Wear 352 D3
Whickham Fell Tyne/Wear 352 E3
Whiddon Devon 55 E6
Whiddon Down Devon 20 B3
Whifflet N Lanarks 393 F6
Whigstreet Angus 421 C4
Whilton Northants 179 F7
Whiltonlocks Northants 179 F7
Whimble Devon 33 F7
Whimple Devon 22 A2
Whimpwell Green Norfolk 234 C4
Whin Lane End Lancs 288 B4
Whinburgh Norfolk 208 B4
Whinfield D'lington 331 C8
Whinhall N Lanarks 393 E7
Whinmoor W Yorks 293 C9
Whinney Hill S Yorks 282 F3
Whinnieliggate Dumf/Gal 402 D1
Whinny Heights Blackb'n 290 E2
Whinny Hill D'lington 332 C2
Whinny Hill Notts 248 B1
Whinnyfold Aberds 437 E7
Whins Wood W Yorks 292 C3
Whipcott Devon 37 C6
Whippingham I/Wight 30 B2
Whipps Cross London 112 E2
Whipsiderry Cornw'l 7 C7
Whipsnade Beds 136 D4
Whipsnade Wild Animal Park, Dunstable Beds 136 D4
Whipton Devon 21 B8
Whirley Grove Ches 266 D4
Whirlow S Yorks 269 C6
Whirlow Brook S Yorks 269 C6
Whisby Lincs 272 F3
Whissendine Rutl'd 226 F3
Whissenthorpe Leics 226 F2
Whissonsett Norfolk 232 D3
Whisterfield Ches 266 E3
Whistlefield Arg/Bute 409 C5
Whistley Green Wokingham 87 B6
Whiston Mersey 264 A4
Whiston Northants 180 F5
Whiston Staffs 221 F7
Whiston Staffs 245 E6
Whiston S Yorks 269 B9
Whiston Cross Mersey 264 A4
Whitacre Heath Warwick 199 E5
Whitbeck Cumb 312 D3
Whitbourne Heref'd 152 A4
Whitbourne Ford Heref'd 152 A4
Whitbread Hop Farm, Beltring Kent 71 B8
Whitburn Tyne/Wear 353 D7
Whitburn W Loth 394 F3
Whitburn Colliery Tyne/Wear 353 D7
Whitby Ches 264 D2
Whitby N Yorks 335 D5
Whitby Abbey N Yorks 335 D5
Whitbyheath Ches 264 E2
Whitchurch Bucks 135 C7
Whitchurch Bristol 80 C4
Whitchurch Card 78 A3
Whitchurch Devon 11 A5
Whitchurch Hants 65 B6
Whitchurch Heref'd 128 D4
Whitchurch Oxon 86 A2
Whitchurch Pembs 118 D3
Whitchurch Shrops 242 F3
Whitchurch Warwick 155 C7
Whitchurch Cannonicorum Dorset 24 A2
Whitchurch Hill Oxon 86 A2
Whitcombe Dorset 26 C1
Whitcott Keysett Shrops 172 B3
White Ball Devon 37 C6
White Colne Essex 141 B6
White Cross Bath/NE Som'set 80 E4
White Cross Cornw'l 4 F1
White Cross Cornw'l 7 D8
White Cross Heref'd 151 D7
White Cross Wilts 61 E7
White End Glos 130 B2
White Gate Gtr Man 279 D6
White Hill Wilts 61 E8
White Hills Northants 180 F2
White Horse Common Norfolk 234 C3
White House Suffolk 165 C7
White Houses Notts 271 D6
White Kirkley Durham 342 D4
White Lackington Dorset 26 A1
White Ladies Aston Worcs 153 B8
White Lee W Yorks 293 E6
White Lund Lancs 301 C7
White Mill Carms 123 C5
White Moor Derby 247 E5
White Moss Cumb 348 D3
White Ness Shetl'd 457 J3
White Notley Essex 140 D4
White Ox Mead Bath/NE Som'set 81 E6
White Pit Lincs 274 D4
White Post Notts 248 C3
White Post Farm Centre, Farnsfield Notts 248 C3
White Rocks Heref'd 128 C2
White Roding Essex 139 E7
White Stake Lancs 289 E7
White Stone Heref'd 152 D1
White Waltham Windsor 87 A7
Whiteacen Moray 435 D7
Whiteacre Kent 74 B2
Whiteash Green Essex 140 A4
Whitebirk Blackb'n 290 E3
Whitebog H'land 434 B2
Whitebridge H'land 425 A6
Whitebrook Monmouths 102 A2
Whiteburn Scot Borders 386 C1
Whitecairn Dumf/Gal 400 D4
Whitecairns Aberds 429 A6
Whitecastle S Lanarks 382 D5
Whitechapel Lancs 289 B8
Whitechapel London 112 F1
Whitechurch Som'set 40 B4
Whitecleat Orkney 453 C6
Whitecliff Glos 128 E5
Whiteclosegate Cumb 348 E2
Whitecote W Yorks 293 C6
Whitecraigs E Renf 380 A3
Whitecroft Glos 102 A4
Whitecrook Renf 392 E2
Whitecross Cornw'l 8 A2
Whitecross Cornw'l 3 D6
Whitecross Dorset 24 A4
Whitecross Falk 394 C4
Whitecross Staffs 221 D7
Whitecross Green Oxon 134 E2
Whiteface H'land 440 E4
Whitefarland N Ayrs 404 B4
Whitefaulds S Ayrs 367 F5
Whitefield Aberds 437 F4
Whitefield Dorset 27 B5
Whitefield Gtr Man 279 C5
Whitefield Perth/Kinr 420 D1
Whitefield Som'set 57 F8
Whitefield Lane End Mersey 264 B4

Whitefield Lane End Mersey 264 B4

Whiteford Aberds 436 F4
Whitegate Ches 265 F7
Whitehall Devon 37 D7
Whitehall Devon 55 D5
Whitehall Hants 66 A4
Whitehall Herts 138 A2
Whitehall Lancs 290 F2
Whitehall W Sussex 48 B2
Whitehall Village Orkney 454 D4
Whitehaven Cumb 324 C4
Whitehaven Shrops 218 D2
Whiteheath Gate W Midlands 197 F8
Whitehill E Sussex 70 F5
Whitehill Hants 67 E5
Whitehill Kent 93 E7
Whitehill Midloth 396 E4
Whitehill Moray 436 C2
Whitehill S Lanarks 381 A6
Whitehills Aberds 436 B3
Whitehills S Lanarks 380 B4
Whitehills Tyne/Wear 352 D4
Whitehough Derby 267 C7
Whitehouse Aberds 428 A3
Whitehouse Arg/Bute 407 F8
Whitehouse Common W Midlands 198 D3
Whitehouse Green W Berks 86 C3
Whiteinch Glasg C 392 E2
Whitekirk E Loth 398 B1
Whiteknights Reading 86 B4
Whiteknowes Aberds 428 B2
Whitelackington Som'set 39 C5
Whitelaw S Lanarks 380 D4
Whiteleaf Bucks 109 B6
Whiteleas Tyne/Wear 353 D6
Whiteleaved Oak Heref'd 153 E5
White-le-Head Durham 352 F2
Whiteless S Ayrs 367 A7
Whiteley Bank I/Wight 30 D3
Whiteley Green Ches 267 D5
Whiteley Village Surrey 88 D3
Whitelye Monmouths 102 B2
Whitemans Green W Sussex 49 A6
Whitemire Moray 434 C4
Whitemoor Nott'ham 247 F8
Whitemoor Cornw'l 8 D2
Whitenap Hants 44 B2
Whiteoak Green Oxon 133 E5
Whiteparish Wilts 43 B8
Whiterashes Aberds 437 F5
Whiterow H'land 445 D7
Whites Som'set 59 E6
Whiteshill Glos 130 F2
Whiteshill S Glos 80 A4
Whiteside W Loth 394 E4
Whitesmith E Sussex 50 D3
Whitestaunton Som'set 38 D3
Whitestone Devon 21 B7
Whitestone Aberds 428 C3
Whitestone Devon 54 B4
Whitestone Warwick 200 F1
Whitestone Cross Devon 21 B8
Whitestones Aberds 437 C5
Whitestreet Green Suffolk 164 E4
Whitewall Common Monmouths 101 E8
Whitewall Corner N Yorks 308 A4
Whiteway Bath/NE Som'set 81 D6
Whiteway Glos 104 C1
Whiteway Glos 130 E4
Whitewayhead Shrops 174 D1
Whitewell Aberds 437 B6
Whitewell H'land 426 B4
Whitewell Lancs 302 F5
Whitewell Bottom Lancs 291 F5
Whiteworks Devon 11 A8
Whitfield Heref'd 128 C5
Whitfield Kent 75 B6
Whitfield Northants 157 E7
Whitfield Northum 350 E2
Whitfield S Glos 103 D5
Whitfield Stoke 244 D2
Whitford Devon 23 A7
Whitford Flints 262 D4
Whitgift ER Yorks 296 F3
Whitgreave Staffs 221 C7
Whithebeir Orkney 454 C3
Whithorn Dumf/Gal 401 E6
Whiting Bay N Ayrs 405 D6
Whitkirk W Yorks 293 D9
Whitland = Hendy-Gwyn Carms 121 D7
Whitle Derby 267 B6
Whitlea Northum 352 A4
Whitleigh Plym'th 10 C5
Whitletts S Ayrs 367 C7
Whitley Gtr Man 277 C8
Whitley N Yorks 295 F5
Whitley Reading 86 B4
Whitley Wilts 82 C2
Whitley W Midlands 178 C2
Whitley Bay Tyne/Wear 353 B6
Whitley Chapel Northum 350 E5
Whitley Heath Staffs 221 C6
Whitley Lower W Yorks 281 A6
Whitley Reed Ches 265 C7
Whitley Row Kent 70 A5
Whitley Thorpe N Yorks 295 F5
Whitley Wood Reading 86 C4
Whitlock's End W Midlands 176 C5
Whitminster Glos 130 F1

Whitmoor Devon 37 D6
Whitmore Dorset 42 E4
Whitmore Staffs 244 F2
Whitmore Heath Staffs 244 F1
Whitmore Park W Midlands 178 B1
Whitnage Devon 37 C5
Whitnash Warwick 178 F1
Whitnell Som'set 58 D4
Whitney Bottom Som'set 38 D4
Whitney-on-Wye Heref'd 150 C3
Whitrigg Cumb 338 D3
Whitrigg Cumb 347 E6
Whitsbury Hants 43 C5
Whitsome Scot Borders 387 B7
Whitsomehill Scot Borders 387 C7
Whitson Newp 101 F7
Whitstable Kent 94 C2
Whitstone Cornw'l 18 A2
Whittaker Gtr Man 279 A7
Whittingham Northum 376 E3
Whittingslow Shrops 194 F4
Whittington Glos 131 C6
Whittington Lancs 315 E6
Whittington Norfolk 207 D5
Whittington Shrops 218 B3
Whittington Staffs 175 B7
Whittington Staffs 198 B4
Whittington Warwick 199 D6
Whittington Moor Derby 269 E7
Whittle Hill Gtr Man 279 C5
Whittlebury Northants 158 D1
Whittleford Warwick 199 E7
Whittle-le-Woods Lancs 289 F8
Whittlesey Cambs 204 D4
Whittlesford Cambs 162 C2
Whittlestone Head Blackb'n 278 A3
Whitton Scot Borders 374 C5
Whitton London 88 B4
Whitton N Lincs 296 F5
Whitton Northum 364 B3
Whitton Powys 172 E3
Whitton Shrops 174 D1
Whitton Suffolk 165 C7
Whitton Stockton 332 B2
Whittonditch Wilts 84 B2
Whittonstall Northum 351 E8
Whitway Hants 85 E6
Whitwell Derby 270 E3
Whitwell Herts 137 C7
Whitwell I/Wight 30 E2
Whitwell N Yorks 318 A4
Whitwell Rutl'd 202 B4
Whitwell Common Norfolk 233 D6
Whitwell Street Norfolk 233 D7
Whitwell-on-the-Hill N Yorks 308 B3
Whitwick Leics 224 E3
Whitwood W Yorks 294 F2
Whitworth Lancs 279 A6
Whixall Shrops 219 B7
Whixley N Yorks 307 D5
Whoberley W Midlands 177 C9
Whome Orkney 452 D4
Whorlton Durham 330 D4
Whorlton N Yorks 332 F4
Whydown E Sussex 51 E7
Whyke W Sussex 46 F5
Whyle Heref'd 173 F9
Whyteleafe Surrey 90 E2
Wibsey W Yorks 292 D4
Wibtoft Warwick 200 F3
Wichenford Worcs 175 F5
Wichling Kent 93 E5
Wick Bournem'th 28 B3
Wick Devon 37 F8
Wick H'land 445 C7
Wick Shetl'd 455 C3
Wick S Glos 81 B6
Wick Som'set 58 C4
Wick Som'set 59 F8
Wick Som'set 60 D2
Wick Som'set 79 F6
Wick V/Glam 77 B5
Wick Wilts 43 B6
Wick Worcs 154 C2
Wick W Sussex 47 F8
Wick Airport H'land 445 C7
Wick End Beds 159 B7
Wick Hill Brackn'l 87 B7
Wick Hill Kent 72 C3
Wick Hill Wokingham 87 D6
Wick Hill Wilts 82 B4
Wick St. Lawrence N Som'set 79 C7
Wick Street Glos 130 F3
Wicken Cambs 184 D4
Wicken Northants 158 E2
Wicken Bonhunt Essex 139 A6
Wicken Green Village Norfolk 231 B8
Wickenby Lincs 273 C6
Wicker Street Green Suffolk 164 D4
Wickersley S Yorks 282 F3
Wickford Essex 114 D1
Wickham Hants 45 D6
Wickham W Berks 84 B4
Wickham Bishops Essex 141 E5
Wickham Green Suffolk 187 E6
Wickham Green W Berks 84 B4
Wickham Heath W Berks 85 C5
Wickham Market Suffolk 166 A3
Wickham St. Paul Essex 164 E1
Wickham Skeith Suffolk 187 E6
Wickham Street Suffolk 187 E6
Wickham Street Suffolk 163 B8
Wickhambreaux Kent 94 E4
Wickhambrook Suffolk 163 B7
Wickhamford Worcs 154 D4
Wickhampton Norfolk 210 B4
Wicklane Bath/NE Som'set 81 E5
Wicklewood Norfolk 209 C5
Wickmere Norfolk 233 B8
Wickridge Street Glos 130 B2
Wicksgreen Glos 130 E1
Wicksteed Park, Kettering Northants 181 C5
Wickstreet E Sussex 50 E3
Wickwar S Glos 103 E6
Widcombe Bath/NE Som'set 81 D7
Widcombe Som'set 38 C2
Widdenham Wilts 82 B1
Widdington Essex 139 A6
Widdop W Yorks 291 D7
Widdrington Northum 365 C7
Widdrington Station Northum 365 D6
Wide Open Tyne/Wear 352 B3
Widecombe in the Moor Devon 20 E4
Widegate's Cornw'l 10 D1
Widemarsh Heref'd 151 D8
Widemouth Bay Cornw'l 32 F4
Widewall Orkney 453 D5
Widewell Plym'th 11 C5
Widford Essex 113 B8
Widford Herts 138 D4
Widford Oxon 132 E4
Widham Wilts 105 E6
Widley Hants 45 E8
Widmer End Bucks 109 C7
Widmerpool Notts 225 C7
Widnes Halton 264 C5
Widworthy Devon 23 A6
Wig Powys 193 F6
Wigan Gtr Man 277 C8
Wigan Pier Gtr Man 277 D8
Wigbeth Dorset 42 E3
Wigborough Som'set 39 C6
Wig-Fach Bridg 76 A3
Wiggaton Devon 22 B4
Wiggenhall St. Germans Norfolk 230 F3
Wiggenhall St. Mary Magdalen Norfolk 206 A2
Wiggenhall St. Mary the Virgin Norfolk 230 F3
Wiggenhall St. Peter Norfolk 206 A3
Wiggens Green Essex 163 D6
Wigginton C/York 307 D8
Wigginton Herts 136 E2
Wigginton Oxon 156 F2
Wigginton Staffs 199 B5
Wigginton Bottom Herts 136 F2
Wigglesworth N Yorks 303 D8
Wiggonby Cumb 347 F7
Wiggonholt W Sussex 47 C9
Wighill N Yorks 307 F6
Wighton Norfolk 256 D1
Wightwick W Midlands 197 D6
Wigley Hants 44 C1
Wigmore Heref'd 173 E6
Wigmore Medway 92 D3
Wigsley Notts 272 E2
Wigsthorpe Northants 181 B8
Wigston Leics 201 D6
Wigston Fields Leics C 201 C5
Wigston Harcourt Leics 201 D6
Wigston Magna Leics 201 D6
Wigston Parva Leics 200 F3
Wigthorpe Notts 270 C3
Wigtoft Lincs 228 A5
Wigton Cumb 338 B4
Wigtown Dumf/Gal 401 D6
Wig Powys 193 A5
Wike W Yorks 293 B8
Wike Well End S Yorks 283 B7
Wilbarston Northants 202 F2
Wilberfoss ER Yorks 308 E3
Wilberlee W Yorks 280 B3
Wilburton Cambs 184 D2
Wilby Norfolk 208 F4
Wilby Northants 180 E5
Wilby Suffolk 188 D2
Wilcot Wilts 83 D7
Wilcot Green Wilts 83 D7
Wilcott Shrops 218 E4
Wilcrick Newp 101 E8
Wild Mill Bridg 99 F5
Wildboarclough Ches 267 F6
Wilde Street Suffolk 185 C7
Wilden Beds 160 A1
Wilden Worcs 175 D6
Wildern Hants 44 D4
Wildernesse Kent 91 E5
Wilderspool Warrington 265 B7
Wildfowl and Wetland Centre, Martin Mere Lancs 277 B5
Wildhern Hants 64 A4
Wildhill Herts 111 A7
Wildlife & Dinosaur Park, Combe Martin Devon 55 C7
Wildmanbridge S Lanarks 381 B8
Wildmoor Hants 86 E3
Wildmoor Oxon 107 C6
Wildmoor Worcs 176 C2
Wildridings Brackn'l 87 C7
Wildsworth Lincs 284 E3
Wildwood Staffs 221 D8
Wilford Notts 225 A6
Wilkesley Ches 243 F5
Wilkhaven H'land 441 E6
Wilkieston W Loth 395 E7
Wilkin Throop Som'set 40 B3
Wilksby Lincs 251 B8
Willacy Lane End Lancs 289 C6
Willand Devon 37 D5
Willand Som'set 38 D1
Willand Moor Devon 37 D5
Willards Hill E Sussex 51 B7
Willaston Ches 243 D6
Willaston Ches 263 D8
Willaston Shrops 220 A1
Willen M/Keynes 158 D5
Willenhall W Midlands 197 D8
Willenhall W Midlands 178 C2
Willerby ER Yorks 297 D7
Willerby N Yorks 322 E4
Willersey Glos 154 E5
Willersley Heref'd 150 C4
Willesborough Kent 73 C7
Willesborough Lees Kent 73 C7
Willesden London 111 E6
Willesden Green London 111 F6
Willesleigh Devon 55 E6
Willesley Glos 104 E2
Willestrew Devon 19 E5
Willett Som'set 58 E1
Willey Shrops 196 D2
Willey Warwick 178 B4
Willey Green Surrey 67 A8
William Herts 137 A8
William's Green Suffolk 164 D4
Williamscot Oxon 156 C4
Williamstown Rh Cyn Taff 99 D7
Williamthorpe Derby 247 A6
Williamwood E Renf 380 A3
Willingale Essex 139 F7
Willingcott Devon 54 C4
Willingdon E Sussex 50 F4
Willingham Cambs 183 C8
Willingham by Stow Lincs 272 B2
Willingham Green Cambs 163 B5
Willington Beds 160 C2
Willington Derby 223 C7
Willington Durham 343 D7
Willington Kent 92 F2
Willington Tyne/Wear 353 C5
Willington Warwick 155 E8
Willington Corner Ches 265 F5
Willington Quay Tyne/Wear 353 C5
Willisham Suffolk 165 B6
Willisham Tye Suffolk 165 B6
Willitoft ER Yorks 296 C1
Williton Som'set 57 C8
Willoughbridge Staffs 243 F7
Willoughby Lincs 275 E6
Willoughby Warwick 179 E5
Willoughby Hills Lincs 252 E3
Willoughby on the Wolds Notts 225 C7
Willoughby Waterleys Leics 201 E5
Willoughton Lincs 272 A3
Willoughton Cliff Lincs 272 A3
Willow Green Ches 265 D7
Willow Holme Cumb 348 E1
Willowbank Bucks 110 E3
Willows Gtr Man 278 C3
Willows Green Essex 140 D3
Willsbridge S Glos 81 B5
Willslock Staffs 222 B3
Willtown Som'set 39 B5
Wilmcote Warwick 155 A6
Wilmington Bath/NE Som'set 81 D5
Wilmington Devon 23 A6
Wilmington E Sussex 50 F4
Wilmington Kent 91 B5
Wilminstone Devon 19 E6
Wilmslow Ches 266 C3
Wilmslow Park Ches 266 C4
Wilnecote Staffs 199 C5
Wilney Green Norfolk 187 B6
Wilpshire Lancs 290 D2
Wilsden W Yorks 292 C3
Wilsford Lincs 250 F3
Wilsford Wilts 63 D7
Wilsford Wilts 83 E6
Wilshaw W Yorks 280 C4
Wilsill N Yorks 305 C7
Wilsley Green Kent 72 D2
Wilsley Pound Kent 72 D2
Wilsom Hants 66 D4
Wilson Heref'd 128 C5
Wilson Leics 224 D3
Wilsontown S Lanarks 382 A3
Wilstead Beds 160 D1
Wilsthorpe Derby 224 B4
Wilsthorpe Lincs 228 F1
Wilstone Herts 136 E2
Wilstone Green Herts 136 E2
Wilthorpe S Yorks 281 C8
Wilton Scot Borders 373 E6
Wilton Cumb 325 D5
Wilton Heref'd 129 C5
Wilton N Yorks 321 D8
Wilton Redcar/Clevel'd 333 C6
Wilton Som'set 38 B2
Wilton Wilts 84 D2
Wilton Wilts 63 E6
Wilton House, Salisbury Wilts 63 E6
Wiltown Devon 37 C8
Wimbish Essex 162 E4
Wimbish Green Essex 162 E5
Wimblebury Staffs 198 A1
Wimbledon London 89 B6
Wimbledon All England Tennis Club London 89 B6
Wimblington Cambs 205 E7
Wimborne Minster Dorset 27 A7
Wimborne Minster Dorset 27 A7
Wimborne St. Giles Dorset 42 D3
Wimbotsham Norfolk 206 B3
Wimpole Hall and Home Farm, Royston Cambs 161 B6
Wimpson S'thampton 44 D2
Wimpstone Warwick 155 C7
Wincanton Som'set 61 F6
Wincanton Racecourse Som'set 61 E6
Winceby Lincs 274 F3
Winch Fawr Merth Tyd 99 A7
Wincham Ches 265 D8
Winchburgh W Loth 395 C6
Winchcombe Glos 131 B6
Winchelsea E Sussex 52 C3
Winchelsea Beach E Sussex 52 C3
Winchester Hants 65 F6
Winchester Cathedral Hants 65 F6
Winchestown Bl Gwent 126 E4
Winchet Hill Kent 72 C1
Winchfield Hants 86 F5
Winchmore Hill Bucks 109 C8
Winchmore Hill London 111 D8
Wincle Ches 244 A5
Wincobank S Yorks 269 A7
Wincombe Wilts 41 B7
Wind Mill Durham 343 F6
Windcross Glos 129 A7
Winder Cumb 325 C6
Windermere Cumb 314 A2
Winderton Warwick 156 D1
Windfallwood Common W Sussex 67 F8
Windhill H'land 433 D7
Windhill S Yorks 282 D3
Windhill W Yorks 292 C5
Windhouse Shetl'd 456 D4
Windle Hill Ches 263 D8
Windlehurst Gtr Man 267 B6
Windlesham Surrey 87 D8
Windley Derby 246 E4
Windmill Cornw'l 16 F2
Windmill Derby 268 D3
Windmill Hill Bristol 80 B3
Windmill Hill E Sussex 51 D6
Windmill Hill Halton 265 C6
Windmill Hill Kent 92 C3
Windmill Hill Som'set 38 C4
Windmill Hill S Yorks 282 C2
Windmill Hill Worcs 153 C8
Windmill Hill W Yorks 282 B1
Windrush Glos 132 E2
Windsor N Lincs 284 B2
Windsor Windsor 87 A8
Windsor Castle Windsor 88 A1
Windsor Green Suffolk 164 B2
Windsor Racecourse Windsor 87 A8
Windsoredge Glos 104 B1
Windy Arbor Mersey 264 B4
Windy Arbour Warwick 177 D8
Windy Hill Wrex 241 D7
Windy Nook Tyne/Wear 352 D4
Windygates Fife 411 B8
Windyharbour Ches 266 E3
Windyknowe W Loth 394 E4
Windywalls Scot Borders 386 F5
Wineham W Sussex 48 B4
Winestead ER Yorks 298 F4
Winewall Lancs 291 C7
Winfarthing Norfolk 187 A7
Winford I/Wight 30 D3
Winford N Som'set 80 C2
Winforton Heref'd 150 C3
Winfrith Newburgh Dorset 26 D3
Wing Bucks 135 C8
Wing Rutl'd 202 C3
Wingate Durham 344 D3
Wingates Gtr Man 278 C2
Wingates Northum 364 C4
Wingerworth Derby 269 F7
Wingfield Beds 136 B4
Wingfield Suffolk 188 C2
Wingfield S Yorks 282 F2
Wingfield Wilts 81 E8
Wingfield Green Suffolk 188 C2
Wingfield Park Derby 247 D5
Wingham Kent 94 E4
Wingham Green Kent 94 E4
Wingham Well Kent 94 E4
Wingmore Kent 74 B3
Wingrave Bucks 135 D8
Winkburn Notts 248 C5
Winkfield Brackn'l 87 B8
Winkfield Row Brackn'l 87 B7
Winkfield Street Brackn'l 87 B8
Winkhill Lincs 251 E5
Winkhill Staffs 245 D7
Winkhurst Green Kent 70 B4
Winklebury Hants 66 A2
Winkleigh Devon 35 E5
Winksley N Yorks 306 A2
Winkton Dorset 28 A3
Winkton Common Dorset 28 B3
Winlaton Tyne/Wear 352 D2
Winlaton Mill Tyne/Wear 352 D2
Winless H'land 445 C7
Winmarleigh Lancs 301 F8
Winnal Heref'd 151 F7
Winnal Common Heref'd 151 F7
Winnall Worcs 175 E6
Winnersh Wokingham 86 B5
Winnington Ches 265 E7
Winnington Shrops 194 A2
Winnothdale Staffs 245 F6
Winscales Cumb 325 A5
Winscombe N Som'set 79 E8
Winsdon Hill Luton 137 C5
Winsford Ches 243 A6
Winsford Som'set 57 E5
Winsham Devon 54 D4
Winsham Som'set 38 E5
Winshill Staffs 223 D7
Winsh-wen Swan 97 C8
Winsick Derby 269 F8
Winskill Cumb 340 E2
Winslade Hants 66 B2
Winsley N Yorks 305 C8
Winsley Wilts 81 D8
Winslow Bucks 135 B6
Winson Glos 131 F7
Winson Green W Midlands 198 F1
Winsor Hants 44 D1
Winstanley Gtr Man 277 D8
Winster Cumb 314 B2
Winster Derby 246 B2
Winston Durham 330 C4
Winston Suffolk 187 F8
Winston Green Suffolk 187 F8
Winstone Glos 131 F5
Winswell Devon 34 D2
Winter Gardens Essex 114 F2
Winter Well Som'set 38 B3
Winterborne Clenston Dorset 41 F6
Winterborne Herrington Dorset 25 C8
Winterborne Houghton Dorset 41 F6
Winterborne Kingston Dorset 26 A4
Winterborne Monkton Dorset 25 C8
Winterborne Stickland Dorset 41 F6
Winterborne Whitechurch Dorset 41 F6
Winterborne Zelston Dorset 26 A4
Winterbourne S Glos 102 E4
Winterbourne W Berks 85 B5
Winterbourne Abbas Dorset 25 B7
Winterbourne Bassett Wilts 83 A6
Winterbourne Dauntsey Wilts 63 E8
Winterbourne Down S Glos 81 A5
Winterbourne Earls Wilts 63 E8
Winterbourne Gunner Wilts 63 D8
Winterbourne Monkton Wilts 83 B6
Winterbourne Steepleton Dorset 25 C7
Winterbourne Stoke Wilts 63 C6
Winterbrook Oxon 108 E1
Winterburn N Yorks 304 D2
Winterhay Green Som'set 38 C5
Winteringham N Lincs 297 F5
Winterley Ches 243 C7
Wintersett W Yorks 282 B1
Wintershill Hants 45 C5
Winterton N Lincs 285 A5
Winterton-on-Sea Norfolk 235 E6
Winthorpe Lincs 253 A7
Winthorpe Notts 249 C7
Winton Bournem'th 28 B1
Winton Cumb 329 D5
Winton E Sussex 50 F3
Winton Gtr Man 278 E4
Winton N Yorks 319 A7
Wintringham N Yorks 309 A6
Winwick Cambs 182 B2
Winwick Northants 179 D7
Winwick Warrington 265 A7
Winwick Quay Warrington 265 A6
Winyates Worcs 176 E4
Winyates Green Worcs 176 E4
Wirksworth Derby 246 D3
Wirksworth Moor Derby 246 D4
Wirswall Ches 242 F3
Wisbech Cambs 205 B8
Wisbech St. Mary Cambs 205 B7
Wisborough Green W Sussex 47 A8
Wiseton Notts 271 B6
Wishanger Glos 130 F4
Wishaw N Lanarks 381 B7
Wishaw Warwick 198 E3
Wisley Surrey 88 E3
Wispington Lincs 273 E9
Wissenden Kent 73 C5
Wissett Suffolk 188 C5
Wistanstow Shrops 173 A6
Wistanswick Shrops 220 C3
Wistaston Ches 243 D6
Wistaston Green Ches 243 D6
Wiston Pembs 117 A6
Wiston S Lanarks 370 A4
Wiston W Sussex 48 D2
Wistow Cambs 183 B5
Wistow Leics 201 D6
Wistow N Yorks 295 C5
Wistow Lordship N Yorks 295 C6
Wiswell Lancs 290 C3
Witcham Cambs 184 C2
Witchampton Dorset 42 E2
Witchford Cambs 184 C2
Witcombe Som'set 39 B7
Withacott Devon 33 C8
Witham Essex 140 E5
Witham Friary Som'set 61 C6
Witham on the Hill Lincs 227 E8
Witham St. Hughes Lincs 249 B8
Withcall Lincs 274 C2
Withdean Brighton/Hove 49 E6
Withecombe Devon 20 C3
Witherenden Hill E Sussex 51 A5
Withergate Norfolk 234 C2
Witheridge Devon 35 D9
Witheridge Hill Oxon 108 F3
Witherley Leics 199 D7
Withermarsh Green Suffolk 165 E5
Withern Lincs 275 C5
Withernsea ER Yorks 299 E5
Withernwick ER Yorks 298 B2
Withersdale Street Suffolk 188 B3
Withersdane Kent 73 B8
Withersfield Suffolk 163 C6
Witherslack Cumb 314 D3
Witherwack Tyne/Wear 353 E6
Withiel Cornw'l 8 B2
Withiel Florey Som'set 57 E6
Withielgoose Mills Cornw'l 8 B3
Withington Ches 266 F3
Withington Glos 131 D6
Withington Gtr Man 266 A4
Withington Heref'd 152 D1
Withington Shrops 195 A7
Withington Staffs 222 A2
Withington Green Ches 266 E3
Withington Marsh Heref'd 151 D9
Withleigh Devon 36 D3
Withnell Lancs 290 F1
Withnell Fold Lancs 289 F9
Withybrook Som'set 61 B5
Withybrook Warwick 178 B3
Withybush Pembs 117 A5
Withycombe Som'set 57 C7
Withycombe Raleigh Devon 22 D2
Withyditch Bath/NE Som'set 81 E6
Withyham E Sussex 70 D4
Withymoor Village W Midlands 175 A8
Withypool Som'set 56 D3
Withywood Bristol 80 C3
Witley Surrey 67 D8
Witnell's End Worcs 175 B5
Witnesham Suffolk 165 B8
Witney Oxon 133 E6
Witney Green Essex 139 F7
Wittensford Hants 43 D8
Wittering Peterbro 203 C7
Wittersham Kent 72 F4
Witton Angus 428 E2
Witton Norfolk 210 B2
Witton Worcs 175 F7
Witton Bridge Norfolk 234 B3
Witton Gilbert Durham 343 B8
Witton le Wear Durham 343 E6
Witton Park Durham 343 E7
Wiveliscombe Som'set 57 F8
Wivelrod Hants 66 D3
Wivelsfield E Sussex 49 B6
Wivelsfield Green E Sussex 49 C7
Wivenhoe Essex 142 C1
Wivenhoe Cross Essex 142 C1
Wiveton Norfolk 256 D3
Wix Essex 142 B4
Wixford Warwick 154 B4
Wixhill Shrops 219 C8
Wixhoe Suffolk 163 D7
Woath Dorset 24 A4
Woburn Beds 136 A2
Woburn Abbey, Woburn Beds 136 A3
Woburn Sands M/Keynes 159 E6
Woburn Wild Animal Kingdom Beds 159 F7
Wofferwood Common Heref'd 152 B3
Woking Surrey 88 E2
Wokingham Wokingham 87 C6
Wolborough Devon 15 A5
Wold Newton ER Yorks 310 A2
Wold Newton NE Lincs 286 E3
Woldingham Surrey 90 E2
Woldingham Garden Village Surrey 90 E2
Wolferlow Heref'd 174 F3
Wolferton Norfolk 231 C5
Wolfhampcote Warwick 179 E5
Wolfhill Perth/Kinr 420 D1
Wolf's Castle Pembs 120 B3
Wolfsdale Pembs 120 C2
Woll Scot Borders 373 C6
Wollaston Northants 181 F6
Wollaston Shrops 194 A2
Wollaston W Midlands 175 B7
Wollaton Nott'ham 224 A5
Wollaton Hall Nott'ham 225 A5
Wolleigh Devon 21 E6
Wollescote W Midlands 175 B8
Wolsingham Durham 343 D5
Wolstanton Staffs 244 E3
Wolstenholme Gtr Man 279 B6
Wolston Warwick 178 C3
Wolsty Cumb 337 A8
Wolterton Norfolk 233 B8
Wolvercote Oxon 133 F8
Wolverham Ches 264 D3
Wolverhampton W Midlands 197 D7
Wolverhampton Racecourse W Midlands 197 C7
Wolverley Shrops 219 B6
Wolverley Worcs 175 C6
Wolverstone Devon 37 F7
Wolverton Hants 85 E8
Wolverton Kent 74 C5
Wolverton M/Keynes 158 D4
Wolverton Shrops 195 F5
Wolverton Warwick 177 F7
Wolverton Wilts 61 E7
Wolverton Common Hants 85 E8
Wolverton Mill M/Keynes 158 D4
Wolvesnewton Monmouths 101 C9
Wolvey Warwick 200 F2
Wolvey Heath Warwick 200 F2
Wolviston Stockton 332 A3
Womaston Powys 172 F3
Wombleton N Yorks 320 D4
Wombourn Staffs 197 E6
Wombridge Telford 196 A2
Wombwell S Yorks 282 D1
Womenswold Kent 74 A4
Womersley N Yorks 282 A4
Wonderstone N Som'set 79 E6
Wonersh Surrey 68 B2
Wonford Devon 21 B8
Wonson Devon 20 C3
Wonston Dorset 40 E4
Wonston Hants 65 D6
Wooburn Bucks 109 E8
Wooburn Common Bucks 109 E8
Wooburn Green Bucks 109 E8
Wooburn Moor Bucks 109 E8
Wood Pembs 118 E5
Wood Som'set 38 C4
Wood Bevington Warwick 154 B4
Wood Burcote Northants 158 C1
Wood Dalling Norfolk 233 C6
Wood Eaton Staffs 221 E6
Wood End Beds 159 C7
Wood End Beds 159 D7
Wood End Beds 159 A9
Wood End Bucks 158 F3
Wood End Bucks 135 A6
Wood End Gtr Man 279 B7
Wood End Heref'd 152 D2
Wood End Herts 138 B2
Wood End London 110 F3
Wood End London 110 F3
Wood End Warwick 177 D5
Wood End Warwick 199 F6
Wood End Warwick 199 D5
Wood End W Midlands 178 B2
Wood End W Midlands 197 C7
Wood End Green London 110 F3
Wood Enderby Lincs 251 B8
Wood Field Surrey 89 E5
Wood Gate Staffs 222 C4
Wood Green Essex 112 C3
Wood Green London 111 D8
Wood Green Norfolk 209 E8
Wood Green W Midlands 197 D8
Wood Green Worcs 175 E6
Wood Hayes W Midlands 197 C7
Wood Hill Kent 75 B7
Wood Kirk W Yorks 293 F7
Wood Laithes S Yorks 282 D1
Wood Lane Staffs 244 D2
Wood Lanes Ches 267 C5
Wood Linkin Derby 247 E6
Wood Nook W Yorks 280 B4
Wood Norton Norfolk 232 C5
Wood Road Gtr Man 278 B4
Wood Row W Yorks 294 E1
Wood Stanway Glos 131 A7
Wood Street Norfolk 234 D4
Wood Street Surrey 67 A9
Wood Street Wilts 83 A6
Woodacott Devon 33 E7
Woodacott Cross Devon 33 E7
Woodale N Yorks 317 E6
Woodall S Yorks 270 C1
Woodbank Arg/Bute 404 E2
Woodbastwick Norfolk 234 F3
Woodbeck Notts 271 D7
Woodborough Notts 248 E3
Woodborough Wilts 83 E7
Woodbridge Dorset 40 D4
Woodbridge Devon 23 A5
Woodbridge Northum 365 E7
Woodbridge Suffolk 166 C3
Woodbridge Hill Surrey 68 A1
Woodbrook Heref'd 150 B4
Woodbury Devon 22 C2
Woodbury Salterton Devon 22 C2
Woodchester Glos 104 B1
Woodchurch Kent 73 E5
Woodchurch Mersey 263 B7
Woodcock Wilts 62 C2
Woodcock Hill Herts 110 D3
Woodcock Hill W Midlands 176 B3
Woodcombe Som'set 57 B5

## Ordnance Survey National Grid

The blue lines which divide the Navigator map pages into squares for indexing match the Ordnance Survey National Grid and correspond to the small squares on the boundary map below. Each side of a grid square measures 10km on the ground.

The National Grid 100-km square letters and kilometre values are indicated for the grid intersection at the outer corners of each page. For example, the intersection SP1020 at the lower right corner of page 99 is 10km East and 20km North of the south-west corner of National Grid square SP.

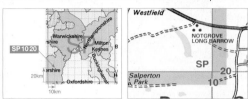

## Using GPS with Navigator mapping

Since Navigator Britain is based on Ordnance Survey mapping, and rectified to the National Grid, it can be used with in-car or handheld GPS for locating identifiable waypoints such as road junctions, bridges, railways and farms, or assessing your position in relation to any of the features shown on the map.

On your receiver, choose British Grid as the location format and for map datum select Ordnance Survey (this may be described as Ord Srvy GB or similar, or more specifically as OSGB36). Your receiver will automatically convert the latitude/longitude co-ordinates transmitted by GPS into compatible National Grid data.

Positional accuracy of any particular feature is limited to 50–100m, due to the limitations of the original survey and the scale of Navigator mapping.

For further information see www.gps.gov.uk

### Greater London

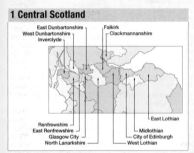

1 City and County of the City of London
2 Hackney
3 Tower Hamlets
4 Southwark
5 Lambeth
6 Wandsworth
7 Hammersmith and Fulham
8 Royal Borough of Kensington and Chelsea
9 City of Westminster
10 Camden
11 Islington
12 Haringey
13 Waltham Forest
14 Newham
15 Greenwich
16 Lewisham
17 Merton
18 Richmond upon Thames
19 Hounslow
20 Ealing
21 Brent
22 Barnet
23 Enfield
24 Redbridge
25 Barking and Dagenham
26 Havering
27 Bexley
28 Bromley
29 Croydon
30 Sutton
31 Kingston upon Thames
32 Hillingdon
33 Harrow

### 1 Central Scotland

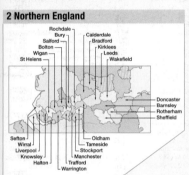

### 2 Northern England

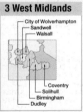

### 3 West Midlands

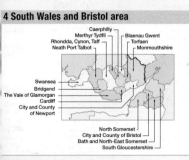

### 4 South Wales and Bristol area

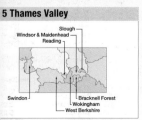

### 5 Thames Valley

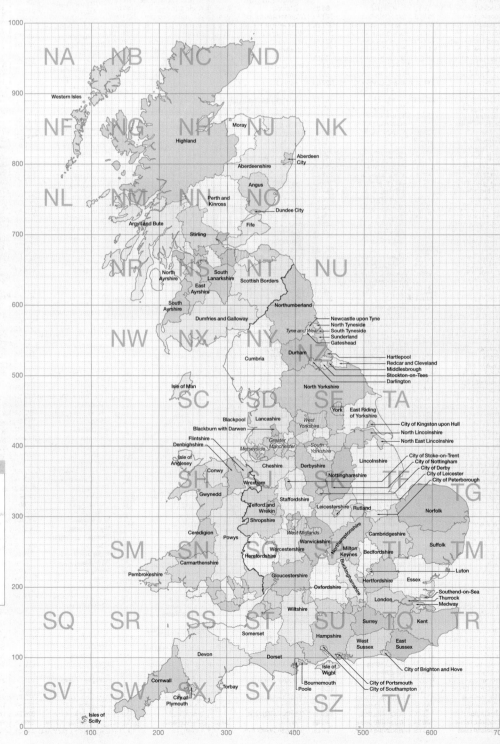

# PHILIP'S MAPS

## the Gold Standard for serious driving

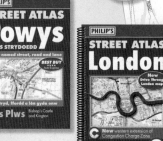
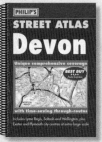
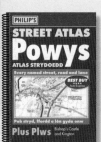
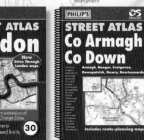
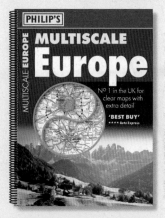
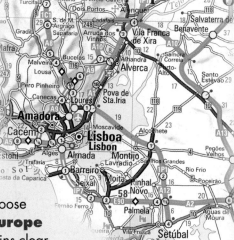
## Bridge heights

This chart converts between metric and Imperial bridge heights. Each small division in blue represents 1cm, each small division in red represents 1 inch.

The range of heights shown starts at the height at which a driver's cab must have a plate indicating vehicle height (3 metres) and ends at the maximum height at which a bridge will have a low bridge warning sign (16ft 6in).

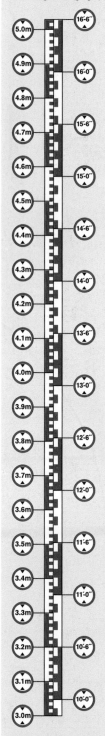

## Conversion factors

To convert from Imperial to metric units, **multiply** by the figure shown. To convert from metric to Imperial units, **divide** by the figure shown.

| Imperial | ✕ | Metric |
|---|---|---|
| inches | 2.54 | centimetres |
| feet | 0.3048 | metres |
| yards | 0.9144 | metres |
| miles | 1.6093 | kilometres |
| cubic feet | 0.0283 | cubic metres |
| cubic yards | 0.7646 | cubic metres |
| pints (UK) | 0.568 | litres |
| gallons (UK) | 4.55 | litres |
| pounds | 0.4536 | kilograms |

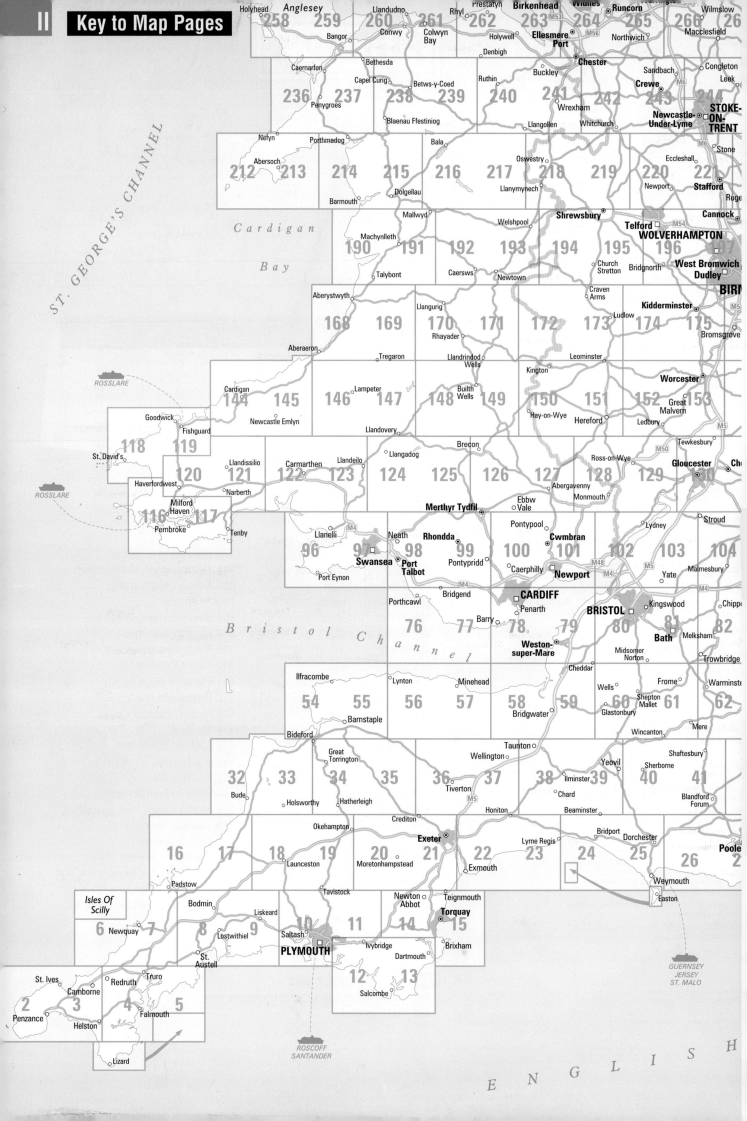

## II Key to Map Pages

# PHILIP'S

# NAVIGATOR® Britain

www.philips-maps.co.uk

First published in 2007 by Philip's
a division of Octopus Publishing Group Ltd
www.octopusbooks.co.uk
2–4 Heron Quays, London E14 4JP
An Hachette Livre UK Company

www.philips-maps.co.uk

First edition 2007
First impression 2007

Cartography by Philip's
Copyright © 2007 Philip's

 Ordnance Survey®

This product includes mapping data licensed from
Ordnance Survey®, with the permission of the Controller
of Her Majesty's Stationery Office. © Crown copyright
2007. All rights reserved. Licence number 100011710

Data for the speed cameras provided by
PocketGPSWorld.com Ltd.

Information for Tourist Attractions in England supplied
by VisitBritain.

Information for National Parks, Areas of Outstanding
Natural Beauty, National Trails and Country Parks in
Wales supplied by the Countryside Council for Wales.

Information for National Parks, Areas of Outstanding
Natural Beauty, National Trails and Country Parks in
England supplied by the Countryside Commission.

Data for Regional Parks, Long Distance Footpaths and
Country Parks in Scotland provided by Scottish Natural
Heritage.

Data for National Scenic Areas in Scotland provided by
the Scottish Executive Office. Crown copyright material
is reproduced with the permission of the Controller of
HMSO and the Queen's Printer for Scotland. Licence
number C02W0003960.

Gaelic name forms used in the Western Isles provided by
Comhairle nan Eilean.

Information for canal bridge numbers supplied by
GEOprojects (UK) Limited.

Printed in Italy by Rotolito

## Contents